MILESTONE DOCUMENTS OF THE SUPREME COURT

Exploring the Cases
That Shaped America

Milestone Documents of the Supreme Court

Exploring the Cases
That Shaped America

Volume 3: 1972–2022

Paul Finkelman

Editor in Chief

Dallas, Texas

Milestone Documents of the Supreme Court: Exploring the Cases That Shaped America

Copyright © 2023 by Schlager Group Inc.

All rights reserved. No part of this book may be reproduced or utilized in any form or by any means, electronic or mechanical, including photocopying, recording, or by any information storage or retrieval systems, without permission in writing from the publisher. For information, contact:

Schlager Group Inc.

10228 E. Northwest HWY, STE 1151
Dallas, TX 75238
USA
(888) 416-5727
info@schlagergroup.com

You can find Schlager Group online at https://www.schlagergroup.com

For Schlager Group:
Vice President, Editorial: Sarah Robertson
Vice President, Operations and Strategy: Benjamin Painter
Founder and President: Neil Schlager

Printed in the United States of America 10 9 8 7 6 5 4 3 2 1
Print ISBN: 9781935306863
eBook: 9781935306870

Library of Congress Control Number: 2023934505

Contents

Reader's Guide..viii
Contributors..x
Introduction..xii

Volume 1: 1803–1908

Marbury v. Madison..2
Martin v. Hunter's Lessee..23
Trustees of Dartmouth College v. Woodward..52
McCulloch v. Maryland...82
Cohens v. Virginia..107
Gibbons v. Ogden..137
Worcester v. Georgia...163
Charles River Bridge v. Warren Bridge..185
United States v. Amistad...193
Prigg v. Pennsylvania..206
Dred Scott v. Sandford..228
Ableman v. Booth..267
Ex parte Milligan..287
Slaughterhouse Cases..310
United States v. Cruikshank..351
Reynolds v. United States..366
Civil Rights Cases...382
Elk v. Wilkins..418
Plessy v. Ferguson...438
United States v. Wong Kim Ark...459
Lochner v. New York...472
Muller v. Oregon...486

Volume 2: 1915-1971

Frank v. Mangum..497
Guinn v. United States..515
Hammer v. Dagenhart...529

Schenck v. United States..542

Abrams v. United States..550

Whitney v. California..563

Olmstead v. United States..575

Powell v. Alabama...593

A.L.A. Schechter Poultry Corporation v. United States..610

United States v. Curtiss-Wright..627

National Labor Relations Board v. Jones & Laughlin Steel Corporation..644

West Coast Hotel v. Parrish...670

Cantwell v. Connecticut...687

Wickard v. Filburn...697

West Virginia State Board of Education v. Barnette...711

Korematsu v. United States..720

Sweatt v. Painter..730

Dennis v. United States..741

Youngstown Sheet and Tube Co. v. Sawyer..761

Brown v. Board of Education..772

Hernandez v. Texas..784

Gomillion v. Lightfoot..793

Mapp v. Ohio...802

Baker v. Carr..815

Engel v. Vitale..822

Gideon v. Wainwright...832

Katzenbach v. McClung...839

New York Times Co. v. Sullivan...850

Griswold v. Connecticut...857

Bond v. Floyd...868

Miranda v. Arizona..884

South Carolina v. Katzenbach..926

Loving v. Virginia..943

Tinker v. Des Moines Independent Community School District..956

New York Times Co. v. United States..967

Volume 3: 1972–2022

Flood v. Kuhn...981

Furman v. Georgia..997

San Antonio Independent School District v. Rodriguez..1010

Sierra Club v. Morton...1049

Roe v. Wade...1061

Milliken v. Bradley..1085

United States v. Nixon..1094

Craig v. Boren...1103

Regents of the University of California v. Bakke..1110

Frontiero v. Richardson...1133

Texas v. Johnson...1143

United States v. Lopez..1152

United States v. Virginia..1164

Clinton v. Jones..1173

Bush v. Gore..1187

Friends of the Earth v. Laidlaw Environmental Services...1219

Zelman v. Simmons-Harris..1234

Lawrence v. Texas...1252

District of Columbia v. Heller...1280

Citizens United v. Federal Election Commission..1322

Shelby County v. Holder..1336

Obergefell v. Hodges..1366

Bostock v. Clayton County...1380

Dobbs v. Jackson Women's Health Organization..1417

Index..1473

Milestone Documents of the Supreme Court

Exploring the Cases
That Shaped America

FLOOD V. KUHN

DATE 1972	**CITATION** 407 U.S. 258
AUTHOR Harry Blackmun	**SIGNIFICANCE** Reasserted that professional baseball's reserve system was exempt from federal and state antitrust laws
VOTE 5–3	

Overview

Argued on March 20, 1972, and decided on June 19, 1972, the case *Flood v. Kuhn* pitted Black St. Louis Cardinals outfielder Curtis C. Flood against the commissioner of baseball, Bowie K. Kuhn, in a decision about the status of the reserve system then in place in professional baseball. The reserve system bound players to continue playing for their current teams even after their contracts expired. It effectively prevented baseball players from participating in decisions about what teams they could play for, putting all power in the hands of baseball club owners.

The essence of the question before the Court was: Did the reserve clause violate existing federal law, in particular the Sherman Antitrust Act of 1890? In a controversial 5–3 decision, Justice Harry Blackmun, writing for the majority, asserted that the reserve clause did not violate the Antitrust Act because baseball was an exhibition sport, subject to state regulations. Chief Justice Warren Burger concurred and called upon Congress rather than the Supreme Court to address the issue. Associate Justice Thurgood Marshall, in a strong dissent joined by William Brennan, pointed out that professional baseball's antitrust exemption was an anomaly among all types of American business and that it was the Supreme Court's responsibility to address the injustices under which baseball players had labored for a century. William O. Douglas also wrote a dissenting opinion, likewise joined by Brennan.

Context

Curtis Flood had been an extraordinarily successful center fielder for the St. Louis Cardinals, leading the team as its co-captain to a World Series victory in 1967 and capturing the National League pennant the following year. When Flood asked the Cardinals' owner, August "Gussie" Busch, for a raise in 1969, Bush refused. In October of that year, Flood received notification that he was being traded to the Philadelphia Phillies. Flood requested of Commissioner Kuhn that he be treated as a free agent, able to sign a contract with any baseball club that wanted his services. Kuhn refused. Flood responded by filing a lawsuit alleging that the reserve clause preventing him from becoming a free agent was a violation of federal antitrust law. Flood,

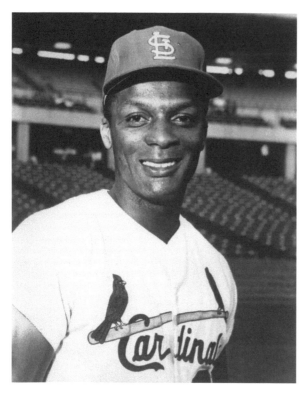

Curt Flood
(St. Louis Cardinals / MLB)

a Black man in a sport long noted for its discrimination, also asserted that the reserve clause made peons of ballplayers, effectively treating them as if they were in bondage—a situation that, Flood said, violated the Thirteenth Amendment that had put an end to slavery.

The problem was this: ever since 1876, baseball club owners had maintained a reserve clause that prevented players from joining whatever teams they liked. When players signed contracts, the reserve clause meant that any given player could play ball only for his current employer. If he objected, he was fired and was effectively banned from playing the game again. Ballplayers saw this as a violation of federal antitrust regulations governing restraint of trade.

The reserve clause was as old as the National League itself. In 1871, a group of team owners met in Manhattan to agree between themselves on the rules that they would follow in managing the game of professional baseball. The problem was that owners with more money could buy the services of the stars of the game, effectively shutting smaller franchises out of competition. When a nationwide depression cut ticket sales, the sport seemed to be on the verge of collapse. To consolidate club owners' control of the game, Chicago White Stockings owner William A. Hulbert reached an agreement with seven other club owners to form the National League. To keep players from moving to whichever team offered them more money or better conditions, Hulbert and his colleagues introduced the reserve clause. It stayed in effect for more than a century.

Players objected to the reserve clause from the start. In 1885, John Montgomery Ward, a New York Giants player who was also a lawyer, helped create the Brotherhood of Professional Base Ball Players, a union intended specifically to wreck the reserve clause. With help from wealthy supporters who had been shut out of ownership of National League teams, in 1890 Ward organized the Players League in an attempt to ensure fair treatment of players. But the Players League only hosted games for a single season before it was forced out of business through the actions of National League president A. G. Spalding.

While the National League was acting to suppress baseball players' attempts to organize, it was also creating and enforcing a color line that locked Black players out of the league altogether. Shortly after the Civil War, an all-Black Philadelphia club called the Pythians played games against all-white teams. The Pythians were refused membership in the National League when they applied in 1867. Bud Fowler of Cooperstown, New York, was one of the first Black players to join a white professional team in 1872. Moses Fleetwood Walker, a graduate of Oberlin College in Ohio, joined the Toledo team in 1884 as a catcher. Racism, virulent at the time, forced him off the team within a few years. By 1887, Black ballplayers in the National League were virtually unknown, and some clubs refused even to take the field against an integrated team.

By the 1890s major league baseball was widely perceived as a monopoly, in which a small number of club owners controlled access to and participation in the sport. As early as 1902, a pitcher named Jack Harper tried to break his contract with the St. Louis Cardinals to join the American League's St. Louis Browns, arguing that the reserve clause amounted to an illegal agreement that prevented free trade. Other cases argued directly that the clause was a violation of the Sherman Antitrust Act. In 1922, however, the U.S. Supreme Court found in *Federal Baseball Club of Baltimore v. National League* that the Antitrust Act did not apply to professional baseball because the game was not a form of interstate commerce. Holmes had claimed that although baseball teams regularly crossed state lines to play one another, travel was incidental to the game itself. He also asserted that if Congress meant to regulate baseball as a trust, it should have passed legislation to do so. Many commentators found the unanimous opinion, written by Justice Oliver Wendell Holmes, to be a distortion of the law. But *Federal Baseball Club of Baltimore v. National League* stood, and it provided a precedent for later challenges to the reserve clause.

George Earl Toolson, a minor league pitcher for the Newark Bears in 1949, challenged the reserve clause in a case that came before the Supreme Court in 1953. The Newark Bears were a minor league team that supplied players to the New York Yankees. The Yankees dissolved the Bears in 1950 and, instead of promoting Toolson, sent him to a smaller minor league team, the Binghamton Triplets. Toolson sued, saying that the reserve clause prevented him from leaving the Triplets to seek employment with another team. In a 7–2 decision, the Court reasserted the game of baseball's exemption from antitrust legislation on the grounds that, since Congress had done nothing to regulate baseball, it must have intended the sport to be exempt from antitrust regulation.

This was where matters stood when Curtis Flood's case came before the Supreme Court in the spring of 1972. The outfielder recognized that he needed high-powered legal help and found it in Major League Baseball Players Association executive director Marvin Miller, in Richard Moss, the general counsel of the Players Association, and in Arthur Goldberg, who was himself a former Supreme Court justice. Flood recognized that suing major league baseball meant an end to his professional career, but he was willing to take that loss—in part because he recognized that the status of players under the reserve clause was analogous to that of enslaved people in the nineteenth century. He even referred to himself on air as "a well-paid slave" on the ABC program *Wide World of Sports*.

And the case came at a time when Black athletes were increasingly willing to stand up for their rights. At the awards ceremony for the 200-meter dash during the 1968 Olympic Games, gold and bronze medalists Tommie Smith and John Carlos famously raised their gloved hands during the playing of the American national anthem in recognition of the racism they faced

Bowie Kuhn
(Major League Baseball)

in the United States. Boxing legend Muhammad Ali, who lost his heavyweight title when he refused to serve in the Vietnam War, compared Black boxers to slaves fighting for the amusement of white masters. Voices like theirs made the claim that the reserve clause violated the Thirteenth Amendment credible.

But the core of Flood's argument lay not in its suggestion that baseball players were treated like slaves but in its challenge to major league baseball's exemption from antitrust laws. It failed, in the opinion of the majority of the Supreme Court justices, to make the point. Harry Blackmun, a lifelong baseball fan, was chosen to record the Court's opinion, reasserting major league baseball's implicit exemption from federal antitrust regulation.

About the Author

Associate Justice Harry Blackmun (1908–1999) is best remembered today for his majority opinion in the groundbreaking *Roe v. Wade* case (1973). Blackmun was appointed to the bench of the nation's highest court in 1970 by President Richard Nixon and remained there until his retirement in 1994. Blackmun had grown up in St. Paul, Minnesota, where one of his classmates and closest friends was Warren Burger, with whom he would later serve on the Supreme Court. Blackmun attended Harvard University on a scholarship, graduating in 1929. He went on to obtain his law degree from Harvard Law School, where he attended classes taught by future associate justice Felix Frankfurter.

After obtaining his degree, Blackmun returned to Minnesota and entered private practice, teaching part-time at the University of Minnesota Law School and the St. Paul College of Law (now the William Mitchell College of Law). In 1959, with Burger's encouragement, Blackmun accepted an appointment to the Eighth Circuit Court of Appeals. In 1970, Richard Nixon appointed Blackmun to the U.S. Supreme Court, filling a vacancy left by the resignation of Associate Justice Abe Fortas.

Blackmun was a Republican, and Nixon apparently expected him to maintain a conservative position. Instead, the Minnesota-raised justice came to embrace very liberal opinions, voting more often with William Brennan than he did with his old friend Burger. Blackmun's change in viewpoint led to a split between the old friends, and the two drifted apart.

Blackmun may have authored the majority opinion in Flood's case, but the dissent authored by Associate Justice Thurgood Marshall (1908–1993) was in its own way just as important. Marshall, the first Black man to be appointed to the U.S. Supreme Court, had been a notable civil rights lawyer before his appointment to the bench. Marshall was a fierce opponent of racial segregation in schools, and he had been the lead attorney in the landmark *Brown v. Board of Education* decision of 1955. He was appointed to the Supreme Court by President Lyndon Johnson in 1967. Although he opposed Blackmun's position in *Flood v. Kuhn*, Marshall and the Minnesota native found themselves on the same side of issues as time went on, notably in *Roe v. Wade* (1973).

Explanation and Analysis of the Document

Blackmun was a lifelong baseball fan, and he opens his opinion with a history of the game, starting with its origins in 1846—the game played between the New York Knickerbockers and a team known as the New York Nine. Blackburn goes on to tell about the creation of the Cincinnati Red Stockings as the first traveling professional team in 1869 and the organization of the National Association of Professional Baseball Players in 1871. For the next few paragraphs, he continues to reminisce on the ways in which the sport evolved from the mid-nineteenth to the mid-twentieth century. One paragraph consists of a list of the names of more than eighty players, followed by another paragraph that talks about the impact of baseball on literature and journalism.

The justice begins the second section of his work with an assessment of the career of petitioner Curtis Flood, emphasizing his successes (Flood won seven Golden Glove awards in the course of his career). Blackmun goes on to outline Flood's complaint and his career after leaving the Cardinals, which included a partial season with the Washington Senators. The justice also emphasizes that Flood was well compensated for his final season with the Senators, receiving a salary of $110,000, which was $10,000 more than he had been offered to play for the Phillies.

In the third section of the opinion, Blackmun explains Flood's journey through the petition and appeal process, beginning with his suit against Commissioner Kuhn and including selections from the opinions rendered in the circuit court. The justice points out that the circuit court's opinion had relied on the precedents set by *Federal Baseball Club v. National League* in 1922 and *Toolson v. New York Yankees* in 1953. The judges who considered the case in circuit court held the decided opinion that Flood did not make a strong case for overturning either of the precedents.

The fourth section of Blackmun's opinion deals specifically with the history of the precedent-making cases of 1922 and 1953. He points out that although baseball as a sport was unusual in its exemption from antitrust regulation, it was not the only entertainment business that was exempt. A 1923 case, *Hart v. B. F. Keith Vaudeville Exchange*, which complained that bookings of acts violated antitrust regulations, cited the *Federal Baseball* decision of the year before. Although petitioners continued to complain about the unfairness of the reserve clause over the next thirty years, in each case the courts found that the sport of baseball needed the reserve clause to survive. Blackmun's opinion makes plain the idea that the courts considered the regulation of baseball to be a matter for Congress, not for the judicial system. Even if they recognized the injustice of the reserve clause, the courts felt that it was a matter that should be addressed through legislation rather than through the judicial process.

Blackmun also shows that the Toolson case served as precedent for several later cases alleging antitrust violations in sports or in entertainment in general. One was *United States v. Shubert* (1955), which was a civil case against the Shubert chain of theaters. Another was *United States v. International Boxing* (1955), and a third was *Haywood v. National Basketball Assn.* (1971). Both undermined the spirit, if not the letter, of the legal ideas behind *Federal Baseball* and *Toolson*. Blackmun concludes that (a) professional baseball was a business engaging in interstate commerce; and (b) court decisions about the status of baseball made it an exception to federal antitrust laws. He reasserts the belief that redress to Flood's grievances should come through legislation from Congress, not from court action. He continues by saying that even though both boxing and basketball had been made subject to federal antitrust laws, the fact that baseball had been deemed exempt by the courts decades earlier meant that it was still up to Congress to act—and since Congress had not done so, the decision as it stood in *Federal Baseball* and *Toolson* should stand as well.

Blackmun does not address Flood's other complaint—that the reserve clause stripped baseball players of their rights to bargain collectively—but Justice Thurgood Marshall does in his dissent. Marshall acknowledges the importance of stare decisis, but he adds that if baseball is a business and it engages in interstate commerce (which Blackburn admits), then it falls under the power of antitrust regulations. He argues that the Court should overrule both *Federal Baseball Club* and *Toolson* and then return the case to the district court from which it came to decide if an antitrust violation had actually occurred.

Impact

Flood lost his case. Embittered by the lack of support he received from his teammates and fellow players, he permanently retired from the game. A few had spoken out in support, notably Jackie Robinson and Hank Greenberg, but most recognized that by supporting Flood they were also risking their own careers if club owners chose to retaliate. And the question he had brought before the Supreme Court had been undermined by a collective bargaining arrangement put in place in 1970, years before Flood's case came to trial. The collective bargaining agreement bound player and owners to arbitration rather than litigation. Marvin Miller, one of Flood's attorneys, argued that the reserve clause only bound a player to continue with his original team for a single season after his contract expired, rather than placing his career at the team owner's whim. In 1975, Miller presented the arguments to arbitrator Peter Seitz. Seitz ruled in favor of Miller and the players. The reserve clause, as interpreted by club owners for more than 100 years, was effectively dead.

Nonetheless, *Flood v. Kuhn* did have an impact on relations between players and owners. The antitrust exemption had been weakened by the Seitz decision, but it was still in place, and various attempts to allege antitrust violations built up in the 1980s and 1990s. In 1998 Congress finally acted by passing the Curt Flood Act, which explicitly placed professional baseball under the scrutiny of antitrust legislation.

Questions for Further Study

1. Was Blackmun's decision to reaffirm the earlier decisions in *Federal Baseball* and *Toolson* justified? Why or why not?

2. How might Marvin Miller's involvement in litigating the Flood case have helped him convince Peter Seitz to decide that the reserve clause was limited to a single year?

3. One of the accusations made against Curt Flood by his opponents in the press and elsewhere was that he was "greedy" for not wanting to play for the Phillies. Do you think that accusation is justified?

4. Does Thurgood Marshall make a good case for sending the Flood case back to the district court where it started?

5. Considering his perspective as a Black man and a Black ballplayer, was Curt Flood justified in comparing the reserve clause to a form of slavery? Why or why not?

Further Reading

Books

Banner, Stuart. *The Baseball Trust: A History of Baseball's Antitrust Exemption*. New York: Oxford University Press, 2013.

Belth, Alex. *Stepping Up: The Story of Curt Flood and His Fight for Baseball Players' Rights*. New York: Persea Books, 2006.

Goldman, Robert Michael. *One Man Out: Curt Flood Versus Baseball*. Lawrence: University Press of Kansas, 2008.

Greenhouse, Linda. *Becoming Justice Blackmun: Harry Blackmun's Supreme Court Journey*. New York: Holt, 2005.

Weiss, Stuart L. *The Curt Flood Story: The Man behind the Myth*. Columbia: University of Missouri Press, 2007

Articles

"Court to Hear Curtis Flood Case." *Oakland Post*, November 4, 1971: 18.

Graham, Christopher P. "Flood at 50: How Curt Flood Changed the Game of Baseball." *Advocate*, November 2022: 30–33.

Websites

Sloope, Terry. "Curt Flood." *Society for American Baseball Research*. Accessed February 18, 2023, https://sabr.org/bioproj/person/curt-flood/.

—Commentary by Kenneth R. Shepherd

Flood v. Kuhn

Document Text

MR. JUSTICE BLACKMUN delivered the opinion of the Court

For the third time in 50 years, the Court is asked specifically to rule that professional baseball's reserve system is within the reach of the federal antitrust laws.

Collateral issues of state law and of federal labor policy are also advanced.

I

The Game

It is a century and a quarter since the New York Nine defeated the Knickerbockers 23 to 1 on Hoboken's Elysian Fields June 19, 1846, with Alexander Jay Cartwright as the instigator and the umpire. The teams were amateur, but the contest marked a significant date in baseball's beginnings. That early game led ultimately to the development of professional baseball and its tightly organized structure.

The Cincinnati Red Stockings came into existence in 1869 upon an outpouring of local pride. With only one Cincinnatian on the payroll, this professional team traveled over 11,000 miles that summer, winning 56 games and tying one. Shortly thereafter, on St. Patrick's Day in 1871, the National Association of Professional Baseball Players was founded and the professional league was born.

The ensuing colorful days are well known. The ardent follower and the student of baseball know of General Abner Doubleday; the formation of the National League in 1876; Chicago's supremacy in the first year's competition under the leadership of Al Spalding and with Cap Anson at third base; the formation of the American Association and then of the Union Association in the 1880's; the introduction of Sunday baseball; inter-league warfare with cut-rate admission prices and player raiding; the development of the reserve "clause"; the emergence in 1885 of the Brotherhood of Professional Ball Players, and in 1890 of the Players League; the appearance of the American League, or "junior circuit," in 1901, rising from the minor Western Association; the first World Series in 1903, disruption in 1904, and the Series' resumption in 1905; the short-lived Federal League on the majors' scene during World War I years; the troublesome and discouraging episode of the 1919 Series; the home run ball; the shifting of franchises; the expansion of the leagues; the installation in 1965 of the major league draft of potential new players; and the formation of the Major League Baseball Players Association in 1966.

Then there are the many names, celebrated for one reason or another, that have sparked the diamond and its environs and that have provided tinder for recaptured thrills, for reminiscence and comparisons, and for conversation and anticipation in-season and off-season: Ty Cobb, Babe Ruth, Tris Speaker, Walter Johnson, Henry Chadwick, Eddie Collins, Lou Gehrig, Grover Cleveland Alexander, Rogers Hornsby, Harry Hooper, Goose Goslin, Jackie Robinson, Honus Wagner, Joe McCarthy, John McGraw, Deacon Phillippe, Rube Marquard, Christy Mathewson, Tommy Leach, Big Ed Delahanty, Davy Jones, Germany Schaefer,

King Kelly, Big Dan Brouthers, Wahoo Sam Crawford, Wee Willie Keeler, Big Ed Walsh, Jimmy Austin, Fred Snodgrass, Satchel Paige, Hugh Jennings, Fred Merkle, Iron Man McGinnity, Three-Finger Brown, Harry and Stan Coveleski, Connie Mack, Al Bridwell, Red Ruffing, Amos Rusie, Cy Young, Smokey Joe Wood, Chief Meyers, Chief Bender, Bill Klem, Hans Lobert, Johnny Evers, Joe Tinker, Roy Campanela, Miller Huggins, Rube Bressler, Dazzy Vance, Edd Roush, Bill Wambsganess, Clark Griffith, Branch Rickey, Frank Chance, Cap Anson, Nap Lajoie, Sad Sam Jones, Bob O'Farrell, Lefty O'Doul, Bobby Veach, Willie Kamm, Heinie Groh, Lloyd and Paul Waner, Stuffy McInnis, Charles Comiske, Roger Bresnahan, Bill Dickey, Zack Wheat, George Sisler, Charlie Gehringer, Eppa Rixey, Harry Heilmann, Fred Clarke, Dizzy Dean, Hank Greenberg, Pie Traynor, Rube Waddell, Bill Terry, Carl Hubbell, Old Hoss Radbourne, Moe Berg, Rabbit Maranville, Jimmie Foxx, Lefty Grove. The list seems endless.

And one recalls the appropriate reference to the "World Serious," attributed to Ring Lardner, Sr.; Ernest L. Thayer's "Casey at the Bat"; the ring of "Tinker to Evers to Chance"; and all the other happenings, habits, and superstitions about and around baseball that made it the "national pastime" or, depending upon the point of view, "the great American tragedy."

II

The Petitioner

The petitioner, Curtis Charles Flood, born in 1938, began his major league career in 1956 when he signed a contract with the Cincinnati Reds for a salary of $4,000 for the season. He had no attorney or agent to advise him on that occasion. He was traded to the St. Louis Cardinals before the 1958 season. Flood rose to fame as a center fielder with the Cardinals during the years 1958-1969. In those 12, seasons he compiled a batting average of .293. His best offensive season was 1967, when he achieved .335. He was .301 or better in six of the 12 St. Louis years. He participated in the 1964, 1967, and 1968 World Series. He played errorless ball in the field in 1966, and once enjoyed 223 consecutive errorless games. Flood has received seven Golden Glove Awards. He was co-captain of his team from 1965-1969. He ranks among the 10 major league outfielders possessing the highest lifetime fielding averages.

Flood's St. Louis compensation for the years shown was:

1961 $13,500 (including a bonus for signing)
1962 $16,000
1963 $17,500
1964 $23,000
1965 $35,000
1966 $45,000
1967 $50,000
1968 $72,500
1969 $90,000

These figures do not include any so-called fringe benefits or World Series shares.

But, at the age of 31, in October, 1969, Flood was traded to the Philadelphia Phillies of the National League in a multi-player transaction. He was not consulted about the trade. He was informed by telephone and received formal notice only after the deal had been consummated. In December, he complained to the Commissioner of Baseball and asked that he be made a free agent and be placed at liberty to strike his own bargain with any other major league team. His request was denied.

Flood then instituted this antitrust suit in January, 1970, in federal court for the Southern District of New York. The defendants (although not all were named in each cause of action) were the Commissioner of Baseball, the presidents of the two major leagues, and the 24 major league clubs. In general, the complaint charged violations of the federal antitrust laws and civil rights statutes, violation of state statutes and the common law, and the imposition of a form of peonage and involuntary servitude contrary to the Thirteenth Amendment and 42 U.S.C. § 1994, 18 U.S.C. § 1581, and 29 U.S.C. §§ 102 and 103. Petitioner sought declaratory and injunctive relief and treble damages.

Flood declined to play for Philadelphia in 1970, despite a $100,000 salary offer, and he sat out the year. After the season was concluded, Philadelphia sold its rights to Flood to the Washington Senators. Washington and the petitioner were able to come to terms for 1971 at a salary of $110,000. Flood started the season but, apparently because he was dissatisfied with his performance, he left the Washington club on April 27, early in the campaign. He has not played baseball since then.

III

The Present Litigation

Judge Cooper, in a detailed opinion, first denied a preliminary injunction, 309 F. Supp. 793 (SDNY 1970), observing on the way:

"Baseball has been the national pastime for over one hundred years, and enjoys a unique place in our American heritage. Major league professional baseball is avidly followed by millions of fans, looked upon with fervor and pride, and provides a special source of inspiration and competitive team spirit, especially for the young."

"Baseball's status in the life of the nation is so pervasive that it would not strain credulity to say the Court can take judicial notice that baseball is everybody's business. To put it mildly and with restraint, it would be unfortunate indeed if a fine sport and profession, which brings surcease from daily travail and an escape from the ordinary to most inhabitants of this land, were to suffer in the least because of undue concentration by any one or any group on commercial and profit considerations. The game is on higher ground; it behooves every one to keep it there."

309 F. Supp. at 797. Flood's application for an early trial was granted. The court next deferred until trial its decision on the defendants' motions to dismiss the primary causes of action, but granted a defense motion for summary judgment on an additional cause of action. 312 F. Supp. 404 (SDNY 1970).

Trial to the court took place in May and June, 1970. An extensive record was developed. In an ensuing opinion, 316 F. Supp. 271 (SDNY 1970), Judge Cooper first noted that:

"Plaintiff's witnesses in the main concede that some form of reserve on players is a necessary element of the organization of baseball as a league sport, but contend that the present all-embracing system is needlessly restrictive, and offer various alternatives which, in their view, might loosen the bonds without sacrifice to the game...."

"* * * *"

"Clearly, the preponderance of credible proof does not favor elimination of the reserve clause. With the sole exception of plaintiff himself, it shows that even plaintiff's witnesses do not contend that it is wholly undesirable; in fact, they regard substantial portions meritorious...."

316 F. Supp. at 275-276. He then held that *Federal Baseball Club v. National League,* 259 U. S. 200 (1922), and *Toolson v. New York Yankees, Inc.,* 346 U. S. 356 (1953), were controlling; that it was not necessary to reach the issue whether exemption from the antitrust laws would result because aspects of baseball now are a subject of collective bargaining; that the plaintiff's state law claims, those based on common law as well as on statute, were to be denied because baseball was not "a matter which admits of diversity of treatment," 316 F. Supp. at 280; that the involuntary servitude claim failed because of the absence of "the essential element of this cause of action, a showing of compulsory service," 316 F.Supp. at 281-282; and that judgment was to be entered for the defendants. Judge Cooper included a statement of personal conviction to the effect that "negotiations could produce an accommodation on the reserve system which would be eminently fair and equitable to all concerned," and that "the reserve clause can be fashioned so as to find acceptance by player and club." 316 F. Supp. at 282 and 284.

On appeal, the Second Circuit felt "compelled to affirm." 443 F.2d 264, 265 (1971). It regarded the issue of state law as one of first impression, but concluded that the Commerce Clause precluded its application. Judge Moore added a concurring opinion in which he predicted, with respect to the suggested overruling of *Federal Baseball* and *Toolson,* that "there is no likelihood that such an event will occur." 443 F.2d at 268, 272.

We granted certiorari in order to look once again at this troublesome and unusual situation. 404 U.S. 880 (1971).

IV

The Legal Background

A. *Federal Baseball Club v. National League,* 259 U. S. 200 (1922), was a suit for treble damages instituted by a member of the Federal League (Baltimore) against the National and American Leagues and others. The plaintiff obtained a verdict in the trial court, but the Court of Appeals reversed. The main brief filed by the plaintiff with this Court discloses that it was strenuously argued, among other things, that the business in which the defendants were engaged was interstate commerce; that the interstate relationship among the several clubs, located as they were in different States, was predominant; that organized baseball represented an investment of colossal wealth; that it was an engagement in moneymaking; that gate receipts were divided by agreement between the home club and the visiting club; and that the business of baseball was to be distinguished from the mere playing of the game as a sport for physical exercise and diversion. *See also* 259 U.S. at 259 U. S. 201-206.

Mr. Justice Holmes, in speaking succinctly for a unanimous Court, said:

> The business is giving exhibitions of baseball, which are purely state affairs.... But the fact that, in order to give the exhibitions, the Leagues must induce free persons to cross state lines and must arrange and pay for their doing so is not enough to change the character of the business.... [T]he transport is a mere incident, not the essential thing. That to which it is incident, the exhibition, although made for money, would not be called trade or commerce in the commonly accepted use of those words. As it is put by the defendants, personal effort, not related to production, is not a subject of commerce. That which, in its consumption, is not commerce does not become commerce among the States because the transportation that we have mentioned takes place. To repeat the illustrations given by the Court below, a firm of lawyers sending out a member to argue a case, or the Chautauqua lecture bureau sending out lecturers, does not engage in such commerce because the lawyer or lecturer goes to another State.

If we are right, the plaintiff's business is to be described in the same way, and the restrictions by contract that prevented the plaintiff from getting players to break their bargains and the other conduct charged against the defendants were not an interference with commerce among the States.

The Court thus chose not to be persuaded by opposing examples proffered by the plaintiff, among them (a) Judge Learned Hand's decision on a demurrer to a Sherman Act complaint with respect to vaudeville entertainers traveling a theater circuit covering several States, *H. B. Marienelli, Ltd. v. United Booking Offices,* 227 F. 165 (SDNY 1914); (b) the first Mr. Justice Harlan's opinion in *International Textbook Co. v. Pigg,* 217 U. S. 91 (1910), to the effect that correspondence courses pursued through the mail constituted commerce among the States; and (c) Mr. Justice Holmes' own opinion, for another unanimous Court, on demurrer in a Sherman Act case, relating to cattle shipment, the interstate movement of which was interrupted for the finding of purchasers at the stockyards, *Swift & Co. v. United States,* 196 U. S. 375 (1905). The only earlier case the parties were able to locate where the question was raised whether organized baseball was within the Sherman Act was *American League Baseball Club v. Chase,* 86 Misc. 441, 149 N.Y.S. 6 (1914). That court had answered the question in the negative.

B. *Federal Baseball* was cited a year later, and without disfavor, in another opinion by Mr. Justice Holmes for a unanimous Court. The complaint charged antitrust violations with respect to vaudeville bookings. It was held, however, that the claim was not frivolous, and that the bill should not have been dismissed. *Hart v. B. F. Keith Vaudeville Exchange,* 262 U. S. 271 (1923).

It has also been cited, not unfavorably, with respect to the practice of law, *United States v. South-Eastern Underwriters Assn.,* 322 U. S. 533, 322 U. S. 573 (1944) (Stone, C.J., dissenting); with respect to out-of-state contractors, *United States v. Employing Plasterers Assn.,* 347 U. S. 186, 347 U. S. 196-197 (1954) (Minton, J., dissenting); and upon a general comparison reference, *North American Co. v. SEC,* 327 U. S. 686, 327 U. S. 694 (1946).

In the years that followed, baseball continued to be subject to intermittent antitrust attack. The courts, however, rejected these challenges on the authority of Federal Baseball. In some cases stress was laid, although unsuccessfully, on new factors such as the development of radio and television, with their substantial additional revenues to baseball. For the most part, however, the Holmes opinion was generally and necessarily accepted as controlling authority. And in the 1952 Report of the Subcommittee on Study of Monopoly Power of the House Committee on the Judiciary, H.R.Rep. No. 2002, 82d Cong., 2d Sess., 229, it was said, in conclusion:

> On the other hand, the overwhelming preponderance of the evidence established baseball's need for some sort of reserve clause. Baseball's history shows that chaotic conditions

prevailed when there was no reserve clause. Experience points to no feasible substitute to protect the integrity of the game or to guarantee a comparatively even competitive struggle. The evidence adduced at the hearings would clearly not justify the enactment of legislation flatly condemning the reserve clause.

C. The Court granted certiorari, 345 U.S. 963 (1953), in the *Toolson, Kowalski,* and *Corbett* cases, cited in nn. | 12 and S. 258fn13|>13, *supra,* and, by a short per curiam (Warren, C.J., and Black, Frankfurter, DOUGLAS, Jackson, Clark, and Minton, JJ.), affirmed the judgments of the respective courts of appeals in those three cases. *Toolson v. New York Yankees, Inc.,* 346 U. S. 356 (1953). *Federal Baseball* was cited as holding

> that the business of providing public baseball games for profit between clubs of professional baseball players was not within the scope of the federal antitrust laws,

346 U.S. at 346 U. S. 357, and:

> Congress has had the ruling under consideration, but has not seen fit to bring such business under these laws by legislation having prospective effect. The business has thus been left for thirty years to develop on the understanding that it was not subject to existing antitrust legislation. The present cases ask us to overrule the prior decision and, with retrospective effect, hold the legislation applicable. We think that, if there are evils in this field which now warrant application to it of the antitrust laws, it should be by legislation. Without reexamination of the underlying issues, the judgments below are affirmed on the authority of Federal Baseball Club of Baltimore v. National League of Professional Baseball Clubs, supra, so far as that decision determines that Congress had no intention of including the business of baseball within the scope of the federal antitrust laws.

Ibid.

This quotation reveals four reasons for the Court's affirmance of *Toolson* and its companion cases: (a) Congressional awareness for three decades of the Court's ruling in *Federal Baseball,* coupled with congressional inaction. (b) The fact that baseball was left alone to develop for that period upon the understanding that the reserve system was not subject to existing federal antitrust laws. (c) A reluctance to overrule Federal Baseball with consequent retroactive effect. (d) A professed desire that any needed remedy be provided by legislation, rather than by court decree. The emphasis in *Toolson* was on the determination, attributed even to *Federal Baseball,* that Congress had no intention to include baseball within the reach of the federal antitrust laws. Two Justices (Burton and Reed, JJ.) dissented, stressing the factual aspects, revenue sources, and the absence of an express exemption of organized baseball from the Sherman Act. 346 U.S. at 346 U. S. 357. The 1952 congressional study was mentioned. *Id.* at 346 U. S. 358, 346 U. S. 359, 346 U. S. 361.

It is of interest to note that, in *Toolson,* the petitioner had argued flatly that *Federal Baseball* "is wrong, and must be overruled," Brief for Petitioner, No. 18, O.T. 1953, p. 19, and that Thomas Reed Powell, a constitutional scholar of no small stature, urged, as counsel for an *amicus,* that "baseball is a unique enterprise," Brief for Boston American League Base Ball Co. as *Amicus Curiae* 2, and that "unbridled competition as applied to baseball would not be in the public interest." *Id.* at 14.

D. *United States v. Shubert,* 348 U. S. 222 (1955), was a civil antitrust action against defendants engaged in the production of legitimate theatrical attractions throughout the United States and in operating theaters for the presentation of such attractions. The District Court had dismissed the complaint on the authority of *Federal Baseball* and *Toolson.* 120 F. Supp. 15 (SDNY 1953). This Court reversed. Mr. Chief Justice Warren noted the Court's broad conception of "trade or commerce" in the antitrust statutes and the types of enterprises already held to be within the reach of that phrase.

He stated that *Federal Baseball* and *Toolson* afforded no basis for a conclusion that businesses built around the performance of local exhibitions are exempt from the antitrust laws. 348 U.S. at 348 U. S. 227. He then went on to elucidate the holding in *Toolson* by meticulously spelling out the factors mentioned above:

> In Federal Baseball, the Court, speaking through Mr. Justice Holmes, was dealing with the business of baseball and nothing else.... The travel, the Court concluded, was 'a mere incident, not the essential thing.' ...

"* * * *"

"In *Toolson,* where the issue was the same as in *Federal Baseball,* the Court was confronted with a unique combination of circumstances. For over 30 years, there had stood a decision of this Court specifically fixing the status of the baseball business under the antitrust laws, and more particularly the validity of the so-called 'reserve clause.' During this period, in reliance on the *Federal Baseball* precedent, the baseball business had grown and developed.... And Congress, although it had actively considered the ruling, had not seen fit to reject it by amendatory legislation. Against this background, the Court in *Toolson* was asked to overrule *Federal Baseball* on the ground that it was out of step with subsequent decisions reflecting present-day concepts of interstate commerce. The Court, in view of the circumstances of the case, declined to do so. But neither did the Court necessarily reaffirm all that was said in *Federal Baseball.* Instead, '[w]ithout reexamination of the underlying issues,' the Court adhered to *Federal Baseball* so far as that decision determines that Congress had no intention of including the business of baseball within the scope of the federal antitrust laws."

346 U.S. at 346 U. S. 357. In short, *Toolson* was a narrow application of the rule of *stare decisis.*

"... If the *Toolson* holding is to be expanded—or contracted—the appropriate remedy lies with Congress."

348 U.S. at 348 U. S. 228-230.

E. *United States v. International Boxing Club,* 348 U. S. 236 (1955), was a companion to *Shubert,* and was decided the same day. This was a civil antitrust action against defendants engaged in the business of promoting professional championship boxing contests. Here again, the District Court had dismissed the complaint in reliance upon *Federal Baseball* and *Toolson.* The Chief Justice observed that,

"if it were not for *Federal Baseball* and *Toolson,* we think that it would be too clear for dispute that the Government's allegations bring the defendants within the scope of the Act."

348 U.S. at 348 U. S. 240-241. He pointed out that the defendants relied on the two baseball cases, but also would have been content with a more restrictive interpretation of them than the *Shubert* defendants, for the boxing defendants argued that the cases immunized only businesses that involve exhibitions of an athletic nature. The Court accepted neither argument. It again noted, 348 U.S. at 348 U. S. 242, that "*Toolson* neither overruled *Federal Baseball* nor necessarily reaffirmed all that was said in *Federal Baseball.*" It stated:

> The controlling consideration in Federal Baseball and Hart was, instead, a very practical one—the degree of interstate activity involved in the particular business under review. It follows that stare decisis cannot help the defendants here; for, contrary to their argument, Federal Baseball did not hold that all businesses based on professional sports were outside the scope of the antitrust laws. The issue confronting us is, therefore, not whether a previously granted exemption should continue, but whether an exemption should be granted in the first instance. And that issue is for Congress to resolve, not this Court.

348 U.S. at 348 U. S. 243.

The Court noted the presence then in Congress of various bills forbidding the application of the antitrust laws to "organized professional sports enterprises"; the holding of extensive hearings on some of these; subcommittee opposition; a postponement recommendation as to baseball; and the fact that "Congress thus left intact the then-existing coverage of the antitrust laws." 348 U.S. at 348 U. S. 243-244.

Mr. Justice Frankfurter, joined by Mr. Justice Minton, dissented. "It would baffle the subtlest ingenuity," he said,

"to find a single differentiating factor between other sporting exhibitions ... and baseball insofar as the conduct of the sport is relevant to the criteria or considerations by which the Sherman Law becomes applicable to a 'trade or commerce.'"

348 U.S. at 348 U. S. 248. He went on:

"The Court decided as it did in the *Toolson* case as an application of the doctrine of *stare decisis.* That doctrine is not, to be sure, an imprisonment of reason. But neither is it a whimsy. It can hardly be that this Court gave a preferred position to baseball because it is the great American sport.... If *stare decisis* be one aspect of law, as it is, to disregard it in identical situations is mere caprice."

"Congress, on the other hand, may yield to sentiment and be capricious, subject only to due process...."

"Between them, this case and *Shubert* illustrate that nice but rational distinctions are inevitable in adjudication. I agree with the Court's opinion in *Shubert* for precisely the reason that constrains me to dissent in this case."

348 U.S. at 348 U. S. 249-250.

Mr. Justice Minton also separately dissented on the ground that boxing is not trade or commerce. He added the comment that "Congress has not attempted" to control baseball and boxing. 348 U.S. at 348 U. S. 251, 348 U. S. 253. The two dissenting Justices, thus, did not call for the overruling of *Federal Baseball* and *Toolson;* they merely felt that boxing should be under the same umbrella of freedom as was baseball and, as Mr. Justice Frankfurter said, 348 U.S. at 348 U. S. 250, they could not exempt baseball "to the exclusion of every other sport different not one legal jot or tittle from it."

F. The parade marched on. *Radovich v. National Football League,* 352 U. S. 445 (1957), was a civil Clayton Act case testing the application of the antitrust laws to professional football. The District Court dismissed. The Ninth Circuit affirmed in part on the basis of *Federal Baseball* and *Toolson.* The court did not hesitate to "confess that the strength of the pull" of the baseball cases and of *International Boxing* "is about equal," but then observed that "[f]ootball is a team sport" and boxing an individual one. 231 F.2d 620, 622.

This Court reversed with an opinion by Mr. Justice Clark. He said that the Court made its ruling in *Toolson*

"because it was concluded that more harm would be done in overruling *Federal Baseball* than in upholding a ruling which, at best, was of dubious validity."

352 U.S. at 352 U. S. 450. He noted that Congress had not acted. He then said:

"All this, combined with the flood of litigation that would follow its repudiation, the harassment that would ensue, and the retroactive effect of such a decision, led the Court to the practical result that it should sustain the unequivocal line of authority reaching over many years."

"[S]ince *Toolson* and *Federal Baseball* are still cited as controlling authority in antitrust actions involving other fields of business, we now specifically limit the rule there established to the facts there involved, *i.e.,* the business of organized professional baseball. As long as the Congress continues to acquiesce, we should adhere to—but not extend—the interpretation of the Act made in those cases...."

"If this ruling is unrealistic, inconsistent, or illogical, it is sufficient to answer, aside from the distinctions between the businesses, that, were we considering the question of baseball for the first time upon a clean slate, we would have no doubts. But *Federal Baseball* held the business of baseball outside the scope of the Act. No other business claiming the coverage of those cases has such an adjudication. We therefore conclude that the orderly way to eliminate error or discrimination, if any there be, is by legislation, and not by court decision. Congressional processes are more accommodative, affording the whole industry hearings and an opportunity to assist in the formulation of new legislation. The resulting product is therefore more likely to protect the industry and the public alike. The whole scope of congressional action would be known long in advance, and effective dates for the legislation could be set in the future without the injustices of retroactivity and surprise which might follow court action."

352 U.S. at 352 U. S. 450-452 (footnote omitted).

Mr. Justice Frankfurter dissented essentially for the reasons stated in his dissent in *International Boxing,* 352 U.S. at 352 U. S. 455. Mr. Justice Harlan, joined by MR. JUSTICE BRENNAN, also dissented because he, too, was "unable to distinguish football from baseball." 352 U.S. at 352 U. S. 456. Here again, the dissenting Justices did not call for the overruling of the baseball decisions. They merely could not distinguish the two sports, and, out of respect for *stare decisis,,* voted to affirm.

G. Finally, in *Haywood v. National Basketball Assn.,* 401 U. S. 1204 (1971), MR. JUSTICE DOUGLAS, in his capacity as Circuit Justice, reinstated a District Court's injunction *pendente lite* in favor of a professional basketball player and said, "Basketball ... does not enjoy exemption from the antitrust laws." 401 U.S. at 401 U. S. 1205.

H. This series of decisions understandably spawned extensive commentary, some of it mildly critical and much of it not; nearly all of it looked to Congress for any remedy that might be deemed essential.

I. Legislative proposals have been numerous and persistent. Since *Toolson,* more than 50 bills have been introduced in Congress relative to the applicability or nonapplicability of the antitrust laws to baseball. A few of these passed one house or the other. Those that did would have expanded, not restricted, the reserve system's exemption to other professional league sports. And the Act of Sept. 30, 1961, Pub.L. 87-331, 75 Stat. 732, and the merger addition thereto effected by the Act of Nov. 8, 1966, Pub.L. 89-800, § 6(b), 80 Stat. 1515, 15 U.S.C. §§ 1291-1295, were also expansive, rather than restrictive, as to antitrust exemption.

V

In view of all this, it seems appropriate now to say that:

1. Professional baseball is a business, and it is engaged in interstate commerce.

2. With its reserve system enjoying exemption from the federal antitrust laws, baseball is, in a very distinct sense, an exception and an anomaly. *Federal Baseball* and *Toolson* have become an aberration confined to baseball.

3. Even though others might regard this as "unrealistic, inconsistent, or illogical," *see Radovich,* 352 U.S. at 352 U. S. 452, the aberration is an established one, and one that has been recognized not only in *Federal Baseball* and *Toolson,* but in *Shubert, International Boxing,* and *Radovich,* as well, a total of five consecutive cases in this Court. It is an aberration that has been with us now for half a century, one heretofore deemed fully entitled to the benefit of *stare decisis,* and one that has survived the Court's expanding concept of interstate commerce. It rests on a recognition and an acceptance of baseball's unique characteristics and needs.

4. Other professional sports operating interstate—football, boxing, basketball, and, presumably, hockey and golf—are not so exempt.

5. The advent of radio and television, with their consequent increased coverage and additional revenues, has not occasioned an overruling of *Federal Baseball* and *Toolson.*

6. The Court has emphasized that, since 1922, baseball, with full and continuing congressional awareness, has been allowed to develop and to expand unhindered by federal legislative action. Remedial legislation has been introduced repeatedly in Congress, but none has ever been enacted. The Court, accordingly, has concluded that Congress as yet has had no intention to subject baseball's reserve system to the reach of the antitrust statutes. This, obviously, has been deemed to be something other than mere congressional silence and passivity. *Cf. Boys Markets, Inc. v. Retail Clerks Union,* 398 U. S. 235, 398 U. S. 241-242 (1970).

7. The Court has expressed concern about the confusion and the retroactivity problems that inevitably would result with a judicial overturning of *Federal Baseball.* It has voiced a preference that, if any change is to be made, it come by legislative action that, by its nature, is only prospective in operation.

8. The Court noted in *Radovich,* 352 U.S. at 352 U. S. 452, that the slate with respect to baseball is not clean. Indeed, it has not been clean for half a century.

This emphasis and this concern are still with us. We continue to be loath, 50 years after *Federal Baseball* and almost two decades after *Toolson,* to overturn those cases judicially when Congress, by its positive inaction, has allowed those decisions to stand for so long and, far beyond mere inference and implication, has clearly evinced a desire not to disapprove them legislatively.

Accordingly, we adhere once again to *Federal Baseball* and *Toolson,* and to their application to professional baseball. We adhere also to *International Boxing* and *Radovich,* and to their respective applications to professional boxing and professional football. If there is any inconsistency or illogic in all this, it is an inconsistency and illogic of long standing that is to be remedied by the Congress, and not by this Court. If we were to act otherwise, we would be withdrawing from the conclusion as to congressional intent made in *Toolson* and from the concerns as to retrospectivity therein expressed. Under these circumstances, there is merit in consistency, even though some might claim that beneath that consistency is a layer of inconsistency.

The petitioner's argument as to the application of state antitrust laws deserves a word. Judge Cooper rejected the state law claims because state antitrust regulation would conflict with federal policy and because national "uniformity [is required] in any regulation of baseball and its reserve system." 316 F. Supp. at 280. The Court of Appeals, in affirming, stated,

"[A]s the burden on interstate commerce outweighs the states' interests in regulating baseball's reserve system, the Commerce Clause precludes the application here of state antitrust law."

443 F.2d at 268. As applied to organized baseball, and in the light of this Court's observations and holdings in *Federal Baseball*, in *Toolson*, in *Shubert*, in *International Boxing*, and in *Radovich*, and despite baseball's allegedly inconsistent position taken in the past with respect to the application of state law, these statements adequately dispose of the state law claims.

The conclusion we have reached makes it unnecessary for us to consider the respondents' additional argument that the reserve system is a mandatory subject of collective bargaining and that federal labor policy therefore exempts the reserve system from the operation of federal antitrust laws.

We repeat for this case what was said in *Toolson*:

"Without reexamination of the underlying issues, the [judgment] below [is] affirmed on the authority of *Federal Baseball Club of Baltimore v. National League of Professional Baseball Clubs, supra,* so far as that decision determines that Congress had no intention of including the business of baseball within the scope of the federal antitrust laws."

346 U.S. at 346 U. S. 357. And what the Court said in *Federal Baseball* in 1922, and what it said in *Toolson* in 1953, we say again here in 1972: the remedy, if any is indicated, is for congressional, and not judicial, action.

The judgment of the Court of Appeals is

Affirmed.

MR. JUSTICE WHITE joins in the judgment of the Court, and in all but Part I of the Court's opinion.

MR. JUSTICE POWELL took no part in the consideration or decision of this case.

MR. JUSTICE DOUGLAS, with whom MR. JUSTICE BRENNAN concurs, dissenting

This Court's decision in *Federal Baseball Club v. National League,* 259 U. S. 200, made in 1922, is a derelict in the stream of the law that we, its creator, should remove. Only a romantic view of a rather dismal business account over the last 50 years would keep that derelict in midstream.

In 1922, the Court had a narrow, parochial view of commerce. With the demise of the old landmarks of that era, particularly *United States v. Knight Co.,* 156 U. S. 1, *Hammer v. Dagenhart,* 247 U. S. 251, and *Paul v. Virginia,* 8 Wall. 168, the whole concept of commerce has changed.

Under the modern decisions such as *Mandeville Island Farms v. American Crystal Sugar Co.,* 334 U. S. 219; *United States v. Darby,* 312 U. S. 100; *Wickard v. Filburn,* 317 U. S. 111; *United States v. South-Eastern Underwriters Assn.,* 322 U. S. 533, the power of Congress was recognized as broad enough to reach all phases of the vast operations of our national industrial system.

An industry so dependent on radio and television as is baseball and gleaning vast interstate revenues (*see* H.R.Rep. No. 2002, 82d Cong., 2d Sess., 4, 5 (1952)) would be hard put today to say with the Court in the *Federal Baseball* Club case that baseball was only a local exhibition, not trade or commerce.

Baseball is today big business that is packaged with beer, with broadcasting, and with other industries. The beneficiaries of the *Federal Baseball* Club decision are not the Babe Ruths, Ty Cobbs, and Lou Gehrigs.

The owners, whose records many say reveal a proclivity for predatory practices, do not come to us with equities. The equities are with the victims of the reserve clause. I use the word "victims" in the Sherman Act sense, since a contract which forbids anyone to practice his calling is commonly called an unreasonable restraint of trade. *Gardella v. Chandler,* 172 F.2d 402 (CA2). *And see Haywood v. National Basketball Assn.,* 401 U. S. 1204 (DOUGLAS, J., in chambers).

If congressional inaction is our guide, we should rely upon the fact that Congress has refused to enact bills broadly exempting professional sports from antitrust regulation. H.R.Rep. No. 2002, 82d Cong., 2d Sess. (1952). The only statutory exemption granted by Congress to professional sports concerns broadcasting rights. 15 U.S.C. §§ 1291-1295. I would not ascribe a broader exemption through inaction than Congress has seen fit to grant explicitly.

There can be no doubt "that, were we considering the question of baseball for the first time upon a clean slate" we would hold it to be subject to federal antitrust regulation. *Radovich v. National Football League*, 352 U. S. 445, 352 U. S. 452. The unbroken silence of Congress should not prevent us from correcting our own mistakes.

Glossary

antitrust laws: laws that prohibit agreements and conspiracies, such as price fixing, boycotts, and rigging bids, that are intended to restrain trade and commerce

commerce clause: a section of the Constitution (Article 1, Section 8, Clause 3) that grants Congress the power to regulate interstate business and trade

stare decisis: the principle of honoring legal precedent

FURMAN V. GEORGIA

DATE 1972 **AUTHOR** William O. Douglas, William Brennan, Thurgood Marshall, Potter Stewart, Byron White **VOTE** 5–4	**CITATION** 408 U.S. 238 **SIGNIFICANCE** Held that held that the imposition of the death penalty in this case constituted cruel and unusual punishment and thus violated the Eighth Amendment of the Constitution

Overview

One of the most monumental and controversial decisions in history, the three cases that made up the *Furman v. Georgia* decision declared that capital punishment, as then practiced, amounted to an unconstitutional violation of the Eighth Amendment's prohibition on cruel and unusual punishments. The decision, which caught the nation by surprise, was so contested within the Supreme Court that nine separate opinions were filed. Five justices—William O. Douglas, William Brennan, Thurgood Marshall, Potter Stewart, and Byron White—agreed that the death penalty as administered was unconstitutional, though for different reasons; none of the five signed any other's concurring opinion. Four justices—Chief Justice Warren Burger, Harry Blackmun, Lewis Powell, and William Rehnquist—found that the death penalty as administered was compatible with the Eighth Amendment and dissented from the majority's opinion.

The petitioners were three African American men convicted for murder and rape in state courts in Georgia and Texas. The issue of federalism, which weighs the relative rights of state governments and the federal government, was important in this case because statutes in the two states mandated that juries determine whether the death sentence was to be applied. The Court took up the question, then, of whether the Eighth Amendment barring "cruel and unusual punishment" applied to the states. The Court sent the case back to the lower courts for reconsideration while holding that the death penalty did, in fact, violate the Eighth and Fourteenth Amendments. The Court's reasoning was that capital punishment was applied in a discretionary, haphazard, and discriminatory way because it was imposed in a small number of total possible cases and primarily against certain minority groups. This case resulted in the suspension of capital punishment in the United States for a few years.

Context

A Georgia resident woke in the middle of the night to find William Henry Furman in the act of burglarizing his house. After his arrest, Furman would state that while he was trying to escape, he tripped and his gun accidentally fired, killing the resident; this statement,

Thurgood Marshall, along with William J. Brennan, concluded that the death penalty was "cruel and unusual punishment."
(Library of Congress)

however, contradicted an earlier statement he made to police that he turned and fired blindly in the direction of the victim. Because the shooting took place during the commission of a felony, the felony murder rule applied. Furman was tried for murder, found guilty, and sentenced to death. At the Supreme Court level, Furman's case was consolidated with that of *Jackson v. Georgia*. The defendant was Lucius Jackson, who committed rape in the process of committing an armed robbery. The third case was *Branch v. Texas*, a case in which Elmer Branch was convicted of rape. In all three cases, the defendants were African Americans, and in all three an appellate court affirmed their convictions and death sentences.

The U.S. Supreme Court agreed to hear the cases and to address the question: "Does the imposition and carrying out of the death penalty in [these cases] constitute cruel and unusual punishment in violation of the Eighth and Fourteenth Amendments?" The Court concluded that it did. Because of the immense significance of the case, each of the Court's nine justices issued an opinion outlining his reasoning. The fact that the Court was fragmented in this way and that it issued a per curiam decision suggests that the coalition that voted to declare the death penalty unconstitutional—at least as it was imposed in these cases—was shaky. Justices William O. Douglas, William J. Brennan Jr., and Thurgood Marshall concluded that *any* application of the death penalty constituted cruel and unusual punishment. Justice Potter Stewart did not reject the death penalty entirely, but he argued that it had to be imposed more fairly and rationally. Justice Byron R. White argued that the infrequency of execution prevented it from functioning as an effective deterrent and from meeting the societal need for retribution. Dissents were filed by Chief Justice Warren E. Burger and Justices Harry A. Blackmun, Lewis F. Powell Jr., and William H. Rehnquist. All argued that the Court was intruding on matters properly delegated to state legislatures and that the justices' private opinions about the morality of the death penalty should not be turned into a matter of public policy.

About the Author

William O. Douglas

In William O. Douglas's years on the bench, a variety of cases came before the Supreme Court that fundamentally affected American public life and the concepts of individual and civil rights. His long tenure was also marked by major international conflicts, such as World War II, the Cold War, and the Vietnam War, as well as major domestic movements, notably the civil rights movement. His opinions demonstrate his judicial priorities—protection of civil and individual rights, including the right to privacy; near-absolute deference to the First Amendment; and environmental protection—and show how he sought to fit his opinions to what he saw as the social reality that underlay the question. Douglas addressed cases not just from within the narrow confines of case-law precedent but also from what he saw as the social ramifications of the particular questions contested in the cases.

Douglas was one of the more idiosyncratic and naturally contrarian justices ever to serve on the Supreme Court. In his more than thirty-six years on the bench, Douglas authored 531 dissents, more than any other justice. His legal philosophy was strongly influenced by Underhill Moore, his professor at Columbia Law School and one of the most prominent of the legal realists, and by Louis D. Brandeis, the justice whose place Douglas took on the Supreme Court. From these two, he learned to draw upon sources as varied as poetry, sociology, agricultural reports, or his own intuition and to use these sources to justify his decisions, reflecting the realist belief that "real world" information needed to be considered in rendering legal decisions rather than relying exclusively on legal precedent. Douglas was known as a liberal throughout his tenure on the Court. In the 1930s he strongly supported President Franklin Roosevelt's New Deal program, the legislative and governmental reorganization measures aimed at alleviating the Great Depression. He also was generally a consistent civil libertarian, though he grew into that role haltingly during World War II.

Douglas is often said to have been an ecologist before there was such a thing, and his love of nature and the unspoiled wilderness was evident in several notable opinions in major Supreme Court cases. Washington's William O. Douglas National Wilderness is named in his honor, in recognition of his efforts on behalf of the environment. Spending so much time in the outdoors sharpened Douglas's appreciation for unspoiled nature, which he maintained for the remainder of his life, intervening personally to save the Chesapeake and Ohio Canal from being turned into a highway and prompting some of Douglas's more controversial opinions on behalf of environmental concerns.

Douglas was born on October 16, 1898, in Maine, Minnesota, the son of Julia Fisk Douglas and the Reverend William Douglas. Following her husband's death in 1904, Julia moved the family to Yakima, Washington, where she purchased a small home before losing much of the family's money in a failed land investment. Growing up poor and working odd jobs from the age of seven on, Douglas developed an appreciation for hard work and a strong sense of class justice that later expressed itself in his belief that all citizens should be entitled to the rights and privileges afforded the wealthy. Douglas went to nearby Whitman College, where he graduated in 1920. After spending time teaching, he enrolled at Columbia Law School in 1922. Douglas took on several jobs at Columbia, including assisting with the compilation of case law books, a task for which he was unqualified. The intellectual vigor he employed in the task was indicative of the engagement with which an interested Douglas would approach problems on the bench.

After graduating from Columbia, Douglas floated through several positions over the next decade, including two stints at a Wall Street law firm and positions on both the Columbia and Yale faculties. There he developed more fully his appreciation for legal realism, which he had first encountered as a student at Columbia. This belief that the law as traditionally practiced was too distant from "real life" and needed to be supplemented with empirical studies from other disciplines, such as sociology, psychology, and economics, strongly influenced Douglas's legal thought process, which in turn influenced his decisions on the Supreme Court. He was appointed to the Supreme Court in 1939, after serving as chairman of the Securities and Exchange Commission.

Douglas's approach and his willingness to sidestep judicial precedent in coming to his decisions made him a frequent—and sometimes justified—target of critics, who charged him with judicial activism. Douglas would set several records while on the bench, including the longest tenure. Throughout that time, he was the most consistently liberal justice, the steadiest civil libertarian, and the justice most willing to rule against corporate interests in favor of individuals or the environment. Nonetheless, he is widely viewed as having done liberal causes as much harm as good because he relied more on his own views in formulating his legal opinions than on case law precedents or an articulated legal philosophy. As a result, his impact was more limited than it otherwise could have been, and he left behind no theoretical legacy that succeeding justices could follow.

Thurgood Marshall

Thurgood Marshall's life spanned a momentous period in American history, from the entrenched segregation of the early twentieth century to the post–civil rights movement after the middle of the century in which discrimination grievances became incorporated into formal legal structures. It is noteworthy that it was Marshall, the grandchild of enslaved African Americans, who played a crucial role in affording civil rights the protection of the law. As an attorney for the National Association for the Advancement of Colored People (NAACP), he was a prime advocate of legal strategies that ushered in an integrated American society. As an associate Supreme Court justice, Marshall continued his passion for correcting some of the practices he viewed as systemically discriminatory.

Marshall, whose grandfathers were both born enslaved but became freemen, was the first African American U.S. Supreme Court justice. He was born on July 2, 1908, in Baltimore, Maryland, and his life spanned years during which segregation existed both in law and in practice. His formative experiences in Baltimore played an important role in his strong belief as an adult in the importance of the rule of law and the possibilities the U.S. Constitution held in advancing integration and protecting the rights of racial minorities. He did as much as perhaps any single American to create a post-segregation society.

In 1925 Marshall enrolled at the historically Black Lincoln University in Pennsylvania. After graduation, he hoped to attend the University of Maryland law school but was denied admission because of his race, so he enrolled in law school at Howard University, where he came under the tutelage of its highly regarded dean, Charles Hamilton Houston. Houston trained his law students in the art of legal argumentation and litigation strategy, focusing on defending the civil rights of African Americans. After graduating from Howard in 1933, Marshall moved to New York City, which was then a dynamic mecca of African American culture and politics. There he was exposed to diverse viewpoints and backgrounds and served first as a staff attorney and then as the legal director of the NAACP. By 1940 Marshall had risen to become the NAACP's chief counsel.

Marshall, an ardent integrationist, was a key architect of the legal strategy behind modern American civil rights. During his years at the NAACP, he litigated dozens of important legal challenges to segregation, building a base of experience as well as court rulings that would eventually lead to the end of legal segregation. It was Marshall's life goal to overturn the "separate but equal" doctrine enshrined in *Plessy v. Ferguson* (1896), a case in which the U.S. Supreme Court ruled that racial segregation of public railroad cars was legal because, presumably, the cars occupied for Blacks were "equal" to those reserved for white travelers. He worked closely with Houston in creating the legal strategy that dismantled the *Plessy* doctrine. A half century after *Plessy*, the Court issued its landmark decision in *Brown v. Board of Education of Topeka* (1954), holding that segregated public schools violated the U.S. Constitution. Marshall built the legal strategy behind *Brown* and, in a watershed moment in American history, successfully argued the case before the U.S. Supreme Court. Although the post-*Brown* years found the civil rights movement battling de facto segregation in the schools (that is, segregation that existed "in fact" rather than by law), Marshall continued to lend a guiding hand first as a justice on the U.S. Court of Appeals for the Second Circuit and later as a Supreme Court justice.

In 1967 President Lyndon B. Johnson nominated Marshall to the U.S. Supreme Court. Although his confirmation hearing was at times contentious, with conservative southern senators attempting to portray Marshall as a Communist sympathizer, his confirmation was secured with some intervention on the part of Johnson, a gifted parliamentarian and backroom dealer. As a member of the highest appeals court in the United States, he would be reviewing cases that would become the legal progeny of holdings he had played a role in as an advocate. At the same time, Marshall's tenure on the Supreme Court, which lasted until 1991, coincided with a powerful backlash against some of the legal gains made during the civil rights movement, which served to create a complex jurisprudence on race. Marshall died on January 24, 1993, in Washington, D.C.

Explanation and Analysis of the Document

William O. Douglas: Concurrence

Douglas's concurrence in *Furman v. Georgia* is typically far-ranging, extending its consideration to the development of English law back to the Norman conquest of 1066. He notes that the English Bill of Rights (1689), from which the Eighth Amendment derives its language, was intended to prohibit discriminatory application of harsh penalties. He further states that the United States had a history of including prohibitions against cruel and unusual punishments in state constitutions and other legally determinative documents prior to the adoption of the Bill of Rights in 1791. Douglas argues, however, that this history is unhelpful in determining what constitutes a cruel or unusual punishment, the question at the center of *Furman*.

For Douglas, the term "cruel and unusual" clearly refers to punishments deemed "barbaric," but he goes further and states that it is cruel and unusual to apply the death penalty disproportionately to minorities or social outcasts. This is a critical insight and one that he bases on the findings of the President's Commission on Law Enforcement and the Administration of Justice, which found that the death penalty was disproportionately imposed on the poor, on African Americans, and on "unpopular groups," groups that Douglas had been defending from the bench for several decades. In driving the point home, he makes sure to mention that each of the defendants in the three cases under consideration was Black and that the victims were white. Douglas also wonders whether anyone can find a wealthy person in American history who was executed for his or her crimes or whether the execution rolls were exclusively populated by those from lower economic classes.

On January 21, 1972, after hearing oral arguments in *Furman*, the nine justices convened to discuss the case among the entire assembled Court, the only time they would do so during their deliberations, speaking in order of seniority. Chief Justice Warren Burger explained that he did not see a constitutional problem with the death penalty and would vote to uphold the sentences. Douglas, speaking second as the longest-serving member of the Court, declared that he did not believe that the death penalty as applied passed constitutional muster and that he would vote against it. In so doing, he was the first justice to cast a vote against the death penalty in *Furman*. By addressing the issue of the racial disparities in application, as Douglas did in that conference and at length in his opinion, he stood far ahead of his colleagues on the bench. Although Brennan and Marshall declared their belief that the death penalty violated the Eighth Amendment and thus was unconstitutional in all cases, neither of them considered the racially discriminatory application of the penalty in their opinions. Neither did White or Stewart, both of whom wrote in concurrence on the basis of the capriciousness with which the death penalty was arbitrarily applied. Only Douglas was willing to look at the facts surrounding the use of the death penalty and declare his opposition based on the inequitable application of the penalty based on race. This discrimination was for him "incontestable," and he declared that any penalty that can be shown to be discriminatorily applied, whether on the basis of the defendant's race, religion, social position, class or wealth, is inherently cruel and unusual and thus unconstitutional.

Thurgood Marshall: Concurrence

In the case of *Furman v. Georgia*, the Supreme Court addressed the legal question of whether the imposition of the death penalty amounted to "cruel and unusual punishment" in violation of the Eighth and Fourteenth Amendments to the Constitution. This was an issue close to Marshall's heart because, as NAACP counsel, he had seen firsthand that the death penalty sentencing rate for African Americans, particularly when the victims were white, was disproportionately high. Marshall expended a significant amount of energy speaking to his colleagues on the Court about this issue and was successful in forming a majority bloc.

In his concurrence, Marshall clarified that his position against the death penalty was not meant to condone or mitigate the conduct for which the petitioners had been convicted. Quoting Austin Gardiner, England's lord chancellor (the head of Britain's legal profession), Marshall states that "the question then is not whether we condone rape or murder, for surely we do not; it is whether capital punishment is 'a punishment no longer consistent with our own self-respect' and, therefore, in violation of the Eighth Amendment." Marshall then argues that the Founding Fathers' original intent in the Eighth Amendment was to prohibit torture and "other cruel punishments." He provides a historical accounting of the emergence of the Eighth Amendment, its derivation from English law, and the practices (such as torture) that led to its passage. He connects the arguments made in the sixteenth century—that the Magna Carta (the English legal charter dating to 1215) prohibited the "cruel and barbarous" practice of torture by English ecclesiastical (church) courts—to what he viewed as such protections in the U.S. Constitution. Marshall notes that the language of the Eighth Amendment's prohibition on "cruel and unusual" punishment originated from the English Bill of Rights of 1689. He states that whether the English Bill of Rights prohibited cruel and unusual punishments because of excessive or illegal punishments, in reaction to barbaric forms of punishment, or both, the Founders of the United States clearly borrowed the language of the English Bill of Rights and included it in the Eighth Amendment to outlaw not only torture but also other cruel punishments. He then reviews historical precedent on the meaning and application of the Eighth Amendment's prohibition on "cruel and unusual" punishment.

Marshall argues that the most important principle in analyzing what was "cruel and unusual" was evolving standards. Thus, a penalty that was permissible at one time in history is not necessarily permissible later. He provides precedent for this concept by arguing that though prior courts may have held that the death penalty was not cruel and unusual, they had allowed that this view could change based on contemporary public opinion. Marshall states that although prior courts and individual justices may have held that the death penalty is constitutional, the current Court was not bound by that view. He emphasizes this point by noting that "the very nature of the Eighth Amendment would dictate that unless a very recent decision existed, *stare decisis* [the obligation of courts to follow precedent] would bow to changing values, and the question of the constitutionality of capital punishment at a given moment in history would remain open." Marshall's early experience at the NAACP in defending cases involving charges of rape against African American men provided some of his motivation for ending what he perceived as an inequitably applied sentencing measure. But in his intricately written concurrence, Marshall emphasizes that this was an argument based on principle, one premised on a lifelong view that the Constitution should be an arbiter of fairness.

Impact

It must be emphasized that the Court's ruling pertained to the particular cases before it and was based on the Court's conclusion that the death penalty was being imposed in an arbitrary and capricious manner. In other words, it was not the death penalty itself that that the Court declared unconstitutional. Rather, it was the seemingly capricious manner in which it was imposed. The decision had the effect of rendering state death penalty statutes void and essentially imposing a moratorium on executions, which fell to historic lows during the mid-1970s—in many states, to zero. That moratorium was in effect lifted in 1976 in the case of *Gregg v. Georgia*. In that case, the Court ruled that death penalty statutes that provided for a bifurcated trial in capital cases—that is, a trial to determine guilt or innocence, and a separate trial to determine the sentence—were constitutional. Meanwhile, states had rewritten their laws in accordance with *Furman* guidelines to make it more likely that sentencing guidelines reflected rational standards for when capital punishment was to be imposed and when it was not.

In the 2010s, the number of persons executed in the United States reached historic lows. The number was just twenty in 2016, twenty-three in 2017. These numbers are down from a modern historic high of ninety-eight executions in 1999. Since the year 1700, nearly 15,800 persons have been executed in the United States.

Questions for Further Study

1. Did the Court prohibit capital punishment as a result of its ruling?

2. On what basis did the Court overturn the conviction of Furman and the other men?

3. What was the connection between this case and the Eighth Amendment to the Constitution? To the Fourteenth Amendment?

4. How did the states respond to the Court's ruling in this case?

Further Reading

Books

Gershman, Gary P. *Death Penalty on Trial: A Handbook with Cases, Laws, and Documents.* Santa Barbara, CA: ABC-CLIO, 2005.

Herda, D. J. *Furman v. Georgia: The Death Penalty Case.* Berkeley Heights, NJ: Enslow Publishers, 2010.

Oshinsky, David M. *Capital Punishment on Trial: Furman v. Georgia and the Death Penalty in Modern America.* Lawrence: University Press of Kansas, 2010.

Roensch, Greg. *Furman v. Georgia: Cruel and Unusual Punishment.* New York: Chelsea House, 2007.

Articles

"Cruel and Unusual Punishment: The Death Penalty Cases: *Furman v. Georgia, Jackson v. Georgia, Branch v. Texas*, 408 U.S. 238 (1972)," *Journal of Criminal Law and Criminology* 63, no. 4 (1973): 484–92.

Lahey, Kathleen A., and Lewis M. Sang. "Constitutional Law—The Remains of the Death Penalty: *Furman v. Georgia.*" *DePaul Law Review* 22, no. 2 (Winter 1973): 481–98.

Tao, L. S. "Beyond *Furman v. Georgia*: The Need for a Morally Based Decision on Capital Punishment. *Notre Dame Law Review* 51 (April 1976): 722–36.

—Commentary by Anthony Santoro, Michael Chang, and Michael J. O'Neal

Furman v. Georgia

Document Text

Per Curiam

Petitioner in No. 69-5003 was convicted of murder in Georgia, and was sentenced to death pursuant to Ga. Code Ann. § 26-1005 (Supp. 1971) (effective prior to July 1, 1969). 225 Ga. 253, 167 S.E.2d 628 (1969). Petitioner in No. 69-5030 was convicted of rape in Georgia, and was sentenced to death pursuant to Ga. Code Ann. § 26-1302 (Supp. 1971) (effective prior to July 1, 1969). 225 Ga. 790, 171 S.D.2d 501 (1969). Petitioner in No. 69-5031 was convicted of rape in Texas, and was sentenced to death pursuant to Tex. Penal Code, Art. 1189 (1961). 447 S.W.2d 932 (Ct. Crim. App. 1969). Certiorari was granted limited to the following question: Does the imposition and carrying out of the death penalty in [these cases] constitute cruel and unusual punishment in violation of the Eighth and Fourteenth Amendments? 403 U.S. 952 (1971). The Court holds that the imposition and carrying out of the death penalty in these cases constitute cruel and unusual punishment in violation of the Eighth and Fourteenth Amendments. The judgment in each case is therefore reversed insofar as it leaves undisturbed the death sentence imposed, and the cases are remanded for further proceedings.

So ordered.

William O. Douglas: Concurrence

In these three cases the death penalty was imposed, one of them for murder, and two for rape. In each, the determination of whether the penalty should be death or a lighter punishment was left by the State to the discretion of the judge or of the jury. In each of the three cases, the trial was to a jury. They are here on petitions for certiorari which we granted limited to the question whether the imposition and execution of the death penalty constitute "cruel and unusual punishment" within the meaning of the Eighth Amendment as applied to the States by the Fourteenth. I vote to vacate each judgment, believing that the exaction of the death penalty does violate the Eighth and Fourteenth Amendments.

That the requirements of due process ban cruel and unusual punishment is now settled....

It has been assumed in our decisions that punishment by death is not cruel, unless the manner of execution can be said to be inhuman and barbarous. It is also said in our opinions that the proscription of cruel and unusual punishments "is not fastened to the obsolete, but may acquire meaning as public opinion becomes enlightened by a humane justice." A like statement was made in *Trop v. Dulles*, that the Eighth Amendment "must draw its meaning from the evolving standards of decency that mark the progress of a maturing society."

The generality of a law inflicting capital punishment is one thing. What may be said of the validity of a law on the books and what may be done with the law in its application do, or may, lead to quite different conclusions.

It would seem to be incontestable that the death penalty inflicted on one defendant is "unusual" if it discriminates against him by reason of his race, religion, wealth, social position, or class, or if it is imposed under a procedure that gives room for the play of such prejudices.

There is evidence that the provision of the English Bill of Rights of 1689, from which the language of the Eighth Amendment was taken, was concerned primarily with selective or irregular application of harsh penalties, and that its aim was to forbid arbitrary and discriminatory penalties of a severe nature:

> Following the Norman conquest of England in 1066, the old system of penalties, which ensured equality between crime and punishment, suddenly disappeared. By the time systematic judicial records were kept, its demise was almost complete. With the exception of certain grave crimes for which the punishment was death or outlawry, the arbitrary fine was replaced by a discretionary amercement. Although amercement's discretionary character allowed the circumstances of each case to be taken into account, and the level of cash penalties to be decreased or increased accordingly, the amercement presented an opportunity for excessive or oppressive fines.

The problem of excessive amercements became so prevalent that three chapters of the Magna Carta were devoted to their regulation. Maitland said of Chapter 14 that, 'very likely, there was no clause in the Magna Carta more grateful to the mass of the people.' Chapter 14 clearly stipulated as fundamental law a prohibition of excessiveness in punishments:

A free man shall not be amerced for a trivial offence, except in accordance with the degree of the offence, and for a serious offence, he shall be amerced according to its gravity, saving his livelihood; and a merchant likewise, saving his merchandise; in the same way, a villein shall be amerced saving his wainage, if they fall into our mercy. And none of the aforesaid amercements shall be imposed except by the testimony of reputable men of the neighborhood.

The English Bill of Rights, enacted December 16, 1689, stated that "excessive bail ought not to be required, nor excessive fines imposed, nor cruel and unusual punishments inflicted." These were the words chosen for our Eighth Amendment. A like provision had been in Virginia's Constitution of 1776, and in the constitutions of seven other States. The Northwest Ordinance, enacted under the Articles of Confederation, included a prohibition of cruel and unusual punishments. But the debates of the First Congress on the Bill of Rights throw little light on its intended meaning. . . .

The words "cruel and unusual" certainly include penalties that are barbaric. But the words, at least when read in light of the English proscription against selective and irregular use of penalties, suggest that it is "cruel and unusual" to apply the death penalty—or any other penalty—selectively to minorities whose numbers are few, who are outcasts of society, and who are unpopular, but whom society is willing to see suffer though it would not countenance general application of the same penalty across the board. . . .

There is increasing recognition of the fact that the basic theme of equal protection is implicit in "cruel and unusual" punishments. "A penalty . . . should be considered unusually imposed if it is administered arbitrarily or discriminatorily." The same authors add that "[t]he extreme rarity with which applicable death penalty provisions are put to use raises a strong inference of arbitrariness." The President's Commission on Law Enforcement and Administration of Justice recently concluded:

> Finally, there is evidence that the imposition of the death sentence and the exercise of dispensing power by the courts and the executive follow discriminatory patterns. The death sentence is disproportionately imposed, and carried out on the poor, the Negro, and the members of unpopular groups.

A study of capital cases in Texas from 1924 to 1968 reached the following conclusions:

"Application of the death penalty is unequal: most of those executed were poor, young, and ignorant." . . .

"Seventy-five of the 460 cases involved codefendants, who, under Texas law, were given separate trials. In several instances where a white and a Negro were co-defendants, the white was sentenced to life imprisonment or a term of years, and the Negro was given the death penalty."

"Another ethnic disparity is found in the type of sentence imposed for rape. The Negro convicted of rape is far more likely to get the death penalty than a term sentence, whereas whites and Latins are far more likely to get a term sentence than the death penalty."

Warden Lewis E. Lawes of Sing Sing said:

> Not only does capital punishment fail in its justification, but no punishment could be invented with so many inherent defects. It is an unequal punishment in the way it is applied to the rich and to the poor. The defendant of wealth and position never goes to the electric chair or to the gallows. Juries do not intentionally favour the rich, the law is theoretically impartial, but the defendant with ample means is able to have his case presented with every favourable aspect, while the poor defendant often has a lawyer assigned by the court. Sometimes such assignment is considered part of political patronage; usually the lawyer assigned has had no experience whatever in a capital case.

Former Attorney General Ramsey Clark has said, "It is the poor, the sick, the ignorant, the powerless and the hated who are executed. One searches our chronicles in vain for the execution of any member of the affluent strata of this society. The Leopolds and Loebs are given prison terms, not sentenced to death.

"Jackson, a black, convicted of the rape of a white woman, was 21 years old...

"Furman, a black, killed a householder while seeking to enter the home at night...

"Branch, a black, entered the rural home of a 65-year-old widow, a white, while she slept and raped her, holding his arm against her throat...

> We cannot say from facts disclosed in these records that these defendants were sentenced to death because they were black. Yet our task is not restricted to an effort to divine what motives impelled these death penalties. Rather, we deal with a system of law and of justice that leaves to the uncontrolled discretion of judges or juries the determination whether defendants committing these crimes should die or be imprisoned. Under these laws, no standards govern the selection of the penalty. People live or die, dependent on the whim of one man or of 12....

Those who wrote the Eighth Amendment knew what price their forebears had paid for a system based not on equal justice, but on discrimination. In those days, the target was not the blacks or the poor, but the dissenters, those who opposed absolutism in government, who struggled for a parliamentary regime, and who opposed governments' recurring efforts to foist a particular religion on the people. But the tool of capital punishment was used with vengeance against the opposition and those unpopular with the regime. One cannot read this history without realizing that the desire for equality was reflected in the ban against "cruel and unusual punishments" contained in the Eighth Amendment.

In a Nation committed to equal protection of the laws there is no permissible "caste" aspect of law enforcement. Yet we know that the discretion of judges and juries in imposing the death penalty enables the penalty to be selectively applied, feeding prejudices against the accused if he is poor and despised, and lacking political clout, or if he is a member of a suspect or unpopular minority, and saving those who by social position may be in a more protected position. In ancient Hindu law, a Brahman was exempt from capital punishment, and, under that law, "[g]enerally, in the law books, punishment increased in severity as social status diminished." We have, I fear, taken in practice the same position, partially as a result of making the death penalty discretionary and partially as a result of the ability of the rich to purchase the services of the most respected and most resourceful legal talent in the Nation.

The high service rendered by the "cruel and unusual" punishment clause of the Eighth Amendment is to require legislatures to write penal laws that are even-handed, nonselective, and nonarbitrary, and to require judges to see to it that general laws are not applied sparsely, selectively, and spottily to unpopular groups.

A law that stated that anyone making more than $50,000 would be exempt from the death penalty would plainly fall, as would a law that in terms said that blacks, those who never went beyond the fifth grade in school, those who made less than $3,000 a year, or those who were unpopular or unstable should be the only people executed. A law which, in the overall view, reaches that result in practice has no more sanctity than a law which in terms provides the same.

Thus, these discretionary statutes are unconstitutional in their operation. They are pregnant with discrimination, and discrimination is an ingredient not compatible with the idea of equal protection of the laws that is implicit in the ban on "cruel and unusual" punishments.

Any law which is nondiscriminatory on its face may be applied in such a way as to violate the Equal Protection Clause of the Fourteenth Amendment. Such conceivably might be the fate of a mandatory death penalty, where equal or lesser sentences were imposed on the elite, a harsher one on the minorities or members of the lower castes. Whether a mandatory death penalty would otherwise be constitutional is a question I do not reach.

I concur in the judgments of the Court.

Thurgood Marshall: Concurrence

These three cases present the question whether the death penalty is a cruel and unusual punishment prohibited by the Eighth Amendment to the United States Constitution....

The elasticity of the constitutional provision under consideration presents dangers of too little or too much self-restraint. Hence, we must proceed with caution to answer the question presented. By first examining the historical derivation of the Eighth Amendment and the construction given it in the past by this Court, and then exploring the history and attributes of capital punishment in this country, we can answer the question presented with objectivity and a proper measure of self-restraint.

Candor is critical to such an inquiry. All relevant material must be marshaled and sorted and forthrightly examined. We must not only be precise as to the standards of judgment that we are utilizing, but exacting in examining the relevant material in light of those standards.

Candor compels me to confess that I am not oblivious to the fact that this is truly a matter of life and death....

I

The Eighth Amendment's ban against cruel and unusual punishments derives from English law....

Cruel punishments were not confined to those accused of crimes, but were notoriously applied with even greater relish to those who were convicted. Blackstone described in ghastly detail the myriad of inhumane forms of punishment imposed on persons found guilty of any of a large number of offenses. Death, of course, was the usual result....

This legislative history has led at least one legal historian to conclude "that the cruel and unusual punishments clause of the Bill of Rights of 1689 was, first, an objection to the imposition of punishments that were unauthorized by statute and outside the jurisdiction of the sentencing court, and second, a reiteration of the English policy against disproportionate penalties," and not primarily a reaction to the torture of the High Commission, harsh sentences, or the assizes.

Whether the English Bill of Rights prohibition against cruel and unusual punishments is properly read as a response to excessive or illegal punishments, as a reaction to barbaric and objectionable modes of punishment, or as both, there is no doubt whatever that in borrowing the language and in including it in the Eighth Amendment, our Founding Fathers intended to outlaw torture and other cruel punishments.

The precise language used in the Eighth Amendment first appeared in America on June 12, 1776, in Virginia's "Declaration of Rights," §9 of which read: "That excessive bail ought not to be required, nor excessive fines imposed, nor cruel and unusual punishments inflicted." This language was drawn verbatim from the English Bill of Rights of 1689. Other States adopted similar clauses, and there is evidence in the debates of the various state conventions that were called upon to ratify the Constitution of great concern for the omission of any prohibition against torture or other cruel punishments.

The Virginia Convention offers some clues as to what the Founding Fathers had in mind in prohibiting cruel and unusual punishments. At one point George Mason advocated the adoption of a Bill of Rights, and Patrick Henry concurred....

> In this business of legislation, your members of Congress will loose the restriction of not imposing excessive fines, demanding excessive bail, and inflicting cruel and unusual punishments. These are prohibited by your declaration of rights. What has distinguished our ancestors?—That they would not admit of tortures, or cruel and barbarous punishment. But Congress may introduce the practice of the civil law, in preference to that of the common law. They

may introduce the practice of France, Spain, and Germany—of torturing, to extort a confession of the crime. They will say that they might as well draw examples from those countries as from Great Britain, and they will tell you that there is such a necessity of strengthening the arm of government, that they must have a criminal equity, and extort confession by torture, in order to punish with still more relentless severity. We are then lost and undone.

Henry's statement indicates that he wished to insure that "relentless severity" would be prohibited by the Constitution. Other expressions with respect to the proposed Eighth Amendment by Members of the First Congress indicate that they shared Henry's view of the need for and purpose of the Cruel and Unusual Punishments Clause....

The fact, therefore, that the Court, or individual Justices, may have in the past expressed an opinion that the death penalty is constitutional is not now binding on us.... There is no holding directly in point, and the very nature of the Eighth Amendment would dictate that unless a very recent decision existed, *stare decisis* would bow to changing values, and the question of the constitutionality of capital punishment at a given moment in history would remain open.

Faced with an open question, we must establish our standards for decision....

In addition, even if capital punishment is not excessive, it nonetheless violates the Eighth Amendment because it is morally unacceptable to the people of the United States at this time in their history.

In judging whether or not a given penalty is morally acceptable, most courts have said that the punishment is valid unless "it shocks the conscience and sense of justice of the people."...

No nation in the recorded history of man has a greater tradition of revering justice and fair treatment for all its citizens in times of turmoil, confusion, and tension than ours. This is a country which stands tallest in troubled times, a country that clings to fundamental principles, cherishes its constitutional heritage, and rejects simple solutions that compromise the values that lie at the roots of our democratic system.

In striking down capital punishment, this Court does not malign our system of government. On the contrary, it pays homage to it. Only in a free society could right triumph in difficult times, and could civilization record its magnificent advancement. In recognizing the humanity of our fellow beings, we pay ourselves the highest tribute. We achieve "a major milestone in the long road up from barbarism" and join the approximately 70 other jurisdictions in the world which celebrate their regard for civilization and humanity by shunning capital punishment.

Glossary

absolutism: complete control by a ruler

according to its gravity: in connection to the seriousness of the case

amerced: fined or charged

Blackstone: William Blackstone, British jurist of the eighteenth century whose *Commentaries on the Laws of England* was highly influential in jurisprudence for generations

Brahman: the highest-ranking group in the caste system of Hinduism

capital cases: cases involving a crime for which the defendant might, if proved guilty, be executed

caste: a rigid form of social class

certiorari: a demand by a higher court that a lower court release its records relating to a particular case

Glossary

discretionary amercement: choice, on the part of the court, in setting fines

disparity: difference, usually with the implication that one individual or group has an unfair advantage over others

due process: the right to proper, fair, and impartial treatment in legal proceedings

elasticity: flexibility; susceptibility to differing interpretations

fastened to the obsolete: tied to something that is or will soon be outmoded

George Mason: author of the Virginia Declaration of Rights

inference of arbitrariness: the conclusion that justice is not being applied fairly

into our mercy: under our jurisdiction

the Leopolds and Loebs: a reference to Nathan Leopold and Richard A. Loeb, rich young men convicted of murdering fourteen-year-old Bobby Franks in Chicago in 1924

Magna Carta: the "Great Charter," signed by King John of England in 1215, which granted specific rights to citizens and required the king to obey the law

Maitland: English historian Frederic William Maitland

"major milestone in the long road up from barbarism": quotation from Attorney General Ramsey Clark in his book *Crime in America*

one legal historian: Anthony Granucci, in a 1969 article in the *California Law Review*

Patrick Henry: an enthusiastic supporter of the American Revolution, best known for his "Give me liberty, or give me death!" speech

stare decisis: the legal principle that courts are obligated to follow precedents established in earlier legal cases

patronage: the exchange of support and favors for political or social advantage

saving his livelihood: with the exception of his means for earning an income (for example, tools)

term sentence: a sentence to serve a particular number of years

our decisions: decisions that the Supreme Court has made as a whole, whether or not Douglas had a role in a particular case

vacate: overrule, strike down

villein: peasant

wainage: carts and carriages

SAN ANTONIO INDEPENDENT SCHOOL DISTRICT V. RODRIGUEZ

DATE 1973 **AUTHOR** Lewis F. Powell Jr. **VOTE** 5–4	**CITATION** 411 U.S. 1 **SIGNIFICANCE** Found that Texas's system of public education financing did not violate the Fourteenth Amendment's Equal Protection Clause because, in the Court's opinion, education was not a basic right guaranteed by the Constitution

Overview

Argued on October 12, 1972, and decided on March 21, 1973, *San Antonio Independent School District v. Rodriguez* stands as one of the major decisions in the history of education reform. Nearly twenty years earlier, in *Brown v. Board of Education* (1954), the Supreme Court had asserted that the "separate but equal" doctrine that had upheld discriminatory racism since the 1890s was unconstitutional. If the *Brown* decision opened a door to ending discrimination based on race in public education, it was feared that *Rodriguez* would close that door, setting limits to the hard-won freedoms of racial minorities.

Rodriguez was presented and argued as a question about funding public education rather than about access to it, and the Court's finding was based on that idea. As a result, challenges to inequitable public funding moved from the federal court system to individual state courts, where it continues to be argued today. The *Rodriguez* decision is widely seen as one of the first cases in which the Supreme Court began to move away from its decade-long protection of civil rights.

Context

The Supreme Court's finding in *Rodriguez* was based on two principles. The first dealt with the Fourteenth Amendment, a change to the Constitution that was put into place following the Civil War. The Fourteenth Amendment, the lawyers who argued the case before the Supreme Court said, made education to citizens as a fundamental right. The amendment has an "equal protection" clause in it that gives the federal government the power to regulate the way states treat their citizens in matters that affect fundamental rights: rights guaranteed to American citizens by the U.S. Constitution.

The second principle said that the inequitable funding of schools benefited white middle-class and wealthy families in ways that did not benefit Latino and poor families. At the time the case was filed in the late 1960s, the student population of the school district was overwhelmingly Latino and Mexican American. Since funding for the school district was based in part on local property taxes, and since the Latino and Mexican American population had a much lower income than other school districts in the area, the student body suffered as a result.

The case was originally filed on July 10, 1968, as a class action by Demetrio Rodriguez (1925–2013) and fifteen other parents who wanted to know why their school district, the Edgewood Independent School District, did not fix problems with its buildings, buy sufficient textbooks for its students, and hire more teachers. Other school districts in and around San Antonio did not seem to have the same sort of problems. Alamo Heights, for instance, a largely Anglo school district in the northeastern suburbs of the city, spent an average of twice as much per student than Edgewood did because the taxable value of the property on the north side was ten times that of property within the Edgewood school district. Rodriguez, who had five children in Edgewood schools and held a job as a sheet metal worker at a U.S. Air Force base, had never been able to complete his education. His parents had been migrant farm workers, and they had been unable to provide him with the kind of education he wanted for his own children. The lawsuit that bears his name was meant to address the educational disparity for future generations.

The original lawsuit that became the *Rodriguez* case was called *Rodriguez et al. v. San Antonio Independent School District* (1968), and it was directed against the Texas State Board of Education plus several other defendants. It made its way through state courts until, in 1971, it found its way into a federal court, which ruled that Texas's system of funding public education was unconstitutional because it violated the "equal protection" clause of the Fourteenth Amendment. At the same time, the Court also ruled that education was a basic right guaranteed by the Constitution. The state of Texas appealed the verdict, and the case proceeded to the U.S. Supreme Court.

Rodriguez's lawyer was Arthur Gochman (1930–2010). When Gochman brought the case before the Supreme Court, he dropped the idea that education was a basic right under the Constitution and instead argued that if a government agreed to fund education for children, that funding needed to be equitable. Huge discrepancies in funding, he argued, were a de facto violation of equal protection.

While Gochman made a strong argument—stronger even than his opponent, a constitutional law expert named Charles Alan Wright (1927–2000)—the Court found that the funding system, although it was unfair, was not unconstitutional. In addition, the Court said, the state of Texas had not used poverty as a label to discriminate against what in legal terminology is called a "suspect class"—a grouping of people who have historically suffered because of some form of discrimination (such as racism). Accordingly, the justices ruled, the case fell under the responsibility of the court system of Texas to decide.

Justice Lewis Powell was the swing vote in the case.
(Library of Congress)

About the Author

The majority opinion in the Rodriguez case was written by Justice Lewis F. Powell Jr. (1907–1998), who had only shortly before been appointed to the Court by Richard Nixon as a replacement for Associate Justice Hugo Black (1886–1971). Black, who had been appointed by Franklin Delano Roosevelt in 1937, had been a strong, mostly liberal voice on the court. However, he felt very ill in 1971, suffered a debilitating stroke in the following month, and died only a couple of days after retiring from the bench. Powell, appointed by Republican Richard Nixon, marked a shift in the Court's outlook from relatively liberal to relatively conservative.

Powell, a native Virginian, earned his law degree from Washington and Lee University School of Law in 1931 and went on to earn a Master of Laws degree from Harvard Law School in 1932. following the bombing of Pearl Harbor in 1941, Powell attempted to join the U.S. Navy but instead served in the Air Force as an intelligence officer. Toward the end of the war, he was on the staff of the Ultra project and helped break the Nazi coding system, which hastened the Allied victory. After leaving the military in 1945, he served as a partner in a Richmond, Virginia, law firm, and in the mid-1960s he became president of the American Bar Association. He also had experience with public education; from 1952 until 1961, he was chairman of the Richmond School Board at a time when the state was attempting to resist the implications of *Brown v. Board of Education*.

Explanation and Analysis of the Document

Powell begins the Supreme Court's case by discussing the opinion delivered by the district court. He points out that Texas funds its primary and secondary public schools through a combination of state and local taxes. Half of that tax is supplied by the state, he says, and the rest derives from an ad valorem tax on property (a tax that is proportionate to the estimated value of properties) within the jurisdiction of each individual school district. Powell says that the district court classified wealth as a suspect classification and asserted that education is a fundamental right guaranteed by the Constitution. Powell points out that the district court's decision found that the state, arguing for the school district, did not show a compelling reason for the existence of the current system of taxation. The district court also said that the state of Texas could not even demonstrate that there was a rational basis for the taxes to be distributed the way they were.

Powell goes on to summarize the Supreme Court's decision in the case. He asserts first that the district court went beyond its mandate in choosing to examine Texas laws on school funding. He says that judicial scrutiny, under which such laws could be examined, only really applies in cases involving "suspect classes." Powell's assumption here is that the Latino and Mexican American citizens who filed the suit do not qualify as a suspect class. He goes on to make this assumption explicit by asserting that the Texas taxation system does not discriminate against any suspect class.

The associate justice continues by saying that education, although an important service provided by the state, is not a right guaranteed by the Constitution. He continues by noting that there is no evidence in the case that demonstrates that Texas does not provide an education that provides the skills that such a right might demand. Thirdly, he says that the case really ought not to be given strict scrutiny because it involves local taxation rather than national taxation as well as educational policy and questions of federalism. As a result, the Court argues for a "restrained" exercise of judicial power.

Finally, he concludes that the Texas system has not violated the equal protection clause of the Fourteenth Amendment. It is not perfect, he says, but it does what it is supposed to do by assuring a basic education for all children in Texas.

Justice Powell goes on to deliver the majority opinion, in which he is joined by Chief Justice Burger and Associate Justices Stewart, Blackmun, and Rehnquist. Justice Stewart filed a concurring opinion, while Justices Byron White, Thurgood Marshall, William Brennan, and William O. Douglas filed dissents.

Justice Powell begins the Court's opinion by summarizing the background of the case in question. After doing so, he goes on to explain the background of the decision with a constitutional history of the state of Texas and an explanation of how the inequities in Texas school funding came to be. He notes that Texas had a provision in its constitution from its entry into the Union that asserted the state's duty to provide free schooling. Later revisions of the constitution maintained importance of free schooling and provided for a dual system of funding, with about half of the funds coming from a permanent fund run by the state and the other half from local taxes on properties within the individual independent school districts.

Problems arose when Texas began to develop significant urban centers, with concentrations of populations not previously seen in the state. As population shifted from largely rural to both rural and urban, so did the concentration of wealth. As discrepancies in property values increased, the state's permanent fund was expected to make up more and more of the difference between different school districts. Powell states that the available school fund provided only $46 per student by the end of World War II. In the late 1940s, the legislature of the state of Texas established a committee to reform the state's school funding to provide for discrepancies in funding between different school districts. Even this was not enough. In the eighteen years between 1949 and 1967, when Rodriguez's lawsuit was initially filed, school spending increased by about 500 percent. From the late 1950s to the late 1960s alone, the total public school budget had to be increased by about 280 percent.

Powell continues by saying that although these discrepancies do undoubtedly exist, the Court's opinion needs to be based on whether Texas school financing is hurting a suspect class or is violating a fundamental right protected by the U.S. Constitution. Texas, he says, does not appear to be suggesting in its appeal that the system of school funding it has in place is perfectly equitable. As a result, the associate justice concludes, the real issue is over whether Texas has violated a constitutional right (real or implied) or the Fourteenth Amendment's due process clause.

The associate justice goes on to examine in detail the issue of wealth discrimination and poverty. Previous cases considered by the Supreme Court have looked at issues of wealth discrimination, but Powell alleges that this one is not similar to those. He says that the appellees have not offered any data to support their contention that the residents of the Edgewood Independent School District constitute a suspect class. He goes on to suggest three ways in which such a class might be defined: by showing that the funding system discriminates against people who fall below an established poverty line; by demonstrating discrimination against those whose incomes are proportionately less than those of their neighbors; or by showing that the funding through property taxes discriminated in some way against people who happen to live in poorer districts.

Justice Powell states that decisions in previous case law rule out the second two of these possibilities. Poorer people in those cases, he says, tended to reside in industrial areas, which would theoretically at least be paying the highest taxes to the school districts. In addition, he says, a total lack of resources did not lead to denial of education. As a result, the state of Texas is in fact fulfilling its self-defined requirement to provide every child in the state with a minimum education. In addition, although a great discrepancy shows up when comparing Edgewood, one of the poorest Independent School Districts in the San Diego region, with Alamo Heights, one of the most affluent, the same discrepancy does not appear when comparing other relatively poor school districts with relatively rich ones. He concludes by saying that, as a result, the Texas system of public education does not discriminate against any definable suspect class.

The second major question before the court, Powell says, is whether education is a fundamental right under the Constitution. Powell cites the decision in *Brown v. Board of Education* as perhaps the closest that the Court had ever come to asserting education as a fundamental right. However, he adds, to exercise strict judicial review of a state's self-taxation for purposes of education falls outside the proper function of the U.S. Supreme Court. Since the original plaintiffs in the case, the parents of the Edgewood Independent School District, have not shown either that education is a constitutionally protected right or that Texas has fallen short of its duty to provide every student with a minimum basic education, the Supreme Court should not challenge the state's case. As a result, the Court finds that even though the finance system is not equal, it does not violate federal law.

Four dissents were filed by Justices Byron White, Thurgood Marshall. William Brennan, and William O. Douglas. All of the dissents broke with the majority opinion on the questions of fundamental rights and of inequalities based on taxation. Together, they make up a document that is almost as long as the Court's majority opinion. Justice White, in a lengthy commentary, demonstrates that Texas's system of taxation has no rational basis and therefore violates the equal protection clause of the Fourteenth Amendment. White, who was a business attorney before being named a judge, looked at the taxation data and concluded that Edgewood lacked enough taxable property to match Alamo Heights in tax dollars per student without violating the state's cap on property taxes. Justice Brennan rejected the majority's assertion that education was not a fundamental right guaranteed by the U.S. Constitution, saying that a good primary education is fundamental to maintaining rights of free speech and association, both of which are explicitly guaranteed.

The longest dissent was filed by Associate Justice Marshall. Thurgood Marshall had made his reputation as a civil rights attorney, and he, more than any of his fellow justices then on the Supreme Court, felt that denying Texas children an equal education through lack of funding was a fundamental violation of the principles of American equality. In his conclusion, Marshall condemns the majority's call for a legislative solution to the funding issue. He points out that as long as wealthy school districts profit at the expense of poorer school districts, students from impoverished areas will continue to suffer. He concludes by asserting that the great disparities in district property taxation, as reflected by the distribution of wealth, is a direct violation of the equal protection clause.

Impact

Reaction to the decision in *San Antonio Independent School District v. Rodriguez* was largely unfavorable. Most proponents of civil rights recognized it as a setback in the effort to achieve fairness and equality in American education. Some states took relatively quick action to amend their constitutions or to change their school funding plans to make them more equitable.

In Texas, however, the struggle went on for decades. In 1984, the Mexican American Legal Defense and Educational Fund (MALDEF) sued Texas commissioner of education William Kirby in *Edgewood Independent School District v. Kirby* on the grounds that the state's reliance on property taxes to fund local education discriminated against students in poorer districts and violated the state constitutional provision for public education. In response, the state legislature reform bill increased state aid—but not enough to address the inequalities that the MALDEF plaintiffs alleged. In 1989, Texas District Court judge Harley Clark ruled in favor of MALDEF and the Edgewood district. The decision was reversed upon appeal, but in 1991 the Supreme Court of Texas ruled 9–0 in favor of Edgewood.

That still did not resolve the situation. Lawsuits attempting to redress student underfunding continued through the end of the twentieth century and well into the twenty-first century. As recently as 2019, more than fifty years after Demetrio Rodriguez filed his initial case, Edgewood Independent School District was still looking for ways to redress its funding disparities through the Texas legal system.

Questions for Further Study

1. What was it, according to the *Rodriguez* case, that made disparities in student funding a question for the U.S. Supreme Court?

2. What was the basis for the Supreme Court's finding that Texas's school funding program did not violate the Fourteenth Amendment?

3. What is a "suspect class" according to the Supreme Court? Can people living in poverty be a "suspect class"?

4. Associate Justice Thurgood Marshall declared in his dissent to *San Antonio School District v. Rodriguez* that education was a right under the Constitution. What was his basis for that claim?

5. Justice Powell, writing for the Supreme Court's majority, said that the proper way to solve the problem of inequitable funding for Texas's schools was for the Texas legislation to pass laws that fixed the issue. Did the legislature do that? If so, did it work?

Further Reading

Books

Heise, Michael R. *The Story of San Antonio Independent School Dist. v. Rodriguez: School Finance, Local Control, and Constitutional Limits*. Ithaca, NY: Cornell Law School, 2007.

Owings, William A. *American Public School Finance*. Belmont, CA: Wadsworth/Cengage Learning, 2013.

Sracic, Paul A. *San Antonio v. Rodriguez and the Pursuit of Equal Education: The Debate over Discrimination and School Funding*. Lawrence: University Press of Kansas, 2006.

Articles

Black, Derek W. "The Constitutional Compromise to Guarantee Education." *Stanford Law Review* 70 (March 2018): 735–837.

Saleh, Matthew. "Modernizing *San Antonio Independent School District v. Rodriguez*: How Evolving Supreme Court Jurisprudence Changes the Face of Education Finance Litigation." *Journal of Education Finance* 37, no. 2 (Fall 2011): 99–129.

Websites

Isensee, Laura. "How a Dad Helped Start the Fight for Better Public School Funding in Texas." *Houston Public Media*. September 7, 2015. Accessed February 20, 2023, https://www.houstonpublicmedia.org/articles/news/2015/09/07/59720/how-a-dad-helped-start-the-fight-for-better-public-school-funding-in-texas-2/.

"Texas School Finance Litigation Archive." *Legislative Reference Library of Texas*. Accessed February 20, 2023, https://lrl.texas.gov/collections/schoolFinance/lrlhome.cfm.

—Commentary by Kenneth R. Shepherd

San Antonio Independent School District v. Rodriguez

Document Text

MR. JUSTICE POWELL delivered the opinion of the Court

This suit attacking the Texas system of financing public education was initiated by Mexican-American parents whose children attend the elementary and secondary schools in the Edgewood Independent School District, an urban school district in San Antonio, Texas. They brought a class action on behalf of school children throughout the State who are members of minority groups or who are poor and reside in school districts having a low property tax base. Named as defendants were the State Board of Education, the Commissioner of Education, the State Attorney General, and the Bexar County (San Antonio) Board of Trustees. The complaint was filed in the summer of 1968, and a three-judge court was impaneled in January, 1969. In December, 1971, the panel rendered its judgment in a per curiam opinion holding the Texas school finance system unconstitutional under the Equal Protection Clause of the Fourteenth Amendment. The State appealed, and we noted probable jurisdiction to consider the far-reaching constitutional questions presented. 406 U.S. 966 (1972). For the reasons stated in this opinion, we reverse the decision of the District Court.

I

The first Texas State Constitution, promulgated upon Texas' entry into the Union in 1845, provided for the establishment of a system of free schools. Early in its history, Texas adopted a dual approach to the financing of its schools, relying on mutual participation by the local school districts and the State. As early as 1883, the state constitution was amended to provide for the creation of local school districts empowered to levy *ad valorem* taxes with the consent of local taxpayers for the "erection . . . of school buildings" and for the "further maintenance of public free schools." Such local funds as were raised were supplemented by funds distributed to each district from the State's Permanent and Available School Funds. The Permanent School Fund, its predecessor established in 1854 with $2,000,000 realized from an annexation settlement, was thereafter endowed with millions of acres of public land set aside to assure a continued source of income for school support. The Available School Fund, which received income from the Permanent School Fund as well as from a state *ad valorem* property tax and other designated taxes, served as the disbursing arm for most state educational funds throughout the late 1800's and first half of this century. Additionally, in 1918, an increase in state property taxes was used to finance a program providing free textbooks throughout the State.

Until recent times, Texas was a predominantly rural State, and its population and property wealth were spread relatively evenly across the State. Sizable differences in the value of assessable property between local school districts became increasingly evident as the State became more industrialized and as rural-to-urban population shifts became more pronounced. The location of commercial and industrial property began to play a significant role in determining the amount of tax resources available to each school district. These growing disparities in population and taxable property between districts were responsible in part for increasingly notable differences in levels of local expenditure for education. In due time, it became apparent to those concerned with financing public education that contributions from the Available School Fund were not sufficient to ameliorate these disparities. Prior to 1939, the Available School Fund contributed money to every school district at a rate of $17.50 per school-age child. Although the amount was increased several times in the early 1940's, the Fund was providing only $46 per student by 1945.

Recognizing the need for increased state funding to help offset disparities in local spending and to meet Texas' changing educational requirements, the state legislature, in the late 1940's, undertook a thorough evaluation of public education with an eye toward major reform. In 1947, an 18-member committee, composed of educators and legislators, was appointed to explore alternative systems in other States and to propose a funding scheme that would guarantee a minimum or basic educational offering to each child and that would help overcome inter-district disparities in taxable resources. The Committee's efforts led to the passage of the Gilmer-Aikin bills, named for the Committee's co-chairmen, establishing the Texas Minimum Foundation School Program. Today, this Program accounts for approximately half of the total educational expenditures in Texas.

The Program calls for state and local contributions to a fund earmarked specifically for teacher salaries, operating expenses, and transportation costs. The State, supplying funds from its general revenues, finances approximately 80% of the Program, and the school districts are responsible—as a unit—for providing the remaining 20%. The districts' share, known as the Local Fund Assignment, is apportioned among the school districts under a formula designed to reflect each district's relative taxpaying ability. The Assignment is first divided among Texas' 254 counties pursuant to a complicated economic index that takes into account the relative value of each county's contribution to the State's total income from manufacturing, mining, and agricultural activities. It also considers each county's relative share of all payrolls paid within the State and, to a lesser extent, considers each county's share of all property in the State. Each county's assignment is then divided among its school districts on the basis of each district's share of assessable property within the county. The district, in turn, finances its share of the Assignment out of revenues from local property taxation.

The design of this complex system was twofold. First, it was an attempt to assure that the Foundation Program would have an equalizing influence on expenditure levels between school districts by placing the heaviest burden on the school districts most capable of paying. Second, the Program's architects sought to establish a Local Fund Assignment that would force every school district to contribute to the education of its children, but that would not, by itself, exhaust any district's resources. Today every school district does impose a property tax from which it derives locally expendable funds in excess of the amount necessary to satisfy its Local Fund Assignment under the Foundation Program.

In the years since this program went into operation in 1949, expenditures for education—from state as well as local sources—have increased steadily. Between 1949 and 1967, expenditures increased approximately 500%. In the last decade alone, the total public school budget rose from $750 million to $2.1 billion, and these increases have been reflected in consistently rising per-pupil expenditures throughout the State. Teacher salaries, by far the largest item in any school's budget, have increased dramatically—the state supported minimum salary for teachers possessing college degrees has risen from $2,400 to $6,000 over the last 20 years.

The school district in which appellees reside, the Edgewood Independent School District, has been compared throughout this litigation with the Alamo Heights Independent School District. This comparison between the least and most affluent districts in the San Antonio area serves to illustrate the manner in which the dual system of finance operates, and to indicate the extent to which substantial disparities exist despite the State's impressive progress in recent years. Edgewood is one of seven public school districts in the metropolitan area. Approximately 22,000 students are enrolled in its 25 elementary and secondary schools. The district is situated in the core-city sector of San Antonio in a residential neighborhood that has little commercial or industrial property. The residents are predominantly of Mexican-American descent: approximately 90% of the student population is Mexican-American and over 6% is Negro. The average assessed property value per pupil is $5,960—the lowest in the metropolitan area—and the median family income ($4,686) is also the lowest. At an equalized tax rate of $1.05 per $100 of assessed property—the highest in the metropolitan area—the district contributed $26 to the education of each child for the 1967-1968 school year above its Local Fund Assignment for the Minimum Foundation Program. The Foundation Program contributed $222 per pupil for a state-local total of $248. Federal funds added another $108, for a total of $356 per pupil.

Alamo Heights is the most affluent school district in San Antonio. Its six schools, housing approximately 5,000 students, are situated in a residential community quite unlike the Edgewood District. The school population is predominantly "Anglo," having only 18% Mexican-Americans and less than 1% Negroes. The assessed property value per pupil exceeds $49,000, and the median family income is $8,001. In 1967-1968 the local tax rate of $.85 per $100 of valuation yielded $333 per pupil over and above its contribution to the Foundation Program. Coupled with the $225 provided from that Program, the district was able to supply $558 per student. Supplemented by a $36 per-pupil grant from federal sources, Alamo Heights spent $594 per pupil.

Although the 1967-1968 school year figures provide the only complete statistical breakdown for each category of aid, more recent partial statistics indicate that the previously noted trend of increasing state aid has been significant. For the 1970-1971 school year, the Foundation School Program allotment for Edgewood was $356 per pupil, a 62% increase over the 1967-1968 school year. Indeed, state aid alone in 1970-1971 equaled Edgewood's entire 1967-1968 school budget from local, state, and federal sources. Alamo Heights enjoyed a similar increase under the Foundation Program, netting $491 per pupil in 1970-1971. These recent figures also reveal the extent to which these two districts' allotments were funded from their own required contributions to the Local Fund Assignment. Alamo Heights, because of its relative wealth, was required to contribute out of its local property tax collections approximately $100 per pupil, or about 20% of its Foundation grant. Edgewood, on the other hand, paid only $8.46 per pupil, which is about 2.4% of its grant. It appears then that, at least as to these two districts, the Local Fund Assignment does reflect a rough approximation of the relative taxpaying potential of each. Despite these recent increases, substantial inter-district disparities in school expenditures found by the District Court to prevail in San Antonio and in varying degrees throughout the State still exist. And it was these disparities, largely attributable to differences in the amounts of money collected through local property taxation, that led the District Court to conclude that Texas' dual system of public school financing violated the Equal Protection Clause. The District Court held that the Texas system discriminates on the basis of wealth in the manner in which education is provided for its people. 337 F. Supp. at 282. Finding that wealth is a "suspect" classification, and that education is a "fundamental" interest, the District Court held that the Texas system could be sustained only if the State could show that it was premised upon some compelling ate interest. *Id.* at 282-284. On this issue the court concluded that

"[n]ot only are defendants unable to demonstrate compelling state interests ... they fail even to establish a reasonable basis for these classifications."

Id. at 284.

Texas virtually concedes that its historically rooted dual system of financing education could not withstand the strict judicial scrutiny that this Court has found appropriate in reviewing legislative judgments that interfere with fundamental constitutional rights or that involve suspect classifications. If, as previous decisions have indicated, strict scrutiny means that the State's system is not entitled to the usual presumption of validity, that the State, rather than the complainants, must carry a "heavy burden of justification," that the State must demonstrate that its educational system has been structured with "precision," and is "tailored" narrowly to serve legitimate objectives, and that it has selected the "less drastic means" for effectuating its objectives, the Texas financing system and its counterpart in virtually every other State will not pass muster. The State candidly admits that "[n]o one familiar with the Texas system would contend that it has yet achieved perfection." Apart from its concession that educational financing in Texas has "defects" and "imperfections," the State defends the system's rationality with vigor, and disputes the District Court's finding that it lacks a "reasonable basis."

This, then, establishes the framework for our analysis. We must decide, first, whether the Texas system of financing public education operates to the disadvantage of some suspect class or impinges upon a fundamental right explicitly or implicitly protected by the Constitution, thereby requiring strict judicial scrutiny. If so, the judgment of the District Court should be affirmed. If not, the Texas scheme must still be examined to determine whether it rationally furthers some legitimate, articulated state purpose, and therefore does not constitute an invidious discrimination in violation of the Equal Protection Clause of the Fourteenth Amendment.

II

The District Court's opinion does not reflect the novelty and complexity of the constitutional questions posed by appellees' challenge to Texas' system of school financing. In concluding that strict judicial scrutiny was required, that court relied on decisions dealing with the rights of indigents to equal treatment in the criminal trial and appellate processes, and on cases disapproving wealth restrictions on the right to vote. Those cases, the District Court concluded, established wealth as a suspect classification. Finding that the local property tax system discriminated on the basis of wealth, it regarded those precedents as controlling. It then reasoned, based on decisions of this Court affirming the undeniable importance of education, that there is a fundamental right to education, and that, absent some compelling state justification, the Texas system could not stand.

We are unable to agree that this case, which in significant aspects is *sui generis,* may be so neatly fitted into the conventional mosaic of constitutional analysis under the Equal Protection Clause. Indeed, for the several reasons that follow, we find neither the suspect classification nor the fundamental interest analysis persuasive.

A

The wealth discrimination discovered by the District Court in this case, and by several other courts that have recently struck down school financing laws in other States, is quite unlike any of the forms of wealth discrimination heretofore reviewed by this Court. Rather than focusing on the unique features of the alleged discrimination, the courts in these cases have virtually assumed their findings of a suspect classification through a simplistic process of analysis: since, under the traditional systems of financing public schools, some poorer people receive less expensive educations than other more affluent people, these systems discriminate on the basis of wealth. This approach largely ignores the hard threshold questions, including whether it makes a difference, for purposes of consideration under the Constitution, that the class of disadvantaged "poor" cannot be identified or defined in customary equal protection terms, and whether the relative—rather than absolute—nature of the asserted deprivation is of significant consequence. Before a State's laws and the justifications for the classifications they create are subjected to strict judicial scrutiny, we think these threshold considerations must be analyzed more closely than they were in the court below.

The case comes to us with no definitive description of the classifying facts or delineation of the disfavored class. Examination of the District Court's opinion and of appellees' complaint, briefs, and contentions at oral argument suggests, however, at least three ways in which the discrimination claimed here might be described. The Texas system of school financing might be regarded as discriminating (1) against "poor" persons whose incomes fall below some identifiable level of poverty or who might be characterized as functionally "indigent," or (2) against those who are relatively poorer than others or (3) against all those who, irrespective of their personal incomes, happen to reside in relatively poorer school districts. Our task must be to ascertain whether, in fact, the Texas system has been shown to discriminate on any of these possible bases and, if so, whether the resulting classification may be regarded as suspect.

The precedents of this Court provide the proper starting point. The individuals, or groups of individuals, who constituted the class discriminated against in our prior cases shared two distinguishing characteristics: because of their impecunity, they were completely unable to pay for some desired benefit, and, as a consequence, they sustained an absolute deprivation of a meaningful opportunity to enjoy that benefit. In *Griffin v. Illinois,* 351 U. S. 12 (1956), and its progeny, the Court invalidated state laws that prevented an indigent criminal defendant from acquiring a transcript, or an adequate substitute for a transcript, for use at several stages of the trial and appeal process. The payment requirements in each case were found to occasion *de facto* discrimination against those who, because of their indigency, were totally unable to pay for transcripts. And the Court in each case emphasized that no constitutional violation would have been shown if the State had provided some "adequate substitute" for a full stenographic transcript. *Britt v. North Carolina,* 404 U. S. 226, 404 U. S. 228 (1971); *Gardner v. California,* 393 U. S. 367 (1969); *Draper v. Washington,* 372 U. S. 487 (1963); *Eskridge v. Washington Prison Board,* 357 U. S. 214 (1958).

Likewise, in *Douglas v. California,* 372 U. S. 353 (1963), a decision establishing an indigent defendant's right to court-appointed counsel on direct appeal, the Court dealt only with defendants who could not pay for counsel from their own resources and who had no other way of gaining representation. *Douglas* provides no relief for those on whom the burdens of paying for a criminal defense are, relatively speaking, great but not insurmountable. Nor does it deal with relative differences in the quality of counsel acquired by the less wealthy.

Williams v. Illinois, 399 U. S. 235 (1970), and *Tate v. Short,* 401 U. S. 395 (1971), struck down criminal penalties that subjected indigents to incarceration simply because of their inability to pay a fine. Again, the disadvantaged class was composed only of persons who were totally unable to pay the demanded sum. Those cases do not touch on the question whether equal protection is denied to persons with relatively less money on whom designated fines impose heavier burdens. The Court has not held that fines must be structured to reflect each person's ability to pay in order to avoid disproportionate burdens. Sentencing judges may, and often do, consider the defendant's ability to pay, but, in such circumstances, they are guided by sound judicial discretion, rather than by constitutional mandate.

Finally, in *Bullock v. Carter,* 405 U. S. 134 (1972), the Court invalidated the Texas filing fee requirement for primary elections. Both of the relevant classifying facts found in the previous cases were present there. The size of the fee, often running into the thousands of dollars and, in at least one case, as high as $8,900, effectively barred all potential candidates who were unable to pay the required fee. As the system provided "no reasonable alternative means of access to the ballot" (*id.* at 405 U. S. 149), inability to pay occasioned an absolute denial of a position on the primary ballot.

Only appellees' first possible basis for describing the class disadvantaged by the Texas school financing system—discrimination against a class of definably "poor" persons—might arguably meet the criteria established in these prior cases. Even a cursory examination, however, demonstrates that neither of the two distinguishing characteristics of wealth classifications can be found here. First, in support of their charge that the system discriminates against the "poor," appellees have made no effort to demonstrate that it operates to the peculiar disadvantage of any class fairly definable as indigent, or as composed of persons whose incomes are beneath any designated poverty level. Indeed, there is reason to believe that the poorest families are not necessarily clustered in the poorest property districts. A recent and exhaustive study of school districts in Connecticut concluded that

"[i]t is clearly incorrect . . . to contend that the 'poor' live in 'poor' districts. . . . Thus, the major factual assumption of *Serrano*—that the educational financing system discriminates against the 'poor'—is simply false in Connecticut."

Defining "poor" families as those below the Bureau of the Census "poverty level," the Connecticut study found, not surprisingly, that the poor were clustered around commercial and industrial areas—those same areas that provide the most attractive sources of property tax income for school districts. Whether a similar pattern would be discovered in Texas is not known, but there is no basis on the record in this case for assuming that the poorest people—defined by reference to any level of absolute impecunity—are concentrated in the poorest districts.

Second, neither appellees nor the District Court addressed the fact that, unlike each of the foregoing cases, lack of personal resources has not occasioned an absolute deprivation of the desired benefit. The argument here is not that the children in districts having relatively low assessable property values are receiving no public education; rather, it is that they are receiving a poorer quality education than that available to children in districts having more assessable wealth. Apart from the unsettled and disputed question whether the quality of education may be determined by the amount of money expended for it, a sufficient answer to appellees' argument is that, at least where wealth is involved, the Equal Protection Clause does not require absolute equality or precisely equal advantages. Nor, indeed, in view of the infinite variables affecting the educational process, can any system assure equal quality of education except in the most relative sense. Texas asserts that the Minimum

Foundation Program provides an "adequate" education for all children in the State. By providing 12 years of free public school education, and by assuring teachers, books, transportation, and operating funds, the Texas Legislature has endeavored to

"guarantee, for the welfare of the state as a whole, that all people shall have at least an adequate program of education. This is what is meant by 'A Minimum Foundation Program of Education.'"

The State repeatedly asserted in its briefs in this Court that it has fulfilled this desire, and that it now assures "every child in every school district an adequate education." No proof was offered at trial persuasively discrediting or refuting the State's assertion.

For these two reasons—the absence of any evidence that the financing system discriminates against any definable category of "poor" people or that it results in the absolute deprivation of education—the disadvantaged class is not susceptible of identification in traditional terms.

As suggested above, appellees and the District Court may have embraced a second or third approach, the second of which might be characterized as a theory of relative or comparative discrimination based on family income. Appellees sought to prove that a direct correlation exists between the wealth of families within each district and the expenditures therein for education. That is, along a continuum, the poorer the family, the lower the dollar amount of education received by the family's children.

The principal evidence adduced in support of this comparative discrimination claim is an affidavit submitted by Professor Joel S. Berke of Syracuse University's Educational Finance Policy Institute. The District Court, relying in major part upon this affidavit and apparently accepting the substance of appellees' theory, noted, first, a positive correlation between the wealth of school districts, measured in terms of assessable property per pupil, and their levels of per-pupil expenditures. Second, the court found a similar correlation between district wealth and the personal wealth of its residents, measured in terms of median family income. 337 F. Supp. at 282 n. 3.

If, in fact, these correlations could be sustained, then it might be argued that expenditures on education—equated by appellees to the quality of education—are dependent on personal wealth. Appellees' comparative discrimination theory would still face serious unanswered questions, including whether a bare positive correlation or some higher degree of correlation is necessary to provide a basis for concluding that the financing system is designed to operate to the peculiar disadvantage of the comparatively poor, and whether a class of this size and diversity could ever claim the special protection accorded "suspect" classes. These questions need not be addressed in this case, however, since appellees' proof fails to support their allegations or the District Court's conclusions.

Professor Berke's affidavit is based on a survey of approximately 10% of the school districts in Texas. His findings, previously set out in the margin, show only that the wealthiest few districts in the sample have the highest median family incomes and spend the most on education, and that the several poorest districts have the lowest family incomes and devote the least amount of money to education. For the remainder of the districts—96 districts composing almost 90% of the sample—the correlation is inverted, *i.e.*, the districts that spend next to the most money on education are populated by families having next to the lowest median family incomes, while the districts spending the least have the highest median family incomes. It is evident that, even if the conceptual questions were answered favorably to appellees, no factual basis exists upon which to found a claim of comparative wealth discrimination.

This brings us, then, to the third way in which the classification scheme might be defined—*district* wealth discrimination. Since the only correlation indicated by the evidence is between district property wealth and expenditures, it may be argued that discrimination might be found without regard to the individual income characteristics of district residents. Assuming a perfect correlation between district property wealth and expenditures from top to bottom, the disadvantaged class might be viewed as encompassing every child in every district except the district that has the most assessable wealth and spends the most on education. Alternatively, as suggested in MR. JUSTICE MARSHALL's dissenting opinion, *post* at 411 U. S. 96, the class might be defined more restrictively to include children in districts with assessable property which falls below the state-wide average, or median, or below some other artificially defined level.

However described, it is clear that appellees' suit asks this Court to extend its most exacting scrutiny to review a system that allegedly discriminates against a large, diverse, and amorphous class, unified only by the common factor of residence in districts that happen to have less taxable wealth than other districts. The system of alleged discrimination and the class it defines have none of the traditional indicia of suspectness: the class is not saddled with such disabilities, or subjected to such a history of purposeful unequal treatment, or relegated to such a position of political powerlessness as to command extraordinary protection from the majoritarian political process.

We thus conclude that the Texas system does not operate to the peculiar disadvantage of any suspect class.

But in recognition of the fact that this Court has never heretofore held that wealth discrimination alone provides an adequate basis for invoking strict scrutiny, appellees have not relied solely on this contention. They also assert that the State's system impermissibly interferes with the exercise of a "fundamental" right, and that, accordingly, the prior decisions of this Court require the application of the strict standard of judicial review. *Graham v. Richardson,* 403 U. S. 365, 403 U. S. 375-376 (1971); *Kramer v. Union School District,* 395 U. S. 621 (1969); *Shapiro v. Thompson,* 394 U. S. 618 (1969). It is this question—whether education is a fundamental right, in the sense that it is among the rights and liberties protected by the Constitution—which has so consumed the attention of courts and commentators in recent years.

B

In *Brown v. Board of Education,* 347 U. S. 483 (1954), a unanimous Court recognized that "education is perhaps the most important function of state and local governments." *Id.* at 347 U. S. 493. What was said there in the context of racial discrimination has lost none of its vitality with the passage of time:

"Compulsory school attendance laws and the great expenditures for education both demonstrate our recognition of the importance of education to our democratic society. It is required in the performance of our most basic public responsibilities, even service in the armed forces. It is the very foundation of good citizenship. Today it is a principal instrument in awakening the child to cultural values, in preparing him for later professional training, and in helping him to adjust normally to his environment. In these days, it is doubtful that any child may reasonably be expected to succeed in life if he is denied the opportunity of an education. Such an opportunity, where the state has undertaken to provide it, is a right which must be made available to all on equal terms."

Ibid. This theme, expressing an abiding respect for the vital role of education in a free society, may be found in numerous opinions of Justices of this Court writing both before and after *Brown* was decided. *Wisconsin v. Yoder,* 406 U. S. 205, 406 U. S. 213 (BURGER, C.J.), 406 U. S. 237, 406 U. S. 238-239 (WHITE, J.), (1972); *Abington School Dist. v. Schempp,* 374 U. S. 203, 374 U. S. 230 (1963) (BRENNAN, J.); *McCollum v. Board of Education,* 333 U. S. 203 212 (1948) (Frankfurter, J.); *Pierce v. Society of Sisters,* 268 U. S. 510 (1925); *Meyer v. Nebraska,* 262 U. S. 390 (1923); *Interstate Consolidated Street R. Co. v. Massachusetts,* 207 U. S. 79 (1907).

Nothing this Court holds today in any way detracts from our historic dedication to public education. We are in complete agreement with the conclusion of the three-judge panel below that "the grave significance of education both to the individual and to our society" cannot be doubted. But the importance of a service performed by the State does not determine whether it must be regarded as fundamental for purposes of examination under the Equal Protection Clause. Mr. Justice Harlan, dissenting from the Court's application of strict scrutiny to a law impinging upon the right of interstate travel, admonished that "[v]irtually every state statute affects important rights." *Shapiro v. Thompson,* 394 U.S. at 394 U. S. 655, 394 U. S. 661. In his view, if the degree of judicial scrutiny of state legislation fluctuated, depending on a majority's view of the importance of the interest affected, we would have gone "far toward making this Court a *super-legislature.*" *Ibid. We would, indeed, then be assuming a legislative role, and one for which the Court lacks both authority and competence. But MR. JUSTICE STEWART s response in Shapiro to Mr. Justice Harlan's concern correctly articulates the limits of the fundamental rights rationale employed in the Court's equal protection decisions:*

"The Court today does *not* "pick out particular human activities, characterize them as *fundamental,*' and give them added protection...." To the contrary, the Court simply recognizes, as it must, an established constitu-

tional right, and gives to that right no less protection than the Constitution itself demands."

Id. at 394 U. S. 642. (Emphasis in original.)

MR. JUSTICE STEWART's statement serves to underline what the opinion of the Court in *Shapiro* makes clear. In subjecting to strict judicial scrutiny state welfare eligibility statutes that imposed a one-year durational residency requirement as a precondition to receiving AFDC benefits, the Court explained:

"[I]n moving from State to State . . . appellees were exercising a constitutional right, and any classification which serves to penalize the exercise of that right, unless shown to be necessary to promote a *compelling* governmental interest, is unconstitutional."

Id. at 394 U. S. 634. (Emphasis in original.)

The right to interstate travel had long been recognized as a right of constitutional significance, and the Court's decision, therefore, did not require an *ad hoc* determination as to the social or economic importance of that right.

Lindsey v. Normet, 405 U. S. 56 (1972), decided only last Term, firmly reiterates that social importance is not the critical determinant for subjecting state legislation to strict scrutiny. The complainants in that case, involving a challenge to the procedural limitations imposed on tenants in suits brought by landlords under Oregon's Forcible Entry and Wrongful Detainer Law, urged the Court to examine the operation of the statute under "a more stringent standard than mere rationality." *Id.* at 405 U. S. 73. The tenants argued that the statutory limitations implicated "fundamental interests which are particularly important to the poor," such as the *"need for decent shelter"* and the *"'right to retain peaceful possession of one's home." Ibid.* MR. JUSTICE WHITE's analysis, in his *opinion for the Court, is instructive:*

"We do not denigrate the importance of decent, safe, and sanitary housing. But the Constitution does not provide judicial remedies for every social and economic ill. We are unable to perceive in that document any constitutional guarantee of access to dwellings of a particular quality or any recognition of the right of a tenant to occupy the real property of his landlord beyond the term of his lease, without the payment of rent. . . . *Absent constitutional mandate,* the assurance of adequate housing and the definition of landlord-tenant relationships are legislative, not judicial, functions."

Id. at 74. (Emphasis supplied.)

Similarly, in *Dandridge v. Williams,* 397 U. S. 471 (1970), the Court's explicit recognition of the fact that the "administration of public welfare assistance . . . involves the most basic economic needs of impoverished human beings," *id.* at 397 U. S. 485, provided no basis for departing from the settled mode of constitutional analysis of legislative classifications involving questions of economic and social policy. As in the case of housing, the central importance of welfare benefits to the poor was not an adequate foundation for requiring the State to justify its law by showing some compelling state interest. *See also Jefferson v. Hackney,* 406 U. S. 535 (1972); *Richardson v. Belcher,* 404 U. S. 78 (1971).

The lesson of these cases in addressing the question now before the Court is plain. It is not the province of this Court to create substantive constitutional rights in the name of guaranteeing equal protection of the laws. Thus, the key to discovering whether education is "fundamental" is not to be found in comparisons of the relative societal significance of education, as opposed to subsistence or housing. Nor is it to be found by weighing whether education is as important as the right to travel. Rather, the answer lies in assessing whether there is a right to education explicitly or implicitly guaranteed by the Constitution.

Eisenstadt v. Baird, 405 U. S. 438 (1972); *Dunn v. Blumstein,* 405 U. S. 330 (1972); *Police Dept. of Chicago v. Mosley,* 408 U. S. 92 (197); *Skinner v. Oklahoma,* 316 U. S. 535 (1942).

Education, of course, is not among the rights afforded explicit protection under our Federal Constitution. Nor do we find any basis for saying it is implicitly so protected. As we have said, the undisputed importance of education will not, alone, cause this Court to depart from the usual standard for reviewing a State's social and economic legislation. It is appellees' contention, however, that education is distinguishable from other services and benefits provided by the State, because it bears a peculiarly close relationship to other rights and liberties accorded protection under the Constitution. Specifically, they insist that education is itself a fundamental personal right, because it is essential to the effective exercise of First Amendment freedoms and to intelligent utilization of the right to vote. In asserting a nexus between speech and education, appellees urge that the right to speak is meaningless unless the speaker is capable of articulating his thoughts intelligently and persuasively. The "marketplace of ideas" is an empty forum for those lacking basic communicative tools. Likewise, they argue that the corollary right to receive information becomes little more than a hollow privilege when the recipient has not been taught to read, assimilate, and utilize available knowledge.

A similar line of reasoning is pursued with respect to the right to vote. Exercise of the franchise, it is contended, cannot be divorced from the educational foundation of the voter. The electoral process, if reality is to conform to the democratic ideal, depends on an informed electorate: a voter cannot cast his ballot intelligently unless his reading skills and thought processes have been adequately developed.

We need not dispute any of these propositions. The Court has long afforded zealous protection against unjustifiable governmental interference with the individual's rights to speak and to vote. Yet we have never presumed to possess either the ability or the authority to guarantee to the citizenry the most effective speech or the most informed electoral choice. That these may be desirable goals of a system of freedom of expression and of a representative form of government is not to be doubted. These are indeed goals to be pursued by a people whose thoughts and beliefs are freed from governmental interference. But they are not values to be implemented by judicial intrusion into otherwise legitimate state activities.

Even if it were conceded that some identifiable quantum of education is a constitutionally protected prerequisite to the meaningful exercise of either right, we have no indication that the present levels of educational expenditures in Texas provide an education that falls short. Whatever merit appellees' argument might have if a State's financing system occasioned an absolute denial of educational opportunities to any of its children, that argument provides no basis for finding an interference with fundamental rights where only relative differences in spending levels are involved and where—as is true in the present case—no charge fairly could be made that the system fails to provide each child with an opportunity to acquire the basic minimal skills necessary for the enjoyment of the rights of speech and of full participation in the political process.

Furthermore, the logical limitations on appellees' nexus theory are difficult to perceive. How, for instance, is education to be distinguished from the significant personal interests in the basics of decent food and shelter? Empirical examination might well buttress an assumption that the ill-fed, ill-clothed, and ill-housed are among the most ineffective participants in the political process, and that they derive the least enjoyment from the benefits of the First Amendment. If so, appellees' thesis would cast serious doubt on the authority of *Dandridge v. Williams, supra,* and *Lindsey v. Normet, supra.*

We have carefully considered each of the arguments supportive of the District Court's finding that education is a fundamental right or liberty, and have found those arguments unpersuasive. In one further respect, we find this a particularly inappropriate case in which to subject state action to strict judicial scrutiny. The present case, in another basic sense, is significantly different from any of the cases in which the Court has applied strict scrutiny to state or federal legislation touching upon constitutionally protected rights. Each of our prior cases involved legislation which "deprived," "infringed," or "interfered" with the free exercise of some such fundamental personal right or liberty. *See Skinner v. Oklahoma, supra,* at 316 U. S. 536; *Shapiro v. Thompson, supra* at 394 U. S. 634; *Dunn v. Blumstein, supra,* at 405 U. S. 338-343. A critical distinction between those cases and the one now before us lies in what Texas is endeavoring to do with respect to education. MR. JUSTICE BRENNAN, writing for the Court in *Katzenbach v. Morgan,* 384 U. S. 641 (1966), expresses well the salient point:

"This is not a complaint that Congress…has unconstitutionally denied or diluted anyone's right to vote, but rather that Congress violated the Constitution by not extending the relief effected [to others similarly situated]…."

"[The federal law in question] does not restrict or deny the franchise, but, in effect, extends the franchise to persons who otherwise would be denied it by state law.… We need only decide whether the challenged limitation on the relief effected … was permissible. In deciding that question, the principle that calls for the closest scrutiny of distinctions in laws *denying* fundamental rights . . . is inapplicable; for the distinction challenged by appellees is presented only as a limitation on a reform measure aimed at eliminating an existing barrier to the exercise of the franchise. Rather, in deciding the constitutional propriety of the limitations in such a reform measure we are guided by the familiar principles that a 'statute is not invalid under the Constitution because it might have gone farther than it did,' . . . that a legislature need not 'strike at all evils at the same time,' . . . and that 'reform may take one step at a time, addressing itself to the phase of the problem which seems most acute to the legislative mind. . . .'"

Id. at 384 U. S. 656-657. (Emphasis in original.) The Texas system of school financing is not unlike the federal legislation involved in *Katzenbach* in this regard. Every step leading to the establishment of the system Texas utilizes today—including the decisions permitting localities to tax and expend locally, and creating and continuously expanding state aid—was implemented in an effort to extend public education and to improve its quality. Of course, every reform that benefits some more than others may be criticized for what it fails to accomplish. But we think it plain that, in substance, the thrust of the Texas system is affirmative and reformatory, and, therefore, should be scrutinized under judicial principles sensitive to the nature of the State's efforts and to the rights reserved to the States under the Constitution.

C

It should be clear, for the reasons stated above and in accord with the prior decisions of this Court, that this is not a case in which the challenged state action must be subjected to the searching judicial scrutiny reserved for laws that create suspect classifications or impinge upon constitutionally protected rights.

We need not rest our decision, however, solely on the inappropriateness of the strict scrutiny test. A century of Supreme Court adjudication under the Equal Protection Clause affirmatively supports the application of the traditional standard of review, which requires only that the State's system be shown to bear some rational relationship to legitimate state purposes. This case represents far more than a challenge to the manner in which Texas provides for the education of its children. We have here nothing less than a direct attack on the way in which Texas has chosen to raise and disburse state and local tax revenues. We are asked to condemn the State's judgment in conferring on political subdivisions the power to tax local property to supply revenues for local interests. In so doing, appellees would have the Court intrude in an area in which it has traditionally deferred to state legislatures. This Court has often admonished against such interferences with the State's fiscal policies under the Equal Protection Clause:

"The broad discretion as to classification possessed by a legislature in the field of taxation has long been recognized. . . . [T]he passage of time has only served to underscore the wisdom of that recognition of the large area of discretion which is needed by a legislature in formulating sound tax policies. . . .

It has . . . been pointed out that in taxation, even more than in other fields, legislatures possess the greatest freedom in classification. Since the members of a legislature necessarily enjoy a familiarity with local conditions which this Court cannot have, the presumption of constitutionality can be overcome only by the most explicit demonstration that a classification is a hostile and oppressive discrimination against particular persons and classes. . . ."

Madden v. Kentucky, 309 U. S. 83, 309 U. S. 87-88 (1940). *See also Lehnhausen v. Lake Shore Auto Parts Co.,* 410 U. S. 356 (1973); *Wisconsin v. J. C. Penney Co.,* 311 U. S. 435, 311 U. S. 445 (1940).

Thus, we stand on familiar ground when we continue to acknowledge that the Justices of this Court lack both the expertise and the familiarity with local problems so necessary to the making of wise decisions with respect to the raising and disposition of public revenues. Yet we are urged to direct the States either to alter drastically the present system or to throw out the property tax altogether in favor of some other form of taxation. No scheme of taxation, whether the tax is imposed on property, income, or purchases of goods and services, has yet been devised which is free of all discriminatory impact. In such a complex arena in which no perfect alternatives exist, the Court does well not to impose too rigorous a standard of scrutiny lest all local fiscal schemes become subjects of criticism under the Equal Protection Clause.

In addition to matters of fiscal policy, this case also involves the most persistent and difficult questions of educational policy, another area in which this Court's lack of specialized knowledge and experience counsels against premature interference with the informed judgments made at the state and local levels. Education, perhaps even more than welfare assistance, presents a myriad of "intractable economic, social, and even philosophical problems." *Dandridge v. Williams,* 397 U.S. at 397 U. S. 487. The very complexity of the problems of financing and managing a state-wide public school system suggests that "there will be more than one constitutionally permissible method of solving them," and that, within the limits of rationality, "the legislature's efforts to tackle the problems" should be entitled to respect. *Jefferson v. Hackney,* 406 U.S. at 406 U. S. 546-547. On even the most basic questions in this area, the scholars and educational experts are divided. Indeed, one of the major sources of controversy concerns the extent to which there is a demonstrable correlation between educational expenditures and the quality of education—an assumed correlation underlying virtually every legal conclusion drawn by the District Court in this case. Related to the questioned relationship between cost and quality is the equally unsettled controversy as to the proper goals of a system of public education. And the question regarding the most effective relationship between state boards of education and local school boards, in terms of their respective responsibilities and degrees of control, is now undergoing searching reexamination. The ultimate wisdom as to these and related problems of education is not likely to be divined for all time even by the scholars who now so earnestly debate the issues. In such circumstances, the judiciary is well advised to refrain from imposing on the States inflexible constitutional restraints that could circumscribe or handicap the continued research and experimentation so vital to finding even partial solutions to educational problems and to keeping abreast of ever-changing conditions.

It must be remembered, also, that every claim arising under the Equal Protection Clause has implications for the relationship between national and state power under our federal system. Questions of federalism are always inherent in the process of determining whether a State's laws are to be accorded the traditional presumption of constitutionality, or are to be subjected instead to rigorous judicial scrutiny. While

"[t]he maintenance of the principles of federalism is a foremost consideration in interpreting any of the pertinent constitutional provisions under which this Court examines state action,"

it would be difficult to imagine a case having a greater potential impact on our federal system than the one now before us, in which we are urged to abrogate systems of financing public education presently in existence in virtually every State.

The foregoing considerations buttress our conclusion that Texas' system of public school finance is an inappropriate candidate for strict judicial scrutiny. These same considerations are relevant to the determination whether that system, with its conceded imperfections, nevertheless bears some rational relationship to a legitimate state purpose. It is to this question that we next turn our attention.

III

The basic contours of the Texas school finance system have been traced at the outset of this opinion. We will now describe in more detail that system and how it operates, as these facts bear directly upon the demands of the Equal Protection Clause.

Apart from federal assistance, each Texas school receives its funds from the State and from its local school district. On a state-wide average, a roughly comparable amount of funds is derived from each source. The State's contribution, under the Minimum Foundation Program, was designed to provide an adequate minimum educational offering in every school in the State. Funds are distributed to assure that there will be one teacher—compensated at the state supported minimum salary—for every 25 students. Each school district's other supportive personnel are provided for: one principal for every 30 teachers; one "special service" teacher—librarian, nurse, doctor, etc.—for every 20 teachers; superintendents, vocational instructors, counselors, and educators for exceptional children are also provided. Additional funds are earmarked for current operating expenses, for student transportation, and for free textbooks. The program is administered by the State Board of Education and by the Central Education Agency, which also have responsibility for school accreditation and for monitoring the statutory teacher-qualification standards. As reflected by the 62 increase in funds allotted to the Edgewood School

District over the last three years, the State's financial contribution to education is steadily increasing. None of Texas' school districts, however, has been content to rely alone on funds from the Foundation Program.

By virtue of the obligation to fulfill its Local Fund Assignment, every district must impose an *ad valorem* tax on property located within its borders. The Fund Assignment was designed to remain sufficiently low to assure that each district would have some ability to provide a more enriched educational program. Every district supplements its Foundation grant in this manner. In some districts, the local property tax contribution is insubstantial, as in Edgewood, where the supplement was only $26 per pupil in 1967. In other districts, the local share may far exceed even the total Foundation grant. In part, local differences are attributable to differences in the rates of taxation or in the degree to which the market value for any category of property varies from its assessed value. The greatest inter-district disparities, however, are attributable to differences in the amount of assessable property available within any district. Those districts that have more property, or more valuable property, have a greater capability for supplementing state funds. In large measure, these additional local revenues are devoted to paying higher salaries to more teachers. Therefore, the primary distinguishing attributes of schools in property-affluent districts are lower pupil-teacher ratios and higher salary schedules.

This, then, is the basic outline of the Texas school financing structure. Because of differences in expenditure levels occasioned by disparities in property tax income, appellees claim that children in less affluent districts have been made the subject of invidious discrimination. The District Court found that the State had failed even "to establish a reasonable basis" for a system that results in different levels of per-pupil expenditure. 337 F. Supp. at 284. We disagree.

In its reliance on state, as well as local, resources, the Texas system is comparable to the systems employed in virtually every other State. The power to tax local property for educational purposes has been recognized in Texas at least since 1883. When the growth of commercial and industrial centers and accompanying shifts in population began to create disparities in local resources, Texas undertook a program calling for a considerable investment of state funds.

The "foundation grant" theory upon which Texas legislators and educators based the Gilmer-Aikin bills was a product of the pioneering work of two New York educational reformers in the 1920's, George D. Strayer and Robert M. Haig. Their efforts were devoted to establishing a means of guaranteeing a minimum statewide educational program without sacrificing the vital element of local participation. The Strayer-Haig thesis represented an accommodation between these two competing forces. As articulated by Professor Coleman:

"The history of education since the industrial revolution shows a continual struggle between two forces: the desire by members of society to have educational opportunity for all children and the desire of each family to provide the best education it can afford for its own children."

The Texas system of school finance is responsive to these two forces. While assuring a basic education for every child in the State, it permits and encourages a large measure of participation in and control of each district's schools at the local level. In an era that has witnessed a consistent trend toward centralization of the functions of government, local sharing of responsibility for public education has survived. The merit of local control was recognized last Term in both the majority and dissenting opinions in *Wright v. Council of the City of Emporia,* 407 U. S. 451 (1972). MR. JUSTICE STEWART stated there that "[d]irect control over decisions vitally affecting the education of one's children is a need that is strongly felt in our society." *Id.* at 407 U. S. 469. THE CHIEF JUSTICE, in his dissent, agreed that

"[l]ocal control is not only vital to continued public support of the schools, but it is of overriding importance from an educational standpoint as well."

Id. at 407 U. S. 478.

The persistence of attachment to government at the lowest level where education is concerned reflects the depth of commitment of its supporters. In part, local control means, as Professor Coleman suggests, the freedom to devote more money to the education of one's children. Equally important, however, is the opportunity it offers for participation in the decision-making process that determines how those local tax dollars will be spent. Each locality is free to tailor local programs to local needs. Pluralism also affords some opportunity for experimentation, innovation, and a healthy competition for educational excellence. An analogy to the Nation-State relationship in our federal system seems uniquely appropriate. Mr. Justice Brandeis identified as one of the peculiar strengths of our form of government each State's freedom to "serve as a laboratory; and try novel social and economic experiments." No area of social concern stands to profit more from a multiplicity of viewpoints and from a diversity of approaches than does public education.

Appellees do not question the propriety of Texas' dedication to local control of education. To the contrary, they attack the school financing system precisely because, in their view, it does not provide the same level of local control and fiscal flexibility in all districts. Appellees suggest that local control could be preserved and promoted under other financing systems that resulted in more equality in educational expenditures. While it is no doubt true that reliance on local property taxation for school revenues provides less freedom of choice with respect to expenditures for some districts than for others, the existence of "some inequality" in the manner in which the State's rationale is achieved is not alone a sufficient basis for striking down the entire system. *McGowan v. Maryland,* 366 U. S. 420, 366 U. S. 425-426 (1961). It may not be condemned simply because it imperfectly effectuates the State's goals. *Dandridge v. Williams,* 397 U.S. at 397 U. S. 485. Nor must the financing system fail because, as appellees suggest, other methods of satisfying the State's interest, which occasion "less drastic" disparities in expenditures, might be conceived. Only where state action impinges on the exercise of fundamental constitutional rights or liberties must it be found to have chosen the least restrictive alternative. *Cf. Dunn v. Blumstein,* 405 U.S. at 405 U. S. 343; *Shelton v. Tucker,* 364 U. S. 479, 364 U. S. 488 (1960). It is also well to remember that even those districts that have reduced ability to make free decisions with respect to how much they spend on education still retain, under the present system, a large measure of authority as to how available funds will be allocated. They further enjoy the power to make numerous other decisions with respect to the operation of the schools. The people of Texas may be justified in believing that other systems of school financing, which place more of the financial responsibility in the hands of the State, will result in a comparable lessening of desired local autonomy. That is, they may believe that along with increased control of the purse strings at the state level will go increased control over local policies.

Appellees further urge that the Texas system is unconstitutionally arbitrary because it allows the availability of local taxable resources to turn on "happenstance." They see no justification for a system that allows, as they contend, the quality of education to fluctuate on the basis of the fortuitous positioning of the boundary lines of political subdivisions and the location of valuable commercial and industrial property. But any scheme of local taxation—indeed the very existence of identifiable local governmental units—requires the establishment of jurisdictional boundaries that are inevitably arbitrary. It is equally inevitable that some localities are going to be blessed with more taxable assets than others. Nor is local wealth a static quantity. Changes in the level of taxable wealth within any district may result from any number of events, some of which local residents can and do influence. For instance, commercial and industrial enterprises may be encouraged to locate within a district by various actions—public and private.

Moreover, if local taxation for local expenditures were an unconstitutional method of providing for education, then it might be an equally impermissible means of providing other necessary services customarily financed largely from local property taxes, including local police and fire protection, public health and hospitals, and public utility facilities of various kinds. We perceive no justification for such a severe denigration of local property taxation and control as would follow from appellees' contentions. It has simply never been within the constitutional prerogative of this Court to nullify state-wide measures for financing public services merely because the burdens or benefits thereof fall unevenly depending upon the relative wealth of the political subdivisions in which citizens live.

In sum, to the extent that the Texas system of school financing results in unequal expenditures between children who happen to reside in different districts, we cannot say that such disparities are the product of a system that is so irrational as to be invidiously discriminatory. Texas has acknowledged its shortcomings, and has persistently endeavored—not without some success—to ameliorate the differences in levels of expenditures without sacrificing the benefits of local participation. The Texas plan is not the result of hurried, ill-conceived legislation. It certainly is not the product of purposeful discrimination against any group or class. On the contrary, it is rooted in decades of experience in Texas and elsewhere, and, in major part, is the product of responsible studies by qualified people. In giving substance to the presumption of validity to which the Texas system is entitled, *Lindsley v. Natural Carbonic Gas Co.,* 220 U. S. 61, 220 U. S. 78 (1911), it is important to remember that, at every stage of its development, it has constituted a "rough accommodation" of interests in an effort to arrive at practical and workable solutions. *Metropolis Theatre Co. v. City of Chicago,* 228 U. S. 61, 228 U. S. 69-70 (1913). One also must remember that the system here challenged is not peculiar to Texas or to any other State. In its essential characteristics, the Texas plan for financing public education reflects what many educators for a half century have thought was an enlightened approach to a problem for which there is no perfect solution. We are unwilling to assume for ourselves a level of wisdom superior to that of legislators, scholars, and educational authorities in 50 States, especially where the alternatives proposed are only recently conceived and nowhere yet tested. The constitutional standard under the Equal Protection Clause is whether the challenged state action rationally furthers a legitimate state purpose or interest. *McGinnis v. Royster,* 410 U. S. 263, 410 U. S. 270 (1973). We hold that the Texas plan abundantly satisfies this standard.

IV

In light of the considerable attention that has focused on the District Court opinion in this case and on its California predecessor, *Serrano v. Priest,* 5 Cal. 3d 584, 487 P.2d 1241 (1971), a cautionary postscript seems appropriate. It cannot be questioned that the constitutional judgment reached by the District Court and approved by our dissenting Brothers today would occasion in Texas and elsewhere an unprecedented upheaval in public education. Some commentators have concluded that, whatever the contours of the alternative financing programs that might be devised and approved, the result could not avoid being a beneficial one. But, just as there is nothing simple about the constitutional issues involved in these cases, there is nothing simple or certain about predicting the consequences of massive change in the financing and control of public education. Those who have devoted the most thoughtful attention to the practical ramifications of these cases have found no clear or dependable answers, and their scholarship reflects no such unqualified confidence in the desirability of completely uprooting the existing system.

The complexity of these problems is demonstrated by the lack of consensus with respect to whether it may be said with any assurance that the poor, the racial minorities, or the children in overburdened core-city school districts would be benefited by abrogation of traditional modes of financing education. Unless there is to be a substantial increase in state expenditures on education across the board—an event the likelihood of which is open to considerable question—these groups stand to realize gains in terms of increased per-pupil expenditures only if they reside in districts that presently spend at relatively low levels, *i.e.,* in those districts that would benefit from the redistribution of existing resources. Yet recent studies have indicated that the poorest families are not invariably clustered in the most impecunious school districts. Nor does it now appear that there is any more than a random chance that racial minorities are concentrated in property-poor districts. Additionally, several research projects have concluded that any financing alternative designed to achieve a greater equality of expenditures is likely to lead to higher taxation and lower educational expenditures in the major urban centers, a result that would exacerbate, rather than ameliorate, existing conditions in those areas.

These practical considerations, of course, play no role in the adjudication of the constitutional issues presented here. But they serve to highlight the wisdom of the traditional limitations on this Court's function. The consideration and initiation of fundamental reforms with respect to state taxation and education are matters reserved for the legislative processes of the various States, and we do no violence to the values of federalism and separation of powers by staying our hand. We hardly need add that this Court's action today is not to be viewed as placing its judicial imprimatur on the *status quo.* The need is apparent for reform in tax systems which may well have relied too long and too heavily on the local property tax. And certainly innovative thinking as to public education, its methods, and its funding is necessary to assure both a higher level of quality and greater uniformity of opportunity. These matters merit the continued attention of the scholars who already have contributed much by their challenges. But the ultimate solutions must come from the lawmakers and from the democratic pressures of those who elect them.

Reversed.

MR. JUSTICE MARSHALL, with whom MR. JUSTICE DOUGLAS concurs, dissenting

The Court today decides, in effect, that a State may constitutionally vary the quality of education which it offers its children in accordance with the amount of taxable wealth located in the school districts within which they reside. The majority's decision represents an abrupt departure from the mainstream of recent state and federal court decisions concerning the unconstitutionality of state educational financing schemes dependent upon taxable local wealth. More unfortunately, though, the majority's holding can only be seen as a retreat from our historic commitment to equality of educational opportunity and as unsupportable acquiescence in a system which deprives children in their earliest years of the chance to reach their full potential as citizens. The Court does this despite the absence of any substantial justification for a scheme which arbitrarily channels educational resources in accordance with the fortuity of the amount of taxable wealth within each district.

In my judgment, the right of every American to an equal start in life, so far as the provision of a state service as important as education is concerned, is far too vital to permit state discrimination on grounds as tenuous as those presented by this record. Nor can I accept the notion that it is sufficient to remit these appellees to the vagaries of the political process which, contrary to the majority's suggestion, has proved singularly unsuited to the task of providing a remedy for this discrimination. I, for one, am unsatisfied with the hope of an ultimate "political" solution sometime in the indefinite future while, in the meantime, countless children unjustifiably receive inferior educations that "may affect their hearts and minds in a way unlikely ever to be undone." *Brown v. Board of Education,* 347 U. S. 483, 347 U. S. 494 (1954). I must therefore respectfully dissent.

I

The Court acknowledges that "substantial inter-district disparities in school expenditures" exist in Texas, *ante* at 411 U. S. 15, and that these disparities are "largely attributable to differences in the amounts of money collected through local property taxation," *ante* at 411 U. S. 16. But instead of closely examining the seriousness of these disparities and the invidiousness of the Texas financing scheme, the Court undertakes an elaborate exploration of the efforts Texas has purportedly made to close the gaps between its districts in terms of levels of district wealth and resulting educational funding. Yet however praiseworthy Texas' equalizing efforts, the issue in this case is not whether Texas is doing its best to ameliorate the worst features of a discriminatory scheme, but rather whether the scheme itself is, in fact, unconstitutionally discriminatory in the face of the Fourteenth Amendment's guarantee of equal protection of the laws. When the Texas financing scheme is taken as a whole, I do not think it can be doubted that it produces a discriminatory impact on substantial numbers of the school-age children of the State of Texas.

A

Funds to support public education in Texas are derived from three sources: local *ad valorem* property taxes; the Federal Government; and the state government. It is enlightening to consider these in order. Under Texas law, the only mechanism provided the local school district for raising new, unencumbered revenues is the power to tax property located within its boundaries. At the same time, the Texas financing scheme effectively restricts the use of monies raised by local property taxation to the support of public education within the boundaries of the district in which they are raised, since any such taxes must be approved by a majority of the property-taxpaying voters of the district.

The significance of the local property tax element of the Texas financing scheme is apparent from the fact that it provides the funds to meet some 40% of the cost of public education for Texas as a whole. Yet the amount of revenue that any particular Texas district can raise is dependent on two factors—its tax rate and its amount of taxable property. The first factor is determined by the property-taxpaying voters of the district. But, regardless of the enthusiasm of the local voters for public education, the second factor—the taxable property wealth of the district—necessarily restricts the district's ability to raise funds to support public education. Thus, even though the voters of two Texas districts may be willing to make the same tax effort, the results for the districts will be substantially different if one is property rich, while the other is property poor. The necessary effect of the Texas local property tax is, in short, to favor property-rich districts and to disfavor property-poor ones.

The seriously disparate consequences of the Texas local property tax, when that tax is considered alone, are amply illustrated by data presented to the District Court by appellees. These data included a detailed study of a sample of 110 Texas school districts for the 1967-1968 school year conducted by Professor Joel S. Berke of Syracuse University's Educational Finance Policy Institute. Among other things, this study revealed that the 10 richest districts examined, each of which had more than $100,000 in taxable property per pupil, raised through local effort an average of $610 per pupil, whereas the four poorest districts studied, each of which had less than $10,000 in taxable property per pupil, were able to raise only an average of $63 per pupil. And, as the Court effectively recognizes, *ante* at 411 U. S. 27, this correlation between the amount of taxable property per pupil and the amount of local revenues per pupil holds true for the 96 districts in between the richest and poorest districts.

It is clear, moreover, that the disparity of per-pupil revenues cannot be dismissed as the result of lack of local effort—that is, lower tax rates by property-poor districts. To the contrary, the data presented below indicate that the poorest districts tend to have the highest tax rates and the richest districts tend to have the lowest tax rates. Yet, despite the apparent extra effort being made by the poorest districts, they are unable even to begin to match the richest districts in terms of the production of local revenues. For example, the 10 richest districts studied by Professor Berke were able to produce $585 per pupil with an equalized tax rate of 31¢ on $100 of equalized valuation, but the four poorest districts studied, with an equalized rate of 70¢ on $100 of equalized valuation, were able to produce only $60 per pupil. Without more, this state-imposed system of educational funding presents a serious picture of widely varying treatment of Texas school districts, and thereby of Texas school children, in terms of the amount of funds available for public education.

Nor are these funding variations corrected by the other aspects of the Texas financing scheme. The Federal Government provides funds sufficient to cover only some 10% of the total cost of public education in Texas. Furthermore, while these federal funds are not distributed in Texas solely on a per-pupil basis, appellants do not here contend that they are used in such a way as to ameliorate significantly the widely varying consequences for Texas school districts and school children of the local property tax element of the state financing scheme.

State funds provide the remaining some 50% of the monies spent on public education in Texas. Technically, they are distributed under two programs. The first is the Available School Fund, for which provision is made in the Texas Constitution. The Available School Fund is composed of revenues obtained from a number of sources, including receipts from the state *ad valorem* property tax, one-fourth of all monies collected by the occupation tax, annual contributions by the legislature from general revenues, and the revenues derived from the Permanent School Fund. For the 1970-1971 school year, the Available School Fund contained $296,000,000. The Texas Constitution requires that this money be distributed annually on a per capita basis to the local school districts. Obviously, such a flat grant could not alone eradicate the funding differentials attributable to the local property tax. Moreover, today the Available School Fund is in reality simply one facet of the second state financing program, the Minimum Foundation School Program, since each district's annual share of the Fund is deducted from the sum to which the district is entitled under the Foundation Program. The Minimum Foundation School Program provides funds for three specific purposes: professional salaries, current operating expenses, and transportation expenses. The State pays, on an overall basis, for approximately 80% of the cost of the Program; the remaining 20% is distributed among the local school districts under the Local Fund Assignment. Each district's share of the Local Fund Assignment is determined by a complex "economic index" which is designed to allocate a larger share of the costs to property-rich districts than to property-poor districts. Each district pays its share with revenues derived from local property taxation.

The stated purpose of the Minimum Foundation School Program is to provide certain basic funding for each local Texas school district. At the same time, the Program was apparently intended to improve, to some degree, the financial position of property-poor districts relative to property-rich districts, since—through the use of the economic index—an effort is made to charge a disproportionate share of the costs of the Program to rich districts. It bears noting, however, that substantial criticism has been leveled at the practical effectiveness of the economic index system of local cost allocation. In theory, the index is designed to ascertain the relative ability of each district to contribute to the Local Fund Assignment from local property taxes. Yet the index is not developed simply on the basis of each district's taxable wealth. It also takes into account the district's relative income from manufacturing, mining, and agriculture, its payrolls, and its scholastic population.

It is difficult to discern precisely how these latter factors are predictive of a district's relative ability to raise revenues through local property taxes. Thus, in 1966, one of the consultants who originally participated in the development of the Texas economic index adopted in 1949 told the Governor's Committee on Public School Education: "The Economic Index approach to evaluating local ability offers a little better measure than sheer chance, but not much."

Moreover, even putting aside these criticisms of the economic index as a device for achieving meaningful district wealth equalization through cost allocation, poor districts still do not necessarily receive more state aid than property-rich districts. For the standards which currently determine the amount received from the Foundation School Program by any particular district favor property-rich districts. Thus, focusing on the same Edgewood Independent and Alamo Heights School Districts which the majority uses for purposes of illustration, we find that, in 1967-1968, property-rich Alamo Heights, which raised $333 per pupil on an equalized tax rate of 85¢ per $100 valuation, received $225 per pupil from the Foundation School Program, while property-poor Edgewood, which raised only $26 per pupil with an equalized tax rate of $1.05 per $100 valuation, received only $222 per pupil from the Foundation School Program. And, more recent data, which indicate that, for the 1970-1971 school year, Alamo Heights received $491 per pupil from the Program while Edgewood received only $356 per pupil, hardly suggest that the wealth gap between the districts is being narrowed by the State Program. To the contrary, whereas, in 1967-1968, Alamo Heights received only $3 per pupil, or about 1%, more than Edgewood in state aid, by 1970-1971, the gap had widened to a difference of $135 per pupil, or about 38%. It was data of this character that prompted the District Court to observe that "the current [state aid] system tends to subsidize the rich at the expense of the poor, rather than the other way around." 337 F. Supp. 280, 282. And even the appellants go no further here than to venture that the Minimum Foundation School Program has "a mildly equalizing effect."

Despite these facts, the majority continually emphasizes how much state aid has, in recent years, been given to property-poor Texas school districts. What the Court fails to emphasize is the cruel irony of how much more state aid is being given to property-rich Texas school districts on top of their already substantial local property tax revenues. Under any view, then, it is apparent that the state aid provided by the Foundation School Program fails to compensate for the large funding variations attributable to the local property tax element of the Texas financing scheme. And it is these stark differences in the treatment of Texas school districts and school children inherent in the Texas financing scheme, not the absolute amount of state aid provided to any particular school district, that are the crux of this case. There can, moreover, be no escaping the conclusion that the local property tax which is dependent upon taxable district property wealth is an essential feature of the Texas scheme for financing public education.

B

The appellants do not deny the disparities in educational funding caused by variations in taxable district property wealth. They do contend, however, that whatever the differences in per-pupil spending among Texas districts, there are no discriminatory consequences for the children of the disadvantaged districts. They recognize that what is at stake in this case is the quality of the public education provided Texas children in the districts in which they live. But appellants reject the suggestion that the quality of education in any particular district is determined by money—beyond some minimal level of funding which they believe to be assured every Texas district by the Minimum Foundation School Program. In their view, there is simply no denial of equal educational opportunity to any Texas school children as a result of the widely varying per-pupil spending power provided districts under the current financing scheme.

In my view, though, even an unadorned restatement of this contention is sufficient to reveal its absurdity. Authorities concerned with educational quality no doubt disagree as to the significance of variations in per-pupil spending. Indeed, conflicting expert testimony was presented to the District Court in this case concerning the effect of spending variations on educational achievement. We sit, however, not to resolve disputes over educational theory, but to enforce our Constitution. It is an inescapable fact that, if one district has more funds available per pupil than another district, the former will have greater choice in educational planning than will the latter. In this regard, I believe the question of discrimination in educational quality must be deemed to be an objective one that looks to what the State provides its children, not to what the children are able to do with what they receive. That a child forced to attend an underfunded school with poorer physical facilities, less experienced teachers, larger classes, and a narrower range of courses than a school with substantially more funds—and thus with greater choice in educational planning—may nevertheless excel is to the credit of the child, not the State, *cf. Missouri ex rel. Gaines v. Canada*, 305 U. S. 337, 305 U. S. 349 (1938). Indeed, who can ever measure for such a child the opportunities lost and the talents wasted for want of a broader, more enriched education? Discrimination in the opportunity to learn that is afforded a child must be our standard.

Hence, even before this Court recognized its duty to tear down the barriers of state-enforced racial segregation in public education, it acknowledged that inequality in the educational facilities provided to students may be discriminatory state action as contemplated by the Equal Protection Clause. As a basis for striking down state-enforced segregation of a law school, the Court in *Sweatt v. Painter*, 339 U. S. 629, 339 U. S. 633-634 (1950), stated:

"[W]e cannot find substantial equality in the educational opportunities offered white and Negro law students by the State. In terms of number of the faculty, variety of courses and opportunity for specialization, size of the student body, scope of the library, availability of law review and similar activities, the [whites-only] Law School is superior. . . . It is difficult to believe that one who had a free choice between these law schools would consider the question close."

See also McLaurin v. Oklahoma State Regents for Higher Education, 339 U. S. 637 (1950). Likewise, it is difficult to believe that, if the children of Texas had a free choice, they would choose to be educated in districts with fewer resources, and hence with more antiquated plants, less experienced teachers, and a less diversified curriculum. In fact, if financing variations are so insignificant to educational quality, it is difficult to understand why a number of our country's wealthiest school districts, which have no legal obligation to argue in support of the constitutionality of the Texas legislation, have nevertheless zealously pursued its cause before this Court.

The consequences, in terms of objective educational input, of the variations in district funding caused by the Texas financing scheme are apparent from the data introduced before the District Court. For example, in 1968-1969, 100% of the teachers in the property-rich Alamo Heights School District had college degrees. By contrast, during the same school year, only 80.02% of the teachers had college degrees in the property poor Edgewood Independent school District. Also, in 1968-1969, approximately 47% of the teachers in the Edgewood District were on emergency teaching permits, whereas only 11% of the teachers in Alamo Heights were on such permits. This is undoubtedly a reflection of the fact that the top of Edgewood's teacher salary scale was approximately 80% of Alamo Heights'. And, not surprisingly, the teacher-student ratio varies significantly between the two districts. In other wards, as might be expected, a difference in the funds available to districts results in a difference in educational inputs available for a child's public education in Texas. For constitutional purposes, I believe this situation, which is directly attributable to the Texas financing scheme, raises a grave question of state-created discrimination in the provision of public education. *Cf. Gaston County v. United States*, 395 U. S. 285, 395 U. S. 293-294 (1969).

At the very least, in view of the substantial inter-district disparities in funding and in resulting educational inputs shown by appellees to exist under the Texas financing scheme, the burden of proving that these disparities do not, in fact, affect the quality of children's education must fall upon the appellants. *Cf. Hobson v. Hansen,* 327 F. Supp. 844, 860-861 (DC 1971). Yet appellants made no effort in the District Court to demonstrate that educational quality is not affected by variations in funding and in resulting inputs. And, in this Court, they have argued no more than that the relationship is ambiguous. This is hardly sufficient to overcome appellees' *prima facie* showing of state-created discrimination between the school children of Texas with respect to objective educational opportunity.

Nor can I accept the appellants' apparent suggestion that the Texas Minimum Foundation School Program effectively eradicates any discriminatory effects otherwise resulting from the local property tax element of the Texas financing scheme. Appellants assert that, despite its imperfections, the Program "does guarantee an adequate education to every child." The majority, in considering the constitutionality of the Texas financing scheme, seems to find substantial merit in this contention, for it tells us that the Foundation Program "was designed to provide an adequate minimum educational offering in every school in the State," *ante* at 411 U. S. 45, and that the Program "assur[es] a basic education for every child," *ante* at 411 U. S. 49. But I fail to understand how the constitutional problems inherent in the financing scheme are eased by the Foundation Program. Indeed, the precise thrust of the appellants' and the Court's remarks are not altogether clear to me.

The suggestion may be that the state aid received via the Foundation Program sufficiently improves the position of property-poor districts *vis-a-vis* property-rich districts—in terms of educational funds—to eliminate any claim of inter-district discrimination in available educational resources which might otherwise exist if educational funding were dependent solely upon local property taxation. Certainly the Court has recognized that to demand precise equality of treatment is normally unrealistic, and thus minor differences inherent in any practical context usually will not make out a substantial equal protection claim. *See, e.g., Mayer v. City of Chicago,* 404 U. S. 189, 404 U. S. 194-195 (1971); *Draper v. Washington,* 372 U. S. 487, 372 U. S. 495-496 (1963); *Bain Peanut Co. v. Pinson,* 282 U. S. 499, 282 U. S. 501 (1931). But, as has already been seen, we are hardly presented here with some *de minimis* claim of discrimination resulting from the play necessary in any functioning system; to the contrary, it is clear that the Foundation Program utterly fails to ameliorate the seriously discriminatory effects of the local property tax.

Alternatively, the appellants and the majority may believe that the Equal Protection Clause cannot be offended by substantially unequal state treatment of persons who are similarly situated so long as the State provides everyone with some unspecified amount of education which evidently is "enough." The basis for such a novel view is far from clear. It is, of course, true that the Constitution does not require precise equality in the treatment of all persons. As Mr. Justice Frankfurter explained:

"The equality at which the 'equal protection' clause aims is not a disembodied equality. The Fourteenth Amendment enjoins 'the equal protection of the laws,' and laws are not abstract propositions. . . . The Constitution does not require things which are different in fact or opinion to be treated in law as though they were the same."

Tigner v. Texas, 310 U. S. 141, 310 U. S. 147 (1940). *See also Douglas v. California,* 372 U. S. 353, 372 U. S. 357 (1963); *Goesaert v. Cleary,* 335 U. S. 464, 335 U. S. 466 (1948).

But this Court has never suggested that, because some "adequate" level of benefits is provided to all, discrimination in the provision of services is therefore constitutionally excusable. The Equal Protection Clause is not addressed to the minimal sufficiency, but rather to the unjustifiable inequalities of state action. It mandates nothing less than that "all persons similarly circumstanced shall be treated alike." *F. S. Royster Guano Co. v. Virginia,* 253 U. S. 412, 253 U. S. 415 (1920).

Even if the Equal Protection Clause encompassed some theory of constitutional adequacy, discrimination in the provision of educational opportunity would certainly seem to be a poor candidate for its application. Neither the majority nor appellants inform us how judicially manageable standards are to be derived for determining how much education is "enough" to excuse constitutional discrimination. One would think that the majority would heed its own fervent affirmation of judicial self-restraint before undertaking the complex task of determining at large what level of education is constitutionally sufficient. Indeed, the majority's apparent reliance upon the adequacy of the educational opportunity assured by the Texas Minimum Foundation School Program seems fundamentally inconsistent with its own recognition that educational authorities are unable to agree upon what makes for educational quality, *see ante* at 411 U. S. 42-43 and n. 86 and at 411 U. S. 47 n. 101. If, as the majority stresses, such authorities are uncertain as to the impact of various levels of funding on educational quality, I fail to see where it finds the expertise to divine that the particular levels of funding provided by the Program assure an adequate educational opportunity—much less an education substantially equivalent in quality to that which a higher level of funding might provide. Certainly appellants' mere assertion before this Court of the adequacy of the education guaranteed by the Minimum Foundation School Program cannot obscure the constitutional implications of the discrimination in educational funding and objective educational inputs resulting from the local property tax—particularly since the appellees offered substantial uncontroverted evidence before the District Court impugning the now much-touted "adequacy" of the education guaranteed by the Foundation Program.

In my view, then, it is inequality—not some notion of gross inadequacy—of educational opportunity that raises a question of denial of equal protection of the laws. I find any other approach to the issue unintelligible, and without directing principle. Here, appellees have made a substantial showing of wide variations in educational funding and the resulting educational opportunity afforded to the school children of Texas. This discrimination is, in large measure, attributable to significant disparities in the taxable wealth of local Texas school districts. This is a sufficient showing to raise a substantial question of discriminatory state action in violation of the Equal Protection Clause.

C

Despite the evident discriminatory effect of the Texas financing scheme, both the appellants and the majority raise substantial questions concerning the precise character of the disadvantaged class in this case. The District Court concluded that the Texas financing scheme draws "distinction between groups of citizens depending upon the wealth of the district in which they live," and thus creates a disadvantaged class composed of persons living in property-poor districts. *See* 337 F. Supp. at 282. *See also id.* at 281. In light of the data introduced before the District Court, the conclusion that the school children of property-poor districts constitute a sufficient class for our purposes seems indisputable to me.

Appellants contend, however, that, in constitutional terms, this case involves nothing more than discrimination against local school districts, not against individuals, since, on its face, the state scheme is concerned only with the provision of funds to local districts. The result of the Texas financing scheme, appellants suggest, is merely that some local districts have more available revenues for education; others have less. In that respect, they point out, the States have broad discretion in drawing reasonable distinctions between their political subdivisions. *See Griffin v. County School Board of Prince Edward County,* 377 U. S. 218, 377 U. S. 231 (1964); *McGowan v. Maryland,* 366 U. S. 420, 366 U. S. 427 (1961); *Salsbury v. Maryland,* 346 U. S. 545, 346 U. S. 550-554 (1954).

But this Court has consistently recognized that, where there is, in fact, discrimination against individual interests, the constitutional guarantee of equal protection of the laws is not inapplicable simply because the discrimination is based upon some group characteristic such as geographic location. *See Gordon v. Lance,* 403 U. S. 1, 403 U. S. 4 (1971); *Reynolds v. Sims,* 377 U. S. 533, 377 U.S. 565-566 (1964); *Gray v. Sanders,* 372 U. S. 368, 372 U. S. 379 (1963). Texas has chosen to provide free public education for all its citizens, and it has embodied that decision in its constitution. Yet, having established public education for its citizens, the State, as a direct consequence of the variations in local property wealth endemic to Texas' financing scheme, has provided some Texas school children with substantially less resources for their education than others. Thus, while, on its face, the Texas scheme may merely discriminate between local districts, the impact of that discrimination falls directly upon the children whose educational opportunity is dependent upon where they happen to live. Consequently, the District Court correctly concluded that the Texas financing scheme discriminates, from a constitutional perspective, between school children on the basis of the amount of taxable property located within their local districts.

In my Brother STEWART's view, however, such a description of the discrimination inherent in this case is apparently not sufficient, for it fails to define the "kind of objectively identifiable classes" that he evidently perceives to be necessary for a claim to be "cognizable under the Equal Protection Clause," *ante* at 411 U. S. 62. He asserts that this is also the view of the majority, but he is unable to cite, nor have I been able to find, any portion of the Court's opinion which remotely suggests that there is no objectively identifiable or definable class in this case. In any event, if he means to suggest that an essential predicate to equal protection analysis is the precise identification of the particular individuals who compose the disadvantaged class, I fail to find the source from which he derives such a requirement. Certainly such precision is not analytically necessary. So long as the basis of the discrimination is clearly identified, it is possible to test it against the State's purpose for such discrimination—whatever the standard of equal protection analysis employed. This is clear from our decision only last Term in *Bullock v. Carter*, 405 U. S. 134 (1972), where the Court, in striking down Texas' primary filing fees as violative of equal protection, found no impediment to equal protection analysis in the fact that the members of the disadvantaged class could not be readily identified. The Court recognized that the filing fee system tended

"to deny some voters the opportunity to vote for a candidate of their choosing; at the same time it gives the affluent the power to place on the ballot their own names or the names of persons they favor."

Id. at 405 U. S. 144. The Court also recognized that

"[t]his disparity in voting power based on wealth cannot be described by reference to discrete and precisely defined segments of the community as is typical of inequities challenged under the Equal Protection Clause...."

Ibid. Nevertheless it concluded that

"we would ignore reality were we not to recognize that this system falls with unequal weight on voters . . . according to their economic status."

Ibid. The nature of the classification in *Bullock* was clear, although the precise membership of the disadvantaged class was not. This was enough in *Bullock* for purposes of equal protection analysis. It is enough here.

It may be, though, that my Brother STEWART is not in fact, demanding precise identification of the membership of the disadvantaged class for purposes of equal protection analysis, but is merely unable to discern with sufficient clarity the nature of the discrimination charged in this case. Indeed, the Court itself displays some uncertainty as to the exact nature of the discrimination and the resulting disadvantaged class alleged to exist in this case. *See ante* at 411 U. S. 120. It is, of course, essential to equal protection analysis to have a firm grasp upon the nature of the discrimination at issue. In fact, the absence of such a clear, articulable understanding of the nature of alleged discrimination in a particular instance may well suggest the absence of any real discrimination. But such is hardly the case here.

A number of theories of discrimination have, to be sure, been considered in the course of this litigation. Thus, the District Court found that, in Texas, the poor and minority group members tend to live in property-poor districts, suggesting discrimination on the basis of both personal wealth and race. *See* 337 F. Supp. at 282 and n. 3. The Court goes to great lengths to discredit the data upon which the District Court relied, and thereby its conclusion that poor people live in property-poor districts.

Although I have serious doubts as to the correctness of the Court's analysis in rejecting the data submitted below, I have no need to join issue on these factual disputes.

I believe it is sufficient that the overarching form of discrimination in this case is between the school children of Texas on the basis of the taxable property wealth of the districts in which they happen to live. To understand both the precise nature of this discrimination and the parameters of the disadvantaged class, it is sufficient to consider the constitutional principle which appellees contend is controlling in the context of educational financing. In their complaint, appellees asserted that the Constitution does not permit local district wealth to be determinative of educational opportunity. This is simply another way of saying, as the District Court concluded, that, consistent with the guarantee of equal protection of the laws, "the quality of public education may not be a function of wealth, other than the wealth of the state as a whole." 337 F. Supp. at 284. Under such a principle, the children of a district are excessively advantaged if that district has more taxable property per pupil than the average amount of taxable property per pupil considering the State as a whole. By contrast, the children of a district are disadvantaged if that district has less taxable property per pupil than the state average. The majority attempts to disparage such a definition of the disadvantaged class as the product of an "artificially defined level" of district wealth. *Ante* at 411 U. S. 28. But such is clearly not the case, for this is the definition unmistakably dictated by the constitutional principle for which appellees have argued throughout the course of this litigation. And I do not believe that a clearer definition of either the disadvantaged class of Texas school children or the allegedly unconstitutional discrimination suffered by the members of that class under the present Texas financing scheme could be asked for, much less needed. Whether this discrimination, against the school children of property-poor districts, inherent in the Texas financing scheme, is violative of the Equal Protection Clause is the question to which we must now turn.

II

To avoid having the Texas financing scheme struck down because of the inter-district variations in taxable property wealth, the District Court determined that it was insufficient for appellants to show merely that the State's scheme was rationally related to some legitimate state purpose; rather, the discrimination inherent in the scheme had to be shown necessary to promote a "compelling state interest" in order to withstand constitutional scrutiny. The basis for this determination was twofold: first, the financing scheme divides citizens on a wealth basis, a classification which the District Court viewed as highly suspect; and second, the discriminatory scheme directly affects what it considered to be a "fundamental interest," namely, education.

This Court has repeatedly held that state discrimination which either adversely affects a "fundamental interest," *see, e.g., Dunn v. Blumstein,* 405 U. S. 330, 405 U. S. 336-342 (1972); *Shapiro v. Thompson,* 394 U. S. 618, 394 U. S. 629-631 (1969), or is based on a distinction of a suspect character, *see, e.g., Graham v. Richardson,* 403 U. S. 365, 403 U. S. 372 (1971); *McLaughlin v. Florida,* 379 U. S. 184, 379 U. S. 191-192 (1964), must be carefully scrutinized to ensure that the scheme is necessary to promote a substantial, legitimate state interest. *See, e.g., Dunn v. Blumstein, supra,* at 405 U. S. 342-343; *Shapiro v. Thompson, supra,* at 394 U. S. 634. The majority today concludes, however, that the Texas scheme is not subject to such a strict standard of review under the Equal Protection Clause. Instead, in its view, the Texas scheme must be tested by nothing more than that lenient standard of rationality which we have traditionally applied to discriminatory state action in the context of economic and commercial matters. *See, e.g., McGowan v. Maryland,* 366 U.S. at 366 U. S. 425-426; *Morey v. Doud,* 354 U. S. 457, 354 U. S. 465-466 (1957); *F. S. Royster Guano Co. v. Virginia,* 253 U.S. at 253 U. S. 415; *Lindsley v. Natural Carbonic Gas Co.,* 220 U. S. 61, 220 U. S. 78-79 (1911). By so doing, the Court avoids the telling task of searching for a substantial state interest which the Texas financing scheme, with its variations in taxable district property wealth, is necessary to further. I cannot accept such an emasculation of the Equal Protection Clause in the context of this case.

A

To begin, I must once more voice my disagreement with the Court's rigidified approach to equal protection analysis. *See Dandridge v. Williams,* 397 U. S. 471, 397 U. S. 519-521 (1970) (dissenting opinion); *Richardson v. Belcher,* 404 U. S. 78, 404 U. S. 90 (1971) (dissenting opinion). The Court apparently seeks to establish today that equal protection cases fall into one of two neat categories which dictate the appropriate standard of review—strict scrutiny or mere rationality. But this Court's decisions in the field of equal protection defy such easy categorization. A principled reading of what this Court has done reveals that it has applied a spectrum of standards in reviewing discrimination allegedly violative of the Equal Protection Clause. This spectrum clearly comprehends variations in the degree of care with which the Court will scrutinize particular classifications, depending, I believe, on the constitutional and societal importance of the interest adversely affected and the recognized invidiousness of the basis upon which the particular classification is drawn. I find, in fact, that many of the Court's recent decisions embody the very sort of reasoned approach to equal protection analysis for which I previously argued—that is, an approach in which

"concentration [is] placed upon the character of the classification in question, the relative importance to individuals in the class discriminated against of the governmental benefits that they do not receive, and the asserted state interests in support of the classification."

Dandridge v. Williams, supra, at 397 U. S. 520-521 (dissenting opinion).

I therefore cannot accept the majority's labored efforts to demonstrate that fundamental interests, which call for strict scrutiny of the challenged classification, encompass only established rights which we are somehow bound to recognize from the text of the Constitution itself. To be sure, some interests which the Court has deemed to be fundamental for purposes of equal protection analysis are themselves constitutionally protected rights. Thus, discrimination against the guaranteed right of freedom of speech has called for strict judicial scrutiny. *See Police Dept. of Chicago v. Mosley,* 408 U. S. 92 (1972). Further, every citizen's right to travel interstate, although nowhere expressly mentioned in the Constitution, has long been recognized as implicit in the premises underlying that document: the right "was conceived from the beginning to be a necessary concomitant of the stronger Union the Constitution created." *United States v. Guest,* 383 U. S. 745, 383 U. S. 758 (1966). *See also Crandall v. Nevada,* 6 Wall. 35, 73 U. S. 48 (1868). Consequently, the Court has required that a state classification affecting the constitutionally protected right to travel must be "shown to be necessary to promote a compelling governmental interest." *Shapiro v. Thompson,* 394 U.S. at 394 U. S. 634. But it will not do to suggest that the "answer" to whether an interest is fundamental for purposes of equal protection analysis is always determined by whether that interest "is a right . . . explicitly or implicitly guaranteed by the Constitution," *ante* at 411 U. S. 33-34.

I would like to know where the Constitution guarantees the right to procreate, *Skinner v. Oklahoma,* 316 U. S. 535 541 (1942) or the right to vote in state elections, *e.g., Reynolds v. Sims,* 377 U. S. 533 (1964) or the right to an appeal from a criminal conviction, *e.g., Griffin v. Illinois,* 351 U. S. 12 (1956). These are instances in which, due to the importance of the interests at stake, the Court has displayed a strong concern with the existence of discriminatory state treatment. But the Court has never said or indicated that these are interests which independently enjoy full-blown constitutional protection.

Thus, in *Buck v. Bell,* 274 U. S. 200 (1927), the Court refused to recognize a substantive constitutional guarantee of the right to procreate. Nevertheless, in *Skinner v. Oklahoma, supra,* at 316 U. S. 541 the Court, without impugning the continuing validity of *Buck v. Bell,* held that "strict scrutiny" of state discrimination affecting procreation "is essential," for "[m]arriage and procreation are fundamental to the very existence and survival of the race." Recently, in *Roe v. Wade,* 410 U. S. 113, 410 U. S. 152-154 (1973), the importance of procreation has, indeed, been explained on the basis of its intimate relationship with the constitutional right of privacy which we have recognized. Yet the limited stature thereby accorded any "right" to procreate is evident from the fact that, at the same time, the Court reaffirmed its initial decision in *Buck v. Bell. See Roe v. Wade, supra,* at 410 U. S. 154.

Similarly, the right to vote in state elections has been recognized as a "fundamental political right," because the Court concluded very early that it is "preservative of all rights." *Yick Wo v. Hopkins,* 118 U. S. 356, 118 U. S. 370 (1886); *see, e.g., Reynolds v. Sims, supra,* at 377 U. S. 561-562. For this reason,

"this Court has made clear that a citizen has a *constitutionally protected right to participate in elections on an equal basis with other citizens in the jurisdiction.*"

Dunn v. Blumstein, 405 U.S. at 405 U. S. 336 (emphasis added). The final source of such protection from inequality in the provision of the state franchise is, of course, the Equal Protection Clause. Yet it is clear that whatever degree of importance has been attached to the state electoral process when unequally distributed, the right to vote in state elections has itself never been accorded the stature of an independent constitutional guarantee. *See Oregon v. Mitchell,* 400 U. S. 112 (1970); *Kramer v. Union School District,* 395 U. S. 621, 395 U. S. 626-629 (1969); *Harper v. Virginia Bd. of Elections,* 383 U. S. 663, 383 U. S. 665 (1966).

Finally, it is likewise "true that a State is not required by the Federal Constitution to provide appellate courts or a right to appellate review at all." *Griffin v. Illinois,* 351 U.S. at 351 U. S. 18. Nevertheless, discrimination adversely affecting access to an appellate process which a State has chosen to provide has been considered to require close judicial scrutiny. *See, e.g., Griffin v. Illinois, supra; Douglas v. California,* 372 U. S. 353 (1963).

The majority is, of course, correct when it suggests that the process of determining which interests are fundamental is a difficult one. But I do not think the problem is insurmountable. And I certainly do not accept the view that the process need necessarily degenerate into an unprincipled, subjective "picking-and-choosing" between various interests, or that it must involve this Court in creating "substantive constitutional rights in the name of guaranteeing equal protection of the laws," *ante* at 411 U. S. 33. Although not all fundamental interests are constitutionally guaranteed, the determination of which interests are fundamental should be firmly rooted in the text of the Constitution. The task in every case should be to determine the extent to which constitutionally guaranteed rights are dependent on interests not mentioned in the Constitution. As the nexus between the specific constitutional guarantee and the nonconstitutional interest draws closer, the nonconstitutional interest becomes more fundamental and the degree of judicial scrutiny applied when the interest is infringed on a discriminatory basis must be adjusted accordingly. Thus, it cannot be denied that interests such as procreation, the exercise of the state franchise, and access to criminal appellate processes are not fully guaranteed to the citizen by our Constitution. But these interests have nonetheless been afforded special judicial consideration in the face of discrimination because they are, to some extent, interrelated with constitutional guarantees. Procreation is now understood to be important because of its interaction with the established constitutional right of privacy. The exercise of the state franchise is closely tied to basic civil and political rights inherent in the First Amendment. And access to criminal appellate processes enhances the integrity of the range of rights implicit in the Fourteenth Amendment guarantee of due process of law. Only if we closely protect the related interests from state discrimination do we ultimately ensure the integrity of the constitutional guarantee itself. This is the real lesson that must be taken from our previous decisions involving interests deemed to be fundamental.

The effect of the interaction of individual interests with established constitutional guarantees upon the degree of care exercised by this Court in reviewing state discrimination affecting such interests is amply illustrated by our decision last Term in *Eisenstadt v. Baird*, 405 U. S. 438 (1972). In *Baird*, the Court struck down as violative of the Equal Protection Clause a state statute which denied unmarried persons access to contraceptive devices on the same basis as married persons. The Court purported to test the statute under its traditional standard whether there is some rational basis for the discrimination effected. *Id.* at 405 U. S. 446-447. In the context of commercial regulation, the Court has indicated that the Equal Protection Clause "is offended only if the classification rests on grounds wholly irrelevant to the achievement of the State's objective." *See, e.g., McGowan v. Maryland*, 366 U.S. at 366 U. S. 425; *Kotch v. Board of River Port Pilot Comm'rs*, 330 U. S. 552, 330 U. S. 557 (1947). And this lenient standard is further weighted in the State's favor by the fact that "[a] statutory discrimination will not be set aside if any state of facts reasonably may be conceived [by the Court] to justify it." *McGowan v. Maryland, supra*, at 366 U. S. 426. But, in *Baird*, the Court clearly did not adhere to these highly tolerant standards of traditional rational review. For although there were conceivable state interests intended to be advanced by the statute—*e.g.*, deterrence of premarital sexual activity and regulation of the dissemination of potentially dangerous articles—the Court was not prepared to accept these interests on their face, but instead proceeded to test their substantiality by independent analysis. *See* 405 U.S. at 405 U. S. 449-454. Such close scrutiny of the State's interests was hardly characteristic of the deference shown state classifications in the context of economic interests. *See, e.g., Goesaert v. Cleary*, 335 U. S. 464 (1948); *Kotch v. Board of River Port Pilot Comm'rs, supra*. Yet I think the Court's action was entirely appropriate, for access to and use of contraceptives bears a close relationship to the individual's constitutional right of privacy. *See* 405 U.S. at 405 U. S. 453-454; *id.* at 405 U. S. 463-464 (WHITE, J., concurring in result). *See also Roe v. Wade*, 410 U.S. at 410 U. S. 152-153.

A similar process of analysis with respect to the invidiousness of the basis on which a particular classification is drawn has also influenced the Court as to the appropriate degree of scrutiny to be accorded any particular case. The highly suspect character of classifications based on race, nationality, or alienage is well established. The reasons why such classifications call for close judicial scrutiny are manifold. Certain racial and ethnic groups have frequently been recognized as "discrete and insular minorities" who are relatively powerless to protect their interests in the political process. *See Graham v. Richardson*, 403 U.S. at 403 U. S. 372; *cf. United States v. Carolene Products Co.*, 304 U. S. 144, 304 U. S. 152-153, n. 4 (1938). Moreover, race, nationality, or alienage is, "'in most circumstances, irrelevant' to any constitutionally acceptable legislative purpose, *Hirabayashi v. United States,* 320 U. S. 81, 320 U. S. 100."

McLaughlin v. Florida, 379 U.S. at 379 U. S. 192. Instead, lines drawn on such bases are frequently the reflection of historic prejudices, rather than legislative rationality. It may be that all of these considerations, which make for particular judicial solicitude in the face of discrimination on the basis of race, nationality, or alienage, do not coalesce—or at least not to the same degree—in other forms of discrimination. Nevertheless, these considerations have undoubtedly influenced the care with which the Court has scrutinized other forms of discrimination.

In *James v. Strange,* 407 U. S. 128 (1972), the Court held unconstitutional a state statute which provided for recoupment from indigent convicts of legal defense fees paid by the State. The Court found that the statute impermissibly differentiated between indigent criminals in debt to the State and civil judgment debtors, since criminal debtors were denied various protective exemptions afforded civil judgment debtors. The Court suggested that, in reviewing the statute under the Equal Protection Clause, it was merely applying the traditional requirement that there be "*some rationality*'" *in the line drawn between the different types of debtors. I.d. at 407 U. S. 140. Yet it then proceeded to scrutinize the statute with less than traditional deference and restraint. Thus, the Court recognized "that state recoupment statutes may betoken legitimate state interests" in recovering expenses and discouraging fraud. Nevertheless, MR. JUSTICE POWELL, speaking for the Court, concluded that*

"these interests are not thwarted by requiring more even treatment of indigent criminal defendants with other classes of debtors to whom the statute itself repeatedly makes reference. State recoupment laws, notwithstanding the state interests they may serve, need not blight in such discriminatory fashion the hopes of indigents for self-sufficiency and self-respect."

Id. at 407 U. S. 141-142. The Court, in short, clearly did not consider the problems of fraud and collection that the state legislature might have concluded were peculiar to indigent criminal defendants to be either sufficiently important or at least sufficiently substantiated to justify denial of the protective exemptions afforded to all civil judgment debtors, to a class composed exclusively of indigent criminal debtors.

Similarly, in *Reed v. Reed,* 404 U. S. 71 (1971), the Court, in striking down a state statute which gave men preference over women when persons of equal entitlement apply for assignment as an administrator of a particular estate, resorted to a more stringent standard of equal protection review than that employed in cases involving commercial matters. The Court indicated that it was testing the claim of sex discrimination by nothing more than whether the line drawn bore "a rational relationship to a state objective," which it recognized as a legitimate effort to reduce the work of probate courts in choosing between competing applications for letters of administration. *Id.* at 404 U. S. 76. Accepting such a purpose, the Idaho Supreme Court had thought the classification to be sustainable on the basis that the legislature might have reasonably concluded that, as a rule, men have more experience than women in business matters relevant to the administration of an estate. 93 Idaho 511, 514, 465 P.2d 635, 638 (1970). This Court, however, concluded that

"[t]o give a mandatory preference to members of either sex over members of the other merely to accomplish the elimination of hearings on the merits is to make the very kind of arbitrary legislative choice forbidden by the Equal Protection Clause of the Fourteenth Amendment...."

404 U.S. at 404 U. S. 76. This Court, in other words, was unwilling to consider a theoretical and unsubstantiated basis for distinction—however reasonable it might appear—sufficient to sustain a statute discriminating on the basis of sex.

James and *Reed* can only be understood as instances in which the particularly invidious character of the classification caused the Court to pause and scrutinize with more than traditional care the rationality of state discrimination. Discrimination on the basis of past criminality and on the basis of sex posed for the Court the specter of forms of discrimination which it implicitly recognized to have deep social and legal roots without necessarily having any basis in actual differences. Still, the Court's sensitivity to the invidiousness of the basis for discrimination is perhaps most apparent in its decisions protecting the interests of children born out of wedlock from discriminatory state action. *See Weber v.*

Aetna Casualty & Surety Co., 406 U. S. 164 (1972); *Levy v. Louisiana,* 391 U. S. 68 (1968).

In *Weber,* the Court struck down a portion of a state workmen's compensation statute that relegated unacknowledged illegitimate children of the deceased to a lesser status with respect to benefits than that occupied by legitimate children of the deceased. The Court acknowledged the true nature of its inquiry in cases such as these: "What legitimate state interest does the classification promote? What fundamental personal rights might the classification endanger?" *Id.* at 406 U. S. 173. Embarking upon a determination of the relative substantiality of the State's justifications for the classification, the Court rejected the contention that the classifications reflected what might be presumed to have been the deceased's preference of beneficiaries as "not compelling... where dependency on the deceased is a prerequisite to anyone's recovery. . . ." *Ibid.* Likewise, it deemed the relationship between the State's interest in encouraging legitimate family relationships and the burden placed on the illegitimates too tenuous to permit the classification to stand. *Ibid.* A clear insight into the basis of the Court's action is provided by its conclusion:

"[I]mposing disabilities on the illegitimate child is contrary to the basic concept of our system that legal burdens should bear some relationship to individual responsibility or wrongdoing. Obviously, no child is responsible for his birth and penalizing the illegitimate child is an ineffectual—as well as an unjust—way of deterring the parent. Courts are powerless to prevent the social opprobrium suffered by these hapless children, but the Equal Protection Clause does enable us to strike down discriminatory laws relating to status of birth. . . ."

Id. at 406 U. S. 175-176. Status of birth, like the color of one's skin, is something which the individual cannot control, and should generally be irrelevant in legislative considerations. Yet illegitimacy has long been stigmatized by our society. Hence, discrimination on the basis of birth—particularly when it affects innocent children—warrants special judicial consideration.

In summary, it seems to me inescapably clear that this Court has consistently adjusted the care with which it will review state discrimination in light of the constitutional significance of the interests affected and the invidiousness of the particular classification. In the context of economic interests, we find that discriminatory state action is almost always sustained, for such interests are generally far removed from constitutional guarantees. Moreover,

"[t]he extremes to which the Court has gone in dreaming up rational bases for state regulation in that area may in many instances be ascribed to a healthy revulsion from the Court's earlier excesses in using the Constitution to protect interests that have more than enough power to protect themselves in the legislative halls."

Dandridge v. Williams, 397 U.S. at 397 U. S. 520 (dissenting opinion). But the situation differs markedly when discrimination against important individual interests with constitutional implications and against particularly disadvantaged or powerless classes is involved. The majority suggests, however, that a variable standard of review would give this Court the appearance of a "super-legislature." *Ante* at 411 U. S. 31. I cannot agree. Such an approach seems to me a part of the guarantees of our Constitution and of the historic experiences with oppression of and discrimination against discrete, powerless minorities which underlie that document. In truth, the Court itself will be open to the criticism raised by the majority so long as it continues on its present course of effectively selecting in private which cases will be afforded special consideration without acknowledging the true basis of its action. Opinions such as those in *Reed* and *James* seem drawn more as efforts to shield, rather than to reveal, the true basis of the Court's decisions. Such obfuscated action may be appropriate to a political body such as a legislature, but it is not appropriate to this Court. Open debate of the bases for the Court's action is essential to the rationality and consistency of our decisionmaking process. Only in this way can we avoid the label of legislature and ensure the integrity of the judicial process.

Nevertheless, the majority today attempts to force this case into the same category for purposes of equal protection analysis as decisions involving discrimination affecting commercial interests. By so doing, the majority ingles this case out for analytic treatment at odds with what seems to me to be the clear trend of recent decisions in this Court, and thereby ignores the constitutional importance of the interest at stake and the invidiousness of the particular classification, factors that call for far more than the lenient scrutiny of the Texas financing scheme which the majority pursues. Yet if the discrimination inherent in the Texas scheme is scrutinized with the care demanded by the interest and classification present in this case, the unconstitutionality of that scheme is unmistakable.

B

Since the Court now suggests that only interests guaranteed by the Constitution are fundamental for purposes of equal protection analysis, and since it rejects the contention that public education is fundamental, it follows that the Court concludes that public education is not constitutionally guaranteed. It is true that this Court has never deemed the provision of free public education to be required by the Constitution. Indeed, it has on occasion suggested that state-supported education is a privilege bestowed by a State on its citizens. *See Missouri ex rel. Gaines v. Canada*, 305 U.S. at 305 U. S. 349. Nevertheless, the fundamental importance of education is amply indicated by the prior decisions of this Court, by the unique status accorded public education by our society, and by the close relationship between education and some of our most basic constitutional values.

The special concern of this Court with the educational process of our country is a matter of common knowledge. Undoubtedly, this Court's most famous statement on the subject is that contained in *Brown v. Board of Education*, 347 U.S. at 347 U. S. 493:

"Today, education is perhaps the most important function of state and local governments. Compulsory school attendance laws and the great expenditures for education both demonstrate our recognition of the importance of education to our democratic society. It is required in the performance of our most basic public responsibilities, even service in the armed forces. It is the very foundation of good citizenship. Today it is a principal instrument in awakening the child to cultural values, in preparing him for later professional training, and in helping him to adjust normally to his environment...."

Only last Term, the Court recognized that "[p]roviding public schools ranks at the very apex of the function of a State." *Wisconsin v. Yoder*, 406 U. S. 205, 406 U. S. 213 (1972). This is clearly borne out by the fact that, in 48 of our 50 States, the provision of public education is mandated by the state constitution. No other state function is so uniformly recognized as an essential element of our society's wellbeing. In large measure, the explanation for the special importance attached to education must rest, as the Court recognized in *Yoder*, id. at 406 U. S. 221, on the facts that "some degree of education is necessary to prepare citizens to participate effectively and intelligently in our open political system . . . ," and that "education prepares individuals to be self-reliant and self-sufficient participants in society." Both facets of this observation are suggestive of the substantial relationship which education bears to guarantees of our Constitution.

Education directly affects the ability of a child to exercise his First Amendment rights, both as a source and as a receiver of information and ideas, whatever interests he may pursue in life. This Court's decision in *Sweezy v. New Hampshire*, 354 U. S. 234, 354 U. S. 250 (1957), speaks of the right of students "to inquire, to study and to evaluate, to gain new maturity and understanding. . . ." Thus, we have not casually described the classroom as the "*marketplace of ideas.*" *Keyishian v. Board of Regents*, 385 U. S. 589, 385 U. S. 603 (1967). *The opportunity for formal education may not necessarily be the essential determinant of an individual's ability to enjoy throughout his life the rights of free speech and association guaranteed to him by the First Amendment. But such an opportunity may enhance the individual's enjoyment of those rights not only during, but also following, school attendance. Thus, in the final analysis,*

"the pivotal position of education to success in American society and its essential role in opening up to the individual the central experiences of our culture lend it an importance that is undeniable."

Of particular importance is the relationship between education and the political process. "Americans regard the public schools as a most vital civic institution for the preservation of a democratic system of government." *Abington School Dist. v. Schempp*, 374 U. S. 203, 374 U. S. 230 (1963) (BRENNAN, J., concurring). Education serves the essential function of instilling in our young an understanding of and appreciation for the principles and operation of our governmental processes. Education may instill the interest and provide the tools necessary for political discourse and debate. Indeed, it has frequently been suggested that education is the dominant factor affecting political consciousness and participation. A system of "[c]ompetition in ideas and governmental policies is at the core of our electoral process and of the First Amendment freedoms."

Williams v. Rhodes, 393 U. S. 23, 393 U. S. 32 (1968). But of most immediate and direct concern must be the demonstrated effect of education on the exercise of the franchise by the electorate. The right to vote in federal elections is conferred by Art. I, § 2, and the Seventeenth Amendment of the Constitution, and access to the state franchise has been afforded special protection because it is "preservative of other basic civil and political rights," *Reynolds v. Sims,* 377 U.S. at 377 U. S. 562. Data from the Presidential Election of 1968 clearly demonstrate a direct relationship between participation in the electoral process and level of educational attainment, and, as this Court recognized in *Gaston County v. United States,* 395 U. S. 285, 395 U. S. 296 (1969), the quality of education offered may influence a child's decision to "enter or remain in school." It is this very sort of intimate relationship between a particular personal interest and specific constitutional guarantees that has heretofore caused the Court to attach special significance, for purposes of equal protection analysis, to individual interests such as procreation and the exercise of the state franchise.

While ultimately disputing little of this, the majority seeks refuge in the fact that the Court has

"never presumed to possess either the ability or the authority to guarantee to the citizenry the most *effective* speech or the most *informed* electoral choice."

Ante at 411 U. S. 36. This serves only to blur what is in fact, at stake. With due respect, the issue is neither provision of the most effective speech nor of the most *informed* vote. Appellees do not now seek the best education Texas might provide. They do seek, however, an end to state discrimination resulting from the unequal distribution of taxable district property wealth that directly impairs the ability of some districts to provide the same educational opportunity that other districts can provide with the same or even substantially less tax effort. The issue is, in other words, one of discrimination that affects the quality of the education which Texas has chosen to provide its children; and, the precise question here is what importance should attach to education for purposes of equal protection analysis of that discrimination. As this Court held in *Brown v. Board of Education,* 347 U.S. at 347 U. S. 493, the opportunity of education, "where the state has undertaken to provide it, is a right which must be made available to all on equal terms." The factors just considered, including the relationship between education and the social and political interests enshrined within the Constitution, compel us to recognize the fundamentality of education and to scrutinize with appropriate care the bases for state discrimination affecting equality of educational opportunity in Texas' school districts—a conclusion which is only strengthened when we consider the character of the classification in this case.

C

The District Court found that, in discriminating between Texas school children on the basis of the amount of taxable property wealth located in the district in which they live, the Texas financing scheme created a form of wealth discrimination. This Court has frequently recognized that discrimination on the basis of wealth may create a classification of a suspect character, and thereby call for exacting judicial scrutiny. *See, e.g., Griffin v. Illinois,* 351 U. S. 12 (1956); *Douglas v. California,* 372 U. S. 353 (1963); *McDonald v. Board of Election Comm'rs of Chicago,* 394 U. S. 802, 394 U. S. 807 (1969). The majority, however, considers any wealth classification in this case to lack certain essential characteristics which it contends are common to the instances of wealth discrimination that this Court has heretofore recognized. We are told that, in every prior case involving a wealth classification, the members of the disadvantaged class have

"shared two distinguishing characteristics: because of their impecunity, they were completely unable to pay for some desired benefit, and as a consequence, they sustained an absolute deprivation of a meaningful opportunity to enjoy that benefit."

Ante at 411 U. S. 20. I cannot agree. The Court's distinctions may be sufficient to explain the decisions in *Williams v. Illinois,* 399 U. S. 235 (1970); *Tate v. Short,* 401 U. S. 395 (1971); and even *Bullock v. Carter,* 405 U. S. 134 (1972). But they are not, in fact, consistent with the decisions in *Harper v. Virginia Bd. of Elections,* 383 U. S. 663 (1966), or *Griffin v. Illinois, supra,* or *Douglas v. California, supra.*

In *Harper,* the Court struck down, as violative of the Equal Protection Clause, an annual Virginia poll tax of $1.50, payment of which by persons over the age of 21 was a prerequisite to voting in Virginia elections. In part, the Court relied on the fact that the poll tax interfered with a fundamental interest—the exercise of the state franchise. In addition, though, the Court emphasized that "[l]ines drawn on the basis of wealth or property... are traditionally disfavored." 383 U.S. at 383 U. S. 668. Under the first part of the theory announced by the majority, the disadvantaged class in *Harper,* in terms of a wealth analysis, should have consisted only of those too poor to afford the $1.50 necessary to vote. But the *Harper* Court did not see it that way. In its view, the Equal Protection Clause "bars a system which excludes [from the franchise] those unable to pay a fee to vote or who *fail to pay." Ibid.* (Emphasis added.) So far as the Court was concerned, the "degree of the discrimination [was] irrelevant." *Ibid.* Thus, the Court struck down the poll tax *in toto;* it did not order merely that those too poor to pay the tax be exempted; complete impecunity clearly was not determinative of the limits of the disadvantaged class, nor was it essential to make an equal protection claim. Similarly, *Griffin* and *Douglas* refute the majority's contention that we have in the past required an absolute deprivation before subjecting wealth classifications to strict scrutiny. The Court characterizes *Griffin* as a case concerned simply with the denial of a transcript or an adequate substitute therefor, and *Douglas* as involving the denial of counsel. But, in both cases, the question was, in fact, whether "a State that [grants] *appellate review* can do so in a way that discriminates against some convicted defendants on account of their poverty." *Griffin v. Illinois, supra,* at 351 U. S. 18 (emphasis added). In that regard, the Court concluded that inability to purchase a transcript denies "the poor an adequate *appellate review* accorded to all who have money enough to pay the costs in advance," *ibid.* (emphasis added), and that "the type of an *appeal* a person is afforded . . . hinges upon whether or not he can pay for the assistance of counsel," *Douglas v. California, supra,* at 372 U. S. 355-356 (emphasis added). The right of appeal itself was not absolutely denied to those too poor to pay, but, because of the cost of a transcript and of counsel, the appeal was a substantially less meaningful right for the poor than for the rich. It was on these terms that the Court found a denial of equal protection, and those terms clearly encompassed degrees of discrimination on the basis of wealth which do not amount to outright denial of the affected right or interest.

This is not to say that the form of wealth classification in this case does not differ significantly from those recognized in the previous decisions of this Court. Our prior cases have dealt essentially with discrimination on the basis of personal wealth. Here, by contrast, the children of the disadvantaged Texas school districts are being discriminated against not necessarily because of their personal wealth or the wealth of their families, but because of the taxable property wealth of the residents of the district in which they happen to live. The appropriate question, then, is whether the same degree of judicial solicitude and scrutiny that has previously been afforded wealth classifications is warranted here.

As the Court points out, *ante* at 411 U. S. 28-29, no previous decision has deemed the presence of just a wealth classification to be sufficient basis to call forth rigorous judicial scrutiny of allegedly discriminatory state action. *Compare, e.g., Harper v. Virginia Bd. of Elections, supra, with, e.g., James v. Valtierra,* 402 U. S. 137 (1971). That wealth classifications alone have not necessarily been considered to bear the same high degree of suspectness as have classifications based on, for instance, race or alienage may be explainable on a number of grounds. The "poor" may not be seen as politically powerless as certain discrete and insular minority groups. Personal poverty may entail much the same social stigma as historically attached to certain racial or ethnic groups. But personal poverty is not a permanent disability; its shackles may be escaped. Perhaps most importantly, though, personal wealth may not necessarily share the general irrelevance as a basis for legislative action that race or nationality is recognized to have. While the "poor" have frequently been a legally disadvantaged group, it cannot be ignored that social legislation must frequently take cognizance of the economic status of our citizens. Thus, we have generally gauged the invidiousness of wealth classifications with an awareness of the importance of the interests being affected and the relevance of personal wealth to those interests. *See Harper v. Virginia Bd. of Elections, supra.*

When evaluated with these considerations in mind, it seems to me that discrimination on the basis of group wealth in this case likewise calls for careful judicial scrutiny. First, it must be recognized that, while local district wealth may serve other interests, it bears no relationship whatsoever to the interest of Texas school children in the educational opportunity afforded them by the State of Texas. Given the importance of that interest, we must be particularly sensitive to the invidious characteristics of any form of discrimination that is not clearly intended to serve it, as opposed to some other distinct state interest. Discrimination on the basis of group wealth may not, to be sure, reflect the social stigma frequently attached to personal poverty. Nevertheless, insofar as group wealth discrimination involves wealth over which the disadvantaged individual has no significant control, it represents in fact, a more serious basis of discrimination than does personal wealth. For such discrimination is no reflection of the individual's characteristics or his abilities. And thus—particularly in the context of a disadvantaged class composed of children—we have previously treated discrimination on a basis which the individual cannot control as constitutionally disfavored. *Cf. Weber v. Aetna Casualty & Surety Co.,* 406 U. S. 164 (1972); *Levy v. Louisiana,* 391 U. S. 68 (1968).

The disability of the disadvantaged class in this case extends as well into the political processes upon which we ordinarily rely a adequate for the protection and promotion of all interests. Here legislative reallocation of the State's property wealth must be sought in the face of inevitable opposition from significantly advantaged districts that have a strong vested interest in the preservation of the *status quo,* a problem not completely dissimilar to that faced by underrepresented districts prior to the Court's intervention in the process of reapportionment, *see Baker v. Carr,* 369 U. S. 186, 369 U. S. 191-192 (1962).

Nor can we ignore the extent to which, in contrast to our prior decisions, the State is responsible for the wealth discrimination in this instance. *Griffin, Douglas, Williams, Tate,* and our other prior cases have dealt with discrimination on the basis of indigency which was attributable to the operation of the private sector. But we have no such simple *de facto* wealth discrimination here. The means for financing public education in Texas are selected and specified by the State. It is the State that has created local school districts, and tied educational funding to the local property tax, and thereby to local district wealth. At the same time, governmentally imposed land use controls have undoubtedly encouraged and rigidified natural trends in the allocation of particular areas for residential or commercial use, and thus determined each district's amount of taxable property wealth. In short, this case, in contrast to the Court's previous wealth discrimination decisions, can only be seen as "unusual in the extent to which governmental action is the cause of the wealth classifications."

In the final analysis, then, the invidious characteristics of the group wealth classification present in this case merely serve to emphasize the need for careful judicial scrutiny of the State's justifications for the resulting inter-district discrimination in the educational opportunity afforded to the school children of Texas.

D

The nature of our inquiry into the justifications for state discrimination is essentially the same in all equal protection cases: we must consider the substantiality of the state interests sought to be served, and we must scrutinize the reasonableness of the means by which the State has sought to advance its interests. *See Police Dept. of Chicago v. Mosley,* 408 U.S. at 408 U. S. 95. Differences in the application of this test are, in my view, a function of the constitutional importance of the interests at stake and the invidiousness of the particular classification. In terms of the asserted state interests, the Court has indicated that it will require, for instance, a "compelling," *Shapiro v. Thompson,* 394 U.S. at 394 U. S. 634, or a "substantial" or "important," *Dunn v. Blumstein,* 405 U.S. at 405 U. S. 343, state interest to justify discrimination affecting individual interests of constitutional significance. Whatever the differences, if any, in these descriptions of the character of the state interest necessary to sustain such discrimination, basic to each is, I believe, a concern with the legitimacy and the reality of the asserted state interests. Thus, when interests of constitutional importance are at stake, the Court does not stand ready to credit the State's classification with any conceivable legitimate purpose, but demands a clear showing that there are legitimate state interests which the classification was in fact, intended to serve. Beyond the question of the adequacy of the State's purpose for the classification, the Court traditionally has become increasingly sensitive to the means by which a State chooses to act as its action affects more directly interests of constitutional significance. *See, e.g., United States v. Robel,* 389 U. S. 258, 389 U. S. 265 (1967); *Shelton v. Tucker,* 364 U. S. 479, 364 U. S. 488 (1960). Thus, by now, "less restrictive alternatives" analysis is firmly established in equal protection jurisprudence. *See Dunn v. Blumstein, supra,* at 405 U. S. 343; *Kramer v. Union School District,* 395 U.S. at 395 U. S. 627. It seems to me that the range of choice we are willing to accord the State in selecting the means by which it will act, and the care with which we scrutinize the effectiveness of the means which the State selects, also must reflect the constitutional importance of the interest affected and the invidiousness of the particular classification. Here, both the nature of the interest and the classification dictate close judicial scrutiny of the purposes which Texas seeks to serve with its present educational financing scheme and of the means it has selected to serve that purpose.

The only justification offered by appellants to sustain the discrimination in educational opportunity caused by the Texas financing scheme is local educational control. Presented with this justification, the District Court concluded that

"[n]ot only are defendants unable to demonstrate compelling state interests for their classifications based upon wealth, they fail even to establish a reasonable basis for these classifications."

337 F. Supp. at 284. I must agree with this conclusion.

At the outset, I do not question that local control of public education, as an abstract matter, constitutes a very substantial state interest. We observed only last Term that "[d]irect control over decisions vitally affecting the education of one's children is a need that is strongly felt in our society." *Wright v. Council of the City of Emporia,* 407 U. S. 451, 407 U. S. 469 (1972). *See also id.* at 407 U. S. 477-478 (BURGER, C.J., dissenting). The State's interest in local educational control—which certainly includes questions of educational funding—has deep roots in the inherent benefits of community support for public education. Consequently, true state dedication to local control would present, I think, a substantial justification to weigh against simply inter-district variations in the treatment of a State's school children. But I need not now decide how I might ultimately strike the balance were we confronted with a situation where the State's sincere concern for local control inevitably produced educational inequality. For, on this record, it is apparent that the State's purported concern with local control is offered primarily as an excuse, rather than as a justification for inter-district inequality.

In Texas, state-wide laws regulate in fact, the most minute details of local public education. For example, the State prescribes required courses. All textbooks must be submitted for state approval, and only approved textbooks may be used. The State has established the qualifications necessary for teaching in Texas public schools and the procedures for obtaining certification. The State has even legislated on the length of the school day. Texas' own courts have said:

"As a result of the acts of the Legislature, our school system is not of mere local concern, but it is state-wide. While a school district is local in territorial limits, it is an integral part of the vast school system which is co-extensive with the confines of the State of Texas."

Treadaway v. Whitney Independent School District, 205 S.W.2d 97, 99 Tex.Ct. Civ.App. (1947). *See also El Dorado Independent School District v. Tisdale,* 3 S.W.2d 420, 422 (Tex. Comm'n App. 1928).

Moreover, even if we accept Texas' general dedication to local control in educational matters, it is difficult to find any evidence of such dedication with respect to fiscal matters. It ignores reality to suggest—as the Court does, *ante* at 411 U. S. 49-50—that the local property tax element of the Texas financing scheme reflects a conscious legislative effort to provide school districts with local fiscal control. If Texas had a system truly dedicated to local fiscal control, one would expect the quality of the educational opportunity provided in each district to vary with the decision of the voters in that district as to the level of sacrifice they wish to make for public education. In fact, the Texas scheme produces precisely the opposite result. Local school districts cannot choose to have the best education in the State by imposing the highest tax rate. Instead, the quality of the educational opportunity offered by any particular district is largely determined by the amount of taxable property located in the district—a factor over which local voters can exercise no control.

The study introduced in the District Court showed a direct inverse relationship between equalized taxable district property wealth and district tax effort with the result that the property-poor districts making the highest tax effort obtained the lowest per-pupil yield. The implications of this situation for local choice are illustrated by again comparing the Edgewood and Alamo Heights School Districts. In 1967-1968, Edgewood, after contributing its share to the Local Fund Assignment, raised only $26 per pupil through its local property tax, whereas Alamo Heights was able to raise $333 per pupil. Since the funds received through the Minimum Foundation School Program are to be used only for minimum professional salaries, transportation costs, and operating expenses, it is not hard to see the lack of local choice with respect to higher teacher salaries to attract more and better teachers, physical facilities, library books, and facilities, special courses, or participation in special state and federal matching funds programs—under which a property-poor district such as Edgewood is forced to labor. In fact, because of the difference in taxable local property wealth, Edgewood would have to tax itself almost nine times as heavily to obtain the same yield as Alamo Heights. At present, then, local control is a myth for many of the local school districts in Texas. As one district court has observed,

"rather than reposing in each school district the economic power to fix its own level of per pupil expenditure, the State has so arranged the structure as to guarantee that some districts will spend low (with high taxes) while others will spend high (with low taxes)."

Van Dusatz v. Hatfield, 334 F. Supp. 870, 876 (Minn.1971).

In my judgment, any substantial degree of scrutiny of the operation of the Texas financing scheme reveals that the State has selected means wholly inappropriate to secure its purported interest in assuring its school districts local fiscal control. At the same time, appellees have pointed out a variety of alternative financing schemes which may serve the State's purported interest in local control as well as, if not better than, the present scheme without the current impairment of the educational opportunity of vast numbers of Texas school children. I see no need, however, to explore the practical or constitutional merits of those suggested alternatives at this time, for, whatever their positive or negative features, experience with the present financing scheme impugns any suggestion that it constitutes a serious effort to provide local fiscal control. If, for the sake of local education control, this Court is to sustain inter-district discrimination in the educational opportunity afforded Texas school children, it should require that the State present something more than the mere sham now before us.

III

In conclusion, it is essential to recognize that an end to the wide variations in taxable district property wealth inherent in the Texas financing scheme would entail none of the untoward consequences suggested by the Court or by the appellants.

First, affirmance of the District Court's decisions would hardly sound the death knell for local control of education. It would mean neither centralized decisionmaking nor federal court intervention in the operation of public schools. Clearly, this suit has nothing to do with local decisionmaking with respect to educational policy or even educational spending. It involves only a narrow aspect of local control—namely, local control over the raising of educational funds. In fact, in striking down inter-district disparities in taxable local wealth, the District Court took the course which is most likely to make true local control over educational decisionmaking a reality for all Texas school districts.

Nor does the District Court's decision even necessarily eliminate local control of educational funding. The District Court struck down nothing more than the continued inter-district wealth discrimination inherent in the present property tax. Both centralized and decentralized plans for educational funding not involving such inter-district discrimination have been put forward. The choice among these or other alternatives would remain with the State, not with the federal courts. In this regard, it should be evident that the degree of federal intervention in matters of local concern would be substantially less in this context than in previous decisions in which we have been asked effectively to impose a particular scheme upon the States under the guise of the Equal Protection Clause. *See, e.g., Dandridge v. Williams*, 397 U. S. 471 (1970); *cf. Richardson v. Belcher*, 404 U. S. 78 (1971).

Still, we are told that this case requires us "to condemn the State's judgment in conferring on political subdivisions the power to tax local property to supply revenues for local interests." *Ante* at 411 U. S. 40. Yet no one in the course of this entire litigation has ever questioned the constitutionality of the local property tax as a device for raising educational funds. The District Court's decision, at most, restricts the power of the State to make educational funding dependent exclusively upon local property taxation so long as there exists inter-district disparities in taxable property wealth. But it hardly eliminates the local property tax as a source of educational funding or as a means of providing local fiscal control.

The Court seeks solace for its action today in the possibility of legislative reform. The Court's suggestions of legislative redress and experimentation will doubtless be of great comfort to the school children of Texas' disadvantaged districts, but, considering the vested interests of wealthy school districts in the preservation of the *status quo,* they are worth little more. The possibility of legislative action is, in all events, no answer to this Court's duty under the Constitution to eliminate unjustified state discrimination. In this case, we have been presented with an instance of such discrimination, in a particularly invidious form, against an individual interest of large constitutional and practical importance. To support the demonstrated discrimination in the provision of educational opportunity the State has offered a justification which, on analysis, takes on, at best, an ephemeral character. Thus, I believe that the wide disparities in taxable district property wealth inherent in the local property tax element of the Texas financing scheme render that scheme violative of the Equal Protection Clause.

I would therefore affirm the judgment of the District Court.

Glossary

ad valorem tax: a tax that is proportionate to an estimated value

de facto: resulting from social or economic factors rather than laws

suspect class: a grouping of people who have historically suffered because of some form of discrimination, such as racism

SIERRA CLUB V. MORTON

DATE 1972 **AUTHOR** Potter Stewart **VOTE** 4–3	**CITATION** 405 U.S. 727 **SIGNIFICANCE** Confirmed that without evidence of a personal stake, a party could not sue the federal government or a business venture

Overview

The case of *Sierra Club v. Morton* involved the question of whether the Sierra Club, an organization dedicated to the conservation of natural landscapes and fighting for environmental justice, had enough stake in the development of the Mineral King valley in the Sequoia National Forest of California to claim a tort against Walt Disney Enterprises' efforts to develop the region. As Walt Disney set about plans to develop a ski lodge on the outer limits of the Mineral King valley, it needed a highway for the tourists to reach the lodges, which would require state and federal funding. The proposed highway would have to cut through this region of the national forest, which led the Sierra Club to file a lawsuit against Secretary of the Interior Ballard Morton, who approved the highway route and the construction of the resort. While a federal district court would allow the lawsuit to proceed, the Ninth Circuit Court of Appeals argued that the Sierra Club would not suffer personal harm by the development and thus was not eligible for a tort claim, so it had no grounds to bring a suit to federal court under the Administrative Procedure Act (APA). The case was granted certiorari and argued in November 1971 while two court seats were vacant (Justices Lewis Powell and William Rehnquist would both join the Court in January 1972) and ultimately would confirm the Ninth Circuit's ruling that without evidence of a personal stake, an individual could not sue the federal government or a business venture.

Context

The end of the 1960s and the 1970s were a period of great liberalization in the United States arising from a confluence of two major events that would shape American views. The first was the coming of age of the Baby Boomers, the children born in the post–World War II era, who helped bring about a socially liberal view of the world that became increasingly critical as the fears of a nuclear war between the United States and the Soviet Union intensified with each newly tested atomic weapon. The voting bloc created by the Baby Boomers helped shape numerous American events and policies, including the election of John F. Kennedy, the passage of the Civil Rights and Voting Rights acts, and the eventual withdrawal of American

Mineral King Valley
(Wikimedia Commons)

forces from Vietnam. The second factor was the Vietnam War, which led many Americans to lose faith in the government, creating what political scientists refer to as a credibility gap. As theories arose about how big businesses like DuPont and Goodyear had influenced American leadership to become involved in the Vietnam War, Americans became increasingly critical of just how much freedom at the expense of the people (and nature) big business was able to achieve as they no longer viewed government as serving the masses but, rather, the elites.

One of the primary concerns of the Baby Boomer generation was that the natural spaces of the United States would be threatened by the increasing actions of big business to gain a profit. Large swaths of land had already been bought up by developers to build the suburban homes that defined the 1950s and 1960s American family, and the rapid gross domestic product (GDP) growth of the United States in the 1950s, coupled with the work of labor unions, led to major increases in wages for industrial workers. By the end of the 1960s, most families owned at least one automobile and had the means to take vacations to locations such as Disneyland in Los Angeles, California. During the end of the 1960s, the United States Forestry Service accepted a $35 billion bid from Walt Disney Enterprises to develop a ski resort capable of handling over a million visitors annually, including 20,000 skiers during the busy winter season. Coupled with Disney's large donations to gubernatorial candidate Ronald Reagan's campaign in 1966, Disney ensured that it would have the support not only of the federal government but of the state of California in the development of the highway leading to the resort.

Historically speaking, the case against Disney was a difficult one for the Sierra Club. The Sierra Club was a nonprofit organization that had an interest in the protection and preservation of wildlife and natural areas, but it didn't have a personal stake in any claim against Walt Disney Enterprises as a whole. America's judicial system had typically favored big business in lawsuits, particularly when no evidence of a personal harm against the petitioner could be found (essentially, when a case lacked a basic tort claim). The Sierra Club saw an opportunity to address this, however, in the Second Circuit Court of Appeals case of *Scenic Hudson Preservation Conference v. Federal Power Commission* (1965), in which the Court ruled that the Scenic Hudson Preservation Conference had grounds to challenge the Federal Power Commission over the creation of a new power plant in Storm King, New York. Subsequently, using the Administrative Procedure Act as their grounds to challenge the procedures and decisions of the Department of the Interior, the Sierra Club filed suit in the Federal District Court of Northern California.

At the lowest level of the courts, the judge concurred with the Sierra Club's standing to file suit and ordered an immediate injunction against Disney's plans to move forward with the construction and property attainment for the project. The U.S. Department of Interior, headed by Secretary Roger C.B. Morton, filed an appeal with the U.S. Ninth Circuit Court of Appeals arguing that the judge had overstepped his authority in granting the injunction as the Sierra Club lacked the capability to sue. Subsequently, on November 17, 1971, the case was heard before the United States Supreme Court, which was still missing two justices (John Marshall Harlan II and Hugo Black having passed away that year and Nixon's nominees not yet sworn in). Many looked at the case with interest as Chief Justice Warren E. Burger had refused to overturn many of the perceived "liberal" precedents established by the Warren Court despite his strong conservative interpretation of legal doctrine.

About the Author

Justice Potter Stewart had been on the Supreme Court bench since his appointment in 1958 by President Dwight D. Eisenhower and had written several opinions in landmark cases during the Earl Warren Court. One of his most notable opinions was for *Katz v. United States*, in which he wrote that the Fourth Amendment protected the "rights of people, not places." This meant that the expectation of privacy was no longer related only to physical objects but also to words. Despite his liberal leanings in support of protecting the accused and those protesting for civil rights in the South (*Shuttlesworth v. City of Birmingham*), he also recognized needs for limiting power and freedom of the people. In *Whalen v. Roe*, for example, he argued that while *Katz* extended protections to the people from government intrusion, it did not prohibit the government from collecting information as the right to privacy was tied to the Fourth Amendment regarding search and seizure. This reflected Stewart's strict interpretation of the Constitution in his writing of legal doctrine.

The three dissenting justices—William O. Douglas, William Brennan Jr., and Harry Blackmun—were often seen as more liberal justices who tended to push for the expansion and protection of individual rights over those of the state. Douglas, who had joined the Court during the New Deal era, often argued against the policies of big business in favor of labor (making him a natural target of the Republican Nixon presidency) and was actively involved in numerous environmental groups around the country. Brennan wrote numerous dissents and opinions during his tenure that expanded the definition of jurisdiction for the courts regarding cases involving business law and often empowered states to have increasing authority to regulate businesses using the judicial arm rather than the legislative one.

Explanation and Analysis of the Document

The final decision of the Supreme Court came in 1972 with a split vote of 4–3. Concurring with Justice Potter Stewart were Chief Justice Burger and Associate Justices Byron White and Thurgood Marshall. William O. Douglas, William Brennan, and Harry Blackmun each wrote dissents. The Court upheld that the Sierra Club did not have grounds to bring suit against the secretary of the interior because it lacked proof that it was independently harmed in the decision to allow Walt Disney Enterprises to construct a resort in the Sequoia National Forest. In his opinion, Justice Stewart referred to the cases of *Data Processing Service v. Camp* and *Barlow v. Collins* as demonstrating instances where the economic impact to the petitioner was real and therefore "the alleged injury was to an interest 'arguably within the zone of interests to be protected or regulated' by the statutes that the agencies were claimed to have violated."

Stewart's opinion opens by discussing the contention that the Sierra Club had grounds for bringing about a tort claim against Disney by looking at past cases the Sierra Club attorneys viewed as pertinent. Stewart uses the same test as was applied in *Baker v. Carr* (1962), in which a party must have a "personal stake in the outcome of the controversy." The Sierra Club claimed that they had met that burden through the APA, which read that "a person suffering legal wrong because of agency action, or adversely affected ... is entitled to judicial review thereof." Stewart counters that in *Data Processing Service v. Camp* (1970) and *Barlow v. Collins* (1970), the Court ruled that the injury must be either direct or as a result of the interests the agency is supposed to protect or regulate. In both *Data Processing* and *Barlow*, there was a direct economic result tied to the decision of the governmental agency involved; this was not the case for the Sierra Club, whose only tie to the decision was related to aesthetic and environmental concerns. This meant that the precedent of enforcing the APA for these two cases did not apply to *Sierra Club v. Morton*.

Stewart addresses this issue in his next section, pointing out that while the Court did not question the importance of environmental and aesthetic well-being to society, these qualities do not in and of themselves represent a natural claim for tort. He defines such a claim specifically as needing to be more cognizable, or tangible, in its effects. This is one of the weaknesses of the Sierra Club's argument: defining aesthetic beauty is difficult to do at a level that can be agreed upon across all subsections of American society, whereas an economic loss can be numerically demonstrated and tangibly experienced. In the case of the Sierra Club, even with the claims that were put forth by the organization, the direct effect of the harm cannot be identifiable to individual members of the Sierra Club but rather only to those who have used the parks and recreational areas. More important, Stewart contended that from a recreational point of view, the increased highway access and the park will provide more opportunities for people to engage with the natural parks, which would make enforcing a claim of harm increasingly difficult.

vDespite affirming that the Sierra Club did not have legal standing to bring suit under the APA, Stewart is careful in his concluding argument to specify that they rendered no other judgments on the merit of this case. This reflected the growing concern in the 1970s regarding the misuse of natural resources and exploitation of land for the economic gain of large corporations such as Disney. This allowed the Sierra Club to reapproach the suit using those who could meet the criteria of the case's decision, which they would do in the summer of 1972. By the fall, however, the governor had withdrawn his support, and the project and the case eventually would die away by the end of the decade.

Justice William O. Douglas counters in his dissent that natural resources should be able to have standing to sue for their protection, an argument that on the surface sounds whimsical but made a strong legal basis to serve in future cases for the Court. He points to examples such as a ship that can become the center of legal disputes or a corporation that takes on the role of an individual when brought to court or when appealing to a court to right a wrong. Douglas acknowledges that the need for economic growth might still see many natural areas bulldozed down for building homes and businesses, but he argues that just as a ship had a nation or business arguing for it, a person who uses the recreational facilities should have claim to represent the trees. He writes that "those who hike the Appalachian Trail into Sunfish Pond, New Jersey, and camp or sleep there, or run the Allagash in Maine, or climb the Guadalupes in West Texas, or who canoe and portage the Quetico Superior in Minnesota, certainly should have standing to defend those natural wonders before courts or agencies, though they live 3,000 miles away."

Douglas's dissent also points out the increasing concern in America over the growing collusion between the regulatory agencies and the industries they were meant to regulate. While Congress has the power and oversight to prevent such events from occurring, the sheer size of the United States (and therefore, its bureaucracy) makes it an impossible feat to achieve. The businesses are able to dictate and control the agencies by helping them navigate the bureaucratic maze as well as facilitate the election of the very representatives who are slated to oversee and protect the interests that the regulatory body is there to shield. As Douglas points out, they are not inherently "venal or corrupt," but rather, they are simply manipulated into seeing only one side of the picture. This type of corruption would be referred to as "regulatory capture," and it would become a target for Washington throughout much of the 1970s and early 1980s.

Impact

Although the Sierra Club lost the battle, ultimately surrendering its case in 1977, it did in fact bring about a powerful victory regarding environmentalism and its relevance in the courts. For an environmental group to achieve the standing needed to bring about a tort claim such as that seen in Mineral King, all they needed to do was produce an individual or group within the organization who could prove they had been harmed by the actions or would face harm from the actions. This could be a simple impact, such as one affecting a person who fishes or hikes in the mountains, or a more advanced impact affecting, for example, a nature photographer. Organizations such as the Sierra Club often had the financial and political resources to fuel a long, extended court battle and thus would better be able to protect the environmental interests than a single individual.

As noted, the case left open the opportunity for the Sierra Club to renew its legal challenge by showing how it would be impacted from the development as local club outings would no longer be able to occur. The courts allowed the challenge to proceed, which put increased pressure on Governor Ronald Reagan to withdraw his approval, and the project died. Eventually, the region would become absorbed as part of the Sequoia National Park and would be added to several acts of Congress, ensuring its protection for the foreseeable future.

Questions for Further Study

1. What is the significance of U.S. courts not siding with a large company such as Disney? How did that differ from American legal practice only a century before?

2. It is sometimes said that the dissenters in Supreme Court cases often set the tone for future case precedent. To what extent did Douglas's arguments help establish not just American jurisprudence regarding environmentalism but global activism as well?

3. How did this case potentially expose the flaws of regulatory agencies operating in Washington, D.C., but tied to congressional budgets and political championing of political action committees and other interest groups? How did this case represent the 1970s "iron triangle" as well as a public outcry against it as well?

Further Reading

Books

McKeown, M. Margaret. "The Trees Are Still Standing—The Backstory of Sierra Club v. Morton." In *Citizen Justice: The Environmental Legacy of William O. Douglas—Public Advocate and Conservation Champion*, 143–58. Lincoln: University of Nebraska Press, 2022. https://doi.org/10.2307/j.ctv2pfq2gh.14.

Selmi, Daniel P. *Dawn at the Mineral King Valley*. Chicago: University of Chicago Press, 2022.

Articles

Niro, William L. "Constitutional Law—Standing to Sue in Environmental Litigation: Sierra Club v. Morton." *DePaul Law Review* 22, no. 2 (Winter 1973) 451–60.

Websites

"Bill of Rights." National Archives "Charters of Freedom&dquo; Website. http://www.archives.gov/national-archives-experience/charters/bill_of_rights.html. Accessed on February 19, 2020.

—Commentary by Ryan Fontanella

Sierra Club v. Morton

Document Text

MR. JUSTICE STEWART delivered the opinion of the Court

I

The Mineral King Valley is an area of great natural beauty nestled in the Sierra Nevada Mountains in Tulare County, California, adjacent to Sequoia National Park. It has been part of the Sequoia National Forest since 1926, and is designated as a national game refuge by special Act of Congress. Though once the site of extensive mining activity, Mineral King is now used almost exclusively for recreational purposes. Its relative inaccessibility and lack of development have limited the number of visitors each year, and at the same time have preserved the valley's quality as a *quasi*-wilderness area largely uncluttered by the products of civilization.

The United States Forest Service, which is entrusted with the maintenance and administration of national forests, began in the late 1940's to give consideration to Mineral King as a potential site for recreational development. Prodded by a rapidly increasing demand for skiing facilities, the Forest Service published a prospectus in 1965, inviting bids from private developers for the construction and operation of a ski resort that would also serve as a summer recreation area. The proposal of Walt Disney Enterprises, Inc., was chosen from those of six bidders, and Disney received a three-year permit to conduct surveys and explorations in the valley in connection with its preparation of a complete master plan for the resort.

The final Disney plan, approved by the Forest Service in January, 1969, outlines a $35 million complex of motels, restaurants, swimming pools, parking lots, and other structures designed to accommodate 14,000 visitors daily. This complex is to be constructed on 80 acres of the valley floor under a 30-year use permit from the Forest Service. Other facilities, including ski lifts, ski trails, a cog-assisted railway, and utility installations, are to be constructed on the mountain slopes and in other parts of the valley under a revocable special use permit. To provide access to the resort, the State of California proposes to construct a highway 20 miles in length. A section of this road would traverse Sequoia National Park, as would a proposed high-voltage power line needed to provide electricity for the resort. Both the highway and the power line require the approval of the Department of the Interior, which is entrusted with the preservation and maintenance of the national parks.

Representatives of the Sierra Club, who favor maintaining Mineral King largely in its present state, followed the progress of recreational planning for the valley with close attention and increasing dismay. They unsuccessfully sought a public hearing on the proposed development in 1965, and, in subsequent correspondence with officials of the Forest Service and the Department of the Interior, they expressed the Club's objections to Disney's plan as a whole and to particular features included in it. In June, 1969, the Club filed the present suit in the United States District Court for the Northern District of California, seeking a declaratory judgment that various aspects of the proposed development contravene federal laws and regulations governing the preservation of national parks, forests, and game refuges, and also seeking preliminary and permanent injunctions restraining the federal officials involved from granting their approval or issuing permits in connection with the Mineral King project. The petitioner Sierra Club sued as a membership corporation with "a special interest in the conservation and the sound maintenance of the national parks, game refuges and forests of the country," and invoked the judicial review provisions of the Administrative Procedure Act, 5 U.S.C. § 701 *et seq.*

After two days of hearings, the District Court granted the requested preliminary injunction. It rejected the respondents' challenge to the Sierra Club's standing to sue, and determined that the hearing had raised questions "concerning possible excess of statutory authority, sufficiently substantial and serious to justify a preliminary injunction. . . ." The respondents appealed, and the Court of Appeals for the Ninth Circuit reversed. 433 F.2d 24. With respect to the petitioner's standing, the court noted that there was

"no allegation in the complaint that members of the Sierra Club would be affected by the actions of [the respondents] other than the fact that the actions are personally displeasing or distasteful to them,"

id. at 33, and concluded:

"We do not believe such club concern without a showing of more direct interest can constitute standing in the legal sense sufficient to challenge the exercise of responsibilities on behalf of all the citizens by two cabinet level officials of the government acting under Congressional and Constitutional authority."

Id. at 30. Alternatively, the Court of Appeals held that the Sierra Club had not made an adequate showing of irreparable injury and likelihood of success on the merits to justify issuance of a preliminary injunction. The court thus vacated the injunction. The Sierra Club filed a petition for a writ of certiorari which we granted, 401 U.S. 907, to review the questions of federal law presented.

II

The first question presented is whether the Sierra Club has alleged facts that entitle it to obtain judicial review of the challenged action. Whether a party has a sufficient stake in an otherwise justiciable controversy to obtain judicial resolution of that controversy is what has traditionally been referred to as the question of standing to sue. Where the party does not rely on any specific statute authorizing invocation of the judicial process, the question of standing depends upon whether the party has alleged such a "personal stake in the outcome of the controversy," *Baker v. Carr,* 369 U. S. 186, 369 U. S. 204, as to ensure that

"the dispute sought to be adjudicated will be presented in an adversary context and in a form historically viewed as capable of judicial resolution."

Flast v. Cohen, 392 U. S. 83, 392 U. S. 101. Where, however, Congress has authorized public officials to perform certain functions according to law, and has provided by statute for judicial review of those actions under certain circumstances, the inquiry as to standing must begin with a determination of whether the statute in question authorizes review at the behest of the plaintiff. The Sierra Club relies upon § 10 of the Administrative Procedure Act (APA), 5 U.S.C. § 702, which provides:

"A person suffering legal wrong because of agency action, or adversely affected or aggrieved by agency action within the meaning of a relevant statute, is entitled to judicial review thereof."

Early decisions under this statute interpreted the language as adopting the various formulations of "legal interest" and "legal wrong" then prevailing as constitutional requirements of standing. But, in *Data Processing Service v. Camp,* 397 U. S. 150, and *Barlow v. Collins,* 397 U. S. 159, decided the same day, we held more broadly that persons had standing to obtain judicial review of federal agency action under § 10 of the APA where they had alleged that the challenged action had caused them "injury in fact," and where the alleged injury was to an interest "arguably within the zone of interests to be protected or regulated" by the statutes that the agencies were claimed to have violated.

In *Data Processing,* the injury claimed by the petitioners consisted of harm to their competitive position in the computer servicing market through a ruling by the Comptroller of the Currency that national banks might perform data processing services for their customers. In *Barlow,* the petitioners were tenant farmers who claimed that certain regulations of the Secretary of Agriculture adversely affected their economic position *vis-a-vis* their landlords. These palpable economic injuries have long been recognized as sufficient to lay the basis for standing, with or without a specific statutory provision for judicial review. Thus, neither *Data Processing* nor *Barlow* addressed itself to the question, which has arisen with increasing frequency in federal courts in recent years, as to what must be alleged by persons who claim injury of a noneconomic nature to interests that are widely shared. That question is presented in this case.

III

The injury alleged by the Sierra Club will be incurred entirely by reason of the change in the uses to which Mineral King will be put, and the attendant change in the aesthetics and ecology of the area. Thus, in referring to the road to be built through Sequoia National Park, the complaint alleged that the development

"would destroy or otherwise adversely affect the scenery, natural and historic objects and wildlife of the park, and would impair the enjoyment of the park for future generations."

We do not question that this type of harm may amount to an "injury in fact" sufficient to lay the basis for standing under § 10 of the APA. Aesthetic and environmental wellbeing, like economic wellbeing, are important ingredients of the quality of life in our society, and the fact that particular environmental interests are shared by the many, rather than the few, does not make them less deserving of legal protection through the judicial process. But the "injury in fact," test requires more than an injury to a cognizable interest. It requires that the party seeking review be himself among the injured.

The impact of the proposed changes in the environment of Mineral King will not fall indiscriminately upon every citizen. The alleged injury will be felt directly only by those who use Mineral King and Sequoia National Park, and for whom the aesthetic and recreational values of the area will be lessened by the highway and ski resort. The Sierra Club failed to allege that it or its members would be affected in any of their activities or pastimes by the Disney development. Nowhere in the pleadings or affidavits did the Club state that its members use Mineral King for any purpose, much less that they use it in any way that would be significantly affected by the proposed action of the respondents.

The Club apparently regarded any allegations of individualized injury as superfluous, on the theory that this was a "public" action involving questions as to the use of natural resources, and that the Club's longstanding concern with and expertise in such matters were sufficient to give it standing as a "representative of the public." This theory reflects a misunderstanding of our cases involving so-called "public actions" in the area of administrative law.

The origin of the theory advanced by the Sierra Club may be traced to a dictum in *Scripps-Howard Radio v. FCC,* 316 U. S. 4, in which the licensee of a radio station in Cincinnati, Ohio, sought a stay of an order of the FCC allowing another radio station in a nearby city to change its frequency and increase its range. In discussing its power to grant a stay, the Court noted that "these private litigants have standing only as representatives of the public interest." *Id.* at 316 U. S. 14. But that observation did not describe the basis upon which the appellant was allowed to obtain judicial review as a "person aggrieved" within the meaning of the statute involved in that case, since Scripps Howard was clearly "aggrieved" by reason of the economic injury that it would suffer as a result of the Commission's action. The Court's statement was, rather, directed to the theory upon which Congress had authorized judicial review of the Commission's actions. That theory had been described earlier in *FCC v. Sanders Bros. Radio Station,* 309 U. S. 470, 309 U. S. 477, as follows:

"Congress had some purpose in enacting § 40(b)(2). It may have been of opinion that one likely to be financially injured by the issue of a license would be the only person having a sufficient interest to bring to the attention of the appellate court errors of law in the action of the Commission in granting the license. It is within the power of Congress to confer such standing to prosecute an appeal."

Taken together, *Sanders* and *Scripps-Howard* thus established a dual proposition: the fact of economic injury is what gives a person standing to seek judicial review under the statute, but, once review is properly invoked, that person may argue the public interest in support of his claim that the agency has failed to comply with its statutory mandate. It was in the latter sense that the "standing" of the appellant in *Scripps-Howard* existed only as a "representative of the public interest." It is in a similar sense that we have used the phrase "private attorney general" to describe the function performed by persons upon whom Congress has conferred the right to seek judicial review of agency action. *See Data Processing, supra,* at 397 U. S. 154.

The trend of cases arising under the APA and other statutes authorizing judicial review of federal agency action has been toward recognizing that injuries other than economic harm are sufficient to bring a person within the meaning of the statutory language, and toward discarding the notion that an injury that is widely shared is *ipso facto* not an injury sufficient to provide the basis for judicial review. We noted this development with approval in *Data Processing,* 397 U.S. at 397 U. S. 154, in saying that the interest alleged to have been injured "may reflect *aesthetic, conservational, and recreational,' as well as economic, values." But broadening the categories of injury that may be alleged in support of standing is a different matter from abandoning the requirement that the party seeking review must himself have suffered an injury.*

Some courts have indicated a willingness to take this latter step by conferring standing upon organizations that have demonstrated "an organizational interest in the problem" of environmental or consumer protection. *Environmental Defense Fund v. Hardin,* 138 U.S.App.D.C. 391, 395, 428 F.2d 1093, 1097. It is clear that an organization whose members are injured may represent those members in a proceeding for judicial review. *See, e.g., NAACP v. Button,* 371 U. S. 415, 371 U. S. 428. But a mere "interest in a problem," no matter how longstanding the interest and no matter how qualified the organization is in evaluating the problem, is not sufficient, by itself, to render the organization "adversely affected" or "aggrieved" within the meaning of the APA. The Sierra Club is a large and long-established organization, with a historic commitment to the cause of protecting our Nation's natural heritage from man's depredations. But if a "special interest" in this subject were enough to entitle the Sierra Club to commence this litigation, there would appear to be no objective basis upon which to disallow a suit by any other *bona fide* "special interest" organization, however small or short-lived. And if any group with a *bona fide* "special interest" could initiate such litigation, it is difficult to perceive why any individual citizen with the same *bona fide* special interest would not also be entitled to do so.

The requirement that a party seeking review must allege facts showing that he is himself adversely affected does not insulate executive action from judicial review, nor does it prevent any public interests from being protected through the judicial process. It does serve as at least a rough attempt to put the decision as to whether review will be sought in the hands of those who have a direct stake in the outcome. That goal would be undermined were we to construe the APA to authorize judicial review at the behest of organizations or individuals who seek to do no more than vindicate their own value preferences through the judicial process. The principle that the Sierra Club would have us establish in this case would do just that.

As we conclude that the Court of Appeals was correct in its holding that the Sierra Club lacked standing to maintain this action, we do not reach any other questions presented in the petition, and we intimate no view on the merits of the complaint. The judgment is

Affirmed.

MR. JUSTICE DOUGLAS, dissenting

I share the views of my Brother BLACKMUN, and would reverse the judgment below.

The critical question of "standing" would be simplified and also put neatly in focus if we fashioned a federal rule that allowed environmental issues to be litigated before federal agencies or federal courts in the name of the inanimate object about to be despoiled, defaced, or invaded by roads and bulldozers, and where injury is the subject of public outrage. Contemporary public concern for protecting nature's ecological equilibrium should lead to the conferral of standing upon environmental objects to sue for their own preservation. *See* Stone, Should Trees Have Standing?— Toward Legal Rights for Natural Objects, 45 S.Cal.L.Rev. 450 (1972). This suit would therefore be more properly labeled as *Mineral King v. Morton.*

Inanimate objects are sometimes parties in litigation. A ship has a legal personality, a fiction found useful for maritime purposes. The corporation sole— a creature of ecclesiastical law— is an acceptable adversary, and large fortunes ride on its cases. The ordinary corporation is a "person" for purposes of the adjudicatory processes, whether it represents proprietary, spiritual, aesthetic, or charitable causes.

So it should be as respects valleys, alpine meadows, rivers, lakes, estuaries, beaches, ridges, groves of trees, swampland, or even air that feels the destructive pressures of modern technology and modern life. The river, for example, is the living symbol of all the life it sustains or nourishes— fish, aquatic insects, water ouzels, otter, fisher, deer, elk, bear, and all other animals, including man, who are dependent on it or who enjoy it for its sight, its sound, or its life. The river as plaintiff speaks for the ecological unit of life that is part of it. Those people who have a meaningful relation to that body of water— whether it be a fisherman, a canoeist, a zoologist, or a logger— must be able to speak for the values which the river represents, and which are threatened with destruction.

I do not know Mineral King. I have never seen it, nor traveled it, though I have seen articles describing its proposed "development" notably Hano, Protectionists vs. recreationists— The Battle of Mineral King, N.Y. Times Mag., Aug. 17, 1969, p. 25; and Browning, Mickey Mouse in the Mountain, Harper's, March 1972, p. 65. The Sierra Club, in its complaint alleges that "[o]ne of the principal purposes of the Sierra Club is to protect and conserve the national resources of the Sierra Nevada Mountains." The District Court held that this uncontested allegation made the Sierra Club "sufficiently aggrieved" to have "standing" to sue on behalf of Mineral King.

Mineral King is doubtless like other wonders of the Sierra Nevada such as Tuolumne Meadows and the John Muir Trail. Those who hike it, fish it, hunt it, camp in it, frequent it, or visit it merely to sit in solitude and wonderment are legitimate spokesmen for it, whether they may be few or many. Those who have that intimate relation with the inanimate object about to be injured, polluted, or otherwise despoiled are its legitimate spokesmen.

The Solicitor General, whose views on this subject are in the Appendix to this opinion, takes a wholly different approach. He considers the problem in terms of "government by the Judiciary." With all respect, the problem is to make certain that the inanimate objects, which are the very core of America's beauty, have spokesmen before they are destroyed. It is, of course, true that most of them are under the control of a federal or state agency. The standards given those agencies are usually expressed in terms of the "public interest." Yet "public interest" has so many differing shades of meaning as to be quite meaningless on the environmental front. Congress accordingly has adopted ecological standards in the National Environmental Policy Act of 1969, Pub.L. 91-190, 83 Stat. 852, 42 U.S.C. § 4321 *et seq.*, and guidelines for agency action have been provided by the Council on Environmental Quality, of which Russell E. Train is Chairman. *See* 36 Fed.Reg. 7724.

Yet the pressures on agencies for favorable action one way or the other are enormous. The suggestion that Congress can stop action which is undesirable is true in theory; yet even Congress is too remote to give meaningful direction, and its machinery is too ponderous to use very often. The federal agencies of which I speak are not venal or corrupt. But they are notoriously under the control of powerful interests who manipulate them through advisory committees, or friendly working relations, or who have that natural affinity with the agency which in time develops between the regulator and the regulated. As early as 1894, Attorney General Olney predicted that regulatory agencies might become "industry-minded," as illustrated by his forecast concerning the Interstate Commerce Commission:

"The Commission . . . is, or can be, made of great use to the railroads. It satisfies the popular clamor for a government supervision of railroads, at the same time that that supervision is almost entirely nominal. Further, the older such a commission gets to be, the more inclined it will be found to take the business and railroad view of things."

M. Josephson, The Politicos 526 (1938).

Years later, a court of appeals observed,

"the recurring question which has plagued public regulation of industry [is] whether the regulatory agency is unduly oriented toward the interests of the industry it is designed to regulate, rather than the public interest it is designed to protect."

Moss v. CAB, 139 U.S.App.D.C. 150, 152, 430 F.2d 891, 893. *See also Office of Communication of the United Church of Christ v. FCC,* 123 U.S.App.D.C. 328, 337-338, 359 F.2d 994, 1003-1004; *Udall v. FPC,* 387 U. S. 428; *Calvert Cliffs' Coordinating Committee, Inc. v. AEC,* 146 U.S.App.D.C. 33, 449 F.2d 1109; *Environmental Defense Fund, Inc. v. Ruckelhaus,* 142 U.S.App.D.C. 74, 439 F.2d 584; *Environmental Defense Fund, Inc. v. HEW,* 138 U.S.App.D.C. 381, 428 F.2d 1083; *Scenic Hudson Preservation Conf. v. FPC,* 354 F.2d

608, 620. *But see* Jaffe, The Federal Regulatory Agencies In Perspective: Administrative Limitations In A Political Setting, 11 B.C.Ind. & Com.L.Rev. 565 (1970) (labels "industry-mindedness" as "devil" theory). The Forest Service— one of the federal agencies behind the scheme to despoil Mineral King— has been notorious for its alignment with lumber companies, although its mandate from Congress directs it to consider the various aspects of multiple use in its supervision of the national forests. The voice of the inanimate object, therefore, should not be stilled. That does not mean that the judiciary takes over the managerial functions from the federal agency. It merely means that, before these priceless bits of Americana (such as a valley, an alpine meadow, a river, or a lake) are forever lost or are so transformed a to be reduced to the eventual rubble of our urban environment, the voice of the existing beneficiaries of these environmental wonders should be heard.

Perhaps they will not win. Perhaps the bulldozers of "progress" will plow under all the aesthetic wonders of this beautiful land. That is not the present question. The sole question is, who has standing to be heard?

Those who hike the Appalachian Trail into Sunfish Pond, New Jersey, and camp or sleep there, or run the Allagash in Maine, or climb the Guadalupes in West Texas, or who canoe and portage the Quetico Superior in Minnesota, certainly should have standing to defend those natural wonders before courts or agencies, though they live 3,000 miles away. Those who merely are caught up in environmental news or propaganda and flock to defend these waters or areas may be treated differently. That is why these environmental issues should be tendered by the inanimate object itself. Then there will be assurances that all of the forms of life which it represents will stand before the court— the pileated woodpecker as well as the coyote and bear, the lemmings as well a the trout in the streams. Those inarticulate members of the ecological group cannot speak. But those people who have so frequented the place as to know its values and wonders will be able to speak for the entire ecological community.

Ecology reflects the land ethic; and Aldo Leopold wrote in A Sand County Almanac 204 (1949), "The land ethic simply enlarges the boundaries of the community to include soils, waters, plants, and animals, or collectively: the land."

That, as I see it, is the issue of "standing" in the present case and controversy.

Glossary

adjudicatory processes: proceedings involved in deciding a legal case

Administrative Procedure Act (APA): a 1946 law that requires agencies, among other duties, to inform the public of their activities and to allow a person who has been adversely affected by an agency's action to sue the agency

certiorari: a superior court's review of a lower court's records

the corporation sole: a business entity, sometimes treated as a "person" under the law

litigated: argued within a legal context

mandate: authorization

nominal: in name only

standing: the right to bring legal action

venal: open to bribery

ROE V. WADE

DATE 1973 **AUTHOR** Harry Blackmun **VOTE** 7–2	**CITATION** 410 U.S. 113 **SIGNIFICANCE** Established abortion as a fundamental right guaranteed in the U.S. Constitution

Overview

Abortion, or the deliberate termination of unwanted pregnancy, has occurred in some form in human society since ancient times. Nevertheless, amid the Victorian morals of the mid-nineteenth century, it became one of Western society's most contentious issues, sparking bitter religious and ethical debates that continued into the twenty-first century. In 1973 the Supreme Court case known as *Roe v. Wade* became the most pivotal moment for the issue in the history of the United States.

In *Roe v. Wade*, the Supreme Court for the first time established abortion as a fundamental right guaranteed in the U.S. Constitution, albeit with some qualifications. Regardless, the case brought a virtual end to illegal, unsanitary "back-alley" abortions and, in broader terms, established new parameters for the concept of a constitutional right to privacy.

Context

Before the nineteenth century, abortion was fairly widely available to women in the United States, though it was extremely hazardous because of the lack of advanced medical procedures and knowledge concerning the need for sterilization. Starting in the 1820s, many states began to restrict access to abortion. The Comstock Act (1873), a federal law named for the nineteenth-century anti-obscenity crusader Anthony Comstock, restricted the distribution of birth control devices and information. Twenty-four states passed similar laws, likewise prohibiting the distribution of birth control information and materials. Women continued to seek illegal abortions when poverty, domestic abuse, or other circumstances made pregnancy unwanted; they often suffered grievous injury or death as a result. In 1950, authorities estimated that from 200,000 to 1.3 million illegal abortions were performed in the United States that year.

To some, the abortion debate hinged on whether women should be forced to surrender control of their own bodies to their states of residence. Others held the religious view that life begins at conception, such that abortion is nothing short of murder. Laws varied from state to state, creating a situation that many decried as fundamentally unfair: a woman's ability to obtain an

Norma McCorvey, "Jane Roe" of the Roe v. Wade decision, shown in 1989 with attorney Gloria Allred.
(Lorie Shaull)

abortion depended upon where she happened to live and whether she had the wealth to travel to wherever facilities were available.

In the years leading up to *Roe v. Wade*, a series of Supreme Court precedents began relaxing restrictions on contraception and paved the way for a claim of a right to privacy under the Constitution. The most significant acknowledgment of a privacy right came in the 1965 case of *Griswold v. Connecticut*, which struck down a statute outlawing the use of birth control by married couples. Estelle Griswold, the executive director of Planned Parenthood of Connecticut, had been prosecuted by the state for giving contraceptives to a married couple. In her appeal, the Supreme Court determined that the Constitution presupposes a class of fundamental rights, among which is privacy in matters of marriage, family, and sex. *Griswold* would be a key precedent for *Roe*. Relying on that and other precedent cases, the attorneys Linda Coffee and Sarah Weddington teamed with the plaintiff Norma McCorvey, a former carnival worker and mother of two previous children—who would be named as Jane Roe—to file the original 1970 lawsuit against the Texas district attorney Henry Wade.

Far from settling the debate on abortion, *Roe v. Wade* further stoked Americans' passions over the issue. Subsequently, legal battles continually swirled around the abortion right, and changes to the composition of the Supreme Court during the presidencies of George W. Bush and Donald Trump raised the question of whether the right to abortion would continue to erode or even be reversed at the federal level and thus revert to the states for regulation.

Court observers and the public indeed sensed that a shift had been taking place in the ideological makeup of the Court as it pertained to the abortion issue. In addition to Justice Brett Kavanaugh, President Trump appointed two other justices regarded as conservative, Neil Gorsuch (2017) and Amy Coney Barrett (2020). The *Roe* case gained considerable national attention in light of the legal battles waged over the 2021 Texas

Heartbeat Act, which was more restrictive than Mississippi's law: the Texas act stated that "a physician may not knowingly perform or induce an abortion on a pregnant woman if the physician detected a fetal heartbeat for the unborn child." Generally, such a heartbeat can be detected at around six weeks (although "heartbeat" is somewhat of a misnomer, since an embryo has not yet developed a heart at that stage but rather a tube that generates electrical impulses). Additionally, the Texas act enabled any person to bring a civil action against anyone who performs an illegal abortion and specified that the abortion provider could face a $10,000 fine for each such abortion.

On June 24, 2022, a seismic event took place: the U.S. Supreme Court, in *Dobbs v. Jackson Women's Health Organization*, issued a landmark ruling that overturned *Roe v. Wade* (and *Planned Parenthood v. Casey*). The essence of the ruling was that the U.S. Constitution does not confer a right to an abortion. The impact of the ruling was that the states, through their elected legislators, had the authority to define abortion rights and restrictions at the state level.

The case involved the question of whether a 2018 state law in Mississippi that banned most abortions after fifteen weeks of pregnancy was constitutional. The law was one of a number of so-called fetal heartbeat laws passed in various states; these laws banned abortion after a cardiac activity in an embryo or fetus could be detected. In Mississippi, the Jackson Women's Health Organization, the state's only abortion clinic, sued Thomas E. Dobbs, an officer with the state department of health, to block enforcement of the law. Its efforts were successful in lower courts, which issued injunctions based on the Supreme Court's ruling in *Planned Parenthood v. Casey*, a 1992 case in which the Court prevented states from banning abortions any time before a fetus was viable, usually within the first twenty-four weeks. In that case, the Court ruled that a woman's right to an abortion was protected by the equal protection clause of the Fourteenth Amendment to the Constitution.

The majority in *Dobbs* emphasized that it was not ruling on the advisability or morality of abortion. The majority saw the matter strictly as a constitutional issue. The Court's syllabus stated that the *Roe* decision was "egregiously wrong and on a collision course with the Constitution from the day it was decided." Justice Kavanaugh wrote:

The issue before this Court, however, is not the policy or morality of abortion. The issue before this Court is what the Constitution says about abortion. The Constitution does not take sides on the issue of abortion. The text of the Constitution does not refer to or encompass abortion.... The Constitution is neutral and leaves the issue for the people and their elected representatives to resolve through the democratic process in the States or Congress—like the numerous other difficult questions of American social and economic policy that the Constitution does not address.

In response to the verdict in *Dobbs*, President Joe Biden pledged to codify the ruling in *Roe v. Wade* into law, essentially nullifying the decision in *Dobbs*. The year 2022 was a midterm election year, and a number of Democrats running for office or for reelection made clear their opposition to the ruling in *Dobbs*.

About the Author

Roe v. Wade was the defining case of Associate Justice Harry Blackmun's twenty-four-year career on the Supreme Court, which stretched from 1970 to 1994. When President Richard Nixon nominated Blackmun for the Court in April 1970, following the Senate rejection of two southern conservative nominees, Blackmun seemed poised to adhere to conventional Republican principles. He and Chief Justice Warren Burger were friends, and newspapers dubbed them the "Minnesota twins" because of their shared history in the state. As Blackmun's career progressed, however, particularly after the *Roe* decision, his opinions drifted toward the Court's liberal side, as he often sided with Justices William Brennan and Thurgood Marshall in finding constitutional protection for individual rights.

Born in Illinois on November 12, 1908, and reared in Minnesota, Blackmun was a 1932 graduate of Harvard Law School. He married Dorothy Clark in 1941 and fathered three daughters. Perhaps the most influential phase of his career before he sat on the federal bench was his service as resident counsel for the Mayo Clinic in Rochester, Minnesota, from 1950 to 1959. That pioneering era for heart surgery exhilarated Blackmun and inspired in him an almost reverential respect for physicians. After joining the Eighth Circuit Court of

Sarah Weddington, along with Linda Coffee, represented Norma McCorvey.
(National Archives and Records Administration)

Appeals upon President Dwight Eisenhower's nomination, he continued to serve on the board of directors of the Rochester Methodist Hospital until ascending to the Supreme Court. He would later state that if he had had the chance to pursue his career over again, he would have become a physician. In the summer of 1972, he did much of his work on the *Roe* opinion from the Mayo Clinic's library.

Blackmun's interest in the practice of medicine resonates throughout the *Roe* opinion, particularly in his examination of the Hippocratic oath and in his footnote citation of medical texts such as Arturo Castiglioni's *History of Medicine*. Blackmun's opinion reflected the Court's 7–2 majority ruling, with Justices Burger, Brennan, William Douglas, Marshall, Lewis Powell, and Potter Stewart joining and with Justices Byron White and William Rehnquist dissenting. After *Roe*, Blackmun received a flood of public response and letters, including some death threats.

Another significant issue addressed by Blackmun during his Supreme Court career was the death penalty. Although he often voted to uphold capital punishment in his early cases, he reversed himself shortly before his retirement in a dissenting opinion in 1994's *Callins v. Collins*, declaring the death penalty unconstitutional in all circumstances. At the time of his retirement from the Court in 1994, he was considered one of the Court's most liberal justices. Blackmun died on March 4, 1999, following complications from hip surgery.

Explanation and Analysis of the Document

Three appellants came before the Court challenging Texas abortion statutes. The first was Jane Roe (Norma McCorvey), a single woman who was pregnant and had been unable to procure a legal abortion at the time she filed action against the Dallas County district attorney Henry Wade in 1970. The second appellant was the licensed physician James Hubert Hallford, who had faced two state prosecutions for performing abortions and argued that the Texas statute was unconstitutionally vague and violated his own and his patients' rights. The third was the married couple John and Mary Doe (David and Marsha King). Mary Doe suffered from a medical disorder that left her unable to use birth control pills and made pregnancy a medical danger; the couple sued on the grounds of potential injury resulting from possible contraceptive failure and pregnancy.

The Majority Opinion

The majority ruling, authored by Justice Harry Blackmun and joined by Justices Burger, Brennan, Douglas, Marshall, Powell, and Stewart, holds that only Roe had the standing to sue. The ruling establishes that the end of Roe's pregnancy—she gave birth and allowed the child to be adopted—did not render the case moot; that Hallford's arguments could be asserted in his defense in state courts and therefore did not belong in federal court; and that the Does' complaint was too "speculative ... to present an actual case or controversy." Then—the part that those in the courtroom in January 1973 were waiting to hear—the ruling declares that abortion is constitutionally protected by the right to privacy implicit in the Fourteenth Amendment. In her cultural and legal history of the case, *Roe v. Wade: Marking the 20th Anniversary of the Landmark Supreme Court Decision That Made Abortion Legal*, Marian Faux states, "A palpable sigh of relief went through the courtroom. That was the crux of the opinion—the victory for pro-choice forces, as it were" (p. 308).

The Court does apply some qualifications to the right to abortion, enumerating them as based on three stages of pregnancy. During the first trimester, the abortion decision is left to the woman and her attending physician; between the end of that trimester and the point where the fetus becomes viable, states may regulate abortion "in ways that are reasonably related to maternal health"; and after fetal viability, states may prohibit abortion except when the procedure is necessary to protect the life or health of the mother.

In the initial paragraphs of his opinion, Blackmun acknowledges the controversial nature of the abortion issue and the need to "resolve the issue by constitutional measurement, free of emotion and of predilection." The first four parts following the brief introduction deal with the issues of jurisdiction, standing, and mootness, dismissing the claims of Hallford and the Does. Blackmun rejects the appellee's argument that the case was moot because Roe was no longer pregnant; because of the 266-day length of the normal human gestation period, virtually no pregnancy-related appellate review could be conducted before the natural end of the pregnancy. Blackmun declares, "Our law should not be that rigid."

After a brief paragraph laying out the appellant's argument, Blackmun embarks in part VI on a lengthy history of abortion laws. He begins with the Persian empire and the classical Greek and Roman eras, when abortion was commonly practiced and not barred by ancient religion. He reviews the history of the Hippocratic oath, an ethical guide to the medical profession that proscribes abortion. Blackmun concludes, based on his research, that the oath's rigidity represented a small minority of Greek opinion. He then examines the treatment of abortion across the centuries under English law, common law, and historic American law. He notes that most states did not have laws proscribing abortion until the Civil War era. Thus, until the mid-nineteenth century, he writes, "a woman enjoyed a substantially broader right to terminate a pregnancy than she does in most States today." He then summarizes the stances of the American Medical Association, the American Public Health Association, and the American Bar Association, all of which accepted abortion to varying degrees.

In part VII, Blackmun raises three legislative purposes for the enactment of criminal abortion laws: the discouragement of illicit sexual conduct for moral reasons; the protection of maternal health in light of the medical hazards of abortion procedures that preceded the advent of sterilization; and the protection of prenatal life. Blackmun also introduces the concept of "potential life," which had not been raised by any parties in the case; the appellees argued that life begins at conception, and the appellants disputed that claim. The historian Faux states that the term "appeared to be the Court's own creation" (p. 309) and raised the question of whether fetuses might have some rights of personhood.

Blackmun begins addressing the constitutional contentions of the case in part VIII. He traces the line of Supreme Court decisions establishing a right of personal privacy, notably including *Griswold v. Connecticut*, and concludes that the constitutional right of privacy found in the Fourteenth Amendment "is broad enough to encompass a woman's decision whether or not to terminate her pregnancy." However, he continues, the right is not unqualified and must be balanced against state interests in its regulation.

In part IX, Blackmun turns his attention to the definition of "person" under the law. Despite the questions raised by his earlier use of the term "potential life," Blackmun states that his duty for the case does not entail answering the question of when human life begins. He concludes that nowhere in the Constitution is the term "person" intended to apply before birth.

Part X delineates the framework for how states will be permitted to regulate abortion, based on the stage of pregnancy involved. As Faux notes, this idea as well had not been raised in either the briefs or the oral arguments and appears to be Blackmun's own creation. He chose to permit abortion during the first trimester of pregnancy based on medical evidence that mortality from abortion during that stage is lower than mortality from normal childbirth. Therefore, he writes, the state cannot claim maternal health as a compelling interest. He establishes that the state's interest in regulation becomes compelling at the point of viability of the fetus outside the mother's womb and that states may proscribe abortion during that period "except when it is necessary to preserve the life or health of the mother." In the final two parts, Blackmun summarizes and repeats his key findings about the stages of pregnancy.

He notes that states may prohibit anyone who is not a physician from performing an abortion. Justice Blackmun instructs that the opinion in the companion case *Doe v. Bolton* should be read together with *Roe* and concludes that the Texas statute must fall.

Byron White and William Rehnquist each wrote dissenting opinions in the case.

Impact

On a personal level, the case in fact had no impact on the outcome of its plaintiff's pregnancy; Norma McCorvey wrote in her autobiography *I Am Roe: My Life, Roe v. Wade, and Freedom of Choice* that she learned of the decision only upon reading about it in the newspaper at home the following day. After more than two decades lobbying in favor of abortion rights, she experienced a religious conversion in 1995 and shifted her efforts to anti-abortion causes. Still later, she said that she had been paid for her anti-abortion activism and in fact continued to support abortion rights.

The uniform legalization of abortion, of course, had far-reaching political and social consequences. The 1973 ruling galvanized the nation's political and religious right wing, sparking the formation of the National Right to Life Committee that same year. Under President Ronald Reagan, a Republican Party platform plank called for a constitutional amendment banning abortions, but the issue was a low priority during the Reagan administration. Anti-abortion forces gained traction with the 1988 election of George H.W. Bush—who, ironically, began his political career as a supporter of Planned Parenthood. His successor, Bill Clinton, vetoed several attempts to further restrict abortion, but the 2000 election of President George W. Bush put abortion policies—and nominations for Supreme Court justices—back under right-wing control.

The issue of abortion was indeed revealed to be far from settled as the composition of the Supreme Court evolved. Subsequent decisions barred the use of public hospitals and clinics for abortions and upheld certain restrictions that were deemed not to impose undue burdens on women. On April 18, 2007, the Court voted to uphold a ban on the late-term abortion procedure of intact dilation and extraction, also known as partial-birth abortion, in *Gonzales v. Carhart*. In 2022, the Court overturned *Roe v. Wade* with its decision in *Dobbs v. Jackson Women's Health Organization*.

Questions for Further Study

1. *Roe v. Wade* and *Brown v. Board of Education*, a 1954 ruling that ended racial segregation in public schools, are considered two of the Supreme Court's most significant landmark cases of the twentieth century. Compare and contrast the social impact of each. Which case do you think has had more importance in American society?

2. For centuries, philosophers and theologians have debated the question of when human life begins. The Supreme Court has examined the question of when human life is constitutionally protected on numerous occasions. In the modern era, scientific advancements have pushed the boundaries regarding what is considered a viable fetus. Consider the perspectives from each of these realms of knowledge. When, in your view, does human life begin?

3. The Supreme Court is integral to the constitutional system of checks and balances instituted in the executive, legislative, and judicial branches of the U.S. government. Examine *Roe v. Wade* in the context of this system, and discuss the positions of each of the three branches of government on the abortion issue both before the decision and since the decision was handed down.

Further Reading

Books

Faux, Marion. *Roe v. Wade: Marking the 20th Anniversary of the Landmark Supreme Court Decision That Made Abortion Legal*. New York: Penguin, 1993.

Garrow, David J. *Liberty and Sexuality: The Right to Privacy and the Making of Roe v. Wade*. Berkeley: University of California Press, 1998.

Gordon, Linda. *Woman's Body, Woman's Right: Birth Control in America*. New York: Penguin, 1990.

Hull, N.E.H., and Peter Charles Hoffer. *Roe v. Wade: The Abortion Rights Controversy in American History*, 3rd ed. Lawrence: University Press of Kansas, 2021.

Landis, Jacquelyn, ed. *Abortion*. San Diego: Greenhaven, 2007.

McCorvey, Norma, with Andy Meisler. *I Am Roe: My Life, Roe v. Wade and Freedom of Choice*. New York: HarperCollins, 1994.

McCorvey, Norma, with Gary Thomas. *Won by Love: Norma McCorvey, Jane Roe of Roe v. Wade, Speaks Out for the Unborn as She Shares Her New Conviction for Life*. Nashville, TN: Thomas Nelson, 1997.

Tompkins, Nancy. *Roe v. Wade and the Fight over Life and Liberty*. New York: Franklin Watts, 1996.

Ziegler, Mary. *Abortion and the Law in America: Roe v. Wade to the Present*. New York: Cambridge University Press, 2020.

Articles

Cohen, I. Glenn, Melissa Murray, and Lawrence O. Gostin. "The End of Roe v Wade and New Legal Frontiers on the Constitutional Right to Abortion." *JAMA* 328, no. 4 (2022): 325–26.

Lawler, Kelly. "Roe v Wade's Jane Roe Says She Was Paid to Speak against Abortion in Shocking FX Documentary." *USA Today*, May 21, 2020. https://www.usatoday.com/story/entertainment/tv/2020/05/21/aka-jane-roe-fx-norma-mccorvey-paid-speak-against-abortion/5236476002/.

Prager, Joshua. "The Roe Baby." *Atlantic*, September 9, 2021. https://www.theatlantic.com/politics/archive/2021/09/jane-roe-v-wade-baby-norma-mccorvey/620009/.

Solly, Meilan. "Who Was Norma McCorvey, the Woman behind Roe v. Wade?" *Smithsonian Magazine*, June 24, 2022. https://www.smithsonianmag.com/smart-news/who-was-norma-mccorvey-the-woman-behind-roe-v-wade-180980311/.

—Commentary by Leigh Dyer and Michael J. O'Neal

ROE V. WADE

Document Text

Mr. Justice Blackmun delivered the opinion of the Court

This Texas federal appeal and its Georgia companion, *Doe v. Bolton*, post, p. 179, present constitutional challenges to state criminal abortion legislation. The Texas statutes under attack here are typical of those that have been in effect in many States for approximately a century. The Georgia statutes, in contrast, have a modern cast, and are a legislative product that, to an extent at least, obviously reflects the influences of recent attitudinal change, of advancing medical knowledge and techniques, and of new thinking about an old issue.

We forthwith acknowledge our awareness of the sensitive and emotional nature of the abortion controversy, of the vigorous opposing views, even among physicians, and of the deep and seemingly absolute convictions that the subject inspires. One's philosophy, one's experiences, one's exposure to the raw edges of human existence, one's religious training, one's attitudes toward life and family and their values, and the moral standards one establishes and seeks to observe, are all likely to influence and to color one's thinking and conclusions about abortion.

In addition, population growth, pollution, poverty, and racial overtones tend to complicate and not to simplify the problem.

Our task, of course, is to resolve the issue by constitutional measurement, free of emotion and of predilection. We seek earnestly to do this, and, because we do, we have inquired into, and in this opinion place some emphasis upon, medical and medical-legal history and what that history reveals about man's attitudes toward the abortion procedure over the centuries. We bear in mind, too, Mr. Justice Holmes' admonition in his now-vindicated dissent in *Lochner v. New York*, 198 U.S. 45, 76 (1905):

> [The Constitution] is made for people of fundamentally differing views, and the accident of our finding certain opinions natural and familiar or novel and even shocking ought not to conclude our judgment upon the question whether statutes embodying them conflict with the Constitution of the United States.

I

The Texas statutes that concern us here are Arts. 1191-1194 and 1196 of the State's Penal Code. These make it a crime to "procure an abortion," as therein defined, or to attempt one, except with respect to "an abortion procured or attempted by medical advice for the purpose of saving the life of the mother." Similar statutes are in existence in a majority of the States.

Texas first enacted a criminal abortion statute in 1854. Texas Laws 1854, c. 49, § 1, set forth in 3 H. Gammel, Laws of Texas 1502 (1898). This was soon modified into language that has remained substantially unchanged to the present time. See Texas Penal Code of 1857, c. 7, Arts. 531-536; G. Paschal, Laws of Texas, Arts. 2192-2197 (1866); Texas Rev.Stat., c. 8, Arts. 536-541 (1879); Texas Rev.Crim.Stat., Arts. 1071-1076 (1911). The final article in each of these compilations provided the same exception, as does the present Article 1196, for an abortion by "medical advice for the purpose of saving the life of the mother."

II

Jane Roe, a single woman who was residing in Dallas County, Texas, instituted this federal action in March 1970 against the District Attorney of the county. She sought a declaratory judgment that the Texas criminal abortion statutes were unconstitutional on their face, and an injunction restraining the defendant from enforcing the statutes.

Roe alleged that she was unmarried and pregnant; that she wished to terminate her pregnancy by an abortion "performed by a competent, licensed physician, under safe, clinical conditions"; that she was unable to get a "legal" abortion in Texas because her life did not appear to be threatened by the continuation of her pregnancy; and that she could not afford to travel to another jurisdiction in order to secure a legal abortion under safe conditions. She claimed that the Texas statutes were unconstitutionally vague and that they abridged her right of personal privacy, protected by the First, Fourth, Fifth, Ninth, and Fourteenth Amendments. By an amendment to her complaint, Roe purported to sue "on behalf of herself and all other women" similarly situated.

James Hubert Hallford, a licensed physician, sought and was granted leave to intervene in Roe's action. In his complaint, he alleged that he had been arrested previously for violations of the Texas abortion statutes, and that two such prosecutions were pending against him. He described conditions of patients who came to him seeking abortions, and he claimed that for many cases he, as a physician, was unable to determine whether they fell within or outside the exception recognized by Article 1196. He alleged that, as a consequence, the statutes were vague and uncertain, in violation of the Fourteenth Amendment, and that they violated his own and his patients' rights to privacy in the doctor-patient relationship and his own right to practice medicine, rights he claimed were guaranteed by the First, Fourth, Fifth, Ninth, and Fourteenth Amendments.

John and Mary Doe, a married couple, filed a companion complaint to that of Roe. They also named the District Attorney as defendant, claimed like constitutional deprivations, and sought declaratory and injunctive relief. The Does alleged that they were a childless couple; that Mrs. Doe was suffering from a "neural-chemical" disorder; that her physician had "advised her to avoid pregnancy until such time as her condition has materially improved" (although a pregnancy at the present time would not present "a serious risk" to her life); that, pursuant to medical advice, she had discontinued use of birth control pills; and that, if she should become pregnant, she would want to terminate the pregnancy by an abortion performed by a competent, licensed physician under safe, clinical conditions. By an amendment to their complaint, the Does purported to sue "on behalf of themselves and all couples similarly situated."

The two actions were consolidated and heard together by a duly convened three-judge district court. The suits thus presented the situations of the pregnant single woman, the childless couple, with the wife not pregnant, and the licensed practicing physician, all joining in the attack on the Texas criminal abortion statutes. Upon the filing of affidavits, motions were made for dismissal and for summary judgment. The court held that Roe and members of her class, and Dr. Hallford, had standing to sue and presented justiciable controversies, but that the Does had failed to allege facts sufficient to state a present controversy, and did not have standing. It concluded that, with respect to the requests for a declaratory judgment, abstention was not warranted. On the merits, the District Court held that the

> fundamental right of single women and married persons to choose whether to have children is protected by the Ninth Amendment, through the Fourteenth Amendment,

and that the Texas criminal abortion statutes were void on their face because they were both unconstitutionally vague and constituted an overbroad infringement of the plaintiffs' Ninth Amendment rights. The court then held that abstention was warranted with respect to the requests for an injunction. It therefore dismissed the Does' complaint, declared the abortion statutes void, and dismissed the application for injunctive relief. 314 F.Supp. 1217, 1225 (ND Tex.1970).

The plaintiffs Roe and Doe and the intervenor Hallford, pursuant to 28 U.S.C. § 1253 have appealed to this Court from that part of the District Court's judgment denying the injunction. The defendant District Attorney has purported to cross-appeal, pursuant to the same statute, from the court's grant of declaratory relief to Roe and Hallford. Both sides also have taken protective appeals to the United States Court of Appeals for the Fifth Circuit. That court ordered the appeals held in abeyance pending decision here. We postponed decision on jurisdiction to the hearing on the merits. 402 U.S. 941 (1971)

III

It might have been preferable if the defendant, pursuant to our Rule 20, had presented to us a petition for certiorari before judgment in the Court of Appeals with respect to the granting of the plaintiffs' prayer for declaratory relief. Our decisions in *Mitchell v. Donovan*, 398 U.S. 427 (1970), and *Gunn v. University Committee*, 399 U.S. 383 (1970), are to the effect that § 1253 does not authorize an appeal to this Court from the grant or denial of declaratory relief alone. We conclude, nevertheless, that those decisions do not foreclose our review of both the injunctive and the declaratory aspects of a case of this kind when it is properly here, as this one is, on appeal under 1253 from specific denial of injunctive relief, and the arguments as to both aspects are necessarily identical. See *Carter v. Jury Comm'n*, 396 U.S. 320 (1970); *Florida Lime Growers v. Jacobsen*, 362 U.S. 73, 80-81 (1960). It would be destructive of time and energy for all concerned were we to rule otherwise. Cf. *Doe v. Bolton*, post, p. 179.

IV

We are next confronted with issues of justiciability, standing, and abstention. Have Roe and the Does established that "personal stake in the outcome of the controversy," *Baker v. Carr*, 369 U.S. 186, 204 (1962), that insures that

> the dispute sought to be adjudicated will be presented in an adversary context and in a form historically viewed as capable of judicial resolution,

Flast v. Cohen, 392 U.S. 83, 101 (1968), and *Sierra Club v. Morton*, 405 U.S. 727, 732 (1972)? And what effect did the pendency of criminal abortion charges against Dr. Hallford in state court have upon the propriety of the federal court's granting relief to him as a plaintiff-intervenor?

A. Jane Roe. Despite the use of the pseudonym, no suggestion is made that Roe is a fictitious person. For purposes of her case, we accept as true, and as established, her existence; her pregnant state, as of the inception of her suit in March 1970 and as late as May 21 of that year when she filed an alias affidavit with the District Court; and her inability to obtain a legal abortion in Texas.

Viewing Roe's case as of the time of its filing and thereafter until as late a May, there can be little dispute that it then presented a case or controversy and that, wholly apart from the class aspects, she, as a pregnant single woman thwarted by the Texas criminal abortion laws, had standing to challenge those statutes. *Abele v. Markle*, 452 F.2d 1121, 1125 (CA2 1971); *Crossen v. Breckenridge*, 446 F.2d 833, 838-839 (CA6 1971); *Poe v. Menghini*, 339 F.Supp. 986, 990-991 (Kan.1972). See *Truax v. Raich*, 239 U.S. 33 (1915). Indeed, we do not read the appellee's brief as really asserting anything to the contrary. The "logical nexus between the status asserted and the claim sought to be adjudicated," *Flast v. Cohen*, 392 U.S. at 102, and the necessary degree of contentiousness, *Golden v. Zwickler*, 394 U.S. 103 (1969), are both present.

The appellee notes, however, that the record does not disclose that Roe was pregnant at the time of the District Court hearing on May 22, 1970, or on the following June 17 when the court's opinion and judgment were filed. And he suggests that Roe's case must now be moot because she and all other members of her class are no longer subject to any 1970 pregnancy.

The usual rule in federal cases is that an actual controversy must exist at stages of appellate or certiorari review, and not simply at the date the action is initiated. *United States v. Munsingwear, Inc.*, 340 U.S. 36 (1950); *Golden v. Zwickler*, supra; *SEC v. Medical Committee for Human Rights*, 404 U.S. 403 (1972).

But when, as here, pregnancy is a significant fact in the litigation, the normal 266-day human gestation period is so short that the pregnancy will come to term before the usual appellate process is complete. If that termination makes a case moot, pregnancy litigation seldom will survive much beyond the trial stage, and appellate review will be effectively denied. Our law should not be that rigid. Pregnancy often comes more than once to the same woman, and in the general population, if man is to survive, it will always be with us. Pregnancy provides a classic justification for a conclusion of nonmootness. It truly could be "capable of repetition, yet evading review." *Southern Pacific Terminal Co. v. ICC*, 219 U.S. 498, 515 (1911). See *Moore v. Ogilvie*, 394 U.S. 814, 816 (1969); *Carroll v. Princess Anne*, 393 U.S. 175, 178-179 (1968); *United States v. W. T. Grant Co.*, 345 U.S. 629, 632-633 (1953).

We, therefore, agree with the District Court that Jane Roe had standing to undertake this litigation, that she presented a justiciable controversy, and that the termination of her 1970 pregnancy has not rendered her case moot.

B. Dr. Hallford. The doctor's position is different. He entered Roe's litigation as a plaintiff-intervenor, alleging in his complaint that he:

> [I]n the past has been arrested for violating the Texas Abortion Laws and at the present time stands charged by indictment with violating said laws in the Criminal
>
> District Court of Dallas County, Texas to-wit: (1) The State of Texas vs. James H. Hallford, No. C-69-5307-IH, and (2) The State of Texas vs. James H. Hallford, No. C-692524-H. In
>
> both cases, the defendant is charged with abortion....

In his application for leave to intervene, the doctor made like representations as to the abortion charges pending in the state court. These representations were also repeated in the affidavit he executed and filed in support of his motion for summary judgment.

Dr. Hallford is, therefore, in the position of seeking, in a federal court, declaratory and injunctive relief with respect to the same statutes under which he stands charged in criminal prosecutions simultaneously pending in state court. Although he stated that he has been arrested in the past for violating the State's abortion laws, he makes no allegation of any substantial and immediate threat to any federally protected right that cannot be asserted in his defense against the state prosecutions. Neither is there any allegation of harassment or bad faith prosecution. In order to escape the rule articulated in the cases cited in the next paragraph of this opinion that, absent harassment and bad faith, a defendant in a pending state criminal case cannot affirmatively challenge in federal court the statutes under which the State is prosecuting him, Dr. Hallford seeks to distinguish his status as a present state defendant from his status as a "potential future defendant," and to assert only the latter for standing purposes here.

We see no merit in that distinction. Our decision in *Samuels v. Mackell*, 401 U.S. 66 (1971), compels the conclusion that the District Court erred when it granted declaratory relief to Dr. Hallford instead of refraining from so doing. The court, of course, was correct in refusing to grant injunctive relief to the doctor. The reasons supportive of that action, however, are those expressed in *Samuels v. Mackell*, supra, and in *Younger v. Harris*, 401 U.S. 37 (1971); *Boyle v. Landry*, 401 U.S. 77 (1971); *Perez v. Ledesma*, 401 U.S. 82 (1971); and *Byrne v. Karaleis*, 401 U.S. 216 (1971). See also *Dombrowski v. Pfister*, 380 U.S. 479 (1965). We note, in passing, that Younger and its companion cases were decided after the three-judge District Court decision in this case.

Dr. Hallford's complaint in intervention, therefore, is to be dismissed. He is remitted to his defenses in the state criminal proceedings against him. We reverse the judgment of the District Court insofar as it granted Dr. Hallford relief and failed to dismiss his complaint in intervention.

C. The Does. In view of our ruling as to Roe's standing in her case, the issue of the Does' standing in their case has little significance. The claims they assert are essentially the same as those of Roe, and they attack the same statutes. Nevertheless, we briefly note the Does' posture.

Their pleadings present them as a childless married couple, the woman not being pregnant, who have no desire to have children at this time because of their having received medical advice that Mrs. Doe should avoid pregnancy, and for "other highly personal reasons." But they "fear . . . they may face the prospect of becoming parents." And if pregnancy ensues, they "would want to terminate" it by an abortion. They assert an inability to obtain an abortion legally in Texas and, consequently, the prospect of obtaining an illegal abortion there or of going outside Texas to some place where the procedure could be obtained legally and competently.

We thus have as plaintiffs a married couple who have, as their asserted immediate and present injury, only an alleged "detrimental effect upon [their] marital happiness" because they are forced to "the choice of refraining from normal sexual relations or of endangering Mary Doe's health through a possible pregnancy." Their claim is that, sometime in the future, Mrs. Doe might become pregnant because of possible failure of contraceptive measures, and, at that time in the future, she might want an abortion that might then be illegal under the Texas statutes.

This very phrasing of the Does' position reveals its speculative character. Their alleged injury rests on possible future contraceptive failure, possible future pregnancy, possible future unpreparedness for parenthood, and possible future impairment of health. Any one or more of these several possibilities may not take place, and all may not combine. In the Does' estimation, these possibilities might have some real or imagined impact upon their marital happiness. But we are not prepared to say that the bare allegation of so indirect an injury is sufficient to present an actual case or controversy. *Younger v. Harris*, 401 U.S. at 41-42; *Golden v. Zwickler*, 394 U.S. at 109-110; *Abele v. Markle*, 452 F.2d at 1124-1125; *Crossen v. Breckenridge*, 446 F.2d at 839. The Does' claim falls far short of those resolved otherwise in the cases that the Does urge upon us, namely, *Investment Co. Institute v. Camp*, 401 U.S. 617 (1971); *Data Processing Service v. Camp*, 397 U.S. 150 (1970); and *Epperson v. Arkansas*, 393 U.S. 97 (1968). See also *Truax v. Raich*, 239 U.S. 33 (1915).

The Does therefore are not appropriate plaintiffs in this litigation. Their complaint was properly dismissed by the District Court, and we affirm that dismissal.

V

The principal thrust of appellant's attack on the Texas statutes is that they improperly invade a right, said to be possessed by the pregnant woman, to choose to terminate her pregnancy. Appellant would discover this right in the concept of personal "liberty" embodied in the Fourteenth Amendment's Due Process Clause; or in personal, marital, familial, and sexual privacy said to be protected by the Bill of Rights or its penumbras, see *Griswold v. Connecticut*, 381 U.S. 479 (1965); *Eisenstadt v. Baird*, 405 U.S. 438 (1972); id. at 460 (WHITE, J., concurring in result); or among those rights reserved to the people by the Ninth Amendment, *Griswold v. Connecticut*, 381 U.S. at 486 (Goldberg, J., concurring). Before addressing this claim, we feel it desirable briefly to survey, in several aspects, the history of abortion, for such insight as that history may afford us, and then to examine the state purposes and interests behind the criminal abortion laws.

VI

It perhaps is not generally appreciated that the restrictive criminal abortion laws in effect in a majority of States today are of relatively recent vintage. Those laws, generally proscribing abortion or its attempt at any time during pregnancy except when necessary to preserve the pregnant woman's life, are not of ancient or even of common law origin. Instead, they derive from statutory changes effected, for the most part, in the latter half of the 19th century.

1. Ancient attitudes. These are not capable of precise determination. We are told that, at the time of the Persian Empire, abortifacients were known, and that criminal abortions were severely punished. We are also told, however, that abortion was practiced in Greek times as well as in the Roman Era, and that "it was resorted to without scruple." The Ephesian, Soranos, often described as the greatest of the ancient gynecologists, appears to have been generally opposed to Rome's prevailing free-abortion practices. He found it necessary to think first of the life of the mother, and he resorted to abortion when, upon this standard, he felt the procedure advisable. Greek and Roman law afforded little protection to the unborn. If abortion was prosecuted in some places, it seems to have been based on a concept of a violation of the father's right to his offspring. Ancient religion did not bar abortion.

2. The Hippocratic Oath. What then of the famous Oath that has stood so long as the ethical guide of the medical profession and that bears the name of the great Greek (460(?)-377(?) B. C.), who has been described as the Father of Medicine, the "wisest and the greatest practitioner of his art," and the "most important and most complete medical personality of antiquity," who dominated the medical schools of his time, and who typified the sum of the medical knowledge of the past? The Oath varies somewhat according to the particular translation, but in any translation the content is clear:

> I will give no deadly medicine to anyone if asked, nor suggest any such counsel; and in like manner, I will not give to a woman a pessary to produce abortion,

or

> I will neither give a deadly drug to anybody if asked for it, nor will I make a suggestion to

this effect. Similarly, I will not give to a woman an abortive remedy.

Although the Oath is not mentioned in any of the principal briefs in this case or in *Doe v. Bolton*, post, p. 179, it represents the apex of the development of strict ethical concepts in medicine, and its influence endures to this day. Why did not the authority of Hippocrates dissuade abortion practice in his time and that of Rome? The late Dr. Edelstein provides us with a theory: [n16] The Oath was not uncontested even in Hippocrates' day; only the Pythagorean school of philosophers frowned upon the related act of suicide. Most Greek thinkers, on the other hand, commended abortion, at least prior to viability. See Plato, Republic, V, 461; Aristotle, Politics, VII, 1335b 25. For the Pythagoreans, however, it was a matter of dogma. For them, the embryo was animate from the moment of conception, and abortion meant destruction of a living being. The abortion clause of the Oath, therefore, "echoes Pythagorean doctrines," and "[i]n no other stratum of Greek opinion were such views held or proposed in the same spirit of uncompromising austerity."

Dr. Edelstein then concludes that the Oath originated in a group representing only a small segment of Greek opinion, and that it certainly was not accepted by all ancient physicians. He points out that medical writings down to Galen (A.D. 130-200) "give evidence of the violation of almost every one of its injunctions." But with the end of antiquity, a decided change took place. Resistance against suicide and against abortion became common. The Oath came to be popular. The emerging teachings of Christianity were in agreement with the Pythagorean ethic. The Oath "became the nucleus of all medical ethics," and "was applauded as the embodiment of truth." Thus, suggests Dr. Edelstein, it is "a Pythagorean manifesto, and not the expression of an absolute standard of medical conduct."

This, it seems to us, is a satisfactory and acceptable explanation of the Hippocratic Oath's apparent rigidity. It enables us to understand, in historical context, a long-accepted and revered statement of medical ethics.

3. The common law. It is undisputed that, at common law, abortion performed before quickening"—the first recognizable movement of the fetus in utero, appearing usually from the 16th to the 18th week of pregnancy—was not an indictable offense. The absence of a common law crime for pre-quickening abortion appears to have developed from a confluence of earlier philosophical, theological, and civil and canon law concepts of when life begins. These disciplines variously approached the question in terms of the point at which the embryo or fetus became "formed" or recognizably human, or in terms of when a "person" came into being, that is, infused with a "soul" or "animated." A loose consensus evolved in early English law that these events occurred at some point between conception and live birth. This was "mediate animation." Although Christian theology and the canon law came to fix the point of animation at 40 days for a male and 80 days for a female, a view that persisted until the 19th century, there was otherwise little agreement about the precise time of formation or animation. There was agreement, however, that, prior to this point, the fetus was to be regarded as part of the mother, and its destruction, therefore, was not homicide. Due to continued uncertainty about the precise time when animation occurred, to the lack of any empirical basis for the 40-80-day view, and perhaps to Aquinas' definition of movement as one of the two first principles of life, Bracton focused upon quickening as the critical point. The significance of quickening was echoed by later common law scholars, and found its way into the received common law in this country.

Whether abortion of a quick fetus was a felony at common law, or even a lesser crime, is still disputed. Bracton, writing early in the 13th century, thought it homicide. But the later and predominant view, following the great common law scholars, has been that it was, at most, a lesser offense. In a frequently cited passage, Coke took the position that abortion of a woman "quick with childe" is "a great misprision, and no murder." Blackstone followed, saying that, while abortion after quickening had once been considered manslaughter (though not murder), "modern law" took a less severe view. A recent review of the common law precedents argues, however, that those precedents contradict Coke, and that even post-quickening abortion was never established as a common law crime. This is of some importance, because, while most American courts ruled, in holding or dictum, that abortion of an unquickened fetus was not criminal under their received common law, others followed Coke in stating that abortion of a quick fetus was a "misprision," a term they translated to mean "misdemeanor." That their reliance on Coke on this aspect of the law was uncritical and, apparently in all the reported cases, dictum (due probably to the paucity of common law prosecutions for post-quickening abortion), makes it now appear doubtful that abortion was ever firmly established as a common law crime even with respect to the destruction of a quick fetus.

4. The English statutory law. England's first criminal abortion statute, Lord Ellenborough's Act, 43 Geo. 3, c. 58, came in 1803. It made abortion of a quick fetus, § 1, a capital crime, but, in § 2, it provided lesser penalties for the felony of abortion before quickening, and thus preserved the "quickening" distinction. This contrast was continued in the general revision of 1828, 9 Geo. 4, c. 31, § 13. It disappeared, however, together with the death penalty, in 1837, 7 Will. 4 & 1 Vict., c. 85. § 6, and did not reappear in the Offenses Against the Person Act of 1861, 24 & 25 Vict., c. 100, § 59, that formed the core of English anti-abortion law until the liberalizing reforms of 1967. In 1929, the Infant Life (Preservation) Act, 19 & 20 Geo. 5, c. 34, came into being. Its emphasis was upon the destruction of "the life of a child capable of being born alive." It made a willful act performed with the necessary intent a felony. It contained a proviso that one was not to be found guilty of the offense

> unless it is proved that the act which caused the death of the child was not done in good faith for the purpose only of preserving the life of the mother.

A seemingly notable development in the English law was the case of *Rex v. Bourne*, [1939] 1 K.B. 687. This case apparently answered in the affirmative the question whether an abortion necessary to preserve the life of the pregnant woman was excepted from the criminal penalties of the 1861 Act. In his instructions to the jury, Judge Macnaghten referred to the 1929 Act, and observed that that Act related to "the case where a child is killed by a willful act at the time when it is being delivered in the ordinary course of nature." Id. at 691. He concluded that the 1861 Act's use of the word "unlawfully," imported the same meaning expressed by the specific proviso in the 1929 Act, even though there was no mention of preserving the mother's life in the 1861 Act. He then construed the phrase "preserving the life of the mother" broadly, that is, "in a reasonable sense," to include a serious and permanent threat to the mother's health, and instructed the jury to acquit Dr. Bourne if it found he had acted in a good faith belief that the abortion was necessary for this purpose. Id. at 693-694. The jury did acquit.

Recently, Parliament enacted a new abortion law. This is the Abortion Act of 1967, 15 & 16 Eliz. 2, c. 87. The Act permits a licensed physician to perform an abortion where two other licensed physicians agree (a)

> that the continuance of the pregnancy would involve risk to the life of the pregnant woman, or of injury to the physical or mental health of the pregnant woman or any existing children of her family, greater than if the pregnancy were terminated,

or (b)

> that there is a substantial risk that, if the child were born it would suffer from such physical or mental abnormalities as to be seriously handicapped.

The Act also provides that, in making this determination, "account may be taken of the pregnant woman's actual or reasonably foreseeable environment." It also permits a physician, without the concurrence of others, to terminate a pregnancy where he is of the good faith opinion that the abortion "is immediately necessary to save the life or to prevent grave permanent injury to the physical or mental health of the pregnant woman."

5. The American law. In this country, the law in effect in all but a few States until mid-19th century was the preexisting English common law. Connecticut, the first State to enact abortion legislation, adopted in 1821 that part of Lord Ellenborough's Act that related to a woman "quick with child." The death penalty was not imposed. Abortion before quickening was made a crime in that State only in 1860. In 1828, New York enacted legislation that, in two respects, was to serve as a model for early anti-abortion statutes. First, while barring destruction of an unquickened fetus as well as a quick fetus, it made the former only a misdemeanor, but the latter second-degree manslaughter. Second, it incorporated a concept of therapeutic abortion by providing that an abortion was excused if it

> shall have been necessary to preserve the life of such mother, or shall have been advised by two physicians to be necessary for such purpose.

By 1840, when Texas had received the common law, only eight American States had statutes dealing with abortion. It was not until after the War Between the States that legislation began generally to replace the common law. Most of these initial statutes dealt severely with abortion after quickening, but were lenient with it before quickening. Most punished attempts equally with completed abortions. While many statutes included the exception for an abortion thought by one or more physicians to be necessary to save the mother's life, that provision soon disappeared, and the typical law required that the procedure actually be necessary for that purpose. Gradually, in the middle and late 19th century, the quickening distinction disappeared from the statutory law of most States and the degree of the offense and the penalties were increased. By the end of the 1950's, a large majority of the jurisdictions banned abortion, however and whenever performed, unless done to save or preserve the life of the mother. The exceptions, Alabama and the District of Columbia, permitted abortion to preserve the mother's health. Three States permitted abortions that were not "unlawfully" performed or that were not "without lawful justification," leaving interpretation of those standards to the courts. In the past several years, however, a trend toward liberalization of abortion statutes has resulted in adoption, by about one-third of the States, of less stringent laws, most of them patterned after the ALI Model Penal Code, § 230.3, set forth as Appendix B to the opinion in *Doe v. Bolton*, post, p. 205.

It is thus apparent that, at common law, at the time of the adoption of our Constitution, and throughout the major portion of the 19th century, abortion was viewed with less disfavor than under most American statutes currently in effect. Phrasing it another way, a woman enjoyed a substantially broader right to terminate a pregnancy than she does in most States today. At least with respect to the early stage of pregnancy, and very possibly without such a limitation, the opportunity to make this choice was present in this country well into the 19th century. Even later, the law continued for some time to treat less punitively an abortion procured in early pregnancy.

6. The position of the American Medical Association. The anti-abortion mood prevalent in this country in the late 19th century was shared by the medical profession. Indeed, the attitude of the profession may have played a significant role in the enactment of stringent criminal abortion legislation during that period.

An AMA Committee on Criminal Abortion was appointed in May, 1857. It presented its report, 12 Trans. of the Am.Med.Assn. 778 (1859), to the Twelfth Annual Meeting. That report observed that the Committee had been appointed to investigate criminal abortion "with a view to its general suppression." It deplored abortion and its frequency and it listed three causes of "this general demoralization":

> The first of these causes is a widespread popular ignorance of the true character of the crime—a belief, even among mothers themselves, that the foetus is not alive till after the period of quickening.
>
> The second of the agents alluded to is the fact that the profession themselves are frequently supposed careless of foetal life....
>
> The third reason of the frightful extent of this crime is found in the grave defects of our laws, both common and statute, as regards the independent and actual existence of the child before birth, as a living being. These errors, which are sufficient in most instances to prevent conviction, are based, and only based, upon mistaken and exploded medical dogmas. With strange inconsistency, the law fully acknowledges the foetus in utero and its inherent rights, for civil purposes; while personally and as criminally affected, it fails to recognize it, and to its life as yet denies all protection.

Id. at 776. The Committee then offered, and the Association adopted, resolutions protesting "against such unwarrantable destruction of human life," calling upon state legislatures to revise their abortion laws, and requesting the cooperation of state medical societies "in pressing the subject." Id. at 28, 78.

In 1871, a long and vivid report was submitted by the Committee on Criminal Abortion. It ended with the observation,

> We had to deal with human life. In a matter of less importance, we could entertain no compromise. An honest judge on the bench would call things by their proper names. We could do no less.

22 Trans. of the Am.Med.Assn. 268 (1871). It proffered resolutions, adopted by the Association, id. at 38-39, recommending, among other things, that it

> be unlawful and unprofessional for any physician to induce abortion or premature labor without the concurrent opinion of at least one respectable consulting physician, and then always with a view to the safety of the child—if that be possible,

and calling

> the attention of the clergy of all denominations to the perverted views of morality entertained by a large class of females—aye, and men also, on this important question.

Except for periodic condemnation of the criminal abortionist, no further formal AMA action took place until 1967. In that year, the Committee on Human Reproduction urged the adoption of a stated policy of opposition to induced abortion except when there is "documented medical evidence" of a threat to the health or life of the mother, or that the child "may be born with incapacitating physical deformity or mental deficiency," or that a pregnancy "resulting from legally established statutory or forcible rape or incest may constitute a threat to the mental or physical health of the patient," two other physicians "chosen because of their recognized professional competence have examined the patient and have concurred in writing," and the procedure "is performed in a hospital accredited by the Joint Commission on Accreditation of Hospitals." The providing of medical information by physicians to state legislatures in their consideration of legislation regarding therapeutic abortion was "to be considered consistent with the principles of ethics of the American Medical Association." This recommendation was adopted by the House of Delegates. Proceedings of the AMA House of Delegates 40-51 (June 1967).

In 1970, after the introduction of a variety of proposed resolutions and of a report from its Board of Trustees, a reference committee noted "polarization of the medical profession on this controversial issue"; division among those who had testified; a difference of opinion among AMA councils and committees; "the remarkable shift in testimony" in six months, felt to be influenced "by the rapid changes in state laws and by the judicial decisions which tend to make abortion more freely available;" and a feeling "that this trend will continue." On June 25, 1970, the House of Delegates adopted preambles and most of the resolutions proposed by the reference committee. The preambles emphasized "the best interests of the patient," "sound clinical judgment," and "informed patient consent," in contrast to "mere acquiescence to the patient's demand." The resolutions asserted that abortion is a medical procedure that should be performed by a licensed physician in an accredited hospital only after consultation with two other physicians and in conformity with state law, and that no party to the procedure should be required to violate personally held moral principles. Proceedings of the AMA House of Delegates 220 (June 1970). The AMA Judicial Council rendered a complementary opinion.

7. The position of the American Public Health Association. In October, 1970, the Executive Board of the APHA adopted Standards for Abortion Services. These were five in number:

> a. Rapid and simple abortion referral must be readily available through state and local public health departments, medical societies, or other nonprofit organizations.

> b. An important function of counseling should be to simplify and expedite the provision of abortion services; it should not delay the obtaining of these services.

> c. Psychiatric consultation should not be mandatory. As in the case of other specialized medical services, psychiatric consultation should be sought for definite indications, and not on a routine basis.

> d. A wide range of individuals from appropriately trained, sympathetic volunteers to highly skilled physicians may qualify as abortion counselors.

> e. Contraception and/or sterilization should be discussed with each abortion patient.

Recommended Standards for Abortion Services, 61 Am.J.Pub.Health 396 (1971). Among factors pertinent to life and health risks associated with abortion were three that "are recognized as important":

a. the skill of the physician,

b. the environment in which the abortion is performed, and above all

c. the duration of pregnancy, as determined by uterine size and confirmed by menstrual history.

Id. at 397.

It was said that "a well equipped hospital" offers more protection

to cope with unforeseen difficulties than an office or clinic without such resources. . . . The factor of gestational age is of overriding importance.

Thus, it was recommended that abortions in the second trimester and early abortions in the presence of existing medical complications be performed in hospitals as inpatient procedures. For pregnancies in the first trimester, abortion in the hospital with or without overnight stay "is probably the safest practice." An abortion in an extramural facility, however, is an acceptable alternative "provided arrangements exist in advance to admit patients promptly if unforeseen complications develop." Standards for an abortion facility were listed. It was said that, at present, abortions should be performed by physicians or osteopaths who are licensed to practice and who have "adequate training." Id. at 398.

8. The position of the American Bar Association. At its meeting in February, 1972, the ABA House of Delegates approved, with 17 opposing votes, the Uniform Abortion Act that had been drafted and approved the preceding August by the Conference of Commissioners on Uniform State Laws. 58 A.B.A.J. 380 (1972). We set forth the Act in full in the margin. The Opinion of the Court Conference has appended an enlightening Prefatory Note.

VII

Three reasons have been advanced to explain historically the enactment of criminal abortion laws in the 19th century and to justify their continued existence.

It has been argued occasionally that these laws were the product of a Victorian social concern to discourage illicit sexual conduct. Texas, however, does not advance this justification in the present case, and it appears that no court or commentator has taken the argument seriously. The appellants and amici contend, moreover, that this is not a proper state purpose, at all and suggest that, if it were, the Texas statutes are overbroad in protecting it, since the law fails to distinguish between married and unwed mothers.

A second reason is concerned with abortion as a medical procedure. When most criminal abortion laws were first enacted, the procedure was a hazardous one for the woman. This was particularly true prior to the development of antisepsis. Antiseptic techniques, of course, were based on discoveries by Lister, Pasteur, and others first announced in 1867, but were not generally accepted and employed until about the turn of the century. Abortion mortality was high. Even after 1900, and perhaps until as late as the development of antibiotics in the 1940's, standard modern techniques such as dilation and curettage were not nearly so safe as they are today. Thus, it has been argued that a State's real concern in enacting a criminal abortion law was to protect the pregnant woman, that is, to restrain her from submitting to a procedure that placed her life in serious jeopardy.

Modern medical techniques have altered this situation. Appellants and various amici refer to medical data indicating that abortion in early pregnancy, that is, prior to the end of the first trimester, although not without its risk, is now relatively safe. Mortality rates for women undergoing early abortions, where the procedure is legal, appear to be as low as or lower than the rates for normal childbirth. Consequently, any interest of the State in protecting the woman from an inherently hazardous procedure, except when it would be equally dangerous for her to forgo it, has largely disappeared. Of course, important state interests in the areas of health and medical standards do remain. The State has a legitimate interest in seeing to it that abortion, like any other medical procedure, is performed under circumstances that insure maximum safety for the patient. This interest obviously extends at least to the performing physician and his staff, to the facilities involved, to the availability of after-care, and to adequate provision for any complication or emergency that might arise. The prevalence of high mortality rates at illegal "abortion mills" strengthens, rather than weakens, the State's interest in regulating the conditions under which abortions are performed. Moreover, the risk to the woman increases as her pregnancy continues. Thus, the State retains a definite interest in protecting the woman's own health and safety when an abortion is proposed at a late stage of pregnancy.

The third reason is the State's interest—some phrase it in terms of duty—in protecting prenatal life. Some of the argument for this justification rests on the theory that a new human life is present from the moment of conception. The State's interest and general obligation to protect life then extends, it is argued, to prenatal life. Only when the life of the pregnant mother herself is at stake, balanced against the life she carries within her, should the interest of the embryo or fetus not prevail. Logically, of course, a legitimate state interest in this area need not stand or fall on acceptance of the belief that life begins at conception or at some other point prior to live birth. In assessing the State's interest, recognition may be given to the less rigid claim that as long as at least potential life is involved, the State may assert interests beyond the protection of the pregnant woman alone.

Parties challenging state abortion laws have sharply disputed in some courts the contention that a purpose of these laws, when enacted, was to protect prenatal life. Pointing to the absence of legislative history to support the contention, they claim that most state laws were designed solely to protect the woman. Because medical advances have lessened this concern, at least with respect to abortion in early pregnancy, they argue that with respect to such abortions the laws can no longer be justified by any state interest. There is some scholarly support for this view of original purpose. The few state courts called upon to interpret their laws in the late 19th and early 20th centuries did focus on the State's interest in protecting the woman's health, rather than in preserving the embryo and fetus. Proponents of this view point out that in many States, including Texas, by statute or judicial interpretation, the pregnant woman herself could not be prosecuted for self-abortion or for cooperating in an abortion performed upon her by another. They claim that adoption of the "quickening" distinction through received common law and state statutes tacitly recognizes the greater health hazards inherent in late abortion and impliedly repudiates the theory that life begins at conception.

It is with these interests, and the eight to be attached to them, that this case is concerned.

VIII

The Constitution does not explicitly mention any right of privacy. In a line of decisions, however, going back perhaps as far as *Union Pacific R. Co. v. Botsford*, 141 U.S. 250, 251 (1891), the Court has recognized that a right of personal privacy, or a guarantee of certain areas or zones of privacy, does exist under the Constitution. In varying contexts, the Court or individual Justices have, indeed, found at least the roots of that right in the First Amendment, *Stanley v. Georgia*, 394 U.S. 557, 564 (1969); in the Fourth and Fifth Amendments, *Terry v. Ohio*, 392 U.S. 1, 8-9 (1968), *Katz v. United States*, 389 U.S. 347, 350 (1967), *Boyd v. United States*, 116 U.S. 616 (1886), see *Olmstead v. United States*, 277 U.S. 438, 478 (1928) (Brandeis, J., dissenting); in the penumbras of the Bill of Rights, *Griswold v. Connecticut*, 381 U.S. at 484-485; in the Ninth Amendment, id. at 486 (Goldberg, J., concurring); or in the concept of liberty guaranteed by the first section of the Fourteenth Amendment, see *Meyer v. Nebraska*, 262 U.S. 390, 399 (1923). These decisions make it clear that only personal rights that can be deemed "fundamental" or "implicit in the concept of ordered liberty," *Palko v. Connecticut*, 302 U.S. 319, 325 (1937), are included in this guarantee of personal privacy. They also make it clear that the right has some extension to activities relating to marriage, *Loving v. Virginia*, 388 U.S. 1, 12 (1967); procreation, *Skinner v. Oklahoma*, 316 U.S. 535, 541-542 (1942); contraception, *Eisenstadt v. Baird*, 405 U.S. at 453-454; id. at 460, 463-465 (WHITE, J., concurring in result); family relationships, *Prince v. Massachusetts*, 321 U.S. 158, 166 (1944); and childrearing and education, *Pierce v. Society of Sisters*, 268 U.S. 510, 535 (1925), *Meyer v. Nebraska*, supra.

This right of privacy, whether it be founded in the Fourteenth Amendment's concept of personal liberty and restrictions upon state action, as we feel it is, or, as the District Court determined, in the Ninth Amendment's reservation of rights to the people, is broad enough to encompass a woman's decision whether or not to terminate her pregnancy. The detriment that the State would impose upon the pregnant woman by denying this choice altogether is apparent. Specific and direct harm medically diagnosable even in early pregnancy may be involved. Maternity, or additional offspring, may force upon the woman a distressful life and future. Psychological harm may be imminent. Mental and physical health may be taxed by child care. There is also the distress, for all concerned, associated with the unwanted child, and there is the problem of bringing a child into a family already unable, psychologically and otherwise, to care for it. In other cases, as in this one, the additional difficulties and continuing stigma of unwed motherhood may be involved. All these are factors the woman and her responsible physician necessarily will consider in consultation.

On the basis of elements such as these, appellant and some amici argue that the woman's right is absolute and that she is entitled to terminate her pregnancy at whatever time, in whatever way, and for whatever reason she alone chooses. With this we do not agree. Appellant's arguments that Texas either has no valid interest at all in regulating the abortion decision, or no interest strong enough to support any limitation upon the woman's sole determination, are unpersuasive. The Court's decisions recognizing a right of privacy also acknowledge that some state regulation in areas protected by that right is appropriate. As noted above, a State may properly assert important interests in safeguarding health, in maintaining medical standards, and in protecting potential life. At some point in pregnancy, these respective interests become sufficiently compelling to sustain regulation of the factors that govern the abortion decision. The privacy right involved, therefore, cannot be said to be absolute. In fact, it is not clear to us that the claim asserted by some amici that one has an unlimited right to do with one's body as one pleases bears a close relationship to the right of privacy previously articulated in the Court's decisions. The Court has refused to recognize an unlimited right of this kind in the past. *Jacobson v. Massachusetts*, 197 U.S. 11 (1905) (vaccination); *Buck v. Bell*, 274 U.S. 200 (1927) (sterilization).

We, therefore, conclude that the right of personal privacy includes the abortion decision, but that this right is not unqualified, and must be considered against important state interests in regulation.

We note that those federal and state courts that have recently considered abortion law challenges have reached the same conclusion. A majority, in addition to the District Court in the present case, have held state laws unconstitutional, at least in part, because of vagueness or because of overbreadth and abridgment of rights. *Abele v. Markle*, 342 F.Supp. 800 (Conn.1972), appeal docketed, No. 72-56; *Abele v. Markle*, 351 F.Supp. 224 (Conn.1972), appeal docketed, No. 72-730; *Doe v. Bolton*, 319 F.Supp. 1048 (ND Ga.1970), appeal decided today, post, p. 179; *Doe v. Scott*, 321 F.Supp. 1385 (ND Ill.1971), appeal docketed, No. 70-105; *Poe v. Menghini*, 339 F.Supp. 986 (Kan.1972); *YWCA v. Kuler*, 342 F.Supp. 1048 (NJ 1972); *Babbitz v. McCann*, 310 F.Supp. 293 (ED Wis.1970), appeal dismissed, 400 U.S. 1 (1970); *People v. Belous*, 71 Cal.2d 954, 458 P.2d 194 (1969), cert. denied, 397 U.S. 915 (1970); *State v. Barquet*, 262 So.2d 431 (Fla.1972).

Others have sustained state statutes. *Crossen v. Attorney General*, 344 F.Supp. 587 (ED Ky.1972), appeal docketed, No. 72-256; *Rosen v. Louisiana State Board of Medical Examiners*, 318 F.Supp. 1217 (ED La.1970), appeal docketed, No. 70-42; *Corkey v. Edwards*, 322 F.Supp. 1248 (WDNC 1971), appeal docketed, No. 71-92; *Steinberg v. Brown*, 321 F.Supp. 741 (ND Ohio 1970); *Doe v. Rampton* (Utah 1971), appeal docketed, No. 71-5666; *Cheaney v. State*, ___ Ind. ___, 285 N.E.2d 265 (1972); *Spears v. State*, 257 So.2d 876 (Miss. 1972); *State v. Munson*, 86 S.D. 663, 201 N.W.2d 123 (1972), appeal docketed, No. 72-631.

Although the results are divided, most of these courts have agreed that the right of privacy, however based, is broad enough to cover the abortion decision; that the right, nonetheless, is not absolute, and is subject to some limitations; and that, at some point, the state interests as to protection of health, medical standards, and prenatal life, become dominant. We agree with this approach.

Where certain "fundamental rights" are involved, the Court has held that regulation limiting these rights may be justified only by a "compelling state interest," *Kramer v. Union Free School District*, 395 U.S. 621, 627 (1969); *Shapiro v. Thompson*, 394 U.S. 618, 634 (1969), *Sherbert v. Verner*, 374 U.S. 398, 406 (1963), and that legislative enactments must be narrowly drawn to express only the legitimate state interests at stake. *Griswold v. Connecticut*, 381 U.S. at 485; *Aptheker v. Secretary of State*, 378 U.S. 500, 508 (1964); *Cantwell v. Connecticut*, 310 U.S. 296, 307-308 (1940); see *Eisenstadt v. Baird*, 405 U.S. at 460, 463-464 (WHITE, J., concurring in result).

In the recent abortion cases cited above, courts have recognized these principles. Those striking down state laws have generally scrutinized the State's interests in protecting health and potential life, and have concluded that neither interest justified broad limitations on the reasons for which a physician and his pregnant patient might decide that she should have an abortion in the early stages of pregnancy. Courts sustaining state laws have held that the State's determinations to protect health or prenatal life are dominant and constitutionally justifiable.

IX

The District Court held that the appellee failed to meet his burden of demonstrating that the Texas statute's infringement upon Roe's rights was necessary to support a compelling state interest, and that, although the appellee presented "several compelling justifications for state presence in the area of abortions," the statutes outstripped these justifications and swept "far beyond any areas of compelling state interest." 314 F.Supp. at 1222-1223. Appellant and appellee both contest that holding. Appellant, as has been indicated, claims an absolute right that bars any state imposition of criminal penalties in the area. Appellee argues that the State's determination to recognize and protect prenatal life from and after conception constitutes a compelling state interest. As noted above, we do not agree fully with either formulation.

A. The appellee and certain amici argue that the fetus is a "person" within the language and meaning of the Fourteenth Amendment. In support of this, they outline at length and in detail the well known facts of fetal development. If this suggestion of personhood is established, the appellant's case, of course, collapses, for the fetus' right to life would then be guaranteed specifically by the Amendment. The appellant conceded as much on reargument. On the other hand, the appellee conceded on reargument that no case could be cited that holds that a fetus is a person within the meaning of the Fourteenth Amendment.

The Constitution does not define "person" in so many words. Section 1 of the Fourteenth Amendment contains three references to "person." The first, in defining "citizens," speaks of "persons born or naturalized in the United States." The word also appears both in the Due Process Clause and in the Equal Protection Clause. "Person" is used in other places in the Constitution: in the listing of qualifications for Representatives and Senators, Art. I, § 2, cl. 2, and § 3, cl. 3; in the Apportionment Clause, Art. I, § 2, cl. 3; in the Migration and Importation provision, Art. I, § 9, cl. 1; in the Emolument Clause, Art. I, § 9, cl. 8; in the Electors provisions, Art. II, § 1, cl. 2, and the superseded cl. 3; in the provision outlining qualifications for the office of President, Art. II, § 1, cl. 5; in the Extradition provisions, Art. IV, § 2, cl. 2, and the superseded Fugitive Slave Clause 3; and in the Fifth, Twelfth, and Twenty-second Amendments, as well as in §§ 2 and 3 of the Fourteenth Amendment. But in nearly all these instances, the use of the word is such that it has application only post-natally. None indicates, with any assurance, that it has any possible pre-natal application.

All this, together with our observation, supra, that, throughout the major portion of the 19th century, prevailing legal abortion practices were far freer than they are today, persuades us that the word "person," as used in the Fourteenth Amendment, does not include the unborn. This is in accord with the results reached in those few cases where the issue has been squarely presented. *McGarvey v. Magee-Womens Hospital*, 340 F.Supp. 751 (WD Pa.1972); *Byrn v. New York City Health & Hospitals Corp.*, 31 N.Y.2d 194, 286 N.E.2d 887 (1972), appeal docketed, No. 72-434; *Abele v. Markle*, 351 F. Supp. 224 (Conn.1972), appeal docketed, No. 72-730. Cf. *Cheaney v. State*, ___ Ind. at ___, 285 N.E.2d at 270; *Montana v. Rogers*, 278 F.2d 68, 72 (CA7 1960), affs' d sub nom. *Montana v. Kennedy*, 366 U.S. 308 (1961); *Keeler v. Superior Court*, 2 Cal.3d 619, 470 P.2d 617 (1970); *State v. Dickinson*, 28 Ohio St.2d 65, 275 N.E.2d 599 (1971). Indeed, our decision in *United States v. Vuitch*, 402 U.S. 62 (1971), inferentially is to the same effect, for we there would not have indulged in statutory interpretation favorable to abortion in specified circumstances if the necessary consequence was the termination of life entitled to Fourteenth Amendment protection.

This conclusion, however, does not of itself fully answer the contentions raised by Texas, and we pass on to other considerations.

B. The pregnant woman cannot be isolated in her privacy. She carries an embryo and, later, a fetus, if one accepts the medical definitions of the developing young in the human uterus. See Dorland's Illustrated Medical Dictionary 478-479, 547 (24th ed.1965). The situation therefore is inherently different from marital intimacy, or bedroom possession of obscene material, or marriage, or procreation, or education, with which Eisenstadt and Griswold, Stanley, Loving, Skinner, and Pierce and Meyer were respectively concerned. As we have intimated above, it is reasonable and appropriate for a State to decide that, at some point in time another interest, that of health of the mother or that of potential human life, becomes significantly involved. The woman's privacy is no longer sole and any right of privacy she possesses must be measured accordingly.

Texas urges that, apart from the Fourteenth Amendment, life begins at conception and is present throughout pregnancy, and that, therefore, the State has a compelling interest in protecting that life from and after conception. We need not resolve the difficult question of when life begins. When those trained in the respective disciplines of medicine, philosophy, and theology are unable to arrive at any consensus, the judiciary, at this point in the development of man's knowledge, is not in a position to speculate as to the answer.

It should be sufficient to note briefly the wide divergence of thinking on this most sensitive and difficult question. There has always been strong support for the view that life does not begin until live birth. This was the belief of the Stoics. It appears to be the predominant, though not the unanimous, attitude of the Jewish faith. It may be taken to represent also the position of a large segment of the Protestant community, insofar as that can be ascertained; organized groups that have taken a formal position on the abortion issue have generally regarded abortion as a matter for the conscience of the individual and her family. As we have noted, the common law found greater significance in quickening. Physician and their scientific colleagues have regarded that event with less interest and have tended to focus either upon conception, upon live birth, or upon the interim point at which the fetus becomes "viable," that is, potentially able to live outside the mother's womb, albeit with artificial aid. Viability is usually placed at about seven months (28 weeks) but may occur earlier, even at 24 weeks. The Aristotelian theory of "mediate animation," that held sway throughout the Middle Ages and the Renaissance in Europe, continued to be official Roman Catholic dogma until the 19th century, despite opposition to this "ensoulment" theory from those in the Church who would recognize the existence of life from the moment of conception. The latter is now, of course, the official belief of the Catholic Church. As one brief amicus discloses, this is a view strongly held by many non-Catholics as well, and by many physicians. Substantial problems for precise definition of this view are posed, however, by new embryological data that purport to indicate that conception is a "process" over time, rather than an event, and by new medical techniques such as menstrual extraction, the "morning-after" pill, implantation of embryos, artificial insemination, and even artificial wombs.

In areas other than criminal abortion, the law has been reluctant to endorse any theory that life, as we recognize it, begins before live birth, or to accord legal rights to the unborn except in narrowly defined situations and except when the rights are contingent upon live birth. For example, the traditional rule of tort law denied recovery for prenatal injuries even though the child was born alive. That rule has been changed in almost every jurisdiction. In most States, recovery is said to be permitted only if the fetus was viable, or at least quick, when the injuries were sustained, though few courts have squarely so held. In a recent development, generally opposed by the commentators, some States permit the parents of a stillborn child to maintain an action for wrongful death because of prenatal injuries. Such an action, however, would appear to be one to vindicate the parents' interest and is thus consistent with the view that the fetus, at most, represents only the potentiality of life. Similarly, unborn children have been recognized as acquiring rights or interests by way of inheritance or other devolution of property, and have been represented by guardians ad litem. Perfection of the interests involved, again, has generally been contingent upon live birth. In short, the unborn have never been recognized in the law as persons in the whole sense.

X

In view of all this, we do not agree that, by adopting one theory of life, Texas may override the rights of the pregnant woman that are at stake. We repeat, however, that the State does have an important and legitimate interest in preserving and protecting the health of the pregnant woman, whether she be a resident of the State or a nonresident who seeks medical consultation and treatment there, and that it has still another important and legitimate interest in protecting the potentiality of human life. These interests are separate and distinct. Each grows in substantiality as the woman approaches term and, at a point during pregnancy, each becomes "compelling."

With respect to the State's important and legitimate interest in the health of the mother, the "compelling" point, in the light of present medical knowledge, is at approximately the end of the first trimester. This is so because of the now-established medical fact, referred to above at 149, that, until the end of the first trimester mortality in abortion may be less than mortality in normal childbirth. It follows that, from and after this point, a State may regulate the abortion procedure to the extent that the regulation reasonably relates to the preservation and protection of maternal health. Examples of permissible state regulation in this area are requirements as to the qualifications of the person who is to perform the abortion; as to the licensure of that person; as to the facility in which the procedure is to be performed, that is, whether it must be a hospital or may be a clinic or some other place of less-than-hospital status; as to the licensing of the facility; and the like.

This means, on the other hand, that, for the period of pregnancy prior to this "compelling" point, the attending physician, in consultation with his patient, is free to determine, without regulation by the State, that, in his medical judgment, the patient's pregnancy should be terminated. If that decision is reached, the judgment may be effectuated by an abortion free of interference by the State.

With respect to the State's important and legitimate interest in potential life, the "compelling" point is at viability. This is so because the fetus then presumably has the capability of meaningful life outside the mother's womb. State regulation protective of fetal life after viability thus has both logical and biological justifications. If the State is interested in protecting fetal life after viability, it may go so far as to proscribe abortion during that period, except when it is necessary to preserve the life or health of the mother.

Measured against these standards, Art. 1196 of the Texas Penal Code, in restricting legal abortions to those "procured or attempted by medical advice for the purpose of saving the life of the mother," sweeps too broadly. The statute makes no distinction between abortions performed early in pregnancy and those performed later, and it limits to a single reason, "saving" the mother's life, the legal justification for the procedure. The statute, therefore, cannot survive the constitutional attack made upon it here.

This conclusion makes it unnecessary for us to consider the additional challenge to the Texas statute asserted on grounds of vagueness. See *United States v. Vuitch*, 402 U.S. at 67-72.

XI

To summarize and to repeat:

1. A state criminal abortion statute of the current Texas type, that excepts from criminality only a lifesaving procedure on behalf of the mother, without regard to pregnancy stage and without recognition of the other interests involved, is violative of the Due Process Clause of the Fourteenth Amendment.

(a) For the stage prior to approximately the end of the first trimester, the abortion decision avnd its effectuation must be left to the medical judgment of the pregnant woman's attending physician.

(b) For the stage subsequent to approximately the end of the first trimester, the State, in promoting its interest in the health of the mother, may, if it chooses, regulate the abortion procedure in ways that are reasonably related to maternal health.

(c) For the stage subsequent to viability, the State in promoting its interest in the potentiality of human life may, if it chooses, regulate, and even proscribe, abortion except where it is necessary, in appropriate medical judgment, for the preservation of the life or health of the mother.

2. The State may define the term "physician," as it has been employed in the preceding paragraphs of this Part XI of this opinion, to mean only a physician currently licensed by the State, and may proscribe any abortion by a person who is not a physician as so defined.

In *Doe v. Bolton*, post, p. 179, procedural requirements contained in one of the modern abortion statutes are considered. That opinion and this one, of course, are to be read together.

This holding, we feel, is consistent with the relative weights of the respective interests involved, with the lessons and examples of medical and legal history, with the lenity of the common law, and with the demands of the profound problems of the present day. The decision leaves the State free to place increasing restrictions on abortion as the period of pregnancy lengthens, so long as those restrictions are tailored to the recognized state interests. The decision vindicates the right of the physician to administer medical treatment according to his professional judgment up to the points where important state interests provide compelling justifications for intervention. Up to those points, the abortion decision in all its aspects is inherently, and primarily, a medical decision, and basic responsibility for it must rest with the physician. If an individual practitioner abuses the privilege of exercising proper medical judgment, the usual remedies, judicial and intra-professional, are available.

XII

Our conclusion that Art. 1196 is unconstitutional means, of course, that the Texas abortion statutes, as a unit, must fall. The exception of Art. 1196 cannot be struck down separately, for then the State would be left with a statute proscribing all abortion procedures no matter how medically urgent the case.

Although the District Court granted appellant Roe declaratory relief, it stopped short of issuing an injunction against enforcement of the Texas statutes. The Court has recognized that different considerations enter into a federal court's decision as to declaratory relief, on the one hand, and injunctive relief, on the other. *Zwickler v. Koota*, 389 U.S. 241, 252-255 (1967); *Dombrowski v. Pfister*, 380 U.S. 479 (1965). We are not dealing with a statute that, on its face, appears to abridge free expression, an area of particular concern under Dombrowski and refined in *Younger v. Harris*, 401 U.S. at 50.

We find it unnecessary to decide whether the District Court erred in withholding injunctive relief, for we assume the Texas prosecutorial authorities will give full credence to this decision that the present criminal abortion statutes of that State are unconstitutional.

The judgment of the District Court as to intervenor Hallford is reversed, and Dr. Hallford's complaint in intervention is dismissed. In all other respects, the judgment of the District Court is affirmed. Costs are allowed to the appellee.

It is so ordered.

Glossary

abortion: voluntary termination of a pregnancy

contraception: deliberate prevention of pregnancy by drugs, techniques, or devices; also known as birth control

eschews: avoids, rejects

embryo: the fertilized egg as implanted in the womb through the first two months of development

fetus: the developing human after the second month of gestation

"formulate a rule of constitutional law …": quotation from Justice Oliver Wendell Holmes in *Chastleton Corporation et al. v. Sinclair et al.* (1924)

gestation: pregnancy

Hippocratic Oath: an oath embodying the duties and obligations of physicians

In toto: entirely, in total

Mr. Justice Holmes: Oliver Wendell Holmes, associate justice of the Supreme Court

Mr. Justice Peckham: Rufus Wheeler Peckham, associate justice of the Supreme Court

pendency: the state of being pending or in process

Glossary

precedents: legal decisions that serve as rules or patterns for future similar cases

predicate: precondition, requirement

quickening: stage of pregnancy at which fetal movement first occurs

"so rooted in the traditions": quotation from Supreme Court Justice Benjamin Cardoza in *Snyder v. Massachusetts* (1934)

trimester: a period of three months

viable: capable of living outside a uterus

Milliken v. Bradley

Date 1974	**Citation** 418 U.S. 717
Author Warren E. Burger	**Significance** Held that school district lines cannot be redrawn for the purpose of combating segregation unless the segregation was the product of discriminatory acts by school districts
Vote 5–4	

Overview

Milliken v. Bradley was a landmark U.S. Supreme Court that took up the issue of desegregation in light of the decision in the desegregation case of *Brown v. Board of Education* (1954). *Brown* had declared unconstitutional state laws establishing separate public schools for Black and white students. The school districts of metropolitan Detroit proposed to bus public school students across district lines as a remedy to segregation. In a 5–4 decision, written by Warren Burger, the Court denied the validity of the plan, ruling that the decision in *Brown* did not require dismantling a "dual school system" to create racial balance. William O. Douglas, Byron White, and Thurgood Marshall issued separate dissents and were joined in opposition to the majority opinion by William J. Brennan.

Context

In the unanimous 1954 opinion in *Brown v. Board of Education*, authored by Earl Warren, the Supreme Court held that legally enforced segregation of schools by race was a violation of the equal protection clause of the Fourteenth Amendment. In a second opinion in the same case, commonly referred to as *Brown II*, the Court considered ways to remedy past segregation but, while outlining various considerations, decided to leave those matters to the district courts that would conduct local trials. Under Chief Justice Warren Burger, the Court preserved *Brown* and generally carried forward its mandate. For example, in *Swann v. Charlotte-Mecklenburg Board of Education* (1971), the Court unanimously affirmed the decision of the district court that required the redrawing of school attendance zones and the use of busing as a remedy to create a racial mix at each school approximating the district's racial composition.

In the wake of *Brown v. Board of Education*, the city of Detroit was becoming increasingly polarized along racial grounds, especially in light of the immense growth of the city's African American population and increasing segregation in the school. In response to the polarization, the city's board of education passed an integration and decentralization plan on April 7, 1970. The state legislature, however, passed Public Act 48, a bill that nullified the April 7 plan and placed the

Integrated busing in 1973
(Library of Congress)

school districts under control of local neighborhoods. On August 18, 1970, the local chapter of the NAACP filed a suit in the Federal District Court for the Eastern District of Michigan against the state's governor, William Milliken, Attorney General Frank J. Kelley, State Superintendent of Public Instruction John W. Porter, the Michigan Board of Education, the Detroit Board of Education, and the Detroit school superintendent on behalf of students Ronald and Richard Bradley, the Detroit branch of the NAACP, and parents of all minority children attending Detroit public schools. The petitioners called Act 48 unconstitutional, argued that official policies had segregated Detroit's schools, and sought to reinstate the April 7 plan.

The case went through two preliminary rounds in district court and the U.S. Court of Appeals for the Sixth Circuit. The Sixth Circuit held that Act 48 was unconstitutional because it nullified the local district's effort to comply with the federal desegregation mandate. In the second round of hearings, the Sixth Circuit affirmed a magnet school integration plan, but it remanded the case to district court for arguments on whether the Detroit board and state government had practiced *de jure* segregation.

The trial began on April 6, 1971. Witnesses testified that African Americans could not live wherever they chose, citing an environment in which the Federal Housing Administration, the Veteran's Administration, the Home Owners' Loan Corporation, and the practices of real estate associations, banks, and other lending institutions fostered a racially segregated housing market in Detroit and in the suburbs. Suburban schools, it was argued, did not have to write policies to keep Black children out because housing policies already accomplished that goal. The NAACP argued that both the Detroit board and state government actively increased school segregation by instituting an optional attendance zone policy, building new schools in white neighborhoods, and drawing boundaries that created racially segregated schools. Their proposal was to integrate Detroit's schools by means of an interdistrict busing desegregation plan that encompassed the suburbs. In September 1971, the Sixth Circuit concluded that school and housing segregation were interdependent and that they were caused by government policies at all levels. The court found the Detroit board of education and the state responsible for school segregation. On June 14, 1972, the Detroit board submitted a proposal for an interdistrict solution, with fifty-three metropolitan school districts taking part in a cross-district busing integration plan. The Sixth Circuit approved this plan, but it would not rule on the relationship between housing discrimination and school segregation. Michigan and the suburbs appealed to the U.S. Supreme Court, arguing that they had not formulated any policies that led to segregation in the schools of metropolitan Detroit.

About the Author

Warren Earl Burger was the fifteenth chief justice of the United States and enjoyed the fourth-longest tenure as head of the Supreme Court. Coming from a working-class family of modest means in Saint Paul, Minnesota, Burger took work at an early age to help out with his family's finances. He was a good student and won a scholarship to Princeton, which he declined because it would not have paid for all of his expenses. While selling insurance, Burger attended evening school, taking extension courses at the University of Minnesota from 1925 to 1927. He worked as an accountant while attending Saint Paul College of Law (now William Mitchell College of Law), from which he graduated magna cum laude in 1931.

For over twenty years Burger worked for the Saint Paul law firm of Boyesen, Otis & Faricy (1931–53), where he became a named partner in 1935. He worked primarily in the fields of probate, real estate, and corporate law, meanwhile gaining experience in political matters. His active role in Republican politics in Minnesota resulted in his leading the delegation that sought to nominate the Minnesota governor Harold Stassen for president at the 1952 Republican National Convention. It was Burger who ultimately announced the transfer of the delegation's votes from Stassen to General Dwight D. Eisenhower, which gave the latter enough votes to win the nomination. Eisenhower proceeded to win the presidential election. Before the end of the year, Burger was named assistant attorney general in charge of the Justice Department's Claims Division (later the Civil Division). Burger did not have the type of practice, national reputation as a lawyer, or experience in government that would have warranted his appointment; although his general competency as a lawyer was no doubt confirmed, Burger's role in the 1952 convention was what brought him to the attention of the Eisenhower administration.

Burger's role within the Claims Division, similarly, was not that of a brilliant trial lawyer who won cases others could not have won, nor was it that of an incisive intellectual who developed creative legal theories that led to victories in the appellate courts. Rather, Burger's role was primarily that of an administrator of a large government office. His role was to supervise the legal work of his office's attorneys, who were often younger than he was, and ensure that the legal positions taken by his office were consistent with the policy preferences of the Eisenhower administration. Burger's administrative ability and political loyalty led President Eisenhower to appoint Burger to the U.S. Court of Appeals for the District of Columbia Circuit in 1956, where he served for thirteen years.

On an appeals court that was often divided over decisions in criminal cases, Burger led the judges opposed to expanding the rights of criminal defendants—that is, persons who were charged with crimes and whose guilt or innocence was to be determined by a jury or court. Burger wanted to give more deference to trial judges, prosecutors, and the police in the proving of guilt and to provide fewer protections for defendants. By taking this position, he established a reputation as a conservative "law and order" judge. He also notably remained untainted by any ethical scandal. In 1969 President Richard Nixon nominated Burger for the position of chief justice of the United States. It was not Burger's legal brilliance that brought him to the attention of President Nixon; rather, it was his speeches— which might be referred to as political speeches—on limiting the rights of defendants. Nixon's nomination of Burger fulfilled a campaign promise to counter the Court's judicial activism under Earl Warren by appointing justices who, in his view, followed conservative philosophy. Burger was confirmed by the U.S. Senate by a vote of seventy-four to three.

Chief Justice Burger served on the Supreme Court for over seventeen years and during that time wrote more than 250 opinions. Under Chief Justice Warren, the Court had extended protections for those charged with crimes and decided cases abolishing school segregation and protecting the right to vote. Burger came to disappoint those who wanted a wholesale repudiation of the Warren Court era. He helped slow the rate at which change took place and in some cases diluted the effects of prior decisions, but he did little to overrule the decisions that had spurred political debate. The Burger Court did take a more limited view of the rights of those accused of crimes and was also more deferential to the states, under the banner of federalism. But it also recognized new rights and expanded others in the areas of welfare, abortion, gender-based discrimination, and affirmative action. This approach continued for Burger's entire term as chief justice. At times he continued the course of the Warren Court, as illustrated by his opinion in segregation cases like *Swann v. Charlotte-Mecklenburg Board of Education* (1971). Yet he also refused to extend the remedy for segregation to surrounding school districts in *Milliken v. Bradley* (1974). In other cases, like his dissent in *Bivens v. Six Unknown Named Agents*, Burger tried to stem the expansion of judicial remedies but was unable to muster a majority on the Court. He served as chief justice until 1986, when he resigned to serve as chair of the Commission on the Bicentennial of the U.S. Constitution. Burger died in 1995 in Washington, D.C.

Explanation and Analysis of the Document

In *Milliken*, the Court denied a plan involving multiple school districts that intended to remedy wrongful segregation within the school system of the city of Detroit. *Milliken v. Bradley* (1974) can be read in two ways, and those readings correspond to the two possibilities presented in the title question of a book edited by Bernard Schwartz: *The Burger Court: Counter-revolution or Confirmation?* This decision can be seen as confirming while in a sense consolidating the decision in *Brown*. Having found that past *Brown*-related cases involved only remedies within the segregated school districts in question, Chief Justice Burger presented his opinion as simply refusing to extend *Brown* to allow or require an interdistrict remedy. From this point of view, Burger's opinion was both a consolidation of the past Warren Court decisions and a refusal to extend the guiding principle in *Brown* to new situations.

The *Milliken* decision can also be viewed a second way. In each of the prior *Brown*-related decisions, the Court had limited the remedy to a single district based not upon the Constitution or law but rather upon the facts of the case. As such, the question of whether to extend the *Brown* remedy to interdistrict circumstances was a new legal issue that could have legitimately been decided in the contrary manner. Indeed, the fact that this was a five-to-four decision highlights the lack of inevitability to the Burger Court's majority opinion and validates the notion that a supportable decision could have been crafted with the opposite conclusion.

The dissenters in *Milliken* make the point that *Brown* required that the effects of segregation be remedied "root and branch," and the Burger Court's opinion did not do this. Indeed, while Burger accused the four dissenters of wanting to crudely balance the school system wholesale by numbers, he never convincingly responded to their claim that the only remedies left to the school district by his decision simply would not accomplish the "root and branch" solution mandated by *Brown II*. Further, as a practical matter, the *Milliken* plaintiffs were surely right that the "state," in the broadest sense of the term, had taken several actions or failed to take actions that led to the segregation of the district schools. As illustrated by the four dissenting justices, a different justice with a different point of view could have used this analysis to create a more effective remedy.

The chief justice refused to consider the entire picture of state actions, in part because he accepted the state argument that it should be allowed to compartmentalize itself into school districts. Burger so valued local school systems and local control that these priorities seemed to trump the duty imposed by *Brown* to provide a "root and branch" remedy. In the long run, then, *Milliken* not only curtailed the mandate of *Brown II* but also led to the resegregation of schools. In this sense, Burger's opinion was not a confirmation of *Brown* but rather a counterrevolution that foreshadowed the resegregation of schools nationwide.

Burger did not always produce such narrow readings of the relevant constitutional and statutory provisions in matters involving claims of racial discrimination. In *Fullilove v. Klutznick* (1980), Burger wrote an opinion upholding the requirement that 10 percent of public works funding be set aside for minority businesses. Similarly, in *Bob Jones University v. United States* (1983), he held that the Internal Revenue Service had the authority to deny tax exemptions to private religious schools that discriminated on the basis of race, a position that was contrary to the views of the Reagan administration.

Impact

The chief impact of the Court's decision was "white flight," the movement of middle-class white residents of Detroit to the suburbs. Busing between neighborhoods within Detroit accelerated this trend. As whites fled the city, the tax base was reduced. The retail sector suffered because of lower incomes among the remaining residents. The number of housing vacancies skyrocketed. The 2020 census reported a population of just over 639,000, down from 1.85 million in 1950 and 1.67 million in 1970. By 1980, African Americans made up more than 60 percent of the city's population. Some observers believed that these trends would have been mitigated if the Supreme Court had sanctioned a regional integration plan, including the suburbs. White flight would have been discouraged, and the Detroit school system, now 84 percent Black, would not have become one of the nation's most segregated systems in the country. A story published by *Michigan Radio* characterized the decision as "a moment in history that sealed the Detroit schools' fate."

Questions for Further Study

1. What was at issue in the *Milliken v. Bradley* case?

2. Why was busing to achieve racial integration such a contentious issue in the 1970s?

3. How did the Court rule in *Milliken v. Bradley*?

4. What constitutional issues arose in this case?

Further Reading

Books

Baugh, Joyce A. *The Detroit School Busing Case: Milliken v. Bradley and the Controversy over Desegregation*. Lawrence: University Press of Kansas, 2011.

Siegel-Hawley, Genevieve. *When the Fences Come Down: Twenty-First-Century Lessons from Metropolitan School Desegregation*. Chapel Hill: University of North Carolina Press, 2016.

Articles

James, David R. "City Limits on Racial Equality: The Effects of City-Suburb Boundaries on Public-School Desegregation, 1968–1976." *American Sociological Review* 54, no. 6 (December 1989): 963–85.

Meinke, Samantha. "*Milliken v. Bradley*: The Northern Battle for Desegregation." *Michigan Bar Journal* 90 (September 2011): 20–2. https://www.michbar.org/file/journal/pdf/pdf4article1911.pdf.

Sedler, Robert A. "The Profound Impact of *Milliken v. Bradley*." *Wayne Law Review* 33 (1987): 1693–1722. https://digitalcommons.wayne.edu/cgi/viewcontent.cgi?article=1076&context=lawfrp.

Taylor, William L. "Desegregating Urban School Systems after *Milliken v. Bradley*." *Wayne Law Review* 21, no. 3 (March 1975): 751–78. https://heinonline.org/HOL/LandingPage?handle=hein.journals/waynlr21&div=42&id=&page=.

Websites

Graham, Lester. "A Moment in History That Sealed the Detroit Schools' Fate." *Michigan Radio*, September 13, 2016. https://www.michiganradio.org/education/2016-09-13/a-moment-in-history-that-sealed-the-detroit-schools-fate.

Nadworny, Elissa, and Cory Turner. "This Supreme Court Case Made School District Lines a Tool for Segregation," NPR, July 25, 2019. https://www.npr.org/2019/07/25/739493839/this-supreme-court-case-made-school-district-lines-a-tool-for-segregation.

—Commentary by Richard L. Aynes and Michael J. O'Neal

Milliken v. Bradley

Document Text

MR. CHIEF JUSTICE BURGER delivered the opinion of the Court

We granted certiorari in these consolidated cases to determine whether a federal court may impose a multidistrict, areawide remedy to a single-district de jure segregation problem absent any finding that the other included school districts have failed to operate unitary school systems within their districts....

Ever since *Brown v. Board of Education* ... (1954), judicial consideration of school desegregation cases has begun with the standard:

"(I)n the field of public education the doctrine of 'separate but equal' has no place. Separate educational facilities are inherently unequal."...

The target of the *Brown* holding was clear and forthright: the elimination of state-mandated or deliberately maintained dual school systems with certain schools for Negro pupils and others for white pupils....

In *Brown v. Board of Education* ... (*Brown II*), the Court's first encounter with the problem of remedies in school desegregation cases, the Court noted:

"In fashioning and effectuating the decrees, the courts will be guided by equitable principles. Traditionally, equity has been characterized by a practical flexibility in shaping its remedies and by a facility for adjusting and reconciling public and private needs."...

While specifically acknowledging that the District Court's findings of a condition of segregation were limited to Detroit, the Court of Appeals approved the use of a metropolitan remedy largely on the grounds that it is

"impossible to declare 'clearly erroneous' the District Judge's conclusion that any Detroit only segregation plan will lead directly to a single segregated Detroit school district overwhelmingly black in all of its schools, surrounded by a ring of suburbs and suburban school districts overwhelmingly white in composition in a State in which the racial composition is 87 per cent white and 13 per cent black."...

Both [the District Court and the Court of Appeals] proceeded on an assumption that the Detroit schools could not be truly desegregated—in their view of what constituted desegregation—unless the racial composition of the student body of each school substantially reflected the racial composition of the population of the metropolitan area....

Here the District Court's approach to what constituted "actual desegregation" raises the fundamental question, not presented in *Swann*, as to the circumstances in which a federal court may order desegregation relief that embraces more than a single school district. The court's analytical starting point was its conclusion that school district lines are no more than arbitrary lines on a map drawn "for political convenience." Boundary lines may be bridged where there has been a constitutional violation calling for interdistrict relief, but the notion that school district lines may be casually ignored or treated as a mere administrative convenience is contrary to the history of public education in our country. No single tradition in public education is more deeply rooted than local control over the operation of schools; local autonomy has long been thought essential both to the maintenance of community concern and support for public schools and to quality of the educational process....

The Michigan educational structure involved in this case, in common with most States, provides for a large measure of local control, and a review of the scope and character of these local powers indicates the extent to which the interdistrict remedy approved by the two courts could disrupt and alter the structure of public education in Michigan. The metropolitan remedy would require, in effect, consolidation of 54 independent school districts historically administered as separate units into a vast new super school district.... Entirely apart from the logistical and other serious problems attending large-scale transportation of students, the consolidation would give rise to an array of other problems in financing and operating this new school system....

It may be suggested that all of these vital operational problems are yet to be resolved by the District Court, and that this is the purpose of the Court of Appeals' proposed remand. But it is obvious from the scope of the interdistrict remedy itself that absent a complete restructuring of the laws of Michigan relating to school districts the District Court will become first, a de facto "legislative authority" to resolve these complex questions, and then the "school superintendent" for the entire area. This is a task which few, if any, judges are qualified to perform and one which would deprive the people of control of schools through their elected representatives.

Of course, no state law is above the Constitution. School district lines and the present laws with respect to local control, are not sacrosanct and if they conflict with the Fourteenth Amendment federal courts have a duty to prescribe appropriate remedies.... But our prior holdings have been confined to violations and remedies within a single school district. We therefore turn to address, for the first time, the validity of a remedy mandating cross-district or interdistrict consolidation to remedy a condition of segregation found to exist in only one district.

The controlling principle consistently expounded in our holdings is that the scope of the remedy is determined by the nature and extent of the constitutional violation. ... Before the boundaries of separate and autonomous school districts may be set aside by consolidating the separate units for remedial purposes or by imposing a cross-district remedy, it must first be shown that there has been a constitutional violation within one district that produces a significant segregative effect in another district. Specifically, it must be shown that racially discriminatory acts of the state or local school districts, or of a single school district have been a substantial cause of interdistrict segregation. Thus an interdistrict remedy might be in order where the racially discriminatory acts of one or more school districts caused racial segregation in an adjacent district, or where district lines have been deliberately drawn on the basis of race. In such circumstances an interdistrict remedy would be appropriate to eliminate the interdistrict segregation directly caused by the constitutional violation. Conversely, without an interdistrict violation and interdistrict effect, there is no constitutional wrong calling for an interdistrict remedy....

With no showing of significant violation by the 53 outlying school districts and no evidence of any interdistrict violation or effect, the court ... mandated a metropolitan area remedy. To approve the remedy ordered by the court would impose on the outlying districts, not shown to have committed any constitutional violation, a wholly impermissible remedy based on a standard not hinted at in *Brown I* and *II* or any holding of this Court.

In dissent, Mr. Justice WHITE and Mr. Justice MARSHALL undertake to demonstrate that agencies having statewide authority participated in maintaining the dual school system found to exist in Detroit.... But the remedy is necessarily designed, as all remedies are, to restore the victims of discriminatory conduct to the position they would have occupied in the absence of such conduct. Disparate treatment of white and Negro students occurred within the Detroit school system, and not elsewhere, and on this record the remedy must be limited to that system....

The constitutional right of the Negro respondents residing in Detroit is to attend a unitary school system in that district.... The view of the dissenters, that the existence of a dual system in Detroit can be made the basis for a decree requiring cross-district transportation of pupils, cannot be supported on the grounds that it represents merely the devising of a suitably flexible remedy for the violation of rights already established by our prior decisions. It can be supported only by drastic expansion of the constitutional right itself, an expansion without any support in either constitutional principle or precedent....

We recognize that the ... record ... contains language and some specific incidental findings thought by the District Court to afford a basis for interdistrict relief. However, these comparatively isolated findings and brief comments concern only one possible interdistrict violation and are found in the context of a proceeding that, as the District Court conceded, included no proof of segregation practiced by any of the 85 suburban school districts surrounding Detroit. The Court of Appeals, for example, relied on five factors which, it held, amounted to unconstitutional state action with respect to the violations found in the Detroit system....

We conclude that the relief ordered by the District Court and affirmed by the Court of Appeals was based upon an erroneous standard and was unsupported by record evidence that acts of the outlying districts effected the discrimination found to exist in the schools of Detroit....

Reversed and remanded.

Glossary

Brown I* and *II: reference to the original *Brown v. Board of Education* case (*Brown I*) and a later case, *Brown II*, in which the Court, to implement *Brown I*, assigned to district courts the task of desegregating schools "with all deliberate speed"

certiorari: a demand by a higher court that a lower court release its records relating to a particular case

de jure: Latin for "in law," meaning that something is established or required by statute, as opposed to *de facto*, or "in fact," meaning that something exists independent of the law

remand: the act of sending a case back to a lower court for reconsideration

Swann: *Swann v. Charlotte-Mecklenburg County* (1971), a key case in the controversy surrounding busing of students to achieve racial desegregation

UNITED STATES v. NIXON

DATE 1974	**CITATION** 418 U.S. 683
AUTHOR Warren Burger	**SIGNIFICANCE** Ordered President Richard M. Nixon to turn over tapes and other subpoenaed materials to the federal court
VOTE 8–0	

Overview

The landmark case of *United States v. Nixon* grew out of the June 1972 break-in at the Democratic National Committee headquarters at the Watergate office complex in Washington, D.C., and the Nixon administration's attempt to cover up its involvement. The special prosecutor in charge of investigating the case issued a subpoena ordering President Richard Nixon to release audiotapes and papers related to meetings between the president and four Nixon aides indicted by the grand jury. Refusing the prosecutor's demands, President Nixon publicly stated that he would abide only by a definitive decision of the Supreme Court. Rejecting Nixon's claim of presidential immunity, the Court's unanimous 8–0 ruling, handed down in July 1974, is considered an important precedent in limiting the powers of the executive branch; it led directly to Nixon's resignation in August of that year.

Context

A landmark in the political and judicial history of the country, the case arose in a very troubled and stormy time for the nation. President Nixon was the first president since Grover Cleveland to have two of his nominees for the Supreme Court rejected by the Senate. Moreover, for the first time in history, a vice president of the United States, Spiro Agnew, had been indicted on a variety of charges of corruption. Agnew ultimately made a plea-bargain agreement under which he pleaded no contest to the charge of failure to report income and pay taxes and resigned from the office of vice president—the first ever to do so.

And, of course, the war in Vietnam was still underway. Nixon had won the presidential election in 1968 with promises that included the ending of the Vietnam War. Although he reduced American troops and shifted their roles to the South Vietnamese, the North Vietnamese responded with more military attacks in the south. President Nixon, in turn, responded by expanding the aerial bombing campaign to Cambodia and Laos, which resulted in increased nationwide antiwar protests. During this time, the *New York Times* obtained copies of a classified analysis of the war that became known as the Pentagon Papers. The Nixon administration was unsuccessful in trying to prevent the publication of these

The Watergate Complex
(Wikimedia Commons)

papers; meanwhile, a group known as the "plumbers," operatives directed by E. Howard Hunt of the White House Special Investigations Unit, was formed to fix leaks of confidential or classified information. Hunt directed the covert operation that led to the scandal involving the Pentagon Papers. Even before Watergate, the whiff of scandal surrounded the president.

On June 17, 1972, five burglars—Virgilio Gonzalez, Bernard Barker, James McCord, Eugenio Martínez, and Frank Sturgis—were caught as they were breaking into the Democratic National Headquarters at the Watergate Office Building in Washington, D.C.; the various scandals that surrounded President Nixon at that time are virtually always referred to under the umbrella term "Watergate," and other scandals affix the syllable "-gate" as a figure of speech. Apparently, the burglars intended to wiretap the headquarters to provide the Nixon reelection campaign with intelligence about Democratic campaign plans. The break-in was extensively investigated by media outlets, principally the *Washington Post*. It was discovered that the burglars were connected with the Committee for the Re-election of the President, ironically often abbreviated as CREEP, and the cash found on the burglars after they were arrested was connected to the committee. As the investigation unfolded and the burglars were tried, the House of Representatives granted the U.S. House Judiciary Committee broad investigative authority, resulting in hearings conducted by the Senate Watergate Committee, headed by Senator Sam Ervin. From May 17 to November 15, 1973, many Americans were glued to their television sets and PBS as a parade of witnesses testified that Nixon had approved plans to cover up the administration's involvement in the matter.

A bombshell revelation was made by Republican staffer Alexander Butterfield on July 13. He testified that a voice-activated taping system had been installed in the Oval Office of the White House. That system recorded conversations that Nixon had with his aides, including White House chief of staff H. R. Haldeman, White House counsel John Dean, White House counsel John Erlichman, and others who played major roles in the scandal. During these conversations, it was clear that Nixon and his aides explored ways to resist the investigations and to use federal officials to turn attention away from the growing scandal. They came up with the expression "modified limited hangout," a technique that involves the release of previously hidden information to prevent exposure of more important and potentially more damning details. As a result of the Senate hearings, the House Judiciary Committee conducted televised hearings that launched the impeachment process against Nixon and ultimately led to three articles of impeachment: obstruction of justice, abuse of power, and contempt of Congress.

The result was a constitutional crisis. The U.S. Supreme Court ordered the president to turn over the tapes to a special prosecutor. Nixon refused, instead turning over edited transcripts of the tapes. His refusal was challenged in federal district court, which ordered the president to comply with all of the requests of the special prosecutor. After the president appealed this decision to the U.S. Circuit Court of Appeals, the special prosecutor asked the U.S. Supreme Court to hear the case. At the Supreme Court, the attorneys for the president argued that because the matter involved a dispute *within* the executive branch, the court system had no jurisdiction. Further, the attorneys argued that the president enjoyed executive privilege, shielding the tapes from being subpoenaed; the concept of executive privilege, based on the constitutional separation of powers, enables the president to take part in confidential communications with aides, particularly on matters of defense and national security, without having to reveal the content of those communications. The special prosecutor countered, however, that executive privilege is not absolute. The case at hand involved a criminal matter, requiring the president to submit to the demands of the legal system. The alternative would be to give the president unchecked power and render him immune to the rule of law.

From President Nixon's point of view, there was some hope that the decision would be less than unanimous. After all, Nixon himself had appointed four members of his own political party to the Court: Burger, Harry A. Blackmun, Lewis F. Powell Jr., and William H. Rehnquist. Furthermore, Justice Rehnquist had served in the attorney general's office during Nixon's presidency. (However, Rehnquist duly excused himself from the case.) It was not unreasonable for the president to think that if his counsel advanced a plausible argument, in a close case, at least some of his appointees might take his side. Still, if Nixon had been emboldened by dissenters to defy a majority of the Supreme Court, it would almost surely have resulted in impeachment and removal from office. Nixon, of course, resigned before he could be impeached.

About the Author

Warren Earl Burger was the fifteenth chief justice of the United States and enjoyed the fourth-longest tenure as head of the Supreme Court. Coming from a working-class family of modest means in Saint Paul, Minnesota, Burger took work at an early age to help out with his family's finances. He was a good student and won a scholarship to Princeton, which he declined because it would not have paid for all of his expenses. While selling insurance, Burger attended evening school, taking extension courses at the University of Minnesota from 1925 to 1927. He worked as an accountant while attending Saint Paul College of Law (now William Mitchell College of Law), from which he graduated magna cum laude in 1931.

For over twenty years Burger worked for the Saint Paul law firm of Boyesen, Otis & Faricy (1931–1953), where he became a named partner in 1935. He worked primarily in the fields of probate, real estate, and corporate law, meanwhile gaining experience in political matters. His active role in Republican politics in Minnesota resulted in his leading the delegation that sought to nominate the Minnesota governor Harold Stassen for president at the 1952 Republican National Convention. It was Burger who ultimately announced the transfer of the delegation's votes from Stassen to General Dwight D. Eisenhower, which gave the latter enough votes to win the nomination. Eisenhower proceeded to win the presidential election. Before the end of the year, Burger was named assistant attorney general in charge of the Justice Department's Claims Division (later the Civil Division). Burger did not have the type of practice, national reputation as a lawyer, or experience in government that would have warranted his appointment; although his general competency as a lawyer was no doubt confirmed, Burger's role in the 1952 convention was what brought him to the attention of the Eisenhower administration.

Burger's role within the Claims Division, similarly, was not that of a brilliant trial lawyer who won cases others could not have won, nor was it that of an incisive intellectual who developed creative legal theories that led to victories in the appellate courts. Rather, Burger's role was primarily that of an administrator of a large government office. His role was to supervise the legal work of his office's attorneys, who were often younger than he was, and ensure that the legal positions taken by his office were consistent with the policy preferences of the Eisenhower administration. Burger's administrative ability and political loyalty led President Eisenhower to appoint Burger to the U.S. Court of Appeals for the District of Columbia Circuit in 1956, where he served for thirteen years.

On an appeals court that was often divided over decisions in criminal cases, Burger led the judges opposed to expanding the rights of criminal defendants—that is, persons who were charged with crimes and whose guilt or innocence was to be determined by a jury or court. Burger wanted to give more deference to trial judges, prosecutors, and the police in the proving of guilt and to provide fewer protections for defendants. By taking this position, he established a reputation as a conservative "law and order" judge. He also notably remained untainted by any ethical scandal. In 1969 President Richard Nixon nominated Burger for the position of chief justice of the United States. It was not Burger's legal brilliance that brought him to the attention of President Nixon; rather, it was his speeches—which might be referred to as political speeches—on limiting the rights of defendants. Nixon's nomination of Burger fulfilled a campaign promise to counter the Court's judicial activism under Earl Warren by appointing justices who, in his view, followed conservative philosophy. Burger was confirmed by the U.S. Senate by a vote of seventy-four to three.

Chief Justice Burger served on the Supreme Court for over seventeen years and during that time wrote more than 250 opinions. Under Chief Justice Warren, the Court had extended protections for those charged

Nixon resigned on August 9, 1974.
(White House Photo Office Collection)

with crimes and decided cases abolishing school segregation and protecting the right to vote. Burger came to disappoint those who wanted a wholesale repudiation of the Warren Court era. He helped slow the rate at which change took place and in some cases diluted the effects of prior decisions, but he did little to overrule the decisions that had spurred political debate. The Burger court did take a more limited view of the rights of those accused of crimes and was also more deferential to the states, under the banner of federalism. But it also recognized new rights and expanded others in the areas of welfare, abortion, gender-based discrimination, and affirmative action. This approach continued for Burger's entire term as chief justice. At times he continued the course of the Warren court, as illustrated by his opinion in segregation cases like *Swann v. Charlotte-Mecklenburg Board of Education* (1971). Yet he also refused to extend the remedy for segregation to surrounding school districts in *Milliken v. Bradley* (1974). In other cases, like his dissent in *Bivens v. Six Unknown Named Agents*, Burger tried to stem the expansion of judicial remedies but was unable to muster a majority on the Court. He served as chief justice until 1986, when he resigned to serve as chair of the Commission on the Bicentennial of the U.S. Constitution. Burger died in 1995 in Washington, D.C.

Explanation and Analysis of the Document

The ruling handed down by the Supreme Court on July 24 was unanimous. Chief Justice Burger assumed the role of writing the opinion, which ordered President Nixon to honor the subpoena and produce the evidence sought by the special prosecutor. For the first time in history, the Court held that there was a constitutional basis for the claim of executive privilege. Its rationale was that "the privilege can be said to be derived from the supremacy of each branch [of government] within its own assigned area of constitutional duties." Nevertheless, the Court found that President Nixon's generalized claim of confidentiality had to be weighed against the more specific duty of the federal courts to ensure that justice was done in a criminal proceeding, the right to call witnesses under the Sixth Amendment, and right to due process of law under the Fifth Amendment. Emphasizing that Nixon had made no claim that the evidence at issue involved any military, diplomatic, or sensitive national security secrets, the Court held that the president's "generalized interest in confidentiality" did not outweigh the "fundamental demands of due process of law in the fair administration of criminal justice."

The Court's unanimous decision indeed led Nixon to turn over the evidence sought by the subpoena, and among the evidence submitted was the proverbial "smoking gun" revealing that the president had been involved in the conspiracy to cover up the crime. Sixteen days after the opinion was announced, Nixon resigned, the only president to do so in the nation's history. There was a certain irony in the fact that Chief Justice Burger's opinion helped lead to the resignation of the very president who had nominated him for the Court. Notably, although Burger's early judicial advancement was based upon his political actions, his role in this case was not influenced by politics.

In many ways, *United States v. Nixon* shows Burger at his best. The opinion was unanimous on an issue of great national importance and was straightforward and easy to understand. While Burger ultimately rules against President Nixon's "generalized claim" of privilege, he nevertheless goes out of his way in the decision to support more specific claims of privilege, to recognize the unique status of the president when subpoenaed, and to protect for future presidents the claim of a robust reading of executive privilege.

A deeper inquiry into this opinion reveals Burger's weaknesses. An examination of the memoranda and draft opinions circulated among the justices reveals that a significant part of the opinion was actually drafted by Justices Potter Stewart, Byron White, and Brennan, with a major initial contribution by Justice William O. Douglas. While a review of the memoranda and drafts of opinions exchanged by the justices before the final decision suggests that all eight participating justices agreed upon the final result from the outset, the unanimous opinion was achieved only by Burger's giving up his own views and language in deference to those of the other justices.

Impact

The impact of the Supreme Court's decision was clear: executive privilege is not unlimited. In a criminal case, the president has to conform to the rulings of the court system just as any other U.S. citizen does. The president cannot hide behind executive privilege to evade the court system—or to evade responsibility for actions taken within his administration.

The chief impact, however, was on Nixon himself. At this point in the scandal, he did not have a leg to stand on. The incriminating tapes had to be turned over, and ultimately, their tawdry revelations led to the threat of impeachment and Nixon's resignation from office.

The matter, however, did not end with the Court's decision. Nixon turned over the tapes, but in the middle of one, made on June 20, three days after the break-in, there was a mysterious eighteen-and-a-half-minute gap, filled with odd clicks and buzzes. The gap was blamed on the actions of the president's loyal private secretary, Rose Mary Woods, as she was transcribing the tapes using a Dictaphone, but in the broader context of the scandal, the gap raised suspicions about what was omitted, adding to the belief in many quarters that the Nixon administration was corrupt.

Questions for Further Study

1. On what basis did the Burger court deny the claims made by the Nixon administration?

2. Why was the doctrine of "executive privilege" not fully applicable in this case?

3. What was the relevance of the constitutional doctrine of "due process" in this case?

4. On what grounds did the Court restate the concept that "the public . . . has a right to every man's evidence"?

5. What does the Court mean when it says "the impediment that an absolute, unqualified privilege would place in the way of the primary constitutional duty of the Judicial Branch to do justice in criminal prosecutions would plainly conflict with the function of the courts."

Further Reading

Books

Graff, Garrett M. *Watergate: A New History*. New York: Simon and Schuster, 2022.

Kutler, Stanley L. *The Wars of Watergate*. New York: Norton, 1992.

Schudson, Michael. *Watergate in American Memory: How We Remember, Forget, and Reconstruct the Past*. New York: Basic Books, 1992.

Articles

Gunther, Gerald. "Judicial Hegemony and Legislative Autonomy: The Nixon Case and the Impeachment Process." *UCLA Law Review* 22, no. 1 (1974): 20–9.

Owens, Dennis J. "The Establishment of a Doctrine: Executive Privilege after United States v. Nixon." *Texas Southern University Law Review* 4, no. 1 (1976): 22–49.

Schwartz, Bernard. "Bad Presidents Make Hard Law: Richard M. Nixon in the Supreme Court." *Rutgers Law Review* 31, no. 1 (1977): 22–40.

Van Alstyne, William W. "A Political and Constitutional Review of *United States v. Nixon*." *UCLA Law Review* 22 (1974): 116–40.

Websites

"Battle for the Tapes: Timeline." The Watergate Files, Ford Library Museum. Accessed February 24, 2023, https://www.fordlibrarymuseum.gov/museum/exhibits/watergate_files/content.php?section=3&page=d.

"Nixon Grand Jury Records." National Archives. Accessed June 13, 2022. https://www.archives.gov/research/investigations/watergate/nixon-grand-jury.

—Commentary by Richard L. Aynes and Michael J. O'Neal

United States v. Nixon

Document Text

MR. CHIEF JUSTICE BURGER delivered the opinion of the Court

... The first contention is a broad claim that the separation of powers doctrine precludes judicial review of a President's claim of privilege. The second contention is that if he does not prevail on the claim of absolute privilege, the court should hold as a matter of constitutional law that the privilege prevails over the subpoena duces tecum.

In the performance of assigned constitutional duties each branch of the Government must initially interpret the Constitution, and the interpretation of its powers by any branch is due great respect from the others.... Many decisions of this Court, however, have unequivocally reaffirmed the holding of *Marbury v. Madison* . . . that "(i)t is emphatically the province and duty of the judicial department to say what the law is." ...

Since this Court has consistently exercised the power to construe and delineate claims arising under express powers, it must follow that the Court has authority to interpret claims with respect to powers alleged to derive from enumerated powers....

Notwithstanding the deference each branch must accord the others, the "judicial Power of the United States" vested in the federal courts by Art. III, §1, of the Constitution can no more be shared with the Executive Branch than the Chief Executive, for example, can share with the Judiciary the veto power, or the Congress share with the Judiciary the power to override a Presidential veto. Any other conclusion would be contrary to the basic concept of separation of powers and the checks and balances that flow from the scheme of a tripartite government....

In support of his claim of absolute privilege, the President's counsel urges two grounds.... The first ground is the valid need for protection of communications between high Government officials and those who advise and assist them in the performance of their manifold duties; the importance of this confidentiality is too plain to require further discussion.... Whatever the nature of the privilege of confidentiality of Presidential communications in the exercise of Art. II powers, the privilege can be said to derive from the supremacy of each branch within its own assigned area of constitutional duties. Certain powers and privileges flow from the nature of enumerated powers; the protection of the confidentiality of Presidential communications has similar constitutional underpinnings.

The second ground asserted by the President's counsel in support of the claim of absolute privilege rests on the doctrine of separation of powers. Here it is argued that the independence of the Executive Branch within its own sphere ... insulates a President from a judicial subpoena in an ongoing criminal prosecution, and thereby protects confidential Presidential communications.

However, neither the doctrine of separation of powers, nor the need for confidentiality of high-level communications, without more, can sustain an absolute, unqualified Presidential privilege of immunity from judicial process under all circumstances. The President's need for complete candor and objectivity from advisers calls for great deference from the courts. However, when the privilege depends solely on the broad, undifferentiated claim of public interest in the confidentiality of such conversations, a confrontation with other values arises. Absent a claim of need to protect military, diplomatic, or sensitive national security secrets, we find it difficult to accept the argument that even the very important interest in confidentiality of Presidential communications is significantly diminished by production of such material for in camera inspection with all the protection that a district court will be obliged to provide.

The impediment that an absolute, unqualified privilege would place in the way of the primary constitutional duty of the Judicial Branch to do justice in criminal prosecutions would plainly conflict with the function of the courts under Art. III. In designing the structure of our Government and dividing and allocating the sovereign power among three co-equal branches, the Framers of the Constitution sought to provide a comprehensive system, but the separate powers were not intended to operate with absolute independence....

To read the Art. II powers of the President as providing an absolute privilege as against a subpoena essential to enforcement of criminal statutes on no more than a generalized claim of the public interest in confidentiality of nonmilitary and nondiplomatic discussions would upset the constitutional balance of "a workable government" and gravely impair the role of the courts under Art. III....

Since we conclude that the legitimate needs of the judicial process may outweigh Presidential privilege, it is necessary to resolve those competing interests in a manner that preserves the essential functions of each branch....

A President and those who assist him must be free to explore alternatives in the process of shaping policies and making decisions and to do so in a way many would be unwilling to express except privately. These are the considerations justifying a presumptive privilege for Presidential communications. The privilege is fundamental to the operation of Government and inextricably rooted in the separation of powers under the Constitution.... We agree with Mr. Chief Justice Marshall's observation, therefore, that "(i)n no case of this kind would a court be required to proceed against the president as against an ordinary individual."...

But this presumptive privilege must be considered in light of our historic commitment to the rule of law. This is nowhere more profoundly manifest than in our view that "the twofold aim (of criminal justice) is that guilt shall not escape or innocence suffer."... The ends of criminal justice would be defeated if judgments were to be founded on a partial or speculative presentation of the facts. The very integrity of the judicial system and public confidence in the system depend on full disclosure of all the facts, within the framework of the rules of evidence. To ensure that justice is done, it is imperative to the function of courts that compulsory process be available for the production of evidence needed either by the prosecution or by the defense.

Only recently the Court restated the ancient proposition of law, albeit in the context of a grand jury inquiry rather than a trial, that "the public . . . has a right to every man's evidence," except for those persons protected by a constitutional, common-law, or statutory privilege.... Whatever their origins, these exceptions to the demand for every man's evidence are not lightly created nor expansively construed, for they are in derogation of the search for truth....

The right to the production of all evidence at a criminal trial similarly has constitutional dimensions. The Sixth Amendment explicitly confers upon every defendant in a criminal trial the right "to be confronted with the witnesses against him" and "to have compulsory process for obtaining witnesses in his favor." Moreover, the Fifth Amendment also guarantees that no person shall be deprived of liberty without due process of law. It is the manifest duty of the courts to vindicate those guarantees, and to accomplish that it is essential that all relevant and admissible evidence be produced.

In this case we must weigh the importance of the general privilege of confidentiality of Presidential communications in performance of the President's responsibilities against the inroads of such a privilege on the fair administration of criminal justice....

On the other hand, the allowance of the privilege to withhold evidence that is demonstrably relevant in a criminal trial would cut deeply into the guarantee of due process of law and gravely impair the basic function of the courts. A President's acknowledged need for confidentiality in the communications of his office is general in nature, whereas the constitutional need for production of relevant evidence in a criminal proceeding is specific and central to the fair adjudication of a particular criminal case in the administration of justice. Without access to specific facts a criminal prosecution may be totally frustrated. The President's broad interest in confidentiality of communications will not be vitiated by disclosure of a limited number of conversations preliminarily shown to have some bearing on the pending criminal cases.

We conclude that when the ground for asserting privilege as to subpoenaed materials sought for use in a criminal trial is based only on the generalized interest in confidentiality, it cannot prevail over the fundamental demands of due process of law in the fair administration of criminal justice. The generalized assertion of privilege must yield to the demonstrated, specific need for evidence in a pending criminal trial....

Affirmed.

Glossary

Chief Justice Marshall: John Marshall (1755–1835), the highly influential fourth chief justice of the United States from 1801 to 1835

derogation: the taking away of the effectiveness of a law

enumerated powers: in Article I, Section 8 of the Constitution, the list of specific powers held by Congress

express powers: powers specifically granted (to the president or Congress, for example) by the U.S. Constitution

in camera: in chambers (a judge's chambers), as opposed to in open court

Marbury v. Madison: a landmark Supreme Court case in 1803 that established the principle of judicial review, that is, that the judicial branch of government has the power to annul acts of the legislature and the executive

subpoena duces tecum: a Latin legal term referring to a command to produce documents

vitiated: diminished; eroded

Craig v. Boren

Date 1976	**Citation** 429 U.S. 190
Author William J. Brennan	**Significance** Held that an Oklahoma statute violated the Fourteenth Amendment's equal protection clause by establishing different drinking ages for men and women.
Vote 7–2	

Overview

The U.S. Supreme Court case of *Craig v. Boren* (1976) introduced the "intermediate scrutiny" test to assess government actions based on gender. Oklahoma had passed a statute prohibiting the sale of "nonintoxicating" 3.2 percent beer to males under the age of twenty-one while permitting females over the age of eighteen to purchase it. Two young men, Mark Walker and Curtis Craig, brought suit, challenging the law as a violation of the Fourteenth Amendment equal protection clause; they were joined by an alcohol vendor, Carolyn Whitener. The lower courts dismissed the case, saying that the state of Oklahoma had the right to regulate commerce in alcoholic beverages. The case was appealed to the Supreme Court. Writing for the majority, William J. Brennan held that the gender classifications set in place by the Oklahoma law were indeed unconstitutional. He went on to enunciate the "intermediate" standard of scrutiny for determining the constitutionality of sex-based classifications in state laws, whereby the state had to prove the existence of specific important governmental objectives and the law had to be substantially related to the achievement of those objectives. The case was decided on a 7–2 vote, with Warren E. Burger and William Rehnquist writing dissenting opinions.

Context

On its face, *Craig v. Boren* seems an unlikely case to cite for its important role in Supreme Court—and U.S.—history. As Ruth Bader Ginsburg (later a Supreme Court justice herself but at the time a litigator for the Women's Rights Project of the American Civil Liberties Union) remarked tongue in cheek to appellants' counsel, "Delighted to see the Supreme Court is interested in beer drinkers." *Craig* concerned an Oklahoma statute permitting eighteen-year-old women to purchase beer with an alcohol content of 3.2 percent but requiring that men who wished to purchase 3.2 percent beer be at least twenty-one years old. Mark Walker, then an eighteen-year-old college freshman, decided to challenge the statute in court. Concerned that he might have difficulty demonstrating damages and thus obtaining standing to sue, his attorney recommended that Walker add a vendor of 3.2 percent beer as a plaintiff. Carolyn Whitener was according-

Justice William J. Brennan Jr. delivered the majority opinion.
(Library of Congress)

ly added. As the case wended its way to court, Walker turned twenty-one, and a third plaintiff, then-eighteen-year-old Curtis Craig, joined the suit.

The federal district court that heard *Craig* dismissed it out of hand, declaring the statute a valid exercise of Oklahoma's right under the Twenty-first Amendment to regulate commerce in alcoholic beverages. Plaintiffs then appealed to the U.S. Supreme Court. By the time the case reached the high court, however, Curtis Craig, too, had attained the age of majority, leaving Carolyn Whitener the only appellant with standing. In his opinion for the Court, Brennan addresses this oddity first, declaring that Whitener can rely upon the equal protection claims of affected eighteen- to twenty-year-old males, whose rights would be affected should her claim fail. Brennan's treatment of the state's Twenty-first Amendment argument is similarly direct: The Twenty-first Amendment, which repealed the Eighteenth Amendment and legalized the sale of alcoholic beverages, was intended to affect interstate commerce in alcohol, not individual rights.

About the Author

William Brennan, U.S. Supreme Court justice, was one of the architects of the constitutional revolution that radically changed American life in the second half of the twentieth century. As Chief Justice Earl Warren's right-hand man, Brennan was responsible for crafting majority opinions such as *Baker v. Carr*, which helped to establish the principle of "one person, one vote" and which Warren always referred to as the most important decision handed down during his momentous tenure on the Court. Brennan, whose politics placed him squarely at the Warren Court's center, was also responsible for crafting majorities for opinions such as the one he wrote in *New York Times Co. v. Sullivan*, which managed to greatly expand the First Amendment while avoiding his more liberal colleagues' wish to make criticism of public officials immune to libel suits. During the Warren years (1953–1969), Brennan was the justice least likely to dissent from the majority's views; but later, during the tenures of Chief Justices Warren Burger and William Rehnquist, he frequently played the role of passionate dissenter, most notably in death penalty cases. Nonetheless, as late as a year before he retired from an increasingly conservative Court, Brennan marshaled a majority in *Texas v. Johnson* and engineered an opinion that expanded the definition of protected speech. It is no accident that Brennan is remembered not only for the law he made but also for his skills as a coalition builder.

Born in Newark, New Jersey, on April 25, 1906, the son of Irish working-class parents, William Joseph Brennan Jr. could be said to have inherited the social activism he later exhibited on the high bench. His father worked as coal stoker at a brewery, hard labor that prompted him to become, first, a leader of the local labor union and, later, a reformer as member of the Newark Board of Commissioners. William Jr. shared many of his father's attitudes, but not—at least not overtly—his father's taste for politics. After graduating with an advanced business degree from the Wharton School at the University of Pennsylvania, Brennan attended Harvard Law School. He practiced law privately for only a short while before commencing a campaign to reform the New Jersey court system. Within a few years, he was sitting on the state supreme court bench, where, seemingly anticipating the role he would later play in connection to Earl Warren, Brennan became New Jersey Chief Justice Arthur Vanderbilt's closest associate.

Brennan arrived at the U.S. Supreme Court on October 16, 1956, appointed by President Dwight D. Eisenhower when Congress was in recess. When the Senate reconvened and voted on Brennan's appointment, only one voice was raised against him: that of Joseph McCarthy, who presumably objected not to Brennan's jurisprudence but to the latter's onetime comparison of McCarthy's Communist-hunting tactics with those employed at the Salem witch trials. Later, Eisenhower would come to regret his choice. Asked if he had made any mistakes as president, he responded, "Yes, two, and they are both sitting on the Supreme Court." Eisenhower grew to dislike Brennan's liberality on the Court almost as much as he disliked Warren's. And, indeed, Warren and Brennan worked together closely throughout Warren's tenure, meeting together privately to discuss strategies for bringing the other justices around to their view of current cases before each weekly judicial conference. Warren valued Brennan not only for his ability to parse and articulate a legal argument but also for his persuasiveness. Achieving unanimity—or, barring that, the clearest majority possible—was of the utmost importance to Warren, who sought to make his Court's precedents stick. Brennan was, in every sense, Warren's ambassador.

During the subsequent tenures of Chief Justices Burger and Rehnquist (respectively, 1969–1986 and 1986–2005), the politics of the Court shifted steadily rightward, and Brennan eventually lost both his leadership role and some of his optimism. Increasingly, he found himself in the minority, and whereas he had written few dissents during the Warren years, after 1969 the number rose steadily. Brennan's closest associate became Thurgood Marshall, one of the few other remaining members of the liberal voting bloc that had been responsible for so many of the Warren Court's momentous decisions. Brennan and Marshall frequently voted together—and they always voted together against imposing the death penalty, which both men believed to be inherently unconstitutional. In later years Brennan was nonetheless still an influential figure, drafting important opinions for the Court on gender discrimination and affirmative action, as well as First Amendment freedoms. He retired on July 20, 1990, having written 1,360 opinions, a number bested only by his fellow Warren Court liberal William O. Douglas.

Explanation and Analysis of the Document

The heart of the case concerned the appropriate standard of review for determining the constitutionality, under the equal protection clause of the Fourteenth Amendment, of a state law having a disparate impact on men and women. Was gender, like income, a "non-suspect" category subject only to the so-called rational basis test, whereby the state had to show only that its statute was reasonably related to a legitimate government interest? The Oklahoma law, which the state declared protected the populace from drunk drivers, might be said to fall under this rubric. Brennan, however, did not find the state's statistics convincing: "Suffice to say that the showing offered by the appellees does not satisfy us that sex represents a legitimate, accurate proxy for the regulation of drinking and driving." While Oklahoma could demonstrate that 0.18 percent of females versus 2 percent of males aged eighteen to twenty had been arrested for alcohol-related driving offenses, what of the 98 percent of young men who were not guilty of such transgressions? What is more, says Brennan, ever since *Reed v. Reed* (a decision mandating that estate executors be appointed in a gender-neutral manner) was decided in 1971, in order to withstand an equal protection challenge, states had been required to show something more than a rational basis for non-gender-neutral laws. Here, however, "the relationship between gender and traffic safety becomes far too tenuous to satisfy *Reed*'s requirement that the gender-based difference be substantially related to achievement of the statutory objective."

Brennan goes on to enunciate the standard for determining the constitutionality of sex-based classifications in state laws. Although the strict scrutiny trained on suspect classifications such as race might not be appropriate, ordinary scrutiny was not rigorous enough when applied to statutes like the one in question. Gender-specific statutes "must serve important governmental objectives and be substantially related to achievement of those objectives" in order to pass constitutional muster. This standard, he avers, is the same one pronounced in *Reed*. As other justices pointed out in a multiplicity of concurring opinions, this last statement was inaccurate. In fact, Brennan—perhaps influenced by the burgeoning feminist movement and the contemporaneous drive for an equal rights amendment to the Constitution—had elaborated on *Reed* to develop a new standard. Ever since *Craig*, the Court has employed Brennan's "intermediate scrutiny" test to assess government actions based on gender.

Impact

Previously, the Court had judged gender distinctions by a "rational basis test." This test asked whether legislatures had reason to believe that gender discrimination in certain instances served the public interest. In *Reed v. Reed* (1971), the Court, by striking down a Utah law that discriminated on account of sex, departed from a century-long trend in Fourteenth Amendment interpretation by finding that "rational basis" was not enough to sustain the discrimination. The *Reed* opinion appeared to signal a shift toward the application of the "strict scrutiny" test not just for racial classifications but for gender classifications as well. These issues were revisited in *Frontiero v. Richardson* (1973), but that case did not clarify whether "strict scrutiny" would apply to gender discrimination. In *Craig v. Boren*, the Court finally established which test would apply in gender classifications. This determination was central to the efforts of the Court to ensure equal protection under the law in the context of the ongoing quest for equal rights in the 1970s.

Questions for Further Study

1. What were Oklahoma's reasons for discriminating on the basis of gender in its regulation of drinking age?

2. Is gender equivalent to race or religion in matters of civil rights?

3. What is the distinction between "strict scrutiny" and "intermediate scrutiny" as a standard of review?

4. What is the relationship between gender and the equal protection clause of the Fourteenth Amendment?

Further Reading

Books

Barnett, Randy E., and Evan D. Bernick. *The Original Meaning of the Fourteenth Amendment: Its Letter and Spirit*. Cambridge, MA: Harvard University Press, 2021.

Hall, Kermit L., and James W. Ely Jr., eds. *The Oxford Guide to United States Supreme Court Decisions*, 2nd ed. New York: Oxford University Press, 2009.

Articles

Darcy, R., and Jenny Sanbrano. "Oklahoma in the Development of Equal Rights: The ERA, 3.2% Beer, Juvenile Justice, and *Craig v. Boren*." *Oklahoma City University Law Review* 22 (1997): 1009–49.

Gryski, Gerard S., and Eleanor C. Main. "Social Backgrounds as Predictors of Votes on State Courts of Last Resort: The Case of Sex Discrimination." *Western Political Quarterly* 39, no. 3 (1986): 528–37.

Segal, Jeffrey A., and Cheryl D. Reedy. "The Supreme Court and Sex Discrimination: The Role of the Solicitor General." *Western Political Quarterly* 41, no. 3 (1988): 553–68.

Websites

Powell, Lewis F., Jr. "Craig v. Boren." Supreme Court Case Files Collection. Box 449. Powell Papers. Lewis F. Powell Jr. Archives, Washington & Lee University School of Law, Virginia. Accessed February 25, 2023, https://scholarlycommons.law.wlu.edu/cgi/viewcontent.cgi?article=1063&context=casefiles.

"Supreme Court Decisions & Women's Rights: Justice for Beer Drinkers—*Craig v. Boren*, 429 U.S. 190 (1976)." Supreme Court Historical Society. Accessed February 25, 2023, https://supremecourthistory.org/classroom-resources-teachers-students/decisions-womens-rights-craig-v-boren/.

—Commentary by Lisa Paddock and Michael J. O'Neal

CRAIG V. BOREN

Document Text

MR. JUSTICE BRENNAN delivered the opinion of the Court

… Analysis may appropriately begin with the reminder that [*Reed v.*] *Reed* emphasized that statutory classifications that distinguish between males and females are "subject to scrutiny under the Equal Protection Clause." … To withstand constitutional challenge, previous cases establish that classifications by gender must serve important governmental objectives and must be substantially related to achievement of those objectives.…

Reed v. Reed has also provided the underpinning for decisions that have invalidated statutes employing gender as an inaccurate proxy for other, more germane bases of classification.… In light of the weak congruence between gender and the characteristic or trait that gender purported to represent, it was necessary that the legislatures choose either to realign their substantive laws in a gender-neutral fashion, or to adopt procedures for identifying those instances where the sex-centered generalization actually comported with fact.…

In this case, too, "*Reed*, we feel, is controlling. . . ." We turn then to the question whether, under *Reed*, the difference between males and females with respect to the purchase of 3.2% beer warrants the differential in age drawn by the Oklahoma statute. We conclude that it does not.…

We accept for purposes of discussion the District Court's identification of the objective underlying 241 and 245 as the enhancement of traffic safety. Clearly, the protection . . . of public health and safety represents an important function of state and local governments. However, appellees' statistics in our view cannot support the conclusion that the gender-based distinction closely serves to achieve that objective and therefore the distinction cannot under *Reed* withstand equal protection challenge.… Even were this statistical evidence accepted as accurate, it nevertheless offers only a weak answer to the equal protection question presented here. The most focused and relevant of the statistical surveys, arrests of 18–20-year-olds for alcohol-related driving offenses, exemplifies the ultimate unpersuasiveness of this evidentiary record. Viewed in terms of the correlation between sex and the actual activity that Oklahoma seeks to regulate—driving while under the influence of alcohol—the statistics broadly establish that .18% of females and 2% of males in that age group were arrested for that offense. While such a disparity is not trivial in a statistical sense, it hardly can form the basis for employment of a gender line as a classifying device. Certainly if maleness . . . is to serve as a proxy for drinking and driving, a correlation of 2% must be considered an unduly tenuous "fit." . . . Moreover, the statistics exhibit a variety of other shortcomings that seriously impugn their value to equal protection analysis. Setting aside the obvious methodological problems, the surveys do not adequately justify the salient . . . features of Oklahoma's gender-based traffic-safety law. None purports to measure the use and dangerousness of 3.2% beer as opposed to alcohol generally, a detail that is of particular importance since, in light of its low alcohol level, Oklahoma apparently considers the 3.2% beverage to be "nonintoxicating." . . . Moreover, many of the studies, while graphically documenting the unfortunate increase in driving while under the influence of alcohol, make no effort to relate their findings to age-sex differential as involved here. Indeed, the only survey that explicitly centered its attention upon young drivers and their use of beer—albeit apparently not of the diluted 3.2% variety—reached results that hardly can be viewed as impressive in justifying either a gender or age classification.

There is no reason to belabor this line of analysis. It is unrealistic to expect either members of the judiciary or state officials to be well versed in the rigors of experimental or statistical technique. But this merely illustrates that proving broad sociological propositions by statistics is a dubious business, and one that inevitably is in tension with the normative philosophy that underlies the Equal Protection Clause. Suffice to say that the showing offered by the appellees does not satisfy us that sex represents a legitimate, accurate proxy for the regulation of drinking and driving. In fact, when it is further recognized that Oklahoma's statute prohibits only the selling of 3.2% beer to young males and not their drinking the beverage once acquired (even after purchase by their 18–20-year-old female companions), the relationship between gender and traffic safety becomes far too tenuous to satisfy *Reed*'s requirement that the gender-based difference be substantially related to achievement of the statutory objective.

We hold, therefore, that under *Reed*, Oklahoma's 3.2% beer statute invidiously discriminates against males 18–20 years of age.

Glossary

appellee: the party against whom a case is appealed by another party (the appellant) in front of a higher court

controlling: carrying the ultimate authority for dealing with a particular legal situation

intermediate scrutiny: a test that requires the state to prove the existence of specific important governmental objectives and that the law must be substantially related to the achievement of those objectives

normative: offering a prescription as to standards

proxy: substitute

rational basis test: tests whether the government's actions are "rationally related" to a "legitimate" government interest; if not, the action is in violation of the equal protection clause of the Fourteenth Amendment

strict scrutiny: a test requiring the government to show that there is a compelling, or very strong, interest in the law, and that the law is either very narrowly tailored or is the least restrictive means available to the government

substantive: defining rights and duties

Regents of the University of California v. Bakke

Date 1978	**Citation** 438 U.S. 265
Author Lewis F. Powell Jr.	**Significance** Upheld affirmative action by allowing educational institutions to give race some special consideration in admissions, but ruled that racial quotas were impermissible
Vote 8–1	

Overview

Regents of the University of California v. Bakke was the first important U.S. Supreme Court decision to test Title VI of the 1964 Civil Rights Act, prohibiting racial discrimination in public education and other endeavors receiving federal funds. In the 1970s, the University of California at Davis School of Medicine had what amounted to dual admission standards based on race. Each year one hundred students were admitted to the medical program, but a number of them were subject to different, more lenient admissions requirements. Sixteen spaces were reserved for "disadvantaged" students, who could identify themselves on the application form as belonging to a minority group or as disadvantaged either economically or educationally. Candidates in this group did not have to meet the same minimum grade point average, and they were compared with one another rather than with the entire pool of applicants.

Allan Bakke, a white male applicant, was rejected by the regular admissions program in 1973 and again in 1974. Both years, applicants with grade-point averages and admissions-test scores lower than Bakke's were admitted under the rules for disadvantaged students. After he was rejected a second time, Bakke sued the university, asking that the Court compel his admission. Bakke based his case on his right to equal protection under the laws, as guaranteed by the Fourteenth Amendment; he also claimed that the university violated Title VI because it had rejected him owing to his race. The Supreme Court ruled in Bakke's favor, ordering the university to admit him, but the Court also held that while Title VI disallowed educational institutions from making racial quotas part of their admissions policies, giving race some special consideration was permissible in order to achieve the important goal of diversity in institutions of higher education and—beyond that—at all levels of society. Thus *Bakke* became, as the Court later characterized it in *Grutter v. Bollinger* (2003), the "touchstone for constitutional analysis of race-conscious admissions policies."

Context

The history of what is known as affirmative action began in March 1961, when President John F. Kennedy, shortly after assuming office, issued Executive Order 10925, establishing the President's Committee on Equal Employment Opportunity. The committee's purpose was to end discrimination in the federal government and any body or organization funded by the federal government. Accordingly, Executive Order 10925 required those contracting with the government to pledge that "the contractor will not discriminate against any employee or applicant for employment because of race, creed, color, or national origin. The contractor will take affirmative action to ensure that applicants are employed, and that employees are treated during employment, without regard to their race, creed, color, or national origin."

Three years later, Title VI of the Civil Rights Act of 1964 expanded upon the original goal of ending discrimination in employment with the following words: "No person in the United States shall, on the ground of race, color or national origin, be excluded from participation in, be denied the benefits of, or be subjected to discrimination under any program or activity receiving federal financial assistance." The Civil Rights Act of 1964 was a product of the civil rights movement that grew out of an education case, *Brown v. Board of Education*, in which the Supreme Court made it clear that racial segregation was no longer the law of the land. *Brown*, decided shortly after Earl Warren took his seat at chief justice, was the first of many socially progressive decisions handed down during Warren's fifteen-year tenure.

The atmosphere of social unrest that characterized the United States in the 1960s had as much to do with the nation's discontent with the conduct of war in Vietnam as it did with the Warren Court, but the turbulent times gave rise to a conservative "silent majority" that in 1968 elected Republican Richard M. Nixon as the thirty-seventh president of the United States. Nixon had run on a platform that emphasized law and order, and when Warren retired in 1969, Nixon nominated another law-and-order Republican, Warren Burger, as the next chief justice. Burger's mission was to help curtail many of the reforms enabled by decisions of the previous Court. He was only marginally successful in achieving this goal, but *Bakke* clearly represented at least a partial retreat from what had up to that time been steady expansion of the doctrine of affirmative action.

Four years before *Bakke*, the Court agreed to hear *DeFunis v. Odegaard*, another education case concerning what came to be known as "reverse discrimination." Marco DeFunis, a white applicant to the University of Washington law school, protested his rejection on

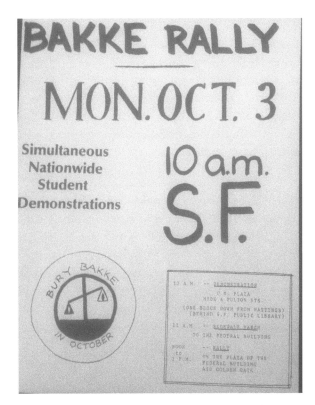

A rally poster in support of overturning the decision in **Regents of the University of California v. Bakke**
(Wikimedia Commons)

ground that his academic record was superior to that of all but one of the African Americans admitted the year he applied. Interim court orders forced the school to admit DeFunis, so that by the time his case was decided by the Supreme Court, he had almost finished his program. The Court declared his case moot, making Bakke's case the first one obliging the justices to struggle with the issue of racial preference in publicly funded education.

About the Author

Lewis Franklin Powell Jr. was born on November 19, 1907, in Suffolk, Virginia, into a family that traced its roots in the state back to the Jamestown colony. He obtained his undergraduate and law degrees from Washington and Lee University in Lexington, Virginia, finally leaving his home state to work on a master of laws degree at Harvard. There, he studied administrative law under Felix Frankfurter, who would leave Harvard shortly thereafter, when President Franklin D. Roosevelt appointed him a U.S. Supreme Court justice.

Powell returned to Virginia, where he practiced law privately until his legal career was interrupted by

World War II, when he enlisted in the Army Air Corps. Serving as an intelligence officer, he rose to the rank of colonel before being demobilized as a decorated veteran. After the war, Powell resumed his legal practice in Richmond, but he became more involved in civic and national affairs, helping the Richmond school board comply with the desegregation requirements spelled out in *Brown v. Board of Education II* (1955) and advising a number of presidential commissions.

When Richard Nixon nominated Powell to the Supreme Court in 1971, he did so in part to fulfill his aim to appoint a southerner to the Court, a goal that had been frustrated when two previous appointments, of the southerners Clement Haynsworth and G. Harold Carswell, were defeated. On December 6, 1971, Powell was confirmed by a nearly unanimous vote in the Senate, becoming, at sixty-four, the second-oldest junior associate justice in Supreme Court history.

Powell was one of the few individuals to come to the Court directly from private practice, and his long years of practice disciplined him to take a pragmatic, lawyerly approach on the high bench, one that included adherence to legal precedents even when he personally disagreed with them. He became a centrist, and he often acted as a swing vote on a Court divided between activist holdovers from the Warren years and more conservative recent appointees. This was the role he played in the *Bakke* case, where he cast the deciding vote and wrote an opinion for the plurality that remains a definitive statement about affirmative action as it pertains to public education. After retiring from the Court in 1987, Powell served occasionally on federal appellate courts until his death in Richmond on August 25, 1998, at the age of ninety.

Explanation and Analysis of the Document

Powell's Opinion Announcing the Judgment of the Court

Justice Powell first restates the essential facts of the case, including the decisions of the lower courts that had heard *Bakke* before it reached the Supreme Court. He also states that Burger, Stewart, Rehnquist, and Stevens agree (albeit in a separate opinion) with his view that the university's admissions policy is unlawful and that Bakke must be admitted to the medical school. Powell's view that the lower court's decision that race cannot play a role in the university's admissions policy is joined (again, in separate opinions) by Brennan, White, Marshall, and Blackmun.

Part I of Powell's opinion details the facts of the case at great length, starting with the history of the University of California Davis School of Medicine and its attempts to diversify its student body, and concluding with the Court's decision to grant the university's petition for certiorari (a term that essentially means that the Court has agreed to hear the case) because of the important constitutional question raised by the case: Are affirmative action programs such as the medical school's permissible under the Fourteenth Amendment and Title VI?

Part II concerns the applicability of Title VI to the case. Although the question of whether a private individual such as Bakke can bring an action under Title VI has not been legally settled, Powell declines to take up this issue, assuming for purposes of this case that Bakke has this right. Powell then revisits the legislative history of Title VI, which was intended to combat discrimination against African Americans by entities in receipt of federal funds, actions that congressional backers of the proposed legislation clearly viewed as unconstitutional. In view of this intent, Powell declares, Title VI must be seen as ruling out only such racial classifications as would violate the Fifth Amendment or the equal protection clause of the Fourteenth Amendment.

Part III opens with the observation that while the university accepts that decisions based on race or ethnic heritage are subject to legal review, and while Bakke agrees that not all considerations of race and ethnicity are not illegal on their face, the two sides disagree about what level of judicial scrutiny should be applied in determining the constitutionality of these categories as used in admissions considerations. In addition, while the university asserts that its special admissions program serves the goal of minority representation in the medical school, Bakke claims that the program promotes a racial quota. Powell declares this last a distinction without a difference, saying that although racial classification is not necessarily illegal, any use of such categorization is subject to "the most exacting judicial examination."

Powell next reviews the history of the equal protection clause. Originally meant to protect African Americans, it was suppressed after the Civil War by a reactionary judiciary. By the time it resumed it proper place in American jurisprudence, the nation had become one made up of many minorities, and over the three decades prior to *Bakke* the Court had interpreted the equal protection clause as a means of extending equal protection of the laws to all persons. The university's contention that discrimination against white applicants to its medical school is not suspect because its purpose is benign must therefore be discarded as outmoded and legally unworkable. The university's contention that the Court has applied a lesser degree of scrutiny when approving preferential classifications is brushed aside, as the cases it cites to support these contentions all concern clear constitutional or statutory violations that can be corrected only through such means. The university, however, was under no legal mandate to preference certain groups over others. "When a classification denies an individual opportunities or benefits enjoyed by others solely because of his race or ethnic background, it must be regarded as suspect"—and subject to strict scrutiny.

In Part IV, Powell states that in order to sanction the use of a suspect classification, the state must be able to demonstrate that it is doing so to advance a goal that is both legal and necessary to achieve a vital interest. The university's interest in maintaining a certain percentage of disadvantaged individuals in its student body is inherently discriminatory and unconstitutional. Remedying the effects of "societal discrimination," which the university declares to be one of its goals, is too unclear to justify discriminating against innocent persons solely because of race. And the university has failed to prove that its stated goal of delivering more and better medical care to minority communities will be achieved through its admissions policies. Furthermore, the university's claim that its pursuit of a diverse student body—and thus a truly free exchange of ideas—is protected by the First Amendment in no way offsets the potential damage its policies can inflict on the equal protection of the rights of such individuals as Allan Bakke.

In Part V, Powell addresses the idea that the university's use of racial quotas is meant to achieve a desirable level of ethnic diversity and then discards it because he refuses to accept the university's argument that quotas are the only means of achieving this goal. While an admissions program that considers race as only one factor might achieve the same goal, the university's special admissions program is purposely racially discriminatory, totally excluding applicants who are not African American, Asian, or Latino from consideration for a set number of places in the medical school, regardless of their qualifications. At the same time, preferred applicants are free to compete for every seat in each entering class. The university's special admissions scheme is for these reasons invalid under the Fourteenth Amendment, although the university is not enjoined from taking race into consideration when weighing applicants.

In Part VI, Powell takes up Bakke's request that the university be ordered to admit him. Because the university admits that absent the requirements of its special admissions program it would have no grounds on which to deny Bakke's application, the Court upholds the lower court's judgment granting Bakke's injunction.

Brennan's Opinion, Concurring in Part and Dissenting in Part

Brennan opens with the statement that the Court's judgment reinforces the constitutional mandate empowering state and federal governments to seek equal opportunity for all citizens. Despite the many and differing opinions recorded in the case, he adds, the fundamental meaning of *Bakke* is that the government may take race into account when seeking to redress past inequality. Justices Burger, Stewart, Rehnquist, and Stevens all agree that the university's special admissions program, however, is impermissible under Title VI and that therefore Bakke must be admitted. Justice Powell looks beyond Title VI to the Constitution, finding the university's program unnecessary to achieve its stated goals. These five form a majority upholding the California Supreme Court's ruling that Bakke must be admitted. The four signatories to this opinion, however, have concluded that the university's program is constitutional and therefore vote to reverse the lower court's opinion in its entirety. But because Powell agrees with these four justices that some consideration of race in admissions policies is permissible, a majority of the Court also votes to reverse the opinion below insofar as it prohibits the university from establishing race-conscious admissions policies in the future.

In Part I, Brennan, like Powell, rehearses the history of the Fourteenth Amendment. In light of its goals and the manner in which they were perverted after the Civil War, Brennan finds it unrealistic and unhelpful to assume that discrimination is a thing of the past and the law color-blind.

Brennan begins Part II of his opinion by declaring that Title VI does not violate the Fourteenth Amendment if it is used to remedy past inequality via methods consonant with the amendment. And the legislative history of Title VI indicates that its whole purpose was to lend government the authority to terminate federal funding when a private program disadvantages members of a minority, just as the Fourteenth Amendment prohibits government from performing in such a manner. Brennan, however, finds that this history does not support Bakke's contention that Title VI was intended to bar affirmative action programs. Instead, he says, Title VI was meant to stop federal funding of programs disadvantaging minority groups through segregation. As support for his contention that Title VI does not require racial neutrality, Brennan cites three reasons: (1) The Court has never said that the Constitution is color-blind; (2) Congress clearly intended to use all remedies, including racial factors, to eliminate unconstitutional discrimination; (3) in drafting Title VI, Congress deliberately avoided defining "discrimination," thus affording considerable latitude in enforcing the legislation as society and the law evolve. Literal application of the plain language of Title VI could, as in the present case, lead to results diametrically opposed to those the Congress intended. Regulations intended as interpretations of Title VI make it clear that race-conscious actions are not only tolerated but also required to fulfill the goals of the statute. Finally, congressional action—as well as decisions of the Court—taken in the aftermath of its passage clearly indicate that racial preferences are an acceptable means of remedying past inequality.

Part III opens with Brennan's assertion that for the Court, human equality has never meant that race is constitutionally irrelevant. Starting with the proposition that racial classifications are not per se invalid under the Fourteenth Amendment, Brennan indicates that "strict scrutiny" of laws compelling affirmative action is necessary only if they violate a fundamental right or contain "suspect classifications." No such right has been violated by the university. What is more, whites do not constitute a group with a history of the kind of unequal treatment the Fourteenth Amendment and Title VI were meant to undo.

The facts in *Bakke*, however, call for something more than the "rational basis" minimal standard of review applied in all affirmative action cases. Instead, Brennan says, gender-discrimination cases suggest a standard that is appropriate here: "Racial classifications designed to further remedial purposes 'must serve important governmental objectives and must be substantially related to achievement of those objectives.'" Racial classifications developed for supposedly benign purposes can and have been misused, so a third, intermediate level of scrutiny is required.

Part IV opens with an endorsement of the university's intention of using racial classifications as a means of redressing long-standing minority underrepresentation in the medical school. Inaction or neutrality in the face of such inequality is insufficient. Brennan cites numerous legal precedents for the proposition that state educational institutions may constitutionally adopt measures—even measures explicitly taking race into account—designed to remedy past racial inequality.

Bakke has asserted that but for the university's special admissions program, he would have been admitted to the medical school. Brennan disputes this claim, adding that the disruption of settled expectations of nonminorities is no argument against affirmative action. Indeed, these expectations are themselves the product of discrimination and therefore "tainted." The special admission program at the medical school was designed to remove pervasive, long-standing inequality; a single admissions standard would only perpetuate underrepresentation of Blacks in medicine born of "the habit of discrimination and the cultural tradition of race prejudice."

"The habit of discrimination and the cultural tradition of race prejudice" constitute the type of indirect, unintentional harm the law calls "disparate impact," and it is often cited as validation for programs like Davis's. In cases such as this, affirmative action that can reasonably be expected to counteract factors that have stigmatized particular groups or individuals are legally permissible. On the other hand, Davis's program has not harmed nonminority groups. It cannot even be said to have harmed Allan Bakke, who probably will not suffer long from having been rejected.

Brennan agrees with the university's assertion that there is no real alternative to special admissions as a means of resolving minority underrepresentation in the medical school. He disagrees with Powell's assertion that there is a qualitative difference between setting aside a fixed number of places for minority applicants and simply using race as one among many considerations determining acceptance. The less-specific Harvard plan for attaining diversity, endorsed by Powell, is to Brennan's way of thinking not superior—only less straightforward. He and his fellow signatories therefore believe that the opinion of the California Supreme Court, declaring the Davis program unconstitutional and ordering Bakke's admission to the medical school, should be reversed in its entirety.

White's Opinion

Justice White chose to write a separate opinion regarding the question of whether or not Title VI allows for private causes of action such as Bakke's suit. While all of the other justices believe it does—either in general or for purposes of this case—White disagrees with this assumption, for if its premise is invalid, then the courts have no jurisdiction to hear *Bakke*. For his part, White feels that private lawsuits brought under Title VI are contrary to legislative intent, owing to the existence of an individual's right to bring suit for discrimination under preexisting laws. Congress would therefore have no reason to—and did not—include such a right as part of Title VI. Termination of funding is the sanction provided for violating Title VI, and allowing an individual to sue to cut off funds sabotages all of the carefully spelled out procedural safeguards intended to promote voluntary compliance. Just because Congress intended Title VI to combat discrimination in both public and private programs, it does not follow that the legislature silently allowed a private right of enforcement. Congress has always required that an inferred private cause of action to enforce a statute be both backed by clear legislative intent and in line with the purposes of the statute. Neither of these requirements is satisfied in this case.

Marshall's Opinion

Justice Marshall agrees with the other members of the Court that the university should be permitted to take race into account in its admissions policy; he does not agree that this policy is unconstitutional. Marshall then rehearses the history of slavery in America, noting the irony of the Founding Fathers' assertion in the Declaration of Independence that "all men are created equal" and "endowed . . . with certain unalienable rights." The implicit protection of slavery found in the Declaration of Independence was reiterated in the Constitution, which counted a slave as three-fifths of a person. Emancipation finally came as a result of the Civil War, but despite passage of the Thirteenth, Fourteenth, and Fifteenth Amendments, African Americans were far from equal to white citizens. The Supreme Court worsened this situation when it began interpreting the Civil Rights amendments in ways that distorted their intended protections, finally declaring in *Plessy v. Ferguson* (1896) that "separate but equal" was the law of the land. And, Marshall maintains, the legacy of this past is still alive in the disfavored position of Blacks in American society.

The Fourteenth Amendment was designed to remedy such discrimination, not stand in the way of measures intended to redress long-standing inequality. The Court has in the past endorsed race-conscious remedial measures, and it is ironic that after several hundred years of class-based discrimination against Blacks, it is unwilling to uphold a class-based remedy for that discrimination. This case affects far more than one individual and one institution. Marshall fears that just as *Plessy* stopped the movement toward equality after the Civil War, this case will stop the progress *Brown v. Board of Education* jump-started in 1954.

Blackmun's Opinion

Justice Blackmun fears that the goal of racial equality may never be achieved if institutions of higher learning are not permitted to preference disadvantaged applicants. He notes the irony of general approval of preferences given college athletes. The original intent of the Fourteenth Amendment, he says, is essentially that of affirmative action. For Blackmun, the Davis program is not unconstitutional. In order to get beyond racism, he says, we must consider race.

Stevens's Opinion, Joined by Burger, Stewart, and Rehnquist, Concurring in the Judgment in Part and Dissenting in Part

The question of racial considerations should not be a part of this case, which concerns a dispute between an individual and an institution of higher learning, which the lower court decided on grounds other than race. As there is no outstanding issue concerning whether race can be used as a factor in an admissions decision, it is also unnecessary to consider the constitutional issue of whether the admissions policy violated the equal protection clause of the Fourteenth Amendment, as resolution of the dispute between the parties rests on interpretation of statute. Because the act in question clearly prohibits the exclusion of anyone from a federally funded program on the ground of race, Allan Bakke must be admitted to the university's medical program.

Impact

Bakke was far from a definitive statement on affirmative action, and when William Rehnquist took over from Warren Burger as chief justice, the Court, guided by its new leader's conservative agenda, seemed determined—and empowered—to roll back affirmative action. In cases such as *Richmond v. J.A. Croson* (1989), for example, the Court applied a more stringent standard in scrutinizing state plans for job set-asides than had been employed to evaluate similar plans at the federal level. And in *Adarand Constructors v. Pena* (1995), the Court retreated even farther from endorsing the use of minority set-asides as a remedy for past discrimination. Clearly, after *Bakke*, anything resembling a quota was suspect.

Because Powell had written alone, with none of the other justices signing on to his opinion and several writing their own, many legal commentators doubted that the plurality decision in *Bakke* would hold much sway as precedent. But when the Rehnquist Court revisited the issue of affirmative action in the academy and promoting a color-blind society through equality of education, the justices followed the bifurcated path Powell laid out a quarter century earlier.

Bakke's flexible criteria had not been bent so far as to break. When two cases with similar facts, *Gratz v. Bollinger* and *Grutter v. Bollinger*, reached the Court in 2003, the rationale carefully explicated by Lewis Powell in the earlier decision held up well. While striking down in *Gratz* the rigid point system used to promote affirmative action at the undergraduate level at the University of Michigan, in *Grutter* the Court upheld the university law school's use of race as one factor in admissions deliberations. In addition, the Court amplified the spirit of the *Bakke* decision by holding for the first time that diversity in a student body is a compelling state interest justifying the use of race in university admissions.

In 2016 in Fisher v. University of Texas, the Court upheld the use of race in admissions. However, by 2023 as the makeup of the Court grew more conservative, new cases before the Court signaled that it might outlaw affirmative action in education.

Questions for Further Study

1. Although his administration submitted an amicus brief supporting both of the petitioners in the Michigan cases, President George W. Bush's response to the Court's decisions in *Grutter* and *Gratz* stressed his hope that America will become a color-blind society. Is it possible to realize this hope if affirmative action were to be outlawed in the education arena?

2. Do you agree that the Harvard plan for achieving student body diversity that Powell holds up as a model is preferable to that of the University of California at Davis Medical School? Why or why not?

3. Do you agree with Justice Brennan that Powell's separation of racial quotas from consideration of race in admissions policies is a distinction without a difference? Why or why not?

Further Reading

Books

Anderson, Terry H. *The Pursuit of Fairness: A History of Affirmative Action.* New York: Oxford University Press, 2004.

Ball, Howard. *The Bakke Case: Race, Education, and Affirmative Action.* Lawrence: University Press of Kansas, 2000.

Beckman, James A., ed. *Controversies in Affirmative Action*, 3 vols. Santa Barbara, CA: Praeger, 2014.

Kellough, J. Edward. *Understanding Affirmative Action: Politics, Discrimination, and the Search for Justice.* Washington, DC: Georgetown University Press, 2006.

Paddock, Lisa. *Facts about the Supreme Court of the United States.* New York: H. W. Wilson, 1996.

Schwartz, Bernard. *A History of the Supreme Court.* New York: Oxford University Press, 1993.

Seeger, Timothy P. "*Regents of the University of California v. Bakke.*" In *The Wiley Blackwell Encyclopedia of Race, Ethnicity, and Nationalism*, edited by John Stone et al. New York: Wiley-Blackwell, 2015.

Wilkinson, J. Harvie. *From Brown to Bakke: The Supreme Court and School Integration, 1954–1978.* New York: Oxford University Press, 1981.

Articles

Johnson, Kevin R. "Foreword: Bakke at 40: The Past, Present, and Future of Affirmative Action." *University of California Davis Law Review* 52, no. 5 (June 2019): 2239+.

—Commentary by Lisa Paddock

Regents of the University of California v. Bakke

Document Text

MR. JUSTICE POWELL announced the judgment of the Court

This case presents a challenge to the special admissions program of the petitioner, the Medical School of the University of California at Davis, which is designed to assure the admission of a specified number of students from certain minority groups. The Superior Court of California sustained respondent's challenge, holding that petitioner's program violated the California Constitution, Title VI of the Civil Rights Act of 1964, 42 U.S.C. 2000d et seq., and the Equal Protection Clause of the Fourteenth Amendment. The court enjoined petitioner from considering respondent's race or the race of any other applicant in making admissions decisions. It refused, however, to order respondent's admission to the Medical School, holding that he had not carried his burden of proving that he would have been admitted but for the constitutional and statutory violations. The Supreme Court of California affirmed those portions of the trial court's judgment declaring the special admissions program unlawful and enjoining petitioner from considering the race of any applicant. It modified that portion of the judgment denying respondent's requested injunction and directed the trial court to order his admission.

For the reasons stated in the following opinion, I believe that so much of the judgment of the California court as holds petitioner's special admissions program unlawful and directs that respondent be admitted to the Medical School must be affirmed. For the reasons expressed in a separate opinion, my Brothers THE CHIEF JUSTICE, MR. JUSTICE STEWART, MR. JUSTICE REHNQUIST, and MR. JUSTICE STEVENS concur in this judgment.

I also conclude for the reasons stated in the following opinion that the portion of the court's judgment enjoining petitioner from according any consideration to race in its admissions process must be reversed. For reasons expressed in separate opinions, my Brothers MR. JUSTICE BRENNAN, MR. JUSTICE WHITE, MR. JUSTICE MARSHALL, and MR. JUSTICE BLACKMUN concur in this judgment.

Affirmed in part and reversed in part.

I

The Medical School of the University of California at Davis opened in 1968 with an entering class of 50 students. In 1971, the size of the entering class was increased to 100 students, a level at which it remains. No admissions program for disadvantaged or minority students existed when the school opened, and the first class contained three Asians but no Blacks, no Mexican-Americans, and no American Indians. Over the next two years, the faculty devised a special admissions program to increase the representation of "disadvantaged" students in each Medical School class. The special program consisted of a separate admissions system operating in coordination with the regular admissions process.

Under the regular admissions procedure, a candidate could submit his application to the Medical School beginning in July of the year preceding the academic year for which admission was sought. Record 149. Because of the large number of applications, the admissions committee screened each one to select candidates for further consideration. Candidates whose overall undergraduate grade point averages fell below 2.5 on a scale of 4.0 were summarily rejected. Id., at 63. About one out of six applicants was invited for a personal interview. Ibid. Following the interviews, each candidate was rated on a scale of 1 to 100 by his interviewers and four other members of the admissions committee. The rating embraced the interviewers' summaries, the candidate's overall grade point average, grade point average in science courses, scores on the Medical College Admissions Test (MCAT), letters of recommendation, extracurricular activities, and other biographical data. Id., at 62. The ratings were added together to arrive at each candidate's "benchmark" score. Since five committee members rated each candidate in 1973, a perfect score was 500; in 1974, six members rated each candidate, so that a perfect score was 600. The full committee then reviewed the file and scores of each applicant and made offers of admission on a "rolling" basis. The chairman was responsible for placing names on the waiting list. They were not placed in strict numerical order; instead, the chairman had discretion to include persons with "special skills." Id., at 63-64.

The special admissions program operated with a separate committee, a majority of whom were members of minority groups. Id., at 163. On the 1973 application form, candidates were asked to indicate whether they wished to be considered as "economically and/or educationally disadvantaged" applicants; on the 1974 form the question was whether they wished to be considered as members of a "minority group," which the Medical School apparently viewed as "Blacks," "Chicanos," "Asians," and "American Indians." Id., at 65-66, 146, 197, 203-205, 216-218. If these questions were answered affirmatively, the application was forwarded to the special admissions committee. No formal definition of "disadvantaged" was ever produced, id., at 163-164, but the chairman of the special committee screened each application to see whether it reflected economic or educational deprivation. Having passed this initial hurdle, the applications then were rated by the special committee in a fashion similar to that used by the general admissions committee, except that special candidates did not have to meet the 2.5 grade point average cutoff applied to regular applicants. About one-fifth of the total number of special applicants were invited for interviews in 1973 and 1974. Following each interview, the special committee assigned each special applicant a benchmark score. The special committee then presented its top choices to the general admissions committee. The latter did not rate or compare the special candidates against the general applicants, id., at 388, but could reject recommended special candidates for failure to meet course requirements or other specific deficiencies. Id., at 171-172. The special committee continued to recommend special applicants until a number prescribed by faculty vote were admitted. While the overall class size was still 50, the prescribed number was 8; in 1973 and 1974, when the class size had doubled to 100, the prescribed number of special admissions also doubled, to 16. Id., at 164, 166.

From the year of the increase in class size—1971—through 1974, the special program resulted in the admission of 21 Black students, 30 Mexican-Americans, and 12 Asians, for a total of 63 minority students. Over the same period, the regular admissions program produced 1 Black, 6 Mexican-Americans, and 37 Asians, for a total of 44 minority students. Although disadvantaged whites applied to the special program in large numbers, see n. 5, supra, none received an offer of admission through that process. Indeed, in 1974, at least, the special committee explicitly considered only "disadvantaged" special applicants who were members of one of the designated minority groups. Record 171.

Allan Bakke is a white male who applied to the Davis Medical School in both 1973 and 1974. In both years Bakke's application was considered under the general admissions program, and he received an interview. His 1973 interview was with Dr. Theodore C. West, who considered Bakke "a very desirable applicant to [the] medical school." Id., at 225. Despite a strong benchmark score of 468 out of 500, Bakke was rejected. His application had come late in the year, and no applicants in the general admissions process with scores below 470 were accepted after Bakke's application was completed. Id., at 69. There were four special admissions slots unfilled at that time, however, for which Bakke was not considered. Id., at 70. After his 1973 rejection, Bakke wrote to Dr. George H. Lowrey, Associate Dean and Chairman of the Admissions Committee, protesting that the special admissions program operated as a racial and ethnic quota. Id., at 259.

Bakke's 1974 application was completed early in the year. Id., at 70. His student interviewer gave him an overall rating of 94, finding him "friendly, well tempered, conscientious and delightful to speak with." Id., at 229. His faculty interviewer was, by coincidence, the same Dr. Lowrey to whom he had written in protest of the special admissions program. Dr. Lowrey found Bakke "rather limited in his approach" to the problems of the medical profession and found disturbing Bakke's "very definite opinions which were based more on his personal viewpoints than upon a study of the total problem." Id., at 226. Dr. Lowrey gave Bakke the lowest of his six ratings, an 86; his total was 549 out of 600. Id., at 230. Again, Bakke's application was rejected. In neither year did the chairman of the admissions committee, Dr. Lowrey, exercise his discretion to place Bakke on the waiting list. Id., at 64. In both years, applicants were admitted under the special program with grade point averages, MCAT scores, and benchmark scores significantly lower than Bakke's.

After the second rejection, Bakke filed the instant suit in the Superior Court of California. He sought mandatory, injunctive, and declaratory relief compelling his admission to the Medical School. He alleged that the Medical School's special admissions program operated to exclude him from the school on the basis of his race, in violation of his rights under the Equal Protection Clause of the Fourteenth Amendment, Art. I, 21, of the California Constitution, and 601 of Title VI of the Civil Rights Act of 1964, 78 Stat. 252, 42 U.S.C. 2000d. The University cross-complained for a declaration that its special admissions program was lawful. The trial court found that the special program operated as a racial quota, because minority applicants in the special program were rated only against one another, Record 388, and 16 places in the class of 100 were reserved for them. Id., at 295-296. Declaring that the University could not take race into account in making admissions decisions, the trial court held the challenged program violative of the Federal Constitution, the State Constitution, and Title VI. The court refused to order Bakke's admission, however, holding that he had failed to carry his burden of proving that he would have been admitted but for the existence of the special program.

Bakke appealed from the portion of the trial court judgment denying him admission, and the University appealed from the decision that its special admissions program was unlawful and the order enjoining it from considering race in the processing of applications. The Supreme Court of California transferred the case directly from the trial court, "because of the importance of the issues involved." 18 Cal. 3d 34, 39, 553 P.2d 1152, 1156 (1976). The California court accepted the findings of the trial court with respect to the University's program. Because the special admissions program involved a racial classification, the Supreme Court held itself bound to apply strict scrutiny. Id., at 49, 553 P.2d, at 1162-1163. It then turned to the goals the University presented as justifying the special program. Although the court agreed that the goals of integrating the medical profession and increasing the number of physicians willing to serve members of minority groups were compelling state interests, id., at 53, 553 P.2d, at 1165, it concluded that the special admissions program was not the least intrusive means of achieving those goals. Without passing on the state constitutional or the federal statutory grounds cited in the trial court's judgment, the California court held that the Equal Protection Clause of the Fourteenth Amendment required that "no applicant may be rejected because of his race, in favor of another who is less qualified, as measured by standards applied without regard to race." Id., at 55, 553 P.2d, at 1166.

Turning to Bakke's appeal, the court ruled that since Bakke had established that the University had discriminated against him on the basis of his race, the burden of proof shifted to the University to demonstrate that he would not have been admitted even in the absence of the special admissions program. Id., at 63-64, 553 P.2d, at 1172. The court analogized Bakke's situation to that of a plaintiff under Title VII of the Civil Rights Act of 1964, 42 U.S.C. 2000e-17 (1970 ed., Supp. V), see, e. g., *Franks v. Bowman Transportation Co.*, 424 U.S. 747, 772 (1976). 18 Cal. 3d, at 63-64, 553 P.2d, at 1172. On this basis, the court initially ordered a remand for the purpose of determining whether, under the newly allocated burden of proof, Bakke would have been admitted to either the 1973 or the 1974 entering class in the absence of the special admissions program. App. A to Application for Stay 48. In its petition for rehearing below, however, the University conceded its inability to carry that burden. App. B to Application for Stay A19-A20. The California court thereupon amended its opinion to direct that the trial court enter judgment ordering Bakke's admission to the Medical School. 18 Cal. 3d, at 64, 553 P.2d, at 1172. That order was stayed pending review in this Court. 429 U.S. 953 (1976). We granted certiorari to consider the important constitutional issue. 429 U.S. 1090 (1977).

II

In this Court the parties neither briefed nor argued the applicability of Title VI of the Civil Rights Act of 1964. Rather, as had the California court, they focused exclusively upon the validity of the special admissions program under the Equal Protection Clause. Because it was possible, however, that a decision on Title VI might obviate resort to constitutional interpretation, see *Ashwander v. TVA*, 297 U.S. 288, 346-348 (1936) (concurring opinion), we requested supplementary briefing on the statutory issue. 434 U.S. 900 (1977).

A

At the outset we face the question whether a right of action for private parties exists under Title VI. Respondent argues that there is a private right of action, invoking the test set forth in *Cort v. Ash*, 422 U.S. 66, 78 (1975). He contends that the statute creates a federal right in his favor, that legislative history reveals an intent to permit private actions, that such actions would further the remedial purposes of the statute, and that enforcement of federal rights under the Civil Rights Act generally is not relegated to the States. In addition, he cites several lower court decisions which have recognized or assumed the existence of a private right of action. Petitioner denies the existence of a private right of action, arguing that the sole function of 601, see n. 11, supra, was to establish a predicate for administrative action under 602, 78 Stat. 252, 42 U.S.C. 2000d-1. In its view, administrative curtailment of federal funds under that section was the only sanction to be imposed upon recipients that violated 601. Petitioner also points out that Title VI contains no explicit grant of a private right of action, in contrast to Titles II, III, IV, and VII, of the same statute, 42 U.S.C. 2000a-3 (a), 2000b-2, 2000c-8, and 2000e-5 (f) (1970 ed. and Supp. V).

We find it unnecessary to resolve this question in the instant case. The question of respondent's right to bring an action under Title VI was neither argued nor decided in either of the courts below, and this Court has been hesitant to review questions not addressed below. *McGoldrick v. Compagnie Generale Transatlantique*, 309 U.S. 430, 434-435 (1940). See also *Massachusetts v. Westcott*, 431 U.S. 322 (1977); *Cardinale v. Louisiana*, 394 U.S. 437, 439 (1969). Cf. *Singleton v. Wulff*, 428 U.S. 106, 121 (1976). We therefore do not address this difficult issue. Similarly, we need not pass upon petitioner's claim that private plaintiffs under Title VI must exhaust administrative remedies. We assume, only for the purposes of this case, that respondent has a right of action under Title VI. See *Lau v. Nichols*, 414 U.S. 563, 571 n. 2 (1974) (STEWART, J., concurring in result).

B

The language of 601, 78 Stat. 252, like that of the Equal Protection Clause, is majestic in its sweep:

> "No person in the United States shall, on the ground of race, color, or national origin, be excluded from participation in, be denied the benefits of, or be subjected to discrimination under any program or activity receiving Federal financial assistance."

The concept of "discrimination," like the phrase "equal protection of the laws," is susceptible of varying interpretations, for as Mr. Justice Holmes declared, "[a] word is not a crystal, transparent and unchanged, it is the skin of a living thought and may vary greatly in color and content according to the circumstances and the time in which it is used." *Towne v. Eisner*, 245 U.S. 418, 425 (1918). We must, therefore, seek whatever aid is available in determining the precise meaning of the statute before us. *Train v. Colorado Public Interest Research Group*, 426 U.S. 1, 10 (1976), quoting *United States v. American Trucking Assns.*, 310 U.S. 534, 543-544 (1940). Examination of the voluminous legislative history of Title VI reveals a congressional intent to halt federal funding of entities that violate a prohibition of racial discrimination similar to that of the Constitution. Although isolated statements of various legislators, taken out of context, can be marshaled in support of the proposition that 601 enacted a purely color-blind scheme, without regard to the reach of the Equal Protection Clause, these comments must be read against the background of both the problem that Congress was addressing and the broader view of the statute that emerges from a full examination of the legislative debates.

The problem confronting Congress was discrimination against Negro citizens at the hands of recipients of federal moneys. Indeed, the color blindness pronouncements cited in the margin at n. 19, generally occur in the midst of extended remarks dealing with the evils of segregation in federally funded programs. Over and over again, proponents of the bill detailed the plight of Negroes seeking equal treatment in such programs. There simply was no reason for Congress to consider the validity of hypothetical preferences that might be accorded minority citizens; the legislators were dealing with the real and pressing problem of how to guarantee those citizens equal treatment.

In addressing that problem, supporters of Title VI repeatedly declared that the bill enacted constitutional principles. For example, Representative Celler, the Chairman of the House Judiciary Committee and floor manager of the legislation in the House, emphasized this in introducing the bill:

> "The bill would offer assurance that hospitals financed by Federal money would not deny adequate care to Negroes. It would prevent abuse of food distribution programs whereby Negroes have been known to be denied food surplus supplies when white persons were given such food. It would assure Negroes the benefits now accorded only white students in programs of high[er] education financed by Federal funds. It would, in short, assure the existing right to equal treatment in the enjoyment of Federal funds. It would not destroy any rights of private property or freedom of association." 110 Cong. Rec. 1519 (1964).

Other sponsors shared Representative Celler's view that Title VI embodied constitutional principles.

In the Senate, Senator Humphrey declared that the purpose of Title VI was "to insure that Federal funds are spent in accordance with the Constitution and the moral sense of the Nation." Id., at 6544. Senator Ribicoff agreed that Title VI embraced the constitutional standard: "Basically, there is a constitutional restriction against discrimination in the use of federal funds; and title VI simply spells out the procedure to be used in enforcing that restriction." Id., at 13333. Other Senators expressed similar views.

Further evidence of the incorporation of a constitutional standard into Title VI appears in the repeated refusals of the legislation's supporters precisely to define the term "discrimination." Opponents sharply criticized this failure, but proponents of the bill merely replied that the meaning of "discrimination" would be made clear by reference to the Constitution or other existing law. For example, Senator Humphrey noted the relevance of the Constitution:

> "As I have said, the bill has a simple purpose. That purpose is to give fellow citizens—Negroes—the same rights and opportunities that white people take for granted. This is no more than what was preached by the prophets, and by Christ Himself. It is no more than what our Constitution guarantees." Id., at 6553.

In view of the clear legislative intent, Title VI must be held to proscribe only those racial classifications that would violate the Equal Protection Clause or the Fifth Amendment.

III

A

Petitioner does not deny that decisions based on race or ethnic origin by faculties and administrations of state universities are reviewable under the Fourteenth Amendment. See, e. g., *Missouri ex rel. Gaines v. Canada*, 305 U.S. 337 (1938); *Sipuel v. Board of Regents*, 332 U.S. 631 (1948); *Sweatt v. Painter*, 339 U.S. 629 (1950); *McLaurin v. Oklahoma State Regents*, 339 U.S. 637 (1950). For his part, respondent does not argue that all racial or ethnic classifications are per se invalid. See, e. g., *Hirabayashi v. United States*, 320 U.S. 81 (1943); *Korematsu v. United States*, 323 U.S. 214 (1944); *Lee v. Washington*, 390 U.S. 333, 334 (1968) (Black, Harlan, and STEWART, JJ., concurring); *United Jewish Organizations v. Carey*, 430 U.S. 144 (1977). The parties do disagree as to the level of judicial scrutiny to be applied to the special admissions program. Petitioner argues that the court below erred in applying strict scrutiny, as this inexact term has been applied in our cases. That level of review, petitioner asserts, should be reserved for classifications that disadvantage "discrete and insular minorities." See *United States v. Carolene Products Co.*, 304 U.S. 144, 152 n. 4 (1938). Respondent, on the other hand, contends that the California court correctly rejected the notion that the degree of judicial scrutiny accorded a particular racial or ethnic classification hinges upon membership in a discrete and insular minority and duly recognized that the "rights established [by the Fourteenth Amendment] are personal rights." *Shelley v. Kraemer*, 334 U.S. 1, 22 (1948).

En route to this crucial battle over the scope of judicial review, the parties fight a sharp preliminary action over the proper characterization of the special admissions program. Petitioner prefers to view it as establishing a "goal" of minority representation in the

Medical School. Respondent, echoing the courts below, labels it a racial quota.

This semantic distinction is beside the point: The special admissions program is undeniably a classification based on race and ethnic background. To the extent that there existed a pool of at least minimally qualified minority applicants to fill the 16 special admissions seats, white applicants could compete only for 84 seats in the entering class, rather than the 100 open to minority applicants. Whether this limitation is described as a quota or a goal, it is a line drawn on the basis of race and ethnic status.

The guarantees of the Fourteenth Amendment extend to all persons. Its language is explicit: "No State shall ... deny to any person within its jurisdiction the equal protection of the laws." It is settled beyond question that the "rights created by the first section of the Fourteenth Amendment are, by its terms, guaranteed to the individual. The rights established are personal rights," *Shelley v. Kraemer*, supra, at 22. Accord, *Missouri ex rel. Gaines v. Canada*, supra, at 351; *McCabe v. Atchison, T. & S. F. R. Co.*, 235 U.S. 151, 161-162 (1914). The guarantee of equal protection cannot mean one thing when applied to one individual and something else when applied to a person of another color. If both are not accorded the same protection, then it is not equal.

Nevertheless, petitioner argues that the court below erred in applying strict scrutiny to the special admissions program because white males, such as respondent, are not a "discrete and insular minority" requiring extraordinary protection from the majoritarian political process. Carolene Products Co., supra, at 152-153, n. 4. This rationale, however, has never been invoked in our decisions as a prerequisite to subjecting racial or ethnic distinctions to strict scrutiny. Nor has this Court held that discreteness and insularity constitute necessary preconditions to a holding that a particular classification is invidious. See, e. g., *Skinner v. Oklahoma ex rel. Williamson*, 316 U.S. 535, 541 (1942); *Carrington v. Rash*, 380 U.S. 89, 94-97 (1965). These characteristics may be relevant in deciding whether or not to add new types of classifications to the list of "suspect" categories or whether a particular classification survives close examination. See, e. g., *Massachusetts Board of Retirement v. Murgia*, 427 U.S. 307, 313 (1976) (age); *San Antonio Independent School Dist. v. Rodriguez*, 411 U.S. 1, 28 (1973) (wealth); *Graham v. Richardson*, 403 U.S. 365, 372 (1971) (aliens). Racial and ethnic classifications, however, are subject to stringent examination without regard to these additional characteristics. We declared as much in the first cases explicitly to recognize racial distinctions as suspect:

> "Distinctions between citizens solely because of their ancestry are by their very nature odious to a free people whose institutions are founded upon the doctrine of equality." Hirabayashi, 320 U.S., at 100.

"[A]ll legal restrictions which curtail the civil rights of a single racial group are immediately suspect. That is not to say that all such restrictions are unconstitutional. It is to say that courts must subject them to the most rigid scrutiny." Korematsu, 323 U.S., at 216.

The Court has never questioned the validity of those pronouncements. Racial and ethnic distinctions of any sort are inherently suspect and thus call for the most exacting judicial examination.

B

This perception of racial and ethnic distinctions is rooted in our Nation's constitutional and demographic history. The Court's initial view of the Fourteenth Amendment was that its "one pervading purpose" was "the freedom of the slave race, the security and firm establishment of that freedom, and the protection of the newly-made freeman and citizen from the oppressions of those who had formerly exercised dominion over him." Slaughter-House Cases, 16 Wall. 36, 71 (1873). The Equal Protection Clause, however, was "[v]irtually strangled in infancy by post-civil-war judicial reactionism." It was relegated to decades of relative desuetude while the Due Process Clause of the Fourteenth Amendment, after a short germinal period, flourished as a cornerstone in the Court's defense of property and liberty of contract. See, e. g., *Mugler v. Kansas*, 123 U.S. 623, 661 (1887); *Allgeyer v. Louisiana*, 165 U.S. 578 (1897); *Lochner v. New York*, 198 U.S. 45 (1905). In that cause, the Fourteenth Amendment's "one pervading purpose" was displaced. See, e. g., *Plessy v. Ferguson*, 163 U.S. 537 (1896). It was only as the era of substantive due process came to a close, see, e. g., *Nebbia v. New York*, 291 U.S. 502 (1934); *West Coast Hotel Co. v. Parrish*, 300 U.S. 379 (1937), that the Equal Protection Clause began to attain a genuine measure of vitality, see, e. g., *United States v. Carolene Products*, 304 U.S. 144 (1938); *Skinner v. Oklahoma ex rel. Williamson*, supra.

By that time it was no longer possible to peg the guarantees of the Fourteenth Amendment to the struggle for equality of one racial minority. During the dormancy of the Equal Protection Clause, the United States had become a Nation of minorities. Each had to struggle—and to some extent struggles still—to overcome the prejudices not of a monolithic majority, but of a "majority" composed of various minority groups of whom it was said—perhaps unfairly in many cases—that a shared characteristic was a willingness to disadvantage other groups. As the Nation filled with the stock of many lands, the reach of the Clause was gradually extended to all ethnic groups seeking protection from official discrimination. See *Strauder v. West Virginia*, 100 U.S. 303, 308 (1880) (Celtic Irishmen) (dictum); *Yick Wo v. Hopkins*, 118 U.S. 356 (1886) (Chinese); *Truax v. Raich*, 239 U.S. 33, 41 (1915) (Austrian resident aliens); Korematsu, supra (Japanese); *Hernandez v. Texas*, 347 U.S. 475 (1954) (Mexican-Americans). The guarantees of equal protection, said the Court in Yick Wo, "are universal in their application, to all persons within the territorial jurisdiction, without regard to any differences of race, of color, or of nationality; and the equal protection of the laws is a pledge of the protection of equal laws." 118 U.S., at 369.

Although many of the Framers of the Fourteenth Amendment conceived of its primary function as bridging the vast distance between members of the Negro race and the white "majority," Slaughter-House Cases, supra, the Amendment itself was framed in universal terms, without reference to color, ethnic origin, or condition of prior servitude. As this Court recently remarked in interpreting the 1866 Civil Rights Act to extend to claims of racial discrimination against white persons, "the 39th Congress was intent upon establishing in the federal law a broader principle than would have been necessary simply to meet the particular and immediate plight of the newly freed Negro slaves." *McDonald v. Santa Fe Trail Transportation Co.*, 427 U.S. 273, 296 (1976). And that legislation was specifically broadened in 1870 to ensure that "all persons," not merely "citizens," would enjoy equal rights under the law. See *Runyon v. McCrary*, 427 U.S. 160, 192-202 (1976) (WHITE, J., dissenting). Indeed, it is not unlikely that among the Framers were many who would have applauded a reading of the Equal Protection Clause that states a principle of universal application and is responsive to the racial, ethnic, and cultural diversity of the Nation. See, e. g., Cong. Globe, 39th Cong., 1st Sess., 1056 (1866) (remarks of Rep. Niblack); id., at 2891-2892 (remarks of Sen. Conness); id., 40th Cong., 2d Sess., 883 (1868) (remarks of Sen. Howe) (Fourteenth Amendment "protect[s] classes from class legislation"). See also Bickel, The Original Understanding and the Segregation Decision, 69 Harv. L. Rev. 1, 60-63 (1955).

Over the past 30 years, this Court has embarked upon the crucial mission of interpreting the Equal Protection Clause with the view of assuring to all persons "the protection of equal laws," Yick Wo, supra, at 369, in a Nation confronting a legacy of slavery and racial discrimination. See, e. g., *Shelley v. Kraemer*, 334 U.S. 1 (1948); *Brown v. Board of Education*, 347 U.S. 483 (1954); *Hills v. Gautreaux*, 425 U.S. 284 (1976). Because the landmark decisions in this area arose in response to the continued exclusion of Negroes from the mainstream of American society, they could be characterized as involving discrimination by the "majority" white race against the Negro minority. But they need not be read as depending upon that characterization for their results. It suffices to say that "[o]ver the years, this Court has consistently repudiated '[d]istinctions between citizens solely because of their ancestry' as being 'odious to a free people whose institutions are founded upon the doctrine of equality.'" *Loving v. Virginia*, 388 U.S. 1, 11 (1967), quoting Hirabayashi, 320 U.S., at 100.

Petitioner urges us to adopt for the first time a more restrictive view of the Equal Protection Clause and hold that discrimination against members of the white "majority" cannot be suspect if its purpose can be characterized as "benign." The clock of our liberties, however, cannot be turned back to 1868. *Brown v. Board of Education*, supra, at 492; accord, *Loving v. Virginia*, supra, at 9. It is far too late to argue that the guarantee of equal protection to all persons permits the recognition of special wards entitled to a degree of protection greater than that accorded others. "The Fourteenth Amendment is not directed solely against discrimination due to a 'two-class theory'—that is, based upon differences between 'white' and Negro." Hernandez, 347 U.S., at 478.

Once the artificial line of a "two-class theory" of the Fourteenth Amendment is put aside, the difficulties entailed in varying the level of judicial review according to a perceived "preferred" status of a particular racial or ethnic minority are intractable. The concepts of "majority" and "minority" necessarily reflect temporary arrangements and political judgments. As observed above, the white "majority" itself is composed of various minority groups, most of which can lay claim to a history of prior discrimination at the hands of the State and private individuals. Not all of these groups can receive preferential treatment and corresponding judicial tolerance of distinctions drawn in terms of race and nationality, for then the only "majority" left would be a new minority of white Anglo-Saxon Protestants. There is no principled basis for deciding which groups would merit "heightened judicial solicitude" and which would not. Courts would be asked to evaluate the extent of the prejudice and consequent harm suffered by various minority groups. Those whose societal injury is thought to exceed some arbitrary level of tolerability then would be entitled to preferential classifications at the expense of individuals belonging to other groups. Those classifications would be free from exacting judicial scrutiny. As these preferences began to have their desired effect, and the consequences of past discrimination were undone, new judicial rankings would be necessary. The kind of variable sociological and political analysis necessary to produce such rankings simply does not lie within the judicial competence—even if they otherwise were politically feasible and socially desirable.

Moreover, there are serious problems of justice connected with the idea of preference itself. First, it may not always be clear that a so-called preference is in fact benign. Courts may be asked to validate burdens imposed upon individual members of a particular group in order to advance the group's general interest. See *United Jewish Organizations v. Carey*, 430 U.S., at 172-173 (BRENNAN, J., concurring in part). Nothing in the Constitution supports the notion that individuals may be asked to suffer otherwise impermissible burdens in order to enhance the societal standing of their ethnic groups. Second, preferential programs may only reinforce common stereotypes holding that certain groups are unable to achieve success without special protection based on a factor having no relationship to individual worth. See *DeFunis v. Odegaard*, 416 U.S. 312, 343 (1974) (Douglas, J., dissenting). Third, there is a measure of inequity in forcing innocent persons in respondent's position to bear the burdens of redressing grievances not of their making.

By hitching the meaning of the Equal Protection Clause to these transitory considerations, we would be holding, as a constitutional principle, that judicial scrutiny of classifications touching on racial and ethnic background may vary with the ebb and flow of political forces. Disparate constitutional tolerance of such classifications well may serve to exacerbate racial and ethnic antagonisms rather than alleviate them. United Jewish Organizations, supra, at 173-174 (BRENNAN, J., concurring in part). Also, the mutability of a constitutional principle, based upon shifting political and social judgments, undermines the chances for consistent application of the Constitution from one generation to the next, a critical feature of its coherent interpretation. *Pollock v. Farmers' Loan & Trust Co.*, 157 U.S. 429, 650-651 (1895) (White, J., dissenting). In expounding the Constitution, the Court's role is to discern "principles sufficiently absolute to give them roots throughout the community and continuity over significant periods of time, and to lift them above the level of the pragmatic political judgments of a particular time and place." A. Cox, The Role of the Supreme Court in American Government 114 (1976).

If it is the individual who is entitled to judicial protection against classifications based upon his racial or ethnic background because such distinctions impinge upon personal rights, rather than the individual only because of his membership in a particular group, then constitutional standards may be applied consistently. Political judgments regarding the necessity for the particular classification may be weighed in the constitutional balance, *Korematsu v. United States*, 323 U.S. 214 (1944), but the standard of justification will remain constant. This is as it should be, since those political judgments are the product of rough compromise struck by contending groups within the democratic process. When they touch upon an individual's race or ethnic background, he is entitled to a judicial determination that the burden he is asked to bear on that basis is precisely tailored to serve a compelling governmental interest. The Constitution guarantees that right to every person regardless of his background. *Shelley v. Kraemer*, 334 U.S., at 22; *Missouri ex rel. Gaines v. Canada*, 305 U.S., at 351.

C

Petitioner contends that on several occasions this Court has approved preferential classifications without applying the most exacting scrutiny. Most of the cases upon which petitioner relies are drawn from three areas: school desegregation, employment discrimination, and sex discrimination. Each of the cases cited presented a situation materially different from the facts of this case.

The school desegregation cases are inapposite. Each involved remedies for clearly determined constitutional violations. E. g., *Swann v. Charlotte-Mecklenburg Board of Education*, 402 U.S. 1 (1971); *McDaniel v. Barresi*, 402 U.S. 39 (1971); *Green v. County School Board*, 391 U.S. 430 (1968). Racial classifications thus were designed as remedies for the vindication of constitutional entitlement. Moreover, the scope of the remedies was not permitted to exceed the extent of the violations. E. g., *Dayton Board of Education v. Brinkman*, 433 U.S. 406 (1977); *Milliken v. Bradley*, 418 U.S. 717 (1974); see *Pasadena City Board of Education v. Spangler*, 427 U.S. 424 (1976). See also *Austin Independent School Dist. v. United States*, 429 U.S. 990, 991-995 (1976) (POWELL, J., concurring). Here, there was no judicial determination of constitutional violation as a predicate for the formulation of a remedial classification.

The employment discrimination cases also do not advance petitioner's cause. For example, in *Franks v. Bowman Transportation Co.*, 424 U.S. 747 (1976), we approved a retroactive award of seniority to a class of Negro truckdrivers who had been the victims of discrimination—not just by society at large, but by the respondent in that case. While this relief imposed some burdens on other employees, it was held necessary "to make [the victims] whole for injuries suffered on account of unlawful employment discrimination." Id., at 763, quoting *Albemarle Paper Co. v. Moody*, 422 U.S. 405, 418 (1975). The Courts of Appeals have fashioned various types of racial preferences as remedies for constitutional or statutory violations resulting in identified, race-based injuries to individuals held entitled to the preference. E. g., *Bridgeport Guardians, Inc. v. Bridgeport Civil Service Commission*, 482 F.2d 1333 (CA2 1973); *Carter v. Gallagher*, 452 F.2d 315 (CA8 1972), modified on rehearing en banc, id., at 327. Such preferences also have been upheld where a legislative or administrative body charged with the responsibility made determinations of past discrimination by the industries affected, and fashioned remedies deemed appropriate to rectify the discrimination. E. g., *Contractors Association of Eastern Pennsylvania v. Secretary of Labor*, 442 F.2d 159 (CA3), cert. denied, 404 U.S. 854 (1971); *Associated General Contractors of Massachusetts, Inc. v. Altshuler*, 490 F.2d 9 (CA1 1973), cert. denied, 416 U.S. 957 (1974); cf. *Katzenbach v. Morgan*, 384 U.S. 641 (1966). But we have never approved preferential classifications in the absence of proved constitutional or statutory violations.

Nor is petitioner's view as to the applicable standard supported by the fact that gender-based classifications are not subjected to this level of scrutiny. E. g., *Califano v. Webster*, 430 U.S. 313, 316-317 (1977); *Craig v. Boren*, 429 U.S. 190, 211 n. (1976) (POWELL, J., concurring). Gender-based distinctions are less likely to create the analytical and practical problems present in preferential programs premised on racial or ethnic criteria. With respect to gender there are only two possible classifications. The incidence of the burdens imposed by preferential classifications is clear. There are no rival groups which can claim that they, too, are entitled to preferential treatment. Classwide questions as to the group suffering previous injury and groups which fairly can be burdened are relatively manageable for reviewing courts. See, e. g., *Califano v. Goldfarb*, 430 U.S. 199, 212-217 (1977); *Weinberger v. Wiesenfeld*, 420 U.S. 636, 645 (1975). The resolution of these same questions in the context of racial and ethnic preferences presents far more complex and intractable problems than gender-based classifications. More importantly, the perception of racial classifications as inherently odious stems from a lengthy and tragic history that gender-based classifications do not share. In sum, the Court has never viewed such classification as inherently suspect or as comparable to racial or ethnic classifications for the purpose of equal protection analysis.

Petitioner also cites *Lau v. Nichols*, 414 U.S. 563 (1974), in support of the proposition that discrimination favoring racial or ethnic minorities has received judicial approval without the exacting inquiry ordinarily accorded "suspect" classifications. In Lau, we held that the failure of the San Francisco school system to provide remedial English instruction for some 1,800 students of oriental ancestry who spoke no English amounted to a violation of Title VI of the Civil Rights Act of 1964, 42 U.S.C. 2000d, and the regulations promulgated thereunder. Those regulations required remedial instruction where inability to understand English excluded children of foreign ancestry from participation in educational programs. 414 U.S., at 568 . Because we found that the students in Lau were denied "a meaningful opportunity to participate in the educational program," ibid., we remanded for the fashioning of a remedial order.

Lau provides little support for petitioner's argument. The decision rested solely on the statute, which had been construed by the responsible administrative agency to reach educational practices "which have the effect of subjecting individuals to discrimination," ibid. We stated: "Under these state-imposed standards there is no equality of treatment merely by providing students with the same facilities, textbooks, teachers, and curriculum; for students who do not understand English are effectively foreclosed from any meaningful education." Id., at 566. Moreover, the "preference" approved did not result in the denial of the relevant benefit—"meaningful opportunity to participate in the educational program"—to anyone else. No other student was deprived by that preference of the ability to participate in San Francisco's school system, and the applicable regulations required similar assistance for all students who suffered similar linguistic deficiencies. Id., at 570-571 (STEWART, J., concurring in result).

In a similar vein, petitioner contends that our recent decision in *United Jewish Organizations v. Carey*, 430 U.S. 144 (1977), indicates a willingness to approve racial classifications designed to benefit certain minorities, without denominating the classifications as "suspect." The State of New York had redrawn its reapportionment plan to meet objections of the Department of Justice under 5 of the Voting Rights Act of 1965, 42 U.S.C. 1973c (1970 ed., Supp. V). Specifically, voting districts were redrawn to enhance the electoral power of certain "nonwhite" voters found to have been the victims of unlawful "dilution" under the original reapportionment plan. United Jewish Organizations, like Lau, properly is viewed as a case in which the remedy for an administrative finding of discrimination encompassed measures to improve the previously disadvantaged group's ability to participate, without excluding individuals belonging to any other group from enjoyment of the relevant opportunity—meaningful participation in the electoral process.

In this case, unlike Lau and United Jewish Organizations, there has been no determination by the legislature or a responsible administrative agency that the University engaged in a discriminatory practice requiring remedial efforts. Moreover, the operation of petitioner's special admissions program is quite different from the remedial measures approved in those cases. It prefers the designated minority groups at the expense of other individuals who are totally foreclosed from competition for the 16 special admissions seats in every Medical School class. Because of that foreclosure, some individuals are excluded from enjoyment of a state-provided benefit—admission to the Medical School—they otherwise would receive. When a classification denies an individual opportunities or benefits enjoyed by others solely because of his race or ethnic background, it must be regarded as suspect. E. g., *McLaurin v. Oklahoma State Regents*, 339 U.S., at 641-642.

IV

We have held that in "order to justify the use of a suspect classification, a State must show that its purpose or interest is both constitutionally permissible and substantial, and that its use of the classification is 'necessary ... to the accomplishment' of its purpose or the safeguarding of its interest." In re Griffiths, 413 U.S. 717, 721-722 (1973) (footnotes omitted); *Loving v. Virginia*, 388 U.S., at 11; *McLaughlin v. Florida*, 379 U.S. 184, 196 (1964). The special admissions program purports to serve the purposes of: (i) "reducing the historic deficit of traditionally disfavored minorities in medical schools and in the medical profession," Brief for Petitioner 32; (ii) countering the effects of societal discrimination; (iii) increasing the number of physicians who will practice in communities currently underserved; and (iv) obtaining the educational benefits that flow from an ethnically diverse student body. It is necessary to decide which, if any, of these purposes is substantial enough to support the use of a suspect classification.

A

If petitioner's purpose is to assure within its student body some specified percentage of a particular group merely because of its race or ethnic origin, such a preferential purpose must be rejected not as insubstantial but as facially invalid. Preferring members of any one group for no reason other than race or ethnic origin is discrimination for its own sake. This the Constitution forbids. E. g., *Loving v. Virginia*, supra, at 11; *McLaughlin v. Florida*, supra, at 196; *Brown v. Board of Education*, 347 U.S. 483 (1954).

B

The State certainly has a legitimate and substantial interest in ameliorating, or eliminating where feasible, the disabling effects of identified discrimination. The line of school desegregation cases, commencing with

Brown, attests to the importance of this state goal and the commitment of the judiciary to affirm all lawful means toward its attainment. In the school cases, the States were required by court order to redress the wrongs worked by specific instances of racial discrimination. That goal was far more focused than the remedying of the effects of "societal discrimination," an amorphous concept of injury that may be ageless in its reach into the past.

We have never approved a classification that aids persons perceived as members of relatively victimized groups at the expense of other innocent individuals in the absence of judicial, legislative, or administrative findings of constitutional or statutory violations. See, e. g., *Teamsters v. United States*, 431 U.S. 324, 367-376 (1977); United Jewish Organizations, 430 U.S., at 155-156; *South Carolina v. Katzenbach*, 383 U.S. 301, 308 (1966). After such findings have been made, the governmental interest in preferring members of the injured groups at the expense of others is substantial, since the legal rights of the victims must be vindicated. In such a case, the extent of the injury and the consequent remedy will have been judicially, legislatively, or administrative defined. Also, the remedial action usually remains subject to continuing oversight to assure that it will work the least harm possible to other innocent persons competing for the benefit. Without such findings of constitutional or statutory violations, it cannot be said that the government has any greater interest in helping one individual than in refraining from harming another. Thus, the government has no compelling justification for inflicting such harm.

Petitioner does not purport to have made, and is in no position to make, such findings. Its broad mission is education, not the formulation of any legislative policy or the adjudication of particular claims of illegality. For reasons similar to those stated in Part III of this opinion, isolated segments of our vast governmental structures are not competent to make those decisions, at least in the absence of legislative mandates and legislatively determined criteria. Cf. *Hampton v. Mow Sun Wong*, 426 U.S. 88 (1976); n. 41, supra. Before relying upon these sorts of findings in establishing a racial classification, a governmental body must have the authority and capability to establish, in the record, that the classification is responsive to identified discrimination. See, e. g., *Califano v. Webster*, 430 U.S., at 316-321; *Califano v. Goldfarb*, 430 U.S., at 212-217. Lacking this capability, petitioner has not carried its burden of justification on this issue.

Hence, the purpose of helping certain groups whom the faculty of the Davis Medical School perceived as victims of "societal discrimination" does not justify a classification that imposes disadvantages upon persons like respondent, who bear no responsibility for whatever harm the beneficiaries of the special admissions program are thought to have suffered. To hold otherwise would be to convert a remedy heretofore reserved for violations of legal rights into a privilege that all institutions throughout the Nation could grant at their pleasure to whatever groups are perceived as victims of societal discrimination. That is a step we have never approved. Cf. *Pasadena City Board of Education v. Spangler*, 427 U.S. 424 (1976).

C

Petitioner identifies, as another purpose of its program, improving the delivery of health-care services to communities currently underserved. It may be assumed that in some situations a State's interest in facilitating the health care of its citizens is sufficiently compelling to support the use of a suspect classification. But there is virtually no evidence in the record indicating that petitioner's special admissions program is either needed or geared to promote that goal. The court below addressed this failure of proof:

> "The University concedes it cannot assure that minority doctors who entered under the program, all of whom expressed an 'interest' in practicing in a disadvantaged community, will actually do so. It may be correct to assume that some of them will carry out this intention, and that it is more likely they will practice in minority communities than the average white doctor. (See Sandalow, Racial Preferences in Higher Education: Political Responsibility and the Judicial Role (1975) 42 U. Chi. L. Rev. 653, 688.) Nevertheless, there are more precise and reliable ways to identify applicants who are genuinely interested in the medical problems of minorities than by race. An applicant of whatever race who has demonstrated his concern for disadvantaged minorities in the past and who declares that practice in such a community is his primary

professional goal would be more likely to contribute to alleviation of the medical shortage than one who is chosen entirely on the basis of race and disadvantage. In short, there is no empirical data to demonstrate that any one race is more selflessly socially oriented or by contrast that another is more selfishly acquisitive." 18 Cal. 3d, at 56, 553 P.2d, at 1167.

Petitioner simply has not carried its burden of demonstrating that it must prefer members of particular ethnic groups over all other individuals in order to promote better health-care delivery to deprived citizens. Indeed, petitioner has not shown that its preferential classification is likely to have any significant effect on the problem.

D

The fourth goal asserted by petitioner is the attainment of a diverse student body. This clearly is a constitutionally permissible goal for an institution of higher education. Academic freedom, though not a specifically enumerated constitutional right, long has been viewed as a special concern of the First Amendment. The freedom of a university to make its own judgments as to education includes the selection of its student body. Mr. Justice Frankfurter summarized the "four essential freedoms" that constitute academic freedom:

> "It is the business of a university to provide that atmosphere which is most conductive to speculation, experiment and creation. It is an atmosphere in which there prevail 'the four essential freedoms' of a university—to determine for itself on academic grounds who may teach, what may be taught, how it shall be taught, and who may be admitted to study." Sweezy v. New Hampshire, 354 U.S. 234, 263 (1957) (concurring in result).

Our national commitment to the safeguarding of these freedoms within university communities was emphasized in *Keyishian v. Board of Regents*, 385 U.S. 589, 603 (1967):

> "Our Nation is deeply committed to safeguarding academic freedom which is of transcendent value to all of us and not merely to the teachers concerned. That freedom is therefore a special concern of the First Amendment.... The Nation's future depends upon leaders trained through wide exposure to that robust exchange of ideas which discovers truth 'out of a multitude of tongues, [rather] than through any kind of authoritative selection.' United States v. Associated Press, 52 F. Supp. 362, 372."

The atmosphere of "speculation, experiment and creation"—so essential to the quality of higher education—is widely believed to be promoted by a diverse student body. As the Court noted in Keyishian, it is not too much to say that the "nation's future depends upon leaders trained through wide exposure" to the ideas and mores of students as diverse as this Nation of many peoples.

Thus, in arguing that its universities must be accorded the right to select those students who will contribute the most to the "robust exchange of ideas," petitioner invokes a countervailing constitutional interest, that of the First Amendment. In this light, petitioner must be viewed as seeking to achieve a goal that is of paramount importance in the fulfillment of its mission.

It may be argued that there is greater force to these views at the undergraduate level than in a medical school where the training is centered primarily on professional competency. But even at the graduate level, our tradition and experience lend support to the view that the contribution of diversity is substantial. In *Sweatt v. Painter*, 339 U.S., at 634, the Court made a similar point with specific reference to legal education:

> "The law school, the proving ground for legal learning and practice, cannot be effective in isolation from the individuals and institutions with which the law interacts. Few students and no one who has practiced law would choose to study in an academic vacuum, removed from the interplay of ideas and the exchange of views with which the law is concerned."

Physicians serve a heterogeneous population. An otherwise qualified medical student with a particular background—whether it be ethnic, geographic, culturally advantaged or disadvantaged—may bring to a professional school of medicine experiences, outlooks, and ideas that enrich the training of its student body and better equip its graduates to render with understanding their vital service to humanity.

Ethnic diversity, however, is only one element in a range of factors a university properly may consider in attaining the goal of a heterogeneous student body. Although a university must have wide discretion in making the sensitive judgments as to who should be admitted, constitutional limitations protecting individual rights may not be disregarded. Respondent urges—and the courts below have held—that petitioner's dual admissions program is a racial classification that impermissibly infringes his rights under the Fourteenth Amendment. As the interest of diversity is compelling in the context of a university's admissions program, the question remains whether the program's racial classification is necessary to promote this interest. In re Griffiths, 413 U.S., at 721-722.

V

A

It may be assumed that the reservation of a specified number of seats in each class for individuals from the preferred ethnic groups would contribute to the attainment of considerable ethnic diversity in the student body. But petitioner's argument that this is the only effective means of serving the interest of diversity is seriously flawed. In a most fundamental sense the argument misconceives the nature of the state interest that would justify consideration of race or ethnic background. It is not an interest in simple ethnic diversity, in which a specified percentage of the student body is in effect guaranteed to be members of selected ethnic groups, with the remaining percentage an undifferentiated aggregation of students. The diversity that furthers a compelling state interest encompasses a far broader array of qualifications and characteristics of which racial or ethnic origin is but a single though important element. Petitioner's special admissions program, focused solely on ethnic diversity, would hinder rather than further attainment of genuine diversity.

Nor would the state interest in genuine diversity be served by expanding petitioner's two-track system into a multitrack program with a prescribed number of seats set aside for each identifiable category of applicants. Indeed, it is inconceivable that a university would thus pursue the logic of petitioner's two-track program to the illogical end of insulating each category of applicants with certain desired qualifications from competition with all other applicants.

The experience of other university admissions programs, which take race into account in achieving the educational diversity valued by the First Amendment, demonstrates that the assignment of a fixed number of places to a minority group is not a necessary means toward that end. An illuminating example is found in the Harvard College program:

> "In recent years Harvard College has expanded the concept of diversity to include students from disadvantaged economic, racial and ethnic groups. Harvard College now recruits not only Californians or Louisianans but also Blacks and Chicanos and other minority students...."

"In practice, this new definition of diversity has meant that race has been a factor in some admission decisions. When the Committee on Admissions reviews the large middle group of applicants who are 'admissible' and deemed capable of doing good work in their courses, the race of an applicant may tip the balance in his favor just as geographic origin or a life spent on a farm may tip the balance in other candidates' cases. A farm boy from Idaho can bring something to Harvard College that a Bostonian cannot offer. Similarly, a Black student can usually bring something that a white person cannot offer.... [See Appendix hereto.]

"In Harvard College admissions the Committee has not set target-quotas for the number of Blacks, or of musicians, football players, physicists or Californians to be admitted in a given year.... But that awareness [of the necessity of including more than a token number of Black students] does not mean that the Committee sets a minimum number of Blacks or of people from west of the Mississippi who are to be admitted. It means only that in choosing among thousands of applicants who are not only 'admissible' academically but have other strong qualities, the Committee, with a number of criteria in mind, pays some attention to distribution among many types and categories of students." App. to Brief for Columbia University, Harvard University, Stanford University, and the University of Pennsylvania, as Amici Curiae 2-3.

In such an admissions program, race or ethnic background may be deemed a "plus" in a particular applicant's file, yet it does not insulate the individual from comparison with all other candidates for the available seats. The file of a particular Black applicant may be examined for his potential contribution to diversity without the factor of race being decisive when compared, for example, with that of an applicant identified as an Italian-American if the latter is thought to exhibit qualities more likely to promote beneficial educational pluralism. Such qualities could include exceptional personal talents, unique work or service experience, leadership potential, maturity, demonstrated compassion, a history of overcoming disadvantage, ability to communicate with the poor, or other qualifications deemed important. In short, an admissions program operated in this way is flexible enough to consider all pertinent elements of diversity in light of the particular qualifications of each applicant, and to place them on the same footing for consideration, although not necessarily according them the same weight. Indeed, the weight attributed to a particular quality may vary from year to year depending upon the "mix" both of the student body and the applicants for the incoming class.

This kind of program treats each applicant as an individual in the admissions process. The applicant who loses out on the last available seat to another candidate receiving a "plus" on the basis of ethnic background will not have been foreclosed from all consideration for that seat simply because he was not the right color or had the wrong surname. It would mean only that his combined qualifications, which may have included similar nonobjective factors, did not outweigh those of the other applicant. His qualifications would have been weighed fairly and competitively, and he would have no basis to complain of unequal treatment under the Fourteenth Amendment.

It has been suggested that an admissions program which considers race only as one factor is simply a subtle and more sophisticated—but no less effective—means of according racial preference than the Davis program. A facial intent to discriminate, however, is evident in petitioner's preference program and not denied in this case. No such facial infirmity exists in an admissions program where race or ethnic background is simply one element—to be weighed fairly against other elements—in the selection process. "A boundary line," as Mr. Justice Frankfurter remarked in another connection, "is none the worse for being narrow." *McLeod v. Dilworth*, 322 U.S. 327, 329 (1944). And a court would not assume that a university, professing to employ a facially nondiscriminatory admissions policy, would operate it as a cover for the functional equivalent of a quota system. In short, good faith would be presumed in the absence of a showing to the contrary in the manner permitted by our cases. See, e. g., *Arlington Heights v. Metropolitan Housing Dev. Corp.*, 429 U.S. 252 (1977); *Washington v. Davis*, 426 U.S. 229 (1976); *Swain v. Alabama*, 380 U.S. 202 (1965).

B

In summary, it is evident that the Davis special admissions program involves the use of an explicit racial classification never before countenanced by this Court. It tells applicants who are not Negro, Asian, or Chicano that they are totally excluded from a specific percentage of the seats in an entering class. No matter how strong their qualifications, quantitative and extracurricular, including their own potential for contribution to educational diversity, they are never afforded the chance to compete with applicants from the preferred groups for the special admissions seats. At the same time, the preferred applicants have the opportunity to compete for every seat in the class.

The fatal flaw in petitioner's preferential program is its disregard of individual rights as guaranteed by the Fourteenth Amendment. *Shelley v. Kraemer*, 334 U.S., at 22. Such rights are not absolute. But when a State's distribution of benefits or imposition of burdens hinges on ancestry or the color of a person's skin, that individual is entitled to a demonstration that the challenged classification is necessary to promote a substantial state interest. Petitioner has failed to carry this burden. For this reason, that portion of the California court's judgment holding petitioner's special admissions program invalid under the Fourteenth Amendment must be affirmed.

C

In enjoining petitioner from ever considering the race of any applicant, however, the courts below failed to recognize that the State has a substantial interest that legitimately may be served by a properly devised admissions program involving the competitive consideration of race and ethnic origin. For this reason, so much of the California court's judgment as enjoins petitioner from any consideration of the race of any applicant must be reversed.

VI

With respect to respondent's entitlement to an injunction directing his admission to the Medical School, petitioner has conceded that it could not carry its burden of proving that, but for the existence of its unlawful special admissions program, respondent still would not have been admitted. Hence, respondent is entitled to the injunction, and that portion of the judgment must be affirmed.

MR. JUSTICE BRENNAN, MR. JUSTICE WHITE, MR. JUSTICE MARSHALL, and MR. JUSTICE BLACKMUN join Parts I and V-C of this opinion. MR. JUSTICE WHITE also joins Part III-A of this opinion.

Glossary

due process: a portion of the Fifth and, later, the Fourteenth Amendment preventing the federal and state governments from depriving any person of life, liberty, or property "without due process of law"

equal protection: clause from the Fourteenth Amendment ensuring that no individual or class of individuals can be denied rights enjoyed by others who exist in similar circumstances

jurisdiction: power to hear and decide cases

FRONTIERO V. RICHARDSON

DATE
1973

AUTHOR
William J. Brennan Jr., Lewis F. Powell (concurrence)

VOTE
8–1

CITATION
411 U.S. 677

SIGNIFICANCE
Held that the military's differing criteria for military spousal dependency based on whether the servicemember was male or female violated the Fifth Amendment's due process clause

Overview

The case of *Frontiero v. Richardson*, argued in January of 1973, brought to light a growing problem related to the increasing numbers of female military personnel serving in the armed forces. Lieutenant Sharron Frontiero had sought to have a dependent's allowance for her husband, something that was automatically allowed for the wife of an active-duty servicemember. For a husband to earn to the dependent's allowance, the active-duty member had to demonstrate that more than one-half of the spouse's support came from the pay and allowances of the member of the armed forces. The government argued to the Court that the policy was designed in such a way as to "save money" as it was far more common for women to receive more than one-half of their support from their husband rather than the other way around, and the rule allowed the government to save time by not having to process every dependent claim to prove the one-half dependency rule. The Court disagreed with this position, responding that the statute itself discriminated against women, which violated the due process clause, and thus required the burden to be the same regardless of gender.

Context

Like all court cases, *Frontiero v. Richardson* did not occur in a political or historical vacuum. In 1971, the case of *Reed v. Reed* had unanimously struck down an Idaho law that mandated "males must be preferred to females" in relation to the heads of estates during probate hearings, setting a sound precedent for the concept of gender equality via the Fourteenth Amendment's equal protection clause. A year later, Congress passed Title IX of the Education Amendments of 1972, which read that "no person in the United States shall, on the basis of sex, be excluded from participation in, be denied the benefits of, or be subjected to discrimination under any education program or activity receiving Federal financial assistance." Also that year, Congress passed the Equal Rights Amendment that aimed to end gender discrimination in all facets of the American workforce. Although the Equal Rights Amendment would never be ratified by the states, its passage helped structure and influence the Court's ruling in *Frontiero v. Richardson*.

While the political context of the case was of significant importance, the historical context cannot be overlooked in relation to this case either. The case represented a growing trend in America of women enter-

Justice William Rehnquist dissented.
(Library of Congress)

ing the military service, something that was allowed only twenty-five years before *Frontiero v. Richardson* with the ratification of the Women's Armed Services Integration Act. This allowed women to serve in many roles in all four branches of service. Even with the passage of this act, however, women found themselves still at a significant disadvantage over their male counterparts serving in the military. Women were excluded from serving in combat roles and from attendance at the military academies, both often seen as prerequisites for promotion to higher levels of command in the military's branches. Generally perceived as possessing moral constitutions that were too weak for the rigors of combat, women were often relegated to administrative or medical roles in military units. Even after *Frontiero*, it would still take years—even decades—for women to achieve greater equality in the military as the armed forces are often one of the slowest parts of the federal government to bring about social change.

This was part of what made *Frontiero v. Richardson* such a unique and precedent-setting case for the Court. The military was often seen as above the traditional judicial and legislative requirements set forth for American society, and therefore bringing about a dramatic change did not occur with ease or frequency. Much of this is a direct result of the Feres doctrine, which barred active-duty members from seeking recourse in federal courts against the military for incidents that occurred during the span of their duties. The military had therefore been allowed to circumnavigate much of the legal doctrine created by the judicial system until a legislative doctrine or executive order directed them otherwise. Throughout American history, the American military establishment had been viewed as largely "above" or "removed" from the traditional views of American society, but the impacts of the war in Vietnam, the draft, and the anti-war movement saw a greater shift to bring the American military systems more in line with America's social and political values. During the 1970s and 1980s, much of that energy would focus on making the military more equitable for women, allowing them access to jobs, benefits, and promotion equal to their male counterparts. *Frontiero* was critical in initiating much of the rapid change that would be seen in the armed forces over the next two decades as it set forth an expectation of equal protection and treatment under the law.

About the Author

Justice William Brennan Jr. was the seventh-longest-serving jurist on the Supreme Court, often representing the liberal voice of the Court between 1956 and 1990. Brennan's path to Supreme Court justice was not a traditional one outside of his attending Harvard Law School, having been the son of Irish immigrants in New Jersey and attending public schools in Newark before finally pursuing an undergraduate degree in economics from the University of Pennsylvania. It was perhaps this unique background that would influence his work serving the Court through three chief justices' tenures.

While serving on the Warren Court, Brennan was often working behind the scenes in an effort to coax his conservative colleagues to vote with the liberal majority, particularly when it came to individual rights. He authored numerous opinions for the Court during this period including some precedent-setting cases such as *Baker v. Carr*, *Roth v. United States*, and *New York Times*

Co. v. Sullivan. His prose and understanding of the power of language in establishing legal doctrine led Chief Justice Earl Warren to appoint him as the writer of the majority opinions and earned him the nickname the "Deputy Chief" among his colleagues.

When Justice Earl Warren left his position in 1969, the Court returned to a more moderate view under Chief Justice Warren Burger. Brennan would continue to fight for the end of the death penalty (*Furman v. Georgia*) as well as access and rights to abortions for women (*Roe v. Wade*), but he found himself facing more battles to convince his conservative colleagues to join him, particularly with the addition of William Rehnquist who would join the Court in 1972 and be the only justice to vote against the majority in the *Frontiero* case.

This dynamic would become the norm once Rehnquist would become chief justice in 1986 and the number of conservative judges would increase, with Justices Antonin Scalia and Anthony Kennedy replacing Burger and Lewis Powell, leaving only Brennan and Thurgood Marshall as the remaining liberal justices of the Warren Court. Despite no longer finding himself among the majority, Brennan's dissents would help to influence and shape the arguments before the Court in the decades following his retirement.

Explanation and Analysis of the Document

In the case, William Brennan outlines the basic question before the Court: does the military's requirement that a male dependent of a female active-duty servicemember prove that they are more than 50 percent supported by their spouse violate the Fifth Amendment due process clause? In essence: can the U.S. military set a requirement for male dependents to receive an allowance that it does not set for female dependents, who receive the allowance automatically?

Brennan begins by looking at the history of the case and reflects a bit on American sociological ideology. He addresses the nature of the law itself, pointing out that if the situation had been reversed (that is, if Frontiero had been a male), the servicemember would have been approved automatically for additional allowances for residence and medical benefits. This raised two charges against the due process clause: first, a female military member must do more to substantiate the spousal dependency than her male counterpart, and second, a female spouse who may not be dependent on her spouse's income is granted an automatic right to benefits whereas the male spouse is not. Brennan contends that the lower courts upheld this ruling in part because of Congress's assumption that the husband is the breadwinner in the family and the wife is the dependent. Brennan subtly attacks this reasoning by bringing out the lower court's ruling that "such differential treatment might conceivably lead to a considerable savings of administrative expense and manpower" given that roughly 99 percent of the armed forces at the time were male.

Brennan's counter to this centers on the concept of judicial scrutiny: that as with race or national origin, any law made to restrict a person's opportunity or financial gain for one of these reasons must be examined by the Court to verify that its merits are in congruence with the Constitution. Brennan references the case *Reed v. Reed* as a precedent established by the Court saying that sexual discrimination subjected any law to scrutiny under the equal protection clause. Brennan points out that despite the seemingly rational arguments of the Idaho Supreme Court in *Reed* regarding the ability of men to serve as the probate, the Court still determined that such a law failed to take into consideration the personal qualifications of an individual, thus making the law unconstitutional in the same manner that the Warren Court had targeted racial discrimination in the previous two decades.

Brennan also counters the government's argument that the measure is cost effective by pointing out that many wives of male active-duty personnel would fail to qualify for the benefits, thus calling into question the claim that the program actually saves money for the government. Further, citing previous Court rulings such as *Shapiro v. Thompson* (1969) and *Stanley v. Illinois* (1972), Brennan contends that convenience and economic savings cannot be the "shibboleth" of determining a law's constitutionality. He concludes by referencing *Reed v. Reed*, stating that such laws are exactly the type of legislative choice that invokes arbitrary conclusions of people and therefore violates the nature of the Constitution.

In a concurring opinion, Justice Lewis Powell states that the uncertainty of the Equal Rights Amendment leaves the idea of automatic scrutiny for questions of sexual discrimination up for debate. Powell contends that by making a decision to automatically review cases of gender discrimination like those of race, national origin, and alienage, the Court is dictating law before it has been written. In this instance, however, Powell agrees that the federal government has failed to meet its responsibility of providing equitable experiences and opportunity for women in the military and that has in fact violated the essence of the due process clause.

The lone dissent, Justice William Rehnquist, agreed with the lower court's conclusion that such a law was a cost-saving measure intended to expedite a process that would be correct for a majority of those in the situation. Rehnquist, a conservative judge who often believed in a strict interpretation of the Constitution, also agreed with the lower court's conclusion that an act of Congress implies a "strong presumption of constitutionality."

Impact

The case of *Frontiero v. Richardson* assured that regardless of gender, the benefits for employees must be equitable in their distribution. As a result of this decision, the military would be forced to reevaluate the applications of any spouse seeking to receive benefits. More significantly, the ruling furthered the efforts of women in the military to advance their opportunities and have equal standing with their male counterparts. Two years after this case, President Gerald Ford would allow women into the U.S. military academies when he signed Public Law 94-106. The case also helped bring attention to a rising lawyer who represented the ACLU's *amicus curiae* brief, Ruth Bader Ginsburg, who would later go on to serve as a justice on the Supreme Court, where she would write the opinion for the case of *United States v. Virginia* (1996), which overturned a century-old law prohibiting women from attending the Virginia Military Institute.

Questions for Further Study

1. How did the rising feminist movement of the 1970s and America's growing distrust of the military system influence the Supreme Court's decision to hear the case and make the decision it did?

2. How did the decision of *Frontiero v. Richardson* help change the civilian labor world in terms of women's competitiveness for jobs? How might it have stayed the same as well?

3. Considering the outcome of this case, why might the Equal Rights Amendment have failed to pass? How might such an amendment have affected American views regarding gender and employment?

Further Reading

Books

Mayeri, Serena. "'When the Trouble Started': The Story of Frontiero v. Richardson." In *Women and the Law: Stories*, edited by Elizabeth M. Schneider and Stephanie M. Wildman. New York: Foundation Press/Thomson Reuters, 2011.

Websites

NCC Staff. "Frontiero v. Richardson: A Landmark Case for Gender Equality." National Constitution Center. Accessed March 2, 2023. https://constitutioncenter.org/blog/frontiero-v.-richardson-a-landmark-case-for-gender-equality.

"Supreme Court Decisions & Women's Rights: A Double Standard for Benefits—Frontiero v. Richardson, 411 U.S. 677 (1973)." Supreme Court Historical Society, April 27, 2022. https://supremecourthistory.org/classroom-resources-teachers-students/decisions-womens-rights-frontiero-v-richardson/.

—Commentary by Ryan Fontanella

FRONTIERO V. RICHARDSON

Document Text

MR. JUSTICE BRENNAN announced the judgment of the Court and an opinion in which MR. JUSTICE DOUGLAS, MR. JUSTICE WHITE, and MR. JUSTICE MARSHALL join

The question before us concerns the right of a female member of the uniformed services to claim her spouse as a "dependent" for the purposes of obtaining increased quarters allowances and medical and dental benefits under 37 U.S.C. §§ 401, 403, and 10 U.S.C. §§ 1072, 1076, on an equal footing with male members. Under these statutes, a serviceman may claim his wife as a "dependent" without regard to whether she is in fact, dependent upon him for any part of her support. 37 U.S.C.§ 401(1); 10 U.S.C.§ 1072(2)(A). A servicewoman, on the other hand, may not claim her husband as a "dependent" under these programs unless he is in fact, dependent upon her for over one-half of his support. 37 U.S.C. § 401; 10 U.S.C. § 1072(2)(C). Thus, the question for decision is whether this difference in treatment constitutes an unconstitutional discrimination against servicewomen in violation of the Due Process Clause of the Fifth Amendment. A three-judge District Court for the Middle District of Alabama, one judge dissenting, rejected this contention and sustained the constitutionality of the provisions of the statutes making this distinction. 341 F. Supp. 201 (1972). We noted probable jurisdiction. 409 U.S. 840 (1972). We reverse.

I

In an effort to attract career personnel through reenlistment, Congress established, in 37 U.S.C. § 401 *et seq.*, and 10 U.S.C. § 1071 *et seq.*, a scheme for the provision of fringe benefits to members of the uniformed services on a competitive basis with business and industry. Thus, under 37 U.S.C. § 403, a member of the uniformed services with dependents is entitled to an increased "basic allowance for quarters" and, under 10 U.S.C. § 1076, a member's dependents are provided comprehensive medical and dental care.

Appellant Sharron Frontiero, a lieutenant in the United States Air Force, sought increased quarters allowances, and housing and medical benefits for her husband, appellant Joseph Frontiero, on the ground that he was her "dependent." Although such benefits would automatically have been granted with respect to the wife of a male member of the uniformed services, appellant's application was denied because she failed to demonstrate that her husband was dependent on her for more than one-half of his support. Appellants then commenced this suit, contending that, by making this distinction, the statutes unreasonably discriminate on the basis of sex in violation of the Due Process Clause of the Fifth Amendment. In essence, appellants asserted that the discriminatory impact of the statutes is twofold: first, as a procedural matter, a female member is required to demonstrate her spouse's dependency, while no such burden is imposed upon male members; and, second, as a substantive matter, a male member who does not provide more than one-half of his wife's support receives benefits, while a similarly situated female member is denied such benefits. Appellants therefore sought a permanent injunction against the continued enforcement of these statutes and an order directing the appellees to provide Lieutenant Frontiero with the same housing and medical benefits that a similarly situated male member would receive.

Although the legislative history of these statutes sheds virtually no light on the purposes underlying the differential treatment accorded male and female members, a majority of the three-judge District Court surmised that Congress might reasonably have concluded that, since the husband in our society is generally the "breadwinner" in the family—and the wife typically the "dependent" partner --

"it would be more economical to require married female members claiming husbands to prove actual dependency than to extend the presumption of dependency to such members."

341 F. Supp. at 207. Indeed, given the fact that approximately 99% of all members of the uniformed services are male, the District Court speculated that such differential treatment might conceivably lead to a "considerable saving of administrative expense and manpower." *Ibid.*

II

At the outset, appellants contend that classifications based upon sex, like classifications based upon race, alienage, and national origin, are inherently suspect, and must therefore be subjected to close judicial scrutiny. We agree, and, indeed, find at least implicit support for such an approach in our unanimous decision only last Term in *Reed v. Reed,* 404 U. S. 71 (1971).

In *Reed,* the Court considered the constitutionality of an Idaho statute providing that, when two individuals are otherwise equally entitled to appointment as administrator of an estate, the male applicant must be preferred to the female. Appellant, the mother of the deceased, and appellee, the father, filed competing petitions for appointment as administrator of their son's estate. Since the parties, as parents of the deceased, were members of the same entitlement class, the statutory preference was invoked, and the father's petition was therefore granted. Appellant claimed that this statute, by giving a mandatory preference to males over females without regard to their individual qualifications, violated the Equal Protection Clause of the Fourteenth Amendment.

The Court noted that the Idaho statute "provides that different treatment be accorded to the applicants on the basis of their sex; it thus establishes a classification subject to scrutiny under the Equal Protection Clause." 404 U.S. at 404 U. S. 75. Under "traditional" equal protection analysis, a legislative classification must be sustained unless it is "patently arbitrary" and bears no rational relationship to a legitimate governmental interest. *See Jefferson v. Hackney,* 406 U. S. 535, 406 U. S. 546 (1972); *Richardson v. Belcher,* 404 U. S. 78, 404 U. S. 81 (1971); *Flemming v. Nestor,* 363 U. S. 603, 363 U. S. 611 (1960); *McGowan v. Maryland,* 366 U. S. 420, 366 U. S. 426 (1961); *Dandridge v. Williams,* 397 U. S. 471, 397 U. S. 485 (1970).

In an effort to meet this standard, appellee contended that the statutory scheme was a reasonable measure designed to reduce the workload on probate courts by eliminating one class of contests. Moreover, appellee argued that the mandatory preference for male applicants was, in itself, reasonable, since "men [are], as a rule, more conversant with business affairs than . . . women." Indeed, appellee maintained that "it is a matter of common knowledge that women still are not engaged in politics, the professions, business or industry to the extent that men are."

And the Idaho Supreme Court, in upholding the constitutionality of this statute, suggested that the Idaho Legislature might reasonably have "concluded that, in general, men are better qualified to act as an administrator than are women."

Despite these contentions, however, the Court held the statutory preference for male applicants unconstitutional. In reaching this result, the Court implicitly rejected appellee's apparently rational explanation of the statutory scheme, and concluded that, by ignoring the individual qualifications of particular applicants, the challenged statute provided "dissimilar treatment for men and women who are . . . similarly situated." 404 U.S. at 404 U. S. 77. The Court therefore held that, even though the State's interest in achieving administrative efficiency "is not without some legitimacy,"

"[t]o give a mandatory preference to members of either sex over members of the other merely to accomplish the elimination of hearings on the merits is to make the very kind of arbitrary legislative choice forbidden by the [Constitution]. . . ."

Id. at 404 U. S. 76. This departure from "traditional" rational basis analysis with respect to sex-based classifications is clearly justified.

There can be no doubt that our Nation has had a long and unfortunate history of sex discrimination. Traditionally, such discrimination was rationalized by an attitude of "romantic paternalism" which, in practical effect, put women not on a pedestal, but in a cage. Indeed, this paternalistic attitude became so firmly rooted in our national consciousness that, 100 years ago, a distinguished Member of this Court was able to proclaim:

"Man is, or should be, woman's protector and defender. The natural and proper timidity and delicacy which belongs to the female sex evidently unfits it for many of the occupations of civil life. The constitution of the family organization, which is founded in the divine ordinance as well as in the nature of things, indicates the domestic sphere as that which properly belongs to the domain and functions of womanhood. The harmony, not to say identity, of interests and views which belong, or should belong, to the family institution is repugnant to the idea of a woman adopting a distinct and independent career from that of her husband...."

"... The paramount destiny and mission of woman are to fulfil the noble and benign offices of wife and mother. This is the law of the Creator."

Bradwell v. State, 16 Wall. 130, 83 U. S. 141 (1873) (Bradley, J., concurring).

As a result of notions such as these, our statute books gradually became laden with gross, stereotyped distinctions between the sexes, and, indeed, throughout much of the 19th century, the position of women in our society was, in many respects, comparable to that of blacks under the pre-Civil War slave codes. Neither slaves nor women could hold office, serve on juries, or bring suit in their own names, and married women traditionally were denied the legal capacity to hold or convey property or to serve as legal guardians of their own children. *See generally* L. Kanowitz, Women and the Law: The Unfinished Revolution 5-6 (1969); G. Myrdal, An American Dilemma 1073 (20th anniversary ed.1962). And although blacks were guaranteed the right to vote in 1870, women were denied even that right—which is itself "preservative of other basic civil and political rights"—until adoption of the Nineteenth Amendment half a century later.

It is true, of course, that the position of women in America has improved markedly in recent decades. Nevertheless, it can hardly be doubted that, in part because of the high visibility of the sex characteristic, women still face pervasive, although at times more subtle, discrimination in our educational institutions, in the job market and, perhaps most conspicuously, in the political arena. *See generally* K. Amundsen, The Silenced Majority: Women and American Democracy (1971); The President's Task Force on Women's Rights and Responsibilities, A Matter of Simple Justice (1970).

Moreover, since sex, like race and national origin, is an immutable characteristic determined solely by the accident of birth, the imposition of special disabilities upon the members of a particular sex because of their sex would seem to violate "the basic concept of our system that legal burdens should bear some relationship to individual responsibility...." *Weber v. Aetna Casualty & Surety Co.*, 406 U. S. 164, 406 U. S. 175 (1972). And what differentiates sex from such nonsuspect statuses as intelligence or physical disability, and aligns it with the recognized suspect criteria, is that the sex characteristic frequently bears no relation to ability to perform or contribute to society. As a result, statutory distinctions between the sexes often have the effect of invidiously relegating the entire class of females to inferior legal status without regard to the actual capabilities of its individual members.

We might also note that, over the past decade, Congress has itself manifested an increasing sensitivity to sex-based classifications. In Tit. VII of the Civil Rights Act of 1964, for example, Congress expressly declared that no employer, labor union, or other organization subject to the provisions of the Act shall discriminate against any individual on the basis of "race, color, religion, *sex*, or national origin." Similarly, the Equal Pay Act of 1963 provides that no employer covered by the Act "shall discriminate . . . between employees on the basis of *sex*." And § 1 of the Equal Rights Amendment, passed by Congress on March 22, 1972, and submitted to the legislatures of the States for ratification, declares that "[e]quality of rights under the law shall not be denied or abridged by the United States or by any State on account of sex." Thus, Congress itself has concluded that classifications based upon sex are inherently invidious, and this conclusion of a coequal branch of Government is not without significance to the question presently under consideration. *Cf. Oregon v. Mitchell,* 400 U. S. 112, 400 U. S. 240, 400 U. S. 248-249 (1970) (opinion of BRENNAN, WHITE, and MARSHALL, JJ.); *Katzenbach v. Moran,* 384 U. S. 641, 384 U. S. 648-649 (1966).

With these considerations in mind, we can only conclude that classifications based upon sex, like classifications based upon race, alienage, or national origin, are inherently suspect, and must therefore be subjected to strict judicial scrutiny. Applying the analysis mandated by that stricter standard of review, it is clear that the statutory scheme now before us is constitutionally invalid.

III

The sole basis of the classification established in the challenged statutes is the sex of the individuals involved. Thus, under 37 U.S.C. §§ 401, 403, and 10 U.S.C. §§ 1072, 1076, a female member of the uniformed services seeking to obtain housing and medical benefits for her spouse must prove his dependency in fact, whereas no such burden is imposed upon male members. In addition, the statutes operate so as to deny benefits to a female member, such as appellant Sharron Frontiero, who provides less than one-half of her spouse's support, while at the same time granting such benefits to a male member who likewise provides less than one-half of his spouse's support. Thus, to this extent, at least, it may fairly be said that these statutes command "dissimilar treatment for men and women who are . . . similarly situated." *Reed v. Reed,* 404 U.S. at 404 U. S. 77.

Moreover, the Government concedes that the differential treatment accorded men and women under these statutes serves no purpose other than mere "administrative convenience." In essence, the Government maintains that, as an empirical matter, wives in our society frequently are dependent upon their husbands, while husbands rarely are dependent upon their wives. Thus, the Government argues that Congress might reasonably have concluded that it would be both cheaper and easier simply conclusively to presume that wives of male members are financially dependent upon their husbands, while burdening female members with the task of establishing dependency in fact.

The Government offers no concrete evidence, however, tending to support its view that such differential treatment in fact saves the Government any money. In order to satisfy the demands of strict judicial scrutiny, the Government must demonstrate, for example, that it is actually cheaper to grant increased benefits with respect to all male members than it is to determine which male members are, in fact, entitled to such benefits, and to grant increased benefits only to those members whose wives actually meet the dependency requirement. Here, however, there is substantial evidence that, if put to the test, many of the wives of male members would fail to qualify for benefits. And in light of the fact that the dependency determination with respect to the husbands of female members is presently made solely on the basis of affidavits, rather than through the more costly hearing process, the Government's explanation of the statutory scheme is, to say the least, questionable.

In any case, our prior decisions make clear that, although efficacious administration of governmental programs is not without some importance, "the Constitution recognizes higher values than speed and efficiency." *Stanley v. Illinois,* 405 U. S. 645, 405 U. S. 656 (1972). And when we enter the realm of "strict judicial scrutiny," there can be no doubt that "administrative convenience" is not a shibboleth, the mere recitation of which dictates constitutionality. *See Shapiro v. Thompson,* 394 U. S. 618 (1969); *Carrington v. Rash,* 380 U. S. 89 (1965). On the contrary, any statutory scheme which draws a sharp line between the sexes, solely for the purpose of achieving administrative convenience, necessarily commands "dissimilar treatment for men and women who are . . . similarly situated," and therefore involves the "very kind of arbitrary legislative choice forbidden by the [Constitution]. . . ." *Reed v. Reed,* 404 U.S. at 404 U. S. 77, 404 U. S. 76. We therefore conclude that, by according differential treatment to male and female members of the uniformed services for the sole purpose of achieving administrative convenience, the challenged statutes violate the Due Process Clause of the Fifth Amendment insofar as they require a female member to prove the dependency of her husband.

Reversed.

Glossary

appellant: person bringing a case on appeal to the Supreme Court

dependent: a person who relies on another person, particularly a family member, for financial or other support

due process clause: a portion of the Fifth and Fourteenth Amendments that states that a person must not be deprived of "life, liberty, or property, without due process of law"

permanent injunction: a court order requiring a party to do or to cease doing something

shibboleth: a saying used by adherents of a party, sect, or belief regarded by others as empty of real meaning

Texas v. Johnson

DATE 1989	**CITATION** 491 U.S. 397
AUTHOR William J. Brennan Jr.	**SIGNIFICANCE** Held that Johnson's burning of a U.S. flag was protected expression under the First Amendment, falling into the category of expressive conduct
VOTE 5–4	

Overview

The 1989 U.S. Supreme Court case of *Texas v. Johnson* invalidated prohibitions on desecrating the American flag that had been in force in forty-eight states. The controversial case began when Gregory Lee Johnson joined in a political demonstration during the 1984 Republican National Convention in Dallas, Texas, and burned a flag. He was eventually convicted of violating a Texas law that prohibits vandalizing respected objects. His conviction was later overturned, whereupon the state of Texas appealed to the Supreme Court. Justice William J. Brennan wrote for a five-justice majority in holding that Johnson's act of flag burning was protected speech under the First Amendment, saying that "the government may not prohibit the expression of an idea simply because society finds the idea itself offensive or disagreeable." William Rehnquist (joined by Byron White and Sandra Day O'Connor) and John P. Stevens wrote dissenting opinions.

Context

Gregory Lee Johnson was a member of the Revolutionary Communist Youth Brigade. On August 22, 1984, he took part in a political demonstration at the Republican National Convention in Dallas, Texas. He and others were protesting the policies of the administration of President Ronald Reagan and opposing his nomination for a second term. The protestors marched through the streets, chanting slogans. Several spray-painted walls. Outside the Mercantile Bank Building, they tore down a U.S. flag, which one of the protestors gave to Johnson. Later, after the protestors reached city hall, Johnson poured kerosene on the flag and ignited it. As it burned, protestors shouted, "America, the red, white, and blue, we spit on you, you stand for plunder, you will go under." Johnson was arrested less than a half hour later. One spectator, a veteran named Daniel Walker, gathered the remains of the flag and buried them in his backyard in Fort Worth. Johnson was charged with violating the Texas flag desecration statute, the only person at the protest to be criminally charged. Initially, he was indicted for disorderly conduct, but that charge was eventually dropped; on December 13, 1984, a jury found Johnson guilty of flag desecration. He was later sentenced to one year in jail and fined $2,000.

Gregory Lee Johnson (right) with his attorney
(Joel Seidenstein)

Johnson appealed his conviction to the Fifth Court of Appeals of Texas, which affirmed the judgment of the lower court. The conviction, however, was overturned by the Texas Court of Criminal Appeals, which found that Johnson's First Amendment rights had been violated—that his actions were symbolic speech and therefore protected by the First Amendment. The court wrote: "A government cannot mandate by fiat a feeling of unity in its citizens. Therefore that very same government cannot carve out a symbol of unity and prescribe a set of approved messages to be associated with that symbol." Texas appealed to the U.S. Supreme Court, asking it to review the case.

About the Author

William Brennan, U.S. Supreme Court justice, was one of the architects of the constitutional revolution that radically changed American life in the second half of the twentieth century. As Chief Justice Earl Warren's right-hand man, Brennan was responsible for crafting majority opinions such as *Baker v. Carr*, which helped to establish the principle of "one person, one vote" and which Warren always referred to as the most important decision handed down during his momentous tenure on the Court. Brennan, whose politics placed him squarely at the Warren Court's center, was also responsible for crafting majorities for opinions such as the one he wrote in *New York Times Co. v. Sullivan*, which managed to greatly expand the First Amendment while avoiding his more liberal colleagues' wish to make criticism of public officials immune to libel suits. During the Warren years (1953–1969), Brennan was the justice least likely to dissent from the majority's views, but later, during the tenures of Chief Justices Warren Burger and William Rehnquist, he frequently played the role of passionate dissenter, most notably in death penalty cases. Nonetheless, as late as a year before he retired from an increasingly conservative Court, Brennan marshaled a majority in *Texas v. Johnson* and engineered an opinion that expanded the definition of protected speech. It is no accident that Brennan is remembered not only for the law he made but also for his skills as a coalition builder.

Born in Newark, New Jersey, on April 25, 1906, the son of Irish working-class parents, William Joseph Brennan Jr. could be said to have inherited the social activism he later exhibited on the high bench. His father worked as coal stoker at a brewery, hard labor that prompted him to become, first, a leader of the local labor union and, later, a reformer as member of the Newark Board of Commissioners. William Jr. shared many of his father's attitudes, but not—at least not overtly—his father's taste for politics. After graduating with an advanced business degree from the Wharton School at the University of Pennsylvania, Brennan attended Harvard Law School. He practiced law privately for only a short while before commencing a campaign to reform the New Jersey court system. Within a few years, he was sitting on the state supreme court bench, where, seemingly anticipating the role he would later play in connection to Earl Warren, Brennan became New Jersey Chief Justice Arthur Vanderbilt's closest associate.

Brennan arrived at the U.S. Supreme Court on October 16, 1956, appointed by President Dwight D. Eisenhower when Congress was in recess. When the Senate reconvened and voted on Brennan's appointment, only one voice was raised against him: that of Joseph McCarthy, who presumably objected not to Brennan's jurisprudence but to the latter's onetime comparison of McCarthy's Communist-hunting tactics with those employed at the Salem witch trials. Later, Eisenhower would come to regret his choice. Asked if he had made any mistakes as president, he responded, "Yes, two, and they are both sitting on the Supreme Court." Eisenhower grew to dislike Brennan's liberality on the Court almost as much as he disliked Warren's. And, indeed, Warren and Brennan worked together closely throughout Warren's tenure, meeting together privately to discuss strategies for bringing the other justices around to their view of current cases before each weekly judicial conference. Warren valued Brennan not only for his ability to parse and articulate a legal argument but also for his persuasiveness. Achieving unanimity—or, barring that, the clearest majority possible—was of the utmost importance to Warren, who sought to make his Court's precedents stick. Brennan was, in every sense, Warren's ambassador.

During the subsequent tenures of Chief Justices Burger and Rehnquist (respectively, 1969–1986 and 1986–2005), the politics of the Court shifted steadily rightward, and Brennan eventually lost both his leadership role and some of his optimism. Increasingly, he found himself in the minority, and whereas he had written few dissents during the Warren years, after 1969 the number rose steadily. Brennan's closest associate became Thurgood Marshall, one of the few other remaining members of the liberal voting bloc that had been responsible for so many of the Warren Court's momentous decisions. Brennan and Marshall frequently voted together—and they always voted together against imposing the death penalty, which both men believed to be inherently unconstitutional. In later years Brennan was nonetheless still an influential figure, drafting important opinions for the Court on gender discrimination and affirmative action, as well as First Amendment freedoms. He retired on July 20, 1990, having written 1,360 opinions, a number bested only by his fellow Warren Court liberal William O. Douglas.

Explanation and Analysis of the Document

Coming near the end of Brennan's tenure on the Court, *Texas v. Johnson* was not a milestone in the sense that many of his earlier opinions were, but it was the most publicly controversial decision of his long career. The case concerned a radical demonstrator, Gregory Lee Johnson, who chose a particularly dramatic means of expressing his criticism of Republican policies during the 1984 Republican National Convention in Dallas: he burned the American flag. Within a half hour, police had arrested Johnson for violating a Texas statute barring violation of venerated objects. A trial jury found Johnson guilty, sentencing him to a year in prison and a $2,000 fine, but the Texas Court of Criminal Appeals overturned his conviction on the ground that Johnson was exercising his right of political dissent. Texas then appealed to the U.S. Supreme Court, confident that the Court's new conservative majority would uphold the state antidesecration statute.

The state of Texas did not, however, understand the power of precedent. While it is true that the Court had not yet ruled definitively on the constitutionality of flag desecration, as Brennan points out in his opinion for the Court, in *West Virginia State Board of Education v. Barnette* (1943) the Court had indicated that failure to demonstrate respect for the flag—in this case, by refusing to salute it—was a permissible exercise of the First Amendment right to express political dissent. For Brennan, such political "statements" made with respect to the flag, itself a symbol, were obviously symbolic. But are they speech of the sort protected by the First Amendment? The Court had found in the past that various forms of expressive conduct were equivalent to protected speech. For example, the Court had upheld as protected symbolic conduct the wearing of black armbands to protest military involvement in Vietnam and a sit-in by Blacks in a "whites only" area to protest racial segregation.

Not every act intended as political dissent—even among those involving flag desecration—is protected, since government may have an overriding interest to protect. Such was the case in *United States v. O'Brien* (1968), where draft-card burning was considered to have combined speech and nonspeech elements and where the government was found to have a legitimate interest—protecting its ability to raise and support an army—that trumped the defendant's right to communicate his antiwar beliefs. When considering expressive conduct, Brennan notes, the Court has always taken context into account. At trial, Johnson had stated the reason for his actions this way: "The American Flag was burned as Ronald Reagan was being renominated as President. And a more powerful statement of symbolic speech, whether you agree with it or not, couldn't have been made at that time." While it is true that the Court has greater latitude in restricting expressive conduct than it does in curtailing words per se, for Brennan, Johnson's rationale certainly supersedes the state's claim that Johnson's arrest was aimed at preventing breaches of the peace. And he is unequivocal in dismissing the state's claim that its statute must be upheld because it is intended to preserve the flag's status as a symbol of nationhood: "If there is a bedrock principle underlying the First Amendment, it is that the government may not prohibit the expression of an idea simply because society finds the idea itself offensive or disagreeable."

Impact

The initial reaction to the Court's ruling reflected the controversial nature of the issue. Justice Brennan's home county in New Jersey was planning to erect a statue honoring his career, but a petition was circulated to halt the project. A few months later, Congress passed the Biden-Roth-Cohen Flag Protection Act of 1989, which amended the federal criminal code to apply criminal penalties for desecration of the U.S. flag; the Senate sponsor of the bill was Joseph Biden, who in 2021 would become the nation's forty-sixth president. The act went into effect on October 28, 1989. In protest, flags were burned throughout the nation; on October 30, 1989, a group set fire to a flag in front of the U.S. Capitol Building and became the first people to be arrested under the new law; among those arrested was Gregory Lee Johnson. The following year, in *United States v. Eichman*, the Court struck down the Flag Protection Act as an unconstitutional violation of the First Amendment. In the years that followed, Congress made a number of attempts to pass a constitutional amendment prohibiting desecration of the flag; in 2006, a vote in the Senate fell one shy of the sixty-seven needed to propose such an amendment to the states.

Questions for Further Study

1. What was the central question presented in *Texas v. Johnson*?

2. What emotional arguments would a jurist need to be aware of and set aside in connection with this case?

3. What other examples of symbolic political speech might be offensive to some but would be protected by the First Amendment?

4. Should flag burning be protected as free speech?

Further Reading

Books

Goldstein, Robert Justin. *Burning the Flag: The Great 1989–1990 American Flag Desecration Controversy*. Kent, OH: Kent State University Press, 1996.

Goldstein, Robert Justin. *Desecrating the American Flag: Key Documents of the Controversy from the Civil War to 1995*. Syracuse, NY: Syracuse University Press, 1996.

Goldstein, Robert Justin. *Flag Burning and Free Speech: The Case of Texas v. Johnson*. Lawrence: University Press of Kansas, 2000.

Vergobbi, David J. "Texas v. Johnson." In *Free Speech on Trial: Communication Perspectives on Landmark Supreme Court Decisions*, edited by Richard A. Parker: 281–97. Tuscaloosa: University of Alabama Press, 2003.

Articles

Blakemore, Erin. "Five Things to Know about the Case That Made Burning the Flag Legal." *Smithsonian Magazine*, November 29, 2016. https://www.smithsonianmag.com/smart-news/five-things-know-about-case-made-burning-flag-legal-180961229/.

Fine, David R. "Symbolic Expression and the Rehnquist Court: The Lessons of the Peculiar Passions of Flag Burning." *University of Toledo Law Review* 22, no. 3 (Spring 1991).

Grosskopf, Anke, and Jeffery J. Mondak. "Do Attitudes toward Specific Supreme Court Decisions Matter? The Impact of *Webster and Texas v. Johnson* on Public Confidence in the Supreme Court." *Political Research Quarterly* 51, no. 3 (1998): 633–54. https://www.jstor.org/stable/3088042.

Lofton, Patricia. "*Texas v. Johnson*: The Constitutional Protection of Flag Desecration." *Pepperdine Law Review* 17, no. 3 (1990): 757–92. https://digitalcommons.pepperdine.edu/cgi/viewcontent.cgi?article=1733&context=plr.

Pollitt, Daniel H. "Reflection on the Bicentennial of the Bill of Rights: The Flag Burning Controversy." *North Carolina Law Review* 70, no. 2 (1992): 552–614.

Websites

Bitzer, J. Michael. "Texas v. Johnson." *First Amendment Encyclopedia*. Accessed February 26, 2023, https://www.mtsu.edu/first-amendment/article/305/texas-v-johnson.

—Commentary by Lisa Paddock and Michael J. O'Neal

Texas v. Johnson

Document Text

JUSTICE BRENNAN delivered the opinion of the Court

... Johnson was convicted of flag desecration for burning the flag rather than for uttering insulting words. This fact somewhat complicates our consideration of his conviction under the First Amendment.... We must first determine whether Johnson's burning of the flag constituted expressive conduct, permitting him to invoke the First Amendment in challenging his conviction.... If his conduct was expressive, we next decide whether the State's regulation is related to the suppression of free expression.... If the State's regulation is not related to expression, then the less stringent standard we announced in *United States v. O'Brien* for regulations of noncommunicative conduct controls.... If it is, then we are outside of *O'Brien*'s test, and we must ask whether this interest justifies Johnson's conviction under a more demanding standard....

The First Amendment literally forbids the abridgment only of "speech," but we have long recognized that its protection does not end at the spoken or written word. While we have rejected "the view that an apparently limitless variety of conduct can be labeled 'speech' whenever the person engaging in the conduct intends thereby to express an idea,"... we have acknowledged that conduct may be "sufficiently imbued with elements of communication to fall within the scope of the First and Fourteenth Amendments."...

In deciding whether particular conduct possesses sufficient communicative elements to bring the First Amendment into play, we have asked whether "[a]n intent to convey a particularized message was present, and [whether] the likelihood was great that the message would be understood by those who viewed it."...

Especially pertinent to this case are our decisions recognizing the communicative nature of conduct relating to flags.... That we have had little difficulty identifying an expressive element in conduct relating to flags should not be surprising. The very purpose of a national flag is to serve as a symbol of our country; it is, one might say, "the one visible manifestation of two hundred years of nationhood."... Pregnant with expressive content, the flag as readily signifies this Nation as does the combination of letters found in "America."

We have not automatically concluded, however, that any action taken with respect to our flag is expressive. Instead, in characterizing such action for First Amendment purposes, we have considered the context in which it occurred.... The State of Texas conceded for purposes of its oral argument in this case that Johnson's conduct was expressive conduct.... Johnson burned an American flag as part—indeed, as the culmination—of a political demonstration that coincided with the convening of the Republican Party and its renomination of Ronald Reagan for President. The expressive, overtly political nature of this conduct was both intentional and overwhelmingly apparent. At his trial, Johnson explained his reasons for burning the flag as follows: "The American Flag was burned as Ronald Reagan was being renominated as President. And a more powerful statement of symbolic speech, whether you agree with it or not, couldn't have been made at that time. It's quite a just position [juxtaposition]. We had new patriotism and no patriotism." ... In these circumstances, Johnson's burning of the flag was conduct "sufficiently imbued with elements of communication" ... to implicate the First Amendment.

The government generally has a freer hand in restricting expressive conduct than it has in restricting the written or spoken word. ... It may not, however, proscribe particular conduct because it has expressive elements. ... It is, in short, not simply the verbal or nonverbal nature of the expression, but the governmental interest at stake, that helps to determine whether a restriction on that expression is valid.

Thus, although we have recognized that where "'speech' and 'nonspeech' elements are combined in the same course of conduct, a sufficiently important governmental interest in regulating the nonspeech element can justify incidental limitations on First Amendment freedoms," ... we have limited the applicability of *O'Brien*'s relatively lenient standard to those cases in which "the governmental interest is unrelated to the suppression of free expression."

In order to decide whether *O'Brien*'s test applies here, therefore, we must decide whether Texas has asserted an interest in support of Johnson's conviction that is unrelated to the suppression of expression. If we find that an interest asserted by the State is simply not implicated on the facts before us, we need not ask whether *O'Brien*'s test applies. ... The State offers two separate interests to justify this conviction: preventing breaches of the peace and preserving the flag as a symbol of nationhood and national unity. We hold that the first interest is not implicated on this record and that the second is related to the suppression of expression. ... The only evidence offered by the State at trial to show the reaction to Johnson's actions was the testimony of several persons who had been seriously offended by the flag burning.

The State's position, therefore, amounts to a claim that an audience that takes serious offense at particular expression is necessarily likely to disturb the peace and that the expression may be prohibited on this basis. Our precedents do not countenance such a presumption. On the contrary, they recognize that a principal "function of free speech under our system of government is to invite dispute. It may indeed best serve its high purpose when it induces a condition of unrest, creates dissatisfaction with conditions as they are, or even stirs people to anger." ... Thus, we have not permitted the government to assume that every expression of a provocative idea will incite a riot, but have instead required careful consideration of the actual circumstances surrounding such expression, asking whether the expression "is directed to inciting or producing imminent lawless action and is likely to incite or produce such action." ...

The State also asserts an interest in preserving the flag as a symbol of nationhood and national unity. In *Spence*, we acknowledged that the government's interest in preserving the flag's special symbolic value "is directly related to expression in the context of activity." ... We are equally persuaded that this interest is related to expression in the case of Johnson's burning of the flag. The State, apparently, is concerned that such conduct will lead people to believe either that the flag does not stand for nationhood and national unity, but instead reflects other, less positive concepts, or that the concepts reflected in the flag do not in fact exist, that is, that we do not enjoy unity as a Nation. These concerns blossom only when a person's treatment of the flag communicates some message, and thus are related "to the suppression of free expression" within the meaning of *O'Brien*. We are thus outside of *O'Brien*'s test altogether.

It remains to consider whether the State's interest in preserving the flag as a symbol of nationhood and national unity justifies Johnson's conviction.

As in *Spence*, "[w]e are confronted with a case of prosecution for the expression of an idea through activity," and "[a]ccordingly, we must examine with particular care the interests ... advanced by [petitioner] to support its prosecution." ... Johnson was not, we add, prosecuted for the expression of just any idea; he was prosecuted for his expression of dissatisfaction with the policies of this country, expression situated at the core of our First Amendment values. ...

Whether Johnson's treatment of the flag violated Texas law thus depended on the likely communicative impact of his expressive conduct. ... Johnson's political expression was restricted because of the content of the message he conveyed. ...

If there is a bedrock principle underlying the First Amendment, it is that the government may not prohibit the expression of an idea simply because society finds the idea itself offensive or disagreeable....

We have not recognized an exception to this principle even where our flag has been involved.... Nothing in our precedents suggests that a State may foster its own view of the flag by prohibiting expressive conduct relating to it. To bring its argument outside our... precedents, Texas attempts to convince us that even if its interest in preserving the flag's symbolic role does not allow it to prohibit words or some expressive conduct critical of the flag, it does permit it to forbid the outright destruction of the flag. The State's argument cannot depend here on the distinction between written or spoken words and nonverbal conduct. That distinction, we have shown, is of no moment where the nonverbal conduct is expressive, as it is here, and where the regulation of that conduct is related to expression, as it is here....

Texas' focus on the precise nature of Johnson's expression, moreover, misses the point of our prior decisions: their enduring lesson, that the government may not prohibit expression simply because it disagrees with its message, is not dependent on the particular mode in which one chooses to express an idea. If we were to hold that a State may forbid flag burning wherever it is likely to endanger the flag's symbolic role, but allow it wherever burning a flag promotes that role—as where, for example, a person ceremoniously burns a dirty flag—we would be saying that when it comes to impairing the flag's physical integrity, the flag itself may be used as... a symbol—as a substitute for the written or spoken word or a "short cut from mind to mind"—only in one direction. We would be permitting a State to "prescribe what shall be orthodox" by saying that one may burn the flag to convey one's attitude toward it and its referents only if one does not endanger the flag's representation of nationhood and national unity.

We never before have held that the Government may ensure that a symbol be used to express only one view of that symbol or its referents.... To conclude that the government may permit designated symbols to be used to communicate only a limited set of messages would be to enter territory having no discernible or defensible boundaries. Could the government, on this theory, prohibit the burning of state flags? Of copies of the Presidential seal? Of the Constitution? In evaluating these choices under the First Amendment, how would we decide which symbols were sufficiently special to warrant this unique status? To do so, we would be forced to consult our own political preferences, and impose them on the citizenry, in the very way that the First Amendment forbids us to do....

There is, moreover, no indication—either in the text of the Constitution or in our cases interpreting it—that a separate juridical category exists for the American flag alone. Indeed, we would not be surprised to learn that the persons... who framed our Constitution and wrote the Amendment that we now construe were not known for their reverence for the Union Jack. The First Amendment does not guarantee that other concepts virtually sacred to our Nation as a whole—such as the principle that discrimination on the basis of race is odious and destructive—will go unquestioned in the marketplace of ideas.... We decline, therefore, to create for the flag an exception to the joust of principles protected by the First Amendment.

It is not the State's ends, but its means, to which we object. It cannot be gainsaid that there is a special place reserved for the flag in this Nation, and thus we do not doubt that the government has a legitimate interest in making efforts to "preserv[e] the national flag as an unalloyed symbol of our country."... We reject the suggestion, urged at oral argument by counsel for Johnson, that the government lacks "any state interest whatsoever" in regulating the manner in which the flag may be displayed.... To say that the government has an interest in encouraging proper treatment of the flag, however, is not to say that it may criminally punish a person for burning a flag as a means of political protest....

We are fortified in today's conclusion by our conviction that forbidding criminal punishment for conduct such as Johnson's will not endanger the special role played by our flag or the feelings it inspires. To paraphrase Justice Holmes, we submit that nobody can suppose that this one gesture of an unknown man will change our Nation's attitude towards its flag.... We are tempted to say, in fact, that the flag's deservedly cherished place in our community will be strengthened, not weakened, by our holding today. Our decision is a reaffirmation of the principles of freedom and inclusiveness that the flag best reflects, and of the conviction that our toleration of criticism such as Johnson's is a sign and source of our strength. Indeed, one of the proudest images of our flag, the one immortalized in our own national anthem, is of the bombardment it survived at Fort McHenry. It is the Nation's resilience, not its rigidity, that Texas sees reflected in the flag—and it is that resilience that we reassert today.

The way to preserve the flag's special role is not to punish those who feel differently about these matters. It is to persuade them that they are wrong.... And, precisely because it is our flag that is involved, one's response to the flag...burner may exploit the uniquely persuasive power of the flag itself. We can imagine no more appropriate response to burning a flag than waving one's own, no better way to counter a flag burner's message than by saluting the flag that burns, no surer means of preserving the dignity even of the flag that burned than by—as one witness here did—according its remains a respectful burial. We do not consecrate the flag by punishing its desecration, for in doing so we dilute the freedom that this cherished emblem represents.

Johnson was convicted for engaging in expressive conduct. The State's interest in preventing breaches of the peace does not support his conviction because Johnson's conduct did not threaten to disturb the peace. Nor does the State's interest in preserving the flag as a symbol of nationhood and national unity justify his criminal conviction for engaging in political expression.

Glossary

desecration: an act of showing disrespect toward an object normally accorded a much higher degree of respect

expressive conduct: actions intended to illustrate a point rather than as an end in themselves

Fort McHenry: a Baltimore military facility where British and American ships fought a naval battle in September 1814, inspiring Francis Scott Key, who observed it firsthand, to write "The Star-Spangled Banner"

gainsaid: denied

implicated on: dependent on

joust of principles: a battle between competing ideas

juridical: relating to the law

moment: importance or significance

noncommunicative conduct: conduct that does not serve to express a political meaning

pregnant with expressive content: filled with symbolic meaning

proscribe: prohibit

referents: those things to which a symbol refers

UNITED STATES V. LOPEZ

DATE
1995

AUTHOR
William Rehnquist

VOTE
5–4

CITATION
514 U.S. 549

SIGNIFICANCE
Held that the 1990 Gun-Free School Zones Act, forbidding individuals from knowingly carrying a gun in a school zone, was unconstitutional because it exceeded the power of Congress to legislate under the commerce clause

Overview

As a new conservative justice on the liberal Court presided over by Chief Justice Warren Burger, William Rehnquist was often the Court's lone voice of dissent. This willingness to disagree with the majority was nowhere more in evidence than in *Roe v. Wade*, the landmark 1973 case that struck down state laws outlawing abortion. Throughout his career, Rehnquist resisted efforts of the Court to expand federal powers—as he did in 1995 in *United States v. Lopez*, a case that reviewed the constitutionality of the Gun-Free School Zones Act of 1990, which made it a federal offense to carry a gun onto school property. When he could, Rehnquist defended the rights of the states against the imposition of federal power. Here he rejected the law because it gave general police power to the federal government, thus usurping the power of the states. Stephen Breyer, John Paul Stevens, and David Souter issued separate dissenting opinions and were joined in opposition by Ruth Bader Ginsburg.

Context

In 1990, Congress enacted the Gun-Free School Zones Act. The act prohibited unauthorized individuals from bringing a loaded or unsecured gun into a school or school zone. The law applied to public, private, and parochial schools, both elementary and high schools, and to non-private property within 1,000 feet of a school. On March 10, however, Alfonso Lopez Jr., a twelfth-grader in San Antonio, Texas, carried an unloaded, concealed .38 caliber revolver and five cartridges to school. School authorities received a tip that he had the gun in his possession. When confronted, he admitted as much and claimed that he had been paid to deliver the gun to another person. Lopez was arrested and charged with violating the Gun-Free School Zones Act.

In court, Lopez argued that the act was unconstitutional because Congress did not have legislative authority over public schools. The trial court rejected this argument, ruling that the law was "a constitutional exercise of Congress' well defined power to regulate activities in and affecting commerce, and the 'business' of elementary, middle, and high schools... affects interstate commerce." After he was convicted, Lopez appeal to the Fifth

Circuit Court of Appeals. He argued that the law exceeded the power of Congress under the commerce clause, which is found in Article I of the Constitution and which gives Congress the power "to regulate commerce with foreign nations, and among the several states, and with the Indian tribes." The Fifth Circuit agreed and reversed Lopez's conviction, finding that the legislative history of the act did not suggest any connection with the commerce clause. The Fifth Circuit added that that it might be possible to write a new act that established a "nexus" with the commerce clause—although doing so would be difficult, because the entire matter had only a "trivial impact" on interstate commerce. The U.S. government appealed to the Supreme Court, arguing that having a gun in an educational setting would lead to violent crime, which in turn would affect the community in two ways. One was by creating expenses and raising insurance costs. The other was by limiting the willingness of people to travel to an area deemed unsafe. Students would be frightened and disturbed, which would impede learning, resulting in a weaker national economy. Thus, in the government's view, the commerce clause was applicable.

About the Author

As chief justice of the United States, William Hubbs Rehnquist oversaw the Supreme Court's profound shift in a conservative direction after the more liberal leadership of his predecessor, Warren Burger. Rehnquist was born on October 1, 1924, in Milwaukee, Wisconsin. After serving in the U.S. Army Air Forces from 1943 to 1946, he attended Stanford University in California, earning bachelor's and master's degrees in political science. After two years at Harvard University, where he earned a second master's degree in government in 1950, he returned to Stanford to attend law school. There he graduated first in his class in 1952; one of his classmates was his future Supreme Court colleague Sandra Day O'Connor.

After serving as a judicial clerk for Supreme Court Justice Robert Jackson during the Court's 1952–1953 term, Rehnquist settled in Phoenix, Arizona, where he worked at a law firm and became active in Republican Party politics. From 1969 to 1971 he was assistant attorney general in the U.S. Justice Department's Office of Legal Counsel. In 1971 President Richard Nixon

The case arose from high-school student Alfonso Lopez Jr.'s challenge to the Gun-Free School Zones Act of 1990.
(Marcus Quigmire)

nominated him for a seat on the Supreme Court; after confirmation by the Senate, Rehnquist assumed his seat in 1972. In 1986 President Ronald Reagan nominated him to the position of chief justice, a position he held, despite ill health in his later years, until his death on September 3, 2005.

As a member of the nation's highest court, Rehnquist wrote primarily decisions in which he explained the legal principles and reasoning that had led to the decision. This type of legal writing requires the justice to outline the facts of the case, cite statutes and legal precedents (previous court decisions) that have a bearing on the case, and then demonstrate how those statutes and precedents should be used to decide the case at hand. Typically, when the Supreme Court arrives at a decision, the chief justice assigns the task of writing the Court's decision to one of the justices who joined the majority, though the chief justice has often reserved that task for himself. In the case of such key Court decisions as *United States v. Lopez* and *George W. Bush et al. v. Albert Gore, Jr., et al.*, Rehnquist himself wrote the decisions. Often, however, justices who do not join with the majority and disagree with the Court's decision file a dissent outlining the basis of their disagreement. In the landmark *Roe v. Wade* abortion decision, Rehnquist disagreed with the majority and wrote such a dissent.

Explanation and Analysis of the Document

The U.S. Supreme Court is the nation's highest court of appeal. As a court of appeal, it does not retry cases but instead reviews cases from lower courts to ensure that the constitutional rights of parties are protected and that the law was applied correctly. In this case, the Supreme Court was asked to review the constitutionality of the Gun-Free School Zones Act of 1990, which made it a federal offense for anyone, including a student, to carry a gun onto school property or the area surrounding it. The respondent in this case—that is, the party who "responds" to the appeal filed by the "petitioner"—was Alfonso Lopez, a student who was charged with carrying a gun to school. Lopez asked a lower district court, which initially heard the case, to dismiss the charge. The district court denied his request. The case was appealed to a U.S. appeals court, which found the 1990 act unconstitutional. In *United States v. Lopez*, the Supreme Court affirmed the ruling of the appeals court.

At issue in this case was the reach of the U.S. Congress under the commerce clause, Article I, Section 8, Clause 3 of the U.S. Constitution. This clause gives Congress the power to regulate interstate commerce, or commerce that crosses state lines. Commerce conducted solely within a state (intrastate commerce) falls under the authority of that state, not the federal government. In modern life, there are few forms of commerce that do not take place over state lines; products are sold in more than one state, suppliers of raw materials come from other states, and so on. Accordingly, there are few types of commerce that the federal government cannot regulate.

The larger question becomes, what is "commerce"? Normally, the word applies to the buying and selling of goods and services. But during the twentieth century, Congress began to regard as commerce any activity that might have a bearing on the economic fortunes of a community. Thus, even though a school would not normally be thought of as a business, its activities can have economic effects that extend across state lines. The level of education of a workforce, for example, can have an impact on whether businesses outside the state will do business in the community served by the school. In the case of guns and schools, Congress essentially decided that because schools can have an impact on interstate commerce, it had the authority to regulate guns in and around school property.

In the view of some legal scholars, Congress has extended its understanding of interstate commerce in ways that the Constitution does not support and never intended. This belief is the essence of Rehnquist's holding in *United States v. Lopez*. In the first sentence, he states explicitly, "The [Gun-Free School Zones] Act exceeds Congress' Commerce Clause authority." He notes that although the Court has sometimes upheld state laws regulating intrastate commerce because they have an impact on interstate commerce, the act in question, as a criminal statute, has nothing to do with economic activity. He goes on to elaborate that sometimes such a statute can be part of a broader set of regulations that can, in fact, affect interstate commerce and that failure to uphold the one regulation would make it difficult for the broader set of laws to succeed in their intent. Rehnquist rejects the view that the Gun-Free School Zones Act is such a law. He continues by noting that the act of carrying a gun to school has nothing to do with interstate commerce or any kind of economic activity that would affect interstate commerce. He concludes that a law such as the one in question turns the commerce clause into a general police power on the part of the federal government, thus usurping the power of the states. It should be noted that Rehnquist was not in any way defending guns in schools. Rather, his view was that the federal government has no authority to regulate guns in schools, at least not on the basis of the commerce clause.

United States v. Lopez was a landmark case. Normally, the Supreme Court is more likely to overturn a law that bears on fundamental rights. The Court will apply the strict scrutiny standard it applied in *Roe v. Wade* to determine whether the state has a compelling interest in regulating the behavior in question. The Court, though, has another test, usually called the "rational basis standard." This standard is less strict and applies in cases that do not involve fundamental rights. In applying the standard, the Court asks whether the state has an important or "rational" interest in controlling the behavior, and most of the time it concludes that it does, so relatively few such laws are declared unconstitutional. Further, because such cases do not involve fundamental rights, the Court will rarely overturn laws that it examines using the rational basis standard. *United States v. Lopez* was just such a case, so the Court's willingness to overturn the law and rein in Congress in its interpretation of the commerce clause was noteworthy. With the case as a precedent, other congressional acts that are justified on the basis of the commerce clause are susceptible to increased scrutiny by the courts.

Impact

The chief significance of *United States v. Lopez* was that it was the first time in a half century that the Court held that Congress had overstepped its authority under the commerce clause by holding that the law was not substantially related to interstate commerce. Following the government's line of reasoning, virtually any matter could be said to affect interstate commerce and thus can be regulated under the commerce clause. But as the Court noted, under the government's theory, "it is difficult to perceive any limitation on federal power, even in areas ... where States historically have been sovereign." It would be impossible to point to any activity that Congress would be powerless to regulate. Since then, numerous attempts have been made to invoke the commerce clause. Some have succeeded, some have failed, but the effort is nearly always controversial.

Questions for Further Study

1. What law was Lopez charged with violating, and what happened to those charges?

2. Why did Lopez challenge his conviction?

3. How did the Supreme Court rule?

4. In a dissent, Justice Breyer argued, "Education, although far more than a matter of economics, has long been inextricably intertwined with the Nation's economy.... [G]uns in the hands of six percent of inner-city high school students and gun-related violence throughout a city's schools must threaten the trade and commerce that those schools support." How convincing is this argument?

Further Reading

Articles

Calabresi, Steven G. "'A Government of Limited and Enumerated Powers': In Defense of *United States v. Lopez*." *Michigan Law Review* 94, no. 3 (December 1995): 752–831.

Graglia, Lino A. "*United States v. Lopez*: Judicial Review under the Commerce Clause." *Texas Law Review* 74 (1995): 719–71. https://heinonline.org/HOL/LandingPage?handle=hein.journals/tlr74&div=38&id=&page=.

Lessig, Lawrence. "Translating Federalism: *United States v Lopez*." *The Supreme Court Review* (1995): 125–215. https://www.docdroid.net/xBtuqCn/lawrence-lessig-translating-federalism-united-states-v-lopez-1996-pdf#page=91.

McJohn, Stephen M. "The Impact of *United States v. Lopez*: The New Hybrid Commerce Clause." *Duquesne Law Review* 34, no. 1 (Fall 1995): 1–40.

Trapp, Michael J. "A Small Step towards Restoring the Balance of Federalism: A Limit to Federal Power under the Commerce Clause—*United States v. Lopez*." *University of Cincinnati Law Review* 64 (1995): 1471ff.

—Commentary by Michael J. O'Neal

UNITED STATES V. LOPEZ

Document Text

After respondent, then a 12th-grade student, carried a concealed handgun into his high school, he was charged with violating the Gun-Free School Zones Act of 1990, which forbids "any individual knowingly to possess a firearm at a place that [he] knows . . . is a school zone," 18 U. S. C. 922(q)(1)(A). The District Court denied his motion to dismiss the indictment, concluding that 922(q) is a constitutional exercise of Congress' power to regulate activities in and affecting commerce. In reversing, the Court of Appeals held that, in light of what it characterized as insufficient congressional findings and legislative history, 922(q) is invalid as beyond Congress' power under the Commerce Clause.

Held:

The Act exceeds Congress' Commerce Clause authority. First, although this Court has upheld a wide variety of congressional Acts regulating intrastate economic activity that substantially affected interstate commerce, the possession of a gun in a local school zone is in no sense an economic activity that might, through repetition elsewhere, have such a substantial effect on interstate commerce. Section 922(q) is a criminal statute that by its terms has nothing to do with "commerce" or any sort of economic enterprise, however broadly those terms are defined. Nor is it an essential part of a larger regulation of economic activity, in which the regulatory scheme could be undercut unless the intrastate activity were regulated. It cannot, therefore, be sustained under the Court's cases upholding regulations of activities that arise out of or are connected with a commercial transaction, which viewed in the aggregate, substantially affects interstate commerce. Second, 922(q) contains no jurisdictional element which would ensure, through case-by-case inquiry, that the firearms possession in question has the requisite nexus with interstate commerce. Respondent was a local student at a local school; there is no indication that he had recently moved in interstate commerce, and there is no requirement that his possession of the firearm have any concrete tie to interstate commerce. To uphold the Government's contention that 922(q) is justified because firearms possession in a local school zone does indeed substantially affect interstate commerce would require this Court to pile inference upon inference in a manner that would bid fair to convert congressional Commerce Clause authority to a general police power of the sort held only by the States.

CHIEF JUSTICE REHNQUIST delivered the opinion of the Court

In the Gun-Free School Zones Act of 1990, Congress made it a federal offense "for any individual knowingly to possess a firearm at a place that the individual knows, or has reasonable cause to believe, is a school zone." The Act neither regulates a commercial activity nor contains a requirement that the possession be connected in any way to interstate commerce. We hold that the Act exceeds the authority of Congress "[t]o regulate Commerce . . . among the several States. . . ." U. S. Const., Art. I, § 8, cl. 3.

On March 10, 1992, respondent, who was then a 12th-grade student, arrived at Edison High School in San

Antonio, Texas, carrying a concealed .38-caliber handgun and five bullets. Acting upon an anonymous tip, school authorities confronted respondent, who admitted that he was carrying the weapon. He was arrested and charged under Texas law with firearm possession on school premises. The next day, the state charges were dismissed after federal agents charged respondent by complaint with violating the Gun-Free School Zones Act of 1990.

A federal grand jury indicted respondent on one count of knowing possession of a firearm at a school zone, in violation of § 922(q). Respondent moved to dismiss his federal indictment on the ground that § 922(q) "is unconstitutional as it is beyond the power of Congress to legislate control over our public schools." The District Court denied the motion, concluding that § 922(q) "is a constitutional exercise of Congress' well-defined power to regulate activities in and affecting commerce, and the 'business' of elementary, middle and high schools ... affects interstate commerce." Respondent waived his right to a jury trial. The District Court conducted a bench trial, found him guilty of violating § 922(q), and sentenced him to six months' imprisonment and two years' supervised release.

On appeal, respondent challenged his conviction based on his claim that § 922(q) exceeded Congress' power to legislate under the Commerce Clause. The Court of Appeals for the Fifth Circuit agreed and reversed respondent's conviction. It held that, in light of what it characterized as insufficient congressional findings and legislative history, "section 922(q), in the full reach of its terms, is invalid as beyond the power of Congress under the Commerce Clause." Because of the importance of the issue, we granted certiorari, and we now affirm.

We start with first principles. The Constitution creates a Federal Government of enumerated powers. See Art. I, § 8. As James Madison wrote: "The powers delegated by the proposed Constitution to the federal government are few and defined. Those which are to remain in the State governments are numerous and indefinite." The Federalist No. 45, pp. 292-293 (C. Rossiter ed. 1961). This constitutionally mandated division of authority "was adopted by the Framers to ensure protection of our fundamental liberties." "Just as the separation and independence of the coordinate branches of the Federal Government serve to prevent the accumulation of excessive power in anyone branch, a healthy balance of power between the States and the Federal Government will reduce the risk of tyranny and abuse from either front."

The Constitution delegates to Congress the power "[t]o regulate Commerce with foreign Nations, and among the several States, and with the Indian Tribes." Art. I, § 8, cl. 3. The Court, through Chief Justice Marshall, first defined the nature of Congress' commerce power in *Gibbons v. Ogden*, 9 Wheat. 1, 189-190 (1824):

> "Commerce, undoubtedly, is traffic, but it is something more: it is intercourse. It describes the commercial intercourse between nations, and parts of nations, in all its branches, and is regulated by prescribing rules for carrying on that intercourse."

The commerce power "is the power to regulate; that is, to prescribe the rule by which commerce is to be governed. This power, like all others vested in congress, is complete in itself, may be exercised to its utmost extent, and acknowledges no limitations, other than are prescribed in the constitution." *Id.*, at 196. The *Gibbons* Court, however, acknowledged that limitations on the commerce power are inherent in the very language of the Commerce Clause.

> "It is not intended to say that these words comprehend that commerce, which is completely internal, which is carried on between man and man in a State, or between different parts of the same State, and which does not extend to or affect other States. Such a power would be inconvenient, and is certainly unnecessary.

> "Comprehensive as the word 'among' is, it may very properly be restricted to that commerce which concerns more States than one. ... The enumeration presupposes something not enumerated; and that something, if we regard the language, or the subject of the sentence, must be the exclusively internal commerce of a State." *Id.*, at 194-195.

For nearly a century thereafter, the Court's Commerce Clause decisions dealt but rarely with the extent of Congress' power, and almost entirely with the Commerce Clause as a limit on state legislation that discriminated against interstate commerce. Under this line of precedent, the Court held that certain categories of activity such as "production," "manufacturing," and "mining" were within the province of state governments, and thus were beyond the power of Congress under the Commerce Clause.

In 1887, Congress enacted the Interstate Commerce Act, 24 Stat. 379, and in 1890, Congress enacted the Sherman Antitrust Act, 26 Stat. 209, as amended, 15 U. S. C. § 1 *et seq.* These laws ushered in a new era of federal regulation under the commerce power. When cases involving these laws first reached this Court, we imported from our negative Commerce Clause cases the approach that Congress could not regulate activities such as "production," "manufacturing," and "mining." Simultaneously, however, the Court held that, where the interstate and intrastate aspects of commerce were so mingled together that full regulation of interstate commerce required incidental regulation of intrastate commerce, the Commerce Clause authorized such regulation.

In *A. L. A. Schechter Poultry Corp. v. United States* (1935), the Court struck down regulations that fixed the hours and wages of individuals employed by an intrastate business because the activity being regulated related to interstate commerce only indirectly. In doing so, the Court characterized the distinction between direct and indirect effects of intrastate transactions upon interstate commerce as "a fundamental one, essential to the maintenance of our constitutional system." Activities that affected interstate commerce directly were within Congress' power; activities that affected interstate commerce indirectly were beyond Congress' reach. The justification for this formal distinction was rooted in the fear that otherwise "there would be virtually no limit to the federal power and for all practical purposes we should have a completely centralized government."

Two years later, in the watershed case of *NLRB v. Jones & Laughlin Steel Corp.* (1937), the Court upheld the National Labor Relations Act against a Commerce Clause challenge, and in the process, departed from the distinction between "direct" and "indirect" effects on interstate commerce. ("The question [of the scope of Congress' power] is necessarily one of degree"). The Court held that intrastate activities that "have such a close and substantial relation to interstate commerce that their control is essential or appropriate to protect that commerce from burdens and obstructions" are within Congress' power to regulate.

In *United States v. Darby* (1941), the Court upheld the Fair Labor Standards Act, stating:

> "The power of Congress over interstate commerce is not confined to the regulation of commerce among the states. It extends to those activities intrastate which so affect interstate commerce or the exercise of the power of Congress over it as to make regulation of them appropriate means to the attainment of a legitimate end, the exercise of the granted power of Congress to regulate interstate commerce."

In *Wickard v. Filburn*, the Court upheld the application of amendments to the Agricultural Adjustment Act of 1938 to the production and consumption of homegrown wheat. The *Wickard* Court explicitly rejected earlier distinctions between direct and indirect effects on interstate commerce, stating:

> "[E]ven if appellee's activity be local and though it may not be regarded as commerce, it may still, whatever its nature, be reached by Congress if it exerts a substantial economic effect on interstate commerce, and this irrespective of whether such effect is what might at some earlier time have been defined as 'direct' or 'indirect.'"

The *Wickard* Court emphasized that although Filburn's own contribution to the demand for wheat may have been trivial by itself, that was not "enough to remove him from the scope of federal regulation where, as here, his contribution, taken together with that of many others similarly situated, is far from trivial."

Jones & Laughlin Steel, *Darby*, and *Wickard* ushered in an era of Commerce Clause jurisprudence that greatly expanded the previously defined authority of Congress under that Clause. In part, this was a recognition of the great changes that had occurred in the way business was carried on in this country. Enterprises that had once been local or at most regional in nature had become national in scope. But the doctrinal change also reflected a view that earlier Commerce Clause cases artificially had constrained the authority of Congress to regulate interstate commerce.

But even these modern-era precedents which have expanded congressional power under the Commerce Clause confirm that this power is subject to outer limits. In *Jones & Laughlin Steel*, the Court warned that the scope of the interstate commerce power "must be considered in the light of our dual system of government and may not be extended so as to embrace effects upon interstate commerce so indirect and remote that to embrace them, in view of our complex society, would effectually obliterate the distinction between what is national and what is local and create a completely centralized government." Since that time, the Court has heeded that warning and undertaken to decide whether a rational basis existed for concluding that a regulated activity sufficiently affected interstate commerce.

Similarly, in *Maryland v. Wirtz* (1968), the Court reaffirmed that "the power to regulate commerce, though broad indeed, has limits" that "[t]he Court has ample power" to enforce, overruled on other grounds In response to the dissent's warnings that the Court was powerless to enforce the limitations on Congress' commerce powers because "[a]ll activities affecting commerce, even in the minutest degree, may be regulated and controlled by Congress," the *Wirtz* Court replied that the dissent had misread precedent as "[n]either here nor in *Wickard* has the Court declared that Congress may use a relatively trivial impact on commerce as an excuse for broad general regulation of state or private activities., . Rather, "[t]he Court has said only that where *a general regulatory statute bears a substantial relation to commerce*, the *de minimis* character of individual instances arising under that statute is of no consequence." (first emphasis added).

Consistent with this structure, we have identified three broad categories of activity that Congress may regulate under its commerce power. First, Congress may regulate the use of the channels of interstate commerce. Second, Congress is empowered to regulate and protect the instrumentalities of interstate commerce, or persons or things in interstate commerce, even though the threat may come only from intrastate activities. Finally, Congress' commerce authority includes the power to regulate those activities having a substantial relation to interstate commerce, i.e., those activities that substantially affect interstate commerce.

Within this final category, admittedly, our case law has not been clear whether an activity must "affect" or "substantially affect" interstate commerce in order to be within Congress' power to regulate it under the Commerce Clause. Compare *Preseault v. ICC*, 494 U. S. 1, 17 (1990), with *Wirtz, supra*, at 196, n. 27 (the Court has never declared that "Congress may use a relatively trivial impact on commerce as an excuse for broad general regulation of state or private activities"). We conclude, consistent with the great weight of our case law, that the proper test requires an analysis of whether the regulated activity "substantially affects" interstate commerce.

We now turn to consider the power of Congress, in the light of this framework, to enact § 922(q). The first two categories of authority may be quickly disposed of: § 922(q) is not a regulation of the use of the channels of interstate commerce, nor is it an attempt to prohibit the interstate transportation of a commodity through the channels of commerce; nor can § 922(q) be justified as a regulation by which Congress has sought to protect an instrumentality of interstate commerce or a thing in interstate commerce. Thus, if § 922(q) is to be sustained, it must be under the third category as a regulation of an activity that substantially affects interstate commerce.

First, we have upheld a wide variety of congressional Acts regulating intrastate economic activity where we have concluded that the activity substantially affected interstate commerce. Examples include the regulation of intrastate coal mining; *Hodel, supra*, intrastate extortionate credit transactions, *Perez, supra*, restaurants utilizing substantial interstate supplies, *McClung, supra*, inns and hotels catering to interstate guests, *Heart of Atlanta Motel, supra*, and production and consumption of homegrown wheat, *Wickard v. Filburn* (1942). These examples are by no means exhaustive, but the pattern is clear. Where economic activity substantially affects interstate commerce, legislation regulating that activity will be sustained.

Even *Wickard*, which is perhaps the most far reaching example of Commerce Clause authority over intrastate activity, involved economic activity in a way that the possession of a gun in a school zone does not. Roscoe Filburn operated a small farm in Ohio, on which, in the year involved, he raised 23 acres of wheat. It was his practice to sow winter wheat in the fall, and after harvesting it in July to sell a portion of the crop, to feed part of it to poultry and livestock on the farm, to use some in making flour for home consumption, and to keep the remainder for seeding future crops. The Secretary of Agriculture assessed a penalty against him under the Agricultural Adjustment Act of 1938 because he harvested about 12 acres more wheat than his allotment under the Act permitted. The Act was designed to regulate the volume of wheat moving in interstate and foreign commerce in order to avoid surpluses and shortages, and concomitant fluctuation in wheat prices, which had previously obtained. The Court said, in an opinion sustaining the application of the Act to Filburn's activity:

> "One of the primary purposes of the Act in question was to increase the market price of wheat and to that end to limit the volume thereof that could affect the market. It can hardly be denied that a factor of such volume and variability as home-consumed wheat would have a substantial influence on price and market conditions. This may arise because being in marketable condition such wheat overhangs the market and, if induced by rising prices, tends to flow into the market and check price increases. But if we assume that it is never marketed, it supplies a need of the man who grew it which would otherwise be reflected by purchases in the open market.
>
> Home-grown wheat in this sense competes with wheat in commerce."

Section 922(q) is a criminal statute that by its terms has nothing to do with "commerce" or any sort of economic enterprise, however broadly one might define those terms. Section 922(q) is not an essential part of a larger regulation of economic activity, in which the regulatory scheme could be undercut unless the intrastate activity were regulated. It cannot, therefore, be sustained under our cases upholding regulations of activities that arise out of or are connected with a commercial transaction, which viewed in the aggregate, substantially affects interstate commerce.

Second, § 922(q) contains no jurisdictional element which would ensure, through case-by-case inquiry, that the firearm possession in question affects interstate commerce. For example, in *United States v. Bass*, (1971), the Court interpreted former 18 U. S. C. § 1202(a), which made it a crime for a felon to "receiv[e], posses[s], or transpor[t] in commerce or affecting commerce . . . any firearm." 404 U. S., at 337. The Court interpreted the possession component of § 1202(a) to require an additional nexus to interstate commerce both because the statute was ambiguous and because "unless Congress conveys its purpose clearly, it will not be deemed to have significantly changed the federal-state balance." The *Bass* Court set aside the conviction because, although the Government had demonstrated that Bass had possessed a firearm, it had failed "to show the requisite nexus with interstate commerce." The Court thus interpreted the statute to reserve the constitutional question whether Congress could regulate, without more, the "mere possession" of firearms. Unlike the statute in *Bass*, § 922(q) has no express jurisdictional element which might limit its reach to a discrete set of firearm possessions that additionally have an explicit connection with or effect on interstate commerce.

Although as part of our independent evaluation of constitutionality under the Commerce Clause we of course consider legislative findings, and indeed even congressional committee findings, regarding effect on interstate commerce, the Government concedes that "[n]either the statute nor its legislative history contain[s] express congressional findings regarding the effects upon interstate commerce of gun possession in a school zone." Brief for United States 5-6. We agree with the Government that Congress normally is not required to make formal findings as to the substantial burdens that an activity has on interstate commerce. But to the extent that congressional findings would enable us to evaluate the legislative judgment that the activity in question substantially affected interstate commerce, even though no such substantial effect was visible to the naked eye, they are lacking here.

The Government argues that Congress has accumulated institutional expertise regarding the regulation of firearms through previous enactments. We agree, however, with the Fifth Circuit that importation of previous findings to justify § 922(q) is especially inappropriate here because the "prior federal enactments or Congressional findings [do not] speak to the subject matter of section 922(q) or its relationship to interstate commerce. Indeed, section 922(q) plows thoroughly new ground and represents a sharp break with the long-standing pattern of federal firearms legislation."

The Government's essential contention, *in fine*, is that we may determine here that § 922(q) is valid because possession of a firearm in a local school zone does indeed substantially affect interstate commerce. The Government argues that possession of a firearm in a school zone may result in violent crime and that violent crime can be expected to affect the functioning of the national economy in two ways. First, the costs of violent crime are substantial, and, through the mechanism of insurance, those costs are spread throughout the population. Second, violent crime reduces the willingness of individuals to travel to areas within the country that are perceived to be unsafe. The Government also argues that the presence of guns in schools poses a substantial threat to the educational process by threatening the learning environment. A handicapped educational process, in turn, will result in a less productive citizenry. That, in turn, would have an adverse effect on the Nation's economic well-being. As a result, the Government argues that Congress could rationally have concluded that § 922(q) substantially affects interstate commerce.

We pause to consider the implications of the Government's arguments. The Government admits, under its "costs of crime" reasoning, that Congress could regulate not only all violent crime, but all activities that might lead to violent crime, regardless of how tenuously they relate to interstate commerce. See Tr. of Oral Arg. 8-9. Similarly, under the Government's "national productivity" reasoning, Congress could regulate any activity that it found was related to the economic productivity of individual citizens: family law (including marriage, divorce, and child custody), for example. Under the theories that the Government presents in support of § 922(q), it is difficult to perceive any limitation on federal power, even in areas such as criminal law enforcement or education where States historically have been sovereign. Thus, if we were to accept the Government's arguments, we are hard pressed to posit any activity by an individual that Congress is without power to regulate.

Although JUSTICE BREYER argues that acceptance of the Government's rationales would not authorize a general federal police power, he is unable to identify any activity that the States may regulate but Congress may not. JUSTICE BREYER posits that there might be some limitations on Congress' commerce power, such as family law or certain aspects of education. These suggested limitations, when viewed in light of the dissent's expansive analysis, are devoid of substance.

JUSTICE BREYER focuses, for the most part, on the threat that firearm possession in and near schools poses to the educational process and the potential economic consequences flowing from that threat. Specifically, the dissent reasons that (1) gun-related violence is a serious problem; (2) that problem, in turn, has an adverse effect on classroom learning; and (3) that adverse effect on classroom learning, in turn, represents a substantial threat to trade and commerce. *Post*, at 623. This analysis would be equally applicable, if not more so, to subjects such as family law and direct regulation of education.

For instance, if Congress can, pursuant to its Commerce Clause power, regulate activities that adversely affect the learning environment, then, *a fortiori*, it also can regulate the educational process directly. Congress could determine that a school's curriculum has a "significant" effect on the extent of classroom learning. As a result, Congress could mandate a federal curriculum for local elementary and secondary schools because what is taught in local schools has a significant "effect on classroom learning," cf. *ibid.*, and that, in turn, has a substantial effect on interstate commerce.

JUSTICE BREYER rejects our reading of precedent and argues that "Congress . . . could rationally conclude that schools fall on the commercial side of the line." Again, JUSTICE BREYER'S rationale lacks any real limits because, depending on the level of generality, any activity can be looked upon as commercial. Under the dissent's rationale, Congress could just as easily look at child rearing as "fall[ing] on the commercial side of the line" because it provides a "valuable service—namely, to equip [children] with the skills they need to survive in life and, more specifically, in the workplace." We do not doubt that Congress has authority under the Commerce Clause to regulate numerous commercial activities that substantially affect interstate commerce and also affect the educational process. That authority, though broad, does not include the authority to regulate each and every aspect of local schools.

Admittedly, a determination whether an intrastate activity is commercial or noncommercial may in some cases result in legal uncertainty. But, so long as Congress' authority is limited to those powers enumerated in the Constitution, and so long as those enumerated powers are interpreted as having judicially enforceable outer limits, congressional legislation under the

Commerce Clause always will engender "legal uncertainty." *Post*, at 630. As Chief Justice Marshall stated in *McCulloch v. Maryland*, :

> "Th[e] [federal] government is acknowledged by all to be one of enumerated powers. The principle, that it can exercise only the powers granted to it ... is now universally admitted. But the question respecting the extent of the powers actually granted, is perpetually arising, and will probably continue to arise, as long as our system shall exist."

The Constitution mandates this uncertainty by withholding from Congress a plenary police power that would authorize enactment of every type of legislation. See Art. I, § 8. Congress has operated within this framework of legal uncertainty ever since this Court determined that it was the Judiciary's duty "to say what the law is." Any possible benefit from eliminating this "legal uncertainty" would be at the expense of the Constitution's system of enumerated powers.

In *Jones & Laughlin Steel*, 301 U. S., at 37, we held that the question of congressional power under the Commerce Clause "is necessarily one of degree." To the same effect is the concurring opinion of Justice Cardozo in *Schechter Poultry*:

> "There is a view of causation that would obliterate the distinction between what is national and what is local in the activities of commerce. Motion at the outer rim is communicated perceptibly, though minutely, to recording instruments at the center. A society such as ours 'is an elastic medium which transmits all tremors throughout its territory; the only question is of their size.'"

These are not precise formulations, and in the nature of things they cannot be. But we think they point the way to a correct decision of this case. The possession of a gun in a local school zone is in no sense an economic activity that might, through repetition elsewhere, substantially affect any sort of interstate commerce. Respondent was a local student at a local school; there is no indication that he had recently moved in interstate commerce, and there is no requirement that his possession of the firearm have any concrete tie to interstate commerce.

To uphold the Government's contentions here, we would have to pile inference upon inference in a manner that would bid fair to convert congressional authority under the Commerce Clause to a general police power of the sort retained by the States. Admittedly, some of our prior cases have taken long steps down that road, giving great deference to congressional action. See *supra*, at 556-558. The broad language in these opinions has suggested the possibility of additional expansion, but we decline here to proceed any further. To do so would require us to conclude that the Constitution's enumeration of powers does not presuppose something not enumerated, and that there never will be a distinction between what is truly national and what is truly local. This we are unwilling to do.

For the foregoing reasons the judgment of the Court of Appeals is

Affirmed.

Glossary

commerce clause: a section of the Constitution (Article 1, Section 8, Clause 3) that grants Congress the power to regulate interstate business and economics

de minimis: minor; insignificant; inconsequential

nexus: connection

respondent: the party against whom a lawsuit is brought by another party, the petitioner

sovereign: autonomous; independent

United States v. Virginia

DATE	CITATION
1996	518 U.S. 515
AUTHOR	**SIGNIFICANCE**
Ruth Bader Ginsburg	Held that the Virginia Military Institute's male-only admissions policy, even with its proposal for a comparable women's-only institute, was a violation of the Fourteenth Amendment's equal protection clause and therefore unconstitutional
VOTE	
7–1 (Clarence Thomas took no part in the case)	

Overview

The Virginia Military Institute (VMI), founded in 1839, was Virginia's only exclusively male undergraduate institution of higher learning and had enjoyed a long tradition as a training ground for military officers. The United States brought suit against VMI and the state of Virginia, arguing that the male-only admissions policy of the school was an unconstitutional violation of the Fourteenth Amendment's equal protection clause. Initially, the district court ruled in favor of VMI, but the Fourth Circuit Court of Appeals reversed the decision of the district court, finding VMI's admissions policy to be unconstitutional. In response, VMI proposed a solution: the creation of the Virginia Women's Institute for Leadership as a parallel program for women. After the district court affirmed the plan, the Fourth Circuit ruled that despite the difference in the prestige of the Women's Institute and VMI, the two would be "substantively comparable" in educational benefits. The United States disagreed and appealed to the Supreme Court, which ruled in *United States v. Virginia* that the VMI admissions policy was unconstitutional.

About the Author

Ruth Bader was born on March 15, 1933, in Brooklyn, New York. She graduated from Cornell University in 1954 and that year married Martin Ginsburg, a classmate. She enrolled at Harvard Law School, but after her husband found employment with a New York City law firm, she transferred to Columbia University, where she graduated tied for first in her class in 1959. That year she accepted a two-year clerkship for U.S. District Court Judge Edmund L. Palmieri in New York. After working on the Columbia Law School Project on International Procedure from 1961 to 1963, Ginsburg accepted a post as a law professor at Rutgers University, where she taught until 1972. She also served as volunteer counsel to the New Jersey chapter of the American Civil Liberties Union (ACLU). At the ACLU, Ginsburg litigated sex discrimination cases and cofounded the Women's Rights Project. Ironically, during her time at Rutgers she became pregnant with her son, James, and because she was not tenured, she concealed her pregnancy with oversized clothes. In 1972 Ginsburg accepted a position at Columbia University, the law school's first woman with the rank of full professor.

Justice Ruth Bader Ginsburg wrote the majority opinion.
(Library of Congress)

In 1980 President Jimmy Carter nominated Ginsburg as a justice on the U.S. Court of Appeals for the District of Columbia. Then, in 1993, President Bill Clinton nominated her to replace Justice Byron White on the U.S. Supreme Court. Ginsburg's reputation as a moderate on the U.S. Court of Appeals was helpful to her confirmation. In her years on the Supreme Court, her written decisions in numerous key cases made her a leading voice in the judicial branch for sex equality, thus expanding the rights of the American public, including both women and men.

Ginsburg was dogged in her determination to remain active on the Court in spite of numerous serious health problems, but ultimately those problems won out. She died on September 18, 2020, in Washington, D.C.

Explanation and Analysis of the Document

In this highly publicized 1996 case, Ginsburg, writing the majority opinion, had the opportunity to apply her knowledge and passion for gender equality to the postsecondary education context. This case involved a Fourteenth Amendment equal protection challenge by the United States to the Commonwealth of Virginia and the Virginia Military Institute (VMI), a public all-male military college. It was prompted by a complaint filed with the attorney general by a female high-school student seeking admission to VMI. After the district court ruled for VMI, the U.S. Court of Appeals for the Fourth Circuit reversed the decision and ordered the state of Virginia to remedy the constitutional violation. Although the district court then found the remedy to be constitutional, the case was appealed to the U.S. Supreme Court.

VMI is the only single-sex public institution of higher education in Virginia. Established in 1839, the school has the mission to create "citizen soldiers" and, as Ginsburg describes it, "to instill physical and mental discipline in its cadets and impart to them a strong moral code." Graduates of the school, Ginsburg writes, "leave VMI with heightened comprehension of their capacity to deal with duress and stress, and a large sense of accomplishment for completing the hazardous course." VMI argued that this type of education, based on the English public school model and once common to military instruction, and which Ginsburg describes as "comparable in intensity to Marine Corps boot camp," was not suitable to a coeducational environment in general and specifically to female cadets.

Ginsburg notes, though, that the attributes needed to succeed in such an environment are not limited to males: "Neither the goal of producing citizen-soldiers nor VMI's implementing methodology is inherently unsuitable to women. And the school's impressive record in producing leaders has made admission desirable to some women." Nonetheless, Ginsburg goes on, "Virginia has elected to preserve exclusively for men the advantages and opportunities a VMI education affords." She notes that at the district court level, experts testified that if VMI admitted women, "the VMI ROTC [Reserve Officers' Training Corps] experience would become a better training program from the perspective of the armed forces, because it would provide training in dealing with a mixed-gender army."

VMI argued that a single-sex, all-male public college (the only one in Virginia) provided diversity to an otherwise coeducational Virginia system and served an important governmental interest. Nevertheless, the state of Virginia proposed a parallel program for women that Ginsburg asserts was akin to the all-Black colleges proposed by segregated southern universities in the 1940s and early 1950s in response to equal protection challenges. Virginia proposed the creation of the Virginia Women's Institute for Leadership, to be located at Mary Baldwin College, a private liberal arts school for women. The district court, treating VMI deferentially, found that Virginia's proposal satisfied the Constitution's equal protection requirement. The Fourth Circuit affirmed, applying the test of whether VMI and Virginia Women's Institute for Leadership students would receive "substantively comparable" benefits. The U.S. Supreme Court, disagreeing with the Fourth Circuit, held that the appropriate standard when a sex-based classification is used is, as Ginsburg states, "an exceedingly persuasive justification."

Ginsburg emphasizes that substantively speaking, the parallel program did not compare with that of VMI. She notes that the program's curriculum was limited in comparison with VMI's, adding that "while VMI offers degrees in liberal arts, the sciences, and engineering, Mary Baldwin, at the time of trial, offered only bachelor of arts degrees." Further, Ginsburg points out that "Mary Baldwin's own endowment is about $19 million; VMI's is $131 million." In addition, Ginsburg notes that "the average combined SAT score of entrants at Mary Baldwin is about 100 points lower than the score for VMI freshmen." She quotes the dean of Mary Baldwin College, who testified that Mary Baldwin's faculty held "significantly fewer Ph.D.'s than the faculty at VMI," and that the faculty "receives significantly lower salaries."

Ginsburg argues that the proposal that female applicants to Virginia Women's Institute for Leadership would have a "substantively comparable" experience and degree was not supported by the numbers or by history. Virginia argued that VMI's all-male student body was an important source of diversity, for it gave the state's students an alternative type of institution to attend. Ginsburg, however, emphasizes that recent history undermines this argument, recalling that it was the standard until relatively recently to segregate women from male university students and that after decades of slow change, Virginia's most prestigious institution of higher education, the University of Virginia, introduced coeducation and in 1972 began to admit women on an equal basis with men.

Referring to precedent, Ginsburg cites *Reed v. Reed*, a 1971 case in which the Court struck down an Idaho law that said that males must be preferred to females where several equally entitled persons are claiming to administer a decedent's estate. She writes: "In 1971, for the first time in our Nation's history, this Court ruled in favor of a woman who complained that her State had denied her the equal protection of its laws." After *Reed*, she says, "the Court has repeatedly recognized that neither federal nor state government acts compatibly with the equal protection principle when a law or official policy denies to women, simply because they are women, full citizenship stature—equal opportunity to aspire, achieve, participate in and contribute to society based on their individual talents and capacities."

Ginsburg notes that the heightened level of scrutiny used for Court review of gender classifications did not equate for all purposes with "classifications based on race or national origin." The Court, in decisions after the *Reed* case, "has carefully inspected official action that closes a door or denies opportunity to women (or to men)." She notes too that the inherent differences between men and women "remain cause for celebration, but not for denigration of the members of either sex or for artificial constraints on an individual's opportunity." Exhibiting a nuanced approach, she concludes that the Court can use gender-based classifications to compensate women for economic inequities but not "to create or perpetuate the legal, social, and economic inferiority of women."

Ginsburg agrees with Virginia that "single-sex education affords pedagogical benefits to at least some students" and notes that those benefits are not contested in this case. She argues, though, that legal precedent requires that Virginia's reasons for using a gender-based classification not be accepted automatically but must be shown to be a "tenable justification" that describes "actual state purposes, not rationalizations for actions in fact differently grounded." She argues that on this important element of the law, Virginia's rationale for the benefits of single-sex education was not tenable and thus was discriminatory, in violation of the equal protection clause.

Ginsburg emphasizes that VMI "offers an educational opportunity no other Virginia institution provides, and the school's 'prestige'—associated with its success in developing 'citizen-soldiers'—is unequaled." But, she writes, "Virginia has closed this facility to its daughters and, instead, has devised for them a 'parallel program'" that fails to approach the standards set by VMI. Thus, she concludes, "Women seeking and fit for a VMI-quality education cannot be offered anything less, under the State's obligation to afford them genuinely equal protection."

Antonin Scalia wrote the sole dissenting opinion.

Impact

The Court's decision in *United States v. Virginia* gave added impetus to the drive to provide equal protection guarantees for men and women. The "skeptical scrutiny" standard placed government actors on notice that gender discrimination would be combatted in the court system. It is worth noting that the Court was not out to dismantle single-sex education in the United States, for numerous private single-sex school continued to exist. The Court's focus in *Virginia* was on public institutions and dubious claims of providing equal opportunity for men and women. In the wake of the Court's decision, proposals were made to turn VMI into a private institution, thus releasing it from the ruling in *Virginia*. The federal government responded by saying that it would withhold ROTC funds from any institution that took such a step. The point became moot when the VMI board voted 9–8 to admit women.

In 1997, one Beth Hogan became the first woman to enroll at VMI, joining 30 other women to be the first to enroll at the school. As of the fall of 2021, VMI had a total of 1,652 students. The student body consisted of 86 percent males and 14 percent females. In the 2022–23 class, enrollment in the freshman class was down in both categories, with 322 entering male freshmen and 53 entering female freshman. As of 2021, 602 women had graduated from VMI.

Questions for Further Study

1. What emotional issues might a jurist need to set aside in reaching a decision in this case?

2. On what basis did the government bring suit against Virginia and VMI?

3. Should VMI's very long tradition as a training ground for male warriors have played any role in the Court's decision?

4. On what basis did the Court find that VMI and the Women's Institute would provide unequal opportunities?

Further Reading

Books

Strum, Philippa. *Women in the Barracks: The VMI Case and Equal Rights*. Lawrence: University Press of Kansas, 2002.

Articles

Bowsher, David K. "Cracking the Code of *United States v. Virginia*." *Duke Law Journal* 48, no. 2 (November 1998): 305–39. https://www.jstor.org/stable/1373108.

Gleason, Christina. "*United States v. Virginia*: Skeptical Scrutiny and the Future of Gender Discrimination Law." *St. John's Law Review* 70, no. 4 (Fall 1996): 801–20. https://scholarship.law.stjohns.edu/cgi/viewcontent.cgi?article=1624&context=lawreview.

Rolando, Kevin N. "A Decade Later: *United States v. Virginia* and the Rise and Fall of 'Skeptical Scrutiny.'" *Roger Williams University Law Review* 12, no. 1 (Fall 2006): 182–228. https://core.ac.uk/download/pdf/56705654.pdf.

Stobaugh, Heather L. "The Aftermath of *United States v. Virginia*: Why Five Justices Are Pulling in the Reins on the 'Exceedingly Persuasive Justification.'" *SMU Law Review* 55, no. 4 (Fall 2002): 1755–79. https://www.academia.edu/22557034/Privilege_Gender_and_the_Fourteenth_Amendment_Reclaiming_Equal_Protection_of_the_Laws.

Stockel, Eric J. "Note, *United States v. Virginia*: Does Intermediate Scrutiny Still Exist?" *Touro Law Review* 13 (1996): 229ff.

—Commentary by Michael Chang and Michael J. O'Neal

UNITED STATES V. VIRGINIA

Document Text

JUSTICE GINSBURG delivered the opinion of the Court

... Founded in 1839, VMI is today the sole single-sex school among Virginia's 15 public institutions of higher learning. VMI's distinctive mission is to produce "citizen-soldiers," men prepared for leadership in civilian life and in military service. VMI pursues this mission through pervasive training of a kind not available anywhere else in Virginia. Assigning prime place to character development, VMI uses an "adversative method" modeled on English public schools and once characteristic of military instruction. VMI constantly endeavors to instill physical and mental discipline in its cadets and impart to them a strong moral code. The school's graduates leave VMI with heightened comprehension of their capacity to deal with duress and stress, and a large sense of accomplishment for completing the hazardous course....

Neither the goal of producing citizen-soldiers nor VMI's implementing methodology is inherently unsuitable to women. And the school's impressive record in producing leaders has made admission desirable to some women. Nevertheless, Virginia has elected to preserve exclusively for men the advantages and opportunities a VMI education affords....

VMI produces its "citizen-soldiers" through "an adversative, or doubting, model of education" which features "[p]hysical rigor, mental stress, absolute equality of treatment, absence of privacy, minute regulation of behavior, and indoctrination in desirable values." As one Commandant of Cadets described it, the adversative method "dissects the young student," and makes him aware of his "limits and capabilities," so that he knows "how far he can go with his anger, ... how much he can take under stress, ... exactly what he can do when he is physically exhausted."

VMI cadets live in spartan barracks where surveillance is constant and privacy nonexistent; they wear uniforms, eat together in the mess hall, and regularly participate in drills. Entering students are incessantly exposed to the rat line, "an extreme form of the adversative model," comparable in intensity to Marine Corps boot camp. Tormenting and punishing, the rat line bonds new cadets to their fellow sufferers and, when they have completed the 7-month experience, to their former tormentors....

In the two years preceding the lawsuit, the District Court noted, VMI had received inquiries from 347 women, but had responded to none of them. "[S]ome women, at least," the court said, "would want to attend the school if they had the opportunity." The court further recognized that, with recruitment, VMI could "achieve at least 10&percent; female enrollment"—a sufficient 'critical mass' to provide the female cadets with a positive educational experience." And it was also established that "some women are capable of all of the individual activities required of VMI cadets." In addition, experts agreed that if VMI admitted women, "the VMI ROTC experience would become a better training program from the perspective of the armed forces, because it would provide training in dealing with a mixed-gender army."

The District Court ruled in favor of VMI, however, and rejected the equal protection challenge pressed by the United States.... The District Court reasoned that education in "a single-gender environment, be it male or female," yields substantial benefits. VMI's school for men brought diversity to an otherwise coeducational Virginia system, and that diversity was "enhanced by VMI's unique method of instruction." If single-gender education for males ranks as an important governmental objective, it becomes obvious, the District Court concluded, that the only means of achieving the objective "is to exclude women from the all-male institution-VMI."...

The Court of Appeals for the Fourth Circuit disagreed and vacated the District Court's judgment. The appellate court held: "The Commonwealth of Virginia has not ... advanced any state policy by which it can justify its determination, under an announced policy of diversity, to afford VMI's unique type of program to men and not to women."...

The parties agreed that "some women can meet the physical standards now imposed on men," and the court was satisfied that "neither the goal of producing citizen soldiers nor VMI's implementing methodology is inherently unsuitable to women." The Court of Appeals, however, accepted the District Court's finding that "at least these three aspects of VMI's program—physical training, the absence of privacy, and the adversative approach—would be materially affected by coeducation." Remanding the case, the appeals court assigned to Virginia, in the first instance, responsibility for selecting a remedial course. The court suggested these options for the State: Admit women to VMI; establish parallel institutions or programs; or abandon state support, leaving VMI free to pursue its policies as a private institution....

In response to the Fourth Circuit's ruling, Virginia proposed a parallel program for women: Virginia Women's Institute for Leadership (VWIL). The 4-year, state-sponsored undergraduate program would be located at Mary Baldwin College, a private liberal arts school for women, and would be open, initially, to about 25 to 30 students. Although VWIL would share VMI's mission-to produce "citizen-soldiers"—the VWIL program would differ, as does Mary Baldwin College, from VMI in academic offerings, methods of education, and financial resources.

The average combined SAT score of entrants at Mary Baldwin is about 100 points lower than the score for VMI freshmen. Mary Baldwin's faculty holds "significantly fewer Ph.D.'s than the faculty at VMI," and receives significantly lower salaries, While VMI offers degrees in liberal arts, the sciences, and engineering, Mary Baldwin, at the time of trial, offered only bachelor of arts degrees. A VWIL student seeking to earn an engineering degree could gain one, without public support, by attending Washington University in St. Louis, Missouri, for two years, paying the required private tuition....

Virginia represented that it will provide equal financial support for in-state VWIL students and VMI cadets, and the VMI Foundation agreed to supply a $5.4625 million endowment for the VWIL program. Mary Baldwin's own endowment is about $19 million; VMI's is $131 million. Mary Baldwin will add $35 million to its endowment based on future commitments; VMI will add $220 million. The VMI Alumni Association has developed a network of employers interested in hiring VMI graduates. The Association has agreed to open its network to VWIL graduates, but those graduates will not have the advantage afforded by a VMI degree....

The court recognized that, as it analyzed the case, means merged into end, and the merger risked "bypass[ing] any equal protection scrutiny." The court therefore added another inquiry, a decisive test it called "substantive comparability." The key question, the court said, was whether men at VMI and women at VWIL would obtain "substantively comparable benefits at their institution or through other means offered by the [S]tate." Although the appeals court recognized that the VWIL degree "lacks the historical benefit and prestige" of a VMI degree, it nevertheless found the educational opportunities at the two schools "sufficiently comparable."...

The Fourth Circuit denied rehearing en banc.... Judge Motz agreed with Judge Phillips that Virginia had not shown an "&thin'exceedingly persuasive justification'" for the disparate opportunities the State supported....

We note, once again, the core instruction of this Court's pathmarking decisions in *J. E. B. v. Alabama ex rel. T. B.*, and *Mississippi Univ. for Women*: Parties who seek to defend gender-based government action must demonstrate an "exceedingly persuasive justification" for that action....

In 1971, for the first time in our Nation's history, this Court ruled in favor of a woman who complained that her State had denied her the equal protection of its laws. Since *Reed*, the Court has repeatedly recognized that neither federal nor state government acts compatibly with the equal protection principle when a law or official policy denies to women, simply because they are women, full citizenship stature—equal opportunity to aspire, achieve, participate in and contribute to society based on their individual talents and capacities.

Without equating gender classifications, for all purposes, to classifications based on race or national origin, the Court, in post-*Reed* decisions, has carefully inspected official action that closes a door or denies opportunity to women (or to men). To summarize the Court's current directions for cases of official classification based on gender: Focusing on the differential treatment or denial of opportunity for which relief is sought, the reviewing court must determine whether the proffered justification is "exceedingly persuasive." The burden of justification is demanding and it rests entirely on the State. The State must show "at least that the [challenged] classification serves 'important governmental objectives and that the discriminatory means employed' are 'substantially related to the achievement of those objectives.'" The justification must be genuine, not hypothesized or invented post hoc in response to litigation. And it must not rely on overbroad generalizations about the different talents, capacities, or preferences of males and females.

The heightened review standard our precedent establishes does not make sex a proscribed classification. Supposed "inherent differences" are no longer accepted as a ground for race or national origin classifications. Physical differences between men and women, however, are enduring: "[T]he two sexes are not fungible; a community made up exclusively of one [sex] is different from a community composed of both."

"Inherent differences" between men and women, we have come to appreciate, remain cause for celebration, but not for denigration of the members of either sex or for artificial constraints on an individual's opportunity. Sex classifications may be used to compensate women "for particular economic disabilities [they have] suffered," to "promot[e] equal employment opportunity," to advance full development of the talent and capacities of our Nation's people. But such classifications may not be used, as they once were, to create or perpetuate the legal, social, and economic inferiority of women.

Measuring the record in this case against the review standard just described, we conclude that Virginia has shown no "exceedingly persuasive justification" for excluding all women from the citizen-soldier training afforded by VMI. . . .

Single-sex education affords pedagogical benefits to at least some students, Virginia emphasizes, and that reality is uncontested in this litigation. Similarly, it is not disputed that diversity among public educational institutions can serve the public good. But Virginia has not shown that VMI was established, or has been maintained, with a view to diversifying, by its categorical exclusion of women, educational opportunities within the State. In cases of this genre, our precedent instructs that "benign" justifications proffered in defense of categorical exclusions will not be accepted automatically; a tenable justification must describe actual state purposes, not rationalizations for actions in fact differently grounded. . . .

Ultimately, in 1970, "the most prestigious institution of higher education in Virginia," the University of Virginia, introduced coeducation and, in 1972, began to admit women on an equal basis with men. A three-judge Federal District Court confirmed: "Virginia may not now deny to women, on the basis of sex, educational opportunities at the Charlottesville campus that are not afforded in other institutions operated by the [S]tate." . . .

VMI, too, offers an educational opportunity no other Virginia institution provides, and the school's "prestige"—associated with its success in developing "citizen-soldiers"—is unequaled. Virginia has closed this facility to its daughters and, instead, has devised for them a "parallel program," with a faculty less impressively credentialed and less well paid, more limited course offerings, fewer opportunities for military training and for scientific specialization. VMI, beyond question, "possesses to a far greater degree" than the VWIL program "those qualities which are incapable of objective measurement but which make for greatness in a . . . school," including "position and influence of the alumni, standing in the community, traditions and prestige." Women seeking and fit for a VMI-quality education cannot be offered anything less, under the State's obligation to afford them genuinely equal protection.

Glossary

en banc: literally, "on the bench"; refers to a case heard with the judges sitting together

endowment: the reserve of money and investments used to help fund an institution such as a college or university

fungible: alike; interchangeable

proscribed: prohibited

remanding: sending back to a lower court for further consideration

spartan: barren, primitive

CLINTON V. JONES

DATE	CITATION
1997	520 U.S. 681

AUTHOR
John Paul Stevens

SIGNIFICANCE
Held that the president did not hold executive immunity to civil litigation for actions prior to his presidency.

VOTE
9-0

Overview

While serving as governor of Arkansas in 1991, President Bill Clinton was accused of making unwanted sexual advances toward Paula Corbin Jones, which she claimed she refused. Jones claimed that she was punished for refusing the governor's advances and that her name was slandered further when a story ran in the *American Spectator* that outlined her as the initiator of the sexual request. She sued in the U.S. District Court for the Eastern District of Arkansas in May 1994, but as a sitting president, Bill Clinton's defense team argued that he was immune from litigation under the doctrine of presidential immunity. The judge agreed that as long as he was president, he was exempt from litigation. The case was appealed to the Eighth Circuit Court of Appeals who ruled in favor of Jones, contending that a president "is subject to the same laws that apply to all members of our society." The case then proceeded to the Supreme Court in 1997, where Clinton's attorneys once again argued that his role as a sitting president granted him immunity from legal prosecution. The Court ruled against Clinton in a unanimous vote.

Context

The case came at a time when Bill Clinton had won the presidential election handily over George H.W. Bush, but his party had lost control of the House of Representatives in the 1994 midterm election by dropping fifty-four seats to the Republicans. The Senate also had a Republican majority. The popularity of Bill Clinton with voters in the 1992 election made him a prime target for Republican political leaders, such as Speaker of the House Newt Gingrich, and any legal distraction would be seen as an opportunity to derail the president's agenda even further. At the Eighth Circuit Court of Appeals hearing, Bill Clinton's attorneys argued that allowing the case to move forward would serve as a distraction for the president, which was made even more significant with both houses in Congress being controlled by the opposition party. Despite these arguments, the Eighth Circuit Court ruled 2-1 in favor of Jones, allowing the case to move forward in 1996—an election year. Fearing that the case would become an opportunity for Clinton's Republican opponent, Senator Bob Dole, to seize on Clinton's moral ambiguity, the president appealed to the Supreme Court to hear the case and stay the litigation until after his presidency. The Court agreed that clarification was needed regard-

eventually lead to his impeachment by the House in 1998. The importance of establishing a precedent on a president's expectation of immunity was viewed as increasingly important for the judicial branch.

About the Author

Justice John Paul Stevens was born in Chicago, Illinois, in 1920 to a wealthy family. He was accused of embezzlement during the Great Depression, but the charges were dropped by the Illinois Supreme Court due to poor prosecution. A graduate of the University of Chicago in 1941 with a major in English, Stevens elected to join the U.S. Navy at the onset of World War II and served as an intelligence officer from 1942 to 1945. During his time in the service, he was awarded the Bronze Star for his codebreaking work that led to the downing of Japanese Admiral Isoroku Yamamoto in 1943 over the Pacific. After the conclusion of the war, Stevens returned to college to pursue a graduate degree in English but was convinced to pursue a law degree by his brother.

Justice John Paul Stevens wrote the majority opinion.
(Steve Petteway)

ing the exact nature of the presidential expectation of immunity and, as a result, granted a hearing for after the November election.

As with any Supreme Court case, this case was not heard in a social or political vacuum. America's 104th Congress put forth a "Contract with America" that called for greater transparency in Washington, particularly that "all laws that apply to the rest of the country also apply to Congress." Clinton's civil litigation and subsequent demand for presidential immunity flew straight in the face of this political promise by the Republicans, a majority of whom were elected in part because of this platform. This made the political quagmire associated with this case increasingly apparent to President Clinton. The Supreme Court also understood the significance of this case in light of the actions of previous presidents, particularly Richard Nixon, who had used his position of executive power to violate federal election laws in the Watergate scandal only two decades earlier. Further complicating matters, following Clinton's election victory in 1996, rumors began to circulate that the president had been involved sexually with a woman named Monica Lewinsky—a witness in *Jones v. Clinton*—since 1995, an allegation that would

Stevens's first brush with the Supreme Court came as a law clerk, from 1947 to 1948, for Justice Wiley Rutledge, who was the last of Franklin Roosevelt's Supreme Court appointees and supported a broad interpretation of the First Amendment and civil liberties statutes. This perhaps influenced and shaped Stevens's judicial interpretation of cases despite his conservative political leanings. By the end of his tenure with the Court in 2010, Stevens was seen as a liberal moderate on the Court despite his being registered as a Republican.

Stevens was a noted legal scholar, earning top marks in Northwestern University's School of Law, but what made him stand out was a dedication to the equal application of the law. In 1969, he was appointed as the special prosecutor for the Greenberg Commission that was to look into allegations of corruption at the Illinois Supreme Court. While many viewed the commission as a publicity stunt that would amount to nothing, Stevens set forth with a prosecutorial zeal that ultimately led to the removal of chief justice Roy Solfisburg. This gained him national fame, particularly from President Richard Nixon, who appointed him to the U.S. Seventh Circuit Court of Appeals in 1970. Five years later, Gerald Ford nominated him to replace William O. Douglas on the Supreme Court, where he served as an associate justice until 2010.

Stevens was noted not only for his longevity on the Court (he served thirty-four and a half years) but also his willingness to change and adapt his views as the needs of the nation's judicial system required. As an early career justice on the Court, Stevens had disapproved of the concept of affirmative action, but by the end of his career, he acknowledged the merits of such an ideology and more openly embraced it in defiance of his political leanings. This earned him a great deal of praise from former presidents and jurists. Stevens was often quoted as saying he preferred not to discuss politics given his role as a jurist on the Supreme Court, which was unsurprising given his desire to read writs of certiorari and draft his opinions initially on his own to help shape his understanding of the legal doctrine he was helping to develop.

Explanation and Analysis of the Document

Stevens opens with a recounting of the facts of the case, reaffirming that the actions in question occurred prior to the assumption of Clinton's role as president. This was an important distinction to the Court because it served to place the extent of the executive immunity in context. Had the infractions occurred during his time as president and as a part of his official role and capacities, it would have potentially changed the narrative of the Court's opinion. This was based on the Court's previous ruling in *Nixon v. Fitzgerald* (1982), in which a former civilian analyst had brought a civil suit against Nixon when he brought reports of inefficiencies regarding defense contracts to the public's attention. The Court held that a president was granted immunity for actions "predicated on his official acts," but as Stevens notes in the ruling, this rule wouldn't apply since Clinton was only the governor at the time of the events in question and therefore not subject to the *Nixon* criteria.

Steven's opinion goes on to discuss the judge's decision to stay the hearing until after the president's term expires, basing it in part on the delay from Jones until two days before the expiration of the statute of limitations for civil damages. The judge, he points out, contended that the effects of the civil trial on the president's ability to conduct his duties and the seeming lack of urgency in Jones's pursuit of a case pointed to a preference that the case be stayed until after the president's term in office expired. The judge would allow the pre-trial motions and discovery to occur so as to keep the statute of limitations from expiring and expedite the case when the time came, but both the Circuit Court and the Supreme Court considered this to be granting a temporary immunity that required reversal on appeal.

Stevens articulates the importance of this case to helping decide the exact extent of the presidential immunity powers. As noted, in *Nixon v. Fitzgerald*, President Nixon's actions were executed as a part of his duties as president, thereby granting him a sovereign protection akin to that of diplomatic immunity for ambassadors operating on foreign soil. This is an understood practice for the executive branch to prevent civil litigation from tying a president's hands in the running of the nation by individuals or even legislative entities such as political action committees and lawmakers. In this situation, however, Stevens points out that there existed no real precedent for a president facing civil litigation for actions that occurred before they were president. In the cases of Teddy Roosevelt and Harry Truman, their cases were dismissed before their inauguration, rendering any decision moot, and in regards to President John Kennedy's civil litigation involving a vehicular accident, the case was settled out of court, granting no opportunity for a judicial precedent to be established.

Stevens next addresses Clinton's legal team's effort to use historical antecedents regarding a president's protection from legal action. In the case against Aaron Burr, Chief Justice John Marshall issued a subpoena for Thomas Jefferson to bring all relevant documents and testimony to the court, which Jefferson opposed on the basis that this action would allow the judicial branch to command the executive branch, thus compromising the separation and balance of powers laid out by the Constitution. Much like the *Nixon* argument, these were related to actions undertaken while the individual held federal office and therefore would be subject to different rules and expectations from those in the Clinton case. Stevens argues that in fact, the historical arguments of those at the Constitutional Convention seem to give more guidance by referencing James Wilson's assessment that "not a single privilege is annexed to his character; far from being above the laws, he is amenable to them in his private character." Stevens essentially concurs with the respondent's argument that the law protects him from civil prosecution for his official acts but not for those committed separate from the office.

This leads Stevens into the second contention of Clinton's legal team: that the case must be suspended until the completion of the president's term. While Stevens acknowledges the difficulty of the role of president, citing the struggles given by President Lyndon Baines Johnson, Stevens is quick to address the constitutional question at hand: does the requirement that the president defend himself in civil litigation while president merit a breach of the judicial doctrine of the separation of powers? For Stevens and the Supreme Court, the answer is an unequivocal "no" simply because the judicial branch is not asserting itself into an executive branch role. The Court is merely allowing a judicial process to continue, not asserting itself into executing a presidential action or role that would interfere with the president's duties. The petitioner's counterargument that the case would divert the president's time holds neither merit nor substance given that no evidence of such a diversion could be found in 200 years of case precedent, and in fact, as evidenced by the Burr treason case, even a president being called to testify is considered within the expectations of the office.

The Court therefore rules to uphold the decision by the Eighth Circuit Court of Appeals and allow Paula Jones's case to proceed against Bill Clinton.

Impact

This case, much like the Nixon cases (*United States v. Nixon* and *Nixon v. Fitzgerald*), served to define the limits of a president's power and indemnity while in office. Whereas in both of Nixon's cases, the actions occurred while he held office, *Clinton v. Jones* established the understanding that a president's actions prior to being president were still subject to civil litigation and offered no shield from the position of his office. As America welcomed and embraced the "Contract with America" promise of Newt Gingrich and his Republican allies to clean up Washington, D.C., this ruling helped solidify that no politician would be above the reaches of the law.

The case returned to district court, where Monica Lewinsky, as a witness in the *Jones v. Clinton* case, denied having sexual relations with Bill Clinton, only to have a taped conversation turned over to Kenneth Starr, a special prosecutor for the Clinton case, that told a very different story. Clinton was found in contempt of the district court for perjury, fined $90,000, and sent before the Arkansas Supreme Court's Committee on Professional Conduct for review of his licensure as an attorney. In the end, Clinton would surrender his license to argue before the U.S. Supreme Court as well as accept a five-year suspension of his license in exchange for the end of a special investigation. As a result of the evidence brought forth in the case, Clinton would be impeached by the House of Representatives and narrowly avoided removal from office following a party-line vote.

Questions for Further Study

1. How did the *Clinton v. Jones* case differ from the *United States v. Nixon* case regarding professional misconduct of the president? In what ways were they similar? How might the similarities have influenced the public's view of the legal proceedings?

2. The idea that the president is above the law has been depicted in many Hollywood movies and novels, but as evidenced by Justice Stevens's opinion, this is hardly the case. What political impacts would a president's immunity have regarding the nature of their decision making?

3. The Founding Fathers emphasized the balance and separation of powers. In the *Marbury v. Madison* case, the judicial branch asserted itself over executive action that violated the nature of the Constitution in order to ensure that balance would remain. Why might opponents of the Court's rulings in *Marbury* and in *Clinton* have felt that this could impede the job of the president and open the door to an unmovable governmental quagmire?

Further Reading

Books

Posner, Richard A. *An Affair of State: The Investigation, Impeachment, and Trial of President Clinton.* Cambridge, MA: Harvard University Press, 1999.

Toobin, Jeffrey. *A Vast Conspiracy: The Real Story of the Sex Scandal That Nearly Brought Down a President.* New York: Penguin Books, 2020.

Websites

"The Impeachment of Bill Clinton." Bill of Rights Institute. Accessed March 2, 2023. https://billofrightsinstitute.org/e-lessons/the-impeachment-of-bill-clinton.

Riley, Russell. "The Clinton Impeachment and Its Fallout." Miller Center, University of Virginia, October 10, 2019. https://millercenter.org/the-presidency/impeachment/clinton-impeachment-and-its-fallout.

"Special Report: Jones v. Clinton Time Line." *Washington Post*, 1998. Accessed March 2, 2023. https://www.washingtonpost.com/wp-srv/politics/special/pjones/timeline.htm.

—Commentary by Ryan Fontanella

CLINTON V. JONES

Document Text

JUSTICE STEVENS delivered the opinion of the Court

This case raises a constitutional and a prudential question concerning the Office of the President of the United States. Respondent, a private citizen, seeks to recover damages from the current occupant of that office based on actions allegedly taken before his term began. The President submits that in all but the most exceptional cases the Constitution requires federal courts to defer such litigation until his term ends and that, in any event, respect for the office warrants such a stay. Despite the force of the arguments supporting the President's submissions, we conclude that they must be rejected.

I

Petitioner, William Jefferson Clinton, was elected to the Presidency in 1992, and reelected in 1996. His term of office expires on January 20, 2001. In 1991 he was the Governor of the State of Arkansas. Respondent, Paula Corbin Jones, is a resident of California. In 1991 she lived in Arkansas, and was an employee of the Arkansas Industrial Development Commission.

On May 6, 1994, she commenced this action in the United States District Court for the Eastern District of Arkansas by filing a complaint naming petitioner and Danny Ferguson, a former Arkansas State Police officer, as defendants. The complaint alleges two federal claims, and two state-law claims over which the federal court has jurisdiction because of the diverse citizenship of the parties. As the case comes to us, we are required to assume the truth of the detailed but as yet untested-factual allegations in the complaint.

Those allegations principally describe events that are said to have occurred on the afternoon of May 8, 1991, during an official conference held at the Excelsior Hotel in Little Rock, Arkansas. The Governor delivered a speech at the conference; respondent—working as a state employee—staffed the registration desk. She alleges that Ferguson persuaded her to leave her desk and to visit the Governor in a business suite at the hotel, where he made "abhorrent" sexual advances that she vehemently rejected. She further claims that her superiors at work subsequently dealt with her in a hostile and rude manner, and changed her duties to punish her for rejecting those advances. Finally, she alleges that after petitioner was elected President, Ferguson defamed her by making a statement to a reporter that implied she had accepted petitioner's alleged overtures, and that various persons authorized to speak for the President publicly branded her a liar by denying that the incident had occurred.

Respondent seeks actual damages of $75,000 and punitive damages of $100,000. Her complaint contains four counts. The first charges that petitioner, acting under color of state law, deprived her of rights protected by the Constitution, in violation of Rev. Stat. § 1979, 42 U. S. C. § 1983. The second charges that petitioner and Ferguson engaged in a conspiracy to violate her federal rights, also actionable under federal law. See Rev. Stat. § 1980, 42 U. S. C. § 1985. The third is a state common-law claim for intentional infliction of emotional distress, grounded primarily on the incident at the hotel. The fourth count, also based on state law, is for defamation, embracing both the comments allegedly made to the press by Ferguson and the statements of petitioner's agents. Inasmuch as the legal sufficiency of the claims has not yet been challenged, we assume, without deciding, that each of the four counts states a cause of action as a matter of law. With the exception of the last charge, which arguably may involve conduct within the outer perimeter of the President's official responsibilities, it is perfectly clear that the alleged misconduct of petitioner was unrelated to any of his official duties as President of the United States and, indeed, occurred before he was elected to that office.

II

In response to the complaint, petitioner promptly advised the District Court that he intended to file a motion to dismiss on grounds of Presidential immunity, and requested the court to defer all other pleadings and motions until after the immunity issue was resolved. Relying on our cases holding that immunity questions should be decided at the earliest possible stage of the litigation, 858 F. Supp. 902, 905 (ED Ark. 1994), our recognition of the "'singular importance of the President's duties,'" *id.*, at 904 (quoting *Nixon* v. *Fitzgerald,* 457 U. S. 731, 751 (1982)), and the fact that the question did not require any analysis of the allegations of the complaint, 858 F. Supp., at 905, the court granted the request. Petitioner thereupon filed a motion "to dismiss . . . without prejudice and to toll any statutes of limitation [that may be applicable] until he is no longer President, at which time the plaintiff may refile the instant suit." Record, Doc. No. 17. Extensive submissions were made to the District Court by the parties and the Department of Justice.

The District Judge denied the motion to dismiss on immunity grounds and ruled that discovery in the case could go forward, but ordered any trial stayed until the end of petitioner's Presidency. 869 F. Supp. 690 (ED Ark. 1994). Although she recognized that a "thin majority" in *Nixon* v. *Fitzgerald,* 457 U. S. 731 (1982), had held that "the President has absolute immunity from civil damage actions arising out of the execution of official duties of office," she was not convinced that "a President has absolute immunity from civil causes of action arising prior to assuming the office." She was, however, persuaded by some of the reasoning in our opinion in *Fitzgerald* that deferring the trial if one were required would be appropriate.7 869 F. Supp., at 699-700. Relying in part on the fact that respondent had failed to bring her complaint until two days before the 3-year period of limitations expired, she concluded that the public interest in avoiding litigation that might hamper the President in conducting the duties of his office outweighed any demonstrated need for an immediate trial. *Id.,* at 698-699.

Both parties appealed. A divided panel of the Court of Appeals affirmed the denial of the motion to dismiss, but because it regarded the order postponing the trial until the President leaves office as the "functional equivalent" of a grant of temporary immunity, it reversed that order. 72 F.3d 1354, 1361, n. 9, 1363 (CA8 1996). Writing for the majority, Judge Bowman explained that "the President, like all other government officials, is subject to the same laws that apply to all other members of our society," *id.*, at 1358, that he could find no "case in which any public official ever has been granted any immunity from suit for his unofficial acts," *ibid.*, and that the rationale for official immunity "is inapposite where only personal, private conduct by a President is at issue," *id.*, at 1360. The majority specifically rejected the argument that, unless immunity is available, the threat of judicial interference with the Executive Branch through scheduling orders, potential contempt citations, and sanctions would violate separation-of-powers principles. Judge Bowman suggested that "judicial case management sensitive to the burdens of the presidency and the demands of the President's schedule" would avoid the perceived danger. *Id.*, at 1361.

In dissent, Judge Ross submitted that even though the holding in *Fitzgerald* involved official acts, the logic of the opinion, which "placed primary reliance on the prospect that the President's discharge of his constitutional powers and duties would be impaired if he were subject to suits for damages," applies with equal force to this case. 72 F. 3d, at 1367. In his view, "unless exigent circumstances can be shown," all private actions for damages against a sitting President must be stayed until the completion of his term. *Ibid.* In this case, Judge Ross saw no reason why the stay would prevent respondent from ultimately obtaining an adjudication of her claims.

In response to the dissent, Judge Beam wrote a separate concurrence. He suggested that a prolonged delay may well create a significant risk of irreparable harm to respondent because of an unforeseeable loss of evidence or the possible death of a party. *Id.,* at 1363-1364. Moreover, he argued that in civil rights cases brought under § 1983 there is a "public interest in an ordinary citizen's timely vindication of . . . her most fundamental right against alleged abuse of power by government officials." *Id.,* at 1365. In his view, the dissent's concern about judicial interference with the functioning of the Presidency was "greatly overstated." *Ibid.* Neither the involvement of prior Presidents in litigation, either as parties or as witnesses, nor the character of this "relatively uncomplicated civil litigation," indicated that the threat was serious. *Id.,* at 1365-1366. Finally, he saw "no basis for staying discovery or trial of the claims against Trooper Ferguson." *Id.,* at 1366.

III

The President, represented by private counsel, filed a petition for certiorari. The Acting Solicitor General, representing the United States, supported the petition, arguing that the decision of the Court of Appeals was "fundamentally mistaken" and created "serious risks for the institution of the Presidency." In her brief in opposition to certiorari, respondent argued that this "one-of-a-kind case is singularly inappropriate" for the exercise of our certiorari jurisdiction because it did not create any conflict among the Courts of Appeals, it "does not pose any conceivable threat to the functioning of the Executive Branch," and there is no precedent supporting the President's position.

While our decision to grant the petition, 518 U. S. 1016 (1996), expressed no judgment concerning the merits of the case, it does reflect our appraisal of its importance. The representations made on behalf of the Executive Branch as to the potential impact of the precedent established by the Court of Appeals merit our respectful and deliberate consideration.

It is true that we have often stressed the importance of avoiding the premature adjudication of constitutional questions. That doctrine of avoidance, however, is applicable to the entire Federal Judiciary, not just to this Court, cf. *Arizonans for Official English* v. *Arizona, ante,* p. 43, and comes into play after the court has acquired jurisdiction of a case. It does not dictate a discretionary denial of every certiorari petition raising a novel constitutional question. It does, however, make it appropriate to identify two important constitutional issues not encompassed within the questions presented by the petition for certiorari that we need not address today.

First, because the claim of immunity is asserted in a federal court and relies heavily on the doctrine of separation of powers that restrains each of the three branches of the Federal Government from encroaching on the domain of the other two, see, *e. g., Buckley* v. *Valeo,* 424 U. S. 1, 122 *(1976) (per curiam),* it is not necessary to consider or decide whether a comparable claim might succeed in a state tribunal. If this case were being heard in a state forum, instead of advancing a separation-of-powers argument, petitioner would presumably rely on federalism and comity concerns, as well as the interest in protecting federal officials from possible local prejudice that underlies the authority to remove certain cases brought against federal officers from a state to a federal court, see 28 U. S. C. § 1442(a); *Mesa* v. *California,* 489 U. S. 121, 125-126 (1989). Whether those concerns would present a more compelling case for immunity is a question that is not before us.

Second, our decision rejecting the immunity claim and allowing the case to proceed does not require us to confront the question whether a court may compel the attendance of the President at any specific time or place. We assume that the testimony of the President, both for discovery and for use at trial, may be taken at the White House at a time that will accommodate his busy schedule, and that, if a trial is held, there would be no necessity for the President to attend in person, though he could elect to do SO.

IV

Petitioner's principal submission—that "in all but the most exceptional cases," Brief for Petitioner i, the Constitution affords the President temporary immunity from civil damages litigation arising out of events that occurred before he took office—cannot be sustained on the basis of precedent.

Only three sitting Presidents have been defendants in civil litigation involving their actions prior to taking office. Complaints against Theodore Roosevelt and Harry Truman had been dismissed before they took office; the dismissals were affirmed after their respective inaugurations. Two companion cases arising out of an automobile accident were filed against John F. Kennedy in 1960 during the Presidential campaign. After taking office, he unsuccessfully argued that his status as Commander in Chief gave him a right to a stay under the Soldiers' and Sailors' Civil Relief Act of 1940, 50 U. S. C. App. §§ 501-525. The motion for a stay was denied by the District Court, and the matter was settled out of court. Thus, none of those cases sheds any light on the constitutional issue before us.

The principal rationale for affording certain public servants immunity from suits for money damages arising out of their official acts is inapplicable to unofficial conduct. In cases involving prosecutors, legislators, and judges we have repeatedly explained that the immunity serves the public interest in enabling such officials to perform their designated functions effectively without fear that a particular decision may give rise to personal liability. We explained in *Ferri* v. *Ackerman,* 444 U. S. 193 (1979):

"As public servants, the prosecutor and the judge represent the interest of society as a whole. The conduct of their official duties may adversely affect a wide variety of different individuals, each of whom may be a potential source of future controversy. The societal interest in providing such public officials with the maximum ability to deal fearlessly and impartially with the public at large has long been recognized as an acceptable justification for official immunity. The point of immunity for such officials is to forestall an atmosphere of intimidation that would conflict with their resolve to perform their designated functions in a principled fashion." *Id.,* at 202-204.

That rationale provided the principal basis for our holding that a former President of the United States was "entitled to absolute immunity from damages liability predicated on his official acts," *Fitzgerald,* 457 U. S., at 749. See *id.,* at 752 (citing *Ferri* v. *Ackerman).* Our central concern was to avoid rendering the President "unduly cautious in the discharge of his official duties." 457 U. S., at 752, n. 32.

This reasoning provides no support for an immunity for *unofficial* conduct. As we explained in *Fitzgerald,* "the sphere of protected action must be related closely to the immunity's justifying purposes." *Id.,* at 755. Because of the President's broad responsibilities, we recognized in that case an immunity from damages claims arising out of official acts extending to the "outer perimeter of his authority." *Id.,* at 757. But we have never suggested that the President, or any other official, has an immunity that extends beyond the scope of any action taken in an official capacity. See *id.,* at 759 (Burger, C. J., concurring) (noting that "a President, like Members of Congress, judges, prosecutors, or congressional aides—all having absolute immunity—are not immune for acts outside official duties"); see also *id.,* at 761, n. 4.

Moreover, when defining the scope of an immunity for acts clearly taken *within* an official capacity, we have applied a functional approach. "Frequently our decisions have held that an official's absolute immunity should extend only to acts in performance of particular functions of his office." *Id.,* at 755. Hence, for example, a judge's absolute immunity does not extend to actions performed in a purely administrative capacity. See *Forrester* v. *White,* 484 U. S. 219, 229-230 (1988). As our opinions have made clear, immunities are grounded in "the nature of the function performed, not the identity of the actor who performed it." *Id.,* at 229.

Petitioner's effort to construct an immunity from suit for unofficial acts grounded purely in the identity of his office is unsupported by precedent.

V

We are also unpersuaded by the evidence from the historical record to which petitioner has called our attention. He points to a comment by Thomas Jefferson protesting the subpoena *duces tecum* Chief Justice Marshall directed to him in the Burr trial, a statement in the diaries kept by Senator William Maclay of the first Senate debates, in which then Vice President John Adams and Senator Oliver Ellsworth are recorded as having said that "the President personally [is] not ... subject to any process whatever," lest it be "put . . . in the power of a common Justice to exercise any Authority over him and Stop the Whole Machine of Government," and to a quotation from Justice Story's Commentaries on the Constitution. None of these sources sheds much light on the question at hand.

Respondent, in turn, has called our attention to conflicting historical evidence. Speaking in favor of the Constitution's adoption at the Pennsylvania Convention, James Wilson, who had participated in the Philadelphia Convention at which the document was drafted—explained that, although the President "is placed [on] high," "not a single privilege is annexed to his character; far from being above the laws, he is amenable to them in his private character as a citizen, and in his public character by impeachment." 2 J. Elliot, Debates on the Federal Constitution 480 (2d ed. 1863) (emphasis deleted). This description is consistent with both the doctrine of Presidential immunity as set forth in *Fitzgerald* and rejection of the immunity claim in this case. With respect to acts taken in his "public character"—that is, official acts—the President may be disciplined principally by impeachment, not by private lawsuits for damages. But he is otherwise subject to the laws for his purely private acts.

In the end, as applied to the particular question before us, we reach the same conclusion about these historical materials that Justice Jackson described when confronted with an issue concerning the dimensions of the President's power.

Maclay went on to point out in his diary that he virulently disagreed with them, concluding that his opponents' view "[s]hows clearly how amazingly fond of the old leven many People are." Diary of Maclay 168.

Finally, Justice Story's comments in his constitutional law treatise provide no substantial support for petitioner's position. Story wrote that because the President's "incidental powers" must include "the power to perform [his duties], without any obstruction," he "cannot, therefore, be liable to arrest, imprisonment, or detention, while he is in the discharge of the duties of his office; *and for this purpose* his person must be deemed, in civil cases at least, to possess an official inviolability." 3 Story § 1563, at 418-419 (emphasis added). Story said only that *"an* official inviolability," *ibid.* (emphasis added), was necessary to preserve the President's ability to perform the functions of the office; he did not specify the dimensions of the necessary immunity. While we have held that an immunity from suits grounded on official acts is necessary to serve this purpose, see *Fitzgerald,* 457 U. S., at 749, it does not follow that the broad immunity from *all* civil damages suits that petitioner seeks is also necessary.

"Just what our forefathers did envision, or would have envisioned had they foreseen modern conditions, must be divined from materials almost as enigmatic as the dreams Joseph was called upon to interpret for Pharoah. A century and a half of partisan debate and scholarly speculation yields no net result but only supplies more or less apt quotations from respected sources on each side.... They largely cancel each other." *Youngstown Sheet & Tube Co.* v. *Sawyer, 343* U. S. 579, 634-635 (1952) (concurring opinion).

VI

Petitioner's strongest argument supporting his immunity claim is based on the text and structure of the Constitution. He does not contend that the occupant of the Office of the President is "above the law," in the sense that his conduct is entirely immune from judicial scrutiny. The President argues merely for a postponement of the judicial proceedings that will determine whether he violated any law. His argument is grounded in the character of the office that was created by Article II of the Constitution, and relies on separation-of-powers principles that have structured our constitutional arrangement since the founding.

As a starting premise, petitioner contends that he occupies a unique office with powers and responsibilities so vast and important that the public interest demands that he devote his undivided time and attention to his public duties. He submits that—given the nature of the office—the doctrine of separation of powers places limits on the authority of the Federal Judiciary to interfere with the Executive Branch that would be transgressed by allowing this action to proceed.

We have no dispute with the initial premise of the argument. Former Presidents, from George Washington to George Bush, have consistently endorsed petitioner's characterization of the office. After serving his term, Lyndon Johnson observed: "Of all the 1,886 nights I was President, there were not many when I got to sleep before 1 or 2 a.m., and there were few mornings when I didn't wake up by 6 or 6:30." In 1967, the Twenty-fifth Amendment to the Constitution was adopted to ensure continuity in the performance of the powers and duties of the office; one of the sponsors of that Amendment stressed the importance of providing that "at all times" there be a President "who has complete control and will be able to perform" those duties. As Justice Jackson has pointed out, the Presidency concentrates executive authority "in a single head in whose choice the whole Nation has a part, making him the focus of public hopes and expectations. In drama, magnitude and finality his decisions so far overshadow any others that almost alone he fills the public eye and ear." *Youngstown Sheet & Tube Co.* v. *Sawyer,* 343 U. S., at 653 (concurring opinion). We have, in short, long recognized the "unique position in the constitutional scheme" that this office occupies. *Fitzgerald,* 457 U. S., at 749. Thus, while we suspect that even in our modern era there remains some truth to Chief Justice Marshall's suggestion that the duties of the Presidency are not entirely "unremitting," *United States* v. *Burr,* 25 F. Cas. 30, 34 (No. 14,692d) (CC Va. 1807), we accept the initial premise of the Executive's argument.

It does not follow, however, that separation-of-powers principles would be violated by allowing this action to proceed. The doctrine of separation of powers is concerned with the allocation of official power among the three coequal branches of our Government. The Framers "built into the tripartite Federal Government . . . a self-executing safeguard against the encroachment or aggrandizement of one branch at the expense of the other." *Buckley* v. *Valeo,* 424 U. S., at 122. Thus, for example, the Congress may not exercise the judicial power to revise final judgments, *Plaut* v. *Spendthrift Farm, Inc.,* 514 U. S. 211 (1995), or the executive power to manage an airport, see *Metropolitan Washington Airports Authority* v. *Citizens for Abatement of Aircraft Noise, Inc.,* 501 U. S. 252, 276 (1991) (holding that "[i]f the power is executive, the Constitution does not permit an agent of Congress to exercise it"). See *J. W Hampton, Jr., & Co.* v. *United States,* 276 U. S. 394, 406 (1928) (Congress may not "invest itself or its members with either executive power or judicial power"). Similarly, the President may not exercise the legislative power to authorize the seizure of private property for public use. *Youngstown,* 343 U. S., at 588. And, the judicial power to decide cases and controversies does not include the provision of purely advisory opinions to the Executive, or permit the federal courts to resolve nonjusticiable questions.

Of course the lines between the powers of the three branches are not always neatly defined. See *Mistretta* v. *United States,* 488 U. S. 361, 380-381 (1989). But in this case there is no suggestion that the Federal Judiciary is being asked to perform any function that might in some way be described as "executive." Respondent is merely asking the courts to exercise their core Article III jurisdiction to decide cases and controversies. Whatever the outcome of this case, there is no possibility that the decision will curtail the scope of the official powers of the Executive Branch. The litigation of questions that relate entirely to the unofficial conduct of the individual who happens to be the President poses no perceptible risk of misallocation of either judicial power or executive power.

Rather than arguing that the decision of the case will produce either an aggrandizement of judicial power or a narrowing of executive power, petitioner contends that—as a byproduct of an otherwise traditional exercise of judicial power—burdens will be placed on the President that will hamper the performance of his official duties. We have recognized that "[e]ven when a branch does not arrogate power to itself . . . the separation-of-powers doctrine requires that a branch not impair another in the performance of its constitutional duties." *Loving* v. *United States,* 517 U. S. 748, 757 (1996); see also *Nixon* v. *Administrator of General Services,* 433 U. S. 425, 443 (1977). As a factual matter, petitioner contends that this particular case—as well as the potential . . . constitutional commitment of the issue to a coordinate political department; or a lack of judicially discoverable and manageable standards for resolving it . . . .' *Baker* v. *Carr,* 369 U. S. 186, 217 (1962). But the courts must, in the first instance, interpret the text in question and determine whether and to what extent the issue is textually committed. See *ibid.; Powell* v. *McCormack,* 395 U. S. 486, 519 (1969)." *Id.,* at 228. additional litigation that an affirmance of the Court of Appeals judgment might spawn—may impose an unacceptable burden on the President's time and energy, and thereby impair the effective performance of his office.

Petitioner's predictive judgment finds little support in either history or the relatively narrow compass of the issues raised in this particular case. As we have already noted, in the more than 200-year history of the Republic, only three sitting Presidents have been subjected to suits for their private actions. See *supra,* at 692. If the past is any indicator, it seems unlikely that a deluge of such litigation will ever engulf the Presidency. As for the case at hand, if properly managed by the District Court, it appears to us highly unlikely to occupy any substantial amount of petitioner's time.

Of greater significance, petitioner errs by presuming that interactions between the Judicial Branch and the Executive, even quite burdensome interactions, necessarily rise to the level of constitutionally forbidden impairment of the Executive's ability to perform its constitutionally mandated functions. "[O]ur ... system imposes upon the Branches a degree of overlapping responsibility, a duty of interdependence as well as independence the absence of which 'would preclude the establishment of a Nation capable of governing itself effectively.'" *Mistretta,* 488 U. S., at 381 (quoting *Buckley,* 424 U. S., at 121). As Madison explained, separation of powers does not mean that the branches "ought to have no *partial agency* in, or no *controul* over the acts of each other." The fact that a federal court's exercise of its traditional Article III jurisdiction may significantly burden the time and attention of the Chief Executive is not sufficient to establish a violation of the Constitution. Two long-settled propositions, first announced by Chief Justice Marshall, support that conclusion.

First, we have long held that when the President takes official action, the Court has the authority to determine whether he has acted within the law. Perhaps the most dramatic example of such a case is our holding that President Truman exceeded his constitutional authority when he issued an order directing the Secretary of Commerce to take possession of and operate most of the Nation's steel mills in order to avert a national catastrophe. *Youngstown Sheet & Tube Co.* v. *Sawyer,* 343 U. S. 579 (1952). Despite the serious impact of that decision on the ability of the Executive Branch to accomplish its assigned mission, and the substantial time that the President must necessarily have devoted to the matter as a result of judicial involvement, we exercised our Article III jurisdiction to decide whether his official conduct conformed to the law. Our holding was an application of the principle established in *Marbury* v. *Madison,* 1 Cranch 137 (1803), that "[i]t is emphatically the province and duty of the judicial department to say what the law is." *Id.,* at 177.

Second, it is also settled that the President is subject to judicial process in appropriate circumstances. Although Thomas Jefferson apparently thought otherwise, Chief Justice Marshall, when presiding in the treason trial of Aaron Burr, ruled that a subpoena *duces tecum* could be directed to the President. *United States* v. *Burr,* 25 F. Cas. 30 (No. 14,692d) (CC Va. 1807). We unequivocally and emphatically endorsed Marshall's position when we held that President Nixon was obligated to comply with a subpoena commanding him to produce certain tape recordings of his conversations with his aides. *United States* v. *Nixon, 418* U. S. 683 (1974). As we explained, "neither the doctrine of separation of powers, nor the need for confidentiality of high-level communications, without more, can sustain an absolute, unqualified Presidential privilege of immunity from judicial process under all circumstances." *Id.,* at 706.

Sitting Presidents have responded to court orders to provide testimony and other information with sufficient frequency that such interactions between the Judicial and Executive Branches can scarcely be thought a novelty. President Monroe responded to written interrogatories, see Rotunda, Presidents and Ex-Presidents as Witnesses: A Brief Historical Footnote, 1975 U. Ill. L. Forum 1, 5-6, President Nixon as noted above—produced tapes in response to a subpoena *duces tecum,* see *United States* v. *Nixon,* President Ford complied with an order to give a deposition in a criminal trial, *United States* v. *Fromme,* 405 F. Supp. 578 (ED Cal. 1975), and President Clinton has twice given videotaped testimony in criminal proceedings, see *United States* v. *McDougal,* 934 F. Supp. 296 (ED Ark. 1996); *United States* v. *Branscum,* No. LRP-CR-96-49 (ED Ark., June 7, 1996). Moreover, sitting Presidents have also voluntarily complied with judicial requests for testimony. President Grant gave a lengthy deposition in a criminal case under such circumstances, 1 R. Rotunda & J. Nowak, Treatise on Constitutional Law § 7.1 (2d ed. 1992), and President Carter similarly gave videotaped testimony for use at a criminal trial, *id.,* § 7.1(b) (Supp. 1997).

In sum, "[i]t is settled law that the separation-of-powers doctrine does not bar every exercise of jurisdiction over the President of the United States." *Fitzgerald,* 457 U. S., at 753-754. If the Judiciary may severely burden the Executive Branch by reviewing the legality of the President's official conduct, and if it may direct appropriate process to the President himself, it must follow that the federal courts have power to determine the legality of his unofficial conduct. The burden on the President's time and energy that is a mere byproduct of such review surely cannot be considered as onerous as the direct burden imposed by judicial review and the occasional invalidation of his official actions. We therefore hold that the doctrine of separation of powers does not require federal courts to stay all private actions against the President until he leaves office.

The reasons for rejecting such a categorical rule apply as well to a rule that would require a stay "in all but the most exceptional cases." Brief for Petitioner i. Indeed, if the Framers of the Constitution had thought it necessary to protect the President from the burdens of private litigation, we think it far more likely that they would have adopted a categorical rule than a rule that required the President to litigate the question whether a specific case belonged in the "exceptional case" subcategory. In all events, the question whether a specific case should receive exceptional treatment is more appropriately the subject of the exercise of judicial discretion than an interpretation of the Constitution. Accordingly, we turn to the question whether the District Court's decision to stay the trial until after petitioner leaves office was an abuse of discretion.

VII

The Court of Appeals described the District Court's discretionary decision to stay the trial as the "functional equivalent" of a grant of temporary immunity. 72 F. 3d, at 1361, n. 9. Concluding that petitioner was not constitutionally entitled to such an immunity, the court held that it was error to grant the stay. *Ibid.* Although we ultimately conclude that the stay should not have been granted, we think the issue is more difficult than the opinion of the Court of Appeals suggests.

Strictly speaking the stay was not the functional equivalent of the constitutional immunity that petitioner claimed, because the District Court ordered discovery to proceed. Moreover, a stay of either the trial or discovery might be justified by considerations that do not require the recognition of any constitutional immunity. The District Court has broad discretion to stay proceedings as an incident to its power to control its own docket. See, *e. g., Landis* v. *North American Co.,* 299 U. S. 248, 254 (1936). As we have explained, "[e]specially in cases of extraordinary public moment, [a plaintiff] may be required to submit to delay not immoderate in extent and not oppressive in its consequences if the public welfare or convenience will thereby be promoted." *Id.,* at 256. Although we have rejected the argument that the potential burdens on the President violate separation-of-powers principles, those burdens are appropriate matters for the District Court to evaluate in its management of the case. The high respect that is owed to the office of the Chief Executive, though not justifying a rule of categorical immunity, is a matter that should inform the conduct of the entire proceeding, including the timing and scope of discovery.

Nevertheless, we are persuaded that it was an abuse of discretion for the District Court to defer the trial until after the President leaves office. Such a lengthy and categorical stay takes no account whatever of the respondent's interest in bringing the case to trial. The complaint was filed within the statutory limitations period—albeit near the end of that period—and delaying trial would increase the danger of prejudice resulting from the loss of evidence, including the inability of witnesses to recall specific facts, or the possible death of a party.

The decision to postpone the trial was, furthermore, premature. The proponent of a stay bears the burden of establishing its need. *Id.,* at 255. In this case, at the stage at which the District Court made its ruling, there was no way to assess whether a stay of trial after the completion of discovery would be warranted. Other than the fact that a trial may consume some of the President's time and attention, there is nothing in the record to enable a judge to assess the potential harm that may ensue from scheduling the trial promptly after discovery is concluded. We think the District Court may have given undue weight to the concern that a trial might generate unrelated civil actions that could conceivably hamper the President in conducting the duties of his office. If and when that should occur, the court's discretion would permit it to manage those actions in such fashion (including deferral of trial) that interference with the President's duties would not occur. But no such impingement upon the President's conduct of his office was shown here.

VIII

We add a final comment on two matters that are discussed at length in the briefs: the risk that our decision will generate a large volume of politically motivated harassing and frivolous litigation, and the danger that national security concerns might prevent the President from explaining a legitimate need for a continuance.

We are not persuaded that either of these risks is serious.

Most frivolous and vexatious litigation is terminated at the pleading stage or on summary judgment, with little if any personal involvement by the defendant. See Fed. Rules Civ. Proc. 12, 56. Moreover, the availability of sanctions provides a significant deterrent to litigation directed at the President in his unofficial capacity for purposes of political gain or harassment. History indicates that the likelihood that a significant number of such cases will be filed is remote. Although scheduling problems may arise, there is no reason to assume that the district courts will be either unable to accommodate the President's needs or unfaithful to the tradition—especially in matters involving national security of giving "the utmost deference to Presidential responsibilities." Several Presidents, including petitioner, have given testimony without jeopardizing the Nation's security. See *supra,* at 704-705. In short, we have confidence in the ability of our federal judges to deal with both of these concerns.

If Congress deems it appropriate to afford the President stronger protection, it may respond with appropriate legislation. As petitioner notes in his brief, Congress has enacted more than one statute providing for the deferral of civil litigation to accommodate important public interests. Brief for Petitioner 34-36. See, *e. g.,* 11 U. S. C. § 362 (litigation against debtor stayed upon filing of bankruptcy petition); Soldiers' and Sailors' Civil Relief Act of 1940, 50 U. S. C. App. §§ 501-525 (provisions governing, *inter alia,* tolling or stay of civil claims by or against military personnel during course of active duty). If the Constitution embodied the rule that the President advocates, Congress, of course, could not repeal it. But our holding today raises no barrier to a statutory response to these concerns.

The Federal District Court has jurisdiction to decide this case. Like every other citizen who properly invokes that jurisdiction, respondent has a right to an orderly disposition of her claims. Accordingly, the judgment of the Court of Appeals is affirmed.

It is so ordered.

Glossary

appeal: a request that a higher court examine the ruling of a lower court

petitioner: a person or group seeking an appeal or other action by a court

presidential immunity: also called executive immunity; the U.S. president's exemption from prosecution; in particular, exemption from prosecution in civil court for acts done while in office or to carry out the duties of office

respondent: the party against whom a lawsuit is brought by another party, the petitioner

Bush v. Gore

DATE 2000 **AUTHOR** U.S. Supreme Court **VOTE** 5–4	**CITATION** 531 U.S. 98 **SIGNIFICANCE** Stopped the recounting of votes in Florida in the 2000 presidential election, leading to George W. Bush being declared the victor and thus the forty-third president of the United States

Overview

Traditionally, the federal courts have refused to become involved in "political question suits," or disputes arising from and revolving around the political process. Foremost among such disputes are questions over electoral outcomes. Election contests tend to be messy; by definition, such events speak directly to the divided will of the people. Especially where certain voting laws have been bent or broken, a "right" or "wrong" solution to a dispute often cannot be determined. Inevitably, judges have to make choices that seem to ignore the will of at least a part of the electorate. As Justice Felix Frankfurter noted in 1946's *Colegrove v. Green*, the democratic state simply presents some "demands on judicial power which . . . [are] not meet for judicial determination," for "it is hostile to a democratic system to involve the judiciary in the politics of the people." He concluded, "Courts ought not to enter this political thicket."

In 2000, nevertheless, the U.S. Supreme Court was obligated to enter the political thicket of electoral outcomes. At issue was the winner of the 2000 presidential election, between the vice president, Albert Gore Jr., and the Texas governor, George W. Bush. The two were separated by only some 200 votes—out of more than five million cast—in Florida, which held the decisive electoral college votes needed by each candidate to win the presidency. Al Gore had challenged the accuracy of the Florida vote totals, calling for selective hand recounts. George W. Bush defended these totals and challenged the validity of recounting votes by hand. Ultimately, the issues raised by the Florida recounts landed in the Supreme Court, which ruled by a 5–4 vote that Florida's methods of recounting votes were so disorganized and diverse from county to county that they amounted to an unconstitutional violation of the equal protection clauses of the Constitution and of the Fourteenth Amendment. In addition, the ruling held that as the time allowed for counting votes had expired, the Florida recounts were finished and the candidate ahead at that time, George W. Bush, was the winner of the Florida vote—and hence became the forty-third president of the United States.

Context

Election Day was November 7, 2000. More than one hundred million Americans voted in this election, with

Gore's decision to contest the Florida vote count extended the 2000 election for weeks. The following thirty-six days of electoral crisis and chaos featured grand political theater, with local county officials attempting to hand recount ballots in an atmosphere of intense pressure, with more than forty separate court cases litigating all aspects of the recount process, and with some ten separate rulings being issued by the Florida Supreme Court, including a controversial order for a statewide recount more than three weeks after the election. At length, the U.S. Supreme Court heard cases on the matter on two occasions. With its ruling in *Bush v. Gore* on December 12, the Supreme Court finally ended the recounts in Florida and effectively named George W. Bush the forty-third president of the United States.

About the Author

Unlike most U.S. Supreme Court opinions, the ruling in *Bush v. Gore* was not signed by a single justice as author. Rather, the opinion was issued as a per curiam ruling, or an unsigned ruling—written by one or more justices but presented as merely being "from the court." Supreme Court justices often issue a per curiam ruling when they wish to express a result that enjoyed the full and total institutional support of all nine justices. At other times, they issue such a ruling when a case is so lacking in complexity that no member of the Court wishes to commit the time to draft and sign his or her own opinion. Per curiam rulings also can provide cover in politically sensitive cases, shielding the writing justice within the protecting arms of the whole Court. Last, a per curiam ruling, especially in a case featuring dissent among the nine justices, can be a means of expressing the barest measure of consensus.

George Bush
(Eric Draper)

tracking polls showing very close totals throughout the day. That evening, the television networks began to announce which candidates had won which states. As the night progressed, the race remained tight; midnight came and passed, but the election still remained too close to call. By early in the morning of November 8, it became clear that the presidential election between Al Gore and George W. Bush had deadlocked in a virtual tie.

The source of this tie was Florida. Out of some five million votes cast in the Sunshine State, about sixteen hundred votes separated the two candidates as of November 8; with less than a 0.005 percent difference between the two, state law required an automatic recount. The law also allowed the losing candidate to request hand recounts. Given that without Florida's twenty-five electoral college votes, neither candidate would have a majority of the all-important electoral votes, the ultimate outcome of the Florida recount would determine which candidate had won the presidency. When the automatic recount lessened the gap between the two candidates to just under two hundred votes, the candidate who was then losing, Al Gore, indeed requested hand recounts.

Most likely, the Court adopted the per curiam approach to authorship in *Bush v. Gore* for all of these reasons. With little time to spare, the opinion was probably written in different chambers and later cobbled together to form a whole—in point of fact, the evidence that exists suggests that most of this ruling was written by Justices Anthony Kennedy and Sandra Day O'Connor working in tandem. The per curiam approach also served as a means to consensus, permitting the members of the 7–2 majority in agreement on equal protection to reach a rough accord on the basic proposition that the Florida recount was flawed and unconstitutional; with this accord expressed in the per curiam statement, the justices were free to write separate concurring and dissenting opinions further detailing their personal views. Of course, the per curiam ruling also spared one of the justices from having to sign his or her name to an opinion that, owing to severe time constraints, was less coherent than the authors might have wished. So, too, it provided protection from the ruling's politically explosive impact. Perhaps above all, the per curiam statement gave the Court's ruling an air of consensus that actually did not exist, implied that the ruling was of modest scope, and supported the assertion that the Court was only reluctantly entering the fray to fulfill its constitutional role.

Explanation and Analysis of the Document

The Per Curiam Ruling

The per curiam statement begins by noting that Bush's petition to the Court presented three interrelated questions: "whether the Florida Supreme Court established new standards for resolving Presidential election contests, thereby violating Art. II, §1, cl. 2, of the United States Constitution and failing to comply with 3 U.S.C. §5, and whether the use of standardless manual recounts violates the Equal Protection and Due Process Clauses." The opinion, however, largely ignores the first two questions, almost immediately moving on to the third topic, equal protection and due process. In fact, other than drawing on Article II of the Constitution and Title 3 of the U.S. Code as a foundation for grounding the ruling on equal protection, the per curiam statement ignores these matters entirely.

The majority starts its discussion of equal protection and voting, ironically, by noting how "the individual citizen has no federal constitutional right to vote for electors for the President of the United States unless and until the state legislature chooses a statewide election as the means to implement its power to appoint members of the Electoral College." With this fundamental constitutional tenet understood, "the State legislature's power to select the manner for appointing electors" was undeniably supreme; if it so chose, the state legislature had the power and the right to "select the electors itself." However, "history has now favored the voter" in the selection of "Presidential electors."

Al Gore
(Wikimedia Commons)

This extension of the right to vote was key in this matter. "When the state legislature vests the right to vote for President in its people," explains the per curiam statement, "the right to vote as the legislature has prescribed is fundamental; and one source of its fundamental nature lies in the equal weight accorded to each vote and the equal dignity owed to each voter." In fact, "the right to vote is protected in more than the initial allocation of the franchise": Equal protection applies as well "to the manner of its exercise." As the per curiam ruling makes clear, having granted to the people the right to vote on equal terms, the state could not, "by later arbitrary and disparate treatment, value one person's vote over that of another." Once granted, in other words, a citizen's right to vote is subject to the full protection of the law, including the equal protection clauses of the Constitution.

With this established, the per curiam statement moves to the issues raised by the Florida recounts, noting, "The question before us... is whether the recount procedures the Florida Supreme Court has adopted" were consistent with the voters' equal protection rights. The Court's consensus on this question is that the Florida courts had not met this burden. To be valid, notes the per curiam ruling, recounts had to be performed in a uniform manner, "to assure" that the determination of voters' intents was "equal [in] application." This had not been the case in Florida: "The standards for accepting or rejecting contested ballots might vary not only from county to county," notes the ruling, but also often "within a single county from one recount team to another." Since the intents of voters were sometimes difficult to determine, what one county called a valid ballot frequently was excluded in another county and vice versa. The Florida Supreme Court's order initiating a statewide recount, in turn, had improperly "ratified this uneven treatment."

Worse yet, continues the per curiam ruling, the recount procedures issued by the Florida court system were, if anything, just as bad as and perhaps worse than the preexisting state standards. The rules issued by the circuit court (under orders from the Florida Supreme Court) "did not specify who would recount the ballots." This omission forced the creation of ad hoc counting teams "who had no previous training in handling and interpreting ballots." Such informal procedures were constitutionally unacceptable, argues the per curiam statement, "inconsistent with the minimum procedures necessary to protect the fundamental right of each voter" in a statewide recount. Further, the state standard regarding the validity of votes simply cited "the intent of the voter" as determined by the totality of the circumstances as presented by the ballot; the deficiency of uniform rules regarding vote validity meant that the "recount mechanisms implemented in response to the decisions of the Florida Supreme Court do not satisfy the minimum requirement for non-arbitrary treatment of voters necessary to secure the fundamental right." Such had been the reason behind the Court's stay order of December 9. Lacking necessary procedural "safeguards," the contest provisions were simply "not well calculated to sustain the confidence that all citizens must have in the outcome of elections." As such, they were in direct violation of the equal protection clause of the Constitution.

Up to this point, the per curiam ruling had the support of seven of the nine justices; only Justices Ruth Bader Ginsburg and John Paul Stevens objected to the application of equal protection requirements to the Florida recounts. This consensus broke when the issue switched to the appropriate remedy for these violations. Only five of the Justices—William Rehnquist, Antonin Scalia, Clarence Thomas, O'Connor, and Kennedy—agreed that the recounts had to end. Thus, with little foundation of agreement to be presented in the rest of the opinion, the per curiam ruling simply states that the time for recounts has run out; the recounts are thus by necessity over and so is the election.

With its bombshell dropped, the per curiam statement ends with an intriguing attempt to minimize the Court's central role in this matter—despite the revolutionary potential of the ruling. The majority, in identifying equal protection as a fundamental entitlement guaranteeing the voters' right to have their votes counted in a manner that avoids "arbitrary and disparate treatment," had enunciated a new equal protection principle, one whose long-term implications for voting in America was explosive. With voting procedures differing not only between states but also within most states, the potential to revolutionize how Americans voted was enormous and intriguing, yet the majority seemed anxious to limit this principle almost as soon as they formulated it. Most explicit in this regard is the statement early in the ruling limiting the scope of the ruling to the current case alone: "Our consideration," writes the majority, "is limited to the present circumstances, for the problem of equal protection in election processes generally presents many complexities." Just why the ruling could so effectively overcome the many complexities of the 2000 postelection debacle and not be fit for application to future cases remains unstated. Nonetheless, with these words the per curiam ruling limited the use of equal protection as a precedent in future cases.

The per curiam statement's conclusion offers a more subtle and encompassing effort at distancing as well. In one of the most striking paragraphs of the opinion, the Court effectively asserts a limitation on its own judicial role:

> None are more conscious of the vital limits on judicial authority than are the members of this Court, and none stand more in admiration of the Constitution's design to leave the selection of the President to the people, through their legislatures, and to the political sphere. When contending parties invoke the process of the courts, however, it becomes our unsought responsibility to resolve the federal and constitutional issues the judicial system has been forced to confront.

Like the equal protection right that the majority created and then confined, this statement both asserts and rejects judicial power in these matters. The Court's opinion thus portrays the justices of the majority as reluctant decision makers, forced to resolve this case but unwilling and unable to extend their unsought authority beyond the minimum required to perform that task.

The Concurrence

If the per curiam statement aims at deemphasizing the Court's powers—and authority—to act in this matter, Chief Justice Rehnquist's concurrence celebrates them. (The concurrence was joined by Justices Scalia and Thomas.) As far as the chief justice is concerned, "We deal here not with an ordinary election, but with an election for the President of the United States," and this made all the difference in the world. It is true, the chief justice explains, that "in most cases, comity and respect for federalism" lead the Supreme Court "to defer to the decisions of state courts on issues of state law." After all, the decisions of state courts are generally seen as "definitive pronouncements of the will of the States as sovereigns." But this situation was different: "In ordinary cases, the distribution of powers among the branches of a State's government raises no questions of federal constitutional law.... But there are a few exceptional cases in which the Constitution imposes a duty or confers a power on a particular branch of a State's government. This is one of them."

With the Court's power to rule established, the chief justice offers an additional—and, though unstated, presumably superior—reason to overturn the Florida Supreme Court's recount order. Article II, Section 1, Clause 2 of the Constitution places authority over presidential elections *exclusively* in the hands of the state legislatures. In Florida the legislature had set up a series of (admittedly inadequate) procedures for counting votes and determining the distribution of presidential electors. The Florida Supreme Court, in turn, had disrupted these legislatively mandated procedures by ordering a statewide recount so late in the vote-counting process. Moreover, federal law had created a "safe harbor" under which a state's determination of its electors could not be challenged so long as the rules applied were set *before* the election and all disputes were settled by December 18, 2000. For its part, the Florida legislature had clearly sought to reach this safe harbor; the Florida Supreme Court's ruling, on the other hand, created new rules *after* the election.

Therefore, the Florida Supreme Court's changing the method of determining presidential electors by calling for a statewide recount was tantamount to neglect of the safe harbor provisions and was thus a violation of Article II's grant of exclusive authority to the state legislature. Hence, the Florida recounts were unconstitutional.

The Dissents

Four justices objected to the per curiam ruling. Justices Stevens and Ginsburg objected to the whole of the per curiam statement in strident terms. The other two, Justices Stephen Breyer and David Souter, agreed with the majority on the equal protection failures of the Florida electoral system but disagreed regarding the proposed remedy of halting all recounts.

Despite his agreement on the issue of equal protection, Justice Breyer complains that the majority is implementing the wrong remedy. "Of course, the selection of the President is of fundamental national importance," Breyer writes. "But that importance is political, not legal." The federal legal questions presented by this case, "with one exception," were "insubstantial." For this reason alone, "this Court should resist the temptation unnecessarily to resolve tangential legal disputes, where doing so threatens to determine the outcome of the election." As Breyer sees it, "The Court was wrong to take this case. It was wrong to grant a stay. It should now vacate that stay and permit the Florida Supreme Court to decide whether the recount should resume." The benefits of the halting of the recounts were tainted by the questionable constitutionalism of the act, explains Breyer, and the costs of the Court acting were simply too great. Breyer writes,

> We run no risk of returning to the days when a President (responding to this Court's efforts to protect the Cherokee Indians) might have said, "John Marshall has made his decision; now let him enforce it!" ... But we do risk a self-inflicted wound—a wound that may harm not just the Court, but the Nation. I fear that in order to bring this agonizingly long election process to a definitive conclusion we have not adequately attended to that necessary "check upon our own exercise of power," "our own sense of self-restraint."

Justice Souter is even more blunt in his conclusions about the majority's proposed remedies when he writes: "If this Court had allowed the State to follow the course indicated by the opinions of its own Supreme Court, it is entirely possible that there would ultimately have been no issue requiring our review, and political tension could have worked itself out in the Congress following the procedure provided in 3 U.S.C. § 15." Sadly, the situation had not been resolved in any such way. And with the Court having wrongly taken up the case, "its resolution by the majority" amounted to "another erroneous decision." The key problem in Souter's eyes is the per curiam ruling's remedy. Souter himself believes that the best option would have been to "remand the case to the courts of Florida with instructions to establish uniform standards for evaluating the several types of ballots that have prompted differing treatments." Unlike the majority, Souter sees "no warrant for this Court to assume that Florida could not possibly comply with this requirement before the date set for the meeting of electors, December 18." For Souter, there is simply "no justification for denying the State the opportunity to try to count all disputed ballots now."

Unlike Breyer and Souter, Justice John Paul Stevens objected to the majority's entire ruling. He asserts that "the Constitution assigns to the States the primary responsibility for determining the manner of selecting the Presidential electors." Hence, "when questions arise about the meaning of state laws, including election laws," it has been the Court's "settled practice to accept the opinions of the highest courts of the States as providing the final answers." This was decidedly not the case here. The per curiam statement's equal protection arguments also did not convince Justice Stevens of the need to act. "Admittedly, the use of differing substandards for determining voter intent in different counties employing similar voting systems may raise serious concerns," he says. However, notes Stevens, "those concerns are alleviated—if not eliminated—by the fact that a single impartial magistrate will ultimately adjudicate all objections arising from the recount process." Actually underlying the entire assault on the Florida election procedures, Justice Stevens argues, was "an unstated lack of confidence in the impartiality and capacity of the state judges who would make the critical decisions if the vote count were to proceed." This was a troubling view, one, he states, that can "only lend credence to the most cynical appraisal of the work of judges throughout the land." "Time will one day heal the wound to that confidence that will be inflicted by today's decision," Justice Stevens concludes. Still, "one thing ... is certain. Although we may never know with complete certainty the identity of the winner of this year's Presidential election, the identity of the loser is perfectly clear. It is the Nation's confidence in the judge as an impartial guardian of the rule of law."

The most angry of the dissenters was Justice Ruth Bader Ginsburg. Ginsburg is especially malcontented with the lack of respect shown the Florida Supreme Court, noting, "The extraordinary setting of this case has obscured the ordinary principle that dictates its proper resolution: Federal courts defer to state high courts' interpretations of their state's own law." This principle was the foundation upon which federalism was built and to which all agreed. The five justices in the majority were normally among the strongest supporters of state authority under federalism. This role reversal frustrates Ginsburg:

> The Chief Justice's solicitude for the Florida Legislature comes at the expense of the more fundamental solicitude we owe to the legislature's sovereign [the State and its people]. ... Were the other members of this Court as mindful as they generally are of our system of dual sovereignty, they would affirm the judgment of the Florida Supreme Court.

Ginsburg also questions the majority's equal protection logic. Ideally, she explains,

> perfection would be the appropriate standard for judging the recount. But we live in an imperfect world, one in which thousands of votes have not been counted. I cannot agree that the recount adopted by the Florida court, flawed as it may be, would yield a result any less fair or precise than the certification that preceded that recount.

Lacking any respect for the majority's logic, and perhaps distrusting their motives, Justice Ginsburg breaks tradition by ending her views bluntly: "I dissent."

Impact

More so than the average Supreme Court case, the ruling in *Bush v. Gore* had a very obvious and significant impact: the naming of a president. Hence, President George W. Bush was the one to face the crises of the following few years. In particular, President Bush, rather than President Gore, responded to the attacks of September 11, 2001; not just America but the world as well, then, might have become a very different place had the Court ruled differently.

On a constitutional level the impact of the case was more ambiguous. On the one hand, the application of equal protection to matters of electoral administration was a major expansion of the doctrine into the realm of voting rights. Florida was not alone in having electoral rules and procedures that permitted the nonstandardized counting of votes in elections; in fact, Florida was not even the worst state in this regard. The per curiam ruling's use of the equal protection doctrine thus promised a new future of ever-increasing federal involvement in the running of elections, as inequitable state voting procedures would seemingly have to be ended under federal supervision. On the other hand, little has come of the case or its promise of enhanced federal involvement in voting since the opinion's writing. The Supreme Court has not mentioned the case even once in any subsequent opinion. Similarly, the lower federal courts have seemed to avoid the case as precedent—even when matters have involved voting rights issues. As a result, while the opinion seemed to promise much, it effectively did nothing to change the existing structural relationship between the states and the national government on the issue of voting.

Questions for Further Study

1. Discuss possible reasons why the Supreme Court in *Bush v. Gore* decided (a) to accept the case, (b) to base the ruling on the concept of equal protection, and (c) to end the recounts by its own fiat.

2. In what ways is the Supreme Court's ruling in *Bush v. Gore* similar to and different from another key document in voting rights history, the Voting Rights Act of 1965?

3. Explore the validity of Justice Stevens's dissenting assertions: "Time will one day heal the wound to that confidence that will be inflicted by today's decision. One thing, however, is certain. Although we may never know with complete certainty the identity of the winner of this year's Presidential election, the identity of the loser is perfectly clear. It is the Nation's confidence in the judge as an impartial guardian of the rule of law." Do you agree with Stevens's assessment? Have perceptions of the Supreme Court and of judges in general changed since 2000? If so, why and how? If not, then how should Justice Stevens's comment be considered?

Further Reading

Books

Boies, David. *Courting Justice: From NY Yankees v. Major League Baseball to Bush v. Gore, 1997–2000.* New York: Hyperion, 2004.

Dionne, E. J., and William Kristol. *Bush v. Gore: The Court Cases and the Commentary.* Washington, DC: Brookings Institution Press, 2010.

Gillman, Howard. *The Votes That Counted: How the Court Decided the 2000 Presidential Election.* Chicago: University of Chicago Press, 2001.

Greene, Abner. *Understanding the 2000 Election: A Guide to the Legal Battles That Decided the Presidency.* New York: New York University Press, 2001.

Kaplan, David A. *The Accidental President: How 413 Lawyers, 9 Supreme Court Justices, and 5,963,110 (Give or Take a Few) Floridians Landed George W. Bush in the White House.* New York: Morrow, 2001.

Merzer, Martin. *The Miami Herald Report: Democracy Held Hostage.* New York: St. Martin's Press, 2001.

Posner, Richard A. *Breaking the Deadlock: The 2000 Election, the Constitution, and the Courts.* Princeton, NJ: Princeton University Press, 2001.

Sunstein, Cass R., and Richard A. Epstein, eds. *The Vote: Bush, Gore, and the Supreme Court.* Chicago: University of Chicago Press, 2001.

Tapper, Jake. Down and Dirty: *The Plot to Steal the Presidency.* Boston: Little, Brown, 2001.

Toobin, Jeffrey. *Too Close to Call: The Thirty-Six-Day Battle to Decide the 2000 Election.* New York: Random House, 2001.

United States Commission on Civil Rights. *Voting Irregularities in Florida during the 2000 Presidential Election.* Washington, DC: Government Printing Office, 2001.

Washington Post. *Deadlock: The Inside Story of America's Closest Election.* New York: PublicAffairs, 2001.

Wells, Charley. *Inside Bush v. Gore.* Gainesville: University Press of Florida, 2013.

Zelden, Charles L. *Bush v. Gore: Exposing the Hidden Crisis in American Democracy.* Lawrence: University Press of Kansas, 2010.

—Commentary by Charles L. Zelden

BUSH v. GORE

Document Text

Per Curiam

I

On December 8, 2000, the Supreme Court of Florida ordered that the Circuit Court of Leon County tabulate by hand 9,000 ballots in Miami-Dade County. It also ordered the inclusion in the certified vote totals of 215 votes identified in Palm Beach County and 168 votes identified in Miami-Dade County for Vice President Albert Gore Jr. and Senator Joseph Lieberman, Democratic Candidates for President and Vice President. The Supreme Court noted that petitioner, Governor George W. Bush asserted that the net gain for Vice President Gore in Palm Beach County was 176 votes, and directed the Circuit Court to resolve that dispute on remand. ___ So.2d, at ___ (slip op., at 4, n.6). The court further held that relief would require manual recounts in all Florida counties where so-called "undervotes" had not been subject to manual tabulation. The court ordered all manual recounts to begin at once. Governor Bush and Richard Cheney, Republican Candidates for the Presidency and Vice Presidency, filed an emergency application for a stay of this mandate. On December 9, we granted the application, treated the application as a petition for a writ of certiorari, and granted certiorari. Post, p.___.

The proceedings leading to the present controversy are discussed in some detail in our opinion in *Bush v. Palm Beach County Canvassing Bd.*, ante, p.___ (per curiam) (BushI). On November 8, 2000, the day following the Presidential election, the Florida Division of Elections reported that petitioner, Governor Bush, had received 2,909,135 votes, and respondent, Vice President Gore, had received 2,907,351 votes, a margin of 1,784 for Governor Bush. Because Governor Bush's margin of victory was less than "one-half of a percent ... of the votes cast," an automatic machine recount was conducted under §102.141(4) of the election code, the results of which showed Governor Bush still winning the race but by a diminished margin. Vice President Gore then sought manual recounts in Volusia, Palm Beach, Broward, and Miami-Dade Counties, pursuant to Florida's election protest provisions. Fla. Stat. §102.166 (2000). A dispute arose concerning the deadline for local county canvassing boards to submit their returns to the Secretary of State (Secretary). The Secretary declined to waive the November 14 deadline imposed by statute. §§102.111, 102.112. The Florida Supreme Court, however, set the deadline at November 26. We granted certiorari and vacated the Florida Supreme Court's decision, finding considerable uncertainty as to the grounds on which it was based. BushI, ante, at ___-___ (slip. op., at 6-7). On December 11, the Florida Supreme Court issued a decision on remand reinstating that date. ___ So.2d ___, ___ (slip op. at 30-31).

On November 26, the Florida Elections Canvassing Commission certified the results of the election and declared Governor Bush the winner of Florida's 25 electoral votes. On November 27, Vice President Gore, pursuant to Florida's contest provisions, filed a complaint in Leon County Circuit Court contesting the certification. Fla. Stat. §102.168 (2000). He sought relief pursuant to §102.168(3)(c), which provides that "[r]eceipt of a number of illegal votes or rejection of a number of legal votes sufficient to change or place in doubt the result of the election" shall be grounds for a contest. The Circuit Court denied relief, stating that Vice President Gore failed to meet his burden of proof. He appealed to the First District Court of Appeal, which certified the matter to the Florida Supreme Court.

Accepting jurisdiction, the Florida Supreme Court affirmed in part and reversed in part. *Gore v. Harris*, ___ So. 2d. ____ (2000). The court held that the Circuit Court had been correct to reject Vice President Gore's challenge to the results certified in Nassau County and his challenge to the Palm Beach County Canvassing Board's determination that 3,300 ballots cast in that county were not, in the statutory phrase, "legal votes."

The Supreme Court held that Vice President Gore had satisfied his burden of proof under §102.168(3)(c) with respect to his challenge to Miami-Dade County's failure to tabulate, by manual count, 9,000 ballots on which the machines had failed to detect a vote for President ("undervotes"). ___ So. 2d., at ___ (slip. op., at 22-23). Noting the closeness of the election, the Court explained that "[o]n this record, there can be no question that there are legal votes within the 9,000 uncounted votes sufficient to place the results of this election in doubt." Id., at ___ (slip. op., at 35). A "legal vote," as determined by the Supreme Court, is "one in which there is a 'clear indication of the intent of the voter.'" Id., at ___ (slip op., at 25). The court therefore ordered a hand recount of the 9,000 ballots in Miami-Dade County. Observing that the contest provisions vest broad discretion in the circuit judge to "provide any relief appropriate under such circumstances," Fla. Stat. §102.168(8) (2000), the Supreme Court further held that the Circuit Court could order "the Supervisor of Elections and the Canvassing Boards, as well as the necessary public officials, in all counties that have not conducted a manual recount or tabulation of the undervotes . . . to do so forthwith, said tabulation to take place in the individual counties where the ballots are located." ___ So.2d, at ___ (slip. op., at 38).

The Supreme Court also determined that both Palm Beach County and Miami-Dade County, in their earlier manual recounts, had identified a net gain of 215 and 168 legal votes for Vice President Gore. Id., at ___ (slip. op., at 33-34). Rejecting the Circuit Court's conclusion that Palm Beach County lacked the authority to include the 215 net votes submitted past the November 26 deadline, the Supreme Court explained that the deadline was not intended to exclude votes identified after that date through ongoing manual recounts. As to Miami-Dade County, the Court concluded that although the 168 votes identified were the result of a partial recount, they were "legal votes [that] could change the outcome of the election." Id., at (slip op., at 34). The Supreme Court therefore directed the Circuit Court to include those totals in the certified results, subject to resolution of the actual vote total from the Miami-Dade partial recount.

The petition presents the following questions: whether the Florida Supreme Court established new standards for resolving Presidential election contests, thereby violating Art.II, §1, cl.2, of the United States Constitution and failing to comply with 3 U.S.C. §5, and whether the use of standardless manual recounts violates the Equal Protection and Due Process Clauses. With respect to the equal protection question, we find a violation of the Equal Protection Clause.

II

A

The closeness of this election, and the multitude of legal challenges which have followed in its wake, have brought into sharp focus a common, if heretofore unnoticed, phenomenon.Nationwide statistics reveal that an estimated 2% of ballots cast do not register a vote for President for whatever reason, including deliberately choosing no candidate at all or some voter error, such as voting for two candidates or insufficiently marking a ballot. See Ho, More Than 2M Ballots Uncounted, AP Online (Nov. 28, 2000); Kelley, Balloting Problems Not Rare But Only In A Very Close Election Do Mistakes And Mismarking Make A Difference, Omaha World-Herald (Nov. 15, 2000). In certifying election results, the votes eligible for inclusion in the certification are the votes meeting the properly established legal requirements.

This case has shown that punch card balloting machines can produce an unfortunate number of ballots which are not punched in a clean, complete way by the voter. After the current counting, it is likely legislative bodies nationwide will examine ways to improve the mechanisms and machinery for voting.

B

The individual citizen has no federal constitutional right to vote for electors for the President of the United States unless and until the state legislature chooses a statewide election as the means to implement its power to appoint members of the Electoral College. U.S. Const., Art.II, §1. This is the source for the statement in *McPherson v. Blacker*, 146 U.S. 1, 35 (1892), that the State legislature's power to select the manner for appointing electors is plenary; it may, if it so chooses, select the electors itself, which indeed was the manner used by State legislatures in several States for many years after the Framing of our Constitution. Id., at 28-33. History has now favored the voter, and in each of the several States the citizens themselves vote for Presidential electors. When the state legislature vests the right to vote for President in its people, the right to vote as the legislature has prescribed is fundamental; and one source of its fundamental nature lies in the equal weight accorded to each vote and the equal dignity owed to each voter. The State, of course, after granting the franchise in the special context of ArticleII, can take back the power to appoint electors. See id., at 35 ("[T]here is no doubt of the right of the legislature to resume the power at any time, for it can neither be taken away nor abdicated") (quoting S.Rep. No. 395, 43d Cong., 1st Sess.).

The right to vote is protected in more than the initial allocation of the franchise. Equal protection applies as well to the manner of its exercise. Having once granted the right to vote on equal terms, the State may not, by later arbitrary and disparate treatment, value one person's vote over that of another. See, e.g., *Harper v. Virginia Bd. of Elections*, 383 U.S. 663, 665 (1966) ("[O]nce the franchise is granted to the electorate, lines may not be drawn which are inconsistent with the Equal Protection Clause of the Fourteenth Amendment"). It must be remembered that "the right of suffrage can be denied by a debasement or dilution of the weight of a citizen's vote just as effectively as by wholly prohibiting the free exercise of the franchise." *Reynolds v. Sims*, 377 U.S. 533, 555 (1964).

There is no difference between the two sides of the present controversy on these basic propositions. Respondents say that the very purpose of vindicating the right to vote justifies the recount procedures now at issue. The question before us, however, is whether the recount procedures the Florida Supreme Court has adopted are consistent with its obligation to avoid arbitrary and disparate treatment of the members of its electorate.

Much of the controversy seems to revolve around ballot cards designed to be perforated by a stylus but which, either through error or deliberate omission, have not been perforated with sufficient precision for a machine to count them. In some cases a piece of the card—a chad—is hanging, say by two corners. In other cases there is no separation at all, just an indentation.

The Florida Supreme Court has ordered that the intent of the voter be discerned from such ballots. For purposes of resolving the equal protection challenge, it is not necessary to decide whether the Florida Supreme Court had the authority under the legislative scheme for resolving election disputes to define what a legal vote is and to mandate a manual recount implementing that definition. The recount mechanisms implemented in response to the decisions of the Florida Supreme Court do not satisfy the minimum requirement for non-arbitrary treatment of voters necessary to secure the fundamental right. Florida's basic command for the count of legally cast votes is to consider the "intent of the voter." *Gore v. Harris*, ___ So.2d, at ___ (slip op., at 39). This is unobjectionable as an abstract proposition and a starting principle. The problem inheres inthe absence of specific standards to ensure its equal application. The formulation of uniform rules to determine intent based on these recurring circumstances is practicable and, we conclude, necessary.

The law does not refrain from searching for the intent of the actor in a multitude of circumstances; and in some cases the general command to ascertain intent is not susceptible to much further refinement. In this instance, however, the question is not whether to believe a witness but how to interpret the marks or holes or scratches on an inanimate object, a piece of cardboard or paper which, it is said, might not have registered as a vote during the machine count. The factfinder confronts a thing, not a person. The search for intent can be confined by specific rules designed to ensure uniform treatment.

The want of those rules here has led to unequal evaluation of ballots in various respects. See *Gore v. Harris*,

___ So.2d, at ___ (slip op., at 51) (Wells, J., dissenting) ("Should a county canvassing board count or not count a 'dimpled chad' where the voter is able to successfully dislodge the chad in every other contest on that ballot? Here, the county canvassing boards disagree"). As seems to have been acknowledged at oral argument, the standards for accepting or rejecting contested ballots might vary not only from county to county but indeed within a single county from one recount team to another.

The record provides some examples. A monitor in Miami-Dade County testified at trial that he observed that three members of the county canvassing board applied different standards in defining a legal vote. 3 Tr. 497, 499 (Dec. 3, 2000). And testimony at trial also revealed that at least one county changed its evaluative standards during the counting process. Palm Beach County, for example, began the process with a 1990 guideline which precluded counting completely attached chads, switched to a rule that considered a vote to be legal if any light could be seen through a chad, changed back to the 1990 rule, and then abandoned any pretense of a per se rule, only to have a court order that the county consider dimpled chads legal. This is not a process with sufficient guarantees of equal treatment.

An early case in our one person, one vote jurisprudence arose when a State accorded arbitrary and disparate treatment to voters in its different counties. *Gray v. Sanders*, 372 U.S. 368 (1963). The Court found a constitutional violation. We relied on these principles in the context of the Presidential selection process in *Moore v. Ogilvie*, 394 U.S. 814 (1969), where we invalidated a county-based procedure that diluted the influence of citizens in larger counties in the nominating process. There we observed that "[t]he idea that one group can be granted greater voting strength than another is hostile to the one man, one vote basis of our representative government." Id., at 819.

The State Supreme Court ratified this uneven treatment. It mandated that the recount totals from two counties, Miami-Dade and Palm Beach, be included in the certified total. The court also appeared to hold sub silentio that the recount totals from Broward County, which were not completed until after the original November 14 certification by the Secretary of State, were to be considered part of the new certified vote totals even though the county certification was not contested by Vice President Gore. Yet each of the counties used varying standards to determine what was a legal vote. Broward County used a more forgiving standard than Palm Beach County, and uncovered almost three times as many new votes, a result markedly disproportionate to the difference in population between the counties.

In addition, the recounts in these three counties were not limited to so-called undervotes but extended to all of the ballots. The distinction has real consequences. A manual recount of all ballots identifies not only those ballots which show no vote but also those which contain more than one, the so-called overvotes. Neither category will be counted by the machine. This is not a trivial concern. At oral argument, respondents estimated there are as many as 110,000 overvotes statewide. As a result, the citizen whose ballot was not read by a machine because he failed to vote for a candidate in a way readable by a machine may still have his vote counted in a manual recount; on the other hand, the citizen who marks two candidates in a way discernable by the machine will not have the same opportunity to have his vote count, even if a manual examination of the ballot would reveal the requisite indicia of intent. Furthermore, the citizen who marks two candidates, only one of which is discernable by the machine, will have his vote counted even though it should have been read as an invalid ballot. The State Supreme Court's inclusion of vote counts based on these variant standards exemplifies concerns with the remedial processes that were under way.

That brings the analysis to yet a further equal protection problem. The votes certified by the court included a partial total from one county, Miami-Dade. The Florida Supreme Court's decision thus gives no assurance that the recounts included in a final certification must be complete. Indeed, it is respondent's submission that it would be consistent with the rules of the recount procedures to include whatever partial counts are done by the time of final certification, and we interpret the Florida Supreme Court's decision to permit this. See ___ So.2d, at ___, n.21 (slip op., at 37, n.21) (noting "practical difficulties" may control outcome of election, but certifying partial Miami-Dade total nonetheless). This accommodation no doubt results from the truncated contest period established by the Florida Supreme Court in BushI, at respondents' own urging. The press of time does not diminish the constitutional concern. A desire for speed is not a general excuse for ignoring equal protection guarantees.

In addition to these difficulties the actual process by which the votes were to be counted under the Florida Supreme Court's decision raises further concerns. That order did not specify who would recount the ballots. The county canvassing boards were forced to pull together ad hoc teams comprised of judges from various Circuits who had no previous training in handling and interpreting ballots. Furthermore, while others were permitted to observe, they were prohibited from objecting during the recount.

The recount process, in its features here described, is inconsistent with the minimum procedures necessary to protect the fundamental right of each voter in the special instance of a statewide recount under the authority of a single state judicial officer. Our consideration is limited to the present circumstances, for the problem of equal protection in election processes generally presents many complexities.

The question before the Court is not whether local entities, in the exercise of their expertise, may develop different systems for implementing elections. Instead, we are presented with a situation where a state court with the power to assure uniformity has ordered a statewide recount with minimal procedural safeguards. When a court orders a statewide remedy, there must be at least some assurance that the rudimentary requirements of equal treatment and fundamental fairness are satisfied.

Given the Court's assessment that the recount process underway was probably being conducted in an unconstitutional manner, the Court stayed the order directing the recount so it could hear this case and render an expedited decision. The contest provision, as it was mandated by the State Supreme Court, is not well calculated to sustain the confidence that all citizens must have in the outcome of elections. The State has not shown that its procedures include the necessary safeguards. The problem, for instance, of the estimated 110,000 overvotes has not been addressed, although Chief Justice Wells called attention to the concern in his dissenting opinion. See ___ So.2d, at ___, n.26 (slip op., at 45, n.26).

Upon due consideration of the difficulties identified to this point, it is obvious that the recount cannot be conducted in compliance with the requirements of equal protection and due process without substantial additional work. It would require not only the adoption (after opportunity for argument) of adequate statewide standards for determining what is a legal vote, and practicable procedures to implement them, but also orderly judicial review of any disputed matters that might arise. In addition, the Secretary of State has advised that the recount of only a portion of the ballots requires that the vote tabulation equipment be used to screen out undervotes, a function for which the machines were not designed. If a recount of overvotes were also required, perhaps even a second screening would be necessary. Use of the equipment for this purpose, and any new software developed for it, would have to be evaluated for accuracy by the Secretary of State, as required by Fla. Stat. §101.015 (2000).

The Supreme Court of Florida has said that the legislature intended the State's electors to "participat[e] fully in the federal electoral process," as provided in 3 U.S.C. §5. ___ So.2d, at ___ (slip op. at 27); see also *Palm Beach Canvassing Bd. v. Harris*, 2000 WL 1725434, *13 (Fla. 2000). That statute, in turn, requires that any controversy or contest that is designed to lead to a conclusive selection of electors be completed by December 12. That date is upon us, and there is no recount procedure in place under the State Supreme Court's order that comports with minimal constitutional standards. Because it is evident that any recount seeking to meet the December 12 date will be unconstitutional for the reasons we have discussed, we reverse the judgment of the Supreme Court of Florida ordering a recount to proceed.

Seven Justices of the Court agree that there are constitutional problems with the recount ordered by the Florida Supreme Court that demand a remedy. See post, at 6 (Souter, J., dissenting); post, at 2, 15 (Breyer, J., dissenting). The only disagreement is as to the remedy. Because the Florida Supreme Court has said that the Florida Legislature intended to obtain the safe-harbor benefits of 3 U. S. C. §5, Justice Breyer's proposed remedy—remanding to the Florida Supreme Court for its ordering of a constitutionally proper contest until December 18-contemplates action in violation of the Florida election code, and hence could not be part of an "appropriate" order authorized by Fla. Stat. §102.168(8) (2000).

* * *

None are more conscious of the vital limits on judicial authority than are the members of this Court, and none stand more in admiration of the Constitution's design to leave the selection of the President to the people, through their legislatures, and to the political sphere. When contending parties invoke the process of the courts, however, it becomes our unsought responsibility to resolve the federal and constitutional issues the judicial system has been forced to confront.

The judgment of the Supreme Court of Florida is reversed, and the case is remanded for further proceedings not inconsistent with this opinion.

Pursuant to this Court's Rule 45.2, the Clerk is directed to issue the mandate in this case forthwith.

It is so ordered.

Chief Justice Rehnquist, with Whom Justice Scalia and Justice Thomas Join, Concurring

We join the per curiam opinion. We write separately because we believe there are additional grounds that require us to reverse the Florida Supreme Court's decision.

I

We deal here not with an ordinary election, but with an election for the President of the United States. In *Burroughs v. United States*, 290 U.S. 534, 545 (1934), we said:

"While presidential electors are not officers or agents of the federal government (Inre Green, 134 U.S. 377, 379), they exercise federal functions under, and discharge duties in virtue of authority conferred by, the Constitution of the United States. The President is vested with the executive power of the nation. The importance of his election and the vital character of its relationship to and effect upon the welfare and safety of the whole people cannot be too strongly stated."

Likewise, in *Anderson v. Celebrezze*, 460 U.S. 780, 794-795 (1983) (footnote omitted), we said: "[I]n the context of a Presidential election, state-imposed restrictions implicate a uniquely important national interest. For the President and the Vice President of the United States are the only elected officials who represent all the voters in the Nation."

In most cases, comity and respect for federalism compel us to defer to the decisions of state courts on issues of state law. That practice reflects our understanding that the decisions of state courts are definitive pronouncements of the will of the States as sovereigns. Cf. *Erie R. Co. v. Tompkins*, 304 U.S. 64 (1938). Of course, in ordinary cases, the distribution of powers among the branches of a State's government raises no questions of federal constitutional law, subject to the requirement that the government be republican in character. See U.S. Const., Art.IV, §4. But there are a few exceptional cases in which the Constitution imposes a duty or confers a power on a particular branch of a State's government. This is one of them. Article II, §1, cl.2, provides that "[e]ach State shall appoint, in such Manner as the *Legislature* thereof may direct," electors for President and Vice President. (Emphasis added.) Thus, the text of the election law itself, and not just its interpretation by the courts of the States, takes on independent significance.

In *McPherson v. Blacker*, 146 U.S. 1 (1892), we explained that Art. II, §1, cl.2, "convey[s] the broadest power of determination" and "leaves it to the legislature exclusively to define the method" of appointment. Id., at 27. A significant departure from the legislative scheme for appointing Presidential electors presents a federal constitutional question.

3 U.S.C. §5 informs our application of Art.II, §1, cl.2, to the Florida statutory scheme, which, as the Florida Supreme Court acknowledged, took that statute into account. Section 5 provides that the State's selection of electors "shall be conclusive, and shall govern in the counting of the electoral votes" if the electors are chosen under laws enacted prior to election day, and if the selection process is completed six days prior to the meeting of the electoral college. As we noted in *Bush v. Palm Beach County Canvassing Bd.*, ante, at 6.

"Since §5 contains a principle of federal law that would assure finality of the State's determination if made pursuant to a state law in effect before the election, a legislative wish to take advantage of the 'safe harbor' would counsel against any construction of the Election Code that Congress might deem to be a change in the law."

If we are to respect the legislature's Article II powers, therefore, we must ensure that postelection state-court actions do not frustrate the legislative desire to attain the "safe harbor" provided by §5.

In Florida, the legislature has chosen to hold statewide elections to appoint the State's 25 electors. Importantly, the legislature has delegated the authority to run the elections and to oversee election disputes to the Secretary of State (Secretary), Fla. Stat. §97.012(1) (2000), and to state circuit courts, §§102.168(1), 102.168(8). Isolated sections of the code may well admit of more than one interpretation, but the general coherence of the legislative scheme may not be altered by judicial interpretation so as to wholly change the statutorily provided apportionment of responsibility among these various bodies. In any election but a Presidential election, the Florida Supreme Court can give as little or as much deference to Florida's executives as it chooses, so far as Article II is concerned, and this Court will have no cause to question the court's actions. But, with respect to a Presidential election, the court must be both mindful of the legislature's role under Article II in choosing the manner of appointing electors and deferential to those bodies expressly empowered by the legislature to carry out its constitutional mandate.

In order to determine whether a state court has infringed upon the legislature's authority, we necessarily must examine the law of the State as it existed prior to the action of the court. Though we generally defer to state courts on the interpretation of state law—see, e.g., *Mullaney v. Wilbur*, 421 U.S. 684 (1975)—there are of course areas in which the Constitution requires this Court to undertake an independent, if still deferential, analysis of state law.

For example, in *NAACP v. Alabama ex rel. Patterson*, 357 U.S. 449 (1958), it was argued that we were without jurisdiction because the petitioner had not pursued the correct appellate remedy in Alabama's state courts. Petitioners had sought a state-law writ of certiorari in the Alabama Supreme Court when a writ of mandamus, according to that court, was proper. We found this state-law ground inadequate to defeat our jurisdiction because we were "unable to reconcile the procedural holding of the Alabama Supreme Court" with prior Alabama precedent. Id., at 456. The purported state-law ground was so novel, in our independent estimation, that "petitioner could not fairly be deemed to have been apprised of its existence." Id., at 457.

Six years later we decided *Bouie v. City of Columbia*, 378 U.S. 347 (1964), in which the state court had held, contrary to precedent, that the state trespass law applied to Black sit-in demonstrators who had consent to enter private property but were then asked to leave. Relying upon NAACP, we concluded that the South Carolina Supreme Court's interpretation of a state penal statute had impermissibly broadened the scope of that statute beyond what a fair reading provided, in violation of due process. See 378 U.S., at 361-362. What we would do in the present case is precisely parallel: Hold that the Florida Supreme Court's interpretation of the Florida election laws impermissibly distorted them beyond what a fair reading required, in violation of Article II.

This inquiry does not imply a disrespect for state courts but rather a respect for the constitutionally prescribed role of state legislatures. To attach definitive weight to the pronouncement of a state court, when the very question at issue is whether the court has actually departed from the statutory meaning, would be to abdicate our responsibility to enforce the explicit requirements of Article II.

II

Acting pursuant to its constitutional grant of authority, the Florida Legislature has created a detailed, if not perfectly crafted, statutory scheme that provides for appointment of Presidential electors by direct election. Fla. Stat. §103.011 (2000). Under the statute, "[v]otes cast for the actual candidates for President and Vice President shall be counted as votes cast for the presidential electors supporting such candidates." Ibid. The legislature has designated the Secretary of State as the "chief election officer," with the responsibility to "[o]btain and maintain uniformity in the application, operation, and interpretation of the election laws." §97.012. The state legislature has delegated to county canvassing boards the duties of administering elections. §102.141. Those boards are responsible for providing results to the state Elections Canvassing Commission, comprising the Governor, the Secretary of State, and the Director of the Division of Elections. §102.111. Cf. *Boardman v. Esteva*, 323 So. 2d 259, 268, n. 5 (1975) ("The election process . . . is committed to the executive branch of government through duly designated officials all charged with specific duties. . . . [The] judgments [of these officials] are entitled to be regarded by the courts as presumptively correct . . .").

After the election has taken place, the canvassing boards receive returns from precincts, count the votes, and in the event that a candidate was defeated by 5% or less, conduct a mandatory recount. Fla. Stat. §102.141(4) (2000). The county canvassing boards must file certified election returns with the Department of State by 5 p.m. on the seventh day following the election. §102.112(1). The Elections Canvassing Commission must then certify the results of the election. §102.111(1).

The state legislature has also provided mechanisms both for protesting election returns and for contesting certified election results. Section 102.166 governs protests. Any protest must be filed prior to the certification of election results by the county canvassing board. §102.166(4)(b). Once a protest has been filed, "the county canvassing board may authorize a manual recount." §102.166(4)(c). If a sample recount conducted pursuant to §102.166(5) "indicates an error in the vote tabulation which could affect the outcome of the election," the county canvassing board is instructed to: "(a) Correct the error and recount the remaining precincts with the vote tabulation system; (b) Request the Department of State to verify the tabulation software; or (c) Manually recount all ballots," §102.166(5). In the event a canvassing board chooses to conduct a manual recount of all ballots, §102.166(7) prescribes procedures for such a recount.

Contests to the certification of an election, on the other hand, are controlled by §102.168. The grounds for contesting an election include "[r]eceipt of a number of illegal votes or rejection of a number of legal votes sufficient to change or place in doubt the result of the election." §102.168(3)(c). Any contest must be filed in the appropriate Florida circuit court, Fla. Stat. §102.168(1), and the canvassing board or election board is the proper party defendant, §102.168(4). Section 102.168(8) provides that "[t]he circuit judge to whom the contest is presented may fashion such orders as he or she deems necessary to ensure that each allegation in the complaint is investigated, examined, or checked, to prevent or correct any alleged wrong, and to provide any relief appropriate under such circumstances." In Presidential elections, the contest period necessarily terminates on the date set by 3 U.S.C. §5 for concluding the State's "final determination" of election controversies.

In its first decision, *Palm Beach Canvassing Bd. v. Harris*, ___ So.2d, ___ (Nov. 21, 2000) (Harris I), the Florida Supreme Court extended the 7-day statutory certification deadline established by the legislature. This modification of the code, by lengthening the protest period, necessarily shortened the contest period for Presidential elections. Underlying the extension of the certification deadline and the shortchanging of the contest period was, presumably, the clear implication that certification was a matter of significance: The certified winner would enjoy presumptive validity, making a contest proceeding by the losing candidate an uphill battle. In its latest opinion, however, the court empties certification of virtually all legal consequence during the contest, and in doing so departs from the provisions enacted by the Florida Legislature.

The court determined that canvassing boards' decisions regarding whether to recount ballots past the certification deadline (even the certification deadline established by Harris I) are to be reviewed de novo, although the election code clearly vests discretion whether to recount in the boards, and sets strict deadlines subject to the Secretary's rejection of late tallies and monetary fines for tardiness. See Fla. Stat. §102.112 (2000). Moreover, the Florida court held that all late vote tallies arriving during the contest period should be automatically included in the certification regardless of the certification deadline (even the certification deadline established by Harris I), thus virtually eliminating both the deadline and the Secretary's discretion to disregard recounts that violate it.

Moreover, the court's interpretation of "legal vote," and hence its decision to order a contest-period recount, plainly departed from the legislative scheme. Florida statutory law cannot reasonably be thought to require the counting of improperly marked ballots. Each Florida precinct before election day provides instructions on how properly to cast a vote, §101.46; each polling place on election day contains a working model of the voting machine it uses, §101.5611; and each voting booth contains a sample ballot, §101.46. In precincts using punch-card ballots, voters are instructed to punch out the ballot cleanly:

AFTER VOTING, CHECK YOUR BALLOT CARD TO BE SURE YOUR VOTING SELECTIONS ARE CLEARLY AND CLEANLY PUNCHED AND THERE ARE NO CHIPS LEFT HANGING ON THE BACK OF THE CARD.

Instructions to Voters, quoted in *Touchston v. McDermott*, 2000 WL 1781942, *6 & n. 19 (CA11) (Tjoflat, J., dissenting). No reasonable person would call it "an error in the vote tabulation," Fla. Stat. §102.166(5), or a "rejection of legal votes," Fla. Stat. §102.168(3)(c), when electronic or electromechanical equipment performs precisely in the manner designed, and fails to count those ballots that are not marked in the manner that these voting instructions explicitly and prominently specify. The scheme that the Florida Supreme Court's opinion attributes to the legislature is one in which machines are required to be "capable of correctly counting votes," §101.5606(4), but which nonetheless regularly produces elections in which legal votes are predictably not tabulated, so that in close elections manual recounts are regularly required. This is of course absurd. The Secretary of State, who is authorized by law to issue binding interpretations of the election code, §§97.012, 106.23, rejected this peculiar reading of the statutes. See DE 00-13 (opinion of the Division of Elections). The Florida Supreme Court, although it must defer to the Secretary's interpretations, see *Krivanek v. Take Back Tampa Political Committee*, 625 So.2d 840, 844 (Fla. 1993), rejected her reasonable interpretation and embraced the peculiar one. See *Palm Beach County Canvassing Board v. Harris*, No. SC00-2346 (Dec. 11, 2000) (Harris III).

But as we indicated in our remand of the earlier case, in a Presidential election the clearly expressed intent of the legislature must prevail. And there is no basis for reading the Florida statutes as requiring the counting of improperly marked ballots, as an examination of the Florida Supreme Court's textual analysis shows. We will not parse that analysis here, except to note that the principal provision of the election code on which it relied, §101.5614(5), was, as the Chief Justice pointed out in his dissent from Harris II, entirely irrelevant. See *Gore v. Harris*, No. SC00-2431, slip op., at 50 (Dec. 8, 2000). The State's Attorney General (who was supporting the Gore challenge) confirmed in oral argument here that never before the present election had a manual recount been conducted on the basis of the contention that "undervotes" should have been examined to determine voter intent. Tr. of Oral Arg. in *Bush v. Palm Beach County Canvassing Bd.*, 39-40 (Dec. 1, 2000); cf. *Broward County Canvassing Board v. Hogan*, 607 So.2d 508, 509 (Fla. Ct. App. 1992) (denial of recount for failure to count ballots with "hanging paper chads"). For the court to step away from this established practice, prescribed by the Secretary of State, the state official charged by the legislature with "responsibility to . . . [o]btain and maintain uniformity in the application, operation, and interpretation of the election laws," §97.012(1), was to depart from the legislative scheme.

III

The scope and nature of the remedy ordered by the Florida Supreme Court jeopardizes the "legislative wish" to take advantage of the safe harbor provided by 3 U.S.C. §5. *Bush v. Palm Beach County Canvassing Bd.*, ante, at 6. December 12, 2000, is the last date for a final determination of the Florida electors that will satisfy §5. Yet in the late afternoon of December 8th—four days before this deadline—the Supreme Court of Florida ordered recounts of tens of thousands of so-called "undervotes" spread through 64 of the State's 67 counties. This was done in a search for elusive—perhaps delusive—certainty as to the exact count of 6 million votes. But no one claims that these ballots have not previously been tabulated; they were initially read by voting machines at the time of the election, and thereafter reread by virtue of Florida's automatic recount provision. No one claims there was any fraud in the election. The Supreme Court of Florida ordered this additional recount under the provision of the election code giving the circuit judge the authority to provide relief that is "appropriate under such circumstances." Fla. Stat. §102.168(8) (2000).

Surely when the Florida Legislature empowered the courts of the State to grant "appropriate" relief, it must have meant relief that would have become final by the cut-off date of 3 U.S.C. §5. In light of the inevitable legal challenges and ensuing appeals to the Supreme Court of Florida and petitions for certiorari to this Court, the entire recounting process could not possibly be completed by that date. Whereas the majority in the Supreme Court of Florida stated its confidence that "the remaining undervotes in these counties can be [counted] within the required time frame," ___ So. 2d. at ___, n. 22 (slip op., at 38, n. 22), it made no assertion that the seemingly inevitable appeals could be disposed of in that time. Although the Florida Supreme Court has on occasion taken over a year to resolve disputes over local elections, see, e.g., *Beckstrom v. Volusia County Canvassing Bd.*, 707 So.2d 720 (1998) (resolving contest of sheriff's race 16 months after the election), it has heard and decided the appeals in the present case with great promptness. But the federal deadlines for the Presidential election simply do not permit even such a shortened process.

As the dissent noted:

"In [the four days remaining], all questionable ballots must be reviewed by the judicial officer appointed to discern the intent of the voter in a process open to the public. Fairness dictates that a provision be made for either party to object to how a particular ballot is counted. Additionally, this short time period must allow for judicial review. I respectfully submit this cannot be completed without taking Florida's presidential electors outside the safe harbor provision, creating the very real possibility of disenfranchising those nearly 6 million voters who are able to correctly cast their ballots on election day." ___ So.2d, at ___ (slip op., at 55) (Wells, C.J., dissenting).

The other dissenters echoed this concern: "[T]he majority is departing from the essential requirements of the law by providing a remedy which is impossible to achieve and which will ultimately lead to chaos." Id., at ___ (slip op., at 67 (Harding, J., dissenting, Shaw, J. concurring).

Given all these factors, and in light of the legislative intent identified by the Florida Supreme Court to bring Florida within the "safe harbor" provision of 3 U.S.C. §5, the remedy prescribed by the Supreme Court of Florida cannot be deemed an "appropriate" one as of December 8. It significantly departed from the statutory framework in place on November 7, and authorized open-ended further proceedings which could not be completed by December 12, thereby preventing a final determination by that date.

For these reasons, in addition to those given in the per curiam, we would reverse.

Justice Stevens, with Whom Justice Ginsburg and Justice Breyer Join, Dissenting

The Constitution assigns to the States the primary responsibility for determining the manner of selecting the Presidential electors. See Art.II, §1, cl.2. When questions arise about the meaning of state laws, including election laws, it is our settled practice to accept the opinions of the highest courts of the States as providing the final answers. On rare occasions, however, either federal statutes or the Federal Constitution may require federal judicial intervention in state elections. This is not such an occasion.

The federal questions that ultimately emerged in this case are not substantial. Article II provides that "[e]ach *State* shall appoint, in such Manner as the Legislature *thereof* may direct, a Number of Electors." Ibid. (emphasis added). It does not create state legislatures out of whole cloth, but rather takes them as they come—as creatures born of, and constrained by, their state constitutions. Lest there be any doubt, we stated over 100 years ago in *McPherson v. Blacker*, 146 U.S. 1, 25 (1892), that "[w]hat is forbidden or required to be done by a State" in the Article II context "is forbidden or required of the legislative power under state constitutions as they exist." In the same vein, we also observed that "[t]he [State's] legislative power is the supreme authority except as limited by the constitution of the State." Ibid.; cf. *Smiley v. Holm*, 285 U.S. 355, 367 (1932). The legislative power in Florida is subject to judicial review pursuant to Article V of the Florida Constitution, and nothing in Article II of the Federal Constitution frees the state legislature from the constraints in the state constitution that created it. Moreover, the Florida Legislature's own decision to employ a unitary code for all elections indicates that it intended the Florida Supreme Court to play the same role in Presidential elections that it has historically played in resolving electoral disputes. The Florida Supreme Court's exercise of appellate jurisdiction therefore was wholly consistent with, and indeed contemplated by, the grant of authority in Article II.

It hardly needs stating that Congress, pursuant to 3 U.S.C. §5, did not impose any affirmative duties upon the States that their governmental branches could "violate." Rather, §5 provides a safe harbor for States to select electors in contested elections "by judicial or other methods" established by laws prior to the election day. Section 5, like Article II, assumes the involvement of the state judiciary in interpreting state election laws and resolving election disputes under those laws. Neither §5 nor Article II grants federal judges any special authority to substitute their views for those of the state judiciary on matters of state law.

Nor are petitioners correct in asserting that the failure of the Florida Supreme Court to specify in detail the precise manner in which the "intent of the voter," Fla. Stat. §101.5614(5) (Supp. 2001), is to be determined rises to the level of a constitutional violation. We found such a violation when individual votes within the same State were weighted unequally, see, e.g., *Reynolds v. Sims*, 377 U.S. 533, 568 (1964), but we have never before called into question the substantive standard by which a State determines that a vote has been legally cast. And there is no reason to think that the guidance provided to the factfinders, specifically the various canvassing boards, by the "intent of the voter" standard is any less sufficient—or will lead to results any less uniform—than, for example, the "beyond a reasonable doubt" standard employed everyday by ordinary citizens in courtrooms across this country.

Admittedly, the use of differing substandards for determining voter intent in different counties employing similar voting systems may raise serious concerns. Those concerns are alleviated—if not eliminated—by the fact that a single impartial magistrate will ultimately adjudicate all objections arising from the recount process. Of course, as a general matter, "[t]he interpretation of constitutional principles must not be too literal. We must remember that the machinery of government would not work if it were not allowed a little play in its joints." *Bain Peanut Co. of Tex. v. Pinson*, 282 U.S. 499, 501 (1931) (Holmes, J.). If it were otherwise, Florida's decision to leave to each county the determination of what balloting system to employ—despite enormous differences in accuracy—might run afoul of equal protection. So, too, might the similar decisions of the vast majority of state legislatures to delegate to local authorities certain decisions with respect to voting systems and ballot design.

Even assuming that aspects of the remedial scheme might ultimately be found to violate the Equal Protection Clause, I could not subscribe to the majority's disposition of the case. As the majority explicitly holds, once a state legislature determines to select electors through a popular vote, the right to have one's vote counted is of constitutional stature. As the majority further acknowledges, Florida law holds that all ballots that reveal the intent of the voter constitute valid votes. Recognizing these principles, the majority nonetheless orders the termination of the contest proceeding before all such votes have been tabulated. Under their own reasoning, the appropriate course of action would be to remand to allow more specific procedures for implementing the legislature's uniform general standard to be established.

In the interest of finality, however, the majority effectively orders the disenfranchisement of an unknown number of voters whose ballots reveal their intent—and are therefore legal votes under state law—but were for some reason rejected by ballot-counting machines. It does so on the basis of the deadlines set forth in Title 3 of the UnitedStates Code. Ante, at 11. But, as I have already noted, those provisions merely provide rules of decision for Congress to follow when selecting among conflicting slates of electors. Supra, at 2. They do not prohibit a State from counting what the majority concedes to be legal votes until a bona fide winner is determined. Indeed, in 1960, Hawaii appointed two slates of electors and Congress chose to count the one appointed on January 4, 1961, well after the Title 3 deadlines. See Josephson & Ross, Repairing the Electoral College, 22 J. Legis. 145, 166, n. 154 (1996). Thus, nothing prevents the majority, even if it properly found an equal protection violation, from ordering relief appropriate to remedy that violation without depriving Florida voters of their right to have their votes counted. As the majority notes, "[a] desire for speed is not a general excuse for ignoring equal protection guarantees." Ante, at 10.

Finally, neither in this case, nor in its earlier opinion in *Palm Beach County Canvassing Bd. v. Harris*, 2000 WL 1725434 (Fla., Nov. 21, 2000), did the Florida Supreme Court make any substantive change in Florida electoral law. Its decisions were rooted in long-established precedent and were consistent with the relevant statutory provisions, taken as a whole. It did what courts do—it decided the case before it in light of the legislature's intent to leave no legally cast vote uncounted. In so doing, it relied on the sufficiency of the general "intent of the voter" standard articulated by the state legislature, coupled with a procedure for ultimate review by an impartial judge, to resolve the concern about disparate evaluations of contested ballots. If we assume—as I do—that the members of that court and the judges who would have carried out its mandate are impartial, its decision does not even raise a colorable federal question.

What must underlie petitioners' entire federal assault on the Florida election procedures is an unstated lack of confidence in the impartiality and capacity of the state judges who would make the critical decisions if the vote count were to proceed. Otherwise, their position is wholly without merit. The endorsement of that position by the majority of this Court can only lend credence to the most cynical appraisal of the work of judges throughout the land. It is confidence in the men and women who administer the judicial system that is the true backbone of the rule of law. Time will one day heal the wound to that confidence that will be inflicted by today's decision. One thing, however, is certain. Although we may never know with complete certainty the identity of the winner of this year's Presidential election, the identity of the loser is perfectly clear. It is the Nation's confidence in the judge as an impartial guardian of the rule of law.

I respectfully dissent.

Justice Souter, with Whom Justice Breyer Joins and with Whom Justice Stevens and Justice Ginsburg Join with Regard to All but Part C, Dissenting

The Court should not have reviewed either *Bush v. Palm Beach County Canvassing Bd.*, ante, p.___ (per curiam), or this case, and should not have stopped Florida's attempt to recount all undervote ballots, see ante at ___, by issuing a stay of the Florida Supreme Court's orders during the period of this review, see *Bush v. Gore*, post at ____ (slip op., at 1). If this Court had allowed the State to follow the course indicated by the opinions of its own Supreme Court, it is entirely possible that there would ultimately have been no issue requiring our review, and political tension could have worked itself out in the Congress following the procedure provided in 3 U.S.C. §15. The case being before us, however, its resolution by the majority is another erroneous decision.

As will be clear, I am in substantial agreement with the dissenting opinions of Justice Stevens, Justice Ginsburg and Justice Breyer. I write separately only to say how straightforward the issues before us really are.

There are three issues: whether the State Supreme Court's interpretation of the statute providing for a contest of the state election results somehow violates 3 U.S.C. §5; whether that court's construction of the state statutory provisions governing contests impermissibly changes a state law from what the State's legislature has provided, in violation of Article II, §1, cl.2, of the national Constitution; and whether the manner of interpreting markings on disputed ballots failing to cause machines to register votes for President (the undervote ballots) violates the equal protection or due process guaranteed by the Fourteenth Amendment. None of these issues is difficult to describe or to resolve.

A

The 3 U.S.C. §5 issue is not serious. That provision sets certain conditions for treating a State's certification of Presidential electors as conclusive in the event that a dispute over recognizing those electors must be resolved in the Congress under 3 U.S.C. §15. Conclusiveness requires selection under a legal scheme in place before the election, with results determined at least six days before the date set for casting electoral votes. But no State is required to conform to §5 if it cannot do that (for whatever reason); the sanction for failing to satisfy the conditions of §5 is simply loss of what has been called its "safe harbor." And even that determination is to be made, if made anywhere, in the Congress.

B

The second matter here goes to the State Supreme Court's interpretation of certain terms in the state statute governing election "contests," Fla. Stat. §102.168 (2000); there is no question here about the state court's interpretation of the related provisions dealing with the antecedent process of "protesting" particular vote counts, §102.166, which was involved in the previous case, *Bush v. Palm Beach County Canvassing Board*. The issue is whether the judgment of the state supreme court has displaced the state legislature's provisions for election contests: is the law as declared by the court different from the provisions made by the legislature, to which the national Constitution commits responsibility for determining how each State's Presidential electors are chosen? See U.S. Const., Art.II, §1, cl.2. Bush does not, of course, claim that any judicial act interpreting a statute of uncertain meaning is enough to displace the legislative provision and violate Article II; statutes require interpretation, which does not without more affect the legislative character of a statute within the meaning of the Constitution. Brief for Petitioners 48, n.22, in *Bush v. Palm Beach County Canvassing Bd.*, etal., 531 U.S. ___ (2000). What Bush does argue, as I understand the contention, is that the interpretation of §102.168 was so unreasonable as to transcend the accepted bounds of statutory interpretation, to the point of being a nonjudicial act and producing new law untethered to the legislative act in question.

The starting point for evaluating the claim that the Florida Supreme Court's interpretation effectively rewrote §102.168 must be the language of the provision on which Gore relies to show his right to raise this contest: that the previously certified result in Bush's favor was produced by "rejection of a number of legal votes sufficient to change or place in doubt the result of the election." Fla. Stat. §102.168(3)(c) (2000). None of the state court's interpretations is unreasonable to the point of displacing the legislative enactment quoted. As I will note below, other interpretations were of course possible, and some might have been better than those adopted by the Florida court's majority; the two dissents from the majority opinion of that court and various briefs submitted to us set out alternatives. But the majority view is in each instance within the bounds of reasonable interpretation, and the law as declared is consistent with ArticleII.

1. The statute does not define a "legal vote," the rejection of which may affect the election. The State Supreme Court was therefore required to define it, and in doing that the court looked to another election statute, §101.5614(5), dealing with damaged or defective ballots, which contains a provision that no vote shall be disregarded "if there is a clear indication of the intent of the voter as determined by a canvassing board." The court read that objective of looking to the voter's intent as indicating that the legislature probably meant "legal vote" to mean a vote recorded on a ballot indicating what the voter intended. *Gore v. Harris*, __ So.2d __ (slip op., at 23-25) (Dec. 8, 2000). It is perfectly true that the majority might have chosen a different reading. See, e.g., Brief for Respondent Harris etal. 10 (defining "legal votes" as "votes properly executed in accordance with the instructions provided to all registered voters in advance of the election and in the polling places"). But even so, there is no constitutional violation in following the majority view; Article II is unconcerned with mere disagreements about interpretive merits.

2. The Florida court next interpreted "rejection" to determine what act in the counting process may be attacked in a contest. Again, the statute does not define the term. The court majority read the word to mean simply a failure to count. ____ So.2d, at___ (slip op., at 26-27). That reading is certainly within the bounds of common sense, given the objective to give effect to a voter's intent if that can be determined. A different reading, of course, is possible. The majority might have concluded that "rejection" should refer to machine malfunction, or that a ballot should not be treated as "reject[ed]" in the absence of wrongdoing by election officials, lest contests be so easy to claim that every election will end up in one. Cf. id., at ____ (slip op., at 48) (Wells, C.J., dissenting). There is, however, nothing nonjudicial in the Florida majority's more hospitable reading.

3. The same is true about the court majority's understanding of the phrase "votes sufficient to change or place in doubt" the result of the election in Florida. The court held that if the uncounted ballots were so numerous that it was reasonably possible that they contained enough "legal" votes to swing the election, this contest would be authorized by the statute. While the majority might have thought (as the trial judge did) that a probability, not a possibility, should be necessary to justify a contest, that reading is not required by the statute's text, which says nothing about probability. Whatever people of good will and good sense may argue about the merits of the Florida court's reading, there is no warrant for saying that it transcends the limits of reasonable statutory interpretation to the point of supplanting the statute enacted by the "legislature" within the meaning of Article II.

In sum, the interpretations by the Florida court raise no substantial question under Article II. That court engaged in permissible construction in determining that Gore had instituted a contest authorized by the state statute, and it proceeded to direct the trial judge to deal with that contest in the exercise of the discretionary powers generously conferred by Fla. Stat. §102.168(8) (2000), to "fashion such orders as he or she deems necessary to ensure that each allegation in the complaint is investigated, examined, or checked, to prevent or correct any alleged wrong, and to provide any relief appropriate under such circumstances." As Justice Ginsburg has persuasively explained in her own dissenting opinion, our customary respect for state interpretations of state law counsels against rejection of the Florida court's determinations in this case.

C

It is only on the third issue before us that there is a meritorious argument for relief, as this Court's Per Curiam opinion recognizes. It is an issue that might well have been dealt with adequately by the Florida courts if the state proceedings had not been interrupted, and if not disposed of at the state level it could have been considered by the Congress in any electoral vote dispute. But because the course of state proceedings has been interrupted, time is short, and the issue is before us, I think it sensible for the Court to address it.

Petitioners have raised an equal protection claim (or, alternatively, a due process claim, see generally *Logan v. Zimmerman Brush Co.*, 455 U.S. 422 (1982)), in the charge that unjustifiably disparate standards are applied in different electoral jurisdictions to otherwise identical facts. It is true that the Equal Protection Clause does not forbid the use of a variety of voting mechanisms within a jurisdiction, even though different mechanisms will have different levels of effectiveness in recording voters' intentions; local variety can be justified by concerns about cost, the potential value of innovation, and so on. But evidence in the record here suggests that a different order of disparity obtains under rules for determining a voter's intent that have been applied (and could continue to be applied) to identical types of ballots used in identical brands of machines and exhibiting identical physical characteristics (such as "hanging" or "dimpled" chads). See, e.g., Tr., at 238-242 (Dec. 2-3, 2000) (testimony of Palm Beach County Canvassing Board Chairman Judge Charles Burton describing varying standards applied to imperfectly punched ballots in Palm Beach County during precertification manual recount); id., at 497-500 (similarly describing varying standards applied in Miami-Dade County); Tr. of Hearing 8-10 (Dec. 8, 2000) (soliciting from county canvassing boards proposed protocols for determining voters' intent but declining to provide a precise, uniform standard). I can conceive of no legitimate state interest served by these differing treatments of the expressions of voters' fundamental rights. The differences appear wholly arbitrary.

In deciding what to do about this, we should take account of the fact that electoral votes are due to be cast in six days. I would therefore remand the case to the courts of Florida with instructions to establish uniform standards for evaluating the several types of ballots that have prompted differing treatments, to be applied within and among counties when passing on such identical ballots in any further recounting (or successive recounting) that the courts might order.

Unlike the majority, I see no warrant for this Court to assume that Florida could not possibly comply with this requirement before the date set for the meeting of electors, December 18. Although one of the dissenting justices of the State Supreme Court estimated that disparate standards potentially affected 170,000 votes, *Gore v. Harris*, supra, ___ So.2d, at ___ (slip op., at 66), the number at issue is significantly smaller. The 170,000 figure apparently represents all uncounted votes, both undervotes (those for which no Presidential choice was recorded by a machine) and overvotes (those rejected because of votes for more than one candidate). Tr. of Oral Arg. 61-62. But as Justice Breyer has pointed out, no showing has been made of legal overvotes uncounted, and counsel for Gore made an uncontradicted representation to the Court that the statewide total of undervotes is about 60,000. Id., at 62. To recount these manually would be a tall order, but before this Court stayed the effort to do that the courts of Florida were ready to do their best to get that job done. There is no justification for denying the State the opportunity to try to count all disputed ballots now.

I respectfully dissent.

Justice Ginsburg, with Whom Justice Stevens Joins, and with Whom Justice Souter and Justice Breyer Join as to Part I, Dissenting

I

The Chief Justice acknowledges that provisions of Florida's Election Code "may well admit of more than one interpretation." Ante, at 3. But instead of respecting the state high court's province to say what the State's Election Code means, The Chief Justice maintains that Florida's Supreme Court has veered so far from the ordinary practice of judicial review that what it did cannot properly be called judging. My colleagues have offered a reasonable construction of Florida's law. Their construction coincides with the view of one of Florida's seven Supreme Court justices. *Gore v. Harris*, ___ So.2d ___, ___ (Fla. 2000) (slip op., at 45-55) (Wells, C.J., dissenting); *Palm Beach County Canvassing Bd. v. Harris*, ___ So.2d ___, ___ (Fla. 2000) (slip op., at 34) (on remand) (confirming, 6-1, the construction of Florida law advanced in Gore). I might join The Chief Justice were it my commission to interpret Florida law. But disagreement with the Florida court's interpretation of its own State's law does not warrant the conclusion that the justices of that court have legislated. There is no cause here to believe that the members of Florida's high court have done less than "their mortal best to discharge their oath of office," *Sumner v. Mata*, 449 U.S. 539, 549 (1981), and no cause to upset their reasoned interpretation of Florida law.

This Court more than occasionally affirms statutory, and even constitutional, interpretations with which it disagrees. For example, when reviewing challenges to administrative agencies' interpretations of laws they implement, we defer to the agencies unless their interpretation violates "the unambiguously expressed intent of Congress." *Chevron U.S.A. Inc. v. Natural Resources Defense Council, Inc.*, 467 U.S. 837, 843 (1984). We do so in the face of the declaration in Article I of the United States Constitution that "All legislative Powers herein granted shall be vested in a Congress of the United States." Surely the Constitution does not call upon us to pay more respect to a federal administrative agency's construction of federal law than to a state high court's interpretation of its own state's law. And not uncommonly, we let stand state-court interpretations of federal law with which we might disagree. Notably, in the habeas context, the Court adheres to the view that "there is 'no intrinsic reason why the fact that a man is a federal judge should make him more competent, or conscientious, or learned with respect to [federal law] than his neighbor in the state courthouse.'" *Stone v. Powell*, 428 U. S. 465, 494, n. 35 (1976) (quoting Bator, Finality in Criminal Law and Federal Habeas Corpus For State Prisoners, 76 Harv. L. Rev. 441, 509 (1963)); see *O'Dell v. Netherland*, 521 U.S. 151, 156 (1997) ("[T]he Teague doctrine validates reasonable, good-faith interpretations of existing precedents made by state courts even though they are shown to be contrary to later decisions.") (citing *Butler v. McKellar*, 494 U.S. 407, 414 (1990)); O'Connor, Trends in the Relationship Between the Federal and State Courts from the Perspective of a State Court Judge, 22 Wm. & Mary L.Rev. 801, 813 (1981) ("There is no reason to assume that state court judges cannot and will not provide a 'hospitable forum' in litigating federal constitutional questions.").

No doubt there are cases in which the proper application of federal law may hinge on interpretations of state law. Unavoidably, this Court must sometimes examine state law in order to protect federal rights. But we have dealt with such cases ever mindful of the full measure of respect we owe to interpretations of state law by a State's highest court. In the Contract Clause case, *General Motors Corp. v. Romein*, 503 U.S. 181 (1992), for example, we said that although "ultimately we are bound to decide for ourselves whether a contract was made," the Court "accord[s] respectful consideration and great weight to the views of the State's highest court." Id., at 187 (citation omitted). And in *Central Union Telephone Co. v. Edwardsville*, 269 U.S. 190 (1925), we upheld the Illinois Supreme Court's interpretation of a state waiver rule, even though that interpretation resulted in the forfeiture of federal constitutional rights. Refusing to supplant Illinois law with a federal definition of waiver, we explained that the state court's declaration "should bind us unless so unfair or unreasonable in its application to those asserting a federal right as to obstruct it." Id., at 195.1

In deferring to state courts on matters of state law, we appropriately recognize that this Court acts as an "'outside[r]' lacking the common exposure to local law which comes from sitting in the jurisdiction." *Lehman Brothers v. Schein*, 416 U. S. 386, 391 (1974). That recognition has sometimes prompted us to resolve doubts about the meaning of state law by certifying issues to a State's highest court, even when federal rights are at stake. Cf. *Arizonans for Official English v. Arizona*, 520 U. S. 43, 79 (1997) ("Warnings against premature adjudication of constitutional questions bear heightened attention when a federal court is asked to invalidate a State's law, for the federal tribunal risks friction-generating error when it endeavors to construe a novel state Act not yet reviewed by the State's highest court."). Notwithstanding our authority to decide issues of state law underlying federal claims, we have used the certification devise to afford state high courts an opportunity to inform us on matters of their own State's law because such restraint "helps build a cooperative judicial federalism." Lehman Brothers, 416 U.S., at 391.

Just last Term, in *Fiore v. White*, 528 U.S. 23 (1999), we took advantage of Pennsylvania's certification procedure. In that case, a state prisoner brought a federal habeas action claiming that the State had failed to prove an essential element of his charged offense in violation of the Due Process Clause. Id., at 25-26. Instead of resolving the state-law question on which the federal claim depended, we certified the question to the Pennsylvania Supreme Court for that court to "help determine the proper state-law predicate for our determination of the federal constitutional questions raised." Id., at 29; id., at 28 (asking the Pennsylvania Supreme Court whether its recent interpretation of the statute under which Fiore was convicted "was always the statute's meaning, even at the time of Fiore's trial"). The Chief Justice's willingness to reverse the Florida Supreme Court's interpretation of Florida law in this case is at least in tension with our reluctance in Fiore even to interpret Pennsylvania law before seeking instruction from the Pennsylvania Supreme Court. I would have thought the "cautious approach" we counsel when federal courts address matters of state law, Arizonans, 520 U.S., at 77, and our commitment to "build[ing] cooperative judicial federalism," Lehman Brothers, 416 U.S., at 391, demanded greater restraint.

Rarely has this Court rejected outright an interpretation of state law by a state high court. *Fairfax's Devisee v. Hunter's Lessee*, 7 Cranch 603 (1813), *NAACP v. Alabama ex rel. Patterson*, 357 U.S. 449 (1958), and *Bouie v. City of Columbia*, 378 U.S. 347 (1964), cited by The Chief Justice, are three such rare instances. See ante, at 4, 5, and n.2. But those cases are embedded in historical contexts hardly comparable to the situation here. Fairfax's Devisee, which held that the Virginia Court of Appeals had misconstrued its own forfeiture laws to deprive a British subject of lands secured to him by federal treaties, occurred amidst vociferous States' rights attacks on the Marshall Court. G. Gunther & K. Sullivan, Constitutional Law 61-62 (13th ed. 1997). The Virginia court refused to obey this Court's Fairfax's Devisee mandate to enter judgment for the British subject's successor in interest. That refusal led to the Court's pathmarking decision in *Martin v. Hunter's Lessee*, 1 Wheat. 304 (1816). Patterson, a case decided three months after *Cooper v. Aaron*, 358 U.S. 1 (1958), in the face of Southern resistance to the civil rights movement, held that the Alabama Supreme Court had irregularly applied its own procedural rules to deny review of a contempt order against the NAACP arising from its refusal to disclose membership lists. We said that "our jurisdiction is not defeated if the nonfederal ground relied on by the state court is without any fair or substantial support." 357 U.S., at 455. Bouie, stemming from a lunch counter "sit-in" at the height of the civil rights movement, held that the South Carolina Supreme Court's construction of its trespass laws—criminalizing conduct not covered by the text of an otherwise clear statute—was "unforeseeable" and thus violated due process when applied retroactively to the petitioners. 378 U.S., at 350, 354.

The Chief Justice's casual citation of these cases might lead one to believe they are part of a larger collection of cases in which we said that the Constitution impelled us to train a skeptical eye on a state court's portrayal of state law. But one would be hard pressed, I think, to find additional cases that fit the mold. As Justice Breyer convincingly explains, see post, at 5-9 (dissenting opinion), this case involves nothing close to the kind of recalcitrance by a state high court that warrants extraordinary action by this Court. The Florida Supreme Court concluded that counting every legal vote was the overriding concern of the Florida Legislature when it enacted the State's Election Code. The court surely should not be bracketed with state high courts of the Jim Crow South.

The Chief Justice says that Article II, by providing that state legislatures shall direct the manner of appointing electors, authorizes federal superintendence over the relationship between state courts and state legislatures, and licenses a departure from the usual deference we give to state court interpretations of state law. Ante, at 5 ("To attach definitive weight to the pronouncement of a state court, when the very question at issue is whether the court has actually departed from the statutory meaning, would be to abdicate our responsibility to enforce the explicit requirements of Article II."). The Framers of our Constitution, however, understood that in a republican government, the judiciary would construe the legislature's enactments. See U.S. Const., Art.III; The Federalist No. 78 (A. Hamilton). In light of the constitutional guarantee to States of a "Republican Form of Government," U.S. Const., Art. IV, §4, Article II can hardly be read to invite this Court to disrupt a State's republican regime. Yet The Chief Justice today would reach out to do just that. By holding that Article II requires our revision of a state court's construction of state laws in order to protect one organ of the State from another, The Chief Justice contradicts the basic principle that a State may organize itself as it sees fit. See, e.g., *Gregory v. Ashcroft*, 501 U. S. 452, 460 (1991) ("Through the structure of its government, and the character of those who exercise government authority, a State defines itself as a sovereign."); *Highland Farms Dairy, Inc. v. Agnew*, 300 U.S. 608, 612 (1937) ("How power shall be distributed by a state among its governmental organs is commonly, if not always, a question for the state itself."). Article II does not call for the scrutiny undertaken by this Court.

The extraordinary setting of this case has obscured the ordinary principle that dictates its proper resolution: Federal courts defer to state high courts' interpretations of their state's own law. This principle reflects the core of federalism, on which all agree. "The Framers split the atom of sovereignty. It was the genius of their idea that our citizens would have two political capacities, one state and one federal, each protected from incursion by the other." *Saenz v. Roe*, 526 U.S. 489, 504, n.17 (1999) (citing *U.S. Term Limits, Inc. v. Thornton*, 514 U.S. 779, 838 (1995) (Kennedy, J., concurring)). The Chief Justice's solicitude for the Florida Legislature comes at the expense of the more fundamental solicitude we owe to the legislature's sovereign. U.S. Const., Art.II, §1, cl.2 ("Each *State* shall appoint, in such Manner as the Legislature *thereof* may direct," the electors for President and Vice President) (emphasis added); ante, at 1-2 (Stevens, J., dissenting). Were the other members of this Court as mindful as they generally are of our system of dual sovereignty, they would affirm the judgment of the Florida Supreme Court.

II

I agree with Justice Stevens that petitioners have not presented a substantial equal protection claim. Ideally, perfection would be the appropriate standard for judging the recount. But we live in an imperfect world, one in which thousands of votes have not been counted. I cannot agree that the recount adopted by the Florida court, flawed as it may be, would yield a result any less fair or precise than the certification that preceded that recount. See, e.g., *McDonald v. Board of Election Comm'rs of Chicago*, 394 U.S. 802, 807 (1969) (even in the context of the right to vote, the state is permitted to reform "one step at a time") (quoting *Williamson v. Lee Optical of Oklahoma, Inc.*, 348 U.S. 483, 489 (1955)).

Even if there were an equal protection violation, I would agree with Justice Stevens, Justice Souter, and Justice Breyer that the Court's concern about "the December 12 deadline," ante, at 12, is misplaced. Time is short in part because of the Court's entry of a stay on December 9, several hours after an able circuit judge in Leon County had begun to superintend the recount process. More fundamentally, the Court's reluctance to let the recount go forward—despite its suggestion that "[t]he search for intent can be confined by specific rules designed to ensure uniform treatment," ante, at 8—ultimately turns on its own judgment about the practical realities of implementing a recount, not the judgment of those much closer to the process.

Equally important, as Justice Breyer explains, post, at 12 (dissenting opinion), the December 12 "deadline" for bringing Florida's electoral votes into 3 U.S.C. §5's safe harbor lacks the significance the Court assigns it. Were that date to pass, Florida would still be entitled to deliver electoral votes Congress must count unless both Houses find that the votes "ha[d] not been . . . regularly given." 3 U.S.C. §15. The statute identifies other significant dates. See, e.g., §7 (specifying December 18 as the date electors "shall meet and give their votes"); §12 (specifying "the fourth Wednesday in December"—this year, December 27—as the date on which Congress, if it has not received a State's electoral votes, shall request the state secretary of state to send a certified return immediately). But none of these dates has ultimate significance in light of Congress' detailed provisions for determining, on "the sixth day of January," the validity of electoral votes. §15.

The Court assumes that time will not permit "orderly judicial review of any disputed matters that might arise." Ante, at 12. But no one has doubted the good faith and diligence with which Florida election officials, attorneys for all sides of this controversy, and the courts of law have performed their duties. Notably, the Florida Supreme Court has produced two substantial opinions within 29 hours of oral argument. In sum, the Court's conclusion that a constitutionally adequate recount is impractical is a prophecy the Court's own judgment will not allow to be tested. Such an untested prophecy should not decide the Presidency of the United States.

I dissent.

Justice Breyer, with Whom Justice Stevens and Justice Ginsburg Join Except as to Part I—A-1, and with Whom Justice Souter Joins as to PartI, Dissenting

The Court was wrong to take this case. It was wrong to grant a stay. It should now vacate that stay and permit the Florida Supreme Court to decide whether the recount should resume.

I

The political implications of this case for the country are momentous. But the federal legal questions presented, with one exception, are insubstantial.

A

1

The majority raises three Equal Protection problems with the Florida Supreme Court's recount order: first, the failure to include overvotes in the manual recount; second, the fact that all ballots, rather than simply the undervotes, were recounted in some, but not all, counties; and third, the absence of a uniform, specific standard to guide the recounts. As far as the first issue is concerned, petitioners presented no evidence, to this Court or to any Florida court, that a manual recount of overvotes would identify additional legal votes. The same is true of the second, and, in addition, the majority's reasoning would seem to invalidate any state provision for a manual recount of individual counties in a statewide election.

The majority's third concern does implicate principles of fundamental fairness. The majority concludes that the Equal Protection Clause requires that a manual recount be governed not only by the uniform general standard of the "clear intent of the voter," but also by uniform subsidiary standards (for example, a uniform determination whether indented, but not perforated, "undervotes" should count). The opinion points out that the Florida Supreme Court ordered the inclusion of Broward County's undercounted "legal votes" even though those votes included ballots that were not perforated but simply "dimpled," while newly recounted ballots from other counties will likely include only votes determined to be "legal" on the basis of a stricter standard. In light of our previous remand, the Florida Supreme Court may have been reluctant to adopt a more specific standard than that provided for by the legislature for fear of exceeding its authority under Article II. However, since the use of different standards could favor one or the other of the candidates, since time was, and is, too short to permit the lower courts to iron out significant differences through ordinary judicial review, and since the relevant distinction was embodied in the order of the State's highest court, I agree that, in these very special circumstances, basic principles of fairness may well have counseled the adoption of a uniform standard to address the problem. In light of the majority's disposition, I need not decide whether, or the extent to which, as a remedial matter, the Constitution would place limits upon the content of the uniform standard.

2

Nonetheless, there is no justification for the majority's remedy, which is simply to reverse the lower court and halt the recount entirely. An appropriate remedy would be, instead, to remand this case with instructions that, even at this late date, would permit the Florida Supreme Court to require recounting all undercounted votes in Florida, including those from Broward, Volusia, Palm Beach, and Miami-Dade Counties, whether or not previously recounted prior to the end of the protest period, and to do so in accordance with a single-uniform substandard.

The majority justifies stopping the recount entirely on the ground that there is no more time. In particular, the majority relies on the lack of time for the Secretary to review and approve equipment needed to separate undervotes. But the majority reaches this conclusion in the absence of any record evidence that the recount could not have been completed in the time allowed by the Florida Supreme Court. The majority finds facts outside of the record on matters that state courts are in a far better position to address. Of course, it is too late for any such recount to take place by December 12, the date by which election disputes must be decided if a State is to take advantage of the safe harbor provisions of 3 U.S.C. §5. Whether there is time to conduct a recount prior to December 18, when the electors are scheduled to meet, is a matter for the state courts to determine. And whether, under Florida law, Florida could or could not take further action is obviously a matter for Florida courts, not this Court, to decide. See ante, at 13 (per curiam).

By halting the manual recount, and thus ensuring that the uncounted legal votes will not be counted under any standard, this Court crafts a remedy out of proportion to the asserted harm. And that remedy harms the very fairness interests the Court is attempting to protect. The manual recount would itself redress a problem of unequal treatment of ballots. As Justice Stevens points out, see ante, at 4 and n.4 (Stevens, J., dissenting opinion), the ballots of voters in counties that use punch-card systems are more likely to be disqualified than those in counties using optical-scanning systems. According to recent news reports, variations in the undervote rate are even more pronounced. See Fessenden, No-Vote Rates Higher in Punch Card Count, N.Y. Times, Dec. 1, 2000, p.A29 (reporting that 0.3% of ballots cast in 30 Florida counties using optical-scanning systems registered no Presidential vote, in comparison to 1.53% in the 15 counties using Votomatic punch card ballots). Thus, in a system that allows counties to use different types of voting systems, voters already arrive at the polls with an unequal chance that their votes will be counted. I do not see how the fact that this results from counties' selection of different voting machines rather than a court order makes the outcome any more fair. Nor do I understand why the Florida Supreme Court's recount order, which helps to redress this inequity, must be entirely prohibited based on a deficiency that could easily be remedied.

B

The remainder of petitioners' claims, which are the focus of the Chief Justice's concurrence, raise no significant federal questions. I cannot agree that the Chief Justice's unusual review of state law in this case, see ante, at 5-8 (Ginsburg, J., dissenting opinion), is justified by reference either to Art.II, §1, or to 3 U.S.C. §5. Moreover, even were such review proper, the conclusion that the Florida Supreme Court's decision contravenes federal law is untenable.

While conceding that, in most cases, "comity and respect for federalism compel us to defer to the decisions of state courts on issues of state law," the concurrence relies on some combination of Art. II, §1, and 3 U.S.C. §5 to justify the majority's conclusion that this case is one of the few in which we may lay that fundamental principle aside. Ante, at 2 (Opinion of Rehnquist, C.J. The concurrence's primary foundation for this conclusion rests on an appeal to plain text: Art. II, §1's grant of the power to appoint Presidential electors to the State "Legislature." Ibid. But neither the text of Article II itself nor the only case the concurrence cites that interprets Article II, *McPherson v. Blacker*, 146 U.S. 1 (1892), leads to the conclusion that Article II grants unlimited power to the legislature, devoid of any state constitutional limitations, to select the manner of appointing electors. See id., at 41 (specifically referring to state constitutional provision in upholding state law regarding selection of electors). Nor, as Justice Stevens points out, have we interpreted the Federal constitutional provision most analogous to Art. II, §1—Art.I, §4—in the strained manner put forth in the concurrence. Ante, at 1-2 and n.1 (dissenting opinion).

The concurrence's treatment of §5 as "inform[ing]" its interpretation of Article II, §1, cl.2, ante, at 3 (Rehnquist, C.J., concurring), is no more convincing. The Chief Justice contends that our opinion in *Bush v. Palm Beach County Canvassing Bd.*, ante, p.___, (per curiam) (BushI), in which we stated that "a legislative wish to take advantage of [§5] would counsel against" a construction of Florida law that Congress might deem to be a change in law, id., (slip op. at 6), now means that this Court "must ensure that post-election state court actions do not frustrate the legislative desire to attain the 'safe harbor' provided by §5." Ante, at 3. However, §5 is part of the rules that govern Congress' recognition of slates of electors. Nowhere in BushI did we establish that this Court had the authority to enforce §5. Nor did we suggest that the permissive "counsel against" could be transformed into the mandatory "must ensure." And nowhere did we intimate, as the concurrence does here, that a state court decision that threatens the safe harbor provision of §5 does so in violation of ArticleII. The concurrence's logic turns the presumption that legislatures would wish to take advantage of §5's "safe harbor" provision into a mandate that trumps other statutory provisions and overrides the intent that the legislature did express.

But, in any event, the concurrence, having conducted its review, now reaches the wrong conclusion. It says that "the Florida Supreme Court's interpretation of the Florida election laws impermissibly distorted them beyond what a fair reading required, in violation of Article II." Ante, at 4-5 (Rehnquist, C.J, concurring). But what precisely is the distortion? Apparently, it has three elements. First, the Florida court, in its earlier opinion, changed the election certification date from

November 14 to November 26. Second, the Florida court ordered a manual recount of "undercounted" ballots that could not have been fully completed by the December 12 "safe harbor" deadline. Third, the Florida court, in the opinion now under review, failed to give adequate deference to the determinations of canvassing boards and the Secretary.

To characterize the first element as a "distortion," however, requires the concurrence to second-guess the way in which the state court resolved a plain conflict in the language of different statutes. Compare Fla. Stat. §102.166 (2001) (foreseeing manual recounts during the protest period) with §102.111 (setting what is arguably too short a deadline for manual recounts to be conducted); compare §102.112(1) (stating that the Secretary "may" ignore late returns) with §102.111(1) (stating that the Secretary "shall" ignore late returns). In any event, that issue no longer has any practical importance and cannot justify the reversal of the different Florida court decision before us now.

To characterize the second element as a "distortion" requires the concurrence to overlook the fact that the inability of the Florida courts to conduct the recount on time is, in significant part, a problem of the Court's own making. The Florida Supreme Court thought that the recount could be completed on time, and, within hours, the Florida Circuit Court was moving in an orderly fashion to meet the deadline. This Court improvidently entered a stay. As a result, we will never know whether the recount could have been completed.

Nor can one characterize the third element as "impermissibl[e] distort[ing]" once one understands that there are two sides to the opinion's argument that the Florida Supreme Court "virtually eliminated the Secretary's discretion." Ante, at 9 (Rehnquist, C.J, concurring). The Florida statute in question was amended in 1999 to provide that the "grounds for contesting an election" include the "rejection of a number of legal votes sufficient to ... place in doubt the result of the election." Fla. Stat. §§102.168(3), (3)(c) (2000). And the parties have argued about the proper meaning of the statute's term "legal vote." The Secretary has claimed that a "legal vote" is a vote "properly executed in accordance with the instructions provided to all registered voters." Brief for Respondent Harris etal. 10. On that interpretation, punchcard ballots for which the machines cannot register a vote are not "legal" votes. Id., at 14. The Florida Supreme Court did not accept her definition. But it had a reason. Its reason was that a different provision of Florida election laws (a provision that addresses damaged or defective ballots) says that no vote shall be disregarded "if there is a clear indication of the intent of the voter as determined by the canvassing board" (adding that ballots should not be counted "if it is impossible to determine the elector's choice"). Fla. Stat. §101.5614(5) (2000). Given this statutory language, certain roughly analogous judicial precedent, e.g., *Darby v. State ex rel. McCollough*, 75 So. 411 (Fla. 1917) (per curiam), and somewhat similar determinations by courts throughout the Nation, see cases cited infra, at 9, the Florida Supreme Court concluded that the term "legal vote" means a vote recorded on a ballot that clearly reflects what the voter intended. *Gore v. Harris*, ___ So.2d ___, ___ (2000) (slip op., at 19). That conclusion differs from the conclusion of the Secretary. But nothing in Florida law requires the Florida Supreme Court to accept as determinative the Secretary's view on such a matter. Nor can one say that the Court's ultimate determination is so unreasonable as to amount to a constitutionally "impermissible distort[ion]" of Florida law.

The Florida Supreme Court, applying this definition, decided, on the basis of the record, that respondents had shown that the ballots undercounted by the voting machines contained enough "legal votes" to place "the results" of the election "in doubt." Since only a few hundred votes separated the candidates, and since the "undercounted" ballots numbered tens of thousands, it is difficult to see how anyone could find this conclusion unreasonable-however strict the standard used to measure the voter's "clear intent." Nor did this conclusion "strip" canvassing boards of their discretion. The boards retain their traditional discretionary authority during the protest period. And during the contest period, as the court stated, "the Canvassing Board's actions [during the protest period] may constitute evidence that a ballot does or does not qualify as a legal vote." Id., at *13. Whether a local county canvassing board's discretionary judgment during the protest period not to conduct a manual recount will be set aside during a contest period depends upon whether a candidate provides additional evidence that the rejected votes contain enough "legal votes" to place the outcome of the race in doubt. To limit the local canvassing board's discretion in this way is not to eliminate that discretion. At the least, one could reasonably so believe.

The statute goes on to provide the Florida circuit judge with authority to "fashion such orders as he or she deems necessary to ensure that each allegation . . . is *investigated, examined, or checked*, . . . and to provide any relief appropriate." Fla. Stat. §102.168(8) (2000) (emphasis added). The Florida Supreme Court did just that. One might reasonably disagree with the Florida Supreme Court's interpretation of these, or other, words in the statute. But I do not see how one could call its plain language interpretation of a 1999 statutory change so misguided as no longer to qualify as judicial interpretation or as a usurpation of the authority of the State legislature. Indeed, other state courts have interpreted roughly similar state statutes in similar ways. See, e.g., Inre Election of U.S. Representative for Second Congressional Dist., 231 Conn. 602, 621, 653 A. 2d 79, 90-91 (1994) ("Whatever the process used to vote and to count votes, differences in technology should not furnish a basis for disregarding the bedrock principle that the purpose of the voting process is to ascertain the intent of the voters"); *Brown v. Carr*, 130 W.Va. 401, 460, 43 S.E.2d 401, 404-405 (1947) ("[W]hether a ballot shall be counted . . . depends on the intent of the voter. . . . Courts decry any resort to technical rules in reaching a conclusion as to the intent of the voter").

I repeat, where is the "impermissible" distortion?

II

Despite the reminder that this case involves "an election for the President of the United States," ante, at 1 (Rehnquist, C.J., concurring), no preeminent legal concern, or practical concern related to legal questions, required this Court to hear this case, let alone to issue a stay that stopped Florida's recount process in its tracks. With one exception, petitioners' claims do not ask us to vindicate a constitutional provision designed to protect a basic human right. See, e.g., *Brown v. Board of Education*, 347 U.S. 483 (1954). Petitioners invoke fundamental fairness, namely, the need for procedural fairness, including finality. But with the one "equal protection" exception, they rely upon law that focuses, not upon that basic need, but upon the constitutional allocation of power. Respondents invoke a competing fundamental consideration—the need to determine the voter's true intent. But they look to state law, not to federal constitutional law, to protect that interest. Neither side claims electoral fraud, dishonesty, or the like. And the more fundamental equal protection claim might have been left to the state court to resolve if and when it was discovered to have mattered. It could still be resolved through a remand conditioned upon issuance of a uniform standard; it does not require reversing the Florida Supreme Court.

Of course, the selection of the President is of fundamental national importance. But that importance is political, not legal. And this Court should resist the temptation unnecessarily to resolve tangential legal disputes, where doing so threatens to determine the outcome of the election.

The Constitution and federal statutes themselves make clear that restraint is appropriate. They set forth a road map of how to resolve disputes about electors, even after an election as close as this one. That road map foresees resolution of electoral disputes by state courts. See 3 U.S.C. §5 (providing that, where a "State shall have provided, by laws enacted prior to [election day], for its final determination of any controversy or contest concerning the appointment of . . . electors . . . by judicial or other methods," the subsequently chosen electors enter a safe harbor free from congressional challenge). But it nowhere provides for involvement by the United States Supreme Court.

To the contrary, the Twelfth Amendment commits to Congress the authority and responsibility to count electoral votes. A federal statute, the Electoral Count Act, enacted after the close 1876 Hayes-Tilden Presidential election, specifies that, after States have tried to resolve disputes (through "judicial" or other means), Congress is the body primarily authorized to resolve remaining disputes. See Electoral Count Act of 1887, 24 Stat. 373, 3 U.S.C. §§5, 6, and 15.

The legislative history of the Act makes clear its intent to commit the power to resolve such disputes to Congress, rather than the courts:

"The two Houses are, by the Constitution, authorized to make the count of electoral votes. They can only count legal votes, and in doing so must determine, from the best evidence to be had, what are legal votes. . . . The power to determine rests with the two Houses, and there is no other constitutional tribunal." H. Rep. No. 1638, 49th Cong., 1st Sess., 2 (1886) (report submitted by Rep. Caldwell, Select Committee on the Election of President and Vice-President).

The Member of Congress who introduced the Act added:

"The power to judge of the legality of the votes is a necessary consequent of the power to count. The existence of this power is of absolute necessity to the preservation of the Government. The interests of all the States in their relations to each other in the Federal Union demand that the ultimate tribunal to decide upon the election of President should be a constituent body, in which the States in their federal relationships and the people in their sovereign capacity should be represented." 18 Cong. Rec. 30 (1886).

"Under the Constitution who else could decide? Who is nearer to the State in determining a question of vital importance to the whole union of States than the constituent body upon whom the Constitution has devolved the duty to count the vote?" Id., at 31.

The Act goes on to set out rules for the congressional determination of disputes about those votes. If, for example, a state submits a single slate of electors, Congress must count those votes unless both Houses agree that the votes "have not been ... regularly given." 3 U.S.C. § 15. If, as occurred in 1876, one or more states submits two sets of electors, then Congress must determine whether a slate has entered the safe harbor of §5, in which case its votes will have "conclusive" effect. Ibid. If, as also occurred in 1876, there is controversy about "which of two or more of such State authorities ... is the lawful tribunal" authorized to appoint electors, then each House shall determine separately which votes are "supported by the decision of such State so authorized by its law." Ibid. If the two Houses of Congress agree, the votes they have approved will be counted. If they disagree, then "the votes of the electors whose appointment shall have been certified by the executive of the State, under the seal thereof, shall be counted." Ibid.

Given this detailed, comprehensive scheme for counting electoral votes, there is no reason to believe that federal law either foresees or requires resolution of such a political issue by this Court. Nor, for that matter, is there any reason to that think the Constitution's Framers would have reached a different conclusion. Madison, at least, believed that allowing the judiciary to choose the presidential electors "was out of the question." Madison, July 25, 1787 (reprinted in 5 Elliot's Debates on the Federal Constitution 363 (2d ed. 1876)).

The decision by both the Constitution's Framers and the 1886 Congress to minimize this Court's role in resolving close federal presidential elections is as wise as it is clear. However awkward or difficult it may be for Congress to resolve difficult electoral disputes, Congress, being a political body, expresses the people's will far more accurately than does an unelected Court. And the people's will is what elections are about.

Moreover, Congress was fully aware of the danger that would arise should it ask judges, unarmed with appropriate legal standards, to resolve a hotly contested Presidential election contest. Just after the 1876 Presidential election, Florida, South Carolina, and Louisiana each sent two slates of electors to Washington. Without these States, Tilden, the Democrat, had 184 electoral votes, one short of the number required to win the Presidency. With those States, Hayes, his Republican opponent, would have had 185. In order to choose between the two slates of electors, Congress decided to appoint an electoral commission composed of five Senators, five Representatives, and five Supreme Court Justices. Initially the Commission was to be evenly divided between Republicans and Democrats, with Justice David Davis, an Independent, to possess the decisive vote. However, when at the last minute the Illinois Legislature elected Justice Davis to the United States Senate, the final position on the Commission was filled by Supreme Court Justice Joseph P. Bradley.

The Commission divided along partisan lines, and the responsibility to cast the deciding vote fell to Justice Bradley. He decided to accept the votes by the Republican electors, and thereby awarded the Presidency to Hayes.

Justice Bradley immediately became the subject of vociferous attacks. Bradley was accused of accepting bribes, of being captured by railroad interests, and of an eleventh-hour change in position after a night in which his house "was surrounded by the carriages" of Republican partisans and railroad officials. C. Woodward, Reunion and Reaction 159-160 (1966). Many years later, Professor Bickel concluded that Bradley was honest and impartial. He thought that "'the great question' for Bradley was, in fact, whether Congress was entitled to go behind election returns or had to accept them as certified by state authorities," an "issue of principle." The Least Dangerous Branch 185 (1962). Nonetheless, Bickel points out, the legal question upon which Justice

Bradley's decision turned was not very important in the contemporaneous political context. He says that "in the circumstances the issue of principle was trivial, it was overwhelmed by all that hung in the balance, and it should not have been decisive." Ibid.

For present purposes, the relevance of this history lies in the fact that the participation in the work of the electoral commission by five Justices, including Justice Bradley, did not lend that process legitimacy. Nor did it assure the public that the process had worked fairly, guided by the law. Rather, it simply embroiled Members of the Court in partisan conflict, thereby undermining respect for the judicial process. And the Congress that later enacted the Electoral Count Act knew it.

This history may help to explain why I think it not only legally wrong, but also most unfortunate, for the Court simply to have terminated the Florida recount. Those who caution judicial restraint in resolving political disputes have described the quintessential case for that restraint as a case marked, among other things, by the "strangeness of the issue," its "intractability to principled resolution," its "sheer momentousness, . . . which tends to unbalance judicial judgment," and "the inner vulnerability, the self-doubt of an institution which is electorally irresponsible and has no earth to draw strength from." Bickel, supra, at 184. Those characteristics mark this case.

At the same time, as I have said, the Court is not acting to vindicate a fundamental constitutional principle, such as the need to protect a basic human liberty. No other strong reason to act is present. Congressional statutes tend to obviate the need. And, above all, in this highly politicized matter, the appearance of a split decision runs the risk of undermining the public's confidence in the Court itself. That confidence is a public treasure. It has been built slowly over many years, some of which were marked by a Civil War and the tragedy of segregation. It is a vitally necessary ingredient of any successful effort to protect basic liberty and, indeed, the rule of law itself. We run no risk of returning to the days when a President (responding to this Court's efforts to protect the Cherokee Indians) might have said, "John Marshall has made his decision; now let him enforce it!" Loth, Chief Justice John Marshall and The Growth of the American Republic 365 (1948). But we do risk a self-inflicted wound—a wound that may harm not just the Court, but the Nation.

I fear that in order to bring this agonizingly long election process to a definitive conclusion, we have not adequately attended to that necessary "check upon our own exercise of power," "our own sense of self-restraint." *United States v. Butler*, 297 U.S. 1, 79 (1936) (Stone, J., dissenting). Justice Brandeis once said of the Court, "The most important thing we do is not doing." Bickel, supra, at 71. What it does today, the Court should have left undone. I would repair the damage done as best we now can, by permitting the Florida recount to continue under uniform standards.

I respectfully dissent.

Glossary

certiorari: a writ of a superior court to review the records of a lesser court

chads: in some voting technologies, the small pieces of paper pushed out of voting cards when a vote is cast

concurrence: a judicial opinion written in support of the result of a majority ruling but providing alternate reasons or justifications for action

dissents: judicial opinions written in objection to or in disagreement with a majority ruling

due process: the concept that all citizens should be treated equally under the law by the terms of a set of known and understandable rules and laws

election contests: procedures organized under state laws for recounting votes to determine the winner of an election

Glossary

Electoral College: the system used to choose the president of the United States, by which states are proportionately assigned electors determined by popular vote, a majority of which are required to win the presidency

equal protection: legal and constitutional concept by which no state law or procedure can treat or affect one segment of the population any differently from any other population segment

overvotes: the results when a voter places marks next to the names of more than one candidate for the same office; such overvotes invalidate a ballot for that electoral race

per curiam: literally, "from the court" as a whole; said of a judicial opinion without a declared author

petitioner: one who asks an appellate court to hear a case; normally the first name listed in a court case title

Presidential electors: members of the Electoral College, assigned by popular vote in each state to determine the winner of the presidential election

safe harbor: provision for upholding a state's electoral votes without challenge in Congress, as set out by Title 3 of the U.S. Code, section 5

sub silentio: without comment

undervotes: the results when no mark is made by a voter for a particular electoral race; such undervotes are not counted in the final vote tallies

Friends of the Earth v. Laidlaw Environmental Services

Date
2000

Author
Ruth Bader Ginsburg

Vote
7–2

Citation
528 U.S. 167

Significance
Determined that even if a company were to bring their violations under the Clean Water Act into compliance after a lawsuit has begun, the petitioner can still sue for damages

Overview

In 1986, Laidlaw Environmental Services purchased a hazardous waste incinerator near South Carolina's North Tyger River, which required them to receive a permit for the disposal of waste under the Clean Water Act. This permit limited the volume of pollutants the company could discharge into the river from the operation of the incinerator. During the period of operation from 1987 to 1995, the company violated the permit's allowable amount of discharge 489 times, leading the Friends of the Earth to file suit under the Clean Water Act. Attempting to avoid a costly lawsuit, Laidlaw petitioned the South Carolina Department of Health and Environmental Control to request a state enforcement that would give them a civil penalty and a timeline to address the issues, thus negating the case of the Friends of the Earth. The District Court did not concur, however, awarding damages for $400,000. Laidlaw appealed the ruling. The Fourth Circuit Court of Appeals agreed with Laidlaw and set aside the ruling, arguing that Friends of the Earth did not have grounds to sue. The Supreme Court, in what some scholars defined as a far reach of their judicial power, overturned the Fourth Circuit ruling, stating that civil penalties served as a deterrent for future violations.

Context

The Clean Water Act began as the 1948 Federal Water Pollution Control Act, but the law was limited, and the powers to enforce it were minimal. After the creation of the Environmental Protection Agency (EPA) in 1970, Congress amended the Water Pollution Control Act to give greater authority to the EPA to enforce violations, and the 1972 amendments became known simply as the Clean Water Act. The act aimed to limit the pollutants that were being discharged into America's river systems and granted the ability for any citizen to sue when violations of the act occurred. The difficulty with the act, however, was that establishing standing in environmental suits was tricky because individuals in these areas often lacked the financial means to bring about a lawsuit, and environmental groups were often viewed as too far removed from the issue to have grounds to sue.

In the 1970s, the Supreme Court greatly expanded the rights of environmental groups and organizations to file suits against industries that were seen as significantly damaging or altering the landscape. In the 1972 *Sierra Club v. Morton*, the Court ruled against the Sierra Club only because the club could not articulate

Ruth Bader Ginsburg wrote for the majority.
(Steve Petteway)

how it had been injured; the Court allowed the case to move through the system once the Sierra Club argued that Disney's development in the Mineral King Valley would disrupt the club's ability to hold meetings and events in the area. A year later, in *United States v. Students Challenging Regulatory Agency Procedure (SCRAP)*, the Court granted standing to sue to SCRAP when the respondent argued that the increased extraction of materials brought about by new rail freight rates would impact their ability to use the streams, mountains, and other natural resources around Washington. The Court would continue to use the *Sierra Club v. Morton* case as its reasoning for not hearing other environmental cases, resulting in a very liberal interpretation of ecological and environmental law for the next twenty years.

With the shift of the Court to a more conservative panel of judges under Presidents Ronald Reagan and George H.W. Bush in the 1980s and 1990s, however, the Court began to reexamine the applicability of *Sierra Club v. Morton*, particularly with regard to standing to bring about a suit. The case of *Lujan v. National Wildlife Federation* (1992) saw the Court essentially override *Sierra Club v. Morton* by stating the that NWF did not prove enough specific harm to have grounds to file suit against the U.S. Bureau of Land Management (USBLM). The Court tightened the standard further in the subsequent case of *Lujan v. Defenders of Wildlife*, in which it set out three specific parameters that must be met for an individual to have standing to sue: injury in fact (direct harm or impact), causation, and redressability. These standards were loosely interpreted in *Bennett v. Spear* (1997), however, when Justice Antonin Scalia ruled that the potential of harm from a USBLM policy to a business owner gave them grounds to sue and enforce change to an executive order.

The shift of the 1990s was seen as a push from conservatives to limit the impact of economic growth in defense of the environment, particularly in situations that were either deemed as aesthetic in nature or unclear in the degree of their dangers and harms to individuals. This was a striking shift in policy from the Court in the 1970s when Justice William O. Douglas noted in his *Sierra* Club dissent that "inanimate objects are sometimes parties in litigation . . . [s]o it should be as respects valleys, alpine meadows, rivers, lakes, estuaries, beaches, ridges, groves of trees, swampland, or even air that feels the destructive pressures of modern technology and modern life." The conservative nature of the Court now shifted their policy to harm needing to be physically tangible, whether in an actual physical injury or an economic impact rather than a perceived danger. Citing *Lujan* in their brief to the 4th Circuit Court of Appeals, Laidlaw had sought to dismiss the case by proving that by entering into an agreement with the South Carolina Department of Health and Environmental Control to rectify the problem, the Friends of the Earth had no standing to sue as they did not have a possible redress for damages.

About the Author

Justice Ruth Bader Ginsburg was born Joan Ruth Bader in Brooklyn, New York, during the Great Depression to Jewish family, including a father who was an immigrant from Russia. She would go by Ruth during school because of the number of female students named "Joan" in her class, and the name would stick with her as she progressed through academia. She graduated from James Madison High School in Brooklyn and went on to Cornell University in upstate New

York, where she met her husband, Martin D. Ginsburg. While her husband was stationed in Oklahoma, Ginsburg worked at the Social Security Administration, where she was demoted after becoming pregnant with their first child. This in part drove her desire to attend law school and would shape a large amount of her legal work early in her career.

Though Ginsburg attended Harvard Law for part of her academic career, her husband's career took them to New York City, where she transferred to Columbia Law School and went on to be the first woman to serve on the *Columbia Law Review*. Tied for first in her class at her graduation in 1959, Ginsburg seemed destined to be a successful lawyer except for the misogynistic nature of the law profession, which made finding employment difficult. These struggles would help her find her voice working on behalf of equality for women in the workplace through the ACLU as the cofounder and lead attorney for the Women's Rights Project. During her time with the ACLU, she wrote amicus curiae briefs in the cases of *Reed v. Reed* (1971), *Frontiero v. Richardson* (1973), and *Weinberger v. Wisenfeld* (1975) that helped expand Fourteenth Amendment protections to women in the United States. These high-profile cases led to her promotion by President Jimmy Carter to the D.C. Circuit Court as the only liberal voice alongside conservative jurists Robert H. Bork and Antonin Scalia. In 1993, President Bill Clinton appointed her to the Supreme Court to replace justice Byron White, making her the first Jewish female justice on the Supreme Court.

Writing the dissent was the staunch conservative, Justice Antonin Scalia, who had served with Ginsburg on the DC Circuit Court and maintained a friendship with Ginsburg until his death in 2016. Ginsburg wrote that despite often finding themselves on opposing sides of many rulings, Scalia's writings gave her what she needed to "strengthen the majority opinion" as he would "nail all the weak spots."

Justice Antonin Scalia was born the son of an Italian immigrant in New Jersey in 1936 and spent much of his life in New York City's boroughs. After graduating from the Jesuit Xavier Military School in Manhattan in 1953, he enrolled in Georgetown University, where he graduated with a major in history; he went on to study law at Harvard and serve as the notes editor for the *Harvard Law Review*. Though he began his career as a civil practice attorney in Cleveland, Ohio, he returned to academia to teach at the University of Virginia Law School in 1967. Under President Richard Nixon, he was appointed to general counsel for the Office of Telecommunications Policy and then nominated as the assistant attorney general for the Office of Legal Counsel (a position he would then be appointed to under Gerald Ford). He would argue once before the Supreme Court on behalf of the U.S. government before going back to academia at the University of Chicago Law School.

Scalia's conservative views and strict interpretation of the Constitution gained the attention of President Reagan, who appointed him to the U.S. Court of Appeals for the D.C. Circuit in 1982 and then as Supreme Court associate justice in 1986, making him the first Italian American justice. With the appointment of Justice William Rehnquist as chief justice on the same day, the Court moved substantially to the political right, with Scalia and, later, Clarence Thomas serving to push a more strict interpretation of the Constitution.

Explanation and Analysis of the Document

Justice Ginsburg's opinion for the Court opens by reviewing the intentions of the Clean Water Act and what the government establishes as an individual with grounds to bring suit against a corporation or entity that violates the law. Of particular importance in her opening is the sixty-day notice that must be filed with the offending party of the intent to pursue litigation, which that act defined as a necessity to give the offender the opportunity to right the wrong before suit is brought before court. Ginsburg acknowledges that traditionally, the courts have held that no legal standing for suit can exist if the offense has been redressed prior to the filing of the lawsuit or if the state or EPA has already commenced action. This position will essentially serve as the foundation of Justice Scalia's dissent (joined by Clarence Thomas), which contends that because Laidlaw received a penalty from the state of South Carolina and was already addressing the concern, the Friends of the Earth had no legal standing to pursue a lawsuit, rendering the case moot.

Ginsburg's opinion contends that the case is in fact about the declaration of the Fourth Court of Appeals that the case was moot, thus leaving the initial question of standing to sue by the Friends of the Earth unanswered. Ginsburg addresses the Court's ruling in *Lujan v. Defenders of Wildlife* that determined that three factors must be met to allow a plaintiff to have standing in court to sue: 1) it has sustained an injury that is either concrete or imminent; 2) the injury must be traceable to the defendant (causation); and 3) there exists a course of remedy from a court's ruling that will address the injury.

Laidlaw contended that the Friends of the Earth had not directly sustained any harm from incident as there was no substantiated scientific evidence that the environment had been irreparably harmed as a result of the pollutants (in this case, mercury), and therefore, no harm was incurred by any member of the Friends of the Earth. Ginsburg contends that injury to the environment does not constitute the same as injury to the plaintiff, which the Friends of Earth had demonstrated using testimony from Kenneth Lee Curtis that he no longer could hunt, camp, or fish along the river due to the smell and sight of the polluted river. Ginsburg contends that this testimony, along with several others given in the initial case, allowed the case to meet the first burden of a concrete or imminent injury of fact. Given that Laidlaw had come to a deal with South Carolina's regulatory agency regarding the problem, the second burden of causation was not up for contest.

Ginsburg then proceeds to address the question of whether a civil redress existed for the Friends of the Earth given that the fine was paid to the state and therefore the individual had no right to seek any damages. Ginsburg acknowledges that while Laidlaw had some merit to the case, the key is that civil penalties also serve as a deterrent, not just as a redress to an injury. Scalia contends that it is the threat of civil penalties as opposed to the administration of the penalties that serves as the deterrent, but Ginsburg counters that a threat has no power to deter until it is in fact carried out. Secondly, in the case of Laidlaw's penalty to the state, the financial penalty was not sufficient as to deter future violations, particularly given that Laidlaw initiated the process only in response to the plaintiff's suit. Therefore, according to Ginsburg, the case met the three criteria established under *Lujan* and thus standing was proven.

The next question the Court needed to address was whether the case was rendered moot by the agreement entered into by the state of South Carolina and Laidlaw. Justice Scalia's dissent argues that not only was a civil penalty administered, but requirements were set in place for the offense to be fixed and monitored as a result. Thus, the petitioner's original claim was now rendered moot because the original problem ended. Ginsburg addresses this by pointing out that the burden of proof lies with the defendant to show that there is no way that the process would continue even without litigation. Scalia's dissent contends that because compliance was met by the company's voluntary compliance (which occurred before the appeals court hearing) or the closing of the plant (which occurred after), the petitioner no longer had legal grounds to pursue any damages as the wrong had been corrected. But Ginsburg asserts that the burden of proof for mootness for a defendant lies in proving that the offense cannot occur in the future, something that Laidlaw could not convince the Court of given its retention of the permits it originally received for the property. In essence, if Laidlaw had surrendered the permits and fully demonstrated that it had no intention of ever reopening the plant's operations, then perhaps the question of mootness could be revisited but at this point, there was no guarantee that the wrong had been permanently righted.

For Scalia's dissent, he added that the precedent being established by the Court in the majority's opinion came close to violating the concept of separation of powers by turning the power of enforcement from the EPA to the people, making them in essence a "self-appointed EPA." The result would be that rather than allowing the regulatory agencies to monitor and respond to violations and infractions, private citizens would use the threat of lawsuit as a tool of bargaining to bring about the change they desire; this would disregard the very due process of law the courts are sworn to protect, particularly in cases like Laidlaw where a suit could move forward even after the original condition of the suit had been addressed and rectified. While Scalia noted that the standard of mootness was not perfect, it was up to the courts to a apply a standard of common-sense interpretation throughout the entirety of the case, not to open up a blanket opportunity as he argued the majority had done in this instance.

Impact

The case of *Friends of Earth v. Laidlaw* had a far-reaching impact for plaintiffs in environmental cases. The heavier burden of proving that they had in fact established grounds to sue had been lightened somewhat by the majority opinion and would result in some cases that had been overturned on appeal to be revisited, such as *Friends of the Earth v. Gaston Copper Recycling Corporation*. In this case, the court's initial ruling before *Laidlaw* was that the petitioner had not proven an actual harm from the pollution and therefore had no grounds to sue; after *Laidlaw*, however, the Court reversed its ruling, citing that no actual evidence of harm to the waterway needed to occur but rather merely the loss recreational value from the perceived damages of the pollution. Though the appeals court in this case would affirm the decision of *Laidlaw* in the application for this case, the judges openly opposed the ruling, with one judge indicating that *Laidlaw* had opened the floodgates for injury cases. Regardless of these views, the lower court's decision to overturn a prior ruling indicated than an added power of enforcement had indeed been granted to private citizens.

Questions for Further Study

1. Compared to *Sierra Club v. Morton*, how did this case address the idea of standing in a case? In what ways did it clarify what degree of injury represents enough harm to bring about a tort claim?

2. The Court has often been viewed as a tool of judicial activism, blurring the lines of balancing power between it and the two other branches to enact a change. In what ways could critics of the Court use the case of *Laidlaw* as proof of judicial activism?

3. Justice Scalia warned of the dangers of setting a lower threshold for mootness by allowing a case to proceed through the system, including financial compensation for damages even after the problem was fixed. Why might this have been a focal point of his dissent? In what ways would granting that power also make a citizen more powerful than the government regulatory bodies?

Further Reading

Books

Ginsburg, Ruth Bader. *Ruth Bader Ginsburg Dissents*. San Diego: Word Cloud Classics, 2022.

Wilson, Grant, Rachelle Adam, Anthony R. Zelle, and Herman F. Greene. *Earth Law: Emerging Ecocentric Law—A Practitioner's Guide*. New York: Wolters Kluwer, 2020.

Articles

Davison, Steven G. "Standing to Sue in Citizen Suits against Air and Water Polluters under Friends of the Earth, Inc. v. Laidlaw Environmental Services (TOC), Inc." *Tulane Environmental Law Journal* 17, no. 1 (Winter 2003).

Deluliis, Nicholas J. "Deterrence Effect of Civil Penalties, Potential Loss of Recreational and Economic Use by Plaintiff Organization's Members, and Absence of a Clear Indication of Eliminating Future Violations Will Meet Article III Mootness and Standing Requirements for Clean Water Act ('CWA') Citizen Suits: Friends of the Earth, Inc. v. Laidlaw Environmental Services (TOC), Inc." *Duquesne Law Review* 39, no. 1 (2000): 267.

—Commentary by Ryan Fontanella

FRIENDS OF THE EARTH V. LAIDLAW ENVIRONMENTAL SERVICES

Document Text

JUSTICE GINSBURG delivered the opinion of the Court

This case presents an important question concerning the operation of the citizen-suit provisions of the Clean Water Act. Congress authorized the federal district courts to entertain Clean Water Act suits initiated by "a person or persons having an interest which is or may be adversely affected." 33 U. S. C. §§ 1365(a), (g). To impel future compliance with the Act, a district court may prescribe injunctive relief in such a suit; additionally or alternatively, the court may impose civil penalties payable to the United States Treasury. § 1365(a). In the Clean Water Act citizen suit now before us, the District Court determined that injunctive relief was inappropriate because the defendant, after the institution of the litigation, achieved substantial compliance with the terms of its discharge permit. 956 F. Supp. 588, 611 (SC 1997). The court did, however, assess a civil penalty of $405,800. *Id.,* at 610. The "total deterrent effect" of the penalty would be adequate to forestall future violations, the court reasoned, taking into account that the defendant "will be required to reimburse plaintiffs for a significant amount of legal fees and has, itself, incurred significant legal expenses." *Id.,* at 610-611.

The Court of Appeals vacated the District Court's order. 149 F.3d 303 *(CA4* 1998). The case became moot, the appellate court declared, once the defendant fully complied with the terms of its permit and the plaintiff failed to appeal the denial of equitable relief. "[C]ivil penalties payable to the government," the Court of Appeals stated, "would not redress any injury Plaintiffs have suffered." *Id.,* at 307. Nor were attorneys' fees in order, the Court of Appeals noted, because absent relief on the merits, plaintiffs could not qualify as prevailing parties. *Id.,* at 307, n. 5.

We reverse the judgment of the Court of Appeals. The appellate court erred in concluding that a citizen suitor's claim for civil penalties must be dismissed as moot when the defendant, albeit after commencement of the litigation, has come into compliance. In directing dismissal of the suit on grounds of mootness, the Court of Appeals incorrectly conflated our case law on initial standing to bring suit, see, *e. g., Steel Co.* v. *Citizens for Better Environment,* 523 U. S. 83 (1998), with our case law on postcommencement mootness, see, *e. g., City of Mesquite* v. *Aladdin's Castle, Inc.,* 455 U. S. 283 (1982). A defendant's voluntary cessation of allegedly unlawful conduct ordinarily does not suffice to moot a case. The Court of Appeals also misperceived the remedial potential of civil penalties. Such penalties may serve, as an alternative to an injunction, to deter future violations and thereby redress the injuries that prompted a citizen suitor to commence litigation.

I

A

In 1972, Congress enacted the Clean Water Act (Act), also known as the Federal Water Pollution Control Act, 86 Stat. 816, as amended, 33 U. S. C. § 1251 *et seq.* Section 402 of the Act, 33 U. S. C. § 1342, provides for the issuance, by the Administrator of the Environmental Protection Agency (EPA) or by authorized States, of

National Pollutant Discharge Elimination System (NPDES) permits. NPDES permits impose limitations on the discharge of pollutants, and establish related monitoring and reporting requirements, in order to improve the cleanliness and safety of the Nation's waters. Noncompliance with a permit constitutes a violation of the Act. § 1342(h).

Under § 505(a) of the Act, a suit to enforce any limitation in an NPDES permit may be brought by any "citizen," defined as "a person or persons having an interest which is or may be adversely affected." 33 U. S. C. §§ 1365(a), (g). Sixty days before initiating a citizen suit, however, the would-be plaintiff must give notice of the alleged violation to the EP A, the State in which the alleged violation occurred, and the alleged violator. § 1365(b)(1)(A). "[T]he purpose of notice to the alleged violator is to give it an opportunity to bring itself into complete compliance with the Act and thus ... render unnecessary a citizen suit." *Gwaltney of Smithfield, Ltd.* v. *Chesapeake Bay Foundation, Inc.*, 484 U. S. 49, 60 (1987). Accordingly, we have held that citizens lack statutory standing under § 505(a) to sue for violations that have ceased by the time the complaint is filed. *Id.*, at 56-63. The Act also bars a citizen from suing if the EPA or the State has already commenced, and is "diligently prosecuting," an enforcement action. 33 U. S. C. § 1365(b)(1)(B).

The Act authorizes district courts in citizen-suit proceedings to enter injunctions and to assess civil penalties, which are payable to the United States Treasury. § 1365(a). In determining the amount of any civil penalty, the district court must take into account "the seriousness of the violation or violations, the economic benefit (if any) resulting from the violation, any history of such violations, any good-faith efforts to comply with the applicable requirements, the economic impact of the penalty on the violator, and such other matters as justice may require." § 1319(d). In addition, the court "may award costs of litigation (including reasonable attorney and expert witness fees) to any prevailing or substantially prevailing party, whenever the court determines such award is appropriate." § 1365(d).

B

In 1986, defendant-respondent Laidlaw Environmental Services (TOC), Inc., bought a hazardous waste incinerator facility in Roebuck, South Carolina, that included a wastewater treatment plant. (The company has since changed its name to Safety-Kleen (Roebuck), Inc., but for simplicity we will refer to it as "Laidlaw" throughout.) Shortly after Laidlaw acquired the facility, the South Carolina Department of Health and Environmental Control (DHEC), acting under 33 U. S. C. § 1342(a)(1), granted Laidlaw an NPDES permit authorizing the company to discharge treated water into the North Tyger River. The permit, which became effective on January 1, 1987, placed limits on Laidlaw's discharge of several pollutants into the river, including—of particular relevance to this case—mercury, an extremely toxic pollutant. The permit also regulated the flow, temperature, toxicity, and pH of the effluent from the facility, and imposed monitoring and reporting obligations.

Once it received its permit, Laidlaw began to discharge various pollutants into the waterway; repeatedly, Laidlaw's discharges exceeded the limits set by the permit. In particular, despite experimenting with several technological fixes, Laidlaw consistently failed to meet the permit's stringent 1.3 ppb (parts per billion) daily average limit on mercury discharges. The District Court later found that Laidlaw had violated the mercury limits on 489 occasions between 1987 and 1995. 956 F. Supp., at 613-621.

On April 10, 1992, plaintiff-petitioners Friends of the Earth (FOE) and Citizens Local Environmental Action Network, Inc. (CLEAN) (referred to collectively in this opinion, together with later joined plaintiff-petitioner Sierra Club, as "FOE") took the preliminary step necessary to the institution of litigation. They sent a letter to Laidlaw notifying the company of their intention to file a citizen suit against it under § 505(a) of the Act after the expiration of the requisite 60-day notice period, i. *e.*, on or after June 10, 1992. Laidlaw's lawyer then contacted DHEC to ask whether DHEC would consider filing a lawsuit against Laidlaw. The District Court later found that Laidlaw's reason for requesting that DHEC file a lawsuit against it was to bar FOE's proposed citizen suit through the operation of 33 U. S. C. § 1365(b)(1)(B). 890 F. Supp. 470, 478 (SC 1995). DHEC agreed to file a lawsuit against Laidlaw; the company's lawyer then drafted the complaint for DHEC and paid the filing fee. On June 9, 1992, the last day before FOE's 60-day notice period expired, DHEC and Laidlaw reached a settlement requiring Laidlaw to pay $100,000 in civil penalties and to make "'every effort'" to comply with its permit obligations. *Id.*, at 479-481.

On June 12, 1992, FOE filed this citizen suit against Laidlaw under § 505(a) of the Act, alleging noncompliance with the NPDES permit and seeking declaratory and injunctive relief and an award of civil penalties. Laidlaw moved for summary judgment on the ground that FOE had failed to present evidence demonstrating injury in fact, and therefore lacked Article III standing to bring the lawsuit. Record, Doc. No. 43. In opposition to this motion, FOE submitted affidavits and deposition testimony from members of the plaintiff organizations. Record, Doc. No. 71 (Exhs. 41-51). The record before the District Court also included affidavits from the organizations' members submitted by FOE in support of an earlier motion for preliminary injunctive relief. Record, Doc. No. 21 (Exhs. 5-10). After examining this evidence, the District Court denied Laidlaw's summary judgment motion, finding—albeit "by the very slimmest of margins"—that FOE had standing to bring the suit. App. in No. 97-1246 *(CA4)*, pp. 207-208 (Tr. of Hearing 39-40 (June 30, 1993)).

Laidlaw also moved to dismiss the action on the ground that the citizen suit was barred under 33 U. S. C. § 1365(b)(1)(B) by DHEC's prior action against the company. The United States, appearing as *amicus curiae*, joined FOE in opposing the motion. After an extensive analysis of the Laidlaw-DHEC settlement and the circumstances under which it was reached, the District Court held that DHEC's action against Laidlaw had not been "diligently prosecuted"; consequently, the court allowed FOE's citizen suit to proceed. 890 F. Supp., at 499. The record indicates that after FOE initiated the suit, but before the District Court rendered judgment, Laidlaw violated the mercury discharge limitation in its permit 13 times. 956 F. Supp., at 621. The District Court also found that Laidlaw had committed 13 monitoring and 10 reporting violations during this period. *Id.,* at 601. The last recorded mercury discharge violation occurred in January 1995, long after the complaint was filed but about two years before judgment was rendered. *Id.,* at 621.

On January 22, 1997, the District Court issued its judgment. 956 F. Supp. 588 (SC). It found that Laidlaw had gained a total economic benefit of $1,092,581 as a result of its extended period of noncompliance with the mercury discharge limit in its permit. *Id.,* at 603. The court concluded, however, that a civil penalty of $405,800 was adequate in light of the guiding factors listed in 33 U. S. C. § 1319(d). 956 F. Supp., at 610. In particular, the District Court stated that the lesser penalty was appropriate taking into account the judgment's "total deterrent effect." In reaching this determination, the court "considered that Laidlaw will be required to reimburse plaintiffs for a significant amount of legal fees." *Id.,* at 610-611. The court declined to grant FOE's request for injunctive relief, stating that an injunction was inappropriate because "Laidlaw has been in substantial compliance with all parameters in its NPDES permit since at least August 1992." *Id.,* at 611. FOE appealed the District Court's civil penalty judgment, arguing that the penalty was inadequate, but did not appeal the denial of declaratory or injunctive relief. Laidlaw cross-appealed, arguing, among other things, that FOE lacked standing to bring the suit and that DHEC's action qualified as a diligent prosecution precluding FOE's litigation. The United States continued to participate as *amicus curiae* in support of FOE.

On July 16, 1998, the Court of Appeals for the Fourth Circuit issued its judgment. 149 F.3d 303. The Court of Appeals assumed without deciding that FOE initially had standing to bring the action, *id.,* at 306, n. 3, but went on to hold that the case had become moot. The appellate court stated, first, that the elements of Article III standing—injury, causation, and redressability—must persist at every stage of review, or else the action becomes moot. *Id.,* at 306. Citing our decision in *Steel Co.,* the Court of Appeals reasoned that the case had become moot because "the only remedy currently available to [FOE]—civil penalties payable to the government—would not redress any injury [FOE has] suffered." 149 F. 3d, at 306-307. The court therefore vacated the District Court's order and remanded with instructions to dismiss the action. In a footnote, the Court of Appeals added that FOE's "failure to obtain relief on the merits of [its] claims precludes any recovery of attorneys' fees or other litigation costs because such an award is available only to a 'prevailing or substantially prevailing party.'" *Id.,* at 307, n. 5 (quoting 33 U. S. C. § 1365(d)).

According to Laidlaw, after the Court of Appeals issued its decision but before this Court granted certiorari, the entire incinerator facility in Roebuck was permanently closed, dismantled, and put up for sale, and all discharges from the facility permanently ceased. Respondent's Suggestion of Mootness 3.

We granted certiorari, 525 U. S. 1176 (1999), to resolve the inconsistency between the Fourth Circuit's decision in this case and the decisions of several other Courts of Appeals, which have held that a defendant's compliance with its permit after the commencement of litigation does not moot claims for civil penalties under the Act. See, e. g., *Atlantic States Legal Foundation, Inc.* v. *Stroh Die Casting Co.,* 116 F. 3d 814, 820 *(CA7),* cert. denied, 522 U. S. 981 (1997); *Natural Resources Defense Council, Inc.* v. *Texaco Rfg. and Mktg., Inc.,* 2 F.3d 493, 503-504 *(CA3* 1993); *Atlantic States Legal Foundation, Inc.* v. *Pan American Tanning Corp.,* 993 F. 2d 1017, 1020-1021 *(CA2* 1993); *Atlantic States Legal Foundation, Inc.* v. *Tyson Foods, Inc.,* 897 F.2d 1128,1135*1136 (CAll 1990).*

II

A

The Constitution's case-or-controversy limitation on federal judicial authority, Art. III, § 2, underpins both our standing and our mootness jurisprudence, but the two inquiries differ in respects critical to the proper resolution of this case, so we address them separately. Because the Court of Appeals was persuaded that the case had become moot and so held, it simply assumed without deciding that FOE had initial standing. See *Arizonans for Official English* v. *Arizona,* 520 U. S. 43, 66-67 (1997) (court may assume without deciding that standing exists in order to analyze mootness). But because we hold that the Court of Appeals erred in declaring the case moot, we have an obligation to assure ourselves that FOE had Article III standing at the outset of the litigation. We therefore address the question of standing before turning to mootness.

In *Lujan* v. *Defenders of Wildlife,* 504 U. S. 555, 560-561 (1992), we held that, to satisfy Article III's standing requirements, a plaintiff must show (1) it has suffered an "injury in fact" that is (a) concrete and particularized and (b) actual or imminent, not conjectural or hypothetical; (2) the injury is fairly traceable to the challenged action of the defendant; and (3) it is likely, as opposed to merely speculative, that the injury will be redressed by a favorable decision. An association has standing to bring suit on behalf of its members when its members would otherwise have standing to sue in their own right, the interests at stake are germane to the organization's purpose, and neither the claim asserted nor the relief requested requires the participation of individual members in the lawsuit. *Hunt* v. *Washington State Apple Advertising Comm'n,* 432 U. S. 333, 343 (1977).

Laidlaw contends first that FOE lacked standing from the outset even to seek injunctive relief, because the plaintiff organizations failed to show that any of their members had sustained or faced the threat of any "injury in fact" from Laidlaw's activities. In support of this contention Laidlaw points to the District Court's finding, made in the course of setting the penalty amount, that there had been "no demonstrated proof of harm to the environment" from Laidlaw's mercury discharge violations. 956 F. Supp., at 602; see also *ibid.* ("[T]he NPDES permit violations at issue in this citizen suit did not result in any health risk or environmental harm.").

The relevant showing for purposes of Article III standing, however, is not injury to the environment but injury to the plaintiff. To insist upon the former rather than the latter as part of the standing inquiry (as the dissent in essence does, *post,* at 199-200) is to raise the standing hurdle higher than the necessary showing for success on the merits in an action alleging noncompliance with an NPDES permit. Focusing properly on injury to the plaintiff, the District Court found that FOE had demonstrated sufficient injury to establish standing. App. in No. 97-1246 *(CA4),* at 207-208 (Tr. of Hearing 39-40). For example, FOE member Kenneth Lee Curtis averred in affidavits that he lived a half-mile from Laidlaw's facility; that he occasionally drove over the North Tyger River, and that it looked and smelled polluted; and that he would like to fish, camp, swim, and picnic in and near the river between 3 and 15 miles downstream from the facility, as he did when he was a teenager, but would not do so because he was concerned that the water was polluted by Laidlaw's discharges. Record, Doc. No. 71 (Exhs. 41, 42). Curtis reaffirmed these statements in extensive deposition testimony. For example, he testified that he would like to fish in the river at a specific spot he used as a boy, but that he would not do so now because of his concerns about Laidlaw's discharges. *Ibid.* (Exh. 43, at 52-53; Exh. 44, at 33).

Other members presented evidence to similar effect.

CLEAN member Angela Patterson attested that she lived two miles from the facility; that before Laidlaw operated the facility, she picnicked, walked, birdwatched, and waded in and along the North Tyger River because of the natural beauty of the area; that she no longer engaged in these activities in or near the river because she was concerned about harmful effects from discharged pollutants; and that she and her husband would like to purchase a home near the river but did not intend to do so, in part because of Laidlaw's discharges. Record, Doc. No. 21 (Exh. 10). CLEAN member Judy Pruitt averred that she lived one-quarter mile from Laidlaw's facility and would like to fish, hike, and picnic along the North Tyger River, but has refrained from those activities because of the discharges. *Ibid.* (Exh. 7). FOE member Linda Moore attested that she lived 20 miles from Roebuck, and would use the North Tyger River south of Roebuck and the land surrounding it for recreational purposes were she not concerned that the water contained harmful pollutants. Record, Doc. No. 71 (Exhs. 45, 46). In her deposition, Moore testified at length that she would hike, picnic, camp, swim, boat, and drive near or in the river were it not for her concerns about illegal discharges. *Ibid.* (Exh. 48, at 29, 36-37, 62-63, 72). CLEAN member Gail Lee attested that her home, which is near Laidlaw's facility, had a lower value than similar homes located farther from the facility, and that she believed the pollutant discharges accounted for some of the discrepancy. Record, Doc. No. 21 (Exh. 9). Sierra Club member Norman Sharp averred that he had canoed approximately 40 miles downstream of the Laidlaw facility and would like to canoe in the North Tyger River closer to Laidlaw's discharge point, but did not do so because he was concerned that the water contained harmful pollutants. *Ibid.* (Exh. 8).

These sworn statements, as the District Court determined, adequately documented injury in fact. We have held that environmental plaintiffs adequately allege injury in fact when they aver that they use the affected area and are persons "for whom the aesthetic and recreational values of the area will be lessened" by the challenged activity. *Sierra Club* v. *Morton,* 405 U. S. 727, 735 (1972). See also *Defenders of Wildlife,* 504 U. S., at 562-563 ("Of course, the desire to use or observe an animal species, even for purely esthetic purposes, is undeniably a cognizable interest for purposes of standing.").

Our decision in *Lujan* v. *National Wildlife Federation,* 497 U. S. 871 (1990), is not to the contrary. In that case an environmental organization assailed the Bureau of Land Management's "land withdrawal review program," a program covering millions of acres, alleging that the program illegally opened up public lands to mining activities. The defendants moved for summary judgment, challenging the plaintiff organization's standing to initiate the action under the Administrative Procedure Act, 5 U. S. C. § 702. We held that the plaintiff could not survive the summary judgment motion merely by offering "averments which state only that one of [the organization's] members uses unspecified portions of an immense tract of territory, on some portions of which mining activity has occurred or probably will occur by virtue of the governmental action." 497 U. S., at 889.

In contrast, the affidavits and testimony presented by FOE in this case assert that Laidlaw's discharges, and the affiant members' reasonable concerns about the effects of those discharges, directly affected those affiants' recreational, aesthetic, and economic interests. These submissions present dispositively more than the mere "general averments" and "conclusory allegations" found inadequate in *National Wildlife Federation. Id.,* at 888. Nor can the affiants' conditional statements—that they would use the nearby North Tyger River for recreation if Laidlaw were not discharging pollutants into it—be equated with the speculative "'some day' intentions" to visit endangered species halfway around the world that we held insufficient to show injury in fact in *Defenders of Wildlife.* 504 U. S., at 564.

Los Angeles v. *Lyons,* 461 U. S. 95 (1983), relied on by the dissent, *post,* at 199, does not weigh against standing in this case. In *Lyons,* we held that a plaintiff lacked standing to seek an injunction against the enforcement of a police chokehold policy because he could not credibly allege that he faced a realistic threat from the policy. 461 U. S., at 107, n. 7. In the footnote from *Lyons* cited by the dissent, we noted that "[t]he reasonableness of Lyons' fear is dependent upon the likelihood of a recurrence of the allegedly unlawful conduct," and that his "subjective apprehensions" that such a recurrence would even *take place* were not enough to support standing. *Id.,* at 108, n. 8. Here, in contrast, it is undisputed that Laidlaw's unlawful conduct—discharging pollutants in excess of permit limits—was occurring at the time the complaint was filed. Under *Lyons,* then, the only "subjective" issue here is "[t]he reasonableness of [the] fear" that led the affiants to respond to that concededly ongoing conduct by refraining from use of the North Tyger River and surrounding areas. Unlike the dissent, *post,* at 200, we see nothing "improbable" about the proposition that a company's continuous and pervasive illegal discharges of pollutants into a river would cause nearby residents to curtail their recreational use of that waterway and would subject them to other economic and aesthetic harms. The proposition is entirely reasonable, the District Court found it was true in this case, and that is enough for injury in fact.

Laidlaw argues next that even if FOE had standing to seek injunctive relief, it lacked standing to seek civil penalties. Here the asserted defect is not injury but redressability. Civil penalties offer no redress to private plaintiffs, Laidlaw argues, because they are paid to the Government, and therefore a citizen plaintiff can never have standing to seek them.

Laidlaw is right to insist that a plaintiff must demonstrate standing separately for each form of relief sought. See, *e. g., Lyons,* 461 U. S., at 109 (notwithstanding the fact that plaintiff had standing to pursue damages, he lacked standing to pursue injunctive relief); see also *Lewis* v. *Casey,* 518 U. S. 343, 358, n. 6 (1996) ("[S]tanding is not dispensed in gross."). But it is wrong to maintain that citizen plaintiffs facing ongoing violations never have standing to seek civil penalties.

We have recognized on numerous occasions that "all civil penalties have some deterrent effect." *Hudson* v. *United States,* 522 U. S. 93, 102 (1997); see also, *e. g., Department of Revenue of Mont.* v. *Kurth Ranch,* 511 U. S. 767, 778 (1994). More specifically, Congress has found that civil penalties in Clean Water Act cases do more than promote immediate compliance by limiting the defendant's economic incentive to delay its attainment of permit limits; they also deter future violations. This congressional determination warrants judicial attention and respect. "The legislative history of the Act reveals that Congress wanted the district court to consider the need for retribution and deterrence, in addition to restitution, when it imposed civil penalties .... [The district court may] seek to deter future violations by basing the penalty on its economic impact." *Tull* v. *United States, 481* U. S. 412, 422-423 (1987).

It can scarcely be doubted that, for a plaintiff who is injured or faces the threat of future injury due to illegal conduct ongoing at the time of suit, a sanction that effectively abates that conduct and prevents its recurrence provides a form of redress. Civil penalties can fit that description. To the extent that they encourage defendants to discontinue current violations and deter them from committing future ones, they afford redress to citizen plaintiffs who are injured or threatened with injury as a consequence of ongoing unlawful conduct.

The dissent argues that it is the *availability* rather than the *imposition* of civil penalties that deters any particular polluter from continuing to pollute. *Post,* at 207-208. This argument misses the mark in two ways. First, it overlooks the interdependence of the availability and the imposition; a threat has no deterrent value unless it is credible that it will be carried out. Second, it is reasonable for Congress to conclude that an actual award of civil penalties does in fact bring with it a significant quantum of deterrence over and above what is achieved by the mere prospect of such penalties. A would-be polluter mayor may not be dissuaded by the existence of a remedy on the books, but a defendant once hit in its pocketbook will surely think twice before polluting again.

We recognize that there may be a point at which the deterrent effect of a claim for civil penalties becomes so insubstantial or so remote that it cannot support citizen standing. The fact that this vanishing point is not easy to ascertain does not detract from the deterrent power of such penalties in the ordinary case. Justice Frankfurter's observations for the Court, made in a different context nearly 60 years ago, hold true here as well:

"How to effectuate policy—the adaptation of means to legitimately sought ends—is one of the most intractable of legislative problems. Whether proscribed conduct is to be deterred by *qui tam* action or triple damages or injunction, or by criminal prosecution, or merely by defense to actions in contract, or by some, or all, of these remedies in combination, is a matter within the legislature's range of choice. Judgment on the deterrent effect of the various weapons in the armory of the law can lay little claim to scientific basis." *Tigner* v. *Texas, 310* U. S. 141, 148 (1940).

In this case we need not explore the outer limits of the principle that civil penalties provide sufficient deterrence to support redressability. Here, the civil penalties sought by FOE carried with them a deterrent effect that made it likely, as opposed to merely speculative, that the penalties would redress FOE's injuries by abating current violations and preventing future ones—as the District Court reasonably found when it assessed a penalty of $405,800. 956 F. Supp., at 610-611.

Laidlaw contends that the reasoning of our decision in *Steel Co.* directs the conclusion that citizen plaintiffs have no standing to seek civil penalties under the Act. We disagree. *Steel Co.* established that citizen suitors lack standing to seek civil penalties for violations that have abated by the time of suit. 523 U. S., at 106-107. We specifically noted in that case that there was no allegation in the complaint of any continuing or imminent violation, and that no basis for such an allegation appeared to exist. *Id.,* at 108; see also *Gwalt*ney, 484 U. S., at 59 ("the harm sought to be addressed by the citizen suit lies in the present or the future, not in the past"). In short, *Steel Co.* held that private plaintiffs, unlike the Federal Government, may not sue to assess penalties for wholly past violations, but our decision in that case did not reach the issue of standing to seek penalties for violations that are ongoing at the time of the complaint and that could continue into the future if undeterred.

B

Satisfied that FOE had standing under Article III to bring this action, we turn to the question of mootness.

The only conceivable basis for a finding of mootness in this case is Laidlaw's voluntary conduct—either its achievement by August 1992 of substantial compliance with its NPDES permit or its more recent shutdown of the Roebuck facility. It is well settled that "a defendant's voluntary cessation of a challenged practice does not deprive a federal court of its power to determine the legality of the practice." *City of Mesquite,* 455 U. S., at 289. "[I]f it did, the courts would be compelled to leave '[t]he defendant ... free to return to his old ways.'" *Id.,* at 289, n. 10 (citing *United States* v. *W T. Grant Co.,* 345 U. S. 629, 632 (1953)). In accordance with this principle, the standard we have announced for determining whether a case has been mooted by the defendant's voluntary conduct is stringent: "A case might become moot if subsequent events made it absolutely clear that the allegedly wrongful behavior could not reasonably be expected to recur." *United States* v. *Concentrated Phosphate Export Assn., Inc.,* 393 U. S. 199, 203 (1968). The "heavy burden of persua[ding]" the court that the challenged conduct cannot reasonably be expected to start up again lies with the party asserting mootness. *Ibid.*

The Court of Appeals justified its mootness disposition by reference to *Steel Co.,* which held that citizen plaintiffs lack standing to seek civil penalties for wholly past violations. In relying on *Steel Co.,* the Court of Appeals confused mootness with standing. The confusion is understandable, given this Court's repeated statements that the doctrine of mootness can be described as "the doctrine of standing set in a time frame: The requisite personal interest that must exist at the commencement of the litigation (standing) must continue throughout its existence (mootness)." *Arizonans for Official English,* 520 U. S., at 68, n. 22 (quoting *United States Parole Comm'n* v. *Geraghty,* 445 U. S. 388, 397 (1980), in turn quoting Monaghan, Constitutional Adjudication: The Who and When, 82 Yale L. J. 1363, 1384 (1973)) (internal quotation marks omitted).

Careful reflection on the long-recognized exceptions to mootness, however, reveals that the description of mootness as "standing set in a time frame" is not comprehensive. As just noted, a defendant claiming that its voluntary compliance moots a case bears the formidable burden of showing that it is absolutely clear the allegedly wrongful behavior could not reasonably be expected to recur. *Concentrated Phosphate Export Assn.,* 393 U. S., at 203. By contrast, in a lawsuit brought to force compliance, it is the plaintiff's burden to establish standing by demonstrating that, if unchecked by the litigation, the defendant's allegedly wrongful behavior will likely occur or continue, and that the "threatened injury [is] certainly impending." *Whitmore* v. *Arkansas,* 495 U. S. 149, 158 (1990) (citations and internal quotation marks omitted). Thus, in *Lyons,* as already noted, we held that a plaintiff lacked initial standing to seek an injunction against the enforcement of a police chokehold policy because he could not credibly allege that he faced a realistic threat arising from the policy. 461 U. S., at 105-110. Elsewhere in the opinion, however, we noted that a citywide moratorium on police chokeholds—an action that surely diminished the already slim likelihood that any particular individual would be choked by police—would not have mooted an otherwise valid claim for injunctive relief, because the moratorium by its terms was not permanent. *Id.,* at 101. The plain lesson of these cases is that there are circumstances in which the prospect that a defendant will engage in (or resume) harmful conduct may be too speculative to support standing, but not too speculative to overcome mootness.

Furthermore, if mootness were simply "standing set in a time frame," the exception to mootness that arises when the defendant's allegedly unlawful activity is "capable of repetition, yet evading review," could not exist. When, for example, a mentally disabled patient files a lawsuit challenging her confinement in a segregated institution, her postcomplaint transfer to a community-based program will not moot the action, *Olmstead* v. *L.* c., 527 U. S. 581, 594, n. 6 (1999), despite the fact that she would have lacked initial standing had she filed the complaint after the transfer. Standing admits of no similar exception; if a plaintiff lacks standing at the time the action commences, the fact that the dispute is capable of repetition yet evading review will not entitle the complainant to a federal judicial forum. See *Steel Co., 523* U. S., at 109 (" 'the mootness exception for disputes capable of repetition yet evading review ... will not revive a dispute which became moot before the action commenced' ") (quoting *Renne* v. *Geary,* 501 U. S. 312, 320 (1991)).

We acknowledged the distinction between mootness and standing most recently in *Steel Co.:*

"The United States ... argues that the injunctive relief does constitute remediation because 'there is a presumption of [future] injury when the defendant has voluntarily ceased its illegal activity in response to litigation,' even if that occurs before a complaint is filed .... This makes a sword out of a shield. The 'presumption' the Government refers to has been applied to refute the assertion of mootness by a defendant who, when sued in a complaint that alleges present or threatened injury, ceases the complained-of activity .... It is an immense and unacceptable stretch to call the presumption into service as a substitute for the allegation of present or threatened injury upon which initial standing must be based." 523 U. S., at 109.

Standing doctrine functions to ensure, among other things, that the scarce resources of the federal courts are devoted to those disputes in which the parties have a concrete stake. In contrast, by the time mootness is an issue, the case has been brought and litigated, often (as here) for years. To abandon the case at an advanced stage may prove more wasteful than frugal. This argument from sunk costs 5 does not license courts to retain jurisdiction over cases in which one or both of the parties plainly lack a continuing interest, as when the parties have settled or a plaintiff pursuing a non surviving claim has died. See, *e. g., DeFunis* v. *Odegaard,* 416 U. S. 312 (1974) *(per curiam)* (non-class-action challenge to constitutionality of law school admissions process mooted when plaintiff, admitted pursuant to preliminary injunction, neared graduation and defendant law school conceded that, as a matter of ordinary school policy, plaintiff would be allowed to finish his final term); *Arizonans, 520* U. S., at 67 (non-class-action challenge to state constitutional amendment declaring English the official language of the State became moot when plaintiff, a state employee who sought to use her bilingual skills, left state employment). But the argument surely highlights an important difference between the two doctrines. See generally *Honig* v. *Doe, 484* U. S. 305, 329-332 (1988) (REHNQUIST, C. J., concurring).

In its brief, Laidlaw appears to argue that, regardless of the effect of Laidlaw's compliance, FOE doomed its own civil penalty claim to mootness by failing to appeal the District Court's denial of injunctive relief. Brief for Respondent 1417. This argument misconceives the statutory scheme. Under § 1365(a), the district court has discretion to determine which form of relief is best suited, in the particular case, to abate current violations and deter future ones. "[A] federal judge sitting as chancellor is not mechanically obligated to grant an injunction for every violation of law."

5 Of course we mean sunk costs to the judicial system, not to the litigants. *Lewis* v. *Continental Bank Corp.,* 494 U. S. 472 (1990) (cited by the dissent, *post,* at 213), dealt with the latter, noting that courts should use caution to avoid carrying forward a moot case solely to vindicate a plaintiff's interest in recovering attorneys' fees.

Weinberger v. *Romero-Barcelo,* 456 U. S. 305, 313 (1982). Denial of injunctive relief does not necessarily mean that the district court has concluded there is no prospect of future violations for civil penalties to deter. Indeed, it meant no such thing in this case. The District Court denied injunctive relief, but expressly based its award of civil penalties on the need for deterrence. See 956 F. Supp., at 610-611. As the dissent notes, *post,* at 205, federal courts should aim to ensure "'the framing of relief no broader than required by the precise facts.'" *Schlesinger* v. *Reservists Comm. to Stop the War,* 418 U. S. 208, 222 (1974). In accordance with this aim, a district court in a Clean Water Act citizen suit properly may conclude that an injunction would be an excessively intrusive remedy, because it could entail continuing superintendence of the permit holder's activities by a federal court—a process burdensome to court and permit holder alike. See *City of Mesquite,* 455 U. S., at 289 (although the defendant's voluntary cessation of the challenged practice does not moot the case, "[s]uch abandonment is an important factor bearing on the question whether a court should exercise its power to enjoin the defendant from renewing the practice").

Laidlaw also asserts, in a supplemental suggestion of mootness, that the closure of its Roebuck facility, which took place after the Court of Appeals issued its decision, mooted the case. The facility closure, like Laidlaw's earlier achievement of substantial compliance with its permit requirements, might moot the case, but—we once more reiterate—only if one or the other of these events made it absolutely clear that Laidlaw's permit violations could not reasonably be expected to recur. *Concentrated Phosphate Export Assn.,* 393 U. S., at 203. The effect of both Laidlaw's compliance and the facility closure on the prospect of future violations is a disputed factual matter. FOE points out, for example—and Laidlaw does not appear to contest—that Laidlaw retains its NPDES permit. These issues have not been aired in the lower courts; they remain open for consideration on remand.

C

FOE argues that it is entitled to attorneys' fees on the theory that a plaintiff can be a "prevailing party" for purposes of 33 U. S. C. § 1365(d) if it was the "catalyst" that triggered a favorable outcome. In the decision under review, the Court of Appeals noted that its Circuit precedent construed our decision in *Farrar* v. *Hobby,* 506 U.S. 103 (1992), to require rejection of that theory. 149 F. 3d, at 307, n. 5 (citing *S-l & S-2* v. *State Bd. of Ed. of* N. c., 21 F.3d 49, 51 *(CA4* 1994) (en banc)). Cf. *Foreman* v. *Dallas County, 193* F. 3d 314, 320 *(CA5* 1999) (stating, in dicta, that "[a]fter *Farrar* ... the continuing validity of the catalyst theory is in serious doubt").

Farrar acknowledged that a civil rights plaintiff awarded nominal damages may be a "prevailing party" under 42 U. S. C. § 1988. 506 U. S., at 112. The case involved no catalytic effect. Recognizing that the issue was not presented for this Court's decision in *Farrar,* several Courts of Appeals have expressly concluded that *Farrar* did not repudiate the catalyst theory. See *Marbley* v. *Bane,* 57 F.3d 224, 234 *(CA2* 1995); *Baumgartner* v. *Harrisburg Housing Authority,* 21 F.3d 541, 546-550 *(CA3* 1994); *Zinn* v. *Shalala,* 35 F.3d 273, 276 *(CA7* 1994); *Little Rock School Dist.* v. *Pulaski County Special Sch. Dist.,* #1, 17 F.3d 260, 263, n. 2 *(CA8 1994); Kilgour* v. *Pasadena,* 53 F.3d 1007, 1010 *(CA9 1995); Beard* v. *Teska,* 31 F.3d 942, 951-952 (CAlO 1994); *Morris* v. *West Palm Beach,* 194 F.3d 1203, 1207 (CAll 1999). Other Courts of Appeals have likewise continued to apply the catalyst theory notwithstanding *Farrar. Paris* v. *United States Dept. of Housing and Urban Development,* 988 F.2d 236, *238 (CA1* 1993); *Citizens Against Tax Waste* v. *Westerville City School,* 985 F.2d 255, 257 *(CA6 1993).*

It would be premature, however, for us to address the continuing validity of the catalyst theory in the context of this case. The District Court, in an order separate from the one in which it imposed civil penalties against Laidlaw, stayed the time for a petition for attorneys' fees until the time for appeal had expired or, if either party appealed, until the appeal was resolved. See 149 F. 3d, at 305 (describing order staying time for attorneys' fees petition). In the opinion accompanying its order on penalties, the District Court stated only that "this court has considered that Laidlaw will be required to reimburse plaintiffs for a significant amount of legal fees," and referred to "potential fee awards." 956 F. Supp., at 610-611. Thus, when the Court of Appeals addressed the availability of counsel fees in this case, no order was before it either denying or awarding fees. It is for the District Court, not this Court, to address in the first instance any request for reimbursement of costs, including fees.

***

For the reasons stated, the judgment of the United States Court of Appeals for the Fourth Circuit is reversed, and the case is remanded for further proceedings consistent with this opinion.

It is so ordered.

Glossary

affiant: a person whose has made an affidavit, or sworn statement

averments: statements

case-or-controversy limitation on federal judicial authority: requirement that the courts hear actual cases and not be called on to settle controversial issues

dispositively: having the quality of bringing about the disposition, or settlement, of a case.

equitable relief: a legal remedy ordered by a court, including an injunction, a restraining order, adherence to the terms of a contract, or other requirement; generally provided only when monetary damages are inappropriate

injunctive relief: a court-ordered prohibition of an act that has been requested by another party

moot: of no legal significance because the matter has been settled or previously decided

vacated: set aside

ZELMAN V. SIMMONS-HARRIS

DATE 2002 **AUTHOR** William Rehnquist (opinion), David Souter (dissent) **VOTE** 5–4	**CITATION** 536 U.S. 639 **SIGNIFICANCE** Narrowly ruled that a tuition voucher program to allow parents in Cleveland to have their children attend the private or religious school of their choice did not violate the establishment clause of the Constitution

Overview

In 1996, the state of Ohio introduced a school tuition voucher program for Cleveland residents in lower income areas to use the funds to enroll students in schools of their choice in the surrounding area. In the 1999–2000 academic year, 82 percent of the schools receiving funding from the voucher program had a religious affiliation, and 96 percent of the students in the program attended religious-based schools. Ohio taxpayers filed suit in the federal district court contending that allowing the monies to go to religiously affiliated schools violated the establishment clause of the Constitution; this was affirmed by both the district court and the Sixth Circuit Court of Appeals. At the Supreme Court, however, Chief Justice William Rehnquist and four others determined that the program did not violate the establishment clause because it did not mandate that a religious school be attended.

Context

The state of Ohio found that schools in the Cleveland City School District were performing well below state and federal standards, particularly those schools that served primarily low-income families. In 1995, a federal court order placed the entire district under state control in an effort to combat high drop-out rates and low performance on standardized assessments. The state of Ohio opted to introduce its Pilot Scholarship Program, aimed at giving parents the opportunity to have their children attend a private or religious school of their choice using state funds. Initially, the program was centered on elementary children, but eventually it included intermediate grade levels as well. For a school to participate in the state-funded program, the school receiving the funds had to agree not to discriminate on any federally protected basis such as religion, race, or ethnic background. Likewise, public schools bordering on the city's school district (that is, in the suburbs) could also participate and receive additional state funding per pupil.

Within the first three years of the program, fifty-six private schools participated in the program, of which forty-six had a religious connection; none of the neighboring public school districts agreed to participate. Of the 3,700 students who participated in the scholarship program, 96 percent attended one of the forty-six religiously affiliated schools.

The question of state funding to private, religiously affiliated schools has seen numerous contests at the Supreme Court and often represented a deep political divide in postwar America. With *Abbington School District v. Schempp* (1963), the Court ruled that publicly funded schools could not mandate a specific religion over another in the school setting, while *Engel v. Vitale* (1962) made school-sponsored prayer unconstitutional in a public school setting as well. Ten years after *Engel*, the Supreme Court ruled in *Lemon v. Kurtzman* (1971) that state funding for private, religious schools violated the Constitution's establishment clause forbidding the establishment of a state-sponsored religion. This precedent became the basis for the *Lemon* test, which dictated that three principles had to be met for a policy or law not to violate the establishment clause: the primary purpose of the policy must be secular; the policy must neither promote or prohibit a religion; and there is no excessive entanglement between the state and church.

With the rise of conservatism in the 1980s and 1990s, many right-wing groups began to push back against the traditional stance of separation of church and state in educational matters and instead attempted to find ways to use federal funding for private education vouchers to offer educational opportunities to minorities. The *Zelman* case represented an opportunity for the conservative-leaning Court to revisit the concept of federal funding for private schools, including religious schools, without necessarily overriding *Lemon v. Kurtzman* completely as precedent.

About the Author

Chief Justice William Rehnquist was born in 1924 in Wisconsin as a second-generation American. After his graduation from high school, he attended Kenyon College in Ohio for a quarter before enlisting in the U.S. Army Air Forces in 1942, where he worked in meteorology until his discharge in 1946. Using the benefits of the G.I. Bill, he enrolled in Stanford University and quickly earned a bachelor's degree and a master's degree in political science before earning another master's degree from Harvard University in 1950. He then returned to Stanford University to attend law school, earning the role of editor of the *Stanford Law Review*. During his time at Stanford, he briefly dated his class-

Chief Justice William Rehnquist delivered the majority opinion.
(Library of Congress)

mate Sandra Day O'Connor, who would go on to become the first female Supreme Court justice and serve with him on the Court for several years.

Rehnquist was a notable conservative, often criticizing the liberal opinions of Justice Hugo Black while he attended Stanford Law. His conservative views put him at odds with many of the more liberal decisions of the Warren Court, particularly the overturning of the principle of "separate but equal" facilities held in *Plessy v. Ferguson*. Rehnquist believed strongly in the power of the people in determining what was law and what wasn't, often taking the side of the states in cases involving civil liberties and the Fourteenth Amendment once he began his tenure on the Court in 1972. Despite being the lone wolf in many of the early cases of his tenure, his dissents would often become the arguments for the majority in future opinions of a more conservative Court under President Ronald Reagan. He supported prayer in schools and protection for big business and dissented in *Roe v. Wade* (1973), making him a justice conservatives held in high regard, a position that would see him promoted to chief justice in 1986 upon the retirement of Warren Burger.

Despite his conservative views, Rehnquist believed that justices should not impart their own feelings and emotions on the legal canon but follow a strict interpretation of the laws established by the will of the people through the Constitution and its amendments. Still, Rehnquist disapproved of the concept of *stare decisis*, or the use of precedent cases to dictate future rulings. In the cases of *Planned Parenthood v. Casey* (1992), for example, he dissented in the 5–4 ruling, arguing that while *Roe v. Wade* may have established a precedent, it was not good legal practice to decide solely based on precedent.

Explanation and Analysis of the Document

The Majority Opinion

Chief Justice Rehnquist's opinion quickly sets to work addressing the concerns of the establishment clause laid out by the *Lemon* test, targeting the primary question of the intent of the Ohio program. Rehnquist notes that the standard burden lies in whether a government program has the purpose or effect of advancing or inhibiting a particular religion. In the case of the Ohio voucher program, there was "no dispute that the program . . . was enacted for the valid secular purpose of providing educational assistance to poor children in a failing school system." Thus, the program met the first component of not advancing a religion, but did it attempt to inhibit or advance the religion as a side effect of the act.

Rehnquist bases his assessment largely on the precedent cases of *Mitchell v. Helms* (2000) and *Mueller v. Allen* (1983) that saw similar questions regarding the intended effects of state financial support that benefitted secular schools. While precedents had established that direct aid to religious schools violated the establishment clause, *Mitchell* and *Mueller* held that it was acceptable for private religious schools to benefit from secular programs that saw the independent choice of the people leading to their monetary gain. Rehnquist emphasizes that it was the choice of the individuals, not the state, that led to the funding of the religious schools and their programs, and therefore they did not violate the intended neutrality of the law. Rehnquist thus contends that the interpretation must be on the neutrality of the law as it is written, not as it is executed by the decisions of the beneficiaries of the program.

In the case of the Ohio law, the opinion of the Court agreed that it met the same standards applied in *Mueller* and *Mitchell* as it was neutral in its design, affording an opportunity for families to take the money to a school of their choice regardless of religious affiliation. The program may not have had equitable participation from other public schools or schools of non-religious affiliation, but that was a choice made by the schools, not the law itself. Families themselves were also not impacted in their funding or opportunity for choice due to religion as the program asked nothing about their religious preference nor dictated terms on their amount of financial benefit, which was determined solely by residence and income. Thus, no religious inhibition existed that would have met the criteria of *Lemon*.

Rehnquist goes on to address several of the dissenting arguments, specifically the argument that barriers to other schools limited the number of secular schools participating in the program. Rehnquist counters this argument by pointing out that while the program only provided a small portion of the funding needed for each student ($2,500 versus the roughly $7,000 that public schools received from a student's attendance), new non-religious charter schools continued to open in the hope of taking advantage of the state-funded program. More important, no evidence of restricting participation by public or private charter schools could be proven, making the decision based on the assumption of low enrollment data at these programs rather than concrete fact. This notion had been rejected in *Mueller* as it did not "provide the certainty . . . nor the principled standards by which statistical evidence might be evaluated."

The Dissenting Opinions

The dissents written by three of the four dissenting justices focused largely on the assertion that state funds being used mostly for religious schools was a direct violation of the establishment clause. Justice David Souter argues that an overwhelming majority of the funding went to religiously affiliated schools that had a clear program of religious indoctrination, which they promoted using tax dollars from individuals who may have had different religious beliefs or no religious beliefs at all. Referencing *Everson v. Board of Education of the Township of Ewing* (1947), Souter contends that in that case, the money went to a city transportation program that then used it to bus children to and from school regardless of religious creed, not to the religious instructional institutions themselves, thus creating a separation as prescribed by the establishment clause. In the case of *Zelman*, however, the money was to be directly paid to the religiously affiliated schools, thereby breaking the gap that had been established by *Everson*.

Souter likewise references *Board of Ed. of Central School Dist. No.1 v. Allen* (1968), in which a New York State law was upheld that allowed for secular textbooks to be loaned to children attending religious schools since it was not a direct support of the school but rather a secular support of a what would be available for any child as part of the government's educational programs. In this case, the Court established that a nonsecular school served two purposes, that of secular education and that of religious education, and without the ability to only influence the secular portion, state and federal funds could not be used to directly support these schools. Rehnquist counters this argument in his opinion by pointing out that public schools and secular private schools were given identical opportunities to participate and public schools elected not to, and that the funds did not go directly to the schools but to the participating families, who in turn chose to use them at religiously affiliated schools, keeping the separation mandated by *Everson* and *Allen*.

Justice Stephen Breyer likewise contends that the Court's primary responsibility in adjudicating cases regarding establishment of a religion and schools is in making sure there is a stark separation between the state and the church. Referencing the dissenting opinion of *Everson*, Breyer points out that allowing state funds to go to religious programs creates a battle of sect against sect for funding and converts, akin to the very religious struggles of Europe that influenced the Founding Fathers in the construction of the Constitution. It was the intent of the Constitution to not serve as an equal opportunity for religion but rather to prevent religious strife.

Breyer also addresses the equal opportunity for individuals to attend these schools regardless of race, ethnicity, or religion as required by Ohio law. Though the law allowed for the suspension of participation in the program if violations were found, Breyer questions to what degree this could be enforced without in turn violating the protection of one religion's rights by putting one religion ahead of another in their own religious program. This in his view violated the third principle of *Lemon* by bringing about an entanglement between the church and the state. Despite a somewhat homogenous theological background in America, recent waves of immigrants from regions like Southwest Asia raised the potential for increased tensions and conflicts in religious schools. Rehnquist and the majority assert, however, that the decision to attend a patriarchal school remained a parent's choice, not a demand, and therefore they had the right not to attend a school that might conflict with their views and use the money elsewhere more suiting to their ideas and beliefs, thus once again returning to the argument that a separation did in fact exist under the Ohio law.

Impact

The case was seen as a significant victory for conservatives, particularly those favoring school choice and a greater expansion of religion in schools. The Ohio program was not necessarily a uniform opportunity for school vouchers, however, as it did not rule on the legality of vouchers as a whole, meaning state constitutions that strictly forbade the use of vouchers still would prevent their usage. Though the majority repeatedly emphasized the power of choice in their opinions, none of the justices tackled the issue of the constitutionality of vouchers or anti-voucher laws, leaving that problem for a future docket. Florida and Milwaukee adopted similar programs in an effort to grant parents in districts that were struggling more options in their children's education, and with this ruling, the religious affiliation of the school was deemed of little import as long as the money's usage was dictated by the parent and not the state.

Questions for Further Study

1. What did opponents of the Ohio law argue was the cause of unconstitutionality of the voucher program? What legal precedents did they cite to try to overturn the law?

2. The idea of separating church and state is seen as a crucial element of American democracy as it is a part of the First Amendment, which many legal scholars contend represents the Founding Fathers' most important rights. In a modern American society that has been populated by immigrants from the around the world throughout its history, what are the risks of using schools to indoctrinate children to one particular belief? What might supporters of a state religion argue is the reason behind allowing religions in schools?

3. Justice Breyer discussed the lack of options for some parents looking for either their specific religion or a secular private school. With the choice between a failing public school and a private religious program that was not in line with the family beliefs, what other options might a low-income family have faced? What was the solution put forth by the majority to alleviate this concern?

Further Reading

Books

MacMullen, Ian. *Faith in Schools? Autonomy, Citizenship, and Religious Education in the Liberal State.* Princeton: Princeton University Press, 2007.

Maranto, Robert, and M. Danish Shakeel, eds. *Educating Believers: Religion and School Choice.* London: Routledge, 2020.

Thomas, R. Murray. *God in the Classroom: Religion and America's Public Schools.* Westport, CT: Praeger, 2007.

Websites

Davis, Derek H. "Aid to Parochial Schools." *The First Amendment Encyclopedia.* 2009. Accessed March 10, 2023. https://www.mtsu.edu/first-amendment/article/902/aid-to-parochial-schools.

Lupu, Ira C., David Masci, and Robert W. Tuttle. "Religion in the Public Schools." Pew Research Center. October 3, 2019. https://www.pewresearch.org/religion/2019/10/03/religion-in-the-public-schools-2019-update/.

Posnick-Goodwin, Sherry. "Teaching about Religion." National Education Association. December 4, 2018. https://www.nea.org/professional-excellence/student-engagement/tools-tips/teaching-about-religion.

—Commentary by Ryan Fontanella

ZELMAN V. SIMMONS-HARRIS

Document Text

CHIEF JUSTICE REHNQUIST delivered the opinion of the Court

The State of Ohio has established a pilot program designed to provide educational choices to families with children who . . . reside in the Cleveland City School District. The question presented is whether this program offends the Establishment Clause of the United States Constitution. We hold that it does not.

There are more than 75,000 children enrolled in the Cleveland City School District. The majority of these children are from low-income and minority families. Few of these families enjoy the means to send their children to any school other than an inner-city public school. For more than a generation, however, Cleveland's public schools have been among the worst performing public schools in the Nation. In 1995, a Federal District Court declared a "crisis of magnitude" and placed the entire Cleveland school district under state control. See Reed v. Rhodes, No. 1:73 CV 1300 (ND Ohio, Mar. 3, 1995). Shortly thereafter, the state auditor found that Cleveland's public schools were in the midst of a "crisis that is perhaps unprecedented in the history of American education." Cleveland City School District Performance Audit 2-1 (Mar. 1996). The district had failed to meet any of the 18 state standards for minimal acceptable performance. Only 1 in 10 ninth graders could pass a basic proficiency examination, and students at all levels performed at a dismal rate compared with students in other Ohio public schools. More than two-thirds of high school students either dropped or failed out before graduation. Of those students who managed to reach their senior year, one of every four still failed to graduate. Of those students who did graduate, few could read, write, or compute at levels comparable to their counterparts in other cities.

It is against this backdrop that Ohio enacted, among other initiatives, its Pilot Project Scholarship Program, Ohio Rev. Code Ann. §§ 3313.974-3313.979 (Anderson 1999 and Supp. 2000) (program). The program provides financial assistance to families in any Ohio school district that is or has been "under federal court order requiring supervision and operational management of the district by the state superintendent." § 3313.975(A). Cleveland is the only Ohio school district to fall within that category.

The program provides two basic kinds of assistance to parents of children in a covered district. First, the program provides tuition aid for students in kindergarten through third grade, expanding each year through eighth grade, to attend a participating public or private school of their parent's choosing. §§ 3313.975(B) and (C)(l). Second, the program provides tutorial aid for students who choose to remain enrolled in public school. § 3313.975(A).

The tuition aid portion of the program is designed to provide educational choices to parents who reside in a covered district. Any private school, whether religious or nonreligious, may participate in the program and accept program students so long as the school is located within the boundaries of a covered district and meets statewide educational standards. § 313.976(A)(3). Participating private schools must agree not to discriminate on the basis of race, religion, or ethnic background, or to "advocate or foster unlawful behavior or teach hatred of any person or group on the basis of race, ethnicity, national origin, or religion." § 3313.976(A)(6). Any public school located in a school district adjacent to the covered district may also participate in the program. § *3313.976(C)*. Adjacent public schools are eligible to receive a $2,250 tuition grant for each program student accepted in addition to the full amount of per-pupil state funding attributable to each additional student. §§ *3313.976(C)*, 3317.03(1)(1). All participating schools, whether public or private, are required to accept students in accordance with rules and procedures established by the state superintendent. §§ 3313.977(A)(1)(a)-(c).

Tuition aid is distributed to parents according to financial need. Families with incomes below 200% of the poverty line are given priority and are eligible to receive 90% of private school tuition up to $2,250. §§ 3313.978(A) and *(C)(l)*. For these lowest income families, participating private schools may not charge a parental copayment greater than $250. § 3313.976(A)(8). For all other families, the program pays 75% of tuition costs, up to $1,875, with no copayment cap. §§ 3313.976(A)(8), 3313.978(A). These families receive tuition aid only if the number of available scholarships exceeds the number of low-income children who choose to participate. Where tuition aid is spent depends solely upon where parents who receive tuition aid choose to enroll their child. If parents choose a private school, checks are made payable to the parents who then endorse the checks over to the chosen school. § 3313.979.

The tutorial aid portion of the program provides tutorial assistance through grants to any student in a covered district who chooses to remain in public school. Parents arrange for registered tutors to provide assistance to their children and then submit bills for those services to the State for payment. §§ 3313.976(D), *3313.979(C)*. Students from low-income families receive 90% of the amount charged for such assistance up to $360. All other students receive 75% of that amount. § 3313.978(B). The number of tutorial assistance grants offered to students in a covered district must equal the number of tuition aid scholarships provided to students enrolled at participating private or adjacent public schools. § 3313.975(A).

The program has been in operation within the Cleveland City School District since the 1996-1997 school year. In the 1999-2000 school year, 56 private schools participated in the program, 46 (or 82%) of which had a religious affiliation. None of the public schools in districts adjacent to Cleveland have elected to participate. More than 3,700 students participated in the scholarship program, most of whom (96%) enrolled in religiously affiliated schools. Sixty percent of these students were from families at or below the poverty line. In the 1998-1999 school year, approximately 1,400 Cleveland public school students received tutorial aid. This number was expected to double during the 1999-2000 school year.

The program is part of a broader undertaking by the State to enhance the educational options of Cleveland's schoolchildren in response to the 1995 takeover. That undertaking includes programs governing community and magnet schools. Community schools are funded under state law but are run by their own school boards, not by local school districts. §§ 3314.01(B), 3314.04. These schools enjoy academic independence to hire their own teachers and to determine their own curriculum. They can have no religious affiliation and are required to accept students by lottery. During the 1999-2000 school year, there were 10 startup community schools in the Cleveland City School District with more than 1,900 students enrolled. For each child enrolled in a community school, the school receives state funding of $4,518, twice the funding a participating program school may receive.

Magnet schools are public schools operated by a local school board that emphasize a particular subject area, teaching method, or service to students. For each student enrolled in a magnet school, the school district receives $7,746, including state funding of $4,167, the same amount received per student enrolled at a traditional public school. As of 1999, parents in Cleveland were able to choose from among 23 magnet schools, which together enrolled more than 13,000 students in kindergarten through eighth grade. These schools provide specialized teaching methods, such as Montessori, or a particularized curriculum focus, such as foreign language, computers, or the arts.

In 1996, respondents, a group of Ohio taxpayers, challenged the Ohio program in state court on state and federal grounds. The Ohio Supreme Court rejected respondents' federal claims, but held that the enactment of the program violated certain procedural requirements of the Ohio Constitution. *Simmons-Harris* v. *Goff,* 86 Ohio St. 3d 1, 8-9, 711 N. E. 2d 203, 211 (1999). The state legislature immediately cured this defect, leaving the basic provisions discussed above intact.

In July 1999, respondents filed this action in United States District Court, seeking to enjoin the reenacted program on the ground that it violated the Establishment Clause of the United States Constitution. In August 1999, the District Court issued a preliminary injunction barring further implementation of the program, 54 F. Supp. 2d 725 (ND Ohio), which we stayed pending review by the Court of Appeals, 528 U. S. 983 (1999). In December 1999, the District Court granted summary judgment for respondents. 72 F. Supp. 2d 834. In December 2000, a divided panel of the Court of Appeals affirmed the judgment of the District Court, finding that the program had the "primary effect" of advancing religion in violation of the Establishment Clause. 234 F.3d 945 *(CA6).* The Court of Appeals stayed its mandate pending disposition in this Court. App. to Pet. for Cert. in No. 00-1779, p. 151. We granted certiorari, 533 U. S. 976 (2001), and now reverse the Court of Appeals.

The Establishment Clause of the First Amendment, applied to the States through the Fourteenth Amendment, prevents a State from enacting laws that have the "purpose" or "effect" of advancing or inhibiting religion. *Agostini* v. *Felton,* 521 U. S. 203, 222-223 (1997) ("[W]e continue to ask whether the government acted with the purpose of advancing or inhibiting religion [and] whether the aid has the 'effect' of advancing or inhibiting religion" (citations omitted)). There is no dispute that the program challenged here was enacted for the valid secular purpose of providing educational assistance to poor children in a demonstrably failing public school system. Thus, the question presented is whether the Ohio program nonetheless has the forbidden "effect" of advancing or inhibiting religion.

To answer that question, our decisions have drawn a consistent distinction between government programs that provide aid directly to religious schools, *Mitchell* v. *Helms, 530* U. S. 793, 810-814 (2000) (plurality opinion); *id.,* at 841-844 (O'CONNOR, J., concurring in judgment); *Agostini, supra,* at *225-227; Rosenberger* v. *Rector and Visitors of Univ. of Va.,* 515 U. S. 819, 842 (1995) (collecting cases), and programs of true private choice, in which government aid reaches religious schools only as a result of the genuine and independent choices of private individuals, *Mueller* v. *Allen,* 463 U. S. 388 *(1983); Witters* v. *Washington Dept. of Servs. for Blind,* 474 U. S. 481 (1986); *Zobrest* v. *Catalina Foothills School Dist.,* 509 U. S. 1 (1993). While our jurisprudence with respect to the constitutionality of direct aid programs has "changed significantly" over the past two decades, *Agostini, supra,* at 236, our jurisprudence with respect to true private choice programs has remained consistent and unbroken. Three times we have confronted Establishment Clause challenges to neutral government programs that provide aid directly to a broad class of individuals, who, in turn, direct the aid to religious schools or institutions of their own choosing. Three times we have rejected such challenges.

In *Mueller,* we rejected an Establishment Clause challenge to a Minnesota program authorizing tax deductions for various educational expenses, including private school tuition costs, even though the great majority of the program's beneficiaries (96%) were parents of children in religious schools. We began by focusing on the class of beneficiaries, finding that because the class included *"all* parents," including parents with "children [who] attend nonsectarian private schools or sectarian private schools," 463 U. S., at 397 (emphasis in original), the program was "not readily subject to challenge under the Establishment Clause," *id.,* at 399 (citing *Widmar* v. *Vincent,* 454 U. S. 263, 274 (1981) ("The provision of benefits to so broad a spectrum of groups is an important index of secular effect")). Then, viewing the program as a whole, we emphasized the principle of private choice, noting that public funds were made available to religious schools "only as a result of numerous, private choices of individual parents of school-age children." 463 U. S., at 399-400. This, we said, ensured that "no 'imprimatur of state approval' can be deemed to have been conferred on any particular religion, or on religion generally." *Id.,* at 399 (quoting *Widmar, supra,* at 274)). We thus found it irrelevant to the constitutional inquiry that the vast majority of beneficiaries were parents of children in religious schools, saying:

"We would be loath to adopt a rule grounding the constitutionality of a facially neutral law on annual reports reciting the extent to which various classes of private citizens claimed benefits under the law." 463 U. S., at 401.

That the program was one of true private choice, with no evidence that the State deliberately skewed incentives toward religious schools, was sufficient for the program to survive scrutiny under the Establishment Clause.

In *Witters,* we used identical reasoning to reject an Establishment Clause challenge to a vocational scholarship program that provided tuition aid to a student studying at a religious institution to become a pastor. Looking at the program as a whole, we observed that "[a]ny aid ... that ultimately flows to religious institutions does so only as a result of the genuinely independent and private choices of aid recipients." 474 U. S., at 487. We further remarked that, as in *Mueller,* "[the] program is made available generally without regard to the sectarian-nonsectarian, or public-nonpublic nature of the institution benefited." 474 U. S., at 487 (internal quotation marks omitted). In light of these factors, we held that the program was not inconsistent with the Establishment Clause. *Id.,* at 488-489.

Five Members of the Court, in separate opinions, emphasized the general rule from *Mueller* that the amount of government aid channeled to religious institutions by individual aid recipients was not relevant to the constitutional inquiry. 474 U. S., at 490-491 (Powell, J., joined by Burger, C. J., and REHNQUIST, J., concurring) (citing *Mueller, supra,* at 398399); 474 U. S., at 493 (O'CONNOR, J., concurring in part and concurring in judgment); *id.,* at 490 (White, J., concurring). Our holding thus rested not on whether few or many recipients chose to expend government aid at a religious school but, rather, on whether recipients generally were empowered to direct the aid to schools or institutions of their own choosing.

Finally, in *Zobrest,* we applied *Mueller* and *Witters* to reject an Establishment Clause challenge to a federal program that permitted sign-language interpreters to assist deaf children enrolled in religious schools. Reviewing our earlier decisions, we stated that "government programs that neutrally provide benefits to a broad class of citizens defined without reference to religion are not readily subject to an Establishment Clause challenge." 509 U. S., at 8. Looking once again to the challenged program as a whole, we observed that the program "distributes benefits neutrally to any child qualifying as 'disabled.'" *Id.,* at 10. Its "primary beneficiaries," we said, were "disabled children, not sectarian schools." *Id.,* at 12.

We further observed that "[b]y according parents freedom to select a school of their choice, the statute ensures that a government-paid interpreter will be present in a sectarian school only as a result of the private decision of individual parents." *Id.,* at 10. Our focus again was on neutrality and the principle of private choice, not on the number of program beneficiaries attending religious schools. *Id.,* at 10-11. See, *e. g., Agostini,* 521 U. S., at 229 *("Zobrest* did not turn on the fact that James Zobrest had, at the time of litigation, been the only child using a publicly funded sign-language interpreter to attend a parochial school"). Because the program ensured that parents were the ones to select a religious school as the best learning environment for their handicapped child, the circuit between government and religion was broken, and the Establishment Clause was not implicated.

Mueller, Witters, and *Zobrest* thus make clear that where a government aid program is neutral with respect to religion, and provides assistance directly to a broad class of citizens who, in turn, direct government aid to religious schools wholly as a result of their own genuine and independent private choice, the program is not readily subject to challenge under the Establishment Clause. A program that shares these features permits government aid to reach religious institutions only by way of the deliberate choices of numerous individual recipients. The incidental advancement of a religious mission, or the perceived endorsement of a religious message, is reasonably attributable to the individual recipient, not to the government, whose role ends with the disbursement of benefits. As a plurality of this Court recentlyobserved:

"[I]f numerous private choices, rather than the single choice of a government, determine the distribution of aid, pursuant to neutral eligibility criteria, then a government cannot, or at least cannot easily, grant special favors that might lead to a religious establishment." *Mitchell,* 530 U. S., at 810. See also *id.,* at 843 (O'CONNOR, J., concurring in judgment) ("[W]hen government aid supports a school's religious mission only because of independent decisions made by numerous individuals to guide their secular aid to that school, 'no reasonable observer is likely to draw from the facts ... an inference that the State itself is endorsing a religious practice or belief'" (quoting *Witters,* 474 U. S., at 493 (O'CONNOR, J., concurring in part and concurring in judgment))). It is precisely for these reasons that we have never found a program of true private choice to offend the Establishment Clause.

We believe that the program challenged here is a program of true private choice, consistent with *Mueller, Witters,* and *Zobrest,* and thus constitutional. As was true in those cases, the Ohio program is neutral in all respects toward religion. It is part of a general and multifaceted undertaking by the State of Ohio to provide educational opportunities to the children of a failed school district. It confers educational assistance directly to a broad class of individuals defined without reference to religion, i. e., any parent of a school-age child who resides in the Cleveland City School District. The program permits the participation of *all* schools within the district, religious or nonreligious. Adjacent public schools also may participate and have a financial incentive to do so. Program benefits are available to participating families on neutral terms, with no reference to religion. The only preference stated anywhere in the program is a preference for low-income families, who receive greater assistance and are given priority for admission at participating schools.

There are no "financial incentive[s]" that "ske[w]" the program toward religious schools. *Witters, supra,* at 487-488. Such incentives "[are] not present ... where the aid is allocated on the basis of neutral, secular criteria that neither favor nor disfavor religion, and is made available to both religious and secular beneficiaries on a nondiscriminatory basis." *Agostini, supra,* at 231. The program here in fact creates financial disincentives for religious schools, with private schools receiving only half the government assistance given to community schools and one-third the assistance given to magnet schools. Adjacent public schools, should any choose to accept program students, are also eligible to receive two to three times the state funding of a private religious school. Families too have a financial disincentive to choose a private religious school over other schools. Parents that choose to participate in the scholarship program and then to enroll their children in a private school (religious or nonreligious) must copay a portion of the school's tuition. Families that choose a community school, magnet school, or traditional public school pay nothing. Although such features of the program are not necessary to its constitutionality, they clearly dispel the claim that the program "creates ... financial incentive[s] for parents to choose a sectarian school." *Zobrest,* 509 U. S., at 10.

Respondents suggest that even without a financial incentive for parents to choose a religious school, the program creates a "public perception that the State is endorsing religious practices and beliefs." Brief for Respondents Simmons-Harris et al. 37-38. But we have repeatedly recognized that no reasonable observer would think a neutral program of private choice, where state aid reaches religious schools solely as a result of the numerous independent decisions of private individuals, carries with it the *imprimatur* of government endorsement. *Mueller,* 463 U. S., at 399; *Witters, supra,* at 488-489; *Zobrest, supra,* at 10-11; *e. g., Mitchell, supra,* at 842-843 (O'CONNOR, J., concurring in judgment) ("In terms of public perception, a government program of direct aid to religious schools ... differs meaningfully from the government distributing aid directly to individual students who, in turn, decide to use the aid at the same religious schools"). The argument is particularly misplaced here since "the reasonable observer in the endorsement inquiry must be deemed aware" of the "history and context" underlying a challenged program. *Good News Club* v. *Milford Central School,* 533 U. S. 98, 119 (2001) (internal quotation marks omitted). See also *Capitol Square Review and Advisory Bd.* v. *Pinette,* 515 U. S. 753, 780 (1995) (O'CONNOR, J., concurring in part and concurring in judgment). Any objective observer familiar with the full history and context of the Ohio program would reasonably view it as one aspect of a broader undertaking to assist poor children in failed schools, not as an endorsement of religious schooling in general.

There also is no evidence that the program fails to provide genuine opportunities for Cleveland parents to select secular educational options for their school-age children. Cleveland schoolchildren enjoy a range of educational choices: They may remain in public school as before, remain in public school with publicly funded tutoring aid, obtain a scholarship and choose a religious school, obtain a scholarship and choose a nonreligious private school, enroll in a community school, or enroll in a magnet school. That 46 of the 56 private schools now participating in the program are religious schools does not condemn it as a violation of the Establishment Clause. The Establishment Clause question is whether Ohio is coercing parents into sending their children to religious schools, and that question must be answered by evaluating *all* options Ohio provides Cleveland schoolchildren, only one of which is to obtain a program scholarship and then choose a religious school.

JUSTICE SOUTER speculates that because more private religious schools currently participate in the program, the program itself must somehow discourage the participation of private nonreligious schools. *Post,* at 703-705 (dissenting opinion). But Cleveland's preponderance of religiously affiliated private schools certainly did not arise as a result of the program; it is a phenomenon common to many American cities. See U. S. Dept. of Ed., National Center for Education Statistics, Private School Universe Survey: 1999-2000, pp. 2-4 (NCES 2001-330, 2001) (hereinafter Private School Universe Survey) (cited in Brief for United States as *Amicus Curiae* 24). Indeed, by all accounts the program has captured a remarkable cross-section of private schools, religious and nonreligious. It is true that 82% of Cleveland's participating private schools are religious schools, but it is also true that 81% of private schools in Ohio are religious schools. See Brief for State of Florida et al. as *Amici Curiae* 16 (citing Private School Universe Survey). To attribute constitutional significance to this figure, moreover, would lead to the absurd result that a neutral school-choice program might be permissible in some parts of Ohio, such as Columbus, where a lower percentage of private schools are religious schools, see Ohio Educational Directory (Lodging of Respondents Gatton et al., available in Clerk of Court's case file), and Reply Brief for Petitioners in No. 00-1751, p. 12, n. 1, but not in inner-city Cleveland, where Ohio has deemed such programs most sorely needed, but where the preponderance of religious schools happens to be greater. Cf. Brief for State of Florida et al. as *Amici Curiae* 17 ("[T]he percentages of sectarian to nonsectarian private schools within Florida's 67 school districts ... vary from zero to 100 percent"). Likewise, an identical private choice program might be constitutional in some States, such as Maine or Utah, where less than 45% of private schools are religious schools, but not in other States, such as Nebraska or Kansas, where over 90% of private schools are religious schools. *Id.,* at 15-16 (citing Private School Universe Survey).

Respondents and JUSTICE SOUTER claim that even if we do not focus on the number of participating schools that are religious schools, we should attach constitutional significance to the fact that 96% of scholarship recipients have enrolled in religious schools. They claim that this alone proves parents lack genuine choice, even if no parent has ever said so. We need not consider this argument in detail, since it was flatly rejected in *Mueller,* where we found it irrelevant that 96% of parents taking deductions for tuition expenses paid tuition at religious schools. Indeed, we have recently found it irrelevant even to the constitutionality of a direct aid program that a vast majority of program benefits went to religious schools. See *Agostini,* 521 U. S., at 229 ("Nor are we willing to conclude that the constitutionality of an aid program depends on the number of sectarian school students who happen to receive the otherwise neutral aid" (citing *Mueller,* 463 U. S., at 401)); see also *Mitchell,* 530 U. S., at 812, n. 6 (plurality opinion) *("[Agostini]* held that the proportion of aid benefiting students at religious schools pursuant to a neutral program involving private choices was irrelevant to the constitutional inquiry"); *id.,* at 848 (O'CONNOR, J., concurring in judgment) (same) (quoting *Agostini, supra,* at 229). The constitutionality of a neutral educational aid program simply does not turn on whether and why, in a particular area, at a particular time, most private schools are run by religious organizations, or most recipients choose to use the aid at a religious school. As we said in *Mueller,* "[s]uch an approach would scarcely provide the certainty that this field stands in need of, nor can we perceive principled standards by which such statistical evidence might be evaluated." 463 U. S., at 401.

This point is aptly illustrated here. The 96% figure upon which respondents and JUSTICE SOUTER rely discounts entirely (1) the more than 1,900 Cleveland children enrolled in alternative community schools, (2) the more than 13,000 children enrolled in alternative magnet schools, and (3) the more than 1,400 children enrolled in traditional public schools with tutorial assistance. See *supra,* at 647-648. Including some or all of these children in the denominator of children enrolled in nontraditional schools during the 1999-2000 school year drops the percentage enrolled in religious schools from 96% to under 20%. See also J. Greene, The Racial, Economic, and Religious Context of Parental Choice in Cleveland 11, Table 4 (Oct. 8, 1999), App. 217a (reporting that only 16.5% of nontraditional schoolchildren in Cleveland choose religious schools). The 96% figure also represents but a snapshot of one particular school year. In the 1997-1998 school year, by contrast, only 78% of scholarship recipients attended religious schools. See App. to Pet. for Cert. in No. 00-1751, p. 5a. The difference was attributable to two private nonreligious schools that had accepted 15% of all scholarship students electing instead to register as community schools, in light of larger per-pupil funding for community schools and the uncertain future of the scholarship program generated by this litigation. See App. 59a-62a, 209a, 223a-227a.5 Many of the students enrolled in these schools as scholarship students remained enrolled as community school students, *id.*, at 145a-146a, thus demonstrating the arbitrariness of counting one type of school but not the other to assess primary effect, *e. g.*, Ohio Rev. Code Ann. § 3314.11 (Anderson 1999) (establishing a single "office of school options" to "provide services that facilitate the management of the community schools program and the pilot project scholarship program"). In spite of repeated questioning from the Court at oral argument, respondents offered no convincing justification for their approach, which relies entirely on such arbitrary classifications. Tr. of Oral Arg. 52-60.

schools. Brief for Wisconsin 11-12. Similarly, the number of program students attending nonreligious private schools increased from 2,048 to 3,582; these students now represent 33% of all program students. *Id.*, at 12-13. There are currently 34 nonreligious private schools participating in the Milwaukee program, a nearly fivefold increase from the 7 nonreligious schools that participated when the program began in 1990. See App. 218a; Brief for Wisconsin 12. And the total number of students enrolled in nonreligious schools has grown from 337 when the program began to 3,582 in the most recent school year. See App. 218a, 234a-236a; Brief for Wisconsin 12-13. These numbers further demonstrate the wisdom of our refusal in *Mueller* v. *Allen*, 463 U. S., at 401, to make the constitutionality of such a program depend on "annual reports reciting the extent to which various classes of private citizens claimed benefits under the law."

Respondents finally claim that we should look to *Committee for Public Ed. & Religious Liberty* v. *Nyquist*, 413 U. S. 756 (1973), to decide these cases. We disagree for two reasons. First, the program in *Nyquist* was quite different from the program challenged here. *Nyquist* involved a New York program that gave a package of benefits exclusively to private schools and the parents of private school enrollees. Although the program was enacted for ostensibly secular purposes, *id.*, at 773-774, we found that its "function" was *"unmistakably* to provide desired financial support for nonpublic, sectarian institutions," *id.*, at 783 (emphasis added). Its genesis, we said, was that private religious schools faced "increasingly grave fiscal problems." *Id.*, at 795. The program thus provided direct money grants to religious schools. *Id.*, at 762-764. It provided tax benefits "unrelated to the amount of money actually expended by any parent on tuition," ensuring a windfall to parents of children in religious schools. *Id.*, at 790. It similarly provided tuition reimbursements designed explicitly to "offe[r] ... an incentive to parents to send their children to sectarian schools." *Id.*, at 786. Indeed, the program flatly prohibited the participation of any public school, or parent of any public school enrollee. *Id.*, at 763-765. Ohio's program shares none of these features.

Second, were there any doubt that the program challenged in *Nyquist* is far removed from the program challenged here, we expressly reserved judgment with respect to "a case involving some form of public assistance *(e. g.,* scholarships) made available generally without regard to the sectarian-nonsectarian, or public-nonpublic nature of the institution benefited." *Id.*, at 782-783, n. 38. That, of course, is the very question now before us, and it has since been answered, first in *Mueller,* 463 U. S., at 398-399 ("[A] program ... that neutrally provides state assistance to a broad spectrum of citizens is not readily subject to challenge under the Establishment Clause" (citing *Nyquist, supra,* at 782-783, n. 38)), then in *Witters,* 474 U. S., at 487 ("Washington's program is 'made available generally without regard to the sectarian-nonsectarian, or public-nonpublic nature of the institution benefited'" (quoting *Nyquist, supra,* at 782-783, n. 38)), and again in *Zobrest,* 509 U. S., at 12-13 ("[T]he function of the [program] is hardly 'to provide desired financial support for nonpublic, sectarian institutions'" (quoting *Nyquist, supra,* at 782-783, n. 38)). To the extent the scope of *Nyquist* has remained an open question in light of these later decisions, we now hold that *Nyquist* does not govern neutral educational assistance programs that, like the program here, offer aid directly to a broad class of individual recipients defined without regard to religion.

In sum, the Ohio program is entirely neutral with respect to religion. It provides benefits directly to a wide spectrum of individuals, defined only by financial need and residence in a particular school district. It permits such individuals to exercise genuine choice among options public and private, secular and religious. The program is therefore a program of true private choice. In keeping with an unbroken line of decisions rejecting challenges to similar programs, we hold that the program does not offend the Establishment Clause.

The judgment of the Court of Appeals is reversed.

It is so ordered.

JUSTICE BREYER, with whom JUSTICE STEVENS and JUSTICE SOUTER join, dissenting

I join JUSTICE SOUTER'S opinion, and I agree substantially with JUSTICE STEVENS. I write separately, however, to emphasize the risk that publicly financed voucher programs pose in terms of religiously based social conflict. I do so because I believe that the Establishment Clause concern for protecting the Nation's social fabric from religious conflict poses an overriding obstacle to the implementation of this well-intentioned school voucher program. And by explaining the nature of the concern, I hope to demonstrate why, in my view, "parental choice" cannot significantly alleviate the constitutional problem. See Part IV, *infra*.

I

The First Amendment begins with a prohibition, that "Congress shall make no law respecting an establishment of religion," and a guarantee, that the government shall not prohibit "the free exercise thereof." These Clauses embody an understanding, reached in the 17th century after decades of religious war, that liberty and social stability demand a religious tolerance that respects the religious views of all citizens, permits those citizens to "worship God in their own way," and allows all families to "teach their children and to form their characters" as they wish. C. Radcliffe, The Law & Its Compass 71 (1960). The Clauses reflect the Framers' vision of an American Nation free of the religious strife that had long plagued the nations of Europe. See, *e. g.*, Freund, Public Aid to Parochial Schools, 82 Harv. L. Rev. 1680, 1692 (1969) (religious strife was "one of the principal evils that the first amendment sought to forestall"); B. Kosmin & S. Lachman, One Nation Under God: Religion in Contemporary American Society 24 (1993) (First Amendment designed in "part to prevent the religious wars of Europe from entering the United States"). Whatever the Framers might have thought about particular 18th-century school funding practices, they undeniably intended an interpretation of the Religion Clauses that would implement this basic First Amendment objective.

In part for this reason, the Court's 20th-century Establishment Clause cases—both those limiting the practice of religion in public schools and those limiting the public funding of private religious education—focused directly upon social conflict, potentially created when government becomes involved in religious education. In *Engel* v. *Vitale*, 370 U. S. 421 (1962), the Court held that the Establishment Clause forbids prayer in public elementary and secondary schools. It did so in part because it recognized the "anguish, hardship and bitter strife that could come when zealous religious groups struggl[e] with one another to obtain the Government's stamp of approval. . . ." *Id.*, at 429. And it added:

"The history of governmentally established religion, both in England and in this country, showed that whenever government had allied itself with one particular form of religion, the inevitable result had been that it had incurred the hatred, disrespect and even contempt of those who held contrary beliefs." *Id.*, at 431.

See also *Lee* v. *Weisman*, 505 U. S. 577, 588 (1992) (striking down school-sanctioned prayer at high school graduation ceremony because "potential for divisiveness" has "particular relevance" in school environment); *School Dist. of Abington Township* v. *Schempp*, 374 U. S. 203, 307 (1963) (Goldberg, J., concurring) (Bible-reading program violated Establishment Clause in part because it gave rise "to those very divisive influences and inhibitions of freedom" that come with government efforts to impose religious influence on "young impressionable [school] children").

In *Lemon* v. *Kurtzman*, 403 U. S. 602 (1971), the Court held that the Establishment Clause forbids state funding, through salary supplements, of religious school teachers. It did so in part because of the "threat" that this funding would create religious "divisiveness" that would harm "the normal political process." *Id.*, at 622. The Court explained:

"[P]olitical debate and division ... are normal and healthy manifestations of our democratic system of government, but political division along religious lines was one of the principal evils against which [the First Amendment's religious clauses were] ... intended to protect." *Ibid.*

And in *Committee for Public Ed. & Religious Liberty* v. *Nyquist,* 413 U. S. 756, 794 (1973), the Court struck down a state statute that, much like voucher programs, provided aid for parents whose children attended religious schools, explaining that the "assistance of the sort here involved carries grave potential for ... continuing political strife over aid to religion."

When it decided these 20th-century Establishment Clause cases, the Court did not deny that an earlier American society might have found a less clear-cut church/state separation compatible with social tranquility. Indeed, historians point out that during the early years of the Republic, American schools—including the first public schools—were Protestant in character. Their students recited Protestant prayers, read the King James version of the Bible, and learned Protestant religious ideals. See, *e. g.,* D. Tyack, Onward Christian Soldiers: Religion in the American Common School, in History and Education 217-226 (P. Nash ed. 1970). Those practices may have wrongly discriminated against members of minority religions, but given the small number of such individuals, the teaching of Protestant religions in schools did not threaten serious social conflict. See Kosmin & Lachman, *supra,* at 45 (Catholics constituted less than 2% of American church-affiliated population at time of founding).

The 20th-century Court was fully aware, however, that immigration and growth had changed American society dramatically since its early years. By 1850, 1.6 million Catholics lived in America, and by 1900 that number rose to 12 million. Jeffries & Ryan, A Political History of the Establishment Clause, 100 Mich. L. Rev. 279, 299-300 (Nov. 2001). There were similar percentage increases in the Jewish population. Kosmin & Lachman, *supra,* at 45-46. Not surprisingly, with this increase in numbers, members of non-Protestant religions, particularly Catholics, began to resist the Protestant domination of the public schools. Scholars report that by the mid-19th century religious conflict over matters such as Bible reading "grew intense," as Catholics resisted and Protestants fought back to preserve their domination. Jeffries & Ryan, *supra,* at 300. "Dreading Catholic domination," native Protestants "terrorized Catholics." P. Hamburger, Separation of Church and State 219 (2002). In some States "Catholic students suffered beatings or expulsions for refusing to read from the Protestant Bible, and crowds ... rioted over whether Catholic children could be released from the classroom during Bible reading." Jeffries & Ryan, 100 Mich. L. Rev., at 300.

The 20th-century Court was also aware that political efforts to right the wrong of discrimination against religious minorities in primary education had failed; in fact they had exacerbated religious conflict. Catholics sought equal government support for the education of their children in the form of aid for private Catholic schools. But the "Protestant position" on this matter, scholars report, "was that public schools must be 'nonsectarian' (which was usually understood to allow Bible reading and other Protestant observances) and public money must not support 'sectarian' schools (which in practical terms meant Catholic)." *Id.,* at 301. And this sentiment played a significant role in creating a movement that sought to amend several state constitutions (often successfully), and to amend the United States Constitution (unsuccessfully) to make certain that government would not help pay for "sectarian" (i. *e.,* Catholic) schooling for children. *Id.,* at 301-305. See also Hamburger, *supra,* at 287.

These historical circumstances suggest that the Court, applying the Establishment Clause through the Fourteenth Amendment to 20th-century American society, faced an interpretive dilemma that was in part practical. The Court appreciated the religious diversity of contemporary American society. See *Schempp, supra,* at 240 (Brennan, J., concurring). It realized that the status quo favored some religions at the expense of others. And it understood the Establishment Clause to prohibit (among other things) any such favoritism. Yet *how* did the Clause achieve that objective? Did it simply require the government to give each religion an equal chance to introduce religion into the primary schools—a kind of "equal opportunity" approach to the interpretation of the Establishment Clause? Or, did that Clause avoid government favoritism of some religions by insisting upon "separation"—that the government achieve equal treatment by removing itself from the business of providing religious education for children? This interpretive choice arose in respect both to religious activities in public schools and government aid to private education.

In both areas the Court concluded that the Establishment Clause required "separation," in part because an "equal opportunity" approach was not workable. With respect to religious activities in the public schools, how could the Clause require public primary and secondary school teachers, when reading prayers or the Bible, *only* to treat all religions alike? In many places there were too many religions, too diverse a set of religious practices, too many whose spiritual beliefs denied the virtue of formal religious training. This diversity made it difficult, if not impossible, to devise meaningful forms of "equal treatment" by providing an "equal opportunity" for all to introduce their own religious practices into the public schools.

With respect to government aid to private education, did not history show that efforts to obtain equivalent funding for the private education of children whose parents did not hold popular religious beliefs only exacerbated religious strife? As Justice Rutledge recognized:

"Public money devoted to payment of religious costs, educational or other, brings the quest for more. It brings too the struggle of sect against sect for the larger share or for any. Here one [religious sect] by numbers [of adherents] alone will benefit most, there another. This is precisely the history of societies which have had an established religion and dissident groups." *Everson* v. *Board of Ed. of Ewing,* 330 U. S. 1,53-54 (1947) (dissenting opinion).

The upshot is the development of constitutional doctrine that reads the Establishment Clause as avoiding religious strife, *not* by providing every religion with an *equal opportunity* (say, to secure state funding or to pray in the public schools), but by drawing fairly clear lines of *separation* between church and state—at least where the heartland of religious belief, such as primary religious education, is at issue.

II

The principle underlying these cases—avoiding religiously based social conflict—remains of great concern. As religiously diverse as America had become when the Court decided its major 20th-century Establishment Clause cases, we are exponentially more diverse today. America boasts more than 55 different religious groups and subgroups with a significant number of members. Graduate Center of the City University of New York, B. Kosmin, E. Mayer, & A. Keysar, American Religious Identification Survey 12-13 (2001). Major religions include, among others, Protestants, Catholics, Jews, Muslims, Buddhists, Hindus, and Sikhs. *Ibid.* And several of these major religions contain different subsidiary sects with different religious beliefs. See Lester, Oh, Gods!, The Atlantic Monthly 37 (Feb. 2002). Newer Christian immigrant groups are "expressing their Christianity in languages, customs, and independent churches that are barely recognizable, and often controversial, for European ancestry Catholics and Protestants." H. Ebaugh & J. Chafetz, Religion and the New Immigrants: Continuities and Adaptations in Immigrant Congregations 4 (abridged student ed. 2002).

Under these modern-day circumstances, how is the "equal opportunity" principle to work—without risking the "struggle of sect against sect" against which Justice Rutledge warned? School voucher programs finance the religious education of the young. And, if widely adopted, they may well provide billions of dollars that will do so. Why will different religions not become concerned about, and seek to influence, the criteria used to channel this money to religious schools? Why will they not want to examine the implementation of the programs that provide this money—to determine, for example, whether implementation has biased a program toward or against particular sects, or whether recipient religious schools are adequately fulfilling a program's criteria? If so, just how is the State to resolve the resulting controversies without provoking legitimate fears of the kinds of religious favoritism that, in so religiously diverse a Nation, threaten social dissension?

Consider the voucher program here at issue. That program insists that the religious school accept students of all religions. Does that criterion treat fairly groups whose religion forbids them to do so? The program also insists that no participating school "advocate or foster unlawful behavior or teach hatred of any person or group on the basis of race, ethnicity, national origin, or religion." Ohio Rev. Code Ann. § 3313.976(A)(6) (West Supp. 2002). And it requires the State to "revoke the registration of any school if, after a hearing, the superintendent determines that the school is in violation" of the program's rules. § 3313.976(B). As one *amicus* argues, "it is difficult to imagine a more divisive activity" than the appointment of state officials as referees to determine whether a particular religious doctrine "teaches hatred or advocates lawlessness."

Brief for National Committee for Public Education and Religious Liberty as *Amic*us Curiae 23.

How are state officials to adjudicate claims that one religion or another is advocating, for example, civil disobedience in response to unjust laws, the use of illegal drugs in a religious ceremony, or resort to force to call attention to what it views as an immoral social practice? What kind of public hearing will there be in response to claims that one religion or another is continuing to teach a view of history that casts members of other religions in the worst possible light? How will the public react to government funding for schools that take controversial religious positions on topics that are of current popular interest—say, the conflict in the Middle East or the war on terrorism? Yet any major funding program for primary religious education will require criteria. And the selection of those criteria, as well as their application, inevitably pose problems that are divisive. Efforts to respond to these problems not only will seriously entangle church and state, see *Lemon*, 403 U. S., at 622, but also will promote division among religious groups, as one group or another fears (often legitimately) that it will receive unfair treatment at the hands of the government.

I recognize that other nations, for example Great Britain and France, have in the past reconciled religious school funding and religious freedom without creating serious strife. Yet British and French societies are religiously more homogeneous—and it bears noting that recent waves of immigration have begun to create problems of social division there as well. See, *e. g.*, The Muslims of France, 75 Foreign Affairs 78 (1996) (describing increased religious strife in France, as exemplified by expulsion of teenage girls from school for wearing traditional Muslim scarves); Ahmed, Extreme Prejudice; Muslims in Britain, The Times of London, May 2, 1992, p. 10 (describing religious strife in connection with increased Muslim immigration in Great Britain).

In a society as religiously diverse as ours, the Court has recognized that we must rely on the Religion Clauses of the First Amendment to protect against religious strife, particularly when what is at issue is an area as central to religious belief as the shaping, through primary education, of the next generation's minds and spirits. See, *e. g.*, Webster, On the Education of Youth in America (1790), in Essays on Education in the Early Republic 43, 53, 59 (F. Rudolph ed. 1965) ("[E]ducation of youth" is "of more consequence than making laws and preaching the gospel, because it lays the foundation on which both law and gospel rest for success"); Pope Paul VI, Declaration on Christian Education (1965) ("[T]he Catholic school can be such an aid to the fulfillment of the mission of the People of God and to the fostering of dialogue between the Church and mankind, to the benefit of both, it retains even in our present circumstances the utmost importance").

III

I concede that the Establishment Clause currently permits States to channel various forms of assistance to religious schools, for example, transportation costs for students, computers, and secular texts. See *Everson* v. *Board of Ed. of Ewing*, 330 U. S. 1 (1947); *Mitchell* v. *Helms*, 530 U. S. 793 (2000). States now certify the nonsectarian educational content of religious school education. See, *e. g.*, *New Life Baptist Church Academy* v. *East Longmeadow*, 885 F.2d 940 *(CA1* 1989). Yet the consequence has not been great turmoil. But see, *e. g.*, May, Charter School's Religious Tone; Operation of South Bay Academy Raises Church-State Questions, San Francisco Chronicle, Dec. 17, 2001, p. A1 (describing increased government supervision of charter schools after complaints that students were "studying Islam in class and praying with their teachers," and Muslim educators complaining of" 'post-Sept. 11 anti-Muslim sentiment' ").

School voucher programs differ, however, in both *kind* and *degree* from aid programs upheld in the past. They differ in kind because they direct financing to a core function of the church: the teaching of religious truths to young children. For that reason the constitutional demand for "separation" is of particular constitutional concern. See, *e. g.*, *Weisman*, 505 U. S., at 592 ("heightened concerns" in context of primary education); *Edwards* v. *Aguillard*, 482 U. S. 578, 583584 (1987) ("Court has been particularly vigilant in monitoring compliance with the Establishment Clause in elementary and secondary schools").

Private schools that participate in Ohio's program, for example, recognize the importance of primary religious education, for they pronounce that their goals are to "communicate the gospel," "provide opportunities to ... experience a faith community," "provide ... for growth in prayer," and "provide instruction in religious truths and values." App. 408a, 487a. History suggests, not that such private school teaching of religion is undesirable, but that *government funding* of this kind of religious endeavor is far more contentious than providing funding for secular textbooks, computers, vocational training, or even funding for adults who wish to obtain a college education at a religious university. See *supra,* at 720-722. Contrary to JUSTICE O'CONNOR'S opinion, *ante,* at 665-666 (concurring opinion), history also shows that government involvement in religious primary education is far more divisive than state property tax exemptions for religious institutions or tax deductions for charitable contributions, both of which come far closer to exemplifying the neutrality that distinguishes, for example, fire protection on the one hand from direct monetary assistance on the other. Federal aid to religiously based hospitals, *ante,* at 666 (O'CONNOR, J., concurring), is even further removed from education, which lies at the heartland of religious belief.

Vouchers also differ in *degree*. The aid programs recently upheld by the Court involved limited amounts of aid to religion. But the majority's analysis here appears to permit a considerable shift of taxpayer dollars from public secular schools to private religious schools. That fact, combined with the use to which these dollars will be put, exacerbates the conflict problem. State aid that takes the form of peripheral secular items, with prohibitions against diversion of funds to religious teaching, holds significantly less potential for social division. In this respect as well, the secular aid upheld in *Mitchell* differs dramatically from the present case. Although it was conceivable that minor amounts of money could have, contrary to the statute, found their way to the religious activities of the recipients, see 530 U. S., at 864 (O'CONNOR, J., concurring in judgment), that case is at worst the camel's nose, while the litigation before us is the camel itself.

IV

I do not believe that the "parental choice" aspect of the voucher program sufficiently offsets the concerns I have mentioned. Parental choice cannot help the taxpayer who does not want to finance the religious education of children. It will not always help the parent who may see little real choice between inadequate nonsectarian public education and adequate education at a school whose religious teachings are contrary to his own. It will not satisfy religious minorities unable to participate because they are too few in number to support the creation of their own private schools. It will not satisfy groups whose religious beliefs preclude them from participating in a government-sponsored program, and who may well feel ignored as government funds primarily support the education of children in the doctrines of the dominant religions. And it does little to ameliorate the entanglement problems or the related problems of social division that Part II, *supra,* describes. Consequently, the fact that the parent may choose which school can cash the government's voucher check does not alleviate the Establishment Clause concerns associated with voucher programs.

V

The Court, in effect, turns the clock back. It adopts, under the name of "neutrality," an interpretation of the Establishment Clause that this Court rejected more than half a century ago. In its view, the parental choice that offers each religious group a kind of equal opportunity to secure government funding overcomes the Establishment Clause concern for social concord. An earlier Court found that "equal opportunity" principle insufficient; it read the Clause as insisting upon greater separation of church and state, at least in respect to primary education. See *Nyquist,* 413 U. S., at 783. In a society composed of many different religious creeds, I fear that this present departure from the Court's earlier understanding risks creating a form of religiously based conflict potentially harmful to the Nation's social fabric. Because I believe the Establishment Clause was written in part to avoid this kind of conflict, and for reasons set forth by JUSTICE SOUTER and JUSTICE STEVENS, I respectfully dissent.

Glossary

amicus curiae: literally, "friend of the court"; referring to a party who is not participating in a lawsuit or action but has a strong interest in the case

establishment clause: the portion of the First Amendment that says, "Congress shall make no law respecting an establishment of religion"

jurisprudence: the theory and philosophy of law

***Lemon* test:** a test based on the case *Lemon v. Kurtzman* (1971) dictating that certain principles have to be met for a policy or law not to violate the establishment clause

nonsectarian: not religious; not relating to a particular religion

sectarian: religious

secular: not religious

LAWRENCE V. TEXAS

DATE 2003 **AUTHOR** Anthony M. Kennedy **VOTE** 6–3	**CITATION** 539 U.S. 558 **SIGNIFICANCE** Ruled that laws banning sodomy were unconstitutional and recognized a constitutional right with regard to private, consensual sexual conduct by adults, including those of the same sex

Overview

In 1986, in *Bowers v. Hardwick* the U.S. Supreme Court upheld as constitutional a Georgia law criminalizing sodomy between consenting adults. The defendant in the case was a gay man who had been convicted under the statute. He argued that he had a constitutional right to privacy that extended to private, consensual sexual conduct. Reframing the legal question as whether the Constitution created "a fundamental right to engage in homosexual sodomy," the Court rejected the defendant's arguments and answered that the Constitution provided no such right.

Seventeen years later, in *Lawrence v. Texas*, the Supreme Court faced a direct challenge to the holding of *Bowers*. In *Lawrence*, two men convicted of illegal sexual intercourse under a Texas statute criminalizing oral and anal sex by consenting same-sex couples argued that the Texas law was unconstitutional for the very reasons rejected by the Court in *Bowers*. In its decision in *Lawrence*, the Court took the unusual step of overruling itself and striking down the Texas statute. Writing for the majority, Justice Anthony M. Kennedy declared *Bowers* to have been wrongly decided and held that the defendants were free as adults to engage in private sexual conduct in the exercise of their liberty rights as guaranteed by the due process clause of the Fourteenth Amendment.

Context

The social and political landscape for gays and lesbians in the United States in 2003, when *Lawrence* was decided, was significantly different from merely seventeen years earlier, when the Court heard *Bowers*. Those seventeen years saw significant shifts in the country's treatment of gay men and women as well as important changes in the composition of the Supreme Court.

In 1986, the year *Bowers* was decided, most gay men and lesbian women maintained their sexual orientation as a closely guarded secret. The public revelation of homosexual orientation was unusual and often harmful to those exposed. Reports that gay men and lesbian women were publicly subjected to vitriol, discrimination, and outright violence were not uncommon, and the law offered little protection. In fact, twenty-four states and the District of Columbia deemed sex between members of the same sex to be criminal activity. Only Wisconsin outlawed discrimination on the basis of sexual orientation. The military prohibited gay men and lesbians from service, and no state offered legal recognition of same-sex unions.

By 2003, lesbians and gay men had become a visible presence in American society unlike at any other time in history. Politicians, teachers, judges, athletes, and movie stars had made public their attractions to people of the same sex. Gay and lesbian couples lived openly in many communities, raising children and serving in civic organizations. Universities and high schools saw the formation of gay student unions, in which young people made their sexual orientations a matter of public record. Gay characters appeared as protagonists on television and in movies. Gay rights activists organized large, public, and effective advocacy campaigns.

Some of these changes were, somewhat paradoxically, a result of the AIDS crisis of the 1980s. *Bowers v. Hardwick* made its way through the courts at the height of the HIV/AIDS epidemic in the United States, an epidemic that decimated the gay community physically and socially. In the 1980s, HIV infection—originally dubbed the "gay cancer"—was widely believed to be transmitted primarily, if not exclusively, by sex between men. Infection with the virus was essentially a death sentence. As a result, HIV stigmatized gay men as potential predators and sex between men as a threat to health and safety. By 2003 medical advances in the treatment of HIV/AIDS had transformed HIV infection from a veritable death sentence into a treatable condition. Educational efforts had successfully informed the public that the virus infected across genders, ages, and sexual orientations, lessening the stigma of the disease. More important, the political activism generated in response to the AIDS epidemic brought gay rights, and the people seeking them, into mainstream U.S. culture.

Laws reflected the social evolution. By 2003, Vermont had recognized legal civil unions between same-sex couples, and California and New York City had adopted domestic partnership laws. A historic case that would ultimately give gay couples the right to marry in Massachusetts was winding its way through the state courts. Many states allowed same-sex couples to adopt children, and half of the states with sodomy statutes on the books in 1986 had decriminalized homosexual behav-

The majority opinion was written by Justice Anthony Kennedy.
(Collection of the Supreme Court of the United States)

ior. Municipalities and states throughout the country were making it illegal to discriminate on the basis of sexual orientation in housing, education, and employment. The military, in turn, permitted gay men and lesbians to serve. To be sure, many antigay laws remained on the books, including the one at issue in *Lawrence v. Texas*, but the changes in the political climate and the social status of gay men and women were undeniable.

In addition to the shifts in the social and legal standing of homosexuality, the composition of the Supreme Court changed dramatically in the seventeen years between the decisions in *Lawrence* and *Bowers*. Of the five justices who joined or concurred with the *Bowers* majority opinion (Byron White, Warren Burger, Lewis F. Powell, William Rehnquist, and Sandra Day O'Connor) and the four dissenters (Harry Blackmun, William J. Brennan, Thurgood Marshall, and John Paul Stevens), only O'Connor, Rehnquist, and Stevens were on the bench when the Court heard *Lawrence*. In the years between the decisions in *Bowers* and *Lawrence*, O'Connor, who would concur with the majority in *Lawrence*, and Kennedy, who would be the author of *Lawrence*, cast pivotal votes reaffirming the existence of a constitutional right to privacy, which was in doubt at the time *Bowers* was decided. The other justices who joined the majority in *Lawrence*—David Souter, Ruth Bader Ginsburg, and Stephen Breyer—were all new to the Court.

About the Author

Justice Anthony M. Kennedy was born on July 23, 1936, in Sacramento, California. He attended Stanford University from 1954 to 1958, with a period of study at the London School of Economics. After receiving his BA from Stanford, he entered Harvard Law School, where he graduated with a bachelor of laws in 1961. Kennedy then entered the private practice of law, meanwhile coming to serve as a professor of constitutional law at the University of the Pacific's McGeorge School of Law. In 1975, President Gerald Ford nominated Kennedy to serve on the U.S. Court of Appeals for the Ninth Circuit, to which he was appointed. In 1988 President Ronald Reagan nominated him to the U.S. Supreme Court, and he took office as an associate justice on February 18, 1988.

Considered a crucial "swing vote" on the Supreme Court, Justice Kennedy cast the decisive vote in decisions ranging from one that upheld the Republican congressional map in Texas to one invalidating planned military tribunals for suspected terrorists. Through the turn of the twenty-first century, his voting record was not predictably partisan; although he was appointed by a conservative Republican, he tended to vote with the liberal bloc of the Court almost as often as with the conservatives.

Explanation and Analysis of the Document

Majority Opinion

Justice Anthony Kennedy's majority opinion, which was joined by Justices Stevens, Souter, Ginsburg, and Breyer, starts with a philosophical description of the concepts of liberty and freedom. Without reference to law, Kennedy notes that liberty protects people from government intrusions in their homes but also reaches beyond the home, to other spheres where the state does not belong. "Freedom," he states, "extends beyond spatial bounds. Liberty presumes an autonomy of self that includes freedom of thought, belief, expression, and certain intimate conduct. The instant case involves liberty of the person both in its spatial and more transcendent dimensions."

Unlike the introduction, part I is all business. Kennedy first defines the specific issue confronting the court: the validity of a Texas statute criminalizing certain sexual conduct between members of the same sex. He then describes the factual situation that gave rise to the case. The petitioners, he explains, are two men who were arrested for deviate sexual intercourse after being observed by two police officers engaging in consensual anal sex in the bedroom of one man's home. Kennedy lists the three questions the Court would consider: Whether the Texas statute was in violation of equal protection, whether convictions for "adult consensual sexual intimacy in the home" violated Fourteenth Amendment due process protections, and whether the 1986 decision in *Bowers v. Hardwick* should be overruled.

In framing the issues, Kennedy emphasizes that the petitioners were adults at the time of the offense and that the conduct occurred in private and was consensual. These emphases—repeated throughout the opinion—may limit the extent to which the liberty interest identified in *Lawrence* applies; that is, it would not necessarily apply to relationships involving minors or to public or nonconsensual acts.

In part II, Kennedy declares that resolving the case requires a rethinking of the analysis applied by the Court in *Bowers v. Hardwick*. In *Bowers*, the Court had rejected the claim that the due process clause protected individuals from criminal sodomy statutes as "at best, facetious." The decision to reevaluate the analytic framework applied in *Bowers* was a marked departure from typical Supreme Court decision making. In the normal course, justices apply established rules and distinguish new cases from older ones by finding that differences in the facts of the cases require new results or reinterpretations of old rules. The Court rarely engages in a wholesale reevaluation of a prior decision.

In this case, Justice Kennedy begins the reevaluation by tracing the "substantive reach of liberty under the Due Process Clause" in relevant circumstances. He finds most instructive the cases that arose in the context of state attempts to regulate human reproductive activity. Collectively, those cases, *Pierce v. Society of the Sisters of the Holy Names of Jesus and Mary*, *Meyer v. Ne-*

braska, *Griswold v. Connecticut*, *Eisenstadt v. Baird*, *Roe v. Wade*, and *Carey v. Population Services International*, firmly establish a right to privacy that includes the right of married and unmarried individuals to make decisions regarding sexual conduct.

Kennedy writes that although *Bowers v. Hardwick* was decided under the law enunciated in the reproductive freedom cases, the Court's analysis was skewed because it misapprehended the issue at hand. By casting *Bowers* as a case turning on whether the "Federal Constitution confers a fundamental right upon homosexuals to engage in sodomy," the Court failed "to appreciate the extent of the liberty at stake." The liberty at stake when laws criminalize private sexual conduct, Kennedy asserts, concerns not only the sexual act but also the private personal relationships to which individuals are entitled as part of the greater liberty protected by the Constitution. The state, says Kennedy, should avoid setting boundaries on relationships "absent injury to a person or abuse of an institution the law protects."

Having established that the Court that heard *Bowers* addressed too narrow a question, Kennedy attacks the reasoning used by that Court. He asserts that the historical foundation used in *Bowers* was not correct. Here, Kennedy recharacterizes common history as not definitively opposed to "homosexual" or same-sex conduct until the last third of the twentieth century. He notes that sodomy is seldom prosecuted even in the remaining states that make it a criminal act and that most states have moved to abolish the criminal prohibitions altogether. Kennedy acknowledges the condemnation of same-sex conduct by "powerful voices" but dismisses that condemnation, quoting *Planned Parenthood of Southeastern Pa. v. Casey*: "The issue is whether the majority may use the power of the State to enforce [its] views on the whole society through operation of the criminal law. 'Our obligation is to define the liberty of all, not to mandate our own moral code.'"

Kennedy directly challenges the conclusion drawn in *Bowers* that sodomy has been condemned throughout the history of Western civilization. He cites the non-enforcement of sodomy laws and the reduction in the number of sodomy laws from twenty-five to thirteen in the years following *Bowers*. Then, in one of the more controversial parts of the decision, he turns to evidence of shifting mores from other countries and from international law. For example, he notes that the European Court of Human Rights held that laws proscribing consensual homosexual conduct were invalid under the European Convention on Human Rights, thus showing that foreign court holdings are at odds with the "the premise in *Bowers* that the claim put forward was insubstantial in our Western civilization."

Kennedy goes on to show that two cases decided after *Bowers* cast its holding into even further doubt. He cites *Planned Parenthood of Southeastern Pa. v. Casey*, a case challenging certain Pennsylvania abortion laws, which confirmed that the constitutional protections of the autonomy of a person to make personal choices considered "central to personal dignity and autonomy, are central to the liberty protected by the Fourteenth Amendment." That case, he reasons, requires the Court to recognize for the first time constitutional rights for gays and lesbians: "Persons in a homosexual relationship may seek autonomy for these purposes, just as heterosexual persons do." This pronouncement of substantive due process rights is presented in language traditionally used in equal protection cases. Kennedy further supports the Court's reassessment with the second relevant post-*Bowers* case, *Romer v. Evans*. In that case the Court cited the equal protection clause in striking down legislation disallowing the protection of gays from discrimination. Kennedy writes that the holding of *Romer* that laws "born of animosity toward [a] class of persons" fulfilled no legitimate government interest applies equally in the due process analysis: "Equality of treatment and the due process right to demand respect for conduct protected by the substantive guarantee of liberty are linked."

Kennedy next rejects the notion that *Bowers* remains viable. *Bowers*, he states, does not reflect "values we share with a wider civilization." He notes that the values established by that case have been rejected around the world, including by the European Court of Human Rights, and that the right at issue in this case has been accepted as an "integral part of human freedom in many other countries." As a last justification of the Court's reassessment of the holdings of *Bowers*, Kennedy explains that the present Court need not apply the doctrine of stare decisis (a policy of following principles set forth in previous judicial decisions) because no one has relied on *Bowers* to protect his or her individual rights in taking a given action. Accordingly, no individual will be disadvantaged if it is overruled.

With the Court free, then, to decide the issue anew, Justice Kennedy offers what is an almost shockingly thin analysis. Most significantly, he does not complete the threshold step taken in other due process cases, which is to identify the degree of scrutiny applicable to the law at issue. That step normally frames the rest of the analysis by dictating how essential the government's purpose must be to justify the law. Instead, Kennedy makes reference to Justice Stevens's dissent from *Bowers*, which recognizes a liberty interest in intimate conduct and rejects the notion that a state's view of a practice as immoral is sufficient to uphold the practice, without fitting the conclusion into a traditional analytic framework.

Thus, Kennedy declares, "*Bowers* was not correct when it was decided, and it is not correct today.... *Bowers v. Hardwick* should be and now is overruled." He concludes that the "petitioners are entitled to respect for their private lives. The State cannot demean their existence or control their destiny by making their private sexual conduct a crime."

Beyond its specific holding, the meaning and reach of *Lawrence* is unclear. While the Court adopted a fundamental invalidation through substantive due process, an open question remains as to the standard used by the Court to invalidate the statute: strict scrutiny appropriate for fundamental constitutional rights under due process or rational-basis scrutiny requiring only a legitimate state interest. An interpretation in favor of strict scrutiny is supported by the number of times the Court uses substantive due process in its argument—and rejects "mere" equal protection—and by the way liberty is discussed in the context of the due process clause throughout.

An interpretation favoring rational-basis scrutiny is supported by the failure of the Court to explicitly state the standard in question or use the words *fundamental right* with respect to the liberty interest identified in *Lawrence*. In addition, Kennedy states that "the Texas statute furthers no legitimate state interest which can justify its intrusion into the personal and private life of the individual." This statement indicates that the Texas statute does not even further a *legitimate* state interest, much less the compelling interest required under substantive due process.

A third interpretation of the decision holds that Kennedy applied some form of intermediate scrutiny, by which the government is required to show more than a rational basis but not so much as a compelling state interest to justify laws regulating private sexual conduct.

The uncertainty in the analysis presented by Kennedy cannot be viewed as anything but deliberate. In fact, the dissent takes the majority to task for having "laid waste the foundations of our rational-basis jurisprudence" by refusing to classify the importance of the right at issue. Justice Kennedy had the opportunity to perhaps respond to the criticism, modify his opinion, or clarify the analytic structure; his decision to leave the threshold questions to another day undermines the usefulness and clarity of an otherwise momentous decision. Of greatest import in the decision, then, is the majority's rejection of morality as a legitimate basis for law, a concept echoed by Justice O'Connor in her concurrence.

Concurrence

Justice Sandra Day O'Connor wrote separately to concur with the Court's judgment. She does not join the majority to explicitly overrule *Bowers* but finds the Texas statute unconstitutional as a matter of equal protection, in that it applies to sodomy between members of the same sex but not the opposite sex.

Most critically, O'Connor expressly identifies and applies "a more searching form of rational basis review" than the Court has applied in relevant cases involving economic or tax legislation. Reviewing a series of cases, she correctly observes, "When a law exhibits such a desire to harm a politically unpopular group, we have applied a more searching form of rational basis review to strike down such laws under the Equal Protection Clause."

In scrutinizing the Texas statute and the rationale proffered in its defense by the state of Texas, she finds no basis for the statute other than moral disapproval of sodomy. Echoing the sentiments of the majority in its due process analysis, O'Connor rejects moral disapproval alone as a legitimate basis for a law that discriminates among groups of persons. The Texas law discriminates, she says, because it "serves more as a statement of dislike and disapproval against homosexuals than as a tool to stop criminal behavior." A law "branding one class of persons as criminals solely based on the State's moral disapproval of that class and conduct associated with that class" cannot stand.

O'Connor goes out of her way to limit the scope of her opinion. She notes, for example, that preserving the traditional institution of marriage is a legitimate state interest. Nevertheless, she admonishes that "other reasons exist to promote the institution of marriage beyond mere moral disapproval of an excluded group."

Dissents

As joined by Justices Rehnquist and Clarence Thomas, Justice Antonin Scalia takes issue with every part of the majority's analysis in a caustic dissent. His introduction accuses the majority of hypocrisy for its willingness to overrule this particular seventeen-year-old precedent when it had refused to reconsider *Roe v. Wade* just the previous year. Scalia then mocks the majority for lacking the courage to identify the liberty interest at stake as fundamental, which, Scalia suggests, might have been wrong but would have at least justified the result reached. He also warns that the majority used an "unheard-of form of rational-basis review," an approach that would have far-reaching implications.

In part I of the dissent, Scalia rants against "the Court's surprising readiness to reconsider a decision rendered a mere 17 years ago in *Bowers v. Hardwick*." Of note in this section is the degree to which Scalia renews old battles. Specifically, he engages in a step-by-step analysis of the legitimacy of the *Roe v. Wade* abortion decision using the analytic framework employed by Justice Kennedy in the majority opinion. Accusing the majority of "manipulating" the analytic framework employed in *Planned Parenthood of Southeastern Pa. v. Casey*, Scalia argues that *Roe* should be overruled. The majority's hypocrisy, he says, has "exposed *Casey*'s extraordinary deference to precedent for the result-oriented expedient that it is."

Part I also sets forth one of the two main threads of argument winding their way through the lengthy dissent: The majority's holding that moral reproach is not a rational basis for regulation will wreak havoc with the law. In Scalia's view, "a governing majority's belief that certain sexual behavior is 'immoral and unacceptable' constitutes a rational basis for regulation." The majority's decision, he claims, calls into question laws against bigamy, same-sex marriage, incest, prostitution, adultery, bestiality, and obscenity.

Part II develops the second main theme of the dissent: The majority's failure to expressly overrule the part of *Bowers* rejecting a claim to a fundamental right in the case of same-sex sodomy renders the rest of the majority opinion's conclusions untenable. Here, Scalia sets forth a primer on substantive due process analysis. While the due process clause "prohibits States from infringing fundamental liberty interests, unless the infringement is narrowly tailored to serve a compelling state interest," something is only a "fundamental right" if it is, as stated in the 1997 case *Washington v. Glucksberg*, "deeply rooted in this Nation's history and tradition." All other liberty interests must merely be rationally related to a legitimate state interest. Scalia declares that the due process clause is not implicated in this case because, as the Court found in *Bowers*, with the majority here seeming to agree, homosexual sodomy is not a fundamental right. That the majority "does not have the boldness to reverse" the conclusion reached in *Bowers* on the fundamental right point, then, means that the only logical conclusion is that the Texas law does not infringe on a constitutionally protected liberty interest. Meanwhile, a rational basis exists here, just as it does with respect to laws criminalizing prostitution or the recreational use of heroin.

In part III, Scalia addresses "some aspersions that the Court casts upon *Bowers* conclusion that homosexual sodomy is not a fundamental right." In particular, Scalia quarrels with the historical analysis conducted by the majority. He states that the conclusion in *Bowers* that "homosexual sodomy is not a fundamental right 'deeply rooted in this Nation's history and tradition' is utterly unassailable" and that the majority's emphasis on proceedings from only the last fifty years is inappropriate. An "emerging awareness," he says, citing a term used in the majority opinion, does not create a fundamental right.

Part IV returns to the moral slippery slope argument. Here, Scalia asserts that the majority opinion "effectively decrees the end of all morals legislation," thus calling into question "criminal laws against fornication, bigamy, adultery, adult incest, bestiality, and obscenity."

In part V, Scalia responds to Justice O'Connor's concurrence by arguing that the law in question indeed applies equally to all people. The Texas statute, he asserts, merely distinguishes "between the sexes insofar as concerns the partner with whom the sexual acts are performed: men can violate the law only with other men, and women only with other women." Such treatment, he says, does not violate the equal protection clause because it is the same distinction used to justify same-sex marriage prohibitions and laws against adultery.

Scalia's rhetoric intensifies in his conclusion. He characterizes the majority ruling thus: "Today's opinion is the product of a Court, which is the product of a law-profession culture, that has largely signed on to the so-called homosexual agenda, by which I mean the agenda promoted by some homosexual activists directed at eliminating the moral opprobrium that has traditionally attached to homosexual conduct." The majority, he says, has departed from its role as neutral observer and imposed its own view of morality on the entire nation, even though "many Americans do not want persons who openly engage in homosexual conduct as partners in their business, as scoutmasters for their children, as teachers in their children's schools, or as boarders in their home."

Justice Clarence Thomas wrote an additional dissent to state that the Constitution does not actually provide a right to privacy, and therefore the Texas law, while "uncommonly silly"—a quote from the dissent of Potter Stewart from the 1965 case *Griswold v. Connecticut*—should stand.

Impact

The *Lawrence v. Texas* decision was greeted by gay rights activists and civil libertarians as monumental, even earthshaking. Gay rights activists predicted that no law penalizing gays and lesbians, even indirectly, such as by limiting the availability of social benefits like marriage and adoption, could stand in the wake of *Lawrence*. Whether that excitement was justified remained to be seen within the half decade after the decision.

Critically, the majority opinion in *Lawrence* did not explicitly recognize private sexual activity as a fundamental right. Indeed, one reading of the case is that a state need only offer a rational basis for regulating such activity. As such, some observers felt that *Lawrence* might not serve as the foundation for a gay rights revolution in the same way that, for example, *Brown v. Board of Education* did for race.

However, *Lawrence* did immediately make illegal the thirteen remaining state sodomy laws. The Court recognized a constitutional right with regard to private, consensual sexual conduct by adults. More significantly, the decision called into question laws founded on the moral disapproval of private actions that do no harm to others. Within twenty years of this decision, the Court built on the foundation for LGBTQ rights by approving nationwide same-sex marriage (*Obergefell v. Hodges*) and ruling that employees could not be discriminated against based on their homosexual or transgender status (*Bostock v. Clayton County*).

Questions for Further Study

1. Which justice presents the best-reasoned analysis in the opinions from *Lawrence v. Texas*? Does Kennedy adequately answer the critiques of his logic put forth by Scalia?

2. Among the most important holdings in *Lawrence* is that moral judgments can no longer serve as a legitimate basis for legislation; other public-interest motivations must be advanced if morality-based legislation is to sustain constitutional attack. What laws might this holding affect? Is there more than a moral basis for outlawing polygamy? Same-sex marriage? Sodomy in the military? Incest? Prostitution? Bestiality? Adoption by gay parents? Obscenity? Recreational drug use?

3. Compare the analysis employed by Justice Kennedy in the majority opinion with that employed by Justice William Rehnquist in *Washington v. Glucksberg* (1997), which rejected the claim that the right to privacy included the right to direct the course of one's own death through physician-assisted suicide. In *Glucksberg* the Court reasoned that access to physician-assisted suicide is not a right deeply rooted in our nation's history and traditions and thus is not protected by the due process clause. Does that analysis withstand scrutiny after *Lawrence*?

4. Does Justice Kennedy's discussion of European and international law have relevance to the proper analysis of the scope of the U.S. due process clause?

Further Reading

Books

Andersen, Ellen Ann. *Out of the Closets and into the Courts: Legal Opportunity Structure and Gay Rights Litigation.* Ann Arbor: University of Michigan Press, 2006.

Carpenter, Dale. *Flagrant Conduct: The Story of Lawrence v. Texas.* New York: Norton, 2012.

Richards, David A. J. *The Case for Gay Rights: From Bowers to Lawrence and Beyond.* Lawrence: University Press of Kansas, 2005.

Richards, David A. J. *The Sodomy Cases: Bowers v. Hardwick and Lawrence v Texas.* Lawrence: University Press of Kansas, 2012.

Roosevelt, Kermit. *The Myth of Judicial Activism: Making Sense of Supreme Court Decisions.* New Haven, CT: Yale University Press, 2006.

Walzer, Lee. *Gay Rights on Trial: A Sourcebook with Cases, Laws, and Documents.* Indianapolis: Hackett Publishing, 2002.

Articles

Gardner, Martin R. "Adoption by Homosexuals in the Wake of *Lawrence v. Texas*." *Journal of Law and Family Studies* 6, no. 1 (2004): 19–58.

Further Reading

Articles

Gong, LiJia, and Rachel Shapiro. "Sexual Privacy after *Lawrence v. Texas*." *Georgetown Journal of Gender and Law* 13 (2012).

Gonzalez, Jessica A. "Decriminalizing Sexual Conduct: The Supreme Court Ruling in *Lawrence v. Texas*." *St. Mary's Law Journal* 35, no. 3 (2004): 685–706.

Greene, Jamal. "Beyond Lawrence: Metaprivacy and Punishment." *Yale Law Journal* 115, no. 8 (June 2006): 1862–1928.

Hassel, Diana. "Sex and Death: Lawrence's Liberty and Physician-Assisted Suicide." *University of Pennsylvania Journal of Constitutional Law* 9 (2007): 1003–1032.

Katyal, Sonia K. "Sexuality and Sovereignty: The Global Limits and Possibilities of Lawrence." *William and Mary Bill of Rights Journal* 14 (April 2006): 1429–1492.

Krotoszynski, Ronald J., Jr. "Dumbo's Feather: An Examination and Critique of the Supreme Court's Use, Misuse, and Abuse of Tradition in Protecting Fundamental Rights." *William and Mary Law Review* 48, no. 3 (2006): 923–1023.

Marcus, Nancy C. "Beyond Romer and Lawrence: The Right to Privacy Comes Out of the Closet." *Columbia Journal of Gender and Law* 15 (2006): 355–436.

Sharum, Jerald A. "Controlling Conduct: The Emerging Protection of Sodomy in the Military." *Albany Law Review* 69, no. 4 (2006): 1195–1236.

Strasser, Mark. "Monogamy, Licentiousness, Desuetude, and Mere Tolerance: The Multiple Misinterpretations of *Lawrence v. Texas*." *Southern California Review of Law and Women's Studies* 15, no. 1 (2005): 95–144.

Susstein, Cass R. "What Did Lawrence Hold? Of Autonomy, Desuetude, Sexuality, and Marriage." *Supreme Court Review* 2003 (2003): 27–74.

Tribe, Laurence H. "*Lawrence v. Texas*: The 'Fundamental Right' That Dare Not Speak Its Name." *Harvard Law Review* 117, no. 6 (2004): 1893–1955.

—Commentary by Alicia R. Ouellette

LAWRENCE V. TEXAS

Document Text

Justice Kennedy Delivered the Opinion of the Court

Liberty protects the person from unwarranted government intrusions into a dwelling or other private places. In our tradition the State is not omnipresent in the home. And there are other spheres of our lives and existence, outside the home, where the State should not be a dominant presence. Freedom extends beyond spatial bounds. Liberty presumes an autonomy of self that includes freedom of thought, belief, expression, and certain intimate conduct. The instant case involves liberty of the person both in its spatial and more transcendent dimensions.

I

The question before the Court is the validity of a Texas statute making it a crime for two persons of the same sex to engage in certain intimate sexual conduct.

In Houston, Texas, officers of the Harris County Police Department were dispatched to a private residence in response to a reported weapons disturbance. They entered an apartment where one of the petitioners, John Geddes Lawrence, resided. The right of the police to enter does not seem to have been questioned. The officers observed Lawrence and another man, Tyron Garner, engaging in a sexual act. The two petitioners were arrested, held in custody over night, and charged and convicted before a Justice of the Peace.

The complaints described their crime as "deviate sexual intercourse, namely anal sex, with a member of the same sex (man)." App. to Pet. for Cert. 127a, 139a. The applicable state law is Tex. Penal Code Ann. §21.06(a) (2003). It provides: "A person commits an offense if he engages in deviate sexual intercourse with another individual of the same sex." The statute defines "[d]eviate sexual intercourse" as follows:

"(A) any contact between any part of the genitals of one person and the mouth or anus of another person; or

"(B) the penetration of the genitals or the anus of another person with an object." §21.01(1).

The petitioners exercised their right to a trial *de novo* in Harris County Criminal Court. They challenged the statute as a violation of the Equal Protection Clause of the Fourteenth Amendment and of a like provision of the Texas Constitution. Tex. Const., Art. 1, §3a. Those contentions were rejected. The petitioners, having entered a plea of *nolo contendere*, were each fined $200 and assessed court costs of $141.25. App. to Pet. for Cert. 107a-110a.

The Court of Appeals for the Texas Fourteenth District considered the petitioners' federal constitutional arguments under both the Equal Protection and Due Process Clauses of the Fourteenth Amendment. After hearing the case en banc the court, in a divided opinion, rejected the constitutional arguments and affirmed the convictions. 41 S. W. 3d 349 (Tex. App. 2001). The majority opinion indicates that the Court of Appeals considered our decision in *Bowers v. Hardwick*, 478 U. S. 186 (1986), to be controlling on the federal due process aspect of the case. *Bowers* then being authoritative, this was proper.

We granted certiorari, 537 U. S. 1044 (2002), to consider three questions:

1. Whether Petitioners' criminal convictions under the Texas "Homosexual Conduct" law—which criminalizes sexual intimacy by same-sex couples, but not identical behavior by different-sex couples—violate the Fourteenth Amendment guarantee of equal protection of laws?

2. Whether Petitioners' criminal convictions for adult consensual sexual intimacy in the home violate their vital interests in liberty and privacy protected by the Due Process Clause of the Fourteenth Amendment?

3. Whether *Bowers v. Hardwick*, 478 U. S. 186 (1986), should be overruled? Pet. for Cert. i.

The petitioners were adults at the time of the alleged offense. Their conduct was in private and consensual.

II

We conclude the case should be resolved by determining whether the petitioners were free as adults to engage in the private conduct in the exercise of their liberty under the Due Process Clause of the Fourteenth Amendment to the Constitution. For this inquiry we deem it necessary to reconsider the Court's holding in *Bowers*.

There are broad statements of the substantive reach of liberty under the Due Process Clause in earlier cases, including *Pierce v. Society of Sisters*, 268 U. S. 510 (1925), and *Meyer v. Nebraska*, 262 U. S. 390 (1923); but the most pertinent beginning point is our decision in *Griswold v. Connecticut*, 381 U. S. 479 (1965).

In *Griswold* the Court invalidated a state law prohibiting the use of drugs or devices of contraception and counseling or aiding and abetting the use of contraceptives. The Court described the protected interest as a right to privacy and placed emphasis on the marriage relation and the protected space of the marital bedroom. *Id.*, at 485.

After *Griswold* it was established that the right to make certain decisions regarding sexual conduct extends beyond the marital relationship. In *Eisenstadt v. Baird*, 405 U. S. 438 (1972), the Court invalidated a law prohibiting the distribution of contraceptives to unmarried persons. The case was decided under the Equal Protection Clause, *id.*, at 454; but with respect to unmarried persons, the Court went on to state the fundamental proposition that the law impaired the exercise of their personal rights, *ibid*. It quoted from the statement of the Court of Appeals finding the law to be in conflict with fundamental human rights, and it followed with this statement of its own:

"It is true that in *Griswold* the right of privacy in question inhered in the marital relationship. . . . If the right of privacy means anything, it is the right of the *individual*, married or single, to be free from unwarranted governmental intrusion into matters so fundamentally affecting a person as the decision whether to bear or beget a child." *Id.*, at 453.

The opinions in *Griswold* and *Eisenstadt* were part of the background for the decision in *Roe v. Wade*, 410 U. S. 113 (1973). As is well known, the case involved a challenge to the Texas law prohibiting abortions, but the laws of other States were affected as well. Although the Court held the woman's rights were not absolute, her right to elect an abortion did have real and substantial protection as an exercise of her liberty under the Due Process Clause. The Court cited cases that protect spatial freedom and cases that go well beyond it. *Roe* recognized the right of a woman to make certain fundamental decisions affecting her destiny and confirmed once more that the protection of liberty under the Due Process Clause has a substantive dimension of fundamental significance in defining the rights of the person.

In *Carey v. Population Services Int'l*, 431 U. S. 678 (1977), the Court confronted a New York law forbidding sale or distribution of contraceptive devices to persons under 16 years of age. Although there was no single opinion for the Court, the law was invalidated. Both *Eisenstadt* and *Carey*, as well as the holding and rationale in *Roe*, confirmed that the reasoning of Griswold could not be confined to the protection of rights of married adults. This was the state of the law with respect to some of the most relevant cases when the Court considered *Bowers v. Hardwick*.

The facts in *Bowers* had some similarities to the instant case. A police officer, whose right to enter seems not to have been in question, observed Hardwick, in his own bedroom, engaging in intimate sexual conduct with another adult male. The conduct was in violation of a Georgia statute making it a criminal offense to engage in sodomy. One difference between the two cases is that the Georgia statute prohibited the conduct whether or not the participants were of the same sex, while the Texas statute, as we have seen, applies only to participants of the same sex. Hardwick was not prosecuted, but he brought an action in federal court to declare the state statute invalid. He alleged he was a practicing homosexual and that the criminal prohibition violated rights guaranteed to him by the Constitution. The Court, in an opinion by Justice White, sustained the Georgia law. Chief Justice Burger and Justice Powell joined the opinion of the Court and filed separate, concurring opinions. Four Justices dissented. 478 U. S., at 199 (opinion of Blackmun, J., joined by Brennan, Marshall, and Stevens, JJ.); *id.*, at 214 (opinion of Stevens, J., joined by Brennan and Marshall, JJ.).

The Court began its substantive discussion in *Bowers* as follows: "The issue presented is whether the Federal Constitution confers a fundamental right upon homosexuals to engage in sodomy and hence invalidates the laws of the many States that still make such conduct illegal and have done so for a very long time." *Id.*, at 190. That statement, we now conclude, discloses the Court's own failure to appreciate the extent of the liberty at stake. To say that the issue in *Bowers* was simply the right to engage in certain sexual conduct demeans the claim the individual put forward, just as it would demean a married couple were it to be said marriage is simply about the right to have sexual intercourse. The laws involved in Bowers and here are, to be sure, statutes that purport to do no more than prohibit a particular sexual act. Their penalties and purposes, though, have more far-reaching consequences, touching upon the most private human conduct, sexual behavior, and in the most private of places, the home. The statutes do seek to control a personal relationship that, whether or not entitled to formal recognition in the law, is within the liberty of persons to choose without being punished as criminals.

This, as a general rule, should counsel against attempts by the State, or a court, to define the meaning of the relationship or to set its boundaries absent injury to a person or abuse of an institution the law protects. It suffices for us to acknowledge that adults may choose to enter upon this relationship in the confines of their homes and their own private lives and still retain their dignity as free persons. When sexuality finds overt expression in intimate conduct with another person, the conduct can be but one element in a personal bond that is more enduring. The liberty protected by the Constitution allows homosexual persons the right to make this choice.

Having misapprehended the claim of liberty there presented to it, and thus stating the claim to be whether there is a fundamental right to engage in consensual sodomy, the Bowers Court said: "Proscriptions against that conduct have ancient roots." *Id.*, at 192. In academic writings, and in many of the scholarly *amicus* briefs filed to assist the Court in this case, there are fundamental criticisms of the historical premises relied upon by the majority and concurring opinions in *Bowers*. Brief for Cato Institute as *Amicus Curiae* 16-17; Brief for American Civil Liberties Union et al. as Amici Curiae 15-21; Brief for Professors of History et al. as *Amici Curiae* 3-10. We need not enter this debate in the attempt to reach a definitive historical judgment, but the following considerations counsel against adopting the definitive conclusions upon which *Bowers* placed such reliance.

At the outset it should be noted that there is no longstanding history in this country of laws directed at homosexual conduct as a distinct matter. Beginning in colonial times there were prohibitions of sodomy derived from the English criminal laws passed in the first instance by the Reformation Parliament of 1533. The English prohibition was understood to include relations between men and women as well as relations between men and men. See, *e.g., King v. Wiseman*, 92 Eng. Rep. 774, 775 (K. B. 1718) (interpreting "mankind" in Act of 1533 as including women and girls). Nineteenth-century commentators similarly read American sodomy, buggery, and crime-against-nature statutes as criminalizing certain relations between men and women and between men and men. See, *e.g.*, 2 J. Bishop, Criminal Law §1028 (1858); 2 J. Chitty, Criminal Law 47-50 (5th Am. ed. 1847); R. Desty, A Compendium of American Criminal Law 143 (1882); J. May, The Law of Crimes §203 (2d ed. 1893). The absence of legal prohibitions focusing on homosexual conduct may be explained in part by noting that according to some scholars the concept of the homosexual as a distinct category of person did not emerge until the late 19th century. See, *e.g.*, J. Katz, *The Invention of Heterosexuality* 10 (1995); J. D'Emilio & E. Freedman, *Intimate Matters: A History of Sexuality in America* 121 (2d ed. 1997) ("The modern terms *homosexuality* and *heterosexuality* do not apply to an era that had not yet articulated these distinctions"). Thus early American sodomy laws were not directed at homosexuals as such but instead sought to prohibit nonprocreative sexual activity more generally. This does not suggest approval of homosexual conduct. It does tend to show that this particular form of conduct was not thought of as a separate category from like conduct between heterosexual persons.

Laws prohibiting sodomy do not seem to have been enforced against consenting adults acting in private. A substantial number of sodomy prosecutions and convictions for which there are surviving records were for predatory acts against those who could not or did not consent, as in the case of a minor or the victim of an assault. As to these, one purpose for the prohibitions was to ensure there would be no lack of coverage if a predator committed a sexual assault that did not constitute rape as defined by the criminal law. Thus the model sodomy indictments presented in a 19th-century treatise, see 2 Chitty, *supra*, at 49, addressed the predatory acts of an adult man against a minor girl or minor boy. Instead of targeting relations between consenting adults in private, 19th-century sodomy prosecutions typically involved relations between men and minor girls or minor boys, relations between adults involving force, relations between adults implicating disparity in status, or relations between men and animals.

To the extent that there were any prosecutions for the acts in question, 19th-century evidence rules imposed a burden that would make a conviction more difficult to obtain even taking into account the problems always inherent in prosecuting consensual acts committed in private. Under then-prevailing standards, a man could not be convicted of sodomy based upon testimony of a consenting partner, because the partner was considered an accomplice. A partner's testimony, however, was admissible if he or she had not consented to the act or was a minor, and therefore incapable of consent. See, *e.g.*, F. Wharton, Criminal Law 443 (2d ed. 1852); 1 F. Wharton, Criminal Law 512 (8th ed. 1880). The rule may explain in part the infrequency of these prosecutions. In all events that infrequency makes it difficult to say that society approved of a rigorous and systematic punishment of the consensual acts committed in private and by adults. The longstanding criminal prohibition of homosexual sodomy upon which the *Bowers* decision placed such reliance is as consistent with a general condemnation of nonprocreative sex as it is with an established tradition of prosecuting acts because of their homosexual character.

The policy of punishing consenting adults for private acts was not much discussed in the early legal literature. We can infer that one reason for this was the very private nature of the conduct. Despite the absence of prosecutions, there may have been periods in which there was public criticism of homosexuals as such and an insistence that the criminal laws be enforced to discourage their practices. But far from possessing "ancient roots," *Bowers*, 478 U. S., at 192, American laws targeting same-sex couples did not develop until the last third of the 20th century. The reported decisions concerning the prosecution of consensual, homosexual sodomy between adults for the years 1880-1995 are not always clear in the details, but a significant number involved conduct in a public place. See Brief for American Civil Liberties Union et al. as *Amici Curiae* 14-15, and n. 18.

It was not until the 1970's that any State singled out same-sex relations for criminal prosecution, and only nine States have done so. See 1977 Ark. Gen. Acts no. 828; 1983 Kan. Sess. Laws p. 652; 1974 Ky. Acts p. 847; 1977 Mo. Laws p. 687; 1973 Mont. Laws p. 1339; 1977 Nev. Stats. p. 1632; 1989 Tenn. Pub. Acts ch. 591; 1973 Tex. Gen. Laws ch. 399; see also *Post v. State*, 715 P. 2d 1105 (Okla. Crim. App. 1986) (sodomy law invalidated as applied to different-sex couples). Post-*Bowers* even some of these States did not adhere to the policy of suppressing homosexual conduct. Over the course of the last decades, States with same-sex prohibitions have moved toward abolishing them. See, *e.g., Jegley v. Picado*, 349 Ark. 600, 80 S. W. 3d 332 (2002); *Gryczan v. State*, 283 Mont. 433, 942 P. 2d 112 (1997); *Campbell v. Sundquist*, 926 S. W. 2d 250 (Tenn. App. 1996); *Commonwealth v. Wasson*, 842 S. W. 2d 487 (Ky. 1992); see also 1993 Nev. Stats. p. 518 (repealing Nev. Rev. Stat. §201.193).

In summary, the historical grounds relied upon in *Bowers* are more complex than the majority opinion and the concurring opinion by Chief Justice Burger indicate. Their historical premises are not without doubt and, at the very least, are overstated.

It must be acknowledged, of course, that the Court in *Bowers* was making the broader point that for centuries there have been powerful voices to condemn homosexual conduct as immoral. The condemnation has been shaped by religious beliefs, conceptions of right and acceptable behavior, and respect for the traditional family. For many persons these are not trivial concerns but profound and deep convictions accepted as ethical and moral principles to which they aspire and which thus determine the course of their lives. These considerations do not answer the question before us, however. The issue is whether the majority may use the power of the State to enforce these views on the whole society through operation of the criminal law. "Our obligation is to define the liberty of all, not to mandate our own moral code." *Planned Parenthood of Southeastern Pa. v. Casey*, 505 U. S. 833, 850 (1992).

Chief Justice Burger joined the opinion for the Court in Bowers and further explained his views as follows: "Decisions of individuals relating to homosexual conduct have been subject to state intervention throughout the history of Western civilization. Condemnation of those practices is firmly rooted in Judeao-Christian moral and ethical standards." 478 U. S., at 196. As with Justice White's assumptions about history, scholarship casts some doubt on the sweeping nature of the statement by Chief Justice Burger as it pertains to private homosexual conduct between consenting adults. See, *e.g.*, Eskridge, Hardwick and Historiography, 1999 U. Ill. L. Rev. 631, 656. In all events we think that our laws and traditions in the past half century are of most relevance here. These references show an emerging awareness that liberty gives substantial protection to adult persons in deciding how to conduct their private lives in matters pertaining to sex. "[H]istory and tradition are the starting point but not in all cases the ending point of the substantive due process inquiry." *County of Sacramento v. Lewis*, 523 U. S. 833, 857 (1998) (Kennedy, J., concurring).

This emerging recognition should have been apparent when *Bowers* was decided. In 1955 the American Law Institute promulgated the Model Penal Code and made clear that it did not recommend or provide for "criminal penalties for consensual sexual relations conducted in private." ALI, Model Penal Code §213.2, Comment 2, p. 372 (1980). It justified its decision on three grounds: (1) The prohibitions undermined respect for the law by penalizing conduct many people engaged in; (2) the statutes regulated private conduct not harmful to others; and (3) the laws were arbitrarily enforced and thus invited the danger of blackmail. ALI, Model Penal Code, Commentary 277-280 (Tent. Draft No. 4, 1955). In 1961 Illinois changed its laws to conform to the Model Penal Code. Other States soon followed. Brief for Cato Institute as *Amicus Curiae* 15-16.

In *Bowers* the Court referred to the fact that before 1961 all 50 States had outlawed sodomy, and that at the time of the Court's decision 24 States and the District of Columbia had sodomy laws. 478 U. S., at 192-193. Justice Powell pointed out that these prohibitions often were being ignored, however. Georgia, for instance, had not sought to enforce its law for decades. *Id.*, at 197-198, n. 2 ("The history of nonenforcement suggests the moribund character today of laws criminalizing this type of private, consensual conduct").

The sweeping references by Chief Justice Burger to the history of Western civilization and to Judeo-Christian moral and ethical standards did not take account of other authorities pointing in an opposite direction. A committee advising the British Parliament recommended in 1957 repeal of laws punishing homosexual conduct. The Wolfenden Report: Report of the Committee on Homosexual Offenses and Prostitution (1963). Parliament enacted the substance of those recommendations 10 years later. Sexual Offences Act 1967, §1.

Of even more importance, almost five years before *Bowers* was decided the European Court of Human Rights considered a case with parallels to *Bowers* and to today's case. An adult male resident in Northern Ireland alleged he was a practicing homosexual who desired to engage in consensual homosexual conduct. The laws of Northern Ireland forbade him that right. He alleged that he had been questioned, his home had been searched, and he feared criminal prosecution. The court held that the laws proscribing the conduct were invalid under the European Convention on Human Rights. *Dudgeon v. United Kingdom*, 45 Eur. Ct. H. R. (1981) ¶;52. Authoritative in all countries that are members of the Council of Europe (21 nations then, 45 nations now), the decision is at odds with the premise in *Bowers* that the claim put forward was insubstantial in our Western civilization.

In our own constitutional system the deficiencies in Bowers became even more apparent in the years following its announcement. The 25 States with laws prohibiting the relevant conduct referenced in the Bowers decision are reduced now to 13, of which 4 enforce their laws only against homosexual conduct. In those States where sodomy is still proscribed, whether for same-sex or heterosexual conduct, there is a pattern of nonenforcement with respect to consenting adults acting in private. The State of Texas admitted in 1994 that as of that date it had not prosecuted anyone under those circumstances. *State v. Morales*, 869 S. W. 2d 941, 943.

Two principal cases decided after *Bowers* cast its holding into even more doubt. In *Planned Parenthood of Southeastern Pa. v. Casey*, 505 U. S. 833 (1992), the Court reaffirmed the substantive force of the liberty protected by the Due Process Clause. The *Casey* decision again confirmed that our laws and tradition afford constitutional protection to personal decisions relating to marriage, procreation, contraception, family relationships, child rearing, and education. *Id.*, at 851. In explaining the respect the Constitution demands for the autonomy of the person in making these choices, we stated as follows:

"These matters, involving the most intimate and personal choices a person may make in a lifetime, choices central to personal dignity and autonomy, are central to the liberty protected by the Fourteenth Amendment. At the heart of liberty is the right to define one's own concept of existence, of meaning, of the universe, and of the mystery of human life. Beliefs about these matters could not define the attributes of personhood were they formed under compulsion of the State." *Ibid.*

Persons in a homosexual relationship may seek autonomy for these purposes, just as heterosexual persons do. The decision in *Bowers* would deny them this right.

The second post-Bowers case of principal relevance is *Romer v. Evans*, 517 U. S. 620 (1996). There the Court struck down class-based legislation directed at homosexuals as a violation of the Equal Protection Clause. *Romer* invalidated an amendment to Colorado's constitution which named as a solitary class persons who were homosexuals, lesbians, or bisexual either by "orientation, conduct, practices or relationships," *id.*, at 624 (internal quotation marks omitted), and deprived them of protection under state antidiscrimination laws. We concluded that the provision was "born of animosity toward the class of persons affected" and further that it had no rational relation to a legitimate governmental purpose. *Id.*, at 634.

As an alternative argument in this case, counsel for the petitioners and some *amici* contend that *Romer* provides the basis for declaring the Texas statute invalid under the Equal Protection Clause. That is a tenable argument, but we conclude the instant case requires us to address whether *Bowers* itself has continuing validity. Were we to hold the statute invalid under the Equal Protection Clause some might question whether a prohibition would be valid if drawn differently, say, to prohibit the conduct both between same-sex and different-sex participants.

Equality of treatment and the due process right to demand respect for conduct protected by the substantive guarantee of liberty are linked in important respects, and a decision on the latter point advances both interests. If protected conduct is made criminal and the law which does so remains unexamined for its substantive validity, its stigma might remain even if it were not enforceable as drawn for equal protection reasons. When homosexual conduct is made criminal by the law of the State, that declaration in and of itself is an invitation to subject homosexual persons to discrimination both in the public and in the private spheres. The central holding of *Bowers* has been brought in question by this case, and it should be addressed. Its continuance as precedent demeans the lives of homosexual persons.

The stigma this criminal statute imposes, moreover, is not trivial. The offense, to be sure, is but a class C misdemeanor, a minor offense in the Texas legal system. Still, it remains a criminal offense with all that imports for the dignity of the persons charged. The petitioners will bear on their record the history of their criminal convictions. Just this Term we rejected various challenges to state laws requiring the registration of sex offenders. *Smith v. Doe*, 538 U. S. __ (2003); *Connecticut Dept. of Public Safety v. Doe*, 538 U. S. 1 (2003). We are advised that if Texas convicted an adult for private, consensual homosexual conduct under the statute here in question the convicted person would come within the registration laws of a least four States were he or she to be subject to their jurisdiction. Pet. for Cert. 13, and n. 12 (citing Idaho Code §§18-8301 to 18-8326 (Cum. Supp. 2002); La. Code Crim. Proc. Ann., §§15:540-15:549 (West 2003); Miss. Code Ann. §§45-33-21 to 45-33-57 (Lexis 2003); S. C. Code Ann. §§23-3-400 to 23-3-490 (West 2002)). This underscores the consequential nature of the punishment and the state-sponsored condemnation attendant to the criminal prohibition. Furthermore, the Texas criminal conviction carries with it the other collateral consequences always following a conviction, such as notations on job application forms, to mention but one example.

The foundations of *Bowers* have sustained serious erosion from our recent decisions in *Casey* and *Romer*. When our precedent has been thus weakened, criticism from other sources is of greater significance. In the United States criticism of *Bowers* has been substantial and continuing, disapproving of its reasoning in all respects, not just as to its historical assumptions. See, *e.g.*, C. Fried, Order and Law: Arguing the Reagan Revolution—A Firsthand Account 81-84 (1991); R. Posner, Sex and Reason 341-350 (1992). The courts of five different States have declined to follow it in interpreting provisions in their own state constitutions parallel to the Due Process Clause of the Fourteenth Amendment, see *Jegley v. Picado*, 349 Ark. 600, 80 S. W. 3d 332 (2002); *Powell v. State*, 270 Ga. 327, 510 S. E. 2d 18, 24 (1998); *Gryczan v. State*, 283 Mont. 433, 942 P. 2d 112 (1997); *Campbell v. Sundquist*, 926 S. W. 2d 250 (Tenn. App. 1996); *Commonwealth v. Wasson*, 842 S. W. 2d 487 (Ky. 1992).

To the extent Bowers relied on values we share with a wider civilization, it should be noted that the reasoning and holding in *Bowers* have been rejected elsewhere. The European Court of Human Rights has followed not *Bowers* but its own decision in *Dudgeon v. United Kingdom*. See *P. G. & J. H. v. United Kingdom*, App. No. 00044787/98, ¶;56 (Eur. Ct. H. R., Sept. 25, 2001); *Modinos v. Cyprus*, 259 Eur. Ct. H. R. (1993); *Norris v. Ireland*, 142 Eur. Ct. H. R. (1988). Other nations, too, have taken action consistent with an affirmation of the protected right of homosexual adults to engage in intimate, consensual conduct. See Brief for Mary Robinson et al. as *Amici Curiae* 11-12. The right the petitioners seek in this case has been accepted as an integral part of human freedom in many other countries. There has been no showing that in this country the governmental interest in circumscribing personal choice is somehow more legitimate or urgent.

The doctrine of *stare decisis* is essential to the respect accorded to the judgments of the Court and to the stability of the law. It is not, however, an inexorable command. *Payne v. Tennessee*, 501 U. S. 808, 828 (1991) ("*Stare decisis* is not an inexorable command; rather, it 'is a principle of policy and not a mechanical formula of adherence to the latest decision'") (quoting *Helvering v. Hallock*, 309 U. S. 106, 119 (1940))). In *Casey* we noted that when a Court is asked to overrule a precedent recognizing a constitutional liberty interest, individual or societal reliance on the existence of that liberty cautions with particular strength against reversing course. 505 U. S., at 855-856; see also *id.*, at 844 ("Liberty finds no refuge in a jurisprudence of doubt"). The holding in *Bowers*, however, has not induced detrimental reliance comparable to some instances where recognized individual rights are involved. Indeed, there has been no individual or societal reliance on *Bowers* of the sort that could counsel against overturning its holding once there are compelling reasons to do so. *Bowers* itself causes uncertainty, for the precedents before and after its issuance contradict its central holding.

The rationale of *Bowers* does not withstand careful analysis. In his dissenting opinion in *Bowers* Justice Stevens came to these conclusions:

> "Our prior cases make two propositions abundantly clear. First, the fact that the governing majority in a State has traditionally viewed a particular practice as immoral is not a sufficient reason for upholding a law prohibiting the practice; neither history nor tradition could save a law prohibiting miscegenation from constitutional attack. Second, individual decisions by married persons, concerning the intimacies of their physical relationship, even when not intended to produce offspring, are a form of 'liberty' protected by the Due Process Clause of the Fourteenth Amendment. Moreover, this protection extends to intimate choices by unmarried as well as married persons." 478 U. S., at 216 (footnotes and citations omitted).

Justice Stevens' analysis, in our view, should have been controlling in Bowers and should control here.

Bowers was not correct when it was decided, and it is not correct today. It ought not to remain binding precedent. *Bowers v. Hardwick* should be and now is overruled.

The present case does not involve minors. It does not involve persons who might be injured or coerced or who are situated in relationships where consent might not easily be refused. It does not involve public conduct or prostitution. It does not involve whether the government must give formal recognition to any relationship that homosexual persons seek to enter. The case does involve two adults who, with full and mutual consent from each other, engaged in sexual practices common to a homosexual lifestyle. The petitioners are entitled to respect for their private lives. The State cannot demean their existence or control their destiny by making their private sexual conduct a crime. Their right to liberty under the Due Process Clause gives them the full right to engage in their conduct without intervention of the government. "It is a promise of the Constitution that there is a realm of personal liberty which the government may not enter." *Casey, supra*, at 847. The Texas statute furthers no legitimate state interest which can justify its intrusion into the personal and private life of the individual.

Had those who drew and ratified the Due Process Clauses of the Fifth Amendment or the Fourteenth Amendment known the components of liberty in its manifold possibilities, they might have been more specific. They did not presume to have this insight. They knew times can blind us to certain truths and later generations can see that laws once thought necessary and proper in fact serve only to oppress. As the Constitution endures, persons in every generation can invoke its principles in their own search for greater freedom.

The judgment of the Court of Appeals for the Texas Fourteenth District is reversed, and the case is remanded for further proceedings not inconsistent with this opinion.

It is so ordered.

Justice O'Connor, Concurring in the Judgment

The Court today overrules *Bowers v. Hardwick*, 478 U. S. 186 (1986). I joined *Bowers*, and do not join the Court in overruling it. Nevertheless, I agree with the Court that Texas' statute banning same-sex sodomy is unconstitutional. See Tex. Penal Code Ann. §21.06 (2003). Rather than relying on the substantive component of the Fourteenth Amendment's Due Process Clause, as the Court does, I base my conclusion on the Fourteenth Amendment's Equal Protection Clause.

The Equal Protection Clause of the Fourteenth Amendment "is essentially a direction that all persons similarly situated should be treated alike." *Cleburne v. Cleburne Living Center, Inc.*, 473 U. S. 432, 439 (1985); see also *Plyler v. Doe*, 457 U. S. 202, 216 (1982). Under our rational basis standard of review, "legislation is presumed to be valid and will be sustained if the classification drawn by the statute is rationally related to a legitimate state interest." *Cleburne v. Cleburne Living Center, supra*, at 440; see also *Department of Agriculture v. Moreno*, 413 U. S. 528, 534 (1973); *Romer v. Evans*, 517 U. S. 620, 632-633 (1996); *Nordlinger v. Hahn*, 505 U. S. 1, 11-12 (1992).

Laws such as economic or tax legislation that are scrutinized under rational basis review normally pass constitutional muster, since "the Constitution presumes that even improvident decisions will eventually be rectified by the democratic processes." *Cleburne v. Cleburne Living Center*, supra, at 440; see also *Fitzgerald v. Racing Assn. of Central Iowa, ante*, p. ___; *Williamson v. Lee Optical of Okla., Inc.*, 348 U. S. 483 (1955). We have consistently held, however, that some objectives, such as "a bare . . . desire to harm a politically unpopular group," are not legitimate state interests. *Department of Agriculture v. Moreno, supra*, at 534. See also *Cleburne v. Cleburne Living Center, supra*, at 446-447; *Romer v. Evans, supra*, at 632. When a law exhibits such a desire to harm a politically unpopular group, we have applied a more searching form of rational basis review to strike down such laws under the Equal Protection Clause.

We have been most likely to apply rational basis review to hold a law unconstitutional under the Equal Protection Clause where, as here, the challenged legislation inhibits personal relationships. In *Department of Agriculture v. Moreno*, for example, we held that a law preventing those households containing an individual unrelated to any other member of the household from receiving food stamps violated equal protection because the purpose of the law was to "discriminate against hippies." 413 U. S., at 534. The asserted governmental interest in preventing food stamp fraud was not deemed sufficient to satisfy rational basis review. *Id.*, at 535-538. In *Eisenstadt v. Baird*, 405 U. S. 438, 447-455 (1972), we refused to sanction a law that discriminated between married and unmarried persons by prohibiting the distribution of contraceptives to single persons. Likewise, in *Cleburne v. Cleburne Living Center, supra*, we held that it was irrational for a State to require a home for the mentally disabled to obtain a special use permit when other residences—like fraternity houses and apartment buildings—did not have to obtain such a permit. And in *Romer v. Evans*, we disallowed a state statute that "impos[ed] a broad and undifferentiated disability on a single named group"—

specifically, homosexuals. 517 U. S., at 632. The dissent apparently agrees that if these cases have *stare decisis* effect, Texas' sodomy law would not pass scrutiny under the Equal Protection Clause, regardless of the type of rational basis review that we apply. See *post*, at 17-18 (opinion of Scalia, J.).

The statute at issue here makes sodomy a crime only if a person "engages in deviate sexual intercourse with another individual of the same sex." Tex. Penal Code Ann. §21.06(a) (2003). Sodomy between opposite-sex partners, however, is not a crime in Texas. That is, Texas treats the same conduct differently based solely on the participants. Those harmed by this law are people who have a same-sex sexual orientation and thus are more likely to engage in behavior prohibited by §21.06.

The Texas statute makes homosexuals unequal in the eyes of the law by making particular conduct—and only that conduct—subject to criminal sanction. It appears that prosecutions under Texas' sodomy law are rare. See *State v. Morales*, 869 S. W. 2d 941, 943 (Tex. 1994) (noting in 1994 that §21.06 "has not been, and in all probability will not be, enforced against private consensual conduct between adults"). This case shows, however, that prosecutions under §21.06 *do* occur. And while the penalty imposed on petitioners in this case was relatively minor, the consequences of conviction are not. As the Court notes, see *ante*, at 15, petitioners' convictions, if upheld, would disqualify them from or restrict their ability to engage in a variety of professions, including medicine, athletic training, and interior design. See, *e.g.*, Tex. Occ. Code Ann. §164.051(a)(2)(B) (2003 Pamphlet) (physician); §451.251 (a)(1) (athletic trainer); §1053.252(2) (interior designer). Indeed, were petitioners to move to one of four States, their convictions would require them to register as sex offenders to local law enforcement. See, *e.g.*, Idaho Code §18-8304 (Cum. Supp. 2002); La. Stat. Ann. §15:542 (West Cum. Supp. 2003); Miss. Code Ann. §45-33-25 (West 2003); S. C. Code Ann. §23-3-430 (West Cum. Supp. 2002); cf. *ante*, at 15.

And the effect of Texas' sodomy law is not just limited to the threat of prosecution or consequence of conviction. Texas' sodomy law brands all homosexuals as criminals, thereby making it more difficult for homosexuals to be treated in the same manner as everyone else. Indeed, Texas itself has previously acknowledged the collateral effects of the law, stipulating in a prior challenge to this action that the law "legally sanctions discrimination against [homosexuals] in a variety of ways unrelated to the criminal law," including in the areas of "employment, family issues, and housing." *State v. Morales*, 826 S. W. 2d 201, 203 (Tex. App. 1992).

Texas attempts to justify its law, and the effects of the law, by arguing that the statute satisfies rational basis review because it furthers the legitimate governmental interest of the promotion of morality. In *Bowers*, we held that a state law criminalizing sodomy as applied to homosexual couples did not violate substantive due process. We rejected the argument that no rational basis existed to justify the law, pointing to the government's interest in promoting morality. 478 U. S., at 196. The only question in front of the Court in *Bowers* was whether the substantive component of the Due Process Clause protected a right to engage in homosexual sodomy. *Id.*, at 188, n. 2. *Bowers* did not hold that moral disapproval of a group is a rational basis under the Equal Protection Clause to criminalize homosexual sodomy when heterosexual sodomy is not punished.

This case raises a different issue than *Bowers*: whether, under the Equal Protection Clause, moral disapproval is a legitimate state interest to justify by itself a statute that bans homosexual sodomy, but not heterosexual sodomy. It is not. Moral disapproval of this group, like a bare desire to harm the group, is an interest that is insufficient to satisfy rational basis review under the Equal Protection Clause. See, *e.g., Department of Agriculture v. Moreno*, *supra*, at 534; *Romer v. Evans*, 517 U. S., at 634-635. Indeed, we have never held that moral disapproval, without any other asserted state interest, is a sufficient rationale under the Equal Protection Clause to justify a law that discriminates among groups of persons.

Moral disapproval of a group cannot be a legitimate governmental interest under the Equal Protection Clause because legal classifications must not be "drawn for the purpose of disadvantaging the group burdened by the law." *Id.*, at 633. Texas' invocation of moral disapproval as a legitimate state interest proves nothing more than Texas' desire to criminalize homosexual sodomy. But the Equal Protection Clause prevents a State from creating "a classification of persons undertaken for its own sake." *Id.*, at 635. And because Texas so rarely enforces its sodomy law as applied to private, consensual acts, the law serves more as a statement of dislike and disapproval against homosexuals than as a tool to stop criminal behavior. The Texas sodomy law "raise[s] the inevitable inference that the disadvantage imposed is born of animosity toward the class of persons affected." *Id.*, at 634.

Texas argues, however, that the sodomy law does not discriminate against homosexual persons. Instead, the State maintains that the law discriminates only against homosexual conduct. While it is true that the law applies only to conduct, the conduct targeted by this law is conduct that is closely correlated with being homosexual. Under such circumstances, Texas' sodomy law is targeted at more than conduct. It is instead directed toward gay persons as a class. "After all, there can hardly be more palpable discrimination against a class than making the conduct that defines the class criminal." *Id.*, at 641 (Scalia, J., dissenting) (internal quotation marks omitted). When a State makes homosexual conduct criminal, and not "deviate sexual intercourse" committed by persons of different sexes, "that declaration in and of itself is an invitation to subject homosexual persons to discrimination both in the public and in the private spheres." *Ante*, at 14.

Indeed, Texas law confirms that the sodomy statute is directed toward homosexuals as a class. In Texas, calling a person a homosexual is slander per se because the word "homosexual" "impute[s] the commission of a crime." *Plumley v. Landmark Chevrolet, Inc.*, 122 F. 3d 308, 310 (CA5 1997) (applying Texas law); see also *Head v. Newton*, 596 S. W. 2d 209, 210 (Tex. App. 1980). The State has admitted that because of the sodomy law, *being* homosexual carries the presumption of being a criminal. See *State v. Morales*, 826 S. W. 2d, at 202-203 ("[T]he statute brands lesbians and gay men as criminals and thereby legally sanctions discrimination against them in a variety of ways unrelated to the criminal law"). Texas' sodomy law therefore results in discrimination against homosexuals as a class in an array of areas outside the criminal law. See *ibid.* In *Romer v. Evans*, we refused to sanction a law that singled out homosexuals "for disfavored legal status." 517 U. S., at 633. The same is true here. The Equal Protection Clause "neither knows nor tolerates classes among citizens." *Id.*, at 623 (quoting *Plessy v. Ferguson*, 163 U. S. 537, 559 (1896) (Harlan, J. dissenting)).

A State can of course assign certain consequences to a violation of its criminal law. But the State cannot single out one identifiable class of citizens for punishment that does not apply to everyone else, with moral disapproval as the only asserted state interest for the law. The Texas sodomy statute subjects homosexuals to "a lifelong penalty and stigma. A legislative classification that threatens the creation of an underclass ... cannot be reconciled with" the Equal Protection Clause. *Plyler v. Doe*, 457 U. S., at 239 (Powell, J., concurring).

Whether a sodomy law that is neutral both in effect and application, see *Yick Wo v. Hopkins*, 118 U. S. 356 (1886), would violate the substantive component of the Due Process Clause is an issue that need not be decided today. I am confident, however, that so long as the Equal Protection Clause requires a sodomy law to apply equally to the private consensual conduct of homosexuals and heterosexuals alike, such a law would not long stand in our democratic society. In the words of Justice Jackson:

"The framers of the Constitution knew, and we should not forget today, that there is no more effective practical guaranty against arbitrary and unreasonable government than to require that the principles of law which officials would impose upon a minority be imposed generally. Conversely, nothing opens the door to arbitrary action so effectively as to allow those officials to pick and choose only a few to whom they will apply legislation and thus to escape the political retribution that might be visited upon them if larger numbers were affected." *Railway Express Agency, Inc. v. New York*, 336 U. S. 106, 112-113 (1949) (concurring opinion).

That this law as applied to private, consensual conduct is unconstitutional under the Equal Protection Clause does not mean that other laws distinguishing between heterosexuals and homosexuals would similarly fail under rational basis review. Texas cannot assert any legitimate state interest here, such as national security or preserving the traditional institution of marriage. Unlike the moral disapproval of same-sex relations—the asserted state interest in this case—other reasons exist to promote the institution of marriage beyond mere moral disapproval of an excluded group.

A law branding one class of persons as criminal solely based on the State's moral disapproval of that class and the conduct associated with that class runs contrary to the values of the Constitution and the Equal Protection Clause, under any standard of review. I therefore concur in the Court's judgment that Texas' sodomy law banning "deviate sexual intercourse" between consenting adults of the same sex, but not between consenting adults of different sexes, is unconstitutional.

Justice Scalia, with Whom the Chief Justice and Justice Thomas Join, Dissenting

"Liberty finds no refuge in a jurisprudence of doubt." *Planned Parenthood of Southeastern Pa. v. Casey*, 505 U. S. 833, 844 (1992). That was the Court's sententious response, barely more than a decade ago, to those seeking to overrule *Roe v. Wade*, 410 U. S. 113 (1973). The Court's response today, to those who have engaged in a 17-year crusade to overrule *Bowers v. Hardwick*, 478 U. S. 186 (1986), is very different. The need for stability and certainty presents no barrier.

Most of the rest of today's opinion has no relevance to its actual holding—that the Texas statute "furthers no legitimate state interest which can justify" its application to petitioners under rational-basis review. *Ante*, at 18 (overruling Bowers to the extent it sustained Georgia's anti-sodomy statute under the rational-basis test). Though there is discussion of "fundamental proposition[s]," *ante*, at 4, and "fundamental decisions," *ibid.* nowhere does the Court's opinion declare that homosexual sodomy is a "fundamental right" under the Due Process Clause; nor does it subject the Texas law to the standard of review that would be appropriate (strict scrutiny) if homosexual sodomy were a "fundamental right." Thus, while overruling the *outcome* of *Bowers*, the Court leaves strangely untouched its central legal conclusion: "[R]espondent would have us announce . . . a fundamental right to engage in homosexual sodomy. This we are quite unwilling to do." 478 U. S., at 191. Instead the Court simply describes petitioners' conduct as "an exercise of their liberty"—which it undoubtedly is—and proceeds to apply an unheard-of form of rational-basis review that will have far-reaching implications beyond this case. *Ante*, at 3.

I

I begin with the Court's surprising readiness to reconsider a decision rendered a mere 17 years ago in *Bowers v. Hardwick*. I do not myself believe in rigid adherence to *stare decisis* in constitutional cases; but I do believe that we should be consistent rather than manipulative in invoking the doctrine. Today's opinions in support of reversal do not bother to distinguish—or indeed, even bother to mention—the paean to *stare decisis* coauthored by three Members of today's majority in *Planned Parenthood v. Casey*. There, when *stare decisis* meant preservation of judicially invented abortion rights, the widespread criticism of *Roe* was strong reason to *reaffirm* it:

"Where, in the performance of its judicial duties, the Court decides a case in such a way as to resolve the sort of intensely divisive controversy reflected in *Roe*[,] . . . its decision has a dimension that the resolution of the normal case does not carry. . . . [T]o overrule under fire in the absence of the most compelling reason . . . would subvert the Court's legitimacy beyond any serious question." 505 U. S., at 866-867.

Today, however, the widespread opposition to *Bowers*, a decision resolving an issue as "intensely divisive" as the issue in *Roe*, is offered as a reason in favor of *overruling* it. See *ante*, at 15-16. Gone, too, is any "enquiry" (of the sort conducted in *Casey*) into whether the decision sought to be overruled has "proven 'unworkable,'" *Casey, supra*, at 855.

Today's approach to *stare decisis* invites us to overrule an erroneously decided precedent (including an "intensely divisive" decision) *if:* (1) its foundations have been "eroded" by subsequent decisions, *ante*, at 15; (2) it has been subject to "substantial and continuing" criticism, *ibid.*; and (3) it has not induced "individual or societal reliance" that counsels against overturning, *ante*, at 16. The problem is that *Roe* itself—which today's majority surely has no disposition to overrule—satisfies these conditions to at least the same degree as *Bowers*.

(1) A preliminary digressive observation with regard to the first factor: The Court's claim that *Planned Parenthood v. Casey, supra*, "casts some doubt" upon the holding in *Bowers* (or any other case, for that matter) does not withstand analysis. *Ante*, at 10. As far as its holding is concerned, *Casey* provided a less expansive right to abortion than did *Roe*, which was already on the books when Bowers was decided. And if the Court is referring not to the holding of *Casey*, but to the dictum of its famed sweet-mystery-of-life passage, *ante*, at 13 ("At the heart of liberty is the right to define one's own concept of existence, of meaning, of the universe, and of the mystery of human life"): That "casts some doubt" upon either the totality of our jurisprudence or else (presumably the right answer) nothing at all.

I have never heard of a law that attempted to restrict one's "right to define" certain concepts; and if the passage calls into question the government's power to regulate *actions based on* one's self-defined "concept of existence, etc.," it is the passage that ate the rule of law.

I do not quarrel with the Court's claim that *Romer v. Evans*, 517 U. S. 620 (1996), "eroded" the "foundations" of *Bowers*' rational-basis holding. See *Romer, supra*, at 640-643 (Scalia, J., dissenting).) But *Roe* and *Casey* have been equally "eroded" by *Washington v. Glucksberg*, 521 U. S. 702, 721 (1997), which held that *only* fundamental rights which are "deeply rooted in this Nation's history and tradition" qualify for anything other than rational basis scrutiny under the doctrine of "substantive due process." *Roe* and *Casey*, of course, subjected the restriction of abortion to heightened scrutiny without even attempting to establish that the freedom to abort *was* rooted in this Nation's tradition.

(2) *Bowers*, the Court says, has been subject to "substantial and continuing [criticism], disapproving of its reasoning in all respects, not just as to its historical assumptions." *Ante*, at 15. Exactly what those nonhistorical criticisms are, and whether the Court even agrees with them, are left unsaid, although the Court does cite two books. See *ibid.* (citing C. Fried, Order and Law: Arguing the Reagan Revolution—A Firsthand Account 81-84 (1991); R. Posner, Sex and Reason 341-350 (1992)). Of course, *Roe* too (and by extension *Casey*) had been (and still is) subject to unrelenting criticism, including criticism from the two commentators cited by the Court today. See Fried, *supra*, at 75 ("Roe was a prime example of twisted judging"); Posner, *supra*, at 337 ("[The Court's] opinion in *Roe* . . . fails to measure up to professional expectations regarding judicial opinions"); Posner, Judicial Opinion Writing, 62 U. Chi. L. Rev. 1421, 1434 (1995) (describing the opinion in *Roe* as an "embarrassing performanc[e]").

(3) That leaves, to distinguish the rock-solid, unamendable disposition of *Roe* from the readily overrulable *Bowers*, only the third factor. "[T]here has been," the Court says, "no individual or societal reliance on *Bowers* of the sort that could counsel against overturning its holding. . . ." *Ante*, at 16. It seems to me that the "societal reliance" on the principles confirmed in *Bowers* and discarded today has been overwhelming. Countless judicial decisions and legislative enactments have relied on the ancient proposition that a governing majority's belief that certain sexual behavior is "immoral and unacceptable" constitutes a rational basis for regulation. See, *e.g., Williams v. Pryor*, 240 F. 3d 944, 949 (CA11 2001) (citing *Bowers* in upholding Alabama's prohibition on the sale of sex toys on the ground that "[t]he crafting and safeguarding of public morality . . . indisputably is a legitimate government interest under rational basis scrutiny"); *Milner v. Apfel*, 148 F. 3d 812, 814 (CA7 1998) (citing *Bowers* for the proposition that "[l]egislatures are permitted to legislate with regard to morality . . . rather than confined to preventing demonstrable harms"); *Holmes v. California Army National Guard* 124 F. 3d 1126, 1136 (CA9 1997) (relying on *Bowers* in upholding the federal statute and regulations banning from military service those who engage in homosexual conduct); *Owens v. State*, 352 Md. 663, 683, 724 A. 2d 43, 53 (1999) (relying on *Bowers* in holding that "a person has no constitutional right to engage in sexual intercourse, at least outside of marriage"); *Sherman v. Henry*, 928 S. W. 2d 464, 469-473 (Tex. 1996) (relying on *Bowers* in rejecting a claimed constitutional right to commit adultery). We ourselves relied extensively on *Bowers* when we concluded, in *Barnes v. Glen Theatre, Inc.*, 501 U. S. 560, 569 (1991), that Indiana's public indecency statute furthered "a substantial government interest in protecting order and morality," *ibid.*, (plurality opinion); see also *id.*, at 575 (Scalia, J., concurring in judgment). State laws against bigamy, same-sex marriage, adult incest, prostitution, masturbation, adultery, fornication, bestiality, and obscenity are likewise sustainable only in light of *Bowers*' validation of laws based on moral choices. Every single one of these laws is called into question by today's decision; the Court makes no effort to cabin the scope of its decision to exclude them from its holding. See *ante*, at 11 (noting "an emerging awareness that liberty gives substantial protection to adult persons in deciding how to conduct their private lives *in matters pertaining to sex*" (emphasis added)). The impossibility of distinguishing homosexuality from other traditional "morals" offenses is precisely why Bowers rejected the rational-basis challenge. "The law," it said, "is constantly based on notions of morality, and if all laws representing essentially moral choices are to be invalidated under the Due Process Clause, the courts will be very busy indeed." 478 U. S., at 196.

What a massive disruption of the current social order, therefore, the overruling of *Bowers* entails. Not so the overruling of *Roe*, which would simply have restored the regime that existed for centuries before 1973, in which the permissibility of and restrictions upon abortion were determined legislatively State-by-State. *Casey*, however, chose to base its *stare decisis* determination on a different "sort" of reliance. "[P]eople," it said, "have organized intimate relationships and made choices that define their views of themselves and their places in society, in reliance on the availability of abortion in the event that contraception should fail." 505 U. S., at 856. This falsely assumes that the consequence of overruling *Roe* would have been to make abortion unlawful. It would not; it would merely have *permitted* the States to do so. Many States would unquestionably have declined to prohibit abortion, and others would not have prohibited it within six months (after which the most significant reliance interests would have expired). Even for persons in States other than these, the choice would not have been between abortion and childbirth, but between abortion nearby and abortion in a neighboring State.

To tell the truth, it does not surprise me, and should surprise no one, that the Court has chosen today to revise the standards of *stare decisis* set forth in *Casey*. It has thereby exposed *Casey*'s extraordinary deference to precedent for the result-oriented expedient that it is.

II

Having decided that it need not adhere to *stare decisis*, the Court still must establish that *Bowers* was wrongly decided and that the Texas statute, as applied to petitioners, is unconstitutional.

Texas Penal Code Ann. §21.06(a) (2003) undoubtedly imposes constraints on liberty. So do laws prohibiting prostitution, recreational use of heroin, and, for that matter, working more than 60 hours per week in a bakery. But there is no right to "liberty" under the Due Process Clause, though today's opinion repeatedly makes that claim. *Ante*, at 6 ("The liberty protected by the Constitution allows homosexual persons the right to make this choice"); *ante*, at 13 ("These matters . . . are central to the liberty protected by the Fourteenth Amendment"); *ante*, at 17 ("Their right to liberty under the Due Process Clause gives them the full right to engage in their conduct without intervention of the government"). The Fourteenth Amendment *expressly allows* States to deprive their citizens of "liberty," *so long as "due process of law" is provided*:

"No state shall . . . deprive any person of life, liberty, or property, *without due process of law*." Amdt. 14 (emphasis added).

Our opinions applying the doctrine known as "substantive due process" hold that the Due Process Clause prohibits States from infringing *fundamental* liberty interests, unless the infringement is narrowly tailored to serve a compelling state interest. *Washington v. Glucksberg*, 521 U. S., at 721. We have held repeatedly, in cases the Court today does not overrule, that *only* fundamental rights qualify for this so-called "heightened scrutiny" protection—that is, rights which are "deeply rooted in this Nation's history and tradition," *ibid*. See *Reno v. Flores*, 507 U. S. 292, 303 (1993) (fundamental liberty interests must be "so rooted in the traditions and conscience of our people as to be ranked as fundamental" (internal quotation marks and citations omitted)); *United States v. Salerno*, 481 U. S. 739, 751 (1987) (same). See also *Michael H. v. Gerald D.*, 491 U. S. 110, 122 (1989) ("[W]e have insisted not merely that the interest denominated as a 'liberty' be 'fundamental' . . . but also that it be an interest traditionally protected by our society"); *Moore v. East Cleveland*, 431 U. S. 494, 503 (1977) (plurality opinion); *Meyer v. Nebraska*, 262 U. S. 390, 399 (1923) (Fourteenth Amendment protects "those privileges *long recognized at common law* as essential to the orderly pursuit of happiness by free men" (emphasis added)). All other liberty interests may be abridged or abrogated pursuant to a validly enacted state law if that law is rationally related to a legitimate state interest.

Bowers held, first, that criminal prohibitions of homosexual sodomy are not subject to heightened scrutiny because they do not implicate a "fundamental right" under the Due Process Clause, 478 U. S., at 191-194. Noting that "[p]roscriptions against that conduct have ancient roots," *id.*, at 192, that "[s]odomy was a criminal offense at common law and was forbidden by the laws of the original 13 States when they ratified the Bill of Rights," *ibid.*, and that many States had retained their bans on sodomy, *id.*, at 193, *Bowers* concluded that a right to engage in homosexual sodomy was not "deeply rooted in this Nation's history and tradition," *id.*, at 192.

The Court today does not overrule this holding. Not once does it describe homosexual sodomy as a "fundamental right" or a "fundamental liberty interest," nor does it subject the Texas statute to strict scrutiny. Instead, having failed to establish that the right to homosexual sodomy is "deeply rooted in this Nation's history and tradition," the Court concludes that the application of Texas's statute to petitioners' conduct fails the rational-basis test, and overrules *Bowers*' holding to the contrary, see *id.*, at 196. "The Texas statute furthers no legitimate state interest which can justify its intrusion into the personal and private life of the individual." *Ante*, at 18.

I shall address that rational-basis holding presently. First, however, I address some aspersions that the Court casts upon Bowers' conclusion that homosexual sodomy is not a "fundamental right"—even though, as I have said, the Court does not have the boldness to reverse that conclusion.

III

The Court's description of "the state of the law" at the time of *Bowers* only confirms that *Bowers* was right. *Ante*, at 5. The Court points to *Griswold v. Connecticut*, 381 U. S. 479, 481-482 (1965). But that case *expressly disclaimed* any reliance on the doctrine of "substantive due process," and grounded the so-called "right to privacy" in penumbras of constitutional provisions *other than* the Due Process Clause. *Eisenstadt v. Baird*, 405 U. S. 438 (1972), likewise had nothing to do with "substantive due process"; it invalidated a Massachusetts law prohibiting the distribution of contraceptives to unmarried persons solely on the basis of the Equal Protection Clause. Of course *Eisenstadt* contains well known dictum relating to the "right to privacy," but this referred to the right recognized in *Griswold*—a right penumbral to the *specific* guarantees in the Bill of Rights, and not a "substantive due process" right.

Roe v. Wade recognized that the right to abort an unborn child was a "fundamental right" protected by the Due Process Clause. 410 U. S., at 155. The *Roe* Court, however, made no attempt to establish that this right was "deeply rooted in this Nation's history and tradition"; instead, it based its conclusion that "the Fourteenth Amendment's concept of personal liberty . . . is broad enough to encompass a woman's decision whether or not to terminate her pregnancy" on its own normative judgment that anti-abortion laws were undesirable. See *id.*, at 153. We have since rejected *Roe*'s holding that regulations of abortion must be narrowly tailored to serve a compelling state interest, see *Planned Parenthood v. Casey*, 505 U. S., at 876 (joint opinion of O'Connor, Kennedy, and Souter, JJ.); id., at 951-953 (Rehnquist, C. J., concurring in judgment in part and dissenting in part)—and thus, by logical implication, *Roe*'s holding that the right to abort an unborn child is a "fundamental right." See 505 U. S., at 843-912 (joint opinion of O'Connor, Kennedy, and Souter, JJ.) (not once describing abortion as a "fundamental right" or a "fundamental liberty interest").

After discussing the history of antisodomy laws, *ante*, at 7-10, the Court proclaims that, "it should be noted that there is no longstanding history in this country of laws directed at homosexual conduct as a distinct matter," *ante*, at 7. This observation in no way casts into doubt the "definitive [historical] conclusion," *id.*, on which *Bowers* relied: that our Nation has a longstanding history of laws prohibiting *sodomy in general*—regardless of whether it was performed by same-sex or opposite-sex couples:

"It is obvious to us that neither of these formulations would extend a fundamental right to homosexuals to engage in acts of consensual sodomy. Proscriptions against that conduct have ancient roots. *Sodomy* was a criminal offense at common law and was forbidden by the laws of the original 13 States when they ratified the Bill of Rights. In 1868, when the Fourteenth Amendment was ratified, all but 5 of the 37 States in the Union had *criminal sodomy laws*. In fact, until 1961, all 50 States outlawed *sodomy*, and today, 24 States and the District of Columbia continue to provide criminal penalties for *sodomy* performed in private and between consenting adults. Against this background, to claim that a right to engage in such conduct is 'deeply rooted in this Nation's history and tradition' or 'implicit in the concept of ordered liberty' is, at best, facetious." 478 U. S., at 192-194 (citations and footnotes omitted; emphasis added).

It is (as *Bowers* recognized) entirely irrelevant whether the laws in our long national tradition criminalizing homosexual sodomy were "directed at homosexual conduct as a distinct matter." *Ante*, at 7. Whether homosexual sodomy was prohibited by a law targeted at same-sex sexual relations or by a more general law prohibiting both homosexual and heterosexual sodomy, the only relevant point is that it *was* criminalized—which suffices to establish that homosexual sodomy is not a right "deeply rooted in our Nation's history and tradition." The Court today agrees that homosexual sodomy was criminalized and thus does not dispute the facts on which *Bowers actually* relied.

Next the Court makes the claim, again unsupported by any citations, that "[l]aws prohibiting sodomy do not seem to have been enforced against consenting adults acting in private." *Ante*, at 8. The key qualifier here is "acting in private"—since the Court admits that sodomy laws *were* enforced against consenting adults (although the Court contends that prosecutions were "infrequent," *ante*, at 9). I do not know what "acting in private" means; surely consensual sodomy, like heterosexual intercourse, is rarely performed on stage. If all the Court means by "acting in private" is "on private premises, with the doors closed and windows covered," it is entirely unsurprising that evidence of enforcement would be hard to come by. (Imagine the circumstances that would enable a search warrant to be obtained for a residence on the ground that there was probable cause to believe that consensual sodomy was then and there occurring.) Surely that lack of evidence would not sustain the proposition that consensual sodomy on private premises with the doors closed and windows covered was regarded as a "fundamental right," even though all other consensual sodomy was criminalized. There are 203 prosecutions for consensual, adult homosexual sodomy reported in the West Reporting system and official state reporters from the years 1880-1995. See W. Eskridge, Gaylaw: Challenging the Apartheid of the Closet 375 (1999) (hereinafter Gaylaw). There are also records of 20 sodomy prosecutions and 4 executions during the colonial period. J. Katz, Gay/Lesbian Almanac 29, 58, 663 (1983). Bowers' conclusion that homosexual sodomy is not a fundamental right "deeply rooted in this Nation's history and tradition" is utterly unassailable.

Realizing that fact, the Court instead says: "[W]e think that our laws and traditions in the past half century are of most relevance here. These references show *an emerging awareness* that liberty gives substantial protection to adult persons in deciding how to conduct their private lives *in matters pertaining to sex*." *Ante*, at 11 (emphasis added). Apart from the fact that such an "emerging awareness" does not establish a "fundamental right," the statement is factually false. States continue to prosecute all sorts of crimes by adults "in matters pertaining to sex": prostitution, adult incest, adultery, obscenity, and child pornography. Sodomy laws, too, have been enforced "in the past half century," in which there have been 134 reported cases involving prosecutions for consensual, adult, homosexual sodomy. Gaylaw 375. In relying, for evidence of an "emerging recognition," upon the American Law Institute's 1955 recommendation not to criminalize "consensual sexual relations conducted in private," *ante*, at 11, the Court ignores the fact that this recommendation was "a point of resistance in most of the states that considered adopting the Model Penal Code." Gaylaw 159.

In any event, an "emerging awareness" is by definition not "deeply rooted in this Nation's history and tradition[s]," as we have said "fundamental right" status requires. Constitutional entitlements do not spring into existence because some States choose to lessen or eliminate criminal sanctions on certain behavior. Much less do they spring into existence, as the Court seems to believe, because *foreign nations* decriminalize conduct. The *Bowers* majority opinion never relied on "values we share with a wider civilization," *ante*, at 16, but rather rejected the claimed right to sodomy on the ground that such a right was not "deeply rooted in *this Nation*'s history and tradition," 478 U. S., at 193-194 (emphasis added). *Bowers*' rational-basis holding is likewise devoid of any reliance on the views of a "wider civilization," see *id.*, at 196. The Court's discussion of these foreign views (ignoring, of course, the many countries that have retained criminal prohibitions on sodomy) is therefore meaningless dicta. Dangerous dicta, however, since "this Court ... should not impose foreign moods, fads, or fashions on Americans." *Foster v. Florida*, 537 U. S. 990, n. (2002) (Thomas, J., concurring in denial of certiorari).

IV

I turn now to the ground on which the Court squarely rests its holding: the contention that there is no rational basis for the law here under attack. This proposition is so out of accord with our jurisprudence—indeed, with the jurisprudence of *any* society we know—that it requires little discussion.

The Texas statute undeniably seeks to further the belief of its citizens that certain forms of sexual behavior are "immoral and unacceptable," *Bowers, supra*, at 196—the same interest furthered by criminal laws against fornication, bigamy, adultery, adult incest, bestiality, and obscenity. *Bowers* held that this was a legitimate state interest. The Court today reaches the opposite conclusion. The Texas statute, it says, "furthers *no legitimate state interest* which can justify its intrusion into the personal and private life of the individual," *ante*, at 18 (emphasis addded). The Court embraces instead Justice Stevens' declaration in his *Bowers* dissent, that "the fact that the governing majority in a State has traditionally viewed a particular practice as immoral is not a sufficient reason for upholding a law prohibiting the practice," *ante*, at 17. This effectively decrees the end of all morals legislation. If, as the Court asserts, the promotion of majoritarian sexual morality is not even a *legitimate* state interest, none of the above-mentioned laws can survive rational-basis review.

V

Finally, I turn to petitioners' equal-protection challenge, which no Member of the Court save Justice O'Connor, *ante*, at 1 (opinion concurring in judgment), embraces: On its face §21.06(a) applies equally to all persons. Men and women, heterosexuals and homosexuals, are all subject to its prohibition of deviate sexual intercourse with someone of the same sex. To be sure, §21.06 does distinguish between the sexes insofar as concerns the partner with whom the sexual acts are performed: men can violate the law only with other men, and women only with other women. But this cannot itself be a denial of equal protection, since it is precisely the same distinction regarding partner that is drawn in state laws prohibiting marriage with someone of the same sex while permitting marriage with someone of the opposite sex.

The objection is made, however, that the antimiscegenation laws invalidated in *Loving v. Virginia*, 388 U. S. 1, 8 (1967), similarly were applicable to whites and Blacks alike, and only distinguished between the races insofar as the *partner* was concerned. In *Loving*, however, we correctly applied heightened scrutiny, rather than the usual rational-basis review, because the Virginia statute was "designed to maintain White Supremacy." *Id.*, at 6, 11. A racially discriminatory purpose is always sufficient to subject a law to strict scrutiny, even a facially neutral law that makes no mention of race. See *Washington v. Davis*, 426 U. S. 229, 241-242 (1976). No purpose to discriminate against men or women as a class can be gleaned from the Texas law, so rational-basis review applies. That review is readily satisfied here by the same rational basis that satisfied it in *Bowers*—society's belief that certain forms of sexual behavior are "immoral and unacceptable," 478 U. S., at 196. This is the same justification that supports many other laws regulating sexual behavior that make a distinction based upon the identity of the partner— for example, laws against adultery, fornication, and adult incest, and laws refusing to recognize homosexual marriage.

Justice O'Connor argues that the discrimination in this law which must be justified is not its discrimination with regard to the sex of the partner but its discrimination with regard to the sexual proclivity of the principal actor.

"While it is true that the law applies only to conduct, the conduct targeted by this law is conduct that is closely correlated with being homosexual. Under such circumstances, Texas' sodomy law is targeted at more than conduct. It is instead directed toward gay persons as a class." *Ante*, at 5.

Of course the same could be said of any law. A law against public nudity targets "the conduct that is closely correlated with being a nudist," and hence "is targeted at more than conduct"; it is "directed toward nudists as a class." But be that as it may. Even if the Texas law *does* deny equal protection to "homosexuals as a class," that denial *still* does not need to be justified by anything more than a rational basis, which our cases show is satisfied by the enforcement of traditional notions of sexual morality.

Justice O'Connor simply decrees application of "a more searching form of rational basis review" to the Texas statute. *Ante*, at 2. The cases she cites do not recognize such a standard, and reach their conclusions only after finding, as required by conventional rational-basis analysis, that no conceivable legitimate state interest supports the classification at issue. See *Romer v. Evans*, 517 U. S., at 635; *Cleburne v. Cleburne Living Center, Inc.*, 473 U. S. 432, 448-450 (1985); *Department of Agriculture v. Moreno*, 413 U. S. 528, 534-538 (1973). Nor does Justice O'Connor explain precisely what her "more searching form" of rational-basis review consists of. It must at least mean, however, that laws exhibiting "a . . . desire to harm a politically unpopular group," *ante*, at 2, are invalid *even though* there may be a conceivable rational basis to support them.

This reasoning leaves on pretty shaky grounds state laws limiting marriage to opposite-sex couples. Justice

O'Connor seeks to preserve them by the conclusory statement that "preserving the traditional institution of marriage" is a legitimate state interest. *Ante*, at 7. But "preserving the traditional institution of marriage" is just a kinder way of describing the State's *moral disapproval* of same-sex couples. Texas's interest in §21.06 could be recast in similarly euphemistic terms: "preserving the traditional sexual mores of our society." In the jurisprudence Justice O'Connor has seemingly created, judges can validate laws by characterizing them as "preserving the traditions of society" (good); or invalidate them by characterizing them as "expressing moral disapproval" (bad).

* * *

Today's opinion is the product of a Court, which is the product of a law-profession culture, that has largely signed on to the so-called homosexual agenda, by which I mean the agenda promoted by some homosexual activists directed at eliminating the moral opprobrium that has traditionally attached to homosexual conduct. I noted in an earlier opinion the fact that the American Association of Law Schools (to which any reputable law school *must* seek to belong) excludes from membership any school that refuses to ban from its job-interview facilities a law firm (no matter how small) that does not wish to hire as a prospective partner a person who openly engages in homosexual conduct. See *Romer, supra*, at 653.

One of the most revealing statements in today's opinion is the Court's grim warning that the criminalization of homosexual conduct is "an invitation to subject homosexual persons to discrimination both in the public and in the private spheres." *Ante*, at 14. It is clear from this that the Court has taken sides in the culture war, departing from its role of assuring, as neutral observer, that the democratic rules of engagement are observed. Many Americans do not want persons who openly engage in homosexual conduct as partners in their business, as scoutmasters for their children, as teachers in their children's schools, or as boarders in their home. They view this as protecting themselves and their families from a lifestyle that they believe to be immoral and destructive. The Court views it as "discrimination" which it is the function of our judgments to deter. So imbued is the Court with the law profession's anti-anti-homosexual culture, that it is seemingly unaware that the attitudes of that culture are not obviously "mainstream"; that in most States what the Court calls "discrimination" against those who engage in homosexual acts is perfectly legal; that proposals to ban such "discrimination" under Title VII have repeatedly been rejected by Congress, see Employment Non-Discrimination Act of 1994, S. 2238, 103d Cong., 2d Sess. (1994); Civil Rights Amendments, H. R. 5452, 94th Cong., 1st Sess. (1975); that in some cases such "discrimination" is *mandated* by federal statute, see 10 U. S. C. §654(b)(1) (mandating discharge from the armed forces of any service member who engages in or intends to engage in homosexual acts); and that in some cases such "discrimination" is a constitutional right, see *Boy Scouts of America v. Dale*, 530 U. S. 640 (2000).

Let me be clear that I have nothing against homosexuals, or any other group, promoting their agenda through normal democratic means. Social perceptions of sexual and other morality change over time, and every group has the right to persuade its fellow citizens that its view of such matters is the best. That homosexuals have achieved some success in that enterprise is attested to by the fact that Texas is one of the few remaining States that criminalize private, consensual homosexual acts. But persuading one's fellow citizens is one thing, and imposing one's views in absence of democratic majority will is something else. I would no more *require* a State to criminalize homosexual acts—or, for that matter, display *any* moral disapprobation of them—than I would *forbid* it to do so. What Texas has chosen to do is well within the range of traditional democratic action, and its hand should not be stayed through the invention of a brand-new "constitutional right" by a Court that is impatient of democratic change. It is indeed true that "later generations can see that laws once thought necessary and proper in fact serve only to oppress," *ante*, at 18; and when that happens, later generations can repeal those laws. But it is the premise of our system that those judgments are to be made by the people, and not imposed by a governing caste that knows best.

One of the benefits of leaving regulation of this matter to the people rather than to the courts is that the people, unlike judges, need not carry things to their logical conclusion. The people may feel that their disapprobation of homosexual conduct is strong enough to disallow homosexual marriage, but not strong enough to criminalize private homosexual acts—and may legislate accordingly. The Court today pretends that it possesses a similar freedom of action, so that that we need not fear judicial imposition of homosexual marriage, as has recently occurred in Canada (in a decision that the Canadian Government has chosen not to appeal). See *Halpern v. Toronto*, 2003 WL 34950 (Ontario Ct. App.); Cohen, Dozens in Canada Follow Gay Couple's Lead, Washington Post, June 12, 2003, p. A25. At the end of its opinion—after having laid waste the foundations of our rational-basis jurisprudence—the Court says that the present case "does not involve whether the government must give formal recognition to any relationship that homosexual persons seek to enter." *Ante*, at 17. Do not believe it. More illuminating than this bald, unreasoned disclaimer is the progression of thought displayed by an earlier passage in the Court's opinion, which notes the constitutional protections afforded to "personal decisions relating to *marriage*, procreation, contraception, family relationships, child rearing, and education," and then declares that "[p]ersons in a homosexual relationship may seek autonomy for these purposes, just as heterosexual persons do." *Ante*, at 13 (emphasis added). Today's opinion dismantles the structure of constitutional law that has permitted a distinction to be made between heterosexual and homosexual unions, insofar as formal recognition in marriage is concerned. If moral disapprobation of homosexual conduct is "no legitimate state interest" for purposes of proscribing that conduct, *ante*, at 18; and if, as the Court coos (casting aside all pretense of neutrality), "[w]hen sexuality finds overt expression in intimate conduct with another person, the conduct can be but one element in a personal bond that is more enduring," *ante*, at 6; what justification could there possibly be for denying the benefits of marriage to homosexual couples exercising "[t]he liberty protected by the Constitution,"

ibid.? Surely not the encouragement of procreation, since the sterile and the elderly are allowed to marry. This case "does not involve" the issue of homosexual marriage only if one entertains the belief that principle and logic have nothing to do with the decisions of this Court. Many will hope that, as the Court comfortingly assures us, this is so.

The matters appropriate for this Court's resolution are only three: Texas's prohibition of sodomy neither infringes a "fundamental right" (which the Court does not dispute), nor is unsupported by a rational relation to what the Constitution considers a legitimate state interest, nor denies the equal protection of the laws. I dissent.

Justice Thomas, Dissenting

I join Justice Scalia's dissenting opinion. I write separately to note that the law before the Court today "is . . . uncommonly silly." *Griswold v. Connecticut*, 381 U. S. 479, 527 (1965) (Stewart, J., dissenting). If I were a member of the Texas Legislature, I would vote to repeal it. Punishing someone for expressing his sexual preference through noncommercial consensual conduct with another adult does not appear to be a worthy way to expend valuable law enforcement resources.

Notwithstanding this, I recognize that as a member of this Court I am not empowered to help petitioners and others similarly situated. My duty, rather, is to "decide cases 'agreeably to the Constitution and laws of the United States.'" *Id.*, at 530. And, just like Justice Stewart, I "can find [neither in the Bill of Rights nor any other part of the Constitution a] general right of privacy," *ibid.*, or as the Court terms it today, the "liberty of the person both in its spatial and more transcendent dimensions," *ante*, at 1.

Glossary

amicus briefs: briefs by friends of the court, submitted by interest groups or others who are not parties to a case but have special knowledge about or a special interest in the case

compelling state interest: an interest of public concern that is so important as to justify limiting fundamental rights

fundamental rights: rights that are enumerated in the Bill of Rights or are inherent in the national concept of liberty; government cannot interfere with the exercise of fundamental rights without demonstrating that the regulation serves a compelling state interest

plea of nolo contendere: plea of no contest—no admission of guilt

rational-basis test: a test, employed in determining the constitutionality of most legislation, that asks if the legislation at issue is reasonably related to a legitimate state interest, such as public safety or the provision of services

stare decisis: the principle holding that courts should follow precedent in the interest of consistency and certainty in the law

substantive due process: the legal theory that rights implicit in the concept of liberty are fundamental and protected under the due process clause of the Constitution even if they are not explicitly mentioned in the Constitution

trial de novo: a form of appeal in which the appeals court holds a trial as if no other trial had been held

District of Columbia v. Heller

Date
2008

Author
Antonin Scalia

Vote
5–4

Citation
554 U.S. 570

Significance
Determined that the Second Amendment guarantees American citizens the right to possess firearms in their home, including handguns, without belonging to a militia, for the purpose of protecting one's life or property.

Overview

One of the seminal cases regarding gun rights, *District of Columbia v. Heller* obligated the Supreme Court to weigh in on a series of provisions enforced in the District of Columbia Code that barred the district's residents from carrying unregistered firearms and banned registering handguns. Gunowners were also obligated to keep their lawfully registered firearms unloaded and disassembled or made unusable by a trigger lock. Under certain conditions, the district's chief of police could issue a one-year license for handguns. Dick Heller, a police officer in the District of Columbia, sought such a license but was denied. Heller then sued the district, insisting that its code violated rights guaranteed by the Second Amendment, specifically that one could keep an operational firearm in one's residence without a license. While the district court opted to dismiss the complaint, the U.S. Court of Appeals for the District of Columbia Circuit declared that the district's condition that firearms kept in a home be nonoperational violated the Second Amendment right to keep firearms in a household for the purpose of self-protection.

The case went before the Supreme Court in 2008 and ended in a 5–4 decision that found the district's code to be unconstitutional. Justices John Paul Stevens and Stephen Breyer wrote dissenting opinions, being joined in opposition by David Souter and Ruth Bader Ginsburg.

The majority based its decision largely on the idea that the Second Amendment's first clause, which refers to a "militia," is a prefatory clause that does not impose restrictions on the amendment's optative clause, which guarantees citizens' right to bear arms. The majority further declared that the amendment should be interpreted in a straightforward manner that is consistent with the legal concepts of the era during which it was written, which is that there exists an individual right to own and carry firearms for the purpose of self-defense. Therefore, the District of Columbia's restrictions are to be considered unconstitutional.

Context

At the time the Supreme Court heard arguments in the *District of Columbia v. Heller* case in 2008, the country had become increasingly divided over the issue of gun rights. The United States' status as the nation with both the greatest number of guns and the highest number of guns per capita draws from numerous traditions and historical events. Supporters of the right to bear arms cite its enshrinement in the Bill of Rights as the Second Amendment as evidence of its central importance. Critics point out the amendment's reference to a "well-regulated militia" as opposed to individual owners and the advancements in firearm technology since the late 1700s as justification for its being restricted or struck down altogether.

Guns were commonplace in colonial America as a means of providing food by hunting and offering protection from hostile Native Americans. Several colonies passed laws requiring heads of households to possess guns and all men capable of doing so to serve in the local militia. There existed some gun control laws, particularly when it came to their ownership by enslaved people, indentured servants, Catholics, and Native Americans. Many of these firearm laws persisted well after the formation of the United States.

The nineteenth century was a period of rather pervasive restrictions on gun ownership. Southern states, which had previously barred enslaved people from owning firearms, passed laws in the years after the Civil War preventing African Americans from owning, using, or carrying firearms. Despite their reputation in popular culture as places of lawlessness and violence, many western communities in the late 1800s, such as Dodge City and Deadwood, heavily curtailed the possession and carrying of firearms within their limits.

Concerns regarding the rise of organized crime and its accompanying gun violence during the 1920s and 1930s helped to motivate legislation that limited access to specific types of guns and accessories. Congress enacted the National Firearms Act in 1934, which required specific firearms and fittings, such as shotguns, machine guns, short-barreled rifles, and silencers, to be registered by their owners and required their manufacturers to pay a $200 excise tax. Congress then passed the Federal Firearms Act of 1938, which prohibited the selling of firearms to specific groups, such as convicted felons, and decreed that those licensed by the federal government to sell firearms keep customer records.

Dick Heller in 2018
(Gage Skidmore)

In 1968, due in part to recent high-profile assassinations, including that of Martin Luther King Jr., Congress enacted the Gun Control Act of 1968. It restricted gun ownership based on age, mental incompetence, drug use, or criminal background, regulated the importation of guns, and placed more responsibility on gun dealers to keep records of sales. This was followed four years later, in 1972, with the creation of the Bureau of Alcohol, Tobacco, and Firearms (ATF), a federal agency tasked with limiting the illegal sale and use of guns and enforcing federal laws on firearms. In 1976 the District of Columbia passed a law prohibiting the buying, selling, or possessing of a handgun by anyone living in the district except for members of law enforcement or the military. The law also required all rifles and shotguns in the District of Columbia to be registered.

A series of high-profile mass shootings in the 1980s and 1990s helped encourage the passage of gun control legislation during these decades. The year 1986 saw the enactment of the Armed Career Criminal Act, the Firearm Owners Protection Act, and the Law Enforcement Officers Protection Act. The first two imposed new penalties on those unqualified to possess firearms or who used them to commit a crime, and the third banned "cop killer" bullets that could penetrate bulletproof vests and clothing. The Undetectable Firearms Act of 1988 banned the production, importation, shipment, and ownership of guns that cannot be detected by walk-through metal detectors at airports, schools, and courthouses. New laws targeted semiautomatic assault weapons, including a ban imposed by California in 1989 and the Crime Control Act of 1990, which prohibited the manufacture or importation of semiautomatic assault weapons and instituted "gun free school zone." The most visible legislation passed during this era was the Brady Handgun Violence Protection Act. This 1993 act mandated a waiting period of five days for the purchase of a handgun and obligated local law enforcement to complete a background check on those seeking to buy a handgun.

The steady stream of gun control legislation resulted in a growing and increasingly organized oppositional movement, with the National Rifle Association (NRA) as leading gun rights advocacy group. By the late 1990s, a gradual rolling back of gun control law got underway. In the 1997 case of *Printz* v. *United States*, the Supreme Court decided that the background check required under the Brady Bill was unconstitutional. In 2004 Congress allowed the Violent Crime Control and Law Enforcement Act of 1994 to expire, ending a decade-long ban on the sale of nearly 20 types of assault rifles. That same year, Congress opted to halt the funding of a recently created gun control program, Project Safe Neighborhoods. And in 2005 President George W. Bush signed the Protection of Lawful Commerce in Arms Act, which made it more difficult for victims of crimes involving guns to sue the weapons' manufacturers and dealers.

With momentum seemingly shifting toward supporters of gun rights, a police officer named Dick Heller challenged the more-than-three-decade ban on selling or owning handguns in the District of Columbia.

About the Author

A dominant figure among conservative judicial leaders, during his thirty-year tenure Antonin Scalia proved one of the most influential justices on the Supreme Court in the modern era. He was born in Trenton, New Jersey, in 1936 to an Italian immigrant father who became a professor at Brooklyn College and a mother who was the daughter of Italian immigrants. Following the family's relocation to Queens, New York, when he was a boy, Scalia attended Xavier High School in Manhattan, where he excelled. His academic excellence continued at Georgetown University, and he graduated as valedictorian of his class with a degree in history in 1957, an accomplishment he repeated when he completed his legal degree at Harvard Law School in 1960.

Scalia worked at the international law firm of Jones Day from 1961 to 1967, focusing on commercial law, before accepting a teaching position at the University of Virginia. His time in academia was brief, ending in 1971 when President Richard Nixon appointed him as general counsel for the Office of Communications Policy. Nixon then nominated Scalia to assistant attorney general for the Office of Legal Counsel in 1974, a position he served in until 1977 when he returned to teaching, this time at the University of Chicago Law School. He returned to the bench in 1982 as the judge for the U.S. Court of Appeals for the District of Columbia Circuit following his nomination by President Ronald Reagan, who in 1986 selected Scalia to take the place of William Rehnquist as associate justice as Rehnquist stepped into the position of chief justice following Warren Burger's retirement.

Scalia's presence on the Supreme Court combined humor and doggedness. His views tended to reflect his originalist beliefs that the Constitution should be interpreted according to its interpretation at the time of its ratification. He proved a staunch supporter of gun rights and a fierce critic of the constitutional right to an abortion. Scalia passed away in 2016 at the age of eighty, a widely revered figure who elicited grudging respect from even his harshest detractors.

Explanation and Analysis of the Document

Justice Scalia opens his opinion with an acknowledgment that the District of Columbia imposes sweeping prohibitions on the possession of firearms, including carrying an unregistered firearm. The district further bars carrying a handgun without a license unless issued a one-year license by the chief of police. This contextualizes the facts of the case subsequently laid out by Scalia, that Dick Heller, a special police office employed in the nation's capital, was authorized to carry his handgun while working at the Federal Judicial Center but was denied a registration certificate for a handgun he desired to keep at his residence. Heller responded with a lawsuit filed in the Federal District Court for the District of Columbia, based on the Second Amendment, that city did not possess the right to enforce the restriction on registering handguns or to prohibit the keeping of a firearm at home. The Court of Appeals for the District of Columbia, believing a firearm kept at home was appropriate for self-defense, sided with Heller before directing the district court to determine its judgment.

Defining a "Well Regulated Militia"

Scalia then cites precedents set by previous courts regarding the nature of the Second Amendment as it applies to who should be allowed access to firearms. He recognizes the two primary sides in the debate, specifically that all citizens possess the individual right to a firearm regardless of service in a militia and that only those affiliated with a "well regulated Militia" should possess access to firearms. Scalia acknowledges the vagueness of the Second Amendment and focuses on its operative clause, "the right of the people to keep and bear arms should not be infringed," which is one of three rights of the people identified in the Constitution (the other being the First Amendment's assembly and petition clause and the Fourth Amendment's search and seizure clause). All three clearly refer to individual rather than "collective" rights exercised by participating in a political community such as a militia.

Defining "the People"

Scalia argues that colonial militias drew from a subgroup of "the people," abled-bodied men within a specific range of ages, which contradicts the idea of "the people" possessing the right to bear arms as stated in the Second Amendment. Therefore, the right "to keep and bear Arms" is held by all Americans. Scalia makes no provisions for modern firearms, contending the meaning of "arms" remains virtually unchanged from definitions of more than two centuries ago when the Constitution was written. He scoffs at the argument that only weapons from the eighteenth century should be protected by the Second Amendment. Scalia also contends that the meaning of "keep arms" is to "have weapons" both inside and outside of military service. This also applies to the meaning of to "bear arms," which can apply to carrying weapons independent of an organized militia, such as defending one's person or home. It is not solely in regard to the use of arms in a military context.

Background on the Second Amendment

The historical background of the Second Amendment then becomes the focus of the opinion. Scalia points out that it, like the First and Fourth Amendments, articulate existing rights. The concept that the Second Amendment "shall not be infringed" draws upon late-seventeenth-century efforts by English monarchs to disarm certain segments of the population for the purposes of protecting their rule. This had the effect of promoting a greater willingness to take steps to prevent such efforts from succeeding and codify the possession of arms as a basic right, an outlook embodied in the Second Amendment. Such a view widely existed in the years leading up to the American Revolution when King George III came increasingly to be seen as a tyrant. More historical background is devoted to the concept of militias and their intended purpose. Scalia argues that the Constitution recognizes colonial militias as already being in existence, thus Congress could only organize rather than create them. Militias possessed a fundamental reason for existing, namely to stand up to poential oppression if the government faltered or collapsed. Scalia insists that "A well regulated Militia, being necessary to the security of a free State," the Amendment's prefatory clause, is clear in the militia's permanent importance.

The Second Amendment reflected similar inclusions in state constitutions of the late eighteenth century, some of which made clear individual rights to bear arms independent of military service. Their notions of "common defense" as extended to the defense of one's person or property came to be adopted in numerous state constitutions ratified during the early nineteenth century. This was the prevailing view among the foremost legal scholars in early America, who collectively rejected the view that the government possessed the right to disarm the people. State cases in the decades prior to the Civil War reinforced the view that the Second Amendment protected the right to bear arms as an individual right separate from militia service. Concerns over formerly enslaved people possessing firearms after the Civil War led to several debates and cases centered on the Second Amendment. Southern states generally blocked African Americans from bearing arms, which led to a flurry of condemnation from the amendment's supporters, who believed that it applied to all regardless of race or previous condition of enslavement. Legal scholars of the late 1800s further supported the amendment by arguing that a functional militia depended upon a population well acquainted with firearms, a condition only possible with the unfettered ability to possess them.

The Question of Gun Ownership

Scalia acknowledges the necessity of restrictions on the ownership of certain weapons and when and where weapons may be carried. Most cases in the nineteenth century related to the carrying of concealed firearms ended in rulings that prohibitions were lawful under the federal and state constitutions. Scalia concedes that such prohibitions continue to have their place in contemporary society.

The opinion returns to the case at hand: the constitutionality of a law that completely bans possessing a handgun in the home and requires that any legal firearm be made inoperable by a trigger lock or always disassembled. Scalia insists that the basic right of self-defense, long central to the Second Amendment, undercuts any laws prohibiting a category of arms used for that purpose, particularly the protection of one's home. It is a law whose severity is virtually without legal precedent. Scalia rejects the notion that such a ban is permissible when the possession of other weapons is an option due to their possible lack of effectiveness or usability; handguns possess innate advantages when it comes to accessibility and ease of use when defending oneself. And the law's insistence that legal firearms be made inoperable makes it impossible to allow for self-defense.

In summary, Scalia finds both the District of Columbia's ban on possessing a firearm in the home and its assertion that any legal firearm in home must be inoperable to be in violation of the Second Amendment. The district is to permit Dick Heller to register his firearm and issue him a license to possess it in his home.

Impact

As the first case to be heard by the Supreme Court since 1939 regarding firearm ownership, the *Heller* decision generated considerable interest in the media and on both sides of the gun control debate. Adrian Fenty, the mayor of Washington, D.C., expressed his disappointment with the court's decision to strike down the nation's toughest handgun law but agreed to respect it and ordered the District of Columbia police department to begin working out a process for the registration of firearms within three weeks. The Brady Campaign to Prevent Gun Violence, a prominent organization advocating for gun control, likewise signaled its disappointment. President George W. Bush commended the Court for its decision, which he stated was consistent with what the Constitution says about the individual right to possess and carry firearms.

The Supreme Court heard another case regarding gun rights the year after the *Heller* decision, 2009's *United States v. Hayes*, which upheld a federal law preventing anyone convicted of a crime involving domestic violence from possessing a firearm. Although the decision made no reference to the *Heller* decision, 2010's *MacDonald v. City of Chicago* helped to clarify some of the ambiguity the previous case left in its wake regarding states' rights to enforce gun laws. The court decided 5–4 that states cannot infringe upon the right to keep and bear arms as guaranteed by the Second and Fourteenth Amendments.

This decision came into play in a 2021 case heard by the court, *New York State Rifle & Pistol Association, Inc. v. Bruen*. In a 6–3 decision, the Court struck down a New York law that required an individual desiring to carry a concealed firearm in public for the purpose of self-protection to provide adequate justification for doing so. Such a state law was judged to be discretionary and superfluous when a number of restrictions on gun ownership in New York already existed.

State governments continued to pass gun control laws, including a ban on the sale of assault-style rifles by the Illinois legislature in early 2023, in the aftermath of a mass shooting the previous year. The law met with accusations that it violated the Second Amendment from the National Rifle Association and other guns rights groups, and it may become the basis for a future case before the Supreme Court.

Questions for Further Study

1. How did historical changes, including advancements in firearms technology, inform the debate over gun control through the centuries?

2. What is the distinction Scalia makes between "a well regulated Militia" and "the people" in terms of justifying the latter's right to bear arms?

3. How does the notion of self-defense factor into the Court's decision?

4. Scalia was a well-known "originalist" when it came to his interpretation of the Constitution. How does that come through in his opinion?

Further Reading

Books

Auster, Paul. *Bloodbath Nation*. New York: Grove Press, 2023.

Charles, Patrick J. *Armed in America: A History of Gun Rights from Colonial Militias to Concealed Carry*. Buffalo: Prometheus, 2018.

Guttenberg, Fred, and Thomas Gabor. *American Carnage: Shattering the Myths That Fuel Gun Violence*. Miami: Mango Publishing, 2023.

Spitzer, Robert J. *The Politics of Gun Control*. New York: Routledge, 2020.

Winkler, Adam. *Gun Fight: The Battle over the Right to Bear Arms in America*. New York: Norton, 2013.

Websites

Kiely, Eugene, D'Angelo Gore, Lori Robertson, and Robert Farley. "The Gun Debate." FactCheck.org. March 5, 2018. https://www.factcheck.org/2018/03/the-gun-debate/.

Schaeffer, Katherine. "Key Facts about Americans and Guns." Pew Research Center. September 13, 2021. https://www.pewresearch.org/fact-tank/2021/09/13/key-facts-about-americans-and-guns/.

"Should More Gun Laws Be Enacted?" Britannica ProCon.org. Accessed February 20, 2023. https://gun-control.procon.org.

—Commentary by Michael Martin Carver

DISTRICT OF COLUMBIA V. HELLER

Document Text

Justice Scalia delivered the opinion of the Court

We consider whether a District of Columbia prohibition on the possession of usable handguns in the home violates the Second Amendment to the Constitution.

I

The District of Columbia generally prohibits the possession of handguns. It is a crime to carry an unregistered firearm, and the registration of handguns is prohibited. See D. C. Code §§7–2501.01(12), 7–2502.01(a), 7–2502.02(a)(4) (2001). Wholly apart from that prohibition, no person may carry a handgun without a license, but the chief of police may issue licenses for 1-year periods. See §§22–4504(a), 22–4506. District of Columbia law also requires residents to keep their lawfully owned firearms, such as registered long guns, "unloaded and dissembled or bound by a trigger lock or similar device" unless they are located in a place of business or are being used for lawful recreational activities. See §7–2507.02.

Respondent Dick Heller is a D. C. special police officer authorized to carry a handgun while on duty at the Federal Judicial Center. He applied for a registration certificate for a handgun that he wished to keep at home, but the District refused. He thereafter filed a lawsuit in the Federal District Court for the District of Columbia seeking, on Second Amendment grounds, to enjoin the city from enforcing the bar on the registration of handguns, the licensing requirement insofar as it prohibits the carrying of a firearm in the home without a license, and the trigger-lock requirement insofar as it prohibits the use of "functional firearms within the home." App. 59a. The District Court dismissed respondent's complaint, see *Parker* v. *District of Columbia*, 311 F. Supp. 2d 103, 109 (2004). The Court of Appeals for the District of Columbia Circuit, construing his complaint as seeking the right to render a firearm operable and carry it about his home in that condition only when necessary for self-defense, reversed, see *Parker* v. *District of Columbia*, 478 F. 3d 370, 401 (2007). It held that the Second Amendment protects an individual right to possess firearms and that the city's total ban on handguns, as well as its requirement that firearms in the home be kept nonfunctional even when necessary for self-defense, violated that right. See *id.*, at 395, 399–401. The Court of Appeals directed the District Court to enter summary judgment for respondent.

We granted certiorari. 552 U. S. ___ (2007).

II

We turn first to the meaning of the Second Amendment.

A

The Second Amendment provides: "A well regulated Militia, being necessary to the security of a free State, the right of the people to keep and bear Arms, shall not be infringed." In interpreting this text, we are guided by the principle that "[t]he Constitution was written to be understood by the voters; its words and phrases were used in their normal and ordinary as distinguished from technical meaning." *United States* v. *Sprague*, 282 U. S. 716, 731 (1931); see also *Gibbons* v. *Ogden*, 9 Wheat.

1, 188 (1824). Normal meaning may of course include an idiomatic meaning, but it excludes secret or technical meanings that would not have been known to ordinary citizens in the founding generation.

The two sides in this case have set out very different interpretations of the Amendment. Petitioners and today's dissenting Justices believe that it protects only the right to possess and carry a firearm in connection with militia service. See Brief for Petitioners 11–12; *post*, at 1 (Stevens, J., dissenting). Respondent argues that it protects an individual right to possess a firearm unconnected with service in a militia, and to use that arm for traditionally lawful purposes, such as self-defense within the home. See Brief for Respondent 2–4.

The Second Amendment is naturally divided into two parts: its prefatory clause and its operative clause. The former does not limit the latter grammatically, but rather announces a purpose. The Amendment could be rephrased, "Because a well regulated Militia is necessary to the security of a free State, the right of the people to keep and bear Arms shall not be infringed." See J. Tiffany, A Treatise on Government and Constitutional Law §585, p. 394 (1867); Brief for Professors of Linguistics and English as *Amici Curiae* 3 (hereinafter Linguists' Brief). Although this structure of the Second Amendment is unique in our Constitution, other legal documents of the founding era, particularly individual-rights provisions of state constitutions, commonly included a prefatory statement of purpose. See generally Volokh, The Commonplace Second Amendment, 73 N. Y. U. L. Rev. 793, 814–821 (1998).

Logic demands that there be a link between the stated purpose and the command. The Second Amendment would be nonsensical if it read, "A well regulated Militia, being necessary to the security of a free State, the right of the people to petition for redress of grievances shall not be infringed." That requirement of logical connection may cause a prefatory clause to resolve an ambiguity in the operative clause ("The separation of church and state being an important objective, the teachings of canons shall have no place in our jurisprudence." The preface makes clear that the operative clause refers not to canons of interpretation but to clergymen.) But apart from that clarifying function, a prefatory clause does not limit or expand the scope of the operative clause. See F. Dwarris, A General Treatise on Statutes 268–269 (P. Potter ed. 1871) (hereinafter Dwarris); T. Sedgwick, The Interpretation and Construction of Statutory and Constitutional Law 42–45 (2d ed. 1874)."It is nothing unusual in acts . . . for the enacting part to go beyond the preamble; the remedy often extends beyond the particular act or mischief which first suggested the necessity of the law." J. Bishop, Commentaries on Written Laws and Their Interpretation §51, p. 49 (1882) (quoting *Rex* v. *Marks*, 3 East, 157, 165 (K. B. 1802)). Therefore, while we will begin our textual analysis with the operative clause, we will return to the prefatory clause to ensure that our reading of the operative clause is consistent with the announced purpose.

1. Operative Clause.

a. "Right of the People." The first salient feature of the operative clause is that it codifies a "right of the people." The unamended Constitution and the Bill of Rights use the phrase "right of the people" two other times, in the First Amendment's Assembly-and-Petition Clause and in the Fourth Amendment's Search-and-Seizure Clause. The Ninth Amendment uses very similar terminology ("The enumeration in the Constitution, of certain rights, shall not be construed to deny or disparage others retained by the people"). All three of these instances unambiguously refer to individual rights, not "collective" rights, or rights that may be exercised only through participation in some corporate body.

Three provisions of the Constitution refer to "the people" in a context other than "rights"—the famous preamble ("We the people"), §2 of Article I (providing that "the people" will choose members of the House), and the Tenth Amendment (providing that those powers not given the Federal Government remain with "the States" or "the people"). Those provisions arguably refer to "the people" acting collectively—but they deal with the exercise or reservation of powers, not rights. Nowhere else in the Constitution does a "right" attributed to "the people" refer to anything other than an individual right.

What is more, in all six other provisions of the Constitution that mention "the people," the term unambiguously refers to all members of the political community, not an unspecified subset. As we said in *United States* v. *Verdugo-Urquidez*, 494 U. S. 259, 265 (1990):

"'[T]he people' seems to have been a term of art employed in select parts of the Constitution.... [Its uses] sugges[t] that 'the people' protected by the Fourth Amendment, and by the First and Second Amendments, and to whom rights and powers are reserved in the Ninth and Tenth Amendments, refers to a class of persons who are part of a national community or who have otherwise developed sufficient connection with this country to be considered part of that community."

This contrasts markedly with the phrase "the militia" in the prefatory clause. As we will describe below, the "militia" in colonial America consisted of a subset of "the people"—those who were male, able bodied, and within a certain age range. Reading the Second Amendment as protecting only the right to "keep and bear Arms" in an organized militia therefore fits poorly with the operative clause's description of the holder of that right as "the people."

We start therefore with a strong presumption that the Second Amendment right is exercised individually and belongs to all Americans.

b. "Keep and bear Arms." We move now from the holder of the right—"the people"—to the substance of the right: "to keep and bear Arms."

Before addressing the verbs "keep" and "bear," we interpret their object: "Arms." The 18th-century meaning is no different from the meaning today. The 1773 edition of Samuel Johnson's dictionary defined "arms" as "weapons of offence, or armour of defence." 1 Dictionary of the English Language 107 (4th ed.) (hereinafter Johnson). Timothy Cunningham's important 1771 legal dictionary defined "arms" as "any thing that a man wears for his defence, or takes into his hands, or useth in wrath to cast at or strike another." 1 A New and Complete Law Dictionary (1771); see also N. Webster, American Dictionary of the English Language (1828) (reprinted 1989) (hereinafter Webster) (similar).

The term was applied, then as now, to weapons that were not specifically designed for military use and were not employed in a military capacity. For instance, Cunningham's legal dictionary gave as an example of usage: "Servants and labourers shall use bows and arrows on *Sundays*, &c. and not bear other arms." See also, *e.g.,* An Act for the trial of Negroes, 1797 Del. Laws ch. XLIII, §6, p. 104, in 1 First Laws of the State of Delaware 102, 104 (J. Cushing ed. 1981 (pt. 1)); see generally *State* v. *Duke*, 42 Tex. 455, 458 (1874) (citing decisions of state courts construing "arms"). Although one founding-era thesaurus limited "arms" (as opposed to "weapons") to "instruments of offence *generally* made use of in war," even that source stated that all firearms constituted "arms." 1 J. Trusler, The Distinction Between Words Esteemed Synonymous in the English Language 37 (1794) (emphasis added).

Some have made the argument, bordering on the frivolous, that only those arms in existence in the 18th century are protected by the Second Amendment. We do not interpret constitutional rights that way. Just as the First Amendment protects modern forms of communications, *e.g., Reno* v. *American Civil Liberties Union*, 521 U. S. 844, 849 (1997), and the Fourth Amendment applies to modern forms of search, *e.g., Kyllo* v. *United States*, 533 U. S. 27, 35–36 (2001), the Second Amendment extends, prima facie, to all instruments that constitute bearable arms, even those that were not in existence at the time of the founding.

We turn to the phrases "keep arms" and "bear arms." Johnson defined "keep" as, most relevantly, "[t]o retain; not to lose," and "[t]o have in custody." Johnson 1095. Webster defined it as "[t]o hold; to retain in one's power or possession." No party has apprised us of an idiomatic meaning of "keep Arms." Thus, the most natural reading of "keep Arms" in the Second Amendment is to "have weapons."

The phrase "keep arms" was not prevalent in the written documents of the founding period that we have found, but there are a few examples, all of which favor viewing the right to "keep Arms" as an individual right unconnected with militia service. William Blackstone, for example, wrote that Catholics convicted of not attending service in the Church of England suffered certain penalties, one of which was that they were not permitted to "keep arms in their houses." 4 Commentaries on the Laws of England 55 (1769) (hereinafter Blackstone); see also 1 W. & M., c. 15, §4, in 3 Eng. Stat. at Large 422 (1689) ("[N]o Papist . . . shall or may have or keep in his House . . . any Arms . . . "); 1 Hawkins, Treatise on the Pleas of the Crown 26 (1771) (similar). Petitioners point to militia laws of the founding period that required militia members to "keep" arms in connection with militia service, and they conclude from this that the phrase "keep Arms" has a militia-related connotation. See Brief for Petitioners 16–17 (citing laws of Delaware, New Jersey, and Virginia). This is rather like saying that, since there are many statutes that authorize aggrieved employees to "file complaints" with federal agencies, the phrase "file complaints" has an employment-related connotation. "Keep arms" was simply a common way of referring to possessing arms, for militiamen *and everyone else.*

At the time of the founding, as now, to "bear" meant to "carry." See Johnson 161; Webster; T. Sheridan, A Complete Dictionary of the English Language (1796); 2 Oxford English Dictionary 20 (2d ed. 1989) (hereinafter Oxford). When used with "arms," however, the term has a meaning that refers to carrying for a particular purpose—confrontation. In *Muscarello* v. *United States*, 524 U. S. 125 (1998), in the course of analyzing the meaning of "carries a firearm" in a federal criminal statute, Justice Ginsburg wrote that "[s]urely a most familiar meaning is, as the Constitution's Second Amendment . . . indicate[s]: 'wear, bear, or carry . . . upon the person or in the clothing or in a pocket, for the purpose . . . of being armed and ready for offensive or defensive action in a case of conflict with another person.'" *Id.*, at 143 (dissenting opinion) (quoting Black's Law Dictionary 214 (6th ed. 1998)). We think that Justice Ginsburg accurately captured the natural meaning of "bear arms." Although the phrase implies that the carrying of the weapon is for the purpose of "offensive or defensive action," it in no way connotes participation in a structured military organization.

From our review of founding-era sources, we conclude that this natural meaning was also the meaning that "bear arms" had in the 18th century. In numerous instances, "bear arms" was unambiguously used to refer to the carrying of weapons outside of an organized militia. The most prominent examples are those most relevant to the Second Amendment: Nine state constitutional provisions written in the 18th century or the first two decades of the 19th, which enshrined a right of citizens to "bear arms in defense of themselves and the state" or "bear arms in defense of himself and the state." It is clear from those formulations that "bear arms" did not refer only to carrying a weapon in an organized military unit. Justice James Wilson interpreted the Pennsylvania Constitution's arms-bearing right, for example, as a recognition of the natural right of defense "of one's person or house"—what he called the law of "self preservation." 2 Collected Works of James Wilson 1142, and n. x (K. Hall & M. Hall eds. 2007) (citing Pa. Const., Art. IX, §21 (1790)); see also T. Walker, Introduction to American Law 198 (1837) ("Thus the right of self-defence [is] guaranteed by the [Ohio] constitution"); see also *id.*, at 157 (equating Second Amendment with that provision of the Ohio Constitution). That was also the interpretation of those state constitutional provisions adopted by pre-Civil War state courts. These provisions demonstrate—again, in the most analogous linguistic context—that "bear arms" was not limited to the carrying of arms in a militia.

The phrase "bear Arms" also had at the time of the founding an idiomatic meaning that was significantly different from its natural meaning: "to serve as a soldier, do military service, fight" or "to wage war." See Linguists' Brief 18; *post*, at 11 (Stevens, J., dissenting). But it *unequivocally* bore that idiomatic meaning only when followed by the preposition "against," which was in turn followed by the target of the hostilities. See 2 Oxford 21. (That is how, for example, our Declaration of Independence ¶28, used the phrase: "He has constrained our fellow Citizens taken Captive on the high Seas to bear Arms against their Country . . . .") Every example given by petitioners' *amici* for the idiomatic meaning of "bear arms" from the founding period either includes the preposition "against" or is not clearly idiomatic. See Linguists' Brief 18–23. Without the preposition, "bear arms" normally meant (as it continues to mean today) what Justice Ginsburg's opinion in *Muscarello* said.

In any event, the meaning of "bear arms" that petitioners and Justice Stevens propose is *not even* the (sometimes) idiomatic meaning. Rather, they manufacture a hybrid definition, whereby "bear arms" connotes the actual carrying of arms (and therefore is not really an idiom) but only in the service of an organized militia. No dictionary has ever adopted that definition, and we have been apprised of no source that indicates that it carried that meaning at the time of the founding. But it is easy to see why petitioners and the dissent are driven to the hybrid definition. Giving "bear Arms" its idiomatic meaning would cause the protected right to consist of the right to be a soldier or to wage war—an absurdity that no commentator has ever endorsed. See L. Levy, Origins of the Bill of Rights 135 (1999). Worse still, the phrase "keep and bear Arms" would be incoherent. The word "Arms" would have two different meanings at once: "weapons" (as the object of "keep") and (as the object of "bear") one-half of an idiom. It would be rather like saying "He filled and kicked the bucket" to mean "He filled the bucket and died." Grotesque.

Petitioners justify their limitation of "bear arms" to the military context by pointing out the unremarkable fact that it was often used in that context—the same mistake they made with respect to "keep arms." It is especially unremarkable that the phrase was often used in a military context in the federal legal sources (such as records of congressional debate) that have been the focus of petitioners' inquiry. Those sources would have had little occasion to use it *except* in discussions about the standing army and the militia. And the phrases used primarily in those military discussions include not only "bear arms" but also "carry arms," "possess arms," and "have arms"—though no one thinks that those *other* phrases also had special military meanings. See Barnett, Was the Right to Keep and Bear Arms Conditioned on Service in an Organized Militia?, 83 Tex. L. Rev. 237, 261 (2004). The common references to those "fit to bear arms" in congressional discussions about the militia are matched by use of the same phrase in the few nonmilitary federal contexts where the concept would be relevant. See, *e.g.*, 30 Journals of Continental Congress 349–351 (J. Fitzpatrick ed. 1934). Other legal sources frequently used "bear arms" in nonmilitary contexts. Cunningham's legal dictionary, cited above, gave as an example of its usage a sentence unrelated to military affairs ("Servants and labourers shall use bows and arrows on *Sundays*, &c. and not bear other arms"). And if one looks beyond legal sources, "bear arms" was frequently used in nonmilitary contexts. See Cramer & Olson, What Did "Bear Arms" Mean in the Second Amendment?, 6 Georgetown J. L. & Pub. Pol'y (forthcoming Sept. 2008), online at http://papers.ssrn.com/abstract=1086176 (as visited June 24, 2008, and available in Clerk of Court's case file) (identifying numerous nonmilitary uses of "bear arms" from the founding period).

Justice Stevens points to a study by *amici* supposedly showing that the phrase "bear arms" was most frequently used in the military context. See *post*, at 12–13, n. 9; Linguists' Brief 24. Of course, as we have said, the fact that the phrase was commonly used in a particular context does not show that it is limited to that context, and, in any event, we have given many sources where the phrase was used in nonmilitary contexts. Moreover, the study's collection appears to include (who knows how many times) the idiomatic phrase "bear arms against," which is irrelevant. The *amici* also dismiss examples such as "'bear arms . . . for the purpose of killing game'" because those uses are "expressly qualified." Linguists' Brief 24. (Justice Stevens uses the same excuse for dismissing the state constitutional provisions analogous to the Second Amendment that identify private-use purposes for which the individual right can be asserted. See *post*, at 12.) That analysis is faulty. A purposive qualifying phrase that contradicts the word or phrase it modifies is unknown this side of the looking glass (except, apparently, in some courses on Linguistics). If "bear arms" means, as we think, simply the carrying of arms, a modifier can limit the purpose of the carriage ("for the purpose of self-defense" or "to make war against the King"). But if "bear arms" means, as the petitioners and the dissent think, the carrying of arms only for military purposes, one simply cannot add "for the purpose of killing game." The right "to carry arms in the militia for the purpose of killing game" is worthy of the mad hatter. Thus, these purposive qualifying phrases positively establish that "to bear arms" is not limited to military use.

Justice Stevens places great weight on James Madison's inclusion of a conscientious-objector clause in his original draft of the Second Amendment: "but no person religiously scrupulous of bearing arms, shall be compelled to render military service in person." Creating the Bill of Rights 12 (H. Veit, K. Bowling, & C. Bickford eds. 1991) (hereinafter Veit). He argues that this clause establishes that the drafters of the Second Amendment intended "bear Arms" to refer only to military service. See *post*, at 26. It is always perilous to derive the meaning of an adopted provision from another provision deleted in the drafting process. In any case, what Justice Stevens would conclude from the deleted provision does not follow. It was not meant to exempt from military service those who objected to going to war but had no scruples about personal gunfights. Quakers opposed the use of arms not just for militia service, but for any violent purpose whatsoever—so much so that Quaker frontiersmen were forbidden to use arms to defend their families, even though "[i]n such circumstances the temptation to seize a hunting rifle or knife in self-defense . . . must sometimes have been almost overwhelming." P. Brock, Pacifism in the United States 359 (1968); see M. Hirst, The Quakers in Peace and War 336–339 (1923); 3 T. Clarkson, Portraiture of Quakerism 103–104 (3d ed. 1807).

The Pennsylvania Militia Act of 1757 exempted from service those *"scrupling the use of arms"*—a phrase that no one contends had an idiomatic meaning. See 5 Stat. at Large of Pa. 613 (J. Mitchell & H. Flanders eds. 1898) (emphasis added). Thus, the most natural interpretation of Madison's deleted text is that those opposed to carrying weapons for potential violent confrontation would not be "compelled to render military service," in which such carrying would be required.

Finally, Justice Stevens suggests that "keep and bear Arms" was some sort of term of art, presumably akin to "hue and cry" or "cease and desist." (This suggestion usefully evades the problem that there is no evidence whatsoever to support a military reading of "keep arms.") Justice Stevens believes that the unitary meaning of "keep and bear Arms" is established by the Second Amendment's calling it a "right" (singular) rather than "rights" (plural). See *post*, at 16. There is nothing to this. State constitutions of the founding period routinely grouped multiple (related) guarantees under a singular "right," and the First Amendment protects the "right [singular] of the people peaceably to assemble, and to petition the Government for a redress of grievances." See, *e.g.*, Pa. Declaration of Rights §§IX, XII, XVI, in 5 Thorpe 3083–3084; Ohio Const., Arts. VIII, §§11, 19 (1802), in *id.*, at 2910–2911. And even if "keep and bear Arms" were a unitary phrase, we find no evidence that it bore a military meaning. Although the phrase was not at all common (which would be unusual for a term of art), we have found instances of its use with a clearly nonmilitary connotation. In a 1780 debate in the House of Lords, for example, Lord Richmond described an order to disarm private citizens (not militia members) as "a violation of the constitutional right of Protestant subjects to keep and bear arms for their own defense." 49 The London Magazine or Gentleman's Monthly Intelligencer 467 (1780). In response, another member of Parliament referred to "the right of bearing arms for personal defence," making clear that no special military meaning for "keep and bear arms" was intended in the discussion. *Id.*, at 467–468.

c. Meaning of the Operative Clause. Putting all of these textual elements together, we find that they guarantee the individual right to possess and carry weapons in case of confrontation. This meaning is strongly confirmed by the historical background of the Second Amendment. We look to this because it has always been widely understood that the Second Amendment, like the First and Fourth Amendments, codified a *pre-existing* right. The very text of the Second Amendment implicitly recognizes the pre-existence of the right and declares only that it "shall not be infringed." As we said in *United States* v. *Cruikshank*, 92 U.S. 542, 553 (1876), "[t]his is not a right granted by the Constitution. Neither is it in any manner dependent upon that instrument for its existence. The Second amendment declares that it shall not be infringed . . . ."

Between the Restoration and the Glorious Revolution, the Stuart Kings Charles II and James II succeeded in using select militias loyal to them to suppress political dissidents, in part by disarming their opponents. See J. Malcolm, To Keep and Bear Arms 31–53 (1994) (hereinafter Malcolm); L. Schwoerer, The Declaration of Rights, 1689, p. 76 (1981). Under the auspices of the 1671 Game Act, for example, the Catholic James II had ordered general disarmaments of regions home to his Protestant enemies. See Malcolm 103–106. These experiences caused Englishmen to be extremely wary of concentrated military forces run by the state and to be jealous of their arms. They accordingly obtained an assurance from William and Mary, in the Declaration of Right (which was codified as the English Bill of Rights), that Protestants would never be disarmed: "That the subjects which are Protestants may have arms for their defense suitable to their conditions and as allowed by law." 1 W. & M., c. 2, §7, in 3 Eng. Stat. at Large 441 (1689). This right has long been understood to be the predecessor to our Second Amendment. See E. Dumbauld, The Bill of Rights and What It Means Today 51 (1957); W. Rawle, A View of the Constitution of the United States of America 122 (1825) (hereinafter Rawle). It was clearly an individual right, having nothing whatever to do with service in a militia. To be sure, it was an individual right not available to the whole population, given that it was restricted to Protestants, and like all written English rights it was held only against the Crown, not Parliament. See Schwoerer, To Hold and Bear Arms: The English Perspective, in Bogus 207, 218; but see 3 J. Story, Commentaries on the Constitution of the United States §1858 (1833) (hereinafter Story) (contending that the "right to bear arms" is a "limitatio[n] upon the power of parliament" as well). But it was secured to them as individuals, according to "libertarian political principles," not as members of a fighting force. Schwoerer, Declaration of Rights, at 283; see also *id.*, at 78; G. Jellinek, The Declaration of the Rights of Man and of Citizens 49, and n. 7 (1901) (reprinted 1979).

By the time of the founding, the right to have arms had become fundamental for English subjects. See Malcolm 122–134. Blackstone, whose works, we have said, "constituted the preeminent authority on English law for the founding generation," *Alden* v. *Maine*, 527 U. S. 706, 715 (1999), cited the arms provision of the Bill of Rights as one of the fundamental rights of Englishmen. See 1 Blackstone 136, 139–140 (1765). His description of it cannot possibly be thought to tie it to militia or military service. It was, he said, "the natural right of resistance and self-preservation," *id.*, at 139, and "the right of having and using arms for self-preservation and defence," *id.*, at 140; see also 3 *id.*, at 2–4 (1768). Other contemporary authorities concurred. See G. Sharp, Tracts, Concerning the Ancient and Only True Legal Means of National Defence, by a Free Militia 17–18, 27 (3d ed. 1782); 2 J. de Lolme, The Rise and Progress of the English Constitution 886–887 (1784) (A. Stephens ed. 1838); W. Blizard, Desultory Reflections on Police 59–60 (1785). Thus, the right secured in 1689 as a result of the Stuarts' abuses was by the time of the founding understood to be an individual right protecting against both public and private violence.

And, of course, what the Stuarts had tried to do to their political enemies, George III had tried to do to the colonists. In the tumultuous decades of the 1760's and 1770's, the Crown began to disarm the inhabitants of the most rebellious areas. That provoked polemical reactions by Americans invoking their rights as Englishmen to keep arms. A New York article of April 1769 said that "[i]t is a natural right which the people have reserved to themselves, confirmed by the Bill of Rights, to keep arms for their own defence." A Journal of the Times: Mar. 17, New York Journal, Supp. 1, Apr. 13, 1769, in Boston Under Military Rule 79 (O. Dickerson ed. 1936); see also, *e.g.*, Shippen, Boston Gazette, Jan. 30, 1769, in 1 The Writings of Samuel Adams 299 (H. Cushing ed. 1968). They understood the right to enable individuals to defend themselves. As the most important early American edition of Blackstone's Commentaries (by the law professor and former Antifederalist St. George Tucker) made clear in the notes to the description of the arms right, Americans understood the "right of self-preservation" as permitting a citizen to "repe[l] force by force" when "the intervention of society in his behalf, may be too late to prevent an injury." 1 Blackstone's Commentaries 145–146, n. 42 (1803) (hereinafter Tucker's Blackstone). See also W. Duer, Outlines of the Constitutional Jurisprudence of the United States 31–32 (1833).

There seems to us no doubt, on the basis of both text and history, that the Second Amendment conferred an individual right to keep and bear arms. Of course the right was not unlimited, just as the First Amendment's right of free speech was not, see, *e.g.*, *United States* v. *Williams*, 553 U. S. ___ (2008). Thus, we do not read the Second Amendment to protect the right of citizens to carry arms for *any sort* of confrontation, just as we do not read the First Amendment to protect the right of citizens to speak for *any purpose*. Before turning to limitations upon the individual right, however, we must determine whether the prefatory clause of the Second Amendment comports with our interpretation of the operative clause.

2. Prefatory Clause.

The prefatory clause reads: "A well regulated Militia, being necessary to the security of a free State . . . ."

a. "Well-Regulated Militia." In *United States* v. *Miller*, 307 U. S. 174, 179 (1939), we explained that "the Militia comprised all males physically capable of acting in concert for the common defense." That definition comports with founding-era sources. See, *e.g.*, Webster ("The militia of a country are the able bodied men organized into companies, regiments and brigades . . . and required by law to attend military exercises on certain days only, but at other times left to pursue their usual occupations"); The Federalist No. 46, pp. 329, 334 (B. Wright ed. 1961) (J. Madison) ("near half a million of citizens with arms in their hands"); Letter to Destutt de Tracy (Jan. 26, 1811), in The Portable Thomas Jefferson 520, 524 (M. Peterson ed. 1975) ("[T]he militia of the State, that is to say, of every man in it able to bear arms").

Petitioners take a seemingly narrower view of the militia, stating that "[m]ilitias are the state- and congressionally-regulated military forces described in the Militia Clauses (art. I, §8, cls. 15–16)." Brief for Petitioners 12. Although we agree with petitioners' interpretive assumption that "militia" means the same thing in Article I and the Second Amendment, we believe that petitioners identify the wrong thing, namely, the organized militia. Unlike armies and navies, which Congress is given the power to create ("to raise . . . Armies"; "to provide . . . a Navy," Art. I, §8, cls. 12–13), the militia is assumed by Article I already to be *in existence*. Congress is given the power to "provide for calling forth the militia," §8, cl. 15; and the power not to create, but to "organiz[e]" it—and not to organize "a" militia, which is what one would expect if the militia were to be a federal creation, but to organize "the" militia, connoting a body already in existence, *ibid.*, cl. 16. This is fully consistent with the ordinary definition of the militia as all able-bodied men. From that pool, Congress has plenary power to organize the units that will make up an effective fighting force. That is what Congress did in the first militia Act, which specified that "each and every free able-bodied white male citizen of the respective states, resident therein, who is or shall be of the age of eighteen years, and under the age of forty-five years (except as is herein after excepted) shall severally and respectively be enrolled in the militia." Act of May 8, 1792, 1 Stat. 271. To be sure, Congress need not conscript every able-bodied man into the militia, because nothing in Article I suggests that in exercising its power to organize, discipline, and arm the militia, Congress must focus upon the entire body. Although the militia consists of all able-bodied men, the federally organized militia may consist of a subset of them.

Finally, the adjective "well-regulated" implies nothing more than the imposition of proper discipline and training. See Johnson 1619 ("Regulate": "To adjust by rule or method"); Rawle 121–122; cf. Va. Declaration of Rights §13 (1776), in 7 Thorpe 3812, 3814 (referring to "a well-regulated militia, composed of the body of the people, trained to arms").

b. "Security of a Free State." The phrase "security of a free state" meant "security of a free polity," not security of each of the several States as the dissent below argued, see 478 F. 3d, at 405, and n. 10. Joseph Story wrote in his treatise on the Constitution that "the word 'state' is used in various senses [and in] its most enlarged sense, it means the people composing a particular nation or community." 1 Story §208; see also 3 *id.*, §1890 (in reference to the Second Amendment's prefatory clause: "The militia is the natural defence of a free country"). It is true that the term "State" elsewhere in the Constitution refers to individual States, but the phrase "security of a free state" and close variations seem to have been terms of art in 18th-century political discourse, meaning a "'free country'" or free polity. See Volokh, "Necessary to the Security of a Free State," 83 Notre Dame L. Rev. 1, 5 (2007); see, *e.g.*, 4 Blackstone 151 (1769); Brutus Essay III (Nov. 15, 1787), in The Essential Antifederalist 251, 253 (W. Allen & G. Lloyd eds., 2d ed. 2002). Moreover, the other instances of "state" in the Constitution are typically accompanied by modifiers making clear that the reference is to the several States—"each state," "several states," "any state," "that state," "particular states," "one state," "no state." And the presence of the term "foreign state" in Article I and Article III shows that the word "state" did not have a single meaning in the Constitution.

There are many reasons why the militia was thought to be "necessary to the security of a free state." See 3 Story §1890. First, of course, it is useful in repelling invasions and suppressing insurrections. Second, it renders large standing armies unnecessary—an argument that Alexander Hamilton made in favor of federal control over the militia. The Federalist No. 29, pp. 226, 227 (B. Wright ed. 1961) (A. Hamilton). Third, when the able-bodied men of a nation are trained in arms and organized, they are better able to resist tyranny.

3. Relationship between Prefatory Clause and Operative Clause

We reach the question, then: Does the preface fit with an operative clause that creates an individual right to keep and bear arms? It fits perfectly, once one knows the history that the founding generation knew and that we have described above. That history showed that the way tyrants had eliminated a militia consisting of all the able-bodied men was not by banning the militia but simply by taking away the people's arms, enabling a select militia or standing army to suppress political opponents. This is what had occurred in England that prompted codification of the right to have arms in the English Bill of Rights.

The debate with respect to the right to keep and bear arms, as with other guarantees in the Bill of Rights, was not over whether it was desirable (all agreed that it was) but over whether it needed to be codified in the Constitution. During the 1788 ratification debates, the fear that the federal government would disarm the people in order to impose rule through a standing army or select militia was pervasive in Antifederalist rhetoric. See, *e.g.*, Letters from The Federal Farmer

III (Oct. 10, 1787), in 2 The Complete Anti-Federalist 234, 242 (H. Storing ed. 1981). John Smilie, for example, worried not only that Congress's "command of the militia" could be used to create a "select militia," or to have "no militia at all," but also, as a separate concern, that "[w]hen a select militia is formed; the people in general may be disarmed." 2 Documentary History of the Ratification of the Constitution 508–509 (M. Jensen ed. 1976) (hereinafter Documentary Hist.). Federalists responded that because Congress was given no power to abridge the ancient right of individuals to keep and bear arms, such a force could never oppress the people. See, *e.g.*, A Pennsylvanian III (Feb. 20, 1788), in The Origin of the Second Amendment 275, 276 (D. Young ed., 2d ed. 2001) (hereinafter Young); White, To the Citizens of Virginia, Feb. 22, 1788, in *id.*, at 280, 281; A Citizen of America, (Oct. 10, 1787) in *id.*, at 38, 40; Remarks on the Amendments to the federal Constitution, Nov. 7, 1788, in *id.*, at 556. It was understood across the political spectrum that the right helped to secure the ideal of a citizen militia, which might be necessary to oppose an oppressive military force if the constitutional order broke down.

It is therefore entirely sensible that the Second Amendment's prefatory clause announces the purpose for which the right was codified: to prevent elimination of the militia. The prefatory clause does not suggest that preserving the militia was the only reason Americans valued the ancient right; most undoubtedly thought it even more important for self-defense and hunting. But the threat that the new Federal Government would destroy the citizens' militia by taking away their arms was the reason that right—unlike some other English rights—was codified in a written Constitution. Justice Breyer's assertion that individual self-defense is merely a "subsidiary interest" of the right to keep and bear arms, see *post*, at 36, is profoundly mistaken. He bases that assertion solely upon the prologue—but that can only show that self-defense had little to do with the right's *codification;* it was the *central component* of the right itself.

Besides ignoring the historical reality that the Second Amendment was not intended to lay down a "novel principl[e]" but rather codified a right "inherited from our English ancestors," *Robertson* v. *Baldwin*, 165 U. S. 275, 281 (1897), petitioners' interpretation does not even achieve the narrower purpose that prompted codification of the right. If, as they believe, the Second Amendment right is no more than the right to keep and use weapons as a member of an organized militia, see Brief for Petititioners 8—if, that is, the *organized* militia is the sole institutional beneficiary of the Second Amendment's guarantee—it does not assure the existence of a "citizens' militia" as a safeguard against tyranny. For Congress retains plenary authority to organize the militia, which must include the authority to say who will belong to the organized force. That is why the first Militia Act's requirement that only whites enroll caused States to amend their militia laws to exclude free blacks. See Siegel, The Federal Government's Power to Enact Color-Conscious Laws, 92 Nw. U. L. Rev. 477, 521–525 (1998). Thus, if petitioners are correct, the Second Amendment protects citizens' right to use a gun in an organization from which Congress has plenary authority to exclude them. It guarantees a select militia of the sort the Stuart kings found useful, but not the people's militia that was the concern of the founding generation.

B

Our interpretation is confirmed by analogous arms-bearing rights in state constitutions that preceded and immediately followed adoption of the Second Amendment. Four States adopted analogues to the Federal Second Amendment in the period between independence and the ratification of the Bill of Rights. Two of them—Pennsylvania and Vermont—clearly adopted individual rights unconnected to militia service. Pennsylvania's Declaration of Rights of 1776 said: "That the people have a right to bear arms *for the defence of themselves*, and the state . . . ." §XIII, in 5 Thorpe 3082, 3083 (emphasis added). In 1777, Vermont adopted the identical provision, except for inconsequential differences in punctuation and capitalization. See Vt. Const., ch. 1, §15, in 6 *id.*, at 3741.

North Carolina also codified a right to bear arms in 1776: "That the people have a right to bear arms, for the defence of the State . . . ." Declaration of Rights §XVII, in *id.*, at 2787, 2788. This could plausibly be read to support only a right to bear arms in a militia—but that is a peculiar way to make the point in a constitution that elsewhere repeatedly mentions the militia explicitly. See §§14, 18, 35, in 5 *id.*, 2789, 2791, 2793. Many colonial statutes required individual arms-bearing for public-safety reasons—such as the 1770 Georgia law that "for the security and *defence of this prov-*

ince from internal dangers and insurrections" required those men who qualified for militia duty individually "to carry fire arms" "to places of public worship." 19 Colonial Records of the State of Georgia 137–139 (A. Candler ed. 1911 (pt. 2)) (emphasis added). That broad public-safety understanding was the connotation given to the North Carolina right by that State's Supreme Court in 1843. See *State* v. *Huntly*, 3 Ired. 418, 422–423.

The 1780 Massachusetts Constitution presented another variation on the theme: "The people have a right to keep and to bear arms for the common defence...." Pt. First, Art. XVII, in 3 Thorpe 1888, 1892. Once again, if one gives narrow meaning to the phrase "common defence" this can be thought to limit the right to the bearing of arms in a state-organized military force. But once again the State's highest court thought otherwise. Writing for the court in an 1825 libel case, Chief Justice Parker wrote: "The liberty of the press was to be unrestrained, but he who used it was to be responsible in cases of its abuse; like the right to keep fire arms, which does not protect him who uses them for annoyance or destruction." *Commonwealth* v. *Blanding*, 20 Mass. 304, 313–314. The analogy makes no sense if firearms could not be used for any individual purpose at all. See also Kates, Handgun Prohibition and the Original Meaning of the Second Amendment, 82 Mich. L. Rev. 204, 244 (1983) (19th-century courts never read "common defence" to limit the use of weapons to militia service).

We therefore believe that the most likely reading of all four of these pre-Second Amendment state constitutional provisions is that they secured an individual right to bear arms for defensive purposes. Other States did not include rights to bear arms in their pre-1789 constitutions—although in Virginia a Second Amendment analogue was proposed (unsuccessfully) by Thomas Jefferson. (It read: "No freeman shall ever be debarred the use of arms [within his own lands or tenements]." The Papers of Thomas Jefferson 344 (J. Boyd ed. 1950)).

Between 1789 and 1820, nine States adopted Second Amendment analogues. Four of them—Kentucky, Ohio, Indiana, and Missouri—referred to the right of the people to "bear arms in defence of themselves and the State." See n. 8, *supra*. Another three States—Mississippi, Connecticut, and Alabama—used the even more individualistic phrasing that each citizen has the "right to bear arms in defence of himself and the State."

See *ibid*. Finally, two States—Tennessee and Maine—used the "common defence" language of Massachusetts. See Tenn. Const., Art. XI, §26 (1796), in 6 Thorpe 3414, 3424; Me. Const., Art. I, §16 (1819), in 3 *id*., at 1646, 1648. That of the nine state constitutional protections for the right to bear arms enacted immediately after 1789 at least seven unequivocally protected an individual citizen's right to self-defense is strong evidence that that is how the founding generation conceived of the right. And with one possible exception that we discuss in Part II–D–2, 19th-century courts and commentators interpreted these state constitutional provisions to protect an individual right to use arms for self-defense. See n. 9, *supra; Simpson* v. *State*, 5 Yer. 356, 360 (Tenn. 1833).

The historical narrative that petitioners must endorse would thus treat the Federal Second Amendment as an odd outlier, protecting a right unknown in state constitutions or at English common law, based on little more than an overreading of the prefatory clause.

C

Justice Stevens relies on the drafting history of the Second Amendment—the various proposals in the state conventions and the debates in Congress. It is dubious to rely on such history to interpret a text that was widely understood to codify a pre-existing right, rather than to fashion a new one. But even assuming that this legislative history is relevant, Justice Stevens flatly misreads the historical record.

It is true, as Justice Stevens says, that there was concern that the Federal Government would abolish the institution of the state militia. See *post*, at 20. That concern found expression, however, *not* in the various Second Amendment precursors proposed in the State conventions, but in separate structural provisions that would have given the States concurrent and seemingly non-pre-emptible authority to organize, discipline, and arm the militia when the Federal Government failed to do so. See Veit 17, 20 (Virginia proposal); 4 J. Eliot, The Debates in the Several State Conventions on the Adoption of the Federal Constitution 244, 245 (2d ed. 1836) (reprinted 1941) (North Carolina proposal); see also 2 Documentary Hist. 624 (Pennsylvania minority's proposal). The Second Amendment precursors, by contrast, referred to the individual English right already codified in two (and probably four) State constitutions. The Federalist-dominated first Congress chose to reject virtually all major structural revisions favored by the Antifederalists, including the proposed militia amendments. Rather, it adopted primarily the popular and uncontroversial (though, in the Federalists' view, unnecessary) individual-rights amendments. The Second Amendment right, protecting only individuals' liberty to keep and carry arms, did nothing to assuage Antifederalists' concerns about federal control of the militia. See, *e.g.*, Centinel, Revived, No. XXIX, Philadelphia Independent Gazetteer, Sept. 9, 1789, in Young 711, 712.

Justice Stevens thinks it significant that the Virginia, New York, and North Carolina Second Amendment proposals were "embedded . . . within a group of principles that are distinctly military in meaning," such as statements about the danger of standing armies. *Post*, at 22. But so was the highly influential minority proposal in Pennsylvania, yet that proposal, with its reference to hunting, plainly referred to an individual right. See 2 Documentary Hist. 624. Other than that erroneous point, Justice Stevens has brought forward absolutely no evidence that those proposals conferred only a right to carry arms in a militia. By contrast, New Hampshire's proposal, the Pennsylvania minority's proposal, and Samuel Adams' proposal in Massachusetts unequivocally referred to individual rights, as did two state constitutional provisions at the time. See Veit 16, 17 (New Hampshire proposal); 6 Documentary Hist. 1452, 1453 (J. Kaminski & G. Saladino eds. 2000) (Samuel Adams' proposal). Justice Stevens' view thus relies on the proposition, unsupported by any evidence, that different people of the founding period had vastly different conceptions of the right to keep and bear arms. That simply does not comport with our longstanding view that the Bill of Rights codified venerable, widely understood liberties.

D

We now address how the Second Amendment was interpreted from immediately after its ratification through the end of the 19th century. Before proceeding, however, we take issue with Justice Stevens' equating of these sources with postenactment legislative history, a comparison that betrays a fundamental misunderstanding of a court's interpretive task. See *post*, at 27, n. 28. "Legislative history," of course, refers to the pre-enactment statements of those who drafted or voted for a law; it is considered persuasive by some, not because they reflect the general understanding of the disputed terms, but because the legislators who heard or read those statements presumably voted with that understanding. *Ibid*. "Postenactment legislative history," *ibid.*, a deprecatory contradiction in terms, refers to statements of those who drafted or voted for the law that are made after its enactment and hence could have had no effect on the congressional vote. It most certainly does not refer to the examination of a variety of legal and other sources to determine *the public understanding* of a legal text in the period after its enactment or ratification. That sort of inquiry is a critical tool of constitutional interpretation. As we will show, virtually all interpreters of the Second Amendment in the century after its enactment interpreted the amendment as we do.

1. Post-ratification Commentary

Three important founding-era legal scholars interpreted the Second Amendment in published writings. All three understood it to protect an individual right unconnected with militia service.

St. George Tucker's version of Blackstone's Commentaries, as we explained above, conceived of the Blackstonian arms right as necessary for self-defense. He equated that right, absent the religious and class-based restrictions, with the Second Amendment. See 2 Tucker's Blackstone 143. In Note D, entitled, "View of the Constitution of the United States," Tucker elaborated on the Second Amendment: "This may be considered as the true palladium of liberty. . . . The right to self-defence is the first law of nature: in most governments it has been the study of rulers to confine the right within the narrowest limits possible. Wherever standing armies are kept up, and the right of the people to keep and bear arms is, under any colour or pretext whatsoever, prohibited, liberty, if not already annihilated, is on the brink of destruction." 1 *id.*, at App. 300 (ellipsis in original). He believed that the English game laws had abridged the right by prohibiting "keeping a gun or other engine for the destruction of game." *Ibid*; see also 2 *id.*, at 143, and nn. 40 and 41. He later grouped the right with some of the individual rights included in the First Amendment and said that if "a law be passed by congress, prohibiting" any of those rights, it would "be the province of the judiciary to pronounce whether any such act were constitutional, or not; and if not, to acquit the accused.

. . ." 1 *id.*, at App. 357. It is unlikely that Tucker was referring to a person's being "accused" of violating a law making it a crime to bear arms in a state militia.

In 1825, William Rawle, a prominent lawyer who had been a member of the Pennsylvania Assembly that ratified the Bill of Rights, published an influential treatise, which analyzed the Second Amendment as follows:

"The first [principle] is a declaration that a well regulated militia is necessary to the security of a free state; a proposition from which few will dissent. . . .

"The corollary, from the first position is, that the right of the people to keep and bear arms shall not be infringed.

"The prohibition is general. No clause in the constitution could by any rule of construction be conceived to give to congress a power to disarm the people. Such a flagitious attempt could only be made under some general pretence by a state legislature. But if in any blind pursuit of inordinate power, either should attempt it, this amendment may be appealed to as a restraint on both." Rawle 121–122.

Like Tucker, Rawle regarded the English game laws as violating the right codified in the Second Amendment. See *id.*, 122–123. Rawle clearly differentiated between the people's right to bear arms and their service in a militia: "In a people permitted and accustomed to bear arms, we have the rudiments of a militia, which properly consists of armed citizens, divided into military bands, and instructed at least in part, in the use of arms for the purposes of war." *Id.*, at 140. Rawle further said that the Second Amendment right ought not "be abused to the disturbance of the public peace," such as by assembling with other armed individuals "for an unlawful purpose"—statements that make no sense if the right does not extend to *any* individual purpose.

Joseph Story published his famous Commentaries on the Constitution of the United States in 1833. Justice Stevens suggests that "[t]here is not so much as a whisper" in Story's explanation of the Second Amendment that favors the individual-rights view. *Post*, at 34. That is wrong. Story explained that the English Bill of Rights had also included a "right to bear arms," a right that, as we have discussed, had nothing to do with militia service. 3 Story §1858. He then equated the English right with the Second Amendment:

"§1891. A similar provision [to the Second Amendment] in favour of protestants (for to them it is confined) is to be found in the bill of rights of 1688, it being declared, 'that the subjects, which are protestants, may have arms for their defence suitable to their condition, and as allowed by law.' But under various pretences the effect of this provision has been greatly narrowed; and it is at present in England more nominal than real, as a defensive privilege." (Footnotes omitted.)

This comparison to the Declaration of Right would not make sense if the Second Amendment right was the right to use a gun in a militia, which was plainly not what the English right protected. As the Tennessee Supreme Court recognized 38 years after Story wrote his Commentaries, "[t]he passage from Story, shows clearly that this right was intended . . . and was guaranteed to, and to be exercised and enjoyed by the citizen as such, and not by him as a soldier, or in defense solely of his political rights." *Andrews* v. *State*, 50 Tenn. 165, 183 (1871). Story's Commentaries also cite as support Tucker and Rawle, both of whom clearly viewed the right as unconnected to militia service. See 3 Story §1890, n. 2; §1891, n. 3. In addition, in a shorter 1840 work Story wrote: "One of the ordinary modes, by which tyrants accomplish their purposes without resistance, is, by disarming the people, and making it an offence to keep arms, and by substituting a regular army in the stead of a resort to the militia." A Familiar Exposition of the Constitution of the United States §450 (reprinted in 1986).

Antislavery advocates routinely invoked the right to bear arms for self-defense. Joel Tiffany, for example, citing Blackstone's description of the right, wrote that "the right to keep and bear arms, also implies the right to use them if necessary in self defence; without this right to use the guaranty would have hardly been worth the paper it consumed." A Treatise on the Unconstitutionality of American Slavery 117–118 (1849); see also L. Spooner, The Unconstitutionality of Slavery 116 (1845) (right enables "personal defence"). In his famous Senate speech about the 1856 "Bleeding Kansas" conflict, Charles Sumner proclaimed:

"The rifle has ever been the companion of the pioneer and, under God, his tutelary protector against the red man and the beast of the forest. Never was this efficient weapon more needed in just self-defence, than now in Kansas, and at least one article in our National

Constitution must be blotted out, before the complete right to it can in any way be impeached. And yet such is the madness of the hour, that, in defiance of the solemn guarantee, embodied in the Amendments to the Constitution, that 'the right of the people to keep and bear arms shall not be infringed,' the people of Kansas have been arraigned for keeping and bearing them, and the Senator from South Carolina has had the face to say openly, on this floor, that they should be disarmed—of course, that the fanatics of Slavery, his allies and constituents, may meet no impediment." The Crime Against Kansas, May 19–20, 1856, in American Speeches: Political Oratory from the Revolution to the Civil War 553, 606–607 (2006).

We have found only one early 19th-century commentator who clearly conditioned the right to keep and bear arms upon service in the militia—and he recognized that the prevailing view was to the contrary. "The provision of the constitution, declaring the right of the people to keep and bear arms, &c. was probably intended to apply to the right of the people to bear arms for such [militia-related] purposes only, and not to prevent congress or the legislatures of the different states from enacting laws to prevent the citizens from always going armed. A different construction however has been given to it." B. Oliver, The Rights of an American Citizen 177 (1832).

2. Pre-Civil War Case Law

The 19th-century cases that interpreted the Second Amendment universally support an individual right unconnected to militia service. In *Houston* v. *Moore*, 5 Wheat. 1, 24 (1820), this Court held that States have concurrent power over the militia, at least where not pre-empted by Congress. Agreeing in dissent that States could "organize, discipline, and arm" the militia in the absence of conflicting federal regulation, Justice Story said that the Second Amendment "may not, perhaps, be thought to have any important bearing on this point. If it have, it confirms and illustrates, rather than impugns the reasoning already suggested." *Id.*, at 51–53. Of course, if the Amendment simply "protect[ed] the right of the people of each of the several States to maintain a well-regulated militia," *post*, at 1 (Stevens, J., dissenting), it would have enormous and obvious bearing on the point. But the Court and Story derived the States' power over the militia from the nonexclusive nature of federal power, not from the Second Amendment, whose preamble merely "confirms and illustrates" the importance of the militia. Even clearer was Justice Baldwin. In the famous fugitive-slave case of *Johnson* v. *Tompkins*, 13 F. Cas. 840, 850, 852 (CC Pa. 1833), Baldwin, sitting as a circuit judge, cited both the Second Amendment and the Pennsylvania analogue for his conclusion that a citizen has "a right to carry arms in defence of his property or person, and to use them, if either were assailed with such force, numbers or violence as made it necessary for the protection or safety of either."

Many early 19th-century state cases indicated that the Second Amendment right to bear arms was an individual right unconnected to militia service, though subject to certain restrictions. A Virginia case in 1824 holding that the Constitution did not extend to free blacks explained that "numerous restrictions imposed on [blacks] in our Statute Book, many of which are inconsistent with the letter and spirit of the Constitution, both of this State and of the United States as respects the free whites, demonstrate, that, here, those instruments have not been considered to extend equally to both classes of our population. We will only instance the restriction upon the migration of free blacks into this State, and upon their right to bear arms." *Aldridge* v. *Commonwealth*, 2 Va. Cas. 447, 449 (Gen. Ct.). The claim was obviously not that blacks were prevented from carrying guns in the militia. See also *Waters* v. *State*, 1 Gill 302, 309 (Md. 1843) (because free blacks were treated as a "dangerous population," "laws have been passed to prevent their migration into this State; to make it unlawful for them to bear arms; to guard even their religious assemblages with peculiar watchfulness"). An 1829 decision by the Supreme Court of Michigan said: "The constitution of the United States also grants to the citizen the right to keep and bear arms. But the grant of this privilege cannot be construed into the right in him who keeps a gun to destroy his neighbor. No rights are intended to be granted by the constitution for an unlawful or unjustifiable purpose." *United States* v. *Sheldon*, in 5 Transactions of the Supreme Court of the Territory of Michigan 337, 346 (W. Blume ed. 1940) (hereinafter Blume). It is not possible to read this as discussing anything other than an individual right unconnected to militia service. If it did have to do with militia service, the limitation upon it would not be any "unlawful or unjustifiable purpose," but any nonmilitary purpose whatsoever.

In *Nunn v. State*, 1 Ga. 243, 251 (1846), the Georgia Supreme Court construed the Second Amendment as protecting the "*natural* right of self-defence" and therefore struck down a ban on carrying pistols openly. Its opinion perfectly captured the way in which the operative clause of the Second Amendment furthers the purpose announced in the prefatory clause, in continuity with the English right:

"The right of the whole people, old and young, men, women and boys, and not militia only, to keep and bear *arms* of every description, and not *such* merely as are used by the *militia*, shall not be *infringed*, curtailed, or broken in upon, in the smallest degree; and all this for the important end to be attained: the rearing up and qualifying a well-regulated militia, so vitally necessary to the security of a free State. Our opinion is, that any law, State or Federal, is repugnant to the Constitution, and void, which contravenes this *right*, originally belonging to our forefathers, trampled under foot by Charles I. and his two wicked sons and successors, re-established by the revolution of 1688, conveyed to this land of liberty by the colonists, and finally incorporated conspicuously in our own Magna Charta!"

Likewise, in *State v. Chandler*, 5 La. Ann. 489, 490 (1850), the Louisiana Supreme Court held that citizens had a right to carry arms openly: "This is the right guaranteed by the Constitution of the United States, and which is calculated to incite men to a manly and noble defence of themselves, if necessary, and of their country, without any tendency to secret advantages and unmanly assassinations."

Those who believe that the Second Amendment preserves only a militia-centered right place great reliance on the Tennessee Supreme Court's 1840 decision in *Aymette v. State*, 21 Tenn. 154. The case does not stand for that broad proposition; in fact, the case does not mention the word "militia" at all, except in its quoting of the Second Amendment. *Aymette* held that the state constitutional guarantee of the right to "bear" arms did not prohibit the banning of concealed weapons. The opinion first recognized that both the state right and the federal right were descendents of the 1689 English right, but (erroneously, and contrary to virtually all other authorities) read that right to refer only to "protect[ion of] the public liberty" and "keep[ing] in awe those in power," *id.*, at 158. The court then adopted a sort of middle position, whereby citizens were permitted to carry arms openly, unconnected with any service in a formal militia, but were given the right to use them only for the military purpose of banding together to oppose tyranny. This odd reading of the right is, to be sure, not the one we adopt—but it is not petitioners' reading either. More importantly, seven years earlier the Tennessee Supreme Court had treated the state constitutional provision as conferring a right "of all the free citizens of the State to keep and bear arms for their defence," *Simpson*, 5 Yer., at 360; and 21 years later the court held that the "keep" portion of the state constitutional right included the right to personal self-defense: "[T]he right to keep arms involves, necessarily, the right to use such arms for all the ordinary purposes, and in all the ordinary modes usual in the country, and to which arms are adapted, limited by the duties of a good citizen in times of peace." *Andrews*, 50 Tenn., at 178; see also *ibid.* (equating state provision with Second Amendment).

3. Post-Civil War Legislation.

In the aftermath of the Civil War, there was an outpouring of discussion of the Second Amendment in Congress and in public discourse, as people debated whether and how to secure constitutional rights for newly free slaves. See generally S. Halbrook, Freedmen, the Fourteenth Amendment, and the Right to Bear Arms, 1866–1876 (1998) (hereinafter Halbrook); Brief for Institute for Justice as *Amicus Curiae*. Since those discussions took place 75 years after the ratification of the Second Amendment, they do not provide as much insight into its original meaning as earlier sources. Yet those born and educated in the early 19th century faced a widespread effort to limit arms ownership by a large number of citizens; their understanding of the origins and continuing significance of the Amendment is instructive.

Blacks were routinely disarmed by Southern States after the Civil War. Those who opposed these injustices frequently stated that they infringed blacks' constitutional right to keep and bear arms. Needless to say, the claim was not that blacks were being prohibited from carrying arms in an organized state militia. A Report of the Commission of the Freedmen's Bureau in 1866 stated plainly: "[T]he civil law [of Kentucky] prohibits the colored man from bearing arms.... Their arms are taken from them by the civil authorities.... Thus, the right of the people to keep and bear arms as provided in the Constitution is *infringed*." H. R. Exec. Doc. No. 70, 39th Cong., 1st Sess., 233, 236. A joint congressional Report decried:

"in some parts of [South Carolina], armed parties are, without proper authority, engaged in seizing all firearms found in the hands of the freemen. Such conduct is in clear and direct violation of their personal rights as guaranteed by the Constitution of the United States, which declares that 'the right of the people to keep and bear arms shall not be infringed.' The freedmen of South Carolina have shown by their peaceful and orderly conduct that they can safely be trusted with firearms, and they need them to kill game for subsistence, and to protect their crops from destruction by birds and animals." Joint Comm. on Reconstruction, H. R. Rep. No. 30, 39th Cong., 1st Sess., pt. 2, p. 229 (1866) (Proposed Circular of Brigadier General R. Saxton).

The view expressed in these statements was widely reported and was apparently widely held. For example, an editorial in The Loyal Georgian (Augusta) on February 3, 1866, assured blacks that "[a]ll men, without distinction of color, have the right to keep and bear arms to defend their homes, families or themselves." Halbrook 19.

Congress enacted the Freedmen's Bureau Act on July 16, 1866. Section 14 stated:

"[T]he right . . . to have full and equal benefit of all laws and proceedings concerning personal liberty, personal security, and the acquisition, enjoyment, and disposition of estate, real and personal, including the constitutional right to bear arms, shall be secured to and enjoyed by all the citizens . . . without respect to race or color, or previous condition of slavery. . . . " 14 Stat. 176–177.

The understanding that the Second Amendment gave freed blacks the right to keep and bear arms was reflected in congressional discussion of the bill, with even an opponent of it saying that the founding generation "were for every man bearing his arms about him and keeping them in his house, his castle, for his own defense." Cong. Globe, 39th Cong., 1st Sess., 362, 371 (1866) (Sen. Davis).

Similar discussion attended the passage of the Civil Rights Act of 1871 and the Fourteenth Amendment. For example, Representative Butler said of the Act: "Section eight is intended to enforce the well-known constitutional provision guaranteeing the right of the citizen to 'keep and bear arms,' and provides that whoever shall take away, by force or violence, or by threats and intimidation, the arms and weapons which any person may have for his defense, shall be deemed guilty of larceny of the same." H. R. Rep. No. 37, 41st Cong., 3d Sess., pp. 7–8 (1871). With respect to the proposed Amendment, Senator Pomeroy described as one of the three "indispensable" "safeguards of liberty . . . under the Constitution" a man's "right to bear arms for the defense of himself and family and his homestead." Cong. Globe, 39th Cong., 1st Sess., 1182 (1866). Representative Nye thought the Fourteenth Amendment unnecessary because "[a]s citizens of the United States [blacks] have equal right to protection, and to keep and bear arms for self-defense." *Id.*, at 1073 (1866).

It was plainly the understanding in the post-Civil War Congress that the Second Amendment protected an individual right to use arms for self-defense.

4. Post-Civil War Commentators.

Every late-19th-century legal scholar that we have read interpreted the Second Amendment to secure an individual right unconnected with militia service. The most famous was the judge and professor Thomas Cooley, who wrote a massively popular 1868 Treatise on Constitutional Limitations. Concerning the Second Amendment it said:

"Among the other defences to personal liberty should be mentioned the right of the people to keep and bear arms. . . . The alternative to a standing army is 'a well-regulated militia,' but this cannot exist unless the people are trained to bearing arms. How far it is in the power of the legislature to regulate this right, we shall not undertake to say, as happily there has been very little occasion to discuss that subject by the courts." *Id.*, at 350.

That Cooley understood the right not as connected to militia service, but as securing the militia by ensuring a populace familiar with arms, is made even clearer in his 1880 work, General Principles of Constitutional Law. The Second Amendment, he said, "was adopted with some modification and enlargement from the English Bill of Rights of 1688, where it stood as a protest against arbitrary action of the overturned dynasty in disarming the people." *Id.*, at 270. In a section entitled "The Right in General," he continued:

"It might be supposed from the phraseology of this provision that the right to keep and bear arms was only guaranteed to the militia; but this would be an interpretation not warranted by the intent. The militia, as has been elsewhere explained, consists of those persons who, under the law, are liable to the performance of military duty, and are officered and enrolled for service when called upon. But the law may make provision for the enrolment of all who are fit to perform military duty, or of a small number only, or it may wholly omit to make any provision at all; and if the right were limited to those enrolled, the purpose of this guaranty might be defeated altogether by the action or neglect to act of the government it was meant to hold in check. The meaning of the provision undoubtedly is, that the people, from whom the militia must be taken, shall have the right to keep and bear arms; and they need no permission or regulation of law for the purpose. But this enables government to have a well-regulated militia; for to bear arms implies something more than the mere keeping; it implies the learning to handle and use them in a way that makes those who keep them ready for their efficient use; in other words, it implies the right to meet for voluntary discipline in arms, observing in doing so the laws of public order." *Id.*, at 271.

All other post-Civil War 19th-century sources we have found concurred with Cooley. One example from each decade will convey the general flavor:

"[The purpose of the Second Amendment is] to secure a well-armed militia.... But a militia would be useless unless the citizens were enabled to exercise themselves in the use of warlike weapons. To preserve this privilege, and to secure to the people the ability to oppose themselves in military force against the usurpations of government, as well as against enemies from without, that government is forbidden by any law or proceeding to invade or destroy the right to keep and bear arms.... The clause is analogous to the one securing the freedom of speech and of the press. Freedom, not license, is secured; the fair use, not the libellous abuse, is protected." J. Pomeroy, An Introduction to the Constitutional Law of the United States 152–153 (1868) (hereinafter Pomeroy).

"As the Constitution of the United States, and the constitutions of several of the states, in terms more or less comprehensive, declare the right of the people to keep and bear arms, it has been a subject of grave discussion, in some of the state courts, whether a statute prohibiting persons, when not on a journey, or as travellers, from *wearing or carrying concealed weapons*, be constitutional. There has been a great difference of opinion on the question." 2 J. Kent, Commentaries on American Law *340, n. 2 (O. Holmes ed., 12th ed. 1873) (hereinafter Kent).

"Some general knowledge of firearms is important to the public welfare; because it would be impossible, in case of war, to organize promptly an efficient force of volunteers unless the people had some familiarity with weapons of war. The Constitution secures the right of the people to keep and bear arms. No doubt, a citizen who keeps a gun or pistol under judicious precautions, practices in safe places the use of it, and in due time teaches his sons to do the same, exercises his individual right. No doubt, a person whose residence or duties involve peculiar peril may keep a pistol for prudent self-defence." B. Abbott, Judge and Jury: A Popular Explanation of the Leading Topics in the Law of the Land 333 (1880) (hereinafter Abbott).

"The right to bear arms has always been the distinctive privilege of freemen. Aside from any necessity of self-protection to the person, it represents among all nations power coupled with the exercise of a certain jurisdiction.... [I]t was not necessary that the right to bear arms should be granted in the Constitution, for it had always existed." J. Ordronaux, Constitutional Legislation in the United States 241–242 (1891).

E

We now ask whether any of our precedents forecloses the conclusions we have reached about the meaning of the Second Amendment.

United States v. *Cruikshank*, 92 U. S. 542, in the course of vacating the convictions of members of a white mob for depriving blacks of their right to keep and bear arms, held that the Second Amendment does not by its own force apply to anyone other than the Federal Government. The opinion explained that the right "is not a right granted by the Constitution [or] in any manner dependent upon that instrument for its existence. The second amendment ... means no more than that it shall not be infringed by Congress." 92 U. S., at 553. States, we said, were free to restrict or protect the right under their police powers. The limited discussion of the Second Amendment in *Cruikshank* supports, if anything, the individual-rights interpretation. There was no claim in *Cruikshank* that the victims had been deprived of their right to carry arms in a militia; indeed, the Governor had disbanded the local militia unit the year before the mob's attack, see C. Lane, The Day Freedom Died 62 (2008). We described the right protected by the Second Amendment as "'bearing arms for a lawful purpose'" and said that "the people [must] look for their protection against any violation by their fellow-citizens of the rights it recognizes" to the States' police power. 92 U. S., at 553. That discussion makes little sense if it is only a right to bear arms in a state militia.

Presser v. *Illinois*, 116 U. S. 252 (1886), held that the right to keep and bear arms was not violated by a law that forbade "bodies of men to associate together as military organizations, or to drill or parade with arms in cities and towns unless authorized by law." *Id.*, at 264–265. This does not refute the individual-rights interpretation of the Amendment; no one supporting that interpretation has contended that States may not ban such groups. Justice Stevens presses *Presser* into service to support his view that the right to bear arms is limited to service in the militia by joining *Presser's* brief discussion of the Second Amendment with a later portion of the opinion making the seemingly relevant (to the Second Amendment) point that the plaintiff was not a member of the state militia. Unfortunately for Justice Stevens' argument, that later portion deals with the *Fourteenth Amendment;* it was the *Fourteenth Amendment* to which the plaintiff's nonmembership in the militia was relevant. Thus, Justice Stevens' statement that *Presser* "suggested that... nothing in the Constitution protected the use of arms outside the context of a militia," *post*, at 40, is simply wrong. *Presser* said nothing about the Second Amendment's meaning or scope, beyond the fact that it does not prevent the prohibition of private paramilitary organizations.

Justice Stevens places overwhelming reliance upon this Court's decision in *United States* v. *Miller*, 307 U. S. 174 (1939). "[H]undreds of judges," we are told, "have relied on the view of the amendment we endorsed there," *post*, at 2, and "[e]ven if the textual and historical arguments on both side of the issue were evenly balanced, respect for the well-settled views of all of our predecessors on this Court, and for the rule of law itself... would prevent most jurists from endorsing such a dramatic upheaval in the law," *post*, at 4. And what is,

according to Justice Stevens, the holding of *Miller* that demands such obeisance? That the Second Amendment "protects the right to keep and bear arms for certain military purposes, but that it does not curtail the legislature's power to regulate the nonmilitary use and ownership of weapons." *Post*, at 2.

Nothing so clearly demonstrates the weakness of Justice Stevens' case. *Miller* did not hold that and cannot possibly be read to have held that. The judgment in the case upheld against a Second Amendment challenge two men's federal convictions for transporting an unregistered short-barreled shotgun in interstate commerce, in violation of the National Firearms Act, 48 Stat. 1236. It is entirely clear that the Court's basis for saying that the Second Amendment did not apply was *not* that the defendants were "bear[ing] arms" not "for . . . military purposes" but for "nonmilitary use," *post*, at 2. Rather, it was that the *type of weapon at issue* was not eligible for Second Amendment protection: "In the absence of any evidence tending to show that the possession or use of a [short-barreled shotgun] at this time has some reasonable relationship to the preservation or efficiency of a well regulated militia, we cannot say that the Second Amendment guarantees the right to keep and bear *such an instrument.*" 307 U. S., at 178 (emphasis added). "Certainly," the Court continued, "it is not within judicial notice that this weapon is any part of the ordinary military equipment or that its use could contribute to the common defense." *Ibid*. Beyond that, the opinion provided no explanation of the content of the right.

This holding is not only consistent with, but positively suggests, that the Second Amendment confers an individual right to keep and bear arms (though only arms that "have some reasonable relationship to the preservation or efficiency of a well regulated militia"). Had the Court believed that the Second Amendment protects only those serving in the militia, it would have been odd to examine the character of the weapon rather than simply note that the two crooks were not militiamen. Justice Stevens can say again and again that *Miller* did "not turn on the difference between muskets and sawed-off shotguns, it turned, rather, on the basic difference between the military and nonmilitary use and possession of guns," *post*, at 42–43, but the words of the opinion prove otherwise. The most Justice Stevens can plausibly claim for *Miller* is that it declined to decide the nature of the Second Amendment right, despite the Solicitor General's argument (made in the alternative) that the right was collective, see Brief for United States, O. T. 1938, No. 696, pp. 4–5. *Miller* stands only for the proposition that the Second Amendment right, whatever its nature, extends only to certain types of weapons.

It is particularly wrongheaded to read *Miller* for more than what it said, because the case did not even purport to be a thorough examination of the Second Amendment. Justice Stevens claims, *post*, at 42, that the opinion reached its conclusion "[a]fter reviewing many of the same sources that are discussed at greater length by the Court today." Not many, which was not entirely the Court's fault. The respondent made no appearance in the case, neither filing a brief nor appearing at oral argument; the Court heard from no one but the Government (reason enough, one would think, not to make that case the beginning and the end of this Court's consideration of the Second Amendment). See Frye, The Peculiar Story of *United States* v. *Miller*, 3 N. Y. U. J. L. & Liberty 48, 65–68 (2008). The Government's brief spent two pages discussing English legal sources, concluding "that at least the carrying of weapons without lawful occasion or excuse was always a crime" and that (because of the class-based restrictions and the prohibition on terrorizing people with dangerous or unusual weapons) "the early English law did not guarantee an unrestricted right to bear arms." Brief for United States, O. T. 1938, No. 696, at 9–11. It then went on to rely primarily on the discussion of the English right to bear arms in *Aymette* v. *State*, 21 Tenn. 154, for the proposition that the only uses of arms protected by the Second Amendment are those that relate to the militia, not self-defense. See Brief for United States, O. T. 1938, No. 696, at 12–18. The final section of the brief recognized that "some courts have said that the right to bear arms includes the right of the individual to have them for the protection of his person and property," and launched an alternative argument that "weapons which are commonly used by criminals," such as sawed-off shotguns, are not protected. See *id.*, at 18–21. The Government's *Miller* brief thus provided scant discussion of the history of the Second Amendment—and the Court was presented with no counterdiscussion. As for the text of the Court's opinion itself, that discusses *none* of the history of the Second Amendment. It assumes from the prologue that the Amendment was designed to preserve the militia, 307 U. S., at 178 (which we do not dispute), and then reviews some historical materials dealing with the nature of the militia, and in particular with the nature of the arms their members were expected to possess, *id.*, at 178–182. Not a word *(not a word)* about the history of the Second Amendment. This is the mighty rock upon which the dissent rests its case.

We may as well consider at this point (for we will have to consider eventually) *what* types of weapons *Miller* permits. Read in isolation, *Miller*'s phrase "part of ordinary military equipment" could mean that only those weapons useful in warfare are protected. That would be a startling reading of the opinion, since it would mean that the National Firearms Act's restrictions on machineguns (not challenged in *Miller*) might be unconstitutional, machineguns being useful in warfare in 1939. We think that *Miller*'s "ordinary military equipment" language must be read in tandem with what comes after: "[O]rdinarily when called for [militia] service [able-bodied] men were expected to appear bearing arms supplied by themselves and of the kind in common use at the time." 307 U. S., at 179. The traditional militia was formed from a pool of men bringing arms "in common use at the time" for lawful purposes like self-defense. "In the colonial and revolutionary war era, [small-arms] weapons used by militiamen and weapons used in defense of person and home were one and the same." *State* v. *Kessler*, 289 Ore. 359, 368, 614 P. 2d 94, 98 (1980) (citing G. Neumann, Swords and Blades of the American Revolution 6–15, 252–254 (1973)). Indeed, that is precisely the way in which the Second Amendment's operative clause furthers the purpose announced in its preface. We therefore read *Miller* to say only that the Second Amendment does not protect those weapons not typically possessed by law-abiding citizens for lawful purposes, such as short-barreled shotguns. That accords with the historical understanding of the scope of the right, see Part III, *infra*.

We conclude that nothing in our precedents forecloses our adoption of the original understanding of the Second Amendment. It should be unsurprising that such a significant matter has been for so long judicially unresolved. For most of our history, the Bill of Rights was not thought applicable to the States, and the Federal Government did not significantly regulate the possession of firearms by law-abiding citizens. Other provisions of the Bill of Rights have similarly remained unilluminated for lengthy periods. This Court first held a law to violate the First Amendment's guarantee of freedom of speech in 1931, almost 150 years after the Amendment was ratified, see *Near* v. *Minnesota ex rel. Olson*, 283 U. S. 697 (1931), and it was not until after World War II that we held a law invalid under the Establishment Clause, see *Illinois ex rel. McCollum* v. *Board of Ed. of School Dist. No. 71, Champaign Cty.*, 333 U. S. 203 (1948). Even a question as basic as the scope of proscribable libel was not addressed by this Court until 1964, nearly two centuries after the founding. See *New York Times Co.* v. *Sullivan*, 376 U. S. 254 (1964). It is demonstrably not true that, as Justice Stevens claims, *post*, at 41–42, "for most of our history, the invalidity of Second-Amendment-based objections to firearms regulations has been well settled and uncontroversial." For most of our history the question did not present itself.

III

Like most rights, the right secured by the Second Amendment is not unlimited. From Blackstone through the 19th-century cases, commentators and courts routinely explained that the right was not a right to keep and carry any weapon whatsoever in any manner whatsoever and for whatever purpose. See, *e.g.*, *Sheldon*, in 5 Blume 346; Rawle 123; Pomeroy 152–153; Abbott 333. For example, the majority of the 19th-century courts to consider the question held that prohibitions on carrying concealed weapons were lawful under the Second Amendment or state analogues. See, *e.g.*, *State* v. *Chandler*, 5 La. Ann., at 489–490; *Nunn* v. *State*, 1 Ga., at 251; see generally 2 Kent *340, n. 2; The American Students' Blackstone 84, n. 11 (G. Chase ed. 1884). Although we do not undertake an exhaustive historical analysis today of the full scope of the Second Amendment, nothing in our opinion should be taken to cast doubt on longstanding prohibitions on the possession of firearms by felons and the mentally ill, or laws forbidding the carrying of firearms in sensitive places such as schools and government buildings, or laws imposing conditions and qualifications on the commercial sale of arms.

We also recognize another important limitation on the right to keep and carry arms. *Miller* said, as we have explained, that the sorts of weapons protected were those "in common use at the time." 307 U. S., at 179. We think that limitation is fairly supported by the historical tradition of prohibiting the carrying of "dangerous and unusual weapons." See 4 Blackstone 148–149 (1769); 3 B. Wilson, Works of the Honourable James Wilson 79 (1804); J. Dunlap, The New-York Justice 8 (1815); C. Humphreys, A Compendium of the Common Law in Force in Kentucky 482 (1822); 1 W. Russell, A Treatise on Crimes and Indictable Misdemeanors 271–272 (1831); H. Stephen, Summary of the Criminal Law 48 (1840); E. Lewis, An Abridgment of the Criminal Law of the United States 64 (1847); F. Wharton, A Treatise on the Criminal Law of the United States 726 (1852). See also *State* v. *Langford*, 10 N. C. 381, 383–384 (1824); *O'Neill* v. *State*, 16 Ala. 65, 67 (1849); *English* v. *State*, 35 Tex. 473, 476 (1871); *State* v. *Lanier*, 71 N. C. 288, 289 (1874).

It may be objected that if weapons that are most useful in military service—M-16 rifles and the like—may be banned, then the Second Amendment right is completely detached from the prefatory clause. But as we have said, the conception of the militia at the time of the Second Amendment's ratification was the body of all citizens capable of military service, who would bring the sorts of lawful weapons that they possessed at home to militia duty. It may well be true today that a militia, to be as effective as militias in the 18th century, would require sophisticated arms that are highly unusual in society at large. Indeed, it may be true that no amount of small arms could be useful against modern-day bombers and tanks. But the fact that modern developments have limited the degree of fit between the prefatory clause and the protected right cannot change our interpretation of the right.

IV

We turn finally to the law at issue here. As we have said, the law totally bans handgun possession in the home. It also requires that any lawful firearm in the home be disassembled or bound by a trigger lock at all times, rendering it inoperable.

As the quotations earlier in this opinion demonstrate, the inherent right of self-defense has been central to the Second Amendment right. The handgun ban amounts to a prohibition of an entire class of "arms" that is overwhelmingly chosen by American society for that lawful purpose. The prohibition extends, moreover, to the home, where the need for defense of self, family, and property is most acute. Under any of the standards of scrutiny that we have applied to enumerated constitutional rights, banning from the home "the most preferred firearm in the nation to 'keep' and use for protection of one's home and family," 478 F. 3d, at 400, would fail constitutional muster.

Few laws in the history of our Nation have come close to the severe restriction of the District's handgun ban. And some of those few have been struck down. In *Nunn* v. *State*, the Georgia Supreme Court struck down a prohibition on carrying pistols openly (even though it upheld a prohibition on carrying concealed weapons). See 1 Ga., at 251. In *Andrews* v. *State*, the Tennessee Supreme Court likewise held that a statute that forbade openly carrying a pistol "publicly or privately, without regard to time or place, or circumstances," 50 Tenn., at 187, violated the state constitutional provision (which the court equated with the Second Amendment). That was so even though the statute did not restrict the carrying of long guns. *Ibid.* See also *State* v. *Reid*, 1 Ala. 612, 616–617 (1840) ("A statute which, under the pretence of regulating, amounts to a destruction of the right, or which requires arms to be so borne as to render them wholly useless for the purpose of defence, would be clearly unconstitutional").

It is no answer to say, as petitioners do, that it is permissible to ban the possession of handguns so long as the possession of other firearms (*i.e.*, long guns) is allowed. It is enough to note, as we have observed, that the American people have considered the handgun to be the quintessential self-defense weapon. There are many reasons that a citizen may prefer a handgun for home defense: It is easier to store in a location that is readily accessible in an emergency; it cannot easily be redirected or wrestled away by an attacker; it is easier to use for those without the upper-body strength to lift and aim a long gun; it can be pointed at a burglar with one hand while the other hand dials the police. Whatever the reason, handguns are the most popular weapon chosen by Americans for self-defense in the home, and a complete prohibition of their use is invalid.

We must also address the District's requirement (as applied to respondent's handgun) that firearms in the home be rendered and kept inoperable at all times. This makes it impossible for citizens to use them for the core lawful purpose of self-defense and is hence unconstitutional. The District argues that we should interpret this element of the statute to contain an exception for self-defense. See Brief for Petitioners 56–57. But we think that is precluded by the unequivocal text, and by the presence of certain other enumerated exceptions: "Except for law enforcement personnel . . . , each registrant shall keep any firearm in his possession unloaded and disassembled or bound by a trigger lock or similar device unless such firearm is kept at his place of business, or while being used for lawful recreational purposes within the District of Columbia." D. C. Code §7–2507.02. The nonexistence of a self-defense exception is also suggested by the D. C. Court of Appeals' statement that the statute forbids residents to use firearms to stop intruders, see *McIntosh* v. *Washington*, 395 A. 2d 744, 755–756 (1978).

Apart from his challenge to the handgun ban and the trigger-lock requirement respondent asked the District Court to enjoin petitioners from enforcing the separate licensing requirement "in such a manner as to forbid the carrying of a firearm within one's home or possessed land without a license." App. 59a. The Court of Appeals did not invalidate the licensing requirement, but held only that the District "may not prevent [a handgun] from being moved throughout one's house." 478 F. 3d, at 400. It then ordered the District Court to enter summary judgment "consistent with [respondent's] prayer for relief." *Id.*, at 401. Before this Court petitioners have stated that "if the handgun ban is struck down and respondent registers a handgun, he could obtain a license, assuming he is not otherwise disqualified," by which they apparently mean if he is not a felon and is not insane. Brief for Petitioners 58. Respondent conceded at oral argument that he does not "have a problem with . . . licensing" and that the District's law is permissible so long as it is "not enforced in an arbitrary and capricious manner." Tr. of Oral Arg. 74–75. We therefore assume that petitioners' issuance of a license will satisfy respondent's prayer for relief and do not address the licensing requirement.

Justice Breyer has devoted most of his separate dissent to the handgun ban. He says that, even assuming the Second Amendment is a personal guarantee of the right to bear arms, the District's prohibition is valid. He first tries to establish this by founding-era historical precedent, pointing to various restrictive laws in the colonial period. These demonstrate, in his view, that the District's law "imposes a burden upon gun owners that seems proportionately no greater than restrictions in existence at the time the

Second Amendment was adopted." *Post*, at 2. Of the laws he cites, only one offers even marginal support for his assertion. A 1783 Massachusetts law forbade the residents of Boston to "take into" or "receive into" "any Dwelling House, Stable, Barn, Out-house, Ware-house, Store, Shop or other Building" loaded firearms, and permitted the seizure of any loaded firearms that "shall be found" there. Act of Mar. 1, 1783, ch. 13, 1783 Mass. Acts p. 218. That statute's text and its prologue, which makes clear that the purpose of the prohibition was to eliminate the danger to firefighters posed by the "depositing of loaded Arms" in buildings, give reason to doubt that colonial Boston authorities would have enforced that general prohibition against someone who temporarily loaded a firearm to confront an intruder (despite the law's application in that case). In any case, we would not stake our interpretation of the Second Amendment upon a single law, in effect in a single city, that contradicts the overwhelming weight of other evidence regarding the right to keep and bear arms for defense of the home. The other laws Justice Breyer cites are gunpowder-storage laws that he concedes did not clearly prohibit loaded weapons, but required only that excess gunpowder be kept in a special container or on the top floor of the home. *Post*, at 6–7. Nothing about those fire-safety laws undermines our analysis; they do not remotely burden the right of self-defense as much as an absolute ban on handguns. Nor, correspondingly, does our analysis suggest the invalidity of laws regulating the storage of firearms to prevent accidents.

Justice Breyer points to other founding-era laws that he says "restricted the firing of guns within the city limits to at least some degree" in Boston, Philadelphia and New York. *Post*, at 4 (citing Churchill, Gun Regulation, the Police Power, and the Right to Keep Arms in Early America, 25 Law & Hist. Rev. 139, 162 (2007)). Those laws provide no support for the severe restriction in the present case. The New York law levied a fine of 20 shillings on anyone who fired a gun in certain places (including houses) on New Year's Eve and the first two days of January, and was aimed at preventing the "great Damages ... frequently done on [those days] by persons going House to House, with Guns and other Firearms and being often intoxicated with Liquor." 5 Colonial Laws of New York 244–246 (1894). It is inconceivable that this law would have been enforced against a person exercising his right to self-defense on New Year's Day against such drunken hooligans. The Pennsylvania law to which Justice Breyer refers levied a fine of 5 shillings on one who fired a gun or set off fireworks in Philadelphia without first obtaining a license from the governor. See Act of Aug. 26, 1721, §4, in 3 Stat. at Large 253–254. Given Justice Wilson's explanation that the right to self-defense with arms was protected by the Pennsylvania Constitution, it is unlikely that this law (which in any event amounted to at most a licensing regime) would have been enforced against a person who used firearms for self-defense. Justice Breyer cites a Rhode Island law that simply levied a 5-shilling fine on those who fired guns in *streets* and *taverns*, a law obviously inapplicable to this case. See An Act for preventing Mischief being done in the town of Newport, or in any other town in this Government, 1731, Rhode Island Session Laws. Finally, Justice Breyer points to a Massachusetts law similar to the Pennsylvania law, prohibiting "discharg[ing] any Gun or Pistol charged with Shot or Ball in the Town of *Boston*." Act of May 28, 1746, ch. X, Acts and Laws of Mass. Bay 208. It is again implausible that this would have been enforced against a citizen acting in self-defense, particularly given its preambulatory reference to "the *indiscreet* firing of Guns." *Ibid.* (preamble) (emphasis added).

A broader point about the laws that Justice Breyer cites: All of them punished the discharge (or loading) of guns with a small fine and forfeiture of the weapon (or in a few cases a very brief stay in the local jail), not with significant criminal penalties. They are akin to modern penalties for minor public-safety infractions like speeding or jaywalking. And although such public-safety laws may not contain exceptions for self-defense, it is inconceivable that the threat of a jaywalking ticket would deter someone from disregarding a "Do Not Walk" sign in order to flee an attacker, or that the Government would enforce those laws under such circumstances. Likewise, we do not think that a law imposing a 5-shilling fine and forfeiture of the gun would have prevented a person in the founding era from using a gun to protect himself or his family from violence, or that if he did so the law would be enforced against him. The District law, by contrast, far from imposing a minor fine, threatens citizens with a year in prison (five years for a second violation) for even obtaining a gun in the first place. See D. C. Code §7–2507.06.

Justice Breyer moves on to make a broad jurisprudential point: He criticizes us for declining to establish a level of scrutiny for evaluating Second Amendment restrictions. He proposes, explicitly at least, none of the traditionally expressed levels (strict scrutiny, intermediate scrutiny, rational basis), but rather a judge-empowering "interest-balancing inquiry" that "asks whether the statute burdens a protected interest in a way or to an extent that is out of proportion to the statute's salutary effects upon other important governmental interests." *Post*, at 10. After an exhaustive discussion of the arguments for and against gun control, Justice Breyer arrives at his interest-balanced answer: because handgun violence is a problem, because the law is limited to an urban area, and because there were somewhat similar restrictions in the founding period (a false proposition that we have already discussed), the interest-balancing inquiry results in the constitutionality of the handgun ban. QED.

We know of no other enumerated constitutional right whose core protection has been subjected to a freestanding "interest-balancing" approach. The very enumeration of the right takes out of the hands of government—even the Third Branch of Government—the power to decide on a case-by-case basis whether the right is *really worth* insisting upon. A constitutional guarantee subject to future judges' assessments of its usefulness is no constitutional guarantee at all. Constitutional rights are enshrined with the scope they were understood to have when the people adopted them, whether or not future legislatures or (yes) even future judges think that scope too broad. We would not apply an "interest-balancing" approach to the prohibition of a peaceful neo-Nazi march through Skokie. See *National Socialist Party of America* v. *Skokie*, 432 U. S. 43 (1977) *(per curiam)*. The First Amendment contains the freedom-of-speech guarantee that the people ratified, which included exceptions for obscenity, libel, and disclosure of state secrets, but not for the expression of extremely unpopular and wrong-headed views. The Second Amendment is no different. Like the First, it is the very *product* of an interest-balancing by the people—which Justice Breyer would now conduct for them anew. And whatever else it leaves to future evaluation, it surely elevates above all other interests the right of law-abiding, responsible citizens to use arms in defense of hearth and home.

Justice Breyer chides us for leaving so many applications of the right to keep and bear arms in doubt, and for not providing extensive historical justification for those regulations of the right that we describe as permissible. See *post*, at 42–43. But since this case represents this Court's first in-depth examination of the Second Amendment, one should not expect it to clarify the entire field, any more than *Reynolds* v. *United States*, 98 U. S. 145 (1879), our first in-depth Free Exercise Clause case, left that area in a state of utter certainty. And there will be time enough to expound upon the historical justifications for the exceptions we have mentioned if and when those exceptions come before us.

In sum, we hold that the District's ban on handgun possession in the home violates the Second Amendment, as does its prohibition against rendering any lawful firearm in the home operable for the purpose of immediate self-defense. Assuming that Heller is not disqualified from the exercise of Second Amendment rights, the District must permit him to register his handgun and must issue him a license to carry it in the home.

*   *   *

We are aware of the problem of handgun violence in this country, and we take seriously the concerns raised by the many *amici* who believe that prohibition of handgun ownership is a solution. The Constitution leaves the District of Columbia a variety of tools for combating that problem, including some measures regulating handguns, see *supra*, at 54–55, and n. 26. But the enshrinement of constitutional rights necessarily takes certain policy choices off the table. These include the absolute prohibition of handguns held and used for self-defense in the home. Undoubtedly some think that the Second Amendment is outmoded in a society where our standing army is the pride of our Nation, where well-trained police forces provide personal security, and where gun violence is a serious problem. That is perhaps debatable, but what is not debatable is that it is not the role of this Court to pronounce the Second Amendment extinct.

We affirm the judgment of the Court of Appeals.

It is so ordered.

Justice Stevens, with whom Justice Souter, Justice Ginsburg, and Justice Breyer join, dissenting

The question presented by this case is not whether the Second Amendment protects a "collective right" or an "individual right." Surely it protects a right that can be enforced by individuals. But a conclusion that the Second Amendment protects an individual right does not tell us anything about the scope of that right.

Guns are used to hunt, for self-defense, to commit crimes, for sporting activities, and to perform military duties. The Second Amendment plainly does not protect the right to use a gun to rob a bank; it is equally clear that it *does* encompass the right to use weapons for certain military purposes. Whether it also protects the right to possess and use guns for nonmilitary purposes like hunting and personal self-defense is the question presented by this case. The text of the Amendment, its history, and our decision in *United States* v. *Miller*, 307 U. S. 174 (1939), provide a clear answer to that question.

The Second Amendment was adopted to protect the right of the people of each of the several States to maintain a well-regulated militia. It was a response to concerns raised during the ratification of the Constitution that the power of Congress to disarm the state militias and create a national standing army posed an intolerable threat to the sovereignty of the several States. Neither the text of the Amendment nor the arguments advanced by its proponents evidenced the slightest interest in limiting any legislature's authority to regulate private civilian uses of firearms. Specifically, there is no indication that the Framers of the Amendment intended to enshrine the common-law right of self-defense in the Constitution.

In 1934, Congress enacted the National Firearms Act, the first major federal firearms law. Upholding a conviction under that Act, this Court held that, "[i]n the absence of any evidence tending to show that possession or use of a 'shotgun having a barrel of less than eighteen inches in length' at this time has some reasonable relationship to the preservation or efficiency of a well regulated militia, we cannot say that the Second Amendment guarantees the right to keep and bear such an instrument." *Miller*, 307 U. S., at 178. The view of the Amendment we took in *Miller*—that it protects the right to keep and bear arms for certain military purposes, but that it does not curtail the Legislature's power to regulate the nonmilitary use and ownership of weapons—is both the most natural reading of the Amendment's text and the interpretation most faithful to the history of its adoption.

Since our decision in *Miller*, hundreds of judges have relied on the view of the Amendment we endorsed there; we ourselves affirmed it in 1980. See *Lewis* v. *United States*, 445 U. S. 55, 65–66, n. 8 (1980). No new evidence has surfaced since 1980 supporting the view that the Amendment was intended to curtail the power of Congress to regulate civilian use or misuse of weapons. Indeed, a review of the drafting history of the Amendment demonstrates that its Framers *rejected* proposals that would have broadened its coverage to include such uses.

The opinion the Court announces today fails to identify any new evidence supporting the view that the Amendment was intended to limit the power of Congress to regulate civilian uses of weapons. Unable to point to any such evidence, the Court stakes its holding on a strained and unpersuasive reading of the Amendment's text; significantly different provisions in the 1689 English Bill of Rights, and in various 19th-century State Constitutions; postenactment commentary that was available to the Court when it decided *Miller*; and, ultimately, a feeble attempt to distinguish *Miller* that places more emphasis on the Court's decisional process than on the reasoning in the opinion itself.

Even if the textual and historical arguments on both sides of the issue were evenly balanced, respect for the well-settled views of all of our predecessors on this Court, and for the rule of law itself, see *Mitchell* v. *W. T. Grant Co.*, 416 U. S. 600, 636 (1974) (Stewart, J., dissenting), would prevent most jurists from endorsing such a dramatic upheaval in the law. As Justice Cardozo observed years ago, the "labor of judges would be increased almost to the breaking point if every past decision could be reopened in every case, and one could not lay one's own course of bricks on the secure foundation of the courses laid by others who had gone before him." The Nature of the Judicial Process 149 (1921).

In this dissent I shall first explain why our decision in *Miller* was faithful to the text of the Second Amendment and the purposes revealed in its drafting history.

I shall then comment on the postratification history of the Amendment, which makes abundantly clear that the Amendment should not be interpreted as limiting the authority of Congress to regulate the use or possession of firearms for purely civilian purposes.

I

The text of the Second Amendment is brief. It provides: "A well regulated Militia, being necessary to the security of a free State, the right of the people to keep and bear Arms, shall not be infringed."

Three portions of that text merit special focus: the introductory language defining the Amendment's purpose, the class of persons encompassed within its reach, and the unitary nature of the right that it protects.

"A well regulated Militia, being necessary to the security of a free State"

The preamble to the Second Amendment makes three important points. It identifies the preservation of the militia as the Amendment's purpose; it explains that the militia is necessary to the security of a free State; and it recognizes that the militia must be "well regulated." In all three respects it is comparable to provisions in several State Declarations of Rights that were adopted roughly contemporaneously with the Declaration of Independence. Those state provisions highlight the importance members of the founding generation attached to the maintenance of state militias; they also underscore the profound fear shared by many in that era of the dangers posed by standing armies. While the need for state militias has not been a matter of significant public interest for almost two centuries, that fact should not obscure the contemporary concerns that animated the Framers.

The parallels between the Second Amendment and these state declarations, and the Second Amendment's omission of any statement of purpose related to the right to use firearms for hunting or personal self-defense, is especially striking in light of the fact that the Declarations of Rights of Pennsylvania and Vermont did expressly protect such civilian uses at the time. Article XIII of Pennsylvania's 1776 Declaration of Rights announced that "the people have a right to bear arms for the defence *of themselves* and the state," 1 Schwartz 266 (emphasis added); §43 of the Declaration assured that "the inhabitants of this state shall have the liberty to fowl and hunt in seasonable times on the lands they hold, and on all other lands therein not inclosed," *id.*, at 274. And Article XV of the 1777 Vermont Declaration of Rights guaranteed "[t]hat the people have a right to bear arms for the defence *of themselves* and the State." *Id.*, at 324 (emphasis added). The contrast between those two declarations and the Second Amendment reinforces the clear statement of purpose announced in the Amendment's preamble. It confirms that the Framers' single-minded focus in crafting the constitutional guarantee "to keep and bear arms" was on military uses of firearms, which they viewed in the context of service in state militias.

The preamble thus both sets forth the object of the Amendment and informs the meaning of the remainder of its text. Such text should not be treated as mere surplusage, for "[i]t cannot be presumed that any clause in the constitution is intended to be without effect." *Marbury* v. *Madison*, 1 Cranch 137, 174 (1803).

The Court today tries to denigrate the importance of this clause of the Amendment by beginning its analysis with the Amendment's operative provision and returning to the preamble merely "to ensure that our reading of the operative clause is consistent with the announced purpose." *Ante*, at 5. That is not how this Court ordinarily reads such texts, and it is not how the preamble would have been viewed at the time the Amendment was adopted. While the Court makes the novel suggestion that it need only find some "logical connection" between the preamble and the operative provision, it does acknowledge that a prefatory clause may resolve an ambiguity in the text. *Ante*, at 4. Without identifying any language in the text that even mentions civilian uses of firearms, the Court proceeds to "find" its preferred reading in what is at best an ambiguous text, and then concludes that its reading is not foreclosed by the preamble. Perhaps the Court's approach to the text is acceptable advocacy, but it is surely an unusual approach for judges to follow.

"The right of the people"

The centerpiece of the Court's textual argument is its insistence that the words "the people" as used in the Second Amendment must have the same meaning, and protect the same class of individuals, as when they are used in the First and Fourth Amendments. According to the Court, in all three provisions—as well as the Constitution's preamble, section 2 of Article I, and the Tenth Amendment—"the term unambiguously refers to all members of the political community, not an unspecified subset." *Ante*, at 6. But the Court *itself* reads the Second Amendment to protect a "subset" significantly narrower than the class of persons protected by the First and Fourth Amendments; when it finally drills down on the substantive meaning of the Second Amendment, the Court limits the protected class to "law-abiding, responsible citizens," *ante,* at 63. But the class of persons protected by the First and Fourth Amendments is *not* so limited; for even felons (and presumably irresponsible citizens as well) may invoke the protections of those constitutional provisions. The Court offers no way to harmonize its conflicting pronouncements.

The Court also overlooks the significance of the way the Framers used the phrase "the people" in these constitutional provisions. In the First Amendment, no words define the class of individuals entitled to speak, to publish, or to worship; in that Amendment it is only the right peaceably to assemble, and to petition the Government for a redress of grievances, that is described as a right of "the people." These rights contemplate collective action. While the right peaceably to assemble protects the individual rights of those persons participating in the assembly, its concern is with action engaged in by members of a group, rather than any single individual. Likewise, although the act of petitioning the Government is a right that can be exercised by individuals, it is primarily collective in nature. For if they are to be effective, petitions must involve groups of individuals acting in concert.

Similarly, the words "the people" in the Second Amendment refer back to the object announced in the Amendment's preamble. They remind us that it is the collective action of individuals having a duty to serve in the militia that the text directly protects and, perhaps more importantly, that the ultimate purpose of the Amendment was to protect the States' share of the divided sovereignty created by the Constitution.

As used in the Fourth Amendment, "the people" describes the class of persons protected from unreasonable searches and seizures by Government officials. It is true that the Fourth Amendment describes a right that need not be exercised in any collective sense. But that observation does not settle the meaning of the phrase "the people" when used in the Second Amendment. For, as we have seen, the phrase means something quite different in the Petition and Assembly Clauses of the First Amendment. Although the abstract definition of the phrase "the people" could carry the same meaning in the Second Amendment as in the Fourth Amendment, the preamble of the Second Amendment suggests that the uses of the phrase in the First and Second Amendments are the same in referring to a collective activity. By way of contrast, the Fourth Amendment describes a right *against* governmental interference rather than an affirmative right *to* engage in protected conduct, and so refers to a right to protect a purely individual interest. As used in the Second Amendment, the words "the people" do not enlarge the right to keep and bear arms to encompass use or ownership of weapons outside the context of service in a well-regulated militia.

"To keep and bear Arms"

Although the Court's discussion of these words treats them as two "phrases"—as if they read "to keep" and "to bear"—they describe a unitary right: to possess arms if needed for military purposes and to use them in conjunction with military activities.

As a threshold matter, it is worth pausing to note an oddity in the Court's interpretation of "to keep and bear arms." Unlike the Court of Appeals, the Court does not read that phrase to create a right to possess arms for "lawful, private purposes." *Parker* v. *District of Columbia,* 478 F. 3d 370, 382 (CADC 2007). Instead, the Court limits the Amendment's protection to the right "to possess and carry weapons in case of confrontation." *Ante,* at 19. No party or *amicus* urged this interpretation; the Court appears to have fashioned it out of whole cloth. But although this novel limitation lacks support in the text of the Amendment, the Amendment's text *does* justify a different limitation: the "right to keep and bear arms" protects only a right to possess and use firearms in connection with service in a state-organized militia.

The term "bear arms" is a familiar idiom; when used unadorned by any additional words, its meaning is "to serve as a soldier, do military service, fight." 1 Oxford English Dictionary 634 (2d ed. 1989). It is derived from the Latin *arma ferre,* which, translated literally, means "to bear *[ferre]* war equipment *[arma]*." Brief for Professors of Linguistics and English as *Amici Curiae* 19.

One 18th-century dictionary defined "arms" as "weapons of offence, or armour of defence," 1 S. Johnson, A Dictionary of the English Language (1755), and another contemporaneous source explained that "[b]y *arms*, we understand those instruments of offence generally made use of in war; such as firearms, swords, & c. By *weapons*, we more particularly mean instruments of other kinds (exclusive of fire-arms), made use of as offensive, on special occasions." 1 J. Trusler, The Distinction Between Words Esteemed Synonymous in the English Language 37 (1794). Had the Framers wished to expand the meaning of the phrase "bear arms" to encompass civilian possession and use, they could have done so by the addition of phrases such as "for the defense of themselves," as was done in the Pennsylvania and Vermont Declarations of Rights. The *unmodified* use of "bear arms," by contrast, refers most naturally to a military purpose, as evidenced by its use in literally dozens of contemporary texts. The absence of any reference to civilian uses of weapons tailors the text of the Amendment to the purpose identified in its preamble. But when discussing these words, the Court simply ignores the preamble.

The Court argues that a "qualifying phrase that contradicts the word or phrase it modifies is unknown this side of the looking glass." *Ante*, at 15. But this fundamentally fails to grasp the point. The stand-alone phrase "bear arms" most naturally conveys a military meaning *unless* the addition of a qualifying phrase signals that a different meaning is intended. When, as in this case, there is no such qualifier, the most natural meaning is the military one; and, in the absence of any qualifier, it is all the more appropriate to look to the preamble to confirm the natural meaning of the text. The Court's objection is particularly puzzling in light of its own contention that the addition of the modifier "against" changes the meaning of "bear arms." Compare *ante*, at 10 (defining "bear arms" to mean "carrying [a weapon] for a particular purpose—confrontation"), with *ante*, at 12 ("The phrase 'bear Arms' also had at the time of the founding an idiomatic meaning that was significantly different from its natural meaning: to serve as a soldier, do military service, fight or to wage war. But it unequivocally bore that idiomatic meaning only when followed by the preposition 'against.'" (citations and some internal quotation marks omitted)).

The Amendment's use of the term "keep" in no way contradicts the military meaning conveyed by the phrase "bear arms" and the Amendment's preamble. To the contrary, a number of state militia laws in effect at the time of the Second Amendment's drafting used the term "keep" to describe the requirement that militia members store their arms at their homes, ready to be used for service when necessary. The Virginia military law, for example, ordered that "every one of the said officers, non-commissioned officers, and privates, shall constantly *keep* the aforesaid arms, accoutrements, and ammunition, ready to be produced whenever called for by his commanding officer." Act for Regulating and Disciplining the Militia, 1785 Va. Acts ch. 1, §3, p. 2 (emphasis added). "[K]eep and bear arms" thus perfectly describes the responsibilities of a framing-era militia member.

This reading is confirmed by the fact that the clause protects only one right, rather than two. It does not describe a right "to keep arms" and a separate right "to bear arms." Rather, the single right that it does describe is both a duty and a right to have arms available and ready for military service, and to use them for military purposes when necessary. Different language surely would have been used to protect nonmilitary use and possession of weapons from regulation if such an intent had played any role in the drafting of the Amendment.

* * *

When each word in the text is given full effect, the Amendment is most naturally read to secure to the people a right to use and possess arms in conjunction with service in a well-regulated militia. So far as appears, no more than that was contemplated by its drafters or is encompassed within its terms. Even if the meaning of the text were genuinely susceptible to more than one interpretation, the burden would remain on those advocating a departure from the purpose identified in the preamble and from settled law to come forward with persuasive new arguments or evidence. The textual analysis offered by respondent and embraced by the Court falls far short of sustaining that heavy burden. And the Court's emphatic reliance on the claim "that the Second Amendment . . . codified a *pre-existing* right," *ante*, at 19, is of course beside the point because the right to keep and bear arms for service in a state militia was also a pre-existing right.

Indeed, not a word in the constitutional text even arguably supports the Court's overwrought and novel description of the Second Amendment as "elevat[ing] above all other interests" "the right of law-abiding, responsible citizens to use arms in defense of hearth and home." *Ante,* at 63.

II

The proper allocation of military power in the new Nation was an issue of central concern for the Framers. The compromises they ultimately reached, reflected in Article I's Militia Clauses and the Second Amendment, represent quintessential examples of the Framers'"splitting the atom of sovereignty."

Two themes relevant to our current interpretive task ran through the debates on the original Constitution. "On the one hand, there was a widespread fear that a national standing Army posed an intolerable threat to individual liberty and to the sovereignty of the separate States." *Perpich* v. *Department of Defense,* 496 U. S. 334, 340 (1990). Governor Edmund Randolph, reporting on the Constitutional Convention to the Virginia Ratification Convention, explained: "With respect to a standing army, I believe there was not a member in the federal Convention, who did not feel indignation at such an institution." 3 J. Elliot, Debates in the Several State Conventions on the Adoption of the Federal Constitution 401 (2d ed. 1863) (hereinafter Elliot). On the other hand, the Framers recognized the dangers inherent in relying on inadequately trained militia members "as the primary means of providing for the common defense," *Perpich,* 496 U. S., at 340; during the Revolutionary War, "[t]his force, though armed, was largely untrained, and its deficiencies were the subject of bitter complaint." Wiener, The Militia Clause of the Constitution, 54 Harv. L. Rev. 181, 182 (1940). In order to respond to those twin concerns, a compromise was reached: Congress would be authorized to raise and support a national Army and Navy, and also to organize, arm, discipline, and provide for the calling forth of "the Militia." U. S. Const., Art. I, §8, cls. 12–16. The President, at the same time, was empowered as the "Commander in Chief of the Army and Navy of the United States, and of the Militia of the several States, when called into the actual Service of the United States." Art. II, §2. But, with respect to the militia, a significant reservation was made to the States: Although Congress would have the power to call forth, organize, arm, and discipline the militia, as well as to govern "such Part of them as may be employed in the Service of the United States," the States respectively would retain the right to appoint the officers and to train the militia in accordance with the discipline prescribed by Congress. Art. I, §8, cl. 16.

But the original Constitution's retention of the militia and its creation of divided authority over that body did not prove sufficient to allay fears about the dangers posed by a standing army. For it was perceived by some that Article I contained a significant gap: While it empowered Congress to organize, arm, and discipline the militia, it did not prevent Congress from providing for the militia's *dis*armament. As George Mason argued during the debates in Virginia on the ratification of the original Constitution:

"The militia may be here destroyed by that method which has been practiced in other parts of the world before; that is, by rendering them useless—by disarming them. Under various pretences, Congress may neglect to provide for arming and disciplining the militia; and the state governments cannot do it, for Congress has the exclusive right to arm them." Elliot 379.

This sentiment was echoed at a number of state ratification conventions; indeed, it was one of the primary objections to the original Constitution voiced by its opponents. The Anti-Federalists were ultimately unsuccessful in persuading state ratification conventions to condition their approval of the Constitution upon the eventual inclusion of any particular amendment. But a number of States did propose to the first Federal Congress amendments reflecting a desire to ensure that the institution of the militia would remain protected under the new Government. The proposed amendments sent by the States of Virginia, North Carolina, and New York focused on the importance of preserving the state militias and reiterated the dangers posed by standing armies. New Hampshire sent a proposal that differed significantly from the others; while also invoking the dangers of a standing army, it suggested that the Constitution should more broadly protect the use and possession of weapons, without tying such a guarantee expressly to the maintenance of the militia. The States of Maryland, Pennsylvania, and Massachusetts sent no relevant proposed amendments to Congress, but in each of those States a minority of the delegates advocated related amendments. While the Maryland minority proposals were exclusively concerned with standing armies and conscientious objectors, the unsuccessful proposals in both Massachusetts and Pennsylvania would have protected a more broadly worded right, less clearly tied to service in a state militia. Faced with all of these options, it is telling that James Madison chose to craft the Second Amendment as he did.

The relevant proposals sent by the Virginia Ratifying Convention read as follows:

"17th, That the people have a right to keep and bear arms; that a well regulated Militia composed of the body of the people trained to arms is the proper, natural and safe defence of a free State. That standing armies are dangerous to liberty, and therefore ought to be avoided, as far as the circumstances and protection of the Community will admit; and that in all cases the military should be under strict subordination to and be governed by the civil power." Elliot 659.

"19th. That any person religiously scrupulous of bearing arms ought to be exempted, upon payment of an equivalent to employ another to bear arms in his stead." *Ibid.*

North Carolina adopted Virginia's proposals and sent them to Congress as its own, although it did not actually ratify the original Constitution until Congress had sent the proposed Bill of Rights to the States for ratification. 2 Schwartz 932–933; see The Complete Bill of Rights 182–183 (N. Cogan ed. 1997) (hereinafter Cogan).

New York produced a proposal with nearly identical language. It read:

"That the people have a right to keep and bear Arms; that a well regulated Militia, including the body of the People capable of bearing Arms, is the proper, natural, and safe defence of a free State. . . . That standing Armies, in time of Peace, are dangerous to Liberty, and ought not to be kept up, except in Cases of necessity; and that at all times, the Military should be kept under strict Subordination to the civil Power." 2 Schwartz 912.

Notably, each of these proposals used the phrase "keep and bear arms," which was eventually adopted by Madison. And each proposal embedded the phrase within a group of principles that are distinctly military in meaning.

By contrast, New Hampshire's proposal, although it followed another proposed amendment that echoed the familiar concern about standing armies, described the protection involved in more clearly personal terms. Its proposal read:

"*Twelfth,* Congress shall never disarm any Citizen unless such as are or have been in Actual Rebellion." *Id.,* at 758, 761.

The proposals considered in the other three States, although ultimately rejected by their respective ratification conventions, are also relevant to our historical inquiry. First, the Maryland proposal, endorsed by a minority of the delegates and later circulated in pamphlet form, read:

"4. That no standing army shall be kept up in time of peace, unless with the consent of two thirds of the members present of each branch of Congress.

.   .   .   .   .

"10. That no person conscientiously scrupulous of bearing arms in any case, shall be compelled personally to serve as a soldier." *Id.,* at 729, 735.

The rejected Pennsylvania proposal, which was later incorporated into a critique of the Constitution titled "The Address and Reasons of Dissent of the Pennsylvania Minority of the Convention of the State of Pennsylvania to Their Constituents (1787)," signed by a minority of the State's delegates (those who had voted against ratification of the Constitution), *id.,* at 628, 662, read:

7. "That the people have a right to bear arms for the defense of themselves and their own State, or the United States, or for the purpose of killing game; and no law shall be passed for disarming the people or any of them unless for crimes committed, or real danger of public injury from individuals; and as standing armies in the time of peace are dangerous to liberty, they ought not to be kept up; and that the military shall be kept under strict subordination to, and be governed by the civil powers." *Id.,* at 665.

Finally, after the delegates at the Massachusetts Ratification Convention had compiled a list of proposed amendments and alterations, a motion was made to add to the list the following language: "[T]hat the said Constitution never be construed to authorize Congress to . . . prevent the people of the United States, who are peaceable citizens, from keeping their own arms." Cogan 181. This motion, however, failed to achieve the necessary support, and the proposal was excluded from the list of amendments the State sent to Congress. 2 Schwartz 674–675.

Madison, charged with the task of assembling the proposals for amendments sent by the ratifying States, was the principal draftsman of the Second Amendment. He had before him, or at the very least would have been aware of, all of these proposed formulations. In addition, Madison had been a member, some years earlier, of the committee tasked with drafting the Virginia Declaration of Rights. That committee considered a proposal by Thomas Jefferson that would have included within the Virginia Declaration the following language: "No freeman shall ever be debarred the use of arms [within his own lands or tenements]." 1 Papers of Thomas Jefferson 363 (J. Boyd ed. 1950). But the committee rejected that language, adopting instead the provision drafted by George Mason.

With all of these sources upon which to draw, it is strikingly significant that Madison's first draft omitted any mention of nonmilitary use or possession of weapons. Rather, his original draft repeated the essence of the two proposed amendments sent by Virginia, combining the substance of the two provisions succinctly into one, which read: "The right of the people to keep and bear arms shall not be infringed; a well armed, and well regulated militia being the best security of a free country; but no person religiously scrupulous of bearing arms, shall be compelled to render military service in person." Cogan 169.

Madison's decision to model the Second Amendment on the distinctly military Virginia proposal is therefore revealing, since it is clear that he considered and rejected formulations that would have unambiguously protected civilian uses of firearms. When Madison prepared his first draft, and when that draft was debated and modified, it is reasonable to assume that all participants in the drafting process were fully aware of the other formulations that would have protected civilian use and possession of weapons and that their choice to craft the Amendment as they did represented a rejection of those alternative formulations.

Madison's initial inclusion of an exemption for conscientious objectors sheds revelatory light on the purpose of the Amendment. It confirms an intent to describe a duty as well as a right, and it unequivocally identifies the military character of both. The objections voiced to the conscientious-objector clause only confirm the central meaning of the text. Although records of the debate in the Senate, which is where the conscientious-objector clause was removed, do not survive, the arguments raised in the House illuminate the perceived problems with the clause: Specifically, there was concern that Congress "can declare who are those religiously scrupulous, and prevent them from bearing arms." The ultimate removal of the clause, therefore, only serves to confirm the purpose of the Amendment—to protect against congressional disarmament, by whatever means, of the States' militias.

The Court also contends that because "Quakers opposed the use of arms not just for militia service, but for any violent purpose whatsoever," *ante*, at 17, the inclusion of a conscientious-objector clause in the original draft of the Amendment does not support the conclusion that the phrase "bear arms" was military in meaning. But that claim cannot be squared with the record. In the proposals cited *supra*, at 21–22, both Virginia and North Carolina included the following language: "That any person religiously scrupulous of bearing arms ought to be exempted, upon payment of an equivalent *to employ another to bear arms in his stead*" (emphasis added). There is no plausible argument that the use of "bear arms" in those provisions was not unequivocally and exclusively military: The State simply does not compel its citizens to carry arms for the purpose of private "confrontation," *ante*, at 10, or for self-defense.

The history of the adoption of the Amendment thus describes an overriding concern about the potential threat to state sovereignty that a federal standing army would pose, and a desire to protect the States' militias as the means by which to guard against that danger. But state militias could not effectively check the prospect of a federal standing army so long as Congress retained the power to disarm them, and so a guarantee against such disarmament was needed. As we explained in *Miller:* "With obvious purpose to assure the continuation and render possible the effectiveness of such forces the declaration and guarantee of the Second Amendment were made. It must be interpreted and applied with that end in view." 307 U. S., at 178. The evidence plainly refutes the claim that the Amendment was motivated by the Framers' fears that Congress might act to regulate any civilian uses of weapons. And even if the historical record were genuinely ambiguous, the burden would remain on the parties advocating a change in the law to introduce facts or arguments "'newly ascertained,'" *Vasquez*, 474 U. S., at 266; the Court is unable to identify any such facts or arguments.

III

Although it gives short shrift to the drafting history of the Second Amendment, the Court dwells at length on four other sources: the 17th-century English Bill of Rights; Blackstone's Commentaries on the Laws of England; postenactment commentary on the Second Amendment; and post-Civil War legislative history. All of these sources shed only indirect light on the question before us, and in any event offer little support for the Court's conclusion.

The English Bill of Rights

The Court's reliance on Article VII of the 1689 English Bill of Rights—which, like most of the evidence offered by the Court today, was considered in *Miller*—is misguided both because Article VII was enacted in response to different concerns from those that motivated the Framers of the Second Amendment, and because the guarantees of the two provisions were by no means coextensive. Moreover, the English text contained no preamble or other provision identifying a narrow, militia-related purpose.

The English Bill of Rights responded to abuses by the Stuart monarchs; among the grievances set forth in the Bill of Rights was that the King had violated the law "[b]y causing several good Subjects being Protestants to be disarmed at the same time when Papists were both armed and Employed contrary to Law." Article VII of the Bill of Rights was a response to that selective disarmament; it guaranteed that "the Subjects which are Protestants may have Armes for their defence, Suitable to their condition and as allowed by Law." L. Schwoerer, The Declaration of Rights, 1689 (App. 1, pp. 295, 297) (1981). This grant did not establish a general right of all persons, or even of all Protestants, to possess weapons. Rather, the right was qualified in two distinct ways: First, it was restricted to those of adequate social and economic status ("suitable to their Condition"); second, it was only available subject to regulation by Parliament ("as allowed by Law").

The Court may well be correct that the English Bill of Rights protected the right of *some* English subjects to use *some* arms for personal self-defense free from restrictions by the Crown (but not Parliament). But that right—adopted in a different historical and political context and framed in markedly different language—tells us little about the meaning of the Second Amendment.

Blackstone's Commentaries

The Court's reliance on *Blackstone's Commentaries on the Laws of England* is unpersuasive for the same reason as its reliance on the English Bill of Rights. Blackstone's invocation of "'the natural right of resistance and self-preservation,'" *ante*, at 20, and "'the right of having and using arms for self-preservation and defence'" *ibid.*, referred specifically to Article VII in the English Bill of Rights. The excerpt from Blackstone offered by the Court, therefore, is, like Article VII itself, of limited use in interpreting the very differently worded, and differently historically situated, Second Amendment.

What is important about Blackstone is the instruction he provided on reading the sort of text before us today. Blackstone described an interpretive approach that gave far more weight to preambles than the Court allows. Counseling that "[t]he fairest and most rational method to interpret the will of the legislator, is by exploring his intentions at the time when the law was made, by *signs* the most natural and probable," Blackstone explained that "[i]f words happen to be still dubious, we may establish their meaning from the context; with which it may be of singular use to compare a word, or a sentence, whenever they are ambiguous, equivocal, or intricate. Thus, the proeme, or preamble, is often called in to help the construction of an act of parliament." 1 Commentaries on the Laws of England 59–60 (1765) (hereinafter Blackstone). In light of the Court's invocation of Blackstone as "'the preeminent authority on English law for the founding generation,'" *ante*, at 20 (quoting *Alden* v. *Maine*, 527 U. S. 706, 715 (1999)), its disregard for his guidance on matters of interpretation is striking.

Postenactment Commentary

The Court also excerpts, without any real analysis, commentary by a number of additional scholars, some near in time to the framing and others post-dating it by close to a century. Those scholars are for the most part of limited relevance in construing the guarantee of the Second Amendment: Their views are not altogether clear, they tended to collapse the Second Amendment with Article VII of the English Bill of Rights, and they appear to have been unfamiliar with the drafting history of the Second Amendment.

The most significant of these commentators was Joseph Story. Contrary to the Court's assertions, however, Story actually supports the view that the Amendment was designed to protect the right of each of the States to maintain a well-regulated militia. When Story used the term "palladium" in discussions of the Second Amendment, he merely echoed the concerns that animated the Framers of the Amendment and led to its adoption. An excerpt from his 1833 Commentaries on the Constitution of the United States—the same passage cited by the Court in *Miller*—merits reproducing at some length:

"The importance of [the Second Amendment] will scarcely be doubted by any persons who have duly reflected upon the subject. The militia is the natural defence of a free country against sudden foreign invasions, domestic insurrections, and domestic usurpations of power by rulers. It is against sound policy for a free people to keep up large military establishments and standing armies in time of peace, both from the enormous expenses with which they are attended and the facile means which they afford to ambitious and unprincipled rulers to subvert the government, or trample upon the rights of the people. The right of the citizens to keep and bear arms has justly been considered as the palladium of the liberties of a republic, since it offers a strong moral check against the usurpation and arbitrary power of rulers, and will generally, even if these are successful in the first instance, enable the people to resist and triumph over them. And yet, though this truth would seem so clear, and the importance of a well-regulated militia would seem so undeniable, it cannot be disguised that, among the American people, there is a growing indifference to any system of militia discipline, and a strong disposition, from a sense of its burdens, to be rid of all regulations. How it is practicable to keep the people duly armed without some organization, it is difficult to see. There is certainly no small danger that indifference may lead to disgust, and disgust to contempt; and thus gradually undermine all the protection intended by the clause of our national bill of rights." 2 J. Story, Commentaries on the Constitution of the United States §1897, pp. 620–621 (4th ed. 1873) (footnote omitted).

Story thus began by tying the significance of the Amendment directly to the paramount importance of the militia. He then invoked the fear that drove the Framers of the Second Amendment—specifically, the threat to liberty posed by a standing army. An important check on that danger, he suggested, was a "well-regulated militia," *id.*, at 621, for which he assumed that arms would have to be kept and, when necessary, borne. There is not so much as a whisper in the passage above that Story believed that the right secured by the Amendment bore any relation to private use or possession of weapons for activities like hunting or personal self-defense.

After extolling the virtues of the militia as a bulwark against tyranny, Story went on to decry the "growing indifference to any system of militia discipline." *Ibid.* When he wrote, "[h]ow it is practicable to keep the people duly armed without some organization it is difficult to see," *ibid.*, he underscored the degree to which he viewed the arming of the people and the militia as indissolubly linked. Story warned that the "growing indifference" he perceived would "gradually undermine all the protection intended by this clause of our national bill of rights," *ibid.* In his view, the importance of the Amendment was directly related to the continuing vitality of an institution in the process of apparently becoming obsolete.

In an attempt to downplay the absence of any reference to nonmilitary uses of weapons in Story's commentary, the Court relies on the fact that Story characterized Article VII of the English Declaration of Rights as a "'similar provision,'" *ante*, at 36. The two provisions were indeed similar, in that both protected some uses of firearms. But Story's characterization in no way suggests that he believed that the provisions had the same scope. To the contrary, Story's exclusive focus on the militia in his discussion of the Second Amendment confirms his understanding of the right protected by the Second Amendment as limited to military uses of arms.

Story's writings as a Justice of this Court, to the extent that they shed light on this question, only confirm that Justice Story did not view the Amendment as conferring upon individuals any "self-defense" right disconnected from service in a state militia. Justice Story dissented from the Court's decision in *Houston* v. *Moore,* 5 Wheat. 1, 24 (1820), which held that a state court "had a concurrent jurisdiction" with the federal courts "to try a militia man who had disobeyed the call of the President, and to enforce the laws of Congress against such delinquent." *Id.,* at 31–32. Justice Story believed that Congress' power to provide for the organizing, arming, and disciplining of the militia was, when Congress acted, plenary; but he explained that in the absence of congressional action, "I am certainly not prepared to deny the legitimacy of such an exercise of [state] authority." *Id.,* at 52. As to the Second Amendment, he wrote that it "may not, perhaps, be thought to have any important bearing on this point. If it have, it confirms and illustrates, rather than impugns the reasoning already suggested." *Id.,* at 52–53. The Court contends that had Justice Story understood the Amendment to have a militia purpose, the Amendment would have had "enormous and obvious bearing on the point." *Ante,* at 38. But the Court has it quite backwards: If Story had believed that the purpose of the Amendment was to permit civilians to keep firearms for activities like personal self-defense, what "confirm[ation] and illustrat[ion]," *Houston,* 5 Wheat., at 53, could the Amendment possibly have provided for the point that States retained the power to organize, arm, and discipline their own militias?

Post-Civil War Legislative History

The Court suggests that by the post-Civil War period, the Second Amendment was understood to secure a right to firearm use and ownership for purely private purposes like personal self-defense. While it is true that some of the legislative history on which the Court relies supports that contention, see *ante,* at 41–44, such sources are entitled to limited, if any, weight. All of the statements the Court cites were made long after the framing of the Amendment and cannot possibly supply any insight into the intent of the Framers; and all were made during pitched political debates, so that they are better characterized as advocacy than good-faith attempts at constitutional interpretation.

What is more, much of the evidence the Court offers is decidedly less clear than its discussion allows. The Court notes that "[b]lacks were routinely disarmed by Southern States after the Civil War. Those who opposed these injustices frequently stated that they infringed blacks' constitutional right to keep and bear arms." *Ante,* at 42. The Court hastily concludes that "[n]eedless to say, the claim was not that blacks were being prohibited from carrying arms in an organized state militia," *ibid.* But some of the claims of the sort the Court cites may have been just that. In some Southern States, Reconstruction-era Republican governments created state militias in which both blacks and whites were permitted to serve. Because "[t]he decision to allow blacks to serve alongside whites meant that most southerners refused to join the new militia," the bodies were dubbed "Negro militia[s]." S. Cornell, A Well-Regulated Militia 176–177 (2006). The "arming of the Negro militias met with especially fierce resistance in South Carolina. . . . The sight of organized, armed freedmen incensed opponents of Reconstruction and led to an intensified campaign of Klan terror. Leading members of the Negro militia were beaten or lynched and their weapons stolen." *Id.,* at 177.

One particularly chilling account of Reconstruction-era Klan violence directed at a black militia member is recounted in the memoir of Louis F. Post, A "Carpetbagger" in South Carolina, 10 Journal of Negro History 10 (1925). Post describes the murder by local Klan members of Jim Williams, the captain of a "Negro militia company," *id.,* at 59, this way:

"[A] cavalcade of sixty cowardly white men, completely disguised with face masks and body gowns, rode up one night in March, 1871, to the house of Captain Williams . . . in the wood [they] hanged [and shot] him . . . [and on his body they] then pinned a slip of paper inscribed, as I remember it, with these grim words: 'Jim Williams gone to his last muster.'" *Id.,* at 61.

In light of this evidence, it is quite possible that at least some of the statements on which the Court relies actually did mean to refer to the disarmament of black militia members.

IV

The brilliance of the debates that resulted in the Second Amendment faded into oblivion during the ensuing years, for the concerns about Article I's Militia Clauses that generated such pitched debate during the ratification process and led to the adoption of the Second Amendment were short lived.

In 1792, the year after the Amendment was ratified,

Congress passed a statute that purported to establish "an Uniform Militia throughout the United States." 1 Stat. 271. The statute commanded every able-bodied white male citizen between the ages of 18 and 45 to be enrolled therein and to "provide himself with a good musket or firelock" and other specified weaponry. *Ibid.* The statute is significant, for it confirmed the way those in the founding generation viewed firearm ownership: as a duty linked to military service. The statute they enacted, however, "was virtually ignored for more than a century," and was finally repealed in 1901. See *Perpich,* 496 U. S., at 341.

The postratification history of the Second Amendment is strikingly similar. The Amendment played little role in any legislative debate about the civilian use of firearms for most of the 19th century, and it made few appearances in the decisions of this Court. Two 19th-century cases, however, bear mentioning.

In *United States* v. *Cruikshank,* 92 U. S. 542 (1876), the Court sustained a challenge to respondents' convictions under the Enforcement Act of 1870 for conspiring to deprive any individual of "'any right or privilege granted or secured to him by the constitution or laws of the United States.'" *Id.,* at 548. The Court wrote, as to counts 2 and 10 of respondents' indictment:

"The right there specified is that of 'bearing arms for a lawful purpose.' This is not a right granted by the Constitution. Neither is it in any manner dependent on that instrument for its existence. The second amendment declares that it shall not be infringed; but this, as has been seen, means no more than that it shall not be infringed by Congress. This is one of the amendments that has no other effect than to restrict the powers of the national government." *Id.,* at 553.

The majority's assertion that the Court in *Cruikshank* "described the right protected by the Second Amendment as '"bearing arms for a lawful purpose,"'" *ante,* at 47 (quoting *Cruikshank,* 92 U. S., at 553), is not accurate. The *Cruikshank* Court explained that the defective *indictment* contained such language, but the Court did not itself describe the right, or endorse the indictment's description of the right.

Moreover, it is entirely possible that the basis for the indictment's counts 2 and 10, which charged respondents with depriving the victims of rights secured by the Second Amendment, was the prosecutor's belief that the victims—members of a group of citizens, mostly black but also white, who were rounded up by the Sheriff, sworn in as a posse to defend the local courthouse, and attacked by a white mob—bore sufficient resemblance to members of a state militia that they were brought within the reach of the Second Amendment. See generally C. Lane, The Day Freedom Died: The Colfax Massacre, The Supreme Court, and the Betrayal of Reconstruction (2008).

Only one other 19th-century case in this Court, *Presser* v. *Illinois,* 116 U. S. 252 (1886), engaged in any significant discussion of the Second Amendment. The petitioner in *Presser* was convicted of violating a state statute that prohibited organizations other than the Illinois National Guard from associating together as military companies or parading with arms. Presser challenged his conviction, asserting, as relevant, that the statute violated both the Second and the Fourteenth Amendments. With respect to the Second Amendment, the Court wrote:

"We think it clear that the sections under consideration, which only forbid bodies of men to associate together as military organizations, or to drill or parade with arms in cities and towns unless authorized by law, do not infringe the right of the people to keep and bear arms. But a conclusive answer to the contention that this amendment prohibits the legislation in question lies in the fact that the amendment is a limitation only upon the power of Congress and the National government, and not upon that of the States." *Id.,* at 264–265.

And in discussing the Fourteenth Amendment, the Court explained:

"The plaintiff in error was not a member of the organized volunteer militia of the State of Illinois, nor did he belong to the troops of the United States or to any organization under the militia law of the United States. On the contrary, the fact that he did not belong to the organized militia or the troops of the United States was an ingredient in the offence for which he was convicted and sentenced. The question is, therefore, had he a right as a citizen of the United States, in disobedience of the State law, to associate with others as a military company, and to drill and parade with arms in the towns and cities of the State? If the plaintiff in error has any such privilege he must be able to point to the provision of the Constitution or statutes of the United States by which it is conferred." *Id.,* at 266.

Presser, therefore, both affirmed *Cruikshank*'s holding that the Second Amendment posed no obstacle to regulation by state governments, and suggested that in any event nothing in the Constitution protected the use of arms outside the context of a militia "authorized by law" and organized by the State or Federal Government.

In 1901 the President revitalized the militia by creating "'the National Guard of the several States,'" *Perpich,* 496 U. S., at 341, and nn. 9–10; meanwhile, the dominant understanding of the Second Amendment's inapplicability to private gun ownership continued well into the 20th century. The first two federal laws directly restricting civilian use and possession of firearms—the 1927 Act prohibiting mail delivery of "pistols, revolvers, and other firearms capable of being concealed on the person," Ch. 75, 44 Stat. 1059, and the 1934 Act prohibiting the possession of sawed-off shotguns and machine guns—were enacted over minor Second Amendment objections dismissed by the vast majority of the legislators who participated in the debates. Members of Congress clashed over the wisdom and efficacy of such laws as crime-control measures. But since the statutes did not infringe upon the military use or possession of weapons, for most legislators they did not even raise the specter of possible conflict with the Second Amendment.

Thus, for most of our history, the invalidity of Second-Amendment-based objections to firearms regulations has been well settled and uncontroversial. Indeed, the Second Amendment was not even mentioned in either full House of Congress during the legislative proceedings that led to the passage of the 1934 Act. Yet enforcement of that law produced the judicial decision that confirmed the status of the Amendment as limited in reach to military usage. After reviewing many of the same sources that are discussed at greater length by the Court today, the *Miller* Court unanimously concluded that the Second Amendment did not apply to the possession of a firearm that did not have "some reasonable relationship to the preservation or efficiency of a well regulated militia." 307 U. S., at 178.

The key to that decision did not, as the Court belatedly suggests, *ante,* at 49–51, turn on the difference between muskets and sawed-off shotguns; it turned, rather, on the basic difference between the military and nonmilitary use and possession of guns. Indeed, if the Second Amendment were not limited in its coverage to military uses of weapons, why should the Court in *Miller* have suggested that some weapons but not others were eligible for Second Amendment protection? If use for self-defense were the relevant standard, why did the Court not inquire into the suitability of a particular weapon for self-defense purposes?

Perhaps in recognition of the weakness of its attempt to distinguish *Miller,* the Court argues in the alternative that *Miller* should be discounted because of its decisional history. It is true that the appellee in *Miller* did not file a brief or make an appearance, although the court below had held that the relevant provision of the National Firearms Act violated the Second Amendment (albeit without any reasoned opinion). But, as our decision in *Marbury* v. *Madison,* 1 Cranch 137, in which only one side appeared and presented arguments, demonstrates, the absence of adversarial presentation alone is not a basis for refusing to accord *stare decisis* effect to a decision of this Court. See Bloch, *Marbury* Redux, in Arguing *Marbury* v. *Madison* 59, 63 (M. Tushnet ed. 2005). Of course, if it can be demonstrated that new evidence or arguments were genuinely not available to an earlier Court, that fact should be given special weight as we consider whether to overrule a prior case. But the Court does not make that claim, because it cannot. Although it is true that the drafting history of the Amendment was not discussed in the Government's brief, see *ante,* at 51, it is certainly not the drafting history that the Court's decision today turns on. And those sources upon which the Court today relies most heavily *were* available to the *Miller* Court. The Government cited the English Bill of Rights and quoted a lengthy passage from *Aymette* detailing the history leading to the English guarantee, Brief for United States in *United States* v. *Miller,* O. T. 1938, No. 696, pp 12–13; it also cited Blackstone, *id.,* at 9, n. 2, Cooley, *id.,* at 12, 15, and Story, *id.,* at 15. The Court is reduced to critiquing the number of *pages* the Government devoted to exploring the English legal sources. Only two (in a brief 21 pages in length)! Would the Court be satisfied with four? Ten?

The Court is simply wrong when it intones that *Miller* contained "*not a word*" about the Amendment's history. *Ante,* at 52. The Court plainly looked to history to construe the term "Militia," and, on the best reading of *Miller,* the entire guarantee of the Second Amendment. After noting the original Constitution's grant of power to Congress and to the States over the militia, the Court explained:

"With obvious purpose to assure the continuation and render possible the effectiveness of such forces the declaration and guarantee of the Second Amendment were made. It must be interpreted and applied with that end in view.

"The Militia which the States were expected to maintain and train is set in contrast with Troops which they were forbidden to keep without the consent of Congress. The sentiment of the time strongly disfavored standing armies; the common view was that adequate defense of country and laws could be secured through the Militia—civilians primarily, soldiers on occasion.

"The signification attributed to the term Militia appears from the debates in the Convention, the history and legislation of Colonies and States, and the writings of approved commentators." *Miller*, 307 U. S., at 178–179.

The majority cannot seriously believe that the *Miller* Court did not consider any relevant evidence; the majority simply does not approve of the conclusion the *Miller* Court reached on that evidence. Standing alone, that is insufficient reason to disregard a unanimous opinion of this Court, upon which substantial reliance has been placed by legislators and citizens for nearly 70 years.

V

The Court concludes its opinion by declaring that it is not the proper role of this Court to change the meaning of rights "enshrine[d]" in the Constitution. *Ante*, at 64. But the right the Court announces was not "enshrined" in the Second Amendment by the Framers; it is the product of today's law-changing decision. The majority's exegesis has utterly failed to establish that as a matter of text or history, "the right of law-abiding, responsible citizens to use arms in defense of hearth and home" is "elevate[d] above all other interests" by the Second Amendment. *Ante*, at 64.

Until today, it has been understood that legislatures may regulate the civilian use and misuse of firearms so long as they do not interfere with the preservation of a well-regulated militia. The Court's announcement of a new constitutional right to own and use firearms for private purposes upsets that settled understanding, but leaves for future cases the formidable task of defining the scope of permissible regulations. Today judicial craftsmen have confidently asserted that a policy choice that denies a "law-abiding, responsible citize[n]" the right to keep and use weapons in the home for self-defense is "off the table." *Ante*, at 64. Given the presumption that most citizens are law abiding, and the reality that the need to defend oneself may suddenly arise in a host of locations outside the home, I fear that the District's policy choice may well be just the first of an unknown number of dominoes to be knocked off the table.

I do not know whether today's decision will increase the labor of federal judges to the "breaking point" envisioned by Justice Cardozo, but it will surely give rise to a far more active judicial role in making vitally important national policy decisions than was envisioned at any time in the 18th, 19th, or 20th centuries.

The Court properly disclaims any interest in evaluating the wisdom of the specific policy choice challenged in this case, but it fails to pay heed to a far more important policy choice—the choice made by the Framers themselves. The Court would have us believe that over 200 years ago, the Framers made a choice to limit the tools available to elected officials wishing to regulate civilian uses of weapons, and to authorize this Court to use the common-law process of case-by-case judicial lawmaking to define the contours of acceptable gun control policy. Absent compelling evidence that is nowhere to be found in the Court's opinion, I could not possibly conclude that the Framers made such a choice.

For these reasons, I respectfully dissent.

Glossary

infringed: breached; violated; encroached upon

militia: citizens organized to serve as a military force; a country's organized armed forces

Second Amendment: a very brief amendment to the U.S. Constitution that states: "A well regulated Militia, being necessary to the security of a free State, the right of the people to keep and bear Arms, shall not be infringed."

CITIZENS UNITED V. FEDERAL ELECTION COMMISSION

DATE
2010

AUTHOR
Anthony M. Kennedy

VOTE
5–4

CITATION
558 U.S. 310

SIGNIFICANCE
Ruled that political spending is a form of free speech, allowing virtually unlimited corporate donations to political campaigns

Overview

In 2010 the U.S. Supreme Court ruled in *Citizens United v. Federal Election Commission* (FEC) that political spending is a form of free speech and thus is protected under the First Amendment of the Constitution. The landmark decision allows corporations and unions to spend unlimited amounts of money on political campaigns as long as those companies and unions are not directly affiliated with the candidates' campaigns. A controversial 5–4 decision by the Court changed the nature of political campaign spending, allowing massive influxes of cash to support candidates on behalf of corporate interests.

Citizens United is a conservative nonprofit organization that, in 2008, created a documentary titled *Hillary: The Movie*. The documentary was designed to negatively portray Hillary Clinton, one of the candidates for the Democratic nomination for president. A 1971 federal law had prohibited corporations from making direct contributions to political campaigns. In 2002 Congress passed the Bipartisan Campaign Reform Act (BCRA), also known as the McCain-Feingold Act, which modified the earlier campaign finance law. BCRA specifically barred unions or corporations from using their general treasuries to fund "electioneering communications" (radio, television, or satellite broadcasts) within sixty days of a general election or thirty days of a primary election. Citizens United filed a lawsuit with the U.S. District Court, in Washington, D.C., to seek exemption from federal legislation. The court ruled against Citizens United, so the nonprofit asked the Supreme Court to review the case, and the Court agreed.

The Court had to assess whether it should strike down two earlier decisions related to campaign finance, *McConnell v. FEC* (2003) and *Austin v. Michigan Chamber of Commerce* (1990). The Court came to a 5–4 decision, with Justice Anthony Kennedy penning the majority opinion. According to this decision, First Amendment protections extend to corporations, and limitations on corporate funding of independent political broadcasts are disallowed. The Court thus overruled the earlier *Austin* verdict and portions of the *McConnell* verdict.

Those critical of the *Citizens United* decision, including Justice John Paul Stevens, argued that unlimited corporate spending in political campaigns violates the interests of the framers of the Constitution, who sought to protect the rights of individuals. The majority decision contends that, in the digital age, the identity of campaign contributors should be easily disclosed. However, following the *Citizens United* decision, a new kind of political finance organization emerged: the super PAC. Political action committees (PACs) previously had been limited in terms of individual donations, but after the Supreme Court's decision, wealthy individuals and corporate interests could pour unlimited amounts of money into targeted super PACs that supported specific candidates or causes—without fear of having their identities revealed. The *Citizens United v. FEC* decision changed the nature of political campaigns in the United States; candidates for public office now need to discuss how they raise money in order to address public concerns with the role of wealthy donors in political campaigns.

Context

Campaign finance reform has long been a topic of concern in the United States. Troubled by the growing influence of industrial corporations in politics, President Theodore Roosevelt called for an end to corporate contributions to campaigns, resulting in the Tillman Act of 1907. President Franklin Delano Roosevelt sought to curtail corporate and union influence in politics and successfully urged Congress to pass legislation to restrict campaign contributions from those entities. After the Watergate scandal during the Richard Nixon administration, campaign reform laws were strengthened. In 1974, Congress amended the earlier 1971 Federal Election Campaign Act to create the FEC, to enforce laws regarding limitations on contributions by individuals, PACs, and political parties. The FEC also established a mechanism for public funding of elections. Four years later, the FEC opened a loophole: people could donate unlimited money if they directed contributions to party activities (voter drives, etc.) that did not support specific candidates. This so-called soft money was nonetheless diverted to specific candidates by both party organizations, despite the rules. President George H. W. Bush vetoed a bill to end this practice, and President Bill Clinton was unsuccessful in his attempts to get Congress to agree on legislation dealing with soft money.

President Barack Obama condemned the decision.
(Pete Souza)

In 1995, Russ Feingold, a Democrat from Wisconsin, and John McCain, a Republican from Arizona, began working on a bill together to address campaign finance reform. The bill died in Congress, but McCain's 2000 campaign for president and a series of corporate scandals brought the issue to the front of public consciousness. Feingold and McCain brought the bill back to life in 2002, and it passed the House and then narrowly in the Senate. The McCain-Feingold Act (Bipartisan Campaign Reform Act, or BCRA) amended the 1971 law to address two key issues. The first issue was to limit "soft money," the money not subjected to federal limits. The second issue, which played a significant role in the *Citizens United* case, was to limit the spread of issue-advocacy ads. These political advertisements did not advocate specifically for or against a candidate's campaign but did mention a candidate by name while targeting another issue. This law defined such ads as "electioneering communications." An example of such an ad would be a television commercial paid for by a Wall Street firm naming a candidate as bad for business. Such advertising was prohibited thirty days from a primary and sixty days from a general election.

In 2008, the conservative nonprofit organization Citizens United produced the documentary *Hillary: The*

Movie. This documentary presented then Senator Hillary Clinton, who was a candidate for the Democratic presidential nomination, in an unfavorable light. Citizens United wanted to promote the movie and make it available for free through video on-demand services offered by cable companies. Concerned that they would be subject to FEC sanctions and penalties under both the Federal Election Campaign Act and BCRA, Citizens United filed a lawsuit in the district court in Washington, D.C., seeking exemption from the BCRA legislation and arguing that a portion of the earlier legislation was unconstitutional. The court denied the Citizens United petition, and the Supreme Court agreed to hear the case when requested by Citizens United's attorneys.

In January of 2010, the Supreme Court handed down its decision in *Citizens United v. FEC.* The 5–4 decision ruled that limitations on contributions to political campaigns made by either corporations or labor unions were a violation of First Amendment rights. Specifically, in his majority opinion, Anthony M. Kennedy stated that First Amendment protections extended to corporations. This essentially eliminated all restrictions on corporate funding for public political broadcasts. Through this decision, the Court overturned part of its previous decision in *McConnell v. FEC* and overturned the decision in *Austin v. Michigan Chamber of Commerce,* which had allowed restrictions on corporate spending related to political speech.

The decision in this case generated considerable reaction from across the political spectrum. Those in favor of the Court's ruling included the National Rifle Association, the U.S. Chamber of Commerce, and the American Civil Liberties Union. Those in opposition included President Barack Obama, who openly criticized the ruling, stating: "Last week, the Supreme Court reversed a century of law to open the floodgates for special interests—including foreign corporations—to spend without limit in our elections." Senator John McCain also expressed his concern that the Court's decision would unleash unprecedented amounts of union and corporate money into political campaigns. *Citizens United v. FEC* did dramatically increase the flow of money into political campaigns. Previously, contributions to PACs had been limited to $5,000 per person per year. *Citizens United* eliminated this cap, resulting in super PACs, which bring in hundreds of millions of dollars from relatively few entities who exert considerable power on elections.

About the Author

Justice Anthony M. Kennedy was born in Sacramento on July 23, 1936. His father was a lobbyist in California, and his mother was a teacher who was also politically active. Kennedy spent three years at Stanford University and then studied abroad at the London School of Economics, graduating with a degree in political science in 1958. He received his law degree from Harvard in 1961. Kennedy worked in private practice, taking over his father's law firm after his father died in 1963. During these years, Kennedy became active in politics. He was a lobbyist associated with Ronald Reagan, which resulted in Reagan's recommending him to President Gerald Ford for a seat on the U.S. Court of Appeals for the Ninth Circuit. Kennedy was the youngest appointee to the bench at age thirty-eight. Following the rejection of Robert Bork's nomination to the Supreme Court, Ronald Reagan nominated Kennedy to the Supreme Court, and he took his seat on February 18, 1988.

Kennedy represented a moderate voice on the Supreme Court, often voting against the expectations of liberals and conservatives. A staunch supporter of individual rights, he served as a swing vote in many key decisions during his tenure. Kennedy was certainly a conservative, but he did not rely on doctrinal conservative positions for his voting decisions. For example, he was the key vote in deciding in favor of same-sex marriage in the *Obergefell v. Hodges* decision (2015), arguing: "No union is more profound than marriage, for it embodies the highest ideals of love, fidelity, devotion, sacrifice, and family. . . . [The petitioners] ask for equal dignity in the eyes of the law. The Constitution grants them that right."

Time magazine named Anthony Kennedy "The Decider" on its June 18, 2012, cover, in part for his decision in key gay rights cases but also for his decision in favor of upholding the tenets of the Affordable Care Act. Kennedy was usually the deciding vote in important cases, from abortion rights to death penalty issues. In *Citizens United,* Justice Anthony M. Kennedy was selected to write the majority opinion precisely because of his role as "The Decider." He was the middle-ground voice who could present a controversial opinion with an even hand. Kennedy retired in 2018 and was succeeded by his former law clerk, Brett Kavanaugh.

Explanation and Analysis of the Document

Justice Kennedy opens the document with a brief summary of federal laws governing corporate contributions to political campaigns and then provides a background of the case. He refers to a subsection of the 1971 Federal Election Campaign Act (441b). This law banned corporations from making direct contributions to political campaigns. However, the law did allow unions and corporations to create PACs. The McCain-Feingold Act, or BCRA, passed in 2002 and amended 441b to prohibit "electioneering communication."

Citizens United filed its case with the district court because it feared that the movie and ads for it would be banned under 441b and that BCRA restrictions on "electioneering communication" also would apply. Citizens United's case argued that 441b's ban and the BCRA requirements were unconstitutional in the case of *Hillary: The Movie*. The lower court rejected Citizens United's arguments, and thus the Supreme Court ended up with the case.

Justice Kennedy then turns to the important discussion of the Court's logic in how it approached deciding the case. The first decision the Court had to make was whether the jurists would have to reassess previous decisions made in cases involving campaign finance contributions made by corporations. Those two cases are *Austin* and *McConnell*. At question here is whether 441b, the ban on direct corporate contributions to political campaigns, has "facial validity." This legal term means that, on its face, the law may appear valid, but circumstances may modify or explain it, changing its validity. In other words, the Court may have to consider whether to overturn previous decisions. The Court first attempts to resolve the issues at hand without doing that.

The Court first addresses Citizens United's claim that the documentary is not a form of "electioneering communication" because each video-on-demand transmission is not public; it is requested by and sent to an individual cable box. The Court rejects this argument, stating that it is not feasible to estimate the number of cable subscribers that might have seen the movie. (Justice Kennedy notes that the cable company had 34.5 million subscribers.) Citizens United cited an earlier case decision to dispute the validity of 441b's ban. "WRTL" is a reference to *Wisconsin Right to Life v. FEC*, a 2007 case in which the Supreme Court ruled that the FEC could not ban "issue ads" months before a campaign. Justice Kennedy refers to the decision in *McConnell v. FEC*, noting that "electioneering communication" had to be "express advocacy" in favor of or against a specific candidate. Citizens United was arguing that *Hillary: The Movie* is not a form of "express advocacy." The Court shuts down this argument, finding the documentary to be a clear example of advocacy against Hillary Clinton.

Another tactic taken by Citizens United was to argue that video-on-demand distribution provides viewers with less potential for exposure to ads that will distort their political views. The Court states that it is dangerous territory for them to determine which types of media are best for a given message; it is not the Court's place to make such decisions. Last, Citizens United pursued an exception based on its nonprofit status, claiming that its ads and movie were funded by individuals. Justice Kennedy refers to "*MCFL*," which was another case (*FEC v. Massachusetts Citizens for Life, Inc.*) that created an exception. However, because Citizens United accepts donations from for-profit corporations, that exemption does not apply to them.

Justice Kennedy explains that the Court has no choice but to revisit the entire concept of restricting corporate speech (the facial validity of 441b). The Court's primary concern is with 441b's violation of First Amendment rights. Justice Kennedy notes that the law allows corporations to use PACs but argues that establishing a PAC may not be possible for every organization. Thus, he concludes that "Section 4441b's prohibition on corporate independent expenditures is thus a ban on speech. . . . The First Amendment protects speech and speaker, and the ideas that flow from each."

Then the Court takes up the issue of whether restrictions on corporate and union contributions are constitutional. Justice Kennedy discusses the history of legal precedence in this area, mentioning the Federal Election Campaign Act and some past Court rulings.

Buckley v. Valeo was a 1976 decision that struck down limitations on campaign spending contained in the 1971 Federal Election Campaign Act. *Austin v. Michigan Chamber of Commerce* was a 1990 decision that upheld the State of Michigan's law prohibiting corporate expenditures in support of political candidates.

The important language in the *Austin* decision is the desire to limit "the corrosive and distorting effects" of corporate contributions on the public's interests. Justice Kennedy notes, however, that there is an exemption for media corporations. Because of this exemption, non-media companies with the same business interests but no media outlets would be denied First Amendment protections. Furthermore, modern technology has blurred the line between "the media" and others who wish to communicate. Restrictions on political speech in the form of contributions, therefore, are violations of First Amendment rights.

Justice Kennedy uses historical context to bolster his opinion, pointing to the role of newspapers in the debates on the Constitution between the Federalists and the Anti-Federalists. He also notes the changing nature of technology in the twenty-first century, commenting that "soon, however, it may be that Internet sources, such as blogs and social networking Web sites, will provide citizens with significant information about political candidates and issues." The Court then overrules the *Austin* decision.

The Court addresses Citizens United's claim that the disclaimer and disclosure provisions required under BCRA are unconstitutional. The Court rejects this claim, stating that such disclaimers "avoid confusion" and provide "transparency." Justice Kennedy closes with his thoughts on free speech: "The civic discourse belongs to the people, and the Government may not prescribe the means used to conduct it."

Impact

The decision in *Citizens United v. FEC* was met with considerable criticism by parties from both ends of the political spectrum. In his public statement following the decision, President Barack Obama opined that the ruling would give "the special interests and their lobbyists even more power in Washington—while undermining the influence of average Americans." Democratic Senator Russ Feingold called the ruling a "terrible mistake," and Republican Senator John McCain stated that he was "disappointed" with the Court's decision. On the contrary, Senate Minority Leader Mitch McConnell praised the decision, stating that "our democracy depends on free speech, not just for some but for all."

The primary concern was that the Court's decision would flood political campaigns with corporate money, allowing corporations to promote their own financial interests and essentially "buy" candidates through campaign contributions. The actual impact of *Citizens United*, however, has been the creation of super PACs, which do not make direct contributions to campaigns or candidates but rather advocate issues. Super PACs may make unlimited expenditures (and collect unlimited donations) independent of individual campaigns. Super PACs played an important role in the 2012 election immediately following the *Citizens United* decision. Republican strategist Karl Rove created super PACs that collected over $300 million in support of Republican candidates. The leading super PAC in early 2012 had raised more money than the total combined spending of the top nine PACs in the 2008 election. However, most of the super PAC contributions did not come from corporations but rather from wealthy individuals. According to the Center for Responsive Politics, less than 0.5 percent of the money given to the most active super PACs came from publicly traded corporations. Some have argued that this impact of *Citizens United* means that a handful of wealthy individuals with specific interests control our election process, selecting their own hand-picked candidates and buying issue-oriented ads to support those candidates.

Another impact of *Citizens United* has been to allow public advocacy groups, 501 (c) (4) organizations, and trade associations to spend money on elections. Unlike super PACs, they do not have to disclose the names of their donors, although their primary purpose cannot be to engage in political advocacy if they wish to maintain their tax-exempt status. Groups like Planned Parenthood and the National Rifle Association may engage in political activity as a result. Furthermore, some partisan groups have registered as 501 (c) (4) organizations and thus do not have to disclose their donors. These groups have spent considerable sums on political purposes. They include 21st Century

Colorado, a liberal organization, and Karl Rove's highly influential Crossroads Grassroots Policy Strategies.

Thus, while the Court expressed its desire to extend free speech protections to unions and corporations in political activities, it appears that the primary impact of *Citizens United v. FEC* has been to strengthen the power and influence of not the corporate sector but instead wealthy private donors. In the 2018 election the top ten PACs donated just under $30 million total to federal candidates. The Campaign Legal Center revealed that the three biggest spenders in the 2018 election were all super PACS; their total expenditures amounted to $345 million. As Justice Kennedy presciently noted in his opinion, information is increasingly disseminated via social media and the internet, which offers the opportunity for super PACs to avoid disclosure rules. The influx of money into political discourse presents challenges, as we balance the need to preserve free speech with the need to maintain transparency and truth.

Questions for Further Study

1. In his dissent, Justice Stevens stated that the Founders did not intend legal entities to be included as "We the People." What do you think of this critique of the decision in this case?

2. Another point raised by the dissenting minority was the potential for "the appearance of corruption" with the rise of corporate money in political activity. Do you think *Citizens United* has eroded public confidence in the electoral process in this country?

3. What role does technology play in elections, and how does it influence the decisions people make? How did Justice Kennedy address this in his opinion?

4. Justice Kennedy refers to the Federalist Papers and the Founders' embrace of diversity of opinion in political discourse. What role does diversity of opinion play in the Court's landmark decision in this case?

Further Reading

Books

Post, Robert. *Citizens Divided: Campaign Finance Reform and the Constitution.* Cambridge, MA: Harvard University Press, 2016.

Youn, Monica. *Money, Politics, and the Constitution: Beyond Citizens United.* New York: Century Foundation Press, 2011.

Articles

Klumpp, Tilman, Hugo M. Mialon, and Michael A. Williams. "The Business of American Democracy: *Citizens United*, Independent Spending, and Elections." *Journal of Law and Economics* 59, no. 1 (February 2016): 1–43.

Levitt, Justin. "Confronting the Impact of Citizens United." *Yale Law and Policy Review* 29, no. 1, 2010: 217–234.

Websites

Citizens United v. Federal Election Commission. SCOTUSblog. Accessed April 7, 2023. https://www.scotusblog.com/case-files/cases/citizens-united-v-federal-election-commission/.

—Commentary by Karen Linkletter

Citizens United v. Federal Election Commission

Document Text

Justice Kennedy delivered the opinion of the Court

Federal law prohibits corporations and unions from using their general treasury funds to make independent expenditures for speech defined as an "electioneering communication" or for speech expressly advocating the election or defeat of a candidate....

I

A

Citizens United is a nonprofit corporation. It brought this action in the United States District Court for the District of Columbia. A three-judge court later convened to hear the cause. The resulting judgment gives rise to this appeal.

Citizens United has an annual budget of about $12 million. Most of its funds are from donations by individuals; but, in addition, it accepts a small portion of its funds from for-profit corporations.

In January 2008, Citizens United released a film entitled *Hillary: The Movie*.... It is a 90-minute documentary about then-Senator Hillary Clinton, who was a candidate in the Democratic Party's 2008 Presidential primary elections. *Hillary* mentions Senator Clinton by name and depicts interviews with political commentators and other persons, most of them quite critical of Senator Clinton. Hillary was released in theaters and on DVD, but Citizens United wanted to increase distribution by making it available through video-on-demand.

... In December 2007, a cable company offered, for a payment of $1.2 million, to make *Hillary* available on a video-on-demand channel called "Elections '08." Some video-on-demand services require viewers to pay a small fee to view a selected program, but here the proposal was to make Hillary available to viewers free of charge.

To implement the proposal, Citizens United was prepared to pay for the video-on-demand; and to promote the film, it produced two 10-second ads and one 30-second ad for *Hillary*. Each ad includes a short (and, in our view, pejorative) statement about Senator Clinton, followed by the name of the movie and the movie's Website address. Citizens United desired to promote the video-on-demand offering by running advertisements on broadcast and cable television.

B

Before the Bipartisan Campaign Reform Act of 2002 (BCRA), federal law prohibited—and still does prohibit—corporations and unions from using general treasury funds to make direct contributions to candidates or independent expenditures that expressly advocate the election or defeat of a candidate, through any form of media, in connection with certain qualified federal elections.... An electioneering communication is defined as "any broadcast, cable, or satellite communication" that "refers to a clearly identified candidate for Federal office" and is made within 30 days of a primary or 60 days of a general election. The Federal Election Commission's (FEC) regulations further define an electioneering communication as a communication that is "publicly distributed." . . . Corporations and unions are barred from using their general treasury funds for express advocacy or electioneering communications. They may establish, however, a "separate segregated fund" (known as a political action committee, or PAC) for these purposes. The moneys received by the segregated fund are limited to donations from stockholders and employees of the corporation or, in the case of unions, members of the union.

C

Citizens United wanted to make *Hillary* available through video-on-demand within 30 days of the 2008 primary elections. It feared, however, that both the film and the ads would be covered by ß441b's ban on corporate-funded independent expenditures, thus subjecting the corporation to civil and criminal penalties under ß437g. In December 2007, Citizens United sought declaratory and injunctive relief against the FEC. It argued that (1) ß441b is unconstitutional as applied to *Hillary*; and (2) BCRA's disclaimer and disclosure requirements, BCRA ßß201 and 311, are unconstitutional as applied to *Hillary* and to the three ads for the movie.

The District Court denied Citizens United's motion for a preliminary injunction . . . and then granted the FEC's motion for summary judgment. . . . The court held that ß441b was facially constitutional under *McConnell, and that ß441b was constitutional as applied to Hillary* because it was "susceptible of no other interpretation than to inform the electorate that Senator Clinton is unfit for office, that the United States would be a dangerous place in a President Hillary Clinton world, and that viewers should vote against her." The court also rejected Citizens United's challenge to BCRA's disclaimer and disclosure requirements. It noted that "the Supreme Court has written approvingly of disclosure provisions triggered by political speech even though the speech itself was constitutionally protected under the First Amendment."

We noted probable jurisdiction. 555 U. S. ___ (2008). The case was reargued in this Court after the Court asked the parties to file supplemental briefs addressing whether we should overrule either or both *Austin and the part of McConnell* which addresses the facial validity of 2 U. S. C. ß441b.

II

Before considering whether *Austin* should be overruled, we first address whether Citizens United's claim that ß441b cannot be applied to *Hillary* may be resolved on other, narrower grounds.

A

Citizens United contends that ß441b does not cover *Hillary,* as a matter of statutory interpretation, because the film does not qualify as an "electioneering communication." . . . Under the definition of electioneering communication, the video-on-demand showing of *Hillary* on cable television would have been a "cable . . . communication" that "refer[red] to a clearly identified candidate for Federal office" and that was made within 30 days of a primary election. Citizens United, however, argues that *Hillary* was not "publicly distributed," because a single video-on-demand transmission is sent only to a requesting cable converter box and each separate transmission, in most instances, will be seen by just one household—not 50,000 or more persons.

This argument ignores the regulation's instruction on how to determine whether a cable transmission "[c]an be received by 50,000 or more persons." The regulation provides that the number of people who can receive a cable transmission is determined by the number of cable subscribers in the relevant area. Here, Citizens United wanted to use a cable video-on-demand system that had 34.5 million subscribers nationwide. Thus, *Hillary* could have been received by 50,000 persons or more.

One *amici* brief asks us, alternatively, to construe the condition that the communication "[c]an be received by 50,000 or more persons," to require "a plausible likelihood that the communication will be viewed by 50,000 or more potential voters"—as opposed to requiring only that the communication is "technologically capable" of being seen by that many people. Whether the population and demographic statistics in a proposed viewing area consisted of 50,000 registered voters—but not "infants, pre-teens, or otherwise electorally ineligible recipients"—would be a required determination, subject to judicial challenge and review, in any case where the issue was in doubt.

In our view the statute cannot be saved by limiting the reach of 2 U. S. C. ß441b through this suggested interpretation. In addition to the costs and burdens of litigation, this result would require a calculation as to the number of people a particular communication is likely to reach, with an inaccurate estimate potentially subjecting the speaker to criminal sanctions. The First Amendment does not permit laws that force speakers to retain a campaign finance attorney, conduct demographic marketing research, or seek declaratory rulings before discussing the most salient political issues of our day. Prolix laws chill speech for the same reason that vague laws chill speech: People "of common intelligence must necessarily guess at [the law's] meaning and differ as to its application." ... The Government may not render a ban on political speech constitutional by carving out a limited exemption through an amorphous regulatory interpretation....

B

Citizens United next argues that ß441b may not be applied to *Hillary* under the approach taken in *WRTL*. *McConnell* decided that ß441b(b)(2)'s definition of an "electioneering communication" was facially constitutional insofar as it restricted speech that was "the functional equivalent of express advocacy" for or against a specific candidate. *WRTL* then found an unconstitutional application of ß441b where the speech was not "express advocacy or its functional equivalent." As explained by The Chief Justice's controlling opinion in *WRTL*, the functional-equivalent test is objective: "a court should find that [a communication] is the functional equivalent of express advocacy only if [it] is susceptible of no reasonable interpretation other than as an appeal to vote for or against a specific candidate."

Under this test, *Hillary* is equivalent to express advocacy. The movie, in essence, is a feature-length negative advertisement that urges viewers to vote against Senator Clinton for President. In light of historical footage, interviews with persons critical of her, and voiceover narration, the film would be understood by most viewers as an extended criticism of Senator Clinton's character and her fitness for the office of the Presidency....

Citizens United argues that *Hillary* is just "a documentary film that examines certain historical events." We disagree. The movie's consistent emphasis is on the relevance of these events to Senator Clinton's candidacy for President....

As the District Court found, there is no reasonable interpretation of *Hillary* other than as an appeal to vote against Senator Clinton. Under the standard stated in *McConnell* and further elaborated in *WRTL*, the film qualifies as the functional equivalent of express advocacy.

C

Citizens United further contends that ß441b should be invalidated as applied to movies shown through video-on-demand, arguing that this delivery system has a lower risk of distorting the political process than do television ads. On what we might call conventional television, advertising spots reach viewers who have chosen a channel or a program for reasons unrelated to the advertising. With video-on-demand, by contrast, the viewer selects a program after taking "a series of affirmative steps": subscribing to cable; navigating through various menus; and selecting the program....

While some means of communication may be less effective than others at influencing the public in different contexts, any effort by the Judiciary to decide which means of communications are to be preferred for the particular type of message and speaker would raise questions as to the courts' own lawful authority. Substantial questions would arise if courts were to begin saying what means of speech should be preferred or disfavored. And in all events, those differentiations might soon prove to be irrelevant or outdated by technologies that are in rapid flux....

Courts, too, are bound by the First Amendment. We must decline to draw, and then redraw, constitutional lines based on the particular media or technology used to disseminate political speech from a particular speaker.... The interpretive process itself would create an inevitable, pervasive, and serious risk of chilling protected speech pending the drawing of fine distinctions that, in the end, would themselves be questionable. First Amendment standards, however, "must give the benefit of any doubt to protecting rather than stifling speech." ...

D

Citizens United also asks us to carve out an exception to ß441b's expenditure ban for nonprofit corporate political speech funded overwhelmingly by individuals. As an alternative to reconsidering *Austin*, the Government also seems to prefer this approach. This line of analysis, however, would be unavailing.

In *MCFL*, the Court found unconstitutional ß441b's restrictions on corporate expenditures as applied to nonprofit corporations that were formed for the sole purpose of promoting political ideas, did not engage in business activities, and did not accept contributions from for-profit corporations or labor unions.... Citizens United does not qualify for the *MCFL* exemption, however, since some funds used to make the movie were donations from for-profit corporations.

The Government suggests we could find BCRA's Wellstone Amendment unconstitutional, sever it from the statute, and hold that Citizens United's speech is exempt from ß441b's ban under BCRA's Snowe-Jeffords Amendment.... Citizens United would not qualify for the Snowe-Jeffords exemption, under its terms as written, because *Hillary* was funded in part with donations from for-profit corporations.

Consequently, to hold for Citizens United on this argument, the Court would be required to revise the text of *MCFL*, sever BCRA's Wellstone Amendment, ß441b(c)(6), and ignore the plain text of BCRA's Snowe-Jeffords Amendment.... There is no principled basis for doing this without rewriting *Austin*'s holding that the Government can restrict corporate independent expenditures for political speech....

E

As the foregoing analysis confirms, the Court cannot resolve this case on a narrower ground without chilling political speech, speech that is central to the meaning and purpose of the First Amendment....

Citizens United has preserved its First Amendment challenge to ß441b as applied to the facts of its case; and given all the circumstances, we cannot easily address that issue without assuming a premise—the permissibility of restricting corporate political speech—that is itself in doubt....

As noted above, Citizens United's narrower arguments are not sustainable under a fair reading of the statute. In the exercise of its judicial responsibility, it is necessary then for the Court to consider the facial validity of ß441b. Any other course of decision would prolong the substantial, nation-wide chilling effect caused by ß441b's prohibitions on corporate expenditures....

The ongoing chill upon speech that is beyond all doubt protected makes it necessary in this case to invoke the earlier precedents that a statute which chills speech can and must be invalidated where its facial invalidity has been demonstrated....

III

The First Amendment provides that "Congress shall make no law ... abridging the freedom of speech."...

The law before us is an outright ban, backed by criminal sanctions. Section 441b makes it a felony for all corporations—including nonprofit advocacy corporations—either to expressly advocate the election or defeat of candidates or to broadcast electioneering communications within 30 days of a primary election and 60 days of a general election. Thus, the following acts would all be felonies under ß441b: The Sierra Club runs an ad, within the crucial phase of 60 days before the general election, that exhorts the public to disapprove of a Congressman who favors logging in national forests; the National Rifle Association publishes a book urging the public to vote for the challenger because the incumbent U.S. Senator supports a handgun ban; and the American Civil Liberties Union creates a Web site telling the public to vote for a Presidential candidate in light of that candidate's defense of free speech. These prohibitions are classic examples of censorship.

Section 441b is a ban on corporate speech notwithstanding the fact that a PAC created by a corporation can still speak.... So the PAC exemption from ß441b's expenditure ban, ß441b(b)(2), does not allow corporations to speak. Even if a PAC could somehow allow a corporation to speak—and it does not—the option to form PACs does not alleviate the First Amendment problems with ß441b....

Given the onerous restrictions, a corporation may not be able to establish a PAC in time to make its views known regarding candidates and issues in a current campaign.

Section 441b's prohibition on corporate independent expenditures is thus a ban on speech....

Speech is an essential mechanism of democracy, for it is the means to hold officials accountable to the people....

For these reasons, political speech must prevail against laws that would suppress it, whether by design or inadvertence. Laws that burden political speech are "subject to strict scrutiny," which requires the Government to prove that the restriction "furthers a compelling interest and is narrowly tailored to achieve that interest." ...

Premised on mistrust of governmental power, the First Amendment stands against attempts to disfavor certain subjects or viewpoints.... As instruments to censor, these categories are interrelated: Speech restrictions based on the identity of the speaker are all too often simply a means to control content.

Quite apart from the purpose or effect of regulating content, moreover, the Government may commit a constitutional wrong when by law it identifies certain preferred speakers. By taking the right to speak from some and giving it to others, the Government deprives the disadvantaged person or class of the right to use speech to strive to establish worth, standing, and respect for the speaker's voice. The Government may not by these means deprive the public of the right and privilege to determine for itself what speech and speakers are worthy of consideration. The First Amendment protects speech and speaker, and the ideas that flow from each....

We find no basis for the proposition that, in the context of political speech, the Government may impose restrictions on certain disfavored speakers. Both history and logic lead us to this conclusion.

A

1

...

At least since the latter part of the 19th century, the laws of some States and of the United States imposed a ban on corporate direct contributions to candidates.... Yet not until 1947 did Congress first prohibit independent expenditures by corporations and labor unions in ß304 of the Labor Management Relations Act 1947....

For almost three decades thereafter, the Court did not reach the question whether restrictions on corporate and union expenditures are constitutional....

2

In *Buckley,* the Court addressed various challenges to the Federal Election Campaign Act of 1971 (FECA) as amended in 1974....

The *Buckley* Court recognized a "sufficiently important" governmental interest in "the prevention of corruption and the appearance of corruption." This followed from the Court's concern that large contributions could be given "to secure a political *quid pro quo.*"

The *Buckley* Court explained that the potential for *quid pro quo* corruption distinguished direct contributions to candidates from independent expenditures. The Court emphasized that "the independent expenditure ceiling ... fails to serve any substantial governmental interest in stemming the reality or appearance of corruption in the electoral process," because "[t]he absence of prearrangement and coordination ... alleviates the danger that expenditures will be given as a *quid pro quo* for improper commitments from the candidate." ...

3

Thus the law stood until *Austin. Austin* "uph[eld] a direct restriction on the independent expenditure of funds for political speech for the first time in [this Court's] history." There, the Michigan Chamber of Commerce sought to use general treasury funds to run a newspaper ad supporting a specific candidate. Michigan law, however, prohibited corporate independent expenditures that supported or opposed any candidate for state office. A violation of the law was punishable as a felony. The Court sustained the speech prohibition.

...

B

The Court is thus confronted with conflicting lines of precedent: a pre-*Austin* line that forbids restrictions on political speech based on the speaker's corporate identity and a post-*Austin* line that permits them. No case before *Austin* had held that Congress could prohibit independent expenditures for political speech based on the speaker's corporate identity.

...

1

...

Austin's antidistortion rationale would produce the dangerous, and unacceptable, consequence that Congress could ban political speech of media corporations....

Media corporations are now exempt from ß441b's ban on corporate expenditures.... Yet media corporations accumulate wealth with the help of the corporate form, the largest media corporations have "immense aggregations of wealth," and the views expressed by media corporations often "have little or no correlation to the public's support" for those views. Thus, under the Government's reasoning, wealthy media corporations could have their voices diminished to put them on par with other media entities. There is no precedent for permitting this under the First Amendment.

The media exemption discloses further difficulties with the law now under consideration. There is no precedent supporting laws that attempt to distinguish between corporations which are deemed to be exempt as media corporations and those which are not. . . . With the advent of the Internet and the decline of print and broadcast media, moreover, the line between the media and others who wish to comment on political and social issues becomes far more blurred.

The law's exception for media corporations is, on its own terms, all but an admission of the invalidity of the antidistortion rationale. And the exemption results in a further, separate reason for finding this law invalid: Again by its own terms, the law exempts some corporations but covers others, even though both have the need or the motive to communicate their views. The exemption applies to media corporations owned or controlled by corporations that have diverse and substantial investments and participate in endeavors other than news. So even assuming the most doubtful proposition that a news organization has a right to speak when others do not, the exemption would allow a conglomerate that owns both a media business and an unrelated business to influence or control the media in order to advance its overall business interest. At the same time, some other corporation, with an identical business interest but no media outlet in its ownership structure, would be forbidden to speak or inform the public about the same issue. This differential treatment cannot be squared with the First Amendment.

There is simply no support for the view that the First Amendment, as originally understood, would permit the suppression of political speech by media corporations. The Framers may not have anticipated modern business and media corporations. . . .

The great debates between the Federalists and the Anti-Federalists over our founding document were pub-lished and expressed in the most important means of mass communication of that era—newspapers owned by individuals. . . . At the founding, speech was open, comprehensive, and vital to society's definition of itself; there were no limits on the sources of speech and knowledge. . . . The Framers may have been unaware of certain types of speakers or forms of communication, but that does not mean that those speakers and media are entitled to less First Amendment protection than those types of speakers and media that provided the means of communicating political ideas when the Bill of Rights was adopted.

. . .

The censorship we now confront is vast in its reach. The Government has "muffle[d] the voices that best represent the most significant segments of the economy." . . . And "the electorate [has been] deprived of information, knowledge and opinion vital to its function." . . . By suppressing the speech of manifold corporations, both for-profit and nonprofit, the Government prevents their voices and viewpoints from reaching the public and advising voters on which persons or entities are hostile to their interests. Factions will necessarily form in our Republic, but the remedy of "destroying the liberty" of some factions is "worse than the disease." . . .

The purpose and effect of this law is to prevent corporations, including small and nonprofit corporations, from presenting both facts and opinions to the public. This makes *Austin*'s antidistortion rationale all the more an aberration. . . .

When Government seeks to use its full power, including the criminal law, to command where a person may get his or her information or what distrusted source he or she may not hear, it uses censorship to control thought. This is unlawful. The First Amendment confirms the freedom to think for ourselves.

. . .

C

. . .

Austin is undermined by experience since its announcement. Political speech is so ingrained in our culture that speakers find ways to circumvent campaign finance laws. . . . Our Nation's speech dynamic is changing, and informative voices should not have to circumvent onerous restrictions to exercise their First Amendment rights. Speakers have become adept at presenting citizens with sound bites, talking points, and scripted messages that dominate the 24-hour news cycle. Corporations, like individuals, do not have monolithic views. On certain topics corporations may possess valuable expertise, leaving them the best equipped to point out errors or fallacies in speech of all sorts, including the speech of candidates and elected officials.

Rapid changes in technology—and the creative dynamic inherent in the concept of free expression—counsel against upholding a law that restricts political speech in certain media or by certain speakers. . . . The First Amendment does not permit Congress to make these categorical distinctions based on the corporate identity of the speaker and the content of the political speech. . . .

Due consideration leads to this conclusion: *Austin* should be and now is overruled. We return to the principle established in *Buckley* and *Bellotti* that the Government may not suppress political speech on the basis of the speaker's corporate identity. No sufficient governmental interest justifies limits on the political speech of nonprofit or for-profit corporations.

D

Austin is overruled, so it provides no basis for allowing the Government to limit corporate independent expenditures. . . .

IV

A

Citizens United next challenges BCRA's disclaimer and disclosure provisions as applied to *Hillary* and the three advertisements for the movie. Under BCRA ß311, televised electioneering communications funded by anyone other than a candidate must include a disclaimer that "'_____ is responsible for the content of this advertising.'" The required statement must be made in a "clearly spoken manner," and displayed on the screen in a "clearly readable manner" for at least four seconds. It must state that the communication "is not authorized by any candidate or candidate's committee"; it must also display the name and address (or Web site address) of the person or group that funded the advertisement. Under BCRA ß201, any person who spends more than $10,000 on electioneering communications within a calendar year must file a disclosure statement with the FEC. 2 U. S. C. ß434(f)(1). That statement must identify the person making the expenditure, the amount of the expenditure, the election to which the communication was directed, and the names of certain contributors. ß434(f)(2).

Disclaimer and disclosure requirements may burden the ability to speak, but they "impose no ceiling on campaign-related activities" and "do not prevent anyone from speaking." . . .

B

Citizens United sought to broadcast one 30-second and two 10-second ads to promote *Hillary*. Under FEC regulations, a communication that "[p]roposes a commercial transaction" was not subject to 2 U. S. C. ß441b's restrictions on corporate or union funding of electioneering communications. The regulations, however, do not exempt those communications from the disclaimer and disclosure requirements in BCRA ßß201 and 311. . . .

Citizens United argues that the disclaimer requirements in ß311 are unconstitutional as applied to its ads. It contends that the governmental interest in providing information to the electorate does not justify requiring disclaimers for any commercial advertisements, including the ones at issue here. We disagree. The ads fall within BCRA's definition of an "electioneering communication": They referred to then-Senator Clinton by name shortly before a primary and contained pejorative references to her candidacy. . . . The disclaimers required by ß311 "provid[e] the electorate with information" and "insure that the voters are fully informed" about the person or group who is speaking. . . . At the very least, the disclaimers avoid confusion by making clear that the ads are not funded by a candidate or political party. . . .

The First Amendment protects political speech; and disclosure permits citizens and shareholders to react to the speech of corporate entities in a proper way. This transparency enables the electorate to make informed decisions and give proper weight to different speakers and messages.

C

For the same reasons we uphold the application of BCRA ßß201 and 311 to the ads, we affirm their application to *Hillary*. We find no constitutional impediment to the application of BCRA's disclaimer and disclosure requirements to a movie broadcast via video-on-demand. And there has been no showing that, as applied in this case, these requirements would impose a chill on speech or expression.

V

…

Modern day movies, television comedies, or skits on Youtube.com might portray public officials or public policies in unflattering ways. Yet if a covered transmission during the blackout period creates the background for candidate endorsement or opposition, a felony occurs solely because a corporation, other than an exempt media corporation, has made the "purchase, payment, distribution, loan, advance, deposit, or gift of money or anything of value" in order to engage in political speech. Speech would be suppressed in the realm where its necessity is most evident: in the public dialogue preceding a real election. Governments are often hostile to speech, but under our law and our tradition it seems stranger than fiction for our Government to make this political speech a crime. Yet this is the statute's purpose and design.

Some members of the public might consider *Hillary* to be insightful and instructive; some might find it to be neither high art nor a fair discussion on how to set the Nation's course; still others simply might suspend judgment on these points but decide to think more about issues and candidates. Those choices and assessments, however, are not for the Government to make. "The First Amendment underwrites the freedom to experiment and to create in the realm of thought and speech. Citizens must be free to use new forms, and new forums, for the expression of ideas. The civic discourse belongs to the people, and the Government may not prescribe the means used to conduct it." …

The judgment of the District Court is reversed with respect to the constitutionality of 2 U. S. C. ß441b's restrictions on corporate independent expenditures. The judgment is affirmed with respect to BCRA's disclaimer and disclosure requirements. The case is remanded for further proceedings consistent with this opinion.

It is so ordered.

Glossary

***amici* brief:** literally, "friends-of-the-court" brief—a legal document filed by parties who are not directly affiliated with a case but who have strong interests associated with the case. Singular: *amicus*.

declaratory relief: the official judgment of a court concerning the status of the matter in question and the rights of the parties to a lawsuit, without an assessment of damages

injunctive relief: a court order requiring that a defendant engage in or refrain from engaging in a specific action

***McConnell*:** *McConnell v. FEC*, a Supreme Court decision (2003) in which the majority of the provisions of the McCain-Feingold Act (Bipartisan Campaign Reform Act) were upheld

Wellstone Amendment: an amendment to the Bipartisan Campaign Reform Act sponsored by Paul Wellstone that extended the advertising ban to nonprofit organizations

Shelby County v. Holder

Date 2013	**Citation** 570 U.S. 529
Author John Roberts	**Significance** Held that Section 4(b) of the Voting Rights Act, which specified which states and municipalities must secure federal permission prior to passing new voting laws or amending existing ones, is unconstitutional
Vote 5–4	

Overview

Following nearly a century of state and local governments, primarily in the South, denying people of color their right to vote through the imposition of various restrictions and regulations, Congress's passage of the Voting Rights Act in 1965 made clear that no citizen could be deprived of their right to vote based on their race. Under the act, states and districts with a history of disregarding the right of enfranchisement of certain groups could no longer utilize certain practices designed to bar these individuals from casting their ballots. The act also forbade these states and districts from passing laws regarding elections or modify existing ones without first acquiring approval from the federal government. Supporters of the act heralded it as a great victory, with the federal government finally enforcing the Fifteenth Amendment long after its ratification. Its impact came to be evident with a marked increase in the voter registration rates of African Americans in the two decades following the act's passage. Despite some controversy over the years, Congress reauthorized the Voting Rights Act on a regular basis with support from both parties.

The act's supporters championed, and its critics denigrated, the primary source of its influence, Section 4 of the act, which established the applicable jurisdictions with a history of race-based voter discrimination. In 2013, the Supreme Court, in the case *Shelby County v. Holder*, determined that the formula used to determine which jurisdictions Section 4 applied to should be struck down. In a 5–4 decision, the majority insisted that the formula reflected an America that no longer existed, as evidenced by the high percentages of African Americans voting in elections and running for elected office in the years since Congress passed the Voting Rights Act. Ruth Bader Ginsburg wrote a lengthy dissent, joined by Stephen Breyer, Sonia Sotomayor, and Elena Kagan.

Context

Although the Constitution does not expressly grant them, voting rights have long been regarded as a fundamental right to be enjoyed by American citizens. Prior to the Civil War, determining who had the right to vote and overseeing elections was largely the responsibility of the states based on Article IV of the Constitution, which guarantees each state's right to self-government, and the Tenth Amendment's assertion that all rights not granted to the federal government belong to the states.

One of the more pivotal pieces of legislation regarding the right to vote in the United States is the Voting Rights Act of 1965. Congress passed this bill after nearly a century of state and local governments across the South denying African Americans their right to vote. The enfranchisement of Black men was a provision for former Confederate states rejoining the Union after the Civil War, and southern African Americans were politically engaged in the early years of Reconstruction, regularly voting in elections and electing representatives of color to serve at the local, state, and national levels. African Americans in the decades after the Civil War overwhelmingly identified as Republicans, the party being identified with the abolition of slavery and passage of legislation intended to guarantee the rights of African Americans.

The Fourteenth Amendment, ratified in 1867, defines citizenship and protects every citizen's right to due process of law. The ratification of the Fifteenth Amendment in 1870 prohibited states from denying prospective voters their right to cast a ballot based on race, color, or prior enslavement but critically did not guarantee the right to vote, a misstep that came to be exploited routinely by local and state governments across the South. The end of Reconstruction in 1877 came at a time when white southern Democrats increasingly reasserted their control over local and state governments, often with the threat or use of violence. Their takeover complete, white southern leaders passed numerous laws intended to deter or prevent Black voters from participating in elections. Such measures included poll taxes that impoverished African American voters struggled to pay and literacy tests that uneducated African Americans struggled to pass. Black people who challenged these blatant efforts to strip them of any political agency faced the prospect of intimidation and out-and-out violence well into the twentieth century.

It was not until the civil rights movement of the 1950s and 1960s that the federal government took steps to challenge discriminatory voting practices. Years of protests and activism culminated in President Lyndon

The first page of the Voting Rights Act of 1965. The Shelby *case ruled that Section 4(b) was unconstitutional.*
(National Archives and Records Administration)

Johnson signing the Voting Rights Act (VRA) in August 1965 after Congress passed it. The VRA struck down the use of any measures or practices intended to deprive African American citizens of their right to vote. It also necessitated that municipalities known for engaging in discriminatory voter suppression acquire permission from the federal government and the Department of Justice prior to the creation of new laws or procedures related to voting. The VRA also decreed that federal examiners who were able to register citizens to vote be assigned to counties with a history of voter suppression.

Congress renewed the VRA with some amendments with minimal resistance on five occasions in the years following its passage. It was expanded to protect the voting rights of those with language barriers and disabilities. The VRA necessitated the predominantly southern states of Alabama, Alaska, Arizona, Georgia, Louisiana, Mississippi, South Carolina, Texas, and

Virginia, and counties located in California, Florida, Michigan, New York, North Carolina, and South Dakota, to provide the Justice Department or a federal court with any plans to alter voting laws to avert voter suppression based on race or other identifier. The states and counties needing to submit proposed changes is laid out in a formula in Section 4 of the VRA, specifically that applicable districts are those that obligated prospective voters to pass a voting test before November 1, 1964, and had a less than 50 percent turnout for the presidential election of 1964.

Section 5 forbids the designated districts from making changes to their election laws without federal approval and explains the process, called preclearance, whereby approval for voting alterations is acquired from the federal government. A district seeking to alter election laws must first explain to either the attorney general or a panel of three judges from a Washington, D.C., district court how the change will avoid adversely affecting the right to vote possessed by anyone belonging to a particular race or minority group.

Although initially enacted for five years, Section 5 was routinely renewed since the VRA's enactment. Challenges emerged periodically, but it wasn't until Shelby County, Alabama, challenged the constitutionality of Sections 4 and 5 of the VRA that the Supreme Court in 2013 was called upon to decide on the issue after a district court and the U.S. Court of Appeals for the District of Columbia Circuit upheld the constitutionality of the sections. In a 5–4 decision, the Court declared Section 4 of the VRA to be unconstitutional by obligating districts to adhere to standards no longer consistent with the current political landscape, which had changed considerably since the VRA first went into effect in the mid-1960s.

About the Author

Following his appointment to the Supreme Court in 2005, Chief Justice John G. Roberts Jr. quickly established himself as a moderating presence on the Court who sought to reassure the American people that the Court was nonpartisan and deserving of their trust. Born in Buffalo, New York, in 1955, Roberts and his family relocated to Long Beach, Indiana, four years later after his father, an executive for a steel company, received a promotion. He proved a standout student at the La Lumiere boarding school in La Porte, Indiana, showing a keen interest in sports, theater, music, and especially academics.

Roberts then completed a degree in history at Harvard University, graduating summa cum laude in three years, in 1976, with the intention of becoming a professor. But he changed his mind and entered Harvard Law School, graduating in 1979 and accepting a clerkship for Supreme Court Justice William Rehnquist the following year. Roberts spent the next two decades working in both the public and private sectors, including a three-year stint as principal deputy solicitor general from 1990 to 1993.

He was working for the law firm of Hogan & Hartson in 2003 when President George W. Bush nominated him to serve as a judge of the U.S. Court of Appeals and then to the Supreme Court two years later. Bush initially intended Roberts to take the place of retiring justice Sandra Day O'Connor but changed his mind following the unexpected death of Chief Justice William Rehnquist; the president consequently switched Roberts's nomination from associate justice to chief justice.

During his confirmation process, Roberts managed to win over most of the senators at the hearings, presenting himself as a level-headed interpreter of the law who believed in judicial restraint and did not see the Court as being responsible for the creation of new laws. His confirmation made Roberts the youngest chief justice in a century. While Roberts routinely avowed that the Court should render decisions free from ideology or bias, his voting record is consistent with that of a political conservative related to such issues as religious liberty, gun rights, and abortion.

Explanation and Analysis of the Document

Roberts's opinion opens with an acknowledgment of the historical significance of the Voting Rights Act of 1965, which obligated some states to require permission from the federal government prior to the enactment of any new laws concerning voting, an arguable deviation from the spirit of federalism. But such measures were deemed necessary by Congress to overturn the many state and local restrictions on voting based on race. Roberts points out the law's continued existence and potential to remain on the books until 2031, which seems unnecessary considering the vastly changed legal landscape over the previous five decades. Roberts acknowledges that while discrimination remains an issue, the turnout of African American voters in five of the six states covered by the Voting Rights Act is greater than that of whites, raising the question of whether the act should be adjusted to reflect current political realities.

Background on Voter Suppression in the United States

The first section provides coverage of the history of voter suppression in the southern United States in the decades following the Civil War. The ratification of the Fifteenth Amendment provided Black men with the right to vote in spirit if not necessarily practice, given the general lack of congressional enforcement. Congressional action to remove obstacles placed between Black voters and the ballot box was generally met by southern states with new means of blocking African American enfranchisement. This changed with the Voting Rights Act of 1965 and its clear assertion in Section 2 that no one should be denied their right to vote based on race or color anywhere in the nation.

Roberts points out that Sections 4(b) and 5 of the act pertained to specific regions, namely states or political subdivisions that had in effect some measure, such as a literacy test or voucher from registered voters, to serve as a prerequisite to voting as of November 1, 1964, and had a voter registration or turnout lower than 50 percent in the presidential election of 1964. This included the states of Alabama, Georgia, Louisiana, Mississippi, South Carolina, and Virginia, and 39 counties in North Carolina and one in Arizona. According to Section 5, no alterations in voting procedures could go into effect until federal authorities gave their approval that the jurisdiction had taken the appropriate steps to ensure no voter was denied their right based on race. This is known as a "bailout." Although the sections were intended to be to expire after five years, the Supreme Court decided to reauthorize the act for five more years and extended Section 4 to include areas with a voting test and a voter registration or turnout for 1968 under 50 percent, which included counties in California, New York, and New Hampshire. Similar reauthorizations and extensions occurred in 1975, 1982, and 2006 despite challenges issues in 1973, 1980, 1999, and 2008.

Analysis of Shelby County's Challenge to the VRA

Roberts's opinion considers circumstances in Shelby County, Alabama, one such jurisdiction covered by the Voting Rights Act. The county, which did not pursue a bailout, sued the attorney general in the Federal District Court in Washington, D.C., in 2010 to challenge the constitutionality of the Sections 4(b) and 5 of the act. The court decided to uphold the act as it existed, a decision supported by the Court of Appeals for the D.C. Circuit. While the circuit court found substantial justification for Section 5's preservation, it determined that Section 4's identification of covered jurisdictions was questionable but did not declare it unconstitutional.

The opinion then gives consideration to a fundamental issue in federalism: that state legislatures cannot contravene federal law while the federal government lacks the general right to review and reject state enactments prior to their going into effect. States possess the general right to structure their governments and implement legislation as they see fit, as guaranteed by the Tenth Amendment, which includes the regulation of elections. The federal government's control over federal elections includes determining the time and manner by which senators and representatives are elected, but states retain the power to determine the proper conditions under which suffrage is granted, to decide where congressional districts are to be drawn, and to assess the proper qualifications of the state's officers and how they are elected. Such powers are the basis for the principle of equal sovereignty shared by the states. By applying to only nine states and a number of counties, the Voting Rights Act arguably challenges this sovereignty.

Assessment of African American Political Participation after the VRA

The opinion recognizes the requirements and tests enacted by southern states specifically to deter Black voters from casting their ballots but points out the Voting Rights Act's initially temporary character. The notable increase in African American voting activity since 1965 calls into question the necessity of retaining a measure whose usefulness is questionable, the means of discriminating and disenfranchising specific voters having long been dismantled.

When Congress reauthorized the act in 2006, it acknowledged the progress made in the previous half century, particularly the marked increase in African American voting and the large number of African Americans elected to serve on behalf of the six states initially covered by the Voting Rights Act. The opinion cites this progress as evidence for easing the restrictions allowed for by Sections 4 and 5 of the act. This is particularly the case for Section 5, which Congress routinely amended to increase its influence.

The opinion notes 2009 as a turning point in members of the Court taking a closer look at the act and concluding it needed considerable revision, in large part because there no longer existed two groups on states, those in which voting tests had previously hindered voter registration and turnout and those without such tests.

Final Summation on the VRA's Unconstitutional Nature

Roberts argues that Congress continues to uphold the act by contending that some level of discrimination continues to exist in the states and counties impacted, giving little heed to the political realities of the present. The congressional interpretation continues to reflect a view of the South as a region dominated by Jim Crow rather than one where Jim Crow's reign ended decades ago as reflected by African American voting rates and attainment of political office.

The opinion asserts that Congress in 2006 drew upon data intended to justify the act's reauthorization, which failed to prove that there existed a level of discrimination as widespread and egregious as what existed in the mid-1960s. It justifies Shelby County's right to challenge the constitutionality of Sections 4 and 5 of the act.

In conclusion, the opinion reiterates the act's uniqueness and usefulness but questions the ways in which it undermines the concept of equal sovereignty and is out of step with the current state of voting in areas it impacts. Congress must untether itself from a piece of legislation more than four decades out of step with contemporary America.

Impact

Shelby County v. Holder's outcome prompted a swift reaction. The day after the Court handed down its decision, the government of Texas declared that it would enforce a strict new law regarding photo identification as a prerequisite to vote. Alabama and Mississippi likewise implemented photo ID laws that the federal government had previously blocked. Texas governor Rick Perry signed Senate Bill (SB) 14 into law, which limited the types of IDs voters needed to produce in order to vote. This had the result of potentially preventing more than 600,000 registered Texas voters from casting their ballots. With the understanding that SB 14 likely violated Section 5 of the VRA, Texas filed a federal lawsuit, which the U.S. District Court for the District of Columbia rejected in August 2012 on the grounds that Texas had failed to prove that the law would not disproportionately impact people of color. Undeterred by the outcome, Texas modified SB 14 and passed SB 5 in early 2017, which was upheld by the Fifth Circuit Court. Like its predecessor, SB 5 requires voters to present an acceptable form of ID prior to casting their ballots.

North Carolina followed in Texas's footsteps with the passage of its own voting bill just two months after the *Shelby* decision, House Bill (HB) 589, which was more far-reaching than SB 14. In addition to requiring a limited range of photo IDs to vote, the bill did away with early voting, abolished same-day registration, limited pre-registration, and took away county boards of elections' ability to keep polls open an additional hour. As was the case with SB 14, a federal court, the U.S. Court of Appeals for the Fourth Circuit, in July 2016 declared HB 589 to be in violation of Section 2 of the VRA and the Constitution. The court declared that the bill, rather than combating voter fraud and restoring public confidence in elections, would primarily succeed in preventing African Americans from voting. Following the ruling, North Carolina filed an emergency appeal in the hope that the Supreme Court would hear the case. The justices decided, in a 5–4 vote, not to hear the case.

While there have been legislative victories and defeats in the aftermath of the *Shelby* decision, there is no denying its far-reaching impact. Evidence suggests that states previously held accountable by Section 4 have purged voters off their rolls at notably higher rates compared to other jurisdictions. Generally, these states are the same one that have also passed laws intended to restrict voting following the *Shelby* decision.

Questions for Further Study

1. Why did Congress find it necessary to pass the Voting Rights Act in 1965? What was happening in the United States at the time that informed its passage?

2. How did Sections 4 and 5 of the Voting Rights Act protect members of minority groups from potentially being denied their right to vote?

3. What changes in American politics since the passage of the Voting Rights Act does Roberts cite as proof that the VRA is out of step with the present day?

4. How does Roberts's opinion frame the debate over the constitutionality of the Voting Rights Act as fundamentally one over federalism?

Further Reading

Books

Berman, Ari. *Give Us the Ballot: The Struggle for Voting Rights in America*. London: Picador, 2016.

Bullock, Charles S. III, et. al. *The Rise and Fall of the Voting Rights Act*. Norman, OK: University of Oklahoma Press, 2016.

Davidson, Chandler, and Bernard Grofman, eds. *Quiet Revolution in the South: The Impact of the Voting Rights Act, 1965–1990*. Princeton, NJ: Princeton University Press, 2021.

Hillstrom, Laurie Collier. *The Voting Rights Act of 1965*. Detroit: Omnigraphics, 2008.

Keyssar, Alexander. *The Right to Vote: The Contested History of Democracy in the United States*. New York: Basic Books, 2009.

May, Gary. *Bending toward Justice: The Voting Rights Act and the Transformation of American Democracy*. Durham, NC: Duke University Press Books, 2014.

Moore, Gregory T. *Beyond the Voting Rights Act: The Untold Story of the Struggle to Reform America's Voter Registration Laws*. Berlin: De Gruyter, 2022.

Rhodes, Jesse H. *Ballot Blocked: The Political Erosion of the Voting Rights Act*. Redwood City, CA: Stanford University Press, 2017.

—Commentary by Michael Martin Carver

SHELBY COUNTY V. HOLDER

Document Text

Chief Justice Roberts delivered the opinion of the Court

The Voting Rights Act of 1965 employed extraordinary measures to address an extraordinary problem. Section 5 of the Act required States to obtain federal permission before enacting any law related to voting—a drastic departure from basic principles of federalism. And §4 of the Act applied that requirement only to some States—an equally dramatic departure from the principle that all States enjoy equal sovereignty. This was strong medicine, but Congress determined it was needed to address entrenched racial discrimination in voting, "an insidious and pervasive evil which had been perpetuated in certain parts of our country through unremitting and ingenious defiance of the Constitution." *South Carolina v. Katzenbach*, 383 U. S. 301, 309 (1966) . As we explained in upholding the law, "exceptional conditions can justify legislative measures not otherwise appropriate." Id., at 334. Reflecting the unprecedented nature of these measures, they were scheduled to expire after five years. See Voting Rights Act of 1965, §4(a), 79Stat. 438.

Nearly 50 years later, they are still in effect; indeed, they have been made more stringent, and are now scheduled to last until 2031. There is no denying, however, that the conditions that originally justified these measures no longer characterize voting in the covered jurisdictions. By 2009, "the racial gap in voter registration and turnout [was] lower in the States originally covered by §5 than it [was] nationwide." *Northwest Austin Municipal Util. Dist. No. One v. Holder*, 557 U. S. 193 –204 (2009). Since that time, Census Bureau data indicate that African-American voter turnout has come to exceed white voter turnout in five of the six States originally covered by §5, with a gap in the sixth State of less than one half of one percent. See Dept. of Commerce, Census Bureau, Re-ported Voting and Registration, by Sex, Race and His-panic Origin, for States (Nov. 2012) (Table 4b).

At the same time, voting discrimination still exists; no one doubts that. The question is whether the Act's extraordinary measures, including its disparate treatment of the States, continue to satisfy constitutional requirements. As we put it a short time ago, "the Act imposes current burdens and must be justified by current needs." *Northwest Austin*, 557 U. S., at 203.

I

A

The Fifteenth Amendment was ratified in 1870, in the wake of the Civil War. It provides that "[t]he right of citizens of the United States to vote shall not be denied or abridged by the United States or by any State on account of race, color, or previous condition of servitude," and it gives Congress the "power to enforce this article by appropriate legislation."

"The first century of congressional enforcement of the Amendment, however, can only be regarded as a failure." Id., at 197. In the 1890s, Alabama, Georgia, Louisiana, Mississippi, North Carolina, South Carolina, and Virginia began to enact literacy tests for voter registration and to employ other methods designed to prevent African-Americans from voting. *Katzenbach*, 383 U. S., at 310. Congress passed statutes outlawing some of these practices and facilitating litigation against them, but litigation remained slow and expensive, and the States came up with new ways to discriminate as soon as existing ones were struck down. Voter registration of African-Americans barely improved. Id., at 313–314.

Inspired to action by the civil rights movement, Congress responded in 1965 with the Voting Rights Act. Section 2 was enacted to forbid, in all 50 States, any "standard, practice, or procedure . . . imposed or applied . . . to deny or abridge the right of any citizen of the United States to vote on account of race or color." 79Stat. 437. The current version forbids any "standard, practice, or procedure" that "results in a denial or abridgement of the right of any citizen of the United States to vote on account of race or color." 42 U. S. C. §1973(a). Both the Federal Government and individuals have sued to enforce §2, see, e.g., *Johnson v. De Grandy*, 512 U. S. 997 (1994), and injunctive relief is available in appropriate cases to block voting laws from going into effect, see 42 U. S. C. §1973j(d). Section 2 is permanent, applies nationwide, and is not at issue in this case.

Other sections targeted only some parts of the country. At the time of the Act's passage, these "covered" jurisdictions were those States or political subdivisions that had maintained a test or device as a prerequisite to voting as of November 1, 1964, and had less than 50 percent voter registration or turnout in the 1964 Presidential election. §4(b), 79Stat. 438. Such tests or devices included literacy and knowledge tests, good moral character requirements, the need for vouchers from registered voters, and the like. §4(c), id., at 438–439. A covered jurisdiction could "bail out" of coverage if it had not used a test or device in the preceding five years "for the purpose or with the effect of denying or abridging the right to vote on account of race or color." §4(a), id., at 438. In 1965, the covered States included Alabama, Georgia, Louisiana, Mississippi, South Carolina, and Virginia. The additional covered subdivisions included 39 counties in North Carolina and one in Arizona. See 28 CFR pt. 51, App. (2012).

In those jurisdictions, §4 of the Act banned all such tests or devices. §4(a), 79Stat. 438. Section 5 provided that no change in voting procedures could take effect until it was approved by federal authorities in Washington, D. C.—either the Attorney General or a court of three judges. Id., at 439. A jurisdiction could obtain such "preclearance" only by proving that the change had neither "the purpose [nor] the effect of denying or abridging the right to vote on account of race or color." Ibid.

Sections 4 and 5 were intended to be temporary; they were set to expire after five years. See §4(a), id., at 438; Northwest Austin, supra, at 199. In *South Carolina v. Katzenbach*, we upheld the 1965 Act against constitutional challenge, explaining that it was justified to address "voting discrimination where it persists on a pervasive scale." 383 U. S., at 308.

In 1970, Congress reauthorized the Act for another five years, and extended the coverage formula in §4(b) to jurisdictions that had a voting test and less than 50 percent voter registration or turnout as of 1968. Voting Rights Act Amendments of 1970, §§3–4, 84Stat. 315. That swept in several counties in California, New Hampshire, and New York. See 28 CFR pt. 51, App. Congress also extended the ban in §4(a) on tests and devices nationwide. §6, 84Stat. 315.

In 1975, Congress reauthorized the Act for seven more years, and extended its coverage to jurisdictions that had a voting test and less than 50 percent voter registration or turnout as of 1972. Voting Rights Act Amendments of 1975, §§101, 202, 89Stat. 400, 401. Congress also amended the definition of "test or device" to include the practice of providing English-only voting materials in places where over five percent of voting-age citizens spoke a single language other than English. §203, id., at 401–402. As a result of these amendments, the States of Alaska, Arizona, and Texas, as well as several counties in California, Flor-ida, Michigan, New York, North Carolina, and South Da-kota, became covered jurisdictions. See 28 CFR pt. 51, App. Congress correspondingly amended sections 2 and 5 to forbid voting discrimination on the basis of membership in a language minority group, in addition to discrimination on the basis of race or color. §§203, 206, 89Stat. 401, 402. Finally, Congress made the nationwide ban on tests and devices permanent. §102, id., at 400.

In 1982, Congress reauthorized the Act for 25 years, but did not alter its coverage formula. See Voting Rights Act Amendments, 96Stat. 131. Congress did, however, amend the bailout provisions, allowing political subdivisions of covered jurisdictions to bail out. Among other prerequisites for bailout, jurisdictions and their subdivisions must not have used a forbidden test or device, failed to receive preclearance, or lost a §2 suit, in the ten years prior to seeking bailout. §2, id., at 131–133.

We upheld each of these reauthorizations against constitutional challenge. See *Georgia v. United States*, 411 U. S. 526 (1973) ; *City of Rome v. United States*, 446 U. S. 156 (1980) ; *Lopez v. Monterey County*, 525 U. S. 266 (1999).

In 2006, Congress again reauthorized the Voting Rights Act for 25 years, again without change to its coverage formula. Fannie Lou Hamer, Rosa Parks, and Coretta Scott King Voting Rights Act Reauthorization and Amendments Act, 120Stat. 577. Congress also amended §5 to prohibit more conduct than before. §5, id., at 580– 581; see *Reno v. Bossier Parish School Bd.*, 528 U. S. 320, 341 (2000) (Bossier II); *Georgia v. Ashcroft*, 539 U. S. 461, 479 (2003) . Section 5 now forbids voting changes with "any discriminatory purpose" as well as voting changes that diminish the ability of citizens, on account of race, color, or language minority status, "to elect their preferred candidates of choice." 42 U. S. C. §§1973c(b)–(d).

Shortly after this reauthorization, a Texas utility district brought suit, seeking to bail out from the Act's cover- age and, in the alternative, challenging the Act's constitutionality. See *Northwest Austin*, 557 U. S., at 200–201. A three-judge District Court explained that only a State or political subdivision was eligible to seek bailout under the statute, and concluded that the utility district was not a political subdivision, a term that encompassed only "counties, parishes, and voter-registering subunits." *Northwest Austin Municipal Util. Dist. No. One v. Mukasey*, 573 F. Supp. 2d 221, 232 (DC 2008). The District Court also rejected the constitutional challenge. Id., at 283.

We reversed. We explained that " 'normally the Court will not decide a constitutional question if there is some other ground upon which to dispose of the case.' " *Northwest Austin*, supra, at 205 (quoting *Escambia County v. McMillan*, 466 U. S. 48, 51 (1984) (per curiam)). Concluding that "underlying constitutional concerns," among other things, "compel[led]

a broader reading of the bailout provision," we construed the statute to allow the utility district to seek bailout. *Northwest Austin*, 557 U. S., at 207. In doing so we expressed serious doubts about the Act's continued constitutionality.

We explained that §5 "imposes substantial federalism costs" and "differentiates between the States, despite our his- toric tradition that all the States enjoy equal sovereignty." Id., at 202, 203 (internal quotation marks omitted). We also noted that "[t]hings have changed in the South. Voter turnout and registration rates now approach parity. Blatantly discriminatory evasions of federal decrees are rare. And minority candidates hold office at unprece-dented levels." Id., at 202. Finally, we questioned whether the problems that §5 meant to address were still "concentrated in the jurisdictions singled out for preclearance." Id., at 203.

Eight Members of the Court subscribed to these views, and the remaining Member would have held the Act unconstitutional. Ultimately, however, the Court's construction of the bailout provision left the constitutional issues for another day.

B

Shelby County is located in Alabama, a covered jurisdiction. It has not sought bailout, as the Attorney General has recently objected to voting changes proposed from within the county. See App. 87a–92a. Instead, in 2010, the county sued the Attorney General in Federal District Court in Washington, D. C., seeking a declaratory judgment that sections 4(b) and 5 of the Voting Rights Act are facially unconstitutional, as well as a permanent injunction against their enforcement. The District Court ruled against the county and upheld the Act. 811 F. Supp. 2d 424, 508 (2011). The court found that the evidence before Congress in 2006 was sufficient to justify reauthorizing §5 and continuing the §4(b) coverage formula.

The Court of Appeals for the D. C. Circuit affirmed. In assessing §5, the D. C. Circuit considered six primary categories of evidence: Attorney General objections to voting changes, Attorney General requests for more information regarding voting changes, successful §2 suits in covered jurisdictions, the dispatching of federal observers to monitor elections in covered jurisdictions, §5 preclearance suits involving covered jurisdictions, and the deterrent effect of §5. See 679 F. 3d 848,

862–863 (2012). After extensive analysis of the record, the court accepted Congress's conclusion that §2 litigation remained inadequate in the covered jurisdictions to protect the rights of minority voters, and that §5 was therefore still necessary. Id., at 873.

Turning to §4, the D. C. Circuit noted that the evidence for singling out the covered jurisdictions was "less robust" and that the issue presented "a close question." Id., at 879. But the court looked to data comparing the number of successful §2 suits in the different parts of the country. Coupling that evidence with the deterrent effect of §5, the court concluded that the statute continued "to single out the jurisdictions in which discrimination is concentrated," and thus held that the coverage formula passed constitutional muster. Id., at 883.

Judge Williams dissented. He found "no positive correlation between inclusion in §4(b)'s coverage formula and low black registration or turnout." Id., at 891. Rather, to the extent there was any correlation, it actually went the other way: "condemnation under §4(b) is a marker of higher black registration and turnout." Ibid. (emphasis added). Judge Williams also found that "[c]overed jurisdictions have far more black officeholders as a proportion of the black population than do uncovered ones." Id., at 892. As to the evidence of successful §2 suits, Judge Williams disaggregated the reported cases by State, and concluded that "[t]he five worst uncovered jurisdictions . . . have worse records than eight of the covered jurisdictions." Id., at 897. He also noted that two covered jurisdictions—Arizona and Alaska—had not had any successful reported §2 suit brought against them during the entire 24 years covered by the data. Ibid. Judge Williams would have held the coverage formula of §4(b) "irrational" and unconstitutional. Id., at 885.

We granted certiorari. 568 U. S. ___ (2012).

II

In Northwest Austin, we stated that "the Act imposes current burdens and must be justified by current needs." 557 U. S., at 203. And we concluded that "a departure from the fundamental principle of equal sovereignty requires a showing that a statute's disparate geographic coverage is sufficiently related to the problem that it targets." Ibid. These basic principles guide our review of the question before us.

A

The Constitution and laws of the United States are "the supreme Law of the Land." U. S. Const., Art. VI, cl. 2. State legislation may not contravene federal law. The Federal Government does not, however, have a general right to review and veto state enactments before they go into effect. A proposal to grant such authority to "negative" state laws was considered at the Constitutional Convention, but rejected in favor of allowing state laws to take effect, subject to later challenge under the Supremacy Clause. See 1 Records of the Federal Convention of 1787, pp. 21, 164–168 (M. Farrand ed. 1911); 2 id., at 27–29, 390–392.

Outside the strictures of the Supremacy Clause, States retain broad autonomy in structuring their governments and pursuing legislative objectives. Indeed, the Constitution provides that all powers not specifically granted to the Federal Government are reserved to the States or citizens. Amdt. 10. This "allocation of powers in our federal system preserves the integrity, dignity, and residual sovereignty of the States." *Bond v. United States*, 564 U. S. ___, ___ (2011) (slip op., at 9). But the federal balance "is not just an end in itself: Rather, federalism secures to citizens the liberties that derive from the diffusion of sovereign power." Ibid. (internal quotation marks omitted).

More specifically, " 'the Framers of the Constitution intended the States to keep for themselves, as provided in the Tenth Amendment, the power to regulate elections.' " *Gregory v. Ashcroft*, 501 U. S. 452 –462 (1991) (quoting *Sugarman v. Dougall*, 413 U. S. 634, 647 (1973) ; some internal quotation marks omitted). Of course, the Federal Government retains significant control over federal elections. For instance, the Constitution authorizes Congress to establish the time and manner for electing Senators and Representatives. Art. I, §4, cl. 1; see also *Arizona v. Inter Tribal Council of Ariz., Inc.*, ante, at 4–6. But States have "broad powers to determine the conditions under which the right of suffrage may be exercised." *Carrington v. Rash*, 380 U. S. 89, 91 (1965) (internal quotation marks omitted); see also *Arizona*, ante, at 13–15. And "[e]ach State has the power to prescribe the qualifications of its officers and the manner in which they shall be chosen." *Boyd v. Nebraska ex rel. Thayer*, 143 U. S. 135, 161 (1892) . Drawing lines for congressional districts is likewise "primarily the duty and responsibility of the State." *Perry v. Perez*,

565 U. S. ___, ___ (2012) (per curiam) (slip op., at 3) (internal quotation marks omitted).

Not only do States retain sovereignty under the Constitution, there is also a "fundamental principle of equal sovereignty" among the States. *Northwest Austin*, supra, at 203 (citing *United States v. Louisiana*, 363 U. S. 1, 16 (1960); *Lessee of Pollard v. Hagan*, 3 How. 212, 223 (1845); and *Texas v. White*, 7 Wall. 700, 725–726 (1869); emphasis added). Over a hundred years ago, this Court explained that our Nation "was and is a union of States, equal in power, dignity and authority." *Coyle v. Smith*, 221 U. S. 559, 567 (1911) . Indeed, "the constitutional equality of the States is essential to the harmonious operation of the scheme upon which the Republic was organized." Id., at 580. *Coyle* concerned the admission of new States, and *Katzenbach* rejected the notion that the principle operated as a bar on differential treatment outside that context. 383 U. S., at 328–329. At the same time, as we made clear in *Northwest Austin*, the fundamental principle of equal sovereignty remains highly pertinent in assessing subsequent disparate treatment of States. 557 U. S., at 203.

The Voting Rights Act sharply departs from these basic principles. It suspends "all changes to state election law—however innocuous—until they have been precleared by federal authorities in Washington, D. C." Id., at 202. States must beseech the Federal Government for permission to implement laws that they would otherwise have the right to enact and execute on their own, subject of course to any injunction in a §2 action. The Attorney General has 60 days to object to a preclearance request, longer if he requests more information. See 28 CFR §§51.9, 51.37. If a State seeks preclearance from a three-judge court, the process can take years.

And despite the tradition of equal sovereignty, the Act applies to only nine States (and several additional counties). While one State waits months or years and expends funds to implement a validly enacted law, its neighbor can typically put the same law into effect immediately, through the normal legislative process. Even if a noncovered jurisdiction is sued, there are important differences between those proceedings and preclearance proceedings; the preclearance proceeding "not only switches the burden of proof to the supplicant jurisdiction, but also applies substantive standards quite different from those governing the rest of the nation." 679 F. 3d, at 884 (Williams, J., dissenting) (case below).

All this explains why, when we first upheld the Act in 1966, we described it as "stringent" and "potent." *Katzenbach*, 383 U. S., at 308, 315, 337. We recognized that it "may have been an uncommon exercise of congressional power," but concluded that "legislative measures not otherwise appropriate" could be justified by "exceptional conditions." Id., at 334. We have since noted that the Act "authorizes federal intrusion into sensitive areas of state and local policymaking," Lopez, 525 U. S., at 282, and represents an "extraordinary departure from the traditional course of relations between the States and the Federal Government," *Presley v. Etowah County Comm'n*, 502 U. S. 491 –501 (1992). As we reiterated in *Northwest Austin*, the Act constitutes "extraordinary legislation otherwise unfamiliar to our federal system." 557 U. S., at 211.

B

In 1966, we found these departures from the basic features of our system of government justified. The "blight of racial discrimination in voting" had "infected the electoral process in parts of our country for nearly a century." *Katzenbach*, 383 U. S., at 308. Several States had enacted a variety of requirements and tests "specifically designed to prevent" African-Americans from voting. Id., at 310. Case-by-case litigation had proved inadequate to prevent such racial discrimination in voting, in part because States "merely switched to discriminatory devices not covered by the federal decrees," "enacted difficult new tests," or simply "defied and evaded court orders." Id., at 314. Shortly before enactment of the Voting Rights Act, only 19.4 percent of African-Americans of voting age were registered to vote in Alabama, only 31.8 percent in Louisiana, and only 6.4 percent in Mississippi. Id., at 313. Those figures were roughly 50 percentage points or more below the figures for whites. Ibid.

In short, we concluded that "[u]nder the compulsion of these unique circumstances, Congress responded in a permissibly decisive manner." Id., at 334, 335. We also noted then and have emphasized since that this extra-ordinary legislation was intended to be temporary, set to expire after five years. Id., at 333; *Northwest Austin*, supra, at 199.

At the time, the coverage formula—the means of linking the exercise of the unprecedented authority with the problem that warranted it—made sense. We found that "Congress chose to limit its attention to the geographic areas where immediate action seemed necessary." *Katzenbach*, 383 U. S., at 328. The areas where Congress found "evidence of actual voting discrimination" shared two characteristics: "the use of tests and devices for voter registration, and a voting rate in the 1964 presidential election at least 12 points below the national average." Id., at 330. We explained that "[t]ests and devices are relevant to voting discrimination because of their long history as a tool for perpetrating the evil; a low voting rate is pertinent for the obvious reason that widespread disenfranchisement must inevitably affect the number of actual voters." Ibid. We therefore concluded that "the coverage formula [was] rational in both practice and theory." Ibid. It accurately reflected those jurisdictions uniquely characterized by voting discrimination "on a pervasive scale," linking coverage to the devices used to effectuate discrimination and to the resulting disenfranchisement. Id., at 308. The formula ensured that the "stringent remedies [were] aimed at areas where voting discrimination ha[d] been most flagrant." Id., at 315.

C

Nearly 50 years later, things have changed dramatically. Shelby County contends that the preclearance requirement, even without regard to its disparate coverage, is now unconstitutional. Its arguments have a good deal of force. In the covered jurisdictions, "[v]oter turnout and registration rates now approach parity. Blatantly discriminatory evasions of federal decrees are rare. And minority candidates hold office at unprecedented levels." Northwest Austin, 557 U. S., at 202. The tests and devices that blocked access to the ballot have been forbidden nationwide for over 40 years. See §6, 84Stat. 315; §102, 89Stat. 400.

Those conclusions are not ours alone. Congress said the same when it reauthorized the Act in 2006, writing that "[s]ignificant progress has been made in eliminating first generation barriers experienced by minority voters, including increased numbers of registered minority voters, minority voter turnout, and minority representation in Congress, State legislatures, and local elected offices." §2(b)(1), 120Stat. 577. The House Report elaborated that "the number of African-Americans who are registered and who turn out to cast ballots has increased significantly over the last 40 years, particularly since 1982," and noted that "[i]n some circumstances, minorities register to vote and cast ballots at levels that surpass those of white voters." H. R. Rep. No. 109–478, p. 12 (2006). That Report also explained that there have been "significant increases in the number of African-Americans serving in elected offices"; more specifically, there has been approximately a 1,000 percent increase since 1965 in the number of African-American elected officials in the six States originally covered by the Voting Rights Act. . . . Id., at 18.

. . . There is no doubt that these improvements are in large part because of the Voting Rights Act. The Act has proved immensely successful at redressing racial discrimination and integrating the voting process. See §2(b)(1), 120Stat. 577. During the "Freedom Summer" of 1964, in Philadelphia, Mississippi, three men were murdered while working in the area to register African-American voters. See *United States v. Price*, 383 U. S. 787, 790 (1966). On "Bloody Sunday" in 1965, in Selma, Alabama, police beat and used tear gas against hundreds marching in sup- port of African-American enfranchisement. See Northwest Austin, supra, at 220, n. 3 (Thomas, J., concurring in judgment in part and dissenting in part). Today both of those towns are governed by African-American mayors. Problems remain in these States and others, but there is no denying that, due to the Voting Rights Act, our Nation has made great strides.

Yet the Act has not eased the restrictions in §5 or narrowed the scope of the coverage formula in §4(b) along the way. Those extraordinary and unprecedented features were reauthorized—as if nothing had changed. In fact, the Act's unusual remedies have grown even stronger. When Congress reauthorized the Act in 2006, it did so for another 25 years on top of the previous 40—a far cry from the initial five-year period. See 42 U. S. C. §1973b(a)(8). Congress also expanded the prohibitions in §5. We had previously interpreted §5 to prohibit only those redistricting plans that would have the purpose or effect of worsening the position of minority groups. See *Bossier II*, 528 U. S., at 324, 335–336. In 2006, Congress amended §5 to prohibit laws that could have favored such groups but did not do so because of a discriminatory purpose, see 42 U. S. C. §1973c(c), even though we had stated that such broadening of §5 coverage would "exacerbate the substantial federalism costs that the preclearance procedure already exacts, perhaps to the extent of raising concerns about §5's constitutionality," *Bossier II*, supra, at 336 (citation and internal quotation marks omitted).

In addition, Congress expanded §5 to prohibit any voting law "that has the purpose of or will have the effect of diminishing the ability of any citizens of the United States," on account of race, color, or language minority status, "to elect their preferred candidates of choice." §1973c(b). In light of those two amendments, the bar that covered jurisdictions must clear has been raised even as the conditions justifying that requirement have dramatically improved.

We have also previously highlighted the concern that "the preclearance requirements in one State [might] be unconstitutional in another." *Northwest Austin*, 557 U. S., at 203; see *Georgia v. Ashcroft*, 539 U. S., at 491 (Kennedy, J., concurring) ("considerations of race that would doom a redistricting plan under the Fourteenth Amendment or §2 [of the Voting Rights Act] seem to be what save it under §5"). Nothing has happened since to alleviate this troubling concern about the current application of §5.

Respondents do not deny that there have been improvements on the ground, but argue that much of this can be attributed to the deterrent effect of §5, which dissuades covered jurisdictions from engaging in discrimination that they would resume should §5 be struck down. Under this theory, however, §5 would be effectively immune from scrutiny; no matter how "clean" the record of covered jurisdictions, the argument could always be made that it was deterrence that accounted for the good behavior.

The provisions of §5 apply only to those jurisdictions singled out by §4. We now consider whether that coverage formula is constitutional in light of current conditions.

III

A

When upholding the constitutionality of the coverage formula in 1966, we concluded that it was "rational in both practice and theory." *Katzenbach*, 383 U. S., at 330. The formula looked to cause (discriminatory tests) and ef- fect (low voter registration and turnout), and tailored the remedy (preclearance) to those jurisdictions exhibiting both.

By 2009, however, we concluded that the "coverage formula raise[d] serious constitutional questions." *Northwest Austin*, 557 U. S., at 204. As we explained, a statute's "current burdens" must be justified by "current needs," and any "disparate geographic coverage" must be "sufficiently related to the problem that it targets." Id., at 203. The coverage formula met that test in 1965, but no longer does so.

Coverage today is based on decades-old data and eradicated practices. The formula captures States by reference to literacy tests and low voter registration and turnout in the 1960s and early 1970s. But such tests have been banned nationwide for over 40 years. §6, 84Stat. 315; §102, 89Stat. 400. And voter registration and turnout numbers in the covered States have risen dramatically in the years since. H. R. Rep. No. 109–478, at 12. Racial disparity in those numbers was compelling evidence justifying the preclearance remedy and the coverage formula. See, e.g., *Katzenbach*, supra, at 313, 329–330. There is no longer such a disparity.

In 1965, the States could be divided into two groups: those with a recent history of voting tests and low voter registration and turnout, and those without those characteristics. Congress based its coverage formula on that distinction. Today the Nation is no longer divided along those lines, yet the Voting Rights Act continues to treat it as if it were.

B

The Government's defense of the formula is limited. First, the Government contends that the formula is "reverse-engineered": Congress identified the jurisdictions to be covered and then came up with criteria to describe them. Brief for Federal Respondent 48–49. Under that reasoning, there need not be any logical relationship be-tween the criteria in the formula and the reason for coverage; all that is necessary is that the formula happen to capture the jurisdictions Congress wanted to single out.

The Government suggests that *Katzenbach* sanctioned such an approach, but the analysis in *Katzenbach* was quite different. *Katzenbach* reasoned that the coverage formula was rational because the "formula ... was relevant to the problem": "Tests and devices are relevant to voting discrimination because of their long history as a tool for perpetuating the evil; a low voting rate is pertinent for the obvious reason that widespread disenfranchisement must inevitably affect the number of actual voters." 383 U. S., at 329, 330.

Here, by contrast, the Government's reverse-engineering argument does not even attempt to demonstrate the continued relevance of the formula to the problem it targets. And in the context of a decision as significant as this one—subjecting a disfavored subset of States to "extraordinary legislation otherwise unfamiliar to our federal system," Northwest Austin, supra, at 211—that failure to establish even relevance is fatal.

The Government falls back to the argument that because the formula was relevant in 1965, its continued use is permissible so long as any discrimination remains in the States Congress identified back then—regardless of how that discrimination compares to discrimination in States unburdened by coverage. Brief for Federal Respondent 49–50. This argument does not look to "current political conditions," Northwest Austin, supra, at 203, but instead relies on a comparison between the States in 1965. That comparison reflected the different histories of the North and South. It was in the South that slavery was upheld by law until uprooted by the Civil War, that the reign of Jim Crow denied African-Americans the most basic freedoms, and that state and local governments worked tirelessly to disenfranchise citizens on the basis of race. The Court invoked that history—rightly so—in sustaining the disparate coverage of the Voting Rights Act in 1966. See *Katzenbach*, supra, at 308 ("The constitutional propriety of the Voting Rights Act of 1965 must be judged with reference to the historical experience which it reflects.").

But history did not end in 1965. By the time the Act was reauthorized in 2006, there had been 40 more years of it. In assessing the "current need[ ]" for a preclearance system that treats States differently from one another today, that history cannot be ignored. During that time, largely because of the Voting Rights Act, voting tests were abolished, disparities in voter registration and turnout due to race were erased, and African-Americans attained political office in record numbers. And yet the coverage formula that Congress reauthorized in 2006 ignores these developments, keeping the focus on decades-old data rel-evant to decades-old problems, rather than current data reflecting current needs.

The Fifteenth Amendment commands that the right to vote shall not be denied or abridged on account of race or color, and it gives Congress the power to enforce that command. The Amendment is not designed to punish for the past; its purpose is to ensure a better future. See *Rice v. Cayetano*, 528 U. S. 495, 512 (2000) ("Consistent with the design of the Constitution, the [Fifteenth] Amendment is cast in fundamental terms, terms transcending the particular controversy which was the immediate impetus for its enactment."). To serve that purpose, Congress—if it is to divide the States—must identify those jurisdictions to be singled out on a basis that makes sense in light of current conditions. It cannot rely simply on the past. We made that clear in Northwest Austin, and we make it clear again today.

C

In defending the coverage formula, the Government, the intervenors, and the dissent also rely heavily on data from the record that they claim justify disparate coverage. Congress compiled thousands of pages of evidence before reauthorizing the Voting Rights Act. The court below and the parties have debated what that record shows—they have gone back and forth about whether to compare covered to noncovered jurisdictions as blocks, how to disaggregate the data State by State, how to weigh §2 cases as evidence of ongoing discrimination, and whether to consider evidence not before Congress, among other issues. Compare, e.g., 679 F. 3d, at 873–883 (case below), with id., at 889–902 (Williams, J., dissenting). Regardless of how to look at the record, however, no one can fairly say that it shows anything approaching the "pervasive," "flagrant," "widespread," and "rampant" discrimination that faced Congress in 1965, and that clearly distinguished the covered jurisdictions from the rest of the Nation at that time. *Katzenbach*, supra, at 308, 315, 331; *Northwest Austin*, 557 U. S., at 201.

But a more fundamental problem remains: Congress did not use the record it compiled to shape a coverage formula grounded in current conditions. It instead reenacted a formula based on 40-year-old facts having no logical relation to the present day. The dissent relies on "second-generation barriers," which are not impediments to the casting of ballots, but rather electoral arrangements that affect the weight of minority votes. That does not cure the problem. Viewing the preclearance requirements as targeting such efforts simply highlights the irrationality of continued reliance on the §4 coverage formula, which is based on voting tests and access to the ballot, not vote dilution. We cannot pretend that we are reviewing an updated statute, or try our hand at updating the statute ourselves, based on the new record compiled by Congress. Contrary to the dissent's contention, see post, at 23, we are not ignoring the record; we are simply recognizing that it played no role in shaping the statutory formula before us today.

The dissent also turns to the record to argue that, in light of voting discrimination in Shelby County, the county cannot complain about the provisions that subject it to preclearance. Post, at 23–30. But that is like saying that a driver pulled over pursuant to a policy of stopping all redheads cannot complain about that policy, if it turns out his license has expired. Shelby County's claim is that the coverage formula here is unconstitutional in all its applications, because of how it selects the jurisdictions subjected to preclearance. The county was selected based on that formula, and may challenge it in court.

D

The dissent proceeds from a flawed premise. It quotes the famous sentence from *McCulloch v. Maryland*, 4 Wheat. 316, 421 (1819), with the following emphasis: "Let the end be legitimate, let it be within the scope of the constitution, and all means which are appropriate, which are plainly adapted to that end, which are not prohibited, but consist with the letter and spirit of the constitution, are constitutional." Post, at 9 (emphasis in dissent). But this case is about a part of the sentence that the dissent does not emphasize—the part that asks whether a legislative means is "consist[ent] with the letter and spirit of the constitution." The dissent states that "[i]t cannot tenably be maintained" that this is an issue with regard to the Voting Rights Act, post, at 9, but four years ago, in an opinion joined by two of today's dissenters, the Court expressly stated that "[t]he Act's preclearance requirement and its coverage formula raise serious constitutional questions." Northwest Austin, supra, at 204. The dissent does not explain how those "serious constitutional questions" became untenable in four short years.

The dissent treats the Act as if it were just like any other piece of legislation, but this Court has made clear from the beginning that the Voting Rights Act is far from ordinary. At the risk of repetition, *Katzenbach* indicated that the Act was "uncommon" and "not otherwise appropriate," but was justified by "exceptional" and "unique" conditions. 383 U. S., at 334, 335. Multiple decisions since have reaffirmed the Act's "extraordinary" nature. See, e.g., *Northwest Austin*, supra, at 211. Yet the dissent goes so far as to suggest instead that the preclearance requirement and disparate treatment of the States should be upheld into the future "unless there [is] no or almost no evidence of unconstitutional action by States." Post, at 33.

In other ways as well, the dissent analyzes the question presented as if our decision in Northwest Austin never happened. For example, the dissent refuses to con- sider the principle of equal sovereignty, despite *Northwest Austin*'s emphasis on its significance. *Northwest Austin* also emphasized the "dramatic" progress since 1965, 557 U. S., at 201, but the dissent describes current levels of discrimination as "flagrant," "widespread," and "pervasive," post, at 7, 17 (internal quotation marks omitted). Despite the fact that Northwest Austin requires an Act's "disparate geographic coverage" to be "sufficiently related" to its targeted problems, 557 U. S., at 203, the dissent maintains that an Act's limited coverage actually eases Congress's burdens, and suggests that a fortuitous relationship should suffice. Although *Northwest Austin* stated definitively that "current burdens" must be justified by "current needs," ibid., the dissent argues that the coverage formula can be justified by history, and that the required showing can be weaker on reenactment than when the law was first passed.

There is no valid reason to insulate the coverage formula from review merely because it was previously enacted 40 years ago. If Congress had started from scratch in 2006, it plainly could not have enacted the present coverage formula. It would have been irrational for Congress to distinguish between States in such a fundamental way based on 40-year-old data, when today's statistics tell an entirely different story. And it would have been irrational to base coverage on the use of voting tests 40 years ago, when such tests have been illegal since that time. But that is exactly what Congress has done.

*   *   *

Striking down an Act of Congress "is the gravest and most delicate duty that this Court is called on to perform." *Blodgett v. Holden*, 275 U. S. 142, 148 (1927) (Holmes, J., concurring). We do not do so lightly. That is why, in 2009, we took care to avoid ruling on the constitutionality of the Voting Rights Act when asked to do so, and instead resolved the case then before us on statutory grounds. But in issuing that decision, we expressed our broader concerns about the constitutionality of the Act. Congress could have updated the coverage formula at that time, but did not do so. Its failure to act leaves us today with no choice but to declare §4(b) unconstitutional. The formula in that section can no longer be used as a basis for subjecting jurisdictions to preclearance.

Our decision in no way affects the permanent, nationwide ban on racial discrimination in voting found in §2. We issue no holding on §5 itself, only on the coverage formula. Congress may draft another formula based on current conditions. Such a formula is an initial prerequisite to a determination that exceptional conditions still exist justifying such an "extraordinary departure from the traditional course of relations between the States and the Federal Government." *Presley*, 502 U. S., at 500–501. Our country has changed, and while any racial discrimination in voting is too much, Congress must ensure that the legislation it passes to remedy that problem speaks to current conditions.

The judgment of the Court of Appeals is reversed.

It is so ordered.

Justice Thomas, concurring

I join the Court's opinion in full but write separately to explain that I would find §5 of the Voting Rights Act unconstitutional as well. The Court's opinion sets forth the reasons.

"The Voting Rights Act of 1965 employed extraordinary measures to address an extraordinary problem." Ante, at 1. In the face of "unremitting and ingenious defiance" of citizens' constitutionally protected right to vote, §5 was necessary to give effect to the Fifteenth Amendment in particular regions of the country. *South Carolina v. Katzenbach*, 383 U. S. 301, 309 (1966) . Though §5's preclearance requirement represented a "shar[p] depart[ure]" from "basic principles" of federalism and the equal sovereignty of the States, ante, at 9, 11, the Court upheld the measure against early constitutional challenges because it was necessary at the time to address "voting discrimination where it persist[ed] on a pervasive scale." *Katzenbach*, supra, at 308.

Today, our Nation has changed. "[T]he conditions that originally justified [§5] no longer characterize voting in the covered jurisdictions." Ante, at 2. As the Court explains: " '[V]oter turnout and registration rates now approach parity. Blatantly discriminatory evasions of federal decrees are rare. And minority candidates hold office at un-precedented levels.' " Ante, at 13–14 (quoting *Northwest Austin Municipal Util. Dist. No. One v. Holder*, 557 U. S. 193, 202 (2009)).

In spite of these improvements, however, Congress increased the already significant burdens of §5. Following its reenactment in 2006, the Voting Rights Act was amended to "prohibit more conduct than before." Ante, at 5. "Section 5 now forbids voting changes with 'any dis-criminatory purpose' as well as voting changes that diminish the ability of citizens, on account of race, color, or language minority status, 'to elect their preferred candidates of choice.' " Ante, at 6. While the pre-2006 version of the Act went well beyond protection guaranteed under the Constitution, see *Reno v. Bossier Parish School Bd.*, 520 U. S. 471 –482 (1997), it now goes even further.

It is, thus, quite fitting that the Court repeatedly points out that this legislation is "extraordinary" and "unprecedented" and recognizes the significant constitutional problems created by Congress' decision to raise "the bar that covered jurisdictions must clear," even as "the conditions justifying that requirement have dramatically improved." Ante, at 16–17. However one aggregates the data compiled by Congress, it cannot justify the considerable burdens created by §5. As the Court aptly notes: "[N]o one can fairly say that [the record] shows anything approaching the 'pervasive,' 'flagrant,' 'widespread,' and 'rampant' discrimination that faced Congress in 1965, and that clearly distinguished the covered jurisdictions from the rest of the Nation at that time." Ante, at 21. Indeed, circumstances in the covered jurisdictions can no longer be characterized as "exceptional" or "unique." "The extensive pattern of discrimination that led the Court to previously uphold §5 as enforcing the Fifteenth Amendment no longer exists." *Northwest Austin*, supra, at 226 (Thomas, J., concurring in judgment in part and dissenting in part). Section 5 is, thus, unconstitutional.

While the Court claims to "issue no holding on §5 itself," ante, at 24, its own opinion compellingly demonstrates that Congress has failed to justify " 'current burdens' " with a record demonstrating " 'current needs.' " See ante, at 9 (quoting *Northwest Austin,* supra, at 203). By leaving the inevitable conclusion unstated, the Court needlessly prolongs the demise of that provision. For the reasons stated in the Court's opinion, I would find §5 unconstitutional.

Justice Ginsburg, with whom Justice Breyer, Justice Sotomayor, and Justice Kagan join, dissenting

In the Court's view, the very success of §5 of the Voting Rights Act demands its dormancy. Congress was of another mind. Recognizing that large progress has been made, Congress determined, based on a voluminous record, that the scourge of discrimination was not yet extirpated. The question this case presents is who decides whether, as currently operative, §5 remains justifiable, this Court, or a Congress charged with the obligation to enforce the post-Civil War Amendments "by appropriate legislation." With overwhelming support in both Houses, Congress concluded that, for two prime reasons, §5 should continue in force, unabated. First, continuance would facilitate completion of the impressive gains thus far made; and second, continuance would guard against backsliding. Those assessments were well within Congress' province to make and should elicit this Court's unstinting approbation.

I

"[V]oting discrimination still exists; no one doubts that." Ante, at 2. But the Court today terminates the remedy that proved to be best suited to block that discrimination. The Voting Rights Act of 1965 (VRA) has worked to combat voting discrimination where other remedies had been tried and failed. Particularly effective is the VRA's requirement of federal preclearance for all changes to voting laws in the regions of the country with the most aggravated records of rank discrimination against minority voting rights.

A century after the Fourteenth and Fifteenth Amendments guaranteed citizens the right to vote free of discrimination on the basis of race, the "blight of racial discrimination in voting" continued to "infec[t] the electoral process in parts of our country." South Carolina v. *Katzenbach,* 383 U. S. 301, 308 (1966) . Early attempts to cope with this vile infection resembled battling the Hydra. Whenever one form of voting discrimination was identified and prohibited, others sprang up in its place. This Court repeatedly encountered the remarkable "variety and persistence" of laws disenfranchising minority citizens. Id., at 311. To take just one example, the Court, in 1927, held unconstitutional a Texas law barring black voters from participating in primary elections, *Nixon v. Herndon,* 273 U. S. 536 ; in 1944, the Court struck down a "reenacted" and slightly altered version of the same law, *Smith v. Allwright,* 321 U. S. 649 ; and in 1953, the Court once again confronted an attempt by Texas to "circumven[t]" the Fifteenth Amendment by adopting yet another variant of the all-white primary, *Terry v. Adams,* 345 U. S. 461 .

During this era, the Court recognized that discrimination against minority voters was a quintessentially political problem requiring a political solution. As Justice Holmes explained: If "the great mass of the white population intends to keep the blacks from voting," "relief from [that] great political wrong, if done, as alleged, by the people of a State and the State itself, must be given by them or by the legislative and political department of the government of the United States." *Giles v. Harris,* 189 U. S. 475, 488 (1903) .

Congress learned from experience that laws targeting particular electoral practices or enabling case-by-case litigation were inadequate to the task. In the Civil Rights Acts of 1957, 1960, and 1964, Congress authorized and then expanded the power of "the Attorney General to seek injunctions against public and private interference with the right to vote on racial grounds." *Katzenbach,* 383 U. S., at 313. But circumstances reduced the ameliorative potential of these legislative Acts:

"Voting suits are unusually onerous to prepare, sometimes requiring as many as 6,000 man-hours spent combing through registration records in preparation for trial. Litigation has been exceedingly slow, in part because of the ample opportunities for delay afforded voting officials and others involved in the proceedings. Even when favorable decisions have finally been obtained, some of the States affected have merely switched to discriminatory devices not covered by the federal decrees or have enacted difficult new tests designed to prolong the existing disparity between white and Negro registration. Alternatively, certain local officials have defied and evaded court orders or have simply closed their registration offices to freeze the voting rolls." Id., at 314 (footnote omitted).

Patently, a new approach was needed.

Answering that need, the Voting Rights Act became one of the most consequential, efficacious, and amply justified exercises of federal legislative power in our Nation's his-tory. Requiring federal preclearance of changes in voting laws in the covered jurisdictions—those States and localities where opposition to the Constitution's commands were most virulent—the VRA provided a fit solution for minority voters as well as for States. Under the preclearance regime established by §5 of the VRA, covered jurisdictions must submit proposed changes in voting laws or procedures to the Department of Justice (DOJ), which has 60 days to respond to the changes. 79Stat. 439, codified at 42 U. S. C. §1973c(a). A change will be approved unless DOJ finds it has "the purpose [or] ... the effect of denying or abridging the right to vote on account of race or color." Ibid. In the alternative, the covered jurisdiction may seek approval by a three-judge District Court in the District of Columbia.

After a century's failure to fulfill the promise of the Fourteenth and Fifteenth Amendments, passage of the VRA finally led to signal improvement on this front. "The Justice Department estimated that in the five years after [the VRA's] passage, almost as many blacks registered [to vote] in Alabama, Mississippi, Georgia, Louisiana, North Carolina, and South Carolina as in the entire century before 1965." Davidson, The Voting Rights Act: A Brief History, in *Controversies in Minority Voting* 7, 21 (B. Grofman & C. Davidson eds. 1992). And in assessing the overall effects of the VRA in 2006, Congress found that "[s]ignificant progress has been made in eliminating first generation barriers experienced by minority voters, including increased numbers of registered minority voters, minority voter turnout, and minority representation in Congress, State legislatures, and local elected offices. This progress is the direct result of the Voting Rights Act of 1965." Fannie Lou Hamer, Rosa Parks, and Coretta Scott King Voting Rights Act Reauthorization and Amendments Act of 2006 (hereinafter 2006 Reauthorization), §2(b)(1),

120Stat. 577. On that matter of cause and effects there can be no genuine doubt.

Although the VRA wrought dramatic changes in the realization of minority voting rights, the Act, to date, surely has not eliminated all vestiges of discrimination against the exercise of the franchise by minority citizens. Jurisdictions covered by the preclearance requirement continued to submit, in large numbers, proposed changes to voting laws that the Attorney General declined to approve, auguring that barriers to minority voting would quickly resurface were the preclearance remedy eliminated. *City of Rome v. United States*, 446 U. S. 156, 181 (1980) . Congress also found that as "registration and voting of minority citizens increas[ed], other measures may be resorted to which would dilute increasing minority voting strength." Ibid. (quoting H. R. Rep. No. 94–196, p. 10 (1975)). See also *Shaw v. Reno*, 509 U. S. 630, 640 (1993) ("[I]t soon became apparent that guaranteeing equal access to the polls would not suffice to root out other racially discriminatory voting practices" such as voting dilution). Efforts to reduce the impact of minority votes, in contrast to direct attempts to block access to the bal- lot, are aptly described as "second-generation barriers" to minority voting.

Second-generation barriers come in various forms. One of the blockages is racial gerrymandering, the redrawing of legislative districts in an "effort to segregate the races for purposes of voting." Id., at 642. Another is adoption of a system of at-large voting in lieu of district-by-district voting in a city with a sizable black minority. By switching to at-large voting, the overall majority could control the election of each city council member, effectively eliminating the potency of the minority's votes. Grofman & Davidson, The Effect of Municipal Election Structure on Black Representation in Eight Southern States, in *Quiet Revolution in the South* 301, 319 (C. Davidson & B. Grofman eds. 1994) (hereinafter *Quiet Revolution*). A similar effect could be achieved if the city engaged in discriminatory annexation by incorporating majority-white areas into city limits, thereby decreasing the effect of VRA-occasioned increases in black voting. Whatever the device employed, this Court has long recognized that vote dilution, when adopted with a discriminatory purpose, cuts down the right to vote as certainly as denial of access to the ballot. Shaw, 509 U. S., at 640–641; *Allen v. State Bd. of Elections*, 393 U. S. 544, 569 (1969) ; *Reyn-*

olds v. Sims, 377 U. S. 533, 555 (1964). See also H. R. Rep. No. 109–478, p. 6 (2006) (although "[d]iscrimination today is more subtle than the visible methods used in 1965," "the effect and results are the same, namely a diminishing of the minority community's ability to fully participate in the electoral process and to elect their preferred candidates").

In response to evidence of these substituted barriers, Congress reauthorized the VRA for five years in 1970, for seven years in 1975, and for 25 years in 1982. Ante, at 4–5. Each time, this Court upheld the reauthorization as a valid exercise of congressional power. Ante, at 5. As the 1982 reauthorization approached its 2007 expiration date, Congress again considered whether the VRA's preclearance mechanism remained an appropriate response to the problem of voting discrimination in covered jurisdictions.

Congress did not take this task lightly. Quite the opposite. The 109th Congress that took responsibility for the renewal started early and conscientiously. In October 2005, the House began extensive hearings, which continued into November and resumed in March 2006. S. Rep. No. 109–295, p. 2 (2006). In April 2006, the Senate followed suit, with hearings of its own. Ibid. In May 2006, the bills that became the VRA's reauthorization were introduced in both Houses. Ibid. The House held further hearings of considerable length, as did the Senate, which continued to hold hearings into June and July. H. R. Rep. 109–478, at 5; S. Rep. 109–295, at 3–4. In mid-July, the House considered and rejected four amendments, then passed the reauthorization by a vote of 390 yeas to 33 nays. 152 Cong. Rec. H5207 (July 13, 2006); Persily, *The Promise and Pitfalls of the New Voting Rights Act*, 117 Yale L. J. 174, 182–183 (2007) (hereinafter Persily). The bill was read and debated in the Senate, where it passed by a vote of 98 to 0. 152 Cong. Rec. S8012 (July 20, 2006). President Bush signed it a week later, on July 27, 2006, recognizing the need for "further work . . . in the fight against injustice," and calling the reauthorization "an example of our continued commitment to a united America where every person is valued and treated with dignity and respect." 152 Cong. Rec. S8781 (Aug. 3, 2006).

In the long course of the legislative process, Congress "amassed a sizable record." *Northwest Austin Municipal Util. Dist. No. One v. Holder*, 557 U. S. 193, 205 (2009). See also 679 F. 3d 848, 865–873 (CADC 2012) (describing the "extensive record" supporting Congress' determination that "serious and widespread intentional discrimination persisted in covered jurisdictions"). The House and Senate Judiciary Committees held 21 hearings, heard from scores of witnesses, received a number of investigative reports and other written documentation of continuing discrimination in covered jurisdictions. In all, the legislative record Congress compiled filled more than 15,000 pages. H. R. Rep. 109–478, at 5, 11–12; S. Rep. 109–295, at 2–4, 15. The compilation presents countless "examples of flagrant racial discrimination" since the last reauthorization; Congress also brought to light systematic evidence that "intentional racial discrimination in voting remains so serious and widespread in covered jurisdictions that section 5 preclearance is still needed." 679 F. 3d, at 866.

After considering the full legislative record, Congress made the following findings: The VRA has directly caused significant progress in eliminating first-generation barriers to ballot access, leading to a marked increase in minority voter registration and turnout and the number of minority elected officials. 2006 Reauthorization §2(b)(1). But despite this progress, "second generation barriers constructed to prevent minority voters from fully participating in the electoral process" continued to exist, as well as racially polarized voting in the covered jurisdictions, which increased the political vulnerability of racial and language minorities in those jurisdictions. §§2(b)(2)–(3), 120Stat. 577. Extensive "[e]vidence of continued discrimination," Congress concluded, "clearly show[ed] the continued need for Federal oversight" in covered jurisdictions. §§2(b)(4)–(5), id., at 577–578. The overall record demonstrated to the federal lawmakers that, "without the continuation of the Voting Rights Act of 1965 protections, racial and language minority citizens will be deprived of the opportunity to exercise their right to vote, or will have their votes diluted, undermining the significant gains made by minorities in the last 40 years." §2(b)(9), id., at 578.

Based on these findings, Congress reauthorized preclearance for another 25 years, while also undertaking to reconsider the extension after 15 years to ensure that the provision was still necessary and effective. 42 U. S. C. §1973b(a)(7), (8) (2006 ed., Supp. V). The question before the Court is whether Congress had the authority under the Constitution to act as it did.

II

In answering this question, the Court does not write on a clean slate. It is well established that Congress' judgment regarding exercise of its power to enforce the Fourteenth and Fifteenth Amendments warrants substantial deference. The VRA addresses the combination of race discrimination and the right to vote, which is "preservative of all rights." *Yick Wo v. Hopkins*, 118 U. S. 356, 370 (1886). When confronting the most constitutionally invidious form of discrimination, and the most fundamental right in our democratic system, Congress' power to act is at its height.

The basis for this deference is firmly rooted in both constitutional text and precedent. The Fifteenth Amendment, which targets precisely and only racial discrimination in voting rights, states that, in this domain, "Congress shall have power to enforce this article by appropriate legislation." In choosing this language, the Amendment's framers invoked Chief Justice Marshall's formulation of the scope of Congress' powers under the Necessary and Proper Clause:

"Let the end be legitimate, let it be within the scope of the constitution, and all means which are appropriate, which are plainly adapted to that end, which are not prohibited, but consist with the letter and spirit of the constitution, are constitutional." *McCulloch v. Maryland*, 4 Wheat. 316, 421 (1819) (emphasis added).

It cannot tenably be maintained that the VRA, an Act of Congress adopted to shield the right to vote from racial discrimination, is inconsistent with the letter or spirit of the Fifteenth Amendment, or any provision of the Constitution read in light of the Civil War Amendments. Nowhere in today's opinion, or in Northwest Austin, is there clear recognition of the transformative effect the Fifteenth Amendment aimed to achieve. Notably, "the Founders' first successful amendment told Congress that it could 'make no law' over a certain domain"; in contrast, the Civil War Amendments used "language [that] authorized transformative new federal statutes to uproot all vestiges of unfreedom and inequality" and provided "sweeping enforcement powers . . . to enact 'appropriate' legislation targeting state abuses." A. Amar, *America's Constitution: A Biography* 361, 363, 399 (2005). See also McConnell, *Institutions and Interpretation: A Critique of City of Boerne v. Flores*, 111 Harv. L. Rev. 153, 182 (1997) (quoting Civil War-era framer that "the remedy for the violation of the fourteenth and fifteenth amendments was expressly not left to the courts. The remedy was legislative.").

The stated purpose of the Civil War Amendments was to arm Congress with the power and authority to protect all persons within the Nation from violations of their rights by the States. In exercising that power, then, Congress may use "all means which are appropriate, which are plainly adapted" to the constitutional ends declared by these Amendments. *McCulloch*, 4 Wheat., at 421. So when Congress acts to enforce the right to vote free from racial discrimination, we ask not whether Congress has chosen the means most wise, but whether Congress has rationally selected means appropriate to a legitimate end. "It is not for us to review the congressional resolution of [the need for its chosen remedy]. It is enough that we be able to perceive a basis upon which the Congress might resolve the conflict as it did." *Katzenbach v. Morgan*, 384 U. S. 641, 653 (1966).

Until today, in considering the constitutionality of the VRA, the Court has accorded Congress the full measure of respect its judgments in this domain should garner. *South Carolina v. Katzenbach* supplies the standard of review: "As against the reserved powers of the States, Congress may use any rational means to effectuate the constitutional prohibition of racial discrimination in voting." 383 U. S., at 324. Faced with subsequent reauthorizations of the VRA, the Court has reaffirmed this standard. E.g., *City of Rome*, 446 U. S., at 178. Today's Court does not purport to alter settled precedent establishing that the dispositive question is whether Congress has employed "rational means."

For three reasons, legislation reauthorizing an existing statute is especially likely to satisfy the minimal requirements of the rational-basis test. First, when reauthorization is at issue, Congress has already assembled a legislative record justifying the initial legislation. Congress is entitled to consider that preexisting record as well as the record before it at the time of the vote on reauthorization. This is especially true where, as here, the Court has repeatedly affirmed the statute's constitutionality and Congress has adhered to the very model the Court has upheld. See id., at 174 ("The appellants are asking us to do nothing less than overrule our decision in *South Carolina v. Katzenbach* . . . , in which we upheld the constitutionality of the Act."); *Lopez v. Monterey County*, 525 U. S. 266, 283 (1999) (similar).

Second, the very fact that reauthorization is necessary arises because Congress has built a temporal limitation into the Act. It has pledged to review, after a span of years (first 15, then 25) and in light of contemporary evidence, the continued need for the VRA. Cf. *Grutter v. Bollinger*, 539 U. S. 306, 343 (2003) (anticipating, but not guaranteeing, that, in 25 years, "the use of racial preferences [in higher education] will no longer be necessary").

Third, a reviewing court should expect the record supporting reauthorization to be less stark than the record originally made. Demand for a record of violations equivalent to the one earlier made would expose Congress to a catch-22. If the statute was working, there would be less evidence of discrimination, so opponents might argue that Congress should not be allowed to renew the statute. In contrast, if the statute was not working, there would be plenty of evidence of discrimination, but scant reason to renew a failed regulatory regime. See Persily 193–194.

This is not to suggest that congressional power in this area is limitless. It is this Court's responsibility to ensure that Congress has used appropriate means. The question meet for judicial review is whether the chosen means are "adapted to carry out the objects the amendments have in view." *Ex parte Virginia*, 100 U. S. 339, 346 (1880) . The Court's role, then, is not to substitute its judgment for that of Congress, but to determine whether the legislative record sufficed to show that "Congress could rationally have determined that [its chosen] provisions were appropriate methods." *City of Rome*, 446 U. S., at 176–177.

In summary, the Constitution vests broad power in Congress to protect the right to vote, and in particular to combat racial discrimination in voting. This Court has repeatedly reaffirmed Congress' prerogative to use any rational means in exercise of its power in this area. And both precedent and logic dictate that the rational-means test should be easier to satisfy, and the burden on the statute's challenger should be higher, when what is at issue is the reauthorization of a remedy that the Court has previously affirmed, and that Congress found, from contemporary evidence, to be working to advance the legislature's legitimate objective.

III

The 2006 reauthorization of the Voting Rights Act fully satisfies the standard stated in *McCulloch*, 4 Wheat., at 421: Congress may choose any means "appropriate" and "plainly adapted to" a legitimate constitutional end. As we shall see, it is implausible to suggest otherwise.

A

I begin with the evidence on which Congress based its decision to continue the preclearance remedy. The surest way to evaluate whether that remedy remains in order is to see if preclearance is still effectively preventing discriminatory changes to voting laws. See *City of Rome*, 446 U. S., at 181 (identifying "information on the number and types of submissions made by covered jurisdictions and the number and nature of objections interposed by the Attorney General" as a primary basis for upholding the 1975 reauthorization). On that score, the record before Congress was huge. In fact, Congress found there were more DOJ objections between 1982 and 2004 (626) than there were between 1965 and the 1982 reauthorization (490). 1 Voting Rights Act: Evidence of Continued Need, Hearing before the Subcommittee on the Constitution of the House Committee on the Judiciary, 109th Cong., 2d Sess., p. 172 (2006) (hereinafter Evidence of Continued Need).

All told, between 1982 and 2006, DOJ objections blocked over 700 voting changes based on a determination that the changes were discriminatory. H. R. Rep. No. 109–478, at 21. Congress found that the majority of DOJ objections included findings of discriminatory intent, see 679 F. 3d, at 867, and that the changes blocked by preclearance were "calculated decisions to keep minority voters from fully participating in the political process." H. R. Rep. 109–478, at 21. On top of that, over the same time period the DOJ and private plaintiffs succeeded in more than 100 actions to enforce the §5 preclearance requirements. 1 Evidence of Continued Need 186, 250.

In addition to blocking proposed voting changes through preclearance, DOJ may request more information from a jurisdiction proposing a change. In turn, the jurisdiction may modify or withdraw the proposed change. The number of such modifications or withdrawals provides an indication of how many discriminatory proposals are deterred without need for formal objection. Congress received evidence that more than 800 proposed changes were altered or withdrawn since the last reauthorization in 1982. H. R. Rep. No. 109–478, at 40–41. Congress also received empirical studies finding that DOJ's requests for more information had a significant effect on the degree to which covered jurisdictions "compl[ied] with their obligatio[n]" to protect minority voting rights. 2 Evidence of Continued Need 2555.

Congress also received evidence that litigation under §2 of the VRA was an inadequate substitute for preclearance in the covered jurisdictions. Litigation occurs only after the fact, when the illegal voting scheme has already been put in place and individuals have been elected pursuant to it, thereby gaining the advantages of incumbency. 1 Evidence of Continued Need 97. An illegal scheme might be in place for several election cycles before a §2 plaintiff can gather sufficient evidence to challenge it. 1 Voting Rights Act: Section 5 of the Act—History, Scope, and Purpose: Hearing before the Subcommittee on the Constitution of the House Committee on the Judiciary, 109th Cong., 1st Sess., p. 92 (2005) (hereinafter Section 5 Hearing). And litigation places a heavy financial burden on minority voters. See id., at 84. Congress also received evidence that preclearance lessened the litigation burden on covered jurisdictions themselves, because the preclearance process is far less costly than defending against a §2 claim, and clearance by DOJ substantially reduces the likelihood that a §2 claim will be mounted. Reauthorizing the Voting Rights Act's Temporary Provisions: Policy Perspectives and Views From the Field: Hearing before the Subcommittee on the Constitution, Civil Rights and Property Rights of the Senate Committee on the Judiciary, 109th Cong., 2d Sess., pp. 13, 120–121 (2006). See also Brief for States of New York, California, Mississippi, and North Carolina as Amici Curiae 8–9 (Section 5 "reduc[es] the likelihood that a jurisdiction will face costly and protracted Section 2 litigation").

The number of discriminatory changes blocked or deterred by the preclearance requirement suggests that the state of voting rights in the covered jurisdictions would have been significantly different absent this remedy. Surveying the type of changes stopped by the preclearance procedure conveys a sense of the extent to which §5 continues to protect minority voting rights. Set out below are characteristic examples of changes blocked in the years leading up to the 2006 reauthorization:

In 1995, Mississippi sought to reenact a dual voter registration system, "which was initially enacted in 1892 to disenfranchise Black voters," and for that reason, was struck down by a federal court in 1987. H. R. Rep. No. 109–478, at 39.

Following the 2000 census, the City of Albany, Georgia, proposed a redistricting plan that DOJ found to be "designed with the purpose to limit and retrogress the increased black voting strength ... in the city as a whole." Id., at 37 (internal quotation marks omitted).

In 2001, the mayor and all-white five-member Board of Aldermen of Kilmichael, Mississippi, abruptly canceled the town's election after "an unprecedented number" of African-American candidates announced they were running for office. DOJ required an election, and the town elected its first black mayor and three black aldermen. Id., at 36–37.

In 2006, this Court found that Texas' attempt to redraw a congressional district to reduce the strength of Latino voters bore "the mark of intentional discrimination that could give rise to an equal protection violation," and ordered the district redrawn in compliance with the VRA. *League of United Latin American Citizens v. Perry,* 548 U. S. 399, 440 (2006) . In response, Texas sought to undermine this Court's order by curtailing early voting in the district, but was blocked by an action to enforce the §5 preclearance requirement. See *Order in League of United Latin American Citizens v. Texas,* No. 06–cv–1046 (WD Tex.), Doc. 8.

In 2003, after African-Americans won a majority of the seats on the school board for the first time in history, Charleston County, South Carolina, proposed an at-large voting mechanism for the board. The proposal, made without consulting any of the African-American members of the school board, was found to be an "'exact replica'" of an earlier voting scheme that, a federal court had determined, violated the VRA. 811 F. Supp. 2d 424, 483 (DDC 2011). See also S. Rep. No. 109–295, at 309. DOJ invoked §5 to block the proposal.

In 1993, the City of Millen, Georgia, proposed to delay the election in a majority-black district by two years, leaving that district without representation on the city council while the neighboring majority-white district would have three representatives. 1 Section 5 Hearing 744. DOJ blocked the proposal. The county then sought to move a polling place from a predominantly black neighborhood in the city to an inaccessible location in a predominantly white neighborhood outside city limits. Id., at 816.

In 2004, Waller County, Texas, threatened to prosecute two black students after they announced their intention to run for office. The county then attempted to reduce the availability of early voting in that election at polling places near a historically black university. 679 F. 3d, at 865–866.

In 1990, Dallas County, Alabama, whose county seat is the City of Selma, sought to purge its voter rolls of many black voters. DOJ rejected the purge as discriminatory, noting that it would have disqualified many citizens from voting "simply because they failed to pick up or return a voter update form, when there was no valid requirement that they do so." 1 Section 5 Hearing 356.

These examples, and scores more like them, fill the pages of the legislative record. The evidence was indeed sufficient to support Congress' conclusion that "racial discrimination in voting in covered jurisdictions [remained] serious and pervasive." 679 F. 3d, at 865.

Congress further received evidence indicating that formal requests of the kind set out above represented only the tip of the iceberg. There was what one commentator described as an "avalanche of case studies of voting rights violations in the covered jurisdictions," ranging from "outright intimidation and violence against minority voters" to "more subtle forms of voting rights deprivations." Persily 202 (footnote omitted). This evidence gave Congress ever more reason to conclude that the time had not yet come for relaxed vigilance against the scourge of race discrimination in voting.

True, conditions in the South have impressively improved since passage of the Voting Rights Act. Congress noted this improvement and found that the VRA was the driving force behind it. 2006 Reauthorization §2(b)(1). But Congress also found that voting discrimination had evolved into subtler second-generation barriers, and that eliminating preclearance would risk loss of the gains that had been made. §§2(b)(2), (9). Concerns of this order, the Court previously found, gave Congress adequate cause to reauthorize the VRA. *City of Rome*, 446 U. S., at 180–182 (congressional reauthorization of the preclearance requirement was jus-

tified based on "the number and nature of objections interposed by the Attorney General" since the prior reauthorization; extension was "necessary to pre-serve the limited and fragile achievements of the Act and to promote further amelioration of voting discrimination") (internal quotation marks omitted). Facing such evidence then, the Court expressly rejected the argument that disparities in voter turnout and number of elected officials were the only metrics capable of justifying reauthorization of the VRA. Ibid.

B

I turn next to the evidence on which Congress based its decision to reauthorize the coverage formula in §4(b). Because Congress did not alter the coverage formula, the same jurisdictions previously subject to preclearance continue to be covered by this remedy. The evidence just described, of preclearance's continuing efficacy in blocking constitutional violations in the covered jurisdictions, itself grounded Congress' conclusion that the remedy should be retained for those jurisdictions.

There is no question, moreover, that the covered jurisdictions have a unique history of problems with racial discrimination in voting. Ante, at 12–13. Consideration of this long history, still in living memory, was altogether appropriate. The Court criticizes Congress for failing to recognize that "history did not end in 1965." Ante, at 20. But the Court ignores that "what's past is prologue." W. Shakespeare, *The Tempest*, act 2, sc. 1. And "[t]hose who cannot remember the past are condemned to repeat it." 1 G. Santayana, *The Life of Reason* 284 (1905). Congress was especially mindful of the need to reinforce the gains already made and to prevent backsliding. 2006 Reauthorization §2(b)(9).

Of particular importance, even after 40 years and thousands of discriminatory changes blocked by preclearance, conditions in the covered jurisdictions demonstrated that the formula was still justified by "current needs." *Northwest Austin*, 557 U. S., at 203.

Congress learned of these conditions through a report, known as the Katz study, that looked at §2 suits between 1982 and 2004. To Examine the Impact and Effectiveness of the Voting Rights Act: Hearing before the Subcommittee on the Constitution of the House Committee on the Judiciary, 109th Cong., 1st Sess., pp. 964–1124 (2005) (hereinafter Impact and Effectiveness). Because the private right of action authorized by §2 of the VRA applies nationwide, a comparison of §2 lawsuits in covered and noncovered jurisdictions provides an appropriate yardstick for measuring differences between covered and noncovered jurisdictions. If differences in the risk of voting discrimination between covered and noncovered jurisdictions had disappeared, one would expect that the rate of successful §2 lawsuits would be roughly the same in both areas. The study's findings, however, indicated that racial discrimination in voting remains "concentrated in the jurisdictions singled out for preclearance." *Northwest Austin*, 557 U. S., at 203.

Although covered jurisdictions account for less than 25 percent of the country's population, the Katz study revealed that they accounted for 56 percent of successful §2 litigation since 1982. Impact and Effectiveness 974. Controlling for population, there were nearly four times as many successful §2 cases in covered jurisdictions as there were in noncovered jurisdictions. 679 F. 3d, at 874. The Katz study further found that §2 lawsuits are more likely to succeed when they are filed in covered jurisdictions than in noncovered jurisdictions. Impact and Effectiveness 974. From these findings—ignored by the Court—Congress reasonably concluded that the coverage formula continues to identify the jurisdictions of greatest concern.

The evidence before Congress, furthermore, indicated that voting in the covered jurisdictions was more racially polarized than elsewhere in the country. H. R. Rep. No. 109–478, at 34–35. While racially polarized voting alone does not signal a constitutional violation, it is a factor that increases the vulnerability of racial minorities to dis-criminatory changes in voting law. The reason is twofold. First, racial polarization means that racial minorities are at risk of being systematically outvoted and having their interests underrepresented in legislatures. Second, "when political preferences fall along racial lines, the natural inclinations of incumbents and ruling parties to entrench themselves have predictable racial effects. Under circumstances of severe racial polarization, efforts to gain political advantage translate into race-specific disadvantages." Ansolabehere, Persily, & Stewart, Regional Differences in Racial Polarization in the 2012 Presidential Election: Implications for the Constitutionality of Section 5 of the Voting Rights Act, 126 *Harv. L. Rev. Forum* 205, 209 (2013).

In other words, a governing political coalition has an incentive to prevent changes in the existing balance of voting power. When voting is racially polarized, efforts by the ruling party to pursue that incentive "will inevitably discriminate against a racial group." Ibid. Just as buildings in California have a greater need to be earthquake-proofed, places where there is greater racial polarization in voting have a greater need for prophylactic measures to prevent purposeful race discrimination. This point was understood by Congress and is well recognized in the academic literature. See 2006 Reauthorization §2(b)(3), 120Stat. 577 ("The continued evidence of racially polarized voting in each of the jurisdictions covered by the [preclearance requirement] demonstrates that racial and language minorities remain politically vulnerable"); H. R. Rep. No. 109–478, at 35; Davidson, The Recent Evolution of Voting Rights Law Affecting Racial and Language Minorities, in *Quiet Revolution* 21, 22.

The case for retaining a coverage formula that met needs on the ground was therefore solid. Congress might have been charged with rigidity had it afforded covered jurisdictions no way out or ignored jurisdictions that needed superintendence. Congress, however, responded to this concern. Critical components of the congressional design are the statutory provisions allowing jurisdictions to "bail out" of preclearance, and for court-ordered "bail ins." See Northwest Austin, 557 U. S., at 199. The VRA permits a jurisdiction to bail out by showing that it has complied with the Act for ten years, and has engaged in efforts to eliminate intimidation and harassment of voters. 42 U. S. C. §1973b(a) (2006 ed. and Supp. V). It also authorizes a court to subject a noncovered jurisdiction to federal preclearance upon finding that violations of the Fourteenth and Fifteenth Amendments have occurred there. §1973a(c) (2006 ed.).

Congress was satisfied that the VRA's bailout mechanism provided an effective means of adjusting the VRA's coverage over time. H. R. Rep. No. 109–478, at 25 (the success of bailout "illustrates that: (1) covered status is neither permanent nor over-broad; and (2) covered status has been and continues to be within the control of the jurisdiction such that those jurisdictions that have a genuinely clean record and want to terminate coverage have the ability to do so"). Nearly 200 jurisdictions have successfully bailed out of the preclearance requirement, and DOJ has consented to every bailout application filed by an eligible jurisdiction since the current bailout procedure became effective in 1984. Brief for Federal Respondent 54. The bail-in mechanism has also worked. Several jurisdictions have been subject to federal preclearance by court orders, including the States of New Mexico and Arkansas. App. to Brief for Federal Respondent 1a–3a.

This experience exposes the inaccuracy of the Court's portrayal of the Act as static, unchanged since 1965. Congress designed the VRA to be a dynamic statute, capable of adjusting to changing conditions. True, many covered jurisdictions have not been able to bail out due to recent acts of noncompliance with the VRA, but that truth reinforces the congressional judgment that these jurisdictions were rightfully subject to preclearance, and ought to remain under that regime.

IV

Congress approached the 2006 reauthorization of the VRA with great care and seriousness. The same cannot be said of the Court's opinion today. The Court makes no genuine attempt to engage with the massive legislative record that Congress assembled. Instead, it relies on increases in voter registration and turnout as if that were the whole story. See supra, at 18–19. Without even identifying a standard of review, the Court dismissively brushes off arguments based on "data from the record," and declines to enter the "debat[e about] what [the] record shows." Ante, at 20–21. One would expect more from an opinion striking at the heart of the Nation's signal piece of civil-rights legislation.

I note the most disturbing lapses. First, by what right, given its usual restraint, does the Court even address Shelby County's facial challenge to the VRA? Second, the Court veers away from controlling precedent regarding the "equal sovereignty" doctrine without even acknowledging that it is doing so. Third, hardly showing the respect ordinarily paid when Congress acts to implement the Civil War Amendments, and as just stressed, the Court does not even deign to grapple with the legislative record.

A

Shelby County launched a purely facial challenge to the VRA's 2006 reauthorization. "A facial challenge to a legislative Act," the Court has other times said, "is, of course, the most difficult challenge to mount successfully, since the challenger must establish that no set of circumstances exists under which the Act would be valid." *United States v. Salerno*, 481 U. S. 739, 745 (1987).

"[U]nder our constitutional system[,] courts are not roving commissions assigned to pass judgment on the validity of the Nation's laws." *Broadrick v. Oklahoma*, 413 U. S. 601 –611 (1973). Instead, the "judicial Power" is limited to deciding particular "Cases" and "Controversies." U. S. Const., Art. III, §2. "Embedded in the traditional rules governing constitutional adjudication is the principle that a person to whom a statute may constitutionally be applied will not be heard to challenge that statute on the ground that it may conceivably be applied unconstitutionally to others, in other situations not before the Court." Broadrick, 413 U. S., at 610. Yet the Court's opinion in this case contains not a word explaining why Congress lacks the power to subject to preclearance the particular plaintiff that initiated this lawsuit—Shelby County, Alabama. The reason for the Court's silence is apparent, for as applied to Shelby County, the VRA's preclearance requirement is hardly contestable.

Alabama is home to Selma, site of the "Bloody Sunday" beatings of civil-rights demonstrators that served as the catalyst for the VRA's enactment. Following those events, Martin Luther King, Jr., led a march from Selma to Montgomery, Alabama's capital, where he called for passage of the VRA. If the Act passed, he foresaw, progress could be made even in Alabama, but there had to be a steadfast national commitment to see the task through to completion. In King's words, "the arc of the moral universe is long, but it bends toward justice." G. May, *Bending Toward Justice: The Voting Rights Act and the Transformation of American Democracy* 144 (2013).

History has proved King right. Although circumstances in Alabama have changed, serious concerns remain. Between 1982 and 2005, Alabama had one of the highest rates of successful §2 suits, second only to its VRA-covered neighbor Mississippi. 679 F. 3d, at 897 (Williams, J., dissenting). In other words, even while subject to the restraining effect of §5, Alabama was found to have "deni[ed] or abridge[d]" voting rights "on account of race or color" more frequently than nearly all other States in the Union. 42 U. S. C. §1973(a). This fact prompted the dissenting judge below to concede that "a more narrowly tailored coverage formula" capturing Alabama and a handful of other jurisdictions with an established track record of racial discrimination in voting "might be defensible." 679 F. 3d, at 897 (opinion of Williams, J.). That is an understatement. Alabama's sorry history of §2 violations alone provides sufficient justification for Congress' determination in 2006 that the State should remain subject to §5's preclearance requirement.

A few examples suffice to demonstrate that, at least in Alabama, the "current burdens" imposed by §5's preclearance requirement are "justified by current needs." *Northwest Austin*, 557 U. S., at 203. In the interim between the VRA's 1982 and 2006 reauthorizations, this Court twice confronted purposeful racial discrimination in Alabama. In *Pleasant Grove v. United States*, 479 U. S. 462 (1987), the Court held that Pleasant Grove—a city in Jefferson County, Shelby County's neighbor—engaged in purposeful discrimination by annexing all-white areas while rejecting the annexation request of an adjacent black neighborhood. The city had "shown unambiguous opposition to racial integration, both before and after the passage of the fed-eral civil rights laws," and its strategic annexations appeared to be an attempt "to provide for the growth of a monolithic white voting block" for "the impermissible purpose of minimizing future black voting strength." Id., at 465, 471–472.

Two years before *Pleasant Grove*, the Court in *Hunter v. Underwood*, 471 U. S. 222 (1985), struck down a provision of the Alabama Constitution that prohibited individuals convicted of misdemeanor offenses "involving moral turpitude" from voting. Id., at 223 (internal quotation marks omitted). The provision violated the Fourteenth Amendment's Equal Protection Clause, the Court unanimously concluded, because "its original enactment was motivated by a desire to discriminate against blacks on account of race[,] and the [provision] continues to this day to have that effect." Id., at 233.

Pleasant Grove and *Hunter* were not anomalies. In 1986, a Federal District Judge concluded that the at-large election systems in several Alabama counties violated §2. *Dillard v. Crenshaw Cty.*, 640 F. Supp. 1347, 1354–1363 (MD Ala. 1986). Summarizing its findings, the court stated that "[f]rom the late 1800's through the present, [Alabama] has consistently erected barriers to keep black persons from full and equal participation in the social, economic, and political life of the state." Id., at 1360.

The Dillard litigation ultimately expanded to include 183 cities, counties, and school boards employing discriminatory at-large election systems. *Dillard v. Baldwin Cty. Bd. of Ed.*, 686 F. Supp. 1459, 1461 (MD Ala. 1988). One of those defendants was Shelby County, which eventually signed a consent decree to resolve the claims against it. See *Dillard v. Crenshaw Cty.*, 748 F. Supp. 819 (MD Ala. 1990).

Although the *Dillard* litigation resulted in overhauls of numerous electoral systems tainted by racial discrimination, concerns about backsliding persist. In 2008, for example, the city of Calera, located in Shelby County, requested preclearance of a redistricting plan that "would have eliminated the city's sole majority-black district, which had been created pursuant to the consent decree in *Dillard*." 811 F. Supp. 2d 424, 443 (DC 2011). Although DOJ objected to the plan, Calera forged ahead with elections based on the unprecleared voting changes, resulting in the defeat of the incumbent African-American councilman who represented the former majority-black district. Ibid. The city's defiance required DOJ to bring a §5 enforcement action that ultimately yielded appropriate redress, including restoration of the majority-black district. Ibid.; Brief for Respondent-Intervenors Earl Cunningham et al. 20.

A recent FBI investigation provides a further window into the persistence of racial discrimination in state politics. See *United States v. McGregor*, 824 F. Supp. 2d 1339, 1344–1348 (MD Ala. 2011). Recording devices worn by state legislators cooperating with the FBI's investigation captured conversations between members of the state legislature and their political allies. The recorded conversations are shocking. Members of the state Senate derisively refer to African-Americans as "Aborigines" and talk openly of their aim to quash a particular gambling-related referendum because the referendum, if placed on the ballot, might increase African-American voter turnout. Id., at 1345–1346 (internal quotation marks omitted). See also id., at 1345 (legislators and their allies expressed concern that if the referendum were placed on the ballot, " '[e]very black, every illiterate' would be 'bused [to the polls] on HUD financed buses' "). These conversations occurred not in the 1870's, or even in the 1960's, they took place in 2010. Id., at 1344–1345. The District Judge presiding over the criminal trial at which the recorded conversations were introduced commented that the "recordings represent compelling evidence that political exclusion through racism remains a real and enduring problem" in Alabama. Id., at 1347. Racist sentiments, the judge observed, "remain regrettably entrenched in the high echelons of state government." Ibid.

These recent episodes forcefully demonstrate that §5's preclearance requirement is constitutional as applied to Alabama and its political subdivisions. And under our case law, that conclusion should suffice to resolve this case. See *United States v. Raines*, 362 U. S. 17 –25 (1960) ("[I]f the complaint here called for an application of the statute clearly constitutional under the Fifteenth Amendment, that should have been an end to the question of constitutionality."). See also *Nevada Dept. of Human Resources v. Hibbs*, 538 U. S. 721, 743 (2003) (Scalia, J., dissenting) (where, as here, a state or local government raises a facial challenge to a federal statute on the ground that it exceeds Congress' enforcement powers under the Civil War Amendments, the challenge fails if the opposing party is able to show that the statute "could constitutionally be applied to some jurisdictions").

This Court has consistently rejected constitutional challenges to legislation enacted pursuant to Congress' enforcement powers under the Civil War Amendments upon finding that the legislation was constitutional as applied to the particular set of circumstances before the Court. See *United States v. Georgia*, 546 U. S. 151, 159 (2006) (Title II of the Americans with Disabilities Act of 1990 (ADA) validly abrogates state sovereign immunity "insofar as [it] creates a private cause of action . . . for conduct that actually violates the Fourteenth Amendment"); *Tennessee v. Lane*, 541 U. S. 509 –534 (2004) (Title II of the ADA is constitutional "as it applies to the class of cases implicating the fundamental right of access to the courts"); *Raines*, 362 U. S., at 24–26 (federal statute proscribing deprivations of the right to vote based on race was constitutional as applied to the state officials before the Court, even if it could not constitutionally be applied to other parties). A similar approach is warranted here.

The VRA's exceptionally broad severability provision makes it particularly inappropriate for the Court to allow Shelby County to mount a facial challenge to §§4(b) and 5 of the VRA, even though application of those provisions to the county falls well within the bounds of Congress' legislative authority. The severability provision states:

"If any provision of [this Act] or the application thereof to any person or circumstances is held invalid, the remainder of [the Act] and the application of the provision to other persons not similarly situated or to other circumstances shall not be affected thereby." 42 U. S. C. §1973p.

In other words, even if the VRA could not constitutionally be applied to certain States—e.g., Arizona and Alaska, see ante, at 8—§1973p calls for those unconstitutional applications to be severed, leaving the Act in place for juris-dictions as to which its application does not transgress constitutional limits.

Nevertheless, the Court suggests that limiting the jurisdictional scope of the VRA in an appropriate case would be "to try our hand at updating the statute." Ante, at 22. Just last Term, however, the Court rejected this very argument when addressing a materially identical severability provision, explaining that such a provision is "Congress' explicit textual instruction to leave unaffected the remainder of [the Act]" if any particular "application is unconstitutional." *National Federation of Independent Business v. Sebelius*, 567 U. S. __, __ (2012) (plurality opinion) (slip op., at 56) (internal quotation marks omitted); id., at __ (Ginsburg, J., concurring in part, concurring in judgment in part, and dissenting in part) (slip op., at 60) (agreeing with the plurality's severability analysis). See also *Raines*, 362 U. S., at 23 (a statute capable of some constitutional applications may nonetheless be susceptible to a facial challenge only in "that rarest of cases where this Court can justifiably think itself able confidently to discern that Congress would not have desired its legislation to stand at all unless it could validly stand in its every application"). Leaping to resolve Shelby County's facial challenge without considering whether application of the VRA to Shelby County is constitutional, or even addressing the VRA's severability provision, the Court's opinion can hardly be described as an exemplar of restrained and moderate decisionmaking. Quite the opposite. Hubris is a fit word for today's demolition of the VRA.

B

The Court stops any application of §5 by holding that §4(b)'s coverage formula is unconstitutional. It pins this result, in large measure, to "the fundamental principle of equal sovereignty." Ante, at 10–11, 23. In *Katzenbach*, however, the Court held, in no uncertain terms, that the principle "applies only to the terms upon which States are admitted to the Union, and not to the remedies for local evils which have subsequently appeared." 383 U. S., at 328–329 (emphasis added).

Katzenbach, the Court acknowledges, "rejected the notion that the [equal sovereignty] principle operate[s] as a bar on differential treatment outside [the] context [of the admission of new States]." Ante, at 11 (citing 383 U. S., at 328–329) (emphasis omitted). But the Court clouds that once clear understanding by citing dictum from *Northwest Austin* to convey that the principle of equal sovereignty "remains highly pertinent in assessing subsequent disparate treatment of States." Ante, at 11 (citing 557 U. S., at 203). See also ante, at 23 (relying on *Northwest Austin*'s "emphasis on [the] significance" of the equal-sovereignty principle). If the Court is suggesting that dictum in *Northwest Austin* silently overruled *Katzenbach*'s limitation of the equal sovereignty doctrine to "the admission of new States," the suggestion is untenable. *Northwest Austin* cited *Katzenbach*'s holding in the course of declining to decide whether the VRA was constitutional or even what standard of review applied to the question. 557 U. S., at 203–204. In today's decision, the Court ratchets up what was pure dictum in *Northwest Austin*, attributing breadth to the equal sovereignty principle in flat contradiction of *Katzenbach*. The Court does so with nary an explanation of why it finds *Katzenbach* wrong, let alone any discussion of whether stare decisis nonetheless counsels adherence to *Katzenbach*'s ruling on the limited "significance" of the equal sovereignty principle.

Today's unprecedented extension of the equal sovereignty principle outside its proper domain—the admission of new States—is capable of much mischief. Federal statutes that treat States disparately are hardly novelties. See, e.g., 28 U. S. C. §3704 (no State may operate or permit a sports-related gambling scheme, unless that State conducted such a scheme "at any time during the period beginning January 1, 1976, and ending August 31, 1990"); 26 U. S. C. §142(l) (EPA required to locate green building project in a State meeting specified population criteria); 42 U. S. C. §3796bb (at least 50 percent of rural drug enforcement assistance funding must be allocated to States with "a population density of fifty-two or fewer persons per square mile or a State in which the largest county has fewer than one hundred and fifty thousand people, based on the decennial census of 1990 through fiscal year 1997"); §§13925, 13971 (similar population criteria for funding to combat rural domestic violence); §10136 (specifying rules applicable to Nevada's Yucca Mountain nuclear waste site, and providing that "[n]o State, other than the State of Nevada, may receive financial assistance under this subsection after December 22, 1987"). Do such provisions remain safe given the Court's expansion of equal sovereignty's sway?

Of gravest concern, Congress relied on our pathmarking *Katzenbach* decision in each reauthorization of the VRA. It had every reason to believe that the Act's limited geographical scope would weigh in favor of, not against, the Act's constitutionality. See, e.g., *United States v. Morrison*, 529 U. S. 598 –627 (2000) (confining preclearance regime to States with a record of discrimination bolstered the VRA's constitutionality). Congress could hardly have foreseen that the VRA's limited geographic reach would render the Act constitutionally suspect. See Persily 195 ("[S]upporters of the Act sought to develop an evidentiary record for the principal purpose of explaining why the covered jurisdictions should remain covered, rather than justifying the coverage of certain jurisdictions but not others.").

In the Court's conception, it appears, defenders of the VRA could not prevail upon showing what the record overwhelmingly bears out, i.e., that there is a need for continuing the preclearance regime in covered States. In addition, the defenders would have to disprove the existence of a comparable need elsewhere. See Tr. of Oral Arg. 61–62 (suggesting that proof of egregious episodes of racial discrimination in covered jurisdictions would not suffice to carry the day for the VRA, unless such episodes are shown to be absent elsewhere). I am aware of no precedent for imposing such a double burden on defenders of legislation.

C

The Court has time and again declined to upset legislation of this genre unless there was no or almost no evidence of unconstitutional action by States. See, e.g., *City of Boerne v. Flores*, 521 U. S. 507, 530 (1997) (legislative record "mention[ed] no episodes [of the kind the legislation aimed to check] occurring in the past 40 years"). No such claim can be made about the congressional record for the 2006 VRA reauthorization. Given a record replete with examples of denial or abridgment of a paramount federal right, the Court should have left the matter where it belongs: in Congress' bailiwick.

Instead, the Court strikes §4(b)'s coverage provision because, in its view, the provision is not based on "current conditions." Ante, at 17. It discounts, however, that one such condition was the preclearance remedy in place in the covered jurisdictions, a remedy Congress designed both to catch discrimination before it causes harm, and to guard against return to old ways. 2006 Reauthorization §2(b)(3), (9). Volumes of evidence supported Congress' de-termination that the prospect of retrogression was real. Throwing out preclearance when it has worked and is continuing to work to stop discriminatory changes is like throwing away your umbrella in a rainstorm because you are not getting wet.

But, the Court insists, the coverage formula is no good; it is based on "decades-old data and eradicated practices." Ante, at 18. Even if the legislative record shows, as engaging with it would reveal, that the formula accurately identifies the jurisdictions with the worst conditions of voting discrimination, that is of no moment, as the Court sees it. Congress, the Court decrees, must "star[t] from scratch." Ante, at 23. I do not see why that should be so.

Congress' chore was different in 1965 than it was in 2006. In 1965, there were a "small number of States ... which in most instances were familiar to Congress by name," on which Congress fixed its attention. Katzenbach, 383 U. S., at 328. In drafting the coverage formula, "Congress began work with reliable evidence of actual voting discrimination in a great majority of the States" it sought to target. Id., at 329. "The formula [Congress] eventually evolved to describe these areas" also captured a few States that had not been the subject of congressional factfinding. Ibid. Nevertheless, the Court upheld the formula in its entirety, finding it fair "to infer a significant danger of the evil" in all places the formula covered. Ibid.

The situation Congress faced in 2006, when it took up reauthorization of the coverage formula, was not the same. By then, the formula had been in effect for many years, and all of the jurisdictions covered by it were "familiar to Congress by name." Id., at 328. The question before Congress: Was there still a sufficient basis to support continued application of the preclearance remedy in each of those already-identified places? There was at that point no chance that the formula might inadvertently sweep in new areas that were not the subject of congressional findings. And Congress could determine from the record whether the jurisdictions captured by the coverage formula still belonged under the preclearance regime. If they did, there was no need to alter the formula. That is why the Court, in addressing prior reauthorizations of the VRA, did not question the continuing "relevance" of the formula.

Consider once again the components of the record before Congress in 2006. The coverage provision identified a known list of places with an undisputed history of serious problems with racial discrimination in voting. Recent evidence relating to Alabama and its counties was there for all to see. Multiple Supreme Court decisions had upheld the coverage provision, most recently in 1999. There was extensive evidence that, due to the preclearance mechanism, conditions in the covered jurisdictions had notably improved. And there was evidence that preclearance was still having a substantial real-world effect, having stopped hundreds of discriminatory voting changes in the covered jurisdictions since the last reauthorization. In addition, there was evidence that racial polarization in voting was higher in covered jurisdictions than elsewhere, increasing the vulnerability of minority citizens in those jurisdictions. And countless witnesses, reports, and case studies documented continuing problems with voting dis-crimination in those jurisdictions. In light of this record, Congress had more than a reasonable basis to conclude that the existing coverage formula was not out of sync with conditions on the ground in covered areas. And certainly Shelby County was no candidate for release through the mechanism Congress provided. See supra, at 22–23, 26–28.

The Court holds §4(b) invalid on the ground that it is "irrational to base coverage on the use of voting tests 40 years ago, when such tests have been illegal since that time." Ante, at 23. But the Court disregards what Congress set about to do in enacting the VRA. That extraordinary legislation scarcely stopped at the particular tests and devices that happened to exist in 1965. The grand aim of the Act is to secure to all in our polity equal citizenship stature, a voice in our democracy undiluted by race. As the record for the 2006 reauthorization makes abundantly clear, second-generation barriers to minority voting rights have emerged in the covered jurisdictions as attempted substitutes for the first-generation barriers that originally triggered preclearance in those jurisdictions. See supra, at 5–6, 8, 15–17.

The sad irony of today's decision lies in its utter failure to grasp why the VRA has proven effective. The Court appears to believe that the VRA's success in eliminating the specific devices extant in 1965 means that preclearance is no longer needed. Ante, at 21–22, 23–24. With that belief, and the argument derived from it, history repeats itself. The same assumption—that the problem could be solved when particular methods of voting discrimination are identified and eliminated—was indulged and proved wrong repeatedly prior to the VRA's enactment. Unlike prior statutes, which singled out particular tests or devices, the VRA is grounded in Congress' recognition of the "variety and persistence" of measures designed to impair minority voting rights. Katzenbach, 383 U. S., at 311; supra, at 2. In truth, the evolution of voting discrimination into more subtle second-generation barriers is powerful evidence that a remedy as effective as preclearance remains vital to protect minority voting rights and prevent backsliding.

Beyond question, the VRA is no ordinary legislation. It is extraordinary because Congress embarked on a mission long delayed and of extraordinary importance: to realize the purpose and promise of the Fifteenth Amendment. For a half century, a concerted effort has been made to end racial discrimination in voting. Thanks to the Voting Rights Act, progress once the subject of a dream has been achieved and continues to be made.

The record supporting the 2006 reauthorization of the VRA is also extraordinary. It was described by the Chairman of the House Judiciary Committee as "one of the most extensive considerations of any piece of legislation that the United States Congress has dealt with in the 27½ years" he had served in the House. 152 Cong. Rec. H5143 (July 13, 2006) (statement of Rep. Sensenbrenner). After exhaustive evidence-gathering and deliberative process, Congress reauthorized the VRA, including the coverage provision, with overwhelming bipartisan support. It was the judgment of Congress that "40 years has not been a sufficient amount of time to eliminate the vestiges of discrimination following nearly 100 years of disregard for the dictates of the 15th amendment and to ensure that the right of all citizens to vote is protected as guaranteed by the Constitution." 2006 Reauthorization §2(b)(7), 120Stat. 577. That determination of the body empowered to enforce the Civil War Amendments "by appropriate legislation" merits this Court's utmost respect. In my judgment, the Court errs egregiously by overriding Congress' decision.

For the reasons stated, I would affirm the judgment of the Court of Appeals.

Glossary

bailout: the removal of a jurisdiction from the preclearance requirements of Section 5 of the Voting Rights Act after meeting certain conditions

federal examiners: officials appointed by the Justice Department to prepare lists of citizens who are qualified to vote and to register them to vote

preclearance: permission from the federal government for a jurisdiction to make a change to voting procedures, having proved that the change would not discriminate against voters on the basis of race

OBERGEFELL V. HODGES

DATE
2015

AUTHOR
Anthony Kennedy

VOTE
5–4

CITATION
576 U.S. 644

SIGNIFICANCE
Established the constitutional right to marry for same-sex couples

Overview

In *Obergefell v. Hodges* (2015), the U.S. Supreme Court held in a 5–4 decision that same-sex couples across the United States had an equal right to marry and that states had to recognize legal marriages performed in other states. *Obergefell* expressly overruled the Court's previous decision in *Baker v. Nelson,* in which the justices rendered a one-sentence dismissal in 1972 of a Minnesota appeals case, which held that the issue of same-sex marriage did not rise to "a substantial federal question" and was not properly to be heard before the Court. *Obergefell* has proved to be a landmark in civil rights legislation and is a reflection of the majority opinion in the United States as the rights of homosexuals and their acceptance as equals has become a legal norm and perhaps a societal norm as well.

Context

In May 1970, a pair of gay rights activists at the University of Minnesota, Richard Baker and John McConnell, went to the county courthouse in Minneapolis to apply for a marriage license. The Stonewall Inn riot in New York City had taken place a year earlier, and the idea of gay civil rights had only recently been broached as a topic in American political culture. Homosexuality was still largely condemned by most Americans; Baker and McConnell were brave for simply admitting their sexual preferences, let alone asking to have their relationship sanctioned by a legal union.

The couple's application for a marriage license was rejected by the county registrar on the ground that the two applicants were of the same sex. Baker and McConnell subsequently filed a lawsuit to demand that their application be accepted and that they be allowed to marry. They charged that their constitutional rights, particularly under the Ninth and Fourteenth Amendments, had been violated. In 1971, the case made its way to the Minnesota Supreme Court, where one of the justices simply spun his chair around so as not to look at the attorney arguing the men's case. Upon the state's dismissal of their case, Baker and McConnell appealed to the U.S. Supreme Court, again arguing that their rights to life, liberty, and property as outlined in the Fourteenth Amendment were being denied and that their right to privacy as granted by the Ninth Amendment had been violated too. In reviewing the case in 1972, the U.S. Supreme Court decided that

James Obergefell (left) with his lawyer
(Elvert Barnes)

the status of marriage was an issue to be determined by the states, making a one-sentence dismissal: "The appeal is dismissed for want of a substantial federal question." The dismissal blocked federal courts from hearing other cases on same-sex marriage, leaving the decision to declare its legality up to the states. In response, Maryland, Virginia, Florida, Michigan, and Wyoming passed laws in the 1970s defining marriage as being between a man and a woman, effectively stifling any argument over the legality of gay marriages for decades.

Over the course of that time, the acceptance of homosexuality in American society and culture grew, but a clear line was drawn as to the legal precedents for its acceptance, especially on a state-by-state basis. Discrimination against gays in the workplace became less and less acceptable, gay characters became a norm in media productions, and the AIDS crisis built sympathy for the gay community in secular culture. Statutes were passed in San Francisco and the District of Columbia that allowed domestic partners of any sexual orientation to register as a couple in order to share benefits. In response to the lawsuit *Baehr v. Lewin*, brought by three same-sex couples, the Hawaii Supreme Court asserted in 1993 that banning same-sex marriage violated the state constitution. Simultaneously, however, the federal government offered little in the way of funding for AIDS research until well into the 1990s. In response to the Hawaii court case, Congress passed the Defense of Marriage Act (DOMA) in 1996, with broad bipartisan support; the bill was signed into law by President Bill Clinton. DOMA specified that only heterosexual couples would receive federal legal benefits, thus defying the relaxed laws passed in San Francisco and the District of Columbia. Moreover, the challenge to gay marriage represented by the decision of the Hawaii Supreme Court was reversed when voters in that state approved a constitutional amendment banning same-sex marriage. In the election year of 2004, ten states enacted state constitutional amendments blocking gay marriages, and nine more followed in the next two years. If Americans in general became more and more tolerant of homosexuality and homosexuals, they were certainly not tolerant of same-sex marriage.

The popularity of civil unions for gay couples grew in specific states, however, and in the eyes of the public in those states. Vermont legalized gay civil unions in 2000, and in 2004 Massachusetts began issuing marriage licenses to same-sex couples. In fact, at the same time as those nineteen states passed laws defining marriage as a union between a man and a woman, another fifteen states passed laws and constitutional amendments accepting the institution of same-sex marriage, setting the stage for a legal and cultural showdown to take place in the Supreme Court. The court had heard a few cases since 1972 that had chipped away at its dismissal of gay marriage as a matter for the states to decide. The most important of them was *United States v. Windsor* (2013), which ruled that section 3 of DOMA, defining marriage as being between a man and a woman, was unconstitutional. Other U.S. circuit courts of appeal ruled against DOMA in other cases, while at the same time public opinion grew more sympathetic to the idea that the makeup of a union between two people was a matter of personal privacy. A court case was needed to turn public and political opinion into a national legal reality.

The challenge centered on a court case heard in Ohio, *Obergefell v. Kasich* (later retitled *Obergefell v. Wymyslo*). John Arthur was suffering from amyotrophic lateral sclerosis, colloquially known as Lou Gehrig's disease, a terminal illness. He was in the late stages of the disease and wanted to have the Ohio registrar recognize his partner, James Obergefell, as his surviving spouse on his death certificate so that Obergefell would be able to receive spousal death benefits. Arthur and Obergefell had married in Maryland two years earlier. The Ohio registrar intended to grant the request. However, the state of Ohio did not recognize same-sex marriage and the Ohio attorney general's office intervened to defend the ban on same-sex marriage rights. In addition, four Ohio same-sex couples brought a claim seeking to list both parents on their children's birth certificates. Three of the couples lived in Ohio, and all of the children had been born in Ohio.

The cases in Ohio challenged the statutes enacted by state legislatures across the nation in opposition to legal same-sex unions and the family and privacy issues that resulted from them. Other cases arose around the same time that mirrored those challenges. In Tennessee four same-sex couples sued to force the state to recognize their marriages, which had been performed in California and New York. In Michigan a same-sex couple, April DeBoer and Jayne Rowse, both nurses, sought to be able to adopt three special needs children. The couple challenged a state law that prohibited same-sex couples from adopting children, limiting second-parent adoption to married couples and defining marriage as only between a man and a woman. In Kentucky, Gregory Bourke and Michael DeLeon brought a claim on behalf of their two adopted children and were joined by three other couples with adopted children. Bourke and DeLeon had been married in Canada, and the other couples had been married in Iowa, California, and Connecticut.

All these legal actions prevailed in the lower federal district courts. In *Obergefell v. Kasich* a temporary restraining order was issued, and a hearing was scheduled to determine whether it should be granted. Arthur died before the hearing could be held, and the state moved within a week to have the case dismissed as moot. Judge Timothy Black of the U.S. District Court for the Southern District of Ohio denied the motion and ruled that Ohio must recognize same-sex marriages performed in other states.

All of these cases were appealed to the U.S. Court of Appeals for the Sixth Circuit, which reversed the trial court on all of the cases and reinstated the same-sex marriage bans. The U.S. Supreme Court, in turn, agreed to hear all of the cases and consolidated them for review. In its ruling in *Obergefell v. Hodges*, the Court reversed the Sixth Circuit, holding that the Fourteenth Amendment requires a state to issue marriage licenses to same-sex couples and that same-sex marriages must be recognized when lawfully licensed and performed in another state. Writing for the majority, Justice Anthony Kennedy noted that the Fourteenth Amendment protected fundamental liberties, which extended to certain personal choices, including personal identity, and that marriage has been recognized as a personal privacy interest. Justices Ruth Bader Ginsburg, Stephen Breyer, Sonia Sotomayor, and Elena Kagan joined the majority opinion.

About the Author

Anthony Kennedy was born on July 23, 1936, in Sacramento, California. His father was an attorney and lobbyist in the California state legislature, and his mother was a teacher and champion of local civics issues. Kennedy worked as a page in the California state senate while he was in high school. Upon graduation, he attended Stanford University. There he became interested in constitutional law. He entered Harvard Law School and graduated in 1961. He then served in the California Army National Guard and in 1962 returned to Sacramento, where he passed the bar exam.

After the death of his father in 1963, Kennedy took over his father's law practice and remained there until 1975. While keeping his private practice, he joined the faculty at the University of the Pacific's McGeorge School of Law, where he taught for over twenty years. He also worked as a lobbyist for the California Republican Party under attorney Ed Meese (who later served as attorney general of the United States). In that position he assisted Governor Ronald Reagan in drafting a ballot initiative to cut state spending. The ballot measure failed to pass, but his assistance to Reagan ultimately led President Gerald Ford to appoint him to the federal Ninth Circuit Court of Appeals in 1975. He was the youngest federal appellate judge in the country at the age of thirty-nine. Kennedy's Republican ideology differentiated him from the more liberal-leaning federal judges appointed during the administration of President Jimmy Carter, but he was known for taking a deliberate case-by-case approach to his opinions on the federal appellate bench, often being a bridge builder between a divided court.

Kennedy was considered as a nominee to replace Supreme Court Justice Lewis Powell in 1987, but Reagan ultimately nominated Robert Bork. Bork's strict adherence to conservative ideology and abrupt personality caused the Senate to reject his nomination. Kennedy was seen as a more amicable choice and was thereafter unanimously confirmed to the Supreme Court and sworn in on February 18, 1988.

Beginning his tenure on the Supreme Court, Justice Kennedy was considered fairly conservative. This perspective changed after Kennedy coauthored the Court's majority opinion in *Planned Parenthood of Southeastern Pennsylvania v. Casey* in 1992. By holding that restrictions on abortion place an "undue burden" on a woman's free exercise of her right to abortion under *Roe v. Wade*, Kennedy established himself as a proponent of individual privacy rights. Kennedy also wrote for the majority in *Romer v. Evans* (1996), which struck down a Colorado state constitutional amendment that prohibited state and local governments from drafting laws to protect members of the LGBTQ community.

Justice Kennedy grew to be known as an important swing vote between conservative and liberal members of the Supreme Court. This was never more prominent than his swing vote in *Obergefell v. Hodges*. In *Obergefell*, Justice Kennedy's long-standing notions of individual liberty rights came to full fruition in his reasoning that same-sex couples were entitled to the same liberty rights as opposite-sex couples. Justice Kennedy retired from the Supreme Court on July 31, 2018.

Explanation and Analysis of the Document

Obergefell is a unique opinion, in that it does not expressly set forth which constitutional test is being applied. Rather, it analyzes several court precedents and Kennedy's own theory of liberty. The majority observed that the purpose of the Constitution itself is to support rights that are too important to have to wait to be recognized, noting that Jim Obergefell's husband had already died and that the children of same-sex unions were growing up without their parents being able to marry.

Justice Kennedy begins by describing the particulars of the cases involved in his decision, observing that they all came from states that had legally declared marriage as a union of one man and one woman. He then sets the parameters of the Court's majority opinion: deciding whether the Fourteenth Amendment protects a same-sex marriage and whether the states must recognize such a marriage whether they grant marriage licenses to same-sex couples or not. He notes that the Court has long protected the right to marry, but it always presumed such rights to be the purview of one man and one woman. In *Baker v. Nelson*, the Court had even denied itself the right to hear such cases, seeing the nature of marriage as a matter for the states to decide.

The White House was lit in rainbow colors on the evening of the ruling in celebration of the decision.
(Flickr)

So where did that leave these cases? Justice Kennedy states that the court has set several precedents on what it believed to be the tenets of a marriage, through numerous court decisions over two hundred years. He comments that "in assessing whether the force and rationale of its cases apply to same-sex couples, the Court must respect the basic reasons why the right to marry has been long protected." He then defines four principles. He first states that individual freedom dictates "the right to personal choice regarding marriage," meaning that the freedoms guaranteed in the Constitution imply freedom of choice that covers the choice concerning whom to marry. Kennedy also recognizes marriage as a unique supportive union, with the right to marry a basic underlying principle, meaning that the choice individuals make in terms of marriage determines their entire lives and therefore their freedoms too. Third, Kennedy observes, marriage protects children and builds families that participate in their communities and provide stability to the community, the state, and the nation as a whole. Fourth, Kennedy finds that "marriage is a keystone of our social order." Here he notes the opinion of the French aristocrat and early commentator on the American republic Alexis de Tocqueville that Americans respect marriage more than any other people in the world as an institution that underpins the stability of society. Kennedy concludes his discussion of the Court's principles toward its decisions on marriage by saying: "Marriage remains a building block of our national community."

Kennedy follows by pointing out that when a couple makes a vow to lend support to each other, "so does society pledge to support the couple, offering symbolic recognition and material benefits" that nurture and sustain the marriage. States, corporations, the federal government, and private institutions of all sorts have long recognized the rights of married couples to be recognized in order to receive benefits related to health, education, welfare, taxation, estates, ethics, compensation, and the like. To deny same-sex couples the right to marry, then, denies them status, fulfillment, and participation in society and thus violates the individual rights of the two people involved in a marriage, whatever their sexual orientation. As Justice Kennedy puts it, "Laws excluding same-sex couples from the marriage right impose stigma and injury of the kind prohibited by our basic charter."

He then addresses the religious, philosophical, and legal opposition to gay marriages. He notes that, though such opinions might be valid and valued on a private institutional basis, the very existence of the Fourteenth Amendment and its due process and equal protection clauses promise a "liberty" that cannot be denied to same-sex couples. The Fourteenth Amendment is a simple restatement of the principles of the Constitution and Bill of Rights, merely asserting that no state law may abridge those purposes for any American regardless of race, creed, ethnicity, or any other distinctions. Kennedy then avers that the state laws challenged by the couples brought before him do take away those rights and therefore contravene the Fourteenth Amendment. He can only conclude that the right to marry is a basic right, "inherent in the liberty of the person." That basic right may not be countermanded. Kennedy explicitly says that *Baker v. Nelson* is thus overruled.

Justice Kennedy then tries to address some of the concerns of the respondents in the cases. One is that the states need more time and legislation to address changes in individual rights. Public opinion might be solicited through elections and state constitutional amendments to address the issue of same-sex unions. To that, Kennedy responds, using a quote from the Supreme Court opinion *West Virginia State Board of Education v. Barnette* (1943), that basic rights do not stand or fall on the outcomes of voting. (That case opinion defended the First Amendment right not to salute the flag or say the Pledge of Allegiance.) In particular, Kennedy notes the urgency of the petitioners' cases before the Court, pointing out that Obergefell and his fellow petitioners cannot wait for public opinion to change to have their rights recognized. He gently denies that granting same-sex marriages will have any impact on opposite-sex marriages and emphasizes that religious denominations may believe anything they like but that constitutional rights are a secular matter for the courts. On a legal and national basis, the Court finds that same-sex couples may marry in every state and that no state may "refuse to recognize" such lawful unions.

Justice Kennedy ends his majority opinion by characterizing the profundity of the marriage bond in its embrace of "the highest ideals of love, fidelity, devotion, sacrifice, and family." The Constitution allows same-sex couples "equal dignity in the eyes of the law." The primary takeaway from *Obergefell* is that a marriage is central to an individual's identity and is connected to other fundamental rights such as procreation, raising children, and education. The majority opinion concludes that state laws that infringe on these rights and violate the liberty rights of same-sex couples harm not just the individuals but also their children and the underlying principles of equality at the core of American society.

The Court also focused on how the institution of marriage has evolved over time from its traditional, religious origins. The Court acknowledged that arranged marriages were largely now abandoned and that society no longer viewed interracial marriages and contraception for married couples as illegal. Thus, following that precedent, the Court held that same-sex marriages are entitled to the same freedom and equality. Last, the Court acknowledged that same-sex couples and their children should not have to await legislative action when it has become clear through the evolution of research, litigation, and debate that fundamental liberty interests are being infringed and that immediate judicial action is required.

Impact

The impact of *Obergefell* cannot be understated, as it has become a landmark ruling advancing equality and liberty rights for individuals in same-sex marriages. Although critics have agreed with the four dissenting justices (John Roberts, Antonin Scalia, Clarence Thomas, and Samuel Alito) that the Court overextended its role as arbiter of the Constitution and should have left the issue to state legislatures, other legal scholars agree that the Court performed its appropriate role: protecting the liberty and equality of those who have been traditionally discriminated against and extending to them the same rights of equality long regarded as fundamental to others. Until the moment before Justice Kennedy read his short summation from the bench, it was unclear exactly how the Court would rule. However, as Justice Kennedy had drafted virtually every Supreme Court majority case regarding the expansion of LGBTQ rights, there was speculation that the outcome would be favorable to the same-sex community.

As *Obergefell* was based firmly in the Constitution, the only way to overturn it would be by an amendment to the Constitution or a reversal by the Supreme Court in a future case. *Obergefell* opened the door to same-sex marriage in the fourteen remaining states that had banned it and gave legal protection to those in other court rulings that were now bound by a decision made by the highest Court.

After the opinion was released, hundreds of thousands of same-sex couples obtained marriage licenses and were married. Just one year after the opinion was released, same-sex marriages increased by 22 percent. Along with those marriages came the corresponding state and federal spousal rights previously enjoyed only by opposite-sex couples. Some of those rights include more favorable tax treatment, equal rights as parents, and certain estate benefits. The legal community began to prepare to address such issues as child-custody rights, adoption, divorce, and estate planning with same-sex couples. Moreover, nationwide employers needed to reconsider healthcare benefits packages, retirement packages, and other employment-related issues. Previously, spousal and family benefits had applied only to opposite-sex couples.

It was estimated that within one year of the decision, the national economy was boosted by approximately $1.58 billion from same-sex weddings alone. An increase of $102 million in state and local tax revenue was realized at the one-year anniversary of the *Obergefell* decision. The economic impact of the expansion of the right to marriage has been substantial. This trend is expected to continue in the areas of estate planning and probate as more married same-sex couples age, particularly within the large baby boomer generation.

Obergefell made the United States the twenty-third country in the world to recognize marriage equality. As of 2020, twenty-eight countries recognize same-sex marriages. Thus the impact of *Obergefell* can be felt on a societal level as the culmination of a decades-long battle for equality by the LGBTQ community.

Questions for Further Study

1. *Obergefell* does not cite a specific provision of the Constitution as the basis for its decision on marriage equality. Rather, Justice Kennedy based his opinion on privacy rights. On what basis of privacy does the majority rely to establish same-sex marriage equality?

2. What four principles and traditions are noted by the Court as demonstrating that marriage is a fundamental right that should apply to same-sex couples?

3. What role does the Court say the First Amendment plays in regard to religion and marriage equality?

Further Reading

Books

Becker, Jo. *Forcing the Spring: Inside the Fight for Marriage Equality.* New York: Penguin Books, 2014.

Boies, David, and Theodore B. Olson. *Redeeming the Dream: The Case for Marriage Equality.* New York: Viking, 2014.

Cenziper, Debbie, and Jim Obergefell. *Love Wins: The Lovers and Lawyers Who Fought the Landmark Case for Marriage Equality.* New York: William Morrow, 2016.

Articles

Banks, Lisa, and Hannah Alejandro. "Changing Definitions of Sex under Title VII." *ABA Journal of Labor & Employment Law* 32, no. 1 (Fall 2016): 25–44.

Websites

Mallory, Christy, and Brad Sears. "Estimating the Economic Impact of Marriage for Same Sex Couples One Year after *Obergefell*." Williams Institute, UCLA School of Law, June 2016. https://williamsinstitute. law.ucla.edu/research/estimating-the-economic-impact-of-marriage-for-same-sex-couples-one-year-after-obergefell/.

—Commentary by David Simonelli

OBERGEFELL V. HODGES

Document Text

Justice Kennedy delivered the opinion of the Court

The Constitution promises liberty to all within its reach, a liberty that includes certain specific rights that allow persons, within a lawful realm, to define and express their identity. The petitioners in these cases seek to find that liberty by marrying someone of the same sex and having their marriages deemed lawful on the same terms and conditions as marriages between persons of the opposite sex.

I

These cases come from Michigan, Kentucky, Ohio, and Tennessee, States that define marriage as a union between one man and one woman. The petitioners are 14 same-sex couples and two men whose same-sex partners are deceased. The respondents are state officials responsible for enforcing the laws in question. The petitioners claim the respondents violate the Fourteenth Amendment by denying them the right to marry or to have their marriages, lawfully performed in another State, given full recognition....

This Court granted review, limited to two questions. The first, presented by the cases from Michigan and Kentucky, is whether the Fourteenth Amendment requires a State to license a marriage between two people of the same sex. The second, presented by the cases from Ohio, Tennessee, and, again, Kentucky, is whether the Fourteenth Amendment requires a State to recognize a same-sex marriage licensed and performed in a State which does grant that right....

III

Under the Due Process Clause of the Fourteenth Amendment, no State shall "deprive any person of life, liberty, or property, without due process of law." The fundamental liberties protected by this Clause include most of the rights enumerated in the Bill of Rights. In addition these liberties extend to certain personal choices central to individual dignity and autonomy, including intimate choices that define personal identity and beliefs.

The identification and protection of fundamental rights is an enduring part of the judicial duty to interpret the Constitution. That responsibility, however, "has not been reduced to any formula." Rather, it requires courts to exercise reasoned judgment in identifying interests of the person so fundamental that the State must accord them its respect. That process is guided by many of the same considerations relevant to analysis of other constitutional provisions that set forth broad principles rather than specific requirements. History and tradition guide and discipline this inquiry but do not set its outer boundaries. That method respects our history and learns from it without allowing the past alone to rule the present.

The nature of injustice is that we may not always see it in our own times. The generations that wrote and ratified the Bill of Rights and the Fourteenth Amendment did not presume to know the extent of freedom in all of its dimensions, and so they entrusted to future generations a charter protecting the right of all persons to enjoy liberty as we learn its meaning. When new insight reveals discord between the Constitution's central protections and a received legal stricture, a claim to liberty must be addressed.

Applying these established tenets, the Court has long held the right to marry is protected by the Constitution. . . . [Yet i]t cannot be denied that this Court's cases describing the right to marry presumed a relationship involving opposite-sex partners. The Court, like many institutions, has made assumptions defined by the world and time of which it is a part. This was evident in *Baker v. Nelson*, 409 U. S. 810, a one-line summary decision issued in 1972, holding the exclusion of same-sex couples from marriage did not present a substantial federal question.

Still, there are other, more instructive precedents. This Court's cases have expressed constitutional principles of broader reach. In defining the right to marry these cases have identified essential attributes of that right based in history, tradition, and other constitutional liberties inherent in this intimate bond. And in assessing whether the force and rationale of its cases apply to same-sex couples, the Court must respect the basic reasons why the right to marry has been long protected.

This analysis compels the conclusion that same-sex couples may exercise the right to marry. The four principles and traditions to be discussed demonstrate that the reasons marriage is fundamental under the Constitution apply with equal force to same-sex couples.

A first premise of the Court's relevant precedents is that the right to personal choice regarding marriage is inherent in the concept of individual autonomy. . . . Like choices concerning contraception, family relationships, procreation, and childrearing, all of which are protected by the Constitution, decisions concerning marriage are among the most intimate that an individual can make. Indeed, the Court has noted it would be contradictory "to recognize a right of privacy with respect to other matters of family life and not with respect to the decision to enter the relationship that is the foundation of the family in our society."

Choices about marriage shape an individual's destiny. . . . The nature of marriage is that, through its enduring bond, two persons together can find other freedoms, such as expression, intimacy, and spirituality. This is true for all persons, whatever their sexual orientation. There is dignity in the bond between two men or two women who seek to marry and, in their autonomy, to make such profound choices.

A second principle in this Court's jurisprudence is that the right to marry is fundamental because it supports a two-person union unlike any other in its importance to the committed individuals. . . . Marriage responds to the universal fear that a lonely person might call out only to find no one there. It offers the hope of companionship and understanding and assurance that while both still live there will be someone to care for the other. . . .

A third basis for protecting the right to marry is that it safeguards children and families and thus draws meaning from related rights of childrearing, procreation, and education. The Court has recognized these connections by describing the varied rights as a unified whole: "[T]he right to 'marry, establish a home and bring up children' is a central part of the liberty protected by the Due Process Clause." Under the laws of the several States, some of marriage's protections for children and families are material. But marriage also confers more profound benefits. By giving recognition and legal structure to their parents' relationship, marriage allows children "to understand the integrity and closeness of their own family and its concord with other families in their community and in their daily lives." Marriage also affords the permanency and stability important to children's best interests.

As all parties agree, many same-sex couples provide loving and nurturing homes to their children, whether biological or adopted. And hundreds of thousands of children are presently being raised by such couples. Most States have allowed gays and lesbians to adopt, either as individuals or as couples, and many adopted and foster children have same-sex parents. This provides powerful confirmation from the law itself that gays and lesbians can create loving, supportive families.

Excluding same-sex couples from marriage thus conflicts with a central premise of the right to marry. Without the recognition, stability, and predictability marriage offers, their children suffer the stigma of knowing their families are somehow lesser. They also suffer the significant material costs of being raised by unmarried parents, relegated through no fault of their own to a more difficult and uncertain family life. The marriage laws at issue here thus harm and humiliate the children of same-sex couples.

That is not to say the right to marry is less meaningful for those who do not or cannot have children. An ability, desire, or promise to procreate is not and has not been a prerequisite for a valid marriage in any State. In light of precedent protecting the right of a married couple not to procreate, it cannot be said the Court or the States have conditioned the right to marry on the capacity or commitment to procreate. The constitutional marriage right has many aspects, of which childbearing is only one.

Fourth and finally, this Court's cases and the Nation's traditions make clear that marriage is a keystone of our social order. Alexis de Tocqueville recognized this truth on his travels through the United States almost two centuries ago:

> There is certainly no country in the world where the tie of marriage is so much respected as in America . . . [W]hen the American retires from the turmoil of public life to the bosom of his family, he finds in it the image of order and of peace. . . .[H]e afterwards carries [that image] with him into public affairs.

. . . Marriage remains a building block of our national community.

For that reason, just as a couple vows to support each other, so does society pledge to support the couple, offering symbolic recognition and material benefits to protect and nourish the union. Indeed, while the States are in general free to vary the benefits they confer on all married couples, they have throughout our history made marriage the basis for an expanding list of governmental rights, benefits, and responsibilities. These aspects of marital status include: taxation; inheritance and property rights; rules of intestate succession; spousal privilege in the law of evidence; hospital access; medical decision-making authority; adoption rights; the rights and benefits of survivors; birth and death certificates; professional ethics rules; campaign finance restrictions; workers' compensation benefits; health insurance; and child custody, support, and visitation rules. Valid marriage under state law is also a significant status for over a thousand provisions of federal law. The States have contributed to the fundamental character of the marriage right by placing that institution at the center of so many facets of the legal and social order.

There is no difference between same- and opposite-sex couples with respect to this principle. Yet by virtue of their exclusion from that institution, same-sex couples are denied the constellation of benefits that the States have linked to marriage. This harm results in more than just material burdens. Same-sex couples are consigned to an instability many opposite-sex couples would deem intolerable in their own lives. As the State itself makes marriage all the more precious by the significance it attaches to it, exclusion from that status has the effect of teaching that gays and lesbians are unequal in important respects. It demeans gays and lesbians for the State to lock them out of a central institution of the Nation's society. Same-sex couples, too, may aspire to the transcendent purposes of marriage and seek fulfillment in its highest meaning.

The limitation of marriage to opposite-sex couples may long have seemed natural and just, but its inconsistency with the central meaning of the fundamental right to marry is now manifest. With that knowledge must come the recognition that laws excluding same-sex couples from the marriage right impose stigma and injury of the kind prohibited by our basic charter. . . .

The right to marry is fundamental as a matter of history and tradition, but rights come not from ancient sources alone. They rise, too, from a better-informed understanding of how constitutional imperatives define a liberty that remains urgent in our own era. Many who deem same-sex marriage to be wrong reach that conclusion based on decent and honorable religious or philosophical premises, and neither they nor their beliefs are disparaged here. But when that sincere, personal opposition becomes enacted law and public policy, the necessary consequence is to put the imprimatur of the State itself on an exclusion that soon demeans or stigmatizes those whose own liberty is then denied. Under the Constitution, same-sex couples seek in marriage the same legal treatment as opposite-sex couples, and it would disparage their choices and diminish their personhood to deny them this right.

The right of same-sex couples to marry that is part of the liberty promised by the Fourteenth Amendment is derived, too, from that Amendment's guarantee of the equal protection of the laws. The Due Process Clause and the Equal Protection Clause are connected in a profound way, though they set forth independent principles. Rights implicit in liberty and rights secured by equal protection may rest on different precepts and are not always co-extensive, yet in some instances each may be instructive as to the meaning and reach of the other. In any particular case one Clause may be thought to capture the essence of the right in a more accurate and comprehensive way, even as the two Clauses may converge in the identification and definition of the right. This interrelation of the two principles furthers our understanding of what freedom is and must become....

It is now clear that the challenged laws burden the liberty of same-sex couples, and it must be further acknowledged that they abridge central precepts of equality. Here the marriage laws enforced by the respondents are, in essence, unequal: same-sex couples are denied all the benefits afforded to opposite-sex couples and are barred from exercising a fundamental right. Especially against a long history of disapproval of their relationships, this denial to same-sex couples of the right to marry works a grave and continuing harm. The imposition of this disability on gays and lesbians serves to disrespect and subordinate them. And the Equal Protection Clause, like the Due Process Clause, prohibits this unjustified infringement of the fundamental right to marry.

These considerations lead to the conclusion that the right to marry is a fundamental right inherent in the liberty of the person, and under the Due Process and Equal Protection Clauses of the Fourteenth Amendment couples of the same-sex may not be deprived of that right and that liberty. The Court now holds that same-sex couples may exercise the fundamental right to marry. No longer may this liberty be denied to them. *Baker v. Nelson* must be and now is overruled, and the State laws challenged by Petitioners in these cases are now held invalid to the extent they exclude same-sex couples from civil marriage on the same terms and conditions as opposite-sex couples.

IV

There may be an initial inclination in these cases to proceed with caution to await further legislation, litigation, and debate. The respondents warn there has been insufficient democratic discourse before deciding an issue so basic as the definition of marriage. In its ruling on the cases now before this Court, the majority opinion for the Court of Appeals made a cogent argument that it would be appropriate for the respondents' States to await further public discussion and political measures before licensing same-sex marriages.

Yet there has been far more deliberation than this argument acknowledges. There have been referenda, legislative debates, and grassroots campaigns, as well as countless studies, papers, books, and other popular and scholarly writings. There has been extensive litigation in state and federal courts. Judicial opinions addressing the issue have been informed by the contentions of parties and counsel, which, in turn, reflect the more general, societal discussion of same-sex marriage and its meaning that has occurred over the past decades. As more than 100 *amici* make clear in their filings, many of the central institutions in American life state and local governments, the military, large and small businesses, labor unions, religious organizations, law enforcement, civic groups, professional organizations, and universities have devoted substantial attention to the question. This has led to an enhanced understanding of the issue, an understanding reflected in the arguments now presented for resolution as a matter of constitutional law.

... The dynamic of our constitutional system is that individuals need not await legislative action before asserting a fundamental right. The Nation's courts are open to injured individuals who come to them to vindicate their own direct, personal stake in our basic charter. An individual can invoke a right to constitutional protection when he or she is harmed, even if the broader public disagrees and even if the legislature refuses to act. The idea of the Constitution "was to withdraw certain subjects from the vicissitudes of political controversy, to place them beyond the reach of majorities and officials and to establish them as legal principles to be applied by the courts." This is why "fundamental rights may not be submitted to a vote; they depend on the outcome of no elections." It is of no moment whether advocates of same-sex marriage now enjoy or lack momentum in the democratic process. The issue before the Court here is the legal question whether the Constitution protects the right of same-sex couples to marry.

... The petitioners' stories make clear the urgency of the issue they present to the Court. James Obergefell now asks whether Ohio can erase his marriage to John Arthur for all time. April DeBoer and Jayne Rowse now ask whether Michigan may continue to deny them the certainty and stability all mothers desire to protect their children, and for them and their children the childhood years will pass all too soon. Ijpe DeKoe and Thomas Kostura now ask whether Tennessee can deny to one who has served this Nation the basic dignity of recognizing his New York marriage. Properly presented with the petitioners' cases, the Court has a duty to address these claims and answer these questions.

Indeed, faced with a disagreement among the Courts of Appeals a disagreement that caused impermissible geographic variation in the meaning of federal law the Court granted review to determine whether same-sex couples may exercise the right to marry. Were the Court to uphold the challenged laws as constitutional, it would teach the Nation that these laws are in accord with our society's most basic compact. Were the Court to stay its hand to allow slower, case-by-case determination of the required availability of specific public benefits to same-sex couples, it still would deny gays and lesbians many rights and responsibilities intertwined with marriage.

The respondents also argue allowing same-sex couples to wed will harm marriage as an institution by leading to fewer opposite-sex marriages. This may occur, the respondents contend, because licensing same-sex marriage severs the connection between natural procreation and marriage. That argument, however, rests on a counterintuitive view of opposite-sex couple's decision-making processes regarding marriage and parenthood. Decisions about whether to marry and raise children are based on many personal, romantic, and practical considerations; and it is unrealistic to conclude that an opposite-sex couple would choose not to marry simply because same-sex couples may do so. The respondents have not shown a foundation for the conclusion that allowing same-sex marriage will cause the harmful outcomes they describe. Indeed, with respect to this asserted basis for excluding same-sex couples from the right to marry, it is appropriate to observe these cases involve only the rights of two consenting adults whose marriages would pose no risk of harm to themselves or third parties.

Finally, it must be emphasized that religions, and those who adhere to religious doctrines, may continue to advocate with utmost, sincere conviction that, by divine precepts, same-sex marriage should not be condoned. The First Amendment ensures that religious organizations and persons are given proper protection as they seek to teach the principles that are so fulfilling and so central to their lives and faiths, and to their own deep aspirations to continue the family structure they have long revered. The same is true of those who oppose same-sex marriage for other reasons. In turn, those who believe allowing same-sex marriage is proper or indeed essential, whether as a matter of religious conviction or secular belief, may engage those who disagree with their view in an open and searching debate. The Constitution, however, does not permit the State to bar same-sex couples from marriage on the same terms as accorded to couples of the opposite sex.

V

These cases also present the question whether the Constitution requires States to recognize same-sex marriages validly performed out of State. As made clear by the case of Obergefell and Arthur, and by that of DeKoe and Kostura, the recognition bans inflict substantial and continuing harm on same-sex couples.

Being married in one State but having that valid marriage denied in another is one of "the most perplexing and distressing complication[s]" in the law of domestic relations. Leaving the current state of affairs in place would maintain and promote instability and uncertainty. For some couples, even an ordinary drive into a neighboring State to visit family or friends risks causing severe hardship in the event of a spouse's hospitalization while across state lines. In light of the fact that many States already allow same-sex marriage and hundreds of thousands of these marriages already have occurred the disruption caused by the recognition bans is significant and ever-growing.

As counsel for the respondents acknowledged at argument, if States are required by the Constitution to issue marriage licenses to same-sex couples, the justifications for refusing to recognize those marriages performed elsewhere are undermined. The Court, in this decision, holds same-sex couples may exercise the fundamental right to marry in all States. It follows that the Court also must hold and it now does hold that there is no lawful basis for a State to refuse to recognize a lawful same-sex marriage performed in another State on the ground of its same-sex character....

No union is more profound than marriage, for it embodies the highest ideals of love, fidelity, devotion, sacrifice, and family. In forming a marital union, two people become something greater than once they were. As some of the petitioners in these cases demonstrate, marriage embodies a love that may endure even past death. It would misunderstand these men and women to say they disrespect the idea of marriage. Their plea is that they do respect it, respect it so deeply that they seek to find its fulfillment for themselves. Their hope is not to be condemned to live in loneliness, excluded from one of civilization's oldest institutions. They ask for equal dignity in the eyes of the law. The Constitution grants them that right.

The judgment of the Court of Appeals for the Sixth Circuit is reversed. It is so ordered.

Glossary

amici: literally, "friends"—here meaning "friends of the Court," or interested and expert parties who file legal briefings on Supreme Court cases, essentially lobbying to guide the Court's opinions in one direction or another toward a decision

Due Process Clause: a guarantee in the Fifth and Fourteenth Amendments that an individual accused of a crime has a right to be formally charged and tried

Fourteenth Amendment: amendment to the U.S. Constitution ratified in 1868 defining national citizenship and forbidding the states to restrict fundamental rights

fundamental rights: a group of rights recognized by the U.S. Supreme Court as requiring protection from government encroachment

Alexis de Tocqueville: a French government official and traveler to the United States who wrote one of the most famous and prescient essays outlining the principles of American life and society, *Democracy in America* (1835)

Bostock v. Clayton County

Date 2020	**Citation** 590 U.S. ___
Author Neil Gorsuch	**Significance** Determined that employees could not be discriminated against based on their homosexual or transgender status.
Vote 6–3	

Overview

The gradual acceptance and viability of homosexual and transgender Americans within mainstream society brought with it a steady number of court cases challenging discrimination based on one's sexual orientation or transgender status. This issue, specifically discrimination in the workplace, became the basis for a case that went before the Supreme Court in 2020, *Bostock v. Clayton County Board of Commissioners*. In a 6–3 vote, the justices decided that Title VII, a section of the Civil Rights Act of 1964 that bans discrimination against an employee based on "sex," should apply to lesbian, gay, bisexual, and transgender workers. Samuel Alito and Brett Kavanaugh both wrote dissenting opinions, with Alito's being joined by Clarence Thomas.

Bostock consolidated three separate cases based on the dismissal of individuals based on their gay or transgender identity in locations where prohibitions against discrimination against LGBTQ employees did not exist. The crux of the case centered on the definition of "sex" as it appears in Title VII and its applicability to gay and transgender employees. In the court's decision, the argument is made that it is not possible to take one's sexual orientation into consideration unless one's sex is considered first. This correlation meant that Title VII provides LGBTQ employees with protection from discrimination. It further meant that it was not necessary to amend Title VII to explicitly prohibit employee discrimination for LGBTQ employees across the country; such prejudice was now considered unlawful regardless of location.

Context

While homosexuality has existed in the United States throughout its entire existence, the recognition of its existence is comparatively recent, and any semblance of tolerance is newer still. Gay and lesbian Americans found urban centers during the 1920s and 1930s to be relative havens where they could live much more freely than in more isolated areas. There were far greater opportunities for members of the LGBT community to interact with one another during World War II, a tumultuous period that saw millions of Americans uprooted due to military service or wartime labor. Cities, particularly those in the West, expanded in population, with many of the new inhabitants being gay or lesbian.

But as more Americans came to acknowledge and explore their LGBT identities, mainstream America exhibited little interest in accepting, let alone acknowledging, them. Many homosexuals working in the federal government, most of them closeted, lost their jobs in the 1950s during the so-called lavender scare. Such dismissals were justified on the basis that homosexuals in the government were more vulnerable to communist operatives who might blackmail them to procure state secrets. Outraged gay men, having lost their jobs, began to organize as a means of pushing back. Harry Hay and Chuck Rowland founded the Mattachine Society in 1950, an early organization committed to giving an oppressed group some agency. Similar groups followed, including One, Inc., founded on the West Coast in 1952, and Daughters of Bilitis, the first lesbian support network, established in San Francisco in 1955.

Efforts by academics provided additional credence to the concept that gay and lesbian Americans were deserving of recognition and acceptance. In 1947 researcher Alfred Kinsey released his famous report on sexuality in America, which revealed homosexuality to be far more prevalent and complicated than most understood it to be. This was further explored by Edward Sagarin, a prominent sociologist who authored *The Homosexual in America* in 1951, a book that chronicles the many challenges faced by gay and lesbians in the United States and insists upon their receiving the same civil rights as heterosexual Americans. But such pleas made little headway; homosexuality continued to be labeled as an "illness" by the American Psychiatric Association in its diagnostic manual until 1973, and it was not uncommon for judges to rule against gay men and lesbians in cases of loss of employment and denial of child custody based on their sexual orientation.

Drawing inspiration from the legislative victories won by the civil rights movement of the 1950s and 1960s, gay Americans began to stage protests of their own, the first ones being in Philadelphia and Washington, D.C. But it was the Stonewall Riots in June 1969, when the patrons of a popular gay bar in New York City clashed with police during a series of raids, that proved most pivotal in starting the gay pride movement. Stonewall

Gerald Bostock
(Elvert Barnes)

came to be commemorated each June with "pride marches" organized across the nation starting in the 1970s, a decade that saw the gay liberation movement gain traction with the establishment of numerous political organizations, churches, and support groups.

The 1980s proved a challenging period due to the AIDS epidemic's particularly devastating impact on the gay male community and the federal government's reluctance to investigate the virus or mitigate its impact. The struggle of gay men during the period inspired greater political activism, including a large march on Washington in 1987, which involved upward of one million supporters of gay rights, and another in 1993.

The gay rights movement experienced setbacks and advancements in the 1990s. An example of the former related to the controversial issue of openly homosexual or bisexual individuals serving in the U.S. armed forces, which was illegal. In 1993 President Bill Clinton attempted to appease both critics and supporters of the policy by announcing a new rule known as "Don't Ask, Don't Tell" (DADT). Under DADT, members of the military were barred from bullying or ostracizing anyone suspected of being non-heterosexual, while openly gay, lesbian, or bisexual individuals were barred from serving in the armed forces. Many service members were discharged because of DADT. But there appeared to be some gradual acceptance of gay Americans largely as the result of a growing number of public figures in politics, sports, and entertainment identifying as lesbian or gay, perhaps the most notable example being comedian Ellen DeGeneres coming out in 1997.

The start of the twenty-first century ushered in a series of legislative victories for gay Americans, particularly in regard to same-sex marriage. The Vermont legislature legalized civil union between gay and lesbian couples in 2000; Massachusetts allowed same-sex marriages to be performed in 2004. The Supreme Court ultimately recognized same-sex marriage in the *Obergefell v. Hodges* decision in 2016. The 2000s also witnessed the growing emergence of transgender activism building upon the solid foundation laid by the gay rights movement.

It was against this backdrop, in 2020, that the Supreme Court heard the case of *Bostock v. Clayton County*, which centered on the question of whether an employer possessed the right to terminate someone's employment because they were gay or transgender.

About the Author

Following his birth and early upbringing in Denver, Colorado in 1967, Neil Gorsuch and his family relocated to Washington, D.C., when his mother was appointed the head of the U.S. Environmental Protection Agency. Young Gorsuch attended Georgetown Preparatory School in Maryland, where he was elected class president in his senior year and stood out as an adherent of conservative views. He then attended Columbia University, graduating Phi Beta Kappa with a degree in political science in 1988 before heading to Harvard Law School, from which he earned a law degree in 1991.

He began his legal career as a clerk for Judge David B. Sentelle of the U.S. Court of Appeals for the District of Columbia Circuit and then became a clerk at the Supreme Court for Justice Anthony M. Kennedy. He became a member of Kellogg, Huber, Hansen, Todd, Evans & Figel, a Washington, D.C., law firm, in 1995,

becoming a partner three years later. Gorsuch went on to complete a doctorate in legal philosophy from Oxford University in 2004 and became principal deputy to the associate attorney general at the U.S. Department of Justice the following year.

He served in the position for one year before his confirmation to the U.S. Court of Appeals for the Tenth Circuit, located in Denver. In the decisions he handed down, Gorsuch displayed originalist leanings (a belief that the Constitution should be interpreted in accordance with its original public meaning), which undoubtedly factored into his being nominated by President Donald Trump to take the place of recently deceased justice Antonin Scalia, a fellow originalist, in 2017.

Gorsuch's confirmation process proved rather contentious; Democratic senators used a partisan filibuster to attempt to prevent Gorsuch from joining the Supreme Court, but the Republicans bypassed the filibuster by lowering the established threshold for nominees to move forward from 60 votes to 50. Gorsuch has proven to be a reliably conservative judge since being sworn in, supporting gun rights and voting to strike down *Roe v. Wade*.

Explanation and Analysis of the Document

Gorsuch opens his opinion by musing whether an employer can dismiss an employee on the basis of their being homosexual or transgender and if doing so violates Title VII of the Civil Rights Act, which outlaws workplace discrimination based on race, color, religion, sex, or national origin. It is acknowledged that the members of Congress who passed the law could not have anticipated its application to the case at hand.

The Three Cases Forming the Basis for Bostock

The opinion then provides a brief overview of the circumstances under which Gerald Bostock, after ten years of exemplary service for Clayton County, Georgia, as a child welfare advocate, came to be fired for conduct considered "unbecoming" one working for the county due to his participation in a gay recreational softball league. A similar situation occurred when Donald Zarda, a skydiving instructor in New York, came to be fired by the company he worked for after

A rally outside of the Supreme Court on the day of the oral hearing
(Elvert Barnes)

mentioning his homosexuality. Aimee Stephens, an employee at a funeral home in Michigan, was fired after choosing to transition from being a man to a woman. Her decision to live full time as a woman in the sixth year of her employment preceded her employers' decision to fire her.

In each instance, the employee brought suit under Title VII claiming they'd been unlawfully discriminated against on the basis of sex. The Eleventh Circuit dismissed Bostock's case because the law doesn't expressly forbid the termination of employment based on sex. The Second Circuit came to the opposite conclusion in regard to Zarda's case, as did the Sixth Circuit when ruling Stephens's case. Gorsuch lays out the Court's task as determining the meaning of Title VII as it relates to its initial adoption in 1964. The focus must be affixed to the notion of "sex," which the fired employees contend was a concept not limited to reproductive biology and anatomy when Title VII was adopted but included gender identity and sexual orientation. The meaning of "discriminate" in 1964 must also be determined, which Gorsuch contends was approximately the same as it is in the present day.

Interpreting the Meaning of Title VII

Gorsuch argues that Title VII focuses on individuals rather than groups when it comes to discrimination based on sex. This means that one's identity as a homosexual or transgender individual is irrelevant to employment decisions because "it is impossible to discriminate against a person for being homosexual or transgender without discriminating against that individual based on sex." An employer engaged in discrimination against homosexual or transgender employees must purposely "discriminate against individual men and women in part because of sex," which Title VII expressly prohibits.

The opinion considers legal precedents, such as those involving a company that would not hire women with young children but did not make same the same exemption when it came to men with young children. Such cases establish the irrelevancy of what the employer designated a discriminatory practice or why it is in place; Title VII makes clear that an employee fired for being homosexual or transgender is a clear discrimination based in part on sex. And an employer can still be found liable even if it asserts that it views men and women comparably as groups.

As far as employers' assertions that discrimination against employees based on their status as homosexuals or transgender individuals is not applicable to Title VII, Gorsuch asserts that such arguments are fundamentally fallacious. The employers assert that in ordinary conversation, discrimination based on being homosexual or transgender is not considered the same as sex discrimination, which should serve as the guide for how employees came to be fired. But this does not change the fundamental meaning of Title VII and its protection of individual rights. And determining one's identity as a homosexual or transgender individual cannot be done without some consideration of the person's sex. Employees further argue that Title VII's failure to explicitly cite homosexuality or transexual status in its list of protected characteristics places them beyond its reach. But this once again violates the principle that discrimination based on one's being homosexual or transexual is by default discrimination based on gender.

Gorsuch insists that the preceding analysis removes any ambiguity as to how Title VII's terms apply in cases involving discrimination. He further insists that the meaning of Title VII's language has remained fundamentally unchanged since the statute's adoption in 1964, a view the employers actually agree with. Gorsuch then rejects the employers' assertions that no one in 1964 could have predicted homosexual or transexual individuals challenging their dismissal under Title VII. Cases held shortly after Congress passed the new law directly contradict such an argument.

Possible Expansion of Title VII

A final argument of the employers concerns where a decision on behalf of the plaintiff would lead. Might Title VII allow for sex-segregated bathrooms and locker rooms to be abolished? But such a question lies beyond the purview of Title VII; the court's sole responsibility is to establish whether the dismissal of someone for being homosexual or transgender is discrimination based on the individual's sex. The employers further voice apprehension that being forced to comply with Title VII will violate their religious convictions. Gorsuch points out such that concerns are long-standing and that the passage of the Religious Freedom Restoration Act (RFRA) of 1993 "prohibits the federal government from substantially burdening a person's exercise of religion unless it demonstrates that doing so both furthers a compelling governmental interest and represents the least restrictive means of furthering that interest." Such concerns may apply to future cases.

Gorsuch concludes that an employer who dismisses an employee for being homosexual or transexual does so in defiance of the law. The previous judgments handed down by the Second and Sixth Circuits are affirmed and that of the Eleventh Circuit is reversed.

Impact

The *Bostock* decision marked a major victory for the LGBTQ rights movement, providing the sort of legal protections against discrimination in employment based on sexual orientation and gender identity for which activists had spent the previous five decades fighting. In addition to providing the legal means of challenging future discrimination, the decision allowed for the revival of earlier lawsuits regarding wrongful dismissal based on sexual orientation and gender identity, dismissed before the Court handed down its decision. There now existed a clear justification for employers to implement policies to deter discrimination and to address it should it take place.

In the two years following the case, more than 250 new cases cited the *Bostock* decision, allowing lower courts to render decisions based on the rationale handed down by the Supreme Court. In the case of *Grimm v. Gloucester County School Board*, the federal U.S. Court of Appeals for the Fourth Circuit cited *Bostock* in its decision that the unfair treatment of transgender students constituted discrimination based on sex, which violates Title IX, a federal law forbidding sex discrimination by schools receiving federal funding. *Bostock*'s influence carried over to *Doe v. Snyder*, whereby the U.S. Court of Appeals for the Ninth Circuit declared that it was illegal for federally funded health-care providers to discriminate against transgender patients.

The Biden administration built upon the foundation laid by the courts in the aftermath of *Bostock*. Shortly after taking office, President Joe Biden issued an executive order that federal agencies implement *Bostock* and ensure that federal prohibitions on discrimination based sexual orientation or transgender identity be enforced. The order has the potential to impact more than a hundred federal statutes that bar discrimination based on sex.

The *Bostock* decision also influenced new nondiscrimination laws regarding sexual orientation and gender identity passed at the state level. Some offer protections that go well beyond those offered by federal laws.

Questions for Further Study

1. In what ways has the LGBTQ rights movement reflected the struggles of the civil rights movement over the decades? Where has there been shared ground?

2. Why was there so much more opposition to homosexuality and other identities judged to be unconventional, particularly before the 1970s?

3. How does the Roberts Court use Title VII as the basis for justifying its decision in *Bostock v. Clayton County*, particularly in regard to the concept of "sex"?

4. How might the dissenting judges have used the concept of "sex" to argue that Title VII does not extend to protections for members of the LGBTQ community?

Further Reading

Books

Bronski, Michael. *A Queer History of the United States*. Boston: Beacon Press, 2012.

Brooks, Adrian. *Right Side of History: 100 Years of LGBTQI Activism*. Jersey City: Cleis Press, 2015.

Faderman, Lillian. *The Gay Revolution: The Story of the Struggle*. New York: Simon & Schuster, 2016.

Garretson, Jeremiah J. *The Path to Gay Rights: How Activism and Coming Out Changed Public Opinion*. New York: NYU Press, 2018.

Kaiser, Charles. *The Gay Metropolis: The Landmark History of Gay Life in America*. New York: Grove Press, 2019.

Marcus, Eric. *Making Gay History: The Half Century Fight for Lesbian and Gay Equal Rights*. New York: Harper Perennial, 2002.

Websites

Downs, Jim. "The Gay Liberation Movement." Bill of Rights Institute. Accessed March 10, 2023, https://billofrightsinstitute.org/essays/the-gay-liberation-movement.

"The Rights of Lesbian, Gay, Bisexual and Transgender People." ACLU. Accessed March 10, 2023, https://www.aclu.org/other/rights-lesbian-gay-bisexual-and-transgender-people.

—Commentary by Michael Martin Carver

Bostock v. Clayton County

Document Text

Justice Gorsuch delivered the opinion of the Court

Sometimes small gestures can have unexpected consequences. Major initiatives practically guarantee them. In our time, few pieces of federal legislation rank in significance with the Civil Rights Act of 1964. There, in Title VII, Congress outlawed discrimination in the workplace on the basis of race, color, religion, sex, or national origin. Today, we must decide whether an employer can fire someone simply for being homosexual or transgender. The answer is clear. An employer who fires an individual for being homosexual or transgender fires that person for traits or actions it would not have questioned in members of a different sex. Sex plays a necessary and undisguisable role in the decision, exactly what Title VII forbids.

Those who adopted the Civil Rights Act might not have anticipated their work would lead to this particular result. Likely, they weren't thinking about many of the Act's consequences that have become apparent over the years, including its prohibition against discrimination on the basis of motherhood or its ban on the sexual harassment of male employees. But the limits of the drafters' imagination supply no reason to ignore the law's demands. When the express terms of a statute give us one answer and extratextual considerations suggest another, it's no contest. Only the written word is the law, and all persons are entitled to its benefit.

I

Few facts are needed to appreciate the legal question we face. Each of the three cases before us started the same way: An employer fired a long-time employee shortly after the employee revealed that he or she is homosexual or transgender—and allegedly for no reason other than the employee's homosexuality or transgender status.

Gerald Bostock worked for Clayton County, Georgia, as a child welfare advocate. Under his leadership, the county won national awards for its work. After a decade with the county, Mr. Bostock began participating in a gay recreational softball league. Not long after that, influential members of the community allegedly made disparaging comments about Mr. Bostock's sexual orientation and participation in the league. Soon, he was fired for conduct "unbecoming" a county employee.

Donald Zarda worked as a skydiving instructor at Altitude Express in New York. After several seasons with the company, Mr. Zarda mentioned that he was gay and, days later, was fired.

Aimee Stephens worked at R. G. & G. R. Harris Funeral Homes in Garden City, Michigan. When she got the job, Ms. Stephens presented as a male. But two years into her service with the company, she began treatment for despair and loneliness. Ultimately, clinicians diagnosed her with gender dysphoria and recommended that she begin living as a woman. In her sixth year with the company, Ms. Stephens wrote a letter to her employer explaining that she planned to " live and work full-time as a woman" after she returned from an upcoming vacation. The funeral home fired her before she left, telling her "this is not going to work out."

While these cases began the same way, they ended differently. Each employee brought suit under Title VII alleging unlawful discrimination on the basis of sex. 78Stat. 255, 42 U. S. C. §2000e–2(a)(1). In Mr. Bostock's case, the Eleventh Circuit held that the law does not prohibit employers from firing employees for being gay and so his suit could be dismissed as a matter of law. 723 Fed. Appx. 964 (2018). Meanwhile, in Mr. Zarda's case, the Second Circuit concluded that sexual orientation discrimination does violate Title VII and allowed his case to proceed. 883 F.3d 100 (2018). Ms. Stephens's case has a more complex procedural history, but in the end the Sixth Circuit reached a decision along the same lines as the Second Circuit's, holding that Title VII bars employers from firing employees because of their transgender status. 884 F.3d 560 (2018). During the course of the proceedings in these long-running disputes, both Mr. Zarda and Ms. Stephens have passed away. But their estates continue to press their causes for the benefit of their heirs. And we granted certiorari in these matters to resolve at last the disagreement among the courts of appeals over the scope of Title VII's protections for homosexual and transgender persons. 587 U. S. ___ (2019).

II

This Court normally interprets a statute in accord with the ordinary public meaning of its terms at the time of its enactment. After all, only the words on the page constitute the law adopted by Congress and approved by the President. If judges could add to, remodel, update, or detract from old statutory terms inspired only by extratextual sources and our own imaginations, we would risk amending statutes outside the legislative process reserved for the people's representatives. And we would deny the people the right to continue relying on the original meaning of the law they have counted on to settle their rights and obligations. See *New Prime Inc. v. Oliveira*, 586 U. S. ___, ___–___ (2019) (slip op., at 6–7).

With this in mind, our task is clear. We must determine the ordinary public meaning of Title VII's command that it is "unlawful . . . for an employer to fail or refuse to hire or to discharge any individual, or otherwise to discriminate against any individual with respect to his compensation, terms, conditions, or privileges of employment, because of such individual's race, color, religion, sex, or national origin." §2000e–2(a)(1). To do so, we orient ourselves to the time of the statute's adoption, here 1964, and begin by examining the key statutory terms in turn before assessing their impact on the cases at hand and then confirming our work against this Court's precedents.

A

The only statutorily protected characteristic at issue in today's cases is "sex"—and that is also the primary term in Title VII whose meaning the parties dispute. Appealing to roughly contemporaneous dictionaries, the employers say that, as used here, the term "sex" in 1964 referred to "status as either male or female [as] determined by reproductive biology." The employees counter by submitting that, even in 1964, the term bore a broader scope, capturing more than anatomy and reaching at least some norms concerning gender identity and sexual orientation. But because nothing in our approach to these cases turns on the outcome of the parties' debate, and because the employees concede the point for argument's sake, we proceed on the assumption that "sex" signified what the employers suggest, referring only to biological distinctions between male and female.

Still, that's just a starting point. The question isn't just what "sex" meant, but what Title VII says about it. Most notably, the statute prohibits employers from taking certain actions "because of " sex. And, as this Court has previously explained, "the ordinary meaning of 'because of ' is 'by reason of ' or 'on account of.'" *University of Tex. Southwestern Medical Center v. Nassar*, 570 U.S. 338, 350 (2013) (citing *Gross v. FBL Financial Services, Inc.*, 557 U.S. 167, 176 (2009); quotation altered). In the language of law, this means that Title VII's "because of " test incorporates the "'simple'" and "traditional" standard of but-for causation. *Nassar*, 570 U. S., at 346, 360. That form of causation is established whenever a particular outcome would not have happened "but for" the purported cause. See *Gross*, 557 U. S., at 176. In other words, a but-for test directs us to change one thing at a time and see if the outcome changes. If it does, we have found a but-for cause.

This can be a sweeping standard. Often, events have multiple but-for causes. So, for example, if a car accident occurred *both* because the defendant ran a red light *and* because the plaintiff failed to signal his turn at the intersection, we might call each a but-for cause of the collision. Cf. *Burrage v. United States*, 571 U.S. 204, 211–212 (2014). When it comes to Title VII, the adoption of the traditional but-for causation standard means a defendant cannot avoid liability just by citing some *other* factor that contributed to its challenged employment decision. So long as the plaintiff's sex was one but-for cause of that decision, that is enough to trigger the law. See *ibid.; Nassar*, 570 U. S., at 350.

No doubt, Congress could have taken a more parsimonious approach. As it has in other statutes, it could have added "solely" to indicate that actions taken "because of" the confluence of multiple factors do not violate the law. Cf. 11 U. S. C. §525; 16 U. S. C. §511. Or it could have written "primarily because of" to indicate that the prohibited factor had to be the main cause of the defendant's challenged employment decision. Cf. 22 U. S. C. §2688. But none of this is the law we have. If anything, Congress has moved in the opposite direction, supplementing Title VII in 1991 to allow a plaintiff to prevail merely by showing that a protected trait like sex was a "motivating factor" in a defendant's challenged employment practice. Civil Rights Act of 1991, §107, 105Stat. 1075, codified at 42 U. S. C. §2000e–2(m). Under this more forgiving standard, liability can sometimes follow even if sex *wasn't* a but-for cause of the employer's challenged decision. Still, because nothing in our analysis depends on the motivating factor test, we focus on the more traditional but-for causation standard that continues to afford a viable, if no longer exclusive, path to relief under Title VII. §2000e–2(a)(1).

As sweeping as even the but-for causation standard can be, Title VII does not concern itself with everything that happens "because of" sex. The statute imposes liability on employers only when they "fail or refuse to hire," "discharge," "or otherwise... discriminate against" someone because of a statutorily protected characteristic like sex. *Ibid*. The employers acknowledge that they discharged the plaintiffs in today's cases, but assert that the statute's list of verbs is qualified by the last item on it: "otherwise... discriminate against." By virtue of the word *otherwise*, the employers suggest, Title VII concerns itself not with every discharge, only with those discharges that involve discrimination.

Accepting this point, too, for argument's sake, the question becomes: What did "discriminate" mean in 1964? As it turns out, it meant then roughly what it means today: "To make a difference in treatment or favor (of one as compared with others)." Webster's New International Dictionary 745 (2d ed. 1954). To "discriminate against" a person, then, would seem to mean treating that individual worse than others who are similarly situated. See *Burlington N. & S. F. R. Co. v. White*, 548 U.S. 53, 59 (2006). In so-called "disparate treatment" cases like today's, this Court has also held that the difference in treatment based on sex must be intentional. See, e.g., *Watson v. Fort Worth Bank & Trust*, 487 U.S. 977, 986 (1988). So, taken together, an employer who intentionally treats a person worse because of sex—such as by firing the person for actions or attributes it would tolerate in an individual of another sex—discriminates against that person in violation of Title VII.

At first glance, another interpretation might seem possible. Discrimination sometimes involves "the act, practice, or an instance of discriminating categorically rather than individually." Webster's New Collegiate Dictionary 326 (1975); see also *post*, at 27–28, n. 22 (Alito, J., dissenting). On that understanding, the statute would require us to consider the employer's treatment of groups rather than individuals, to see how a policy affects one sex as a whole versus the other as a whole. That idea holds some intuitive appeal too. Maybe the law concerns itself simply with ensuring that employers don't treat women generally less favorably than they do men. So how can we tell which sense, individual or group, "discriminate" carries in Title VII?

The statute answers that question directly. It tells us three times—including immediately after the words "discriminate against"—that our focus should be on individuals, not groups: Employers may not "fail or refuse to hire or . . . discharge any *individual*, or otherwise . . . discriminate against any *individual* with respect to his compensation, terms, conditions, or privileges of employment, because of such *individual's* . . . sex." §2000e–2(a)(1) (emphasis added). And the meaning of "individual" was as uncontroversial in 1964 as it is today: "A particular being as distinguished from a class, species, or collection." Webster's New International Dictionary, at 1267. Here, again, Congress could have written the law differently. It might have said that "it shall be an unlawful employment practice to prefer one sex to the other in hiring, firing, or the terms or conditions of employment." It might have said that there should be no "sex discrimination," perhaps implying a focus on differential treatment between the two sexes as groups. More narrowly still, it could have forbidden only "sexist policies" against women as a class. But, once again, that is not the law we have.

The consequences of the law's focus on individuals rather than groups are anything but academic. Suppose an employer fires a woman for refusing his sexual advances. It's no defense for the employer to note that, while he treated that individual woman worse than he would have treated a man, he gives preferential treatment to female employees overall. The employer is liable for treating *this* woman worse in part because of her sex. Nor is it a defense for an employer to say it discriminates against both men and women because of sex. This statute works to protect individuals of both sexes from discrimination, and does so equally. So an employer who fires a woman, Hannah, because she is insufficiently feminine and also fires a man, Bob, for being insufficiently masculine may treat men and women as groups more or less equally. But in *both* cases the employer fires an individual in part because of sex. Instead of avoiding Title VII exposure, this employer doubles it.

B

From the ordinary public meaning of the statute's language at the time of the law's adoption, a straightforward rule emerges: An employer violates Title VII when it intentionally fires an individual employee based in part on sex. It doesn't matter if other factors besides the plaintiff's sex contributed to the decision. And it doesn't matter if the employer treated women as a group the same when compared to men as a group. If the employer intentionally relies in part on an individual employee's sex when deciding to discharge the employee—put differently, if changing the employee's sex would have yielded a different choice by the employer—a statutory violation has occurred. Title VII's message is "simple but momentous": An individual employee's sex is "not relevant to the selection, evaluation, or compensation of employees." *Price Waterhouse v. Hopkins*, 490 U.S. 228, 239 (1989) (plurality opinion).

The statute's message for our cases is equally simple and momentous: An individual's homosexuality or transgender status is not relevant to employment decisions. That's because it is impossible to discriminate against a person for being homosexual or transgender without discriminating against that individual based on sex. Consider, for example, an employer with two employees, both of whom are attracted to men. The two individuals are, to the employer's mind, materially identical in all respects, except that one is a man and the other a woman. If the employer fires the male employee for no reason other than the fact he is attracted to men, the employer discriminates against him for traits or actions it tolerates in his female colleague. Put differently, the employer intentionally singles out an employee to fire based in part on the employee's sex, and the affected employee's sex is a but-for cause of his discharge. Or take an employer who fires a transgender person who was identified as a male at birth but who now identifies as a female. If the employer retains an otherwise identical employee who was identified as female at birth, the employer intentionally penalizes a person identified as male at birth for traits or actions that it tolerates in an employee identified as female at birth. Again, the individual employee's sex plays an unmistakable and impermissible role in the discharge decision.

That distinguishes these cases from countless others where Title VII has nothing to say. Take an employer who fires a female employee for tardiness or incompetence or simply supporting the wrong sports team. Assuming the employer would not have tolerated the same trait in a man, Title VII stands silent. But unlike any of these other traits or actions, homosexuality and transgender status are inextricably bound up with sex. Not because homosexuality or transgender status are related to sex in some vague sense or because discrimination on these bases has some disparate impact on one sex or another, but because to discriminate on these grounds requires an employer to intentionally treat individual employees differently because of their sex.

Nor does it matter that, when an employer treats one employee worse because of that individual's sex, other factors may contribute to the decision. Consider an employer with a policy of firing any woman he discovers to be a Yankees fan. Carrying out that rule because an employee is a woman *and* a fan of the Yankees is a firing "because of sex" if the employer would have tolerated the same allegiance in a male employee. Likewise here. When an employer fires an employee because she is homosexual or transgender, two causal factors may be in play—*both* the individual's sex *and* something else (the sex to which the individual is attracted or with which the individual identifies). But Title VII doesn't care. If an employer would not have discharged an employee but for that individual's sex, the statute's causation standard is met, and liability may attach.

Reframing the additional causes in today's cases as additional intentions can do no more to insulate the employers from liability. Intentionally burning down a neighbor's house is arson, even if the perpetrator's ultimate intention (or motivation) is only to improve the view. No less, intentional discrimination based on sex violates Title VII, even if it is intended only as a means to achieving the employer's ultimate goal of discriminating against homosexual or transgender employees. There is simply no escaping the role intent plays here: Just as sex is necessarily a but-for *cause* when an employer discriminates against homosexual or transgender employees, an employer who discriminates on these grounds inescapably *intends* to rely on sex in its decisionmaking. Imagine an employer who has a policy of firing any employee known to be homosexual. The employer hosts an office holiday party and invites employees to bring their spouses. A model employee arrives and introduces a manager to Susan, the employee's wife. Will that employee be fired? If the policy works as the employer intends, the answer depends entirely on whether the model employee is a man or a woman. To be sure, that employer's ultimate goal might be to discriminate on the basis of sexual orientation. But to achieve that purpose the employer must, along the way, intentionally treat an employee worse based in part on that individual's sex.

An employer musters no better a defense by responding that it is equally happy to fire male *and* female employees who are homosexual or transgender. Title VII liability is not limited to employers who, through the sum of all of their employment actions, treat the class of men differently than the class of women. Instead, the law makes each instance of discriminating against an individual employee because of that individual's sex an independent violation of Title VII. So just as an employer who fires both Hannah and Bob for failing to fulfill traditional sex stereotypes doubles rather than eliminates Title VII liability, an employer who fires both Hannah and Bob for being gay or transgender does the same.

At bottom, these cases involve no more than the straightforward application of legal terms with plain and settled meanings. For an employer to discriminate against employees for being homosexual or transgender, the employer must intentionally discriminate against individual men and women in part because of sex. That has always been prohibited by Title VII's plain terms—and that "should be the end of the analysis." 883 F. 3d, at 135 (Cabranes, J., concurring in judgment).

C

If more support for our conclusion were required, there's no need to look far. All that the statute's plain terms suggest, this Court's cases have already confirmed. Consider three of our leading precedents.

In *Phillips v. Martin Marietta Corp.*, 400 U.S. 542 (1971) (per curiam), a company allegedly refused to hire women with young children, but did hire men with children the same age. Because its discrimination depended not only on the employee's sex as a female but also on the presence of another criterion—namely, being a parent of young children—the company contended it hadn't engaged in discrimination "because of" sex. The company maintained, too, that it hadn't violated the law because, as a whole, it tended to favor hiring women over men. Unsurprisingly by now, these submissions did not sway the Court. That an employer discriminates intentionally against an individual only in part because of sex supplies no defense to Title VII. Nor does the fact an employer may happen to favor women as a class.

In *Los Angeles Dept. of Water and Power v. Manhart*, 435 U.S. 702 (1978), an employer required women to make larger pension fund contributions than men. The employer sought to justify its disparate treatment on the ground that women tend to live longer than men, and thus are likely to receive more from the pension fund over time. By everyone's admission, the employer was not guilty of animosity against women or a "purely habitual assumptio[n] about a woman's inability to perform certain kinds of work"; instead, it relied on what appeared to be a statistically accurate statement about life expectancy. *Id.*, at 707–708. Even so, the Court recognized, a rule that appears evenhanded at the group level can prove discriminatory at the level of individuals. True, women as a class may live longer than men as a class. But "[t]he statute's focus on the individual is unambiguous," and any individual woman might make the larger pension contributions and still die as early as a man. *Id.*, at 708. Likewise, the Court dismissed as irrelevant the employer's insistence that its actions were motivated by a wish to achieve classwide equality between the sexes: An employer's intentional discrimination on the basis of sex is no more permissible when it is prompted by some further intention (or motivation), even one as prosaic as seeking to account for actuarial tables. *Ibid.* The employer violated Title VII because, when its policy worked exactly as planned, it could not "pass the simple test" asking whether an individual female employee would have been treated the same regardless of her sex. *Id.*, at 711.

In *Oncale v. Sundowner Offshore Services, Inc.*, 523 U.S. 75 (1998), a male plaintiff alleged that he was singled out by his male co-workers for sexual harassment. The Court held it was immaterial that members of the same sex as the victim committed the alleged discrimination. Nor did the Court concern itself with whether men as a group were subject to discrimination or whether something in addition to sex contributed to the discrimination, like the plaintiff's conduct or personal attributes. "[A]ssuredly," the case didn't involve "the principal evil Congress was concerned with when it enacted Title VII." *Id.*, at 79. But, the Court unanimously explained, it is "the provisions of our laws rather than the principal concerns of our legislators by which we are governed." *Ibid.* Because the plaintiff alleged that the harassment would not have taken place but for his sex—that is, the plaintiff would not have suffered similar treatment if he were female—a triable Title VII claim existed.

The lessons these cases hold for ours are by now familiar.

First, it's irrelevant what an employer might call its discriminatory practice, how others might label it, or what else might motivate it. In *Manhart*, the employer called its rule requiring women to pay more into the pension fund a "life expectancy" adjustment necessary to achieve sex equality. In *Phillips*, the employer could have accurately spoken of its policy as one based on "motherhood." In much the same way, today's employers might describe their actions as motivated by their employees' homosexuality or transgender status. But just as labels and additional intentions or motivations didn't make a difference in *Manhart* or *Phillips*, they cannot make a difference here. When an employer fires an employee for being homosexual or transgender, it necessarily and intentionally discriminates against that individual in part because of sex. And that is all Title VII has ever demanded to establish liability.

Second, the plaintiff's sex need not be the sole or primary cause of the employer's adverse action. In *Phillips, Manhart*, and *Oncale*, the defendant easily could have pointed to some other, nonprotected trait and insisted it was the more important factor in the adverse employment outcome. So, too, it has no significance here if another factor—such as the sex the plaintiff is attracted to or presents as—might also be at work, or even play a more important role in the employer's decision.

Finally, an employer cannot escape liability by demonstrating that it treats males and females comparably as groups. As *Manhart* teaches, an employer is liable for intentionally requiring an individual female employee to pay more into a pension plan than a male counterpart even if the scheme promotes equality at the group level. Likewise, an employer who intentionally fires an individual homosexual or transgender employee in part because of that individual's sex violates the law even if the employer is willing to subject all male and female homosexual or transgender employees to the same rule.

III

What do the employers have to say in reply? For present purposes, they do not dispute that they fired the plaintiffs for being homosexual or transgender. Sorting out the true reasons for an adverse employment decision is often a hard business, but none of that is at issue here. Rather, the employers submit that even intentional discrimination against employees based on their homosexuality or transgender status supplies no basis for liability under Title VII.

The employers' argument proceeds in two stages. Seeking footing in the statutory text, they begin by advancing a number of reasons why discrimination on the basis of homosexuality or transgender status doesn't involve discrimination because of sex. But each of these arguments turns out only to repackage errors we've already seen and this Court's precedents have already rejected. In the end, the employers are left to retreat beyond the statute's text, where they fault us for ignoring the legislature's purposes in enacting Title VII or certain expectations about its operation. They warn, too, about consequences that might follow a ruling for the employees. But none of these contentions about what the employers think the law was meant to do, or should do, allow us to ignore the law as it is.

A

Maybe most intuitively, the employers assert that discrimination on the basis of homosexuality and transgender status aren't referred to as sex discrimination in ordinary conversation. If asked by a friend (rather than a judge) why they were fired, even today's plaintiffs would likely respond that it was because they were gay or transgender, not because of sex. According to the employers, that conversational answer, not the statute's strict terms, should guide our thinking and suffice to defeat any suggestion that the employees now before us were fired because of sex. Cf. *post,* at 3 (Alito, J., dissenting); *post,* at 8–13 (Kavanaugh, J., dissenting).

But this submission rests on a mistaken understanding of what kind of cause the law is looking for in a Title VII case. In conversation, a speaker is likely to focus on what seems most relevant or informative to the listener. So an employee who has just been fired is likely to identify the primary or most direct cause rather than list literally every but-for cause. To do otherwise would be tiring at best. But these conversational conventions do not control Title VII's legal analysis, which asks simply whether sex was a but-for cause. In *Phillips,* for example, a woman who was not hired under the employer's policy might have told her friends that her application was rejected because she was a mother, or because she had young children. Given that many women could be hired under the policy, it's unlikely she would say she was not hired because she was a woman. But the Court did not hesitate to recognize that the employer in *Phillips* discriminated against the plaintiff because of her sex. Sex wasn't the only factor, or maybe even the main factor, but it was one but-for cause—and that was enough. You can call the statute's but-for causation test what you will—expansive, legalistic, the dissents even dismiss it as wooden or literal. But it is the law.

Trying another angle, the defendants before us suggest that an employer who discriminates based on homosexuality or transgender status doesn't *intentionally* discriminate based on sex, as a disparate treatment claim requires. See *post,* at 9–12 (Alito, J., dissenting); *post,* at 12–13 (Kavanaugh, J., dissenting). But, as we've seen, an employer who discriminates against homosexual or transgender employees necessarily and intentionally applies sex-based rules. An employer that announces it will not employ anyone who is homosexual, for example, intends to penalize male employees for being attracted to men and female employees for being attracted to women.

What, then, do the employers mean when they insist intentional discrimination based on homosexuality or transgender status isn't intentional discrimination based on sex? Maybe the employers mean they don't intend to harm one sex or the other as a class. But as should be clear by now, the statute focuses on discrimination against individuals, not groups. Alternatively, the employers may mean that they don't perceive themselves as motivated by a desire to discriminate based on sex. But nothing in Title VII turns on the employer's labels or any further intentions (or motivations) for its conduct beyond sex discrimination. In *Manhart,* the employer intentionally required women to make higher pension contributions only to fulfill the further purpose of making things more equitable between men and women as groups. In *Phillips,* the employer may have perceived itself as discriminating based on motherhood, not sex, given that its hiring policies as a whole *favored* women. But in both cases, the Court set all this aside as irrelevant. The employers' policies involved intentional discrimination because of sex, and Title VII liability necessarily followed.

Aren't these cases different, the employers ask, given that an employer could refuse to hire a gay or transgender individual without ever learning the applicant's sex? Suppose an employer asked homosexual or transgender applicants to tick a box on its application form. The employer then had someone else redact any information that could be used to discern sex. The resulting applications would disclose which individuals are homosexual or transgender without revealing whether they also happen to be men or women. Doesn't that possibility indicate that the employer's discrimination against homosexual or transgender persons cannot be sex discrimination?

No, it doesn't. Even in this example, the individual applicant's sex still weighs as a factor in the employer's decision. Change the hypothetical ever so slightly and its flaws become apparent. Suppose an employer's application form offered a single box to check if the applicant is either black or Catholic. If the employer refuses to hire anyone who checks that box, would we conclude the employer has complied with Title VII, so long as it studiously avoids learning any particular applicant's race or religion? Of course not: By intentionally setting out a rule that makes hiring turn on race or religion, the employer violates the law, whatever he might know or not know about individual applicants.

The same holds here. There is no way for an applicant to decide whether to check the homosexual or transgender box without considering sex. To see why, imagine an applicant doesn't know what the words homosexual or transgender mean. Then try writing out instructions for who should check the box without using the words man, woman, or sex (or some synonym). It can't be done. Likewise, there is no way an employer can discriminate against those who check the homosexual or transgender box without discriminating in part because of an applicant's sex. By discriminating against homosexuals, the employer intentionally penalizes men for being attracted to men and women for being attracted to women. By discriminating against transgender persons, the employer unavoidably discriminates against persons with one sex identified at birth and another today. Any way you slice it, the employer intentionally refuses to hire applicants in part because of the affected individuals' sex, even if it never learns any applicant's sex.

Next, the employers turn to Title VII's list of protected characteristics—race, color, religion, sex, and national origin. Because homosexuality and transgender status can't be found on that list and because they are conceptually distinct from sex, the employers reason, they are implicitly excluded from Title VII's reach. Put another way, if Congress had wanted to address these matters in Title VII, it would have referenced them specifically. Cf. *post,* at 7–8 (Alito, J., dissenting); *post,* at 13–15 (Kavanaugh, J., dissenting).

But that much does not follow. We agree that homosexuality and transgender status are distinct concepts from sex. But, as we've seen, discrimination based on homosexuality or transgender status necessarily entails discrimination based on sex; the first cannot happen without the second. Nor is there any such thing as a "canon of donut holes," in which Congress's failure to speak directly to a specific case that falls within a more general statutory rule creates a tacit exception. Instead, when Congress chooses not to include any exceptions to a broad rule, courts apply the broad rule. And that is exactly how this Court has always approached Title VII. "Sexual harassment" is conceptually distinct from sex discrimination, but it can fall within Title VII's sweep. *Oncale,* 523 U. S., at 79–80. Same with "motherhood discrimination." See *Phillips,* 400 U. S., at 544. Would the employers have us reverse those cases on the theory that Congress could have spoken to those problems more specifically? Of course not. As enacted, Title VII prohibits all forms of discrimination because of sex, however they may manifest themselves or whatever other labels might attach to them.

The employers try the same point another way. Since 1964, they observe, Congress has considered several proposals to add sexual orientation to Title VII's list of protected characteristics, but no such amendment has become law. Meanwhile, Congress has enacted other statutes addressing other topics that do discuss sexual orientation. This postenactment legislative history, they urge, should tell us something. Cf. *post,* at 2, 42–43 (Alito, J., dissenting); *post,* at 4, 15–16 (Kavanaugh, J., dissenting).

But what? There's no authoritative evidence explaining why later Congresses adopted other laws referencing sexual orientation but didn't amend this one. Maybe some in the later legislatures understood the impact Title VII's broad language already promised for cases like ours and didn't think a revision needed. Maybe others knew about its impact but hoped no one else would notice. Maybe still others, occupied by other concerns, didn't consider the issue at all. All we can know for certain is that speculation about why a later Congress declined to adopt new legislation offers a "particularly dangerous" basis on which to rest an interpretation of an existing law a different and earlier Congress did adopt. *Pension Benefit Guaranty Corporation v. LTV Corp.,* 496 U.S. 633, 650 (1990); see also *United States v. Wells,* 519 U.S. 482, 496 (1997); *Sullivan v. Finkelstein,* 496 U.S. 617, 632 (1990) (Scalia, J., concurring) ("Arguments based on subsequent legislative history . . . should not be taken seriously, not even in a footnote").

That leaves the employers to seek a different sort of exception. Maybe the traditional and simple but-for causation test should apply in all other Title VII cases, but it just doesn't work when it comes to cases involving homosexual and transgender employees. The test is too blunt to capture the nuances here. The employers illustrate their concern with an example. When we apply the simple test to Mr. Bostock—asking whether Mr. Bostock, a man attracted to other men, would have been fired had he been a woman—we don't just change his sex. Along the way, we change his sexual orientation too (from homosexual to heterosexual). If the aim is to isolate whether a plaintiff's sex caused the dismissal, the employers stress, we must hold sexual orientation constant—meaning we need to change both his sex and the sex to which he is attracted. So for Mr. Bostock, the question should be whether he would've been fired if he were a woman attracted to women. And because his employer would have been as quick to fire a lesbian as it was a gay man, the employers conclude, no Title VII violation has occurred.

While the explanation is new, the mistakes are the same. The employers might be onto something if Title VII only ensured equal treatment between groups of men and women or if the statute applied only when sex is the sole or primary reason for an employer's challenged adverse employment action. But both of these premises are mistaken. Title VII's plain terms and our precedents don't care if an employer treats men and women comparably as groups; an employer who fires both lesbians and gay men equally doesn't diminish but doubles its liability. Just cast a glance back to *Manhart*, where it was no defense that the employer sought to equalize pension contributions based on life expectancy. Nor does the statute care if other factors besides sex contribute to an employer's discharge decision. Mr. Bostock's employer might have decided to fire him only because of the confluence of two factors, his sex and the sex to which he is attracted. But exactly the same might have been said in *Phillips*, where motherhood was the added variable.

Still, the employers insist, something seems different here. Unlike certain other employment policies this Court has addressed that harmed only women or only men, the employers' policies in the cases before us have the same adverse consequences for men and women. How could sex be necessary to the result if a member of the opposite sex might face the same outcome from the same policy?

What the employers see as unique isn't even unusual. Often in life and law two but-for factors combine to yield a result that could have also occurred in some other way. Imagine that it's a nice day outside and your house is too warm, so you decide to open the window. Both the cool temperature outside and the heat inside are but-for causes of your choice to open the window. That doesn't change just because you also would have opened the window had it been warm outside and cold inside. In either case, no one would deny that the window is open "because of" the outside temperature. Our cases are much the same. So, for example, when it comes to homosexual employees, male sex and attraction to men are but-for factors that can combine to get them fired. The fact that female sex and attraction to women can *also* get an employee fired does no more than show the same outcome can be achieved through the combination of different factors. In either case, though, sex plays an essential but-for role.

At bottom, the employers' argument unavoidably comes down to a suggestion that sex must be the sole or primary cause of an adverse employment action for Title VII liability to follow. And, as we've seen, that suggestion is at odds with everything we know about the statute. Consider an employer eager to revive the workplace gender roles of the 1950s. He enforces a policy that he will hire only men as mechanics and only women as secretaries. When a qualified woman applies for a mechanic position and is denied, the "simple test" immediately spots the discrimination: A qualified man would have been given the job, so sex was a but-for cause of the employer's refusal to hire. But like the employers before us today, this employer would say not so fast. By comparing the woman who applied to be a mechanic to a man who applied to be a mechanic, we've quietly changed two things: the applicant's sex and her trait of failing to conform to 1950s gender roles. The "simple test" thus overlooks that it is really the applicant's bucking of 1950s gender roles, not her sex, doing the work. So we need to hold that second trait constant: Instead of comparing the disappointed female applicant to a man who applied for the same position, the employer would say, we should compare her to a man who applied to be a secretary. And because that jobseeker would be refused too, this must not be sex discrimination.

No one thinks *that*, so the employers must scramble to justify deploying a stricter causation test for use only in cases involving discrimination based on sexual orientation or transgender status. Such a rule would create a curious discontinuity in our case law, to put it mildly. Employer hires based on sexual stereotypes? Simple test. Employer sets pension contributions based on sex? Simple test. Employer fires men who do not behave in a sufficiently masculine way around the office? Simple test. But when that same employer discriminates against women who are attracted to women, or persons identified at birth as women who later identify as men, we suddenly roll out a new and more rigorous standard? Why are *these* reasons for taking sex into account different from all the rest? Title VII's text can offer no answer.

B

Ultimately, the employers are forced to abandon the statutory text and precedent altogether and appeal to assumptions and policy. Most pointedly, they contend that few in 1964 would have expected Title VII to apply to discrimination against homosexual and transgender persons. And whatever the text and our precedent indicate, they say, shouldn't this fact cause us to pause before recognizing liability?

It might be tempting to reject this argument out of hand. This Court has explained many times over many years that, when the meaning of the statute's terms is plain, our job is at an end. The people are entitled to rely on the law as written, without fearing that courts might disregard its plain terms based on some extratextual consideration. See, e.g., *Carcieri v. Salazar*, 555 U.S. 379, 387 (2009); *Connecticut Nat. Bank v. Germain*, 503 U.S. 249, 253–254 (1992); *Rubin v. United States*, 449 U.S. 424, 430 (1981). Of course, some Members of this Court have consulted legislative history when interpreting *ambiguous* statutory language. Cf. *post*, at 40 (Alito, J., dissenting). But that has no bearing here. "Legislative history, for those who take it into account, is meant to clear up ambiguity, not create it." *Milner v. Department of Navy*, 562 U.S. 562, 574 (2011). And as we have seen, no ambiguity exists about how Title VII's terms apply to the facts before us. To be sure, the statute's application in these cases reaches "beyond the principal evil" legislators may have intended or expected to address. *Oncale*, 523 U. S., at 79. But "'the fact that [a statute] has been applied in situations not expressly anticipated by Congress'" does not demonstrate ambiguity; instead, it simply "'demonstrates [the] breadth'" of a legislative command. *Sedima, S. P. R. L. v. Imrex Co.*, 473 U.S. 479, 499 (1985). And "it is ultimately the provisions of " those legislative commands "rather than the principal concerns of our legislators by which we are governed." *Oncale*, 523 U. S., at 79; see also A. Scalia & B. Garner, Reading Law: The Interpretation of Legal Texts 101 (2012) (noting that unexpected applications of broad language reflect only Congress's "presumed point [to] produce general coverage—not to leave room for courts to recognize ad hoc exceptions").

Still, while legislative history can never defeat unambiguous statutory text, historical sources can be useful for a different purpose: Because the law's ordinary meaning at the time of enactment usually governs, we must be sensitive to the possibility a statutory term that means one thing today or in one context might have meant something else at the time of its adoption or might mean something different in another context. And we must be attuned to the possibility that a statutory phrase ordinarily bears a different meaning than the terms do when viewed individually or literally. To ferret out such shifts in linguistic usage or subtle distinctions between literal and ordinary meaning, this Court has sometimes consulted the understandings of the law's drafters as some (not always conclusive) evidence. For example, in the context of the National Motor Vehicle Theft Act, this Court admitted that the term "vehicle" in 1931 could literally mean "a conveyance working on land, water or air." *McBoyle v. United States*, 283 U.S. 25, 26 (1931). But given contextual clues and "everyday speech" at the time of the Act's adoption in 1919, this Court concluded that "vehicles" in that statute included only things "moving on land," not airplanes too. *Ibid.* Similarly, in *New Prime*, we held that, while the term "contracts of employment" today might seem to encompass only contracts with employees, at the time of the statute's adoption the phrase was ordinarily understood to cover contracts with independent contractors as well. 586 U. S., at ___–___ (slip op., at 6–9). Cf. *post*, at 7–8 (Kavanaugh, J., dissenting) (providing additional examples).

The employers, however, advocate nothing like that here. They do not seek to use historical sources to illustrate that the meaning of any of Title VII's language has changed since 1964 or that the statute's terms, whether viewed individually or as a whole, ordinarily carried some message we have missed. To the contrary, as we have seen, the employers *agree* with our understanding of all the statutory language—"discriminate against any individual . . . because of such individual's . . . sex." Nor do the competing dissents offer an alternative account about what these terms mean either when viewed individually or in the aggregate. Rather than suggesting that the statutory language bears some other *meaning*, the employers and dissents merely suggest that, because few in 1964 expected today's *result*, we should not dare to admit that it follows ineluctably from the statutory text. When a new application emerges that is both unexpected and important, they would seemingly have us merely point out the question, refer the subject back to Congress, and decline to enforce the plain terms of the law in the meantime.

That is exactly the sort of reasoning this Court has long rejected. Admittedly, the employers take pains to couch their argument in terms of seeking to honor the statute's "expected applications" rather than vindicate its "legislative intent." But the concepts are closely related. One could easily contend that legislators only intended expected applications or that a statute's purpose is limited to achieving applications foreseen at the time of enactment. However framed, the employer's logic impermissibly seeks to displace the plain meaning of the law in favor of something lying beyond it.

If anything, the employers' new framing may only add new problems. The employers assert that "no one" in 1964 or for some time after would have anticipated today's result. But is that really true? Not long after the law's passage, gay and transgender employees began filing Title VII complaints, so at least *some* people foresaw this potential application. See, e.g., *Smith v. Liberty Mut. Ins. Co.*, 395 F. Supp. 1098, 1099 (ND Ga. 1975) (addressing claim from 1969); *Holloway v. Arthur Andersen & Co.*, 566 F.2d 659, 661 (CA9 1977) (addressing claim from 1974). And less than a decade after Title VII's passage, during debates over the Equal Rights Amendment, others counseled that its language—which was strikingly similar to Title VII's—might also protect homosexuals from discrimination. See, e.g., Note, The Legality of Homosexual Marriage, 82 Yale L. J. 573, 583–584 (1973).

Why isn't that enough to demonstrate that today's result isn't totally unexpected? How many people have to foresee the application for it to qualify as "expected"? Do we look only at the moment the statute was enacted, or do we allow some time for the implications of a new statute to be worked out? Should we consider the expectations of those who had no reason to give a particular application any thought or only those with reason to think about the question? How do we account for those who change their minds over time, after learning new facts or hearing a new argument?

How specifically or generally should we frame the "application" at issue? None of these questions have obvious answers, and the employers don't propose any.

One could also reasonably fear that objections about unexpected applications will not be deployed neutrally. Often lurking just behind such objections resides a cynicism that Congress could not *possibly* have meant to protect a disfavored group. Take this Court's encounter with the Americans with Disabilities Act's directive that no "'public entity'" can discriminate against any "'qualified individual with a disability.'" *Pennsylvania Dept. of Corrections v. Yeskey*, 524 U.S. 206, 208 (1998). Congress, of course, didn't list every public entity the statute would apply to. And no one batted an eye at its application to, say, post offices. But when the statute was applied to *prisons*, curiously, some demanded a closer look: Pennsylvania argued that "Congress did not 'envisio[n] that the ADA would be applied to state prisoners.'" *Id.*, at 211–212. This Court emphatically rejected that view, explaining that, "in the context of an unambiguous statutory text," whether a specific application was anticipated by Congress "is irrelevant." *Id.*, at 212. As *Yeskey* and today's cases exemplify, applying protective laws to groups that were politically unpopular at the time of the law's passage—whether prisoners in the 1990s or homosexual and transgender employees in the 1960s—often may be seen as unexpected. But to refuse enforcement just because of that, because the parties before us happened to be unpopular at the time of the law's passage, would not only require us to abandon our role as interpreters of statutes; it would tilt the scales of justice in favor of the strong or popular and neglect the promise that all persons are entitled to the benefit of the law's terms. Cf. *post*, at 28–35 (Alito, J., dissenting); *post*, at 21–22 (Kavanaugh, J., dissenting).

The employer's position also proves too much. If we applied Title VII's plain text only to applications some (yet-to-be-determined) group expected in 1964, we'd have more than a little law to overturn. Start with *Oncale*. How many people in 1964 could have expected that the law would turn out to protect male employees? Let alone to protect them from harassment by other male employees? As we acknowledged at the time, "male-on-male sexual harassment in the workplace was assuredly not the principal evil Congress was concerned with when it enacted Title VII." 523

U. S., at 79. Yet the Court did not hesitate to recognize that Title VII's plain terms forbade it. Under the employer's logic, it would seem this was a mistake.

That's just the beginning of the law we would have to unravel. As one Equal Employment Opportunity Commission (EEOC) Commissioner observed shortly after the law's passage, the words of "'the sex provision of Title VII [are] difficult to ... control.'" Franklin, Inventing the "Traditional Concept" of Sex Discrimination, 125 Harv. L. Rev. 1307, 1338 (2012) (quoting Federal Mediation Service To Play Role in Implementing Title VII, [1965–1968 Transfer Binder] CCH Employment Practices ¶8046, p. 6074). The "difficult[y]" may owe something to the initial proponent of the sex discrimination rule in Title VII, Representative Howard Smith. On some accounts, the congressman may have wanted (or at least was indifferent to the possibility of) broad language with wide-ranging effect. Not necessarily because he was interested in rooting out sex discrimination in all its forms, but because he may have hoped to scuttle the whole Civil Rights Act and thought that adding language covering sex discrimination would serve as a poison pill. See C. Whalen & B. Whalen, The Longest Debate: A Legislative History of the 1964 Civil Rights Act 115–118 (1985). Certainly nothing in the meager legislative history of this provision suggests it was meant to be read narrowly.

Whatever his reasons, thanks to the broad language Representative Smith introduced, many, maybe most, applications of Title VII's sex provision were "unanticipated" at the time of the law's adoption. In fact, many now-obvious applications met with heated opposition early on, even among those tasked with enforcing the law. In the years immediately following Title VII's passage, the EEOC officially opined that listing men's positions and women's positions separately in job postings was simply helpful rather than discriminatory. Franklin, 125 Harv. L. Rev., at 1340 (citing Press Release, EEOC (Sept. 22, 1965)). Some courts held that Title VII did not prevent an employer from firing an employee for refusing his sexual advances. See, e.g., *Barnes v. Train*, 1974 WL 10628, *1 (D DC, Aug. 9, 1974). And courts held that a policy against hiring mothers but not fathers of young children wasn't discrimination because of sex. See *Phillips v. Martin Marietta Corp.*, 411 F.2d 1 (CA5 1969), rev'd, 400 U.S. 542 (1971) (per curiam).

Over time, though, the breadth of the statutory language proved too difficult to deny. By the end of the 1960s, the EEOC reversed its stance on sex-segregated job advertising. See Franklin, 125 Harv. L. Rev., at 1345. In 1971, this Court held that treating women with children differently from men with children violated Title VII. *Phillips*, 400 U. S., at 544. And by the late 1970s, courts began to recognize that sexual harassment can sometimes amount to sex discrimination. See, e.g., *Barnes v. Costle*, 561 F.2d 983, 990 (CADC 1977). While to the modern eye each of these examples may seem "plainly [to] constitut[e] discrimination because of biological sex," *post*, at 38 (Alito, J., dissenting), all were hotly contested for years following Title VII's enactment. And as with the discrimination we consider today, many federal judges long accepted interpretations of Title VII that excluded these situations. Cf. *post*, at 21–22 (Kavanaugh, J., dissenting) (highlighting that certain lower courts have rejected Title VII claims based on homosexuality and transgender status). Would the employers have us undo every one of these unexpected applications too?

The weighty implications of the employers' argument from expectations also reveal why they cannot hide behind the no-elephants-in-mouseholes canon. That canon recognizes that Congress "does not alter the fundamental details of a regulatory scheme in vague terms or ancillary provisions." *Whitman v. American Trucking Assns., Inc.*, 531 U.S. 457, 468 (2001). But it has no relevance here. We can't deny that today's holding—that employers are prohibited from firing employees on the basis of homosexuality or transgender status—is an elephant. But where's the mousehole? Title VII's prohibition of sex discrimination in employment is a major piece of federal civil rights legislation. It is written in starkly broad terms. It has repeatedly produced unexpected applications, at least in the view of those on the receiving end of them. Congress's key drafting choices—to focus on discrimination against individuals and not merely between groups and to hold employers liable whenever sex is a but-for cause of the plaintiff 's injuries—virtually guaranteed that unexpected applications would emerge over time. This elephant has never hidden in a mousehole; it has been standing before us all along.

With that, the employers are left to abandon their concern for expected applications and fall back to the last line of defense for all failing statutory interpretation arguments: naked policy appeals. If we were to apply the statute's plain language, they complain, any number of undesirable policy consequences would follow. Cf. *post*, at 44–54 (Alito, J., dissenting). Gone here is any pretense of statutory interpretation; all that's left is a suggestion we should proceed without the law's guidance to do as we think best. But that's an invitation no court should ever take up. The place to make new legislation, or address unwanted consequences of old legislation, lies in Congress. When it comes to statutory interpretation, our role is limited to applying the law's demands as faithfully as we can in the cases that come before us. As judges we possess no special expertise or authority to declare for ourselves what a self-governing people should consider just or wise. And the same judicial humility that requires us to refrain from adding to statutes requires us to refrain from diminishing them.

What are these consequences anyway? The employers worry that our decision will sweep beyond Title VII to other federal or state laws that prohibit sex discrimination. And, under Title VII itself, they say sex-segregated bathrooms, locker rooms, and dress codes will prove unsustainable after our decision today. But none of these other laws are before us; we have not had the benefit of adversarial testing about the meaning of their terms, and we do not prejudge any such question today. Under Title VII, too, we do not purport to address bathrooms, locker rooms, or anything else of the kind. The only question before us is whether an employer who fires someone simply for being homosexual or transgender has discharged or otherwise discriminated against that individual "because of such individual's sex." As used in Title VII, the term "'discriminate against'" refers to "distinctions or differences in treatment that injure protected individuals." *Burlington N. & S. F. R.*, 548 U. S., at 59. Firing employees because of a statutorily protected trait surely counts. Whether other policies and practices might or might not qualify as unlawful discrimination or find justifications under other provisions of Title VII are questions for future cases, not these.

Separately, the employers fear that complying with Title VII's requirement in cases like ours may require some employers to violate their religious convictions. We are also deeply concerned with preserving the promise of the free exercise of religion enshrined in our Constitution; that guarantee lies at the heart of our pluralistic society. But worries about how Title VII may intersect with religious liberties are nothing new; they even predate the statute's passage. As a result of its deliberations in adopting the law, Congress included an express statutory exception for religious organizations. §2000e–1(a). This Court has also recognized that the First Amendment can bar the application of employment discrimination laws "to claims concerning the employment relationship between a religious institution and its ministers." *Hosanna-Tabor Evangelical Lutheran Church and School v. EEOC*, 565 U.S. 171, 188 (2012). And Congress has gone a step further yet in the Religious Freedom Restoration Act of 1993 (RFRA), 107Stat. 1488, codified at 42 U. S. C. §2000bb *et seq*. That statute prohibits the federal government from substantially burdening a person's exercise of religion unless it demonstrates that doing so both furthers a compelling governmental interest and represents the least restrictive means of furthering that interest. §2000bb–1. Because RFRA operates as a kind of super statute, displacing the normal operation of other federal laws, it might supersede Title VII's commands in appropriate cases. See §2000bb–3.

But how these doctrines protecting religious liberty interact with Title VII are questions for future cases too. Harris Funeral Homes did unsuccessfully pursue a RFRA-based defense in the proceedings below. In its certiorari petition, however, the company declined to seek review of that adverse decision, and no other religious liberty claim is now before us. So while other employers in other cases may raise free exercise arguments that merit careful consideration, none of the employers before us today represent in this Court that compliance with Title VII will infringe their own religious liberties in any way.

*

Some of those who supported adding language to Title VII to ban sex discrimination may have hoped it would derail the entire Civil Rights Act. Yet, contrary to those intentions, the bill became law. Since then, Title VII's effects have unfolded with far-reaching consequences, some likely beyond what many in Congress or elsewhere expected.

But none of this helps decide today's cases. Ours is a society of written laws. Judges are not free to overlook plain statutory commands on the strength of nothing more than suppositions about intentions or guesswork about expectations. In Title VII, Congress adopted broad language making it illegal for an employer to rely on an employee's sex when deciding to fire that employee. We do not hesitate to recognize today a necessary consequence of that legislative choice: An employer who fires an individual merely for being gay or transgender defies the law.

The judgments of the Second and Sixth Circuits in Nos. 17–1623 and 18–107 are affirmed. The judgment of the Eleventh Circuit in No. 17–1618 is reversed, and the case is remanded for further proceedings consistent with this opinion.

It is so ordered.

Justice Alito, with whom Justice Thomas joins, dissenting

There is only one word for what the Court has done today: legislation. The document that the Court releases is in the form of a judicial opinion interpreting a statute, but that is deceptive.

Title VII of the Civil Rights Act of 1964 prohibits employment discrimination on any of five specified grounds: "race, color, religion, sex, [and] national origin." 42 U. S. C. §2000e–2(a)(1). Neither "sexual orientation" nor "gender identity" appears on that list. For the past 45 years, bills have been introduced in Congress to add "sexual orientation" to the list, and in recent years, bills have included "gender identity" as well. But to date, none has passed both Houses.

Last year, the House of Representatives passed a bill that would amend Title VII by defining sex discrimination to include both "sexual orientation" and "gender identity," H. R. 5, 116th Cong., 1st Sess. (2019), but the bill has stalled in the Senate. An alternative bill, H. R. 5331, 116th Cong., 1st Sess. (2019), would add similar prohibitions but contains provisions to protect religious liberty. This bill remains before a House Subcommittee.

Because no such amendment of Title VII has been enacted in accordance with the requirements in the Constitution (passage in both Houses and presentment to the President, Art. I, §7, cl. 2), Title VII's prohibition of discrimination because of "sex" still means what it has always meant. But the Court is not deterred by these constitutional niceties. Usurping the constitutional authority of the other branches, the Court has essentially taken H. R. 5's provision on employment discrim-

ination and issued it under the guise of statutory interpretation. A more brazen abuse of our authority to interpret statutes is hard to recall.

The Court tries to convince readers that it is merely enforcing the terms of the statute, but that is preposterous. Even as understood today, the concept of discrimination because of "sex" is different from discrimination because of "sexual orientation" or "gender identity." And in any event, our duty is to interpret statutory terms to "mean what they conveyed to reasonable people *at the time they were written.*" A. Scalia & B. Garner, Reading Law: The Interpretation of Legal Texts 16 (2012) (emphasis added). If every single living American had been surveyed in 1964, it would have been hard to find any who thought that discrimination because of sex meant discrimination because of sexual orientation—not to mention gender identity, a concept that was essentially unknown at the time.

The Court attempts to pass off its decision as the inevitable product of the textualist school of statutory interpretation championed by our late colleague Justice Scalia, but no one should be fooled. The Court's opinion is like a pirate ship. It sails under a textualist flag, but what it actually represents is a theory of statutory interpretation that Justice Scalia excoriated—the theory that courts should "update" old statutes so that they better reflect the current values of society. See A. Scalia, A Matter of Interpretation 22

(1997). If the Court finds it appropriate to adopt this theory, it should own up to what it is doing.

Many will applaud today's decision because they agree on policy grounds with the Court's updating of Title VII. But the question in these cases is not whether discrimination because of sexual orientation or gender identity *should be* outlawed. The question is *whether Congress did that in 1964.*

It indisputably did not.

I

A

Title VII, as noted, prohibits discrimination "because of . . . sex," §2000e–2(a)(1), and in 1964, it was as clear as clear could be that this meant discrimination because of the genetic and anatomical characteristics that men and women have at the time of birth. Determined searching has not found a single dictionary from that time that defined "sex" to mean sexual orientation, gender identity, or "transgender status." *Ante*, at 2. (Appendix A, *infra*, to this opinion includes the full definitions of "sex" in the unabridged dictionaries in use in the 1960s.)

In all those dictionaries, the primary definition of "sex" was essentially the same as that in the then-most recent edition of Webster's New International Dictionary 2296 (def. 1) (2d ed. 1953): "[o]ne of the two divisions of organisms formed on the distinction of male and female." See also American Heritage Dictionary 1187 (def. 1(a)) (1969) ("The property or quality by which organisms are classified according to their reproductive functions"); Random House Dictionary of the English Language 1307 (def. 1) (1966) (Random House Dictionary) ("the fact or character of being either male or female"); 9 Oxford English Dictionary 577 (def. 1) (1933) ("Either of the two divisions of organic beings distinguished as male and female respectively").

The Court does not dispute that this is what "sex" means in Title VII, although it coyly suggests that there is at least some support for a different and potentially relevant definition. *Ante*, at 5. (I address alternative definitions below. See Part I-B-3, *infra*.) But the Court declines to stand on that ground and instead "proceed[s] on the assumption that 'sex' . . . refer[s] only to biological distinctions between male and female." *Ante*, at 5.

If that is so, it should be perfectly clear that Title VII does not reach discrimination because of sexual orientation or gender identity. If "sex" in Title VII means biologically male or female, then discrimination because of sex means discrimination because the person in question is biologically male or biologically female, not because that person is sexually attracted to members of the same sex or identifies as a member of a particular gender.

How then does the Court claim to avoid that conclusion? The Court tries to cloud the issue by spending many pages discussing matters that are beside the point. The Court observes that a Title VII plaintiff need not show that "sex" was the sole or primary motive for a challenged employment decision or its sole or primary cause; that Title VII is limited to discrimination with respect to a list of specified actions (such as hiring, firing, etc.); and that Title VII protects individual rights, not group rights. See *ante*, at 5–9, 11.

All that is true, but so what? In cases like those before us, a plaintiff must show that sex was a "motivating factor" in the challenged employment action, 42 U. S. C. §2000e–2(m), so the question we must decide comes down to this: if an individual employee or applicant for employment shows that his or her sexual orientation or gender identity was a "motivating factor" in a hiring or discharge decision, for example, is that enough to establish that the employer discriminated "because of . . . sex"? Or, to put the same question in different terms, if an employer takes an employment action solely because of the sexual orientation or gender identity of an employee or applicant, has that employer necessarily discriminated because of biological sex?

The answers to those questions must be no, unless discrimination because of sexual orientation or gender identity inherently constitutes discrimination because of sex. The Court attempts to prove that point, and it argues, not merely that the terms of Title VII *can* be interpreted that way but that they *cannot reasonably be interpreted any other way*. According to the Court, the text is unambiguous. See *ante*, at 24, 27, 30.

The arrogance of this argument is breathtaking. As I will show, there is not a shred of evidence that any Member of Congress interpreted the statutory text that way when Title VII was enacted. See Part III-B, *infra*. But the Court apparently thinks that this was because the Members were not "smart enough to realize" what its language means. *Hively v. Ivy Tech Community College of Ind.*, 853 F.3d 339, 357 (CA7 2017) (Posner, J., concurring). The Court seemingly has the same opinion about our colleagues on the Courts of Appeals, because until 2017, every single Court of Appeals to consider the question interpreted Title VII's prohibition against sex discrimination to mean discrimination on the basis of biological sex. See Part III-C, *infra*. And for good measure, the Court's conclusion that Title VII unambiguously reaches discrimination on the basis of sexual orientation and gender identity necessarily means that the EEOC failed to see the obvious for the first 48 years after Title VII became law. Day in and day out, the Commission enforced Title VII but did not grasp what discrimination "because of . . . sex" unambiguously means. See Part III-C, *infra*.

The Court's argument is not only arrogant, it is wrong. It fails on its own terms. "Sex," "sexual orientation," and "gender identity" are different concepts, as the Court concedes. *Ante*, at 19 ("homosexuality and transgender status are distinct concepts from sex"). And neither "sexual orientation" nor "gender identity" is tied to either of the two biological sexes. See *ante*, at 10 (recognizing that "discrimination on these bases" does not have "some disparate impact on one sex or another"). Both men and women may be attracted to members of the opposite sex, members of the same sex, or members of both sexes. And individuals who are born with the genes and organs of either biological sex may identify with a different gender.

Using slightly different terms, the Court asserts again and again that discrimination because of sexual orientation or gender identity inherently or necessarily entails discrimination because of sex. See *ante*, at 2 (When an employer "fires an individual for being homosexual or transgender," "[s]ex plays a necessary and undisguisable role in the decision"); *ante*, at 9 ("[I]t is impossible to discriminate against a person for being homosexual or transgender without discriminating against that individual based on sex"); *ante*, at 11 ("[W]hen an employer discriminates against homosexual or transgender employees, [the] employer . . . inescapably *intends* to rely on sex in its decisionmaking"); *ante*, at 12 ("For an employer to discriminate against employees for being homosexual or transgender, the employer must intentionally discriminate against individual men and women in part because of sex"); *ante*, at 14 ("When an employer fires an employee for being homosexual or transgender, it necessarily and intentionally discriminates against that individual in part because of sex"); *ante*, at 19 ("[D]iscrimination based on homosexuality or transgender status necessarily entails discrimination based on sex"). But repetition of an assertion does not make it so, and the Court's repeated assertion is demonstrably untrue.

Contrary to the Court's contention, discrimination because of sexual orientation or gender identity does not in and of itself entail discrimination because of sex. We can see this because it is quite possible for an employer to discriminate on those grounds without taking the sex of an individual applicant or employee into account. An employer can have a policy that says: "We do not hire gays, lesbians, or transgender individuals." And an employer can implement this policy without paying any attention to or even knowing the biological sex of gay, lesbian, and transgender applicants. In fact, at the time of the enactment of Title VII, the United States military had a blanket policy of refusing to enlist gays or lesbians, and under this policy for years thereafter, applicants for enlistment were required to complete a form that asked whether they were "homosexual." Appendix D, *infra*, at 88, 101.

At oral argument, the attorney representing the employees, a prominent professor of constitutional law, was asked if there would be discrimination because of sex if an employer with a blanket policy against hiring gays, lesbians, and transgender individuals implemented that policy without knowing the biological sex of any job applicants. Her candid answer was that this would "not" be sex discrimination. And she was right.

The attorney's concession was necessary, but it is fatal to the Court's interpretation, for if an employer discriminates against individual applicants or employees without even knowing whether they are male or female, it is impossible to argue that the employer intentionally discriminated because of sex. Contra, *ante*, at 19. An employer cannot intentionally discriminate on the basis of a characteristic of which the employer has no knowledge. And if an employer does not violate Title VII by discriminating on the basis of sexual orientation or gender identity without knowing the sex of the affected individuals, there is no reason why the same employer could not lawfully implement the same policy even if it knows the sex of these individuals. If an employer takes an adverse employment action for a perfectly legitimate reason—for example, because an employee stole company property—that action is not converted into sex discrimination simply because the employer knows the employee's sex. As explained, a disparate treatment case requires proof of intent—i.e., that the employee's sex motivated the firing. In short, what this example shows is that discrimination because of sexual orientation or gender identity does not inherently or necessarily entail discrimination because of sex, and for that reason, the Court's chief argument collapses.

Trying to escape the consequences of the attorney's concession, the Court offers its own hypothetical:

"Suppose an employer's application form offered a single box to check if the applicant is either black or

Catholic. If the employer refuses to hire anyone who checks that box, would we conclude the employer has complied with Title VII, so long as it studiously avoids learning any particular applicant's race or religion? Of course not." *Ante*, at 18.

How this hypothetical proves the Court's point is a mystery. A person who checked that box would presumably be black, Catholic, or both, and refusing to hire an applicant because of race or religion is prohibited by Title VII. Rejecting applicants who checked a box indicating that they are homosexual is entirely different because it is impossible to tell from that answer whether an applicant is male or female.

The Court follows this strange hypothetical with an even stranger argument. The Court argues that an applicant could not answer the question whether he or she is homosexual without knowing something about sex. If the applicant was unfamiliar with the term "homosexual," the applicant would have to look it up or ask what the term means. And because this applicant would have to take into account his or her sex and that of the persons to whom he or she is sexually attracted to answer the question, it follows, the Court reasons, that an employer could not reject this applicant without taking the applicant's sex into account. See *ante*, at 18–19.

This is illogical. Just because an applicant cannot say whether he or she is homosexual without knowing his or her own sex and that of the persons to whom the applicant is attracted, it does not follow that an employer cannot reject an applicant based on homosexuality without knowing the applicant's sex.

While the Court's imagined application form proves nothing, another hypothetical case offered by the Court is telling. But what it proves is not what the Court thinks. The Court posits:

"Imagine an employer who has a policy of firing any employee known to be homosexual. The employer hosts an office holiday party and invites employees to bring their spouses. A model employee arrives and introduces a manager to Susan, the employee's wife. Will that employee be fired? If the policy works as the employer intends, the answer depends entirely on whether the model employee is a man or a woman." *Ante*, at 11.

This example disproves the Court's argument because it is perfectly clear that the employer's motivation in firing the female employee had nothing to do with that employee's sex. The employer presumably knew that this employee was a woman before she was invited to the fateful party. Yet the employer, far from holding her biological sex against her, rated her a "model employee." At the party, the employer learned something new, her sexual orientation, and it was this new information that motivated her discharge. So this is another example showing that discrimination because of sexual orientation does not inherently involve discrimination because of sex.

In addition to the failed argument just discussed, the Court makes two other arguments, more or less in passing. The first of these is essentially that sexual orientation and gender identity are closely related to sex. The Court argues that sexual orientation and gender identity are "inextricably bound up with sex," *ante*, at 10, and that discrimination on the basis of sexual orientation or gender identity involves the application of "sex-based rules," *ante*, at 17. This is a variant of an argument found in many of the briefs filed in support of the employees and in the lower court decisions that agreed with the Court's interpretation. All these variants stress that sex, sexual orientation, and gender identity are related concepts. The Seventh Circuit observed that "[i]t would require considerable calisthenics to remove 'sex' from 'sexual orientation.'" *Hively*, 853 F. 3d, at 350. The Second Circuit wrote that sex is necessarily "a factor in sexual orientation" and further concluded that "sexual orientation is a function of sex." 883 F.3d 100, 112–113 (CA2 2018) (en banc). Bostock's brief and those of amici supporting his position contend that sexual orientation is "a sex-based consideration." Other briefs state that sexual orientation is "a function of sex" or is "intrinsically related to sex." Similarly, Stephens argues that sex and gender identity are necessarily intertwined: "By definition, a transgender person is someone who lives and identifies with a sex different than the sex assigned to the person at birth."

It is curious to see this argument in an opinion that purports to apply the purest and highest form of textualism because the argument effectively amends the statutory text. Title VII prohibits discrimination because of *sex itself,* not everything that is related to, based on, or defined with reference to, "sex." Many things are related to sex. Think of all the nouns other than "orientation" that are commonly modified by the adjective "sexual." Some examples yielded by a quick computer search are "sexual harassment," "sexual assault," "sexual violence," "sexual intercourse," and "sexual content."

Does the Court really think that Title VII prohibits discrimination on all these grounds? Is it unlawful for an employer to refuse to hire an employee with a record of sexual harassment in prior jobs? Or a record of sexual assault or violence?

To be fair, the Court does not claim that Title VII prohibits discrimination because of *everything* that is related to sex. The Court draws a distinction between things that are "inextricably" related and those that are related in "some vague sense." *Ante*, at 10. Apparently the Court would graft onto Title VII some arbitrary line separating the things that are related closely enough and those that are not. And it would do this in the name of high textualism. An additional argument made in passing also fights the text of Title VII and the policy it reflects. The Court proclaims that "[a]n individual's homosexuality or transgender status is not relevant to employment decisions." *Ante*, at 9. That is the policy view of many people in 2020, and perhaps Congress would have amended Title VII to implement it if this Court had not intervened. But that is not the policy embodied in Title VII in its current form. Title VII prohibits discrimination based on five specified grounds, and neither sexual orientation nor gender identity is on the list. As long as an employer does not discriminate based on one of the listed grounds, the employer is free to decide for itself which characteristics are "relevant to [its] employment decisions." Ibid. By proclaiming that sexual orientation and gender identity are "not relevant to employment decisions," the Court updates Title VII to reflect what it regards as 2020 values.

The Court's remaining argument is based on a hypothetical that the Court finds instructive. In this hypothetical, an employer has two employees who are "attracted to men," and "*to the employer's mind*" the two employees are "materially identical" except that one is a man and the other is a woman. *Ante*, at 9 (emphasis added). The Court reasons that if the employer fires the man but not the woman, the employer is necessarily motivated by the man's biological sex. *Ante*, at 9–10. After all, if two employees are identical in every respect but sex, and the employer fires only one, what other reason could there be?

The problem with this argument is that the Court loads the dice. That is so because in the mind of an employer who does not want to employ individuals who are attracted to members of the same sex, these two employees are not materially identical in every respect but sex. On the contrary, they differ in another way that the employer thinks is quite material. And until Title VII is amended to add sexual orientation as a prohibited ground, this is a view that an employer is permitted to implement. As noted, other than prohibiting discrimination on any of five specified grounds, "race, color, religion, sex, [and] national origin." 42 U. S. C. §2000e–2(a)(1), Title VII allows employers to decide whether two employees are "materially identical." Even idiosyncratic criteria are permitted; if an employer thinks that Scorpios make bad employees, the employer can refuse to hire Scorpios. Such a policy would be unfair and foolish, but under Title VII, it is permitted. And until Title VII is amended, so is a policy against employing gays, lesbians, or transgender individuals.

Once this is recognized, what we have in the Court's hypothetical case are two employees who differ in *two* ways—sex and sexual orientation—and if the employer fires one and keeps the other, all that can be inferred is that the employer was motivated either entirely by sexual orientation, entirely by sex, or in part by both. We cannot infer with any certainty, as the hypothetical is apparently meant to suggest, that the employer was motivated even in part by sex. The Court harps on the fact that under Title VII a prohibited ground need not be the sole motivation for an adverse employment action, see *ante*, at 10–11, 14–15, 21, but its example does not show that sex necessarily played *any* part in the employer's thinking.

The Court tries to avoid this inescapable conclusion by arguing that sex is really the only difference between the two employees. This is so, the Court maintains, because both employees "are attracted to men." *Ante*, at 9–10. Of course, the employer would couch its objection to the man differently. It would say that its objection was his sexual orientation. So this may appear to leave us with a battle of labels. If the employer's objection to the male employee is characterized as attraction to men, it seems that he is just like the woman in all respects except sex and that the employer's disparate treatment must be based on that one difference. On the other hand, if the employer's objection is sexual orientation or homosexuality, the two employees differ in two respects, and it cannot be inferred that the disparate treatment was due even in part to sex.

The Court insists that its label is the right one, and that presumably is why it makes such a point of arguing that an employer cannot escape liability under Title VII by giving sex discrimination some other name. See *ante*, at 14, 17. That is certainly true, but so is the opposite. Something that is *not* sex discrimination cannot be converted into sex discrimination by slapping on that label. So the Court cannot prove its point simply by labeling the employer's objection as "attract[ion] to men." *Ante*, at 9–10. Rather, the Court needs to show that its label is the correct one.

And a labeling standoff would not help the Court because that would mean that the bare text of Title VII does not unambiguously show that its interpretation is right. The Court would have no justification for its stubborn refusal to look any further.

As it turns out, however, there is no standoff. It can easily be shown that the employer's real objection is not "attract[ion] to men" but homosexual orientation.

In an effort to prove its point, the Court carefully includes in its example just two employees, a homosexual man and a heterosexual woman, but suppose we add two more individuals, a woman who is attracted to women and a man who is attracted to women. (A large employer will likely have applicants and employees who fall into all four categories, and a small employer can potentially have all four as well.) We now have the four exemplars listed below, with the discharged employees crossed out:

Man attracted to men

Woman attracted to men

Woman attracted to women

Man attracted to women

The discharged employees have one thing in common. It is not biological sex, attraction to men, or attraction to women. It is attraction to members of their own sex—in a word, sexual orientation. And that, we can infer, is the employer's real motive.

In sum, the Court's textual arguments fail on their own terms. The Court tries to prove that "it is impossible to discriminate against a person for being homosexual or transgender without discriminating against that individual based on sex," *ante*, at 9, but as has been shown, it is entirely possible for an employer to do just that. "[H]omosexuality and transgender status are distinct concepts from sex," *ante*, at 19, and discrimination because of sexual orientation or transgender status does not inherently or necessarily constitute discrimination because of sex. The Court's arguments are squarely contrary to the statutory text.

But even if the words of Title VII did not definitively refute the Court's interpretation, that would not justify the Court's refusal to consider alternative interpretations. The Court's excuse for ignoring everything other than the bare statutory text is that the text is unambiguous and therefore no one can reasonably interpret the text in any way other than the Court does. Unless the Court has met that high standard, it has no justification for its blinkered approach. And to say that the Court's interpretation is the only possible reading is indefensible.

B

Although the Court relies solely on the arguments discussed above, several other arguments figure prominently in the decisions of the lower courts and in briefs submitted by or in support of the employees. The Court apparently finds these arguments unpersuasive, and so do I, but for the sake of completeness, I will address them briefly.

1

One argument, which relies on our decision in *Price Waterhouse v. Hopkins*, 490 U.S. 228 (1989) (plurality opinion), is that discrimination because of sexual orientation or gender identity violates Title VII because it constitutes prohibited discrimination on the basis of sex stereotypes. See 883 F. 3d, at 119–123; *Hively*, 853 F. 3d, at 346; 884 F.3d 560, 576–577 (CA6 2018). The argument goes like this. Title VII prohibits discrimination based on stereotypes about the way men and women should behave; the belief that a person should be attracted only to persons of the opposite sex and the belief that a person should identify with his or her biological sex are examples of such stereotypes; therefore, discrimination on either of these grounds is unlawful.

This argument fails because it is based on a faulty premise, namely, that Title VII forbids discrimination based on sex stereotypes. It does not. It prohibits discrimination because of "sex," and the two concepts are not the same. See *Price Waterhouse*, 490 U. S., at 251. That does not mean, however, that an employee or applicant for employment cannot prevail by showing that a challenged decision was based on a sex stereotype. Such evidence is relevant to prove discrimination because of sex, and it may be convincing where the trait that is inconsistent with the stereotype is one that would be tolerated and perhaps even valued in a person of the opposite sex. See ibid.

Much of the plaintiff's evidence in *Price Waterhouse* was of this nature. The plaintiff was a woman who was passed over for partnership at an accounting firm, and some of the adverse comments about her work appeared to criticize her for being forceful and insufficiently "feminin[e]." Id., at 235–236.

The main issue in *Price Waterhouse*—the proper allocation of the burdens of proof in a so-called mixed motives Title VII case—is not relevant here, but the plurality opinion, endorsed by four Justices, commented on the issue of sex stereotypes. The plurality observed that "sex stereotypes do not inevitably prove that gender played a part in a particular employment decision" but "can certainly be *evidence* that gender played a part." Id., at 251. And the plurality made it clear that "[t]he plaintiff must show that the employer actually relied on her gender in making its decision." Ibid.

Plaintiffs who allege that they were treated unfavorably because of their sexual orientation or gender identity are not in the same position as the plaintiff in *Price Waterhouse*. In cases involving discrimination based on sexual orientation or gender identity, the grounds for the employer's decision—that individuals should be sexually attracted only to persons of the opposite biological sex or should identify with their biological sex—apply equally to men and women. "[H]eterosexuality is not a *female* stereotype; it not a *male* stereotype; it is not a *sex- specific* stereotype at all." *Hively*, 853 F. 3d, at 370 (Sykes, J., dissenting).

To be sure, there may be cases in which a gay, lesbian, or transgender individual can make a claim like the one in *Price Waterhouse*. That is, there may be cases where traits or behaviors that some people associate with gays, lesbians, or transgender individuals are tolerated or valued in persons of one biological sex but not the other. But that is a different matter.

2

A second prominent argument made in support of the result that the Court now reaches analogizes discrimination against gays and lesbians to discrimination against a person who is married to or has an intimate relationship with a person of a different race. Several lower court cases have held that discrimination on this ground violates Title VII. See, e.g., *Holcomb v. Iona College*, 521 F.3d 130 (CA2 2008); *Parr v. Woodmen of World Life Ins. Co.*, 791 F.2d 888 (CA11 1986). And the logic of these decisions, it is argued, applies equally where an employee or applicant is treated unfavorably because he or she is married to, or has an intimate relationship with, a person of the same sex.

This argument totally ignores the historically rooted reason why discrimination on the basis of an interracial relationship constitutes race discrimination. And without taking history into account, it is not easy to see how the decisions in question fit the terms of Title VII.

Recall that Title VII makes it unlawful for an employer to discriminate against an individual "because of *such individual's race*." 42 U. S. C. §2000e–2(a) (emphasis added). So if an employer is happy to employ whites and blacks but will not employ any employee in an interracial relationship, how can it be said that the employer is discriminating against either whites or blacks "because of such individual's race"? This employer would be applying the same rule to all its employees regardless of their race.

The answer is that this employer is discriminating on a ground that history tells us is a core form of race discrimination. "It would require absolute blindness to the history of racial discrimination in this country not to understand what is at stake in such cases . . . . A prohibition on 'race-mixing' was . . . grounded in bigotry against a particular race and was an integral part of preserving the rigid hierarchical distinction that denominated members of the black race as inferior to whites." 883 F. 3d, at 158–159 (Lynch, J., dissenting).

Discrimination because of sexual orientation is different. It cannot be regarded as a form of sex discrimination on the ground that applies in race cases since discrimination because of sexual orientation is not historically tied to a project that aims to subjugate either men or women. An employer who discriminates on this ground might be called "homophobic" or "transphobic," but not sexist. See *Wittmer v. Phillips 66 Co.*, 915 F.3d 328, 338 (CA5 2019) (Ho, J., concurring).

3

The opinion of the Court intimates that the term "sex" was not universally understood in 1964 to refer just to the categories of male and female, see *ante*, at 5, and while the Court does not take up any alternative definition as a ground for its decision, I will say a word on this subject.

As previously noted, the definitions of "sex" in the unabridged dictionaries in use in the 1960s are reproduced in Appendix A, *infra*. Anyone who examines those definitions can see that the primary definition in every one of them refers to the division of living things into two groups, male and female, based on biology, and most of the definitions further down the list are the same or very similar. In addition, some definitions refer to heterosexual sex acts. See Random House Dictionary 1307 ("coitus," "sexual intercourse" (defs. 5–6)); American Heritage Dictionary, at 1187 ("sexual intercourse" (def. 5)).

Aside from these, what is there? One definition, "to neck passionately," Random House Dictionary 1307 (def. 8), refers to sexual conduct that is not necessarily heterosexual. But can it be seriously argued that one of the aims of Title VII is to outlaw employment discrimination against employees, whether heterosexual or homosexual, who engage in necking? And even if Title VII had that effect, that is not what is at issue in cases like those before us.

That brings us to the two remaining subsidiary definitions, both of which refer to sexual urges or instincts and their manifestations. See the fourth definition in the American Heritage Dictionary, at 1187 ("the sexual urge or instinct as it manifests itself in behavior"), and the fourth definition in both Webster's Second and Third ("[p]henomena of sexual instincts and their manifestations," Webster's New International Dictionary, at 2296 (2d ed.); Webster's Third New International Dictionary 2081 (1966)). Since both of these come after three prior definitions that refer to men and women, they are most naturally read to have the same association, and in any event, is it plausible that Title VII prohibits discrimination based on *any* sexual urge or instinct and its manifestations? The urge to rape?

Viewing all these definitions, the overwhelming impact is that discrimination because of "sex" was understood during the era when Title VII was enacted to refer to men and women. (The same is true of current definitions, which are reproduced in Appendix B, *infra*.) This no doubt explains why neither this Court nor any of the lower courts have tried to make much of the dictionary definitions of sex just discussed.

II

A

So far, I have not looked beyond dictionary definitions of "sex," but textualists like Justice Scalia do not confine their inquiry to the scrutiny of dictionaries. See Manning, Textualism and the Equity of the Statute, 101 Colum. L. Rev. 1, 109 (2001). Dictionary definitions are valuable because they are evidence of what people at the time of a statute's enactment would have understood its words to mean. Ibid. But they are not the only source of relevant evidence, and what matters in the end is the answer to the question that the evidence is gathered to resolve: How would the terms of a statute have been understood by ordinary people at the time of enactment?

Justice Scalia was perfectly clear on this point. The words of a law, he insisted, "mean *what they conveyed to reasonable people at the time.*" Reading Law, at 16 (emphasis added).

Leading proponents of Justice Scalia's school of textualism have expounded on this principle and explained that it is grounded on an understanding of the way language works. As Dean John F. Manning explains, "the meaning of language depends on the way a linguistic community uses words and phrases in context." What Divides Textualists From Purposivists? 106 Colum. L. Rev. 70, 78 (2006). "[O]ne can make sense of others' communications only by placing them in their appropriate social and linguistic context," id., at 79–80, and this is no less true of statutes than any other verbal communications. "[S]tatutes convey meaning only because members of a relevant linguistic community apply shared background conventions for understanding how particular words are used in particular contexts."

Manning, The Absurdity Doctrine, 116 Harv. L. Rev. 2387, 2457 (2003). Therefore, judges should ascribe to the words of a statute "what a reasonable person conversant with applicable social conventions would have understood them to be adopting." Manning, 106 Colum. L. Rev., at 77. Or, to put the point in slightly different terms, a judge interpreting a statute should ask "'what one would ordinarily be understood as saying, given the circumstances in which one said it.'" Manning, 116 Harv. L. Rev., at 2397–2398.

Judge Frank Easterbrook has made the same points:

"Words are arbitrary signs, having meaning only to the extent writers and readers share an understanding.... Language in general, and legislation in particular, is a social enterprise to which both speakers and listeners contribute, drawing on background understandings and the structure and circumstances of the utterance." *Herrmann v. Cencom Cable Assocs., Inc., 978* F.2d 978, 982 (CA7 1992).

Consequently, "[s]licing a statute into phrases while ignoring ... the setting of the enactment ... is a formula for disaster." Ibid.; see also *Continental Can Co. v. Chicago Truck Drivers, Helpers and Warehouse Workers Union (Independent) Pension Fund*, 916 F.2d 1154, 1157 (CA7 1990) ("You don't have to be Ludwig Wittgenstein or Hans-Georg Gadamer to know that successful communication depends on meanings shared by interpretive communities").

Thus, when textualism is properly understood, it calls for an examination of the social context in which a statute was enacted because this may have an important bearing on what its words were understood to mean at the time of enactment. Textualists do not read statutes as if they were messages picked up by a powerful radio telescope from a distant and utterly unknown civilization. Statutes consist of communications between members of a particular linguistic community, one that existed in a particular place and at a particular time, and these communications must therefore be interpreted as they were understood by that community at that time.

For this reason, it is imperative to consider how Americans in 1964 would have understood Title VII's prohibition of discrimination because of sex. To get a picture of this, we may imagine this scene. Suppose that, while Title VII was under consideration in Congress, a group of average Americans decided to read the text of the bill with the aim of writing or calling their representatives in Congress and conveying their approval or disapproval. What would these ordinary citizens have taken "discrimination because of sex" to mean? Would they have thought that this language prohibited discrimination because of sexual orientation or gender identity?

B

The answer could not be clearer. In 1964, ordinary Americans reading the text of Title VII would not have dreamed that discrimination because of sex meant discrimination because of sexual orientation, much less gender identity. The *ordinary meaning* of discrimination because of "sex" was discrimination because of a person's biological sex, not sexual orientation or gender identity. The possibility that discrimination on either of these grounds might fit within some exotic understanding of sex discrimination would not have crossed their minds.

1

In 1964, the concept of prohibiting discrimination "because of sex" was no novelty. It was a familiar and well-understood concept, and what it meant was equal treatment for men and women.

Long before Title VII was adopted, many pioneering state and federal laws had used language substantively indistinguishable from Title VII's critical phrase, "discrimination because of sex." For example, the California Constitution of 1879 stipulated that no one, "*on account of sex*, [could] be disqualified from entering upon or pursuing any lawful business, vocation, or profession." Art. XX, §18 (emphasis added). It also prohibited a student's exclusion from any state university department "on account of sex." Art. IX, §9; accord, Mont. Const., Art. XI, §9 (1889).

Wyoming's first Constitution proclaimed broadly that "[b]oth male and female citizens of this state shall equally enjoy all civil, political and religious rights and privileges," Art. VI, §1 (1890), and then provided specifically that "[i]n none of the public schools . . . shall distinction or discrimination be made *on account of sex*," Art. VII, §10 (emphasis added); see also §16 (the "university shall be equally open to students of both sexes"). Washington's Constitution likewise required "ample provision for the education of all children . . . without distinction or preference *on account of. . . sex*." Art. IX, §1 (1889) (emphasis added).

The Constitution of Utah, adopted in 1895, provided that the right to vote and hold public office "shall not be denied or abridged *on account of sex*." Art. IV, §1 (emphasis added). And in the next sentence it made clear what "on account of sex" meant, stating that "[b]oth male and female citizens . . . shall enjoy equally all civil, political and religious rights and privileges." Ibid.

The most prominent example of a provision using this language was the Nineteenth Amendment, ratified in 1920, which bans the denial or abridgment of the right to vote "on account of sex." U. S. Const., Amdt. 19. Similar language appeared in the proposal of the National Woman's Party for an Equal Rights Amendment. As framed in 1921, this proposal forbade all "political, civil or legal disabilities or inequalities *on account of sex*, [o]r on account of marriage." Women Lawyers Meet: Representatives of 20 States Endorse Proposed Equal Rights Amendment, N. Y. Times, Sept. 16, 1921, p. 10.

Similar terms were used in the precursor to the Equal Pay Act. Introduced in 1944 by Congresswoman Winifred C. Stanley, it proclaimed that "[d]iscrimination against employees, in rates of compensation paid, *on account of sex*" was "contrary to the public interest." H. R. 5056, 78th Cong., 2d Sess.

In 1952, the new Constitution for Puerto Rico, which was approved by Congress, 66Stat. 327, prohibited all "discrimination . . . *on account of . . . sex*," Art. II, Bill of Rights §1 (emphasis added), and in the landmark Immigration and Nationality Act of 1952, Congress outlawed discrimination in naturalization "*because of. . . sex*." 8 U. S. C. §1422 (emphasis added).

In 1958, the International Labour Organisation, a United Nations agency of which the United States is a member, recommended that nations bar employment discrimination "made *on the basis of . . . sex*." Convention (No. 111) Concerning Discrimination in Respect of Employment and Occupation, Art. 1(a), June 25, 1958, 362 U. N. T. S. 32 (emphasis added).

In 1961, President Kennedy ordered the Civil Service Commission to review and modify personnel policies "to assure that selection for any career position is hereinafter made solely on the basis of individual merit and fitness, *without regard to sex*." He concurrently established a "Commission on the Status of Women" and directed it to recommend policies "for overcoming discriminations in government and private employment *on the basis of sex*." Exec. Order No. 10980, 3 CFR 138 (1961 Supp.) (emphasis added).

In short, the concept of discrimination "because of," "on account of," or "on the basis of " sex was well understood. It was part of the campaign for equality that had been waged by women's rights advocates for more than a century, and what it meant was equal treatment for men and women.

2

Discrimination "because of sex" was not understood as having anything to do with discrimination because of sexual orientation or transgender status. Any such notion would have clashed in spectacular fashion with the societal norms of the day.

For most 21st-century Americans, it is painful to be reminded of the way our society once treated gays and lesbians, but any honest effort to understand what the terms of Title VII were understood to mean when enacted must take into account the societal norms of that time. And the plain truth is that in 1964 homosexuality was thought to be a mental disorder, and homosexual conduct was regarded as morally culpable and worthy of punishment.

In its then-most recent Diagnostic and Statistical Manual of Mental Disorders (1952) (DSM–I), the American Psychiatric Association (APA) classified same-sex attraction as a "sexual deviation," a particular type of "sociopathic personality disturbance," id., at 38–39, and the next edition, issued in 1968, similarly classified homosexuality as a "sexual deviatio[n]," Diagnostic and Statistical Manual of Mental Disorders 44 (2d ed.) (DSM–II). It was not until the sixth printing of the DSM–II in 1973 that this was changed.

Society's treatment of homosexuality and homosexual conduct was consistent with this understanding. Sodomy was a crime in every State but Illinois, see W. Eskridge, Dishonorable Passions 387–407 (2008), and in the District of Columbia, a law enacted by Congress made sodomy a felony punishable by imprisonment for up to 10 years and permitted the indefinite civil commitment of "sexual psychopath[s],", Act of June 9, 1948, §§104, 201–207, 62Stat. 347–349.

This view of homosexuality was reflected in the rules governing the federal work force. In 1964, federal "[a]gencies could deny homosexual men and women employment because of their sexual orientation," and this practice continued until 1975. GAO, D. Heivilin, Security Clearances: Consideration of Sexual Orientation in the Clearance Process 2 (GAO/NSIAD-95-21, 1995). See, e.g., *Anonymous v. Macy*, 398 F.2d 317, 318 (CA5 1968) (affirming dismissal of postal employee for homosexual acts).

In 1964, individuals who were known to be homosexual could not obtain security clearances, and any who possessed clearances were likely to lose them if their orientation was discovered. A 1953 Executive Order provided that background investigations should look for evidence of "sexual perversion," as well as "[a]ny criminal, infamous, dishonest, immoral, or notoriously disgraceful conduct." Exec. Order No. 10450, §8(a)(1)(iii), 3 CFR 938 (1949–1953 Comp.). "Until about 1991, when agencies began to change their security policies and practices regarding sexual orientation, there were a number of documented cases where defense civilian or contractor employees' security clearances were denied or revoked because of their sexual orientation." GAO, Security Clearances, at 2. See, e.g., *Adams v. Laird*, 420 F.2d 230, 240 (CADC 1969) (upholding denial of security clearance to defense contractor employee because he had "engaged in repeated homosexual acts"); see also *Webster v. Doe*, 486 U.S. 592, 595, 601 (1988) (concluding that decision to fire a particular individual because he was homosexual fell within the "discretion" of the Director of Central Intelligence under the National Security Act of 1947 and thus was unreviewable under the APA).

The picture in state employment was similar. In 1964, it was common for States to bar homosexuals from serving as teachers. An article summarizing the situation *15 years after Title VII became law* reported that "[a]ll states have statutes that permit the revocation of teaching certificates (or credentials) for immorality, moral turpitude, or unprofessionalism," and, the survey added, "[h]omosexuality is considered to fall within all three categories."

The situation in California is illustrative. California laws prohibited individuals who engaged in "immoral conduct" (which was construed to include homosexual behavior), as well as those convicted of "sex offenses" (like sodomy), from employment as teachers. Cal. Educ. Code Ann. §§13202, 13207, 13209, 13218, 13255 (West 1960). The teaching certificates of individuals convicted of engaging in homosexual acts were revoked. See, e.g., *Sarac v. State Bd. of Ed.*, 249 Cal. App. 2d 58, 62–64, 57 Cal. Rptr. 69, 72–73 (1967) (upholding revocation of secondary teaching credential from teacher who was convicted of engaging in homosexual conduct on public beach), overruled in part, *Morrison v. State Bd. of Ed.*, 1 Cal. 3d 214, 461 P.2d 375 (1969).

In Florida, the legislature enacted laws authorizing the revocation of teaching certificates for "misconduct involving moral turpitude," Fla. Stat. Ann. §229.08(16) (1961), and this law was used to target homosexual conduct. In 1964, a legislative committee was wrapping up a 6-year campaign to remove homosexual teachers from public schools and state universities. As a result of these efforts, the state board of education apparently revoked at least 71 teachers' certificates and removed at least 14 university professors. Eskridge, Dishonorable Passions, at 103.

Individuals who engaged in homosexual acts also faced the loss of other occupational licenses, such as those needed to work as a "lawyer, doctor, mortician, [or] beautician." See, e.g., *Florida Bar v. Kay*, 232 So. 2d 378 (Fla. 1970) (attorney disbarred after conviction for homosexual conduct in public bathroom).

In 1964 and for many years thereafter, homosexuals were barred from the military. See, e.g., Army Reg. 635–89, §I(2)(a) (July 15, 1966) ("Personnel who voluntarily engage in homosexual acts, irrespective of sex, will not be permitted to serve in the Army in any capacity, and their prompt separation is mandatory"); Army Reg. 600–443, §I(2) (April 10, 1953) (similar). Prohibitions against homosexual conduct by members of the military were not eliminated until 2010. See Don't Ask, Don't Tell Repeal Act of 2010, 124Stat. 3515 (repealing 10 U. S. C. §654, which required members of the Armed Forces to be separated for engaging in homosexual conduct).

Homosexuals were also excluded from entry into the United States. The Immigration and Nationality Act of 1952 (INA) excluded aliens "afflicted with psychopathic personality." 8 U. S. C. §1182(a)(4) (1964 ed.). In *Boutilier v. INS*, 387 U.S. 118, 120–123 (1967), this Court, relying on the INA's legislative history, interpreted that term to encompass homosexuals and upheld an alien's deportation on that ground. Three Justices disagreed with the majority's interpretation of the phrase "psychopathic personality." But it apparently did not occur to anyone to argue that the Court's interpretation was inconsistent with the INA's express prohibition of discrimination "because of sex." That was how our society—and this Court—saw things a half century ago. Discrimination because of sex and discrimination because of sexual orientation were viewed as two entirely different concepts.

To its credit, our society has now come to recognize the injustice of past practices, and this recognition provides the impetus to "update" Title VII. But that is not our job. Our duty is to understand what the terms of Title VII were understood to mean when enacted, and in doing so, we must take into account the societal norms of that time. We must therefore ask whether ordinary Americans in 1964 would have thought that discrimination because of "sex" carried some exotic meaning under which private-sector employers would be prohibited from engaging in a practice that represented the official policy of the Federal Government with respect to its own employees. We must ask whether Americans at that time would have thought that Title VII banned discrimination against an employee for engaging in conduct that Congress had made a felony and a ground for civil commitment.

The questions answer themselves. Even if discrimination based on sexual orientation or gender identity could be squeezed into some arcane understanding of sex discrimination, the context in which Title VII was enacted would tell us that this is not what the statute's terms were understood to mean at that time. To paraphrase something Justice Scalia once wrote, "our job is not to scavenge the world of English usage to discover whether there is any possible meaning" of discrimination because of sex that might be broad enough to encompass discrimination because of sexual orientation or gender identity. *Chisom v. Roemer*, 501 U.S. 380, 410 (1991) (dissenting opinion). Without strong evidence to the contrary (and there is none here), our job is to ascertain and apply the "*ordinary* meaning" of the statute. Ibid. And in 1964, ordinary Americans most certainly would not have understood Title VII to ban discrimination because of sexual orientation or gender identity.

The Court makes a tiny effort to suggest that at least some people in 1964 might have seen what Title VII really means. *Ante*, at 26. What evidence does it adduce? One complaint filed in 1969, another filed in 1974, and arguments made in the mid-1970s about the meaning of the Equal Rights Amendment. Ibid. To call this evidence merely feeble would be generous.

C

While Americans in 1964 would have been shocked to learn that Congress had enacted a law prohibiting sexual orientation discrimination, they would have been bewildered to hear that this law also forbids discrimination on the basis of "transgender status" or "gender identity," terms that would have left people at the time scratching their heads. The term "transgender" is said to have been coined "'in the early 1970s,'" and the term "gender identity," now understood to mean "[a]n internal sense of being male, female or something else," apparently first appeared in an academic article in 1964. Certainly, neither term was in common parlance; indeed, dictionaries of the time still primarily defined the word "gender" by reference to grammatical classifications. See, *e.g.*, American Heritage Dictionary, at 548 (def. 1(a)) ("Any set of two or more categories, such as masculine, feminine, and neuter, into which words are divided . . . and that determine agreement with or the

selection of modifiers, referents, or grammatical forms").

While it is likely true that there have always been individuals who experience what is now termed "gender dysphoria," i.e., "[d]iscomfort or distress related to an incongruence between an individual's gender identity and the gender assigned at birth," the current understanding of the concept postdates the enactment of Title VII. Nothing resembling what is now called gender dysphoria appeared in either DSM–I (1952) or DSM–II (1968). It was not until 1980 that the APA, in DSM–III, recognized two main psychiatric diagnoses related to this condition, "Gender Identity Disorder of Childhood" and "Transsexualism" in adolescents and adults. DSM–III, at 261–266.

The first widely publicized sex reassignment surgeries in the United States were not performed until 1966, and the great majority of physicians surveyed in 1969 thought that an individual who sought sex reassignment surgery was either "'severely neurotic'" or "'psychotic.'"

It defies belief to suggest that the public meaning of discrimination because of sex in 1964 encompassed discrimination on the basis of a concept that was essentially unknown to the public at that time.

D

1

The Court's main excuse for entirely ignoring the social context in which Title VII was enacted is that the meaning of Title VII's prohibition of discrimination because of sex is clear, and therefore it simply does not matter whether people in 1964 were "smart enough to realize" what its language means. *Hively*, 853 F. 3d, at 357 (Posner, J., concurring). According to the Court, an argument that looks to the societal norms of those times represents an impermissible attempt to displace the statutory language. *Ante*, at 25–26.

The Court's argument rests on a false premise. As already explained at length, the text of Title VII does not prohibit discrimination because of sexual orientation or gender identity. And what the public thought about those issues in 1964 is relevant and important, not because it provides a ground for departing from the statutory text, but because it helps to explain what the text was understood to mean when adopted.

In arguing that we must put out of our minds what we know about the time when Title VII was enacted, the Court relies on Justice Scalia's opinion for the Court in *Oncale v. Sundowner Offshore Services, Inc.*, 523 U.S. 75 (1998). But *Oncale* is nothing like these cases, and no one should be taken in by the majority's effort to enlist Justice Scalia in its updating project.

The Court's unanimous decision in *Oncale* was thoroughly unremarkable. The Court held that a male employee who alleged that he had been sexually harassed at work by other men stated a claim under Title VII. Although the impetus for Title VII's prohibition of sex discrimination was to protect women, anybody reading its terms would immediately appreciate that it applies equally to both sexes, and by the time *Oncale* reached the Court, our precedent already established that sexual harassment may constitute sex discrimination within the meaning of Title VII. See *Meritor Savings Bank, FSB v. Vinson*, 477 U.S. 57 (1986). Given these premises, syllogistic reasoning dictated the holding.

What today's decision latches onto are *Oncale*'s comments about whether "'male-on-male sexual harassment'" was on Congress's mind when it enacted Title VII. *Ante*, at 28 (quoting 523 U. S., at 79). The Court in *Oncale* observed that this specific type of behavior "was assuredly not the *principal evil* Congress was concerned with when it enacted Title VII," but it found that immaterial because "statutory prohibitions often go beyond the *principal evil* to cover reasonably comparable evils, and it is ultimately the provisions of our laws rather than the *principal concerns* of our legislators by which we are governed." 523 U. S., at 79 (emphasis added).

It takes considerable audacity to read these comments as committing the Court to a position on deep philosophical questions about the meaning of language and their implications for the interpretation of legal rules. These comments are better understood as stating mundane and uncontroversial truths. Who would argue that a statute applies only to the "principal evils" and not lesser evils that fall within the plain scope of its terms? Would even the most ardent "purposivists" and fans of legislative history contend that congressional intent is restricted to Congress's "*principal* concerns"?

Properly understood, *Oncale* does not provide the slightest support for what the Court has done today. For one thing, it would be a wild understatement to say that discrimination because of sexual orientation and transgender status was not the "principal evil" on Congress's mind in 1964. Whether we like to admit it now or not, in the thinking of Congress and the public at that time, such discrimination would not have been evil at all.

But the more important difference between these cases and *Oncale* is that here the interpretation that the Court adopts does not fall within the ordinary meaning of the statutory text as it would have been understood in 1964. To decide for the defendants in *Oncale*, it would have been necessary to carve out an exception to the statutory text. Here, no such surgery is at issue. Even if we totally disregard the societal norms of 1964, the text of Title VII does not support the Court's holding. And the reasoning of *Oncale* does not preclude or counsel against our taking those norms into account. They are relevant, not for the purpose of creating an exception to the terms of the statute, but for the purpose of better appreciating how those terms would have been understood at the time.

2

The Court argues that two other decisions—*Phillips v. Martin Marietta Corp.*, 400 U.S. 542 (1971) (per curiam), and *Los Angeles Dept. of Water and Power v. Manhart*, 435 U.S. 702 (1978)—buttress its decision, but those cases merely held that Title VII prohibits employer conduct that plainly constitutes discrimination because of biological sex. In *Philips*, the employer treated women with young children less favorably than men with young children. In *Manhart*, the employer required women to make larger pension contributions than men. It is hard to see how these holdings assist the Court.

The Court extracts three "lessons" from *Phillips, Manhart,* and *Oncale*, but none sheds any light on the question before us. The first lesson is that "it's irrelevant what an employer might call its discriminatory practice, how others might label it, or what else might motivate it." *Ante*, at 14. This lesson is obviously true but proves nothing. As to the label attached to a practice, has anyone ever thought that the application of a law to a person's conduct depends on how it is labeled? Could a bank robber escape conviction by saying he was engaged in asset enhancement? So if an employer discriminates because of sex, the employer is liable no matter what it calls its conduct, but if the employer's conduct is not sex discrimination, the statute does not apply. Thus, this lesson simply takes us back to the question whether discrimination because of sexual orientation or gender identity is a form of discrimination because of biological sex. For reasons already discussed, see Part I–A, supra, it is not.

It likewise proves nothing of relevance here to note that an employer cannot escape liability by showing that discrimination on a prohibited ground was not its sole motivation. So long as a prohibited ground was a motivating factor, the existence of other motivating factors does not defeat liability.

The Court makes much of the argument that "[i]n *Phillips*, the employer could have accurately spoken of its policy as one based on 'motherhood.'" *Ante*, at 14; see also *ante*, at 16. But motherhood, by definition, is a condition that can be experienced only by women, so a policy that distinguishes between motherhood and parenthood is necessarily a policy that draws a sex-based distinction. There was sex discrimination in *Phillips*, because women with children were treated disadvantageously compared to men with children.

Lesson number two—"the plaintiff's sex need not be the sole or primary cause of the employer's adverse action," *ante*, at 14—is similarly unhelpful. The standard of causation in these cases is whether sex is necessarily a "motivating factor" when an employer discriminates on the basis of sexual orientation or gender identity. 42 U. S. C. §2000e–2(m). But the essential question—whether discrimination because of sexual orientation or gender identity constitutes sex discrimination—would be the same no matter what causation standard applied. The Court's extensive discussion of causation standards is so much smoke.

Lesson number three—"an employer cannot escape liability by demonstrating that it treats males and females comparably as groups," *ante*, at 15, is also irrelevant. There is no dispute that discrimination against an individual employee based on that person's sex cannot be justified on the ground that the employer's treatment of the average employee of that sex is at least as favorable as its treatment of the average employee of the opposite sex. Nor does it matter if an employer discriminates against only a subset of men or women, where the same subset of the opposite sex is treated differently, as in *Phillips*. That is not the issue here. An employer who discriminates equally on the basis of sexual orientation or gender identity applies the same criterion to every affected *individual* regardless of sex. See Part I–A, supra.

III

A

Because the opinion of the Court flies a textualist flag, I have taken pains to show that it cannot be defended on textualist grounds. But even if the Court's textualist argument were stronger, that would not explain today's decision. Many Justices of this Court, both past and present, have not espoused or practiced a method of statutory interpretation that is limited to the analysis of statutory text. Instead, when there is ambiguity in the terms of a statute, they have found it appropriate to look to other evidence of "congressional intent," including legislative history.

So, why in these cases are congressional intent and the legislative history of Title VII totally ignored? Any assessment of congressional intent or legislative history seriously undermines the Court's interpretation.

B

As the Court explained in *General Elec. Co. v. Gilbert*, 429 U.S. 125, 143 (1976), the legislative history of Title VII's prohibition of sex discrimination is brief, but it is nevertheless revealing. The prohibition of sex discrimination was "added to Title VII at the last minute on the floor of the House of Representatives," *Meritor Savings Bank*, 477 U.S., at 63, by Representative Howard Smith, the Chairman of the Rules Committee. See 110 Cong. Rec. 2577 (1964). Representative Smith had been an ardent opponent of the civil rights bill, and it has been suggested that he added the prohibition against discrimination on the basis of "sex" as a poison pill. See, e.g., *Ulane v. Eastern Airlines, Inc.*, 742 F.2d 1081, 1085 (CA7 1984). On this theory, Representative Smith thought that prohibiting employment discrimination against women would be unacceptable to Members who might have otherwise voted in favor of the bill and that the addition of this prohibition might bring about the bill's defeat. But if Representative Smith had been looking for a poison pill, prohibiting discrimination on the basis of sexual orientation or gender identity would have been far more potent. However, neither Representative Smith nor any other Member said one word about the possibility that the prohibition of sex discrimination might have that meaning. Instead, all the debate concerned discrimination on the basis of biological sex. See 110 Cong. Rec. 2577–2584.

Representative Smith's motivations are contested, 883 F. 3d, at 139–140 (Lynch, J., dissenting), but whatever they were, the meaning of *the adoption of the prohibition* of sex discrimination is clear. It was no accident. It grew out of "a long history of women's rights advocacy that had increasingly been gaining mainstream recognition and acceptance," and it marked a landmark achievement in the path toward fully equal rights for women. Id., at 140. "Discrimination against gay women and men, by contrast, was not on the table for public debate . . . [i]n those dark, pre-Stonewall days." Ibid.

For those who regard congressional intent as the touchstone of statutory interpretation, the message of Title VII's legislative history cannot be missed.

C

Post-enactment events only clarify what was apparent when Title VII was enacted. As noted, bills to add "sexual orientation" to Title VII's list of prohibited grounds were introduced in every Congress beginning in 1975, see supra, at 2, and two such bills were before Congress in 1991 when it made major changes in Title VII. At that time, the three Courts of Appeals to reach the issue had held that Title VII does not prohibit discrimination because of sexual orientation, two other Circuits had endorsed that interpretation in dicta, and no Court of Appeals had held otherwise. Similarly, the three Circuits to address the application of Title VII to transgender persons had all rejected the argument that it covered discrimination on this basis. These were also the positions of the EEOC. In enacting substantial changes to Title VII, the 1991 Congress abrogated numerous judicial decisions with which it disagreed. If it also disagreed with the decisions regarding sexual orientation and transgender discrimination, it could have easily overruled those as well, but it did not do so.

After 1991, six other Courts of Appeals reached the issue of sexual orientation discrimination, and until 2017, every single Court of Appeals decision understood Title VII's prohibition of "discrimination because of sex" to mean discrimination because of biological sex. . . . Similarly, the other Circuit to formally address whether Title VII applies to claims of discrimination based on transgender status had also rejected the argument, creating unanimous consensus prior to the Sixth Circuit's decision below. See *Etsitty v. Utah Transit Authority*, 502 F.3d 1215, 1220–1221 (CA10 2007).

The Court observes that "[t]he people are entitled to rely on the law as written, without fearing that courts might disregard its plain terms," *ante*, at 24, but it has no qualms about disregarding over 50 years of uniform judicial interpretation of Title VII's plain text. Rather, the Court makes the jaw-dropping statement that its decision exemplifies "judicial humility." *Ante*, at 31. Is it humble to maintain, not only that Congress did not understand the terms it enacted in 1964, but that all the Circuit Judges on all the pre-2017 cases could not see what the phrase discrimination "because of sex" really means? If today's decision is humble, it is sobering to imagine what the Court might do if it decided to be bold.

IV

What the Court has done today—interpreting discrimination because of "sex" to encompass discrimination because of sexual orientation or gender identity—is virtually certain to have far-reaching consequences. Over 100 federal statutes prohibit discrimination because of sex. See Appendix C, infra; *e.g.*, 20 U. S. C. §1681(a) (Title IX); 42 U. S. C. §3631 (Fair Housing Act); 15 U. S. C. 1691(a)(1) (Equal Credit Opportunity Act). The briefs in these cases have called to our attention the potential effects that the Court's reasoning may have under some of these laws, but the Court waves those considerations aside. As to Title VII itself, the Court dismisses questions about "bathrooms, locker rooms, or anything else of the kind." *Ante*, at 31. And it declines to say anything about other statutes whose terms mirror Title VII's.

The Court's brusque refusal to consider the consequences of its reasoning is irresponsible. If the Court had allowed the legislative process to take its course, Congress would have had the opportunity to consider competing interests and might have found a way of accommodating at least some of them. In addition, Congress might have crafted special rules for some of the relevant statutes. But by intervening and proclaiming categorically that employment discrimination based on sexual orientation or gender identity is simply a form of discrimination because of sex, the Court has greatly impeded—and perhaps effectively ended—any chance of a bargained legislative resolution. Before issuing today's radical decision, the Court should have given some thought to where its decision would lead.

As the briefing in these cases has warned, the position that the Court now adopts will threaten freedom of religion, freedom of speech, and personal privacy and safety. No one should think that the Court's decision represents an unalloyed victory for individual liberty.

I will briefly note some of the potential consequences of the Court's decision, but I do not claim to provide a comprehensive survey or to suggest how any of these issues should necessarily play out under the Court's reasoning.

"[B]athrooms, locker rooms, [and other things] of [that] kind." The Court may wish to avoid this subject, but it is a matter of concern to many people who are reticent about disrobing or using toilet facilities in the presence of individuals whom they regard as members of the opposite sex. For some, this may simply be a question of modesty, but for others, there is more at stake. For women who have been victimized by sexual assault or abuse, the experience of seeing an unclothed person with the anatomy of a male in a confined and sensitive location such as a bathroom or locker room can cause serious psychological harm.

Under the Court's decision, however, transgender persons will be able to argue that they are entitled to use a bathroom or locker room that is reserved for persons of the sex with which they identify, and while the Court does not define what it means by a transgender person, the term may apply to individuals who are "gender fluid," that is, individuals whose gender identity is mixed or changes over time. Thus, a person who has not undertaken any physical transitioning may claim the right to use the bathroom or locker room assigned to the sex with which the individual identifies at that particular time. The Court provides no clue why a transgender person's claim to such bathroom or locker room access might not succeed.

A similar issue has arisen under Title IX, which prohibits sex discrimination by any elementary or secondary school and any college or university that receives federal financial assistance. In 2016, a Department of Justice advisory warned that barring a student from a bathroom assigned to individuals of the gender with which the student identifies constitutes unlawful sex discrimination, and some lower court decisions have agreed....

Women's sports. Another issue that may come up under both Title VII and Title IX is the right of a transgender individual to participate on a sports team or in an athletic competition previously reserved for members of one biological sex. This issue has already arisen under Title IX, where it threatens to undermine one of that law's major achievements, giving young women an equal opportunity to participate in sports. The effect of the Court's reasoning may be to force young women to compete against students who have a very significant biological advantage, including students who have the size and strength of a male but identify as female and students who are taking male hormones in order to transition from female to male. See, e.g., *Complaint in Soule v. Connecticut Assn. of Schools*, No. 3:20–cv–00201 (D Conn., Apr. 17, 2020) (challenging Connecticut policy allowing transgender students to compete in girls' high school sports); Complaint in *Hecox v. Little*, No. 1:20–cv–00184 (D Idaho, Apr. 15, 2020) (challenging state law that bars transgender students from participating in school sports in accordance with gender identity). Students in these latter categories have found success in athletic competitions reserved for females.

The logic of the Court's decision could even affect professional sports. Under the Court's holding that Title VII prohibits employment discrimination because of transgender status, an athlete who has the physique of a man but identifies as a woman could claim the right to play on a women's professional sports team. The owners of the team might try to claim that biological sex is a bona fide occupational qualification (BFOQ) under 42 U. S. C. §2000e–2(e), but the BFOQ exception has been read very narrowly. See *Dothard v. Rawlinson*, 433 U.S. 321, 334 (1977).

Housing. The Court's decision may lead to Title IX cases against any college that resists assigning students of the opposite biological sex as roommates. A provision of Title IX, 20 U. S. C. §1686, allows schools to maintain "separate living facilities for the different sexes," but it may be argued that a student's "sex" is the gender with which the student identifies. Similar claims may be brought under the Fair Housing Act. See 42 U. S. C. §3604.

Employment by religious organizations. Briefs filed by a wide range of religious groups—Christian, Jewish, and Muslim—express deep concern that the position now adopted by the Court "will trigger open conflict with faith-based employment practices of numerous churches, synagogues, mosques, and other religious institutions." They argue that "[r]eligious organizations need employees who actually live the faith," and that compelling a religious organization to employ individuals whose conduct flouts the tenets of the organization's faith forces the group to communicate an objectionable message.

This problem is perhaps most acute when it comes to the employment of teachers. A school's standards for its faculty "communicate a particular way of life to its students," and a "violation by the faculty of those precepts" may undermine the school's "moral teaching." Thus, if a religious school teaches that sex outside marriage and sex reassignment procedures are immoral, the message may be lost if the school employs a teacher who is in a same-sex relationship or has undergone or is undergoing sex reassignment. Yet today's decision may lead to Title VII claims by such teachers and applicants for employment.

At least some teachers and applicants for teaching positions may be blocked from recovering on such claims by the "ministerial exception" recognized in *Hosanna-Tabor Evangelical Lutheran Church and School v. EEOC*, 565 U.S. 171 (2012). Two cases now pending before the Court present the question whether teachers who provide religious instruction can be considered to be "ministers." But even if teachers with those responsibilities qualify, what about other very visible school employees who may not qualify for the ministerial exception? Provisions of Title VII provide exemptions for certain religious organizations and schools "with respect to the employment of individuals of a particular religion to perform work connected with the carrying on" of the "activities" of the organization or school, 42 U. S. C. §2000e–1(a); see also §2000e–2(e)(2), but the scope of these provisions is disputed, and as interpreted by some lower courts, they provide only narrow protection.

Healthcare. Healthcare benefits may emerge as an intense battleground under the Court's holding. Transgender employees have brought suit under Title VII to challenge employer-provided health insurance plans that do not cover costly sex reassignment surgery. Similar claims have been brought under the Affordable Care Act (ACA), which broadly prohibits sex discrimination in the provision of healthcare.

Such claims present difficult religious liberty issues because some employers and healthcare providers have strong religious objections to sex reassignment procedures, and therefore requiring them to pay for or to perform these procedures will have a severe impact on their ability to honor their deeply held religious beliefs.

Freedom of speech. The Court's decision may even affect the way employers address their employees and the way teachers and school officials address students. Under established English usage, two sets of sex-specific singular personal pronouns are used to refer to someone in the third person (he, him, and his for males; she, her, and hers for females). But several different sets of gender-neutral pronouns have now been created and are preferred by some individuals who do not identify as falling into either of the two traditional categories. Some jurisdictions, such as New York City, have ordinances making the failure to use an individual's preferred pronoun a punishable offense, and some colleges have similar rules. After today's decision, plaintiffs may claim that the failure to use their preferred pronoun violates one of the federal laws prohibiting sex discrimination. See *Prescott v. Rady Children's Hospital San Diego*, 265 F. Supp. 3d 1090, 1098–1100 (SD Cal. 2017) (hospital staff's refusal to use preferred pronoun violates ACA).

The Court's decision may also pressure employers to suppress any statements by employees expressing disapproval of same-sex relationships and sex reassignment procedures. Employers are already imposing such restrictions voluntarily, and after today's decisions employers will fear that allowing employees to express their religious views on these subjects may give rise to Title VII harassment claims.

Constitutional claims. Finally, despite the important differences between the Fourteenth Amendment and Title VII, the Court's decision may exert a gravitational pull in constitutional cases. Under our precedents, the Equal Protection Clause prohibits sex-based discrimination unless a "heightened" standard of review is met.... By equating discrimination because of sexual orientation or gender identity with discrimination because of sex, the Court's decision will be cited as a ground for subjecting all three forms of discrimination to the same exacting standard of review.

Under this logic, today's decision may have effects that extend well beyond the domain of federal anti- discrimination statutes. This potential is illustrated by pending and recent lower court cases in which transgender individuals have challenged a variety of federal, state, and local laws and policies on constitutional grounds.... Although the Court does not want to think about the consequences of its decision, we will not be able to avoid those issues for long. The entire Federal Judiciary will be mired for years in disputes about the reach of the Court's reasoning.

* * *

The updating desire to which the Court succumbs no doubt arises from humane and generous impulses. Today, many Americans know individuals who are gay, lesbian, or transgender and want them to be treated with the dignity, consideration, and fairness that everyone deserves. But the authority of this Court is limited to saying what the law *is*.

The Court itself recognizes this:

"The place to make new legislation ... lies in Congress. When it comes to statutory interpretation, our role is limited to applying the law's demands as faithfully as we can in the cases that come before us." *Ante*, at 31.

It is easy to utter such words. If only the Court would live by them.

I respectfully dissent.

Glossary

homosexual: characterized by romantic or sexual attraction to a person of one's own sex

legislative intent: the presumed or apparent goals of legislators at the time they passed a law

Title VII: a section of the Civil Rights Act of 1964 that outlaws discrimination against an employee based on race, color, religion, sex, or national origin

transgender: referring to a person whose gender identity differs from the one they were assigned at birth

Dobbs v. Jackson Women's Health Organization

Date
2022

Author
Samuel Alito

Vote
6–3

Citation
597 U.S. _

Significance
Held that the U.S. Constitution does not provide a right to abortion, overturning the court's previous decision *Roe v. Wade* (1973)

Overview

The Supreme Court's decision in 1973's *Roe v. Wade* proved to be one of its most contentious in the modern era. Reflecting the influence of the sexual revolution and the women's rights movement, *Roe* decriminalized abortion across the nation and protected the right to access abortion legally in all fifty states, most of which banned abortion except under specific circumstances. The Court based its decision largely on its interpretation of the Fourteenth Amendment, specifically its guarantee of individual privacy, which extended to the right to an abortion up to the point of fetal viability at roughly twenty-four weeks. But the decision offered no explicit protections for access to abortion, only the right to one, a limitation some states exploited by passing laws that made abortion extremely difficult to obtain.

While a majority of Americans came to accept the right to an abortion as one protected by the Constitution, opponents of *Roe* devised various strategies intended to bring about its overturning. One of the most effective proved to be the appointment of anti-abortion judges and justices across the nation, including on the Supreme Court. By June 2022, when the Court was prepared to revisit *Roe* and determine its constitutionality, six of the nine justices were consistently conservative in their rulings, which indicated to anti-abortion activists that the moment had arrived.

The case that resulted in the overturning of *Roe*, *Dobbs v. Jackson Women's Health Organization*, centered on a challenge to a ban on most abortions at fifteen weeks of pregnancy that was passed by the Mississippi legislature in 2018. The law banned abortion roughly two months earlier in gestation than *Roe* and subsequent decisions allowed, but it failed to go into effect due to a swift legal challenge from the Jackson Women's Health Organization, the state's only abortion clinic. In response to the challenge, a federal appellate court blocked the new law's enforcement on the grounds that *Roe v. Wade* did not allow states to ban abortions before viability, and the state could not prove a fetus's viability at fifteen weeks. Mississippi waited until the fall of 2020 to appeal the lower court's ruling to the U.S. Supreme Court, which agreed in May 2021 to hear the case. By this time, Justice Anthony M. Kennedy, a moderate supporter of abortion rights, had retired, and

Justice Ruth Bader Ginsburg, a staunch defender of abortion rights, had passed away. Their replacements, Brett Kavanaugh and Amy Coney Barrett, joined four other members of the Court in deciding that the Constitution failed to support the viability of *Roe*, and it was subsequently repealed. Justices Stephen Breyer, Elena Kagan, and Sonia Sotomayor wrote a joint dissenting opinion.

Context

When the Supreme Court heard the case of *Dobbs v. Jackson Women's Health Organization* in June 2022, it was the culmination of decades of turmoil and controversy that emerged following 1973's *Roe v. Wade*, one of the most controversial cases to be argued before the court. Abortion generated little controversy in the United States prior to 1840; they were relatively easy, if often risky, to obtain prior to the fourth to sixth month of pregnancy, after which point abortion was considered a misdemeanor. This changed by the mid-nineteenth century when an anti-abortion campaign emerged, initially led by physicians seeking to improve the reputation of their profession by denying that women knew what was best for their health. By the start of the twentieth century, nearly every state legislature had passed laws prohibiting abortion, with some exceptions, at any phase of a pregnancy. This remained the state of things until the mid-1960s and the start of the sexual revolution, a period of women reclaiming control over their bodies and challenging the decisions made by doctors on their behalf. More and more Americans insisted that adjustments be made to state laws to make an abortion easier to obtain, including in cases of rape and fetuses with extreme deformities. The rise of the feminist movement by the end of the 1960s provided additional momentum to the call for the reform of abortion laws, as women argued that they could not be considered full Americans until they regulated their own reproduction. States gradually changed their laws, starting with Colorado and California in 1967 and New York three years later.

As one state legislature after another reformed their abortion laws to make the procedure more accessible, the anti-abortion movement began to take shape. Its first members were primarily Catholics, supported by some Protestant Christians, who founded the National Right to Life Committee in 1967 and several other anti-abortion groups. The movement then sought to present itself as more secular to avoid alienating those who saw it as imposing Catholic morals onto the entirety of the United States. Preliminary efforts by these activists helped to dissuade some states from altering their abortion laws, but the *Roe v. Wade* decision of 1973, which legalized abortion across the entire country, completely changed the debate over abortion. Anti-abortion groups began to focus their efforts at the national, rather than state, level, advocating for a constitutional amendment banning abortion. They also sought to call attention to how abortion affected the fetus, shifting focus away from the mother, by distributing graphic images of aborted fetuses in pamphlets, books, and posters.

Efforts to give greater humanity to unborn fetuses turned out to be an effective strategy that helped the anti-abortion movement to acquire more members throughout the 1970s and 1980s, particularly members of the growing evangelical Christian movement, some of whom formed their own organizations, many of which proved far more confrontational than those that came before. These new groups disdained any chance for legislative reform and instead emphasized dramatic tactics, the goal being to stop abortion by any and all means. The most visible of these radical groups was Operation Rescue, which staged protests and blockades, known as "rescues," in front of abortion clinics to dissuade women from getting an abortion. Some took a more violent approach to their activism during the 1980s and 1990s, assaulting, threatening, and occasionally killing individuals associated with providing abortions. The anti-abortion movement also advanced messages that abortion was harmful to the women who had them, potentially harming their bodies and leaving emotional scars comparable to PTSD.

The more the abortion issue grabbed headlines and compelled Americans to choose a side, the more it came to be politicized by both of the major parties. The Republicans, in making themselves the party emphasizing morality and forging an alliance with evangelical Christians, took up the elimination of abortion as a prominent part of their party platform, although most Republican leaders, including Presidents Ronald Reagan and George H. W. Bush, showed little enthusiasm for endorsing legislation that would strike down *Roe*. At the same time, Democrats em-

Protesters outside of the Supreme Court after the Dobbs *announcement*
(Wikimedia Commons)

braced their identity as the party defending what many saw, by the 1980s, as a fundamental right for American women. Both sides recognized the importance of appointing judges to the Supreme Court who would possess the power to either preserve the *Roe* decision or eliminate it. In 1992, the Supreme Court, in the *Planned Parenthood of Southeastern Pennsylvania v. Casey* ruling, made it less difficult for state legislatures to pass laws restricting abortion.

The election of Donald Trump as president in 2016 set into motion an increased zealousness to have *Roe* overturned by anti-abortion activists. Because he made statements critical of abortion while on the campaign trail, anti-abortion supporters grasped that Trump would, if given the opportunity, nominate judges to the Supreme Court inclined to strike down *Roe v. Wade*. He ultimately nominated three new judges endorsed by a number of conservative organizations: Neil Gorsuch, Brett Kavanaugh, and Amy Coney Barrett. Their appointments resulted in the Court being dominated by a bloc of five reliably conservative justices, which was just what the anti-abortion movement had been hoping for in the preceding decades.

About the Author

Nominated by President George W. Bush in 2005 to take the place of retiring justice Sandra Day O'Connor, Samuel Alito has proven to be a reliably conservative figure on the Supreme Court. Born in 1950 in Trenton, New Jersey, to parents who were teachers, his father being an Italian immigrant, Alito attended Steinert High School, where he showed an early an early interest in politics and participated on the debate team.

Upon graduating at the top of his class, Alito went to Princeton University, from which he earned degrees in history and political science, and then Yale Law School in 1975, hoping to fulfill his ambition of becoming a Supreme Court justice. He edited the *Yale Law Journal* while pursuing his legal studies and then in 1977, two years after graduating law school, became a clerk under Leonard Garth, a judge in the U.S. Court of Appeals for the Third Circuit. He served as an assistant to the U.S. solicitor general and then U.S. attorney for the District of New Jersey before being nominated to the U.S. Court of Appeals for the Third Circuit by President George H. W. Bush in 1990.

As a judge, he generally adhered to his conservative principles, but he handed down his rulings with consideration for the unique specifics of each case. Following his appointment to the bench in 2006, he continued to approach each case as distinctive, often drawing upon a deep sense of empathy while consistently agreeing with his fellow conservative justices. He voted in favor of maintaining the federal Partial-Birth Abortion Ban Act of 2003 in *Gonzales v. Carhart* (2007) and supported the concept of the Second Amendment protecting an individual right to own firearms in *District of Columbia v. Heller* (2008). He wrote the majority opinion in *Dobbs v. Jackson Women's Health Organization* (2022), which struck down the landmark decision from 1973, *Roe v. Wade*, which guaranteed women's access to abortion.

Explanation and Analysis of the Document

Alito recognizes the complexity and divisiveness of the abortion debate in the opening paragraph, with a wide range of opinions as to when life begins. The legality of abortion was left to be decided by each state until the 1973 *Roe v. Wade* decision, in which the Supreme Court, despite the Constitution making no reference to abortion, generally allowed for nationwide access to abortion until the end of the second trimester. Alito states that the Court failed to make clear why it was restricting what it recognized as states' concern in protecting "potential life." *Roe* "imposed the same highly restrictive regime on the entire Nation, and it effectively struck down the abortion laws of every single State" and set into motion five decades of political acrimony.

Background on the *Roe* and *Casey* Decisions

The 1992 case *Planned Parenthood of Southeastern Pa. v. Casey* revisited *Roe* and exposed divisions within the Supreme Court over its constitutionality. The case overturned *Roe*'s trimester scheme and introduced a new rule under which states were prohibited from adopting any regulation that imposed an "undue burden" on a woman's right to an abortion without clarifying its meaning. The case also did little to reduce existing tensions over the abortion debate.

Alito begins consideration of the case at hand, which hinges on the state of Mississippi requesting the Supreme Court to uphold the constitutionality of a law that typically blocks an abortion fifteen weeks after conception, several weeks before the fetus is generally viewed as "viable" outside the mother. Mississippi argued that the Court should reconsider the constitutionality of the *Roe* and *Casey* decisions, overturning both and allowing states to regulate abortion according to the wishes of their citizens. The respondents on the other side requested that *Roe* and *Casey* be reaffirmed and to strike down Mississippi's law, which effectively overturns the two cases.

The opinion makes clear that *Roe* and *Casey* should be overruled based on the absence of any mention of abortion in the Constitution or explicit protection of the right to one. It rejects the arguments that link the right to an abortion to the due process clause of the Fourteenth Amendment, which guarantees some rights not stated in the Constitution that draw upon America's history and its traditions, as being inconsistent with the existing laws at the time of the amendment's adoption, when most states made abortion a crime. Alito condemns *Roe* as "egregiously wrong" with "exceptionally weak" reasoning from the start, and responsible for considerable damage in its aftermath.

The opinion assesses the content of Mississippi's Gestational Age Act, which prohibits abortion after fifteen weeks except in instances of medical emergency or severe fetal abnormality. On the same day of the act's enactment, the respondents, Jackson Women's Health Organization, an abortion clinic, and one of its physicians filed suit in federal district court, contending it restricted a constitutional right to abortion. The district court ruled in favor of the respondents, and the case went before the Supreme Court.

Alito delves into the constitutional history as it pertains to abortion, reiterating the Constitution's lack of "express reference to a right to obtain an abortion." He criticizes the looseness of the *Roe* decision's interpretation of the Constitution, which also makes no mention of a right to privacy, a tenet *Roe* relies upon heavily. Alito similarly dismisses *Casey*'s contention that the right to an abortion is a part of the "liberty" guaranteed by the due process clause of the Fourteenth Amendment.

The Question of Abortion's Place in America's History and Its Traditions

The opinion examines the right to an abortion being guaranteed due to its roots in American history and tradition and finds it lacking. It also identifies the amorphous nature of the term "liberty" in considering its appearance in the Fourteenth Amendment, cautioning it being used too freely by the Court to justify rights not guaranteed by the Constitution. Alito scoffs at the notion of the Fourteenth Amendment protecting the right to an abortion. He also points out the relativeness newness of support for abortion as a constitutional right; throughout the majority of its history, the United States was a nation where abortion was a criminal offense in nearly all the states. This was the case at the time of the Fourteenth Amendment's adoption, a fact overlooked by those who decided both *Roe* and *Casey*.

Alito covers in detail the overwhelming perception of abortion as an abomination and a crime throughout the centuries, during the colonial era and well after, to dismiss the notion of it being either a legal right or allowed by common law, or deeply rooted in American history or tradition. This was reflected in the preponderance of the states prohibiting abortion except in cases involving the life of the mother at the time of the *Roe* decision. Many of these states continued to regulate abortion more rigorously than *Roe* called for. And Alito argues that the states have different views when it comes to measuring the interests of a woman seeking an abortion against those of an unborn child; some want even greater access while others favor less. The opinion argues that women not wishing to raise the children they bear have options to put them up for adoption.

Alito rejects the dissenters' view that a long-standing foundation for abortion rights ever existed, which fundamentally undermines its position. Abortion was only allowed under very specific circumstances in most states well before the *Roe* decision. Alito takes issue with the dissenters' overwhelming concern for the mother and relatively little consideration for "a State's interest in protecting prenatal life." He argues that the many flaws in the dissenters' arguments place *Roe* in the category of "overruled decisions that wrongly removed an issue from the people and the democratic process."

The Viability Question

A fundamental weakness in the *Roe* decision identified by Alito is its resemblance to a statute or regulation. The Court decided in *Roe* to divide pregnancy into three trimesters and "imposed special rules for each" based on the health of the mother at each stage, only taking the life of the unborn child into consideration at the start of the trimester. The Court refrained from explaining how it arrived at the rules, nor did it devote much of its deliberation to how the states regulated abortion in the past. It instead based its decision largely on a constitutional "right of personal privacy" without g overnmental interference.

Alito then addresses the question of the viability of a fetus, which, thanks to medical advancements, had changed since the *Roe* decision from twenty-eighth to the twenty-third or twenty-fourth week of gestation, potentially deepening a state's commitment to protecting the fetus. Given the challenges of determining the viability of a fetus, Alito further rejects the Court's ability to make such determinations, which was further underscored in the *Casey* decision, which did little to clarify what constituted viability.

The opinion addresses the question of how the right to abortion impacts society and the lives of women, a topic that Alito contends the Court lacks the authority or ability to adjudicate effectively. Returning the abortion issue to state legislatures would enable women on both sides of the debate to engage in the legislative process as voters and candidates for elected office. Alito notes that women tend to be more politically engaged than their male counterparts and thus more likely to make an impact.

Impact

The *Dobbs* decision resonated powerfully across the United States and around the world. For supporters of abortion rights, the decision represented the Supreme Court striking down a fundamental right and threatening to turn women into second-class citizens. Opponents of abortion heralded the decision as a triumph decades in the making that would be the first of subsequent victories that would roll back all abortion laws.

The Supreme Court's elimination of the federal constitutional right to abortion enabled numerous states to impose restrictions on abortion or outlaw the practice altogether. More than half of the fifty states may very well choose the latter option in coming years or have already done so; before the *Dobbs* case went before the court, thirteen states passed "trigger bans" designed to ban abortion when *Roe* was overturned.

Critics of the decision warn that its impact will be felt most keenly by some the nation's most vulnerable populations, including rural inhabitants, African Americans, Indigenous Americans, individuals with disabilities, and those living in poverty. For members of such groups, having access to abortion was often disproportionately challenging when *Roe* was still in effect. But numerous state bans going into effect and clinics closing their doors will necessitate traveling to other states where abortion is still legal and may prove a financial and logistical challenge that many will be unable to overcome.

The *Dobbs* decision also highlighted concerns that new bans and restrictions on abortion will limit the availability of reproductive healthcare to pregnant women, even those not seeking an abortion. Fears of being prosecuted have resulted in medical professionals being unable or unwilling to provide fertility care or treatment for pregnancy complications, including miscarriages or pregnancies that impact the health of the mother.

A final round of criticism regarding *Dobbs* concerns its possible ramifications on other constitutional rights. The justices' assertion that *Roe* overstepped the appropriate boundaries of federalism has been seen as the possible basis for eliminating laws that protect one's right to marry someone of a different race or the same sex, access to contraception, and other basic rights.

Questions for Further Study

1. How did the anti-abortion movement's strategy evolve in the aftermath of the Court's decision in *Roe v. Wade*?

2. What aspects of the *Dobbs* decision will likely impact certain groups of American women more profoundly than others?

3. How does Alito argue that abortion rights are inconsistent with the history and traditions of the United States?

4. In what ways does the abortion debate reflect the tensions that have long existed within the United States' federal system of government?

Further Reading

Books

Balkin, Jack M. *What Roe v. Wade Should Have Said: The Nation's Top Legal Experts Rewrite America's Most Controversial Decision.* New York: NYU Press, 2023.

Ginsburg, Faye D. *Contested Lives: The Abortion Debate in an American Community.* Berkeley: University of California Press, 1998.

Reagan, Leslie J. *When Abortion Was a Crime: Women, Medicine, and Law in the United States, 1867–1973.* Berkeley: University of California Press, 2022.

Risen, James, and Judy L. Thomas. *Wrath of Angels: The American Abortion War.* New York: Basic Books, 1998.

Schoen, Johanna. *Abortion after Roe.* Chapel Hill: University of North Carolina Press, 2015.

Williams, Daniel K. *Defenders of the Unborn: The Pro-Life Movement Before Roe v. Wade.* Oxford, UK: Oxford University Press, 2016.

Ziegler, Mary. *Abortion and the Law in America: Roe v. Wade to the Present.* Cambridge, UK: Cambridge University Press, 2020.

Ziegler, Mary. *After Roe: The Lost History of the Abortion Debate.* Cambridge, MA: Harvard University Press, 2015.

—Commentary by Michael Martin Carver

Dobbs v. Jackson Women's Health Organization

Document Text

Justice Alito delivered the opinion of the Court

Abortion presents a profound moral issue on which Americans hold sharply conflicting views. Some believe fervently that a human person comes into being at conception and that abortion ends an innocent life. Others feel just as strongly that any regulation of abortion invades a woman's right to control her own body and prevents women from achieving full equality. Still others in a third group think that abortion should be allowed under some but not all circumstances, and those within this group hold a variety of views about the particular restrictions that should be imposed.

For the first 185 years after the adoption of the Constitution, each State was permitted to address this issue in accordance with the views of its citizens. Then, in 1973, this Court decided *Roe* v. *Wade*, 410 U.S. 113. Even though the Constitution makes no mention of abortion, the Court held that it confers a broad right to obtain one. It did not claim that American law or the common law had ever recognized such a right, and its survey of history ranged from the constitutionally irrelevant (*e.g.*, its discussion of abortion in antiquity) to the plainly incorrect (*e.g.*, its assertion that abortion was probably never a crime under the common law). After cataloging a wealth of other information having no bearing on the meaning of the Constitution, the opinion concluded with a numbered set of rules much like those that might be found in a statute enacted by a legislature.

Under this scheme, each trimester of pregnancy was regulated differently, but the most critical line was drawn at roughly the end of the second trimester, which, at the time, corresponded to the point at which a fetus was thought to achieve "viability," *i.e.*, the ability to survive outside the womb. Although the Court acknowledged that States had a legitimate interest in protecting "potential life," it found that this interest could not justify any restriction on pre-viability abortions. The Court did not explain the basis for this line, and even abortion supporters have found it hard to defend *Roe*'s reasoning. One prominent constitutional scholar wrote that he "would vote for a statute very much like the one the Court end[ed] up drafting" if he were "a legislator," but his assessment of *Roe* was memorable and brutal: *Roe* was "not constitutional law" at all and gave "almost no sense of an obligation to try to be."

At the time of *Roe*, 30 States still prohibited abortion at all stages. In the years prior to that decision, about a third of the States had liberalized their laws, but *Roe* abruptly ended that political process. It imposed the same highly restrictive regime on the entire Nation, and it effectively struck down the abortion laws of every single State. As Justice Byron White aptly put it in his dissent, the decision represented the "exercise of raw judicial power," 410 U. S., at 222, and it sparked a national controversy that has embittered our political culture for a half century.

Eventually, in *Planned Parenthood of Southeastern Pa.* v. *Casey*, 505 U.S. 833 (1992), the Court revisited *Roe*, but the Members of the Court split three ways. Two Justices expressed no desire to change *Roe* in any way. Four others wanted to overrule the decision in its entirety. And the three remaining Justices, who jointly signed the controlling opinion, took a third position. Their opinion did not endorse *Roe*'s reasoning, and it even hinted that one or more of its authors might have "reservations" about whether the Constitution protects a right to abortion. But the opinion concluded that *stare decisis*, which calls for prior decisions to be followed in most instances, required adherence to what it called *Roe*'s "central holding"—that a State may not constitutionally protect fetal life before "viability"—even if that holding was wrong. Anything less, the opinion claimed, would undermine respect for this Court and the rule of law.

Paradoxically, the judgment in *Casey* did a fair amount of overruling. Several important abortion decisions were overruled *in toto*, and *Roe* itself was overruled in part. *Casey* threw out *Roe*'s trimester scheme and substituted a new rule of uncertain origin under which States were forbidden to adopt any regulation that imposed an "undue burden" on a woman's right to have an abortion. The decision provided no clear guidance about the difference between a "due" and an "undue" burden. But the three Justices who authored the controlling opinion "call[ed] the contending sides of a national controversy to end their national division" by treating the Court's decision as the final settlement of the question of the constitutional right to abortion.

As has become increasingly apparent in the intervening years, *Casey* did not achieve that goal. Americans continue to hold passionate and widely divergent views on abortion, and state legislatures have acted accordingly. Some have recently enacted laws allowing abortion, with few restrictions, at all stages of pregnancy. Others have tightly restricted abortion beginning well before viability. And in this case, 26 States have expressly asked this Court to overrule *Roe* and *Casey* and allow the States to regulate or prohibit pre-viability abortions.

Before us now is one such state law. The State of Mississippi asks us to uphold the constitutionality of a law that generally prohibits an abortion after the 15th week of pregnancy—several weeks before the point at which a fetus is now regarded as "viable" outside the womb. In defending this law, the State's primary argument is that we should reconsider and overrule *Roe* and *Casey* and once again allow each State to regulate abortion as its citizens wish. On the other side, respondents and the Solicitor General ask us to reaffirm *Roe* and *Casey*, and they contend that the Mississippi law cannot stand if we do so. Allowing Mississippi to prohibit abortions after 15 weeks of pregnancy, they argue, "would be no different than overruling *Casey* and *Roe* entirely." Brief for Respondents 43. They contend that "no half-measures" are available and that we must either reaffirm or overrule *Roe* and *Casey*. Brief for Respondents 50.

We hold that *Roe* and *Casey* must be overruled. The Constitution makes no reference to abortion, and no such right is implicitly protected by any constitutional provision, including the one on which the defenders of *Roe* and *Casey* now chiefly rely—the Due Process Clause of the Fourteenth Amendment. That provision has been held to guarantee some rights that are not mentioned in the Constitution, but any such right must be "deeply rooted in this Nation's history and tradition" and "implicit in the concept of ordered liberty." *Washington v. Glucksberg*, 521 U.S. 702, 721 (1997) (internal quotation marks omitted).

The right to abortion does not fall within this category. Until the latter part of the 20th century, such a right was entirely unknown in American law. Indeed, when the Fourteenth Amendment was adopted, three quarters of the States made abortion a crime at all stages of pregnancy. The abortion right is also critically different from any other right that this Court has held to fall within the Fourteenth Amendment's protection of "liberty." *Roe*'s defenders characterize the abortion right as similar to the rights recognized in past decisions involving matters such as intimate sexual relations, contraception, and marriage, but abortion is fundamentally different, as both *Roe* and *Casey* acknowledged, because it destroys what those decisions called "fetal life" and what the law now before us describes as an "unborn human being."

Stare decisis, the doctrine on which *Casey*'s controlling opinion was based, does not compel unending adherence to *Roe*'s abuse of judicial authority. *Roe* was egregiously wrong from the start. Its reasoning was exceptionally weak, and the decision has had damaging consequences. And far from bringing about a national settlement of the abortion issue, *Roe* and *Casey* have enflamed debate and deepened division.

It is time to heed the Constitution and return the issue of abortion to the people's elected representatives. "The permissibility of abortion, and the limitations, upon it, are to be resolved like most important questions in our democracy: by citizens trying to persuade one another and then voting." *Casey*, 505 U. S., at 979 (Scalia, J., concurring in judgment in part and dissenting in part). That is what the Constitution and the rule of law demand.

I

The law at issue in this case, Mississippi's Gestational Age Act, see Miss. Code Ann. §41–41–191 (2018), contains this central provision: "Except in a medical emergency or in the case of a severe fetal abnormality, a person shall not intentionally or knowingly perform . . . or induce an abortion of an unborn human being if the probable gestational age of the unborn human being has been determined to be greater than fifteen (15) weeks." §4(b).

To support this Act, the legislature made a series of factual findings. It began by noting that, at the time of enactment, only six countries besides the United States "permit[ted] nontherapeutic or elective abortion-on-demand after the twentieth week of gestation." §2(a). The legislature then found that at 5 or 6 weeks' gestational age an "unborn human being's heart begins beating"; at 8 weeks the "unborn human being begins to move about in the womb"; at 9 weeks "all basic physiological functions are present"; at 10 weeks "vital organs begin to function," and "[h]air, fingernails, and toenails . . . begin to form"; at 11 weeks "an unborn human being's diaphragm is developing," and he or she may "move about freely in the womb"; and at 12 weeks the "unborn human being" has "taken on 'the human form' in all relevant respects." §2(b)(i) (quoting *Gonzales* v. *Carhart*, 550 U.S. 124, 160 (2007)). It found that most abortions after 15 weeks employ "dilation and evacuation procedures which involve the use of surgical instruments to crush and tear the unborn child," and it concluded that the "intentional commitment of such acts for nontherapeutic or elective reasons is a barbaric practice, dangerous for the maternal patient, and demeaning to the medical profession." §2(b)(i)(8).

Respondents are an abortion clinic, Jackson Women's Health Organization, and one of its doctors. On the day the Gestational Age Act was enacted, respondents filed suit in Federal District Court against various Mississippi officials, alleging that the Act violated this Court's precedents establishing a constitutional right to abortion. The District Court granted summary judgment in favor of respondents and permanently enjoined enforcement of the Act, reasoning that "viability marks the earliest point at which the State's interest in fetal life is constitutionally adequate to justify a legislative ban on nontherapeutic abortions" and that 15 weeks' gestational age is "prior to viability." *Jackson Women's Health Org.* v. *Currier*, 349 F. Supp. 3d 536, 539–540 (SD Miss. 2019) (internal quotation marks omitted). The Fifth Circuit affirmed. 945 F.3d 265 (2019).

We granted certiorari, 593 U. S. ___ (2021), to resolve the question whether "all pre-viability prohibitions on elective abortions are unconstitutional," Pet. for Cert. i. Petitioners' primary defense of the Mississippi Gestational Age Act is that *Roe* and *Casey* were wrongly decided and that "the Act is constitutional because it satisfies rational-basis review." Brief for Petitioners 49. Respondents answer that allowing Mississippi to ban pre-viability abortions "would be no different than overruling *Casey* and *Roe* entirely." Brief for Respondents 43. They tell us that "no half-measures" are available: We must either reaffirm or overrule *Roe* and *Casey*. Brief for Respondents 50.

II

We begin by considering the critical question whether the Constitution, properly understood, confers a right to obtain an abortion. Skipping over that question, the controlling opinion in *Casey* reaffirmed *Roe*'s "central holding" based solely on the doctrine of *stare decisis*, but as we will explain, proper application of *stare decisis* required an assessment of the strength of the grounds on which *Roe* was based. See *infra*, at 45–56.

We therefore turn to the question that the *Casey* plurality did not consider, and we address that question in three steps. First, we explain the standard that our cases have used in determining whether the Fourteenth Amendment's reference to "liberty" protects a particular right. Second, we examine whether the right at issue in this case is rooted in our Nation's history and tradition and whether it is an essential component of what we have described as "ordered liberty." Finally, we consider whether a right to obtain an abortion is part of a broader entrenched right that is supported by other precedents.

A

1

Constitutional analysis must begin with "the language of the instrument," *Gibbons* v. *Ogden*, 9 Wheat. 1, 186–189 (1824), which offers a "fixed standard" for ascertaining what our founding document means, 1 J. Story, Commentaries on the Constitution of the United States §399, p. 383 (1833). The Constitution makes no express reference to a right to obtain an abortion, and therefore those who claim that it protects such a right must show that the right is somehow implicit in the constitutional text.

Roe, however, was remarkably loose in its treatment of the constitutional text. It held that the abortion right, which is not mentioned in the Constitution, is part of a right to privacy, which is also not mentioned. See 410 U. S., at 152–153. And that privacy right, *Roe* observed, had been found to spring from no fewer than five different constitutional provisions—the First, Fourth, Fifth, Ninth, and Fourteenth Amendments. *Id.*, at 152.

The Court's discussion left open at least three ways in which some combination of these provisions could protect the abortion right. One possibility was that the right was "founded . . . in the Ninth Amendment's reservation of rights to the people." *Id.*, at 153. Another was that the right was rooted in the First, Fourth, or Fifth Amendment, or in some combination of those provisions, and that this right had been "incorporated" into the Due Process Clause of the Fourteenth Amendment just as many other Bill of Rights provisions had by then been incorporated. *Ibid*; see also *McDonald* v. *Chicago*, 561 U.S. 742, 763–766 (2010) (majority opinion) (discussing incorporation). And a third path was that the First, Fourth, and Fifth Amendments played no role and that the right was simply a component of the "liberty" protected by the Fourteenth Amendment's Due Process Clause. *Roe*, 410 U. S., at 153. *Roe* expressed the "feel[ing]" that the Fourteenth Amendment was the provision that did the work, but its message seemed to be that the abortion right could be found *somewhere* in the Constitution and that specifying its exact location was not of paramount importance. The *Casey* Court did not defend this unfocused analysis and instead grounded its decision solely on the theory that the right to obtain an abortion is part of the "liberty" protected by the Fourteenth Amendment's Due Process Clause.

We discuss this theory in depth below, but before doing so, we briefly address one additional constitutional provision that some of respondents' *amici* have now offered as yet another potential home for the abortion right: the Fourteenth Amendment's Equal Protection Clause. See Brief for United States as *Amicus Curiae* 24 (Brief for United States); see also Brief for Equal Protection Constitutional Law Scholars as *Amici Curiae*. Neither *Roe* nor *Casey* saw fit to invoke this theory, and it is squarely foreclosed by our precedents, which establish that a State's regulation of abortion is not a sex-based classification and is thus not subject to the "heightened scrutiny" that applies to such classifications. The regulation of a medical procedure that only one sex can undergo does not trigger heightened constitutional scrutiny unless the regulation is a "mere pretex[t] designed to effect an invidious discrimination against members of one sex or the other." *Geduldig* v. *Aiello*, 417 U.S. 484, 496, n. 20 (1974). And as the Court has stated, the "goal of preventing abortion" does not constitute "invidiously discriminatory animus" against women. *Bray* v. *Alexandria Women's Health Clinic*, 506 U.S. 263, 273–274 (1993) (internal quotation marks omitted). Accordingly, laws regulating or prohibiting abortion are not subject to heightened scrutiny. Rather, they are governed by the same standard of review as other health and safety measures.

With this new theory addressed, we turn to *Casey's* bold assertion that the abortion right is an aspect of the "liberty" protected by the Due Process Clause of the Fourteenth Amendment. 505 U. S., at 846; Brief for Respondents 17; Brief for United States 21–22.

2

The underlying theory on which this argument rests— that the Fourteenth Amendment's Due Process Clause provides substantive, as well as procedural, protection for "liberty"—has long been controversial. But our decisions have held that the Due Process Clause protects two categories of substantive rights.

The first consists of rights guaranteed by the first eight Amendments. Those Amendments originally applied only to the Federal Government, *Barron ex rel. Tiernan* v. *Mayor of Baltimore*, 7 Pet. 243, 247–251 (1833) (opinion for the Court by Marshall, C. J.), but this Court has held that the Due Process Clause of the Fourteenth Amendment "incorporates" the great majority of those rights and thus makes them equally applicable to the States. See *McDonald*, 561 U. S., at 763–767, and nn. 12–13. The second category—which is the one in question here—comprises a select list of fundamental rights that are not mentioned anywhere in the Constitution.

In deciding whether a right falls into either of these categories, the Court has long asked whether the right is "deeply rooted in [our] history and tradition" and whether it is essential to our Nation's "scheme of ordered liberty." *Timbs* v. *Indiana*, 586 U. S. ___, ___ (2019) (slip op., at 3) (internal quotation marks omitted); *McDonald*, 561 U. S., at 764, 767 (internal quotation marks omitted); *Glucksberg*, 521 U. S., at 721 (internal quotation marks omitted). And in conducting this inquiry, we have engaged in a careful analysis of the history of the right at issue.

Justice Ginsburg's opinion for the Court in *Timbs* is a recent example. In concluding that the Eighth Amendment's protection against excessive fines is "fundamental to our scheme of ordered liberty" and "deeply rooted in this Nation's history and tradition," 586 U. S., at ___ (slip op., at 7) (internal quotation marks omitted), her opinion traced the right back to Magna Carta, Blackstone's Commentaries, and 35 of the 37 state constitutions in effect at the ratification of the Fourteenth Amendment. 586 U. S., at ___–___ (slip op., at 3–7).

A similar inquiry was undertaken in *McDonald*, which held that the Fourteenth Amendment protects the right to keep and bear arms. The lead opinion surveyed the origins of the Second Amendment, the debates in Congress about the adoption of the Fourteenth Amendment, the state constitutions in effect when that Amendment was ratified (at least 22 of the 37 States protected the right to keep and bear arms), federal laws enacted during the same period, and other relevant historical evidence. 561 U. S., at 767–777. Only then did the opinion conclude that "the Framers and ratifiers of the Fourteenth Amendment counted the right to keep and bear arms among those fundamental rights necessary to our system of ordered liberty." *Id.*, at 778; see also *id.*, at 822–850 (Thomas, J., concurring in part and concurring in judgment) (surveying history and reaching the same result under the Fourteenth Amendment's Privileges or Immunities Clause).

Timbs and *McDonald* concerned the question whether the Fourteenth Amendment protects rights that are expressly set out in the Bill of Rights, and it would be anomalous if similar historical support were not required when a putative right is not mentioned anywhere in the Constitution. Thus, in *Glucksberg*, which held that the Due Process Clause does not confer a right to assisted suicide, the Court surveyed more than 700 years of "Anglo-American common law tradition," 521 U. S., at 711, and made clear that a fundamental right must be "objectively, deeply rooted in this Nation's history and tradition," *id.*, at 720–721.

Historical inquiries of this nature are essential whenever we are asked to recognize a new component of the "liberty" protected by the Due Process Clause because the term "liberty" alone provides little guidance. "Liberty" is a capacious term. As Lincoln once said: "We all declare for Liberty; but in using the same word we do not all mean the same thing." In a well-known essay, Isaiah Berlin reported that "[h]istorians of ideas" had cataloged more than 200 different senses in which the term had been used.

In interpreting what is meant by the Fourteenth Amendment's reference to "liberty," we must guard against the natural human tendency to confuse what that Amendment protects with our own ardent views about the liberty that Americans should enjoy. That is why the Court has long been "reluctant" to recognize rights that are not mentioned in the Constitution. *Collins* v. *Harker Heights*, 503 U.S. 115, 125 (1992). "Substantive due process has at times been a treacherous field for this Court," *Moore* v. *East Cleveland*, 431 U.S. 494, 503 (1977) (plurality opinion), and it has sometimes led the Court to usurp authority that the Constitution entrusts to the people's elected representatives. See *Regents of Univ. of Mich.* v. *Ewing*, 474 U.S. 214, 225–226 (1985). As the Court cautioned in *Glucksberg*, "[w]e must . . . exercise the utmost care whenever we are asked to break new ground in this field, lest the liberty protected by the Due Process Clause be subtly transformed into the policy preferences of the Members of this Court." 521 U. S., at 720 (internal quotation marks and citation omitted).

On occasion, when the Court has ignored the "[a]ppropriate limits" imposed by "'respect for the teachings of history,'" *Moore*, 431 U. S., at 503 (plurality opinion), it has fallen into the freewheeling judicial policymaking that characterized discredited decisions such as *Lochner* v. *New York*, 198 U.S. 45 (1905). The Court must not fall prey to such an unprincipled approach. Instead, guided by the history and tradition that map the essential components of our Nation's concept of ordered liberty, we must ask what the *Fourteenth Amendment* means by the term "liberty." When we engage in that inquiry in the present case, the clear answer is that the Fourteenth Amendment does not protect the right to an abortion.

B

1

Until the latter part of the 20th century, there was no support in American law for a constitutional right to obtain an abortion. No state constitutional provision had recognized such a right. Until a few years before *Roe* was handed down, no federal or state court had recognized such a right. Nor had any scholarly treatise of which we are aware. And although law review articles are not reticent about advocating new rights, the earliest article proposing a constitutional right to abortion that has come to our attention was published only a few years before *Roe*.

Not only was there no support for such a constitutional right until shortly before *Roe*, but abortion had long been a *crime* in every single State. At common law, abortion was criminal in at least some stages of pregnancy and was regarded as unlawful and could have very serious consequences at all stages. American law followed the common law until a wave of statutory restrictions in the 1800s expanded criminal liability for abortions. By the time of the adoption of the Fourteenth Amendment, three-quarters of the States had made abortion a crime at any stage of pregnancy, and the remaining States would soon follow.

Roe either ignored or misstated this history, and *Casey* declined to reconsider *Roe*'s faulty historical analysis. It is therefore important to set the record straight.

2

a

We begin with the common law, under which abortion was a crime at least after "quickening"—*i.e.*, the first felt movement of the fetus in the womb, which usually occurs between the 16th and 18th week of pregnancy.

The "eminent common-law authorities (Blackstone, Coke, Hale, and the like)," *Kahler* v. *Kansas*, 589 U. S. ___, ___ (2020) (slip op., at 7), *all* describe abortion after quickening as criminal. Henry de Bracton's 13th-century treatise explained that if a person has "struck a pregnant woman, or has given her poison, whereby he has caused abortion, if the foetus be already formed and animated, and particularly if it be animated, he commits homicide." 2 De Legibus et Consuetudinibus Angliae 279 (T. Twiss ed. 1879); see also 1 Fleta, c. 23, reprinted in 72 Selden Soc. 60–61 (H. Richardson & G. Sayles eds. 1955) (13th-century treatise).

Sir Edward Coke's 17th-century treatise likewise asserted that abortion of a quick child was "murder" if the "childe be born alive" and a "great misprision" if the "childe dieth in her body." 3 Institutes of the Laws of England 50–51 (1644). ("Misprision" referred to "some heynous offence under the degree of felony." *Id.*, at 139.) Two treatises by Sir Matthew Hale likewise described abortion of a quick child who died in the womb as a "great crime" and a "great misprision." Pleas of the Crown 53 (P. Glazebrook ed. 1972); 1 History of the Pleas of the Crown 433 (1736) (Hale). And writing near the time of the adoption of our Constitution, William Blackstone explained that abortion of a "quick" child was "by the ancient law homicide or manslaughter" (citing Bracton), and at least a very "heinous misdemeanor" (citing Coke). 1 Commentaries on the Laws of England 129–130 (7th ed. 1775) (Blackstone).

English cases dating all the way back to the 13th century corroborate the treatises' statements that abortion was a crime. See generally J. Dellapenna, Dispelling the Myths of Abortion History 126, and n. 16, 134–142, 188–194, and nn. 84–86 (2006) (Dellapenna); J. Keown, Abortion, Doctors and the Law 3–12 (1988) (Keown). In 1732, for example, Eleanor Beare was convicted of "destroying the Foetus in the Womb" of another woman and "thereby causing her to miscarry." For that crime and another "misdemeanor," Beare was sentenced to two days in the pillory and three years' imprisonment.

Although a pre-quickening abortion was not itself considered homicide, it does not follow that abortion was *permissible* at common law—much less that abortion was a legal *right*. Cf. *Glucksberg*, 521 U. S., at 713 (removal of "common law's harsh sanctions did not represent an acceptance of suicide"). Quite to the contrary, in the 1732 case mentioned above, the judge said of the charge of abortion (with no mention of quickening) that he had "never met with a case so barbarous and unnatural." Similarly, an indictment from 1602, which did not distinguish between a pre-quickening and post-quickening abortion, described abortion as "pernicious" and "against the peace of our Lady the Queen, her crown and dignity." Keown 7 (discussing *R.* v. *Webb*, Calendar of Assize Records, Surrey Indictments 512 (1980)).

That the common law did not condone even pre-quickening abortions is confirmed by what one might call a proto-felony-murder rule. Hale and Blackstone explained a way in which a pre-quickening abortion could rise to the level of a homicide. Hale wrote that if a physician gave a woman "with child" a "potion" to cause an abortion, and the woman died, it was "murder" because the potion was given "*unlawfully* to destroy her child within her." 1 Hale 429–430 (emphasis added). As Blackstone explained, to be "murder" a killing had to be done with "malice aforethought, . . . either express or implied." 4 Blackstone 198 (emphasis deleted). In the case of an abortionist, Blackstone wrote, "the law will imply [malice]" for the same reason that it would imply malice if a person who intended to kill one person accidentally killed a different person:

"[I]f one shoots at A and misses *him*, but kills B, this is murder; because of the previous felonious intent, which the law transfers from one to the other. The same is the case, where one lays poison for A; and B, against whom the prisoner had no malicious intent, takes it, and it kills him; this is likewise murder. *So also*, if one gives *a woman with child* a medicine to procure abortion, and it operates so violently as to kill the woman, *this is murder* in the person who gave it." *Id.*, at 200–201 (emphasis added; footnote omitted).

Notably, Blackstone, like Hale, did not state that this proto-felony-murder rule required that the woman be "with quick child"—only that she be "with child." *Id.*, at 201. And it is revealing that Hale and Blackstone treated abortionists differently from *other* physicians or surgeons who caused the death of a patient "without any intent of doing [the patient] any bodily hurt." Hale 429; see 4 Blackstone 197. These other physicians—even if "unlicensed"—would not be "guilty of murder or manslaughter." Hale 429. But a physician performing an abortion would, precisely because his aim was an "unlawful" one.

In sum, although common-law authorities differed on the severity of punishment for abortions committed at different points in pregnancy, none endorsed the practice. Moreover, we are aware of no common-law case or authority, and the parties have not pointed to any, that remotely suggests a positive *right* to procure an abortion at any stage of pregnancy.

b

In this country, the historical record is similar. The "most important early American edition of Blackstone's Commentaries," *District of Columbia* v. *Heller*, 554 U.S. 570, 594 (2008), reported Blackstone's statement that abortion of a quick child was at least "a heinous misdemeanor," 2 St. George Tucker, Blackstone's Commentaries 129–130 (1803), and that edition also included Blackstone's discussion of the proto-felony-murder rule, 5 *id.*, at 200–201. Manuals for justices of the peace printed in the Colonies in the 18th century typically restated the common-law rule on abortion, and some manuals repeated Hale's and Blackstone's statements that anyone who prescribed medication "unlawfully to destroy the child" would be guilty of murder if the woman died. See, *e.g.*, J. Parker, Conductor Generalis 220 (1788); 2 R. Burn, Justice of the Peace, and Parish Officer 221–222 (7th ed. 1762) (English manual stating the same).

The few cases available from the early colonial period corroborate that abortion was a crime. See generally Dellapenna 215–228 (collecting cases). In Maryland in 1652, for example, an indictment charged that a man "Murtherously endeavoured to destroy or Murther the Child by him begotten in the Womb." *Proprietary* v. *Mitchell*, 10 Md. Archives 80, 183 (1652) (W. Browne ed. 1891). And by the 19th century, courts frequently explained that the common law made abortion of a quick child a crime. See, *e.g.*, *Smith* v. *Gaffard*, 31 Ala. 45, 51 (1857); *Smith* v. *State*, 33 Me. 48, 55 (1851); *State* v. *Cooper*, 22 N. J. L. 52, 52–55 (1849); *Commonwealth* v. *Parker*, 50 Mass. 263, 264–268 (1845).

c

The original ground for drawing a distinction between pre- and post-quickening abortions is not entirely clear, but some have attributed the rule to the difficulty of proving that a pre-quickening fetus was alive. At that time, there were no scientific methods for detecting pregnancy in its early stages, and thus, as one court put it in 1872: "[U]ntil the period of quickening there is no *evidence* of life; and whatever may be said of the feotus, the law has fixed upon this period of gestation as the time when the child is endowed with life" because "foetal movements are the first clearly marked and well defined *evidences of life*." *Evans* v. *People*, 49 N.Y. 86, 90 (emphasis added); *Cooper*, 22 N. J. L., at 56 ("In contemplation of law life commences at the moment of quickening, at that moment when the embryo gives *the first physical proof of life*, no matter when it first received it" (emphasis added)).

The Solicitor General offers a different explanation of the basis for the quickening rule, namely, that before quickening the common law did not regard a fetus "as having a 'separate and independent existence.' " Brief for United States 26 (quoting *Parker*, 50 Mass., at 266). But the case on which the Solicitor General relies for this proposition also suggested that the criminal law's quickening rule was out of step with the treatment of prenatal life in other areas of law, noting that "to many purposes, in reference to civil rights, an infant *in ventre sa mere* is regarded as a person in being." *Ibid.* (citing 1 Blackstone 129); see also *Evans*, 49 N. Y., at 89; *Mills* v. *Commonwealth*, 13 Pa. 631, 633 (1850); *Morrow* v. *Scott*, 7 Ga. 535, 537 (1849); *Hall* v. *Hancock*, 32 Mass. 255, 258 (1834); *Thellusson* v. *Woodford*, 4 Ves. 227, 321–322, 31 Eng. Rep. 117, 163 (1789).

At any rate, the original ground for the quickening rule is of little importance for present purposes because the rule was abandoned in the 19th century. During that period, treatise writers and commentators criticized the quickening distinction as "neither in accordance with the result of medical experience, nor with the principles of the common law." F. Wharton, Criminal Law §1220, p. 606 (rev. 4th ed. 1857) (footnotes omitted); see also J. Beck, Researches in Medicine and Medical Jurisprudence 26–28 (2d ed. 1835) (describing the quickening distinction as "absurd" and "injurious"). In 1803, the British Parliament made abortion a crime at all stages of pregnancy and authorized the imposition of severe punishment. See Lord Ellenborough's Act, 43 Geo. 3, c. 58 (1803). One scholar has suggested that Parliament's decision "may partly have been attributable to the medical man's concern that fetal life should be protected by the law at all stages of gestation." Keown 22.

In this country during the 19th century, the vast majority of the States enacted statutes criminalizing abortion at all stages of pregnancy. See Appendix A, *infra* (listing state statutory provisions in chronological order). By 1868, the year when the Fourteenth Amendment was ratified, three-quarters of the States, 28 out of 37, had enacted statutes making abortion a crime even if it was performed before quickening. See *ibid*. Of the nine States that had not yet criminalized abortion at all stages, all but one did so by 1910. See *ibid*.

The trend in the Territories that would become the last 13 States was similar: All of them criminalized abortion at all stages of pregnancy between 1850 (the Kingdom of Hawaii) and 1919 (New Mexico). See Appendix B, *infra*; see also *Casey*, 505 U. S., at 952 (Rehnquist, C. J., concurring in judgment in part and dissenting in part); Dellapenna 317–319. By the end of the 1950s, according to the *Roe* Court's own count, statutes in all but four States and the District of Columbia prohibited abortion "however and whenever performed, unless done to save or preserve the life of the mother." 410 U. S., at 139.

This overwhelming consensus endured until the day *Roe* was decided. At that time, also by the *Roe* Court's own count, a substantial majority—30 States—still prohibited abortion at all stages except to save the life of the mother. See *id.*, at 118, and n. 2 (listing States). And though *Roe* discerned a "trend toward liberalization" in about "one-third of the States," those States still criminalized some abortions and regulated them more stringently than *Roe* would allow. *Id.*, at 140, and n. 37; Tribe 2. In short, the "Court's opinion in *Roe* itself convincingly refutes the notion that the abortion liberty is deeply rooted in the history or tradition of our people." *Thornburgh* v. *American College of Obstetricians and Gynecologists*, 476 U.S. 747, 793 (1986) (White, J., dissenting).

d

The inescapable conclusion is that a right to abortion is not deeply rooted in the Nation's history and traditions. On the contrary, an unbroken tradition of prohibiting abortion on pain of criminal punishment persisted from the earliest days of the common law until 1973. The Court in *Roe* could have said of abortion exactly what *Glucksberg* said of assisted suicide: "Attitudes toward [abortion] have changed since Bracton, but our laws have consistently condemned, and continue to prohibit, [that practice]." 521 U. S., at 719.

3

Respondents and their *amici* have no persuasive answer to this historical evidence.

Neither respondents nor the Solicitor General disputes the fact that by 1868 the vast majority of States criminalized abortion at all stages of pregnancy. See Brief for Petitioners 12–13; see also Brief for American Historical Association et al. as *Amici Curiae* 27–28, and nn. 14–15 (conceding that 26 out of 37 States prohibited abortion before quickening); Tr. of Oral Arg. 74–75 (respondents' counsel conceding the same). Instead, respondents are forced to argue that it "does [not] matter that some States prohibited abortion at the time *Roe* was decided or when the Fourteenth Amendment was adopted." Brief for Respondents 21. But that argument flies in the face of the standard we have applied in determining whether an asserted right that is nowhere mentioned in the Constitution is nevertheless protected by the Fourteenth Amendment.

Not only are respondents and their *amici* unable to show that a constitutional right to abortion was established when the Fourteenth Amendment was adopted, but they have found no support for the existence of an abortion right that predates the latter part of the 20th century—no state constitutional provision, no statute, no judicial decision, no learned treatise. The earliest sources called to our attention are a few district court and state court decisions decided shortly before *Roe* and a small number of law review articles from the same time period.

A few of respondents' *amici* muster historical arguments, but they are very weak. The Solicitor General repeats *Roe*'s claim that it is " 'doubtful' . . . 'abortion was ever firmly established as a common-law crime even with respect to the destruction of a quick fetus.' " Brief for United States 26 (quoting *Roe*, 410 U. S., at 136). But as we have seen, great common-law authorities like Bracton, Coke, Hale, and Blackstone all wrote that a post-quickening abortion was a crime—and a serious one at that. Moreover, Hale and Blackstone (and many other authorities following them) asserted that even a pre-quickening abortion was "unlawful" and that, as a result, an abortionist was guilty of murder if the woman died from the attempt.

Instead of following these authorities, *Roe* relied largely on two articles by a pro-abortion advocate who claimed that Coke had intentionally misstated the common law because of his strong anti-abortion views. These articles have been discredited, and it has come to light that even members of Jane Roe's legal team did not regard them as serious scholarship. An internal memorandum characterized this author's work as donning "the guise of impartial scholarship while advancing the proper ideological goals." Continued reliance on such scholarship is unsupportable.

The Solicitor General next suggests that history supports an abortion right because the common law's failure to criminalize abortion before quickening means that "at the Founding and for decades thereafter, women generally could terminate a pregnancy, at least in its early stages." Brief for United States 26–27; see also Brief for Respondents 21. But the insistence on quickening was not universal, see *Mills*, 13 Pa., at 633; *State* v. *Slagle*, 83 N. C. 630, 632 (1880), and regardless, the fact that many States in the late 18th and early 19th century did not criminalize pre-quickening abortions does not mean that anyone thought the States lacked the authority to do so. When legislatures began to exercise that authority as the century wore on, no one, as far as we are aware, argued that the laws they enacted violated a fundamental right. That is not surprising since common-law authorities had repeatedly condemned abortion and described it as an "unlawful" act without regard to whether it occurred before or after quickening. See *supra*, at 16–21.

Another *amicus* brief relied upon by respondents (see Brief for Respondents 21) tries to dismiss the significance of the state criminal statutes that were in effect when the Fourteenth Amendment was adopted by suggesting that they were enacted for illegitimate reasons. According to this account, which is based almost entirely on statements made by one prominent proponent of the statutes, important motives for the laws were the fear that Catholic immigrants were having more babies than Protestants and that the availability of abortion was leading White Protestant women to "shir[k their] maternal duties." Brief for American Historical Association et al. as *Amici Curiae* 20.

Resort to this argument is a testament to the lack of any real historical support for the right that *Roe* and *Casey* recognized. This Court has long disfavored arguments based on alleged legislative motives. See, *e.g.*, *Erie* v. *Pap's A. M.*, 529 U.S. 277, 292 (2000) (plurality opinion); *Turner Broadcasting System, Inc.* v. *FCC*, 512 U.S. 622, 652 (1994); *United States* v. *O'Brien*, 391 U.S. 367, 383 (1968); *Arizona* v. *California*, 283 U.S. 423, 455 (1931) (collecting cases). The Court has recognized that inquiries into legislative motives "are a hazardous matter." *O'Brien*, 391 U. S., at 383. Even when an argument about legislative motive is backed by statements made by legislators who voted for a law, we have been reluctant to attribute those motives to the legislative body as a whole. "What motivates one legislator to make a speech about a statute is not necessarily what motivates scores of others to enact it." *Id., at 384.*

Here, the argument about legislative motive is not even based on statements by legislators, but on statements made by a few supporters of the new 19th-century abortion laws, and it is quite a leap to attribute these motives to all the legislators whose votes were responsible for the enactment of those laws. Recall that at the time of the adoption of the Fourteenth Amendment, over three-quarters of the States had adopted statutes criminalizing abortion (usually at all stages of pregnancy), and that from the early 20th century until the day *Roe* was handed down, every single State had such a law on its books. Are we to believe that the hundreds of lawmakers whose votes were needed to enact these laws were motivated by hostility to Catholics and women?

There is ample evidence that the passage of these laws was instead spurred by a sincere belief that abortion kills a human being. Many judicial decisions from the late 19th and early 20th centuries made that point. See, *e.g., Nash* v. *Meyer*, 54 Idaho 283, 301, 31 P.2d 273, 280 (1934); *State* v. *Ausplund*, 86 Ore. 121, 131–132, 167 P. 1019, 1022–1023 (1917); *Trent* v. *State*, 15 Ala. App. 485, 488, 73 S. 834, 836 (1916); *State* v. *Miller*, 90 Kan. 230, 233, 133 P. 878, 879 (1913); *State* v. *Tippie*, 89 Ohio St. 35, 39–40, 105 N.E. 75, 77 (1913); *State* v. *Gedicke*, 43 N. J. L. 86, 90 (1881); *Dougherty* v. *People*, 1 Colo. 514, 522–523 (1873); *State* v. *Moore*, 25 Iowa 128, 131–132 (1868); *Smith*, 33 Me., at 57; see also *Memphis Center for Reproductive Health* v. *Slatery*, 14 F. 4th 409, 446, and n. 11 (CA6 2021) (Thapar, J., concurring in judgment in part and dissenting in part) (citing cases).

One may disagree with this belief (and our decision is not based on any view about when a State should regard prenatal life as having rights or legally cognizable interests), but even *Roe* and *Casey* did not question the good faith of abortion opponents. See, *e.g., Casey*, 505 U. S., at 850 ("Men and women of good conscience can disagree . . . about the profound moral and spiritual implications of terminating a pregnancy even in its earliest stage"). And we see no reason to discount the significance of the state laws in question based on these *amici*'s suggestions about legislative motive.

C

1

Instead of seriously pressing the argument that the abortion right itself has deep roots, supporters of *Roe* and *Casey* contend that the abortion right is an integral part of a broader entrenched right. *Roe* termed this a right to privacy, 410 U. S., at 154, and *Casey* described it as the freedom to make "intimate and personal choices" that are "central to personal dignity and autonomy," 505 U. S., at 851. *Casey* elaborated: "At the heart of liberty is the right to define one's own concept of existence, of meaning, of the universe, and of the mystery of human life." *Ibid.*

The Court did not claim that this broadly framed right is absolute, and no such claim would be plausible. While individuals are certainly free *to think* and *to say* what they wish about "existence," "meaning," the "universe," and "the mystery of human life," they are not always free *to act* in accordance with those thoughts. License to act on the basis of such beliefs may correspond to one of the many understandings of "liberty," but it is certainly not "ordered liberty."

Ordered liberty sets limits and defines the boundary between competing interests. *Roe* and *Casey* each struck a particular balance between the interests of a woman who wants an abortion and the interests of what they termed "potential life." *Roe*, 410 U. S., at 150 (emphasis deleted); *Casey*, 505 U. S., at 852. But the people of the various States may evaluate those interests differently. In some States, voters may believe that the abortion right should be even more extensive than the right that *Roe* and *Casey* recognized. Voters in other States may wish to impose tight restrictions based on their belief that abortion destroys an "unborn human being." Miss. Code Ann. §41–41–191(4)(b). Our

Nation's historical understanding of ordered liberty does not prevent the people's elected representatives from deciding how abortion should be regulated.

Nor does the right to obtain an abortion have a sound basis in precedent. *Casey* relied on cases involving the right to marry a person of a different race, *Loving* v. *Virginia*, 388 U.S. 1 (1967); the right to marry while in prison, *Turner* v. *Safley*, 482 U.S. 78 (1987); the right to obtain contraceptives, *Griswold* v. *Connecticut*, 381 U.S. 479 (1965), *Eisenstadt* v. *Baird*, 405 U.S. 438 (1972), *Carey* v. *Population Services Int'l*, 431 U.S. 678 (1977); the right to reside with relatives, *Moore* v. *East Cleveland*, 431 U.S. 494 (1977); the right to make decisions about the education of one's children, *Pierce* v. *Society of Sisters*, 268 U.S. 510 (1925), *Meyer* v. *Nebraska*, 262 U.S. 390 (1923); the right not to be sterilized without consent, *Skinner* v. *Oklahoma ex rel. Williamson*, 316 U.S. 535 (1942); and the right in certain circumstances not to undergo involuntary surgery, forced administration of drugs, or other substantially similar procedures, *Winston* v. *Lee*, 470 U.S. 753 (1985), *Washington* v. *Harper*, 494 U.S. 210 (1990), *Rochin* v. *California*, 342 U.S. 165 (1952). Respondents and the Solicitor General also rely on post-*Casey* decisions like *Lawrence* v. *Texas*, 539 U.S. 558 (2003) (right to engage in private, consensual sexual acts), and *Obergefell* v. *Hodges*, 576 U.S. 644 (2015) (right to marry a person of the same sex). See Brief for Respondents 18; Brief for United States 23–24.

These attempts to justify abortion through appeals to a broader right to autonomy and to define one's "concept of existence" prove too much. *Casey*, 505 U. S., at 851. Those criteria, at a high level of generality, could license fundamental rights to illicit drug use, prostitution, and the like. See *Compassion in Dying* v. *Washington*, 85 F.3d 1440, 1444 (CA9 1996) (O'Scannlain, J., dissenting from denial of rehearing en banc). None of these rights has any claim to being deeply rooted in history. *Id.*, at 1440, 1445.

What sharply distinguishes the abortion right from the rights recognized in the cases on which *Roe* and *Casey* rely is something that both those decisions acknowledged: Abortion destroys what those decisions call "potential life" and what the law at issue in this case regards as the life of an "unborn human being." See *Roe*, 410 U. S., at 159 (abortion is "inherently different"); *Casey*, 505 U. S., at 852 (abortion is "a unique act"). None of the other decisions cited by *Roe* and *Casey* involved the critical moral question posed by abortion. They are therefore inapposite. They do not support the right to obtain an abortion, and by the same token, our conclusion that the Constitution does not confer such a right does not undermine them in any way.

2

In drawing this critical distinction between the abortion right and other rights, it is not necessary to dispute *Casey's* claim (which we accept for the sake of argument) that "the specific practices of States at the time of the adoption of the Fourteenth Amendment" do not "mar[k] the outer limits of the substantive sphere of liberty which the Fourteenth Amendment protects." 505 U. S., at 848. Abortion is nothing new. It has been addressed by lawmakers for centuries, and the fundamental moral question that it poses is ageless.

Defenders of *Roe* and *Casey* do not claim that any new scientific learning calls for a different answer to the underlying moral question, but they do contend that changes in society require the recognition of a constitutional right to obtain an abortion. Without the availability of abortion, they maintain, people will be inhibited from exercising their freedom to choose the types of relationships they desire, and women will be unable to compete with men in the workplace and in other endeavors.

Americans who believe that abortion should be restricted press countervailing arguments about modern developments. They note that attitudes about the pregnancy of unmarried women have changed drastically; that federal and state laws ban discrimination on the basis of pregnancy; that leave for pregnancy and childbirth are now guaranteed by law in many cases; that the costs of medical care associated with pregnancy are covered by insurance or government assistance; that States have increasingly adopted "safe haven" laws, which generally allow women to drop off babies anonymously; and that a woman who puts her newborn up for adoption today has little reason to fear that the baby will not find a suitable home. They also claim that many people now have a new appreciation of fetal life and that when prospective parents who want to have a child view a sonogram, they typically have no doubt that what they see is their daughter or son.

Both sides make important policy arguments, but supporters of *Roe* and *Casey* must show that this Court has the authority to weigh those arguments and decide how abortion may be regulated in the States. They have failed to make that showing, and we thus return the power to weigh those arguments to the people and their elected representatives.

D

1

The dissent is very candid that it cannot show that a constitutional right to abortion has any foundation, let alone a " 'deeply rooted' " one, " 'in this Nation's history and tradition.' " *Glucksberg*, 521 U. S., at 721; see *post*, at 12–14 (joint opinion of Breyer, Sotomayor, and Kagan, JJ.). The dissent does not identify *any* pre-*Roe* authority that supports such a right—no state constitutional provision or statute, no federal or state judicial precedent, not even a scholarly treatise. Compare *post*, at 12–14, n. 2, with *supra*, at 15–16, and n. 23. Nor does the dissent dispute the fact that abortion was illegal at common law at least after quickening; that the 19th century saw a trend toward criminalization of pre-quickening abortions; that by 1868, a supermajority of States (at least 26 of 37) had enacted statutes criminalizing abortion at all stages of pregnancy; that by the late 1950s at least 46 States prohibited abortion "however and whenever performed" except if necessary to save "the life of the mother," *Roe*, 410 U. S., at 139; and that when *Roe* was decided in 1973 similar statutes were still in effect in 30 States. Compare *post*, at 12–14, nn. 2–3, with *supra*, at 23–25, and nn. 33–34.

The dissent's failure to engage with this long tradition is devastating to its position. We have held that the "established method of substantive-due-process analysis" requires that an unenumerated right be " 'deeply rooted in this Nation's history and tradition' " before it can be recognized as a component of the "liberty" protected in the Due Process Clause. *Glucksberg*, 521 U. S., at 721; cf. *Timbs*, 586 U. S., at ___ (slip op., at 7). But despite the dissent's professed fidelity to *stare decisis*, it fails to seriously engage with that important precedent—which it cannot possibly satisfy.

The dissent attempts to obscure this failure by misrepresenting our application of *Glucksberg*. The dissent suggests that we have focused only on "the legal status of abortion in the 19th century," *post*, at 26, but our review of this Nation's tradition extends well past that period. As explained, for more than a century after 1868—including "another half-century" after women gained the constitutional right to vote in 1920, see *post*, at 15; Amdt. 19—it was firmly established that laws prohibiting abortion like the Texas law at issue in *Roe* were permissible exercises of state regulatory authority. And today, another half century later, more than half of the States have asked us to overrule *Roe* and *Casey*. The dissent cannot establish that a right to abortion has *ever* been part of this Nation's tradition.

2

Because the dissent cannot argue that the abortion right is rooted in this Nation's history and tradition, it contends that the "constitutional tradition" is "not captured whole at a single moment," and that its "meaning gains content from the long sweep of our history and from successive judicial precedents." *Post*, at 18 (internal quotation marks omitted). This vague formulation imposes no clear restraints on what Justice White called the "exercise of raw judicial power," *Roe*, 410 U. S., at 222 (dissenting opinion), and while the dissent claims that its standard "does not mean anything goes," *post*, at 17, any real restraints are hard to discern.

The largely limitless reach of the dissenters' standard is illustrated by the way they apply it here. First, if the "long sweep of history" imposes any restraint on the recognition of unenumerated rights, then *Roe* was surely wrong, since abortion was never allowed (except to save the life of the mother) in a majority of States for over 100 years before that decision was handed down. Second, it is impossible to defend *Roe* based on prior precedent because all of the precedents *Roe* cited, including *Griswold* and *Eisenstadt*, were critically different for a reason that we have explained: None of those cases involved the destruction of what *Roe* called "potential life." See *supra*, at 32.

So without support in history or relevant precedent, *Roe*'s reasoning cannot be defended even under the dissent's proposed test, and the dissent is forced to rely solely on the fact that a constitutional right to abortion was recognized in *Roe* and later decisions that accepted *Roe*'s interpretation. Under the doctrine of *stare decisis*, those precedents are entitled to careful and respectful consideration, and we engage in that analysis below. But as the Court has reiterated time and time again, adherence to precedent is not "'an inexorable command.'" *Kimble* v. *Marvel Entertainment, LLC*, 576 U.S. 446, 455 (2015). There are occasions when past decisions should be overruled, and as we will explain, this is one of them.

3

The most striking feature of the dissent is the absence of any serious discussion of the legitimacy of the States' interest in protecting fetal life. This is evident in the analogy that the dissent draws between the abortion right and the rights recognized in *Griswold* (contraception), *Eisenstadt* (same), *Lawrence* (sexual conduct with member of the same sex), and *Obergefell* (same-sex marriage). Perhaps this is designed to stoke unfounded fear that our decision will imperil those other rights, but the dissent's analogy is objectionable for a more important reason: what it reveals about the dissent's views on the protection of what *Roe* called "potential life." The exercise of the rights at issue in *Griswold*, *Eisenstadt*, *Lawrence*, and *Obergefell* does not destroy a "potential life," but an abortion has that effect. So if the rights at issue in those cases are fundamentally the same as the right recognized in *Roe* and *Casey*, the implication is clear: The Constitution does not permit the States to regard the destruction of a "potential life" as a matter of any significance.

That view is evident throughout the dissent. The dissent has much to say about the effects of pregnancy on women, the burdens of motherhood, and the difficulties faced by poor women. These are important concerns. However, the dissent evinces no similar regard for a State's interest in protecting prenatal life. The dissent repeatedly praises the "balance," *post*, at 2, 6, 8, 10, 12, that the viability line strikes between a woman's liberty interest and the State's interest in prenatal life. But for reasons we discuss later, see *infra*, at 50–54, 55–56, and given in the opinion of The Chief Justice, *post*, at 2–5 (opinion concurring in judgment), the viability line makes no sense. It was not adequately justified in *Roe*, and the dissent does not even try to defend it today. Nor does it identify any other point in a pregnancy after which a State is permitted to prohibit the destruction of a fetus.

Our opinion is not based on any view about if and when prenatal life is entitled to any of the rights enjoyed after birth. The dissent, by contrast, would impose on the people a particular theory about when the rights of personhood begin. According to the dissent, the Constitution *requires* the States to regard a fetus as lacking even the most basic human right—to live—at least until an arbitrary point in a pregnancy has passed. Nothing in the Constitution or in our Nation's legal traditions authorizes the Court to adopt that "'theory of life.'" *Post*, at 8.

III

We next consider whether the doctrine of *stare decisis* counsels continued acceptance of *Roe* and *Casey*. *Stare decisis* plays an important role in our case law, and we have explained that it serves many valuable ends. It protects the interests of those who have taken action in reliance on a past decision. See *Casey*, 505 U. S., at 856 (joint opinion); see also *Payne* v. *Tennessee*, 501 U.S. 808, 828 (1991). It "reduces incentives for challenging settled precedents, saving parties and courts the expense of endless relitigation." *Kimble*, 576 U. S., at 455. It fosters "evenhanded" decisionmaking by requiring that like cases be decided in a like manner. *Payne*, 501 U. S., at 827. It "contributes to the actual and perceived integrity of the judicial process." *Ibid*. And it restrains judicial hubris and reminds us to respect the judgment of those who have grappled with important questions in the past. "Precedent is a way of accumulating and passing down the learning of past generations, a font of established wisdom richer than what can be found in any single judge or panel of judges." N. Gorsuch, A Republic, If You Can Keep It 217 (2019).

We have long recognized, however, that *stare decisis* is "not an inexorable command," *Pearson* v. *Callahan*, 555 U.S. 223, 233 (2009) (internal quotation marks omitted), and it "is at its weakest when we interpret the Constitution," *Agostini* v. *Felton*, 521 U.S. 203, 235 (1997). It has been said that it is sometimes more important that an issue "'be settled than that it be settled right.'" *Kimble*, 576 U. S., at 455 (quoting *Burnet* v. *Coronado Oil & Gas Co.*, 285 U.S. 393, 406 (1932) (Brandeis, J., dissenting)). But when it comes to the interpretation of the Constitution—the "great charter of our liberties," which was meant "to endure through a long lapse of ages," *Martin* v. *Hunter's Lessee*, 1 Wheat. 304, 326 (1816) (opinion for the Court by Story, J.)—we place a high value on having the matter "settled right." In addition, when one of our constitutional decisions goes astray, the country is usually stuck with the bad decision unless we correct our own mistake. An erroneous constitutional decision can be fixed by amending the Constitution, but our Constitution is notoriously hard to amend. See Art. V; *Kimble*, 576 U. S., at 456. Therefore, in appropriate circumstances we must be willing to reconsider and, if necessary, overrule constitutional decisions.

Some of our most important constitutional decisions have overruled prior precedents. We mention three. In *Brown* v. *Board of Education*, 347 U.S. 483 (1954), the Court repudiated the "separate but equal" doctrine, which had allowed States to maintain racially segregated schools and other facilities. *Id.*, at 488 (internal quotation marks omitted). In so doing, the Court overruled the infamous decision in *Plessy* v. *Ferguson*, 163 U.S. 537 (1896), along with six other Supreme Court precedents that had applied the separate-but-equal rule. See *Brown*, 347 U. S., at 491.

In *West Coast Hotel Co.* v. *Parrish*, 300 U.S. 379 (1937), the Court overruled *Adkins* v. *Children's Hospital of D. C.*, 261 U.S. 525 (1923), which had held that a law setting minimum wages for women violated the "liberty" protected by the Fifth Amendment's Due Process Clause. *Id.*, at 545. *West Coast Hotel* signaled the demise of an entire line of important precedents that had protected an individual liberty right against state and federal health and welfare legislation. See *Lochner* v. *New York*, 198 U.S. 45 (1905) (holding invalid a law setting maximum working hours); *Coppage* v. *Kansas*, 236 U.S. 1 (1915) (holding invalid a law banning contracts forbidding employees to join a union); *Jay Burns Baking Co.* v. *Bryan*, 264 U.S. 504 (1924) (holding invalid laws fixing the weight of loaves of bread).

Finally, in *West Virginia Bd. of Ed.* v. *Barnette*, 319 U.S. 624 (1943), after the lapse of only three years, the Court overruled *Minersville School Dist.* v. *Gobitis*, 310 U.S. 586 (1940), and held that public school students could not be compelled to salute the flag in violation of their sincere beliefs. *Barnette* stands out because nothing had changed during the intervening period other than the Court's belated recognition that its earlier decision had been seriously wrong.

On many other occasions, this Court has overruled important constitutional decisions. (We include a partial list in the footnote that follows.) Without these decisions, American constitutional law as we know it would be unrecognizable, and this would be a different country.

No Justice of this Court has ever argued that the Court should *never* overrule a constitutional decision, but overruling a precedent is a serious matter. It is not a step that should be taken lightly. Our cases have attempted to provide a framework for deciding when a precedent should be overruled, and they have identified factors that should be considered in making such a decision. *Janus* v. *State, County, and Municipal Employees*, 585 U. S. ___, ___–___ (2018) (slip op., at 34–35); *Ramos* v. *Louisiana*, 590 U. S. ___, ___–___ (2020) (Kavanaugh, J., concurring in part) (slip op., at 7–9).

In this case, five factors weigh strongly in favor of overruling *Roe* and *Casey*: the nature of their error, the quality of their reasoning, the "workability" of the rules they imposed on the country, their disruptive effect on other areas of the law, and the absence of concrete reliance.

A

The nature of the Court's error. An erroneous interpretation of the Constitution is always important, but some are more damaging than others.

The infamous decision in *Plessy* v. *Ferguson*, was one such decision. It betrayed our commitment to "equality before the law." 163 U. S., at 562 (Harlan, J., dissenting). It was "egregiously wrong" on the day it was decided, see *Ramos*, 590 U. S., at ___ (opinion of Kavanaugh, J.) (slip op., at 7), and as the Solicitor General agreed at oral argument, it should have been overruled at the earliest opportunity, see Tr. of Oral Arg. 92–93.

Roe was also egregiously wrong and deeply damaging. For reasons already explained, *Roe*'s constitutional analysis was far outside the bounds of any reasonable interpretation of the various constitutional provisions to which it vaguely pointed.

Roe was on a collision course with the Constitution from the day it was decided, *Casey* perpetuated its errors, and those errors do not concern some arcane corner of the law of little importance to the American people. Rather, wielding nothing but "raw judicial power," *Roe*, 410 U. S., at 222 (White, J., dissenting), the Court usurped the power to address a question of profound moral and social importance that the Constitution unequivocally leaves for the people. *Casey* described itself as calling both sides of the national controversy to resolve their debate, but in doing so, *Casey* necessarily declared a winning side. Those on the losing side—those who sought to advance the State's interest in fetal life—could no longer seek to persuade their elected representatives to adopt policies consistent with their views. The Court short-circuited the democratic process by closing it to the large number of Americans who dissented in any respect from *Roe*. "*Roe* fanned into life an issue that has inflamed our national politics in general, and has obscured with its smoke the selection of Justices to this Court in particular, ever since." *Casey*, 505 U. S., at 995–996 (opinion of Scalia, J.). Together, *Roe* and *Casey* represent an error that cannot be allowed to stand.

As the Court's landmark decision in *West Coast Hotel* illustrates, the Court has previously overruled decisions that wrongly removed an issue from the people and the democratic process. As Justice White later explained, "decisions that find in the Constitution principles or values that cannot fairly be read into that document usurp the people's authority, for such decisions represent choices that the people have never made and that they cannot disavow through corrective legislation. For this reason, it is essential that this Court maintain the power to restore authority to its proper possessors by correcting constitutional decisions that, on reconsideration, are found to be mistaken." *Thornburgh*, 476 U. S., at 787 (dissenting opinion).

B

The quality of the reasoning. Under our precedents, the quality of the reasoning in a prior case has an important bearing on whether it should be reconsidered. See *Janus*, 585 U. S., at ___ (slip op., at 38); *Ramos*, 590 U. S., at ___–___ (opinion of Kavanaugh, J.) (slip op., at 7–8). In Part II, *supra*, we explained why *Roe* was incorrectly decided, but that decision was more than just wrong. It stood on exceptionally weak grounds.

Roe found that the Constitution implicitly conferred a right to obtain an abortion, but it failed to ground its decision in text, history, or precedent. It relied on an erroneous historical narrative; it devoted great attention to and presumably relied on matters that have no bearing on the meaning of the Constitution; it disregarded the fundamental difference between the precedents on which it relied and the question before the Court; it concocted an elaborate set of rules, with different restrictions for each trimester of pregnancy, but it did not explain how this veritable code could be teased out of anything in the Constitution, the history of abortion laws, prior precedent, or any other cited source; and its most important rule (that States cannot protect fetal life prior to "viability") was never raised by any party and has never been plausibly explained. *Roe*'s reasoning quickly drew scathing scholarly criticism, even from supporters of broad access to abortion.

The *Casey* plurality, while reaffirming *Roe*'s central holding, pointedly refrained from endorsing most of its reasoning. It revised the textual basis for the abortion right, silently abandoned *Roe*'s erroneous historical narrative, and jettisoned the trimester framework. But it replaced that scheme with an arbitrary "undue burden" test and relied on an exceptional version of *stare decisis* that, as explained below, this Court had never before applied and has never invoked since.

1

a

The weaknesses in *Roe*'s reasoning are well-known. Without any grounding in the constitutional text, history, or precedent, it imposed on the entire country a detailed set of rules much like those that one might expect to find in a statute or regulation. See 410 U. S., at 163–164. Dividing pregnancy into three trimesters, the Court imposed special rules for each. During the first trimester, the Court announced, "the abortion decision and its effectuation must be left to the medical judgment of the pregnant woman's attending physician." *Id.*, at 164. After that point, a State's interest in regulating abortion for the sake of a woman's health became compelling, and accordingly, a State could "regulate the abortion procedure in ways that are reasonably related to maternal health." *Ibid*. Finally, in "the stage subsequent to viability," which in 1973 roughly coincided with the beginning of the third trimester, the State's interest in "the potentiality of human life" became compelling, and therefore a State could "regulate, and even proscribe, abortion except where it is necessary, in appropriate medical judgment, for the preservation of the life or health of the mother." *Id.*, at 164–165.

This elaborate scheme was the Court's own brainchild. Neither party advocated the trimester framework; nor did either party or any *amicus* argue that "viability" should mark the point at which the scope of the abortion right and a State's regulatory authority should be substantially transformed. See Brief for Appellant and Brief for Appellee in *Roe* v. *Wade*, O. T. 1972, No. 70–18; see also C. Forsythe, Abuse of Discretion: The Inside Story of *Roe* v. *Wade* 127, 141 (2012).

b

Not only did this scheme resemble the work of a legislature, but the Court made little effort to explain how these rules could be deduced from any of the sources on which constitutional decisions are usually based. We have already discussed *Roe*'s treatment of constitutional text, and the opinion failed to show that history, precedent, or any other cited source supported its scheme.

Roe featured a lengthy survey of history, but much of its discussion was irrelevant, and the Court made no effort to explain why it was included. For example, multiple paragraphs were devoted to an account of the views and practices of ancient civilizations where infanticide was widely accepted. See 410 U. S., at 130–132 (discussing ancient Greek and Roman practices). When it came to the most important historical fact—how the States regulated abortion when the Fourteenth Amendment was adopted—the Court said almost nothing. It allowed that States had tightened their abortion laws "in the middle and late 19th century," *id.*, at 139, but it implied that these laws might have been enacted not to protect fetal life but to further "a Victorian social concern" about "illicit sexual conduct," *id.*, at 148.

Roe's failure even to note the overwhelming consensus of state laws in effect in 1868 is striking, and what it said about the common law was simply wrong. Relying on two discredited articles by an abortion advocate, the Court erroneously suggested—contrary to Bracton, Coke, Hale, Blackstone, and a wealth of other authority—that the common law had probably never really treated post-quickening abortion as a crime. See *id.*, at 136 ("[I]t now appear[s] doubtful that abortion was ever firmly established as a common-law crime even with respect to the destruction of a quick fetus"). This erroneous understanding appears to have played an important part in the Court's thinking because the opinion cited "the lenity of the common law" as one of the four factors that informed its decision. *Id.*, at 165.

After surveying history, the opinion spent many paragraphs conducting the sort of fact-finding that might be undertaken by a legislative committee. This included a lengthy account of the "position of the American Medical Association" and "[t]he position of the American Public Health Association," as well as the vote by the American Bar Association's House of Delegates in February 1972 on proposed abortion legislation. *Id.*, at 141, 144, 146 (emphasis deleted). Also noted were a British judicial decision handed down in 1939 and a new British abortion law enacted in 1967. *Id.*, at 137–138. The Court did not explain why these sources shed light on the meaning of the Constitution, and not one of them adopted or advocated anything like the scheme that *Roe* imposed on the country.

Finally, after all this, the Court turned to precedent. Citing a broad array of cases, the Court found support for a constitutional "right of personal privacy," *id.*, at 152, but it conflated two very different meanings of the term: the right to shield information from disclosure and the right to make and implement important personal decisions without governmental interference. See *Whalen* v. *Roe*, 429 U.S. 589, 599–600 (1977). Only the cases involving this second sense of the term could have any possible relevance to the abortion issue, and some of the cases in that category involved personal decisions that were obviously very, very far afield. See *Pierce*, 268 U.S. 510 (right to send children to religious school); *Meyer*, 262 U.S. 390 (right to have children receive German language instruction).

What remained was a handful of cases having something to do with marriage, *Loving*, 388 U.S. 1 (right to marry a person of a different race), or procreation, *Skinner*, 316 U.S. 535 (right not to be sterilized); *Griswold*, 381 U.S. 479 (right of married persons to obtain contraceptives); *Eisenstadt*, 405 U.S. 438 (same, for unmarried persons). But none of these decisions involved what is distinctive about abortion: its effect on what *Roe* termed "potential life."

When the Court summarized the basis for the scheme it imposed on the country, it asserted that its rules were "consistent with" the following: (1) "the relative weights of the respective interests involved," (2) "the lessons and examples of medical and legal history," (3) "the lenity of the common law," and (4) "the demands of the profound problems of the present day." *Roe*, 410 U. S., at 165. Put aside the second and third factors, which were based on the Court's flawed account of history, and what remains are precisely the sort of considerations that legislative bodies often take into account when they draw lines that accommodate competing interests. The scheme *Roe* produced *looked* like legislation, and the Court provided the sort of explanation that might be expected from a legislative body.

c

What *Roe* did not provide was any cogent justification for the lines it drew. Why, for example, does a State have no authority to regulate first trimester abortions for the purpose of protecting a woman's health? The Court's only explanation was that mortality rates for abortion at that stage were lower than the mortality rates for childbirth. *Id.*, at 163. But the Court did not explain why mortality rates were the only factor that a State could legitimately consider. Many health and safety regulations aim to avoid adverse health consequences short of death. And the Court did not explain why it departed from the normal rule that courts defer to the judgments of legislatures "in areas fraught with medical and scientific uncertainties." *Marshall* v. *United States*, 414 U.S. 417, 427 (1974).

An even more glaring deficiency was *Roe*'s failure to justify the critical distinction it drew between pre- and post-viability abortions. Here is the Court's entire explanation:

"With respect to the State's important and legitimate interest in potential life, the 'compelling' point is at viability. This is so because the fetus then presumably has the capability of meaningful life outside the womb." 410 U. S., at 163.

As Professor Laurence Tribe has written, "[c]learly, this mistakes 'a definition for a syllogism.' " Tribe 4 (quoting Ely 924). The definition of a "viable" fetus is one that is capable of surviving outside the womb, but why is this the point at which the State's interest becomes compelling? If, as *Roe* held, a State's interest in protecting prenatal life is compelling "after viability," 410 U. S., at 163, why isn't that interest "equally compelling before viability"? *Webster* v. *Reproductive Health Services*, 492 U.S. 490, 519 (1989) (plurality opinion) (quoting *Thornburgh*, 476 U. S., at 795 (White, J., dissenting)). *Roe* did not say, and no explanation is apparent.

This arbitrary line has not found much support among philosophers and ethicists who have attempted to justify a right to abortion. Some have argued that a fetus should not be entitled to legal protection until it acquires the characteristics that they regard as defining what it means to be a "person." Among the characteristics that have been offered as essential attributes of "personhood" are sentience, self-awareness, the ability to reason, or some combination thereof. By this logic, it would be an open question whether even born individuals, including young children or those afflicted with certain developmental or medical conditions, merit protection as "persons." But even if one takes the view that "personhood" begins when a certain attribute or combination of attributes is acquired, it is very hard to see why viability should mark the point where "personhood" begins.

The most obvious problem with any such argument is that viability is heavily dependent on factors that have nothing to do with the characteristics of a fetus. One is the state of neonatal care at a particular point in time. Due to the development of new equipment and improved practices, the viability line has changed over the years. In the 19th century, a fetus may not have been viable until the 32d or 33d week of pregnancy or even later. When *Roe* was decided, viability was gauged at roughly 28 weeks. See 410 U. S., at 160. Today, respondents draw the line at 23 or 24 weeks. Brief for Respondents 8. So, according to *Roe*'s logic, States now have a compelling interest in protecting a fetus with a gestational age of, say, 26 weeks, but in 1973 States did not have an interest in protecting an identical fetus. How can that be?

Viability also depends on the "quality of the available medical facilities." *Colautti* v. *Franklin*, 439 U.S. 379, 396 (1979). Thus, a 24-week-old fetus may be viable if a woman gives birth in a city with hospitals that provide advanced care for very premature babies, but if the woman travels to a remote area far from any such hospital, the fetus may no longer be viable. On what ground could the constitutional status of a fetus depend on the pregnant woman's location? And if viability is meant to mark a line having universal moral significance, can it be that a fetus that is viable in a big city in the United States has a privileged moral status not enjoyed by an identical fetus in a remote area of a poor country?

In addition, as the Court once explained, viability is not really a hard-and-fast line. *Ibid*. A physician determining a particular fetus's odds of surviving outside the womb must consider "a number of variables," including "gestational age," "fetal weight," a woman's "general health and nutrition," the "quality of the available medical facilities," and other factors. *Id.*, at 395–396. It is thus "only with difficulty" that a physician can estimate the "probability" of a particular fetus's survival. *Id.*, at 396. And even if each fetus's probability of survival could be ascertained with certainty, settling on a "probabilit[y] of survival" that should count as "viability" is another matter. *Ibid*. Is a fetus viable with a 10 percent chance of survival? 25 percent? 50 percent? Can such a judgment be made by a State? And can a State specify a gestational age limit that applies in all cases? Or must these difficult questions be left entirely to the individual "attending physician on the particular facts of the case before him"? *Id.*, at 388.

The viability line, which *Casey* termed *Roe*'s central rule, makes no sense, and it is telling that other countries almost uniformly eschew such a line. The Court thus asserted raw judicial power to impose, as a matter of constitutional law, a uniform viability rule that allowed the States less freedom to regulate abortion than the majority of western democracies enjoy.

d

All in all, *Roe*'s reasoning was exceedingly weak, and academic commentators, including those who agreed with the decision as a matter of policy, were unsparing in their criticism. John Hart Ely famously wrote that *Roe* was "not constitutional law and g[ave] almost no sense of an obligation to try to be." Ely 947 (emphasis deleted). Archibald Cox, who served as Solicitor General under President Kennedy, commented that *Roe* "read[s] like a set of hospital rules and regulations" that "[n]either historian, layman, nor lawyer will be persuaded . . . are part of . . . the Constitution." The Role of the Supreme Court in American Government 113–114 (1976). Laurence Tribe wrote that "even if there is a need to divide pregnancy into several segments with lines that clearly identify the limits of governmental power, 'interest-balancing' of the form the Court pursues fails to justify any of the lines actually drawn." Tribe 4–5. Mark Tushnet termed *Roe* a "totally unreasoned judicial opinion." Red, White, and Blue: A Critical Analysis of Constitutional Law 54 (1988). See also P. Bobbitt, Constitutional Fate 157 (1982); A. Amar, Foreword: The Document and the Doctrine, 114 Harv. L. Rev. 26, 110 (2000).

Despite *Roe*'s weaknesses, its reach was steadily extended in the years that followed. The Court struck down laws requiring that second-trimester abortions be performed only in hospitals, *Akron* v. *Akron Center for Reproductive Health, Inc.*, 462 U.S. 416, 433–439 (1983); that minors obtain parental consent, *Planned Parenthood of Central Mo.* v. *Danforth*, 428 U.S. 52, 74 (1976); that women give written consent after being informed of the status of the developing prenatal life and the risks of abortion, *Akron*, 462 U. S., at 442–445; that women wait 24 hours for an abortion, *id.*, at 449–451; that a physician determine viability in a particular manner, *Colautti*, 439 U. S., at 390–397; that a physician performing a post-viability abortion use the technique most likely to preserve the life of the fetus, *id.*, at 397–401; and that fetal remains be treated in a humane and sanitary manner, *Akron*, 462 U. S., at 451–452.

Justice White complained that the Court was engaging in "unrestrained imposition of its own extraconstitutional value preferences." *Thornburgh*, 476 U. S., at 794 (dissenting opinion). And the United States as *amicus curiae* asked the Court to overrule *Roe* five times in the decade before *Casey*, see 505 U. S., at 844 (joint opinion), and then asked the Court to overrule it once more in *Casey* itself.

2

When *Casey* revisited *Roe* almost 20 years later, very little of *Roe*'s reasoning was defended or preserved. The Court abandoned any reliance on a privacy right and instead grounded the abortion right entirely on the Fourteenth Amendment's Due Process Clause. 505 U. S., at 846. The Court did not reaffirm *Roe*'s erroneous account of abortion history. In fact, none of the Justices in the majority said anything about the history of the abortion right. And as for precedent, the Court relied on essentially the same body of cases that *Roe* had cited. Thus, with respect to the standard grounds for constitutional decisionmaking—text, history, and precedent—*Casey* did not attempt to bolster *Roe*'s reasoning.

The Court also made no real effort to remedy one of the greatest weaknesses in *Roe*'s analysis: its much-criticized discussion of viability. The Court retained what it called *Roe*'s "central holding"—that a State may not regulate pre-viability abortions for the purpose of protecting fetal life—but it provided no principled defense of the viability line. 505 U. S., at 860, 870–871. Instead, it merely rephrased what *Roe* had said, stating that viability marked the point at which "the independent existence of a second life can in reason and fairness be the object of state protection that now overrides the rights of the woman." 505 U. S., at 870. Why "reason and fairness" demanded that the line be drawn at viability the Court did not explain. And the Justices who authored the controlling opinion conspicuously failed to say that they agreed with the viability rule; instead, they candidly acknowledged "the reservations [some] of us may have in reaffirming [that] holding of *Roe*." *Id.*, at 853.

The controlling opinion criticized and rejected *Roe*'s trimester scheme, 505 U. S., at 872, and substituted a new "undue burden" test, but the basis for this test was obscure. And as we will explain, the test is full of ambiguities and is difficult to apply.

Casey, in short, either refused to reaffirm or rejected important aspects of *Roe*'s analysis, failed to remedy glaring deficiencies in *Roe*'s reasoning, endorsed what it termed *Roe*'s central holding while suggesting that a majority might not have thought it was correct, provided no new support for the abortion right other than *Roe*'s status as precedent, and imposed a new and problematic test with no firm grounding in constitutional text, history, or precedent.

As discussed below, *Casey* also deployed a novel version of the doctrine of *stare decisis*. See *infra*, at 64–69. This new doctrine did not account for the profound wrongness of the decision in *Roe*, and placed great weight on an intangible form of reliance with little if any basis in prior case law. *Stare decisis* does not command the preservation of such a decision.

C

Workability. Our precedents counsel that another important consideration in deciding whether a precedent should be overruled is whether the rule it imposes is workable—that is, whether it can be understood and applied in a consistent and predictable manner. *Montejo* v. *Louisiana*, 556 U.S. 778, 792 (2009); *Patterson* v. *McLean Credit Union*, 491 U.S. 164, 173 (1989); *Gulfstream Aerospace Corp.* v. *Mayacamas Corp.*, 485 U.S. 271, 283–284 (1988). *Casey*'s "undue burden" test has scored poorly on the workability scale.

1

Problems begin with the very concept of an "undue burden." As Justice Scalia noted in his *Casey* partial dissent, determining whether a burden is "due" or "undue" is "inherently standardless." 505 U. S., at 992; see also *June Medical Services L. L. C.* v. *Russo*, 591 U. S. ___, ___ (2020) (Gorsuch, J., dissenting) (slip op., at 17) ("[W]hether a burden is deemed undue depends heavily on which factors the judge considers and how much weight he accords each of them" (internal quotation marks and alterations omitted)).

The *Casey* plurality tried to put meaning into the "undue burden" test by setting out three subsidiary rules, but these rules created their own problems. The first rule is that "a provision of law is invalid, if its purpose or effect is to place a *substantial obstacle* in the path of a woman seeking an abortion before the fetus attains viability." 505 U. S., at 878 (emphasis added); see also *id.*, at 877. But whether a particular obstacle qualifies as "substantial" is often open to reasonable debate. In the sense relevant here, "substantial" means "of ample or considerable amount, quantity, or size." Random House Webster's Unabridged Dictionary 1897 (2d ed. 2001). Huge burdens are plainly "substantial," and trivial ones are not, but in between these extremes, there is a wide gray area.

This ambiguity is a problem, and the second rule, which applies at all stages of a pregnancy, muddies things further. It states that measures designed "to ensure that the woman's choice is informed" are constitutional so long as they do not impose "an undue burden on the right." *Casey*, 505 U. S., at 878. To the extent that this rule applies to pre-viability abortions, it overlaps with the first rule and appears to impose a different standard. Consider a law that imposes an insubstantial obstacle but serves little purpose. As applied to a pre-viability abortion, would such a regulation be constitutional on the ground that it does not impose a "*substantial* obstacle"? Or would it be unconstitutional on the ground that it creates an *"undue* burden" because the burden it imposes, though slight, outweighs its negligible benefits? *Casey* does not say, and this ambiguity would lead to confusion down the line. Compare *June Medical*, 591 U. S., at ___-___ (plurality opinion) (slip op., at 1–2), with *id.,* at ___-___ (Roberts, C. J., concurring) (slip op., at 5–6).

The third rule complicates the picture even more. Under that rule, *"[u]nnecessary health* regulations that have the purpose or effect of presenting a *substantial obstacle* to a woman seeking an abortion impose an *undue burden* on the right." *Casey*, 505 U. S., at 878 (emphasis added). This rule contains no fewer than three vague terms. It includes the two already discussed—"undue burden" and "substantial obstacle"—even though they are inconsistent. And it adds a third ambiguous term when it refers to *"unnecessary* health regulations." The term "necessary" has a range of meanings—from "essential" to merely "useful." See Black's Law Dictionary 928 (5th ed. 1979); American Heritage Dictionary of the English Language 877 (1971). *Casey* did not explain the sense in which the term is used in this rule.

In addition to these problems, one more applies to all three rules. They all call on courts to examine a law's effect on women, but a regulation may have a very different impact on different women for a variety of reasons, including their places of residence, financial resources, family situations, work and personal obligations, knowledge about fetal development and abortion, psychological and emotional disposition and condition, and the firmness of their desire to obtain abortions. In order to determine whether a regulation presents a substantial obstacle to women, a court needs to know which set of women it should have in mind and how many of the women in this set must find that an obstacle is "substantial."

Casey provided no clear answer to these questions. It said that a regulation is unconstitutional if it imposes a substantial obstacle "in a large fraction of cases in which [it] is relevant," 505 U. S., at 895, but there is obviously no clear line between a fraction that is "large" and one that is not. Nor is it clear what the Court meant by "cases in which" a regulation is "relevant." These ambiguities have caused confusion and disagreement. Compare *Whole Woman's Health* v. *Hellerstedt*, 579 U.S. 582, 627–628 (2016), with *id.,* at 666–667, and n. 11 (Alito, J., dissenting).

2

The difficulty of applying *Casey*'s new rules surfaced in that very case. The controlling opinion found that Pennsylvania's 24-hour waiting period requirement and its informed-consent provision did not impose "undue burden[s]," *Casey*, 505 U. S., at 881–887, but Justice Stevens, applying the same test, reached the opposite result, *id.,* at 920–922 (opinion concurring in part and dissenting in part). That did not bode well, and then-Chief Justice Rehnquist aptly observed that "the undue burden standard presents nothing more workable than the trimester framework." *Id.,* at 964–966 (dissenting opinion).

The ambiguity of the "undue burden" test also produced disagreement in later cases. In *Whole Woman's Health*, the Court adopted the cost-benefit interpretation of the test, stating that "[t]he rule announced in *Casey* . . . requires that courts consider the burdens a law imposes on abortion access *together with the benefits those laws confer."* 579 U. S., at 607 (emphasis added). But five years later, a majority of the Justices rejected that interpretation. See *June Medical*, 591 U. S. ___. Four Justices reaffirmed *Whole Woman's Health*'s instruction to "weigh" a law's "benefits" against "the burdens it imposes on abortion access." 591 U. S., at ___ (plurality opinion) (slip op., at 2) (internal quotation marks omitted). But The Chief Justice—who cast the deciding vote—argued that "[n]othing about *Casey* suggested that a weighing of costs and benefits of an abortion regulation was a job for the courts." *Id.,* at ___ (opinion concurring in judgment) (slip op., at 6). And the four Justices in dissent rejected the plurality's interpretation of *Casey*. See 591 U. S., at ___ (opinion of Alito, J., joined in relevant part by Thomas, Gorsuch, and Kavanaugh, JJ.) (slip op., at 4); *id.,* at ___-___ (opinion of Gorsuch, J.) (slip op., at 15–18); *id.,* at ___-___ (opinion of Kavanaugh, J.) (slip op., at 1–2) ("[F]ive Members of the Court reject the *Whole Woman's Health* cost-benefit standard").

This Court's experience applying *Casey* has confirmed Chief Justice Rehnquist's prescient diagnosis that the undue-burden standard was "not built to last." *Casey*, 505 U. S., at 965 (opinion concurring in judgment in part and dissenting in part).

3

The experience of the Courts of Appeals provides further evidence that *Casey*'s "line between" permissible and unconstitutional restrictions "has proved to be impossible to draw with precision." *Janus*, 585 U. S., at ___ (slip op., at 38).

Casey has generated a long list of Circuit conflicts. Most recently, the Courts of Appeals have disagreed about whether the balancing test from *Whole Woman's Health* correctly states the undue-burden framework. They have disagreed on the legality of parental notification rules. They have disagreed about bans on certain dilation and evacuation procedures. They have disagreed about when an increase in the time needed to reach a clinic constitutes an undue burden. And they have disagreed on whether a State may regulate abortions performed because of the fetus's race, sex, or disability.

The Courts of Appeals have experienced particular difficulty in applying the large-fraction-of-relevant-cases test. They have criticized the assignment while reaching unpredictable results. And they have candidly outlined *Casey*'s many other problems.

Casey's "undue burden" test has proved to be unworkable. "[P]lucked from nowhere," 505 U. S., at 965 (opinion of Rehnquist, C. J.), it "seems calculated to perpetuate give-it-a-try litigation" before judges assigned an unwieldy and inappropriate task. *Lehnert* v. *Ferris Faculty Assn.*, 500 U.S. 507, 551 (1991) (Scalia, J., concurring in judgment in part and dissenting in part). Continued adherence to that standard would undermine, not advance, the "evenhanded, predictable, and consistent development of legal principles." *Payne*, 501 U. S., at 827.

D

Effect on other areas of law. *Roe* and *Casey* have led to the distortion of many important but unrelated legal doctrines, and that effect provides further support for overruling those decisions. See *Ramos*, 590 U. S., at ___ (opinion of Kavanaugh, J.) (slip op., at 8); *Janus*, 585 U. S., at ___ (slip op., at 34).

Members of this Court have repeatedly lamented that "no legal rule or doctrine is safe from ad hoc nullification by this Court when an occasion for its application arises in a case involving state regulation of abortion." *Thornburgh*, 476 U. S., at 814 (O'Connor, J., dissenting); see *Madsen* v. *Women's Health Center, Inc.*, 512 U.S. 753, 785 (1994) (Scalia, J., concurring in judgment in part and dissenting in part); *Whole Woman's Health*, 579 U. S., at 631–633 (Thomas, J., dissenting); *id.*, at 645–666, 678–684 (Alito, J., dissenting); *June Medical*, 591 U. S., at ___–___ (Gorsuch, J., dissenting) (slip op., at 1–15).

The Court's abortion cases have diluted the strict standard for facial constitutional challenges. They have ignored the Court's third-party standing doctrine. They have disregarded standard *res judicata* principles. They have flouted the ordinary rules on the severability of unconstitutional provisions, as well as the rule that statutes should be read where possible to avoid unconstitutionality. And they have distorted First Amendment doctrines.

When vindicating a doctrinal innovation requires courts to engineer exceptions to longstanding background rules, the doctrine "has failed to deliver the 'principled and intelligible' development of the law that *stare decisis* purports to secure." *Id.*, at ___ (Thomas, J., dissenting) (slip op., at 19) (quoting *Vasquez* v. *Hillery*, 474 U.S. 254, 265 (1986)).

E

Reliance interests. We last consider whether overruling *Roe* and *Casey* will upend substantial reliance interests. See *Ramos*, 590 U. S., at ___ (opinion of Kavanaugh, J.) (slip op., at 15); *Janus*, 585 U. S., at ___–___ (slip op., at 34–35).

1

Traditional reliance interests arise "where advance planning of great precision is most obviously a necessity." *Casey*, 505 U. S., at 856 (joint opinion); see also *Payne*, 501 U. S., at 828. In *Casey*, the controlling opinion conceded that those traditional reliance interests were not implicated because getting an abortion is generally "unplanned activity," and "reproductive planning could take virtually immediate account of any sudden restoration of state authority to ban abortions." 505 U. S., at 856. For these reasons, we agree with the *Casey* plurality that conventional, concrete reliance interests are not present here.

2

Unable to find reliance in the conventional sense, the controlling opinion in *Casey* perceived a more intangible form of reliance. It wrote that "people [had] organized intimate relationships and made choices that define their views of themselves and their places in society . . . in reliance on the availability of abortion in the event that contraception should fail" and that "[t]he ability of women to participate equally in the economic and social life of the Nation has been facilitated by their ability to control their reproductive lives." *Ibid*. But this Court is ill-equipped to assess "generalized assertions about the national psyche." *Id*., at 957 (opinion of Rehnquist, C. J.). *Casey*'s notion of reliance thus finds little support in our cases, which instead emphasize very concrete reliance interests, like those that develop in "cases involving property and contract rights." *Payne*, 501 U. S., at 828.

When a concrete reliance interest is asserted, courts are equipped to evaluate the claim, but assessing the novel and intangible form of reliance endorsed by the *Casey* plurality is another matter. That form of reliance depends on an empirical question that is hard for anyone—and in particular, for a court—to assess, namely, the effect of the abortion right on society and in particular on the lives of women. The contending sides in this case make impassioned and conflicting arguments about the effects of the abortion right on the lives of women. Compare Brief for Petitioners 34–36; Brief for Women Scholars et al. as *Amici Curiae* 13–20, 29–41, with Brief for Respondents 36–41; Brief for National Women's Law Center et al. as *Amici Curiae* 15–32. The contending sides also make conflicting arguments about the status of the fetus. This Court has neither the authority nor the expertise to adjudicate those disputes, and the *Casey* plurality's speculations and weighing of the relative importance of the fetus and mother represent a departure from the "original constitutional proposition" that "courts do not substitute their social and economic beliefs for the judgment of legislative bodies." *Ferguson* v. *Skrupa*, 372 U.S. 726, 729–730 (1963).

Our decision returns the issue of abortion to those legislative bodies, and it allows women on both sides of the abortion issue to seek to affect the legislative process by influencing public opinion, lobbying legislators, voting, and running for office. Women are not without electoral or political power. It is noteworthy that the percentage of women who register to vote and cast ballots is consistently higher than the percentage of men who do so. In the last election in November 2020, women, who make up around 51.5 percent of the population of Mississippi, constituted 55.5 percent of the voters who cast ballots.

3

Unable to show concrete reliance on *Roe* and *Casey* themselves, the Solicitor General suggests that overruling those decisions would "threaten the Court's precedents holding that the Due Process Clause protects other rights." Brief for United States 26 (citing *Obergefell*, 576 U.S. 644; *Lawrence*, 539 U.S. 558; *Griswold*, 381 U. S. 479). That is not correct for reasons we have already discussed. As even the *Casey* plurality recognized, "[a]bortion is a unique act" because it terminates "life or potential life." 505 U. S., at 852; see also *Roe*, 410 U. S., at 159 (abortion is "inherently different from marital intimacy," "marriage," or "procreation"). And to ensure that our decision is not misunderstood or mischaracterized, we emphasize that our decision concerns the constitutional right to abortion and no other right. Nothing in this opinion should be understood to cast doubt on precedents that do not concern abortion.

IV

Having shown that traditional *stare decisis* factors do not weigh in favor of retaining *Roe* or *Casey*, we must address one final argument that featured prominently in the *Casey* plurality opinion.

The argument was cast in different terms, but stated simply, it was essentially as follows. The American people's belief in the rule of law would be shaken if they lost respect for this Court as an institution that decides important cases based on principle, not "social and political pressures." 505 U. S., at 865. There is a special danger that the public will perceive a decision as having been made for unprincipled reasons when the Court overrules a controversial "watershed" decision, such as *Roe*. 505 U. S., at 866–867. A decision overruling *Roe* would be perceived as having been made "under fire" and as a "surrender to political pressure," 505 U. S., at 867, and therefore the preservation of public approval of the Court weighs heavily in favor of retaining *Roe*, see 505 U. S., at 869.

This analysis starts out on the right foot but ultimately veers off course. The *Casey* plurality was certainly right that it is important for the public to perceive that our decisions are based on principle, and we should make every effort to achieve that objective by issuing opinions that carefully show how a proper understanding of the law leads to the results we reach. But we cannot exceed the scope of our authority under the Constitution, and we cannot allow our decisions to be affected by any extraneous influences such as concern about the public's reaction to our work. Cf. *Texas v. Johnson*, 491 U.S. 397 (1989); *Brown*, 347 U.S. 483. That is true both when we initially decide a constitutional issue *and* when we consider whether to overrule a prior decision. As Chief Justice Rehnquist explained, "The Judicial Branch derives its legitimacy, not from following public opinion, but from deciding by its best lights whether legislative enactments of the popular branches of Government comport with the Constitution. The doctrine of *stare decisis* is an adjunct of this duty, and should be no more subject to the vagaries of public opinion than is the basic judicial task." *Casey*, 505 U. S., at 963 (opinion concurring in judgment in part and dissenting in part). In suggesting otherwise, the *Casey* plurality went beyond this Court's role in our constitutional system.

The *Casey* plurality "call[ed] the contending sides of a national controversy to end their national division," and claimed the authority to impose a permanent settlement of the issue of a constitutional abortion right simply by saying that the matter was closed. *Id.,* at 867. That unprecedented claim exceeded the power vested in us by the Constitution. As Alexander Hamilton famously put it, the Constitution gives the judiciary "neither Force nor Will." The Federalist No. 78, p. 523 (J. Cooke ed. 1961). Our sole authority is to exercise "judgment"—which is to say, the authority to judge what the law means and how it should apply to the case at hand. *Ibid*. The Court has no authority to decree that an erroneous precedent is *permanently* exempt from evaluation under traditional *stare decisis* principles. A precedent of this Court is subject to the usual principles of *stare decisis* under which adherence to precedent is the norm but not an inexorable command. If the rule were otherwise, erroneous decisions like *Plessy* and *Lochner* would still be the law. That is not how *stare decisis* operates.

The *Casey* plurality also misjudged the practical limits of this Court's influence. *Roe* certainly did not succeed in ending division on the issue of abortion. On the contrary, *Roe* "inflamed" a national issue that has remained bitterly divisive for the past half century. *Casey*, 505 U. S., at 995 (opinion of Scalia, J.); see also R. Ginsburg, Speaking in a Judicial Voice, 67 N. Y. U. L. Rev. 1185, 1208 (1992) (*Roe* may have "halted a political process," "prolonged divisiveness," and "deferred stable settlement of the issue"). And for the past 30 years, *Casey* has done the same.

Neither decision has ended debate over the issue of a constitutional right to obtain an abortion. Indeed, in this case, 26 States expressly ask us to overrule *Roe* and *Casey* and to return the issue of abortion to the people and their elected representatives. This Court's inability to end debate on the issue should not have been surprising. This Court cannot bring about the permanent resolution of a rancorous national controversy simply by dictating a settlement and telling the people to move on. Whatever influence the Court may have on public attitudes must stem from the strength of our opinions, not an attempt to exercise "raw judicial power." *Roe*, 410 U. S., at 222 (White, J., dissenting).

We do not pretend to know how our political system or society will respond to today's decision overruling *Roe* and *Casey*. And even if we could foresee what will happen, we would have no authority to let that knowledge influence our decision. We can only do our job, which is to interpret the law, apply longstanding principles of *stare decisis*, and decide this case accordingly.

We therefore hold that the Constitution does not confer a right to abortion. *Roe* and *Casey* must be overruled, and the authority to regulate abortion must be returned to the people and their elected representatives.

V

A

1

The dissent argues that we have "abandon[ed]" *stare decisis, post,* at 30, but we have done no such thing, and it is the dissent's understanding of *stare decisis* that breaks with tradition. The dissent's foundational contention is that the Court should never (or perhaps almost never) overrule an egregiously wrong constitutional precedent unless the Court can "poin[t] to major legal or factual changes undermining [the] decision's original basis." *Post*, at 37. To support this contention, the dissent claims that *Brown* v. *Board of Education*, 347 U.S. 483, and other landmark cases overruling prior precedents "responded to changed law and to changed facts and attitudes that had taken hold throughout society." *Post*, at 43. The unmistakable implication of this argument is that only the passage of time and new developments justified those decisions. Recognition that the cases they overruled were egregiously wrong on the day they were handed down was not enough.

The Court has never adopted this strange new version of *stare decisis*—and with good reason. Does the dissent really maintain that overruling *Plessy* was not justified until the country had experienced more than a half-century of state-sanctioned segregation and generations of Black school children had suffered all its effects? *Post*, at 44–45.

Here is another example. On the dissent's view, it must have been wrong for *West Virginia Bd. of Ed.* v. *Barnette*, 319 U.S. 624, to overrule *Minersville School Dist.* v. *Gobitis*, 310 U.S. 586, a bare three years after it was handed down. In both cases, children who were Jehovah's Witnesses refused on religious grounds to salute the flag or recite the pledge of allegiance. The *Barnette* Court did not claim that its reexamination of the issue was prompted by any intervening legal or factual developments, so if the Court had followed the dissent's new version of *stare decisis*, it would have been compelled to adhere to *Gobitis* and countenance continued First Amendment violations for some unspecified period.

Precedents should be respected, but sometimes the Court errs, and occasionally the Court issues an important decision that is egregiously wrong. When that happens, *stare decisis* is not a straitjacket. And indeed, the dissent eventually admits that a decision *could* "be overruled just because it is terribly wrong," though the dissent does not explain when that would be so. *Post*, at 45.

2

Even if the dissent were correct in arguing that an egregiously wrong decision should (almost) never be overruled unless its mistake is later highlighted by "major legal or factual changes," reexamination of *Roe* and *Casey* would be amply justified. We have already mentioned a number of post-*Casey* developments, see *supra*, at 33–34, 59–63, but the most profound change may be the failure of the *Casey* plurality's call for "the contending sides" in the controversy about abortion "to end their national division," 505 U. S., at 867. That has not happened, and there is no reason to think that another decision sticking with *Roe* would achieve what *Casey* could not.

The dissent, however, is undeterred. It contends that the "very controversy surrounding *Roe* and *Casey*" is an important *stare decisis* consideration that requires upholding those precedents. See *post*, at 55–57. The dissent characterizes *Casey* as a "precedent about precedent" that is permanently shielded from further evaluation under traditional *stare decisis* principles. See *post*, at 57. But as we have explained, *Casey* broke new ground when it treated the national controversy provoked by *Roe* as a ground for refusing to reconsider that decision, and no subsequent case has relied on that factor. Our decision today simply applies longstanding *stare decisis* factors instead of applying a version of the doctrine that seems to apply only in abortion cases.

3

Finally, the dissent suggests that our decision calls into question *Griswold*, *Eisenstadt*, *Lawrence*, and *Obergefell*. *Post*, at 4–5, 26–27, n. 8. But we have stated unequivocally that "[n]othing in this opinion should be understood to cast doubt on precedents that do not concern abortion." *Supra*, at 66. We have also explained why that is so: rights regarding contraception and same-sex relationships are inherently different from the right to abortion because the latter (as we have stressed) uniquely involves what *Roe* and *Casey* termed "potential life." *Roe*, 410 U. S., at 150 (emphasis deleted); *Casey*, 505 U. S., at 852. Therefore, a right to abortion cannot be justified by a purported analogy to the rights recognized in those other cases or by "appeals to a broader right to autonomy." *Supra*, at 32. It is hard to see how we could be clearer. Moreover, even putting aside that these cases are distinguishable, there is a further point that the dissent ignores: Each precedent is subject to its own *stare decisis* analysis, and the factors that our doctrine instructs us to consider like reliance and workability are different for these cases than for our abortion jurisprudence.

B

1

We now turn to the concurrence in the judgment, which reproves us for deciding whether *Roe* and *Casey* should be retained or overruled. That opinion (which for convenience we will call simply "the concurrence") recommends a "more measured course," which it defends based on what it claims is "a straightforward *stare decisis* analysis." *Post*, at 1 (opinion of Roberts, C. J.). The concurrence would "leave for another day whether to reject any right to an abortion at all," *post*, at 7, and would hold only that if the Constitution protects any such right, the right ends once women have had "a reasonable opportunity" to obtain an abortion, *post*, at 1. The concurrence does not specify what period of time is sufficient to provide such an opportunity, but it would hold that 15 weeks, the period allowed under Mississippi's law, is enough—at least "absent rare circumstances." *Post*, at 2, 10.

There are serious problems with this approach, and it is revealing that nothing like it was recommended by either party. As we have recounted, both parties and the Solicitor General have urged us either to reaffirm or overrule *Roe* and *Casey*. See *supra*, at 4–5. And when the specific approach advanced by the concurrence was broached at oral argument, both respondents and the Solicitor General emphatically rejected it. Respondents' counsel termed it "completely unworkable" and "less principled and less workable than viability." Tr. of Oral Arg. 54. The Solicitor General argued that abandoning the viability line would leave courts and others with "no continued guidance." *Id.*, at 101. What is more, the concurrence has not identified any of the more than 130 *amicus* briefs filed in this case that advocated its approach. The concurrence would do exactly what it criticizes *Roe* for doing: pulling "out of thin air" a test that "[n]o party or *amicus* asked the Court to adopt." *Post*, at 3.

2

The concurrence's most fundamental defect is its failure to offer any principled basis for its approach. The concurrence would "discar[d]" "the rule from *Roe* and *Casey* that a woman's right to terminate her pregnancy extends up to the point that the fetus is regarded as 'viable' outside the womb." *Post*, at 2.

But this rule was a critical component of the holdings in *Roe* and *Casey*, and *stare decisis* is "a doctrine of preservation, not transformation," *Citizens United* v. *Federal Election Comm'n*, 558 U.S. 310, 384 (2010) (Roberts, C. J., concurring). Therefore, a new rule that discards the viability rule cannot be defended on *stare decisis* grounds.

The concurrence concedes that its approach would "not be available" if "the rationale of *Roe* and *Casey* were inextricably entangled with and dependent upon the viability standard." *Post*, at 7. But the concurrence asserts that the viability line is separable from the constitutional right they recognized, and can therefore be "discarded" without disturbing any past precedent. *Post*, at 7–8. That is simply incorrect.

Roe's trimester rule was expressly tied to viability, see 410 U. S., at 163–164, and viability played a critical role in later abortion decisions. For example, in *Planned Parenthood of Central Mo.* v. *Danforth*, 428 U.S. 52, the Court reiterated *Roe*'s rule that a "State may regulate an abortion to protect the life of the fetus and even may proscribe abortion" at "the stage *subsequent to viability*." 428 U. S., at 61 (emphasis added). The Court then rejected a challenge to Missouri's definition of viability, holding that the State's definition was consistent with *Roe*'s. 428 U. S., at 63–64. If viability was not an essential part of the rule adopted in *Roe*, the Court would have had no need to make that comparison.

The holding in *Colautti* v. *Franklin*, 439 U.S. 379, is even more instructive. In that case, the Court noted that prior cases had "stressed viability" and reiterated that "[v]iability is the critical point" under *Roe*. 439 U. S., at 388–389. It then struck down Pennsylvania's definition of viability, *id.*, at 389–394, and it is hard to see how the Court could have done that if *Roe*'s discussion of viability was not part of its holding.

When the Court reconsidered *Roe* in *Casey*, it left no doubt about the importance of the viability rule. It described the rule as *Roe*'s "central holding," 505 U. S., at 860, and repeatedly stated that the right it reaffirmed was "the right of the woman to choose to have an abortion *before viability*." *Id.*, at 846 (emphasis added). See *id.*, at 871 ("The woman's right to terminate her pregnancy *before viability* is the most central principle of *Roe* v. *Wade*. It is a rule of law and a component of liberty we cannot renounce" (emphasis added)); *id.*, at 872 (A "woman has a right to choose to terminate or continue her pregnancy *before viability*" (emphasis added)); *id.*, at 879 ("[A] State may not prohibit any woman from making the ultimate decision to terminate her pregnancy *before viability*" (emphasis added)).

Our subsequent cases have continued to recognize the centrality of the viability rule. See *Whole Women's Health*, 579 U. S., at 589–590 ("[A] provision of law is constitutionally invalid, if the 'purpose or effect' of the provision 'is to place a substantial obstacle in the path of a woman seeking an abortion *before the fetus attains viability*'" (emphasis deleted and added)); *id.*, at 627 ("[W]e now use *'viability'* as the relevant point at which a State may begin limiting women's access to abortion for reasons unrelated to maternal health" (emphasis added)).

Not only is the new rule proposed by the concurrence inconsistent with *Casey*'s unambiguous "language," *post*, at 8, it is also contrary to the judgment in that case and later abortion cases. In *Casey*, the Court held that Pennsylvania's spousal-notification provision was facially unconstitutional, not just that it was unconstitutional as applied to abortions sought prior to the time when a woman has had a reasonable opportunity to choose. See 505 U. S., at 887–898. The same is true of *Whole Women's Health*, which held that certain rules that required physicians performing abortions to have admitting privileges at a nearby hospital were facially unconstitutional because they placed "a substantial obstacle in the path of women seeking *a previability abortion*." 579 U. S., at 591 (emphasis added).

For all these reasons, *stare decisis* cannot justify the new "reasonable opportunity" rule propounded by the concurrence. If that rule is to become the law of the land, it must stand on its own, but the concurrence makes no attempt to show that this rule represents a correct interpretation of the Constitution. The concurrence does not claim that the right to a reasonable opportunity to obtain an abortion is "'deeply rooted in this Nation's history and tradition'" and "'implicit in the concept of ordered liberty.'" *Glucksberg*, 521 U. S., at 720–721. Nor does it propound any other theory that could show that the Constitution supports its new rule. And if the Constitution protects a woman's right to obtain an abortion, the opinion does not explain why that right should end after the point at which all "reasonable" women will have decided whether to seek an abortion. While the concurrence is moved by a desire for judicial minimalism, "we cannot embrace a narrow ground of decision simply because it is narrow; it must also be right." *Citizens United*, 558 U. S., at 375 (Roberts, C. J., concurring). For the reasons that we have explained, the concurrence's approach is not.

3

The concurrence would "leave for another day whether to reject any right to an abortion at all," *post*, at 7, but "another day" would not be long in coming. Some States have set deadlines for obtaining an abortion that are shorter than Mississippi's. See, *e.g., Memphis Center for Reproductive Health* v. *Slatery*, 14 F. 4th, at 414 (considering law with bans "at cascading intervals of two to three weeks" beginning at six weeks), reh'g en banc granted, 14 F. 4th 550 (CA6 2021). If we held only that Mississippi's 15-week rule is constitutional, we would soon be called upon to pass on the constitutionality of a panoply of laws with shorter deadlines or no deadline at all. The "measured course" charted by the concurrence would be fraught with turmoil until the Court answered the question that the concurrence seeks to defer.

Even if the Court ultimately adopted the new rule suggested by the concurrence, we would be faced with the difficult problem of spelling out what it means. For example, if the period required to give women a "reasonable" opportunity to obtain an abortion were pegged, as the concurrence seems to suggest, at the point when a certain percentage of women make that choice, see *post*, at 1–2, 9–10, we would have to identify the relevant percentage. It would also be necessary to explain what the concurrence means when it refers to "rare circumstances" that might justify an exception. *Post*, at 10. And if this new right aims to give women a reasonable opportunity to get an abortion, it would be necessary to decide whether factors other than promptness in deciding might have a bearing on whether such an opportunity was available.

In sum, the concurrence's quest for a middle way would only put off the day when we would be forced to confront the question we now decide. The turmoil wrought by *Roe* and *Casey* would be prolonged. It is far better—for this Court and the country—to face up to the real issue without further delay.

VI

We must now decide what standard will govern if state abortion regulations undergo constitutional challenge and whether the law before us satisfies the appropriate standard.

A

Under our precedents, rational-basis review is the appropriate standard for such challenges. As we have explained, procuring an abortion is not a fundamental constitutional right because such a right has no basis in the Constitution's text or in our Nation's history. See *supra,* at 8–39.

It follows that the States may regulate abortion for legitimate reasons, and when such regulations are challenged under the Constitution, courts cannot "substitute their social and economic beliefs for the judgment of legislative bodies." *Ferguson,* 372 U. S., at 729–730; see also *Dandridge* v. *Williams,* 397 U.S. 471, 484–486 (1970); *United States* v. *Carolene Products Co.,* 304 U.S. 144, 152 (1938). That respect for a legislature's judgment applies even when the laws at issue concern matters of great social significance and moral substance. See, *e.g., Board of Trustees of Univ. of Ala.* v. *Garrett,* 531 U.S. 356, 365–368 (2001) ("treatment of the disabled"); *Glucksberg,* 521 U. S., at 728 ("assisted suicide"); *San Antonio Independent School Dist.* v. *Rodriguez,* 411 U.S. 1, 32–35, 55 (1973) ("financing public education").

A law regulating abortion, like other health and welfare laws, is entitled to a "strong presumption of validity." *Heller* v. *Doe,* 509 U.S. 312, 319 (1993). It must be sustained if there is a rational basis on which the legislature could have thought that it would serve legitimate state interests. *Id.,* at 320; *FCC* v. *Beach Communications, Inc.,* 508 U.S. 307, 313 (1993); *New Orleans* v. *Dukes,* 427 U.S. 297, 303 (1976) (*per curiam*); *Williamson* v. *Lee Optical of Okla., Inc.,* 348 U.S. 483, 491 (1955). These legitimate interests include respect for and preservation of prenatal life at all stages of development, *Gonzales,* 550 U. S., at 157–158; the protection of maternal health and safety; the elimination of particularly gruesome or barbaric medical procedures; the preservation of the integrity of the medical profession; the mitigation of fetal pain; and the prevention of discrimination on the basis of race, sex, or disability. See *id.,* at 156–157; *Roe,* 410 U. S., at 150; cf. *Glucksberg,* 521 U. S., at 728–731 (identifying similar interests).

B

These legitimate interests justify Mississippi's Gestational Age Act. Except "in a medical emergency or in the case of a severe fetal abnormality," the statute prohibits abortion "if the probable gestational age of the unborn human being has been determined to be greater than fifteen (15) weeks." Miss. Code Ann. §41-41-191(4)(b). The Mississippi Legislature's findings recount the stages of "human prenatal development" and assert the State's interest in "protecting the life of the unborn." §2(b)(i). The legislature also found that abortions performed after 15 weeks typically use the dilation and evacuation procedure, and the legislature found the use of this procedure "for nontherapeutic or elective reasons [to be] a barbaric practice, dangerous for the maternal patient, and demeaning to the medical profession." §2(b)(i)(8); see also *Gonzales,* 550 U. S., at 135–143 (describing such procedures). These legitimate interests provide a rational basis for the Gestational Age Act, and it follows that respondents' constitutional challenge must fail.

VII

We end this opinion where we began. Abortion presents a profound moral question. The Constitution does not prohibit the citizens of each State from regulating or prohibiting abortion. *Roe* and *Casey* arrogated that authority. We now overrule those decisions and return that authority to the people and their elected representatives.

The judgment of the Fifth Circuit is reversed, and the case is remanded for further proceedings consistent with this opinion.

It is so ordered.

Justice Breyer, Justice Sotomayor, and Justice Kagan, dissenting

For half a century, *Roe* v. *Wade,* 410 U.S. 113 (1973), and *Planned Parenthood of Southeastern Pa.* v. *Casey,* 505 U.S. 833 (1992), have protected the liberty and equality of women. *Roe* held, and *Casey* reaffirmed, that the Constitution safeguards a woman's right to decide for herself whether to bear a child. *Roe* held, and *Casey* reaffirmed, that in the first stages of pregnancy, the government could not make that choice for women. The government could not control a woman's body or the course of a woman's life: It could not determine what the woman's future would be. See *Casey*, 505 U. S., at 853; *Gonzales* v. *Carhart*, 550 U.S. 124, 171–172 (2007) (Ginsburg, J., dissenting). Respecting a woman as an autonomous being, and granting her full equality, meant giving her substantial choice over this most personal and most consequential of all life decisions.

Roe and *Casey* well understood the difficulty and divisiveness of the abortion issue. The Court knew that Americans hold profoundly different views about the "moral[ity]" of "terminating a pregnancy, even in its earliest stage." *Casey*, 505 U. S., at 850. And the Court recognized that "the State has legitimate interests from the outset of the pregnancy in protecting" the "life of the fetus that may become a child." *Id*., at 846. So the Court struck a balance, as it often does when values and goals compete. It held that the State could prohibit abortions after fetal viability, so long as the ban contained exceptions to safeguard a woman's life or health. It held that even before viability, the State could regulate the abortion procedure in multiple and meaningful ways. But until the viability line was crossed, the Court held, a State could not impose a "substantial obstacle" on a woman's "right to elect the procedure" as she (not the government) thought proper, in light of all the circumstances and complexities of her own life. *Ibid*.

Today, the Court discards that balance. It says that from the very moment of fertilization, a woman has no rights to speak of. A State can force her to bring a pregnancy to term, even at the steepest personal and familial costs. An abortion restriction, the majority holds, is permissible whenever rational, the lowest level of scrutiny known to the law. And because, as the Court has often stated, protecting fetal life is rational, States will feel free to enact all manner of restrictions. The Mississippi law at issue here bars abortions after the 15th week of pregnancy. Under the majority's ruling, though, another State's law could do so after ten weeks, or five or three or one—or, again, from the moment of fertilization. States have already passed such laws, in anticipation of today's ruling. More will follow. Some States have enacted laws extending to all forms of abortion procedure, including taking medication in one's own home. They have passed laws without any exceptions for when the woman is the victim of rape or incest. Under those laws, a woman will have to bear her rapist's child or a young girl her father's—no matter if doing so will destroy her life. So too, after today's ruling, some States may compel women to carry to term a fetus with severe physical anomalies—for example, one afflicted with Tay-Sachs disease, sure to die within a few years of birth. States may even argue that a prohibition on abortion need make no provision for protecting a woman from risk of death or physical harm. Across a vast array of circumstances, a State will be able to impose its moral choice on a woman and coerce her to give birth to a child.

Enforcement of all these draconian restrictions will also be left largely to the States' devices. A State can of course impose criminal penalties on abortion providers, including lengthy prison sentences. But some States will not stop there. Perhaps, in the wake of today's decision, a state law will criminalize the woman's conduct too, incarcerating or fining her for daring to seek or obtain an abortion. And as Texas has recently shown, a State can turn neighbor against neighbor, enlisting fellow citizens in the effort to root out anyone who tries to get an abortion, or to assist another in doing so.

The majority tries to hide the geographically expansive effects of its holding. Today's decision, the majority says, permits "each State" to address abortion as it pleases. *Ante*, at 79. That is cold comfort, of course, for the poor woman who cannot get the money to fly to a distant State for a procedure. Above all others, women lacking financial resources will suffer from today's decision. In any event, interstate restrictions will also soon be in the offing. After this decision, some States may block women from traveling out of State to obtain abortions, or even from receiving abortion medications from out of State. Some may criminalize efforts, including the provision of information or funding, to help women gain access to other States' abortion services. Most threatening of all, no language in today's decision stops the Federal Government from prohibiting abortions nationwide, once again from the moment of conception and without exceptions for rape or incest. If that happens, "the views of [an individual State's] citizens" will not matter. *Ante*, at 1. The challenge for a woman will be to finance a trip not to "New York [or] California" but to Toronto. *Ante*, at 4 (Kavanaugh, J., concurring).

Whatever the exact scope of the coming laws, one result of today's decision is certain: the curtailment of women's rights, and of their status as free and equal citizens.

Yesterday, the Constitution guaranteed that a woman confronted with an unplanned pregnancy could (within reasonable limits) make her own decision about whether to bear a child, with all the life-transforming consequences that act involves. And in thus safeguarding each woman's reproductive freedom, the Constitution also protected "[t]he ability of women to participate equally in [this Nation's] economic and social life." *Casey*, 505 U. S., at 856. But no longer. As of today, this Court holds, a State can always force a woman to give birth, prohibiting even the earliest abortions. A State can thus transform what, when freely undertaken, is a wonder into what, when forced, may be a nightmare. Some women, especially women of means, will find ways around the State's assertion of power. Others—those without money or childcare or the ability to take time off from work—will not be so fortunate. Maybe they will try an unsafe method of abortion, and come to physical harm, or even die. Maybe they will undergo pregnancy and have a child, but at significant personal or familial cost. At the least, they will incur the cost of losing control of their lives. The Constitution will, today's majority holds, provide no shield, despite its guarantees of liberty and equality for all.

And no one should be confident that this majority is done with its work. The right *Roe* and *Casey* recognized does not stand alone. To the contrary, the Court has linked it for decades to other settled freedoms involving bodily integrity, familial relationships, and procreation. Most obviously, the right to terminate a pregnancy arose straight out of the right to purchase and use contraception. See *Griswold* v. *Connecticut*, 381 U.S. 479 (1965); *Eisenstadt* v. *Baird*, 405 U.S. 438 (1972). In turn, those rights led, more recently, to rights of same-sex intimacy and marriage. See *Lawrence* v. *Texas*, 539 U.S. 558 (2003); *Obergefell* v. *Hodges*, 576 U.S. 644 (2015). They are all part of the same constitutional fabric, protecting autonomous decision-making over the most personal of life decisions. The majority (or to be more accurate, most of it) is eager to tell us today that nothing it does "cast[s] doubt on precedents that do not concern abortion." *Ante*, at 66; cf. *ante*, at 3 (Thomas, J., concurring) (advocating the overruling of *Griswold*, *Lawrence*, and *Obergefell*). But how could that be? The lone rationale for what the majority does today is that the right to elect an abortion is not "deeply rooted in history": Not until *Roe*, the majority argues, did people think abortion fell within the Constitution's guarantee of liberty. *Ante*, at 32. The same could be said, though, of most of the rights the majority claims it is not tampering with. The majority could write just as long an opinion showing, for example, that until the mid-20th century, "there was no support in American law for a constitutional right to obtain [contraceptives]." *Ante*, at 15. So one of two things must be true. Either the majority does not really believe in its own reasoning. Or if it does, all rights that have no history stretching back to the mid-19th century are insecure. Either the mass of the majority's opinion is hypocrisy, or additional constitutional rights are under threat. It is one or the other.

One piece of evidence on that score seems especially salient: The majority's cavalier approach to overturning this Court's precedents. *Stare decisis* is the Latin phrase for a foundation stone of the rule of law: that things decided should stay decided unless there is a very good reason for change. It is a doctrine of judicial modesty and humility. Those qualities are not evident in today's opinion. The majority has no good reason for the upheaval in law and society it sets off. *Roe* and *Casey* have been the law of the land for decades, shaping women's expectations of their choices when an unplanned pregnancy occurs. Women have relied on the availability of abortion both in structuring their relationships and in planning their lives. The legal framework *Roe* and *Casey* developed to balance the competing interests in this sphere has proved workable in courts across the country. No recent developments, in either law or fact, have eroded or cast doubt on those precedents. Nothing, in short, has changed. Indeed, the Court in *Casey* already found all of that to be true. *Casey* is a precedent about precedent. It reviewed the same arguments made here in support of overruling *Roe*, and it found that doing so was not warranted. The Court reverses course today for one reason and one reason only: because the composition of this Court has changed. *Stare decisis*, this Court has often said, "contributes to the actual and perceived integrity of the judicial process" by ensuring that decisions are "founded in the law rather than in the proclivities of individuals." *Payne* v. *Ten- nessee*, 501 U.S. 808, 827 (1991); *Vasquez* v. *Hillery*, 474 U.S. 254, 265 (1986). Today, the proclivities of individuals rule. The Court departs from its obligation to faithfully and impartially apply the law. We dissent.

I

We start with *Roe* and *Casey*, and with their deep connections to a broad swath of this Court's precedents. To hear the majority tell the tale, *Roe* and *Casey* are aberrations: They came from nowhere, went nowhere—and so are easy to excise from this Nation's constitutional law. That is not true. After describing the decisions themselves, we explain how they are rooted in—and themselves led to—other rights giving individuals control over their bodies and their most personal and intimate associations. The majority does not wish to talk about these matters for obvious reasons; to do so would both ground *Roe* and *Casey* in this Court's precedents and reveal the broad implications of today's decision. But the facts will not so handily disappear. *Roe* and *Casey* were from the beginning, and are even more now, embedded in core constitutional concepts of individual freedom, and of the equal rights of citizens to decide on the shape of their lives. Those legal concepts, one might even say, have gone far toward defining what it means to be an American. For in this Nation, we do not believe that a government controlling all private choices is compatible with a free people. So we do not (as the majority insists today) place everything within "the reach of majorities and [government] officials." *West Virginia Bd. of Ed.* v. *Barnette*, 319 U.S. 624, 638 (1943). We believe in a Constitution that puts some issues off limits to majority rule. Even in the face of public opposition, we uphold the right of individuals—yes, including women—to make their own choices and chart their own futures. Or at least, we did once.

A

Some half-century ago, *Roe* struck down a state law making it a crime to perform an abortion unless its purpose was to save a woman's life. The *Roe* Court knew it was treading on difficult and disputed ground. It understood that different people's "experiences," "values," and "religious training" and beliefs led to "opposing views" about abortion. 410 U. S., at 116. But by a 7-to-2 vote, the Court held that in the earlier stages of pregnancy, that contested and contestable choice must belong to a woman, in consultation with her family and doctor. The Court explained that a long line of precedents, "founded in the Fourteenth Amendment's concept of personal liberty," protected individual decisionmaking related to "marriage, procreation, contraception, family relationships, and child rearing and education." *Id.*, at 152–153 (citations omitted). For the same reasons, the Court held, the Constitution must protect "a woman's decision whether or not to terminate her pregnancy." *Id.*, at 153. The Court recognized the myriad ways bearing a child can alter the "life and future" of a woman and other members of her family. *Ibid.* A State could not, "by adopting one theory of life," override all "rights of the pregnant woman." *Id.*, at 162.

At the same time, though, the Court recognized "valid interest[s]" of the State "in regulating the abortion decision." *Id.*, at 153. The Court noted in particular "important interests" in "protecting potential life," "maintaining medical standards," and "safeguarding [the] health" of the woman. *Id.*, at 154. No "absolut[ist]" account of the woman's right could wipe away those significant state claims. *Ibid.*

The Court therefore struck a balance, turning on the stage of the pregnancy at which the abortion would occur. The Court explained that early on, a woman's choice must prevail, but that "at some point the state interests" become "dominant." *Id.*, at 155. It then set some guideposts. In the first trimester of pregnancy, the State could not interfere at all with the decision to terminate a pregnancy. At any time after that point, the State could regulate to protect the pregnant woman's health, such as by insisting that abortion providers and facilities meet safety requirements. And after the fetus's viability—the point when the fetus "has the capability of meaningful life outside the mother's womb"—the State could ban abortions, except when necessary to preserve the woman's life or health. *Id.*, at 163–164.

In the 20 years between *Roe* and *Casey*, the Court expressly reaffirmed *Roe* on two occasions, and applied it on many more. Recognizing that "arguments [against *Roe*] continue to be made," we responded that the doctrine of *stare decisis* "demands respect in a society governed by the rule of law." *Akron* v. *Akron Center for Reproductive Health, Inc.*, 462 U.S. 416, 419–420 (1983). And we avowed that the "vitality" of "constitutional principles cannot be allowed to yield simply because of disagreement with them." *Thornburgh* v. *American College of Obstetricians and Gynecologists*, 476 U.S. 747, 759 (1986). So the Court, over and over, enforced the constitutional principles *Roe* had declared. See, *e.g., Ohio* v. *Akron Center for Reproductive Health*, 497 U.S. 502 (1990); *Hodgson* v. *Minneso-*

ta, 497 U.S. 417 (1990); *Simopoulos v. Virginia*, 462 U.S. 506 (1983); *Planned Parenthood Assn. of Kansas City, Mo., Inc. v. Ashcroft*, 462 U.S. 476 (1983); *H. L. v. Matheson*, 450 U.S. 398 (1981); *Bellotti v. Baird*, 443 U.S. 622 (1979); *Planned Parenthood of Central Mo. v. Danforth*, 428 U.S. 52 (1976).

Then, in *Casey*, the Court considered the matter anew, and again upheld *Roe*'s core precepts. *Casey* is in significant measure a precedent about the doctrine of precedent—until today, one of the Court's most important. But we leave for later that aspect of the Court's decision. The key thing now is the substantive aspect of the Court's considered conclusion that "the essential holding of *Roe* v. *Wade* should be retained and once again reaffirmed." 505 U. S., at 846.

Central to that conclusion was a full-throated restatement of a woman's right to choose. Like *Roe*, *Casey* grounded that right in the Fourteenth Amendment's guarantee of "liberty." That guarantee encompasses realms of conduct not specifically referenced in the Constitution: "Marriage is mentioned nowhere" in that document, yet the Court was "no doubt correct" to protect the freedom to marry "against state interference." 505 U. S., at 847–848. And the guarantee of liberty encompasses conduct today that was not protected at the time of the Fourteenth Amendment. See *id.*, at 848. "It is settled now," the Court said—though it was not always so—that "the Constitution places limits on a State's right to interfere with a person's most basic decisions about family and parenthood, as well as bodily integrity." *Id.*, at 849 (citations omitted); see *id.*, at 851 (similarly describing the constitutional protection given to "personal decisions relating to marriage, procreation, contraception, [and] family relationships"). Especially important in this web of precedents protecting an individual's most "personal choices" were those guaranteeing the right to contraception. *Ibid.*; see *id.*, at 852–853. In those cases, the Court had recognized "the right of the individual" to make the vastly consequential "decision whether to bear" a child. *Id.*, at 851 (emphasis deleted). So too, *Casey* reasoned, the liberty clause protects the decision of a woman confronting an unplanned pregnancy. Her decision about abortion was central, in the same way, to her capacity to chart her life's course. See *id.*, at 853.

In reaffirming the right *Roe* recognized, the Court took full account of the diversity of views on abortion, and the importance of various competing state interests. Some Americans, the Court stated, "deem [abortion] nothing short of an act of violence against innocent human life." 505 U. S., at 852. And each State has an interest in "the protection of potential life"—as *Roe* itself had recognized. 505 U. S., at 871 (plurality opinion). On the one hand, that interest was not conclusive. The State could not "resolve" the "moral and spiritual" questions raised by abortion in "such a definitive way that a woman lacks all choice in the matter." *Id.*, at 850 (majority opinion). It could not force her to bear the "pain" and "physical constraints" of "carr[ying] a child to full term" when she would have chosen an early abortion. *Id.*, at 852. But on the other hand, the State had, as *Roe* had held, an exceptionally significant interest in disallowing abortions in the later phase of a pregnancy. And it had an ever-present interest in "ensur[ing] that the woman's choice is informed" and in presenting the case for "choos[ing] childbirth over abortion." 505 U. S., at 878 (plurality opinion).

So *Casey* again struck a balance, differing from *Roe*'s in only incremental ways. It retained *Roe*'s "central holding" that the State could bar abortion only after viability. 505 U. S., at 860 (majority opinion). The viability line, *Casey* thought, was "more workable" than any other in marking the place where the woman's liberty interest gave way to a State's efforts to preserve potential life. *Id.*, at 870 (plurality opinion). At that point, a "second life" was capable of "independent existence." *Ibid.* If the woman even by then had not acted, she lacked adequate grounds to object to "the State's intervention on [the developing child's] behalf." *Ibid.* At the same time, *Casey* decided, based on two decades of experience, that the *Roe* framework did not give States sufficient ability to regulate abortion prior to viability. In that period, *Casey* now made clear, the State could regulate not only to protect the woman's health but also to "promot[e] prenatal life." 505 U. S., at 873 (plurality opinion). In particular, the State could ensure informed choice and could try to promote childbirth. See *id.*, at 877–878. But the State still could not place an "undue burden"—or "substantial obstacle"—"in the path of a woman seeking an abortion." *Id.*, at 878. Prior to viability, the woman, consistent with the constitutional "meaning of liberty," must "retain the ultimate control over her destiny and her body." *Id.*, at 869.

We make one initial point about this analysis in light of the majority's insistence that *Roe* and *Casey*, and we in defending them, are dismissive of a "State's interest in protecting prenatal life." *Ante*, at 38. Nothing could get those decisions more wrong. As just described, *Roe* and *Casey* invoked powerful state interests in that protection, operative at every stage of the pregnancy and overriding the woman's liberty after viability. The strength of those state interests is exactly why the Court allowed greater restrictions on the abortion right than on other rights deriving from the Fourteenth Amendment. But what *Roe* and *Casey* also recognized—which today's majority does not—is that a woman's freedom and equality are likewise involved. That fact—the presence of countervailing interests—is what made the abortion question hard, and what necessitated balancing. The majority scoffs at that idea, castigating us for "repeatedly prais[ing] the 'balance'" the two cases arrived at (with the word "balance" in scare quotes). *Ante*, at 38. To the majority "balance" is a dirty word, as moderation is a foreign concept. The majority would allow States to ban abortion from conception onward because it does not think forced childbirth at all implicates a woman's rights to equality and freedom. Today's Court, that is, does not think there is anything of constitutional significance attached to a woman's control of her body and the path of her life. *Roe* and *Casey* thought that one-sided view misguided. In some sense, that is the difference in a nutshell between our precedents and the majority opinion. The constitutional regime we have lived in for the last 50 years recognized competing interests, and sought a balance between them. The constitutional regime we enter today erases the woman's interest and recognizes only the State's (or the Federal Government's).

B

The majority makes this change based on a single question: Did the reproductive right recognized in *Roe* and *Casey* exist in "1868, the year when the Fourteenth Amendment was ratified"? *Ante*, at 23. The majority says (and with this much we agree) that the answer to this question is no: In 1868, there was no nationwide right to end a pregnancy, and no thought that the Fourteenth Amendment provided one.

Of course, the majority opinion refers as well to some later and earlier history. On the one side of 1868, it goes back as far as the 13th (the 13th!) century. See *ante*, at 17. But that turns out to be wheel-spinning. First, it is not clear what relevance such early history should have, even to the majority. See *New York State Rifle & Pistol Assn., Inc.* v. *Bruen*, 597 U. S. ___, ___ (2022) (slip op., at 26) ("Historical evidence that long predates [ratification] may not illuminate the scope of the right"). If the early history obviously supported abortion rights, the majority would no doubt say that only the views of the Fourteenth Amendment's ratifiers are germane. See *ibid.* (It is "better not to go too far back into antiquity," except if olden "law survived to become our Founders' law"). Second—and embarrassingly for the majority—early law in fact does provide some support for abortion rights. Common-law authorities did not treat abortion as a crime before "quickening"—the point when the fetus moved in the womb. And early American law followed the common-law rule. So the criminal law of that early time might be taken as roughly consonant with *Roe*'s and *Casey*'s different treatment of early and late abortions. Better, then, to move forward in time. On the other side of 1868, the majority occasionally notes that many States barred abortion up to the time of *Roe*. See *ante*, at 24, 36. That is convenient for the majority, but it is window dressing. As the same majority (plus one) just informed us, "post-ratification adoption or acceptance of laws that are *inconsistent* with the original meaning of the constitutional text obviously cannot overcome or alter that text." *New York State Rifle & Pistol Assn., Inc.*, 597 U. S., at ___–___ (slip op., at 27–28). Had the pre-*Roe* liberalization of abortion laws occurred more quickly and more widely in the 20th century, the majority would say (once again) that only the ratifiers' views are germane.

The majority's core legal postulate, then, is that we in the 21st century must read the Fourteenth Amendment just as its ratifiers did. And that is indeed what the majority emphasizes over and over again. See *ante*, at 47 ("[T]he most important historical fact [is] how the States regulated abortion when the Fourteenth Amendment was adopted"); see also *ante*, at 5, 16, and n. 24, 23, 25, 28. If the ratifiers did not understand something as central to freedom, then neither can we. Or said more particularly: If those people did not understand reproductive rights as part of the guarantee of liberty conferred in the Fourteenth Amendment, then those rights do not exist.

As an initial matter, note a mistake in the just preceding sentence. We referred there to the "people" who ratified the Fourteenth Amendment: What rights did those "people" have in their heads at the time? But, of course, "people" did not ratify the Fourteenth Amendment. Men did. So it is perhaps not so surprising that the ratifiers were not perfectly attuned to the importance of reproductive rights for women's liberty, or for their capacity to participate as equal members of our Nation. Indeed, the ratifiers—both in 1868 and when the original Constitution was approved in 1788—did not understand women as full members of the community embraced by the phrase "We the People." In 1868, the first wave of American feminists were explicitly told—of course by men—that it was not their time to seek constitutional protections. (Women would not get even the vote for another half-century.) To be sure, most women in 1868 also had a foreshortened view of their rights: If most men could not then imagine giving women control over their bodies, most women could not imagine having that kind of autonomy. But that takes away nothing from the core point. Those responsible for the original Constitution, including the Fourteenth Amendment, did not perceive women as equals, and did not recognize women's rights. When the majority says that we must read our foundational charter as viewed at the time of ratification (except that we may also check it against the Dark Ages), it consigns women to second-class citizenship.

Casey itself understood this point, as will become clear. See *infra*, at 23–24. It recollected with dismay a decision this Court issued just five years after the Fourteenth Amendment's ratification, approving a State's decision to deny a law license to a woman and suggesting as well that a woman had no legal status apart from her husband. See 505 U. S., at 896–897 (majority opinion) (citing *Bradwell* v. *State*, 16 Wall. 130 (1873)). "There was a time," *Casey* explained, when the Constitution did not protect "men and women alike." 505 U. S., at 896. But times had changed. A woman's place in society had changed, and constitutional law had changed along with it. The relegation of women to inferior status in either the public sphere or the family was "no longer consistent with our understanding" of the Constitution. *Id.*, at 897. Now, "[t]he Constitution protects all individuals, male or female," from "the abuse of governmental power" or "unjustified state interference." *Id.*, at 896, 898.

So how is it that, as *Casey* said, our Constitution, read now, grants rights to women, though it did not in 1868? How is it that our Constitution subjects discrimination against them to heightened judicial scrutiny? How is it that our Constitution, through the Fourteenth Amendment's liberty clause, guarantees access to contraception (also not legally protected in 1868) so that women can decide for themselves whether and when to bear a child? How is it that until today, that same constitutional clause protected a woman's right, in the event contraception failed, to end a pregnancy in its earlier stages?

The answer is that this Court has rejected the majority's pinched view of how to read our Constitution. "The Founders," we recently wrote, "knew they were writing a document designed to apply to ever-changing circumstances over centuries." *NLRB* v. *Noel Canning*, 573 U.S. 513, 533–534 (2014). Or in the words of the great Chief Justice John Marshall, our Constitution is "intended to endure for ages to come," and must adapt itself to a future "seen dimly," if at all. *McCulloch* v. *Maryland*, 4 Wheat. 316, 415 (1819). That is indeed why our Constitution is written as it is. The Framers (both in 1788 and 1868) understood that the world changes. So they did not define rights by reference to the specific practices existing at the time. Instead, the Framers defined rights in general terms, to permit future evolution in their scope and meaning. And over the course of our history, this Court has taken up the Framers' invitation. It has kept true to the Framers' principles by applying them in new ways, responsive to new societal understandings and conditions.

Nowhere has that approach been more prevalent than in construing the majestic but open-ended words of the Fourteenth Amendment—the guarantees of "liberty" and "equality" for all. And nowhere has that approach produced prouder moments, for this country and the Court. Consider an example *Obergefell* used a few years ago. The Court there confronted a claim, based on *Washington* v. *Glucksberg*, 521 U.S. 702 (1997), that the Fourteenth Amendment "must be defined in a most circumscribed manner, with central reference to specific historical practices"—exactly the view today's majority follows. *Obergefell*, 576 U. S., at 671. And the Court specifically rejected that view. In doing so, the Court reflected on what the proposed, historically circumscribed approach would have meant for interracial marriage. See *ibid.* The Fourteenth Amendment's ratifiers did not think it gave black and white people a right to marry each other. To the contrary, contemporaneous practice deemed that act quite as unprotected as abortion. Yet the Court in *Loving* v. *Virginia*, 388 U.S. 1 (1967), read the

Fourteenth Amendment to embrace the Lovings' union. If, *Obergefell* explained, "rights were defined by who exercised them in the past, then received practices could serve as their own continued justification"—even when they conflict with "liberty" and "equality" as later and more broadly understood. 576 U. S., at 671. The Constitution does not freeze for all time the original view of what those rights guarantee, or how they apply.

That does not mean anything goes. The majority wishes people to think there are but two alternatives: (1) accept the original applications of the Fourteenth Amendment and no others, or (2) surrender to judges' "own ardent views," ungrounded in law, about the "liberty that Americans should enjoy." *Ante*, at 14. At least, that idea is what the majority *sometimes* tries to convey. At other times, the majority (or, rather, most of it) tries to assure the public that it has no designs on rights (for example, to contraception) that arose only in the back half of the 20th century—in other words, that it is happy to pick and choose, in accord with individual preferences. See *ante*, at 32, 66, 71–72; *ante*, at 10 (Kavanaugh, J., concurring); but see *ante*, at 3 (Thomas, J., concurring). But that is a matter we discuss later. See *infra*, at 24–29. For now, our point is different: It is that applications of liberty and equality can evolve while remaining grounded in constitutional principles, constitutional history, and constitutional precedents. The second Justice Harlan discussed how to strike the right balance when he explained why he would have invalidated a State's ban on contraceptive use. Judges, he said, are not "free to roam where unguided speculation might take them." *Poe* v. *Ullman*, 367 U.S. 497, 542 (1961) (dissenting opinion). Yet they also must recognize that the constitutional "tradition" of this country is not captured whole at a single moment. *Ibid.* Rather, its meaning gains content from the long sweep of our history and from successive judicial precedents—each looking to the last and each seeking to apply the Constitution's most fundamental commitments to new conditions. That is why Americans, to go back to *Obergefell*'s example, have a right to marry across racial lines. And it is why, to go back to Justice Harlan's case, Americans have a right to use contraceptives so they can choose for themselves whether to have children.

All that is what *Casey* understood. *Casey* explicitly rejected the present majority's method. "[T]he specific practices of States at the time of the adoption of the Fourteenth Amendment," *Casey* stated, do not "mark[ ] the outer limits of the substantive sphere of liberty which the Fourteenth Amendment protects." 505 U. S., at 848. To hold otherwise—as the majority does today—"would be inconsistent with our law." *Id.*, at 847. Why? Because the Court has "vindicated [the] principle" over and over that (no matter the sentiment in 1868) "there is a realm of personal liberty which the government may not enter"—especially relating to "bodily integrity" and "family life." *Id.*, at 847, 849, 851. *Casey* described in detail the Court's contraception cases. See *id.*, at 848–849, 851–853. It noted decisions protecting the right to marry, including to someone of another race. See *id.*, at 847–848 ("[I]nterracial marriage was illegal in most States in the 19th century, but the Court was no doubt correct in finding it to be an aspect of liberty protected against state interference"). In reviewing decades and decades of constitutional law, *Casey* could draw but one conclusion: Whatever was true in 1868, "[i]t is settled now, as it was when the Court heard arguments in *Roe* v. *Wade*, that the Constitution places limits on a State's right to interfere with a person's most basic decisions about family and parenthood." *Id.*, at 849.

And that conclusion still held good, until the Court's intervention here. It was settled at the time of *Roe*, settled at the time of *Casey*, and settled yesterday that the Constitution places limits on a State's power to assert control over an individual's body and most personal decisionmaking. A multitude of decisions supporting that principle led to *Roe*'s recognition and *Casey*'s reaffirmation of the right to choose; and *Roe* and *Casey* in turn supported additional protections for intimate and familial relations. The majority has embarrassingly little to say about those precedents. It (literally) rattles them off in a single paragraph; and it implies that they have nothing to do with each other, or with the right to terminate an early pregnancy. See *ante*, at 31–32 (asserting that recognizing a relationship among them, as addressing aspects of personal autonomy, would ineluctably "license fundamental rights" to illegal "drug use [and] prostitution"). But that is flat wrong. The Court's precedents about bodily autonomy, sexual and familial relations, and procreation are all interwoven—all part of the fabric of our constitutional law, and because that is so, of our lives. Especially women's lives, where they safeguard a right to self-determination.

And eliminating that right, we need to say before further describing our precedents, is not taking a "neutral" position, as Justice Kavanaugh tries to argue. *Ante*, at 2–3, 5, 7, 11–12 (concurring opinion). His idea is that neutrality lies in giving the abortion issue to the States, where some can go one way and some another. But would he say that the Court is being "scrupulously neutral" if it allowed New York and California to ban all the guns they want? *Ante*, at 3. If the Court allowed some States to use unanimous juries and others not? If the Court told the States: Decide for yourselves whether to put restrictions on church attendance? We could go on—and in fact we will. Suppose Justice Kavanaugh were to say (in line with the majority opinion) that the rights we just listed are more textually or historically grounded than the right to choose. What, then, of the right to contraception or same-sex marriage? Would it be "scrupulously neutral" for the Court to eliminate those rights too? The point of all these examples is that when it comes to rights, the Court does not act "neutrally" when it leaves everything up to the States. Rather, the Court acts neutrally when it protects the right against all comers. And to apply that point to the case here: When the Court decimates a right women have held for 50 years, the Court is not being "scrupulously neutral." It is instead taking sides: against women who wish to exercise the right, and for States (like Mississippi) that want to bar them from doing so. Justice Kavanaugh cannot obscure that point by appropriating the rhetoric of even-handedness. His position just is what it is: A brook-no-compromise refusal to recognize a woman's right to choose, from the first day of a pregnancy. And that position, as we will now show, cannot be squared with this Court's longstanding view that women indeed have rights (whatever the state of the world in 1868) to make the most personal and consequential decisions about their bodies and their lives.

Consider first, then, the line of this Court's cases protecting "bodily integrity." *Casey*, 505 U. S., at 849. "No right," in this Court's time-honored view, "is held more sacred, or is more carefully guarded," than "the right of every individual to the possession and control of his own person." *Union Pacific R. Co.* v. *Botsford*, 141 U.S. 250, 251 (1891); see *Cruzan* v. *Director, Mo. Dept. of Health*, 497 U.S. 261, 269 (1990) (Every adult "has a right to determine what shall be done with his own body"). Or to put it more simply: Everyone, including women, owns their own bodies. So the Court has restricted the power of government to interfere with a person's medical decisions or compel her to undergo medical procedures or treatments. See, *e.g.*, *Winston* v. *Lee*, 470 U.S. 753, 766–767 (1985) (forced surgery); *Rochin* v. *California*, 342 U.S. 165, 166, 173–174 (1952) (forced stomach pumping); *Washington* v. *Harper*, 494 U.S. 210, 229, 236 (1990) (forced administration of antipsychotic drugs).

Casey recognized the "doctrinal affinity" between those precedents and *Roe*. 505 U. S., at 857. And that doctrinal affinity is born of a factual likeness. There are few greater incursions on a body than forcing a woman to complete a pregnancy and give birth. For every woman, those experiences involve all manner of physical changes, medical treatments (including the possibility of a cesarean section), and medical risk. Just as one example, an American woman is 14 times more likely to die by carrying a pregnancy to term than by having an abortion. See *Whole Woman's Health* v. *Hellerstedt*, 579 U.S. 582, 618 (2016). That women happily undergo those burdens and hazards of their own accord does not lessen how far a State impinges on a woman's body when it compels her to bring a pregnancy to term. And for some women, as *Roe* recognized, abortions are medically necessary to prevent harm. See 410 U. S., at 153. The majority does not say—which is itself ominous—whether a State may prevent a woman from obtaining an abortion when she and her doctor have determined it is a needed medical treatment.

So too, *Roe* and *Casey* fit neatly into a long line of decisions protecting from government intrusion a wealth of private choices about family matters, child rearing, intimate relationships, and procreation. See *Casey*, 505 U. S., at 851, 857; *Roe*, 410 U. S., at 152–153; see also *ante*, at 31–32 (listing the myriad decisions of this kind that *Casey* relied on). Those cases safeguard particular choices about whom to marry; whom to have sex with; what family members to live with; how to raise children—and crucially, whether and when to have children. In varied cases, the Court explained that those choices—"the most intimate and personal" a person can make—reflect fundamental aspects of personal identity; they define the very "attributes of personhood." *Casey*, 505 U. S., at 851. And they inevitably shape the nature and future course of a person's life (and often the lives of those closest to her). So, the Court held, those choices belong to the individual, and not the government. That is the essence of what liberty requires.

And liberty may require it, this Court has repeatedly said, even when those living in 1868 would not have recognized the claim—because they would not have seen the person making it as a full-fledged member of the community. Throughout our history, the sphere of protected liberty has expanded, bringing in individuals formerly excluded. In that way, the constitutional values of liberty and equality go hand in hand; they do not inhabit the hermetically sealed containers the majority portrays. Compare *Obergefell*, 576 U. S., at 672–675, with *ante*, at 10–11. So before *Roe* and *Casey*, the Court expanded in successive cases those who could claim the right to marry—though their relationships would have been outside the law's protection in the mid-19th century. See, *e.g., Loving*, 388 U.S. 1 (interracial couples); *Turner* v. *Safley*, 482 U.S. 78 (1987) (prisoners); see also, *e.g., Stanley* v. *Illinois*, 405 U.S. 645, 651–652 (1972) (offering constitutional protection to untraditional "family unit[s]"). And after *Roe* and *Casey*, of course, the Court continued in that vein. With a critical stop to hold that the Fourteenth Amendment protected same-sex intimacy, the Court resolved that the Amendment also conferred on same-sex couples the right to marry. See *Lawrence*, 539 U.S. 558; *Obergefell*, 576 U. S. 644. In considering that question, the Court held, "[h]istory and tradition," especially as reflected in the course of our precedent, "guide and discipline [the] inquiry." *Id.*, at 664. But the sentiments of 1868 alone do not and cannot "rule the present." *Ibid.*

Casey similarly recognized the need to extend the constitutional sphere of liberty to a previously excluded group. The Court then understood, as the majority today does not, that the men who ratified the Fourteenth Amendment and wrote the state laws of the time did not view women as full and equal citizens. See *supra*, at 15. A woman then, *Casey* wrote, "had no legal existence separate from her husband." 505 U. S., at 897. Women were seen only "as the center of home and family life," without "full and independent legal status under the Constitution." *Ibid.* But that could not be true any longer: The State could not now insist on the historically dominant "vision of the woman's role." *Id.*, at 852. And equal citizenship, *Casey* realized, was inescapably connected to reproductive rights. "The ability of women to participate equally" in the "life of the Nation"—in all its economic, social, political, and legal aspects—"has been facilitated by their ability to control their reproductive lives." *Id.*, at 856. Without the ability to decide whether and when to have children, women could not—in the way men took for granted—determine how they would live their lives, and how they would contribute to the society around them.

For much that reason, *Casey* made clear that the precedents *Roe* most closely tracked were those involving contraception. Over the course of three cases, the Court had held that a right to use and gain access to contraception was part of the Fourteenth Amendment's guarantee of liberty. See *Griswold*, 381 U.S. 479; *Eisenstadt*, 405 U.S. 438; *Carey* v. *Population Services Int'l*, 431 U.S. 678 (1977). That clause, we explained, necessarily conferred a right "to be free from unwarranted governmental intrusion into matters so fundamentally affecting a person as the decision whether to bear or beget a child." *Eisenstadt*, 405 U. S., at 453; see *Carey*, 431 U. S., at 684–685. *Casey* saw *Roe* as of a piece: In "critical respects the abortion decision is of the same character." 505 U. S., at 852. "[R]easonable people," the Court noted, could also oppose contraception; and indeed, they could believe that "some forms of contraception" similarly implicate a concern with "potential life." *Id.*, at 853, 859. Yet the views of others could not automatically prevail against a woman's right to control her own body and make her own choice about whether to bear, and probably to raise, a child. When an unplanned pregnancy is involved—because either contraception or abortion is outlawed—"the liberty of the woman is at stake in a sense unique to the human condition." *Id.*, at 852. No State could undertake to resolve the moral questions raised "in such a definitive way" as to deprive a woman of all choice. *Id.*, at 850.

Faced with all these connections between *Roe/Casey* and judicial decisions recognizing other constitutional rights, the majority tells everyone not to worry. It can (so it says) neatly extract the right to choose from the constitutional edifice without affecting any associated rights. (Think of someone telling you that the Jenga tower simply will not collapse.) Today's decision, the majority first says, "does not undermine" the decisions cited by *Roe* and *Casey*—the ones involving "marriage, procreation, contraception, [and] family relationships"—"in any way." *Ante*, at 32; *Casey*, 505 U. S., at 851. Note that this first assurance does not extend to rights recognized after *Roe* and *Casey*, and partly based on them—in particular, rights to same-sex intimacy and marriage. See *supra*, at 23. On its later tries, though, the majority includes those too: "Nothing in this opinion should be understood to cast doubt on precedents that do not concern abortion." *Ante*, at 66; see *ante*, at 71–72. That right is unique, the majority asserts, "because [abortion] terminates life or potential life." *Ante*, at 66 (internal quotation marks omitted); see *ante*, at 32, 71–72. So the majority depicts today's decision as "a restricted railroad ticket, good for this day and train only." *Smith* v. *Allwright*, 321 U.S. 649, 669 (1944) (Roberts, J., dissenting). Should the audience for these too-much-repeated protestations be duly satisfied? We think not.

The first problem with the majority's account comes from Justice Thomas's concurrence—which makes clear he is not with the program. In saying that nothing in today's opinion casts doubt on non-abortion precedents, Justice Thomas explains, he means only that they are not at issue in this very case. See *ante*, at 7 ("[T]his case does not present the opportunity to reject" those precedents). But he lets us know what he wants to do when they are. "[I]n future cases," he says, "we should reconsider all of this Court's substantive due process precedents, including *Griswold*, *Lawrence*, and *Obergefell*." *Ante*, at 3; see also *supra*, at 25, and n. 6. And when we reconsider them? Then "we have a duty" to "overrul[e] these demonstrably erroneous decisions." *Ante*, at 3. So at least one Justice is planning to use the ticket of today's decision again and again and again.

Even placing the concurrence to the side, the assurance in today's opinion still does not work. Or at least that is so if the majority is serious about its sole reason for overturning *Roe* and *Casey*: the legal status of abortion in the 19th century. Except in the places quoted above, the state interest in protecting fetal life plays no part in the majority's analysis. To the contrary, the majority takes pride in not expressing a view "about the status of the fetus." *Ante*, at 65; see *ante*, at 32 (aligning itself with *Roe*'s and *Casey*'s stance of not deciding whether life or potential life is involved); *ante*, at 38–39 (similar). The majority's departure from *Roe* and *Casey* rests instead—and only—on whether a woman's decision to end a pregnancy involves any Fourteenth Amendment liberty interest (against which *Roe* and *Casey* balanced the state interest in preserving fetal life). According to the majority, no liberty interest is present—because (and only because) the law offered no protection to the woman's choice in the 19th century. But here is the rub. The law also did not then (and would not for ages) protect a wealth of other things. It did not protect the rights recognized in *Lawrence* and *Obergefell* to same-sex intimacy and marriage. It did not protect the right recognized in *Loving* to marry across racial lines. It did not protect the right recognized in *Griswold* to contraceptive use. For that matter, it did not protect the right recognized in *Skinner* v. *Oklahoma ex rel. Williamson*, 316 U.S. 535 (1942), not to be sterilized without consent. So if the majority is right in its legal analysis, all those decisions were wrong, and all those matters properly belong to the States too—whatever the particular state interests involved. And if that is true, it is impossible to understand (as a matter of logic and principle) how the majority can say that its opinion today does not threaten—does not even "undermine"—any number of other constitutional rights. *Ante*, at 32.

Nor does it even help just to take the majority at its word. Assume the majority is sincere in saying, for whatever reason, that it will go so far and no further. Scout's honor. Still, the future significance of today's opinion will be decided in the future. And law often has a way of evolving without regard to original intentions—a way of actually following where logic leads, rather than tolerating hard-to- explain lines. Rights can expand in that way. Dissenting in *Lawrence*, Justice Scalia explained why he took no comfort in the Court's statement that a decision recognizing the right to same-sex intimacy did "not involve" same-sex marriage. 539 U. S., at 604. That could be true, he wrote, "only if one entertains the belief that principle and logic have nothing to do with the decisions of this Court." *Id.*, at 605. Score one for the dissent, as a matter of prophecy. And logic and principle are not one-way ratchets. Rights can contract in the same way and for the same reason—because whatever today's majority might say, one thing really does lead to another. We fervently hope that does not happen because of today's decision. We hope that we will not join Justice Scalia in the book of prophets. But we cannot understand how anyone can be confident that today's opinion will be the last of its kind.

Consider, as our last word on this issue, contraception. The Constitution, of course, does not mention that word. And there is no historical right to contraception, of the kind the majority insists on. To the contrary, the American legal landscape in the decades after the Civil War was littered with bans on the sale of contraceptive devices. So again, there seem to be two choices. See *supra*, at 5, 26–27. If the majority is serious about its historical approach, then *Griswold* and its progeny are in the line of fire too. Or if it is not serious, then . . . what *is* the basis of today's decision? If we had to guess, we suspect the prospects of this Court approving bans on contraception are low. But once again, the future significance of today's opinion will be decided in the future. At the least, today's opinion will fuel the fight to get contraception, and any other issues with a moral dimension, out of the Fourteenth Amendment and into state legislatures.

Anyway, today's decision, taken on its own, is catastrophic enough. As a matter of constitutional method, the majority's commitment to replicate in 2022 every view about the meaning of liberty held in 1868 has precious little to recommend it. Our law in this constitutional sphere, as in most, has for decades upon decades proceeded differently. It has considered fundamental constitutional principles, the whole course of the Nation's history and traditions, and the step-by-step evolution of the Court's precedents. It is disciplined but not static. It relies on accumulated judgments, not just the sentiments of one long-ago generation of men (who themselves believed, and drafted the Constitution to reflect, that the world progresses). And by doing so, it includes those excluded from that olden conversation, rather than perpetuating its bounds.

As a matter of constitutional substance, the majority's opinion has all the flaws its method would suggest. Because laws in 1868 deprived women of any control over their bodies, the majority approves States doing so today. Because those laws prevented women from charting the course of their own lives, the majority says States can do the same again. Because in 1868, the government could tell a pregnant woman—even in the first days of her pregnancy—that she could do nothing but bear a child, it can once more impose that command. Today's decision strips women of agency over what even the majority agrees is a contested and contestable moral issue. It forces her to carry out the State's will, whatever the circumstances and whatever the harm it will wreak on her and her family. In the Fourteenth Amendment's terms, it takes away her liberty. Even before we get to *stare decisis*, we dissent.

II

By overruling *Roe*, *Casey*, and more than 20 cases reaffirming or applying the constitutional right to abortion, the majority abandons *stare decisis*, a principle central to the rule of law. "*Stare decisis*" means "to stand by things decided." Black's Law Dictionary 1696 (11th ed. 2019). Blackstone called it the "established rule to abide by former precedents." 1 Blackstone 69. *Stare decisis* "promotes the evenhanded, predictable, and consistent development of legal principles." *Payne*, 501 U. S., at 827. It maintains a stability that allows people to order their lives under the law. See H. Hart & A. Sacks, The Legal Process: Basic Problems in the Making and Application of Law 568–569 (1994).

Stare decisis also "contributes to the integrity of our constitutional system of government" by ensuring that decisions "are founded in the law rather than in the proclivities of individuals." *Vasquez*, 474 U. S., at 265. As Hamilton wrote: It "avoid[s] an arbitrary discretion in the courts." The Federalist No. 78, p. 529 (J. Cooke ed. 1961) (A. Hamilton). And as Blackstone said before him: It "keep[s] the scale of justice even and steady, and not liable to waver with every new judge's opinion." 1 Blackstone 69. The "glory" of our legal system is that it "gives preference to precedent rather than . . . jurists." H. Humble, Departure From Precedent, 19 Mich. L. Rev. 608, 614 (1921). That is why, the story goes, Chief Justice John Marshall donned a plain black robe when he swore the oath of office. That act personified an American tradition. Judges' personal preferences do not make law; rather, the law speaks through them.

That means the Court may not overrule a decision, even a constitutional one, without a "special justification." *Gamble* v. *United States*, 587 U. S. ___, ___ (2019) (slip op., at 11). *Stare decisis* is, of course, not an "inexorable command"; it is sometimes appropriate to overrule an earlier decision. *Pearson* v. *Callahan*, 555 U.S. 223, 233 (2009). But the Court must have a good reason to do so over and above the belief "that the precedent was wrongly decided." *Halliburton Co.* v. *Erica P. John Fund, Inc.*, 573 U.S. 258, 266 (2014). "[I]t is not alone sufficient that we would decide a case differently now than we did then." *Kimble* v. *Marvel Entertainment, LLC*, 576 U.S. 446, 455 (2015).

The majority today lists some 30 of our cases as overruling precedent, and argues that they support overruling *Roe* and *Casey*. But none does, as further described below and in the Appendix. See *infra*, at 61–66. In some, the Court only partially modified or clarified a precedent. And in the rest, the Court relied on one or more of the traditional *stare decisis* factors in reaching its conclusion. The Court found, for example, (1) a change in legal doctrine that undermined or made obsolete the earlier decision; (2) a factual change that had the same effect; or (3) an absence of reliance because the earlier decision was less than a decade old. (The majority is wrong when it says that we insist on a test of changed law or fact alone, although that is present in most of the cases. See *ante*, at 69.) None of those factors apply here: Nothing—and in particular, no significant legal or factual change—supports overturning a half-century of settled law giving women control over their reproductive lives. First, for all the reasons we have given, *Roe* and *Casey* were correct. In holding that a State could not "resolve" the debate about abortion "in such a definitive way that a woman lacks all choice in the matter," the Court protected women's liberty and women's equality in a way comporting with our Fourteenth Amendment precedents. *Casey*, 505 U. S., at 850. Contrary to the majority's view, the legal status of abortion in the 19th century does not weaken those decisions. And the majority's repeated refrain about "usurp[ing]" state legislatures' "power to address" a publicly contested question does not help it on the key issue here. *Ante*, at 44; see *ante*, at 1. To repeat: The point of a right is to shield individual actions and decisions "from the vicissitudes of political controversy, to place them beyond the reach of majorities and officials and to establish them as legal principles to be applied by the courts." *Barnette*, 319 U. S., at 638; *supra*, at 7. However divisive, a right is not at the people's mercy.

In any event "[w]hether or not we . . . agree" with a prior precedent is the beginning, not the end, of our analysis—and the remaining "principles of *stare decisis* weigh heavily against overruling" *Roe* and *Casey*. *Dickerson* v. *United States*, 530 U.S. 428, 443 (2000). *Casey* itself applied those principles, in one of this Court's most important precedents about precedent. After assessing the traditional *stare decisis* factors, *Casey* reached the only conclusion possible—that *stare decisis* operates powerfully here. It still does. The standards *Roe* and *Casey* set out are perfectly workable. No changes in either law or fact have eroded the two decisions. And tens of millions of American women have relied, and continue to rely, on the right to choose. So under traditional *stare decisis* principles, the majority has no special justification for the harm it causes.

And indeed, the majority comes close to conceding that point. The majority barely mentions any legal or factual changes that have occurred since *Roe* and *Casey*. It suggests that the two decisions are hard for courts to implement, but cannot prove its case. In the end, the majority says, all it must say to override *stare decisis* is one thing: that it believes *Roe* and *Casey* "egregiously wrong." *Ante*, at 70. That rule could equally spell the end of any precedent with which a bare majority of the present Court disagrees. So how does that approach prevent the "scale of justice" from "waver[ing] with every new judge's opinion"? 1 Blackstone 69. It does not. It makes radical change too easy and too fast, based on nothing more than the new views of new judges. The majority has overruled *Roe* and *Casey* for one and only one reason: because it has always despised them, and now it has the votes to discard them. The majority thereby substitutes a rule by judges for the rule of law.

A

Contrary to the majority's view, there is nothing unworkable about *Casey*'s "undue burden" standard. Its primary focus on whether a State has placed a "substantial obstacle" on a woman seeking an abortion is "the sort of inquiry familiar to judges across a variety of contexts." *June Medical Services L. L. C.* v. *Russo*, 591 U. S. ___, ___ (2020) (slip op., at 6) (Roberts, C. J., concurring in judgment). And it has given rise to no more conflict in application than many standards this Court and others unhesitatingly apply every day.

General standards, like the undue burden standard, are ubiquitous in the law, and particularly in constitutional adjudication. When called on to give effect to the Constitution's broad principles, this Court often crafts flexible standards that can be applied case-by-case to a myriad of unforeseeable circumstances. See *Dickerson*, 530 U. S., at 441 ("No court laying down a general rule can possibly foresee the various circumstances" in which it must apply). So, for example, the Court asks about undue or substantial burdens on speech, on voting, and on interstate commerce. See, *e.g., Arizona Free Enterprise Club's Freedom Club PAC* v. *Bennett*, 564 U.S.

721, 748 (2011); *Burdick* v. *Takushi*, 504 U.S. 428, 433–434 (1992); *Pike* v. *Bruce Church, Inc.*, 397 U.S. 137, 142 (1970). The *Casey* undue burden standard is the same. It also resembles general standards that courts work with daily in other legal spheres—like the "rule of reason" in antitrust law or the "arbitrary and capricious" standard for agency decisionmaking. See *Standard Oil Co. of N. J.* v. *United States*, 221 U.S. 1, 62 (1911); *Motor Vehicle Mfrs. Assn. of United States, Inc.* v. *State Farm Mut. Automobile Ins. Co.*, 463 U.S. 29, 42–43 (1983). Applying general standards to particular cases is, in many contexts, just what it means to do law.

And the undue burden standard has given rise to no unusual difficulties. Of course, it has provoked some disagreement among judges. *Casey* knew it would: That much "is to be expected in the application of any legal standard which must accommodate life's complexity." 505 U. S., at 878 (plurality opinion). Which is to say: That much is to be expected in the application of any legal standard. But the majority vastly overstates the divisions among judges applying the standard. We count essentially two. The Chief Justice disagreed with other Justices in the *June Medical* majority about whether *Casey* called for weighing the benefits of an abortion regulation against its burdens. See 591 U. S., at ___–___ (slip op., at 6–7); *ante*, at 59, 60, and n. 53. We agree that the *June Medical* difference is a difference—but not one that would actually make a difference in the result of most cases (it did not in *June Medical*), and not one incapable of resolution were it ever to matter. As for lower courts, there is now a one-year-old, one-to-one Circuit split about how the undue burden standard applies to state laws that ban abortions for certain reasons, like fetal abnormality. See *ante*, at 61, and n. 57. That is about it, as far as we can see. And that is not much. This Court mostly does not even grant certiorari on one-year-old, one-to-one Circuit splits, because we know that a bit of disagreement is an inevitable part of our legal system. To borrow an old saying that might apply here: Not one or even a couple of swallows can make the majority's summer.

Anyone concerned about workability should consider the majority's substitute standard. The majority says a law regulating or banning abortion "must be sustained if there is a rational basis on which the legislature could have thought that it would serve legitimate state interests." *Ante*, at 77. And the majority lists interests like "respect for and preservation of prenatal life," "protection of maternal health," elimination of certain "medical procedures," "mitigation of fetal pain," and others. *Ante*, at 78. This Court will surely face critical questions about how that test applies. Must a state law allow abortions when necessary to protect a woman's life and health? And if so, exactly when? How much risk to a woman's life can a State force her to incur, before the Fourteenth Amendment's protection of life kicks in? Suppose a patient with pulmonary hypertension has a 30-to-50 percent risk of dying with ongoing pregnancy; is that enough? And short of death, how much illness or injury can the State require her to accept, consistent with the Amendment's protection of liberty and equality? Further, the Court may face questions about the application of abortion regulations to medical care most people view as quite different from abortion. What about the morning-after pill? IUDs? In vitro fertilization? And how about the use of dilation and evacuation or medication for miscarriage management? See generally L. Harris, Navigating Loss of Abortion Services—A Large Academic Medical Center Prepares for the Overturn of *Roe* v. *Wade*, 386 New England J. Med. 2061 (2022).

Finally, the majority's ruling today invites a host of questions about interstate conflicts. See *supra*, at 3; see generally D. Cohen, G. Donley, & R. Rebouché, The New Abortion Battleground, 123 Colum. L. Rev. (forthcoming 2023), https://ssrn.com/abstract=4032931. Can a State bar women from traveling to another State to obtain an abortion? Can a State prohibit advertising out-of-state abortions or helping women get to out-of-state providers? Can a State interfere with the mailing of drugs used for medication abortions? The Constitution protects travel and speech and interstate commerce, so today's ruling will give rise to a host of new constitutional questions. Far from removing the Court from the abortion issue, the majority puts the Court at the center of the coming "interjurisdictional abortion wars." *Id.*, at ___ (draft, at 1).

In short, the majority does not save judges from unwieldy tests or extricate them from the sphere of controversy. To the contrary, it discards a known, workable, and predictable standard in favor of something novel and probably far more complicated. It forces the Court to wade further into hotly contested issues, including moral and philosophical ones, that the majority criticizes *Roe* and *Casey* for addressing.

B

When overruling constitutional precedent, the Court has almost always pointed to major legal or factual changes undermining a decision's original basis. A review of the Appendix to this dissent proves the point. See *infra*, at 61–66. Most "successful proponent[s] of overruling precedent," this Court once said, have carried "the heavy burden of persuading the Court that changes in society or in the law dictate that the values served by *stare decisis* yield in favor of a greater objective." *Vasquez*, 474 U. S., at 266. Certainly, that was so of the main examples the majority cites: *Brown* v. *Board of Education*, 347 U.S. 483 (1954), and *West Coast Hotel Co.* v. *Parrish*, 300 U.S. 379 (1937). But it is not so today. Although nodding to some arguments others have made about "modern developments," the majority does not really rely on them, no doubt seeing their slimness. *Ante*, at 33; see *ante*, at 34. The majority briefly invokes the current controversy over abortion. See *ante*, at 70–71. But it has to acknowledge that the same dispute has existed for decades: Conflict over abortion is not a change but a constant. (And as we will later discuss, the presence of that continuing division provides more of a reason to stick with, than to jettison, existing precedent. See *infra*, at 55–57.) In the end, the majority throws longstanding precedent to the winds without showing that anything significant has changed to justify its radical reshaping of the law. See *ante*, at 43.

1

Subsequent legal developments have only reinforced *Roe* and *Casey*. The Court has continued to embrace all the decisions *Roe* and *Casey* cited, decisions which recognize a constitutional right for an individual to make her own choices about "intimate relationships, the family," and contraception. *Casey*, 505 U. S., at 857. *Roe* and *Casey* have themselves formed the legal foundation for subsequent decisions protecting these profoundly personal choices. As discussed earlier, the Court relied on *Casey* to hold that the Fourteenth Amendment protects same-sex intimate relationships. See *Lawrence*, 539 U. S., at 578; *supra*, at 23. The Court later invoked the same set of precedents to accord constitutional recognition to same-sex marriage. See *Obergefell*, 576 U. S., at 665–666; *supra*, at 23. In sum, *Roe* and *Casey* are inextricably interwoven with decades of precedent about the meaning of the Fourteenth Amendment. See *supra*, at 21–24. While the majority might wish it otherwise, *Roe* and *Casey* are the very opposite of " 'obsolete constitutional thinking.' " *Agostini* v. *Felton*, 521 U.S. 203, 236 (1997) (quoting *Casey*, 505 U. S., at 857).

Moreover, no subsequent factual developments have undermined *Roe* and *Casey*. Women continue to experience unplanned pregnancies and unexpected developments in pregnancies. Pregnancies continue to have enormous physical, social, and economic consequences. Even an uncomplicated pregnancy imposes significant strain on the body, unavoidably involving significant physiological change and excruciating pain. For some women, pregnancy and childbirth can mean life-altering physical ailments or even death. Today, as noted earlier, the risks of carrying a pregnancy to term dwarf those of having an abortion. See *supra*, at 22. Experts estimate that a ban on abortions increases maternal mortality by 21 percent, with white women facing a 13 percent increase in maternal mortality while black women face a 33 percent increase. Pregnancy and childbirth may also impose large-scale financial costs. The majority briefly refers to arguments about changes in laws relating to healthcare coverage, pregnancy discrimination, and family leave. See *ante*, at 33–34. Many women, however, still do not have adequate healthcare coverage before and after pregnancy; and, even when insurance coverage is available, healthcare services may be far away. Women also continue to face pregnancy discrimination that interferes with their ability to earn a living. Paid family leave remains inaccessible to many who need it most. Only 20 percent of private-sector workers have access to paid family leave, including a mere 8 percent of workers in the bottom quartile of wage earners.

The majority briefly notes the growing prevalence of safe haven laws and demand for adoption, see *ante*, at 34, and nn. 45–46, but, to the degree that these are changes at all, they too are irrelevant. Neither reduces the health risks or financial costs of going through pregnancy and childbirth. Moreover, the choice to give up parental rights after giving birth is altogether different from the choice not to carry a pregnancy to term. The reality is that few women denied an abortion will choose adoption. The vast majority will continue, just as in *Roe* and *Casey*'s time, to shoulder the costs of childrearing. Whether or not they choose to parent, they will experience the profound loss of autonomy and dignity that coerced pregnancy and birth always impose.

Mississippi's own record illustrates how little facts on the ground have changed since *Roe* and *Casey*, notwithstanding the majority's supposed "modern developments." *Ante*, at 33. Sixty-two percent of pregnancies in Mississippi are unplanned, yet Mississippi does not require insurance to cover contraceptives and prohibits educators from demonstrating proper contraceptive use. The State neither bans pregnancy discrimination nor requires provision of paid parental leave. Brief for Yale Law School Information Society Project as *Amicus Curiae* 13 (Brief for Yale Law School); Brief for National Women's Law Center et al. as *Amici Curiae* 32. It has strict eligibility requirements for Medicaid and nutrition assistance, leaving many women and families without basic medical care or enough food. See Brief for 547 Deans, Chairs, Scholars and Public Health Professionals et al. as *Amici Curiae* 32–34 (Brief for 547 Deans). Although 86 percent of pregnancy-related deaths in the State are due to postpartum complications, Mississippi rejected federal funding to provide a year's worth of Medicaid coverage to women after giving birth. See Brief for Yale Law School 12–13. Perhaps unsurprisingly, health outcomes in Mississippi are abysmal for both women and children. Mississippi has the highest infant mortality rate in the country, and some of the highest rates for preterm birth, low birthweight, cesarean section, and maternal death.] It is approximately 75 times more dangerous for a woman in the State to carry a pregnancy to term than to have an abortion. See Brief for 547 Deans 9–10. We do not say that every State is Mississippi, and we are sure some have made gains since *Roe* and *Casey* in providing support for women and children. But a state-by-state analysis by public health professionals shows that States with the most restrictive abortion policies also continue to invest the least in women's and children's health. See Brief for 547 Deans 23–34.

The only notable change we can see since *Roe* and *Casey* cuts in favor of adhering to precedent: It is that American abortion law has become more and more aligned with other nations. The majority, like the Mississippi Legislature, claims that the United States is an extreme outlier when it comes to abortion regulation. See *ante*, at 6, and n. 15. The global trend, however, has been toward increased provision of legal and safe abortion care. A number of countries, including New Zealand, the Netherlands, and Iceland, permit abortions up to a roughly similar time as *Roe* and *Casey* set. See Brief for International and Comparative Legal Scholars as *Amici Curiae* 18–22. Canada has decriminalized abortion at any point in a pregnancy. See *id.*, at 13–15. Most Western European countries impose restrictions on abortion after 12 to 14 weeks, but they often have liberal exceptions to those time limits, including to prevent harm to a woman's physical or mental health. See *id.*, at 24–27; Brief for European Law Professors as *Amici Curiae* 16–17, Appendix. They also typically make access to early abortion easier, for example, by helping cover its cost. Perhaps most notable, more than 50 countries around the world—in Asia, Latin America, Africa, and Europe—have expanded access to abortion in the past 25 years. See Brief for International and Comparative Legal Scholars as *Amici Curiae* 28–29. In light of that worldwide liberalization of abortion laws, it is American States that will become international outliers after today.

In sum, the majority can point to neither legal nor factual developments in support of its decision. Nothing that has happened in this country or the world in recent decades undermines the core insight of *Roe* and *Casey*. It continues to be true that, within the constraints those decisions established, a woman, not the government, should choose whether she will bear the burdens of pregnancy, childbirth, and parenting.

2

In support of its holding, see *ante*, at 40, the majority invokes two watershed cases overruling prior constitutional precedents: *West Coast Hotel Co.* v. *Parrish* and *Brown* v. *Board of Education*. But those decisions, unlike today's, responded to changed law and to changed facts and attitudes that had taken hold throughout society. As *Casey* recognized, the two cases are relevant only to show—by stark contrast—how unjustified overturning the right to choose is. See 505 U. S., at 861–864.

West Coast Hotel overruled *Adkins* v. *Children's Hospital of D. C.*, 261 U.S. 525 (1923), and a whole line of cases beginning with *Lochner* v. *New York*, 198 U.S. 45 (1905). *Adkins* had found a state minimum-wage law unconstitutional because, in the Court's view, the law interfered with a constitutional right to contract. 261 U. S., at 554–555. But then the Great Depression hit, bringing with it unparalleled economic despair. The experience undermined—in fact, it disproved—

Adkins's assumption that a wholly unregulated market could meet basic human needs. As Justice Jackson (before becoming a Justice) wrote of that time: "The older world of *laissez faire* was recognized everywhere outside the Court to be dead." The Struggle for Judicial Supremacy 85 (1941). In *West Coast Hotel*, the Court caught up, recognizing through the lens of experience the flaws of existing legal doctrine. See also *ante*, at 11 (Roberts, C. J., concurring in judgment). The havoc the Depression had worked on ordinary Americans, the Court noted, was "common knowledge through the length and breadth of the land." 300 U. S., at 399. The *laissez-faire* approach had led to "the exploiting of workers at wages so low as to be insufficient to meet the bare cost of living." *Ibid*. And since *Adkins* was decided, the law had also changed. In several decisions, the Court had started to recognize the power of States to implement economic policies designed to enhance their citizens' economic well-being. See, *e.g.*, *Nebbia* v. *New York*, 291 U.S. 502 (1934); *O'Gorman & Young, Inc.* v. *Hartford Fire Ins. Co.*, 282 U.S. 251 (1931). The statements in those decisions, *West Coast Hotel* explained, were "impossible to reconcile" with *Adkins*. 300 U. S., at 398. There was no escaping the need for *Adkins* to go.

Brown v. *Board of Education* overruled *Plessy* v. *Ferguson*, 163 U.S. 537 (1896), along with its doctrine of "separate but equal." By 1954, decades of Jim Crow had made clear what *Plessy*'s turn of phrase actually meant: "inherent[ ] [in]equal[ity]." *Brown*, 347 U. S., at 495. Segregation was not, and could not ever be, consistent with the Reconstruction Amendments, ratified to give the former slaves full citizenship. Whatever might have been thought in *Plessy*'s time, the *Brown* Court explained, both experience and "modern authority" showed the "detrimental effect[s]" of state-sanctioned segregation: It "affect[ed] [children's] hearts and minds in a way unlikely ever to be undone." 347 U. S., at 494. By that point, too, the law had begun to reflect that understanding. In a series of decisions, the Court had held unconstitutional public graduate schools' exclusion of black students. See, *e.g.*, *Sweatt* v. *Painter*, 339 U.S. 629 (1950); *Sipuel* v. *Board of Regents of Univ. of Okla.*, 332 U.S. 631 (1948) (*per curiam*); *Missouri ex rel. Gaines* v. *Canada*, 305 U.S. 337 (1938). The logic of those cases, *Brown* held, "appl[ied] with added force to children in grade and high schools." 347 U. S., at 494. Changed facts and changed law required *Plessy*'s end.

The majority says that in recognizing those changes, we are implicitly supporting the half-century interlude between *Plessy* and *Brown*. See *ante*, at 70. That is not so. First, if the *Brown* Court had used the majority's method of constitutional construction, it might not ever have overruled *Plessy*, whether 5 or 50 or 500 years later. *Brown* thought that whether the ratification-era history supported desegregation was "[a]t best ... inconclusive." 347 U. S., at 489. But even setting that aside, we are not saying that a decision can *never* be overruled just because it is terribly wrong. Take *West Virginia Bd. of Ed.* v. *Barnette*, 319 U.S. 624, which the majority also relies on. See *ante*, at 40–41, 70. That overruling took place just three years after the initial decision, before any notable reliance interests had developed. It happened as well because individual Justices changed their minds, not because a new majority wanted to undo the decisions of their predecessors. Both *Barnette* and *Brown*, moreover, share another feature setting them apart from the Court's ruling today. They protected individual rights with a strong basis in the Constitution's most fundamental commitments; they did not, as the majority does here, take away a right that individuals have held, and relied on, for 50 years. To take *that* action based on a new and bare majority's declaration that two Courts got the result egregiously wrong? And to justify that action by reference to *Barnette*? Or to *Brown*—a case in which the Chief Justice also wrote an (11-page) opinion in which the entire Court could speak with one voice? These questions answer themselves.

Casey itself addressed both *West Coast Hotel* and *Brown*, and found that neither supported *Roe*'s overruling. In *West Coast Hotel*, *Casey* explained, "the facts of economic life" had proved "different from those previously assumed." 505 U. S., at 862. And even though "*Plessy* was wrong the day it was decided," the passage of time had made that ever more clear to ever more citizens: "Society's understanding of the facts" in 1954 was "fundamentally different" than in 1896. *Id.*, at 863. So the Court needed to reverse course. "In constitutional adjudication as elsewhere in life, changed circumstances may impose new obligations." *Id.*, at 864. And because such dramatic change had occurred, the public could understand why the Court was acting. "[T]he Nation could accept each decision" as a "response to the Court's constitutional duty." *Ibid*. But that would not be true of a reversal of *Roe*—"[b]ecause neither the factual underpinnings of *Roe*'s central holding nor our understanding of it has changed." 505 U. S., at 864.

That is just as much so today, because *Roe* and *Casey* continue to reflect, not diverge from, broad trends in American society. It is, of course, true that many Americans, including many women, opposed those decisions when issued and do so now as well. Yet the fact remains: *Roe* and *Casey* were the product of a profound and ongoing change in women's roles in the latter part of the 20th century. Only a dozen years before *Roe*, the Court described women as "the center of home and family life," with "special responsibilities" that precluded their full legal status under the Constitution. *Hoyt* v. *Florida*, 368 U.S. 57, 62 (1961). By 1973, when the Court decided *Roe*, fundamental social change was underway regarding the place of women—and the law had begun to follow. See *Reed* v. *Reed*, 404 U.S. 71, 76 (1971) (recognizing that the Equal Protection Clause prohibits sex-based discrimination). By 1992, when the Court decided *Casey*, the traditional view of a woman's role as only a wife and mother was "no longer consistent with our understanding of the family, the individual, or the Constitution." 505 U. S., at 897; see *supra*, at 15, 23–24. Under that charter, *Casey* understood, women must take their place as full and equal citizens. And for that to happen, women must have control over their reproductive decisions. Nothing since *Casey*—no changed law, no changed fact—has undermined that promise.

C

The reasons for retaining *Roe* and *Casey* gain further strength from the overwhelming reliance interests those decisions have created. The Court adheres to precedent not just for institutional reasons, but because it recognizes that stability in the law is "an essential thread in the mantle of protection that the law affords the individual." *Florida Dept. of Health and Rehabilitative Servs.* v. *Florida Nursing Home Assn.*, 450 U.S. 147, 154 (1981) (Stevens, J., concurring). So when overruling precedent "would dislodge [individuals'] settled rights and expectations," *stare decisis* has "added force." *Hilton* v. *South Carolina Public Railways Comm'n*, 502 U.S. 197, 202 (1991). *Casey* understood that to deny individuals' reliance on *Roe* was to "refuse to face the fact[s]." 505 U. S., at 856. Today the majority refuses to face the facts. "The most striking feature of the [majority] is the absence of any serious discussion" of how its ruling will affect women. *Ante*, at 37. By characterizing *Casey*'s reliance arguments as "generalized assertions about the national psyche," *ante*, at 64, it reveals how little it knows or cares about women's lives or about the suffering its decision will cause.

In *Casey*, the Court observed that for two decades individuals "have organized intimate relationships and made" significant life choices "in reliance on the availability of abortion in the event that contraception should fail." 505 U. S., at 856. Over another 30 years, that reliance has solidified. For half a century now, in *Casey*'s words, "[t]he ability of women to participate equally in the economic and social life of the Nation has been facilitated by their ability to control their reproductive lives." *Ibid.*; see *supra*, at 23–24. Indeed, all women now of childbearing age have grown up expecting that they would be able to avail themselves of *Roe*'s and *Casey*'s protections.

The disruption of overturning *Roe* and *Casey* will therefore be profound. Abortion is a common medical procedure and a familiar experience in women's lives. About 18 percent of pregnancies in this country end in abortion, and about one quarter of American women will have an abortion before the age of 45. Those numbers reflect the predictable and life-changing effects of carrying a pregnancy, giving birth, and becoming a parent. As *Casey* understood, people today rely on their ability to control and time pregnancies when making countless life decisions: where to live, whether and how to invest in education or careers, how to allocate financial resources, and how to approach intimate and family relationships. Women may count on abortion access for when contraception fails. They may count on abortion access for when contraception cannot be used, for example, if they were raped. They may count on abortion for when something changes in the midst of a pregnancy, whether it involves family or financial circumstances, unanticipated medical complications, or heartbreaking fetal diagnoses. Taking away the right to abortion, as the majority does today, destroys all those individual plans and expectations. In so doing, it diminishes women's opportunities to participate fully and equally in the Nation's political, social, and economic life. See Brief for Economists as *Amici Curiae* 13 (showing that abortion availability has "large effects on women's education, labor force participation, occupations, and earnings" (footnotes omitted)).

The majority's response to these obvious points exists far from the reality American women actually live. The majority proclaims that " 'reproductive planning could take virtually immediate account of any sudden restoration of state authority to ban abortions.'" *Ante*, at 64 (quoting *Casey*, 505 U. S., at 856). The facts are: 45 percent of pregnancies in the United States are unplanned. See Brief for 547 Deans 5. Even the most effective contraceptives fail, and effective contraceptives are not universally accessible. Not all sexual activity is consensual and not all contraceptive choices are made by the party who risks pregnancy. See Brief for Legal Voice et al. as *Amici Curiae* 18–19. The Mississippi law at issue here, for example, has no exception for rape or incest, even for underage women. Finally, the majority ignores, as explained above, that some women decide to have an abortion because their circumstances change during a pregnancy. See *supra*, at 49. Human bodies care little for hopes and plans. Events can occur after conception, from unexpected medical risks to changes in family circumstances, which profoundly alter what it means to carry a pregnancy to term. In all these situations, women have expected that they will get to decide, perhaps in consultation with their families or doctors but free from state interference, whether to continue a pregnancy. For those who will now have to undergo that pregnancy, the loss of *Roe* and *Casey* could be disastrous.

That is especially so for women without money. When we "count[ ] the cost of [*Roe*'s] repudiation" on women who once relied on that decision, it is not hard to see where the greatest burden will fall. *Casey*, 505 U. S., at 855. In States that bar abortion, women of means will still be able to travel to obtain the services they need. It is women who cannot afford to do so who will suffer most. These are the women most likely to seek abortion care in the first place. Women living below the federal poverty line experience unintended pregnancies at rates five times higher than higher income women do, and nearly half of women who seek abortion care live in households below the poverty line. See Brief for 547 Deans 7; Brief for Abortion Funds and Practical Support Organizations as *Amici Curiae* 8 (Brief for Abortion Funds). Even with *Roe*'s protection, these women face immense obstacles to raising the money needed to obtain abortion care early in their pregnancy. See Brief for Abortion Funds 7–12. After today, in States where legal abortions are not available, they will lose any ability to obtain safe, legal abortion care. They will not have the money to make the trip necessary; or to obtain childcare for that time; or to take time off work. Many will endure the costs and risks of pregnancy and giving birth against their wishes. Others will turn in desperation to illegal and unsafe abortions. They may lose not just their freedom, but their lives.

Finally, the expectation of reproductive control is integral to many women's identity and their place in the Nation. See *Casey*, 505 U. S., at 856. That expectation helps define a woman as an "equal citizen[ ]," with all the rights, privileges, and obligations that status entails. *Gonzales*, 550 U. S., at 172 (Ginsburg, J., dissenting); see *supra*, at 23–24. It reflects that she is an autonomous person, and that society and the law recognize her as such. Like many constitutional rights, the right to choose situates a woman in relationship to others and to the government. It helps define a sphere of freedom, in which a person has the capacity to make choices free of government control. As *Casey* recognized, the right "order[s]" her "thinking" as well as her "living." 505 U. S., at 856. Beyond any individual choice about residence, or education, or career, her whole life reflects the control and authority that the right grants.

Withdrawing a woman's right to choose whether to continue a pregnancy does not mean that no choice is being made. It means that a majority of today's Court has wrenched this choice from women and given it to the States. To allow a State to exert control over one of "the most intimate and personal choices" a woman may make is not only to affect the course of her life, monumental as those effects might be. *Id.*, at 851. It is to alter her "views of [herself]" and her understanding of her "place[ ] in society" as someone with the recognized dignity and authority to make these choices. *Id.*, at 856. Women have relied on *Roe* and *Casey* in this way for 50 years. Many have never known anything else. When *Roe* and *Casey* disappear, the loss of power, control, and dignity will be immense.

The Court's failure to perceive the whole swath of expectations *Roe* and *Casey* created reflects an impoverished view of reliance. According to the majority, a reliance interest must be "very concrete," like those involving "property" or "contract." *Ante*, at 64. While many of this Court's cases addressing reliance have been in the "commercial context," *Casey*, 505 U. S., at 855, none holds that interests must be analogous to commercial ones to warrant *stare decisis* protection. This unprecedented assertion is, at bottom, a radical claim to power. By disclaiming any need to consider broad swaths of individuals' interests, the Court arrogates to itself the authority to overrule established legal principles without even acknowledging the costs of its decisions for the individuals who live under the law, costs that this Court's *stare decisis* doctrine instructs us to privilege when deciding whether to change course.

The majority claims that the reliance interests women have in *Roe* and *Casey* are too "intangible" for the Court to consider, even if it were inclined to do so. *Ante*, at 65. This is to ignore as judges what we know as men and women. The interests women have in *Roe* and *Casey* are perfectly, viscerally concrete. Countless women will now make different decisions about careers, education, relationships, and whether to try to become pregnant than they would have when *Roe* served as a backstop. Other women will carry pregnancies to term, with all the costs and risk of harm that involves, when they would previously have chosen to obtain an abortion. For millions of women, *Roe* and *Casey* have been critical in giving them control of their bodies and their lives. Closing our eyes to the suffering today's decision will impose will not make that suffering disappear. The majority cannot escape its obligation to "count[ ] the cost[s]" of its decision by invoking the "conflicting arguments" of "contending sides." *Casey*, 505 U. S., at 855; *ante*, at 65. *Stare decisis* requires that the Court calculate the costs of a decision's repudiation on those who have relied on the decision, not on those who have disavowed it. See *Casey*, 505 U. S., at 855.

More broadly, the majority's approach to reliance cannot be reconciled with our Nation's understanding of constitutional rights. The majority's insistence on a "concrete," economic showing would preclude a finding of reliance on a wide variety of decisions recognizing constitutional rights—such as the right to express opinions, or choose whom to marry, or decide how to educate children. The Court, on the majority's logic, could transfer those choices to the State without having to consider a person's settled understanding that the law makes them hers. That must be wrong. All those rights, like the right to obtain an abortion, profoundly affect and, indeed, anchor individual lives. To recognize that people have relied on these rights is not to dabble in abstractions, but to acknowledge some of the most "concrete" and familiar aspects of human life and liberty. *Ante*, at 64.

All those rights, like the one here, also have a societal dimension, because of the role constitutional liberties play in our structure of government. See, *e.g.*, *Dickerson*, 530 U. S., at 443 (recognizing that *Miranda* "warnings have become part of our national culture" in declining to overrule *Miranda* v. *Arizona*, 384 U.S. 436 (1966)). Rescinding an individual right in its entirety and conferring it on the State, an action the Court takes today for the first time in history, affects all who have relied on our constitutional system of government and its structure of individual liberties protected from state oversight. *Roe* and *Casey* have of course aroused controversy and provoked disagreement. But the right those decisions conferred and reaffirmed is part of society's understanding of constitutional law and of how the Court has defined the liberty and equality that women are entitled to claim.

After today, young women will come of age with fewer rights than their mothers and grandmothers had. The majority accomplishes that result without so much as considering how women have relied on the right to choose or what it means to take that right away. The majority's refusal even to consider the life-altering consequences of reversing *Roe* and *Casey* is a stunning indictment of its decision.

D

One last consideration counsels against the majority's ruling: the very controversy surrounding *Roe* and *Casey*. The majority accuses *Casey* of acting outside the bounds of the law to quell the conflict over abortion—of imposing an unprincipled "settlement" of the issue in an effort to end "national division." *Ante*, at 67. But that is not what *Casey* did. As shown above, *Casey* applied traditional principles of *stare decisis*—which the majority today ignores—in reaffirming *Roe*. *Casey* carefully assessed changed circumstances (none) and reliance interests (profound). It considered every aspect of how *Roe*'s framework operated. It adhered to the law in its analysis, and it reached the conclusion that the law required. True enough that *Casey* took notice of the "national controversy" about abortion: The Court knew in 1992, as it did in 1973, that abortion was a "divisive issue." *Casey*, 505 U. S., at 867–868; see *Roe*, 410 U. S., at 116. But *Casey*'s reason for acknowledging public conflict was the exact opposite of what the majority insinuates. *Casey* addressed the national controversy in order to emphasize how important it was, in that case of all cases, for the Court to stick to the law. Would that today's majority had done likewise.

Consider how the majority itself summarizes this aspect of *Casey*:

"The American people's belief in the rule of law would be shaken if they lost respect for this Court as an institution that decides important cases based on principle, not 'social and political pressures.' There is a special danger that the public will perceive a decision as having been made for unprincipled reasons when the Court overrules a controversial 'watershed' decision, such as *Roe*. A decision overruling *Roe* would be perceived as having been made 'under fire' and as a 'surrender to political pressure.'" *Ante*, at 66–67 (citations omitted).

That seems to us a good description. And it seems to us right. The majority responds (if we understand it correctly): well, yes, but we have to apply the law. See *ante*, at 67. To which *Casey* would have said: That is exactly the point. Here, more than anywhere, the Court needs to apply the law—particularly the law of *stare decisis*. Here, we know that citizens will continue to contest the Court's decision, because "[m]en and women of good conscience" deeply disagree about abortion. *Casey*, 505 U. S., at 850. When that contestation takes place—but when there is no legal basis for reversing course—the Court needs to be steadfast, to stand its ground. That is what the rule of law requires. And that is what respect for this Court depends on.

"The promise of constancy, once given" in so charged an environment, *Casey* explained, "binds its maker for as long as" the "understanding of the issue has not changed so fundamentally as to render the commitment obsolete." *Id.*, at 868. A breach of that promise is "nothing less than a breach of faith." *Ibid.* "[A]nd no Court that broke its faith with the people could sensibly expect credit for principle." *Ibid.* No Court breaking its faith in that way would *deserve* credit for principle. As one of *Casey*'s authors wrote in another case, "Our legitimacy requires, above all, that we adhere to *stare decisis*" in "sensitive political contexts" where "partisan controversy abounds." *Bush* v. *Vera*, 517 U.S. 952, 985 (1996) (opinion of O'Connor, J.).

Justice Jackson once called a decision he dissented from a "loaded weapon," ready to hand for improper uses. *Korematsu* v. *United States*, 323 U.S. 214, 246 (1944). We fear that today's decision, departing from *stare decisis* for no legitimate reason, is its own loaded weapon. Weakening *stare decisis* threatens to upend bedrock legal doctrines, far beyond any single decision. Weakening *stare decisis* creates profound legal instability. And as *Casey* recognized, weakening *stare decisis* in a hotly contested case like this one calls into question this Court's commitment to legal principle. It makes the Court appear not restrained but aggressive, not modest but grasping. In all those ways, today's decision takes aim, we fear, at the rule of law.

III

"Power, not reason, is the new currency of this Court's decisionmaking." *Payne*, 501 U. S., at 844 (Marshall, J., dissenting). *Roe* has stood for fifty years. *Casey*, a precedent about precedent specifically confirming *Roe*, has stood for thirty. And the doctrine of *stare decisis*—a critical element of the rule of law—stands foursquare behind their continued existence. The right those decisions established and preserved is embedded in our constitutional law, both originating in and leading to other rights protecting bodily integrity, personal autonomy, and family relationships. The abortion right is also embedded in the lives of women—shaping their expectations, influencing their choices about relationships and work, supporting (as all reproductive rights do) their social and economic equality. Since the right's recognition (and affirmation), nothing has changed to support what the majority does today. Neither law nor facts nor attitudes have provided any new reasons to reach a different result than *Roe* and *Casey* did. All that has changed is this Court.

Mississippi—and other States too—knew exactly what they were doing in ginning up new legal challenges to *Roe* and *Casey*. The 15-week ban at issue here was enacted in 2018. Other States quickly followed: Between 2019 and 2021, eight States banned abortion procedures after six to eight weeks of pregnancy, and three States enacted all-out bans. Mississippi itself decided in 2019 that it had not gone far enough: The year after enacting the law under review, the State passed a 6-week restriction. A state senator who championed both Mississippi laws said the obvious out loud. "[A] lot of people thought," he explained, that "finally, we have" a conservative Court "and so now would be a good time to start testing the limits of *Roe*." In its petition for certiorari, the State had exercised a smidgen of restraint. It had urged the Court merely to roll back *Roe* and *Casey*, specifically assuring the Court that "the questions presented in this petition do not require the Court to overturn" those precedents. Pet. for Cert. 5; see *ante*, at 5–6 (Roberts, C. J., concurring in judgment). But as Mississippi grew ever more confident in its prospects, it resolved to go all in. It urged the Court to overrule *Roe* and *Casey*. Nothing but everything would be enough.

Earlier this Term, this Court signaled that Mississippi's stratagem would succeed. Texas was one of the fistful of States to have recently banned abortions after six weeks of pregnancy. It added to that "flagrantly unconstitutional" restriction an unprecedented scheme to "evade judicial scrutiny." *Whole Woman's Health* v. *Jackson*, 594 U. S. ___, ___ (2021) (Sotomayor, J., dissenting) (slip op., at 1). And five Justices acceded to that cynical maneuver. They let Texas defy this Court's constitutional rulings, nullifying *Roe* and *Casey* ahead of schedule in the Nation's second largest State.

And now the other shoe drops, courtesy of that same five-person majority. (We believe that The Chief Justice's opinion is wrong too, but no one should think that there is not a large difference between upholding a 15-week ban on the grounds he does and allowing States to prohibit abortion from the time of conception.) Now a new and bare majority of this Court—acting at practically the first moment possible—overrules *Roe* and *Casey*. It converts a series of dissenting opinions expressing antipathy toward *Roe* and *Casey* into a decision greenlighting even total abortion bans. See *ante*, at 57, 59, 63, and nn. 61–64 (relying on former dissents). It eliminates a 50-year-old constitutional right that safeguards women's freedom and equal station. It breaches a core rule-of-law principle, designed to promote constancy in the law. In doing all of that, it places in jeopardy other rights, from contraception to same-sex intimacy and marriage. And finally, it undermines the Court's legitimacy.

Casey itself made the last point in explaining why it would not overrule *Roe*—though some members of its majority might not have joined *Roe* in the first instance. Just as we did here, *Casey* explained the importance of *stare decisis*; the inappositeness of *West Coast Hotel* and *Brown*; the absence of any "changed circumstances" (or other reason) justifying the reversal of precedent. 505 U. S., at 864; see *supra*, at 30–33, 37–47. "[T]he Court," *Casey* explained, "could not pretend" that overruling *Roe* had any "justification beyond a present doctrinal disposition to come out differently from the Court of 1973." 505 U. S., at 864. And to overrule for that reason? Quoting Justice Stewart, *Casey* explained that to do so—to reverse prior law "upon a ground no firmer than a change in [the Court's] membership"—would invite the view that "this institution is little different from the two political branches of the Government." *Ibid.* No view, *Casey* thought, could do "more lasting injury to this Court and to the system of law which it is our abiding mission to serve." *Ibid.* For overruling *Roe*, *Casey* concluded, the Court would pay a "terrible price." 505 U. S., at 864.

The Justices who wrote those words—O'Connor, Kennedy, and Souter—they were judges of wisdom. They would not have won any contests for the kind of ideological purity some court watchers want Justices to deliver. But if there were awards for Justices who left this Court better than they found it? And who for that reason left this country better? And the rule of law stronger? Sign those Justices up.

They knew that "the legitimacy of the Court [is] earned over time." *Id.*, at 868. They also would have recognized that it can be destroyed much more quickly. They worked hard to avert that outcome in *Casey*. The American public, they thought, should never conclude that its constitutional protections hung by a thread—that a new majority, adhering to a new "doctrinal school," could "by dint of numbers" alone expunge their rights. *Id.*, at 864. It is hard—no, it is impossible—to conclude that anything else has happened here. One of us once said that "[i]t is not often in the law that so few have so quickly changed so much." S. Breyer, Breaking the Promise of *Brown*: The Resegregation of America's Schools 30 (2022). For all of us, in our time on this Court, that has never been more true than today. In overruling *Roe* and *Casey*, this Court betrays its guiding principles.

With sorrow—for this Court, but more, for the many millions of American women who have today lost a fundamental constitutional protection—we dissent.

Glossary

abortion: the ending of a pregnancy, whether induced or naturally occurring, after or resulting in the death of the embryo or fetus

due process clause: Section 1, sentence 2 of the Fourteenth Amendment, which states, in part: "nor shall any State deprive any person of life, liberty, or property, without due process of law"

invidiously discriminatory animus: hostile discrimination that is irrational and serves no legitimate purpose

pre-viability abortions: abortions that take place before a fetus is able to survive outside the womb

stare decisis: the principle of honoring legal precedent

viability: the ability of a fetus to survive outside the womb

INDEX

Main entries are listed in bold. Here is a guide to the volume page numbering:

Volume 1: pp. 2–496
Volume 2: pp. 497–980
Volume 3: pp. 981–1486

A

Abbington School District v. Schempp 1235
Abington School District v. Schempp 826
Ableman v. Booth 267-286, 387
abortion rights 674, 857, 861, 890, 1061-1084, 1097, 1135, 1152, 1154, 1257, 1282, 1338, 1369, 1417-1472
Abrams v. United States 542, 544, 550-562, 564
actual malice standard 853
Adair v. United States 499
Adams, John 54, 82, 139, 165, 631
Adams, John Quincy 196, 208, 209
Adamson v. California 723, 834
Adarand Constructors v. Pena 1116
Adkins v. Children's Hospital 578, 671, 672, 673
Administrative Procedure Act 701, 1049
affirmative action 852, 1088, 1097, 1110, 1111, 1114, 1115, 1175
Affordable Care Act 1324
African Americans, rights of 369, 382, 419, 438, 502, 515, 517, 793, 795, 804, 839, 840, 869, 926, 928, 1000, 1001, 1284, 1336, 1337, 1339
Agassiz, Louis 420
Agnew, Spiro 1094
Agricultural Adjustment Act of 1938 670, 697, 698, 699, 701, 839
A.L.A. Schechter Poultry Corp. v. United States 141, 610-626, 646, 670
Alexander II (Tsar of Russia) 551
Ali, Muhammad 983
Alito, Samuel 1371, 1380
　Dobbs v. Jackson Women's Health Organization 1417-1472
Allen v. State Board of Elections 931
Allgeyer v. Louisiana 489, 499
American Communications Association v. Douds 743
American flag 711, 713, 1143, 1145
Anderson, John C. 596
anti-Semitism 497

antitrust laws 981, 983, 984
Argersinger v. Hamlin 835
Armed Career Criminal Act 1281
Arthur, Chester A. 420, 461, 462, 577
Articles of Confederation 140, 228, 365, 631
assembly and petition clause 1283
Associated Press v. Walker 853
Austin v. Michigan Chamber of Commerce 1322, 1324, 1326

B

Baehr v. Lewin 1367
Baer v. United States and Frohwerk v. United States 553
Bailey v. Drexel Furniture Co. 533
Baker v. Carr 796, 815-821, 1052, 1104, 1134, 1144
Baker v. Nelson 948, 1366, 1369, 1371
Baker v. State of Vermont 949
Bakeshop Act 472, 473, 476, 477
Baldridge, Holmes 761, 764
Baldwin, Henry 166, 196
Baldwin, Roger 196
Bao Dai 968
Barbour, Philip 111, 196
Barbour, William T. 313
Barlow v. Collins 1051
Barrett, Amy Coney 1062, 1418, 1419
Barron v. City of Baltimore 803
baseball 981, 985
Bates, Edward 287
Bazile, Leon M. 945, 948
Beckwith, James R. 353
Bennett v. Spear 1220
Bethel School District v. Fraser 960
Betts v. Brady 834
Biden, Joe 1063, 1146, 1385
Biden-Roth-Cohen Flag Protection Act of 1989 1146
Bingham, John 383
birth control 774, 1061
Bivens v. Six Unknown Named Agents 1088, 1097
Black Codes 310, 439
Black, Hugo L. 631, 741, 744, 795, 805, 861, 885, 958,

959, 960, 970, 1011, 1051, 1235
Engel v. Vitale 822-831
Gideon v. Wainwright 832-838
Griswold v. Connecticut 857-867
Korematsu v. United States 720-729
New York Times Co. v. United States 967-980
South Carolina v. Katzenbach 926-942
Youngstown Sheet and Tube Co. v. Sawyer 761-771
Black, Jerimiah 289
Blackmun, Harry A. 971, 997, 1012, 1051, 1096, 1112, 1115, 1253
   Flood v. Kuhn 981-996
   Roe v. Wade 1061-1084
Blackstone, William 1008
Black, Timothy 1368
Blatchford, Samuel 384
Bleecker, Harmanus 313
Board of Ed. of Central School Dist. No.1 v. Allen 1237
Bob Jones University v. United States 1088
Bond, Julian 868, 870
Bond v. Floyd 868-883
Bork, Robert H. 1221, 1324, 1369
Bostock v. Clayton County 1380-1416
Bowers v. Hardwick 1252, 1254, 1257
Boyd v. United States 578
Bradley, Joseph P. 315, 351, 353
   Civil Rights Cases 382-417
Bradwell v. Illinois 313
Brady Handgun Violence Protection Act 1282
Bram v. United States 887, 889
Brandeis, Louis D. 487, 489, 490, 491, 532, 552, 554, 566, 579, 775, 794, 859, 999
Brandenburg v. Ohio 554, 563, 745
Brennan, William J., Jr. 805, 858, 885, 984, 1012, 1051, 1063, 1085, 1098, 1112, 1114, 1253
   Baker v. Carr 815-821
   Craig v. Boren 1103-1109
   Frontiero v. Richardson 1133-1142
   Furman v. Georgia 997-1009
   New York Times Co. v. Sullivan 850-856, 981
   New York Times Co. v. United States 967-980
   Texas v. Johnson 1143-1151
Brewer, David J. 438
   Muller v. Oregon 486-496
Breyer, Stephen 960, 1152, 1191, 1254, 1280, 1336, 1368, 1418
   Zelman v. Simmons-Harris 1237
Broderick, David 313
Brown, Henry Billings 732
   Plessy v. Ferguson 438-458
Brown, Joseph M. 502
Brown v. Board of Education 274, 438, 445, 490, 598, 699, 735, 736, 772-783, 785, 786, 788, 840, 871, 943, 945, 948, 949, 984, 1000, 1010, 1012, 1013,
1066, 1085, 1088, 1111, 1115, 1258
Bryan, William Jennings 530, 578, 629
Buchanan, James 231, 234, 269, 273
Buchanan v. Warley 517
Buckley v. Valeo 1326
Bunting v. Oregon 490
Buren, Martin Van 195, 196, 198, 231
Burger, Warren E. 816, 817, 851, 852, 890, 970, 981, 984, 997, 1012, 1051, 1063, 1103, 1111, 1116, 1135, 1144, 1152, 1235, 1253, 1282
   Milliken v. Bradley 1085-1093
   United States v. Nixon 1094-1102
Burleson, Albert 543
Burlingame-Seward Treaty 460
Burr, Aaron 2, 1175
Burton, Harold 764
Bush, George H.W. 1066, 1173, 1220, 1323, 1418, 1420
Bush, George W. 632, 1062, 1066, 1116, 1187, 1188, 1193, 1282, 1284, 1338, 1419
Bush v. Gore 1154, 1187-1218
Butler, Pierce 579, 596, 597, 644, 673
Butterfield, Alexander 1095
Byrnes, James F. 699

C

Calhoun, John 166
California Criminal Syndicalism Act of 1919 563, 564, 566
Callins v. Collins 1064
campaign finance 1322, 1323, 1326
Campbell, James Valentine 628
Campbell, John Archibald 289, 312
Cannon v. United States 367
Canovas del Castillo, Antonio 551
Cantwell v. Connecticut 687-696
Cardoza, Benjamin 1084
Cardozo, Benjamin 795
Carey v. Population Services International 861, 1255
Carlos, John 983
Carnegie, Andrew 472
Carnot, Sadi 551
Carswell, G. Harold 1112
Carter, Jimmy 1165, 1221, 1369
Carter v. Carter Coal 644
Catron, John 196, 231, 233
Chae Chan Ping v. United States 314
Champion v. Ames 532, 533
Charles River Bridge v. Warren Bridge 185-192
Charles Whittaker 796
Chase, Jeremiah 187
Chase, Salmon P. 209, 312, 315, 355, 368, 388
   Ex Parte Milligan 287-309
Chastleton Corporation et al. v. Sinclair et al. 1083
Cherokee Nation 4, 163

Cherokee Nation v. Georgia 164, 168, 169, 418
Chew Heong v. United States 314
child labor 497, 529, 530, 673
Child Labor Tax Act 534
children and minors, rights of 958, 959, 960
Chinese Exclusion Act 459, 461, 463
Chinese immigrants 314, 459, 460
Christ's Church Hospital v. County of Philadelphia 312
Church of Jesus Christ of Latter-day Saints (LDS) 366, 368, 371
Cinqué, Joseph 194, 197
Cisneros v. Corpus Christi Independent School District 788
Citizenship Act of 1919 422
Citizens United v. Federal Election Commission 1322-1335
Civil Rights Act of 1866 383, 419, 462
Civil Rights Act of 1875 274, 382, 383, 385, 387, 388, 389, 439, 440, 441, 731
Civil Rights Act of 1957 840, 928, 929
Civil Rights Act of 1960 928, 929
Civil Rights Act of 1964 382, 389, 839, 841, 869, 872, 928, 929, 943, 1049, 1110, 1111, 1382
Civil Rights Cases 274, 313, 382-417, 440, 441, 731
civil rights movement 784, 788, 850, 853, 857, 875, 959, 999, 1000, 1001, 1111, 1145, 1337, 1381, 1385
Civil War 1283
Clarke, John H. 532
　Abrams v. United States 550-562, 802
Clark, Harley 1014
Clark, Kenneth 777
Clark, Ramsey 804
Clark, Tom C. 764, 888
　Katzenbach v. McClung 839-849
　Mapp v. Ohio 802-814
　Miranda v. Arizona 884-925
Clawson v. United States 367
Clay, Henry 229, 384
Clayton Antitrust Act 473, 530
Clean Water Act 1219, 1221
clear and present danger doctrine 742, 743
Cleveland, Grover 367, 474, 1094
Clifford, Nathan 312
　United States v. Cruikshank 351-365
Clifton v. Puente 787
Clinton, Bill 1066, 1165, 1173, 1221, 1323, 1367, 1381
Clinton, DeWitt 138
Clinton, Hillary 1322, 1324, 1325
Clinton v. Jones 1173-1186
Cohen, Bernard S. 945
Cohens v. Virginia 107-136, 268, 272
Cold War 741, 745, 857, 968, 969, 999
Colegrove v. Green 795, 796, 816, 818, 1187
Colfax massacre 353, 354, 355

commerce clause 107, 108, 136, 139, 140, 388, 389, 532, 534, 541, 610, 644, 646, 648, 697, 700, 839, 843, 1152, 1153, 1154, 1155
Communism 563, 564, 733, 741, 743, 744, 745, 762, 763
Compromise of 1850 231
Compromise of 1877 357
Comstock Act 1061
contraception 861
contract clause 52, 55, 185, 186
Cooley, Thomas M. 628
Coolidge, Calvin 688
Cooper v. Aaron 274
Coppage v. Kansas 500
Craig v. Boren 1103-1109
Crescent City Case 386, 387
Crime Control Act of 1990 1282
Curtis, Benjamin R. 232, 234, 270
Curtis Publishing Co. v. Butts 853
Cushing, Luther S. 420
Czolgosz, Leon 551

D

Dallas, Alexander 166
Daniel Webster 112
Data Processing Service v. Camp 1051
Davis, David 312, 351, 354
　Ex parte Milligan 287-309
Davis, Jefferson 275, 312
Davis, John 518
Davis v. Beason 368
Dawes, Henry 422
Dawes Severalty Act 422
Day, William R. 476, 553
　Hammer v. Dagenhart 529-541
Dean, John 1096
death penalty 851, 852, 997, 998, 1001, 1064, 1135, 1324
Debs v. United States 544
Declaration of Independence 630, 968, 1115
defendants' rights 593, 598, 832, 834, 884, 886, 1088, 1097
Defense of Marriage Act 1367
DeFunis v. Odegaard 1111
DeGeneres, Ellen 1382
Delgado v. Bastrop Independent School District 785
Dennis v. United States 554, 741-760, 763
Devanter, Willis Van 553, 596
Dewey, Thomas 774, 871, 946
District of Columbia v. Heller 1280-1321, 1420
Dobbs v. Jackson Women's Health Organization 1063, 1066, 1417-1472
Dodge v. Woolsey 312
Doe v. Snyder 1384
Dole, Bob 1173

Dorsey, Hugh M. 498
Douglas, Stephen A. 234, 289
Douglas, William O. 314, 722, 741, 744, 764, 805, 817,
　　　825, 834, 852, 885, 981, 1012, 1051, 1052, 1064,
　　　1085, 1098, 1105, 1145, 1174, 1220
　Furman v. Georgia 997-1009
　Griswold v. Connecticut 857-867
　New York Times Co. v. United States 967-980
Dred Scott v. Sandford 2, 187, 188, 193, 206, 209, 228-
　　　266, 270, 271, 272, 312, 325, 335, 383, 387, 401,
　　　414, 419, 438, 443, 445, 455, 461, 468, 944
due process clause 316, 351, 488, 497, 499, 529, 534,
　　　597, 612, 724, 772, 801, 802, 803, 867, 958, 1133,
　　　1135, 1142, 1189, 1252, 1254, 1256, 1257, 1420
Durham, William J. 730
Duvall, Gabriel 52, 56

E

Edgewood Independent School District v. Kirby 1014
Edmunds Act 367
Edmunds, George F. 367, 368
Edmunds-Tucker Act 368
Eighteenth Amendment 576, 1104
Eighth Amendment 997, 1001
Eisenhower, Dwight D. 774, 786, 817, 840, 852, 871,
　　　885, 946, 1051, 1064, 1087, 1096, 1105, 1144
Eisenstadt v. Baird 858, 861, 1255
Elizabeth (Empress of Austria-Hungary) 551
Elk v. Wilkins 418-437
Ellsberg, Daniel 967, 969
Emancipation Proclamation 384
Embry, John 517
Emerson, Ralph Waldo 420, 543
Emmet, Thomas Addis 137
enemy combatants 291
Enforcement Act of 1870 352, 353, 355, 356, 357, 365
Engelhardt, Samuel, Jr. 794
Engel v. Vitale 822-831, 860, 1235
English Bill of Rights 1001, 1002
environmental protection 857, 859, 999, 1049, 1051,
　　　1053, 1219, 1222
equal protection clause 351, 382, 383, 444, 488, 489,
　　　720, 724, 730, 734, 735, 736, 772, 786, 787, 788,
　　　796, 819, 861, 1010, 1011, 1013, 1085, 1103,
　　　1105, 1106, 1110, 1113, 1133, 1164, 1165, 1187,
　　　1189, 1190, 1192, 1258
Equal Rights Amendment 1133, 1135, 1136
Erlichman, John 1096
Ervin, Sam 1095
Escobedo v. Illinois 884, 886
Espionage Act of 1917 542, 544, 550, 552, 553, 564, 567
establishment clause 824, 826, 827, 1234, 1235, 1236
Evers, Medgar 840
Everson v. Board of Education 824, 825

Everson v. Board of Education of the Township of Ewing
　　　1236
evidence, illegal seizure of 802, 804
exclusionary rule 802, 803, 804, 805, 806
executive branch powers 1094, 1175
Executive Order 9066 720, 723, 724, 725
Executive Order 9981 732, 943
Executive Order 10925 1110
Executive Order No. 10340 761
executive privilege 1098
Ex Parte Crow Dog 419
Ex parte Merryman 188
Ex parte Milligan 287-309
Ex parte Quirin 291, 722
Ex parte Siebold 274
Ex parte Vallandigham 289
Ex parte Virginia 387
Ex parte Yarbrough 313

F

Fairfax, Thomas 23
Fair Labor Standards Act 534, 673
Fall, Albert 688
False Claims Act of 1863 613
Faubus, Orville 274
FEC v. Massachusetts Citizens for Life, Inc. 1325
Federal Baseball Club of Baltimore v. National League
　　　982
Federal Baseball Club v. National League 984
Federal Election Campaign Act 1325
Federal Firearms Act of 1938 1281
Federalist Papers 633, 1327
Feingold, Russ 1323, 1326
Fenton, William D. 488
Fenty, Adrian 1284
Ferrer, José 832
Field, David 289, 313, 355, 487
Field, Stephen J. 289, 312, 354, 384, 487
　Slaughterhouse Cases 310-350
Fifteenth Amendment 310, 315, 352, 353, 355, 356,
　　　383, 387, 389, 418, 419, 438, 443, 515, 516, 518,
　　　519, 520, 526, 793, 796, 926, 927, 930, 1115, 1336,
　　　1337, 1339
Fifth Amendment 232, 233, 234, 314, 531, 575, 578,
　　　612, 699, 700, 724, 772, 774, 803, 805, 806, 860,
　　　884, 886, 888, 889, 926, 1098, 1133, 1135
Fillmore, Millard 312
Firearm Owners Protection Act 1281
First Amendment 366-367, 370, 542, 544, 550-554,
　　　687, 689, 711, 713-714, 723, 741-744, 763, 802,
　　　804, 816, 822, 824, 825, 833, 851, 857, 861, 868,
　　　870, 874, 956, 958, 967, 970, 971, 999, 1104, 1113,
　　　1143, 1144, 1145, 1174, 1238, 1283, 1322, 1324,
　　　1325, 1371

First Bank of the United States 83
First Battle of Bull Run 288
Fiske, Jim 474
Fitch, John 138
flag burning 1146
Fletcher v. Peck 53, 139, 387
Flood v. Kuhn 981-996
Fonda, Henry 832
Ford, Gerald 1136, 1174, 1221, 1254, 1324, 1369
foreign-affairs powers 627, 630
Forsyth, John 198
Fortas, Abe 833, 835, 885, 946, 984
   Tinker v. Des Moines Independent Community School District 956-966
Fourteenth Amendment 108, 234, 274, 310, 312-316, 351, 353-356, 362, 382-389, 418-422, 438, 441-445, 459-472, 476, 488, 489, 499, 500, 518, 534, 563, 593, 597, 613, 670, 687-690, 723, 724, 730, 734-736, 763, 772-775, 784-788, 796, 802, 818, 834, 852, 858, 861, 884, 927, 929, 943, 947, 958, 997, 1001, 1010, 1013, 1064, 1085, 1103-1106, 1110, 1112, 1133, 1164, 1165, 1187, 1221, 1235, 1252, 1337, 1366, 1369, 1371, 1417, 1420, 1421
Fourth Amendment 356, 575, 576, 578, 774, 802, 803, 804, 806, 860, 884, 1051, 1283
Frankfurter, Felix 631, 711, 741, 744, 764, 805, 815, 816, 818, 822, 824, 984, 1187
   Gomillion v. Lightfoot 793-801
Frank Murphy 722, 841
Frank v. Mangum 497-514
freedom of contract 670, 671, 672, 674
freedom of speech 563, 565, 687, 690, 711, 714, 741, 742, 744, 745, 763, 786, 804, 851, 852, 860, 956, 960, 1145, 1322
freedom of the press 850, 852
free exercise clause 826, 827
Frémont, John C. 231
Friends of the Earth v. Gaston Copper Recycling Corporation 1223
Friends of the Earth v. Laidlaw Environmental Services 1219-1233
Frohwerk v. United States 544
Frontiero v. Richardson 1106, 1133-1142, 1221
Fugitive Slave Act of 1793 196, 206, 269
Fugitive Slave Act of 1850 267, 269, 272, 387
Fuller, Melville 460
Fullilove v. Klutznick 1088
Fulton, Robert 137, 142
Furman v. Georgia 997-1009, 1135

G

Garcia v. San Antonio Metropolitan Transit Authority 141, 534
Garfield, James 289
Garth, Leonard 1420
Geary Act 461, 463
Gedney, Thomas 195, 197
Gelb, Leslie H. 969
gender-based discrimination 1103, 1105, 1135, 1145, 1164, 1165, 1167
George III 52, 53
George III (King of England) 1283
Gerry, Elbridge 139
Gertz v. Robert Welch, Inc. 853
Gestational Age Act 1420
Gibbons, Thomas 137
Gibbons v. Ogden 114, 137-162, 532, 700
G.I. Bill 1235
Giddings, Joshua 208
Gideon v. Wainwright 804, 832-838, 860, 884
Gilmer, George 164
Gingrich, Newt 1173, 1176
Ginsburg, Ruth Bader 1103, 1136, 1152, 1190, 1191, 1192, 1254, 1280, 1336, 1368, 1418
   Friends of the Earth v. Laidlaw Environmental Services 1219-1233
   United States v. Virginia 1164-1172
Gitlow v. New York 564, 565, 804
Gochman, Arthur 1011
Goldberg, Arthur 858, 861, 885, 983
Goldmark, Josephine 489, 490, 491
Gold Rush of 1848 313
Gomillion v. Lightfoot 786, 793-801
Gonzales v. Carhart 1066, 1420
Goodridge v. Department of Public Health 890
Gore, Al 1187, 1188, 1193
Gorsuch, Neil 1062, 1419
   Bostock v. Clayton County 1380-1416
Gould, Jay 474
Graham v. Folsom 801
grandfather clause 515, 517, 518, 519, 520, 521
Grant, Ulysses S. 313, 352, 354, 355, 368, 577
Gratz v. Bollinger 1116
Gray, Horace 384
   Elk v. Wilkins 418-437
   United States v. Wong Kim Ark 459-471
Gray v. Sanders 817
Great Depression 89, 594, 610, 645, 648, 671, 673, 687, 697
Greenberg, Hank 985
Greenwood riots 594
Greenwood v. Fright Company 55
Gregg v. Georgia 1002
Gregg, William R. 517
Grier, Robert C. 231, 234
Grimm v. Gloucester County School Board 1384
Griswold v. Connecticut 723, 834, 857-867, 1062, 1065, 1255, 1258

Groves v. Slaughter 141, 166
Grutter v. Bollinger 1110, 1116
Guinn v. United States 515-528
Gulf of Tonkin resolution 869
Gulf of Tonkin Resolution 969
Gun Control Act of 1968 1281
Gun-Free School Zone Act of 1990 843
Gun-Free School Zones Act of 1990 1152, 1154
gun rights 141, 1152, 1153, 1155, 1280, 1281, 1282, 1285, 1338, 1382, 1420

H

habeas corpus 188, 288, 312, 352, 497, 500
Habeas Corpus Suspension Act 289
Haldeman, H. R. 1096
Hamdi v. Rumsfeld 291
Hamilton, Alexander 2, 24, 82, 83, 88
Hammer v. Dagenhart 529-541
Harding, Warren G. 553, 565, 578, 596, 629
Harlan, John Marshall 274, 384, 422, 460, 476, 491, 500, 732, 779, 886
   Civil Rights Cases 382-417
   Plessy v. Ferguson 438-458
Harlan, John Marshall, II 805, 806, 815, 819, 824, 858, 861, 888, 971, 1051
   Miranda v. Arizona 884-925
Harlem Renaissance 594
Harrison, Benjamin 291, 487, 577
Harrison, William Henry 198
Hart v. B. F. Keith Vaudeville Exchange 984
Hawthorne, Nathaniel 420
Hayes, Rutherford B. 313, 357, 385, 439
Hay, Harry 1381
Haymarket Square Bombing 551
Haynsworth, Clement 1112
Haywood v. National Basketball Assn. 985
Heart of Atlanta Motel, Inc. v. United States 141, 841
Hells Canyon massacre 461
Henry, Patrick 54, 165, 1009
Hepburn Act 530
Hepburn v. Griswold 289
Hernandez v. Texas 784-792
Hess v. Indiana 554
Hipolite Egg Co. v. United States 532, 533
Hirabayashi v. United States 724, 725
Hirschkop, Philip J. 945
Hispanics, rights of 785, 787, 788
Hitchman Coal and Coke Co. v. Mitchell 500
Ho Chi Minh 956, 967
Hoke v. United States 532
Holabird, William S. 196
Holden v. Hardy 489
Holder v. Humanitarian Law Project 545
Holmes, Oliver Wendell, Jr. 552, 565, 579, 801, 983, 1083
   Abrams v. United States 550-562
   Frank v. Mangum 497-514
   Hammer v. Dagenhart 529-541
   Schenck v. United States 542-549
Holmes, Oliver Wendell, Sr. 420
Hoover, Herbert 610, 646, 672, 689
Hornblower, Joseph 208
Houseman, John 832
Houston, Charles Hamilton 597, 732, 736, 773, 1000
Hughes, Charles Evans 500, 501, 596, 689, 698, 722, 834
   A.L.A. Schechter Poultry Corporation v. United States 610-626
   National Labor Relations Board v. Jones & Laughlin Steel Corporation 644-669
   West Coast Hotel v. Parrish 670-686
Hunt, E. Howard 1095
Hunter v. Pittsburgh 801
Hunt, Ward 312, 351

I

Immigration Act of 1924 723
incorporation doctrine 825
Indian Citizenship Act 422
Indian Civilization Act 167
Indian Removal Act of 1830 418
Industrial Workers of the World 564
In re Burrus 313
In re Gault 958
In re Look Tin Sing 314
In re Neagle 313
Internal Revenue Service 699
internet speech 960
interracial marriage 943, 944
interstate commerce 137, 140, 141, 701
Interstate Commerce Act 700

J

Jackson, Andrew 166, 168, 187, 196, 209, 231, 270, 418
Jackson, Howell 474
Jackson, Robert H. 632, 720, 724, 741, 744, 761, 764, 766, 824, 1153
   West Virginia State Board of Education v. Barnette 711-719
   Wickard v. Filburn 697-710
James, Henry 543
James, William 543
Japanese internment 720, 723, 724, 725, 763, 774, 824, 834, 871
Jay Treaty 631
Jefferson, Thomas 2, 82, 83, 85, 114, 139, 165, 370, 632, 823, 825, 827, 1175

Jim Crow laws 310, 316, 438, 440, 444, 445, 472, 594, 731, 732, 772, 778, 840, 928, 943, 945, 1337, 1340
Johnson, Andrew 287, 289
Johnson, Lyndon B. 775, 841, 869, 946, 957, 958, 967, 968, 984, 1000, 1176, 1337
Johnson v. Zerbst 722, 834
Johnson, William 114, 137, 139, 365
Juarez v. State 787
Judiciary Act of 1789 23, 232, 290
Judiciary Act of 1801 3
Judson, Andrew T. 195

K

Kagan, Elena 1336, 1368, 1418
Kansas-Nebraska Act 231, 234
Katzenbach v. McClung 839-849
Katz v. United States 577, 1051
Kavanaugh, Brett 1062, 1325, 1380, 1418, 1419
Keating-Owen Child Labor Act 529, 531, 532
Kelley, Frank J. 1086
Kennedy, Anthony M. 1135, 1188, 1190, 1324, 1382, 1417
  Citizens United v. Federal Election Commission 1322-1335
  Lawrence v. Texas 1252-1279
  Obergefell v. Hodges 1366-1379
Kennedy, John F. 775, 840, 871, 886, 946, 957, 968, 1049, 1110, 1175
Kennedy, Robert F. 945, 957, 969
Kennedy v. Bremerton School District 826
Kent, James 137
Kentucky v. Dennison 271, 273
Key, Francis Scott 270, 1151
King, Martin Luther, Jr. 784, 840, 850, 869, 875, 1281
Kinsey, Alfred 1381
Korean War 741, 742, 743, 745, 762
Korematsu v. United States 699, 720-729, 763, 824, 834
Ku Klux Klan 594, 596, 722, 723, 763, 824, 833, 927
Ku Klux Klan Act 352, 389

L

labor rights 1051
laissez-faire capitalism 628
laissez-faire doctrine 487
Landon, Alf 670
Late Corporation of the Church of Jesus Christ of Latter-day Saints v. United States 368
Law Enforcement Officers Protection Act 1282
Lawrence v. Texas 861, 1252-1279
Le Duan 968
Leisy v. Hardin 533
Lemon v. Kurtzman 826, 1235

Lewinsky, Monica 1174, 1176
Lewis, Anthony 853
LGBTQ rights 1252, 1255, 1257, 1258, 1324, 1366, 1369, 1371, 1380, 1381, 1382, 1384, 1385
libel law 850, 852, 853, 1144
License Cases 141
Lincoln, Abraham 188, 228, 287, 288, 289, 290, 312, 313, 354, 384, 516, 944
  "House Divided" Speech 207, 234
  Second Inaugural Address 383
Lippmann, Walter 795
Livingston, Robert R. 137
Lochner v. New York 472-485, 487, 488, 489, 490, 491, 499, 534, 671
Longfellow, Henry Wadsworth 420
Louisiana Purchase 83, 228
Loving v. Virginia 598, 871, 943-955
Lowell, James Russell 420
Lujan v. Defenders of Wildlife 1220, 1222
Lujan v. National Wildlife Federation 1220
Lumpkin, Wilson 168

M

MacDonald v. City of Chicago 1284
Madison, James 2, 3, 82, 83, 84, 85, 87, 111, 165, 196, 370, 631, 823, 825, 827
Magna Carta 1009
Magnuson Act of 1943 461, 463
Mahanoy Area School District v. B.L. 960
Major Crimes Act 420
Malloy v. Hogan 887
Mann Act 532
Mapp v. Ohio 786, 802-814, 861, 884
Marbury v. Madison 2-22, 54, 87, 166, 232, 274, 1176
Marshall, John 2, 3, 23, 25, 53, 54, 56, 82, 83, 84, 90, 91, 109, 110, 137, 138, 139, 140, 142, 164, 165, 185, 187, 196, 209, 365, 384, 387, 418, 532, 628, 631, 633, 942, 1175
  Cohens v. Virginia 107-136
  Gibbons v. Ogden 137-162
  Marbury v. Madison 2-22
  McCulloch v. Maryland 82-106
  Trustees of Dartmouth College v. Woodward 52-81
  Worcester v. Georgia 163-184
Marshall, Thurgood 597, 730, 732, 735, 773, 817, 852, 885, 981, 984, 985, 1012, 1014, 1063, 1085, 1105, 1112, 1115, 1135, 1145, 1253
  Furman v. Georgia 997-1009
  New York Times Co. v. United States 967-980
Marshall v. Baltimore & Ohio Railroad Company 312
Martin v. Hunter's Lessee 23-51, 109, 113, 139, 268
Maryland v. Wirtz 534
Mason, George 1009
Masterpiece Cakeshop, Ltd. v. Colorado Civil Rights

INDEX 1479

Commission 714
Matthews, Stanley 384
Maxwell v. Dow 500
Maynard v. Hill 945, 947, 948
Mayor of New York v. Miln 141
McCain-Feingold Act 1322, 1323
McCain, John 1323, 1326
McCarthy, Joseph 742, 744, 817, 852, 1105, 1144
McConnell, Mitch 1326
McConnell v. FEC 1322, 1324, 1325
McCulloch v. Maryland 2, 4, 82-106, 109, 112, 113, 942
McKenna, Joseph 532, 553
McKinley, John 196
McKinley, William 530, 531, 551, 577
McLaughlin v. Florida 945, 946
McLaurin v. Oklahoma State Regents 733, 735, 841
McLean, John 196, 222, 234
   *Prigg v. Pennsylva*nia 206-227
McNamara, Robert 967, 969
McNaughton, John 969
McReynolds, James Clark 552, 553, 596, 597, 644, 646, 647, 673
Meese, Ed 1369
Meredith, James 840
Mexican American rights 784, 787
Mexican Cession 231
Meyer v. Nebraska 947, 1255
Miles v. United States 367
Miller, Andrew G. 268
Miller, Marvin 983, 985
Miller, Samuel F. 354
   Slaughterhouse Cases 310-350
Miller, Samuel Freeman 384
Millers, Andrew G. 271
Miller v. State 55
*Milligan v. Hove*y 291
Milliken v. Bradley 1085-1093, 1097
Milliken, William 1086
Minersville School District v. Gobitis 711, 713
minimum wage standards 578, 648, 670, 673
Miranda v. Arizona 598, 786, 804, 871, 884-925
Missouri Compromise 196, 228, 229, 231, 232, 234, 272
Missouri ex rel. Gaines v. Canada 732, 735, 773
Mitchell, John 958, 967
Mitchell v. Helms 1236
Mobile v. Bolden 796
Monroe, James 209
Montgomery Bus Boycott 840, 943
Moody, William 565
Mooney, Thomas 795
Moore, Underhill 859, 999
Moore v. Dempsey 502

Morehead v. New York ex rel. Tipaldo 670, 671, 672
Morgan, J. P. 472
Morrill Anti-Bigamy Act 366
Mueller v. Allen 1236
Mugler v. Kansas 314
Muller v. Oregon 486-496, 671, 775
Munn v. Illinois 314, 368, 388
Murdock v. Memphis 313
Murphy, Frank 834
Murphy v. Ramsey 367
Murray v. Maryland 732
Myrdal, Gunnar 773

N

NAACP v. Alabama 862
Naim v. Naim 947
National Firearms Act 1281
National Industrial Recovery Act 610, 611, 645
National Labor Relations Act 644, 646, 647, 671, 673
National Labor Relations Board v. Jones & Laughlin Steel Corporation 644-669, 671
National League of Cities v. Usury 534
National Prohibition Enforcement Act 575
Native Americans, rights of 56, 163, 164, 167, 418, 419
Naturalization Act of 1790 459, 460, 462
Naturalization Act of 1870 459, 460
Naturalization Law of 1802 460, 462
Neal v. Delaware 369
Nelson, Samuel 234
New Deal 610, 611, 613, 644, 646, 647, 670, 672, 673, 687, 698, 722, 733, 763, 795, 833, 842, 859, 860, 999, 1051
New York State Rifle & Pistol Association, Inc. v. Bruen 1284
New York Times Co. v. Sullivan 816, 850-856, 1104, 1135, 1144
New York Times Co. v. United States 723, 763, 766, 834, 860, 967-980
Ngo Dinh Diem 957, 968
Nguyen Van Thieu 969
Nicholas II (Tsar of Russia) 552
Nineteenth Amendment 490
Ninth Amendment 860, 1366
Nixon, Richard M. 766, 890, 946, 967, 969, 983, 1011, 1063, 1087, 1094, 1098, 1111, 1153, 1174, 1175, 1221, 1282, 1323
Nixon v. Fitzgerald 1175, 1176
Nixon v. Herndon 801
Norris v. Alabama 597
Northern Securities Co. v. United States 141, 530
Northwest Ordinance 228, 232
Nuremberg trials 699, 713

O

Oakley, Thomas 137
Obama, Barack 1324, 1326
Obergefell v. Hodges 316, 861, 1324, 1366-1379, 1382
O'Connor, Sandra Day 1143, 1153, 1188, 1190, 1234, 1235, 1256, 1338, 1419
   Lawrence v. Texas 1252-1279
Ogden, Aaron 137
Ogden, David B. 111
Olmstead v. United States 575-592
Omnibus Crime Control and Safe Streets Act of 1968 889

P

Pace v. Alabama 944, 948
Packers and Stockyards Act of 1921 578
Page Act of 1875 460
Palmer, A. Mitchell 545, 563
Palmieri, Edmund L. 1164
Panic of 1837 270
Papish v. Board of Curators of the University of Missouri 959
Parks, Rosa 840
Partial-Birth Abortion Ban Act of 2003 1420
Passenger Cases 141
Patterson, Haywood 595
Pearl Harbor attack 689, 720, 721, 723
Peckham, Rufus W. 1083
   Lochner v. New York 472-485
Pennoyer v. Neff 314
Pennsylvania College Cases 55
Pentagon Papers 967, 969, 970. *See also New York Times Co. v. United States*
Perez v. Sharp 944
Perry, Rick 1340
Pham Van Dong 968
Phillips, Samuel F. 385, 388
physician-assisted suicide 1259
Pierce, Franklin 268
Pierce v. Society of the Sisters of the Holy Names of Jesus and Mary 1254
Pinckney, Charles 139
Pinckney's Treaty 197
Pine, David A. 761, 764
Pinkney, William 111
Piqua Branch of the State Bank of Ohio v. Knoop 312
Pitney, Mahlon 553, 565
   Frank v. Mangum 497-514
Planned Parenthood of Southeastern Pennsylvania v. Casey 1063, 1236, 1255, 1257, 1369, 1419, 1420
Pledge of Allegiance 711
Plessy v. Ferguson 314, 438-458, 499, 500, 517, 730, 732, 734, 735, 772, 776, 777, 779, 886, 945, 1000, 1115, 1235
Pocahontas 945
Pocket Veto Case 565
political spending. *See* campaign finance
Pollock v. Farmer's Loan and Trust Company 314
Porter, John W. 1086
Powell, Lewis F., Jr. 997, 1049, 1064, 1096, 1135, 1253, 1369
   Frontiero v. Richardson 1133-1142
   Regents of the University of California v. Bakke 1110-1132
   San Antonio Independent School District v. Rodriguez 1010-1048
Powell v. Alabama 593-609, 629
presidential immunity 1173, 1174, 1175, 1176
Prigg v. Pennsylvania 196, 206-227, 269, 270, 387
Printz v. United States 1282
privileges or immunities clause 312, 315, 316, 350, 354, 386
Progressive Era 472, 473, 486, 529, 530, 671. *See* Gilded Age
Prohibition 575, 576
Protection of Lawful Commerce in Arms Act 1282
public education 1010, 1012, 1013
Pullman Strike 551
Pure Food and Drug Act 530, 532

R

Racial Integrity Act of 1924 947
Randolph, A. Philip 850
Rankin, J. Lee 775
Reagan, Ronald 1053, 1066, 1145, 1153, 1220, 1221, 1235, 1254, 1282, 1324, 1369, 1418
Reconstruction Acts 351
redistricting 815, 818, 869
Red Summer of 1919 594
Reed, Stanley F. 711
Reed v. Reed 1105, 1133, 1135, 1166, 1221
Regents of the University of California v. Bakke 1110-1132
Rehnquist, William H. 2, 141, 816, 817, 851, 852, 890, 997, 1012, 1049, 1064, 1096, 1103, 1112, 1116, 1135, 1136, 1143, 1144, 1190, 1191, 1221, 1253, 1257, 1259, 1282, 1338
   United States v. Lopez 1152-1163
   Zelman v. Simmons-Harris 1234-1251
Reid v. Covert 631
religious beliefs 366
religious freedom 689, 711, 713, 714, 786, 1338
Religious Freedom Restoration Act (RFRA) of 1993 1384
religious speech 687
reproductive rights 857, 861
Reynolds v. Sims 871

Reynolds v. United States 366-381, 714
Richmond v. J.A. Croson 1116
right to privacy 674, 774, 834, 857, 860, 1051, 1061, 1064, 1253, 1255, 1258, 1259, 1369, 1372, 1417
Roane, Spencer 114
Roberts, John 725, 1371, 1385
   Shelby County v. Holder 1336-1375
Roberts, Owen 648, 711
   Cantwell v. Connecticut 687-696
Roberts v. City of Boston 441, 776
Robinson, Jackie 840, 850, 985
Rockefeller, John D. 472
Rock Springs massacre 461
Roddenbery, Seaborn 944
Roe v. Wade 861, 890, 983, 1061-1084, 1135, 1152, 1154, 1235, 1255, 1257, 1369, 1382, 1417, 1419, 1420, 1421, 1422
Rolfe, John 945
Romer v. Evans 1255, 1369
Roosevelt, Eleanor 850
Roosevelt, Franklin D. 141, 553, 596, 610, 611, 614, 628, 632, 644, 647, 670, 672, 674, 698, 699, 712, 720, 722, 723, 725, 732, 733, 763, 795, 804, 824, 833, 841, 859, 929, 958, 970, 999, 1011, 1111, 1174, 1323
Roosevelt, Theodore 420, 530, 531, 543, 553, 565, 577, 595, 794, 1175, 1323
Rosewood Massacre of 1923 594
Ross, John 164, 168
Roth v. United States 1134
Rove, Karl 1326
Rowland, Chuck 1381
Rumsey, James 138
Rutledge, Wiley 1174
Rutledge, Wiley B. 818

S

Sacco-Vanzetti case 563
Sagarin, Edward 1381
same-sex marriage 316, 861, 890, 948, 1253, 1258, 1259, 1324, 1366-1379, 1382
San Antonio Independent School District v. Rodriguez 1010-1048
Sanford, Edward Terry
   Whitney v. California 563-574
Santa Fe Independent School District v. Doe 826
Sawyer, Charles 761
Scalia, Antonin 1135, 1167, 1190, 1191, 1371, 1382
   District of Columbia v. Heller 1280-1321
   Friends of the Earth v. Laidlaw Environmental Services 1219-1233
   Lawrence v. Texas 1252-1279
Schenck v. Ohio 554
Schenck v. United States 542-549, 550, 553, 564, 566, 742, 743, 744
school prayer 822, 824, 825, 860, 1235
school vouchers 1234, 1235
Scott Act 461, 463
Scottsboro Nine trials of 1931 593
search and seizure clause 1051, 1283
Second Amendment 1280, 1283, 1284, 1420
Second Bank of the United States 83
Sedition Act of 1798 852
Sedition Act of 1918 550, 553, 564
segregation 141, 597, 699, 731, 735, 772, 773, 775, 785, 786, 842, 943, 945, 984, 1000, 1066, 1085, 1089, 1097, 1145
Selective Service Act 542
Seminole Wars 166, 169, 229
Sentelle, David B. 1382
separate but equal doctrine 438, 445, 517, 730, 736, 776, 777, 1000, 1010
Separate Car Act 440, 442, 731
separation of powers 761, 766, 767
Seventeenth Amendment 629
Seward, William H. 208
Shapiro v. Thompson 1135
Shaw, Lemuel 441
Shay's Rebellion 54, 165
Sheehan, Neil 969
Shelby County v. Holder 1336-1365
Shelley v. Kraemer 519, 733, 735, 773
Sherbert v. Verner 714
Sherman Antitrust Act 473, 530, 531, 565, 981, 982
Sherman, John 531
Shields v. Ohio 55
Shuttlesworth v. City of Birmingham 1051
Sierra Club v. Morton 1049-1060, 1219, 1223
Silverman v. United States 576
Silverthorne Lumber Company v. United States 578, 803
Sipuel v. Board of Regents of the University of Oklahoma 732, 735, 840
Sixth Amendment 593, 722, 774, 832, 834, 884, 886, 1098
Skinner v. State of Oklahoma 948
Slaton, John 501
Slaughterhouse Cases 310-350, 354, 355, 385, 387
slavery 111, 114, 141, 142, 150, 193, 194, 206, 207, 210, 228, 229, 267, 269, 270, 312, 366, 422, 461, 730, 1115
Smith, Abram D. 268, 271
Smith Act 741, 742, 743, 744, 745
Smith, Tommie 983
Smyth, Alexander 111
Smythe v. Ames 499
Snyder v. Massachusetts 1084
sodomy laws 1252, 1254, 1255, 1257

sole organ doctrine 631, 632, 633
Solfisburg, Roy 1174
Sotomayor, Sonia 1336, 1368, 1418
Souter, David 1152, 1191, 1236, 1254, 1280
South Carolina v. Katzenbach 926-942
Spanish-American War 531, 577
Spencer, Herbert 628
Spencer Roane 88
Stafford v. Wallace 578
Stanley v. Illinois 1135
Starr, Kenneth 1176
Stassen, Harold 1087, 1096
Steel Seizure Case. See Youngstown Sheet and Tube Co. v. Sawyer
Steiner, Mollie 554
Stevens, John Paul 312, 1112, 1143, 1152, 1190, 1191, 1193, 1253, 1256, 1322, 1327
  Clinton v. Jones 1173-1186
  District of Columbia v. Heller 1280-1321
Stevens, Thaddeus 383
Stewart, Potter 576, 805, 818, 826, 886, 888, 959, 1012, 1064, 1098, 1112, 1258
  Furman v. Georgia 997-1009
  New York Times Co. v. United States 967-980
  Sierra Club v. Morton 1049-1060
Stimson, Henry L. 794
Stone, Harlan F. 141, 579, 698, 733
Story, Joseph 110, 164, 188, 193, 196, 206, 208, 212, 214, 269
  Martin v. Hunter's Lessee 23-51
  Prigg v. Pennsylvania 206-227
  United States v. Amistad 193-205
Strauder v. West Virginia 314, 369, 387, 443, 786
strict scrutiny test 720, 724
Strong, William 312
Sturgis v. Crowninshield 110
substantive due process 674
Sumner, Charles 383
supremacy clause 108, 109
Sutherland, George 644, 672
  Powell v. Alabama 593-609
  United States v. Curtiss-Wright 627-643
Swann v. Charlotte-Mecklenburg Board of Education 1085, 1088, 1097
Swayne, Noah H. 315, 354
Sweatt v. Painter 730-740, 840, 841
Swift & Co. v. United States 530

T

Taft-Hartley Act 764, 766
Taft, Robert 762
Taft, William Howard 500, 530, 565, 595, 612, 794
  Olmstead v. United States 575-592
Taney, Roger B. 141, 193, 196, 208, 209, 211, 212, 221, 228, 231, 232, 233, 234, 235, 236, 269, 270, 271, 272, 273, 274, 275, 288, 296, 328, 387, 401, 419, 426, 436, 468
  Ableman v. Booth 267-286
  Charles River Bridge v. Warren Bridge 185-192
  Dred Scott v. Sandford 228-266
  Prigg v. Pennsylvania 206
Tarble's Case 273
Tassel v. Georgia 165, 169
taxation, power of 533
Taylor, John 114
Taylor, Zachary 231
Tenth Amendment 4, 311, 394, 531, 532, 533, 536, 538, 947, 1337, 1339
Terrett v. Taylor 55
territories clause 232
Terry, David 313
Terry v. Ohio 806, 871
Texas Heartbeat Act 1063
Texas v. Johnson 816, 851, 1104, 1143-1151
Third Amendment 860
Thirteenth Amendment 234, 310, 312, 315, 353, 382, 387, 396, 397, 404, 406, 438, 439, 441, 442, 730, 927, 983, 1115
Thomas, Clarence 312, 1164, 1190, 1191, 1221, 1257, 1258, 1371, 1380
Thompson, Smith 195, 196
Thurmond, Strom 958
Tibbles, T. H. 419
Tilden, Samuel J. 357, 385, 439
Till, Emmett 840
Tillman Act of 1907 1323
Tinker v. Des Moines Independent Community School District 956-966
Title IX 1133
Tocqueville, Alexis de 1370
Toolson v. New York Yankees 984
total incorporation theory 834
Trail of Tears 168
Treaty of Brest-Litovsk 552
Treaty of Guadalupe Hidalgo 231
Treaty of Paris 23, 24, 109
Treaty of Versailles 967
Truman, Harry S. 713, 732, 733, 742, 761, 764, 765, 767, 804, 824, 840, 841, 886, 943, 946, 958, 968, 1175
Trump, Donald 725, 1062, 1382, 1419
Trustees of Dartmouth College v. Woodward 52-81, 109, 110, 112, 139
Tucker, John Randolph 368
Turner, Nat 194
Tweed, Boss 472
Twenty-first Amendment 576, 1104
two-class theory 785, 787
Tyler, John 231

INDEX 1483

U

Umberto I (King of Italy) 551
Undetectable Firearms Act of 1988 1282
United States v. Amistad 168, 193-205
United States v. Belmont 632
United States v. Butler 141, 670, 698
United States v. Cruikshank 351-365, 369, 387, 389
United States v. Curtiss-Wright 627-643
United States v. Darby 534
United States v. Darby Lumber Co. 534
United States v. E.C. Knight Company 141, 314
United States v. Eichman 1146
United States v. Hayes 1284
United States v. International Boxing 985
United States v. Kagama 313, 422
United States v. Lopez 141, 534, 843, 1152-1163
United States v. Morrison 843
United States v. Nixon 766, 1094-1102, 1176
United States v. O'Brien 545, 1145
United States v. Pink 632
United States v. Reese 355, 357, 369, 387
United States v. Shubert 985
United States v. Students Challenging Regulatory Agency Procedure (SCRAP) 1220
United States v. Virginia 1136, 1164-1172
United States v. Windsor 1368
United States v. Wong Kim Ark 459-471
Universal Declaration of Human Rights 732
U.S. War with Mexico 231

V

Vanderbilt, Arthur 817, 852, 1104, 1144
Vanderbilt, Cornelius 472
Van Devanter, Willis 644, 647, 673
Veazie Bank v. Fenno 533
Vesey, Denmark 194
Vietnam War 763, 857, 868, 870, 872, 956, 957, 959, 960, 967, 969, 971, 983, 999, 1050, 1094, 1111, 1134, 1145
Vinson, Fred M. 766, 774, 804, 871, 946
  Dennis v. United States 741-760
  Sweatt v. Painter 730-740
Violence Against Women Act of 1994 843
Violent Crime Control and Law Enforcement Act of 1994 1282
Virginia Declaration of Rights 1009
Virginia's Act III: Baptism Does Not Exempt Slaves from Bondage 949
Virginia Slave Code 949
Virginia Statute for Religious Freedom of 1785 825
Volstead Act. *See* National Prohibition Enforcement Act
voting rights 515, 517, 520, 793, 795, 1088, 1097, 1193, 1336, 1341

Voting Rights Act of 1965 520, 793, 796, 869, 872, 926, 928, 930, 931, 943, 1049, 1193, 1336, 1337, 1338

W

Wabash, St. Louis & Pacific Railroad Co. v. Illinois 141
Wabash v. Illinois 313
Waite, Morrison R. 368, 384
  Reynolds v. United States 366-381
  United States v. Cruikshank 351-365
Wallace, George C. 598, 840
Ware v. Hylton 2, 4
War of 1812 83, 107, 138, 166, 207
Warren, Earl 723, 735, 745, 804, 805, 816, 818, 819, 824, 834, 851, 852, 858, 958, 1051, 1085, 1087, 1097, 1104, 1111, 1135, 1144
  Bond v. Floyd 868-883
  Brown v. Board of Education 772-783
  Hernandez v. Texas 784-792
  Loving v. Virginia 943-955
  Miranda v. Arizona 884-925
  South Carolina v. Katzenbach 926-942
Washington, George 2, 3, 54, 82, 83, 85, 109, 165
Washington v. Glucksberg 1257, 1259
Watergate affair 1094, 1323
Water Pollution Control Act 1219
Watson, Thomas 497
Wayne, James 196
Webster, Daniel 52, 111, 137, 188
Weeks v. United States 578, 802, 805
Weinberger v. Wisenfeld 1221
welfare 1097
Wells, Robert 230
Wellstone, Paul 1335
West Coast Hotel v. Parrish 474, 644, 670-686
West Virginia State Board of Education v. Barnette 711-719, 1145, 1371
West Virginia v. Environmental Protection Agency 701
Weyl, Walter 795
Whalen v. Roe 1051
Wheelock, Eleazar 52
Wheelock, John 53
White, Byron 822, 858, 861, 888, 889, 959, 1012, 1064, 1085, 1098, 1112, 1115, 1143, 1165, 1221, 1253
  Furman v. Georgia 997-1009
  Miranda v. Arizona 884-925
  New York Times Co. v. United States 967-980
White, Edward D. 476, 553, 578
  Guinn v. United States 515-528
Whitney v. California 554, 563-574
Whittaker, Charles Evans 805, 818, 822
Wickard v. Filburn 697-710, 839
Williams, George H. 354
Williams v. Mississippi 499
Wilson, James 1175

Wilson, Woodrow 487, 530, 542, 551, 552, 576, 612, 629, 646, 672
wiretapping 575, 577, 579
Wirt, William 111, 112, 137, 164
Wisconsin Right to Life v. FEC 1325
Wisconsin v. Yoder 714
Wolfson, Louis 958
Wolf v. Colorado 803, 804, 805
women, rights of 486, 490, 530, 673, 852, 1088, 1097, 1133, 1134, 1135, 1136, 1164, 1166, 1167, 1221, 1417
Women's Armed Services Integration Act 1134
Woods, William B. 353, 384, 422
Worcester, Samuel A. 163
Worcester v. Georgia 2, 4, 163-184, 418
World War I 763, 795, 875

World War II 713, 714, 720, 723, 732, 741, 742, 762, 773, 804, 824, 840, 857, 875, 967, 999, 1112, 1174, 1380
Wright, Charles Alan 1011

X

XYZ Affair 4, 54, 139, 165

Y

Yates v. United States 745
Youngstown Sheet and Tube Co. v. Sawyer 631, 632, 633, 743, 761-771

Z

Zelman v. Simmons-Harris 1234-1251
Zimmermann telegram 542, 552